European Union Law

As the preferred choice of both teachers and students, this textbook offers an unrivalled combination of expertise, accessibility and comprehensive coverage. The new edition reflects the way the economic crisis has impacted the shape and nature of European Union Law. Materials from case law, legislation and academic literature are integrated throughout to expose the student to the broadest range of views. Additional online material on the application of EU law in non-member states and on rulings on the Fiscal Compact ensures the material is completely current. The new edition includes a timeline which charts the evolution of the EU project. Written in a way which encourages sophisticated analysis, the book ensures the student's full engagement with sometimes complex material. More importantly, it offers the clarity which is essential to understanding. A required text for all interested in European Union law.

Damian Chalmers is Professor of European Law at the London School of Economics and Political Science.

Gareth Davies is Professor of European Law at VU University, Amsterdam.

Giorgio Monti is Professor of Competition Law at the European University Institute, Florence.

European Union Law

TEXT AND MATERIALS

THIRD EDITION

Damian Chalmers
Gareth Davies
Giorgio Monti

CAMBRIDGE
UNIVERSITY PRESS

University Printing House, Cambridge CB2 8BS, United Kingdom

Cambridge University Press is part of the University of Cambridge.

It furthers the University's mission by disseminating knowledge in the pursuit of
education, learning and research at the highest international levels of excellence.

www.cambridge.org
Information on this title: www.cambridge.org/9781107664340

© Damian Chalmers, Gareth Davies and Giorgio Monti 2014

First published 2006
Second edition 2010
Third edition 2014

Printed in the United Kingdom by Bell and Bain Ltd

A catalogue record for this publication is available from the British Library

Library of Congress Cataloguing in Publication data
Chalmers, Damian, author.
European Union law : text and materials / Damian Chalmers, Gareth Davies,
Giorgio Monti. – Third edition.
    pages   cm
Includes bibliographical references and index.
ISBN 978-1-107-66434-0 (paperback)
1. Law – European Union countries.   2. European Union.   I. Davies, Gareth, author.
II. Monti, Giorgio, author.   III. Title.
KJE947.E883 2014
341.242'2 – dc23   2014007621

ISBN 978-1-107-66434-0 Paperback

Contents

ICELAND

EU member countries

Candidate countries

ICELAND

NORWAY

SWEDEN

FINLAND

ESTONIA

LATVIA

LITHUANIA

RUSSIA

BELARUS

IRELAND

DENMARK

UNITED
KINGDOM

NETHERLANDS

GERMANY

POLAND

BELGIUM

LUXEMBOURG

CZECH
REP.

SLOVAKIA

UKRAINE

FRANCE

SWITZERLAND

AUSTRIA

LIECHTENSTEIN

HUNGARY

MOLDOVA

SLOVENIA

CROATIA

ROMANIA

PORTUGAL

ANDORRA

MONACO

SAN
MARINO

BOSNIA
HERZEGOVINA

SERBIA

BULGARIA

SPAIN

ITALY

MONTENEGRO

KOSOVO*

VATICAN
CITY
STATE

ALBANIA

FYROM

GREECE

RUSSIA

GEORGIA

AZERBAIJAN

ARMENIA

IRAN

TURKEY

SYRIA

IRAQ

MOROCCO

ALGERIA

TUNISIA

MALTA

CYPRUS

LEBANON

KAZAKHSTAN

MADEIRA
(Portugal)

AZORES
(Portugal)

CANARY ISLANDS
(Spain)

GUADELOUPE
(France)

MARTINIQUE
(France)

GUIANA
(France)

RÉUNION
(France)

* Recognised by all member states of the European Union except Cyprus, Greece, Romania, Slovakia and Spain

Preface

The cover of this book portrays the *Myth of Europa*. The story has it that Europa, a Phoenician princess, was abducted by Zeus, the god of thunder, disguised as a bull. Zeus had been searching for a wife beautiful enough to become Queen of his native Crete. When he saw Europa he was smitten. Europa was gathering flowers by the seaside with her friends when she came upon the bull. Uncommonly gentle, the bull inspired no fear. Decking its horns with flowers, Europa climbed upon its back, whereupon the bull – Zeus – took off at a trot and dived into the sea. Europa was carried off to Crete, where she became the mother of Minos, the mythical King of Crete, who periodically demanded a tribute of young men and women of Athens to be sacrificed to the Minotaur.

This myth has not died with the ancients. In 1956, the six countries that were to sign the EEC Treaty appropriated her name to issue a set of Europa stamps to symbolise a community of interests and objectives. And today, Zeus's kidnap of Europa is depicted on the Greek 2 euro coin. The myth has been understood in a variety of ways. On one level it is a story of virtue, innocence and romance; on another, it is a warning of violence and exclusion. As with many of the ancient myths, misunderstanding and contestation lie at its very heart. The Roman depiction on our cover is one of the first depictions and, insofar as the human participants are depicted as Romans, reminds us too that the myth has been repeatedly appropriated and reinvented. We have also here a tale with its origins in modern Lebanon, which was told by the Ancient Greeks, and which then became a central fable of Ancient Rome. Yet Europa's myth is now seen as the origin of a territory whose cultural heartland lies somewhere in central Europe, *Mitteleuropa*, perhaps in the modern Czech Republic, perhaps in Vienna, but certainly somewhere in a nation that became a Member State of the European Union only very recently.

In today's Europe, misunderstanding, contestation, appropriation and reinvention permeate not only its founding myth, but also its most modern institution, the European Union, the law of which is this book's subject. European Union law is often seen as embodying new ideals, new rights and new forms of welfare. Equally, however, it is portrayed as being intrusive, divisive and costly. On the one hand, EU law is said to bring an international comity and to provide a powerful counter to the narrow (and historically dangerous) parochialism that has marked so much of Europe's bloody past. On the other hand, critics point to an overweening, inflexible, even pernicious European-ness, that is intolerant of national diversity and that stymies local democracy.

It is exactly this anxious fragility that gives European Union law its peculiar vitality and interest. It brings both a sceptical eye to the analysis of EU law and a constant demand to revisit old assumptions. As such, debates about EU law have in recent years been central in reconsidering ideas of the state, political community, the market, tradition and society.

This book owes a number of large debts. A particularly strong imprint and contribution has been left by Professors Adam Tomkins and Cristos Hadjiemmanuil, who contributed to the first edition. The efficiency, the friendliness and patience of Cambridge University Press continue to be a hallmark of our relationship with them. We would like to thank Elizabeth Davison, Sinead Moloney and Jessica Ann Murphy. An extra word must be said for Sinead. She has now left Cambridge University Press, but she has been with us since the genesis of this project. She believed in it, and has been fantastic to work with over a period of about ten years. We will miss her and wish her well. Another big debt of gratitude is owed to Sarah Trotter. Sarah was the research assistant for this edition, and she was simply wonderful! She was incredibly efficient, meticulous, friendly, and frighteningly good at picking up errors and omissions and suggesting improvements.

The division of responsibility for the book is as follows. Damian Chalmers wrote Chapters 1–10, 12, 14 and 16. Giorgio Monti wrote Chapters 13, 21, 22 and 23. Gareth Davies wrote Chapters 11, 15, 17, 18, 19 and 20. Finally, there are a number of personal debts. Damian Chalmers would like to thank Juliana Cardinale once again for patience, support and jokes. Gareth Davies wishes to thank Marjolein van Wieringen again for her tolerance and good humour during the writing of his chapters. Giorgio Monti continues to thank Ayako for her common sense and support, and Giulia and Sofia for being constant sources of wonder and laughter. Giorgio and Gareth would also like to thank Damian for his wise leadership and guidance during the writing process.

The Treaties were renumbered by the Treaty of Lisbon and we have used the Treaty numbers set by it throughout. A Table of Equivalent is included for reference's sake. We have aimed to state the law as at 31 December 2013.

DC, GD, GM

ACKNOWLEDGEMENTS

Every attempt has been made to secure permission to reproduce copyright material in this title and grateful acknowledgement is made to the authors and publishers of all reproduced material. In particular, the publisher would like to acknowledge the following for granting permission to reproduce material from the following publications:

L. v. Middelaar, *The Passage to Europe: How a Continent Became a Union*, Yale University Press (2013); G. Majone, 'Unity in Diversity: European Integration and the Enlargement Process' *European Law Review* (2008); M. Wilkinson, 'The Specter of Authoritarian Liberalism: Reflections on the Constitutional Crisis of the European Union' *German Law Journal* (2013); M. Shapiro, 'The Problems of Independent Agencies in the United States and the European Union' *Journal of European Public Policy* (1997); J. Tallberg, 'Bargaining Power in the European Council' *Journal of Common Market Studies* (2008); D. Grimm, 'Does Europe Need a Constitution?' *European Law Journal* (1995); P. Dann, 'European Parliament and Executive

Federalism: Approaching a Parliament in a Semi-Parliamentary Democracy' *European Law Journal* (2003); C. Joerges and J. Neyer, 'Transforming Strategic Interaction into Deliberative Problem-solving: European Comitology in the Foodstuffs Sector' *Journal of European Public Policy* (1997); A. Héritier, 'Elements of Democratic Legitimation in Europe: An Alternative Perspective' *Journal of European Public Policy* (1999); K. Alter, 'The European Court's Political Power' *West European Politics* (1996); M. Kumm, 'The Jurisprudence of Constitutional Conflict: Constitutional Supremacy in Europe Before and After the Constitutional Treaty' *European Law Journal* (2005); M. Cartabia, 'Europe and Rights: Taking Dialogue Seriously' *European Constitutional Law Review* (2009); H. Scott and N. Barber, 'State Liability under *Francovich* for Decisions of National Courts' *Law Quarterly Review* (2004); G. Davies, 'Subsidiarity: the Wrong Idea, in the Wrong Place, at the Wrong Time' *Common Market Law Review* (2006); J. Weiler, 'The Commission as Euro-Skeptic' in C. Joerges *et al.* (eds.), *Symposium: Mountain or Molehill? A Critical Appraisal of the Commission White Paper on Governance* (2002); L. García, 'New Rules, New Players? The ECI as a Source of Competition and Contention in the European Public Sphere' *Perspectives on European Politics and Society* (2012); E. Guild, 'Seeking Asylum: Storm Clouds between International Commitments and Legislative Measures' *European Law Review* (2004); S. Deakin, 'Legal Diversity and Regulatory Competition: Which Model for Europe?' *European Law Journal* (2006); D. Chalmers, 'The European Redistributive State and a European Law of Struggle' *European Law Journal* (2012); C. Newdick, 'Disrupting the Community: Saving Public Health Ethics from the EU Internal Market' in J. van de Gronden *et al.*, *Health Care and EU Law*, Asser Press (2011); C. O'Brien, 'Social Blind Spots and Monocular Policy Making: the ECJ's Migrant Worker Model' *Common Market Law Review* (2009); G. Majone, *Evidence, Argument and Persuasion in the Policy Process*, Yale University Press (1989); M. de la Mano, *For the Customer's Sake: The Competitive Effects of Efficiencies in European Merger Control*, Enterprise Papers No. 11, Enterprise Directorate-General (2002); M. S. Jacobs, 'An Essay on the Normative Foundations of Antitrust Economics' *North Carolina Law Review* (1995–1996); R. Wesseling, *The Modernisation of EC Antitrust Law*, Hart (2000); L. Laudati, 'The European Commission as Regulator: the Uncertain Pursuit of the Competitive Market' in G. Majone (ed.), *Regulating Europe*, Routledge (1996); D. J. Gerber, 'Law and the Abuse of Economic Power in Europe' *Tulane Law Review* (1987); B. Jack, 'Article 260(2) TFEU: An Effective Judicial Procedure for the Enforcement of Judgments?' *European Law Journal* (2013).

Abbreviations

AFSJ	Area of Freedom, Security and Justice
BER	Block Exemption Regulation
BSE	bovine spongiform encephalopathy
CAP	Common Agricultural Policy
CESR	Committee of European Securities Regulators
CFI	Court of First Instance
CFSP	Common Foreign and Security Policy
CISA	Schengen Implementing Convention
COR	Committee of the Regions
COREPER	Committee of Permanent Representatives
COSAC	Conference of Parliamentary Committees for Union Affairs of Parliaments of the European Union
CPVO	Community Plant Variety Office
CT	Constitutional Treaty
DCT	Draft Constitutional Treaty
DG	Directorate-General
EAW	European Arrest Warrant
EC	European Communities
ECB	European Central Bank
ECHA	European Chemicals Agency
ECHR	European Convention on Human Rights
ECI	European Citizens' Initiative
ECN	European Competition Network
ECOWAS	Economic Community of West African States
ECSC	European Coal and Steel Community
ECtHR	European Court of Human Rights
ECU	European Currency Unit
EDC	European Defence Community
EDP	excessive deficit procedure
EEA	European Economic Area
EEC	European Economic Community
EFSA	European Food Safety Authority
EFSF	European Financial Stability Facility
EFTA	European Free Trade Area
EMI	European Monetary Institute
EMS	European Monetary System
EMU	economic and monetary union
ENP	European Neighbourhood Policy
EO	European Ombudsman
ERDF	European Regional Development Fund
ERM	exchange rate mechanism
ERT	European Round Table
ESC	Economic and Social Committee
ESCB	European System of Central Banks
ESDP	European Security and Defence Policy
ESecC	European Securities Committee
ESF	European Social Fund
ESM	European Stability Mechanism
EUCFR	European Union Charter of Fundamental Rights
EURATOM	European Atomic Energy Community
EUROPOL	European Police Office
FSA	Financial Services Authority
FSAP	Financial Services Action Plan
GBER	General Block Exemption Regulation
GDP	gross domestic product
IGC	intergovernmental conference
IMF	International Monetary Fund
ISO	International Standards Organisation
JHA	Justice and Home Affairs
MCA	monetary compensation amount
MEP	Member of the European Parliament
MEQR	measure of equivalent effect
MiFiD	Markets in Financial Instruments Directive
MOU	Memorandum of Understanding
MTBO	Medium Term Budgetary Objective
NAAT	no appreciable affectation of trade
NCA	national competition authority
NCB	national central bank
NGO	non-governmental organisation
OHIM	Office for Harmonisation in the Internal Market
OLAF	European Anti-Fraud Office
OMC	open method of coordination
OMT	Outright Monetary Transaction

PASP Protocol on the Application of the Principles of Subsidiarity and Proportionality
PJCC police and judicial cooperation in criminal matters
QMV qualified majority voting
SBC Schengen Borders Code
SEA Single European Act
SGEI services of general economic interest
SIA Schengen Implementing Agreement
SIS Schengen Information System
SMP Securities Market Programme
SSM Single Supervisory Mechanism

StCF Standing Committee on Foodstuffs
TEU Treaty on European Union
TEU(M) Treaty on European Union (Maastricht)
TFEU Treaty on the Functioning of the European Union
TSCG Treaty on Stability, Coordination and Governance in the Economic and Monetary Union
UNCRPD UN Convention on the Rights of Persons with Disabilities
UPC United Patent Court
VIS Visa Information System
WTO World Trade Organization

Table of Cases

EC Commission Competition Decisions

European Ombudsman Decisions

European Commission of Human Rights

European Court of Human Rights

EFTA Court

National Courts

European Court of Justice: alphabetical order

European Court of Justice: Opinions

Table of Treaties, Instruments and Legislation

Treaties and Analogous Instruments

Declarations Annexed to the Lisbon Treaty Final Act

Declarations in Connection with the Lisbon Treaty

Protocols Annexed to the TEU and EC Treaty

EU Legislation and Policy Documents

Table of Equivalents

TREATY ON EUROPEAN UNION

Lisbon Treaty numbers and their Amsterdam and Pre-Amsterdam equivalents (Amsterdam and Pre-Amsterdam is TEU unless specified otherwise)

Lisbon	Amsterdam	Pre-Amsterdam	Lisbon	Amsterdam	Pre-Amsterdam
1	1	A	29	15	J.5
2			30	22	J.12
3	2	B	31	23	J.13
4	10 EC	5 EC	32	16	J.6
5	5 EC	3b EC	33	18	J.8
6	6	F	34	19	J.9
7	7	F.1	35	20	J.10
8			36	21	J.11
9			37	24	J.14
10	191(1) EC	138a	38	25	J.15
11	191(1) EC	138a	39		
12			40	47	M
13	3, 5, 7, 8, 10 EC	C, D 4, 4a. 5 EC	41	28	J.18
14	189/190/192/197 EC	137, 138, 138b, 140 EC	42	17	J.7
15	4	D	43		
16	202/203/205 EC	145, 146, 148 EC	44		
17	211/214/217 EC	155, 158, 161 EC	45		
18			46		
19	220/221/224 EC	164, 165, 168 EC	47	281 EC	210 EC
20	11/11A EC		48	48	N
	27A-27E, 40–40B, 43–45		49	49	O
21	3	C			
22			50		
23			51	311 EC	239 EC
24	11	J.1	52	299(1) EC	227(1) EC
25	12	J.2	53	51	Q
26	13	J.3	54	52	R
27			55	53	S
28	14	J.4		314 EC	248 EC

TREATY ON THE FUNCTIONING OF THE EUROPEAN UNION

Lisbon Treaty numbers and their Amsterdam and Pre-Amsterdam equivalents (Amsterdam and Pre-Amsterdam is EC Treaty unless specified otherwise)

Lisbon	Amsterdam	Pre-Amsterdam	Lisbon	Amsterdam	Pre-Amsterdam
1			49	43	52
2			50	44	54
3			51	45	55
4			52	46	56
5			53	47	57
6			54	48	58
7	3 TEU	C TEU	55	294	221
8	3(2)	3(2)	56	49	59
9			57	50	60
10			58	51	61
11	6	3c	59	52	63
12	153(2)	129a	60	53	64
13			61	54	65
14	16	7d	62	55	66
15	255	191a	63	56	73b
16	286	213b	64	57	73c
17			65	58	73d
18	12	6	66	59	73f
19	13	6a	67	61	73i
20	17	8		29 TEU	K.1 TEU
21	18	8a	68		
22	19	8b	69		
23	20	8c	70		
24	21	8d	71	36 TEU	K.8 TEU
25	22	8e	72	64(1)	73l(1)
26	14	7a		33 TEU	K.4 TEU
27	15	7c	73		
28	23	9	74		
29	24	10	75	60	73g
30	25	12	76		
31	26	28	77	62	73j
32	27	29	78	63(1, 2), 64(2)	73k(1, 2), 73l(2)
33	135	116	79	63(3, 4)	73k(3, 4)
34	28	30	80		
35	29	34	81	65	73m
36	30	36	82	31 TEU	K.3 TEU
37	31	37	83	31 TEU	K.3 TEU
38	32	38	84		
39	33	39	85	31 TEU	K.3 TEU
40	34	40	86		
41	35	41	87	30 TEU	K.2 TEU
42	36	42	88	30 TEU	K.2 TEU
43	37	43	89	32 TFEU	K.4 TEU
44	38	46	90	70	74
45	39	48	91	71	75
46	40	49	92	72	76
47	41	50	93	73	77
48	42	51	94	74	78

Lisbon	Amsterdam	Pre-Amsterdam	Lisbon	Amsterdam	Pre-Amsterdam
95	75	79	147	127	109p
96	76	80	148	128	109q
97	77	81	149	129	109r
98	78	82	150	130	109s
99	79	83	151	136	117
100	80	84	152		
101	81	85	153	137	118
102	82	86	154	138	118a
103	83	87	155	139	118b
104	84	88	156	140	118c
105	85	89	157	141	119
106	86	90	158	142	119a
107	87	92	159	143	120
108	88	93	160	144	121
109	89	94	161	145	122
110	90	95	162	146	123
111	91	96	163	147	124
112	92	98	164	148	125
113	93	99	165	149	126
114	95	100a	166	150	127
115	96	101	167	151	128
116	96	101	168	152	129
117	97	102	169	153(1, 3, 4, 5)	129a
118			170	154	129b
119	4	3a	171	155	129c
120	98	102a	172	156	129d
121	99	103	173	157	130
122	100	103a	174	158	130a
123	101	104	175	159	130b
124	102	104a	176	160	130c
125	103	104b	177	161	130d
126	104	104c	178	162	130e
127	105	105	179	163	130f
128	106	105a	180	164	130g
129	107	106	181	165	130h
130	108	107	182	166	130i
131	109	108	183	167	130j
132	110	108a	184	168	130k
133			185	169	130l
134	114	109c	186	170	130m
135	115	109d	187	171	130n
136			188	172	130o
137			189		
138	111(4)	109(4)	190	173	130p
139			191	174	130r
140	121(1), 122(2), 123(5)	109j, 109k, 109l	192	175	130s
141	123(3), 117(2)	109l(3), 109f(2)	193	176	130t
142	124(1)	109m(1)	194		
143	119	109h	195		
144	120	109i	196		
145	125	109n	197		
146	126	109o	198	182	131

Lisbon	Amsterdam	Pre-Amsterdam	Lisbon	Amsterdam	Pre-Amsterdam
199	183	132	251	221(2), (3)	165
200	184	133	252	222	166
201	185	134	253	223	167
202	186	135	254	224	168
203	187	136	255		
204	188	136a	256	225	168a
205			257	225a	168a
206	131	110	258	226	169
207	133	113	259	227	170
208	177/178	130u/130v	260	228	171
209	179	130w	261	229	172
210	180	130x	262	229a	172
211	181	130y	263	230	173
212	181a	130y	264	231	174
213			265	232	175
214			266	233	176
215			267	234	177
216			268	235	178
217	310	238	269		
218			270	236	179
219	111(1, 3, 5)	109(1, 3, 5)	271	237	180
220	302, 303, 304	229, 230, 231	272	238	181
221			273	239	182
222			274	240	183
223	190(4, 5)	138(3)	275		
224	191(2)	138(3)	276		
225	192(2)	138b	277	241	184
226	193	138c	278	242	185
227	194	138d	279	243	186
228	195	138e	280	244	187
229	196	139	281	245	188
230	197(2)–(4)	140	282	8	4a
231	198	141	283	112	109a
232	199	142	284	113	109b
233	200	143	285	246	188a
234	201	144	286	247	188b
235			287	248	188c
236			288	249	189
237	204	147	289		
238	205(1, 3)	148(1, 3)	290	202	145
239	206	150	291	202	145
240	207	151	292		
241	208	152	293	250	189a
242	209	153	294	251	189b
243	210	154	295		
244			296	253	190
245	213	157	297	254	191
246	215	159	298		
247	216	160	299	256	192
248	217(2)	161	300	257/258/263	193/194/198a
249	218(2)	162(2)	301	258(1), (2), (4)	194(1), (2), (4)
250	219	163	302	259	195
			303	260	196

Lisbon	Amsterdam	Pre-Amsterdam	Lisbon	Amsterdam	Pre-Amsterdam
304	262	198	332		
305	263(2), (3), (4)	198a(2), (3), (4)	333		
306	264	198b	334		
307	265	198c	335	282	211
308	266	198d	336	283	212
309	267	198e	337	284	213
310	268/270	199/201a	338	285	213a
311	269	200	339	287	214
312			340	288	215
313	272(1)	203	341	289	216
314	272(2–10)	203	342	290	217
315	273	204	343	291	218
316	271	202	344	292	219
317	274	205	345	295	222
318	275	205a	346	296	223
319	276	206	347	297	224
320	277	207	348	298	225
321	278	208	349	299(2)–(4)	227
322	279	209	350	306	233
323			351	307	234
324			352	308	235
325	280	210	353		
326			354	309	236
327			355	299(2)–(6)	227
328			356	312	240
329			357	313	247
330			358		
331					

Electronic Working Paper Series

ARENA Working Papers: www.sv.uio.no/arena/

Constitutionalism Web (CONWeb) Papers:
http://eiop.or.at/erpa/conweb.htm

Centre for Advanced Study in Social Sciences (CEACS) Working Papers:
www.march.es/ceacs/publicaciones/?1=2

Center for Culture, Organization and Politics Working Papers:
www.irle.berkeley.edu/culture/papers.html

Jean Monnet Papers: www.jeanmonnetprogram.org/papers/index.html

European Research Papers Archive: http://eiop.or.at/erpa/

European Integration Online Papers: http://eiop.or.at/eiop/

EUI Online Papers: www.iue.it/PUB/

Max Planck Institut für Gesellschaftsforschung (MPIfG) Working Papers:
www.mpifg.de/pu/workpapers_en.asp

Mannheim Zentrum für Europäische Sozialforschung (MZES) Working Papers:
www.mzes.uni-mannheim.de/frame.php?oben=titel_e.html&links=n_publikationen_e.
php&inhalt=publications/wp/workpap_e.php

Nuffield College Working Papers in Politics: www.nuffield.ox.ac.uk/Research/Politics%20Group/
Working%20Papers/Pages/Working-papers.aspx

Queens Papers on Europeanisation:
www.qub.ac.uk/schools/SchoolofPoliticsInternationalStudiesandPhilosophy/
Research/PaperSeries/EuropeanisationPapers/

University of Edinburgh Europa Institute Mitchell Working Papers: www.europa.ed.ac.uk/research_
activity/edinburgh_europa_paper_series/mitchell_working-papers

Time Line

19 September 1946	Speech by Winston Churchill at University of Zurich calling for a 'United States of Europe'.
4 April 1949	Treaty establishing the North Atlantic Treaty Organisation (NATO).
5 May 1949	Treaty of London establishing the Council of Europe.
9 May 1950	Schuman Declaration.
24 October 1950	Pleven Plan proposing a European Defence Community.
4 November 1950	European Convention for the Protection of Human Rights and Fundamental Freedoms (ECHR).
18 April 1951	Treaty of Paris establishing the European Coal and Steel Community (Belgium, France, Germany, Italy, Luxembourg, Netherlands).
27 May 1952	Treaty establishing a European Defence Community (Belgium, France, Germany, Italy, Luxembourg, Netherlands).
30 August 1954	French Assembly vote down European Defence Community.
20 May 1955	BENELUX Memorandum proposing customs union presented to ECSC Heads of Government (Beyen Plan).
1–3 June 1955	Messina Conference discussing steps for further European integration.
21 April 1956	Presentation of Spaak Report to ECSC Heads of Government.
25 March 1957	Signing of Treaty of Rome establishing the European Economic Community (EEC) and European Atomic Energy Community (Euratom) (Belgium, France, Germany, Italy, Luxembourg, Netherlands).
4 January 1960	Treaty of Stockholm establishing European Free Trade Association (EFTA) (Austria, Denmark, Norway, Portugal, Sweden, Switzerland and United Kingdom).
14 January 1963	British application for EEC membership vetoed by French Government and negotiations with Denmark, Ireland, Norway and United Kingdom end.
5 February 1963	*Van Gend en Loos* judgment of Court of Justice.
15 July 1963	*Plaumann* judgment of Court of Justice.
15 July 1964	*Costa* v *ENEL* judgment of Court of Justice.
8 April 1965	Merger Treaty creating common institutions for three Communities.

30 June 1965	'Empty chair crisis'. Refusal of French Government to take its seat in the Council.
29 January 1966	Luxembourg Accords ending 'empty chair crisis' and agreeing not to vote on any measure where any Member State raises 'very important interests'.
13 July 1966	*Consten and Grundig* judgment of the Court of Justice.
27 November 1967	Second British application to join the European Economic Community vetoed by the French Government.
31 December 1969	End of the Transitional Period.
21 April 1970	Own Resources Decision establishing independent Community Budget.
17 December 1970	*Internationale Handelsgesellschaft* judgment of the Court of Justice.
19–21 October 1972	Paris Summit establishing social and environment policy as objectives of European integration and creating the 'snake in the tunnel', the first system of European monetary cooperation.
1 January 1973	Denmark, Ireland and United Kingdom accede to the EEC. Norway refuses to do so after referendum.
21 February 1973	*Continental Can* judgment of the Court of Justice.
29 May 1974	*Internationale Handelsgesellschaft* judgment of German Constitutional Court.
4 December 1974	*Van Duyn* judgment of the Court of Justice.
10–11 March 1975	First European Council held in Dublin.
8 April 1976	*Defrenne* judgment of Court of Justice.
6 December 1978	Brussels European Council establishing European Monetary System and Exchange Rate Mechanism.
20 February 1979	*Cassis de Dijon* judgment of the Court of Justice.
7–10 June 1979	First direct elections to European Parliament.
1 January 1981	Greece joins the European Community.
19 June 1983	Stuttgart European Council Solemn Declaration on European Union.
14 February 1984	European Parliament Draft Treaty on European Union.
1 February 1985	Greenland leaves the European Economic Community.
14 June 1985	Commission White Paper on Completing the Internal Market.
14 June 1985	Schengen Convention for the gradual abolition of checks at common borders (Belgium, France, Germany, Luxembourg, Netherlands).
8–29 June 1985	Milan European Council opening Intergovernmental Conference (IGC) which leads to Single European Act.
1 January 1986	Portugal and Spain accede to the European Economic Community.
17 and 18 February 1986	Single European Act signed committing the European Economic Community to complete the internal market by 31 December 1992.
1 July 1987	Single European Act enters into effect. The European Economic Community henceforth known as the European Community.
22 October 1987	*Foto-Frost* judgment of the Court of Justice.
27–28 June 1988	Hannover European Council asks the President of the Commission, Jacques Delors, to chair a committee comprising the national central

	bankers to examine practical steps to realise economic and monetary union.
20 September 1988	Speech by British Prime Minister at the College of Europe, Bruges, criticising the direction and pace of European integration.
24 October 1988	Council establishes Court of First Instance (now the General Court).
9 November 1989	Fall of the Berlin Wall.
8–9 December 1989	Strasbourg European Council agree to convene an IGC to amend the EC Treaty to enable economic and monetary union.
19 June 1990	Convention implementing the Schengen Agreement.
25–26 June 1990	Dublin European Council agree to convene an IGC on political union.
18 June 1991	*ERT* judgment of the Court of Justice.
19 November 1991	*Francovich* judgment of the Court of Justice.
7 February 1992	Treaty on European Union (TEU) signed at Maastricht.
2 May 1992	Treaty of Oporto establishing the European Economic Area between the European Community and the EFTA States.
2 June 1992	Danish referendum rejects TEU by 50 to 49.7 per cent.
20 September 1992	French referendum approves TEU by 51 to 49 per cent.
11 December 1992	Edinburgh European Council set out principles which allow second Danish referendum to be held on TEU (which approves the TEU in 1993, with 56.8 per cent of votes in favour).
22 June 1993	Copenhagen European Council sets criteria for membership for states from Central and Eastern Europe ('Copenhagen criteria').
15 October 1993	*Brunner* judgment of the German Constitutional Court on the constitutionality of the TEU.
1 November 1993	TEU enters into force. European Union comes into being.
24 November 1993	*Keck* judgment of the Court of Justice.
1 January 1995	Austria, Finland and Sweden accede to the European Union. Norway refuses to do so after a referendum.
15 December 1995	*Bosman* judgment of the Court of Justice.
2 October 1997	Treaty of Amsterdam signed establishing, inter alia, the Area of Freedom, Security and Justice.
12 May 1998	*Martinez Sala* judgment of the Court of Justice.
1 January 1999	Eleven Member States (all Member States other than Denmark, Greece, Sweden and United Kingdom) enter into the third stage of EMU, the single currency arrangements.
15 March 1999	Resignation of Santer Commission following allegations of maladministration and corruption.
1 May 1999	Treaty of Amsterdam enters into force.
12 May 2000	Speech by German Foreign Minister, Joschka Fischer, at Humboldt University, Berlin, in which he calls for a need to determine the final point ('finality') of European integration.
2 October 2000	Charter of Fundamental Rights of the European Union (EUCFR) proclaimed by European Convention drafting it.

26 February 2001	Treaty of Nice signed.
7 June 2001	Irish referendum rejects Treaty of Nice by 53.87 per cent of the votes.
25 July 2001	Adoption of Commission White Paper on European Governance.
20 September 2001	*Courage* v *Crehan* judgment of the Court of Justice.
15 December 2001	Laeken Declaration of the European Council on the Future of the European Union establishes the Future of Europe Convention to propose treaty amendments allowing for institutional reform and constitutionalisation of the Treaties.
1 January 2002	Euro banknotes are circulated for the first time.
21 June 2002	Seville Declaration offers Ireland certain guarantees, on which basis a second referendum is held ratifying the Treaty of Nice in 2002 (with 62.9 per cent in favour).
1 February 2003	Treaty of Nice comes into force.
18 July 2003	Future of Europe Convention proposes a Draft Treaty Establishing a Constitution for Europe.
1 May 2004	Czech Republic, Cyprus, Estonia, Hungary, Latvia, Lithuania, Malta, Poland, Slovenia and Slovakia accede to the European Union.
29 October 2004	Following on from the Future of Europe Convention, the Member States sign the Constitutional Treaty.
29 May and 1 June 2005	Constitutional Treaty rejected in French and Dutch referendums by 54.68 per cent and 61.54 per cent of votes, respectively.
22 November 2005	*Mangold* judgment of the Court of Justice.
1 January 2007	Bulgaria and Romania accede to the European Union.
13 December 2007	Signing of Lisbon Treaty.
12 June 2008	Irish referendum rejects Lisbon Treaty by 53.4 per cent.
3 September 2008	*Kadi I* judgment of the Court of Justice.
19 June 2009	Declaration adopted by the European Council on the 'concerns of the Irish people' on which basis a second referendum ratified the Lisbon Treaty by 67.1 per cent.
30 June 2009	*Lisbon Treaty* judgment of the German Constitutional Court.
21 October 2009	Greek Government announces that its budget deficit is not 3.5 per cent of GDP as initially estimated but 12.5 per cent.
1 December 2009	Entry into force of the Lisbon Treaty.
2 May 2010	IMF and euro area governments agree €110 billion loan to Greece.
9 May 2010	European Financial Stability Facility (EFSF) established to provide €440 billion of conditional loans to euro area states experiencing public financing difficulties.
14 May 2010	Securities Market Programme (SMP) established by European Central Bank to purchase securities of euro area states having difficulties raising capital.
28 November 2010	€85 billion conditional loan facility provided to Ireland.
8 March 2011	*Zambrano* judgment of the Court of Justice.
4 May 2011	€78 billion conditional loan facility provided to Portugal.

31 January 2012	*Slovak Pensions* judgment of the Czech Constitutional Court.
2 February 2012	European Stability Mechanism Treaty (ESM) signed between euro area states, subsuming EFSF and offering up to €500 billion conditional loans to euro area states experiencing public financing difficulties.
2 March 2012	Treaty on Stability, Coordination and Governance in the Economic and Monetary Union (TSCG) signed by all Member States other than Czech Republic and United Kingdom.
13 May 2012	Second conditional loan facility of €130 billion provided to Greece.
9 June 2012	€100 billion conditional loan facility offered to Spanish banks.
6 September 2012	European Central Bank replaces SMP with Outright Monetary Transaction (OMT) Programme committing itself to potentially unlimited purchase of euro area government securities.
12 September 2012	*European Stability Mechanism (Temporary Injunctions)* judgment of the German Constitutional Court.
8 October 2012	ESM Treaty enters into effect.
27 November 2012	*Pringle* judgment of the Court of Justice.
1 January 2013	TSCG enters into effect.
23 January 2013	British Prime Minister, David Cameron, commits the Conservative Party, if re-elected, to renegotiate the United Kingdom's relationship with the European Union and to submit it to a referendum by 31 December 2017.
5 April 2013	*Fransson* judgment of the Court of Justice.
13 May 2013	€10 billion conditional loan facility provided to Cyprus.
1 July 2013	Croatia accedes to the European Union.
18 July 2013	*Kadi II* judgment of the Court of Justice.
8 December 2013	Ireland successfully exits its EFSF loan arrangement.
31 December 2013	Spain successfully exits the ESM loan arrangement for its banks.

1

European Integration and the Treaty on European Union

CONTENTS

1 INTRODUCTION

This chapter sets out the central features of the European integration process, which provide the historical and political context for European Union law. It also introduces some of the central concepts, ideas and developments in EU law.

Section 2 explores how EU law is centred around an interplay between two themes. The first is the government of many contemporary problems through law. The second is the development of the ideals of Europe and European union. This interplay lays the ground for many of its debates. The European ideal conceives of Europe as the central place of progress, learning and civilisation, placing faith in humanity and its capacity to improve. Its dark side is its arrogance and its dismissal of 'un-European' ways of life or thought as violating these virtues. The idea of European union sets up a political community in competition with the nation-state but one, nevertheless, through which government policy is carried out.

Section 3 considers the establishment of the three Communities, the European Economic Community (EEC), the European Coal and Steel Community (ECSC) and the European Atomic Energy Community (EURATOM). It sets out the central institutions: the Commission, the Parliament, the Council and the Court of Justice. It also considers the central policies, most notably the common market. This section also compares two developments of the 1960s that set out the two dominant models of political authority in EU law: the Luxembourg Accords which set out an intergovernmental vision with political authority and democracy vested in the nation-state, and *Van Gend en Loos* which set out a supranational one in which these are vested in supranational institutions and the rights of European citizens. Finally, this section evaluates the Single European Act (SEA). This established the internal market, and transformed the legislative and political culture surrounding the European Communities by setting out both an ambitious legislative programme and providing for significant amounts of legislation to be adopted free from the national veto.

Section 4 looks at the establishment and early years of the European Union. It considers the three dominant strategies used to justify the authority of the Union, and how these were deployed in the various treaty reforms. These strategies involve increasing EU competencies to allow it to offer more benefits to its subjects, attempting to generate a sense of common identity, and democratic reform of its institutions. At Maastricht, the treaty which instituted the European Union, the central elements of each was, respectively, the establishment of economic and monetary union, European Union citizenship and increased powers for the European Parliament. The Treaty of Amsterdam, signed in 1997 to deal with unfinished business from Maastricht, established the area of freedom, security and justice. Its central features were the abolition of internal border controls between all Member States other than the United Kingdom and Ireland; the establishment of a supranational immigration and asylum policy; and police cooperation and judicial cooperation in criminal and civil matters. Amsterdam sought to orient Union identity more strongly around fundamental rights. In terms of democratic reform, it increased the powers of both the European Parliament and national parliaments.

These strategies were only partially successful. Devices were also introduced to offset tensions generated by the increased centralisation and supranationalisation of law-making. The subsidiarity principle provides that the Union should only act when Member States cannot realise its objectives unilaterally and by reason of the nature or scale of the action, these are better realised through Union action. Differentiated integration was also introduced. In some instances, such as economic and monetary union, it took the form of special regimes for individual Member States. At Amsterdam, a more general form of differentiation was adopted, enhanced cooperation, which allowed a majority of Member States to enact EU laws where others were unwilling.

Section 5 considers the enlargement of the Union. Initially agreed between six Member States, the Union had grown to fifteen Member States by the mid-1990s. Almost all were prosperous and almost all came from Western Europe. The accessions from 2004 onwards brought the number of Member States to twenty-eight, with most of the new Member States being from Central and East Europe and having a post-communist past. This has made the Union a genuinely pan-European organisation but it has made it much more heterogeneous, posing new preferences and challenges, and raising the question of whether it is possible to have a 'one size fits all' EU law.

Section 6 analyses the period of institutional reform which led up to the Lisbon Treaty. It looks, first, at the European Union Charter of Fundamental Rights (EUCFR). This pioneered the convention method for institutional reform, where instead of everything being decided by governments behind closed doors a body was established meeting in open session, taking evidence from civil society, to put forward proposals. The section then goes on to consider the limited institutional reforms agreed at the Treaty of Nice in 2004 and the failure of the Constitutional Treaty. It is then given over to discussion of the Lisbon Treaty.

The Treaty settles the European Union around two treaties, the Treaty on European Union and the Treaty on the Functioning of the European Union. The Treaty catalogues EU competencies, for the first time. In addition, whilst special arrangements are made for foreign and defence policy, all other policies are brought within a common supranational framework. The Treaty next orients the collective identity of the European Union around a particular mission, respect for democratic values and democratic identities. In this regard, the Union must now respect the values set out in the EUCFR and is to be founded on representative democracy. It must also respect the fundamental democratic structures of Member States. Finally, the Lisbon Treaty continues the process of democratic reform with yet further powers for both the European Parliament and significant power for national parliaments, who can now police the subsidiarity principle. As a counter-weight, it accelerates the process of differentiated integration, with a number of special regimes provided for under both the EUCFR and the area of freedom, security and justice.

Section 7, finally, considers how the financial crisis has affected the European Union and led to its re-evaluation. It, first, considers the mechanisms, notably the European Stability Mechanism Treaty, set up outside the formal structures of EU law to provide financial support to those Member States which were no longer able to sustain their public finances. It looks at the limited controls on these, and how these have moved the Union more directly into the world of fiscal and welfare policy, albeit in an asymmetric way where some Member States have considerably more influence than others. It then looks at the more general vision now set out by both EU legislation (the 'six-pack') and by the Treaty on Stability, Coordination and Governance in the Economic and Monetary Union (the fiscal compact). These put in place a series of extensive controls on fiscal and macro-economic policy for the euro area Member States in particular. It ponders the nature of this vision in these, and the challenges posed for democratic politics by it. Finally, the crisis has led to a re-evaluation of the Union. Some see the crisis as a reason for stronger EU institutions with wider competencies whilst others consider the crisis exposes the difficulties of European integration and throws the project into further doubt.

2 EUROPE AND THE EUROPEAN UNION

This book is about the European Union. The phrase itself suggests an interplay between two things. On the one hand, the European Union has been established to deal with a series of contemporary problems and realise a set of goals that individual Member States feel unable to manage alone. That idea is conveyed by the word *Union*. Its other feature is its claim to be *European*. In this, its mission is to lay claim to and further a European heritage. This is contentious. Some may disagree with its interpretation of this heritage, the need to further it or that the European Union should claim ownership of it. Nevertheless, the opening words of the Preamble to the Treaty on European Union establishing the European Union state:

> RESOLVED to mark a new stage in the process of European integration undertaken with the establishment of the European Communities,
>
> DRAWING INSPIRATION from the cultural, religious and humanist inheritance of Europe, from which have developed the universal values of the inviolable and inalienable rights of the human person, freedom, democracy, equality and the rule of law.

To understand EU law, one has to realise that at its core is a constant interplay between these two agendas: the claim to develop European ideals and the government of the problems of contemporary Europe. Elements of both permeate all the chapters of this book. In some areas, there is a tension, imbalance or dysfunction between the two. In other areas, each is being revised in the light of concerns provoked by the other. The balance is constantly changing as political beliefs change, the European Union's institutional settlement evolves and the challenges of the outside world alter. However, each development is considered in the light of a long legacy: be this the history of the European ideal, the institutional settlement of the European Union or a policy whose inception and development goes back many years.

Different chapters of this book consider different legal problems and goals. Yet it is worth pausing at the beginning of the book to consider some of the central elements of this European inheritance, so we know the sort of venture upon which the European Union is embarked. If discussion of the Ancient Greeks and Charlemagne seems rather removed from that of discussion of the single currency, it is, however, worth considering what broader vision of life that currency is tapping into. Is it somehow distinct because it is European and, in turn, does it change our understandings of Europe that 'Europe' is now associated with a series of laws and policies established by the European Union?

(i) The idea of Europe

There is nothing fixed about the meaning of the term 'Europe'. It has been used for a variety of purposes. Its roots, like many things, are curious. The first references to 'Europe' depict it as a woman and the sun. The most famous early reference to Europe is that found in Greek mythology. Europa was a Phoenician woman seduced by the Greek god, Zeus, to come from Lebanon to Crete.[1] Europa was also, however, a Phoenician word that referred to the setting sun. From this, Europe was associated in Ancient Greece with the idea of 'the West'. Originally used to designate the lands to the west of Greece, usage shifted as the Ancient Greek territorial

[1] D. De Rougemont, *The Idea of Europe* (New York, Macmillan, 1965) 6–19.

centre of gravity changed with incursions into modern Turkey and Iran. In his wars, Alexander the Great used it to denote non-Persians and it became associated with the lands in Greece and Asia Minor (today's Turkish Mediterranean coastline). Following this, the term was to lie largely dormant for many centuries. The Roman Empire and Christianity dominated in the organisation of political life, and neither had much use for the term.

Europe re-emerged as an important political idea from the eighth century AD onwards. It was here that it began to acquire many of the associations that we currently make when we use the word 'European'. In part, it became an expression of a siege mentality. The advance of Islam from the South and the East led to Europe being associated with resistance to the religion. An army of Franks, which fought against the Moors, was referred to as a 'European army'.[2] At this time Europe also became associated with the idea of Western Christianity. The Frankish Empire stretched across much of West Europe under the rule of Charlemagne in the ninth century AD. He styled himself as the father of Europe and sought to impose a political system across the region, based on communication between a large number of political and administrative centres. Alongside this, common economic practices were developed: shared accounting standards, price controls and a currency. Finally, he also sought to build a common Christian culture, which fostered learning, Christian morality, the building of churches and the imposition of a single interpretation of Christianity.[3]

These elements are all associated with a European identity. However, it was only from the twelfth century onwards that Europe was used to refer to a place whose inhabitants enjoyed a shared way of life based on Christian humanism, revolving around images of God and Christ portrayed as human.[4] Alongside particular religious beliefs, Europe also became associated with a particular form of political economy, namely, that of rural trade.[5] Increasingly, the rural town became the centre of the local economy. Trade relations between towns expanded across Europe, so that from the fifteenth century onwards, trade flourished between the Italian ports in the South and Flanders in the North, in which the role of the merchant was pivotal. The final feature of this European region was the persecution of non-Christians, be they pagans or followers of other faiths, such as Judaism or Islam. Those whose conduct offended the central values of Christianity were also maltreated, such as heretics and homosexuals, as were those perceived as socially unproductive, in particular, lepers.

Developments in the sixteenth and seventeenth centuries were to set out the dominant institutional context for the subsequent evolution of the European idea. The establishment of the modern nation-state consolidated power in centralised, impersonal bureaucracies and led to certain core policies, such as tax, law and order and foreign policy being the exclusive competence of these bureaucracies.[6] This hegemony of the nation-state over political life led

---

[2] D. Lewis, *God's Crucible: Islam and the Making of Europe 570–1215* (Norton, New York, 2008).

[3] The most extensive exposition is to be found in R. McKitterick, *Charlemagne: The Formation of a European Identity* (Cambridge, Cambridge University Press, 2008).

[4] J. Le Goff, *The Birth of Europe* (Oxford, Blackwell, 2005) 76–80.

[5] On the earlier origins of this in the developments of crops of rye and oats which led both to new divisions of labour within agriculture, to trade and to sustaining centres of population see M. Mitterauer, *Why Europe? The Mediaeval Origins of Its Special Path* (G. Chapple (trans.), Chicago, IL, Chicago University Press, 2010) ch. 1.

[6] C. Tilly (ed.), *The Formation of Nation-States in Europe* (Princeton, NJ, Princeton University Press, 1975); G. Poggi, *The Development of the Modern State: A Sociological Introduction* (Stanford, CA, Stanford University Press, 1978); M. Mann, 'The Autonomous Power of the State: Its Origins, Mechanisms and Results' (1984) 25 *European Journal of Sociology* 185; H. Spruyt, *The Sovereign State and Its Competitors: An Analysis of Systems Change* (Princeton, NJ, Princeton University Press, 1994).

to Europe acquiring new associations in the eighteenth and nineteenth centuries. It became, increasingly, an 'aesthetic category, romantic and nostalgic', associated with utopian ideals. Authors such as Rousseau and Kant saw Europe as an expression of certain ideals: be it a social contract between nations or as a form of perpetual peace. Europe was also considered to represent a shared aesthetic tradition:[7] be this a common form of high culture, institutionalised through the growth of elite tourism in Europe at that time, or that of a historical civilisation, distinguishing it from the New World and justifying its colonialism.

The final twist came in the twentieth century and derives from the United States' involvement in Europe. The role of the United States in two World Wars, the Cold War and in the regeneration of Europe after the Second World War heavily influenced European identity.[8] For those reverting to market democracy after forty-five years of communism, a 'return to Europe' means a turn to the West and to values that are associated, unashamedly, with the United States, namely, those of free markets and constitutional democracy. In today's Western Europe, Europe has acquired an alternate meaning where its values are similar to, but different from those of the United States. Although there is a shared commitment to markets and constitutional democracy, these take a different form from those in the United States. There is an emphasis on the social market and on supposedly 'European' values, such as opposition to the death penalty, which are not present in the United States.

J. Habermas and J. Derrida, 'February 15, or, What Binds Europeans Together: Plea for a Common Foreign Policy Beginning in Core Europe' in D. Levy et al., Old Europe, New Europe, Core Europe: Transatlantic Relations after the Iraq War (London, Verso, 2005) 5, 10–12

...the spread of the ideals of the French revolution throughout Europe explains, among other things, why politics in both of its forms – as organizing power and as a medium for the institutionalization of political liberty – has been welcomed in Europe. By contrast, the triumph of capitalism was bound up with sharp class conflicts, and this fact has hindered an equally positive appraisal of free markets. That differing evaluation of politics and markets may explain Europeans' trust in the civilizing power of the state, and their expectations for it to correct market failures.

The party system that emerged from the French revolution has often been copied. But only in Europe does this system also serve an ideological competition that subjects the socio-pathological results of capitalist modernization to an ongoing political evaluation. This fosters the sensitivities of citizens to the paradoxes of progress. The contest between conservative, liberal and socialist agendas comes down to the weighing of two aspects: Do the benefits of a chimerical progress outweigh the losses that come with the disintegration of protective, traditional forms of life? Or do the benefits that today's processes of 'creative destruction' promise for tomorrow outweigh the pain of modernity's losers?

In Europe, those affected by class distinctions, and their enduring consequences, understood these burdens as a fate that can be averted only through collective action. In the context of workers' movements and the Christian socialist traditions, an ethics of solidarity, the struggle for 'more social

---

[7] A. Chebel d'Appollonia, 'European Nationalism and European Union' and J. Tully, 'The Kantian Idea of Europe: Critical and Cosmopolitan Perspectives' in A. Pagden (ed.), *The Idea of Europe: From Antiquity to the European Union* (Cambridge, Cambridge University Press, 2002). Recent examples of this tradition are Z. Bauman, *Europe: An Unfinished Adventure* (Cambridge, Polity, 2004); U. Beck, *Cosmopolitan Europe* (Cambridge, Polity, 2005).

[8] G. Delanty, *Inventing Europe: Idea, Identity, Reality* (Basingstoke, Macmillan, 1995) 115–55.

justice', with the goal of equal provision for all, asserted itself against the individualist ethos of market justice that accepts glaring social inequalities as part of the bargain.

Contemporary Europe has been shaped by the experience of the totalitarian regimes of the twentieth century and by the Holocaust – the persecution and annihilation of European Jews in which the National Socialist regime made the societies of the conquered countries complicit as well. Self-critical controversies about the past remind us of the moral basis of politics. A heightened sensitivity to injuries to personal and bodily integrity reflects itself, among other ways, in the fact both the Council of Europe and the EU made the ban on capital punishment a condition for membership.

The excerpt from Habermas and Derrida conveys, amongst other things, the view that, since the eighth century, Europe has been seen as a place where there are multiple political communities with a shared way of life. For them, this shared way of life involves both a questioning of the excesses of the market and, since the Second World War, the excesses of the nation-state.[9] This questioning and commitment to pluralism is attractive. However, this way of life is also based on a commitment to progress, civilisation, learning and culture and a belief in the value of humanity and its capacity to better itself and to resolve any problems.[10] Europe is not only associated with this commitment and this belief, but they are often seen as something particularly European, to the irritation of many non-Europeans. Europe has, thus, historically posited itself as the centre of the world.[11] It has been its job to civilise others, to spread progress or human values. There is also an intolerance of things 'non-European'. For if they are not European, there is a chance that they do not represent the good things Europe represents. At its worse, this arrogance and intolerance has led to racism and colonialism, yet it is also present in the European integration process. Time and again, the *sui generis* nature or specialness of the process is emphasised as a form of particularly enlightened cooperation between nations. This leads to an assumption about the desirability of its policies, with opponents of integration, thus, often dismissed as unreasonable or nationalistic (i.e. un-European). It may be, however, that they simply disagree with the policy or the procedure, or that they believe there to exist other forms of value or ways of life beyond those expressed in the European ideal.

(ii) The idea of 'European Union'

The idea of European union has different associations from that of Europe. After all, many self-avowed Europeans oppose European union! Independent proposals for a 'united Europe' first emerged at the end of the seventeenth century. However, they were still firmly confederal in nature. Ultimate authority was vested in the state, with pan-European structures acting as little more than a fetter upon the autonomy of the states. In 1693, the English Quaker, William

---

[9] J.-W. Müller, *Constitutional Patriotism* (Princeton, NJ, Princeton University Press, 2007) ch. 3.

[10] This contradiction is present in the famous 1935 lecture presented by E. Husserl, 'Philosophy and the Crisis of European Humanity' reprinted in E. Husserl, *The Crisis of European Sciences and Transcendental Phenomenology* (Chicago, IL, North Western University Press, 1970) Appendix I.

[11] On the hegemonic force of this see R. Kanth (ed.), *The Challenge of Eurocentrism: Global Perspectives, Policy and Prospects* (Basingstoke, Palgrave, 2009).

Penn, wrote *An Essay Towards the Present and Future Peace of Europe*. Penn suggested that a European Parliament be established, consisting of representatives of the Member States. Its primary purposes would be to prevent wars breaking out between states and to promote justice. A more far-reaching proposal was put forward by John Bellers in 1710. Bellers proposed a cantonal system based upon the Swiss model whereby Europe would be divided into 100 cantons, each of which would be required to contribute to a European army and send representatives to a European Senate.

The first proposal for a Europe which replaced the state system with a sovereign central body came from the Frenchman, Saint-Simon, and was published in a pamphlet in 1814, entitled *Plan for the Reorganisation of the European Society*. Saint-Simon considered that all European states should be governed by national parliaments, but that a European Parliament should be created to decide on common interests. This Parliament would consist of a House of Commons peopled by representatives of local associations and a House of Lords consisting of peers appointed by a European monarch. Saint-Simon's views enjoyed considerable attention during the first part of the nineteenth century. Mazzini, the *éminence grise* of Italian nationalism, allied himself with Proudhon and Victor Hugo in declaring himself in favour of a United Europe. Yet, the nineteenth century represented the age of the nation-state and the relationship between that structure and that of a united Europe was never fully explored.

The balance was altered by the First World War, which acted as a stimulus for those who saw European union as the only means both to prevent war breaking out again between the nation-states and as a means of responding to increased competition from the United States, Argentina and Japan. Most prominent was the pan-European movement set up in the 1920s by the Czech, Count Coudenhove-Kalergi.[12] This movement not only enjoyed considerable support amongst many of Europe's intellectuals and some politicians, but was genuinely transnational, having 'Economic Councils' both in Berlin and in Paris. During the 1920s, the idea of European unity received governmental support in the shape of the 1929 Briand Memorandum. This Memorandum, submitted by the French Foreign Minister to twenty-six other European states, considered the League of Nations to be too weak a body to regulate international relations, and proposed a European Federal Union, which would better police states, whilst not 'in any way affect[ing] the sovereign rights of the States which are members of such an association'. This proposal, despite acknowledging the authority of the nation-states, was still regarded as too radical and received only a lukewarm response from the other states.

A further shock, in the form of the Second World War, was needed to arouse greater governmental interest in the idea of a united Europe. The coming into being of the European Communities and its transformation into the European Union are explored in greater depth in the rest of this chapter. It is useful to consider for a moment how the creation of this powerful organisation, which now adopted the term of 'European Union' for itself, changed the context within which the idea was understood.

In the first place, the European Union has become an independent centre of government in its own right, generating it own understandings about European union and European values and symbols. In some instances, to do this, it has tried to replicate the symbols and tools of nationhood at a pan-European level – be it through the (re)discovery of European flags, anthems,

---

[12] N. Coudenhove-Kalergi, *Pan-Europe* (New York, Knopf, 1926). An excellent discussion can be found in C. Pegg, *Evolution of the European Idea 1914–1932* (Chapel Hill, NC, University of North Carolina Press, 1983).

Cities of Culture or common passports.[13] Other activities cannot be characterised in this way. We shall see in Chapter 11 that the European Union idea of citizenship, for example, takes a very different trajectory from that of national citizenship. The European Union is projected as a model of political community which is an alternative to the nation-state and not a mimic of it.[14] Both understandings of European union, that as mimic and that as alternate to the nation-state, are opposed by 'Euro-sceptic' groups, who see each as something equally destructive of local self-government.[15]

In the second place, European union has become a vehicle through which national governments pursue their understanding of the national interest. Here it does not sit in opposition to national governments, but is used to justify and redefine national government policy. Bickerton has argued that this has led to a subtle and not unproblematic shift in national government understandings of what they are about. They have moved from being nation-states to Member States.

C. Bickerton, *European Integration: From Nation States to Member States* (Oxford, Oxford University Press, 2012) 60, 68–9

The more traditional elements of statehood remain – central government, identifiable territory and a population – and member states retain a monopoly on the legitimate exercise of violence. But the integrated state-society relationship of the modern nation state is increasingly relativized and seen as only part of what makes up the state. The other part is membership of international organizations, regional organizations, and generally the participation in a multitude of activities that appear as external to the state itself and function as material constraints upon its liberty...

...we can point to two critical features of member statehood that stand out in terms of how they contrast with dominant assumptions and practices of modern nation states. The first is that central to member statehood is a presumed *opposition* between state and society. The purpose of limiting national power in ways that appear external to the national polity is in order that domestic populations are distanced from policy-making and decision-making. National elites seek to insulate themselves from the force and compulsion of public opinion because of the risk that 'vile people', as Weiler puts it, will generate vile policies. The idea of membership thus belongs to this sought-for separation between state and society. The contrast with modern nation states is striking: here the goal was to achieve a unity in what was a fractious and divided social space. Problems of economic and ideological conflict have generally been sublimated through unifying categories such as the people and the nation, even if those categories have themselves been subject to long-standing disagreements about their precise meaning.

Whilst modern nation states have sought unity, member states assume division. The state-society relationship is thus reconfigured in a way very alien from traditional thinking about the state: a presumed relationship of representation is replaced by one of insulation and separation.

---

[13] C. Shore, *Building Europe: The Cultural Politics of European Integration* (London/New York, Routledge, 2000).

[14] U. Beck and E. Grande, *Cosmopolitan Europe* (Cambridge, Polity, 2007) 225–40; J. Habermas, *The Crisis of the European Union: A Response* (Cambridge, Polity, 2012) 1–53. In some cases, EU policies adopt elements of both models. For a discussion of the European Cities of Culture and European Landscape Convention see M. Sassatelli, *Becoming Europeans: Cultural Identity and Cultural Policies* (Basingstoke, Palgrave, 2009).

[15] A flavour is provided in M. Holmes (ed.), *The Eurosceptical Reader* (Basingstoke, Macmillan, 1996).

The second feature is the way constraints upon the exercise of national power are based not upon a political ideal or principle but rather on an institutional and bureaucratic understanding of such limits. The picture we thus have of the member state, where its central principle of legitimization resides in the actions of public officials, is one of an administrative machine rather than a political community.

European union, for Bickerton, is thus something which allows national governments to distance themselves from their citizens and thereby acquire a stronger say in controlling and imposing different policies by saying that these are both necessary and externally required. It is a divisive notion.

The third vision of European union flows in the opposite direction. It argues that debates about European union invariably also involve debates about national identity and what it means. These debates act as vehicles for citizens and communities to articulate understandings of themselves and their place in the world through asking themselves how they relate to Europe.[16] This, in turn, shifts their ideas of national identity. The extract below considers the case of Finland, in which the authors argue that by placing itself within the European Union many Finns were able to resolve a prior dichotomy about whether Finland was more 'Western' or more Russian.

M. Malmborg and B. Stråth, 'Introduction: The National Meanings of Europe' in M. Malmborg and B. Stråth (eds.), *The Meaning of Europe* (Oxford/New York, Berg, 2002) 1, 20

Finland's national history has been characterized by a strong awareness of being either on the brink of Europe or on the margins of Russia or somewhere in between...Meinander traces two basic conceptions of Finnish national identity: the Fennoman that stresses the indigenous features of Finnish culture and sees Finland as a cooperative borderland between the West and Russia, and the liberal that is akin to the Russian *zapadniki* in the sense that it prescribes close integration with the Western and European cultures.[17] For the Fennomans, Russia was in a cultural sense never outside Europe, but the feeling of standing at the edge of Europe was reinforced by the Russian revolution, the Finnish civil war and the foundation of the Soviet Union, which effectively precluded any acknowledgement of the eastern layers of Finnish identity. The Finnish notion of Europe became increasingly polarized not least due to the experiences of Finland being left very much alone in the Second World War. Forced into a policy of friendly neutrality with the Soviet Union after the war Finland rediscovered its role as a mediator between East and West. The Finns began to admit that Russia, even in its Soviet manifestation, was a part of European civilization.

The accession to the EU in 1995 was supported by a feeling that the Finns had at last found an answer to two centuries of uncertainty and identity-searching. Finland had, as it were, ultimately found a synthesis of its two historical roles, to be both on the brink of Western Europe and serve as a bridge-builder toward a Europe that stretched to include Russia and Slavonic Europe. EU membership implies both an improvement of national security and an emotional homecoming.

---

16 See J. Diez Medrano, *Framing Europe: Attitudes to European Integration in Germany, Spain and the United Kingdom* (Princeton, NJ, Princeton University Press, 2003).

17 H. Meinander, 'On the Brink or In Between? The Conception of Europe in Finnish Identity' in M. Malmborg and B. Stråth (eds.), *The Meaning of Europe* (Oxford/New York, Berg, 2002).

If ideas of European union may shape our understandings of national identity, the reverse is also true. Long-standing narratives about national identity can shape citizens' feelings about European union, and their understandings of what it means. A study of debates about Europe within the United Kingdom, Spain and Germany found these all to be informed by understandings of recent national histories.[18] The British perception of themselves as heirs to the British Empire, its successor the Commonwealth, and their sense of being at the centre of an Anglophone world led to particular concerns about the intrusiveness of Europe and its effect on national traditions. Spanish debates, by contrast, were informed by a sense of that country's isolation and lack of modernisation during the Franco period. The association of European union with economic progress was particularly resonant there. In Germany, particularly in the west part, European union symbolised securing democracy and restoring the trust of their neighbours. Debates focused, as a consequence, particularly strongly on the democratic qualities of the European Union.

To argue that understandings of European union and feelings about it are informed by national histories is still too simple. Research suggests that the way in which individuals relate to their own community also informs feelings and understandings about European union.[19] Individuals proud to be part of a political community as opposed to seeing it as a constraint are often those who are most engaged by the ideal of European union. This pride is only likely to turn into support for European union where they perceive it as enlarging this political community or as threatening it. In this regard, whether the European Union is seen as doing one or the other will often depend on how a debate is framed by opinion-formers in that state.[20]

3 THE EUROPEAN COMMUNITIES

(i) From the Treaty of Paris to the Treaty of Rome

The origins of the European Union lie in a crisis provoked by the establishment of the Federal Republic of Germany. In 1949, the Ruhr and the Saar, then under the administration of the International High Commission, were due to be handed back to the Federal Republic. French fears of emerging German industrial might were compounded by Germany's increasing share of European steel production. The French response was a plan drafted by the French civil servant, Jean Monnet, which was known as the Schuman Plan, after the French Finance Minister, Robert Schuman.[21]

Robert Schuman, Declaration of 9 May 1950[22]

Europe will not be made all at once or according to a single plan. It will be built through concrete achievements which first create a de facto solidarity. The coming together of the nations of Europe requires the elimination of the age-old opposition of France and Germany. Any action which must

---

[18] Díez Medrano, n. 16 above, chs. 5–10.

[19] S. Duchesne and A.-P. Frognier, 'National and European Identifications: A Dual Relationship' (2008) 6 *Comparative Political Studies* 143.

[20] S. Hobolt, *Europe in Question: Referendums on European Integration* (Oxford, Oxford University Press, 2009).

[21] W. Diebold, *The Schuman Plan: A Study in International Cooperation* (Oxford, Oxford University Press, 1959).

[22] European Parliament, *Selection of Texts Concerning Institutional Matters of the Community for 1950–1982* (Luxembourg, Office for Official Publications of the European Communities, 1982) 47.

be taken in the first place must concern these two countries. With this aim in view, the French Government proposes that action be taken immediately on one limited but decisive point. It proposes that Franco-German production of coal and steel as a whole be placed under a common High Authority, within the framework of an organisation open to the participation of the other countries of Europe.

The pooling of coal and steel production should immediately provide for the setting up of common foundations for economic development as a first step in the federation of Europe, and will change the destinies of those regions which have long been devoted to the manufacture of munitions of war, of which they have been the most constant victims.

The solidarity in production thus established will make it plain that any war between France and Germany becomes not merely unthinkable, but materially impossible. The setting up of this powerful productive unit, open to all countries willing to take part and bound ultimately to provide all the member countries with the basic elements of industrial production on the same terms, will lay a true foundation for their economic unification.

This Plan formed the basis of the Treaty of Paris in 1951, which established the European Coal and Steel Community (ECSC).[23] This Treaty entered into force on 23 July 1952 and ran for fifty years.[24] It set up a common market in coal and steel, which was supervised by the High Authority, a body independent from the Member States and composed of international civil servants, which had considerable powers to determine the conditions of production and price for coal and steel.[25] The High Authority was, in turn, supervised by a Council, which consisted of Member State representatives. The Treaty of Paris was signed by only six states: the BEN-ELUX states (Netherlands, Belgium and Luxembourg), Italy, France and Germany. The United Kingdom had been invited to the negotiations, but refused to participate, as it opposed both the idea of the High Authority and the remit of its powers.[26]

In 1950, during negotiations for the Treaty of Paris, the Korean War began. The United States, perceiving an increased threat from Stalin's Soviet Union, pressed for German rearmament and its entry into NATO, something which was unwelcome to the French.[27] As a response, the French Defence Minister, Pléven, proposed a European Defence Community. There would be a European army under a European Minister of Defence, administered by a European Commissariat. Once again, Britain was invited to join, but declined on the basis that it preferred an expansion of NATO to the establishment of a European Defence Community (EDC). Nevertheless, a treaty establishing the EDC was signed between the same six states which had

---

[23] On the negotiations, see P. Gerbet, 'The Origins: Early Attempts and the Emergence of the Six (1945–52)' in R. Pryce (ed.), *The Dynamics of European Union* (London, Croom Helm, 1987); R. Bullen, 'An Idea Enters Diplomacy: The Schuman Plan, May 1950' in R. Bullen (ed.), *Ideas into Politics: Aspects of European History 1880–1950* (London, Croom Helm, 1984).

[24] The ECSC expired on 23 July 2002. Decision of the representatives of the Member States meeting within the Council on the consequences of the expiry of the European Coal and Steel Community [2002] OJ L194/35.

[25] A good history is D. Spierenburg and R. Poidevin, *The History of the High Authority of the European Coal and Steel Community: Supranationality in Operation* (London, Weidenfeld & Nicholson, 1994).

[26] E. Dell, *The Schuman Plan and the British Abdication of Leadership in Europe* (Oxford, Clarendon, 1995); C. Lord, '"With But Not Of": Britain and the Schuman Plan, a Reinterpretation' (1998) 4 *Journal of European Integration History* 23.

[27] T. Schwartz, 'The Skeleton Key: American Foreign Policy, European Unity, and German Rearmament, 1949–54' (1986) 19 *Central European History* 369.

signed the ECSC in 1952. However, in 1954, the French National Assembly refused to ratify the treaty.[28]

The failure of the EDC marked a moment of considerable political fluidity. The BENELUX states were increasingly worried by the nationalist policies of the government in France, in particular, its attempt to upgrade bilateral relations with Germany. In 1955, the Belgian Foreign Minister, Henri-Paul Spaak, suggested that there should be integration in a limited number of sectors, notably transport and energy. This worried the Netherlands as it threatened to restrict its efficiencies, particularly in the transport sector. The Dutch Government responded by reactivating the 1953 Beyen Plan, which proposed a common market that would lead to economic union. A meeting of Foreign Ministers was held in Messina, Italy, in 1955. The British were invited, in addition to the six ECSC Member States, but did no more than send a Board of Trade Official. Despite considerable French scepticism, a Resolution was tabled, calling for an Intergovernmental Committee under the chairmanship of Spaak, to be set up to examine the establishment of a common market. As a carrot to the French, it was agreed that this should be done in tandem with examining the possibility of integration in the field of atomic energy. British objections to the supranational elements required for a common market entailed that they were unable to participate in the project.

The Spaak Report, published in 1956, laid the basis for the Treaty Establishing the European Economic Community (EEC Treaty). The Report made a pragmatic distinction between matters affecting the functioning of the common market, which would require a supranational decision-making framework and some supranational supervision of Member States' compliance with their obligations, and more general matters of budgetary, monetary and social policy, which would remain within the reserved competence of the Member States. Where these policies had a significant effect on the functioning of the common market, however, Member States should endeavour to coordinate these policies. An intergovernmental conference (IGC) was convened in Venice, with the Spaak Report as the basis for negotiations. The result was the signing of the Treaties of Rome in 1957 between Germany, France, Italy and the BENELUX states: one establishing the European Economic Community (EEC), the other the European Atomic Energy Community (EURATOM). The treaties duly entered into force on 1 January 1958.[29]

(ii) EEC Treaty

The dominant aim of the EEC Treaty was the establishment of a common market. This can be divided into a number of different elements. The first was the customs union, which required the abolition of all customs duties (taxes levied on imports or exports for crossing a national frontier) or charges having equivalent effect on the movement of goods between Member States and the establishment of a common external tariff. Secondly, the heart of the common market comprised the 'four freedoms'. Restrictions on the free movement of goods, workers,

---

[28] On this ill-fated enterprise, see E. Fursdon, *The European Defence Community: A History* (London, Macmillan, 1980); R. Cardozo, 'The Project for a Political Community (1952–4)' in R. Pryce (ed.), *The Dynamics of European Union* (London, Croom Helm, 1987); R. Dwan, 'Jean Monnet and the Failure of the European Defence Community' (2001) 1 *Cold War History* 141.

[29] The literature on the negotiations is voluminous. E. di Nolfo (ed.), *Power in Europe? Britain, France, Germany, Italy, and the Origins of the EEC, 1952–1957* (Berlin/New York, de Gruyter, 1992); E. Serra (ed.), *The Relaunching of Europe and the Treaties of Rome* (Baden Baden, Nomos, 1989).

services and capital were also prohibited subject to a number of exceptions where a Member State could show that these were threatening a public good (i.e. public health) protected by the Treaty. A procedure was put in place for harmonising national laws where this was the case. An EEC law would be adopted setting out a certain level of protection of that public good. If goods, services and so forth complied with it, they could circulate around the community. Thirdly, a competition policy was set up to ensure that private market barriers and cartels did not undermine the prohibition on state barriers. Fourthly, state intervention in the economy, such as state aids and public undertakings, was closely regulated. Fifthly, Member States' fiscal regimes on goods were regulated so that they could not discriminate against imports. Sixthly, a common commercial policy was established to regulate the Community's trade relations with third states. Finally, provision was made for more general cooperation in the field of economic policy in order that broader economic policy-making did not disrupt the common market.

A number of other policies were established. Arguably, the most famous is the Common Agricultural Policy. At the time, agriculture accounted for about 20 per cent of the European labour force and the memory of the severe deflation in the agricultural sector during the 1930s recession had led to considerable government intervention in the sector. A separate policy was, therefore, required in order to Europeanise the system of state intervention currently in place. A common transport policy was established. As with agriculture, this required a separate heading due to the heavy intervention by Member States in their transport sectors. The EEC Treaty also contained a limited social policy, whose central feature was the establishment of a principle of equal pay for work of equal value for men and women.[30] Finally, an association policy was included to provide for the economic and social development of dependent or formerly dependent territories of the Member States.

The most remarkable feature of the EEC Treaty was the institutional arrangement set up to realise these objectives. There were four central institutions. The Commission, a body of officials independent from the Member States, was responsible, inter alia, for proposing legislation and checking that the Member States and other institutions complied with the Treaty and any secondary legislation. The Assembly, later to develop into the European Parliament, was composed, initially, of national parliamentarians. It was to be consulted in most fields of legislative activity and was the body responsible for holding the Commission to account. The Council was the body in which national governments were represented. It had the power of final decision in almost all areas of EEC activity. It voted by unanimity or, in only a few areas initially, by a weighted form of voting, known as qualified majority voting (QMV). Finally, the Eureopan Court of Justice was established to monitor compliance with EEC law by the Member States and EEC institutions and to rule on references to it made by national courts where a point of EEC law came up in a dispute before them.

(iii) Emergence of two visions of EU law: intergovernmental and supranational

1958 marked not only the coming into force of the Treaties, but also Charles de Gaulle becoming President of France.[31] De Gaulle's vision of European integration was an

---

[30] C. Barnard, 'The Economic Objectives of Article 119' in T. Hervey and D. O'Keeffe (eds.), *Sex Equality Law in the European Union* (Chichester, John Wiley, 1996) 321, 322–4.

[31] An excellent overview of this period is N. Ludlow, *The European Community and the Crises of the 1960s: Negotiating the Gaullist Challenge* (Abingdon, Routledge, 2006).

intergovernmental one. At its heart is a vision that democracy rests upon certain social and political institutions and forms of political community. These must have a certain pedigree and strength if democracy is to be sustained. Currently, these qualities exist only at the level of the nation-state. On such a view, supranationalism – be it decisions of the Court of Justice, majority voting by national governments or proposals by the Commission – is invariably a threat to democracy insofar as it limits the autonomy and power of these national institutions, and has insufficient authority of its own to fall back upon. At a press conference on 15 May 1962, he declared:

> These ideas [supranationalism] might appeal to certain minds but I entirely fail to see how they could be put into practice, even with six signatures at the foot of a document. Can we imagine France, Germany, Italy, the Netherlands, Belgium, Luxembourg being prepared on matters of importance to them in the national or international sphere, to do something that appeared wrong to them, merely because others had ordered them to do so? Would the peoples of France, of Germany, of Italy, of the Netherlands, of Belgium, or of Luxembourg ever dream of submitting to laws passed by foreign parliamentarians if such laws run counter to their deepest convictions? Clearly not.[32]

As early as 1961, De Gaulle had attempted to put this into practice through the Fouchet Plan. This proposed a European Political Community whose remit would cover not only economic, but also political and social affairs. It would be based on intergovernmental cooperation, with each Member State retaining a veto. This failed to gain the support of the other Member States.[33] Tensions were raised further in 1963 when De Gaulle vetoed the accession of the United Kingdom, which, along with Denmark, Norway and Ireland, had applied for membership in 1961.

Matters came to a head in 1965. The Commission had made three proposals: first, increased powers for the Assembly; secondly, a system of 'own resources' so that the Communities were financially independent and not dependent on national contributions; and finally, a series of financial regulations, which would allow the common agricultural policy to make progress. France favoured the third proposal, but was strongly opposed to the first two. The Commission insisted on a 'package deal', however, where Member States either accepted all or none. When negotiations broke down, the French walked out, refusing to take part in further EEC business. De Gaulle came under considerable domestic criticism for this drastic move.[34] Yet, the Commission was also perceived as having adopted a very high-handed approach. The crisis was eventually diffused in January 1966 in Luxembourg, but in a way that would cast a shadow over the development of the EEC for the next twenty years. The Luxembourg Accords, as they came to be known, were an 'agreement to disagree'. If a Member State raised 'very important interests' before a vote in the Council was taken, it was agreed that the matter would not be put to a vote. In essence, it gave every Member State a veto in all fields of decision-making. Whilst

---

[32] This can be found at D. Weigall and P. Stirk, *The Origins and Development of the European Community* (Leicester, Leicester University Press, 1992) 134.

[33] P. Gerbet, 'The Fouchet Negotiations (1960–2)' in R. Pryce, *Dynamics of Political Union* (London, Croom Helm, 1987); N. Ludlow, 'Challenging French Leadership in Europe: Germany, Italy and the Netherlands and the Origins of the Empty Chair Crisis of 1965' (1999) 8 *Contemporary European History* 231.

[34] On De Gaulle's Europe see W. Loth (ed.), *Crises and Compromises: The European Project, 1963–9* (Baden Baden, Nomos, 2001); C. Parsons, *A Certain Idea of Europe* (Ithaca, NY, Cornell University Press, 2003).

this veto was developed at the behest of France, once in place, it was invoked equally freely by all the Member States,[35] even where the interest in question was insignificant.[36]

The early 1960s was also remarkable for another vision of political community – the supranational one – taking hold. The place where this was to happen most visibly was in the Court of Justice, in *Van Gend en Loos*, arguably the most important decision ever given by that court. The facts were arcane. Van Gend en Loos, a Dutch road haulier, was charged an import duty on chemicals imported from Germany by the Dutch authorities.[37] It considered this to be in breach of what is now Article 30 TFEU, which prohibits customs duties or charges having equivalent effect being placed on the movement of goods between Member States. It sought to invoke the provisions in legal proceedings before a Dutch tax court, the Tariefcommissie. The question for the Court of Justice was whether a party could invoke and rely on Treaty provisions in proceedings before a national court. Historically, the justiciability of an international treaty was a matter for the relevant Member State to decide as this went to its internal effects within the latter's sovereign territory. For the Court to state that this was not the case, it had to argue that the EEC Treaty was unlike any other international treaty.[38]

Case 26/62 Van Gend en Loos v Nederlandse Administratie der Belastingen [1963] ECR 1

The first question of the Tariefcommissie is whether Article [30 TFEU] has direct application in national law in the sense that nationals of Member States may on the basis of this Article lay claim to rights which the national court must protect.

To ascertain whether the provisions of an international treaty extend so far in their effects it is necessary to consider the spirit, the general scheme and the wording of those provisions.

The objective of the EEC Treaty, which is to establish a common market, the functioning of which is of direct concern to interested parties in the community, implies that this Treaty is more than an agreement which merely creates mutual obligations between the contracting States. This view is confirmed by the preamble to the Treaty which refers not only to governments but to peoples. It is also confirmed more specifically by the establishment of institutions endowed with sovereign rights, the exercise of which affects Member States and also their citizens. Furthermore, it must be noted that the nationals of the States brought together in the Community are called upon to cooperate in the functioning of this Community through the intermediary of the European Parliament and the Economic and Social Committee.

In addition the task assigned to the Court of Justice under Article [267 TFEU][39] the object of which is to secure uniform interpretation of the Treaty by national courts and tribunals, confirms

---

[35] W. Nicholl, 'The Luxembourg Compromise' (1984) 23 *JCMS* 35. For a modern perspective, see J.-M. Palavret *et al.* (eds.), *Visions, Votes and Vetoes: Reassessing the Luxembourg Compromise 40 Years On* (Brussels, Peter Lang, 2006).

[36] In 1985, they were invoked by Germany to prevent a 1.8 per cent decrease in the price of colza, a cooking oil grain. M. Vasey, 'The 1985 Farm Price Negotiations and the Reform of the Common Agriculture Policy' (1985) 22 *CMLRev.* 649, 664–6.

[37] It was no coincidence that the case came from the Netherlands. The Dutch branch of FIDE, the main European law association, had been pushing for some years for test cases on this. A. Vauchez, 'The Transnational Politics of Judicialization. *Van Gend en Loos* and the Making of EU Polity' (2010) 16 *ELJ* 1, 9–10.

[38] The details of the Court's rulings as regards supremacy and direct effect are considered more fully in Chapters 5 and 7, respectively.

[39] Article 267 TEU enables national courts and tribunals to refer questions of the interpretation of Community law to the Court of Justice. The relationships between national courts and the Court of Justice are considered in detail in Chapter 4.

that the States have acknowledged that Community law has an authority which can be invoked by their nationals before those courts and tribunals. The conclusion to be drawn from this is that the Community constitutes a new legal order of international law for the benefit of which the States have limited their sovereign rights, albeit within limited fields, and the subjects of which comprise not only Member States but also their nationals. Independently of the legislation of Member States, Community law therefore not only imposes obligations on individuals but is also intended to confer upon them rights which become part of their legal heritage. These rights arise not only where they are expressly granted by the Treaty, but also by reason of obligations which the Treaty imposes in a clearly defined way upon individuals as well as upon the Member States and upon the institutions of the Community.

Historians have now discovered that the Court was split down the middle over this judgment, and it was adopted by the barest majority.[40] There were, however, two remarkable features about this terse passage.

The first is a claim about power. It is contained in the statement that: 'the Community constitutes a new legal order of international law for the benefit of which the States have limited their sovereign rights, albeit within limited fields'. At one level, this parroted the language of a number of national constitutions of the time, which, following the Second World War, allowed sovereignty to be limited by treaties or transferred to international institutions.[41] However, it was one thing for a national constitution to state this, and another for the Court of Justice. As stated by the latter, the EEC Treaty has created not merely a legal order that is independent but one claiming to limit the power of national law. National legal systems no longer form the central building block for legal authority within Europe. Rather, legal authority flows from the Treaty with national legal systems having to adapt as sub-units to it.

The second is a claim about the nature of political community within Europe. The justification for the authority of the Treaty is that the EEC exists to benefit not merely the governments but also the peoples of Europe. This characterises the EU legal community as a wider, more plural legal community than other international legal communities. If traditional international law governs mutual obligations between states, EU law recognises other subjects: private parties, be they EU citizens, non-EU nationals or corporations. These are to hold a direct relationship with EU law through its conferring both rights and obligations on them. These rights and obligations, in turn, set up legal relations between them independently of national law. A new legal community was thereby born generating its own mutual commitments and sense of right and wrong. These peoples also act as the justification for the authority of EU law. It is to act in their name, and although *Van Gend en Loos* does not say this explicitly, it conveys the following founding myth, namely, that the European Union may be seen as a settlement between the peoples of Europe that binds their governments, and not simply as an agreement between the governments of Europe that binds their peoples.

---

[40] M. Rasmussen, 'The Origins of a Legal Revolution: The Early History of the European Court of Justice' (2008) 14 *Journal of European Integration History* 77, 93–5.

[41] B. de Witte, 'The European Union as an International Legal Experiment' in G. de Búrca and J. Weiler (eds.), *The Worlds of European Constitutionalism* (Cambridge, Cambridge University Press, 2012) 19, 26–8; K v. Leeuwen, 'On Democratic Concerns and Legal Traditions: The Dutch 1953 and 1956 Constitutional Reforms "Towards" Europe' (2012) 21 *Contemporary European History* 357.

The tension between these two visions of political authority and political community permeate every chapter of this book. In the 1960s and 1970s, the vesting of one vision, the Gaullist one, in the political institutions through the Luxembourg Accords and the other, that of a pan-European political community, in the Court of Justice, led to a peculiar dynamic.[42]

The presence of the veto stymied law-making by the political institutions, albeit that some significant institutional developments did take place. At the signing of the Treaty of Rome, the Convention relating to Certain Institutions Common to the European Communities established a single Court and a single Assembly for the three Communities. In 1963, it was agreed that the other institutions – the Council and the Commission – should be merged, and this took place with the Merger Treaty in 1965.[43] In 1970 the Communities were provided with their own Budget and autonomous revenue stream with the Own Resources Decision.[44] Finally, it was agreed in 1976 that there should be direct elections for the European Parliament.[45] These were first held in 1979 and have since been held at five-year intervals.

By contrast, buoyed by *Van Gend en Loos*, networks of lawyers, academics and Commission officials burgeoned.[46] These pushed European integration forward through litigation. From the 1960s onwards, prompted by their demands, the Court gave a series of integrationist judgments, which developed treaty-making powers for the Community, elaborated rights which could be invoked by individuals against national governments, and detailed the content of the economic freedoms and the competition provisions of the Treaty.[47] Juxtaposed with the inertia of the legislature, this led to the development of a deregulatory bias whereby national policies were prohibited or tightly restricted by the Court, without there being any substitute EEC legislation available to take their place.[48] If this tension gave rise to difficulties, others have noted that it can also give rise to the Union's genius: namely, it has to confront these poles and resolve them in a way that creates a new type of legal authority and political community.

J. Weiler, 'In Defence of the Status Quo: Europe's Constitutional Sonderweg' in J. Weiler and M. Wind (eds.), *European Constitutionalism beyond the State* (Cambridge, Cambridge University Press, 2003) 19–22

There are, it seems to me, two basic strategies for dealing with the alien…One strategy is to remove the boundaries. It is the spirit of 'come, be one of us'. It is noble since it involves, of course, elimination of prejudice, of the notion that there are boundaries that cannot be eradicated. But

---

[42] See J. Weiler, 'The Community System: The Dual Character of Supranationalism' (1981) 1 *YBEL* 267.

[43] P.-H. Houben, 'The Merger of the Executives of the European Communities' (1965) 3 *CMLRev.* 37.

[44] Decision 70/243/EEC [1970] OJ English Special Edition (I) 224.

[45] Decision 76/287/EEC [1976] OJ L278/1. Until 1979 it consisted of representatives of national parliaments.

[46] A. Vauchez and A. Cohen, 'The Social Construction of Law: The European Court of Justice and Its Legal Revolution Revisited' (2011) 7 *Annual Review of Law and Society* 417; A. Bernier, 'Constructing and Legitimating: Transnational Jurist Networks and the Making of a Constitutional Practice of European Law, 1950–70' (2012) 21 *Contemporary European History* 399; M. Rasmussen, 'Establishing a Constitutional Practice: The Role of the European Law Associations' in W. Kaiser and J.-H. Meyer (eds.), *Societal Actors in European Integration: Polity-Building and Policy-Making 1958–1992* (Basingstoke, Palgrave, 2013).

[47] It also led to political tensions. B. Davies, *Resisting the European Court of Justice: West Germany's Confrontation with European Law, 1949–1979* (Cambridge, Cambridge University Press, 2012) chs. 3 and 4.

[48] F. Scharpf, 'Negative and Positive Integration in the Political Economy of European Welfare States' in G. Marks *et al.*, *Governance in the European Union* (London, Sage, 1996).

the 'be one of us', however well intentioned, is often an invitation to the alien to be one of us, by being us. Vis-à-vis the alien, it risks robbing him of his identity. Vis-à-vis oneself, it may be a subtle manifestation of both arrogance and belief in my superiority as well as intolerance. If I cannot tolerate the alien, one way of resolving the dilemma is to make him like me, no longer an alien. This is, of course, infinitely better than the opposite: exclusion, repression, and worse. But it is still a form of dangerous internal and external intolerance.

The alternative strategy of dealing with the alien is to acknowledge the validity of certain forms of non-ethnic bounded identity but simultaneously to reach across boundaries. We acknowledge and respect difference, and what is special and unique about ourselves as individuals and groups; and yet we reach across differences in recognition of our essential humanity. What is significant in this are the two elements I have mentioned. On the one hand, the identity of the alien, as such, is maintained. One is not invited to go out and, say, 'save him' by inviting him to be one of us. One is not invited to recast the boundary. On the other hand, despite the boundaries which are maintained, and constitute the I and the Alien, one is commanded to reach over the boundary and accept him, in his alienship, as oneself. The alien is accorded human dignity. The soul of the I is tended to not by eliminating the temptation to oppress but by learning humility and overcoming it.

The European current constitutional architecture represents this alternative, civilizing strategy of dealing with the 'other'. Constitutional Tolerance is encapsulated in that most basic articulation of its meta-political objective in the preamble to the EC Treaty...: 'Determined to lay the foundations of an ever closer union among the *peoples* of Europe'. No matter how close the Union, it is to remain a union among distinct peoples, distinct political identities, distinct political communities. An ever closer union could be achieved by an amalgam of distinct peoples into one which is both the ideal and/or the de facto experience of most federal and non-federal states. The rejection by Europe of that One Nation ideal or destiny is...intended to preserve the rich diversity, cultural and other, of the distinct European peoples...

[I]n the Community, we subject the European peoples to constitutional discipline even though the European polity is composed of distinct peoples. It is a remarkable instance of civic tolerance to accept being bound by precepts articulated not by 'my people' but by a community composed of distinct political communities...

Constitutional actors in the Member States accept the European constitutional discipline not because, as a matter of legal doctrine, as is the case in the federal state, they are subordinate to a higher sovereignty and authority attaching to norms validated by the federal people, the constitutional demos. They accept it as an autonomous voluntary act, endlessly renewed on each occasion, of subordination, in the discrete areas governed by Europe, to a norm which is the aggregate expression of other wills, other political identities, other political communities. Of course, to do so creates in itself a different type of political community, one unique feature of which is that very willingness to accept a binding discipline which is rooted in and derives from a community of others. The Quebecois are told: in the name of the people of Canada, you are obliged to obey. The French or the Italians or the Germans are told: in the name of the peoples of Europe, you are invited to obey...

This process operates also at Community level. Think of the European judge or the European public official who must understand that, in the peculiar constitutional compact of Europe, his decision will take effect only if obeyed by national courts, if executed faithfully by a national public official [who] belongs to a national administration which claims from them a particularly strong form of loyalty and habit. This, too, will instil a measure of caution and tolerance.

(iv) Early enlargements

The United Kingdom was all too aware that the establishment of a common market left it economically isolated. From 1956 onwards, it pushed for the establishment of a free trade area with other European states, which culminated in its setting up of the European Free Trade Area (EFTA) with Austria, Denmark, Norway, Sweden, Switzerland and Portugal in 1960. By 1961, however, Member States within the EEC were experiencing faster economic growth rates than Britain and the latter's failure to prevent South Africa's expulsion from the Commonwealth, following the Sharpeville massacres, brought home Britain's relative decline on the international stage. As discussed earlier,[49] it applied for membership in 1961 but the French President, De Gaulle, vetoed its entry in 1963. Four years later, the United Kingdom, plus Ireland, Denmark and Norway, reapplied. The application was once again vetoed by De Gaulle. This use of the veto left France increasingly isolated and French policy changed in 1969 with the resignation of De Gaulle. The Six agreed in The Hague to open negotiations with the applicants, with a view to extending membership. The United Kingdom, Denmark and Ireland formally became members on 1 January 1973.[50] However, following a referendum, where 53 per cent voted against membership, Norway did not accede to the EEC.

The next state to join was Greece. Greece applied for membership in 1975, following its establishment of a democratic government. For the Greeks, accession was not only economically attractive, but symbolised modernisation and democratic stability. For the Member States, Greece was important geopolitically during the Cold War because of its strategic location in the Aegean. Membership was, therefore, seen as tying Greece more firmly to the West. Greece became a member in 1981. Like Greece, Spain and Portugal emerged from dictatorships and isolationism in the mid-1970s. They made applications to join the Communities only two years after Greece, in 1977. Yet, accession was more problematic in their cases. The size of the agricultural sector in Spain resulted in initial French resistance to entry due to the likely negative effects on the French agricultural sector. It was, thus, not until 1986 that Spain and Portugal became members.

(v) Single European Act

Things changed in the 1980s. The recession of the early 1980s led national governments to confront their relative economic decline and prompted a relaunch of the integration process, as a way of combating this decline. A Solemn Declaration on European Union was adopted by the Heads of Government in 1983. This proposed few concrete reforms, but declared that there should be a 'renewed impetus' towards completion of the internal market, in particular the removal of obstacles to the free movement of goods, services and capital.[51] This Declaration occurred against the backdrop of a number of significant developments. 1983 marked the collapse of the Keynesian economic policies, which had been adopted in France. This collapse

---

[49] See p. 15.
[50] U. Kitzinger, *Diplomacy and Persuasion: How Britain Joined the Common Market* (London, Thames & Hudson, 1973); C. O'Neill, *Britain's Entry into the European Community: Report on the Negotiations of 1970–1972* (London, Frank Cass, 2000).
[51] For critical comment see J. Weiler, 'The Genscher-Colombo Draft European Act: the Politics of Indecision' (1983) 6 *Journal of European Integration* 129.

led to some convergence between national governments that economic policy-making had to focus on 'supply-side' measures which stimulated competition and trade. Market integration fitted this new consensus.[52] Alongside this, since the 1970s, transnational pressure groups had begun to locate themselves in Brussels. The number of these groups expanded in the early 1980s, leading to the growth of an organised industrial constituency that was increasingly rallying for European solutions.[53] From the early 1980s onwards, major industrialists mobilised through organisations such as the European Round Table (ERT) and UNICE. These groups lobbied aggressively across Europe, arguing for the completion of the common market as a means of promoting European competitiveness.[54] Finally, direct elections had also produced a more aggressive European Parliament. Under the chairmanship of Alfiero Spinelli, it produced a draft Treaty on European Union, which proposed a fully federal Europe with common foreign, macro-economic and trade policies and a developed system of central institutions.[55]

These developments all pressed towards further European integration, but were fragmented and uncoordinated. The final piece in the jigsaw fell into place with the appointment of a new Commission in 1984, headed by the charismatic, former French Finance Minister, Jacques Delors. Delors, in lobbying for the post, had already seized upon the goal of market unity as the principal task of the new Commission to be achieved by the end of 1992. In November 1984, he gave the national governments four choices for recapturing momentum: monetary policy, foreign policy and defence, institutional reform or the internal market.[56] All agreed that the internal market was the way forward.

The Commission was instructed by the Member States to consider the practical steps necessary to realise this. In truth, the idea had been kicking around the Commission for a few years. In 1981, the German Commissioner, Karl-Heinz Narjes, had looked into the idea of creating an 'internal market' in which there were no barriers to the exchange of goods, services and labour, but this had met with opposition from the French Government in 1982.[57] The new British Commissioner, Lord Cockfield, took up Narjes' work, and in June 1985, presented the White Paper on Completion of the Internal Market to the Heads of Government at Milan.[58] The paper was a clever piece of work, suggesting that 279 measures were necessary to realise the internal market. Member States were not, therefore, committing themselves to an open-ended set of

---

[52] On the convergence of national government preferences see K. Middlemas, *Orchestrating Europe: The Informal Politics of European Union 1973–1995* (London, Fontana, 1995) 115–35; A. Moravscik, *The Choice for Europe: Social Purpose and State Power from Messina to Maastricht* (Ithaca, NY, Cornell University Press, 1998) ch. 5; J. Gillingham, *European Integration 1950–2003: Superstate or New Market Economy* (Cambridge, Cambridge University Press, 2003) ch. 9.

[53] N. Fligstein and J. McNichol, 'The Institutional Terrain of the European Union' in W. Sandholtz and A. Stone Sweet (eds.), *European Integration and Supranational Governance* (Oxford, Oxford University Press, 1998) 59, 75–80; N. Fligstein and P. Brantley, 'The Single Market Program and the Interests of Business' in B. Eichengreen and J. Frieden (eds.), *Politics and Institutions in an Integrated Europe* (Berlin, Springer, 1995).

[54] W. Sandholtz and J. Zysman, '1992: Recasting the European Bargain' (1989) 42 *World Politics* 95, 116; M. Cowles, 'Setting the Agenda for a New Europe: The ERT and EC 1992' (1995) 33 *JCMS* 527; Middlemas, n. 52 above, 136–40.

[55] [1984] OJ C77/33. For comment, see R. Bieber *et al.*, *An Ever Closer Union: A Critical Analysis of the Draft Treaty Establishing the European Union* (Luxembourg, Office for Official Publications of the European Communities, 1985).

[56] Middlemas, n. 52 above, 141.

[57] N. Fligstein and I. Mara-Drita, 'How to Make a Market: Reflections on the Attempt to Create a Single Market in the European Union' (1996) 102 *American Journal of Sociology* 1, 11–13.

[58] European Commission, *Completing the Internal Market*, COM(85)310.

obligations, but to a finite and limited project. The project was also cast as largely a technical mission rather than having broader panoramas of greater integration.[59] For all this, the goal of the internal market was unattainable whilst unanimity voting prevailed in the Council. This was firmly opposed by Britain, Denmark and Greece. Notwithstanding this, the Italian Government called for a conference to amend the Treaties.[60] Despite their opposing stance, all three states attended. The result was the signing of the Single European Act in 1986.

The principal achievements of the SEA appeared modest at the time. They were described as a victory for minimalism,[61] and both the Commission and the Parliament were relaxed about the Act.[62] Much of the SEA was therefore about giving formal recognition to policies and practices which were already being carried out, albeit under other headings. Provision was made for express competencies in health and safety at work, economic and social cohesion, research and development and environmental protection. A Title was added codifying intergovernmental cooperation in foreign policy. The European Council, the meetings of Heads of Government, was formally acknowledged.[63] However, there had been regular summits from 1961 and it was agreed in 1974 that these should meet twice a year to discuss internal difficulties within the European Communities, broader issues about the future of European integration, and the place of the European Communities in the world order.

There were two reforms, which were to mark the SEA, with hindsight, as the most significant treaty reform in the Union's history. The first was the commitment to establish the internal market by 31 December 1992. The internal market is now set out in Article 46(2) TFEU:

> The internal market shall comprise an area without internal frontiers in which the free movement of goods, persons, services and capital is ensured in accordance with the provisions of the Treaties.

The second was the institutional reform to realise this objective. A new legislative procedure, the cooperation procedure, was introduced, which provided for QMV in the Council and increased powers for the European Parliament.[64]

Neither reform seemed radical at the time. The internal market project seemed simply a restatement of the old dream of establishing a common market. The new voting procedures did not apply to core areas such as taxation and freedom of persons, and their effect upon the Luxembourg Accords was uncertain, particularly as the United Kingdom, Greece and Denmark insisted upon a Declaration being appended to the SEA claiming that nothing within it affected Member States' rights to invoke the Accords. However, the SEA confounded expectations and changed both the legislative and political culture of the Union. In legislative terms, Member States became less tolerant of attempts to invoke the Luxembourg Accords. This was reflected in the 1987 Council Decision on the 'vote to go to a vote', where it was agreed that if a simple majority of Member States voted to go to a formal vote, then a vote should be taken.[65]

---

[59] Sandholtz and Zysman, n. 54 above, 114–15.
[60] On the controversial manner in which it did this see L. v. Middelaar, *The Passage to Europe: How a Continent Became a Union* (New Haven, CT, Yale University Press, 2013) 100–11.
[61] G. Bermann, 'The Single European Act: A New Constitution for the European Community?' (1989) 27 *Columbia Journal of Transnational Law* 529; A. Moravscik, 'Negotiating the Single European Act' (1991) 45 *IO* 19.
[62] C.-D. Ehlermann, 'The Internal Market Following the Single European Act' (1987) 24 *CMLRev.* 361.
[63] Article 2 SEA.
[64] This legislative procedure no longer exists. It has been superseded by the ordinary legislative procedure.
[65] Council Rules of Procedure, Art. 5 [1987] OJ L291/27.

The legislative processes became energised. By the end of 1990, all the measures contained in the White Paper had been formally proposed by the Commission.[66] By the end of 1992, almost 95 per cent of the measures had been enacted and 77 per cent had entered into force in the Member States.[67] Alongside this, the Commission had vastly understated the legislative output of the European Communities. Legislative output increased to 2,500 binding acts per year by 1994.[68] 53 per cent of the legislative measures adopted in France in 1991 were inspired by its Treaty obligations and 30 per cent of all Dutch legislation during the 1990s implemented Union legislation.[69]

4 ESTABLISHMENT OF THE EUROPEAN UNION

(i) Road to Maastricht

The transformation brought about by the SEA in both the levels of law-making done by the Communities and in their political salience generated a far more widespread belief in their capacities. Combined with the end of the division of Europe with the collapse of the Berlin Wall, it also instigated an outbreak of pan-European idealism in many policy-makers and citizens[70] as well as increased anxieties about the Communities overreaching themselves.[71] The economic context was a more uncertain one. The later 1980s marked a period of relaxation of currency controls. Free movement of capital created instability both for weaker states' currencies and for their public finances.[72] It also appeared to threaten the single market. As early as 1987, the Commission indicated that due to the uncertainty generated by national currency instability, the gains anticipated for the single market could not be fully realised without some form of economic and monetary union.[73]

Monetary union thus fitted the aspirations of those, notably President Mitterand of France and President Kohl of Germany, who saw it as the cantilever to open the door to greater political integration and those wishing protection against currency volatility. In June 1988, at Hanover, the Heads of State asserted that 'the Single European Act confirmed the objective of progressive realisation of economic and monetary union'.[74] The Delors Committee, a committee of central

---

[66] *Twenty Fourth Report on the General Activities of the European Communities 1990* (Luxembourg, Office for Official Publications of the European Communities, 1991) 53. For an insight into how the Commission operated during this period see G. Ross, *Jacques Delors and European Integration* (London, Polity, 1995).

[67] *Twenty Sixth General Report on the Activities of the European Communities 1992* (Luxembourg, Office for Official Publications of the European Communities, 1993) 35.

[68] W. Wessels, 'An Ever Closer Fusion? A Dynamic Macropolitical View on Integration Processes' (1997) 35 *JCMS* 267, 276.

[69] G. Mancini, 'Europe: The Case for Statehood' (1998) 4 *ELJ* 29, 40.

[70] This idealism is well captured in the first lines of J. Weiler, 'The Transformation of Europe' (1991) 100 *Yale Law Journal* 2403, 2405–6.

[71] This is most famously captured in the speech given by Margaret Thatcher, the British Prime Minister, at the College of Europe where she expressed opposition to the ideological direction taken by the Communities and their levels of intervention. See www.margaretthatcher.org/speeches/displaydocument.asp%3F;docid=107332. However, others expressed concern. On the worries of François Mitterand see L. v. Middelaar, n. 60 above, 186–7.

[72] K. Mcnamara, 'Consensus and Constraint: Ideas and Capital Mobility in European Monetary Integration' (1999) 37 *JCMS* 455.

[73] T. Padoa-Schioppa *et al.*, *Efficiency, Stability and Equity: A Strategy for the Evolution of the Economic System of the European Community* (Oxford, Oxford University Press, 1987).

[74] Conclusions of Hanover European Council, *EU Bulletin*, 6–1988, 1.1.1–1.1.5.

bank governors chaired by the Commission President, Jacques Delors, was mandated to examine the concrete steps required to realise this goal.

In June 1989, at Madrid, the Delors Report on economic and monetary union was submitted to the Heads of State in Madrid. This Report suggested a gradualist approach to monetary union, which was to be completed in three stages. The final stage would necessitate a European Central Bank fully taking over national central bank functions and assuming a monopoly over the money supply.[75] In December 1989, in Strasbourg, it was agreed that an intergovernmental conference should be held to amend the Treaties, with a view to securing economic and monetary union. Presidents Kohl and Mitterand considered that such a union would be unsustainable without further political integration, and launched an initiative to that effect in April 1990.[76] In June 1990, it was agreed that a separate conference should be held on political union.[77] These parallel conferences culminated in the signing of the Treaty on European Union, at Maastricht, on 10 December 1991.[78]

(ii) Maastricht and the Union's three legitimation strategies

The Treaty on European Union (TEU) was a different beast from the SEA. The latter was presented as largely finishing unfinished business of the common market promised at the Treaty of Rome in 1957, even if the level of legal integration required to meet this had surprised many. The TEU, by contrast, created a new form of political project. Its central institution, monetary union, was traditionally viewed as one of the core prerogatives of the modern nation-state, namely, the right to print its own money. It was, furthermore, not simply setting up a new project, but also proclaiming its own set of political values and political communities. This shift is reflected in the first Article of the TEU, the first two paragraphs of which stand unaltered from those agreed at Maastricht.

Article 1 TEU

By this Treaty, the HIGH CONTRACTING PARTIES establish among themselves a EUROPEAN UNION, hereinafter called 'the Union' on which the Member States confer competences to attain objectives they have in common.

This Treaty marks a new stage in the process of creating an ever closer union among the peoples of Europe, in which decisions are taken as openly as possible and as closely as possible to the citizen.

---

[75] European Commission, *Report on Economic and Monetary Union in the European Community by Committee for the Study of Economic and Monetary Union* (Luxembourg, Office for Official Publications of the European Communities, 1989).

[76] On the negotiations leading to Maastricht see C. Mazzucelli, *France and Germany at Maastricht: Politics and Negotiations to Create the European Union* (New York, Garland, 1997); K. Dyson and K. Featherstone, *The Road to Maastricht: Negotiating Economic and Monetary Union* (Oxford, Oxford University Press, 1999).

[77] Political union was added very much as an afterthought to economic and monetary union and negotiations were not well prepared. R. Corbett, 'The Intergovernmental Conference on Political Union' (1992) 30 *JCMS* 271.

[78] The most detailed analysis of the negotiations is F. Laursen and S. Vanhoonacker, *The Intergovernmental Conference on Political Union: Institutional Reforms, New Policies and International Identity of the European Community* (Dordrecht, Martijnus Nijhoff, 1992).

In short, a new political system was to be created. Such a system would not merely need to be acceptable to the citizens it ruled, it would also have to engage them and give them some sense of co-authorship over it. For all this, the European Union would need a strategy. Luuk van Middelaar has observed that such a strategy has three different elements.

> **L. v. Middelaar, *The Passage to Europe: How a Continent Became a Union* (New Haven, CT, Yale University Press, 2013) 223–4**
>
> There are three basic forms, three notions that can lend credibility to a sense of 'we Europeans'. These are 'our people', 'to our advantage' and 'our decisions'. With a nod to history we might call them the 'German', 'Roman' and 'Greek' strategies. European politics has taken shape by deploying these three strategies by turns.
>
> The 'German' strategy relies on a cultural or historical identity shared by rulers and ruled. They speak the same language, or believe in the same values and holy scriptures, or have the same customs, or ancestors who fought the same wars. The public is supposed to feel that 'they' (the rulers) and 'we' (the ruled) belong to the same people. Around 1800, German thinkers such as Herder, Schlegel and Fichte turned nationalism (which emerged with and in the wake of the French revolution) into an intellectual narrative. They felt they were part of a single German culture, which regrettably lacked a state. In their work they wanted to arouse a sense of being a nation. State power would follow. This ideological programme found imitators all over Europe. From London to Belgrade and from Paris to Palermo people used the same strategies to make a national identity visible, or indeed to generate one. A national history, a flag and anthem, national holidays, conscription and compulsory education, the codification of an official language, monuments to heroes, the 'invention of traditions' – these are all familiar elements.
>
> The 'Roman' strategy bases its appeal on the benefits that people derive from a functioning political system. Rulers offer protection. They create opportunities or distribute money. The public they have in mind consists of clients. The reference is therefore not to republican Rome but to imperial Rome – to the Rome in which the citizen has no voice and the populace was mollified with 'bread and circuses'. Of all the benefits that imperial Rome offered its people, security was the most fundamental. The *pax romana* – along with more material benefits such as aqueducts or baths – was a trump card for an empire attempting to bind foreign peoples to its authority.
>
> The 'Greek' strategy, finally, rests on periodic appraisal by the population of representatives who take decisions on its behalf. Sometimes this is supplemented by a direct vote by the people on specific matters. The aim is to ensure that rules and decisions are felt to be 'our concern'. To this end, a democracy gives the public a vote. The origins of the majority principle (on which rest both direct democracy and its modern, representative version) lie in Ancient Greece. In the 'Greek' strategy, the public is allocated a remarkably powerful role, and in the long run this increases a state's political capacity to respond to an open future.

Altering their sequence, it is possible to identify these strategies coming into play at Maastricht and most of the Treaty reforms subsequent to it. The Roman strategy of securing advantage for the Union's citizens and by showing them that the Union was responsible for it was played out through the acquisition and formalisation of new Union competencies. The justification in all cases was that Union action in a new field of activity brings advantages for these citizens which they did not currently enjoy. The Greek strategy involved reforming the institutional sphere to make the decision-making process (as the Treaty makers saw it) more effective and more democratic.

At Maastricht, these three strategies of *additional competencies, collective identity formation* and *institutional reform* all came into play.

A wide array of competencies was added to the Union's formal powers. In addition to those already enjoyed, the Union was to enjoy new competencies in the fields of visas, education, culture, public health, social policy, consumer protection, the establishment of trans-European networks in transport, energy and telecommunications, industrial policy and development cooperation. In addition, there was a common foreign and security policy, and cooperation in justice and home affairs: a ragbag field focused on migration of non-EU nationals, judicial cooperation in civil and criminal matters and common policing arrangements to combat international crime.

The most high profile new policy was that of economic and monetary union. The Treaty followed the three stage structure of the Delors Report, with the third stage of economic and monetary union beginning on 1 January 1999.[79] The third stage involved monetary policy becoming the responsibility of an independent European Central Bank, established in Frankfurt, which was to be exclusively responsible for authorising the issue of the new European currency, the euro, and for the setting of short-term interest rates. Constraints were also to be placed on national fiscal policy through the limiting of the size of the deficits that governments could run. A procedure was established whereby governments participating in the euro could be heavily sanctioned if they ran an excessive deficit.

The strategy of collective identity formation centred on one significant innovation: European citizenship. All EU nationals were now to be EU citizens. The rights were much more limited than those granted by national citizenship, however. Citizens were granted new rights to free movement around the Union and to access to social benefits in other Member States. New possibilities for democratic participation at both local and European Parliament elections were also created. Beyond the formal rights generated by Union citizenship lay its symbolism, however. It suggested a community of citizens, with mutual expectations of one another, and ties which lay beyond the nation-state, and offered an alternate model for political identity.

Finally, Maastricht gave far more serious consideration to the 'democratic' nature of the Union decision-making processes than the SEA. A new legislative procedure was introduced, today called the ordinary legislative procedure, which gave the European Parliament the power to veto legislation, albeit that this procedure applied in a limited number of fields of EU competence. The place of national parliaments was recognised for the first time, albeit in a fairly minimal manner with a Declaration committing governments to involving them more within the integration process. New stake-holders were introduced, most notably the Committee of the Regions which, whilst only being given consultative powers, created a voice for the European regions within the Community policy process. The TEU was also concerned with administrative accountability. To that end, an Ombudsman was established to consider acts of maladministration by the EU institutions.

Each of these strategies faces challenges. The strategy of additional competencies appeals to people's sense of self-advancement. However, any policy or law will generate winners and

---

[79] It was initially envisaged that the third stage could begin as early as 31 December 1996 if the convergence criteria were met by sufficient Member States: Article 109j(3) EC. At the Cannes Summit, in 1995, it was agreed that the date for the third stage should be 1 January 1999, *EU Bulletin*, 6–1995, 1.11.

losers. In some cases, even beneficiaries will perceive themselves as hard done by as they do not benefit as much as others.[80] The strategy provides nothing for these losers, and certainly no reason to accept the authority of the Union other than personal self-sacrifice. Furthermore, these effects and the consequent feelings of hostility are likely to grow as a result of the distributive consequences of EU law, something that will happen as more EU law is adopted. Collective identity formation faces the difficulty that it is problematic to create common identities. They can appear fake and propagandist.[81] They can also be built on ethically problematic foundations or, alternately, appropriate values and good things that are seen in more general terms, such as fundamental rights, as their own. Finally, inevitably, even if they can complement them, they also compete with other identities.[82] The strategy of popular engagement through institutional reform, van Middelaar has noted, is particularly difficult to realise. A feature of Europe's public is that they are free, diverse and contradictory. This freedom implies a freedom not to become engaged and to disagree violently. Furthermore, insofar as it invites them to be above all an audience for decisions taken by Union legislatures and administrators, they may acquire a sense that this is all that is being asked of them and become correspondingly disenchanted.[83]

Already, at Maastricht, these pressures were apparent in three different ways.

In the first place, there was opposition to all fields of the Union being brought under a single supranational framework. To this end, a three pillar structure was introduced.[84] The first pillar, that of the European Communities, within which the vast majority of activities took place (including economic and monetary union), was to be subject to the full force of supranational rules. This was not to be the case in the two other pillars which were to be much more intergovernmental in nature. The second pillar comprised foreign and security policy, and the third, Justice and Home Affairs. The Parliament and the Court of Justice were only minimally associated with either the second or third pillars. Whilst the Commission was associated quite strongly with the work of the third pillar on Justice and Home Affairs, it was almost completely excluded from the second pillar. This structure, most notably the third pillar, was not uncontroversial, and there was, consequently, a commitment to a further IGC to reconsider them in 1996.

The second response was the development of the subsidiarity principle. In areas of joint competence between the Union and the Member States, the Union was only to act if the objectives of the proposed action could not be sufficiently achieved by the Member States and by reason of its scale or effects the action could be better achieved by the Community.

The final response was the move towards differentiation in the participation of the various Member States in the integration process. The most notable was in regard to economic and monetary union (EMU) where Protocols were agreed reserving the right of the United Kingdom and Denmark not to participate in the third stage of EMU. All Member States, other than the

---

[80] F. Scharpf, *Governing in Europe: Effective and Democratic?* (Oxford, Oxford University Press, 1999) 8–9.

[81] C. Shore, *Building Europe: The Cultural Politics of European Integration* (London, Routledge, 2000) chs. 1–4.

[82] Just over half of the Union's citizens see themselves as having a dual identity, national and European. Just under half see themselves as being either European or national. R. Rose, *Representing Europeans: A Pragmatic Approach* (Oxford, Oxford University Press, 2013) 64–6.

[83] L. v. Middelaar, *The Passage to Europe: How a Continent Became a Union* (New Haven, CT, Yale University Press, 2013) 291–307.

[84] Allegedly, the idea was first suggested by a French negotiator, Pierre de Boissieu, and was constructed around the metaphor of a temple based on three pillars: Middlemas, n. 52 above, 188.

United Kingdom, also wished to extend EU social policy to all main areas of labour law. The compromise was a Protocol, which authorised all the Member States, apart from the United Kingdom, to establish an Agreement on Social Policy that would bind only those Member States, but would allow them access to existing EU machinery and resources. Finally, Ireland and Denmark respectively obtained Protocols protecting their abortion law and legislation on ownership of second homes from EU law.

For all this, the Maastricht provisions on subsidiarity and differentiated participation were brief. There was little recognition at the time that they were manifestations of a more general condition of the European Union, namely, the presence of deep-seated differences about both the level and form of intervention in which it should engage and about the policies it should develop. These differences existed between societies and within societies. The Union would have to return time and again after Maastricht to address this condition.

(iii) Ratification of Treaty on European Union and end of permissive consensus

On 2 June 1992, the Danes voted against ratification of the TEU by 50.7 per cent to 49.3 per cent. This shook the process to the core as the Treaty could not enter into effect unless all Member States ratified it. However, the belief that integration benefited from a permissive consensus for it was shattered. To boost the credibility of the ratification process, President Mitterand decided to hold a referendum in France. It soon became a very close contest, with only 51 per cent of the vote being in favour of ratification. The Danish referendum also signalled the beginning of a bitter legislative fight in the British Parliament, in which legislation was only adopted in July 1993 – a year and a half after the Treaty had been agreed – after the Government had put it forward as a motion of confidence, with the consequence that if it had fallen, the Government would have had to resign.[85]

The Treaty was salvaged at Edinburgh, in December 1992. A Decision was adopted 'interpreting' the Treaty giving the Danish Government guarantees about the autonomy on citizenship and defence as well as setting out in more detail the subsidiarity principle.[86] This gave the Danish Government the necessary breadth to hold a second referendum. This was duly held in May 1993, with 56 per cent voting in favour of ratification. The drama of ratification now simply moved to the courts. Challenges to the Treaty were made before the British, French, Danish and Spanish courts.[87] It was the challenge before the German Constitutional Court, in October 1993, which was to have the most far-reaching consequences.[88] In its judgment, the German Constitutional Court placed markers on the nature and limits of European integration. It ruled that democratic legitimacy is constituted above all at a national level. Within this setting, the constitutionality of the European Union rests on its being an organisation with limited powers

---

[85] R. Rawlings, 'Legal Politics: The United Kingdom and Ratification of the Treaty on European Union' (1994) *PL* 254 and 367; D. Baker, A. Gamble and S. Ludlum, 'The Parliamentary Siege of Maastricht: Conservative Divisions and British Ratification' (1994) 47 *Parliamentary Affairs* 37.

[86] D. Howarth, 'The Compromise on Denmark and the Treaty on European Union: A Legal and Political Analysis' (1994) 31 *CMLRev.* 465.

[87] *R v Secretary of State for Foreign and Commonwealth Affairs ex parte Rees-Mogg* [1994] QB 552 (Britain); *Re Treaty on European Union* (Decision 92–308), Journal Officiel de la République Française 1992, No. 5354 (France); *Re Treaty on European Union* [1994] 3 CMLR 101 (Spain).

[88] *Brunner* v. *European Union* [1994] 1 CMLR 57.

operated in a democratically accountable fashion. Further integration would only be possible if it did not fundamentally undermine national self-government.

The TEU entered into force on 1 November 1993 but the environment was now heavily polarised. Public support for the European Union had diminished[89] and deep divisions had emerged between national governments about which direction to take.[90] Member States had, however, committed themselves at Maastricht to a further IGC in 1996.[91] Negotiations began in earnest in the latter half of 1996. The Treaty of Amsterdam was signed on 2 October 1997.

(iv) Treaty of Amsterdam

Amsterdam adopted the same strategy as Maastricht of extending Union competencies. New policies in the field of employment and equal opportunities were added. With a change of government in the United Kingdom, the Protocol on Social Policy was abolished, and social policy was placed on the same footing as other EU policies. However, the central monument of the Treaty of Amsterdam was the Area of Freedom, Security and Justice (AFSJ). The AFSJ is now set out in the following terms.

Article 67 TFEU

1. The Union shall constitute an area of freedom, security and justice with respect for fundamental rights and the different legal systems and traditions of the Member States.
2. It shall ensure the absence of internal border controls for persons and shall frame a common policy on asylum, immigration and external border control, based on solidarity between Member States, which is fair towards third-country nationals. For the purpose of this Title, stateless persons shall be treated as third-country nationals.
3. The Union shall endeavour to ensure a high level of security through measures to prevent and combat crime, racism and xenophobia, and through measures for coordination and cooperation between police and judicial authorities and other competent authorities, as well as through the mutual recognition of judgments in criminal matters and, if necessary, through the approximation of criminal laws.
4. The Union shall facilitate access to justice, in particular through the principle of mutual recognition of judicial and extra-judicial decisions in civil matters.

To realise the AFSJ, the Treaty of Amsterdam first integrated the Schengen Agreements and their acquis into the legal framework of the TEU. These Agreements, signed in 1985 and 1990, between all the Member States other than Ireland and the United Kingdom, provided for the abolition of frontier checks between parties and a common external frontier. To realise this, the 1990 Convention had provided for intergovernmental cooperation in the fields of migration of non-EU nationals, crime and policing.[92] Secondly, the AFSJ brought immigration, asylum,

---

[89] Opinion polls showed that those who considered the European Union a 'good thing' had dropped from 72 per cent in 1990 to 48 per cent in autumn 1996. *Eurobarometer, Public Opinion in the EU, Report No. 46, Autumn 1996* (Luxembourg, Office for Official Publications of the European Communities, 1997).

[90] A summary of all the positions taken by the Member States at the 1996 Intergovernmental Conference can be found at www.europarl.europa.eu/igc1996/fiches/fiche36_en.htm%23;4.

[91] This had initially been intended to foreclose some of the intergovernmental arrangements agreed at Maastricht.

[92] This is now to be found at [2000] OJ L239/19. Iceland, Switerland, Liechtenstein and Norway are also members.

the rights of non-EU nationals and judicial cooperation on civil matters within the first pillar of the European Communities. Policing and judicial cooperation on criminal matters remained subject to the predominantly intergovernmental procedures of the third pillar.

In terms of collective identity formation, Amsterdam oriented Union identity much more strongly around fundamental rights. This was marked most strongly in a new Article 6 TEU, which stated that the Union was to be founded on the 'principles of liberty, democracy, respect for human rights and fundamental freedoms, and the rule of law'. Furthermore, provision was made for a Member State to have its rights suspended under the TEU or to be expelled from the European Union, where it was deemed to have seriously and persistently breached these ideals.

There was also significant reform of the decision-making processes. Extension of QMV led to a majority of activities now being decided by that form of voting.[93] The most notable feature, however, was the increase in parliamentary involvement provided by the Treaty. The scope of the ordinary legislative procedure was extended considerably. Alongside this, a Protocol on National Parliaments granted national parliaments legal entitlements within the decision-making process for the first time, most notably a six-week period between proposals being announced and their being placed on the legislative agenda to allow them to consider these. Finally, administrative accountability was strengthened by the principle of transparency being formally incorporated into the Treaty.

However, Amsterdam also reflected the growing multiplicity of tensions surrounding the pace, direction and form of European integration. A Protocol on the Application of the Principles of Subsidiarity and Proportionality was agreed, entrenching in Treaty law the Declarations agreed at Edinburgh. It was clear, however, that a 'one size fits all' approach was becoming harder to manage as disagreements about the fields and intensity of the integration process became more entrenched. Provision was made, therefore, for a majority of Member States to engage, as a last resort, in 'enhanced cooperation':[94] adoption of EU laws amongst themselves where agreement was not possible involving all the EU Member States. Alongside this, the United Kingdom and Ireland obtained Protocols preserving their right to decide whether to opt-in to individual pieces of legislation on immigration, asylum and other policies concerning free movement of persons, as well as Protocols preserving their rights to impose frontier controls on persons coming from other Member States. In like vein, Denmark negotiated a Protocol stating that it would only be bound by such legislation under its general obligations in international law, as a Schengen signatory, and not by virtue of EU law.

5 RECASTING THE BORDERS OF THE EUROPEAN UNION

The shape of the European Union was modified by two events at the end of the 1980s. The success of the SEA entailed that exclusion from the world's largest trading bloc posed significant economic risks for neighbouring states. At the same time, communism collapsed in Central and Eastern Europe. Many of these states now saw Union membership as the anchor around which changes in their societies could be made.

The process of expansion began with the EFTA states (Norway, Sweden, Finland, Iceland, Austria, Liechtenstein and Switzerland). In 1991, the Treaty of Oporto was signed, establishing

---

[93] A. Maurer, 'The Legislative Powers and Impact of the European Parliament' (2003) 41 *JCMS* 227, 229.
[94] See pp. 135–9.

the European Economic Area (EEA).[95] The EFTA states were required to adopt all EU legislation in the fields of the internal market, research and development policy, social policy, education, consumer protection and environmental protection in return for access to the internal market.

In June 1993, the European Union agreed that membership be offered to Austria, Finland, Sweden and Norway.[96] Referendums were held in all four states. In Austria and Finland, comfortable majorities voted in favour of membership. However, that in Sweden was narrow. The Norwegians voted narrowly against membership. The three new Member States acceded to the TEU on 2 January 1995.

More challenging was the question of possible membership of the former communist States of Central and Eastern Europe. By the early 1990s, twelve of these had applied for membership.[97] This would almost double the size of the Union with a corresponding reduction of political influence for existing Member States. It would create a financial burden on current members as the applicants were poorer than the Western European states and many had large agricultural populations, which could press claims for support from the Union Budget. Nevertheless, in 1993, at Copenhagen, the European Union agreed that the states of Central and Eastern Europe could become members of the European Union once able to satisfy the obligations of membership. These obligations required new Member States to have:

- stable institutions guaranteeing democracy, the rule of law, human rights and respect for and protection of minorities;
- a functioning market economy as well as the capacity to cope with competitive pressure and market forces within the Union;
- the ability to assume the obligations of membership, including both adherence to the aims of the EU and adoption of all existing Union legislation;
- the legislative and administrative capacity to transpose Union legislation into national legislation and to implement it effectively through appropriate administrative and judicial structures.[98]

In 1997, the Commission, in a 1,300 page document, assessed how far the applicant states met the criteria agreed in Copenhagen. On the basis of that report, it recommended the opening of membership negotiations with the Czech Republic, Poland, Hungary, Slovenia, Estonia and Cyprus in March 1998 and with Bulgaria, Romania, Latvia, Lithuania, Malta and Slovakia in 2000. In Copenhagen, in December 2002, the Member States agreed that all these states, other than Bulgaria and Romania, should become members of the European Union from 1 May 2004. The latter two acceded to the Union on 1 January 2007, bringing the size of the Union to twenty-seven Member States. The final state to join was Croatia. Accession negotiations began at the end of 2005 and an accession treaty was signed in December 2011. Croatia duly joined the Union on 1 July 2013.

The list of states still applying to join the Union is considerable. The Former Yugoslav Republic of Macedonia (FYROM) has candidate status. This is a status where the state has applied to

---

[95] Although Switzerland signed the Treaty, following a referendum, it decided not to ratify it.

[96] M. Jorna, 'The Accession Negotiations with Austria, Finland, Sweden and Norway: A Guided Tour' (1995) 20 *ELRev.* 131; F. Granell, 'The European Union's Enlargement Negotiations with Austria, Finland, Norway and Sweden' (1995) 33 *JCMS* 117.

[97] These were Bulgaria, Cyprus, Czech Republic, Estonia, Hungary, Latvia, Lithuania, Malta, Poland, Romania, Slovenia and Slovakia.

[98] This last condition was added at Madrid in December 1995.

join the Union. The European Union believes that the state in question can meet and is committed to meeting the Copenhagen criteria, but indicates a number of further steps must be taken
before accession negotiations can be opened. Four states are currently in accession negotiations
with the Union: Iceland, Montenegro, Turkey and Serbia.

This relationship is seldom straightforward for either party. FYROM was granted candidate
status only a year later than Croatia in 2005, but accession negotiations have still not begun
despite a Commission recommendation in 2009 that they begin. Concerns continue to be expressed by the Union about the commitment to the rule of law, levels of political conflict, the
quality of public administration and FYROM's relations with other states.[99] The most tortuous
relationship has been between the Union and Turkey. Formal relations go back over fifty years
to the signing of an Association Agreement in 1963. In 1987, Turkey applied for membership
of the European Union. It was not until 1999 that the Member States recognised Turkey's eligibility for membership and that this should be assessed according to the Copenhagen criteria.
In December 2004, it was agreed that accession negotiations should open in October 2005. In
December 2006, these were disrupted over the refusal by Turkey to admit ships or planes flying
the Cypriot flag into its ports or airports. This refusal was influenced by a perception that the
European Union was not doing enough to improve the lot of the Turkish Cypriot community
in the north of Cyprus. As a consequence, the European Union decided that there would be no
negotiations in eight fields[100] and it would not consider negotiations in any field closed until
this matter was resolved. Negotiations have effectively stalled since then.

The expansion of the Union to twenty-eight Member States has transformed it. It can now
claim to be a pan-European organisation rather than predominantly a West European one.
This, in turn, raises acute questions about the identity of the European Union. Turkey would be
the largest state to join the Union since 1957. It would be the first predominantly Islamic state
and would extend the Union's borders far into Asia.[101] Commission surveys have regularly
shown that only just over 30 per cent of EU citizens favour Turkish membership.[102] Analysis
suggests that the economic costs or benefits of Turkish membership play only a small role.
Instead, views are shaped by the perception that Turkey is too culturally different from the
European Union by those opposed to Turkish membership, or the perception that the Union
should be a liberal order capable of embracing all those who sign up to its values by those
supportive of Turkish membership.[103] These views have as much to do with (mis)conceptions
about European identity as about the nature of Turkey: whether Europe should still be seen as
a Christian club, an evangelising force for liberal values, or, as some have argued, a place not
to minimise differences but to mediate between them.[104]

The political economies of the Member States are also now very diverse. Economically, the
GDP per capita (even after rescaling it to account for purchasing power parity) of Luxembourg

---

[99] European Commission, *The Former Yugoslav Republic of Macedonia: Implementation of Reforms Within the Framework of the High Level Accession Dialogue and Promotion of Good Neighbourly Relations*, COM(2013)205.

[100] These were free movement of goods, right of establishment and freedom to provide services, financial services, agriculture and rural development, fisheries, transport policy, customs union and external relations.

[101] European Commission, *Staff Working Paper on Issues Arising from Turkey's Membership Perspective*, COM(2004)656.

[102] See www.publications.parliament.uk/pa/cm201012/cmselect/cmfaff/1567/156710.htm.

[103] A. Ruiz-Jiménez and J. Torreblanca, *European Public Opinion and Turkey's Accession: Making Sense of Arguments For and Against* (Brussels, Centre for European Policy Studies, 2007) 16–23.

[104] E. Balibar, 'Europe as Vanishing Mediator' (2003) *Constellations* 312, 332–3.

is just under six times that of Bulgaria.[105] Trust in democratic institutions varies considerably. In September 2012, only 9 per cent of Czechs, for example, trusted their national parliament whereas the equivalent figure for Swedes was 68 per cent.[106] This is not to be decried but, inevitably, reshapes the European Union. This diversity raises questions about whether it is possible to press forward with common policies across so many different fields. Majone, in particular, has argued that this is increasingly unrealistic and that we will increasingly witness arrangements involving some Member States but not others.

G. Majone, 'Unity in Diversity: European Integration and the Enlargement Process' (2008) 33 *European Law Review* 457, 470–1

An association established to provide excludable public goods is a *club*. Two elements determine the optimal size of a club. One is the cost of producing the club good – in a large club this cost is shared over more members. The second element is the cost to each club member of a good not meeting precisely his or her individual needs or preferences. The latter cost is likely to increase with the size of the club. Therefore the optimal size is determined by the point at which the marginal benefit from the addition of one new member, i.e. the reduction in the per capita cost of producing the good, equals the marginal cost caused by a mismatch between the characteristics of the good and the preferences of the individual club members…

Think now of a society composed, not of individuals but of independent states. Associations of independent states (alliances, leagues, confederations) are typically voluntary, and their members are exclusively entitled to enjoy certain benefits produced by the association, so that the economic theory of clubs is applicable. In fact, since excludability is more easily enforced in such a context, many goods which are purely public at the national level become club goods at the international level. The club goods in question could be collective security, policy coordination, common technical standards, or tax harmonization. In these and many other cases, countries which are not willing to share the costs are usually excluded from the benefits of inter-state cooperation. Now, as an association of states expands, becoming more diverse in its preferences, the cost of uniformity in the provision of such goods – harmonization – can escalate dramatically. The theory predicts a growing number of voluntary associations to meet the increased demand of club goods more precisely tailored to the different requirements of various subsets of more homogeneous states. It will be noted that the model sketched here is inspired by a pluralist philosophy quite different from the one-dimensional philosophy of enhanced cooperation as discussed in a previous section. It is not a question of states working closely together for the sake of the Union. Rather, the underlying idea is that variety in preferences should be matched by a corresponding variety in institutional arrangements.

…'integration à la carte' and 'variable geometry' come closest to the situation modelled by the economic theory of clubs. The expression 'variable geometry' has been used in several meanings. In the meaning most relevant here, it refers to a situation where a subset of Member States undertake some project, for instance an industrial or technological project in which other members of the Union

---

[105] See http://epp.eurostat.ec.europa.eu/tgm/table.do?tab=table&init=1&language=en&pcode=tec00114&plugin=1. There has been some convergence. The difference was sevenfold for the second edition.

[106] European Commission, *Public Opinion in the European Union Fieldwork: Standard Eurobarometer 78, November 2012* (Luxembourg, European Commission, 2013) T41.

are not interested, or to which they are unable to make a positive contribution. Since, by assumption, not all Member States are willing to participate in all EU programmes, this model combines the criterion of differentiation by country, as in multi-speed integration, and by activity or project – as in integration à la carte…

Majone's theory of club goods is that the Union would involve a series of policies in which not all states would participate in all policies. Instead, individual Member States would only participate in those policies which corresponded to their needs. The attractiveness of this is its flexibility, the choice offered to Member States and the sense that policies will work better if they are confined to those who can both meet their demands and are committed to the policy. However, entrants since 2004 have not had the same choices as the first fifteen members, and there is also debate about whether they should be excluded from full participation in all Union policies.

This exclusion takes a number of forms. One is of very long transitional regimes after accession, which either deny their nationals EU law rights or subject these states to extra policing by the EU institutions. The most prominent example of the former concerns free movement of persons. Nationals of the 2004 and 2007 entrants were only granted the same rights to live and work in other EU Member States as other EU citizens seven years after their entry into the Union.[107] An example of the latter is the Cooperation and Verification Mechanism which allows the Commission to monitor observance of Bulgarian and Romanian obligations under EU law and against a number of further benchmarks with regard to anti-corruption, rule of law and independence of the judiciary. During the first three years of membership, if the states failed to meet these commitments or benchmarks, the Commission was able to adopt measures against them, notably suspending their rights.[108]

Another form is the presence of additional hurdles to be met before a state can participate in an EU policy. In December 2007, all the post-2004 Member States acceded to the Schengen Convention. It was not implemented in three, Cyprus, Romania and Bulgaria, with the result that border-free travel does not exist between these states and other Schengen area states.[109] In Cyprus, this was a consequence of the conflict on the island which made it impossible for the government to secure the external frontiers of the island. With Bulgaria and Romania, there were more generalised concerns about their policing of their external frontiers, and it is only when there is confidence that these are secured that these will participate as full members of the Schengen zone. Membership of the euro area has also proved challenging. Every state joining the euro area has to meet tough assessments on its budgetary and economic performance prior to entry.[110] Eleven Member States joined the euro in 1999, with Greece joining three

---

[107] S. Currie, '"Free" Movers? The Post Accession Experience of Accession-8 Migrant Workers in the United Kingdom' (2006) 31 *ELRev.* 207. The period is for five years in the case of Croatia.

[108] In 2008, Commission concerns with Bulgarian maladministration led it to suspend payments of €220 million structural funds to Bulgaria. European Commission, *On the Management of EU Funds in Bulgaria*, COM(2008)496.

[109] Croatia acceded to the Schengen Convention on 1 July 2013. The Convention is unlikely to be implemented there until 2015 at the earliest.

[110] See p. 713.

years later in 2002. To date, a further six states have joined, with the total number of members standing at eighteen in 2014.[111]

All these restrictions still allow the prospect of eventual participation in a policy. It is not clear that this will be available in the future. It has been suggested, most influentially, by Jean-Claude Piris, the former head of the Council Legal Service, that the size and diversity of the Union has affected its cohesion, adaptiveness and identity.[112] This prevents it (in his view) realising the full potential of the integration project. He has, therefore, argued that further steps in integration in fields such as budgetary and economic policy or foreign and defence policy should be taken by an avant-garde. The possibility of participation by others is held out but the terms and processes under which these may join are unspecified, suggesting that the commitment to their eventual participation is not that strong. Piris accepts that this would re-establish divisions and create a periphery but believes this to be a price worth paying for a more integrated core.

6 DECADE OF INSTITUTIONAL REFORM

(i) European Union Charter of Fundamental Rights and Treaty of Nice

The achievements of the Treaty of Amsterdam were seen at the time as limited.[113] There were two areas, in particular, that were seen as unfinished.

First, there had been much discussion about whether the European Union should have its own Bill of Rights. The Member States agreed, in 1999, that an EU Charter of Fundamental Rights should be established, at least cataloguing such rights. Instead of this being left to intergovernmental negotiations, a special Convention was established to agree the Charter.[114] Chaired by Roman Herzog, formerly the German President, the Convention was composed of fifteen representatives of national governments, thirty representatives of national parliaments, sixteen representatives of the European Parliament and one representative of the Commission. It met in open session, decided upon matters by consensus rather than by voting and received extensive representations from civil society. Parliamentarians were not only more numerous in the Convention than government representatives, but also more vocal. A total of 805 amendments were put forward by parliamentarians whilst only 356 were put forward by government representatives.[115] It constituted a move away from negotiations between governments to a new form of deliberative decision-making. It was also successful in terms of its outcome: the Convention drafted the European Union Charter of Fundamental Rights (EUCFR) which was wide-ranging in the entitlements and was adopted by the Convention in October 2000.

---

[111] The euro area states are Austria, Belgium, Cyprus, Estonia, France, Finland, Germany, Greece, Ireland, Italy, Latvia, Luxembourg, Malta, the Netherlands, Portugal, Slovenia, Slovakia and Spain.

[112] J.-C. Piris, *The Future of Europe: Towards a Two-Speed EU?* (Cambridge, Cambridge University Press, 2012) Conclusion.

[113] K. Hughes, 'The 1996 Intergovernmental Conference and EU Enlargement' (1996) 72 *International Affairs* 1; A. Teasdale, 'The Politics of Qualified Majority Voting in Europe' (1996) *Political Quarterly* 101, 110–15.

[114] G. de Búrca, 'The Drafting of the EU Charter of Fundamental Rights' (2001) 26 *ELRev.* 126.

[115] A. Maurer, 'The Convention, the IGC 2004 and European System Development: A Challenge for Parliamentary Democracy' in *Democracy and Accountability in the Enlarged European Union*, Joint Conference of SWP and the Austrian Academy of Sciences, 7–8 March 2003, www.swp-berlin.org/common/get_document.php?asset_id=689.

The second area concerned the institutional pressures generated by possible enlargement of the Union. A Protocol had been signed at Amsterdam, agreeing that a conference be convened at least one year before membership of the EU reached twenty, to review the composition and functioning of the institutions. Discussions began on 1 May 1999. Notwithstanding its technicality, this task was a challenging one as reallocation of power within the EU institutions entailed that for every winner there would be an equivalent loser. The Treaty of Nice was finally signed on 11 December 2000, after over ninety hours of acrimonious, direct negotiations between the Heads of Government.[116] Even within governmental circles, the agreement was seen as limited and unsatisfactory. Agreement was not reached on many of the items for discussion: most notably the legal status of the EUCFR. Instead, limited reforms were made to the four main institutions: the Commission, the Council, the Parliament and the Court of Justice. QMV was extended into thirty-one further areas, almost all of which were procedural and were concerned with the appointment of EU officials. The reforms were not only insubstantial but the Treaties were now a confusing mess. The Union now had a bewildering array of legislative procedures. There were thirty-eight combinations of 'possible voting modalities in the Council and participation opportunities of the European Parliament of which twenty-two were "legislative"'.[117] The Member States announced that there would be yet another IGC in 2004 to consider the unresolved issues. Whilst, therefore, there did not seem to be many strong reasons to vote against the Treaty of Nice, there did not seem to be many reasons to vote for it. In June 2001, the Irish voted 53.87 per cent against ratification of the Treaty of Nice.[118] A Declaration was added that nothing in the TEU affected Irish military neutrality, something that had been raised as a concern amongst a small number of Irish voters. On the basis of this, a second referendum was held in September 2002, and the Treaty of Nice was approved by 62.89 per cent of the vote.[119]

(ii) Constitutional Treaty

Dissatisfaction with the Treaty of Nice concerned, first, the process. There was considerable unhappiness with the closed negotiations between governments which ran up against deadlines late into the night that seemed to be brought by every intergovernmental conference. This seemed neither an effective nor a democratic way to secure deep-seated institutional reforms. In a Declaration at Nice, the Member States called, therefore 'for a deeper and wider debate about the future of the European Union' which would involve 'wide-ranging discussions with all interested parties: representatives of national parliaments and all those reflecting public opinion, namely political, economic and university circles, representatives of civil society, etc.'.[120]

Dissatisfaction also focused on the managerial ambitions of the reforms. They were concerned with securing the working of the institutions in the face of the challenge of increased membership. This concern with technical effectiveness and the institutional tinkering accompanying it was seen as neither ambitious enough to equip the Union for the challenges

---

[116] M. Gray and A. Stubb, 'The Treaty of Nice: Negotiating a Poisoned Chalice?' (2001) 39S *JCMS* 5.
[117] W. Wessels, 'The Millennium IGC in the EU's Evolution' (2001) 39 *JCMS* 197, 201.
[118] K. Gilland, 'Ireland's (First) Referendum on the Treaty of Nice' (2002) 40 *JCMS* 527.
[119] The Treaty of Nice came into force on 2 February 2003.
[120] Declaration 23 to the Treaty of Nice on the Future of the Union.

it faced – one treaty reform always left unfinished business for another treaty reform – nor sufficient to engender the popular affinity necessary for the Union to sustain any kind of wider authority amongst its citizenry. In 2000, at the Humboldt University in Berlin, Joschka Fischer, the German Foreign Minister, suggested that European integration had to have a '*finalité*', an end-point, and that this should be a European constitution:

> These three reforms – the solution of the democracy problem and the need for fundamental reordering of competences both horizontally, i.e. among the European institutions, and vertically, i.e. between Europe, the nation-state and the regions – will only be able to succeed if Europe is established anew with a constitution. In other words: through the realisation of the project of a European Constitution centred around basic, human and civil rights, an equal division of powers between the European institutions and a precise delineation between European and nation-state level. The main axis for such a European Constitution will be the relationship between the Federation and the nation-state.[121]

A number of Heads of Government picked up on this. Within two months, Jacques Chirac, the French President, talked of a 'first European Constitution'. Tony Blair, the British Prime Minister, suggested that there should be a new statement of principles about the Union. And in June 2000 Paavo Lipponen, the Finnish Prime Minister, suggested that a special Convention be established to launch a 'constitutionalisation process'.[122]

The ground was prepared for the decision taken in December 2001, at Laeken in Belgium, to abandon the traditional IGC process. The draft Treaty would be formulated by a Convention modelled on that used to draft the EU Charter of Fundamental Rights. Furthermore, that Convention was to have big ambitions. It was to be one on the 'Future of Europe'. Chaired by Giscard d'Estaing, the Convention opened in February 2002.[123] Although its initial mandate was merely to identify options for the subsequent IGC, Giscard discarded this idea at the first session stating that its purpose should be a single proposal opening the way for a Constitution for Europe.[124] Sixteen months later, he presented this proposal, the Draft Constitutional Treaty (DCT), with much pomp and fanfare to the Member States.

The DCT was concerned to establish the Union as an autonomous constitutional democracy. In addition to many substantive reforms, it, thus, also included many of the symbols associated with national constitutional democracies. There was provision for a European Union flag, anthem, motto and holiday. Union instruments were now to be known as 'laws' or 'framework laws'. There was a primacy clause asserting the precedence of EU law over national law within the limits of the Treaty. A Bill of Rights of sorts was established with the incorporation of the EUCFR into the Treaty, and the Union was to have its own legal personality and Foreign Minister.

---

[121] J. Fischer, 'From Confederacy to Federation: Thoughts on the Finality of European Integration', Humboldt University, Berlin, 12 May 2000, http://centers.law.nyu.edu/jeanmonnet/archive/papers/00/joschka_fischer_en.rtf.

[122] P. Norman, *The Accidental Constitution: The Story of the European Convention* (Brussels, Eurocomment, 2003) 11–24.

[123] For accounts of the Convention, in addition to Norman, n. 122 above, see G. Stuart, *The Making of Europe's Constitution* (London, Fabian Society, 2002); C. Closa, *Improving Constitutional Politics? A Preliminary Assessment of the Convention*, CONWEB Paper No. 1/2003; M. Kleine 'Leadership in the European Convention' (2007) 14 *JEPP* 1227; D. Finke *et al.*, *Reforming the European Union: Realizing the Impossible* (Princeton, NJ, Princeton University Press, 2012) chs. 2 and 3.

[124] P. Magnette, 'In the Name of Simplification: Coping with Constitutional Conflicts in the Convention on the Future of Europe' (2005) 11 *ELJ* 432, 436.

The IGC following the Convention was short. There was only one significant point of debate. Spain and Poland were unhappy about the voting rights accorded to them in the EU law-making process. However, after a change of government in Spain and a series of small but important amendments to the text, the Member States signed the Constitutional Treaty, at a ceremony in Rome, in October 2004. To mark both the significance of the Constitutional Treaty and the spirit of democratic renewal, ten Member States arranged for referendums to determine whether or not they should ratify it.

(iii) Road to the Lisbon Treaty

The first referendum was held in Spain, where the Treaty was approved by 72 per cent of those who voted. However, in the next referendums, held in France (on 29 May 2005) and in the Netherlands (three days later, on 1 June 2005), the Treaty was roundly rejected, with 55 per cent voting against it in France and 62 per cent voting against it in the Netherlands. Analysis of the reasons for the 'No' vote in the Netherlands and France showed the Constitutional Treaty had little hold or meaning for public debate. Despite voters being reasonably well-informed about the details of the Constitutional Treaty, the reasons for their vote had little to do, in most cases, with its legal details. Opponents were protesting against globalisation, the consequences of the 2004 enlargement, fears about Turkish membership of the Union, and in the Netherlands there was anger amongst voters at the perceived power of the large Member States in the Union.[125]

With hindsight, these referendums exposed the difficulties in the strategy behind the Constitutional Treaty. Processes of collective identity formation are complicated and difficult to formulate. They rely on feelings of co-identification, solidarity and trust developing between members of a group. Within the national context, this has been helped because the cultural, economic and politico-administrative boundaries of most modern states reinforce each other.[126] There is a *national* system of law and order, a *national* community with its own myths and symbols, a *national* welfare system, a *national* economy and a *national* administration. For better or worse, this reinforcement generates common identities. This is absent within the Union, and to imagine a convention in a hall in Brussels could establish it was highly optimistic. More telling, however, was the failure of the other strategy. It might be thought that, in the absence of a common identity, Europeans might still welcome the chance offered through institutional reform to engage with each other on matters of common concern. However, Europe's publics saw themselves as, at best, a chorus for the Constitutional Treaty, who were given the chance to comment on it, but, for most people, little more.[127] It did not engage them, and Dutch and French electorates consequently turned to other considerations when voting on it.

By the end of June 2005, ratification of the Constitutional Treaty had reached an impasse. A significant majority of Member States, eighteen, had ratified the Treaty, with Luxembourg

---

[125] *Flash Eurobarometer 171 and 172, European Constitution: Post-Referendum Survey in France and in The Netherlands.* This was all notwithstanding that 88 per cent of the French and 82 per cent of the Dutch still had positive perceptions of the Union in the period after the referendum. European Commission, *The Period of Reflection and Plan D*, COM(2006)212, 2.

[126] S. Bartolini, *Restructuring Europe: Centre Formation, System Building, and Political Structuring Between the Nation State and the European Union* (Oxford, Oxford University Press, 2005) 410.

[127] On this see v. Middelaar, n. 83 above, 273–4 and 289–91.

also having held a positive referendum. Of the remaining seven Member States, six (Czech Republic, Denmark, Ireland, Poland, Portugal and the United Kingdom), were scheduled to hold their own referendums. Of these, there was a significant chance of a 'No' vote in all bar Portugal. The popular vote was out on the European Union. The Union was also now faced not with a single recalcitrant state, such as Denmark and Ireland, as with previous amending Treaties, but with a deep divide in which two-thirds of Member States wished to press ahead whilst one-third did not. In late 2006, the Finnish Government prepared the ground by engaging in a series of consultations on how to achieve institutional reform. In March 2007, at the fiftieth anniversary of the Treaty of Rome, the German Government obtained a commitment from the other Member States to place 'the European Union on a renewed common basis before the European Parliament elections in 2009'.[128] In other words, they had committed to a deadline for ratifying a new treaty.

The process for reaching agreement was very different from that for the Constitutional Treaty. 'Political agreement' on the central points of disagreement was reached in confidential negotiations between ministries, named 'sherpas'. Only when political agreement was reached on the main points would the second stage, an IGC, be opened. Its tasks, however, would be limited by the mandate of the political agreement, and so restricted to translating the political agreement into legal detail and resolving any ambiguities. In terms of substance, the strategy involved the use of the Constitutional Treaty as a starting point for discussion alongside that of what had to be offered to make the Treaty acceptable to those national governments constituting the recalcitrant third. The Heads of Government met between 21 and 23 June 2007 to conclude the first stage of the process: a sixteen-page mandate for the IGC. On 13 December 2007, the new text, the Lisbon Treaty, was formally signed.

The conclusion of the Treaty was a significant negotiating coup. It involved amendments to all of the Articles in the TEU and to 216 provisions in the EC Treaty.[129] Yet it created a double bind. If the Lisbon Treaty differed significantly from the Constitutional Treaty, its nature of reform was more closed and more accelerated than any other to date. There was a lack of transparency and an exclusion of national parliaments from the process which was never explained or justified. If the Lisbon Treaty was not substantially different from the Constitutional Treaty, it would open negotiators to charges of arrogance for ignoring the referendum results in France and the Netherlands.[130] It would also beg the question as to why referendums were not to be held in those states which had promised to hold a referendum on the Constitutional Treaty. For only one state, Ireland, was to hold a referendum on the Lisbon Treaty.

(iv) Lisbon Treaty

The Lisbon Treaty followed the same three-headed strategy as the Treaties of Maastricht and Amsterdam of adding and formalising competencies, collective identity formation and institutional reform.

---

[128] EU Council, *Declaration on the Occasion of the Fiftieth Anniversary of the Signature of the Treaty of Rome* (Brussels, 25 March 2007) para. 3.

[129] Statewatch: www.statewatch.org/news/2007/oct/eu-refrom-treaty-tec-external-relations-3–5.pdf.

[130] For a thoughtful comparison see House of Commons, *EU Reform: A New Treaty or an Old Constitution*, Research Paper 07/64 (London, House of Commons, 2007).

(a) Two Treaties of equal value: Treaty on European Union and Treaty on the Functioning of the European Union

The Lisbon Treaty established new Union competencies in the fields of energy, intellectual property, space, humanitarian aid, sport, civil protection and climate change. The significance of these was belied by the Union already taking significant measures in these fields under other legal bases. A more important reform was replacement of the three pillar structure with a single framework, which made provision for discrete treatment of the Common Foreign and Security Policy, but extended supranational disciplines to all other activities, most notably policing and judicial cooperation in criminal matters which had, hitherto, been subject to limited oversight by the supranational institutions.

As was noted earlier, a central part of the Roman strategy is not merely to be providing benefits but to be seen to be responsible for the provision of those benefits. In that regard, the Lisbon Treaty rationalised and catalogued Union competencies in a manner that allowed them to be more visible and more easily understood. Two treaties, the Treaty on European Union (TEU) and the Treaty on the Functioning of the European Union (TFEU) were to replace the previous framework.[131] Each treaty was to have 'the same legal value'.[132]

The central items set out by the TEU are:

- the mission and values of the European Union: respect for the rule of law, the principle of limited powers, respect for national identities and upholding democracy and fundamental rights;
- the democratic principles of the Union and provision for the active contribution of national parliaments to the functioning of the European Union;
- a neighbourhood policy, whereby the Union is to develop a special relationship with neighbouring countries;
- the composition and central functions of the EU institutions;
- detailed provisions on the Union's external action in the TEU, in particular both its Common Foreign and Security Policy and its Common Security and Defence Policy;
- procedures for amendment of the two Treaties;
- legal personality for the Union;
- the circumstances in which a Member State may leave or be expelled from the Union and when Member States may engage in enhanced cooperation.

The TFEU sets out the explicit competencies of the Union and, with the exception of the Common Foreign and Security Policy, the detailed procedures to be used in each policy field. The competencies are catalogued at the beginning of the TFEU.[133]

---

[131] On the Treaty of Lisbon see House of Lords European Union Committee, *The Treaty of Lisbon: An Impact Assessment* (London, HL, 10th Report, Session 2007–8, 2008); P. Craig, *The Lisbon Treaty: Law, Politics and Treaty Reform* (Oxford, Oxford University Press, 2010); J.-C. Piris, *The Lisbon Treaty: A Legal and Political Analysis* (Cambridge, Cambridge University Press, 2010); D. Ashiagbor *et al.* (eds.), *The European Union After the Treaty of Lisbon* (Cambridge, Cambridge University Press, 2012).

[132] Article 1(2) TFEU.

[133] The discussion is set out in more detail at pp. 108–11.

Article 3 TFEU

1. The Union shall have exclusive competence in the following areas:
   (a) customs union;
   (b) the establishing of the competition rules necessary for the functioning of the internal market;
   (c) monetary policy for the Member States whose currency is the euro;
   (d) the conservation of marine biological resources under the common fisheries policy;
   (e) common commercial policy.
2. The Union shall also have exclusive competence for the conclusion of an international agreement when its conclusion is provided for in a legislative act of the Union or is necessary to enable the Union to exercise its internal competence, or insofar as its conclusion may affect common rules or alter their scope.

Article 4 TFEU

1. The Union shall share competence with the Member States where the Treaties confer on it a competence which does not relate to the areas referred to in Articles 3 and 6.
2. Shared competence between the Union and the Member States applies in the following principal areas:
   (a) internal market;
   (b) social policy, for the aspects defined in this Treaty;
   (c) economic, social and territorial cohesion;
   (d) agriculture and fisheries, excluding the conservation of marine biological resources;
   (e) environment;
   (f) consumer protection;
   (g) transport;
   (h) trans-European networks;
   (i) energy;
   (j) area of freedom, security and justice;
   (k) common safety concerns in public health matters, for the aspects defined in this Treaty.
3. In the areas of research, technological development and space, the Union shall have competence to carry out activities, in particular to define and implement programmes; however, the exercise of that competence shall not result in Member States being prevented from exercising theirs.
4. In the areas of development cooperation and humanitarian aid, the Union shall have competence to carry out activities and conduct a common policy; however, the exercise of that competence shall not result in Member States being prevented from exercising theirs.

Article 5 TFEU

1. The Member States shall coordinate their economic policies within the Union. To this end, the Council shall adopt measures, in particular broad guidelines for these policies. Specific provisions shall apply to those Member States whose currency is the euro.
2. The Union shall take measures to ensure coordination of the employment policies of the Member States, in particular by defining guidelines for these policies.
3. The Union may take initiatives to ensure coordination of Member States' social policies.

> **Article 6 TFEU**
>
> The Union shall have competence to carry out actions to support, coordinate or supplement the actions of the Member States. The areas of such action shall, at European level, be:
> (a) protection and improvement of human health;
> (a) industry;
> (b) culture;
> (c) tourism;
> (d) education, vocational training, youth and sport;
> (e) civil protection;
> (f) administrative cooperation.

(b) Lisbon Treaty and a democratic identity for Europe?

The Lisbon Treaty abandoned the 'constitutional concept'.[134] The flag, the anthem, the motto and the holiday all disappeared. The provisions establishing the primacy of EU law and the detailed elaboration of the Charter were removed from the main text of the Treaty. Union legislative measures were returned to their traditional designation as Regulations and Directives. The Foreign Minister was to be known as the High Representative. There was still a concern, however, to set out a shared identity which set out a reason, beyond mutual advantage, why citizens in the Union should accept its authority.[135] The Lisbon Treaty anchored this identity around the Union respecting and building upon a European heritage of democratic values. The nature of these values is set out in the first substantive provision of the TEU.

> **Article 2 TEU**
>
> The Union is founded on the values of respect for human dignity, freedom, democracy, equality, the rule of law and respect for human rights, including the rights of persons belonging to minorities. These values are common to the Member States in a society in which pluralism, non-discrimination, tolerance, justice, solidarity and equality between women and men prevail.

There is tentativeness in this statement. The Union commits itself to respecting these values. It does not commit itself to promoting or securing them. Nevertheless, the shift was significant. The Union committed itself to recognising the rights and freedom in the EUCFR and to acceding to the European Convention for the Protection of Human Rights and Fundamental Freedoms. In addition, there was a stronger commitment to both citizenship and democracy.

---

[134] EU Council, *IGC 2007 Mandate* (Brussels, 26 June 2007) para. 1.
[135] G. Morgan, 'European Political Integration and the Need for Justification' (2007) 14 *Constellations* 332. See also the distinction made between performance legitimacy and polity legitimacy in N. Walker, 'Constitutionalizing Enlargement, Enlarging Constitutionalism' (2003) 9 *ELJ* 365, 368–70.

> **Article 9 TEU**
>
> In all its activities, the Union shall observe the principle of the equality of its citizens, who shall receive equal attention from its institutions, bodies, offices and agencies.
>
> Every national of a Member State shall be a citizen of the Union. Citizenship of the Union shall be additional to national citizenship and shall not replace it.

> **Article 10 TEU**
>
> 1. The functioning of the Union shall be founded on representative democracy.
> 2. Citizens are directly represented at Union level in the European Parliament. Member States are represented in the European Council by their Heads of State or Government and in the Council by their governments, themselves democratically accountable either to their national Parliaments, or to their citizens.
> 3. Every citizen shall have the right to participate in the democratic life of the Union. Decisions shall be taken as openly and as closely as possible to the citizen.
> 4. Political parties at European level contribute to forming European political awareness and to expressing the will of citizens of the Union.

The commitment to respect these values ties the Union's hands in a manner which happened neither with Maastricht nor Amsterdam. With those treaties, the symbols of common identification were either very vague or served to create new institutions, such as Union citizenship. This is not the case with Lisbon. The commitment to respect is also a commitment not to violate well-established values. These values are, thus, set up not just as a hallmark of the Union but as a benchmark by which to measure it and a stick with which to beat it. If it breaches these values, this can be condemned not simply because these values are cherished but because they go to the reason for the Union's being.

A corollary is that the Union does not claim a monopoly over these values. Values such as democracy, the rule of law, citizenship and fundamental rights are clearly protected by political settlements other than the Union. A commitment to respect these values should, therefore, involve a commitment to cede where these other settlements can protect these values better than the Union. This is, indeed, partially recognised by the 'democratic identity' provision.

> **Article 4(2) TEU**
>
> 2. The Union shall respect the equality of Member States before the Treaties as well as their national identities, inherent in their fundamental structures, political and constitutional, inclusive of regional and local self-government. It shall respect their essential State functions, including ensuring the territorial integrity of the State, maintaining law and order and safeguarding national security. In particular, national security remains the sole responsibility of each Member State.

This idea that the principle of democracy should not only guide how the Union acts but also restrict its authority came up in a number of forms.

First, lines in the sand were laid down in relation to certain fields of activity. National security was deemed to be the sole responsibility of Member States. In addition, a Protocol was added stating that nothing affected the competence of Member States to provide, commission or organise non-economic services of a general interest. With other fields of activity, 'brake' procedures were added. A national government could insist that a Union matter be discussed at European Council level if a measure touched fundamental aspects of their social security or criminal justice systems. In other words, it could insist that such matters be resolved at the highest political level, and then only with the agreement of its Heads of Government.

Secondly, differentiated integration increased to reflect different national sensitivities. In all cases, this went to the democratic values which make up a political community, and whether these should be governed at pan-Union or national level. The special provision for the United Kingdom and Ireland granted at Amsterdam was extended to the whole of the area of freedom, security and justice to cover, most notably, policing and judicial cooperation in criminal justice. These states choose whether to participate in individual pieces of legislation prior to their adoption. If they do not, they are not bound by these. The other central differentiation concerns fundamental rights. A Protocol was added, which stated that the EUCFR did not *extend* the ability of any court to declare Polish or British measures incompatible with EU fundamental rights law. As these states had particular concerns about the development of EU social rights, the Protocol provided that Title IV of the Charter, in which most of these rights were incorporated, was only justiciable in these states insofar as the latter provided for them in national law. Prior to the coming into force of the Lisbon Treaty, the Czech Government requested that the same treatment be applied to it. In later 2011, this was recommended by the European Council. However, in May 2013, when consulted, the European Parliament voted against it. The matter is still outstanding.

These issues rose most sharply in Ireland, the only Member State to hold a referendum on the Lisbon Treaty. On 12 June 2008, 53.4 per cent of the voters rejected the Lisbon Treaty. The basis for holding a second referendum was three guarantees.[136] Nothing in the Lisbon Treaty should:

(i) affect the scope or applicability of the rights to life, protection of the family or in respect of education as set out in the Irish Constitution;
(ii) change in any way, for any Member State, the extent or operation of EU competence in respect to taxation;
(iii) prejudice the security and defence policy of any Member State, provide for the creation of a European army or conscription, or affect a Member State's right to decide whether or not to participate in a military operation.[137]

Thirdly, the most widespread engagement with the question of 'democratic identity' was, however, in the challenges to the Lisbon Treaty in different national constitutional courts. In a

---

[136] In addition, notwithstanding the apparent intent of the Lisbon Treaty, there was agreement that there should continue to be one national from each Member State as a Commissioner. Conclusions of the Brussels European Council, 11/12 December 2008, I.2, EU Council, 17271/1/08 Rev. 1.

[137] This was formally adopted as a Protocol to the Treaty on the accession of Croatia to the European Union. Protocol on the concerns of the Irish people on the Treaty of Lisbon [2013] OJ L60/131.

number of Member States, the principle was seen as setting out a certain core of activities so central to the constitution of a domestic society that, for the moment, they had to be governed by domestic legislatures, irrespective of the content of the Treaties.[138] The reasons were elaborated in most detail by the German Constitutional Court.

---

2 BvE 2/08 *Treaty of Lisbon*, Judgment of 30 June 2009

248. The safeguarding of sovereignty, demanded by the principle of democracy in the valid constitutional system prescribed by the Basic Law in a manner that is open to integration and to international law, does not mean that a pre-determined number or certain types of sovereign rights should remain in the hands of the state. The participation of Germany in the development of the European Union... also comprises a political union, in addition to the creation of an economic and monetary union. Political union means the joint exercise of public authority, including legislative authority, even reaching into the traditional core areas of the state's area of competence. This is rooted in the European idea of peace and unification especially when dealing with the coordination of cross-border aspects of life and when guaranteeing a single economic area and area of justice in which citizens of the Union can freely develop...

249. European unification on the basis of a treaty union of sovereign states may, however, not be achieved in such a way that not sufficient space is left to the Member States for the political formation of the economic, cultural and social living conditions. This applies in particular to areas which shape the citizens' living conditions, in particular the private sphere of their own responsibility and of political and social security, protected by fundamental rights, as well as to political decisions that rely especially on cultural, historical and linguistic perceptions and which develop in public discourse in the party political and parliamentary sphere of public politics. Essential areas of democratic formative action comprise, inter alia, citizenship, the civil and the military monopoly on the use of force, revenue and expenditure including external financing and all elements of encroachment that are decisive for the realisation of fundamental rights, above all in major encroachments on fundamental rights such as deprivation of liberty in the administration of criminal law or placement in an institution. These important areas also include cultural issues such as the disposition of language, the shaping of circumstances concerning the family and education, the ordering of the freedom of opinion, press and of association and the dealing with the profession of faith or ideology.

This shielding of certain fields of activity from Union authority has not been uncontroversial. It has been argued that it fails to consider the democratic qualities of domestic processes in these areas or the possibilities offered by EU law to augment the quality of democratic life, by opening up new possibilities or ways of seeing things.[139] To be sure, too rigid protection of

---

[138] With regard to the other two decisions see Pl ÚS 19/08 *Lisbon Treaty I*, Czech Constitutional Court, Judgment of 26 November 2008; K 32/09 *Lisbon Treaty*, Polish Constitutional Tribunal, Judgment of 24 November 2010; The French Constitutional Council talked of matters 'inherent to national sovereignty', *Re Ratification of the Lisbon Treaty* [2010] 2 CMLR 26, paras. 7–9.

[139] See the debate between F. Mayer, 'Rashomon in Karlsruhe: A Reflection on Democracy and Identity in the European Union: The German Constitutional Court's Lisbon Decision and the Changing Landscape of European Constitutionalism' (2011) 9 *I-CON* 757; K. Nicolaidis, 'Germany as Europe: How the Constitutional Court Unwittingly Embraced EU Demoi-cracy: A Comment on Franz Mayer' (2011) 9 *I-CON* 786.

domestic laws, under a guise of protection of domestic democratic identity, may do just that. However, considering when national processes offer democratic opportunities absent in EU law or when they sensitise the Union to new ways of seeing things, seems both attractive and in keeping with a stage of Union development less concerned about ever greater construction of the European project and more about securing a happy co-existence between the Union and the nation-states which combines to augment the democratic quality of life of the Union's citizens.

(c) Lisbon and the recasting of the Union public sphere

The central thrust of Lisbon was institutional reform. QMV was extended to about fifty new areas. Beyond this, the central reforms were dominated by three trends. First, the process of greater parliamentary involvement that had begun at Amsterdam continued. The ordinary legislative procedure was applied to a further forty areas. National parliaments were given additional time and reinforced entitlements to consider EU legislative proposals. Of greater significance was a power granted to review, although not veto, legislative proposals to see whether these complied with the subsidiarity principle, the principle which requires that Union measures only be adopted if their objectives cannot be sufficiently achieved by Member States and can, instead, be better realised through Union action. Secondly, Lisbon concerned itself both with reforms to all the main EU institutions and with considerable institutional innovation. The size of the Commission and the European Parliament were changed, as was the method for calculating QMV within the Council. Most significantly, the European Council was brought far more into the formal Treaty structures and given a central Treaty role as a political agenda-setter. It was, for the first time, recognised as a formal EU institution, and, to consolidate this institutionalisation, a President was established whose job is to drive forward and prepare its work. A further institutional innovation was the High Representative. A member of both the Council and the Commission, her duty is to represent the Union in matters relating to the Common Foreign and Security Policy and ensure the consistency of the Union's external action. The final theme was greater citizen engagement. A citizens' initiative was established whereby the Commission is obliged to consider proposals for legal measures made by petitions of one million citizens coming from at least seven Member States.

7 SOVEREIGN DEBT CRISIS AND THE EUROPEAN UNION

The Irish Government held a second referendum on the Treaty on 2 October 2009 which was approved by 67 per cent of the vote. The Lisbon Treaty duly entered into force on 1 December 2009. Any thoughts that the Treaty marked a new equilibrium for European integration were blown away by the onset of the financial crisis. The origins of the crisis lay in massive lending by financial institutions on the United States' housing market.[140] This led, in turn, to a large secondary market between financial institutions in the sale and purchase of these housing loans. This secondary market led to the risks from a fall in the price of US housing being amplified and being carried across the global financial system. When the price of US housing, indeed, began to fall from 2006 onwards, the scale of the

---

[140] More detailed discussion of the response to the crisis is in Chapter 16.

losses was staggering. The International Monetary Fund (IMF) estimated the write downs on bad debts between 2007 and 2010 to be US$4.1 trillion,[141] and, following the collapse of the Lehman Brothers bank in autumn 2008, this threatened to bring the whole financial system down.

The crisis posed a number of challenges for EU governments, of which the most visible was financing their sovereign debt. This became difficult for three reasons. First, lending not only slowed as there was less capital, it was also redirected. Lenders, increasingly, re-evaluated the risks of certain borrowers with certain traditionally low-risk investments, such as national governments, now seen as higher risk. The consequence was that the cost of borrowing increased for governments whose public finances were perceived as weak. Secondly, the reduction in lending led to a shrivelling of the economy, and consequently tax receipts, putting further pressure on public finances. This was particularly so for economies that relied heavily on the financial sector and on expansive lending by it to sectors such as property. Thirdly, many states had to bail out a number of their commercial banks to prevent these going bankrupt, with catastrophic consequences for their economies.[142] This added to the national debt.

The first states to experience difficulties were outside the euro area. Latvia and Hungary had to seek financial support from the IMF and the European Union in 2008, with Romania doing likewise in 2009. These difficulties, furthermore, were not confined to the European Union. In autumn 2008, all of Iceland's three major commercial banks went bankrupt and had to be nationalised. The sovereign debt crisis became a crisis on a pan-Union scale in October 2009 when the new Greek Government announced that its budget deficit for 2009 was not 3.7 per cent of GDP, as previously stated, but 12.5 per cent.[143] This led lenders to have doubts about Greece's ability to repay its debt, and to a downgrading of its credit rating in February 2010. Notwithstanding the introduction of an austerity programme by Greece and a ringing endorsement by the European Council in March 2010 that the programme would be sufficient for Greece to regain financial stability, these doubts intensified. In April 2010, Greece had to seek a bailout from the European Union and IMF, which was approved in May for €110 billion. By then, its bonds had been rated by all major agencies as having junk status, meaning it could effectively no longer borrow on capital markets. If the initial Greek loan was a bilateral one, May 2010 marked the beginning of a series of institutional developments which have changed the face of the European Union.

These developments can be categorised into three. There are, first, the institutional arrangements established to govern the terms of lending to states who have asked for financial support. In addition, there are, secondly, a series of EU disciplines governing public finances and economic performance, which are to be applied in some form to all EU Member States, but with full force to all euro area states. Finally, a number of implications, often very different, about the future of the European integration process have been drawn as a result of the crisis.

---

[141] IMF, *Global Financial Stability Report: Responding to the Financial Crisis and Measuring Systemic Risks* (Washington, IMF, April 2009) 30.

[142] By 2012, the Commission estimated that €4.5 trillion had been spent rescuing banks in the EU. European Commission, *A Roadmap towards a Banking Union*, COM(2012)510, 3.

[143] European Commission, *Report on Greek Government Debt and Deficit Statistics*, COM(2010)1.

(i) European Stability Mechanism

In May 2010, it was already clear that Greece was unlikely to be the only state experiencing difficulties financing its public debt. With financial backing from the euro area states, the European Financial Stability Facility (EFSF) was established.[144] A fund set up as a private company in Luxembourg, it was authorised to lend €440 billion to underpin loans to states experiencing financing difficulties. Alongside it, a European Financial Stabilisation Mechanism of €60 billion of Union funds was established to offer direct support to these states.[145] These two instruments were eventually consolidated into a single enterprise, the European Stability Mechanism (ESM) in October 2012.[146] As with the EFSF, it is established as a private company in Luxembourg. Established by two treaties, one in 2011 and the other in 2012, it can lend states seeking support up to €500 billion of guarantees at rates of 3 per cent per annum. Any loan involves the agreement of a Memorandum of Understanding (MOU) between the state seeking support and the ESM which will set up conditions that the state must meet to restore (in the ESM's eyes) its public finances. Invariably, these will include a mixture of privatisations, tax increases, cuts in public spending and measures to improve tax collection. Compliance is typically monitored by a mixture of European Central Bank (ECB), Commission and IMF officials. To date, five states have requested support from the ESM: Greece, Ireland, Portugal, Spain and Cyprus.[147]

The ESM is not the only form of financial support provided. In May 2010 the ECB established the Securities Market Programme (SMP), which allowed it to offer assistance to states experiencing severe tensions in the money markets through purchasing their securities on secondary markets.[148] The programme lasted until September 2012, and was used to purchase €218 billion of debt, of which nearly €103 billion was from Italy.[149] It was replaced by the Outright Monetary Transactions (OMT) programme. This gives the ECB an unlimited right to purchase securities on the secondary markets, but only for states receiving assistance from the ESM. As part of this, OMT was only to be provided if the state in question met conditions similar to those set out in the MOU agreed between it and the ESM.[150] To all intents and purposes, the ESM and OMT, thus, now form a combined package of support in which states in difficulties can receive guarantees and purchase of their securities in return for implementing often quite swingeing austerity programmes.

The consequence has been that the European Union has moved far more actively into a politics of distribution. The levels of fiscal support are considerable, therefore acting as a constraint on the fiscal policy of those states offering support. By contrast, the constraints imposed on those states receiving support affect all areas of public spending – welfare policy, defence, policing – as well as their fiscal policies. This all raises questions about the legal framework

---

[144] See www.efsf.europa.eu/about/index.htm.

[145] Regulation 407/2010/EU establishing a European Financial Stabilisation Mechanism [2010] OJ L118/1.

[146] See www.esm.europa.eu/; M. Ruffert, 'The European Debt Crisis and EU Law' (2011) 48 *CMLRev.* 1790.

[147] Most provide direct support to the government concerned. The exception is the Spanish MOU where support is to a dedicated Spanish fund whose sole responsibility is to recapitalise Spanish banks.

[148] Decision 2010/5/ECB establishing a securities markets programme [2010] OJ L124/8.

[149] The other states who benefited from intervention were Greece, Spain, Portugal and Ireland, see www.ecb.int/press/pr/date/2013/html/pr130221_1.en.html.

[150] OMT has so far not been used. See www.ecb.int/press/pr/date/2012/html/pr120906_1.en.html.

surrounding such momentous decisions, and national constitutional courts have questioned the legal conditions surrounding both the grant of support and the conditions attached to it.[151]

The legal nature of the ESM was addressed in *Pringle*. Pringle, an Irish MP, challenged the introduction of Article 136(3) TFEU by European Council Decision 2011/199. This stated that:

> The Member States whose currency is the euro may establish a stability mechanism to be activated if indispensable to safeguard the stability of the euro area as a whole. The granting of any required financial assistance under the mechanism will be made subject to strict conditionality.

Pringle argued that the Treaty amendment procedure, known as the simplified revision procedure, could not be used to extend Union competences and that is what was happening with the ESM.[152] The Court of Justice disagreed.

Case C–370/12 *Pringle* v *Government of Ireland*, Judgment of 27 November 2012

58. It must next be stated that, as is confirmed moreover by the conclusions of the European Council of 16 and 17 December 2010 to which reference is made in recital 4 of the preamble to Decision 2011/199, the stability mechanism whose establishment is envisaged by Article 1 of Decision 2011/199 serves to complement the new regulatory framework for strengthened economic governance of the Union. Constituted by various regulations of the European Parliament and the Council adopted on 16 November 2011…that framework establishes closer coordination and surveillance of the economic and budgetary policies conducted by the Member States and is intended to consolidate macroeconomic stability and the sustainability of public finances.

59. While the provisions of the regulatory framework referred to in the preceding paragraph and the provisions in the chapter of the TFEU relating to economic policy, in particular Articles 123 TFEU and 125 TFEU, are essentially preventive, in that their objective is to reduce so far as possible the risk of public debt crises, the objective of establishing the stability mechanism is the management of financial crises which, notwithstanding such preventive action as might have been taken, might nonetheless arise.

    In the light of the objectives to be attained by the stability mechanism the establishment of which is envisaged by Article 1 of Decision 2011/199, the instruments provided in order to achieve those objectives and the close link between that mechanism, the provisions of the FEU Treaty relating to economic policy and the regulatory framework for strengthened economic governance of the Union, it must be concluded that the establishment of that mechanism falls within the area of economic policy…

64. Secondly, as regards whether Decision 2011/199 affects the Union's competence in the area of the coordination of the Member States' economic policies, it must be observed that, since Articles 2(3) and 5(1) TFEU restrict the role of the Union in the area of economic policy to the adoption of coordinating measures, the provisions of the EU and FEU Treaties do not confer any specific power on the Union to establish a stability mechanism of the kind envisaged by Decision 2011/199…

---

[151] On the wealth of litigation emerging see E. Fahey and S. Bardutky, 'Judicial Review of Eurozone Law: The Adjudication of Postnational Norms in EU Courts, Plural – A Case Study of the European Stability Mechanism' (2013) 34 *Michigan Journal of International Law* 101.

[152] This is set out in Article 48(6) TEU.

68. Consequently, having regard to Articles 4(1) TEU and 5(2) TEU, the Member States whose currency is the euro are entitled to conclude an agreement between themselves for the establishment of a stability mechanism of the kind envisaged by Article 1 of Decision 2011/199...

69. However, those Member States may not disregard their duty to comply with European Union law when exercising their competences in that area...However, the reason why the grant of financial assistance by the stability mechanism is subject to strict conditionality under paragraph 3 of Article 136 TFEU, the article affected by the revision of the TFEU, is in order to ensure that that mechanism will operate in a way that will comply with European Union law, including the measures adopted by the Union in the context of the coordination of the Member States' economic policies.

The ESM constitutes, therefore, a strange animal. It contributes to EU policy, must comply with EU law, but it is not part of EU law. In reality, as we shall see throughout this book, this has allowed it a space to develop its own balance of power and modus operandi, and granted it some latitude from the normal disciplines of EU law.[153] These weak controls are particularly problematic when the relationship between the parties is so imbalanced. The ESM generates new forms of dependency and hierarchy, whereby, through the conditions established in the MOU, donor states have the possibility to impose their own vision of economic life on recipient states. This has provoked mistrust, as this polemical piece by a German academic illustrates.

U. Beck, *German Europe* (Cambridge, Polity, 2013) 62–3

Today, however given the power constellation of a German Europe, we can see that Europeanization can assume two opposed forms, two varieties of integration and cooperation: either participation on terms of equality (reciprocity) or hierarchical dependence (hegemony). We have to relate the distribution of power and risk in Europe to the scope for action on the part of large States and smaller ones, powerful states and poor States, states that give credit and states that take it, if we are to assess the dynamics and potential for conflict between countries and societies that threaten to split Europe apart.

What then does it mean to speak of a 'German Europe'? The alleged coercion implicit in the austerity programme prescribed by Germany has meant that equitable participation has been sidelined and replaced with increasing frequency by forms of hierarchical dependency. By linking credits to rigorous reforms and the corresponding control mechanisms, entire regions have been plunged into social decline and countless people have been deprived of livelihoods, their dignity, their future – and, not least their faith in Europe.

This immense loss of trust can be measured by the fury of ordinary citizens and the protest and demonstrations in Greece, Spain and Italy.

(ii) Fiscal compact and the 'six-pack'

A broader vision also took hold as to the origins of the crisis and the future mission of the European Union. In October 2010, a Task Force chaired by the President of the European Council,

---

[153] On this see M. Dawson and F. de Witte, 'Constitutional Balance in the EU after the Euro-Crisis' (2013) 76 *MLR* 817.

Herman van Rompuy, and comprising all EU finance ministers reported to the European Council that there needed, on the one hand, to be greater fiscal discipline within the European Union, and, on the other, more done to secure competitiveness and prevent individual economies being imbalanced. To this end, the Task Force recommended both a more wide-ranging regime of economic governance and stronger processes to secure compliance.[154]

This regime was instituted into law in November 2011 by six pieces of legislation: the so-called 'six-pack'.[155] At the heart of this economic governance regime were three goals. First, states should avoid *excessive deficits*. To that end, they should avoid budget deficits of more than 3 per cent of GDP and should bring their total debt down to 60 per cent of GDP. Secondly, states should strive for *balanced budgets*. In principle, taking account of the place of the state in the economic cycle, only a small budget deficit should be incurred.[156] Finally, they should avoid *excessive macro-economic imbalances*. There was a perception that some states' problems had been generated by excessive reliance on one or two industries or were too vulnerable to external shocks. States were, therefore, required to rebalance their economies. An annual meeting, the European Semester for Economic Policy Coordination, would take place to evaluate the performance of each state. In addition, to secure stronger compliance with these goals, states were required to bring in reforms to ensure better statistics, public accounts, and fiscal rules setting levels of expenditure in different areas. Furthermore, procedures provide for states to be fined eye-watering amounts, between 0.1 per cent and 0.5 per cent of GDP in the first instance, if they breach any of these three goals.[157]

Concerns about compliance and whether the existing Treaty allowed for such wide-ranging review led Germany, in particular, to push for a new Treaty amendment. Its central provision would be a new balanced budget rule. This would require euro area states to have a structural deficit of not greater than 0.5 per cent of GDP for states with total debt of more than 60 per cent and 1 per cent in the case of states whose total debt was lower than that. Furthermore, this balanced budget rule was not to exist merely as a Treaty obligation but be enshrined in a permanent and binding domestic law preferably of a constitutional nature. The Treaty, informally known as the fiscal compact, was intended to be a formal amendment to the TFEU. However, in December 2011, the British and Czech Governments indicated that they were not willing to

---

[154] *Strengthening Economic Governance in the EU: Report of the Task Force to the European Council* (October 2010), www.consilium.europa.eu/uedocs/cms_data/docs/pressdata/en/ec/117236.pdf.

[155] Regulation 1173/2011 on the effective enforcement of budgetary surveillance in the euro area [2011] OJ 2011 L306/1; Regulation 1174/2011 on enforcement measures to correct excessive macro-economic imbalances in the euro area [2011] OJ L306/8; Regulation 1175/2011 amending Regulation 1466/97 on the strengthening of the surveillance of budgetary positions and the surveillance and coordination of economic policies [2011] OJ L306/12; Regulation 1176/2011 on the prevention and correction of macro-economic imbalances [2011] OJ L306/25; Regulation 1177/2011 amending Regulation 1467/97 on speeding up and clarifying the implementation of the excessive deficit procedure [2011] OJ L306/33; Directive 2011/85/EU on requirements for budgetary frameworks of the Member States [2011] OJ L306/41.

A further two measures, the 'two pack', were subsequently adopted going to budgetary procedures and budgetary supervision. Regulation 472/2013 on the strengthening of economic and budgetary surveillance of Member States in the euro area experiencing or threatened with serious difficulties with respect to their financial stability [2013] OJ L140/1; Regulation 473/2013 on common provisions for monitoring and assessing draft budgetary plans and ensuring the correction of excessive deficit of the Member States in the euro area [2013] OJ L140/11.

[156] In times of boom, this requires states to run surpluses as taxes receipts are up and welfare spending down. They can incur deficits at moments of recession because of the reduction in tax receipts and increases in spending.

[157] The procedures are complicated in whom they bind. The procedures sanctioning states only apply to euro area states other than that on excessive deficits which applies to all states who are in the euro area or committed to joining it. All states commit themselves to the three goals and to participation in the European Semester.

sign it. It was, therefore signed as an international treaty, the Treaty on Stability, Coordination and Governance in the Economic and Monetary Union (TSCG), by twenty-five Member States in January 2012, and entered into force on 1 January 2013.[158]

With Union total debt standing at 85.3 per cent of GDP at the end of 2012,[159] this regime puts in place an unprecedented system of fiscal retrenchment and welfare reform. This vision of life has, moreover, emerged against a very turbulent backdrop.[160] Governments have collapsed across the Union. There has been a decline in faith in traditionally dominant political parties, the European Union and domestic political institutions.[161] The social consequences have been enormous. Youth unemployment stood at 22.8 per cent for the Union at the end of 2012, with its being over 50 per cent in Greece and Spain.[162] Surveys also showed declines in the provision of public health, and a significant decline in mental health.[163] The disciplining of populations to realise a series of targets in which there seems little place for consideration of alternatives or representative institutions appears deeply authoritarian.[164]

M. Wilkinson, 'The Specter of Authoritarian Liberalism: Reflections on the Constitutional Crisis of the European Union' (2013) 14 *German Law Journal* 527, 542–3 and 551–2

Authoritarian liberalism is outlined here only in stylized form in order to provide some background to its emergence as a transnational phenomenon. Its key characteristic is to curtail or to conceal the conflict between democracy and capitalism rather than to confront it head on through building strong political institutions or reconcile it by supporting social projects. Instead, conflict is managed – successfully or unsuccessfully – from above, in an elite-led attempt to maintain economic stability in the absence of any collective unity or social solidarity. The methods utilized to maintain stability might be formal or informal, coercive or consensual but constitutional principles and legal norms – written and unwritten – are set aside, ignored or distorted in order to maintain the economic credibility of the polity and assuage the pressure exerted by the financial markets. Underlying this constitutional mutation is the attempted depoliticization of the polity, based on a re-conceptualisation of constitutionalism where the economic becomes foundational of the political.

The authoritarian liberal distrust of democracy is based not on a concern for the rights of religious, ethnic or cultural minorities, or the values considered essential for the democratic process, such as freedom of expression or of assembly, but on the perceived need to contain

---

[158] On the details see P. Craig, 'The Stability, Coordination and Governance Treaty: Principle, Politics and Pragmatism' (2012) 37 *ELRev.* 231.

[159] See http://epp.eurostat.ec.europa.eu/tgm/table.do?tab=table&init=1&language=en&pcode=tsdde410&plug in=1.

[160] For an account of the different dimensions to the crisis see A. Menéndez, 'The Existential Crisis of the European Union' (2013) 14 *German Law Journal* 453.

[161] In Spring 2007, trust in the European Union, national parliaments and national governments stood at 57 per cent, 43 per cent and 41 per cent, respectively. In September 2012, the figures were 33 per cent, 28 per cent and 27 per cent. *Standard Eurobarometer, 78 Autumn 2012: Public Opinion in the European Union, First Results* (Luxembourg, European Commission, 2013) 14.

[162] See http://epp.eurostat.ec.europa.eu/portal/page/portal/eurostat/home.

[163] D. Stuckler *et al.*, 'Effects of the 2008 Recession on Health: A First Look at European Data' (2011) 378 *Lancet* 124.

[164] On the particular economic orthodoxy underpinning it see W. Streeck, 'The Crisis in Context: Democratic Capitalism and its Contradictions' in A. Schäfer and W. Streeck (eds.), *Politics in the Age of Austerity* (Cambridge, Polity, 2013).

public interference with private market freedoms and immunities, such as the right to accumulate wealth, to contract and dismiss freely, to dispose of one's property and to exploit, wherever possible, the privatization of public assets. It is concerned with creating as great an area of economic freedom as possible through promoting the values of unbridled competition and private entrepreneurship. This encapsulates the ideology of the market state, the twenty-first century political form that is destined, in one influential account, to replace the twentieth century paradigm of the nation-state...

Depoliticization in the EU is only a symptom of a larger crisis of ideology that follows 'the end of history', even if a particularly acute example. Because of the dominance of the neo-liberal economic model – and its attempted, and to a large extent successful, cooption of other domains, disciplines and fields of enquiry – certain issues are simply removed from the table of democratic contestation. The question of how far, for example, to socialize the economy is largely excluded from the realm of our democratic collective choices, even if imposed wholesale, in an executive manner, in order to rescue financial institutions deemed essential to the capitalist economy. The characterization of the current market liberalism in the EU as authoritarian is strongly confirmed by the language typically used in its support: '[T]here is no alternative' to monetary union. The Euro cannot fail, we are told; the consequences would be too grim for all concerned and would signal the end of the EU itself. What we are now offered by the political Messianism of European elites is not integration through law, let alone integration through concrete achievements of actual solidarity, but integration through necessity.

The point about such eschatological sentiment is that if there is truly 'no alternative', then why bother going through the motions of political democracy at all? Beyond the instrumental utility for those in power of even a sham constitution attaining a certain level of unreflective popular support in order to increase compliance, democratic politics becomes superfluous in these circumstances. Necessity tranquilizes politics in an atmosphere where decision has become more important than judgment.

Instead of encouraging the building of a strong democracy, authoritarian liberalism is content with a weak, deracinated public, one that can be better managed and controlled by the technocratic and political elites at national and supranational level. The emergence of what might be termed a novel form of supranational Machtstaat favors, in other words, no more than a partial democracy, and is content with a limited one, in which any transnational elements of political democracy, or solidarity beyond the market are tamed, if not erased. Publics, to the extent they survive the onslaught of austerity measures, are pitted against each other rather than against the ruling elites. Core is pitted against periphery, nation against nation; it is, as certain political leaders now urge in the climate of economic austerity, sink or swim.

(iii) Integration and disintegration beyond the crisis

The crisis has prompted a number of questions. These include whether the Union contributed to the crisis; whether it has the necessary tools to deal with external challenges; the levels of responsibility different citizens should be expected to have for each other; and whether all EU Member States were ready or willing to assume all the challenges of membership. The initial institutional reaction was to argue that the Union had insufficient tools to protect its citizens from poor national performance and financial markets.

On 26 June 2012, the Presidents of the European Commission, the European Council and the Eurogroup[165] set out a joint report calling for a genuine economic and monetary union.[166] It was to comprise a strengthening of economic and monetary union based around four themes: stronger pan-Union regulation of banks; a more integrated budgetary framework involving stronger oversight of national budgets and possibly issuance of common debt; stronger economic policy coordination; and greater democratic accountability of EMU decision-makers. On the basis of this, the European Council instructed the Commission to set out a roadmap for the achievement of such a union. In addition the Foreign Ministers of eleven Member States came together to form the Future of Europe group whose report argued for a strengthening of economic and monetary union along similar lines.[167]

There was a tension in all this, namely, whether this project was a technical one or something more. In September 2012, the President of the Commission, Jose Manuel Barroso, suggested it was both, by calling for stronger economic and monetary union, which would involve a banking union and a political union in which both the European Parliament and national parliaments would have a stronger role.[168]

In December 2012, the roadmap was presented to the European Union.[169] The thrust of the project was technical. Its first stage was to be a banking union within the euro area. At the heart of this banking union would be a Single Supervisory Mechanism in which the European Central Bank would exercise key regulatory powers over euro area banks, and establish a single rule book setting out the terms under which commercial banking transactions were to take place. There was also to be a Single Resolution Mechanism, a pan-Union process for winding up banks and their liabilities when they went bankrupt. The second stage would involve euro area states making contracts with the EU institutions governing central elements of their economic policies (i.e. competitiveness, labour markets, pensions). These contracts could be underpinned by financial support from the Union. The third stage, after 2014, would involve a central fund to provide support to states who experience shocks, such as the crisis, and to act as a carrot for these to pursue desired fiscal and economic policies. It would also include much more oversight of domestic budgets, as well as some common budgetary decisions.

At the time of writing, agreement on the central elements of banking union has been reached. Although the roadmap argues for a greater role for the European Parliament, the project is above all a functional one that will be dominated by Union and national administrators and bankers. It has been criticised as putting in play a form of executive federalism. The German philosopher, Jürgen Habermas, has, in particular, argued that, instead, what is needed now is a genuine supranational democracy where a convention is held to establish a more genuine political union with the supranational institutions at its heart.[170]

---

[165] The latter is the finance ministers of the euro area.
[166] Report by President of the European Council, Herman Van Rompuy, *Towards a Genuine Economic and Monetary Union*, EUCO 120/12.
[167] These were from Austria, Belgium, Denmark, France, Germany, Italy, Luxembourg, the Netherlands, Poland, Portugal and Spain.
[168] 'State of the Union 2012 Address', Strasbourg, 12 September 2012, http://europa.eu/rapid/press-release_SPEECH-12-596_en.htm.
[169] H. v. Rompuy, J. M. Barroso, J.-C. Juncker and M. Draghi, *Towards a Genuine Economic and Monetary Union* (Brussels, European Council, 2012).
[170] J. Habermas, 'Democracy, Solidarity and the European Crisis', Lecture delivered at Catholic University of Leuven, 26 April 2013. www.kuleuven.be/communicatie/evenementen/evenementen/jurgen-habermas/en/democracy-solidarity-and-the-european-crisis. For a similar but more polemic argument see G. Verhofstadt and D. Cohen-Bendit, *For Europe!* (Munich, Carl Hanser Verlag, 2012).

Even Habermas has had to concede that there is little popular enthusiasm for such a supranational democracy.[171] In part, this is because debates have increased about whether the European Union is more the problem than the solution. In December 2012, the United Kingdom began a two-year review of the balance of competencies between the United Kingdom and the European Union to examine how EU policies affected the United Kingdom, and what that entails for the British national interest. The clear purpose of such a review was to seek reform or even renegotiation where a particular policy did not work to Britain's interest.[172] In June 2013, the Dutch Government published a similar, albeit more limited exercise, where it went through fifty-four pieces of legislation or proposals setting out items it would either oppose or seek to reform, and nine principles for curbing excessive EU intervention.[173]

The most dramatic step was taken in January 2013. David Cameron, the British Prime Minister, sought to negotiate a new multilateral settlement with the other Member States, involving less EU regulation, more room for national parliaments in Union decision-making processes, and more openness both in terms of the trade arrangements with non-EU states and in accepting new members. He promised, with or without this settlement, to put British membership of the European Union to a referendum by 2017 if re-elected.[174] Yet Cameron's speech revealed a paradox which brings us back to the beginning of the chapter. His case for the nature of the United Kingdom's relationship with the Union ultimately rested on an understanding of what it meant to be British and how it has been affected by Europe.

D. Cameron, 'EU Speech at Bloomberg', 23 January 2013

For us, the European Union is a means to an end – prosperity, stability, the anchor of freedom and democracy both within Europe and beyond her shores – not an end in itself.

We insistently ask: How? Why? To what end? But all this doesn't make us somehow un-European. The fact is that ours is not just an island story – it is also a continental story. For all our connections to the rest of the world – of which we are rightly proud – we have always been a European power – and we always will be.

From Caesar's legions to the Napoleonic Wars. From the Reformation, the Enlightenment and the Industrial Revolution to the defeat of Nazism. We have helped to write European history, and Europe has helped write ours.

Over the years, Britain has made her own, unique contribution to Europe. We have provided a haven to those fleeing tyranny and persecution. And in Europe's darkest hour, we helped keep the flame of liberty alight. Across the continent, in silent cemeteries, lie the hundreds of thousands of British servicemen who gave their lives for Europe's freedom.

In more recent decades, we have played our part in tearing down the Iron Curtain and championing the entry into the EU of those countries that lost so many years to Communism. And contained in this history is the crucial point about Britain, our national character, our attitude to Europe.

Britain is characterised not just by its independence but, above all, by its openness.

---

[171] J. Habermas, *The Crisis of the European Union: A Response* (Polity, Cambridge, 2012) 132.

[172] *Review of the Balance of Competences between the United Kingdom and the European Union*, Cm 8415 (London, SO, 2012).

[173] The press release and the link to the English translation is available at www.government.nl/news/2013/06/21/european-where-necessary-national-where-possible.html.

[174] See www.gov.uk/government/speeches/eu-speech-at-bloomberg.

There is much that can be debated and contested in this section. However, it sets out a series of symbols, values and stories by which both national and European identities are understood. In part, they reinforce each other. In part, they compete. Yet when citizens and decision-makers talk about what the European Union, the nation-state or EU law should be doing they are harking back to these. It is how these come to be understood over the next few years, as much as the playing out of the crisis, that is likely to shape the future of the European Union.

FURTHER READING

S. Bartolini, *Restructuring Europe: Centre Formation, System Building, and Political Structuring Between the Nation State and the European Union* (Oxford, Oxford University Press, 2005)

C. Bickerton, *European Integration: From Nation States to Member States* (Oxford, Oxford University Press, 2012)

P. Craig, *The Lisbon Treaty: Law, Politics and Treaty Reform* (Oxford, Oxford University Press, 2010)

N. Fligstein, *Euro-Clash: The EU, European Identity and the Future of Europe* (Oxford, Oxford University Press, 2008)

J. Habermas, *The Crisis of the European Union: A Response* (Cambridge, Polity, 2012)

M. Hartmann and F. de Witte, 'Regeneration Europe' (2013) 14 *German Law Journal*, Issue 5

J. Le Goff, *The Birth of Europe* (Oxford, Blackwell, 2005)

G. Majone, *Dilemmas of European Integration: The Ambiguities and Pitfalls of Integration by Stealth* (Oxford, Oxford University Press, 2005)

L. v. Middelaar, *The Passage to Europe: How a Continent Became a Union* (New Haven, CT, Yale University Press, 2013)

A. Milward, *The Reconstruction of Western Europe 1945–51* (London, Methuen, 1984)

J.-C. Piris, *The Future of Europe: Towards a Two-Speed EU?* (Cambridge, Cambridge University Press, 2012)

F. Scharpf, *Governing in Europe: Effective and Democratic?* (New York, Oxford University Press, 1999)

C. Shore, *Building Europe: The Cultural Politics of European Integration* (London/New York, Routledge, 2000)

J. Zielonka, *Europe as Empire: The Nature of the Enlarged European Union* (Oxford, Oxford University Press, 2006)

2

The EU Institutions

CONTENTS

1 INTRODUCTION

This chapter looks at the institutional settlement governing the European Union.

Section 2 looks at the institutional framework governing the European Union. This framework is subject to two different visions. One is that of institutional balance. EU institutions are only to have the powers provided for them by the EU Treaties. This is both to limit institutional power and to protect the prerogatives of other EU institutions. The other is that EU institutions are to promote the policies of the Union, its interests and those of its citizens. National governments can grant EU institutions any powers for this purpose, even outside the framework of the EU Treaties. If the initial vision was traditionally predominant, the latter has emerged strongly with the onset of the financial crisis. The powers of the EU institutions can no longer be understood simply through the lens of the EU Treaties. If this gives them greater capacities, it also raises concerns about their judicial and democratic control.

Section 3 considers the European Commission. An independent administration, the Commission has four central powers: legislative and quasi-legislative, agenda-setting, executive and supervisory. These extensive powers have increasingly proved too much for it, and so a wide array of its powers have been transferred to specialised European Regulatory Agencies, of which there are now thirty-six. However, even these powers are insufficient to secure the full administration and implementation of EU law and policy, which is predominantly done by national administrations with the Commission supervising them. The consequence is a pan-Union executive order made up of the Commission, European Regulatory Agencies and national administrations which carries out a large number of quasi-legislative, regulatory and executive tasks, and which is relatively unaccountable to broader democratic constituencies, either at a national or pan-Union level.

Section 4 looks at the Council of Ministers ('Council'). Comprised of national ministers, it has the final power of decision over almost all fields of EU law. It has two dominant forms of voting: unanimity, where each national government has a veto, and qualified majority vote (QMV), a weighted form of voting in which different Member States are allocated different numbers of votes, with 260 out of a possible 352 votes required for a measure to be adopted. The Council sits in ten configurations with the minster responsible for a particular field representing the Member State in that field. This specialisation and its floating membership limit what can be decided and debated in Council meetings. This has led to its being particularly dependent on the Committee of Permanent Representatives (COREPER). These are national civil servants, based in Brussels, who prepare the Council's work. Frequently, this will be done through the establishment of Working Groups of civil servants in the different national capitals to formulate common positions. This underworld of COREPER and Working Groups results in few items being discussed, and even fewer votes, within the Council. This raises questions about the balance of power between politicians and civil servants, on the one hand, and the transparency and accountability of this administrative machinery, on the other.

Section 5 assesses the European Council. Comprising the Heads of Government, the central role of the European Council is to provide political direction to the Union. The Lisbon Treaty headlined the European Council's pivotal role within the EU institutional settlement by making it a formal EU institution. However, it is not clear how strongly EU law regulates its activities. The Lisbon Treaty also established the post of President of the European Council. Formally, the President's role is similar to that of COREPER in relation to the Council of Ministers. He is to prepare and ensure follow-up to the European Council's meetings. There were initial doubts about how effective the post would be. The President would have to mediate between the wishes of the different Member States, and the tension between the European Council and other EU institutions, which saw it as treading on their prerogatives. Initial experience is that the post is a powerful one. The President is highly trusted to mediate between both EU institutions and between national governments. The latter have also come to realise that it is only through the President that the European Council can act. They prefer this to inaction or action by the other EU institutions. The presence and workings of the European Council bring out particularly strongly the tensions between supranationalism and intergovernmentalism. With most of its members strongly accountable to their national parliaments, the European Council unsettles the balance of power within the rest of the (supranational) EU institutional settlement.

Section 6 looks at the European Parliament (Parliament). The Parliament will comprise, from November 2014, 751 directly elected Members of the European Parliament (MEPs). Established to represent EU citizens, there is controversy about how effectively it does this. There are no European political parties and Members of the European Parliament (MEPs) are not elected on a pan-Union 'one citizen one vote' principle, but on the basis of quotas allocated to each Member State. Furthermore, less than half of EU citizens vote in European Parliament elections and there is little evidence that voting goes to past or future performance by the European Parliament. Notwithstanding this, the Parliament remains the forum where there is most open public debate about EU decision-making. The Parliament has three forms of power: legislative, budgetary and holding the other EU institutions to account. Its legislative powers vary according to the field of activity. There are, however, three main legislative procedures. In the central one, the ordinary legislative procedure, it can veto legislative proposals. Under the other two, the consultation and consent procedures, it has, respectively, the power to propose amendments and to have to agree to a proposal before it can become law. Its central power in relation to the budget is a power of veto. Finally, its powers over the other EU institutions allow it to bring these to the Court of Justice for breaking EU law and to ask questions. However, its central power here is the power to co-appoint the Commission with the European Council and then also to sack it.

2 EU INSTITUTIONS AND THE INSTITUTIONAL FRAMEWORK

The central EU institutions and their collective mission are set out in Article 13 TEU.

Article 13

1. The Union shall have an institutional framework which shall aim to promote its values, advance its objectives, serve its interests, those of its citizens and those of the Member States, and ensure the consistency, effectiveness and continuity of its policies and actions. This institutional framework comprises:
   - the European Parliament,
   - the European Council,
   - the Council,
   - the European Commission,
   - the Court of Justice of the European Union,
   - the European Central Bank,
   - the Court of Auditors.
2. Each institution shall act within the limits of the powers conferred on it in the Treaties, and in conformity with the procedures, conditions and objectives set out in them. The institutions shall practise mutual sincere cooperation.

All these institutions are considered in this chapter with the exception of the Court of Justice and the European Central Bank, which are considered in more detail in Chapters 4 and 16, respectively. There are three features which are striking about EU institutions.

The first is that they cannot be seen in stand-alone terms. The Union institutional framework exists to promote a particular mission: namely, Union policies and values and the interests of the Member States and its citizens. It is a purposive association. This is different from a state where institutions might have limited powers. With the latter, the exercise of these powers is not tied to realising a particular policy or value. The legislature is simply engaged in law-making rather than to promote a particular policy. The authority of EU institutions is, thus, tied much more strongly to the authority of these policies and the Union's success in realising them. If one does not believe in market liberalisation, for example, the establishment of a legislative machinery to realise it can never be legitimate as it curtails the debate about whether market liberalisation should take place at all.

Secondly, although EU institutions exist independently from one another and have a distinct presence, they also have to act with each other. The Union is based on a division of power which tries to ensure that power is not concentrated in any single institution. The legislative process, for example, involves three institutions: the Commission, Parliament and Council. The power of each makes no sense without regard to the power of the other. The presence of an institutional framework requires EU institutions to be seen not simply in terms of their powers but in terms of their relationship to one another. In some cases, this relationship will be one of cooperation. In other instances, it will be one of competition.

The third issue to arise is the limits to their powers. Article 13(2) TEU indicates that they operate under the doctrine of conferred powers. This doctrine states that public institutions are constrained by law, in this case the treaties, but are creatures of law. They only have the powers granted to them by law. The traditional reason for this is that administrative power should be seen as something exceptional which requires justification and constraint in a liberal society.

This position was adopted in *Safe Countries of Origin*. An EU law set minimum standards for granting and withdrawing refugee status. This law allowed for certain states to be designated safe countries of origin. The presumption was that a national of these states could not be a refugee as these states were safe. The Directive granted the Council implementing powers to draw up lists of which countries were safe. The Treaty did not grant the Council direct implementing powers other than in exceptional circumstances which it had to justify. This had not taken place here.

Case C-133/06 *Parliament v Council (Safe Countries of Origin)* [2008] ECR I-3189

44. It should be borne in mind that ... each institution is to act within the limits of the powers conferred upon it by the Treaty ...

54. ... it has already been held that the rules regarding the manner in which the Community institutions arrive at their decisions are laid down in the Treaty and are not at the disposal of the Member States or of the institutions themselves ...

55. The Treaty alone may ... empower an institution to amend a decision-making procedure established by the Treaty.

56. To acknowledge that an institution can establish secondary legal bases, whether for the purpose of strengthening or easing the detailed rules for the adoption of an act, is tantamount to according that institution a legislative power which exceeds that provided for by the Treaty.

57. It would also enable the institution concerned to undermine the principle of institutional balance which requires that each of the institutions must exercise its powers with due regard for the powers of the other institutions ...

59. Nor can the adoption of secondary legal bases be justified on the basis of considerations relating to the politically sensitive nature of the issue concerned or to a concern to ensure the effectiveness of a Community action.

60. Furthermore, the existence of an earlier practice of establishing secondary legal bases cannot reasonably be relied upon. Even on the assumption that there is such a practice, it cannot derogate from the rules laid down in the Treaty and cannot therefore create a precedent binding on the institutions.

Institutional balance and the need to limit public powers are the reasons, therefore, why EU institutions should only have those powers granted to them by the Treaties. This position was, historically, subject to a limited exception whereby the Commission could handle development aid provided from national development aid budgets that fell outside the EU Budget.[1] This exception was widened considerably in *Pringle*. Pringle challenged an EU Decision authorising ratification of the European Stability Mechanism Treaty, an international agreement between seventeen euro area states which offered financial support to those euro area states otherwise unable to finance themselves. As paragraphs 156 and 157 below explain, EU institutions were central to its administration. The Commission and European Central Bank both assessed terms for granting support and monitored the meeting of those conditions on which the support was offered. Pringle argued, inter alia, that this violated the doctrine of conferred powers in Article 13(2) TEU.

Case C–370/12 *Pringle* v *Government of Ireland*, Judgment of 27 November 2012

155. The ESM Treaty allocates various tasks to the Commission and to the ECB.

156. As regards the Commission, those tasks consist of assessing requests for stability support (Article 13(1)), assessing their urgency (Article 4(4)), negotiating a [Memorandum of Understanding (MoU)] detailing the conditionality attached to the financial assistance granted (Article 13(3)), monitoring compliance with the conditionality attached to the financial assistance (Article 13(7)), and participating in the meetings of the Board of Governors and the Board of Directors as an observer (Articles 5(3) and 6(2)).

157. The tasks allocated to the ECB consist of assessing the urgency of requests for stability support (Article 4(4)), participating in the meetings of the Board of Governors and the Board of Directors as an observer (Articles 5(3) and 6(2)) and, in liaison with the Commission, assessing requests for stability support (Article 13(1)), negotiating an MoU (Article 13(3)) and monitoring compliance with the conditionality attached to the financial assistance (Article 13(7)).

---

[1] Joined Cases C-181/91 and C-248/91 *Parliament* v *Council* [1993] ECR I-3713; Case C-316/91 *Parliament* v *Council* [1994] ECR I-653.

158. In that regard, it is apparent from the case-law of the Court that the Member States are entitled, in areas which do not fall under the exclusive competence of the Union, to entrust tasks to the institutions, outside the framework of the Union, such as the task of coordinating a collective action undertaken by the Member States or managing financial assistance … provided that those tasks do not alter the essential character of the powers conferred on those institutions by the TEU and TFEU …

159. The duties allocated to the Commission and to the ECB in the ESM Treaty constitute tasks of the kind referred to in the preceding paragraph.

160. First, the activities of the ESM fall under economic policy. The Union does not have exclusive competence in that area.

161. Secondly, the duties conferred on the Commission and ECB within the ESM Treaty, important as they are, do not entail any power to make decisions of their own. Further, the activities pursued by those two institutions within the ESM Treaty solely commit the ESM.

162. Thirdly, the tasks conferred on the Commission and the ECB do not alter the essential character of the powers conferred on those institutions by the TEU and TFEU.

163. As regards the Commission, it is stated in Article 17(1) TEU that the Commission 'shall promote the general interest of the Union' and 'shall oversee the application of Union law'.

164. It must be recalled that the objective of the ESM Treaty is to ensure the financial stability of the euro area as a whole. By its involvement in the ESM Treaty, the Commission promotes the general interest of the Union. Further, the tasks allocated to the Commission by the ESM Treaty enable it, as provided in Article 13(3) and (4) of that treaty, to ensure that the memoranda of understanding concluded by the ESM are consistent with European Union law.

165. As regards the tasks allocated to the ECB by the ESM Treaty, they are in line with the various tasks which the TFEU … confer on that institution. By virtue of its duties within the ESM Treaty, the ECB supports the general economic policies in the Union, in accordance with Article 282(2) TFEU …

Although this chapter focuses on the powers granted to the EU institutions by the EU Treaties, it is important to be aware, particularly since the onset of the crisis, that EU institutions can be granted additional powers beyond these, provided this does not alter their 'essential character'. This last phrase is understood very broadly, however. In the case of the Commission, for example, it is understood as promoting the 'general interest of the Union': something which allows it to be granted almost any legislative, executive or judicial power. The rationale, set out in Article 13(1) TEU, is that the institutions have an instrumental role, namely, to promote the interests, policies and values of the Union. This allows a relaxation of controls and for this to be contracted out by groups of Member States. However, it conflicts deeply with the ethos set out in *Safe Countries of Origin* of limiting institutional power and maintaining institutional balance. There is little sense of a democratic balance within the ESM Treaty, as we shall see,[2] about how financial support is dispensed, conditioned and monitored.[3] Contracting out in this way can also avoid judicial controls and fundamental rights guarantees, as these arrangements often are subject to very limited review.[4]

---

[2] See pp. 740–4.

[3] F. de Witte and M. Dawson, 'Constitutional Balance in the EU after the Euro-Crisis' (2013) 77 *MLR* 817.

[4] J. Tomkin, 'Contradiction, Circumvention and Conceptual Gymnastics: The Impact of the Adoption of the ESM Treaty on the State of European Democracy' (2013) 14 *German Law Journal* 169.

3 THE COMMISSION

(i) The Commission bureaucracy

Although the Commission is, legally, a single body, its institutional reality is more complex. It performs a large number of tasks, employs more than 32,000 people and is composed of three tiers: the College of Commissioners, the Directorates-General (DGs) and the Cabinets.

(a) College of Commissioners

Formally, the Commission consists of twenty-eight Commissioners, with one Commissioner from each Member State.[5] These Commissioners make up the College of Commissioners: the body that, formally at least, takes all Commission decisions. The Commission is appointed for a five-year term.[6] Once appointed, the Commissioners are allocated portfolios by the President. Each Commissioner is the primary person responsible for the work of the Commission that falls within that policy area.[7] The Commissioners are to be persons whose 'independence is beyond doubt'.[8] They are required not to seek or take instructions from any government or any other body and a duty is imposed on Member States to respect this principle.[9] In addition, Commissioners must not find themselves in a position where a 'conflict of interest' arises. They must not, therefore, engage in any other occupation during their period of office. If any Commissioner fails to observe these rules, the Court of Justice may, on application by either the Council or the Commission, compulsorily retire that Commissioner.[10]

This independence should not be seen in too absolute terms. Sanctions for breach of this principle can only be applied to the most severe breaches where the behaviour of the Commissioner is manifestly inappropriate.[11] Furthermore, chosen because of distinguished and well-connected prior careers, Commissioners have a list of professional and political contacts, with over two-thirds chosen from a party in government at the time of appointment.[12]

---

[5] Article 17(4) TEU. It was initially anticipated that from 1 November 2014 the Commission should comprise only two-thirds of that number, unless the European Council decided to alter this via Article 17(5) TEU. A condition for Ireland having a second referendum on the Lisbon Treaty was that the principle of one Commissioner per Member State should continue. In May 2013, it was agreed that it would continue at least until the accession of the thirtieth state or until the appointment of the Commission succeeding that beginning its term in November 2014 (whichever was earlier). EU Council, 'The European Council decides on the number of members of the European Commission', EUCO 119/13.

[6] Article 17(3) TEU.

[7] The current portfolios are President; High Representative for Foreign Affairs and Security Policy; Justice, Fundamental Rights and Citizenship; Competition; Transport; Digital Agenda; Industry and Entrepreneurship; Inter-Institutional Relations and Administration; Economic and Monetary Affairs and the Euro; Environment; Development; Internal Market and Services; Education, Culture, Multilingualism and Youth; Taxation, Customs, Statistics, Audit and Anti-Fraud; Trade; Research, Innovation and Science; Financial Programming and Budget; Maritime Affairs and Fisheries; International Cooperation, Humanitarian Aid and Crisis Response; Energy; Regional Policy; Climate Action; Enlargement and European Neighbourhood Policy; Employment, Social Affairs and Inclusion; Home Affairs; Agriculture and Rural Development; Health; Consumer Policy.

[8] Article 17(3) TEU.

[9] There is one exception to this, the High Representative of the Union for Foreign Affairs and Security Policy. She has the portfolio of both the Common Foreign and Security Policy and the Security and Defence Policy within the Commission. She has a 'double hat' which involves her also acting under a mandate from the Council, Article 18(2) TEU.

[10] Article 245 TFEU.

[11] Case C-432/04 *Commission* v *Cresson* [2006] ECR I-6387.

[12] A. Wonka, 'Technocratic and Independent? The Appointment of European Commissioners and its Policy Implications' (2007) 14 *JEPP* 169, 178.

Usually, they are members – and appointees – of the major parties in their Member State and continue some involvement with national politics after becoming Commissioners. Frequent trips to speak before (and to lecture to) national audiences are common. Again, the metaphor of gate-keeping is perhaps most useful: Commissioners are an easy and efficient way for the Commission to maintain a link with Member State governments and domestic political systems. They will know what legislative proposals are politically acceptable in national capitals, while at the same time being in an ideal position to communicate to national elites the requirements of efficient European policy-making.[13]

That said, this networking and gate-keeping role should not be overstated. Research has found little evidence of partisanship by Commissioners either in favour of their respective Member States or sectors with which they have an association.[14]

The other feature of the College is the principle of *collegiality*. The Commission is collectively responsible for all decisions taken and all Commission decisions should be taken collectively. In principle, these decisions should take place at the weekly meetings of the Commission by a simple majority vote of the College. Meetings of each Commissioner's Cabinet (staff) occur two days before the weekly meeting. If there is agreement, it will be formally adopted as an 'A' item and there will be no formal discussion of the matter at the meeting. However, the reality is that there is little discussion within the College about the majority of the Commission's business. Studies are dated, but a 2008 survey of legislative proposals between 2000 and 2004 found that only 17.4 per cent even made it to the agenda of the meeting.[15] Of these, very few are discussed. Between 2000 and 2003, of 1,344 Decisions, there was a vote on only 11 measures, and there was discussion on less than 3 per cent.[16]

The only Commissioner without a portfolio, the President, is the most powerful of all the Commissioners.[17] He has six important roles.

- He is involved in the appointment of the other Commissioners. With the Heads of Government, he nominates the other Commissioners, who are then subject to a collective vote of approval by the Parliament and then appointed by the European Council.[18]
- He decides on the internal organisation of the Commission. He allocates individual portfolios at the beginning of the term, which can then be shifted by him during the term of office.
- Individual Commissioners are responsible to him. The President can request individual Commissioners to resign.[19]
- He is to provide 'political guidance' to the Commission. At its most formal, this involves chairing and setting the agenda for the weekly meetings of the Commission. More substantively, it means proposing the political priorities of the Commission through pushing forward one proposal rather than another for adoption by the Commission.

---

[13] T. Christiansen, 'Tensions of European Governance: Politicised Bureaucracy and Multiple Accountability in the European Commission' (1997) 4 *JEPP* 73, 82; A. Smith, 'Why Commissioners Matter' (2003) 41 *JCMS* 137, 143–5.

[14] R. Thomson, 'National Actors in International Organizations: The Case of the European Commission' (2008) 41 *Comparative Political Studies* 169.

[15] A. Wonka, 'Decision-making Dynamics in the European Commission: Partisan, National or Sectoral?' (2008) 15 *JEPP* 1145, 1151.

[16] EU Commission, *A Constitution for the Union*, COM(2003)548, Annex I.

[17] The current President is a Portuguese national, Manuel Barroso.

[18] Article 17(7) TEU.   [19] Article 17(6) TEU.

- He has a roving policy brief. Although this causes tensions with the individual Commissioner concerned, the President may seek to take over a particular issue and drive Commission policy on that issue.
- He has a representative role. He represents the Commission at meetings involving the Heads of Government and must account to other institutions when there is a questioning of the general conduct of the institution or a particular issue raises broader questions.

(b) Directorates-General

The majority of Commission employees work for the Directorates-General (DGs). These are the equivalent of ministries within a national government. In 2013, there were thirty-three DGs, although the number and organisation is subject to frequent change.[20] In addition, there are eleven services, which provide support to these DGs.[21] Whilst all DGs fall within the portfolio of at least one Commissioner and are answerable to (at least) that Commissioner, with thirty-three DGs and twenty-eight Commissioners, there is no neat dovetailing. Furthermore, DGs' duties are to the Commission rather than the Commissioner. Individual Commissioners have complained about the autonomy DGs enjoy and the lack of loyalty they show.[22]

The variety of Commission activities results in little cohesion between the different DGs.[23] Commission officials tend rather to identify strongly with their DGs and the values promoted by it.[24] As a consequence, the interests and values of officials working for the Environment DG are likely to be very different from those working in the Competition DG. In addition, each DG may focus on very different tasks. The bulk of the work of the Environment DG will be concentrated around the proposal and enforcement of legislation. By contrast, in the fields of education and culture the Union has no law-making powers. The work of officials in that DG focuses on the development of programmes, administration of Union funding and bringing different public and private actors together. This leads to different DGs having quite distinct cultures. This distinctiveness is reinforced by poor central coordinating mechanisms, which

[20] Agriculture and Rural Development; Budget; Climate Action; Communication; Communications Networks, Content and Technology; Competition; Economic and Financial Affairs; Education and Culture; Employment, Social Affairs and Inclusion; Energy; Enlargement; Enterprise and Industry; Environment; EuropeAid Development and Cooperation; Eurostat; Health and Consumers; Home Affairs; Humanitarian Aid; Human Resources and Security; Informatics; Internal Market and Services; Interpretation; Joint Research Centre; Justice; Maritime Affairs and Fisheries; Mobility and Transport; Regional Policy; Research and Innovation; Secretariat-General; Service for Foreign Policy Instruments; Taxation and Customs Union; Trade; Translation.

[21] Bureau of European Policy Advisers; Central Library European Anti-Fraud Office; European Commission Data Protection Officer Historical Archives Infrastructures and Logistics, Brussels; Infrastructures and Logistics, Luxembourg; Internal Audit Service; Legal Service; Office for Administration and Payment of Individual Entitlements; Publications Office.

[22] D. Curtin and M. Egeberg, 'Tradition and Innovation: Europe's Accumulated Executive Order' (2008) 31 *West European Politics* 639, 657. Civil servants working in the DGs also perceive that, because of their number and expertise, they have the upper hand over Commissioners. A. Elinas and E. Suleiman, *The European Commission and Bureaucratic Autonomy* (Cambridge, Cambridge University Press, 2012) 65–73.

[23] L. Cram, 'The European Commission as a Multi-Organization: Social Policy and IT Policy in the EU' (1994) 1 *JEPP* 195.

[24] H. Kassim *et al.*, *The European Commission of the Twenty First Century* (Oxford, Oxford University Press, 2013) 115–18; M. Egeberg, 'Experiments in Supranational Institution Building: The European Commission as Laboratory' (2012) 19 *JEPP* 939, 941–4.

lead, arguably, to insufficient exchange between the DGs and to poor policy coherence because different DGs are often working in very different directions.[25]

(c) Cabinets

If the College of Commissioners represents the political arm of the Commission and the DGs the administrative arm, between them sit the Cabinets. Formally appointed by the President, each Cabinet is the Office of a Commissioner. Composed of seven to eight officials,[26] the Cabinets act, first, as the interface between the Commissioner and the DGs under her aegis.[27] They enable liaison between the two, and they help the Commissioner with formulating priorities and policies. They also act as the eyes and ears for the Commissioner, keeping her informed about what is happening elsewhere in the Commission. Finally, they combine with other Cabinets to prepare the weekly meetings for the College of Commissioners.

These tasks place the Cabinets in a very strong position within the Commission. The preparation of the meetings between the Commissioners forecloses a great deal of debate in the College, because in reality, much is negotiated between the Cabinets. Similarly, by acting as the interface between the Commission and the DG, they inevitably become gate-keepers to the Commissioner, who must be negotiated with by DG officials wishing to put forward particular ideas. Their role is, thus, controversial. DGs have seen them at times as Machiavellian, bypassing normal procedures and sabotaging perfectly acceptable proposals.[28]

(d) Modus operandi of the Commission

The Commission deploys three procedures for conducting its business. Two start with a proposal drawn up by a lead DG or, sometimes, a group involving several DGs. This is circulated to other interested DGs, the Legal Service and the Secretariat General, who have fifteen days to respond. The lead DG may then negotiate, take on board comments, withdraw the proposal or seek resolution by the Cabinets of the Commissioners. Once there is consensus, the proposal may be adopted by the *written procedure*. It has to be approved by the Commissioner responsible for the relevant portfolio who circulates it to the Cabinets of the other Commissioners. If there is no objection, the proposal is adopted as a Commission Decision. The 'ordinary' written procedure gives the Cabinets five working days to consider the proposal. The expedited written procedure must be authorised by the President. In such circumstances, the Cabinets are only given three working days. Alternately, the proposal may be adopted by an *oral procedure* whereby a meeting is held of all the members of the different Cabinets which have responsibility for this activity. If they agree unanimously, it is passed to the College of Commissioners for notification. If there is no agreement, it has to be resolved by the College of Commissioners. The written and oral procedures both give considerable power to the lead DG at the expense of other DGs and even the Commissioners. It can decide how to formulate the proposal, how

---

[25] L. Hooghe, *The European Commission and the Integration of Europe* (Cambridge, Cambridge University Press, 2001) 201–5.

[26] The President's Cabinet is larger, with thirteen officials.

[27] On the functioning and composition see M. Egeberg and A. Heskestad, 'The Denationalization of *Cabinets* in the European Commission' (2010) 48 *JCMS* 775.

[28] J. Peterson, 'The Santer Era: The European Commission in Normative, Historical and Theoretical Perspective' (1999) 6 *JEPP* 46.

to incorporate suggestions, and, most importantly, when to put a proposal forward. It can thus choose the most opportune time to suggest it, and it is not unknown for proposals to be left dormant for many years until the right political opportunity arises.[29]

The third procedure, used for managerial matters, is *internal delegation*. The Commission can delegate a straightforward 'act of management' to particular members.[30] The nature of such an act is unclear. A Decision requiring undertakings to submit to a Commission investigation into anti-competitive practices was considered to be an act of management, which could be delegated. By contrast, a decision finding a violation of EU competition law was not considered to be administrative in nature and was considered too wide to be delegated.[31]

(ii) Powers of the Commission

The powers of the Commission are headlined in a single article.

Article 17(1) TEU

1. The Commission shall promote the general interest of the Union and take appropriate initiatives to that end. It shall ensure the application of the Treaties, and of measures adopted by the institutions pursuant to the Treaties. It shall oversee the application of Union law under the control of the Court of Justice of the European Union. It shall execute the budget and manage programmes. It shall exercise coordinating, executive and management functions, as laid down in the Treaties. With the exception of the common foreign and security policy, and other cases provided for in the Treaties, it shall ensure the Union's external representation. It shall initiate the Union's annual and multiannual programming with a view to achieving interinstitutional agreements.

2. Union legislative acts may only be adopted on the basis of a Commission proposal, except where the Treaties provide otherwise. Other acts shall be adopted on the basis of a Commission proposal where the Treaties so provide.

The Article is however, terse about the scope and detail of these powers which are scattered around the rest of the Treaty. It makes sense to consider them in the light of the central roles enjoyed by the Commission.

(a) Legislative and quasi-legislative powers

The Commission has direct legislative powers in only two limited fields: ensuring that public undertakings comply with the rules contained in the Treaty[32] and determining the conditions under which Union nationals may reside in another Member State after having worked there.[33] It has more significant quasi-legislative powers. These are powers granted to it by EU legislation to adopt general rules, which, whilst not legislative in nature, have binding legal

---

[29] M. Hartlapp, J. Metz and C. Rauh, 'Linking Agenda Setting to Coordination Structures: Bureaucratic Politics inside the European Commission' (2013) 35 *Journal of European Integration* 425.
[30] This practice was upheld in Case 5/85 *AKZO v Commission* [1986] ECR 2585.
[31] Case C-137/92P *Commission v BASF* [1994] ECR I-2555.
[32] Article 106(3) TFEU.   [33] Article 45(3)(d) TFEU.

effects. The number of such measures adopted is considerable. One study found 14,522 to be adopted in the period between 2004 and 2009.[34] The measures in question are often highly significant. For example, the 1996 measure prompting the Bovine Spongiform Encephalopathy (BSE) crisis, the prohibition on the export of beef and bovine products from the United Kingdom, was instigated under powers granted to the Commission to make veterinary and zootechnical checks on live animals and products with a view to the completion of the internal market.[35] This measure had huge implications for animal welfare, public health, public finances and the livelihood of farmers across the Union, and prompted a crisis in relations between the United Kingdom and the rest of the European Union.[36]

At the Lisbon Treaty, a distinction was made between two forms of quasi-legislation: delegated measures and implementing measures. Delegated measures are to be used to amend or supplement non-essential elements of legislation.

Article 290(1) TFEU

1. A legislative act may delegate to the Commission the power to adopt non-legislative acts to supplement or amend certain non-essential elements of the legislative act.

    The objectives, content, scope and duration of the delegation of power shall be explicitly defined in the legislative acts. The essential elements of an area shall be reserved for the legislative act and accordingly shall not be the subject of a delegation of power.

By contrast, implementing measures are to provide greater uniformity to the application and implementation of EU legislation by setting out in greater detail its implications, be this through further rules or individual decisions.

Article 291(2) TFEU

2. Where uniform conditions for implementing legally binding Union acts are needed, those acts shall confer implementing powers on the Commission ...

Justifications for these powers include the legislative procedures not taking pressing decisions sufficiently quickly; legislatures neither having the expertise nor a sufficiently long-term view of matters; and, finally, they liberate other institutions to spend more time on matters of greater political significance.[37] For all this, the widespread grant of such powers raises

---

[34] M. Kaeding and A. Hardacre, 'The European Parliament and the Future of Comitology after Lisbon' (2013) 19 *ELJ* 382.

[35] The measure was Decision 96/239/EC [1966] OJL78/47. The principal basis for it was Directive 90/425/EEC [1990] OJ L224/29, article 10(4). On the subsequent political crisis see M. Westlake, 'Mad Cows and Englishmen: The Institutional Consequences of the BSE Crisis' (1997) 35 *JCMS (Annual Review)* 11; S. Jasonoff, 'Civilization and Madness: The Great BSE Scare of 1996' (1997) 6 *Public Understanding of Science* 221.

[36] See J. Neyer, 'The Regulation of Risks and the Power of the People: Lessons from the BSE Crisis' (2000) 4 *EIOP* 6.

[37] G. Majone, 'Two Logics of Delegation: Agency and Fiduciary Relations in EU Governance' (2001) 2 *EUP* 103; F. Franchino, 'Efficiency or Credibility? Testing the Two Logics of Delegation to the European Commission' (2002) 9 *JEPP* 1; M. Pollack, *The Engines of European Integration: Delegation, Agency and Agenda-Setting in the EU* (Oxford, Oxford University Press, 2003) 101–7.

questions of democratic accountability as it supplants the legislative process.[38] It would be worrying, for example, if the power of delegation allowed the Commission to rewrite almost all the EU legislation. Equally concerning would be if the parent legislation was substantively empty and granted the Commission the power effectively to determine all its content through implementation.[39]

The remit of these quasi-legislative powers is thus very important. The 'essential' elements which could not be delegated had been interpreted as only those elements which 'give concrete shape to the fundamental guidelines of [Union] policy'.[40] It was not until September 2012, therefore, that any piece of EU legislation was found illegal for granting the Commission excessive powers.

This was changed in the *Schengen Borders Code* judgment. The EU legislation in question, the Schengen Borders Code (SBC), provided for surveillance of the Union external frontiers to prevent unauthorised border crossings. To this end, article 12(5) SBC authorised additional measures to be taken governing surveillance which amended or supplement the legislation, albeit it was silent on what these were. In 2010, a Decision was taken under article 12(5) concerning surveillance of maritime frontiers. Two aspects were challenged as too broad.[41] The first allowed officials to board and inspect ships, detain those on board and return non-EU nationals to their home state. The second governed measures to be taken when a ship was in distress. A priority was to be given, in such circumstances, to returning non-EU nationals to their state of origin.

Case C–355/10 *Parliament v Council (Schengen Borders Code)*, Judgment of 5 September 2012

64. According to settled case-law, the adoption of rules essential to the subject-matter envisaged is reserved to the legislature of the European Union ... The essential rules governing the matter in question must be laid down in the basic legislation and may not be delegated ...

65. Thus, provisions which, in order to be adopted, require political choices falling within the responsibilities of the European Union legislature cannot be delegated.

66. It follows from this that implementing measures cannot amend essential elements of basic legislation or supplement it by new essential elements.

67. Ascertaining which elements of a matter must be categorised as essential is not – contrary to what the Council and the Commission claim – for the assessment of the European Union legislature alone, but must be based on objective factors amenable to judicial review.

68. In that connection, it is necessary to take account of the characteristics and particularities of the domain concerned.

---

[38] M. Cini, 'The Commission: An Unelected Legislator?' (2002) 8(4) *Journal of Legislative Studies* 14.

[39] There is some evidence of this taking place as European Parliament powers increased. A. Héritier and C. Moury, 'Contested Delegation: The Impact of Co-decision on Comitology' (2011) 34 *WEP* 145.

[40] Case C-240/90 *Germany v Commission* [1992] ECR I-5383, para. 37; Case C-14/01 *Niemann v Bezirksregierung Hannover* [2003] ECR I-2279, para. 33.

[41] The implementing Decision was taken by the Council not the Commission because of the rules concerning implementing powers at the time which allowed the Council to take the decision if the Commission did not receive a positive opinion from a committee of national representatives.

69. As to whether the Council was empowered to adopt the contested decision as a measure implementing Article 12 of the SBC on border surveillance ... it is first of all necessary to assess the meaning of that article.

70. Article 12(1) and (4) of the SBC provides that the purpose of border surveillance is to prevent unauthorised border crossings, to counter cross-border criminality and to take measures against persons who have crossed the border illegally and to apprehend such persons. Recital 6 of the SBC states, in addition, that border control is intended to help to 'combat illegal immigration and trafficking in human beings and to prevent any threat to the Member States' internal security, public policy, public health and international relations'....

73. Although the SBC, which is the basic legislation in the matter, states in Article 12(4) thereof, that the aim of such surveillance is to apprehend individuals crossing the border illegally, it does not contain any rules concerning the measures which border guards are authorised to apply against persons or ships when they are apprehended and subsequently – such as the application of enforcement measures, the use of force or conducting the persons apprehended to a specific location – or even measures against persons implicated in human trafficking.

74. ... the Annex of the contested decision lays down the measures which border guards may take against ships detected and persons on board. In that connection, [it] allows, inter alia, ships to be stopped, boarded, searched and seized, the persons on board to be searched and stopped, the ship or persons on board to be conducted to another Member State, and thus enforcement measures to be taken against persons and ships which could be subject to the sovereignty of the State whose flag they are flying.

75. In addition, ... the Annex of the contested decision lays down, inter alia, the obligation of the units participating in sea external border operations coordinated by the Agency to provide assistance to any vessel or person in distress at sea. [It] lays down rules on the disembarkation of the persons intercepted or rescued ... stating that priority should be given to disembarkation in the third country from where the ship carrying the persons departed.

76. First, the adoption of rules on the conferral of enforcement powers on border guards, referred to in paragraphs 74 and 75 above, entails political choices falling within the responsibilities of the European Union legislature, in that it requires the conflicting interests at issue to be weighed up on the basis of a number of assessments. Depending on the political choices on the basis of which those rules are adopted, the powers of the border guards may vary significantly, and the exercise of those powers require authorisation, be an obligation or be prohibited, for example, in relation to applying enforcement measures, using force or conducting the persons apprehended to a specific location. In addition, where those powers concern the taking of measures against ships, their exercise is liable, depending on the scope of the powers, to interfere with the sovereign rights of third countries according to the flag flown by the ships concerned. Thus, the adoption of such rules constitutes a major development in the SBC system.

77. Second, it is important to point out that provisions on conferring powers of public authority on border guards – such as the powers conferred in the contested decision, which include stopping persons apprehended, seizing vessels and conducting persons apprehended to a specific location – mean that the fundamental rights of the persons concerned may be interfered with to such an extent that the involvement of the European Union legislature is required.

78. Thus, the adoption of [these] provisions, requires political choices to be made as referred to in paragraphs 76 and 77 above. Accordingly, the adoption of such provisions goes beyond the scope of the additional measures within the meaning of Article 12(5) of the SBC and, in the context of the European Union's institutional system, is a matter for the legislature.

The judgment suggests fewer powers can now be granted to the Commission, as it cannot be granted powers over matters requiring 'political choices'. The question as to when a choice will be 'political' will be informed by the degree of latitude, so whether a wide exercise of discretion is involved, and the subject matter. It was relevant in this case, therefore, that the activities involved fundamental rights and relations with non-EU states.

The other issue concerns the distinction between delegated and implementing powers.[42] It is an obscure one. Implementation will involve some interpretation (and therefore amendment) of the parent legislation just as amendments, the central feature of delegated measures, set out uniform prescriptions as to how the parent legislation is to be implemented.[43] As a consequence, it was deliberately left obscure by the Treaty of Lisbon.[44] The distinction matters because each subjects the Commission to different institutional controls. The consequent obscurity allows the legislature a freedom over the controls to which it can subject the Commission, with it able to determine these not by reference to the risks or the nature of the task but simply by designating measures as 'delegated' or 'implementing'.[45]

Delegated measures are subject to less restrictive controls. They can be revoked by either of the other two institutions involved in EU legislation and may only enter into force if these have not objected within a time frame set out in the legislation.

Article 290(2) TFEU

2. Legislative acts shall explicitly lay down the conditions to which the delegation is subject; these conditions may be as follows:
   (a) the European Parliament or the Council may decide to revoke the delegation;
   (b) the delegated act may enter into force only if no objection has been expressed by the European Parliament or the Council within a period set by the legislative act.

For the purposes of (a) and (b), the European Parliament shall act by a majority of its component members, and the Council by a qualified majority.

In March 2011, a Common Understanding was agreed between the EU institutions on the operation of these powers.[46] It requires the Commission to circulate drafts to the two other EU institutions and to consult more generally, particularly with experts, before drawing up any measure. In exchange, subsequent controls have been interpreted quite leniently. In principle, therefore, whilst it is to be determined by each piece of legislation, the period of initial

---

[42] H. Hofmann et al., *Administrative Law and Policy of the European Union* (Oxford, Oxford University Press, 2013) 525–35.

[43] On this obscurity see H. Hofmann, 'Legislation, Delegation and Implementation under the Treaty of Lisbon: Typology Meets European Reality' (2009) 15 *ELJ* 482. It has been suggested that delegated measures are those which appear more obviously legislative in nature. This does not accord with existing practice, however, and it is difficult to see how such an imprecise characterisation would work, cf. J. Bast, 'New Categories of Acts after the Lisbon Reform: Dynamics of Parliamentarization in EU Law' (2012) 49 *CMLRev.* 885, 893–4.

[44] T. Christiansen and M. Dobbels, 'Comitology and Delegated Acts after Lisbon: How the European Parliament Lost the Implementation Game' (2012) 16 *EIOP* 13.

[45] For a comparison see T. Christiansen and M. Dobbels 'Non-Legislative Rule Making after the Lisbon Treaty: Implementing the New System of Comitology and Delegated Acts' (2013) 19 *ELJ* 42.

[46] EU Council, *Common Understanding: Delegated Acts*, EU Council 8753/11.

objection allowed to the other institutions is to be two months. In addition, parent acts may empower the Commission to adopt delegated acts for an unlimited time. If a determined period of time is set out, the presumption is that it will be extended by a period of identical duration unless one of the other institutions objects. The most likely constraint, particularly for the European Parliament, is resources and expertise to monitor this. It is unlikely that the power of objection or revocation will be used other than exceptionally.[47]

Implementing measures are subject to a system of controls which has a heritage going back to the 1960s.[48] The exercise of Commission powers is monitored by committees composed of representatives of the national governments who may block it. Furthermore, both the other two EU legislative institutions can seek to secure that implementing measures do not exceed the mandate in the parent legislation. This process, known as comitology, is dealt with in more detail in Chapter 3.[49] Insofar as these controls are ongoing, they are more constraining than those for delegated measures. However, they are exercised by a relative range of actors, national government experts, and are modest controls when put next to those in the United States to control similar powers.[50]

(b) Agenda-setting

The Commission has responsibility for initiating the policy process in a number of ways. It first decides the legislative programme for each year.[51] Secondly, in most fields, it has a monopoly over the power of legislative initiative.[52] Thirdly, it also has the power of financial initiative, and starts the budgetary process by placing a draft budget before the Parliament and the Council.[53] Finally, the Commission is responsible for stimulating policy debate more generally. The most celebrated example of this was the White Paper on Completion of the Internal Market, which set out an agenda and timetable for completing the internal market by the end of 1992.[54]

Very few proposals are put forward by the Commission off its own back. It enjoys, instead, a gate-keeper role, where different interests – national governments, industry, NGOs – come to it with legislative suggestions.[55] A breakdown of this has only ever been provided for 1998, where the Commission estimated that 35 per cent of its proposals were adapting legislation to new economic, scientific or social data; 31 per cent were because of international obligations; 12 per cent were tasks required by the Treaty where it enjoyed no discretion; and 17 per cent were responding to requests by national governments, EU institutions or economic operators. Only 5 per cent were taken at its own behest.[56]

---

[47] Christiansen and Dobbels, n. 44 above, section 4.2; Kaeding and Hardacre, n. 34 above, 400.

[48] J. Blom-Hansen, 'The Origins of EU Comitology System: A Case of Informal Agenda-Setting by the Commission' (2008) 15 *JEPP* 208, 213–18.

[49] The regime is now set out in Regulation 182/2011 laying down the rules and general principles concerning mechanisms for control by Member States of the Commission's exercise of implementing powers [2011] OJ L55/13. See pp. 144–51.

[50] These include time limits on delegation, appeal procedures, public hearings and requirements for explicit legislative approval. F. Franchino, 'Delegating Powers in the European Community' (2004) 34 *BJPS* 269.

[51] For 2009, see European Commission, *Commission Work Programme 2013*, COM(2012)629.

[52] The main exception is Common Foreign and Security Policy where it has only an ancillary role. In this field initiatives or proposals may be made by any Member State, the High Representative or the High Representative with Commission support, Article 30(1) TEU.

[53] Article 314(2) TFEU.   [54] COM(85)310.

[55] On the strategies deployed see S. Princen, 'Agenda-Setting Strategies in EU Policy Processes' (2011) 18 *JEPP* 927.

[56] House of Lords European Union Committee, *Initiation of EU Legislation* (22nd Report, 2007–08 Session, HL, London) 15.

This results in the Commission being far more politicised than a traditional civil service. It becomes a marketplace for the development of ideas and accommodation of interests, with a variety of parties, both public and private, seeking to influence it.[57] In addition, it is both an agenda-setter and a veto-player. Nothing can happen without the Commission deciding to make a proposal and this proposal, furthermore, will frame the terms of the legislation. It also gives the Commission significant influence in the subsequent debates. Because it can withdraw a proposal at any time, parties cannot ignore its views even after the proposal has been made. However, its power should not be overestimated. Its influence depends upon a number of variables. Central is institutional context. In areas where a unanimity vote by Member States is not required, the Commission can act as a broker between some actors and to outmanoeuvre others.[58] In some areas, it can induce other institutions to adopt its proposal as the 'lesser evil' by threatening other powers at its disposal, such as bringing a Member State before the Court of Justice, which would lead to more draconian consequences.[59] There is also a temporal dimension. If the Commission is impatient, its influence is weakened, as it has to accept more readily the views of the other institutions. By contrast, if the other institutions are impatient for a measure to be adopted, the Commission's power increases.[60]

The traditional justification for the Commission's powers was that its autonomy would result in its being best able to represent the common European interest.[61] Over time, this justification has come to carry less weight. Increasingly, national governments have taken an interest in agenda-setting and limiting the Commission's discretion.[62] A range of measures have also been taken, as we shall see in the rest of this chapter, by all the other EU institutions to place constraints on this power. There are also now well-established procedures which require it to consult widely and consider the impacts of a significant legislative proposal.[63] To open up the power of agenda-setting further, the Lisbon Treaty establishes a citizens' initiative which requires the Commission to consider petitions for proposals where these come from at least 1 million citizens from at least seven Member States.[64]

It is doubtful whether this is sufficient. A feature of democracies is the presence of elections to elect governments, whose central role is agenda-setting. Elections are typically about the agenda that different candidates promise to present before parliaments. Follesdal and Hix have suggested that, as the Commission holds this role within the Union, there should be elections for the President of the Commission in the same way as there are for domestic governments.

---

[57] G. Peters, 'Agenda-Setting in the European Community' (1994) 1 *JEPP* 9.

[58] S. Schmidt, 'Only an Agenda-Setter? The Commission's Power over the Council of Ministers' (2000) 1 *EUP* 37.

[59] S. Schmidt, 'The European Commission's Powers in Shaping Policies' in D. Dimitrakopoulos (ed.), *The Changing Commission* (Manchester, Manchester University Press, 2004).

[60] M. Pollack, 'Delegation, Agency and Agenda Setting in the European Community' (1997) 51 *IO* 99, 121–4.

[61] K. Featherstone, 'Jean Monnet and the "Democratic Deficit" in the European Union' (1994) 32 *JCMS* 149, 154–5.

[62] G. Majone, *Dilemmas of European Integration: The Ambiguities and Pitfalls of Stealth by Integration* (Oxford, Oxford University Press, 2005) 51–3.

[63] This is dealt with in more detail in Chapter 9. See pp. 406–12.

[64] Article 11(4) TEU. The details are established in Regulation 211/2011 on the citizens' initiative [2011] OJ L65/1. See pp. 388–93.

A. Follesdal and S. Hix, 'Why there is a Democratic Deficit in the EU: A Response to Majone and Moravcsik' (2006) 44 *Journal of Common Market Studies* 533, 554

... the Commission's designated role regarding the European interest should not be formulated in such a way as to imply that the content of this term is uncontested, or that the Commission is the only institution able and willing to identify and pursue it. Now that the basic policy-competence architecture of the EU has been confirmed – in terms of the regulation of the market at the European level and the provision of spending-based public goods at the national level – the role of the Commission is not fundamentally different from other political executives. The purely Pareto-improving functions of the Commission, such as the merger control authority or the monitoring of legislative enforcement, could easily be isolated in new independent agencies. Then, the expressly 'political' functions of the Commission, in terms of defining a work programme for five years, initiating social, economic and environmental laws, and preparing and negotiating the multi-annual and annual budgets, should be open to rigorous contestation and criticism. Such criticism should not be interpreted as euroscepticism or anti-federalism, but rather as an essential element of democratic politics at the European level ...

Related to these two ideas, an institutional mechanism needs to be found for generating debate and contestation about politics *in*, not only *of*, the EU. The most obvious way of doing this is contestation of the office of the Commission President – the most powerful executive position in the EU. For example, there could be a direct election of the Commission President by the citizens or by national parliaments. Alternatively, a less ambitious proposal would be for government leaders to allow a more open battle for this office without any further treaty reform. Now that the Commission President is elected by a qualified-majority vote (after the Nice Treaty), a smaller majority is needed in the European Council for a person to be nominated. This led to a dramatic increase in the number of candidates in the battle to succeed Romano Prodi and a linking of the nomination of a candidate to the majority in the newly elected European Parliament. However, the process could have been much more open and transparent – with candidates declaring themselves before the European elections, issuing manifestos for their term in office, and the transnational parties and the governments then declaring their support for one or other of the candidates well before the horse-trading began.

(c) Executive powers

The Commission is responsible for ensuring that the Union's revenue is collected and passed on by national authorities and that the correct rates are applied. It is also responsible for overseeing and coordinating a large part of Union expenditure. Secondly, it is responsible for administering Union aid to third countries. Thirdly, the High Representative is to represent the Union for matters relating to the common foreign and security policy. Notably, she shall conduct political dialogue with third parties on the Union's behalf and shall express the Union's position in international organisations and at international conferences.[65] To that end, she is assisted by a European External Action Service comprising officials from the Council Secretariat and the Commission.[66] The High Representative occupies a unique position. Responsible for the

[65] Article 27(2) TEU.   [66] Article 27(3) TEU.

conduct of the Union Common Foreign and Security Policy and its Security and Defence Policy, she is both one of the Commissioners[67] and acts under the mandate of the Council.[68] The intention of this 'double hat' is to create a more integrated and coordinated external policy,[69] as well as to give the EU a more salient international profile.[70] Straddling the Commission and the Council, she is subject to a double chain of accountability. She, thus, cannot be dismissed unilaterally by the President of the Commission, who requires the agreement of the European Council, the body representing the Heads of Government, to carry this out.[71] Finally, the Commission handles applications for membership of the European Union by carrying out an investigation of the implications of membership and submitting an opinion to the Council.[72]

(d) Supervisory powers

The Commission polices the Union. It enjoys, first, certain regulatory powers. It can declare illegal state aids provided by Member States[73] or measures enacted in favour of public undertakings which breach the Treaty.[74] It has also been granted powers to declare anti-competitive practices by private undertakings illegal and to fine those firms,[75] as well as the power to impose duties on goods coming from third states, which are benefiting from 'unfair' trade practices, such as dumping or export subsidies.[76] Secondly, it may bring Member States before the Court of Justice for breaching EU law.[77] It uses this power extensively.[78] The Commission is also responsible for monitoring compliance by Member States with judgments of the Court of Justice. It can bring those Member States, which it considers to have failed to comply, back before the Court to have them fined.[79] This was done nine times in 2011.[80]

Its most wide-ranging supervisory powers are, arguably, over euro area states in the fields of economic and fiscal policy. Although, formally, it is the Council which sanctions states in these fields it is on the basis of a Commission finding that states have breached EU limits with regard to their public finances or more general state of their economy. It is also for the Commission to indicate whether states have rectified the situation, and, finally, for it also to make recommendations as to the level of sanction. These powers give it some oversight over almost all areas of fiscal, welfare and economic policy. Furthermore, the sanctions which it can recommend are huge.[81]

---

[67] Article 17(4) TEU.
[68] Article 18(2) TEU. She, consequently, also chairs the Foreign Affairs configuration of the Council, Article 18(3) TEU.
[69] Article 18(4) TEU.
[70] She, consequently also takes part in the work of the European Council as a consequence of its pre-eminence in this field, Article 15(2) TEU.
[71] Article 18(1) TEU. However, if the Parliament passes a motion of censure over the whole Commission, she must resign with the other Commission members, Article 17(8) TEU.
[72] Article 49 TEU.   [73] Article 108(2) TFEU.   [74] Article 106(3) TFEU.
[75] Regulation 1/2003 [2001] OJ L1/1, articles 7 and 23, respectively.
[76] In relation to dumping see Regulation 1225/2009 on protection against dumped imports from countries not members of the European Community [2009] OJ L343/51, especially articles 6–13.
[77] Article 258 TFEU.
[78] At the end of 2011, for example, 1,175 infringement proceedings against Member States were open. European Commission, *Twenty Ninth Annual Report on Monitoring the Application of EU Law*, COM(2012)714, 9.
[79] Article 260(2) TFEU.
[80] European Commission, *Twenty Ninth Annual Report*, n. 78 above, 5.
[81] For more detail see pp. 748–52.

This supervision is even more intense for those euro area states which ask for financial support from the European Stability Mechanism (ESM).[82] This is a €700 billion fund offering financial support to euro area states unable to support their public finances following the financial crisis. Any financial support is subject to conditionality, typically a programme of action to be undertaken by the state to reduce its borrowing needs and debt levels.[83] Within this process, the Commission is entrusted, alongside the European Central Bank, to negotiate a Memorandum of Understanding with the state which sets out the conditions and the timescale for meeting these conditions.[84] In addition, it has to check that these conditions are met.

Article 13(7) ESM

7. The European Commission – in liaison with the ECB and, wherever possible, together with the IMF – shall be entrusted with monitoring compliance with the conditionality attached to the financial assistance facility.

The financial support is staggered so that amounts only become available as conditions are met. The ESM can, thus, cut off support if it is unhappy with the level of state compliance. Monitoring compliance will typically involve Commission officials being on the ground in the state concerned, checking that the state is implementing, inter alia, the competitiveness reforms, privatisations, tax increases and public spending cuts that the MoU will require. The Commission will also publish extensive reviews of the state's performance every three months.[85]

A feature of Commission supervisory powers in economic and fiscal policy is not simply their wide-ranging nature. They are less and less about policing compliance with EU law. The MoU requirements are thus, at best, contractual ones. Similarly, if the Treaty and secondary legislation does establish some legal limits on states' budgetary and economic powers, these are so ill-defined that they allow considerable scope not simply for Commission interpretation but also reformulation.[86] Consequently, for the euro area at least, these supervisory powers in economic and budgetary policy should be seen as less about policing, as it is often not clear what is best policing. Instead, they have allowed a shared government to emerge where Commission officials and national ministers, increasingly, formulate policy jointly.

In other areas, Commission supervision of the national administration of EU law leads to an ongoing engagement between the Commission and its national counterparts about how to administer EU policies.[87] This engagement creates a new executive order, which is responsible for large fields of policy-making. It is neither simply Union nor national in nature, and is one

---

[82] For more detail see pp. 740–4.   [83] ESM Treaty, Article 12(1).

[84] Article 13(3) ESM. The Commission also signs this Memorandum, Article 13(4) ESM, having secured approval from the ESM's Board of Governors, comprising the euro area Finance Ministers, which is also responsible for approving releases of aid, Article 9(6)(f) ESM.

[85] The one for Portugal for June 2013, a typical review, therefore ran to 122 pages. See http://ec.europa.eu/economy_finance/publications/occasional_paper/2013/op153_en.htm.

[86] See pp. 749–53.

[87] H. Hofmann and A. Türk, 'Conclusion: Europe's Integrated Administration' in H. Hofmann and A. Türk (eds.), *EU Administrative Governance* (Cheltenham, Edward Elgar, 2006); D. Curtin, *Executive Power of the European Union: Law, Practices and the Living Constitution* (Oxford, Oxford University Press, 2009) 166–72.

in which national administrators increasingly see themselves as having two masters: their national ones and their European Union ones.[88]

D. Curtin and M. Egeberg, 'Tradition and Innovation: Europe's Accumulated Executive Order' (2008) 31 *West European Politics* 639, 649–50

Since the Commission does not possess its own agencies at the Member State level, it (and EU-level agencies) seems to establish a kind of partnership with those national bodies responsible for the application of EU legislation as well as some involvement in the development of EU policies. Such bodies may be found among national agencies that are already somewhat detached from their respective ministerial departments.

The term 'Europe's integrated administration' takes on board the situation where in contemporary European integration processes the traditional distinction of direct and indirect administration has become blurred, with the levels being interwoven to form a more unitary pattern of 'integrated administration'. The EU level is also involved in implementing activities undertaken by Member State authorities, while Member States' administrations are involved in creating EU legislation and implementing acts. Case studies within five different policy fields have shown that national agencies in fact seem to act in a 'double-hatted' manner, constituting parts of national administrations while at the same time becoming parts of a multi-level Union administration in which the Commission in particular forms the new executive centre. As parts of national administrations, serving their respective ministerial departments, agency officials play a crucial role in transposition of EU legislation as well as in Council working parties and comitology committees. However, when it comes to the application of EU legislation in particular, agencies also cooperate rather closely with their respective directorates in the Commission, often by-passing their ministerial departments.

Not surprisingly, in this situation agencies may face competing policy expectations from their two 'masters' that may be hard to reconcile. A questionnaire study showed that the importance of the 'parent ministry' partly depends on its organisational capacity in the field and the extent to which the legislative area is politically contested. Obviously, the role of the Commission will tend to vary as well depending on, for example, the relative strength of the DG involved. Also, lack of knowledge and novelty make national agencies in new member states more receptive to inputs from the Commission. 'Double-hattedness' entails new patterns of cooperation and conflict in executive politics, evoking conflicts that cut across national boundaries as well. It could also be expected to lead to more even implementation across countries compared to indirect implementation, although not as even as if the Commission had its own agencies or if the application of EU law was in the hands of EU-level bodies.

The presence of such an executive order raises real questions about accountability. A world in which national administrations justify themselves to the Commission can create mixed loyalties and loosen their duty to other constituencies. This is particularly worrisome if the relationship with the Commission is essentially a cosy one based on mutual trust, as then it becomes not so much a duty to account to another master as a duty not to hold oneself out too strongly to account at all.

[88] K. Yesilkagit, 'Institutional Compliance, European Networks of Regulation and the Bureaucratic Autonomy of National Regulatory Authorities' (2011) 18 *JEPP* 962.

(iii) Regulatory agencies and the Commission

The concentration of so many functions in the Commission has placed pressure on its resources. A preference emerged for delegating specialised and time-consuming tasks to independent agencies and offices rather than for using the Commission as a repository for further regulatory competencies. This preference took on a new intensity following two scandals in the late 1990s: first, the BSE scandal in which the Commission had been found to cover up knowledge relating to the risks of BSE and new variant Creutzfeldt–Jakob disease; and secondly, evidence of mismanagement by the Santer Commission. In 1999, a Task Force for Administrative Reform recommended that the Commission was administering too much and more needed to be delegated to specialised agencies.[89] This theme was taken up a year later in the Commission *White Paper on Governance*, which advocated the creation of independent EU regulatory agencies in any field marked by specialisation, complexity and where a single public interest predominates.[90]

To date, thirty-six European regulatory agencies plus a further six executive agencies[91] have been established. The remit of these agencies is wide, ranging from fundamental rights, environment, transport, financial services and external frontiers, to pharmaceuticals, intellectual property and energy. Their powers vary considerably, but in some cases are highly significant. Chiti has proposed a helpful threefold categorisation:[92]

- *Agencies with the power to take decisions.* The Office for Harmonisation in the Internal Market (OHIM) can grant Community trademarks and registered designs, and the Community Plant Variety Office (CPVO) Community plant variety rights. The EU chemicals regime has a 'no data, no market' rule which requires manufacturers to register a dossier assessing the risks of these chemicals with the European Chemicals Agency (ECHA). The most wide-ranging powers are those enjoyed by the European Supervisory Authorities: the European Banking Authority (EBA), European Insurance and Occupational Pensions Authority (EIOPA) and European Securities and Markets Authority (ESMA). These can adopt draft technical standards which the Commission can either adopt or reject, but cannot amend, as delegated law.
- *Agencies with instrumental powers.* These are powers to provide expert opinions to the European Commission which will either be used in granting market authorisations[93] or preparing legislation.[94] Whilst the Commission is not bound by their opinion, there is invariably a duty to consult them and the Commission can then only depart from the opinion where it can provide an alternative, equally authoritative, contradictory opinion.[95]
- *Agencies whose responsibility is to disseminate information.* The least powerful of all the agencies, these include the European Environment Agency (EEA), the European Agency for Safety and Health at Work and the European Union Agency for Fundamental Rights.

---

[89] European Commission, *Reforming the Commission*, COM(2000)200, Part I, 6.

[90] European Commission, *European Governance: A White Paper*, COM(2001)428, 24.

[91] See http://europa.eu/about-eu/agencies/regulatory_agencies_bodies/index_en.htm. Executive agencies differ from other agencies in that they are more managerial in nature, being responsible for the administration of a Union programme. Their mandate is set out in Regulation 58/2003 [2003] OJ L11/1.

[92] E. Chiti, 'European Agencies' Rulemaking: Powers, Procedures and Assessment' (2013) 19 *ELJ* 93, 94–9.

[93] Agencies with this role include ECHA, the European Food Safety Authority (EFSA) and the European Medicines Agency (EMA).

[94] Agencies doing this include the European Network and Information Security Agency (ENISA), the European Maritime Safety Agency (EMSA) and the European Railways Agency (ERA).

[95] Case T-13/99 *Pfizer* v *Council* [2002] ECR II-3305.

Combined, these powers are substantial and wide-ranging. The Commission almost always follows agency opinions, for example, in taking decisions or preparing legislation. The agencies have also been found to operate with a strong degree of independence.[96] The development of this regime has therefore led to the Union acquiring new capacities by the back-door and the development of a wide-ranging technocracy.

M. Shapiro, 'The Problems of Independent Agencies in the United States and the European Union' (1997) 4 *Journal of European Public Policy* 262, 281–2

The standard, overt rationale for the creation of EU agencies is that they ought to be partially or wholly independent of the Commission because they are 'managerial', perform 'technical' tasks or are engaged in 'information' gathering and analysis only. In the US it may make sense to say that managerial, technical, informational functions should be separated from the regular cabinet departments or ministries because those departments are part of the Executive Branch which is political, both in the sense that it is headed by a democratically elected President and in the sense that the President is his political party's leader. This is the get-technology-out-of-politics theme. But the separation of powers in the EU is entirely different. The Commission-Council separation is itself a supposed separation of technocracy (the Commission) from intergovernmental politics (the Council). Therefore, to assert a managerial-technical-informational rationale for separating the agencies from the Commission is, in a certain sense, absurd. It is the assertion that the technical ought to be separated from the technical.

Is all this managerial-technical-informational talk simply a smoke screen for the more fundamental argument that, because Europeans don't like the technocrats in Brussels and fear concentrating even more governance there, if we want more EU technocrats, we need to split them up and scatter them about Europe? I think the answer to this question is largely yes but not entirely.

A second motive is, I believe, a kind of 'neo-functionalism'. If currently direct routes to further political integration of the Union are blocked, following Haas's old arguments about the World Health Organisation and the UN, further growth can be achieved indirectly through the proliferation of small, limited jurisdictions, allegedly 'technical agencies' that will appear politically innocuous. That is why it is not enough to say that the agencies are not in Brussels. It must also be said that they are merely technical or informational.

A third motive is about technocracy. The Member State composed management boards were no doubt a political necessity. But by stressing the technical and informational functions of these agencies, by making each highly specialised to a particular technology and by incorporating large components of scientific personnel, there is undoubtedly the hope that the technocrats will take over these agencies from the politicians. And the technocrats for each of these agencies, it is hoped, will create Europe-wide epistemic communities whose technical truths transcend intergovernmental politics. As Americans say 'there is no Republican or Democratic way to pave a street', Europeans may be able to say there is no French or Greek way. Thus, while the proffered technocratic rationales do not really explain why the agencies should be independent of the Commission, they do explain why the agencies should each take a small slice of allegedly technical-informational activity. That kind of organisation is most likely, over time, to assure the internal dominance within each agency of its transnational technocrats over its national politicians.

---

[96] M. Egeberg and J. Trondal, 'EU-level Agencies: New Executive Centre Formation or Vehicles for National Control?' (2011) 18 *JEPP* 868.

A response has been to strengthen the forms of accountability to which these agencies are subject.[97] All agencies have a management board, comprising representatives from each national government, which, typically, approves their work programme and budget, and ensures that they do not go beyond their mandate.[98] In 2012, the Commission, the Parliament and the Council issued a joint statement establishing an alert system.[99] The Commission activates this where it believes the agency is violating EU law or its mandate or is not complying with EU policy objectives. It formally requests the agency to refrain and, if there is no compliance with this request, it formally raises the issue with the other two EU institutions.

4 COUNCIL OF MINISTERS

(i) Powers and workings of the Council

The Council, alongside the European Council, is the institution that represents national governments. Its powers are rather unsatisfactorily paraphrased in Article 16 TEU.

Article 16(1) TEU

1. The Council shall, jointly with the European Parliament, exercise legislative and budgetary functions. It shall carry out policy-making and coordinating functions as laid down in the Treaties.

In fact, ranged across the Treaties, the Council's powers are multifaceted and varied. They include the following:

- In areas of policy where responsibility lies with the Member States, such as general economic policy, the Council acts as a forum within which Member States can consult with each other and coordinate their behaviour.[100]
- It can take the other institutions before the Court for failure to comply with EU law[101] or for failure to act when required by EU law.[102]
- It can request the Commission to undertake studies or submit legislative proposals. The Commission must provide reasons for not submitting the proposal.[103]
- It prepares the work for the European Council meetings and ensures their follow-up.[104]
- It polices the fiscal and economic policies of euro area states. It can find that states are running excessive budget deficits, excessive macro-economic imbalances or significantly deviating

---

[97] For criticism that the focus on piling up accountability mechanisms has led to insufficient thought about the quality of accountability being asked from agencies, see M. Busuioc, *European Agencies: Law and Practices of Accountability* (Oxford, Oxford University Press, 2013) 270–83.

[98] On these see *Ibid.* ch. 5.

[99] Joint Statement and Common Approach (Parliament, Council and Commission, 2012), see http://europa.eu/about-eu/agencies/regulatory_agencies_bodies/index_en.htm.

[100] Article 121 TFEU.   [101] Article 263 TFEU.   [102] Article 265 TFEU.

[103] Article 241 TFEU.   [104] Article 16(6) TEU.

from their commitment to securing a balanced budget.[105] If states persist, notwithstanding this finding, the Council can impose significant fines.[106]

- It frames the Common Foreign and Security Policy and takes the decisions necessary for defining and implementing it on the basis of the general guidelines and strategic lines defined by the European Council.[107]
- It has power of final decision on the adoption of legislation in most areas of Union policy.

The last power is particularly significant. Whilst it is shared with the Parliament in certain fields, it leads to the Council being perceived as the most important institution in the law-making process.

The Council comprises a minister from each Member State authorised to commit the government of that state on that matter.[108] Environmental Ministers will, thus, sit in the Environmental Council and Agriculture or Fisheries Ministers in the Agriculture and Fisheries Council. Since 2002, it has been agreed that more than one minister from each Member State may sit in a Council meeting, particularly where an issue crosses different ministerial portfolios.[109] The specialisation of the Council into different configurations led to a perception that it was too fragmented, had too weak a collective identity, and lacked sufficient overall vision. Provision was made in the Lisbon Treaty for all configurations other than General and Foreign Affairs to be revisited.[110] However, the subsequent Decisions largely retained the prior configurations.[111] The Council, thus, now sits in ten configurations:

- General Affairs;
- Foreign Affairs;
- Economic and Financial Affairs;
- Justice and Home Affairs;
- Employment, Social Policy, Health and Consumer Affairs;
- Competitiveness (Internal Market, Industry, Research and Space);
- Transport, Telecommunications and Energy;
- Agriculture and Fisheries;
- Environment;
- Education, Youth, Culture and Sport.

---

[105] These terms are explored in more detail in Chapter 16, see pp. 717–20. See, respectively, Article 126(6) TFEU; Regulation 1176/2011 on the prevention and correction of macro-economic imbalances [2011] OJ L306/25, article 7(2); Regulation 1466/97 on the strengthening of the surveillance of budgetary positions and the surveillance and coordination of economic policies [1997] OJ L2091/1 as amended by Regulation 1175/2011 [2011] OJ L306/12, article 6(2).

[106] Article 126(11) TFEU; Regulation 1174/2011 on enforcement measures to correct excessive macro-economic imbalances in the euro area [2011] OJ L306/8, article 3; Regulation 1173/2011 on the effective enforcement of budgetary surveillance in the euro area [2011] OJ L306/1, article 6.

[107] Article 26(2) TEU.   [108] Article 16(2) TEU.

[109] The rules for the Council are set out in Decision 2002/682/EC, EURATOM adopting the Council's Rules of Procedure [2002] OJ L230/7.

[110] Article 236(a) TFEU. Protocol No. 10 on Transitional Provisions, article 4.

[111] Decision 2009/878/EU establishing the list of Council configurations in addition to those referred to in the second and third sub-paragraphs of Article 16(6) TEU [2009] OJ L315/46, as amended by European Council Decision 2010/594/EU amending the list of Council configurations [2010] OJ L263/12.

A word should be added about the General Affairs Council. Comprised of Foreign Ministers, it considers matters straddling different EU policies and is responsible for coordinating work done by the other Council configurations. In this, it is to secure consistency in the work of the different configurations and to prepare and ensure the follow-up to meetings of the European Council, in liaison with the Presidents of the European Council and the Commission.[112] It is questionable whether this overcomes the difficulties of fragmentation. The initial draft for the Constitutional Treaty proposed a permanent General and Legislative Affairs Council based in Brussels comprised of Ministers of Europe which would assume the role performed by the General Affairs Council.[113] This proposal was rejected by the national governments who were concerned that such a Council might become too autonomous and powerful. Yet, the original initiative suggests that Foreign Ministers, meeting every now and then in Brussels, as is the case now, may have neither the required level of interest nor resources to do the job expected of them.

(ii) Decision-making within the Council

The first form of voting is the *simple majority* vote. Under this system, each member of the Council has one vote, and fifteen votes are required for a measure to be adopted. This procedure is used in only a few areas, principally procedural ones, as it fails to protect national interests and undue weight is given to the interests of small states at the expense of larger ones. The only area of real significance subject to a simple majority vote is the decision to convene an intergovernmental conference to amend the TEU.[114] The converse of simple majority voting is voting by *unanimity*. Every Member State has a veto on any legislation being considered. It must actively vote against a measure for it to be vetoed; abstention is insufficient. Unanimity voting is used in those areas which are more politically sensitive. Its requirement is still widespread in the Treaty.[115] The final form of voting frequently used is *qualified majority voting (QMV)*. This is a weighted system of voting, in which each Member State is allocated a number of votes. If the measure is proposed by the Commission, it requires 260 out of 352 possible votes to be adopted and at least fifteen states must vote for it. In the rare circumstances where a measure is not proposed by the Commission, it requires 260 votes and at least two-thirds of the Member States must vote for it.[116] In either case, any Member State can ask to verify that states representing at least 62 per cent of the total EU population supported it. The respective votes and population sizes[117] are shown in Table 2.1.

The weighting of votes seeks a delicate balance between preserving individual national voice and reflecting the different population sizes of the Member States. Since 2004, however, the majority of EU Member States are 'small' states with populations of less than

---

[112] Article 16(6) TEU.   [113] Article 23(1) DCT.

[114] This is taken by the European Council, Article 48(3) TEU. The others are adoption of the Council's own rules of procedure (Article 240(3) TFEU and 235(3) TFEU for European Council) and request for the Commission to undertake studies or submit proposals (Article 241 TFEU).

[115] This is particularly so with any measure which touches on taxation or social security.

[116] Protocol on Transitional Provisions, article 3(3).

[117] Except for states with population of less than 1 million, these are rounded up or down to the nearest million.

Table 2.1   Votes and population sizes of Member States

Member State	Votes	Population
Germany	29	82 million
France	29	65 million
United Kingdom	29	63 million
Italy	29	61 million
Spain	27	46 million
Poland	27	39 million
Romania	14	21 million
Netherlands	13	17 million
Greece	12	11 million
Belgium	12	11 million
Portugal	12	11 million
Czech Republic	12	10 million
Hungary	12	10 million
Sweden	10	9 million
Austria	10	8 million
Bulgaria	10	7 million
Denmark	7	6 million
Slovakia	7	5 million
Finland	7	5 million
Ireland	7	5 million
Croatia	7	4 million
Lithuania	7	3 million
Latvia	4	2 million
Slovenia	4	2 million
Estonia	4	1 million
Cyprus	4	0.9 million
Luxembourg	4	0.5 million
Malta	3	0.4 million

10 million. This results in a situation where the fifteen smallest Member States have a combined population of 67.6 million citizens, just over 14 million citizens less than the German population, but combined, they have 95 votes, over three times the number of votes of Germany. This is not the only anomaly, as each Member State's voting strength depended as much upon its perseverance in Treaty negotiations as anything else. France has, therefore, equal votes to Germany, despite having a population only two-thirds the size of the latter. An almost identical situation exists between Belgium and the Netherlands, even if the latter does have one more vote.

This balance was hotly contested at both the 'Future of Europe' Convention leading up to the Constitutional Treaty and during the negotiations for the Lisbon Treaty. The larger Member States wished a weighting more based on population. Despite an absence of evidence that this happened,[118] smaller Member States were worried that this would allow a small number of large Member States to veto any measure, as the four largest Member States comprise just over 50 per cent of the population. There was agreement that the pre-Lisbon Treaty arrangements would prevail until November 2014.

Article 16(4) TEU

4. As from 1 November 2014, a qualified majority shall be defined as at least 55% of the members of the Council, comprising at least fifteen of them and representing Member States comprising at least 65% of the population of the Union.
   A blocking minority must include at least four Council members, failing which the qualified majority shall be deemed attained.[119]

The new formula rewards the larger Member States by introducing a much stronger population requirement. It provides safeguards for the smaller Member States by providing that at least fifteen states must vote for it. The possibility of a large state veto is constrained by the requirement that at least four states must vote against the measure, although it will be unlikely to be difficult for two large Member States to find two smaller states as partners if they try hard enough.[120]

Poland was unhappy with the new formula. It benefited disproportionately from the status quo as it has only two votes less than Germany whilst having less than half the population. It was thus hit hard by the new weighting for QMV. A transitional regime was therefore agreed. Until 31 March 2017, a Member State can ask for the pre-Lisbon Treaty formula to be used.[121] This formula is likely to prevail until the latter date as Member States with a winning majority under it will want it to prevail, as will states who would wish to block a measure under it. Perhaps even more significantly, a Decision was added indicating a new blocking minority. From 1 November 2014 to 31 March 2017, if Member States representing three-quarters of either the population or number of states necessary to form a blocking majority indicate their opposition to a measure, the Council shall do all in its power to reach 'a satisfactory solution': a euphemism for resolving the matter through unanimity. Translated, that means that during that period, only 33.8 per cent of Member States (three-quarters of the blocking majority of 45.1 per cent of the Member States) or states representing 26.3 per cent of the Union population (three-quarters of the blocking majority of 35.1 per cent of the population) have to indicate their opposition to a measure for it not to be adopted. From 1 April 2017, the position is even more drastic. If states representing 55 per cent of the blocking minority indicate opposition, the Council must seek a satisfactory solution. This means only 24.8 per cent of the Member States or states representing 19.3 per cent of the population have to oppose a measure for it not to be adopted. To put this in perspective, Germany alone currently has about 17.5 per cent of the Union population. This Decision makes it significantly easier

[118] M. Mattila and J. Lane, 'Why Unanimity in the Council? A Roll-Call Analysis of Council Voting' (2001) 2 *EUP* 31.
[119] This is also reproduced in Article 238(3) TFEU.
[120] On the differences in respective influence between the Treaty of Nice and the new formula, see D. Cameron, 'The Stalemate in the Constitutional IGC' (2004) 5 *EUP* 373, 383.
[121] Protocol to the Treaty of Lisbon on Transitional Provisions, article 3(2).

for Member States, particularly those with large populations, to block measures than under the current regime.

The debate about vote weighting may be overblown. Historically, the distinction between unanimity and QMV was seen as axiomatic to the climate of negotiation. Under unanimity, it was argued that Member States, aware of their veto, are inclined to have a heightened sense of self-interest and look for matching concessions.[122] In circumstances where Member States do not have a veto, they are aware of the possibility of outmanoeuvre. As a consequence, Member States have looked far more towards constructing common solutions and are less protective of their initial positions except on matters of real political salience.[123] Even in fields where QMV is allowed, therefore, the central modus operandi is consensus with no state voting against a measure, and a study of QMV between 2009 and 2012 found that 65 per cent of measures were passed with full agreement.[124] Indeed, this figure was lower than earlier periods where 82 per cent of measures were passed without contestation,[125] and seems largely to have resulted from the policy of one Member State, the United Kingdom, to use its vote more actively, with the consequence that it voted against the measure in just under 30 per cent of the cases.[126]

Consensus reshapes the balance of power with the position of central players central to its dynamics.[127] Coalitions clustering around these have the resources and networks to articulate common views and mediate between positions. These tend to be the large Member States and the Commission, with other states seeing themselves as having to mediate with these and rarely negotiating with other partners. Consensus not only thus protects states from being outmanoeuvred by it, but also tends to redress the balance between small and large states, with the former empowered by the voting rules and the latter by their wider capacities to influence.[128]

It also shapes the content of the legislation. One strategy has simply been to incorporate individual national concerns, wherever possible, into the text. The 2004 enlargement led, for example, to the length of legislative documents increasing by approximately 15 per cent.[129] This, of course, increases the complexity, cumbersomeness and internal contradiction within EU legislation. The other strategy adopted is the opposite one. Legislation is kept as general as possible so as not to open up possibilities for disagreement.[130] This, of course, can obstruct EU legislation from realising the goals behind its proposal.

---

[122] F. Scharpf, 'The Joint Decision Trap: Lessons from German Federalism and European Integration' (1988) 66 *Public Administration* 239.

[123] D. Naurin, 'Most Common When Least Important: Deliberation in the European Union Council of Ministers' (2010) 40 *BJPS* 31.

[124] Votewatch Europe, *Agreeing to Disagree: The Voting Records of EU Member States in the Council since 2009* (Brussels, Creative Commons, 2012) figure 3.

[125] M. Mattila, 'Voting and Coalitions in the Council after Enlargement' in D. Naurin and H. Wallace (eds.), *Unveiling the Council of the European Union: Games Governments Play in Brussels* (Basingstoke, Palgrave, 2008).

[126] This was nearly twice as much as anybody else, with Austria and Germany being the next states to voice disagreement most frequently. Votewatch Europe, n. 124 above, figure 7.

[127] J. Beyers and G. Dierickx, 'The Working Groups of the Council of the European Union: Supranational or Intergovernmental Negotiations?' (1998) 36 *JCMS* 289.

[128] D. Naurin and R. Lindahl, 'East-North-South: Coalition Building in the Council Before and After Enlargement' in D. Naurin and H. Wallace (eds.), *Unveiling the Council of the European Union: Games Governments Play in Brussels* (Basingstoke, Palgrave, 2008).

[129] E. Best and P. Settembri, 'Legislative Output after Enlargement: Similar Number, Shifting Nature' in E. Best *et al.* (eds.), *The Institutions of the Enlarged European Union: Change and Continuity* (Cheltenham, Edward Elgar, 2008).

[130] G. Tsebelis, 'Bridging Qualified Majority and Unanimity Decisionmaking in the EU' (2013) 20 *JEPP* 1083.

This focus on consensus has led to concerns about the quality of debate in the Council. The Lisbon Treaty has opened up all deliberations and votes on legislative acts to the public.

Article 16(8) TEU

8. The Council shall meet in public when it deliberates and votes on a draft legislative act. To this end, each Council meeting shall be divided into two parts, dealing respectively with deliberations on Union legislative acts and on non-legislative activities.

One response sees this reform as overdue as it will allow national publics and parliaments to hold governments more fully to account. Such a view would presumably wish this access to extend to non-legislative activities as well. The other response is to see this provision as containing risks. It has led to grandstanding by individual ministers for the benefit of their home constituencies, thereby obstructing problem-solving.[131] Furthermore, as it would only be the formal meetings that are made public, there is a fear that the real decision-making processes will be driven elsewhere, out of sight, with the Council becoming no more than a ratifying body designed for public show.[132]

(iii) Management of the Council: the Presidency, the Secretariat and COREPER

The Presidency of the Council rotates between the Member States. It is held by pre-established groups of three Member States for a period of eighteen months with each of those chairing the Council configurations for six months.[133] It is held on the basis of equal rotation.[134] The Presidency has a number of duties:

- it arranges, chairs and sets the agenda for Council meetings;[135]
- it represents the Council both before the other EU institutions and in the world more generally;
- it acts as a 'neutral broker' between other Member States in order to secure legislation;
- it sets the legislative agenda for its six-month term of office. This will be done in consultation with the Commission and the Presidencies preceding and succeeding it.

There is some debate about the power of the Presidency. The short term of office and the need not to appear too partisan prevent the Presidency from hijacking the agenda of the Council to further national priorities.[136] Nevertheless, a study of eight Presidencies found that whilst these had to stay within the mandates set by their predecessors or the Commission, they have

---

[131] J. Cross, 'Striking a Pose: Transparency and Position Taking in the Council of the European Union' (2013) 52 *EJPR* 291.

[132] On the two views see House of Lords European Union Committee, *The Treaty of Lisbon: An Impact Assessment* (10th Report, 2007–8 Session, London, TSO) 56–7.

[133] Decision 2009/881/EU on the exercise of the Presidency of the Council [2009] OJ L315/50, article 1.

[134] Article 16(9) TEU, Article 236(b) TFEU. The sequence is set out in Decision 2009/908/EU laying down measures for the implementation of the European Council Decision on the exercise of the Presidency of the Council, and on the chairmanship of preparatory bodies of the Council [2009] OJ L322/28, Annex I.

[135] Decision 2002/682/EC, EURATOM adopting the Council's Rules of Procedure [2002] OJ L230/7, article 20.

[136] P. Alexandrova and A. Timmermans, 'National Interest versus the Common Good: The Presidency in European Council Agenda Setting' (2013) 52 *EJPR* 316.

some discretion to shape these agendas.[137] If they had been given only a vague mandate to re-alise a task, they could choose, instead, to make it a priority for their Presidency. Unanticipated events also provide opportunities for agenda-setting. As they require new forms of response from the Union, reliance is placed on the Presidency to organise that response and set out the framework for future action. Conversely, they also seem to have some influence when negotiations are closed. At this moment, they have to bring views together, and whilst this must be done even-handedly, empirical studies show that decisions reached during State Presidencies are usually closer to what they want than decisions taken outside them.[138]

Whilst the Presidency sets out the overall framework for Council meetings, the mundane details are carried out by the Secretariat.[139] Based in Brussels, the central functions of the Secretariat are conference organisation and committee servicing. It produces documents, arranges translation, takes notes and organises meeting rooms.[140] It also provides advice to the Council on the legality of its actions and will represent the Council before the other institutions. It will thus be the Council Secretariat who will litigate on behalf of the Council or represent the Council before Parliament Committees.

However, the central body in the preparation of Council meetings is COREPER. The formal duties of COREPER are merely to prepare the work of the Council and carry out any tasks assigned to it.[141] It has no power to take formal decisions other than ones on Council procedure.[142] It is divided into COREPER I, which is composed of deputy permanent representatives and is responsible for issues such as the environment, social affairs, the internal market and transport; and COREPER II, which consists of permanent representatives of ambassadorial rank responsible for the more sensitive issues, such as economic and financial affairs and external relations. Each meets weekly.

Successive reports have found COREPER essential both to alleviating Council workload and coordinating its work.[143] The heart of COREPER's power lies in its setting the agenda for Council meetings and its dividing that agenda into 'A' and 'B' matters. 'A' items are technical matters, on which there is agreement. These are nodded through in the Council meeting, without discussion. 'B' items, by contrast, are considered more contentious, requiring discussion. COREPER, therefore, decides on what the Council is to decide on. An 'A' item is effectively decided by COREPER, and a 'B' item by the Council of Ministers. The level of ministerial involvement varies considerably, both from year to year and between Councils. However, between 2004 and 2007, depending on the year, between 15 per cent and 30 per cent of items were discussed in some way by ministers.[144]

---

[137] E. Bailleul and H. Versluys, 'The EU Rotating Presidency: "Hostage Taker" of the European Agenda?', paper presented at EUSA Conference, 30 March 2005. A similar conclusion is reached by study of the Presidency of Environmental Councils. A. Warntjen, 'Steering the Union: The Impact of the EU Presidency on Legislative Activity' (2007) 45 *JCMS* 1135.

[138] R. Thomson, 'The Council Presidency of the European Union: Responsibility with Power' (2008) 46 *JCMS* 593, 604–11.

[139] Article 240(2) TFEU.

[140] It is to perform this role also for the European Council. Article 235(4) TFEU.

[141] Article 16(7) TEU, Article 240(1) TFEU.

[142] Case C-25/94 *Commission* v *Council* [1996] ECR I-1469.

[143] *Report on the European Institutions by the Committee of Three to the European Council* (Tindemans Report) (Brussels, EC Council, 1979) 49–54; *Report from the Ad Hoc Committee on Institutional Affairs to the European Council* (Dooge Report) *EC Bulletin*, 3–1985, 3.5.1.

[144] F. Häge, 'Politicising Council Decision-making: The Effect of European Parliament Empowerment' (2011) 34 *WEP* 18, 33–4.

If the vast majority of Council business is resolved within COREPER, it does not act as a loose cannon, but rather as a conduit for informing national capitals of the work of the European Union and for enabling national positions to be properly defended.[145] It is, thus, assisted by about 250 Working Groups of national civil servants. A Commission proposal is first passed to these Groups for analysis. These Groups provide Reports which set the agenda for COREPER meetings by indicating points on which there has been agreement within the Working Group (Roman I points) and points which need discussion within COREPER (Roman II points). It is best to see COREPER as the tip of complex networks of national administrations working together to agree legislation.[146] Furthermore, there is evidence that, within this network of civil servants, ministers are consulted on matters of political salience.[147] Even in this light, COREPER raises some concerns. There is disagreement about whether representatives always articulate national interests or whether they are concerned with solving problems and reaching agreement, wherever possible.[148] The other concern raised by COREPER is government by 'moonlight'. Meetings of the COREPER are not public. Its minutes are not published and it is not accountable to any parliamentary assembly. To be sure, many decisions taken in any national government are taken by civil servants, but it is the unprecedented extent of COREPER's influence that raises particular concerns about accountability and transparency.[149]

5 EUROPEAN COUNCIL

The European Council comprises the Heads of Government of the Member States, its President and the President of the Commission.[150] It is to meet at least four times per year, although additional meetings can be convened if necessary.[151] The Lisbon Treaty set out a change of gear for it by formally recognising it as an EU institution.[152] This was to signal its central place directing Union activities and priorities:

Article 15(1) TEU

1. The European Council shall provide the Union with the necessary impetus for its development and shall define the general political directions and priorities thereof. It shall not exercise legislative functions.

To describe the European Council's powers solely in those terms is not to ignore, however, their multifaceted nature. For the European Council enjoys a wide range of powers across a number of activities.

---

[145] F. Hayes-Renshaw, C. Lequesne and P. Lopez, 'The Permanent Representatives of the Member States of the European Union' (1989) 28 *JCMS* 119, 129–31.
[146] D. Bostock, 'COREPER Revisited' (2002) 40 *JCMS* 215, 231–2.
[147] F. Häge, *Bureaucrats as Law-makers: Committee Decision-making in the EU Council of Ministers* (Abingdon, Routledge, 2013) especially chs. 13 and 14.
[148] Cf. J. Lewis, 'National Interests: COREPER' in J. Peterson and M. Shackleton (eds.), *The Institutions of the European Union* (Oxford, Oxford University Press, 2002); F. Häge, 'Committee Decision-making in the Council of the European Union' (2007) 8 *EUP* 299.
[149] Individuals can now ask for disclosure on the position of governments during negotiations, Case T-233/09 *Access Info Europe v Council* [2011] ECR II-1073. This has been appealed, however, by the Council, Case C-280/11P *Council v Access Info Europe*, Opinion of Advocate General Villalón, 16 May 2013.
[150] Article 15(2) TEU.   [151] Article 15(3) TEU.   [152] Article 13 TEU.

(i) Powers of the European Council

It, first, makes decisions about the future shape and membership of the European Union. It is the European Council, therefore, which takes the decision to suspend the membership of a Member State.[153] It is also the European Council which sets the criteria to be met by a state wishing to join the Union.[154] Perhaps the most important power enjoyed by the European Council is the power to instigate Treaty reform.

There are two procedures for this.

Under the ordinary revision procedure, after consulting other EU institutions, it can call, by simple majority, either a convention along the lines of the 'Future of Europe' Convention or an intergovernmental conference. These will put forward amendments which have to be ratified by all Member States in accordance with their constitutional requirements.[155]

More controversial is the simplified revision procedure. On the one hand, this allows the European Council, after consulting the other EU institutions, to amend Part III of the TFEU, the part of the TFEU comprising all the internal policies of the European Union.[156] Any such amendment must not increase EU competences, and it cannot enter into force until ratified by all Member States in accordance with their constitutional requirements.[157] On the other, it establishes a *passerelle* procedure, whereby the European Council can amend a Treaty requirement of Council unanimity to that of QMV and any legislative procedure can be replaced by the ordinary legislative procedure.[158] This passerelle procedure can be applied to any part of the TFEU and to Title V of the TEU (which governs external action).[159] Any amendment must be notified to national parliaments and if any national parliament indicates its opposition, the amendment must be dropped.

The proponents of the simplified revision procedure argue that it grants the Union added responsiveness.[160] Whilst this argument can be made for QMV, as it allows the Union to take action without the shadow of the national veto, it is less convincing in the case of the ordinary legislative procedure, which simply adds a further veto-player, the European Parliament, to the legislative process.[161] Its opponents worry that it could be a stalking horse for further integration. In its *Lisbon Treaty* judgment, the German Constitutional Court noted that the use of the simplified revision procedure for Part III of the TFEU gave the possibility to amend 172 Articles of primary law in unpredictable ways. However, it reserved its full ire for the passerelle procedure noting that it made it difficult to predict the degree of power granted to the Union or the loss of influence for an individual Member State.[162]

The second set of powers are those to make appointments and determine the composition of some of the other EU institutions. Within the limits set by the Treaties, the European Council

---

[153] Article 7(3) TEU.   [154] Article 49 TEU.   [155] Article 48(2)–(4) TEU.

[156] It excludes Common Foreign and Security Policy, common commercial policy, development policy, association policy, humanitarian aid, economic, financial and technical cooperation with non-EU states, sanctions, internal agreements and customs union. It also excludes the flexibility provision, Article 352 TFEU.

[157] Article 48(6) TEU.   [158] This procedure is discussed in Chapter 3.

[159] Article 48(7) TEU. There is an exclusion for anything that has defence or military implications.

[160] House of Lords, *The Treaty of Lisbon: An Impact Assessment*, n. 132 above, 37–8.

[161] See pp. 117–19.

[162] 2 BvE 2/08 *Treaty of Lisbon*, Judgment of 30 June 2009, paras. 311–21.

can determine the composition of the Parliament and the Commission.[163] It appoints its own President and the President of the Commission, the Commission, the High Representative, and the Executive Board of the European Central Bank.[164] To be sure, this is often done in tandem with other EU institutions but almost every non-elected office involves appointment by the European Council.[165] Even judges of the Court of Justice, while not appointed by the European Council, are appointed by common accord of the governments of the Member States, which is essentially the same thing.[166]

Thirdly, the European Council resolves issues which have reached an impasse within the Council of Ministers. It can do this informally in all fields by virtue of the domestic authority of Heads of Government. Difficult issues too controversial or significant for a minister to concede can sometimes be resolved by the Head of Government. In particularly sensitive fields, the European Council is deployed where a Member State feels insufficient sensitivity is being shown to matters of particular significance for it. There are 'brake procedures' which allow a member of the Council to refer a legislative proposal to the European Council for resolution if the proposal affects important aspects of its social security system[167] or fundamental aspects of its criminal justice system.[168] In the Common Foreign and Security Policy (CFSP), on activities where there is provision for QMV, a Member State may refer the matter to the European Council for 'vital and stated' reasons.[169]

Fourthly, the European Council has a prominent role in the CFSP. It defines and identifies the strategic objectives and interests of CFSP and sets out guidelines.[170] It also acts as a forum where Member States can consult each other about matters of general interest in this field.[171]

The final, and most significant form of power, is an agenda-setting power. In some fields this is explicitly mandated,[172] but the European Council will agree programmes of legislation across all areas of EU policy. This agenda-setting is limited by the final sentence of Article 15(1) TEU, which indicates that the European Council is not to trespass on the Commission's traditional prerogatives to propose legislation. Instead, its role is to direct and prompt the course of the Union more generally. A division of labour, thus, takes place, in which the European Council will usually set out broad principles and ask the Commission to develop an Action Plan to implement these principles. The most pre-eminent recent example was the Taskforce on Economic Governance comprising national Finance Ministers, whose report provided the basis for the fiscal compact and the 'six-pack' disciplining national budgetary and economic policies.[173] In some instances, this agenda-setting is shared with other institutions. The follow-up to the fiscal compact, the report which paves the way for greater institutional and fiscal integration within the euro area, was thus prepared in collaboration with the Commission, the European Council and the European Central Bank.[174]

---

[163] Articles 14(2) and 17(5) TEU, respectively.
[164] Articles 15(5), 17(7) (both President and Commission as a whole), 18(1) TEU and 283(2) TFEU, respectively.
[165] The most significant exception is the Ombudsman, see Article 228 TFEU.
[166] Article 19(2) TEU.   [167] Article 48 TFEU.   [168] Articles 82(3) and 83(3) TFEU.
[169] Article 31(2) TEU.   [170] Articles 22 and 26 TEU.   [171] Article 32 TEU.
[172] Article 68 TFEU (freedom, security and justice); Article 148 TFEU (employment).
[173] *Strengthening Economic Governance in the EU: Final Report of The Task Force to the European Council* (European Council, October 2010), available at www.european-council.europa.eu/the-president/taskforce.aspx.
[174] *Towards a Genuine Economic and Monetary Union* (European Council, December 2012), available at www.consilium.europa.eu/uedocs/cms_data/docs/ … /en/ec/134069.pdf.

This agenda-setting power often transcends the Treaty by going to activities which fall beyond the Union's competence. It is also used not just for legislative initiatives but also for supervision. The central example of this is the European Semester for Economic Policy Coordination. In the Spring European Council, on the basis of an Annual Growth Survey by the Commission setting out fiscal, economic and social priorities, the European Council agrees pan-Union policy orientations across a range of economic, social and environmental fields. Member States develop individual national reform plans in the light of these which are then subject to evaluation and tailored recommendations by the Commission and the Council, and are then, finally, endorsed by the European Council. The legal instruments governing the European Semester indicate the uncomfortable relationship between EU law and the European Council. The position of the other EU institutions within the Semester is governed by Regulation 1175/2011.[175] However, despite being arguably the central actor within the Semester, the European Council is not governed in any way by the Regulation.

(ii) European Council President

There is a mismatch between the time spent by Heads of Government in the European Council, formally only four meetings per year, and its wide-ranging tasks. The General Affairs configuration of the Council is to support the European Council by preparing its meetings and ensuring follow-up to them.[176] However, it meets only periodically and has a floating membership. It is unclear whether it has time, authority or resources either to coordinate policy across such a wide array of fields or to meet often very ambitious targets. To that end, the Lisbon Treaty created a new office: President of the European Council.[177] Elected by the European Council by QMV for a two and a half year term which may be renewed once,[178] the President sits as an additional member of the European Council.[179] His tasks are to:

- chair and drive forward the work of the European Council whilst endeavouring to facilitate consensus and cohesion within it;
- ensure the preparation and continuity of the work of the European Council in cooperation with the President of the Commission, and on the basis of the work of the General Affairs Council;
- present a report to the Parliament after each of the meetings of the European Council;
- ensure the external representation of the Union on issues concerning its Common Foreign and Security Policy, without prejudice to the powers of the High Representative of the Union for Foreign Affairs and Security Policy.[180]

The mission of the President has both an ex ante and an ex post dimension. Ex ante, he is to organise, coordinate and secure direction for the European Council, building alliances and facilitating agendas. Ex post, he is to see that European Council decisions are implemented. However, a number of features appear to constrain this. The President has only a very small

---

[175] Regulation 1175/2011 amending Council Regulation 1466/97 on the strengthening of the surveillance of budgetary positions and the surveillance and coordination of economic policies [2011] OJ L306/12, article 2A.
[176] Article 16(6) TEU. It is to work with the Commission and the President of the European Council on this.
[177] The first incumbent was the Belgian, Herman van Rompuy.
[178] Article 15(5) TEU.   [179] Article 15(2) TEU.   [180] Article 15(6) TEU.

administration of his own. The relationship with the different Member States is delicate. The larger Member States will expect more attention by virtue of their greater economic weight and larger populations, and the smaller Member States will expect equal treatment of all Member States regardless of size. Finally, if the President is expected to cooperate with the Commission, the essential structure of the relationship is a competitive one. Each will have an agenda-setting role and will be keen to assert its preferences and prerogatives.

Notwithstanding all this, the first President of the European Council seems to have carved out a significant role for himself. His unique role allows him to be trusted to mediate between Member States and between Member States and the other EU institutions, as he has no obvious institutional axe to grind. He has emerged as a powerful external figurehead for the European Union in a way that no national leader or supranational institution could: the former being too associated with their own state, and the latter mistrusted by national governments. His greatest source of influence lay, however, in persuading Heads of Government that they had to work together through him if the European Council was to secure an agenda-setting role rather than leaving this exclusively to the Commission. The possibility of this less attractive alternative has allowed him to build European Council positions, most notably during the economic crisis.[181]

(iii) European Council within the EU institutional settlement

The formalisation by the Lisbon Treaty of the European Council's position as the 'Queen Bee' of the EU setting out, through its political directions,[182] what the other EU institutions should do, moves the tectonic plates of power in two ways.

First, it shifts power between the Member States, as the extract below illustrates. The personal authority of a Head of Government and whether a Member State has a particular interest are central to the level of influence of a Member State within the European Council,[183] as are its size and wealth.

> **J. Tallberg, 'Bargaining Power in the European Council' (2008) 46 *Journal of Common Market Studies* 685, 690–1**
>
> In Europe of today, gun-boat diplomacy is not an option and aggregate structural power affects negotiations in considerably more subtle ways. The interviews suggest that resources and capabilities rarely are actively deployed in the bargaining process. Rather, asymmetries in aggregate structural power matter indirectly, by affecting a state's range of alternatives, the resources it can commit to an issue and the legitimacy of its claims to influence. A large home market makes a state more influential in economic negotiations, military capabilities enable a state to exercise leadership in the EU's foreign and security policy and population size grants voice in an EU conceiving of itself as a democratic community.

---

[181] On these dimensions to the President's power see H. de Waele and H. Broeksteeg, 'The Semi-permanent European Council Presidency: Some Reflections on the Law and Early Practice' (2012) 49 *CMLRev.* 1039, 1070–1. On its role in the crisis see U. Puetter, 'Europe's Deliberative Intergovernmentalism: The Role of the Council and European Council in EU Economic Governance' (2012) 19 *JEPP* 161.

[182] This metaphor is taken from D. Curtin, *Executive Power of the European Union: Law, Practices and the Living Constitution* (Oxford, Oxford University Press, 2009) 72–6.

[183] On this first two see J. Tallberg, 'Bargaining Power in the European Council' (2008) 46 *JCMS* 685, 692–4 and 698–9.

According to the interviewees, national executives representing structurally advantaged states are allowed greater latitude in the negotiations. Jean-Claude Juncker explains: 'If you are representing a medium-sized country, you can never say "Denmark thinks …". You can only say "I would submit to your considerations, if not…". Those who are speaking for greater Member States, by opening their mouth and by referring to their national flag, they are immediately indicating that, behind their words, you have to accept size and demography. "La France pense que …" and "Deutschland denkt …" that is something different'. Göran Persson, former prime minister of Sweden, points to a parallel dynamic: 'If you are the prime minister of a country with five to ten million people, you simply cannot monopolize 20 per cent of the time devoted to the conclusions.' Furthermore, differences in structural power are perceived to affect the legitimacy of wielding the veto. According to one prime minister, it is a simple reality of politics that 'Luxemburg can issue a veto once in a decade and Britain once per week'. By the same token, the veto of large Member States is perceived to carry more weight than that of the small or medium-sized states, according to David O'Sullivan, former secretary general of the Commission: 'The veto of Cyprus is not the same as the veto of Germany'. Interviewees also testify that large Member States may get away with tactics that otherwise are considered inappropriate, such as exploiting the inadequate preparation of an issue to push through their own proposal, or launching entirely new initiatives at the negotiation table.

As a result, the interests of the larger Member States tend to set the framework for European Council negotiations. Where the interests of France, Germany and the UK conflict, they nevertheless set the terms within which agreements must be sought. Where these states see eye-to-eye on an issue, or even have arrived at pre-agreements, it is extremely difficult to achieve outcomes that diverge from this position. Frequently cited examples in recent years of France, Germany and the UK dominating negotiations and outcomes in the European Council include the provisions on a semi-permanent president of the European Council in the 2004 Constitutional Treaty, the deal in December 2005 on the new financial perspective for 2007–13 and the political agreement in July 2007 on the subsequent Lisbon Treaty.

These fluid and unstructured power relations raise questions about the quality of decisions reached in the European Council and about its power vis-à-vis other EU institutions. Supra-national controls are addressed half-heartedly. The European Council can now be subject to review by the Court of Justice[184] and the President must submit reports after each meeting to the Parliament.[185] It is far-fetched to imagine the circumstances in which a court would strike down a decision by twenty-eight Heads of Government, and how seriously the latter will take any critical views of the Parliament is also open to question.[186]

In recent times, the European Council has become increasingly accountable to national parliaments. A study by Notre Europe discovered that in only three states (Hungary, Romania and Luxembourg) was there little interest in European Council meeting.[187] In a further six, there was no more than an ad hoc interest.[188] In the remaining eighteen parliaments surveyed,

---

[184] Articles 263 and 265 TFEU.   [185] Article 15(6)(d) TEU.

[186] Cf. B. Crum, 'Accountability and Personalisation of the European Council Presidency' (2009) 31 *Journal of European Integration* 685.

[187] C. Hefftler *et al.*, *National Parliaments: Their Emerging Control over the European Council*, Notre Europe Policy Paper 89 (Paris, 2013).

[188] These were the Czech Republic, Estonia, Italy, Latvia, Poland and Slovakia.

there was strong involvement through either specialised parliamentary committees or plenary sessions of the parliament before and/or after every European Council meeting. In most cases, this went to holding the Head of Government to account for what took place in the meeting. In Germany and Denmark, it went further, to formulating the position for him or her to take in the European Council. Whilst significant, these controls do not address the inevitable asymmetries of powers within the European Council. Furthermore, as the European Council is a secretive body with discussions kept confidential, it is difficult to know how strong an effect they have on each Head of Government.

6 EUROPEAN PARLIAMENT

(i) Composition and authority of the European Parliament

The Parliament was initially set up as the European Assembly and was only formally recognised as a Parliament in the Single European Act (SEA).[189] Prior to 1979, it consisted of representatives from national assemblies or parliaments. Since then, MEPs have been elected by direct universal suffrage at five-yearly intervals.[190] There are a number of features which distinguish the Parliament from national counterparts.

In December 2013, Parliament comprised 766 members.[191] This number is a transitional number, as there was already an elected parliament in sitting when the Lisbon Treaty came into force with the result that its amendments do not come into force until the November 2014 European Parliament elections. From that election onwards, the Parliament must not exceed 751 members. Representation is to be on the basis of degressive proportionality, whereby the principle of per head representation is combined with the principle that the larger the population of a Member State, the lower the weighting per head. Additionally, no state should receive less than six MEPs and no state may have more than ninety-six MEPs.[192] An apportionment was made on that basis, but it did not take into account the accession of Croatia. At the time of writing, a proposal on this has been made by the European Parliament,[193] but it awaits adoption by the European Council.[194] The principle of degressive proportionality results in an unequal representation of European Union citizens, with every vote in Malta and Luxembourg counting for over ten times that in Germany.

There are no uniform procedures for election. Common procedures were used for the first time in the 2004 elections with all MEPs required to be elected by proportional representation.

---

[189] Article 3 SEA. On the history of the European Parliament see B. Rittberger, *Building Europe's Parliament: Democratic Representation Beyond the Nation-State* (Oxford, Oxford University Press, 2005) chs. 3–6.

[190] Article 14(3) TEU.

[191] The apportionment is: Austria 17; Belgium 22; Bulgaria 17; Croatia 12; Czech Republic 22; Cyprus 6; Denmark 13; Estonia 6; Finland 13; France 72; Germany 99; Greece 22; Hungary 22; Ireland 12; Italy 72; Latvia 8; Lithuania 12; Luxembourg 6; Malta 5; the Netherlands 25; Poland 50; Portugal 22; Romania 33; Slovakia 13; Slovenia 7; Spain 50; Sweden 18; United Kingdom 72.

[192] Article 14(2) TEU.

[193] The proposed numbers are: Austria 18; Belgium 21; Bulgaria 17; Croatia 11; Czech Republic 21; Cyprus 6; Denmark 13; Estonia 6; Finland 13; France 74; Germany 96; Greece 21; Hungary 21; Ireland 11; Italy 73; Latvia 8; Lithuania 11; Luxembourg 6; Malta 6; the Netherlands 26; Poland 51; Portugal 21; Romania 32; Slovakia 13; Slovenia 8; Spain 54; Sweden 20; United Kingdom 73. European Parliament Resolution of 13 March 2013 on the composition of the European Parliament with a view to the 2014 elections, A7–0041/2013.

[194] The procedure for seat apportionment involves the European Parliament making a proposal which is adopted by the European Council with the European Parliament's consent, Article 14(2) TEU.

However, Member States can decide on the system of proportional representation to be used. This discretion goes to matters such as the size and shape of voting constituencies, minimum ages for voting and the voting entitlements of non-EU nationals; whether voting is compulsory and whether parties need to achieve up to 5 per cent of the national vote before being allocated seats.[195] Furthermore, the European Parliament cannot challenge the administration of these elections even where it believes that Member States have not followed their own electoral procedures or some dubious practice has taken place.[196]

Finally, there are no European political parties. MEPs are elected as representatives of national political parties. Instead, most MEPs sit in European party groupings.[197] There are seven groupings covering a wide political spectrum, of which the two largest are the European Peoples Party (right-of-centre parties) and the Progressive Alliance of Socialists and Democrats (left-of-centre parties).[198] These groupings are important in the organisation of the Parliament,[199] as they affect voting behaviour. MEPs within groupings vote reasonably cohesively, and this cohesion has increased over time.[200]

These traits have generated concerns about the representative qualities of the European Parliament, as they all seem to go against the idea of the vote of each citizen having equal weight. It has been argued, most notably by the German Constitutional Court in its *Treaty of Lisbon* judgment, that this belies the European Parliament's claim to be a representative assembly.

---

2 BvE 2/08 *Gauweiler* v *Treaty of Lisbon*, Judgment of 30 June 2009

280. Measured against requirements in a constitutional state, the European Union lacks, even after the entry into force of the Treaty of Lisbon, a political decision-making body which has come into being by equal election of all citizens of the Union and which is able to uniformly represent the will of the people. What is also lacking in this connection is a system of organisation of political rule in which a will of the European majority carries the formation of the government in such a way that the will goes back to free and equal electoral decisions and a genuine competition between government and opposition which is transparent for the citizens, can come about ... contrary to the claim that Article 10.1 TEU Lisbon[201] seems to make according to its wording, the European Parliament is not a body of representation of a sovereign European people. This is reflected in the fact that it, as the representation of the peoples in their respectively assigned national contingents of Members, is not laid out as a body of representation of the citizens of the Union as an undistinguished unity according to the principle of electoral equality.

---

[195] Decision 2002/772/EURATOM/EC, concerning the election of the members of the European Parliament by direct universal suffrage [2002] OJ L283/1.

[196] Joined Cases C-393/07 and C-9/08 *Italy v Parliament* [2009] ECR I-3679.

[197] On the evolution of these see A. Kreppel, *The European Parliament and the Supranational Party System* (Cambridge, Cambridge University Press, 2002).

[198] For the 2009–2014 Parliament, the groupings are European Peoples Party (265 MEPs); Progressive Alliance of Socialists and Democrats (184 MEPs); Alliance of Liberals and Democrats for Europe (84 MEPs); the Greens and European Free Alliance (55 MEPs); European Conservatives and Reformists (54 MEPs); European United Left and Nordic Green Left (35 MEPs); Europe of Freedom and Democracy (35 MEPs). There are 27 non-attached MEPs.

[199] Membership of a grouping also entitles a national party to funding. Regulation 2004/2003/EC on the regulations governing political parties at European level and the rules regarding their funding [2003] OJ L297/1.

[200] S. Hix, A. Noury and G. Roland, *Democratic Politics within the European Parliament* (Cambridge, Cambridge University Press, 2007) 87–105; G. McElroy and K. Benoit, 'Policy Positioning in the European Parliament' (2012) 13 *EUP* 150.

[201] This states that the functioning of the Union is to be founded on representative democracy.

281. Also in their elaboration by the Treaty of Lisbon, no independent people's sovereignty of the citizens of the Union in their entirety results from the competences of the European Union. If a decision between political lines in the European Parliament receives a narrow majority, there is no guarantee of the majority of votes cast representing a majority of the citizens of the Union. Therefore the formation, from within Parliament, of an independent government vested with the competences that are usual in states would meet with fundamental objections. Possibly, a numerical minority of citizens existing according to the ratio of representation could govern, through a majority of Members of Parliament, against the political will of an opposition majority of citizens of the Union, which does not find itself represented as a majority. It is true that the principle of electoral equality only ensures a maximum degree of exactness as regards the will of the people under the conditions of a system of strict proportional representation. But also in majority voting systems, there is a sufficient guarantee of electoral equality for the votes at any rate as regards the value counted and the chance of success, whereas it is missed if any contingent that is not merely insignificant is established.

282. For a free democratic fundamental order of a state ..., the equality of all citizens when making use of their right to vote is one of the essential foundations of state order ...

288. It is true that the democracy of the European Union is approximated to federalised state concepts; measured against the principle of representative democracy, however, it would to a considerable degree show excessive federalisation. With the personal composition of the European Council, of the Council, the Commission and the Court of Justice of the European Union, the principle of the equality of states remains linked to national rights of determination, rights which are, in principle, equal. Even for a European Parliament elected with due account to equality, this structure would be a considerable obstacle for asserting a representative will of the parliamentary majority with regard to persons or subject-matters. Also after the entry into force of the Treaty of Lisbon, the Court of Justice, for instance, must always be staffed according to the principle 'one state, one judge' and under the determining influence of the Member States regardless of their number of inhabitants. The functioning of the European Union continues to be characterised by the influence of the negotiating governments and the subject-related administrative and formative competence of the Commission even though the rights of participation of the European Parliament have been strengthened on the whole. Within this system, the parliamentary influence has been consistently further developed with Parliament's being accorded the right to veto in central areas of legislation. With the ordinary legislative procedure, the Treaty of Lisbon makes a norm what is already factually decisive under the currently applicable law in many areas: in the codecision procedure, a directive or a regulation cannot be adopted against the will of the European Parliament.

289. The deficit of European public authority that exists when measured against requirements on democracy in states cannot be compensated by other provisions of the Treaty of Lisbon and to that extent, it cannot be justified.

A counter-argument is that representation also involves allowing as wide a range of viewpoints to be represented as possible. This would be foreclosed by a model based too strongly on majoritarian principles as the size and economic weight of the large Member States would result in views from these becoming predominant, with those from less populated regions or smaller Member States becoming marginalised.[202] Such a justification goes, however, to the quality and range of debate which takes place within and surrounds the European Parliament.

[202] C. Lord and J. Pollak, 'Unequal but Democratic? Equality According to Karlsruhe' (2013) 20 *JEPP* 190.

A second critique is that both this range of debate and the responsiveness of the European Parliament to voters is too weak. Political parties, media and civil society are, thus, all organised along predominantly national lines.[203] Whilst, over time, a certain level of political debate about EU issues has developed, it is still not as plural or vigorous as those on national issues. Most importantly, for the European Parliament, there is very weak political engagement between it and voters. Turn-out for European Parliament elections has steadily declined from 62 per cent in 1979 to 43 per cent in 2009. Over half of EU citizens do not choose to vote for it with only 19.6 per cent and 21 per cent casting their 2009 votes in Slovakia and Lithuania, respectively.[204] Furthermore, there is no evidence that voters cast their votes in relation to what they anticipate it will do or on the basis of its past performance.[205]

D. Grimm, 'Does Europe Need a Constitution?' (1995) 1 *European Law Journal* 282, 293–4, 296–7

The democratic nature of a political system is attested not so much by the existence of elected parliaments … as by the pluralism, internal representativity, freedom and capacity for compromise of the intermediate area of parties, associations, citizens movements and communication media. Where a parliament does not rest on such a structure, which guarantees constant interaction between people and State, democratic substance is lacking even if democratic forms are present.

… At European level, though, even the prerequisites are largely lacking. Mediatory structures have hardly been even formed here yet. There is no Europeanised party system, just European groups in the Strasbourg parliament, and apart from that, loose cooperation among programmatically related parties. This does not bring any integration of the European population, even at the moment of European elections. Nor have European associations or citizens' movements arisen, even though cooperation among national associations is further advanced than with parties. A search for European media, whether in print or broadcast, would be completely fruitless. This makes the European Union fall far short not just of ideal conceptions of a model democracy but even of the already deficient situation in Member States …

The absence of a European communication system, due chiefly, to language diversity, has the consequence that for the foreseeable future there will be neither a European public nor a European political discourse. Public discourse instead remains for the time bound by national frontiers, while the European sphere will remain dominated by professional and interest discourses conducted remotely from the public. European decisional processes are accordingly not under public observation in the same way as national ones. The European level of politics lacks a matching public. The feedback to European officials and representatives is therefore only weakly developed, while national politicians orient themselves even in the case of Council decisions to their national publics, because effective sanctions can come only from them. These circumstances give professional and technical viewpoints, particularly of an economic nature, excessive weight in European politics, while the social consequences and side-effects remain in the dark. This shortcoming cannot be made up for even by

---

[203] On its emergent qualities see T. Risse, *A Community of Europeans? Transnational Identities and Public Spheres* (Ithaca, NY, Cornell University Press, 2010).

[204] On this and possible reason see R. Corbett *et al.*, *The European Parliament*, 8th edn (London, John Harper, 2011) 31–3.

[205] S. Hobolt and J. Tilley, *Blaming Europe? Responsibility without Accountability in the European Union* (Oxford, Oxford University Press, 2014).

growing national attention to European policy themes, since the European dimension is just what is lacking there.

If this is true, the conclusion may be drawn that the full parliamentarisation of the European Union on the model of the national constitutional State will rather aggravate than solve the problem. On the one hand it would loosen the Union's ties back to the Member States, since the European Parliament is by its construction not a federal organ but a central one. Strengthening it would be at the expense of the Council and therefore inevitably have centralising effects. On the other hand the weakened ties back to the Member States would not be compensated by any increased ties back to the Union population. The European Parliament does not meet with any European mediatory structure in being: still less does it constitute a European popular representative body, since there is yet no European people. This is not an argument against any expansion of Parliament's powers. That might even enhance participation opportunities in the Union, provide greater transparency and create a counterweight to the dominance of technical and economic viewpoints. Its objective ought not, however, to be full parliamentarisation on the national model, since political decisions would otherwise move away to where they can be only democratically accountable.

The suspicion that this assessment is a front for the idea that democracy is possible only on the basis of a homogenous 'Volksgemeinschaft' [ethnic community] is, after all that, baseless. The requirements for democracy are here developed not out of the people, but out of the society that wants to constitute itself as a political unit. It is true that this requires a collective identity, if it wants to settle its conflicts non-violently, accept majority rule and practise solidarity. But this identity need by no means be rooted in ethnic conflict, but must also have other bases. All that is necessary is for the society to have formed an awareness of belonging together that can support majority decisions and solidarity efforts, and for it to have the capacity to communicate about its goals and problems discursively. What obstructs democracy is accordingly not the lack of cohesion of Union citizens as a people, but their weakly developed collective identity and low capacity for transnational discourse. This certainly means that the European democracy deficit is structurally determined. It can therefore not be removed by institutional reforms in any short term. The achievement of the democratic constitutional State can for the time being be adequately recognised only in the national framework.

(ii) Powers of the European Parliament

In considering the powers of the European Parliament, it is worth evaluating these against three forms of power traditionally associated with parliaments: law-making, powers over the executive and budgetary powers. These are all mentioned in the description of the Parliament's powers set out in Article 14 TEU.

Article 14(1) TEU

1. The European Parliament shall, jointly with the Council, exercise legislative and budgetary functions. It shall exercise functions of political control and consultation as laid down in the Treaties. It shall elect the President of the Commission.

With regard to law-making, stronger parliaments are seen as controlling law-making whereas weaker parliaments are seen as only ratifying or influencing legislation.[206] With regard to legislature-executive relations, in stronger parliamentary systems, executive power is derived from the legislature. The legislature appoints the executive and sets the conditions for the exercise of its powers.[207] In weaker systems, parliaments exercise powers of scrutiny over the executive and it is accountable to them. Finally, in terms of the budget, stronger parliaments have control over both revenue and expenditure. Weaker parliaments have no effective power to amend or reject budgets proposed to them by the executive.[208]

It is not simply the strength of European Parliament powers which should be considered. There are two styles of parliament, which Dann has termed debating and working parliaments. The central role of the former, of which the British House of Commons is an example, is to debate government policy and translate it into law. Although it is formally supreme, as the government has a majority in it, it can be controlled by the executive. In a working parliament, of which the US Congress is an example, the legislature is separate from the executive. It centres around reviewing the work of the executive and this is usually done by strong committees, which, free from the executive, can be powerful. Dann notes that the European Parliament is very much a working parliament. The extract below sets out the structure and work of the Committees.

> **P. Dann, 'European Parliament and Executive Federalism: Approaching a Parliament in a Semi-Parliamentary Democracy' (2003) 9 *European Law Journal* 549, 564–5**
>
> First, their role in acquiring information, discussing and analysing it, and finally formulating the political position of the European Parliament is absolutely central. The committees have the right to interrogate the Commission and to hold hearings with special experts. Building on these instruments, the committees can (and do) acquire specific expertise in their fields. On this basis, it is their task to file reports for the plenary, thereby formulating and pre-determining most of the final outcomes. These powers are a sword with two sharp sides: they not only facilitate the European Parliament's role in legislative procedures, but also contribute to the European Parliament's ability to competently scrutinise the executive, especially when it comes to implementation.
>
> There is a second aspect which allows the committees to play such a pivotal part in the institution: their internal structure. They are not only small, but also specialised and oriented in their scope towards the division of subject matters in the Commission. Of salient importance is their special leadership structure. This consists of a chairman and a *rapporteur*. The latter is responsible for presenting a matter to the committee, drafting the report for the committee and arguing it in plenary and with other institutions. Therefore a highly influential figure, he is chosen in a complicated and hotly contested procedure. Besides, this position creates clear responsibilities, giving the committee a distinct voice to communicate to the inside (between different committees and party groups) as well as to the outside (to other institutions). It renders the committee especially suited to negotiate with

---

[206] P. Norton, *Legislatures* (Oxford, Oxford University Press, 1990) 179.

[207] P. Raworth, 'A Timid Step Forwards: Maastricht and the Democratisation of the European Community' (1994) 19 *ELRev.* 16.

[208] A. Schick, 'Can National Legislatures Regain an Effective Voice in Budget Policy?' (2002) 1(3) *OECD Journal on Budgeting* 15; P. Posner and C.-K. Park, 'Role of the Legislature in the Budget Process: Recent Trends and Innovations' (2007) 7(3) *OECD Journal on Budgeting* 1.

other institutions through an expert representative. It also contributes to the European Parliament's chances to fit into the consensus system of the EU, where different institutions have to constantly negotiate.

There is one more parameter to qualify a parliament as working or debating type and that is the size and organisation of its staff: whereas the *working parliament* can acquire its expertise and level of scrupulous scrutiny of the executive only because of the support of an extensive staff, the *debating parliament* traditionally has very little of it. Its approach is based more on the rhetorical skill of the single parliamentarian to surprise the government and disclose its weakness in debate than on counter-weighing governmental bureaucracies.

Looking at the European Parliament, the staff is yet another factor which underlines its basic nature as a working parliament. Compared to the US Congress of course, it looks petty. But compared to all national parliaments in Europe, it has one of the largest staffs. The EP staff is organised on different levels: on an individual level, every MEP has at least one full time assistant which she can freely employ. On a party level, every party group in the EP is ascribed a number of assistants according to their size and the number of languages spoken. Finally, there is the General Secretariat of the European Parliament in Luxembourg which provides further assistance for the parliamentarians.

Altogether, the staff of the European Parliament totals 4,100 persons. In sum: the European Parliament is also in respect to its oversight function clearly a working parliament with well-structured committees having prominent rights, providing an infrastructure to seriously scrutinize the executive, and with the number and organisation of the staff displaying once again the basic character of the European Parliament as a working parliament.

The party groups exert their strongest influence over determining the composition of Parliament Committees. Although Committee membership is intended to reflect the ideological and territorial composition of the full Parliament,[209] the Chairs of the Committees are determined by negotiation between the groups. Thus for the 2009 Parliament, there are twenty-two Committees. Of these eighteen are chaired either by a MEP belonging to the European Peoples Party or to the Progressive Alliance of Socialists and Democrats.[210]

(a) Legislative powers of the European Parliament

On their face, the legislative powers of the Parliament seem weaker than national parliaments. The Parliament has neither a monopoly of adoption over any legislative proposal nor power of legislative initiative in any significant field of law-making. Instead, its legislative powers vary according to the legislative procedure adopted and this will depend on the policy field in question. There are three dominant procedures: the consultation, consent and ordinary legislative procedures. Under the first, the Parliament is consulted on a proposal and has the right to propose amendments. Under the second, it must actively agree to a proposal before it can become law. The most common is the third, the ordinary legislative procedure. The European

---

[209] G. Mcelroy, 'Committee Representation in the European Parliament' (2006) 7 *EUP* 5.
[210] See www.europarl.europa.eu/committees/en/full-list.html. All the other groupings other than the grouping of Europe of Freedom and Democracy (the most Euro-sceptic grouping) have one chair.

Parliament's central powers here are a power of veto over any proposal and the power to negotiate joint texts with the Council. The significance of its input is addressed in more detail in Chapter 3.

The Parliament does have, however, informal, general powers of agenda-setting under all procedures. One route is to request the Commission to submit a proposal.[211] This is not true of the other route for agenda-setting available under both legislative procedures, which is to propose amendments to Commission proposals for legislation. As we shall see, under all procedures, significant numbers of these amendments are accepted by the other EU institutions.[212]

(b) Powers over the Executive

Parliament has a variety of tools to hold the other EU institutions to account, including un-limited powers to challenge the acts and failures to act of the other EU institutions before the Court of Justice.[213] However, its central powers over the executive are its powers of appoint-ment and dismissal, on the one hand, and its powers of enquiry, on the other.

Powers of appointment and dismissal: The Parliament is exclusively responsible for ap-pointing the European Ombudsman[214] and can apply for her to be dismissed by the Court of Justice if she no longer fulfils the conditions required for the performance of her duties or is guilty of serious misconduct.[215] Of greater political significance are the Parliament's powers over the appointment of the Commission. The Parliament has a double power of approval. It must approve the President of the Commission, who has been nominated by the Heads of Government. If the nomination is accepted, it must also approve the Col-lege of Commissioners nominated by the President of the Commission and the Heads of Government.[216] Since 1999, the term of the Commission has been synchronised with that of the Parliament. This has allowed the Parliament to use its powers of assent extremely effectively. All prospective Commissioners are subject to questioning by Parliamentary Committees before assent is given to their appointment. They must answer questions about their professional past, their views on European integration and their legislative agenda for their term in office.

That Parliament has used its power of assent when dissatisfied with individual nominees. In 2004, it disapproved of the Italian, Rocco Buttiglione, because of his views on women and homosexuality; the Latvian, Ingride Udre, because of allegations surrounding corruption in her party; and the Hungarian, László Kovács, who was deemed to have insufficient knowl-edge about the Energy portfolio allocated to him. When it became clear that there was not a majority for the Commission because of these nominations, Manuel Barroso, the Commission President, had to arrange for the Italian and Latvian nominations to be replaced, and Kovács was reallocated the Taxation and Customs Union portfolio. In 2009, the Bulgarian, Rumiana Jeleva, had to be replaced, because of allegations over her financial interests.

For the 2014 European Parliament elections, both the Parliament and the Commission have asked all the main political groupings to put forward their own nominees for the post of

---

[211] Article 225 TFEU. The Commission must provide reasons if it does not submit a proposal.
[212] See pp. 119–21.   [213] Articles 263 and 265 TFEU.   [214] Article 228(1) TFEU.
[215] Article 228(2) TFEU.   [216] Article 17(7) TEU.

President of the Commission.[217] They have expressed the hope that the person nominated as the President of the Commission will be the nominee of the grouping which receives the most votes in the European Parliament elections. In this way, the hope, via this power of co-appointment, is to transform the Parliamentary elections into a form of Presidential election, in which rival candidates put forward their own slates of policies to be voted on by the Union's electorate.[218] At the time of writing, it is unclear whether this will be accepted by the European Council.

The Parliament also has important powers to dismiss the Commission. If a motion of censure is passed by a two-thirds majority of the votes cast representing a majority of the total members of the Parliament, the Commission is obliged to resign as a body.[219] This is an 'all or nothing' power. It does not allow the Parliament to criticise or dismiss individual Commissioners. Nevertheless, it was threatened against the Santer Commission in 1998 following allegations of corruption and maladministration against some of its members.[220] The Commission resigned the day before a vote would have been taken sacking the entire College. Following this, a Framework Agreement was made between the Commission and Parliament which allows the Parliament to hold individual Commissioners more to censure. Under this, if the Parliament expresses no confidence in an individual Commissioner, the President must either sack the individual or justify not doing so to the Parliament.[221]

Powers of enquiry: EU citizens and residents of the Union are entitled to petition the Parliament.[222] In 1987, the Parliament set up a Committee of Petitions, consisting of MEPs, to consider the petitions. In 2011 the Committee received 1,414 petitions of which 998 were admissible.[223] These petitions express views on an issue, such as ecological degradation, which may have been caused by an EU institution, national authority or private body. The process serves a number of functions. In cases where a political issue is raised, it allows the possibility for a hearing to be organised by the Parliament, thereby securing a voice for parties who might otherwise be disenfranchised. In cases where maladministration by an EU institution is alleged, the Parliament may take the matter up itself. In cases where a failure of a Member State is alleged, it will ask the Commission to take the matter up with the Member State concerned.

In addition, Parliament has the power to ask questions of or receive reports from most of the EU institutions. The European Commission, European Central Bank and Ombudsman must all submit Annual Reports to the Parliament.[224] In addition, the President of the European Council must report to the Parliament after each of its meetings.[225] Whilst there is no formal obligation

---

[217] *European Parliament on the Elections to the European Parliament in 2014*, 2012/2829(RSP); European Commission, *Preparing for the 2014 European Elections: Further Enhancing their Democratic and Efficient Conduct*, COM(2013)126, 6.

[218] This has been suggested for some time as providing a way for voters to exercise voice about the Commission. S. Hix, 'Executive Selection in the European Union: Does the Commission President Investiture Procedure Reduce the Democratic Deficit?' (1997) 1 *EIoP* No. 21.

[219] Article 17(8) TEU, Article 234 TFEU.

[220] D. Judge and D. Earnshaw, 'The European Parliament and the Commission Crisis: A New Assertiveness?' (2002) 15 *Governance* 345.

[221] Framework Agreement on relations between the European Parliament and the European Commission [2010] OJ L304/47, para. 5.

[222] Articles 20(2)(d), 24 and 227 TFEU.

[223] The petition must relate to matters which fall within the EU's sphere of activity. European Parliament, *Report on the Activities of the Committee on Petitions 2011*, 2011/2317(INI, Statistical Annex).

[224] Articles 249, 284(3) and 228 TFEU.   [225] Article 15(6)(d) TEU.

to do so, it is also customary for the Member State holding the Presidency of the Council to present the proposed work of the Council during its Presidency before the Parliament. Commissioners are also required to reply to questions put by MEPs.[226] A convention has also grown whereby the Council will answer questions put to it by MEPs.[227] A corollary of this is that the Council and the European Council have a right to be heard by the Parliament.[228] Finally, the President of the ECB and members of the Executive Council may, at the request of the Parliament, or on their own initiative, be heard by the competent Committees of the Parliament.[229]

(c) Financial powers of the Parliament

Parliament has significant powers over the EU Budget and is the central player with the Council. A five-year multi-annual framework for expenditure sets out the limits on total expenditure and ceilings for each heading of expenditure to be set by the Council after obtaining the consent of the Parliament.[230] Annual budgets are then set each year. These have to be in balance, comply with the multi-annual framework and be based on individual institutions' estimates of expenditure. Within these constraints, the Commission sets a draft Budget, which may then be adopted by the Council. The Parliament then has the right to veto the Budget should it wish.[231]

7 COURT OF AUDITORS

Comprising twenty-eight members appointed for a six-year term, the Court of Auditors audits the revenue and expenditure of the Union.[232] The audit is to be based on the records of the Union and if necessary, performed on the spot on the premises of any body that manages EU revenue or receives any payments from the EU Budget.[233] Despite these investigative powers, it has no powers to prosecute for fraud, but is obliged to report any irregularity to the appropriate body. For these purposes, the Court of Auditors is required to liaise with national audit bodies or, where appropriate, with national departments. The Court of Auditors can submit observations or deliver opinions on specific matters at the request of the other EU institutions and it can also assist the Parliament and the Council in exercising their powers of control over the implementation of the EU Budget. However, its greatest voice comes from the Annual Report it publishes on EU finances at the end of each financial year.[234] The Parliament can only give a discharge to the Commission in respect of implementation of the Budget on the basis of this Report.[235]

FURTHER READING

M. Busuioc, *European Agencies: Law and Practices of Accountability* (Oxford, Oxford University Press, 2013)

R. Corbett, F. Jacobs and M. Shackleton *The European Parliament*, 8th edn (London, John Harper, 2011)

[226] Article 230 TFEU. [227] It is formally obliged to answer questions in the field of CFSP, Article 36 TEU.
[228] Article 230 TFEU. [229] Article 284(3) TFEU. [230] Article 312(1) and (2) TFEU.
[231] Article 314 TFEU. A process of conciliation takes place similar to that in the ordinary legislative procedure.
[232] Article 287(1) TFEU. [233] Article 287(3) TFEU. [234] Article 287(4) TFEU.
[235] Article 319(1) TFEU. The Annual Report for 2011 is at [2012] OJ C44/1.

Table 2.2   Overview of the powers of the EU institutions

	European Commission	Council of Ministers	European Council	European Parliament
Legislative	Limited direct legislative powers but broader quasi-legislative powers to adopt implementing and delegated measures with binding legal effects	Power of final decision over most fields of EU law. Assisted by COREPER which prepares meetings. Limited quasi-legislative powers	Informal resolution of issues which have reached an impasse within the Council of Ministers	Power of veto, assent or right to consultation depending on legislative procedure
Budgetary	Proposes the Budget Oversees collection of revenue and expenditure	Approves the Budget		Approves the Budget
Agenda-setting	Power of legislative initiative (excluding CFSP). Stimulates policy debate	Forum for consultation and coordination of policies. Can request the Commission to submit a proposal. Agrees six-monthly legislative timetables with the Commission	Provides political directions and guidelines to the Union	Can request the Commission to submit a proposal
Holding other actors to account	Power to bring other EU institutions before the Court of Justice for failure to comply with EU law. Power to bring national governments to Court for failure to comply with EU law. Power to fine undertakings for breach of EU competition law and orders. Imposes duties (financial levies) on non-EU undertakings for breaking EU trade law	Power to bring other EU institutions before the Court of Justice for failure to comply with EU law. Sanctions Member States for failure of economic and fiscal policies		Power to bring other EU institutions before the Court of Justice for failure to comply with EU law. Power to censure the Commission. Asks questions of Commission, Council, European Council. Powers of inquiry
Shaping future direction of the EU	Handles applications for EU membership	Approves accession of new Member States. Suspends Member States' rights under Treaties where serious breach of EU values	Provides political direction to the Union. Makes decisions about the future shape and membership of the Union. Convenes intergovernmental conference for Treaty revision. Instigates Treaty revision through simplified revision procedure. Determines serious breach of EU values by Member State (requisite for suspension of rights)	Power of consent over Treaty amendments or accession of new Member States. Determines serious breach of EU values by Member State (requisite for suspension of rights)

Table 2.2   (*Cont.*)

	European Commission	Council of Ministers	European Council	European Parliament
Appointment and dismissal of other institutions			Power to make appointments and determine the composition of the Commission and Parliament	Power of appointment and dismissal over the Commission
External relations	Represents European Union internationally. Negotiates international agreements	Frames and develops the CFSP on the basis of general guidelines defined by the European Council. Signs international agreements	Defines guidelines and strategic interests of CFSP. Forum for Member State consultation	Power of consultation or veto over international agreement depending on field

D. Curtin, *Executive Power of the European Union: Law, Practices and the Living Constitution* (Oxford, Oxford University Press, 2009)

F. Häge, *Bureaucrats as Law-makers: Committee Decision-Making in the EU Council of Ministers* (Abingdon, Routledge, 2013)

S. Hix, A. Noury and G. Roland, *Democratic Politics within the European Parliament* (Cambridge, Cambridge University Press, 2007)

H. Hofmann and A. Türk (eds.), *EU Administrative Governance* (Cheltenham, Edward Elgar, 2006)

H. Kassim, J. Peterson, M. Bauer, S. Connolly, R. Dehousse, L. Hooghe and A. Thompson, *The European Commission of the Twenty First Century* (Oxford, Oxford University Press, 2013)

T. Risse, *A Community of Europeans? Transnational Identities and Public Spheres* (Ithaca, NY, Cornell University Press, 2010)

B. Rittberger, *Building Europe's Parliament: Democratic Representation Beyond the Nation-State* (Oxford, Oxford University Press, 2005)

J. Werts, *The European Council*, 2nd edn (London, John Harper, 2008)

3

Union Law-making

CONTENTS

1 INTRODUCTION

This chapter considers the different forms of law and regulatory acts in EU law, the legislative and regulatory procedures deployed to enact them and the debate about the democratic legitimacy of the Union. It is organised as follows.

Section 2 looks at the allocation of law-making power within the Treaties. The Treaties provide a series of legal bases which both grant the European Union authority to legislate in a particular field and determine the procedures and instruments which can be used. In cases of contestation reference will be had to the predominant aim and content of the measure to determine the base. If the measure is inextricably and equally associated with more than one base the Court of Justice will then apply a formal hierarchy between legal bases.

Section 3 discusses the types of legal instrument in EU law. There are four types of binding legislative instrument in EU law: Regulations, Directives, Decisions and international agreements. Problems have emerged because these legislative instruments have been used interchangeably. In addition, recent years has seen the growth of soft law: non-binding instruments which are used for a variety of purposes. These include setting out how EU institutions will apply EU law, and interpretations of EU law. This has led to hybrid situations where parties' understanding of their rights and obligations is governed by a mix of hard and soft law.

Section 4 considers the central legislative procedures. The ordinary legislative procedure grants the Parliament the power of veto and the Council, acting by qualified majority voting (QMV), the power of assent over any Commission proposal. Under the assent procedure Parliament has the power of assent, a requirement for it actively to approve a proposal before it becomes law. Under the consultation procedure, Parliament is merely consulted on a Commission proposal with the Council taking the final decision. Increasingly, the formal features of the legislative procedures have been blurred by the development of trilogies: informal meetings between representatives from the three institutions, usually first taking place before the Council first considers the proposal, in which agreement is sought on the proposal.

Section 5 considers the role of national parliaments within the EU law-making process. The European Union claims to be founded on representative democracy but there are representative difficulties with all the main EU law-making institutions. In recent years, national parliaments, from a position of almost complete exclusion, are increasingly incorporated into EU law-making. At the pre-legislative stage, prior to the proposal, there is a dialogue between them and the Commission. After the proposal, there is an eight-week period for them to exercise influence on their national governments. In addition, under the Early Warning Mechanism, national parliaments can police legislative proposal for compliance with the subsidiarity principle: the principle which requires the Union only to legislate when it can show added value. Whilst they cannot formally veto a measure, where the threshold is met, it is very unlikely that a measure will be adopted. This has raised a debate about whether these act as a virtual third legislative chamber, in addition to the Council and the European Parliament.

Section 6 discusses differentiated law-making in which a group of Member States enact laws or other binding instruments between themselves. The central procedure envisaged by the Treaties is enhanced cooperation. This enables as few as nine Member States to adopt laws but the procedural and substantial constraints on use of these procedures are stringent. Other procedures have thus emerged in specific sectors such as economic and monetary union or the Area of Freedom, Security and Justice which avoid these constraints. In addition, differentiated law-making is increasingly taking place through international agreements outside the structures of the Treaties. Some are subsequently incorporated into EU law as other states become aware of the costs of exclusion. Others, more problematically, are used as a substitute for EU law.

Section 7 considers comitology. This concerns the procedures which govern the adoption of implementing measures by the Commission: the advisory procedure, examination procedure and regulatory procedure with scrutiny. All these procedures involve consideration of a draft Commission measure by a committee of national government representatives. Under the advisory procedure, this committee advises. Under the examination procedure, it can veto, or, in some fields, positively approve the draft. The regulatory procedure with scrutiny allows for the measure to be referred to the European Parliament or Council. Some accounts see these committees as exercising a form of control over the Commission. Others see them as working in tandem with it to engage in a form of deliberate problem-solving.

Section 8 discusses how the democratic qualities of EU law-making should be considered. Some accounts see supranational law-making as inherently undemocratic as there is no pan-European political community sustaining it. Democracy requires for these some level of mutual commitment, common public debate and political parties which is not present at Union level. Others argue that national political communities have limits in terms of their capacities and a tendency to neglect or oppress marginalised groups or outsiders. EU law's democratic qualities stem from its rectification of this. Both these views act as a critique of the other. A third view has emerged which claims a limited democratic authority for EU law-making on three grounds. It requires respect and recognition of a wide array of interests and identities. It asks people to come together for common tasks. Its law-making is dispersed amongst a number of institutions. It can be debated whether the EU settlement actually does this, and how much authority is granted to it, as a consequence, when it comes into conflict with other democratic processes.

2 ALLOCATION OF LEGISLATIVE PROCEDURES

Prior to the Lisbon Treaty, it was possible to identify twenty-two different legislative procedures in EU law[1]. The Treaty has reduced this down to three main legislative procedures. Their relationship is set out in Article 289 TFEU.

Article 289 TFEU

1. The ordinary legislative procedure shall consist in the joint adoption by the European Parliament and the Council of a regulation, directive or decision on a proposal from the Commission. This procedure is defined in Article 294.
2. In the specific cases provided for by the Treaties, the adoption of a regulation, directive or decision by the European Parliament with the participation of the Council, or by the latter with the participation of the European Parliament, shall constitute a special legislative procedure.

Article 289 TFEU mentions the ordinary legislative procedure, known as the co-decision procedure prior to the Lisbon Treaty, and special legislative procedures. There are two dominant special legislative procedures: the consultation procedure and the consent procedure.

The choice of procedure is determined by a legal base set out in the Treaties. This legal base (e.g. Article 114 TFEU on the internal market) entitles the Union to legislate in the given field in question. It also governs the legislative procedures and the types of laws that can be adopted which, in turn, determines the respective powers of the EU institutions and national governments.[2] Often, the choice of legal base will not be self-evident. A law may address multifarious matters which seem to cut across many legal bases. A measure prescribing sanctions for dumping

---

[1] European Convention, *Legislative Procedures (including the Budgetary Procedure): Current Situation*, CONV 216/02, Annex I.
[2] R. Barents, 'The Internal Market Unlimited: Some Observations on the Legal Basis of Community Legislation' (1993) 30 *CMLRev.* 85, 92.

waste, for example, has a criminal dimension insofar as it applies penalties; an ecological dimension insofar as it seeks to protect the environment; and a single market dimension insofar as it will govern what sort of services may be offered by waste management service providers across the European Union.[3] Different institutions will seek to exploit this by arguing for the legal base which provides the procedure most advantageous to them.[4]

As both the TEU and TFEU have 'the same legal value',[5] a unitary approach operates across the two Treaties to determine the appropriate legal base for a measure. The starting point is to look at the predominant aim and content of the measure, and ascribe it accordingly to the appropriate legal base.[6] An example is the *Recovery of Indirect Taxes* judgment. The Commission and Parliament challenged the adoption of Directive 2001/44/EC, which provided for mutual assistance between Member States in the recovery of unpaid indirect taxation. The Council had adopted it under Article 113 TFEU, which concerned harmonisation of indirect taxes,[7] rather than under Article 114 TFEU, the internal market provision. The latter requires the use of the ordinary legislative procedure, which provides for QMV in the Council and a veto for the Parliament. The former, by contrast, provides for a unanimity vote in the Council and a reduced role for the Parliament. If tax measures could be agreed by QMV, recalcitrant Member States could be outmanoeuvred and bargained down. If the process were to be subject to a veto, fiscal integration would be held hostage to the wishes of the least integrationist Member State.

Case C-338/01 *Commission v Council (Recovery of Indirect Taxes)* [2004] ECR I-4829

54. ... the choice of the legal basis for a [Union] measure must rest on objective factors amenable to judicial review, which include in particular the aim and the content of the measure.

55. If examination of a [Union] measure reveals that it pursues a twofold purpose or that it has a twofold component and if one of these is identifiable as the main or predominant purpose or component whereas the other is merely incidental, the act must be based on a single legal basis, namely that required by the main or predominant purpose or component ...

56. By way of exception, if it is established that the measure simultaneously pursues several objectives which are inseparably linked without one being secondary and indirect in relation to the other, the measure must be founded on the corresponding legal bases ...

57. However, no dual legal basis is possible where the procedures laid down for each legal basis are incompatible with each other ...

58. In the present case, the procedures set out under [Article 113 TFEU], on the one hand, and that set out under [Article 114 TFEU], on the other, mean that the latter article cannot be applied in conjunction with one of the other two articles mentioned above in order to serve as the legal basis for a measure such as Directive 2001/44. Whereas unanimity is required for the adoption of a measure on the basis of [Article 113 TFEU], a qualified majority is sufficient for a measure to be capable of valid adoption on the basis of [Article 114 TFEU] ...

---

[3] Directive 2008/98/EC on waste and repealing certain Directives [2008] OJ L312/3, article 36(2). The measure is based on Article 192(1) TFEU, the environmental base.

[4] H. Cullen and H. Charlesworth, 'Diplomacy by Other Means: The Use of Legal Basis Litigation as a Political Strategy by the European Parliament and Member States' (1999) 36 *CMLRev.* 1243.

[5] Article 1 TEU and Article 1(2) TFEU.

[6] For a more recent example see Case C-130/10 *Parliament v Council (Sanctions against Osama Bin Laden)*, Judgment of 19 July 2012.

[7] It also based it on a now defunct provision, Article 93 EC, which relates to realisation of the common market.

59. So far as concerns the scope of Article [114 TFEU], which the Commission and Parliament argue ought to have been used as the legal basis for the adoption of Directive 2001/44, it must be pointed out that it is clear from the very wording of Article [114(1) TFEU] that that article applies only if the Treaty does not provide otherwise.

60. It follows that, if the Treaty contains a more specific provision that is capable of constituting the legal basis for the measure in question, that measure must be founded on such provision. That is, in particular, the case with regard to Article [113 TFEU] so far as concerns the harmonisation of legislation concerning turnover taxes, excise duties and other forms of indirect taxation.

61. It must also be pointed out that Article [114(2) TFEU] expressly excludes certain areas from the scope of that article. This is in particular the case with regard to 'fiscal provisions', the approximation of which cannot therefore take place on the basis of that article.

To ascertain the predominant aim and content of a measure, the Court of Justice will look at the principles on which it is based and its ideological content rather than its effects. In *Framework Directive on Waste*,[8] the Commission challenged the adoption of Directive 91/156/EC, the Framework Directive on Waste, on the basis of Article 192(2) TFEU, the environmental base, arguing that it should have been based on Article 114 TFEU, the internal market provision, as it affected the free movement of waste.[9] The Court disagreed. Instead of securing the internal market objectives of free movement of waste, the Directive implemented the ecological principles that environmental damage should be rectified at source and that waste should be disposed of as close as possible to the place of production in order to keep transport to a minimum. The central tenets of the Directive were, thus, those of environmental management rather than those of market liberalisation, and, correspondingly, it had to be based on Article 192(2) TFEU.

The 'predominant purpose' test does not apply where two objectives are so inextricably and equally associated that the Court cannot ascertain a predominant purpose. In such circumstances, where the two legal bases involved prescribe different legislative procedures, it moves to a different test in which it operates a formal hierarchy between the different legal bases, looking to the relationship specified in the Treaties between each. Article 114 TFEU, the internal market provision, thus, enjoys a precedence over Article 192(2) TFEU, the provision governing Union environmental action, on, inter alia, measures primarily of a fiscal nature because the latter indicates that it is 'without prejudice to Article 114'. At the bottom of the pecking order of legal bases sits Article 352 TFEU, the flexibility provision, which allows the Union to take measures to meet its objectives where no other legal base provides the requisite power.[10]

However, it will be rare that a measure pursues inextricably and equally associated objectives. In *Linguistic Diversity in the Information Society*, the Court of Justice had to consider a Decision, which set up a programme to promote linguistic diversity in the information society. It had been adopted under Article 173(3) TFEU, the legal base for industrial policy. The Commission argued that this was because the principal object of the programme was to enable companies to offer

---

8 Case C-155/91 *Commission* v *Council* [1993] ECR I-939.
9 At the time the former provided only for consultation of the Parliament and unanimity voting in the Council.
10 Case C-295/90 *Parliament* v *Council* [1992] ECR I-4193.

multilingual services. The Parliament challenged this, arguing that it should have also been based on Article 166(5) TFEU, the legal base for culture. It argued, and this was not contested, that linguistic wealth was central to the Union's cultural heritage. The Court stated that the presence of twin objectives was insufficient to bring the measure outside the 'predominant purpose' rule. Each component had to be equally essential to the measure and each had to be indissociable for the 'inextricably associated' rule to apply. This was not the case here as the predominant purpose was industrial. The beneficiaries of the programme were, almost exclusively, small and medium-sized enterprises, who might lose competitiveness because of the costs associated with linguistic diversity.[11]

Neither rule is easy to apply to particular sets of circumstances. The 'predominant aim and content' rule assumes each legal base is characterised by a distinctive set of principles which it is possible to identify in all legislation founded on it.[12] This is rarely the case and the Court has to engage in highly selective analysis to justify a particular legal base. The 'inextricably associated' rule, if applied literally, is so narrow as to be almost redundant as it requires two purposes to have equal weight and be completely entwined. However, its occasional use suggests that, sometimes, for ulterior motives, the Court simply wishes to discard the 'predominant purpose' rule. However, this problem is likely to remain whatever test is adopted by the Court. The underlying difficulty is the Byzantine structure of the Treaties, with their proliferation of legal bases.[13]

3 EU LEGISLATION

(i) Binding instruments in EU law

All legislative acts must be published in the *Official Journal* and enter into force twenty days after publication or on the date specified in the instrument.[14] The central provision setting out the types of legislative act is Article 288 TFEU.

Article 288 TFEU

To exercise the Union's competences, the institutions shall adopt regulations, directives, decisions, recommendations and opinions.

A regulation shall have general application. It shall be binding in its entirety and directly applicable in all Member States.

A directive shall be binding, as to the result to be achieved, upon each Member State to which it is addressed, but shall leave to the national authorities the choice of form and methods.

A decision shall be binding in its entirety. A decision which specifies those to whom it is addressed shall be binding only on them.

Recommendations and opinions shall have no binding force.

---

[11] Case C-42/97 *Parliament v Council* [1999] ECR I-869.
[12] D. Chalmers, 'The Single Market: From Prima Donna to Journeyman' in J. Shaw and G. More (eds.), *New Legal Dynamics of the European Union* (Oxford, Clarendon, 1995) 55, 69–71.
[13] S. Weatherill, 'Regulating the Internal Market: Result Orientation in the House of Lords' (1992) 17 *ELRev.* 299, 312–13.
[14] Article 297(1) TFEU.

The provision is not exhaustive and international agreements with non-EU states, although not mentioned in Article 288 TFEU, are regarded as secondary legislation, binding both the Union and the Member States.[15] The different legislative instruments have different traits.

Regulations are the most centralising of all Union instruments and are used wherever there is a need for uniformity. As they are to have general application, they do not apply to individual sets of circumstances, but to an 'objectively determined situation and produce(s) legal effects with regard to categories of persons described in a generalised and abstract manner'.[16] The other hallmark of Regulations is their direct applicability. From the date that they enter into force, they automatically form part of the domestic legal order of each Member State and require no further transposition. Indeed, unless permitted by the Regulation,[17] it is illegal for a Member State to adopt implementing legislation because such measures might contain changes which affect the uniform application of the Regulation[18] or obscure from citizens the fact that it is the Regulation which is the direct source of their rights and obligations.[19] However, there is a caveat. In some cases, Regulations will require national authorities to adopt implementing measures. If there is such a requirement, a failure to implement the Regulation will be a breach of Union law.[20]

Directives are binding as to the result to be achieved. They leave the choice as to form and methods used to implement them to the discretion of Member States. Although, like other legislative instruments, a Directive comes into force twenty days after publication or on the date stipulated in the Directive, it will give a deadline (usually eighteen or twenty-four months after publication) by which Member States must transpose its obligations into national law.

Decisions are binding upon those to whom they are addressed. For this reason the addressee must be notified of any Decision.[21] The majority of Decisions are addressed to Member States, with only a small number addressed to private parties, with almost all of the latter being in the field of competition law, where the Commission can impose fines on parties or require them to desist from certain practices. The Lisbon Treaty introduces an amendment by stipulating that Decisions which specify those to whom they are addressed shall be binding only on them. In this, it makes a distinction found in Germany, which distinguishes these types of Decisions from Decisions which have no addressee ('Beschluss'). If the former are seen more as directions to particular individuals, the latter impose general obligations which bind the Union as an organisational entity and Member States, as part of that entity. However, as they are not addressed to private parties, they are thought not to impose obligations on them.[22]

International agreements will only have legal effects within EU law for that part of the agreement that falls within Union competence. Their legal effects will also depend upon the phrasing of the agreement. If these agreements impose precise obligations, they will not require implementation by either Member States or EU institutions but will enter directly into

---

[15] Article 216(2) TFEU.
[16] Joined Cases 789/79 and 790/79 *Calpak* v *Commission* [1980] ECR 1949.
[17] Case C-606/10 *ANAFE* v *Ministre de l'Intérieur*, Judgment of 14 June 2012.
[18] Case 39/72 *Commission* v *Italy* [1973] ECR 101; Joined Cases C-539/10P and C-550/10P *Stichting Al-Aqsa* v *Council*, Judgment of 15 November 2012.
[19] Case 34/73 *Variola* v *Amministrazione delle Finanze* [1973] ECR 981.
[20] Case 128/78 *Commission* v *United Kingdom* [1978] ECR 2429.
[21] Article 297(2) TFEU.
[22] A. v. Bogdandy, F. Arndt and J. Bast, 'Legal Instruments in European Union Law and Their Reform: A Systematic Approach on an Empirical Basis' (2004) 23 *YBEL* 91, 103–6.

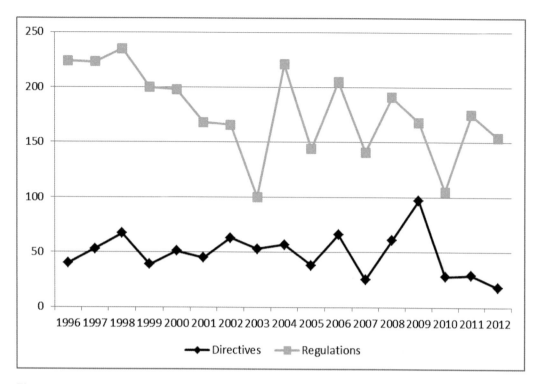

Figure 3.1   Union annual output of Regulations and Directives

force in EU and national law. More vaguely phrased provisions will necessitate implementation. Interpretation of the provisions of an international agreement will be carried out in the light of the object and purpose of that agreement. Provisions identically worded to EU law provisions may be interpreted differently, on the ground that the objective of the agreement differs from that of the Treaties.[23]

A 2004 study found Regulations were the most widely used, accounting for 31 per cent of all legislation. Decisions addressed to a party accounted for a further 27 per cent, with Decisions not addressed to anybody accounting for 10 per cent of all measures. Directives and international agreements each accounted for 9 per cent of all legislation.[24] At least between Regulations and Directives, these proportions have remained the same even as legislative output has declined.

The justification for this wide array of legislative instruments is to allow EU law a different legal bite in different policy fields and also to grant the legislator some discretion over that bite. This rationale has been undermined by the legislative instruments being substitutable for one another. One finds Regulations which substitute for Decisions, in that they apply to individual sets of circumstances rather than generally.[25] There are, conversely, Directives which look like Regulations, because they are so detailed that they vitiate the discretion granted to

[23] Case 104/81 *Kupferberg* [1982] ECR 364; Case C-102/09 *Camar v Presidenza del Consiglio dei Ministri* [2010] ECR I-4045.
[24] Bogdandy *et al.*, n. 22 above, 97.
[25] See e.g. Joined Cases 41–44/70 *International Fruit Company v Commission* [1971] ECR 411.

Member States and must be transposed into national law verbatim.[26] Finally, Decisions without addressees act as a substitute for Directives in that they require Member States to realise certain results without specifying the means. In no instance has any of this been declared illegal.

The Lisbon Treaty introduced a distinction between legislative and non-legislative measures. Legislative acts are those adopted by the procedures set out in Article 289 TFEU.[27] The legislature may, however, grant the Commission the power to take two types of measure: 'delegated' measures and 'implementing' measures.[28] These measures may take the form of Regulations, Directives or Decisions. However, any such measures must identify itself in its title as either a 'delegated' or 'implementing' measure.[29] These are 'non-legislative' in nature,[30] and there is thus clearly a hierarchy between them and all legislative acts.

(ii) Soft law

Recommendations and Opinions are mentioned in Article 288 TFEU, but have no binding force. They must be viewed alongside a variety of other instruments, which include Resolutions and Declarations, Action Programmes and Plans, Communications by the Commission, guidelines and inter-institutional arrangements. These all come under the generic heading of 'soft law': 'rules of conduct which, in principle, have no legally binding force but which nevertheless may have practical effects'.[31] These instruments are used for a variety of purposes:[32]

Commitments about the conduct of institutions: These are commonly used to organise relations between the EU institutions.[33] A good example is the Joint Declaration on Practical Arrangements for the Co-Decision Procedure, which sets out a series of working methods governing the ordinary legislative procedure and the EU institutions' common understanding of their rights and duties under it.[34]

Commitments to respect certain values: Declarations, in particular, are used to commit EU institutions to pursuing certain values. Declarations are not merely commitments to future conduct, but also seek to redefine the political identity of the Union. The most obvious example is the Joint Declaration by the European Parliament, the Council and the Commission on Fundamental Rights, where the EU institutions were asserting for the first time that observance of fundamental rights norms was a goal of the EU institutions, thereby admitting that the Union was not merely concerned with economic integration, but also had an incipient civil identity.[35]

---

[26] Case 38/77 *ENKA* v *Inspecteur der Invoerrechten* [1977] ECR 2203.

[27] Article 289(3) TFEU.

[28] The distinction between delegated and implementing measures is obscure. See pp. 68–9.

[29] Article 290(3) TFEU and Article 291(4) TFEU.

[30] Only delegated measures are described in this way in the Treaty, but it is safe to assume that this is also the case with implementing measures. Article 290(1) TFEU.

[31] F. Snyder, 'The Effectiveness of European Community Law: Institutions, Processes, Tools and Techniques' (1993) 56 *MLR* 19, 32. For an exhaustive discussion see L. Senden, *Soft Law in European Community Law* (Oxford/Portland, Hart, 2004) ch. 5.

[32] On how soft law is coming to supersede hard law in many fields see S. Smismans, 'From Harmonisation to Coordination? EU Law in the Lisbon Governance Architecture' (2011) 18 *JEPP* 504.

[33] H. Hofmann, G. Rowe and A. Türk, *Administrative Law and Policy of the European Union* (Oxford University Press, Oxford, 2011) 536–66.

[34] [2007] OJ C145/2.   [35] [1977] OJ C103/1.

Programming legislation: The instrument, *par excellence*, for this is the Action Plan. Action Plans set out objectives and timetables for particular EU policies, which are used to justify specific legislation and which provide a wider background against which this legislation is understood and interpreted. A good example is the Single Market Act, an Action Plan to relaunch the single market.[36] This identified twelve priority areas for action. These included easier access to finance for small and medium-sized enterprises; easier mutual recognition of professional qualifications; a unitary patent system; a pan-Union framework for Alternate Dispute Resolution; a digital single market allowing secure and seamless electronic interaction across the single market; and clarification of the right to strike. The legal measures needed to realise this Action Plan total fifty.

Regulatory communications: In areas such as nuclear energy and competition, the Commission will issue Opinions as an informal way of indicating to undertakings whether they are complying with EU law. It will also issue Notices, setting out its general enforcement policy on what infractions it will pursue.[37] It cannot depart from these without giving reasons for this which are non-discriminatory in nature.[38]

Interpretation of legislation: Communications or guidelines are used to elaborate understandings of a provision of EU law. These can neither amend binding EU law nor bind EU or national courts.[39] However, insofar as they are seen as settling understandings of underlying hard law, authors have talked of 'legal hybrids' being created where actors' understandings of their EU legal obligations and how EU and national institutions will treat them is informed by a mix of hard and soft law.[40] If this can sometimes generate increased certainty, concerns have also been raised about the limited controls on these hybrids.[41] There is limited possibility for judicial review of these interpretations.[42]

Model law making: In some areas of EU law, harmonising measures involving the setting of common standards through Regulations, Directives and Decisions are excluded. In such fields, norm-setting is done exclusively through soft law.[43] Soft law is also used in many fields where there is the option of harmonising measures. The Secretariat at the 'Future of Europe' Convention identified three circumstances where the former is likely to be preferred:

[36] European Commission, *Single Market Act*, COM(2011)206. This has been followed by European Commission, *Single Market Act II*, COM(2012)573.

[37] E.g. Commission Notice on agreements of minor importance which do not appreciably restrict competition [2001] OJ C368/13.

[38] Case C-167/04P *JCB Service* v *Commission* [2006] ECR I-8935.

[39] Case C-360/09 *Pfleiderer* v *Bundeskartellamt* [2011] ECR I-5161.

[40] D. Trubek and L. Trubek, 'New Governance and Legal Regulation: Complementarity, Rivalry and Transformation' (2007) 13 *CJEL* 539; O. Stefan, 'Hybridity before the Court: A Hard Look at Soft Law in the EU Competition and State Aid Case Law' (2012) 37 *ELRev.* 49.

[41] S. Lefevre, 'Interpretative Communications and the Implementation of Community Law at National Level' (2004) 29 *ELRev.* 808; J. Scott, 'In Legal Limbo: Post-legislative Guidance as a Challenge for European Administrative Law' (2011) 48 *CMLRev.* 329; L. Senden, 'Soft Post-Legislative Rulemaking: A Time for More Stringent Control' (2013) 19 *ELJ* 57.

[42] They must be seen as doing no more than fleshing out existing obligations. Typically, this will be where they use imperative language, Case C-325/91 *France* v *Commission* [1993] ECR I-3283. They will only occasionally be worded in this way. On this see Scott, n. 41 above, 344–53.

[43] The fields include Common Foreign and Security Policy (Article 24(1) TEU); economic policy (Article 121(2) TFEU); employment (Article 148(2) TFEU); education, vocational training, youth and sport (Article 165(4) TFEU); culture (Article 166(5) TFEU); most areas of public health (Article 168(4), (5) TFEU); industry (Article 173(3) TFEU); space (Article 189(2) TFEU); tourism (Article 195(2) TFEU); civil protection (Article 196(2) TFEU); administrative cooperation (Article 197(2) TFEU).

- where the area of work is closely connected with national identity or culture, e.g. culture or education;
- where the instruments for implementing national policies are so diverse and/or complex that harmonisation seemed disproportionate in relation to the objectives pursued, e.g. employment;
- where there is no political will for EU legislation amongst the Member States, but there is a desire to make progress together.[44]

There has been a recent fierce debate over the value of soft law. The arguments of each side have been well set out by Trubek, Cottrell and Nance.[45] Some of the criticisms of soft law they observe are that:

- it lacks the clarity and precision needed to provide predictability and a reliable framework for action;
- soft law cannot really have any effect, but is a covert tactic to enlarge the Union's legislative hard law competence;
- soft law bypasses normal systems of accountability;
- soft law undermines EU legitimacy because it creates expectations, but cannot bring about change.

They argue, however, that soft law has some advantages over traditional law:

- hard law tends toward uniformity of treatment while many current issues demand tolerance for significant diversity among Member States;
- hard law presupposes a fixed condition based on prior knowledge while situations of uncertainty may demand constant experimentation and adjustment;
- hard law is very difficult to change yet in many cases frequent change of norms may be essential to achieve optimal results;
- if actors do not internalise the norms of hard law, enforcement may be difficult; if they do, it may be unnecessary.

From this, it would appear that in areas where uniformity is not important and there is a need for experimentation, soft law has some advantages. Even in these fields, some of the criticisms of soft law still persist: namely, the manner in which it has been used to expand Union involvement, its blurring of institutional rules and its lack of concern with asymmetries of power so that compliance with soft law only tends to occur when it suits vested interests.[46] To meet these difficulties, advocates of soft law have increasingly argued for it to be subject to controls which allow for increased 'political contestation and public scrutiny' of it.[47] Such controls would include duties, enforced by courts, to offer hearings before EU institutions adopt a measure; duties to base it on the best expertise available; duties to give reasons; and public access to documents surrounding its formulation.[48]

---

[44] European Commission, *Coordination of National Policies: The Open Method of Coordination*, WG VI WD015 (Brussels, 26 September 2002).

[45] D. Trubek *et al.*, 'Hard and Soft Law in European Integration' in J. Scott and G. de Búrca (eds.), *New Governance and Constitutionalism* (Oxford/Portland, Hart, 2005).

[46] See, in particular, Senden, n. 31 above, 477–98.

[47] M. Dawson, *New Governance and the Transformation of European Law: Coordinating EU Social Law and Policy* (Cambridge University Press, Cambridge, 2011) 238.

[48] Dawson, n. 47 above, 254–66. See also J. Scott and S. Sturm, 'Courts as Catalysts: Rethinking the Judicial Role in New Governance' (2007) 13 *CJEL* 3.

4 UNION LEGISLATIVE PROCEDURES

(i) Ordinary legislative procedure

(a) Central features of the ordinary legislative procedure

The ordinary legislative procedure is set out in Article 294 TFEU. Its central elements are set out below.

Article 294 TFEU

1. Where reference is made in the Treaties to the ordinary legislative procedure for the adoption of an act, the following procedure shall apply.
2. The Commission shall submit a proposal to the European Parliament and the Council.

First reading

3. The European Parliament shall adopt its position at first reading and communicate it to the Council.
4. If the Council approves the European Parliament's position, the act concerned shall be adopted in the wording which corresponds to the position of the European Parliament.
5. If the Council does not approve the European Parliament's position, it shall adopt its position at first reading and communicate it to the European Parliament.
6. The Council shall inform the European Parliament fully of the reasons which led it to adopt its position at first reading. The Commission shall inform the European Parliament fully of its position.

Second reading

7. If, within three months of such communication, the European Parliament:
   (a) approves the Council's position at first reading or has not taken a decision, the act concerned shall be deemed to have been adopted in the wording which corresponds to the position of the Council;
   (b) rejects, by a majority of its component members, the Council's position at first reading, the proposed act shall be deemed not to have been adopted;
   (c) proposes, by a majority of its component members, amendments to the Council's position at first reading, the text thus amended shall be forwarded to the Council and to the Commission, which shall deliver an opinion on those amendments.
8. If, within three months of receiving the European Parliament's amendments, the Council, acting by a qualified majority:
   (a) approves all those amendments, the act in question shall be deemed to have been adopted;
   (b) does not approve all the amendments, the President of the Council, in agreement with the President of the European Parliament, shall within six weeks convene a meeting of the Conciliation Committee.
9. The Council shall act unanimously on the amendments on which the Commission has delivered a negative opinion.

Conciliation

10. The Conciliation Committee, which shall be composed of the members of the Council or their representatives and an equal number of members representing the European Parliament, shall have the task of reaching agreement on a joint text, by a qualified majority of the members of the Council or

their representatives and by a majority of the members representing the European Parliament within six weeks of its being convened, on the basis of the positions of the European Parliament and the Council at second reading.

11. The Commission shall take part in the Conciliation Committee's proceedings and shall take all necessary initiatives with a view to reconciling the positions of the European Parliament and the Council.

12. If, within six weeks of its being convened, the Conciliation Committee does not approve the joint text, the proposed act shall be deemed not to have been adopted.

Third reading

13. If, within that period, the Conciliation Committee approves a joint text, the European Parliament, acting by a majority of the votes cast, and the Council, acting by a qualified majority, shall each have a period of six weeks from that approval in which to adopt the act in question in accordance with the joint text. If they fail to do so, the proposed act shall be deemed not to have been adopted.

14. The periods of three months and six weeks referred to in this Article shall be extended by a maximum of one month and two weeks respectively at the initiative of the European Parliament or the Council.

The length of this provision makes the procedure look intimidating. It is best to think of the procedure as having four key features.

Joint agreement: Joint adoption of legislation by the Council and Parliament can happen at three junctures during the procedure.

- *First reading by the Parliament*: The Commission makes a proposal. The Parliament issues an opinion on it (the first reading). The Council can adopt the act by QMV if either the Parliament has made no amendments or it agrees with its amendments.
- *Second reading by the Parliament*: If there is no agreement after the first reading the Council can adopt a 'common position'. If it is adopting the Commission proposal, it does this by QMV. If it makes amendments of its own, it does this by unanimity. This common position is referred back to the Parliament for a second reading. If the Parliament does nothing for three months or agrees with the common position, the measure is adopted. Alternately, it may propose amendments. If the amendments have been approved by the Commission, they may be adopted by the Council by QMV. If, however, the Commission expresses a negative view of the Parliament's amendments, these have to be adopted by unanimity in the Council.
- *Third reading*: If there is no agreement following the second reading, a Conciliation Committee is established. It has six weeks to approve a joint text. This text must be adopted within six weeks, by both the Council by QMV and the Parliament to become law.

Double veto of the Parliament: The ordinary legislative procedure grants the Parliament a veto over legislation. The veto can be exercised at the second reading if the Parliament decides to reject the common position of the Council. The other possibility is at the third reading after the Conciliation Committee has provided a joint text. Technically speaking, it is not a veto being exercised here, but Parliamentary assent. It must positively agree to it at this point for it to become law.

Assent of the Council: A measure will only become law if the Council agrees to it. The number of votes required will either be QMV or unanimity. If the measure has been approved by the Commission or by the Conciliation Committee, it will be QMV.[49] If the Council is proposing its own amendments, it must act by unanimity to adopt these amendments.

Conciliation Committee: As mentioned under 'Joint agreement' above, this is convened following the Parliament's second reading, where the Council is unable to accept the amendments proposed by the Parliament. Modelled on the German Mediations Committee,[50] it comprises twenty-eight members from the Council and twenty-eight MEPs. The Council members vote by QMV and the MEPs by simple majority.

(b) Legislative practice and the ordinary legislative procedure

The most dramatic power enjoyed by the European Parliament appears to be the veto. However, it has made only limited use of this. Between 1 May 1999 and 1 January 2013, Parliament only used the veto five times in 1,166 procedures: about 0.4 per cent of the time.[51] There are a number of reasons for this. The veto can bring the worst outcome because, often, from the Parliament's perspective, imperfect EU legislation is better than no legislation. Regular exercise of the veto would also be bad politics. Other parties will not communicate with the Parliament if, in the end, its position is inflexible, as there is nothing to talk about.

For the Parliament, it is rather the shadow of the veto which is important. By threatening to thwart other parties' objectives, it can secure influence for itself to realise outcomes it desires. This role is reinforced by a quirk in the legislative procedure. If the Commission agrees with the Parliament, it is easier for the Council to accept Parliamentary amendments than to produce its own.

Article 293(1) TFEU

1. Where, pursuant to the Treaties, the Council acts on a proposal from the Commission, it may amend that proposal only by acting unanimously, except in the cases referred to in paragraphs 10 and 13 of Articles 294, in Articles 310, 312 and 314 and in the second paragraph of Article 315.[52]

Acceptance of amendments proposed by the Parliament only requires a QMV in the Council, whilst it requires unanimity to produce its own amendments. To be sure, the Commission must agree with the Parliament's suggestions but, importantly, it cannot propose amendments of its own without withdrawing the proposal and starting again. Parliament is the only institution that has the opportunity to 'improve' the text. There are, however, different forms of amendment. In some cases, the Parliament is not the source of the amendment. It puts forward something suggested by an interest group, national government or even one of the other EU institutions.[53]

---

[49] Without Commission approval, European Parliament amendments can only be adopted by unanimity. The measure falls if there is no agreement in the Conciliation Committee.

[50] N. Foster, 'The New Conciliation Committee under Article 189b' (1994) 19 *ELRev.* 185.

[51] These statistics are from the EU Council website, www.consilium.europa.eu/policies/ordinary-legislative-procedure/other-information?lang=en.

[52] These last four provisions are budgetary provisions.

[53] S. Hix and B. Høyland, 'Empowerment of the European Parliament' (2013) 16 *Annual Review of Political Science* 171, 176. These authors also observe that since the growth of the trilogue, it is increasingly difficult to measure Parliamentary influence by amendments as the trilogue results in face-to-face bargaining. For this reason, more recent studies do not look at the level of amendments.

Furthermore, the importance of these amendments varies. Some just dot 'Is'. Others radically change policy. Some clump amendments together, whilst others are put through at the behest of the Council or the Member States. Careful research by Kardasheva of 470 proposals between 1999 and 2007 found that, allowing for this, Parliamentary input was high. It amended 87 per cent of the proposals with amendments per proposal varying from 1 to 322. Instead of looking at formal amendments, Kardasheva identified 1,567 issues raised by the Parliament (discrete matters that were not tidying up exercises) and found Parliamentary success in 65.2 per cent of the cases: a high rate.[54]

The position of the Commission under the ordinary legislative procedure is curious. Its influence diminishes as the procedure continues. As it plays no active role in the Conciliation Committee, it would be possible for the Council and Parliament to rearrange its proposals at that point.[55] In practice, its influence remains significant. This is because very few proposals require conciliation.[56] In the majority of instances, agreement is reached at first or second reading. At this point in the procedure, the Commission's influence is considerable. Almost all successful Parliamentary amendments require the Commission's agreement. Very few are adopted by the Council where there has not been prior approval by the Commission. Early studies found that there was an 88 per cent probability that a Parliament amendment will be rejected by the Council if the Commission rejects it, with, by contrast, an 83 per cent probability that it will be accepted if the Commission approves it.[57]

A further counter-intuitive feature of the procedure is the effectiveness of the Conciliation Committee. The Committee would appear to have little mandate, as any decision requires the subsequent approval of both Parliament and Council and it might be thought that, by the time it meets, institutional positions would be entrenched. Yet, in almost all procedures,[58] the Committee had been able to propose a joint text accepted by both the Parliament and the Council. This might be because the Council is able to behave more proactively and recapture the agenda within the Committee, as it is able to make its own amendments and accept amendments by QMV.[59] An alternative might be that, as parties are aware of each other's positions, negotiation is easier. New amendments are not continually being thrown in, but there are a stable set of issues on which discussion can proceed.[60] Whatever the reason, the effect is an increase in the influence of COREPER, as it is members of COREPER, not Council ministers, who sit in the Conciliation Committee. COREPER is not just preparing the meeting here, but also adopting the Joint Text.

(c) First reading and the trilogue

The greatest change to the ordinary legislative procedure was heralded by a Joint Declaration on practical arrangements for the procedure, subsequently updated by a 2007 Joint

---

[54] R. Kardasheva, *Legislative Package Deals in EU Decision-Making 1999–2007* (Ph.D, London School of Economics and Political Science, 2009) 242–4.
[55] C. Crombez, 'The Codecision Procedure in the European Union' (1997) 22 *Legislative Studies Quarterly* 97.
[56] In 2010–2012 only 6 out of 230 dossiers went to conciliation. EU Council, n. 51 above.
[57] G. Tsebelis *et al.*, 'Legislative Procedures in the European Union: An Empirical Analysis' (2001) 31 *BJPS* 573. For a case study see C. Burns, 'Codecision and the European Commission: A Study of Declining Influence?' (2004) 11 *JEPP* 1.
[58] Between 1 July 1999 and 30 June 2009, 112 proposals went successfully through conciliation. Only three failed. EU Council, n. 51 above.
[59] G. Tsebelis, 'Maastricht and the Democratic Deficit' (1997) 52 *Aussenwirtschaft* 26, 43–5.
[60] A. Rasmussen, 'The EU Conciliation Committee: One or Several Principals' (2008) 9 *EUP* 7.

Declaration.[61] This Joint Declaration formalises two developments that have become a central part of institutional practice and have reshaped understandings in this area: the commitment to reach agreement at first reading and the trilogue.

The Joint Declaration commits the EU institutions to clear the way, where appropriate, for the adoption of the act concerned at an early stage of the procedure.[62] This is understood to mean that, wherever possible, they should try to secure agreement at first reading.[63] In the early days of this arrangement they were only partially successful, with only about 28 per cent of the total agreed at first reading between 1999 and 30 June 2004.[64] Recent enlargements had a significant effect on these figures, however. Concerns about the difficulties of getting twenty-eight Member States to agree have led to an impetus to get agreement by first reading, so that between 1 July 2004 and 31 December 2012, 577 of 726 agreed dossiers (79.5 per cent) were agreed at first reading.[65]

This telescopes the procedure and forecloses spaces for public debate. A study of the Dutch and UK Parliaments found, therefore, that there was less scrutiny within these parliaments of proposals agreed at first reading compared to those which progressed further along the legislative process.[66] It also changes the opportunity structures. Parties seeking influence have to do so as early as possible. For first reading is no longer what it says: an opportunity for initial consideration. It is usually the moment of final decision.

This position is exacerbated by the dominance of the trilogue. Trilogues first emerged in 1995 to prepare the work of the Conciliation Committee.[67] A trilogue is composed of three parties: two or three MEPs, normally from the respective committee, a Deputy Permanent Representative, normally from the Member State holding the Presidency, and a senior Commission official. The job of the trilogue is to act as a forum where each side can explain its position to the other and, if possible, where agreement can be reached. They now operate at all stages of the procedure: before all the readings, after the Council common position and before the Conciliation Committee. Kardasheva has estimated that trilogues take place, in some form, on 76 per cent of Commission proposals under the ordinary legislative procedure.[68] Their value to the EU institutions is set out in the Joint Declaration.

Joint Declaration on practical arrangements for the [ordinary legislative] procedure [2007] OJ C145/2

7. Cooperation between the institutions in the context of [the ordinary legislative procedure] often takes the form of tripartite meetings ('trilogues'). This trilogue system has demonstrated its vitality and flexibility in increasing significantly the possibilities for agreement at first and second reading stages, as well as contributing to the preparation of the work of the Conciliation Committee.

---

[61] [1999] OJ C148/1 and [2007] OJ C145/2.   [62] *Ibid.* para. 4.   [63] *Ibid.* para. 11.
[64] European Parliament, *Activity Report for Fifth Parliamentary Term*, PE 287.644, 12–13.
[65] EU Council, 'Consilium', n. 51 above.
[66] R. de Ruiter, 'Under the Radar? National Parliaments and the Ordinary Legislative Procedure in the European Union' (2013) 20 *JEPP* 1196.
[67] On the trilogue see M. Shackleton, 'The Politics of Codecision' (2000) 38 *JCMS* 325, 334–6; M. Shackleton and T. Raunio, 'Codecision since Amsterdam: A Laboratory for Institutional Innovation and Change' (2003) 10 *JEPP* 171, 177–9.
[68] Kardasheva, n. 54 above, 25.

8. Such trilogues are usually conducted in an informal framework. They may be held at all stages of the procedure and at different levels of representation, depending on the nature of the expected discussion. Each institution, in accordance with its own rules of procedure, will designate its participants for each meeting, define its mandate for the negotiations and inform the other institutions of arrangements for the meetings in good time.

9. As far as possible, any draft compromise texts submitted for discussion at a forthcoming meeting shall be circulated in advance to all participants. In order to enhance transparency, trilogues taking place within the European Parliament and Council shall be announced, where practicable.

Trilogues cover all sectors, ranging from the politically salient to the technical and from those with significant distributive consequences to those with narrower ones.[69] In practice, for three-quarters of law-making under the ordinary legislative procedure, law-making is very simple. Representatives of the Commission, Parliament and Council meet to negotiate a Commission proposal in a closed room. This is then ratified by the Council and the Parliament. The rest of the procedure simply spells out the consequences if there is no agreement.

The growth of the trilogue has implications for the balance of power between and within the EU institutions.[70] In instances where the trilogue is successful, Parliament and COREPER are acting as genuine co-legislators. Within the Council, this enhances the power of national civil servants at the expense of ministers. It also has more subversive effects, with research suggesting that ministers involve themselves less in negotiations leading up to the trilogue precisely because they know it is likely to be resolved by civil servants, with a corresponding weakening of ministerial accountability.[71] Within the Parliament, there was a concern that trilogues would enhance the power of the *relais*, the individuals representing the European Parliament, and the interests these stand for.[72] This appears to be unfounded. There is a desire to seek consensus, as one grouping is aware that if its *relai* attempts to push its interests on one dossier, this might come back to haunt it with other dossiers. The European Parliament has also tried to mitigate these risks by sending representatives from different committees and groupings to negotiate. For all this, small parties poorly represented in the European Parliament committees still feel bypassed.[73]

---

[69] C. Reh et al., 'The Informal Politics of Legislation: Explaining Secluded Decision Making in the European Union' (2013) 46 *Comparative Political Studies* 1112.

[70] H. Farrell and A. Héritier, 'Interorganizational Negotiation and Intraorganizational Power in Shared Decision Making: Early Agreements under Codecision and their Impact on the European Parliament and the Council' (2004) 37 *Comparative Political Studies* 1184; F. Häge and M. Kaeding, 'Reconsidering the European Parliament's Legislative Influence: Formal vs. Informal Procedures' (2007) 29 *Journal of European Integration* 341.

[71] F. Häge and D. Naurin, 'The Effect of Codecision on Council Decision-making: Informalization, Politicization and Power' (2013) 20 *JEPP* 953.

[72] D. Judge and D. Earnshaw, '"Relais Actors" and First-Reading Agreements in the European Parliament: The Case of the Advanced Therapies Regulation' (2011) 18 *JEPP* 53.

[73] C. Burns, 'Consensus and Compromise Become Ordinary – But at What Cost? A Critical Analysis of the Impact of the Changing Norms of Codecision upon European Parliament Committees' (2013) 20 *JEPP* 988. Council Presidencies are aware of this issue within the Council and therefore go out of their way to represent the interests of all Member States rather than their own. A. Rasmussen and C. Reh, 'The Consequences of Concluding Codecision Early: Trilogues and Intra-institutional Bargaining Success' (2013) 20 *JEPP* 1006.

In terms of inter-institutional power, the big winner of trilogues is the Commission. It not only makes the proposal but also forms one side of the triangle which thrashes out deals. Previously, it did not have that role. Insofar as the Commission is an administrative actor, this has clear implications for the democratic quality of the process. That said, it is dangerous to overstate the position of all three EU institutions as equal partners in the negotiations in the trilogue. Studies have shown that outcomes are usually closer to Council positions and preferences than to European Parliament ones.[74] There seems to be recognition by the other EU institutions that, ultimately, it represents twenty-eight Member States and has a corresponding authority not enjoyed by them. Solutions presented by it, which they can live with, will usually be accepted. It is only when it asks for more that agreement will not be reached.

The biggest challenge to democratic legitimacy posed by the trilogue is their sidelining of checks and balances and lack of formality and transparency. Formal procedures do no more than rubber stamp prior agreements. Only very well connected actors have the opportunity to lobby these informal processes because only they can know where they are taking place or who is important within them. Furthermore, only they will have the resources to arbitrage between these centres of power, lobbying both central protagonists in the trilogue and other important actors in the Council, the Parliament and the Commission.

(ii) Consultation procedure

The consultation procedure follows three stages:

(a) the Commission submits a proposal to the Council;
(b) the Council consults the Parliament;
(c) the Council adopts the measure, either by qualified majority or by unanimity, depending upon the field in question.

The most salient feature of the consultation procedure is the duty to consult the Parliament. In *Roquette Frères*, the Court of Justice stated that consultation was an expression of the cardinal principle of institutional balance:

> [Consultation] … allows the Parliament to play an actual part in the legislative process of the [Union], such power represents an essential factor in the institutional balance intended by the Treaty. Although limited, it reflects at [Union] level the fundamental democratic principle that the peoples should take part in the exercise of power through the intermediary of a representative assembly. Due consultation of the Parliament in the cases provided for by the Treaty therefore constitutes an essential formality disregard of which means that the measure concerned is void.[75]

From this principle of institutional balance, the Court of Justice has crafted a number of mutual obligations between Parliament and the Council. On the one hand, the Council is obliged to reconsult Parliament if the text is significantly amended. This ensures that the text adopted by the Council does not differ substantially from the one on which the Parliament has been

---

[74] A. Ripoll Servent, 'Holding the European Parliament Responsible: Policy Shift in the Data Retention Directive from Consultation to Codecision' (2013) 20 *JEPP* 972. R. Costello and R. Thomson, 'The Distribution of Power among EU Institutions: Who Wins under Codecision and Why?'(2013) 20 *JEPP* 1025.
[75] Case 138/79 *Roquette Frères* v *Council* [1980] ECR 3333.

ORDINARY LEGISLATIVE PROCEDURE

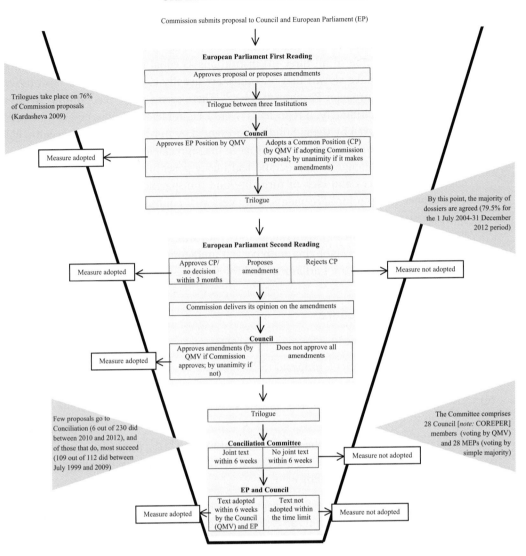

Table 3.1   The Ordinary Legislative Procedure

consulted, unless these amendments correspond essentially to the wishes of the Parliament.[76] By contrast, Parliament must not abuse its right of consultation. In *General Tariff Preferences*,[77] the Council sought to consult Parliament on a proposal to extend the Regulation on General Tariff Preferences, which gave preferential tax treatment to imports from less developed countries, to the states which had emerged from the collapse of the Soviet Union. The request was made in October 1992 and the dossier was marked 'urgent' by the Council,

---

[76] Case C-65/90 *Parliament* v *Council* (*Cabotage II*) [1992] ECR I-4593.
[77] Case C-65/93 *Parliament* v *Council* [1995] ECR I-643.

but the full decision was postponed until a further debate in January 1993, on the grounds that the Parliament's Committee on Development was not happy about including these states. The Council adopted the Regulation in December 1992, without further consultation on the grounds that the matter was urgent. The Court noted that there was a duty on the Council to consult the Parliament but, correspondingly, duties of mutual cooperation also governed relations between the EU institutions. It noted that Parliament had failed to discharge these duties by refusing to take heed of the urgency of the file and by having regard to what the Court considered to be extraneous factors.

Parliament's powers under the consultation procedure are clearly more limited than under the ordinary legislative procedure. The Council is not required to take account of the Parliament's views and the lack of leverage over the Council also harms Parliament's relations with the Commission. As Parliament's views count for little, there are no incentives for the Commission to coordinate with it. This marginalisation is further increased by the fact that the Council is not required to wait until Parliament has been consulted, before it considers a proposal. The Court has even stated that the Council is making good use of time if it considers the matter pending consultation of the Parliament.[78]

The consultation procedure revolves, therefore, around the Commission-Council axis. Both the Commission and the Council are executive-dominated and the current safeguards for national parliamentary input are limited.[79] There is still the question of which 'executive' holds the balance of power in these procedures. Everything hinges on the vote required in the Council. If a unanimity vote is required, power would seem to remain in the hands of individual national governments, as any government can veto the measure. However, the position is more complicated. Twenty-seven national governments do not have the power to push through a measure if one national government resists it. Power is, therefore, concentrated in the government that is most resistant to the measure, as it holds the decision on whether or not to go forward.[80] However, power is also strongly vested in the Commission. As the Council can only amend its proposals by unanimity,[81] its proposals have a 'take it or leave it quality' given that it will be rare that there will be the consensus on the part of, or the resources available, for the Member States to put forward an alternative proposal that secures the agreement of all of them.

Yet, it is wrong to argue that the Parliament's presence does not matter at all. At the very least, Parliamentary hearings bring greater transparency to the process and provide an arena for actors, whose voice might otherwise have been excluded, to express their views. In addition, Parliament does make significant inputs of its own. It submits amendments to about 54 per cent of proposals and about 19 per cent of its amendments are accepted: not an insignificant proportion.[82] The leverage necessary to secure this level of success has been made possible by two strategies.

---

[78] Case C-417/93 *Parliament* v *Council* [1995] ECR I-1185.

[79] See pp. 128–31.

[80] On this see *Report by the Ad Hoc Group Examining the Question of Increasing the Parliament's Powers* (Vedel Report), *EU Bulletin*, Suppl. 4/72; Committee of Three, *Report on the European Institutions* (Luxembourg, Office for Official Publications of the European Communities, 1980) 74–5.

[81] Article 293(1) TFEU.

[82] R. Kardasheva, 'The Power to Delay: The European Parliament's Influence in the Consultation Procedure' (2009) 47 *JCMS* 385, 392–4.

The first is, notwithstanding the *General Tariff Preferences* judgment, the deployment of delay. The Parliament invites the Commission to withdraw a proposal or to accept amendments. When the latter refuses, the Parliament refers it back to a Parliamentary Committee to consider its response.

R. Kardasheva, 'The Power to Delay: The European Parliament's Influence in the Consultation Procedure' (2009) 47 *Journal of Common Market Studies* 385, 404–5

The power to delay allows the EP [European Parliament] to enjoy important benefits in the legislative system. First, through delay the Parliament manages to force concessions from the Council and the Commission. Delay allows the Parliament to see many of its preferences incorporated in the final legislative texts. Second, delay opens the door for informal negotiations between the Council and Parliament. While informal negotiations have become a typical element of Council–Parliament legislative work under co-decision, there are few incentives for Member States to seek informal contacts in consultation. However, when the EP delays its opinion and Member States need an urgent decision, the Council has an incentive to speed up the procedure through informal contacts. Third, delay gives the consultation procedure two readings. Formally, the consultation procedure consists of only one reading. However, by delaying its final vote, the EP gains an additional reading. The EP makes its position on the Commission proposal known, but the plenary refrains from issuing an opinion. Once aware of the EP's preferences, the Council and Commission negotiate with MEPs and adjust their positions in order to speed up the decision-making process. Thus, through delay, the EP transforms the simple consultation procedure into a decision-making procedure with two readings.

The second is through the agreement of multi-proposal package deals with the Council. Package deals involve the considering of a number of legislative proposals together and securing simultaneous political agreement about the central features of all of them. The deals will cover discrete fields (i.e. agriculture, asylum) but often they will straddle legislative measures which involve both the ordinary legislative procedure and the consultation procedure. To secure its preferences in relation to activities covered by the ordinary legislative procedure, the Council will have to make concessions in the field covered by the consultation procedure. These multi-proposal package deals are widespread, covering about 25 per cent of all legislation.[83]

(iii) Consent procedure

The consent procedure is the procedure in which Parliament enjoys greatest formal powers and brings together a number of heterogeneous procedures.

- The Commission does not enjoy a monopoly of initiative. Depending on the field, a proposal can also be made by the Parliament, Member States or the European Council.
- The proposal may come direct to the Parliament. Alternately, there may be other EU institutions that have either to be consulted or to give their consent to the proposal first. The procedures depend on the legal base in question.

---

[83] R. Kardasheva, 'Package Deals in EU Legislative Politics' (2013) 57 *AJPS* 858.

- The Parliament will then have to consent to the measure.
- In some instances, the Council or the European Council then has to consent to the measure before it can become law.

The common features of all these procedures are, first, that Parliament has to affirm a legislative proposal before it can be adopted. This is different from the ordinary legislative procedure in that Parliament must actively say 'yes' to a proposal whereas the latter merely uses its veto. Secondly, it has an indefinite time in which to do this. There must be a strong majority in Parliament in favour of immediate action, therefore, if a measure is to be agreed. The Lisbon Treaty widened the scope of this procedure. It now governs significant fields, which include EU anti-discrimination policy;[84] significant parts of EU criminal justice policy;[85] the Budget;[86] many international agreements;[87] and, perhaps most prominently, the flexibility principle, which allows measures to be taken to realise Union objectives where there is no other legal base.[88] In all these fields the consent of the Council or European Council is also needed.[89] As a consequence, although the powers of the European Parliament are greater than in the ordinary legislative procedure, the process is not so different. The two institutions invariably negotiate to agree a common text.[90]

5 NATIONAL PARLIAMENTS AND REPRESENTATIVE DEMOCRACY

The Lisbon Treaty set out representative democracy as the central model of democracy for the European Union.

Article 10(1) TEU

1. The functioning of the Union shall be founded on representative democracy.

The institutions embodying this ideal are set out in the subsequent paragraph.

Article 10(2) TEU

2. Citizens are directly represented at Union level in the European Parliament. Member States are represented in the European Council by their Heads of State or Government and in the Council by their governments, themselves democratically accountable either to their national Parliaments, or to their citizens.

This is problematic. The weak representative qualities of the European Parliament, in terms of both its make-up and citizen engagement with it, were set out earlier in Chapter 2. Governments

---

[84] Article 19(1) TFEU.   [85] Articles 82(2)(d), 83(1) and Article 86(1), (4) TFEU.

[86] Articles 311 and 312 TFEU.   [87] Article 218(6)(a) TFEU   [88] Article 352 TFEU.

[89] The circumstances where the European Council are involved are rare. These include extension of the European Prosecutor Office's powers (Article 86(4) TFEU); use of the *passarelles* (Article 48(7) TEU); or convening an IGC without holding a convention (Article 47(3) TEU).

[90] On the procedure see R. Corbett *et al.*, *The European Parliament* (8th edn, London, John Harper, 2011) 250–7.

sit in the Council and European Council. Historically, these are not seen as representative institutions. Indeed, the history of representative democracy is of the development of assemblies to curb and hold accountable the growth of these executives. Curbing the 'representative deficit' also turned to the role of national parliaments in the law-making processes.[91] Significantly, this is in a separate provision, suggesting these are not to be at the heart of this representative democracy, but are rather to be secondary players within it. It outlines, inter alia, their contribution to the law-making process.

Article 12 TEU

National Parliaments contribute actively to the good functioning of the Union:

(a) through being informed by the institutions of the Union and having draft legislative acts of the Union forwarded to them in accordance with the Protocol on the role of national Parliaments in the European Union;

(b) by seeing to it that the principle of subsidiarity is respected in accordance with the procedures provided for in the Protocol on the application of the principles of subsidiarity and proportionality …

The powers of national parliaments in EU law-making are thus vested in two Protocols. The Protocol on National Parliaments governs their positive input into the EU legislative process. The Protocol on the application of the principles of subsidiarity and proportionality is the central instrument granting them a guardianship role over compliance with the subsidiarity principle: the principle whereby the Union is only to legislate if the objects of a measure cannot be realised by Member States acting unilaterally and could be better realised by Union action.[92] However, in reality, their contribution to law-making is wider than the formal role set out there. Furthermore, just as with the European Parliament's veto, their role as enforcers of the subsidiarity principle casts a shadow, which secures them broader influence within EU law-making. As a result, it has to be seen hand-in-hand with national parliaments' other powers.

(i) National parliaments and political dialogue

National parliaments' contribution to the content of EU legislation takes place at both the pre-legislative and legislative stage. Pre-legislative involvement was instigated in 2006 under the sobriquet of the 'Barroso initiative'.[93]

D. Jančić, 'The Barroso Initiative: Window Dressing or Democracy Boost?' (2012) 8 *Utrecht Law Review* 78, 81

It operates in two main modes: (a) in the early phase of the Commission's policy-making cycle in order to impart national concerns to its draft legislative proposals; and (b) at any other time through

---

[91] A. Maurer and W. Wessels (eds.), *National Parliaments on their Ways to Europe: Losers or Latecomers?* (Baden Baden, Nomos, 2001); A. Maurer, *National Parliaments in the European Architecture*, Federal Trust Online Paper 06/02 (2002).

[92] On subsidiarity see pp. 393–9.

[93] European Commission, *A Citizens' Agenda: Delivering Results for Europe*, COM(2006)211.

a motley array of visits to national parliaments by Commission officials, meetings with national parliamentary committees and permanent parliamentary representatives to the EU, and gatherings in various interparliamentary forums.

The first mode is generally considered more advantageous to national parliaments as it encourages the *ex ante* pronouncement of MPs and senators, i.e. prior to the onset of the applicable decision-making procedure at EU level. It functions as follows. If, after receiving draft EU acts directly from the Commission, any parliamentary chamber detects an infringement of any of the aforesaid principles that govern the existence and use of EU competences, it may send a reasoned opinion to the Commission explaining why it considers that there has been an infringement. The Commission is not obliged to reply, but does so in practice whenever parliamentarians raise crucial points of law or policy. Where reasoned opinions are positive about the proposed EU measure, the Commission either takes no action or returns an acknowledgment or take-note letter.

This political dialogue allows parliamentarians to provide feedback to the Commission from the perspective of their Member State and to express any possible concerns about the direction that the Commission intends to take. However, only rarely should one expect the Commission to alter its policy choices due to parliamentary opposition, because the Initiative is geared towards discussion and consultation rather than strict enforcement. The Initiative is indeed a unilateral, informal and non-binding commitment of the Commission. No legal instrument exists to sanction the Commission for disregarding the national parliaments' reasoned opinions. The Commission is, therefore, in a win-win situation, whereby national parliamentary participation may increase the legitimacy of EU policies without posing too great a risk of jeopardising the Commission's original blueprint.

The intention of the Barroso initiative is to grant national parliamentary influence over the Commission and its agenda-setting power. This is distinct from the formal consultative entitlements set out by the Protocol on the Role of National Parliaments. These require that:

- all draft legislative acts will be sent directly to national parliaments, rather than to national governments to pass onto national parliaments;[94]
- national parliaments will also be sent the annual legislative programme, as well as any policy or legislative planning instrument;[95]
- all agendas and minutes of Council meetings will be sent to national parliaments;[96]
- an eight week period will elapse between a draft legislative act being sent to national parliaments and its being placed on the agenda of the Council.[97]

The Protocol requirements kick in later, namely, after the formal adoption of the Commission proposal, and they have a different target. They are to give national parliaments influence over their respective governments and, through them, the Council.

Two types of procedure have emerged for the expression of this influence. The *document-based* procedure does not mandate the national minister to take a position in the Council. Instead, on important proposals, it requires the minister not to agree to any proposal until a parliamentary committee has scrutinised it and published its findings. The *mandate* procedure involves the

---

[94] Protocol on the Role of National Parliaments in the European Union, article 2.
[95] *Ibid.* article 1.   [96] *Ibid.* article 5.   [97] *Ibid.* article 4.

national parliament authorising the government to take a position and the national government cannot deviate from that, or must provide reasons if it intends to do so.[98] Auel and Benz have argued that the suitability of either depends on the nature of government-parliament relations. They observed that in the United Kingdom, the document-based system worked well, as the party in government also usually had a large majority in parliament. If the mandate procedure were to be used, the party in government would just fill the committee with sympathetic MPs. The document-based procedure allowed parliamentary committees to be relatively non-partisan, and this allowed these to work well as fora in which stakeholders and experts could set out their views and be considered. This led to considered reports which gained these committees some influence. By contrast, the mandate procedure worked well in Denmark as coalition governments, in which all the main parliamentary parties are represented, has been a feature of the post-war settlement. The mandate procedure allows all coalition partners, as well as public debate, to inform the position of the minister.[99]

For all this, both procedures allow national governments considerable latitude. The document-based procedure does not limit what concessions can be made by a national government in the Council. The parliamentary committee merely tweaks out issues and interests. The mandate procedure allows parliaments to constrain government but its weakness is its lack of flexibility. Awareness that it can disempower governments in negotiations often leads the parliament to soften the mandate so it is very vague, or to use it selectively for only the most salient issues with the government given a free hand elsewhere.

This has led to concerns that, particularly where the European Union exercises its most wide-ranging powers, these controls are insufficient. In its *Treaty of Lisbon* judgment, the German Constitutional Court stated that treaty provisions with an open-ended quality could only be deployed if there was national parliamentary approval in each case.[100] A statute must be adopted by the German Parliament in such cases.[101] A similar requirement has been adopted in the United Kingdom.[102] These requirements affect only one legislative competence which has been frequently used historically, namely, Article 352 TFEU, the flexibility provision, which allows the Union to legislate to realise its objectives where no other legal competence enables this. However, this, in turn, raises a further issue, namely, whether parliamentary approval should be required more broadly. For the issue would seem to be not whether it is core or peripheral to Union competencies but its level of importance to the citizens of the Member State concerned, and that issue can crop up in any field of EU law.

---

[98] Austria, Belgium, Bulgaria, Cyprus, France, Germany, Ireland, Italy, Luxembourg, Netherlands, Portugal, Slovakia, Spain and the United Kingdom all adopt document-based systems. Denmark, Estonia, Finland, Latvia, Lithuania, Poland, Romania, Slovakia, Slovenia and Sweden use mandate-based systems. Other Member States use a mix of the two. COSAC, *Eighth Biannual Report: Developments in European Union Procedures and Practices Relevant to Parliamentary Scrutiny* (Luxembourg, 2007) 7–9.

[99] K. Auel and A. Benz, 'The Politics of Adaptation: The Europeanization of National Parliamentary Systems' (2005) 11 *Journal of Legislative Studies* 372.

[100] 2 BvE 2/08 *Treaty of Lisbon*, Judgment of 30 June 2009, paras. 238–9. These provisions breach the requirement that only limited powers be granted to the Union, and therefore the principle of democratic self-government protected by the German Basic Law. This is examined in more detail at pp. 229–40.

[101] On the German legislation implementing this see D. Jan i, 'Caveats from Karlsruhe and Berlin: Whither Democracy after Lisbon?' (2010) 16 *CJEL* 339, 371–81.

[102] European Union Act 2011, ss. 7 and 8.

(ii) National parliamentary policing of the subsidiarity principle

The rationales for national parliaments policing the legislative process for compliance with the subsidiarity principle are twofold. They are, on the one hand, the institutions whose powers are most encroached upon by EU legislation, and, on the other, domestic representative assemblies well-placed to pick up local concerns about the intrusiveness of EU law.[103] The Protocol on the Application of the Principles of Subsidiarity and Proportionality establishes an Early Warning Mechanism which allows any national parliament or parliament chamber to issue a reasoned opinion within eight weeks of transmission of the draft legislative act stating why the proposal does not comply with the subsidiarity principle.[104] National parliaments are given two votes, which are shared out between chambers in bicameral systems.

For all legislative procedures, the Protocol establishes the so-called 'yellow card' procedure whereby one-third of national parliamentary chambers (or one-quarter in the Area of Freedom, Security and Justice) can ask for the proposal to be reconsidered.

Protocol on the Application of the Principles of Subsidiarity and Proportionality, Article 7(2)

Where reasoned opinions on a draft legislative act's non-compliance with the principle of subsidiarity represent at least one third of all the votes allocated to the national Parliaments ..., the draft must be reviewed. This threshold shall be a quarter in the case of a draft legislative act submitted on the basis of Article 76 TFEU on the area of freedom, security and justice.

After such review, the Commission or, where appropriate, the group of Member States, the European Parliament, the Court of Justice, the European Central Bank or the European Investment Bank, if the draft legislative act originates from them, may decide to maintain, amend or withdraw the draft. Reasons must be given for this decision.

This yellow card was seen as too weak as the Commission, on paper at least, can ignore it. For the ordinary legislative procedure, an orange card procedure was introduced.

Protocol on the Application of the Principles of Subsidiarity and Proportionality, Article 7(3)

... under the ordinary legislative procedure, where reasoned opinions on the non-compliance of a proposal for a legislative act with the principle of subsidiarity represent at least a simple majority of the votes allocated to the national Parliaments ..., the proposal must be reviewed. After such review, the Commission may decide to maintain, amend or withdraw the proposal.

---

[103] I. Cooper, 'Bicameral or Tricameral? National Parliaments and Representative Democracy in the European Union' (2013) 35 *JEI* 531, 536–9.
[104] Protocol on the Application of the Principles of Subsidiarity and Proportionality, article 6.

If it chooses to maintain the proposal, the Commission will have, in a reasoned opinion, to justify why it considers that the proposal complies with the principle of subsidiarity. This reasoned opinion, as well as the reasoned opinions of the national Parliaments, will have to be submitted to the Union's legislator, for consideration in the procedure:

(a) before concluding the first reading, the legislator (the European Parliament and the Council) shall consider whether the legislative proposal is compatible with the principle of subsidiarity, taking particular account of the reasons expressed and shared by the majority of national Parliaments as well as the reasoned opinion of the Commission;

(b) if, by a majority of 55% of the members of the Council or a majority of the votes cast in the European Parliament, the legislator is of the opinion that the proposal is not compatible with the principle of subsidiarity, the legislative proposal shall not be given further consideration.

It is not clear why the orange card only applies to the ordinary legislative procedure. It also states an odd principle. If a majority of national parliaments, the Council and the European Parliament all believe that a measure should not be introduced because Member States are better placed to do it, then it will not be introduced. There would not be a legislative majority for it in such an instance, anyway, so the procedure is otiose. Indeed, it is highly unlikely that the Commission could push ahead even under the yellow card procedure as, with one third or quarter of national parliamentary chambers against it, it would be unlikely to be a qualified majority vote within the Council. The one instance of a yellow card resulted, therefore, in the proposal being withdrawn by the Commission.[105]

(iii) National parliaments: a third legislative chamber?

The overwhelming majority of parliamentary opinions under the Early Warning Mechanism have not confined themselves to verifying whether a proposal complies with the subsidiarity principle. Instead, they have gone to the merits of the proposal's content with parliamentary chambers issuing opinions where they dislike the proposal.[106] This being the case, the distinction between the political dialogue and the Early Warning Mechanism has blurred so that a continuum has emerged whereby national parliaments can put forward their views at an early stage, and, insofar as these are not taken into account, can exert political muscle at a later stage by showing a yellow or orange card. As intimated earlier, any proposal receiving these will have weak prospects in the Council. It has therefore been argued that national parliaments are emerging as an informal virtual third legislative chamber, with the Council and the European Parliament being the other two.

[105] Commission Decision to withdraw the Proposal for a Council Regulation on the exercise of the right to take collective action within the context of the freedom of establishment and the freedom to provide services, COM(2012)130, http://ec.europa.eu/dgs/secretariat_general/relations/relations_other/npo/letter_to_nal_parl_en.htm.

[106] F. Fabbrini and K. Granat, '"Yellow Card, but No Foul": The Role of the National Parliaments under the Subsidiarity Protocol and the Commission Proposal for an EU Regulation on the Right to Strike' (2013) 50 *CMLRev.* 115.

I. Cooper, 'A "Virtual Third Chamber" for the European Union? National Parliaments after the Treaty of Lisbon' (2012) 35 *West European Politics* 441, 445–6

The Virtual Chamber represents a new model of parliamentary involvement in international relations, different from the three existing models of Domestic Oversight, Parliamentary Assembly, and Supranational Parliament. Domestic Oversight refers to the traditional indirect role of the national parliament in international affairs, overseeing the executive arm of government in its conduct of foreign policy. A Parliamentary Assembly (e.g. the pre-1979 EP) is an international gathering of members of different NPs who meet periodically, often within the aegis of an existing international organisation; it is a prominent deliberative forum for the discussion of common issues but has little or no legislative power ... A Supranational Parliament (e.g. the post-1979 EP) is a directly elected, transnational chamber which may have substantial legislative powers; it is essentially a federal parliament transposed to the international level. A Virtual Chamber is a 'meta-parliament' made up of a group of national parliaments that directly participate in a collective decision-making procedure within an international organisation.

These models appeared in historical sequence in Europe, with each new model compensating in some way for deficiencies in its predecessor. The European Parliament (originally the Common Assembly of the European Coal and Steel Community) was created in 1952 as a Parliamentary Assembly to facilitate direct parliamentary oversight of an international organisation – something unfeasible under the Domestic Oversight model. With direct elections in 1979 the EP became a Supranational Parliament; in the process it gained collective democratic legitimacy, overcoming a deficiency of the Parliamentary Assembly model, where national parliamentarians individually enjoyed democratic legitimacy (borrowed from their elected status in their 'home' parliament) but the body as a whole did not; another deficiency, its relative powerlessness, was overcome gradually as it gained new powers with further revisions of the Treaty of Rome.

Finally, the Virtual Chamber model was introduced to compensate for a side effect of the creation of the Supranational Parliament – that is, NPs' loss of their channel of direct influence in the EU; yet it also avoids a democratic deficiency of the Parliamentary Assembly model in that it revives the involvement of NPs in EU affairs through the participation not of individual MPs but of whole parliaments.

There remains, however, the quality of this legislative chamber. Concerns have been expressed that national parliaments cannot issue a 'red card'. If one third/quarter of national parliamentary chambers oppose it, it is argued, this should be sufficient to rob the proposal of authority. The vote should act as a formal veto.[107] It is unclear how much this would alter matters, as a de facto veto probably already exists. Stronger constraints on national parliamentary influence come from a number of other sources.

First, the thresholds for showing any kind of 'card' are high. Typically, EU legislation will not violate some bright red line drawn by all national parliaments. Traditions cherished or values deeply felt in one state often arise precisely because of their idiosyncrasy. It will be difficult, in such circumstances, for the national parliament of that state to mobilise other

---

[107] This view was expressed by the British Foreign Minister in May 2013, see www.gov.uk/government/speeches/britain-and-germany-partners-in-reform.

parliaments. In 2012, therefore, seventy reasoned opinions were provided by national parliamentary chambers. Twelve of these related to the Commission proposal on the right to take collective action, which was shown the yellow card and withdrawn. There were a further six proposals which received three or more reasoned opinions, of which one received five such opinions. None were withdrawn.[108]

Secondly, the Early Warning Mechanism may ask the wrong question. National parliaments are granted an unusual role, namely, to gate-keep and to monitor. They can seek to block the legislation of others.[109] However, a traditional feature of parliaments is that legislation does not take place without action by them, and it is their blessing which grants legislation its authority. More genuine involvement of national parliaments would require these to have to give assent to legislation. If national parliaments were to be an effective 'third chamber', the rule would have to be reversed so that two-thirds or three-quarters would have to say 'yes' before legislation could be adopted. It is furthermore not clear why, like the European Parliament or Council, a certain quorum (e.g. one-third) should not be able to ask the Commission to propose legislation, be it new legislation or repealing or amending existing legislation.[110]

The final issue is resources. In 2012, 663 opinions were received by the Commission within the context of the political dialogue. However, these were very asymmetrically distributed. Only thirteen chambers from eleven Member States issued ten or more opinions. Furthermore, nearly half of all opinions (326) came from just two parliamentary chambers, the Portuguese Assembly of the Republic and the Italian Senate. There is, thus, a very uneven representation of citizens with six parliamentary chambers offering not a single opinion. This might, of course, be a lack of interest. However, there are also resource problems. Historically, it is difficult for national parliaments to formulate a position as national parliaments often have few supporting staff.[111] We have already seen that if legislation is agreed at early stages in the procedure, this tends to restrict debate.[112] When questioned in 2011, twenty-four parliamentary chambers felt that the eight-week period to make observations before the matter was formally considered by the Council was too short.[113]

COSAC has become increasingly central to rectifying this. The Conference of Parliamentary Committees for Union Affairs of Parliaments of the European Union (COSAC) was established in 1989. It is a forum in which national parliaments and the European Parliament meet biannually, to discuss the business of the forthcoming Council Presidency and to exchange information and best practice.[114] Since 2007, it has become a more proactive forum for mutual assistance. All national parliaments commit themselves to an early exchange of information,

---

[108] European Commission, *Annual Report 2012 on Relations between the European Commission and National Parliaments*, COM(2013)565, 9–10. The situation was worse in 2011, with three proposals receiving five or more reasoned opinions and one receiving nine. None were withdrawn. European Commission, *Annual Report 2011 on Relations between the European Commission and National Parliaments*, COM(2012)375, 11.

[109] C. Sprungk, 'A New Type of Representative Democracy? Reconsidering the Role of National Parliaments in the European Union' (2013) 35 *JEI* 547, 551–2.

[110] D. Chalmers, *Democratic Self-Government in Europe* (London, Policy Network, 2013) 7–10.

[111] Future of Europe Convention, *Final Report of the Working Group IV on the Role of National Parliaments*, CONV 353/02, 4–5.

[112] de Ruiter, n. 66 above.

[113] COSAC, *Sixteenth Bi-annual Report: Developments in European Union Procedures and Practices Relevant to Parliamentary Scrutiny* (Warsaw, COSAC, 2011) 7.

[114] Its position is formalised in the Protocol on the Role of National Parliaments in the European Union, article 10. See also Article 12(f) TEU.

particular subsidiarity concerns, to each other. This is now commonplace.[115] In addition, in 2006, a platform, IPEX, was established which grants access not only to relevant EU documents but also to (most of) the positions and opinions of other national parliaments.[116]

6 DIFFERENTIATED LAW-MAKING

(i) Enhanced cooperation

Enhanced cooperation grew out of a debate prior to the Treaty of Amsterdam in which deep-seated differences emerged about both the pace and ideological direction of integration. In some instances, some Member States wished to integrate further than others. In others, there was a simple objection, on the part of some, to the types of policy being proposed. As a consequence, it was agreed that some Member States should not be held back from developing common laws between themselves, should they so wish. This raised the possibility of a 'hard-core Europe' developing laws for itself, thereby excluding other Member States and creating a two-tier Union. It could result in the Union becoming a legal and political rump with the centre of political energy and legal commitments revolving around this new core.[117] To mediate this, procedures going under the unappealing title of 'enhanced cooperation' were established. These put in place a number of safeguards.

Article 20 TEU

1. Member States which wish to establish enhanced cooperation between themselves within the framework of the Union's non-exclusive competences may make use of its institutions and exercise those competences by applying the relevant provisions of the Treaties, subject to the limits and in accordance with the detailed arrangements laid down in this Article and in Articles 326 to 334 TFEU.

   Enhanced cooperation shall aim to further the objectives of the Union, protect its interests and reinforce its integration process. Such cooperation shall be open at any time to all Member States, in accordance with Article 328 TFEU.
2. The decision authorising enhanced cooperation shall be adopted by the Council as a last resort, when it has established that the objectives of such cooperation cannot be attained within a reasonable period by the Union as a whole, and provided that at least nine Member States participate in it. The Council shall act in accordance with the procedure laid down in Article 329 TFEU.

---

[115] COSAC, *Tenth Bi-annual Report: Developments in European Union Procedures and Practices Relevant to Parliamentary Scrutiny* (Paris, COSAC, 2008) 17–18.

[116] See www.ipex.eu/IPEXL-WEB/home/home.do. On the robustness of IPEX see COSAC, *Sevententh Bi-annual Report: Developments in European Union Procedures and Practices Relevant to Parliamentary Scrutiny* (Copenhagen, COSAC, 2012) 12–14.

[117] On the debate see A. Stubb, 'The 1996 Intergovernmental Conference and the Management of Flexible Integration' (1997) 4 *JEPP* 37; F. Tuytschaever, *Differentiation in European Union Law* (Oxford/Portland, Hart, 1999) 1–48; E. Phillipart, 'From Uniformity to Flexibility: The Management of Diversity and Its Impact on the EU System of Governance' in G. de Búrca and J. Scott (eds.), *Constitutional Change in the EU: From Uniformity to Flexibility?* (Oxford/Portland, Hart, 2000).

Article 326 TFEU

Any enhanced cooperation shall comply with the Treaties and Union law. Such cooperation shall not undermine the internal market or economic, social and territorial cohesion. It shall not constitute a barrier to or discrimination in trade between Member States, nor shall it distort competition between them.

Article 327 TFEU

Any enhanced cooperation shall respect the competences, rights and obligations of those Member States which do not participate in it. Those Member States shall not impede its implementation by the participating Member States.

The provisions suggest six substantive constraints:

- there must be nine Member States;
- it must not be in a field where the Union has exclusive competence;[118]
- the measure must only be adopted as a matter of last resort;
- enhanced cooperation must comply with other EU law;
- it must not undermine the internal market or economic or social cohesion; in particular, it must not constitute a barrier to or discrimination in trade between Member States or distort competition between them;
- it must respect the rights, competences and obligations of other Member States.

The most loaded of these conditions is that the measure can only be adopted as a last resort. Interpreted broadly, it could subject the procedure to endless prevarication by one Member State. Interpreted narrowly, it would allow aggressive states to threaten to go ahead without a state unless it caved into their demands. In the *Unitary Patent* judgment, twenty-five Member States proceeded without Spain and Italy to set up a unitary patent enjoying protection across the Union. Whilst the initial Commission proposal was in 2000, an accompanying proposal on translation arrangements was only made in 2010. There was a period of only six months between this latter proposal and the Decision authorising enhanced cooperation. Italy and Spain argued that this was insufficient time to secure agreement.

Joined Cases C-274/11 and C-295/11 *Spain and Italy v Council (Unitary Patent)*, Judgment of 16 April 2013

47. In accordance with Article 20(2) TEU, the Council may not authorise enhanced cooperation except 'as a last resort, when it has established that the objectives of such cooperation cannot be attained within a reasonable period by the Union as a whole'.
48. This condition is particularly important and must be read in the light of the second paragraph of Article 20(1) TEU, which provides that enhanced cooperation is to 'aim to further the objectives of the Union, protect its interests and reinforce its integration process'.

---

[118] On the scope of this see Article 3 TFEU.

49. The Union's interests and the process of integration would, quite clearly, not be protected if all fruitless negotiations could lead to one or more instances of enhanced cooperation, to the detriment of the search for a compromise enabling the adoption of legislation for the Union as a whole.

50. In consequence ... the expression 'as a last resort' highlights the fact that only those situations in which it is impossible to adopt such legislation in the foreseeable future may give rise to the adoption of a decision authorising enhanced cooperation.

51. The applicants claim that both at the date on which the Commission presented its proposal for authorisation to the Council and at the date of the contested decision, there still existed real chances of reaching a compromise. They maintain too that the negotiations for reaching agreement on the unitary patent and its language arrangements were not as various or as thorough as claimed by the Council and the parties intervening in its support.

52. In this respect, it is to be borne in mind that taking part in the procedure leading to the adoption of a decision authorising enhanced cooperation are the Commission, which submits a proposal to that effect, the European Parliament, which approves the proposal, and the Council, which takes the final decision authorising enhanced cooperation.

53. The Council, in taking that final decision, is best placed to determine whether the Member States have demonstrated any willingness to compromise and are in a position to put forward proposals capable of leading to the adoption of legislation for the Union as a whole in the foreseeable future.

54. The Court, in exercising its review of whether the condition that a decision authorising enhanced cooperation must be adopted only as a last resort has been satisfied, should therefore ascertain whether the Council has carefully and impartially examined those aspects that are relevant to this point and whether adequate reasons have been given for the conclusion reached by the Council.

55. In this instance, the Council correctly took into account the fact that the legislative process undertaken with a view to the establishing of a unitary patent at Union level was begun during the year 2000 and covered several stages ...

56. It is apparent too that a considerable number of different language arrangements for the unitary patent were discussed among all the Member States within the Council and that none of those arrangements, with or without the addition of elements of compromise, found support capable of leading to the adoption at Union level of a full 'legislative package' relating to that patent.

57. Furthermore, the applicants have adduced no specific evidence that could disprove the Council's assertion that when the requests for enhanced cooperation were made, and when the proposal for authorisation was sent by the Commission to the Council, and at the date on which the contested decision was adopted, there was still insufficient support for any of the language arrangements proposed or possible to contemplate.

The judgment suggests these constraints will not curtail the scope of enhanced cooperation too strongly. It is only when the Council has taken an interpretation of them which is excessively relaxed that it will intervene. Furthermore, additional procedural constraints have been put in place, which require enhanced cooperation to secure the consent of all three main EU institutions.[119]

---

[119] Slightly different procedures apply in CFSP. The proposal is notified to the Council. It obtains an opinion from the Commission and the High Representative. Parliament is also notified. The Council then makes a decision by unanimity with only its having a veto, Article 329(2) TFEU.

> ### Article 329(1) TFEU
>
> 1. Member States which wish to establish enhanced cooperation between themselves in one of the areas covered by the Treaties, with the exception of fields of exclusive competence and the common foreign and security policy, shall address a request to the Commission, specifying the scope and objectives of the enhanced cooperation proposed. The Commission may submit a proposal to the Council to that effect. In the event of the Commission not submitting a proposal, it shall inform the Member States concerned of the reasons for not doing so. Authorisation to proceed with the enhanced cooperation referred to in the first subparagraph shall be granted by a decision of the Council,[120] on a proposal from the Commission and after obtaining the consent of the European Parliament.

The value of the process to the participating states is further eroded by any measure adopted under it not being part of the EU legislative acquis.[121] Furthermore, they do not have freedom to negotiate between themselves as they must allow non-participating states to participate in the deliberations leading up to the adoption of legislation even if they cannot vote on it.[122] Finally, non-participating states can free-ride by waiting to see the effects of the measure and then joining later. Any initial non-participant can apply subsequently and is free to participate subject to verification that it meets the conditions for participation.[123]

In the light of this, it is unsurprising that only three measures have been adopted under 'enhanced cooperation'.[124] Instead, resort has been made to other arrangements, some within the Union legal framework and some without. These arrangements have thrown up real concerns both about fragmentation of the Union and about protecting the integrity of the Union decision-making processes.

(ii) Other differentiated law-making within the EU Treaty framework

The three central examples of differentiated law-making within the EU legal framework are the Protocol on the Position of the United Kingdom and Ireland in respect of the Area of Freedom, Security and Justice; the Protocol on the Schengen Acquis integrated into the Framework of the European Union, and the third stage of economic and monetary union.

The most straightforward is the first of these. This provides that neither the United Kingdom nor Ireland are required to take part in[125] or be bound by any EU legislation adopted in the field of the Area of Freedom, Security and Justice nor by any judgment of the Court of Justice in that field.[126] However, there is the possibility of opt-in for these states. Within three months of any proposal, either of these states may indicate that they wish to take part in the subsequent measure which it is

---

[120] This is by QMV, Article 16(3) TEU.   [121] Article 20(4) TEU.   [122] Article 20(3) TEU and Article 330 TFEU.

[123] This is to be done by Commission authorisation in all fields other than CFSP. In CFSP it is done by the Council in consultation with the High Representative, Article 331 TFEU.

[124] Decision 2010/405/EU authorising enhanced cooperation in the area of the law applicable to divorce and legal separation [2010] OJ L189/12; Decision 2011/167/EU authorising enhanced cooperation in the area of the creation of unitary patent protection [2011] OJ L76/53; Decision 2013/52/EU authorising enhanced cooperation in the area of financial transaction tax [2013] OJ L22/11.

[125] Protocol on the Position of the United Kingdom and Ireland in respect of the Area of Freedom, Security and Justice, article 1.

[126] *Ibid.* article 2.

anticipated may be adopted.[127] After any acts have been adopted, these states may still accede to the legislation in question. In which case, the conditions are the same as for those adopted under enhanced cooperation. The Commission and Council will verify whether they meet the 'conditions for participation', namely, that they have the necessary legislation in place.[128]

The Protocol on the Schengen Acquis integrated the Schengen Conventions of 1985 and 1990 into the EU legal framework. The Conventions are international agreements now signed, inter alia, by all EU Member States other than the United Kingdom and Ireland. They provide for the abolition of frontier checks, a common external frontier, a common visa policy and cooperation in the fields of migration of non-EU nationals, crime and policing.[129] A large number of measures were agreed under the Schengen Conventions (the 'Schengen Acquis') which the Protocol integrates into EU law. It also defines the relationship between participating and non-participating states. Article 4 of the Protocol provides that non-participants may request to take part in any part or all of the acquis, so long as all other Member States consent.

This begs the question of the relationship between this Protocol and the general EU provisions on immigration, asylum, policing, visas and frontier controls to which all Member States are party, as these activities are covered by both the Schengen Acquis and these general provisions. Could a Member State be excluded from participation in these because it has not signed up to the Schengen Convention? The United Kingdom brought a case against two measures: one establishing the European Agency for the Management of Operational Cooperation at the External Borders of the Member States and the other introducing common security features and biometric identifiers into passports.[130] These had been adopted under the Schengen Protocol, thereby excluding the United Kingdom, even though Article 77(2) TFEU provides for the Union to develop legislation on external borders and the United Kingdom is party to that.

Case C-77/05 *United Kingdom* v *Council* [2007] ECR I-11459

77. ... by analogy with what applies in relation to the choice of the legal basis of a [Union] act, it must be concluded that in a situation such as that at issue in the present case the classification of a [Union] act as a proposal or initiative to build upon the Schengen acquis ... must rest on objective factors which are amenable to judicial review, including in particular the aim and the content of the act ...

83. It should be recalled ... that both the title of the Schengen Agreement and the fourth recital in its preamble and Article 17 of the agreement show that its principal objective was the abolition of checks on persons at the common borders of the Member States and the transfer of those checks to their external borders. The importance of that objective in the context of the Schengen Agreements is underlined by the place occupied in the Implementing Convention by the provisions on the crossing of external borders, and by the fact that, under Articles 6 and 7 of that convention, checks at external borders are to be carried out in accordance with uniform principles, with the Member States having to implement constant and close cooperation in order to ensure that those checks are carried out effectively.

---

[127] *Ibid.* article 3(1). If negotiations stall, after a 'reasonable period of time' the measures may be adopted without their participation, article 3(2).
[128] *Ibid.* article 4.   [129] For more on this see pp. 521–3.
[130] Case C-137/05 *United Kingdom* v *Council* [2007] ECR I-11593. These cases have been reaffirmed in Case C-482/08 *United Kingdom* v *Council* [2010] ECR I-10413.

84. It follows that checks on persons at the external borders of the Member States and consequently the effective implementation of the common rules on standards and procedures for those checks must be regarded as constituting elements of the Schengen acquis.

85. Since ... Regulation No. 2007/2004 is intended, as regards both its purpose and its content, to improve those checks, that regulation must be regarded as constituting a measure to build upon the Schengen acquis ...

This reasoning is open to criticism. The responsibility of the Court of Justice was to mediate a conflict between two bases, the Protocol and Article 77(2) TFEU. Elsewhere, its starting point is to look at the predominant aim and content of the measure. In this case it did not do this. If the measure fell within the aegis of the Protocol, it would be governed by the Protocol, as this should prevail over other parts of the Treaty. No reasons were given for this, and it is a peculiar view of European integration, in which fragmentation and exclusion are chosen over commonality and inclusion.

The third field is economic and monetary union. Currently, ten Member States do not participate in the third stage of economic and monetary union (i.e. have the euro as their currency). There is no detailed Treaty regime mediating the different interests of euro area and non-euro area states. This posed limited issues prior to the crisis as the regime did not involve significant law-making but rather a series of disciplines applied to euro area states. However, the weakness of the financial sector was seen as contributing to the crisis. This led to calls for much more stringent financial regulation across the Union and a more integrated system of financial supervision within the euro area. This has raised two concerns.

The first is that euro area states will form a voting bloc within the Council to secure financial services legislation which benefits the euro area at the expense of non-euro area states. This concern has been prompted, in particular, by the presence of the euro group. Comprised of Finance Ministers of the euro area states and the Commission, with the European Central Bank invited to take part, it meets to discuss euro area state responsibilities relating to the single currency.[131] Regulation of the financial services sector falls fully within its remit. It acts, therefore, as a forum where eighteen Member States, if they wish, can agree common positions without consulting other Member States or having regard to their wishes.

The second is the grant of increased supervisory powers to regulate the financial services sector to the European Central Bank. These supervisory powers include the power to take decisions and regulations on matters such as authorisation of banks, their governance arrangements, exposure, and acquisition and disposal of holdings.[132] Although it is only to do this for banks and branches based in the euro area,[133] inevitably there will be a spillover effect. Banks with a head office in a non-euro state but with a large number of branches or subsidiaries in the euro area will find a large, possibly dominant, part of their activities governed by the ECB.

---

[131] Article 137 TFEU. Protocol on the Euro Group, article 1.
[132] European Commission, *Proposal for a Council Regulation Conferring Specific Tasks on the European Central Bank concerning Policies relating to the Prudential Supervision of Credit Institutions*, COM(2012) 511, article 4.
[133] *Ibid.* article 4(2).

These effects combine so that there is a risk that non-euro area states will find themselves subject to pan-Union legislation whose shape was largely determined by euro group finance ministers. Many of their banks may then find that it is the ECB which implements and supervises it, as well as adding its own measures, over much of their activities. Strong concerns have, therefore, been raised about the regime's failing to accommodate non-euro area state interests.[134]

(iii) Differentiated law-making outside the EU Treaty framework

The European Union is not a closed system in the sense that it has no police force to stop national governments making agreements between themselves outside its structures. Insofar as enhanced cooperation places restrictions on cooperation, it increases, furthermore, the incentives to do this. Concluding an international agreement is much easier. However, it generates all the issues for the Union and non-participating states which enhanced cooperation was designed to prevent.

These issues have manifested themselves in two ways.

First, international agreements have been concluded between limited numbers of states with significant exclusionary costs for non-participants. Awareness of these costs leads others to join subsequently and for the international agreement to be transformed eventually into EU law. This took place with the Schengen Convention.[135] A more recent example was the 2005 Prüm Convention.[136] Signed between Austria, Belgium, France, Germany, Luxembourg, Netherlands and Spain, this provided for greater exchange of DNA, fingerprint and vehicle data between security agencies than was previously possible. It is controversial as there are no common rules on collection of the data or (arguably) sufficient common rules on its protection.[137] Other security agencies were, of course, eager to have access to this pool of data as they saw it as a huge resource. Denial to them of this was a huge cost. In 2008, the Prüm Convention was, therefore, made part of EU law binding all Member States.[138] The challenge is not simply the feeling that other states were bounced into something but also the short-circuiting of public debate. A document was agreed between seven interior ministries with little discussion in their own countries. It was then presented as a *fait accompli* to the EU legislative process in such a way that few amendments could be made, given the momentum behind the process.

Secondly, Member States have used international agreements as a substitute for EU law. One example of this is the Treaty on Stability, Coordination and Governance (TSCG) signed between twenty-five Member States as an international agreement. This establishes the fiscal compact which sets a series of disciplines for euro area public finances. This was only signed as an international agreement because two states, the Czech Republic and the United Kingdom,

---

[134] House of Lords European Union Committee, *European Banking Union: Key Issues and Challenges* (7th Report 2012–13, London, SO, 2012) paras. 128–42.

[135] See p. 139.   [136] EU Council, *Prüm Convention*, EU Council Doc. 10900/05.

[137] House of Lords European Union Committee, *Prüm: An Effective Weapon against Terrorism and Crime?* (18th Report, London, SO, Session 2006–7).

[138] Decision 2008/615/JHA on the stepping up of cross-border cooperation, particularly in combating terrorism and cross-border crime [2008] OJ L209/1; Decision 2008/616/JHA on the implementation of Decision 2008/615/JHA on the stepping up of cross-border cooperation, particularly in combating terrorism and cross-border crime [2008] OJ L210/12.

refused to sign it. It is expressly subject to EU law.[139] There is a commitment to integrate it back into the EU Treaty framework within five years of its entry into force.[140] Other states are also free to accede to it.[141]

A more complex case is the European Stability Mechanism Treaty. Signed between seventeen euro area states, it offered financial support to those euro area states otherwise unable to finance themselves. Albeit an international agreement, EU institutions were central to its administration. The Commission assessed the terms for granting support and the Commission and the ECB, with the IMF, monitored the meeting of the conditions on which the support was offered. Decision 2011/199 authorising this treaty was challenged in *Pringle* on the ground, inter alia, that it fell within the field of monetary policy, which was an exclusive Union competence and would, therefore preclude national activity of this kind. The Court of Justice rejected this on the grounds that the treaty fell within the field of economic policy. This is a policy in which all twenty-eight Member States participate. The Treaty was therefore a form of differential integration. Pringle also argued that the treaty conflicted with Article 122(2) TFEU, which allows the Union to grant aid to states hit by exceptional occurrences beyond their control. Indeed, €60 billion of support had been granted by Regulation 407/2010 (establishing a confusingly named European Financial Stability Mechanism (EFSM)) under this Treaty provision. The Court rejected this argument.

Case C-370/12 *Pringle* v *Government of Ireland*, Judgment of 27 November 2012

64. ... whether Decision 2011/199 affects the Union's competence in the area of the coordination of the Member States' economic policies, it must be observed that, since Articles 2(3) and 5(1) TFEU restrict the role of the Union in the area of economic policy to the adoption of coordinating measures, the provisions of the EU and TFEU do not confer any specific power on the Union to establish a stability mechanism of the kind envisaged by Decision 2011/199.

65. Admittedly, Article 122(2) TFEU confers on the Union the power to grant ad hoc financial assistance to a Member State which is in difficulties or is seriously threatened with severe difficulties caused by natural disasters or exceptional occurrences beyond its control. However, as emphasised by the European Council in recital 4 of the preamble to Decision 2011/199, Article 122(2) TFEU does not constitute an appropriate legal basis for the establishment of a stability mechanism of the kind envisaged by that decision. The fact that the mechanism envisaged is to be permanent and that its objectives are to safeguard the financial stability of the euro area as a whole means that such action cannot be taken by the Union on the basis of that provision of the TFEU ...

67. As to whether the Union could establish a stability mechanism comparable to that envisaged by Decision 2011/199 on the basis of Article 352 TFEU, suffice it to say that the Union has not used its powers under that article and that, in any event, that provision does not impose on the Union any obligation to act ...

68. Consequently, having regard to Articles 4(1) TEU and 5(2) TEU, the Member States whose currency is the euro are entitled to conclude an agreement between themselves for the establishment of a stability mechanism of the kind envisaged by Article 1 of Decision 2011/199 ...

69. However, those Member States may not disregard their duty to comply with European Union law when exercising their competences in that area ... However, the reason why the grant of financial assistance

---

[139] TSCG, article 2(2).   [140] TSCG, article 16.   [141] TSCG, article 15.

by the stability mechanism is subject to strict conditionality under paragraph 3 of Article 136 TFEU, the article affected by the revision of the FEU Treaty, is in order to ensure that that mechanism will operate in a way that will comply with European Union law, including the measures adopted by the Union in the context of the coordination of the Member States' economic policies. ...

103. ... even if it is apparent from recital 1 of the preamble to the ESM Treaty that the ESM will, among other tasks, assume the tasks hitherto allocated temporarily to the EFSM, established on the basis of Article 122(2) TFEU, that fact is not such as to affect common rules of the Union or alter their scope.

104. The establishment of the ESM does not affect the power of the Union to grant, on the basis of Article 122(2) TFEU, ad hoc financial assistance to a Member State when it is found that that Member State is in difficulties or is seriously threatened with severe difficulties caused by natural disasters or exceptional occurrences beyond its control.

105. Moreover, since neither Article 122(2) TFEU nor any other provision of the EU and TFEU confers a specific power on the Union to establish a permanent stability mechanism such as the ESM ... the Member States are entitled, in the light of Articles 4(1) TEU and 5(2) TEU, to act in this area.

106. The conclusion and ratification of the ESM Treaty by the Member States whose currency is the euro therefore does not jeopardise in any way the objective pursued by Article 122(2) TEU or by Council Regulation (EU) No. 407/2010 ... adopted on the basis of that provision, and does not prevent the Union from exercising its own competences in the defence of the common interest ...

Groups of Member States are, thus, free to establish international agreements between themselves to carry out tasks falling within the scope of EU law, and even use EU institutions to execute these tasks. This freedom is subject to a number of conditions. They cannot do this where the EU Treaties confer *specific powers* on the Union or where the activity is already governed by common rules. Any international agreement must still observe more general requirements of EU law. This is still a considerable relaxation of the rules governing enhanced cooperation.

The principle established in the judgment is questionable. The presence of a Union competence indicates that economic policy is a matter of common concern in which Member States have a shared interest in the activities of other Member States. This judgment flouts this. Unless the Treaty grants a specific task, a select group of states is free to agree things amongst themselves, use EU institutions, irrespective of its consequences for other Member States and their Treaty commitment to treat EU policies as a shared interest. If this should not give other Member States a veto, the judgment is disturbingly silent on the interests of other states.

There is also the operability of the constraints mentioned by the Court of Justice. The judgment is vague as to when a task is sufficiently specific to preclude action outside the Treaty framework. For example, Article 115 TFEU allows the Union to harmonise any taxes which 'directly affect the establishment or functioning of the internal market'. It is not clear whether this provision could be used to harmonise corporate or income taxes, and therefore whether it would preclude agreements on this by Member States. Similarly, the judgment indicates that there can be no agreements on matters where there are common rules. There were common rules here, however, in the form of Regulation 407/2010. However, because this was judged to be a form of short-term assistance rather than the long-term assistance being provided by the ESM Treaty, it was irrelevant that both were carrying out the same activity, namely, providing financial support to states in difficulties.

7 COMITOLOGY

We saw in Chapter 2 that the Commission could be granted powers to adopt implementing and delegated measures. The latter was considered in some detail there.[142] Implementing measures are adopted under a set of procedures, known as comitology, in which the Commission works in tandem with a committee of representatives of national governments whose role is to oversee it. Comitology governs not merely 'technical' but highly significant measures, and it is used extensively.[143] At the end of 2011, there were 268 committees in operation.[144] 1,625 measures were adopted that year.[145] These measures are regulatory acts which, when adopted as Regulations or Decisions, will have legally binding effects.

There are now three procedures: the advisory procedure, the examination procedure and the regulatory procedure with scrutiny. The first two were established by Regulation 182/2011, whilst it left the last one intact.[146] It is easiest to consider the advisory and examination procedures first. The criteria for determining when each is to be used are set out in article 2 of the Regulation.

Regulation 182/2011, article 2

1. A basic act may provide for the application of the advisory procedure or the examination procedure, taking into account the nature or the impact of the implementing act required.
2. The examination procedure applies, in particular, for the adoption of:
   (a) implementing acts of general scope;
   (b) other implementing acts relating to:
      (i)   programmes with substantial implications;
      (ii) the common agricultural and common fisheries policies;
      (iii) the environment, security and safety, or protection of the health or safety, of humans, animals or plants;
      (iv) the common commercial policy;
      (v)   taxation.
3. The advisory procedure applies, as a general rule, for the adoption of implementing acts not falling within the ambit of paragraph 2. However, the advisory procedure may apply for the adoption of the implementing acts referred to in paragraph 2 in duly justified cases.

The ethos of article 2 is clear. The most significant and contentious measures should be taken according to the examination procedure.

---

[142] See pp. 67–72.

[143] On the history see C. Bergström, *Comitology: Delegation of Powers in the European Union System* (Oxford, Oxford University Press, 2005).

[144] European Commission, *Report from the Commission on the Working of the Committees during 2011*, COM(2012)685, 7.

[145] *Ibid.* 8.

[146] Regulation 182/2011 laying down the rules and general principles concerning mechanisms for control by Member States of the Commission's exercise of implementing powers [2011] OJ L55/13. On the negotiation see G. Brandsma and J. Blom-Hansen, 'Negotiating the Post-Lisbon Comitology System: Institutional Battles over Delegated Decision-Making' (2012) 50 *JCMS* 939, 948–52.

Both procedures begin, however, in a similar manner. A committee of representatives of national governments is convened and chaired by the Commission.[147] It submits a draft implementing measure to this committee, who will meet not less than fourteen days after submission of the draft. The committee will then submit an opinion on the draft. The time limit for this opinion is set by the Commission according to the urgency of the measure. However, it must be proportionate and allow committee members 'early and effective opportunities to examine the draft implementing act and express their views'.[148]

The consequences of this opinion vary according to the procedure. The Commission is granted most leeway by the advisory procedure.

Regulation 182/2011, article 4

1. Where the advisory procedure applies, the committee shall deliver its opinion, if necessary by taking a vote. If the committee takes a vote, the opinion shall be delivered by a simple majority of its component members.
2. The Commission shall decide on the draft implementing act to be adopted, taking the utmost account of the conclusions drawn from the discussions within the committee and of the opinion delivered.

In principle, the committee is only to advise the Commission. The Commission can ignore its views and does not have to justify this to the committee. However, this needs to be qualified. The Commission does undertake to take 'utmost account' of the committee's conclusions. As we shall see, there is some evidence that this does take place. Furthermore, as we shall also see, the advisory procedure can be subject to an Appeal Committee which can block a Commission measure. A failure by the Commission to give due regard to the views of national governments within the advisory procedure may count against it at appeal.

The examination procedure grants the committee more powers. With the examination procedure, the committee votes on any opinion by QMV. The vote, or absence of it, has a number of implications.

Regulation 182/2011, article 5

2. Where the committee delivers a positive opinion, the Commission shall adopt the draft implementing act.
3. Without prejudice to Article 7,[[149]] if the committee delivers a negative opinion, the Commission shall not adopt the draft implementing act. Where an implementing act is deemed to be necessary, the chair may either submit an amended version of the draft implementing act to the same committee within 2 months of delivery of the negative opinion, or submit the draft implementing act within 1 month of such delivery to the appeal committee for further deliberation.

---

[147] Regulation 182/2011, article 3(2).   [148] *Ibid.* article 3(3).

[149] This provision allows acts to be adopted if delay would entail significant disruption to agricultural markets or the Union's financial interests. In such circumstances, the measure is passed to the Appeal Committee. A negative opinion by it requires the immediate repeal of the measure. More generally, in cases of urgency, the Commission can adopt measures. These are then considered retroactively by the Committee, *Ibid.* article 8.

4. Where no opinion is delivered, the Commission may adopt the draft implementing act, except in the cases provided for in the second subparagraph. Where the Commission does not adopt the draft implementing act, the chair may submit to the committee an amended version thereof.

   Without prejudice to Article 7, the Commission shall not adopt the draft implementing act where:
   (a) that act concerns taxation, financial services, the protection of the health or safety of humans, animals or plants, or definitive multilateral safeguard measures;
   (b) the basic act provides that the draft implementing act may not be adopted where no opinion is delivered; or
   (c) a simple majority of the component members of the committee opposes it.
   In any of the cases referred to in the second subparagraph, where an implementing act is deemed to be necessary, the chair may either submit an amended version of that act to the same committee within 2 months of the vote, or submit the draft implementing act within 1 month of the vote to the appeal committee for further deliberation.

With the examination procedure, the committee can always veto the draft implementing measure. Furthermore, the effect of article 5(4)(c) is that a simple majority of Member States acting within the Committee can veto the measure. However, for many measures, the procedure goes further and requires the committee to approve the measure before it can be adopted. This will be the case where either the parent legislation requires this or in the fields set out in article 5(4) (a) (i.e. financial services, taxation, etc.) which are seen as particularly sensitive.

Both the advisory and examination procedure are subject to two forms of control.

The first is the Appeal Committee. The parent legislation determines whether there shall be such an Appeal Committee and the terms under which a party (be it the Commission or national government(s)) may refer a measure to this Appeal Committee. It meets within fourteen days of referral and must deliver an opinion within two months of referral.[150] It votes by QMV.[151] If its opinion is positive or if gives no opinion, the Commission may adopt the measure. If it is negative, the Commission is blocked from adopting the measure.[152]

The second control is that the Parliament and Council may police the limits of the procedures to check that the measure is not ultra vires.

Regulation 182/2011, article 11

Where a basic act is adopted under the ordinary legislative procedure, either the European Parliament or the Council may at any time indicate to the Commission that, in its view, a draft implementing act exceeds the implementing powers provided for in the basic act. In such a case, the Commission shall review the draft implementing act, taking account of the positions expressed, and shall inform the European Parliament and the Council whether it intends to maintain, amend or withdraw the draft implementing act.

---

[150] *Ibid.* article 3(7).   [151] *Ibid.* article 6(1).
[152] *Ibid.* article 6(3). There is one exception to this. Definitive safeguard measures against imports from non-EU states can only be adopted if there is a positive opinion from the Committee. *Ibid.* article 6(4).

This control goes only to the limits of the act and not to its content. Furthermore, in an unsatisfactory quirk, it only applies to acts adopted under the ordinary legislative procedure and not to measures adopted under other legislative procedures. The reasons for this are historical. With the growth of the ordinary legislative procedure, the Parliament became increasingly uneasy about granting powers to the Commission that would displace that procedure, and, consequently, the European Parliament's influence.

There is a third comitology procedure, the regulatory procedure with scrutiny. The background to its establishment was a 2005 Commission admission of over fifty instances where it had failed to respect Parliament's rights under comitology.[153] The Parliament, consequently, pushed for greater involvement in fields where it exercised more legislative power. The regulatory procedure with scrutiny applies only in the field of the ordinary legislative procedure, therefore, and only to measures amending or supplementing non-essential elements of legislation adopted under that procedure.[154] It is not subject to the controls of the Appeal Committee.

Under the regulatory procedure with scrutiny, the committee gives an opinion by QMV on a Commission draft implementing measure in the same way as under the examination procedure.[155] If the opinion is positive, the European Parliament and the Council each have three months to voice their opposition to the measure. If either does this, the measure will not be adopted. However, opposition may only be based on the Commission exceeding its powers or breach of the subsidiarity or proportionality principles. Furthermore, they have high thresholds to meet to register their opposition: an absolute majority of members and QMV, respectively.[156] If the opinion is negative or there is no opinion, the measure is referred to the Council, which has two months to veto the measure. If it proposes adopting the measure, the proposal is passed to the European Parliament, which has four months to veto the measure on the same grounds as where the committee gave a positive opinion.[157] This procedure always gives the Council and the European Parliament the power to veto an implementing measure. However, the Council is in a stronger position as, in the absence of a positive opinion of the Committee, it can veto the draft implementing measure for any reason. That said, use of the veto is rare. In 2011, only two measures were vetoed (both by the Council), whereas 163 measures were adopted under the procedure.[158]

Comitology is seen by some as simply a series of controls to constrain Commission executive discretion. These include, in the first place, the committees themselves, where representatives of national governments act to patrol the Commission and the content of the measure. These have now been reinforced by the Appeal Committee, to which an outvoted national representative can take the matter if unhappy with the outcome of an advisory and examination procedure. There are, in the second place, the controls granted to the European Parliament and to the Council under the regulatory procedure with scrutiny to veto measures and, under all measures, to check that they are not ultra vires. To facilitate this, the Commission is to keep

---

[153] K. Bradley, 'Halfway House: The 2006 Comitology Reforms and the European Parliament' (2008) 31 *WEP* 837, 842–3.

[154] Decision 1999/468/EC laying down the procedures for the exercise of implementing powers conferred on the Commission [1999] OJ L184/23 as amended by Decision 2006/512 [2006] OJ L200/11, article 5a. J. Blom-Hansen, 'Interests, Instruments and Institutional Preferences in the EU Comitology System: The 2006 Comitology Reform' (2011) 17 *ELJ* 344.

[155] *Ibid.* article 5a(2).   [156] *Ibid.* article 5a(3).

[157] *Ibid.* article 5a(4).   [158] *Report from the Commission*, n. 144 above, 9–10.

a register which includes draft measures placed before the committee, agendas and voting records of the committee, and final implementing measures.[159] These are to be immediately available to the European Parliament and the Council,[160] and drafts are to be sent to these at the same time as to the committees.[161]

Analyses viewing comitology in this manner have undoubtedly helped to explain the reasons for its design and establishment. Unsurprisingly, the Council seeks the tightest controls, and the level of control agreed tends to be determined by the complexity of the measure[162] and the degree of political conflict between the EU institutions, with the strongest controls where these are greatest.[163] However, this vision does not explain the operation of these procedures well at all. If the committees acted as strong national constraints on the Commission, it would be important that national representatives both received strong mandates from their governments beforehand, and reported back to their government superiors directly afterwards. The reality shows many of them to be extremely isolated. A study found 43 per cent of participants to believe that their superiors were not interested in their work, and 84 per cent believed that their minister and government were not interested.[164] The committees escape below the radar of national interest. The same author found similarly low levels of interest by MEPs. Between 1999 and 2010, the European Parliament only indicated that a measure had exceeded Commission powers nine times, less than one time per thousand uses, and in the first five years of use of the regulatory procedure with scrutiny, the European Parliament exercised a veto three times (less than 1 per cent of the time).[165] Even the register was something of a hollow commitment with 95 per cent of draft measures and 35 per cent of agendas not published.[166]

Comitology has therefore been examined by others through the style of interaction between the Commission and the committees. Regulation 178/2011, in particular, imposes a duty on all actors to act by consensus and to allow amendments to be proposed right up until the moment of the adoption of the opinion by the Committee.

Regulation 178/2011, article 3(4)

4. Until the committee delivers an opinion, any committee member may suggest amendments and the chair may present amended versions of the draft implementing act. The chair shall endeavour to find solutions which command the widest possible support within the committee. The chair shall inform the committee of the manner in which the discussions and suggestions for amendments have been taken into account, in particular as regards those suggestions which have been largely supported within the committee.

---

[159] Regulation 182/2011, n. 146 above, article 10(1).   [160] *Ibid.* article 10(3).   [161] *Ibid.* article 10(4).

[162] J. Blom-Hansen, 'Comitology Choices in the EU Legislative Process: Contested or Consensual Decisions?' (2014) 92 *Public Administration* (forthcoming).

[163] J. Blom-Hansen, 'Legislative Control of Powers Delegated to the Executive: The Case of the EU' (2013) 26 *Governance* 425.

[164] G. Brandsma, *Backstage Europe: Comitology, Accountability and Democracy in the European Union* (Ph.D, Utrecht, 2010) 197.

[165] G. Brandsma, 'The Effect of Information on Oversight: The European Parliament's Response to Increasing Information on Comitology Decision-making' (2012) 78 *International Review of Administrative Sciences* 74, 86–7. For similar findings see M. Kaeding and A. Hardacre, 'The European Parliament and the Future of Comitology after Lisbon' (2013) 19 *ELJ* 382.

[166] G. Brandsma *et al.*, 'How Transparent are EU "Comitology" Committees in Practice' (2008) 14 *ELJ* 819, 833.

This is, moreover, not merely a paper obligation. In pioneering work, Joerges and Neyer studied the interaction between the Commission and one such committee, the Standing Committee on Food Stuffs (StCF). They found a settlement centred on deliberative problem-solving in which actors took on board the suggestions and interests of each other, and concern focused on finding the optimal solution rather than representing different interests.[167]

C. Joerges and J. Neyer, 'Transforming Strategic Interaction into Deliberative Problem-solving: European Comitology in the Foodstuffs Sector' (1997) 4 *Journal of European Public Policy* 609, 618–20

(a) The proposals which the Commission presents to the StCF are in general the result of extensive consultations with individual national administrations and independent experts. Particularly in committees like the StCF which act under qualified majority voting, proposals not only reflect the Commission's interest but also what it assumes to be in the interest of *more than a qualified majority* of the other parties involved. This becomes of crucial importance as the effectiveness of any measure adopted depends on Member States transposing the measure adequately into their national legal systems without leaving too many opportunities for evasion and – more importantly – not invoking safeguard procedures. However, in an institutional environment without effective means of hierarchical enforcement, this is only likely to happen if delegates see their own legitimate concerns acknowledged and protected in decision-making.

(b) The importance of the SCF[168] in supporting certain arguments does not derive from any formal power to decide issues of conflict (it has only an advisory status) but from the legal fiction of its scientific expertise and neutrality … Why do Member State delegates nevertheless adhere to the fiction of objective science? To understand this, one needs to consider the functions of legal fictions: scientific findings are supposed to be accepted by all the parties concerned; science-based discourses have the power to discipline arguments; and they allow a clear distinction between legitimate and illegitimate arguments in cases of conflict over competing proposals. Therefore, the fact that the opinions of the SCF have never been seriously challenged by the StCF may be grounded less in the objectivity of its opinions than in the function of scientific discourses as a mechanism that is helpful in overcoming politically constituted preferences by relying on the fiction of objective science. …

… in negotiations in the StCF – and even more so in the SCF – the particular economic costs of policies cannot be explicitly discussed, and information is primarily provided on nondistributional issues. *Ceteris paribus*, therefore, the knowledge of delegates about adequate problem-solving strategies will increase with the duration of negotiations, whereas their *relative* knowledge about economic effects will decline. This change in the perceptions and preferences of delegates becomes increasingly important for shaping national preferences as their informational advantage over their

---

[167] Others found similar modes of interaction elsewhere. J. Trondal, 'Beyond the EU Membership-Non Membership Dichotomy? Supranational Identities among National EU Decision-makers' (2002) 9 *JEPP* 468; J. Blom-Hansen and G. Brandsma, 'The EU Comitology System Intergovernmental Bargaining *and* Deliberative Supranationalism?' (2009) 47 *JCMS* 719. A recent study suggests that there is more conflict than perhaps these studies appreciate, noting that 27 per cent of committees take a vote, suggesting the absence of agreement. R. Dehousse, A. Fernández Pasarín and J. Plaza, 'How Consensual is Comitology', EUSA Biennial Conference, 9–11 May 2013.

[168] This was a separate committee of experts appointed by the Commission. It has now been replaced by the European Food Safety Authority.

national administration increases over time. It is also important to note that negotiations sometimes last for years among nearly the same set of delegates. Moreover, delegates have frequent contacts outside the sessions of the Standing Committee, and have often previously met working on the preparation of a legislative proposal in negotiations about its adoption in Council working groups. During the course of this collaboration, delegates not only learn to reduce differences between national legal provisions but also to develop converging definitions of problems and philosophies for their solution. They slowly proceed from being representatives of national interests to being representatives of a Europeanized inter-administrative discourse characterized by mutual learning and an understanding of each other's difficulties in the implementation of specific solutions.

Understandings of comitology as an interactive network of administrators and experts have provoked fierce debate about its democratic qualities.[169] There have been two central concerns. One is that its language is too technocratic. Delicate political and social questions are reduced to questions of expertise and risk assessment.[170] The other is that its make-up is insufficiently pluralistic. Administrators may 'up their game' by having to respond to other administrators' arguments but, as Gerstenberg and Sabel artfully put it, this may only 'improve government performance and renovate the role of the bureaucrat without much changing the role of the citizen'.[171] The rights of audience or participation of private parties before these committees, for example, is notoriously unclear.[172] Joerges has observed, in defence of the processes, that they contain many checks and balances that are generally unappreciated.

C. Joerges, 'Deliberative Supranationalism: A Defence' (2001) 5(8) *European Integration online Papers (EIoP)* 8–9

... comitology ... interested us because of its links not just with the bureaucracies but also with the polities of the Member States, because of its complex internal structure in which government representatives, the representatives of social interests and 'the' economy all interact. Risk regulation in the internal market seemed to us to document the weaknesses of expertocratic models adequately, because the normative, political and ethical dimensions of risk assessments resist a merely technocratic treatment. Admittedly, in the debates about the tensions between the ideals of democracy and the constraints of the 'knowledge society', Columbus' egg has not been sighted so far. My mere status as a citizen does not qualify me for a qualitatively convincing (to me at least) technical decision, nor can it be seen how 'all' the citizens affected by such decisions are really to participate in them. What is true of risk policy is present as a problem in practically every corner of modern law. And what is true of risk policy in an EU Member State in which (relatively) dense communicative processes guarantee the ongoing political debate is true *a fortiori* for such a polymorphic entity as the EU.

---

[169] R. Dehousse, 'Comitology? Who Watches the Watchmen?' (2003) 10 *JEPP* 798.

[170] J. Weiler, 'Epilogue – "Comitology" as Revolution – Infranationalism, Constitutionalism and Democracy' in C. Joerges and E. Vos (eds.), *EU Committees: Social Regulation, Law and Politics* (Oxford/Portland, Hart, 1999) 339, 345–6.

[171] O. Gerstenberg and C. Sabel, 'Directly-Deliberative Polyarchy: An Institutional Ideal for Europe' in C. Joerges and R. Dehousse (eds.), *Good Governance in Europe's Integrated Market* (Oxford, Oxford University Press, 2002) 289, 320.

[172] F. Bignami, 'The Democratic Deficit in European Community Rulemaking: A Call for Notice and Comment in Comitology' (1999) 40 *Harvard International Law Journal* 451.

8 EU LAW-MAKING: THE MEASURE OF ITS DEMOCRACY

For some, the presence of any supranational element in EU law-making is enough to render it undemocratic. The heart of this critique is that democracy is not something that we share with the whole world. A democratic community is necessarily something limited which is shared with some and not with others. It relies, in particular, on a mutual commitment by participants which is instituted through their all being free and equal members of a political community. The European Union, it is argued, does not possess this sense of political community (*demos*). Most of its citizens do not see themselves as sharing a sufficiently strong identity (i.e. being European). There is insufficient common political debate amongst citizens across the Union about matters of EU law. There is, thus, no strong pan-European media and news of the Union is always reported through a national perspective. Finally, there are no common political parties to articulate different European positions between which voters could choose.[173] By contrast, these elements are, by and large, present at a national level.[174] Critics would, therefore, argue that anything which allows national choices to be obstructed is undemocratic: be it the Commission's right of proposal, decision-making by ministers, particularly by QMV, or veto by the European Parliament.

The difficulties with such arguments, even on their own terms, are twofold.

First, they assume a national self-sufficiency, which allows nation-states to realise what they wish through their parliaments. This may not be the case. There may be harms or risks – be it pollution, pandemics, financial chaos or transnational crime – which come from another territory which no amount of unilateral legislation can prevent. Some shared rules governing what activities can take place in the state of origin enhance national capacity in such cases. There may, alternately, be certain goods that a state cannot realise unilaterally. These might be international trade, migration, communications or transport. Working together can also increase states' collective capacities and strengths to have presence on the international arena or to have additional resources to monitor more obscure risks. Traditional arrangements in which one state imposes its model on others or where this is agreed by bureaucratic fiat do not seem to mediate this issue of national insufficiency very democratically.

Secondly, there is no problematisation of this idea of *demos*. The sense of a shared identity as a precondition for democracy is a dangerous, even fascistic, idea if it implies that individuals must have certain common traits or ways of seeing the world before there can be a democracy.[175] Furthermore, even where this is not the case, representative institutions have proved traditionally weak at protecting certain interests which have mobilised only weakly before them. These might be diffuse interests, such as the environment, consumer interests or the financial interests of future generations. They might also be the interests of groups too small in number or insufficiently united to exercise strong influence within a legislative assembly (i.e. racial, ethnic and religious minorities, LGBT groups, women, foreigners, people with disabilities, or regional interests). A case can be made for an external check in such cases to protect

---

[173] On the absence of these see F. Cheneval and F. Schimmelfennig, 'The Case for Demoicracy in the European Union' (2013) 51 *JCMS* 334, 337–8.

[174] On what is necessary to secure this see L.-E. Cederman, 'Nationalism and Bounded Integration: What it Would Take to Create a European Demos' (2001) 7 *European Journal of International Relations* 139.

[175] J. Weiler, 'Does Europe Need a Constitution? Demos, Telos and the German Maastricht Decision' (1995) 1 *ELJ* 219.

majoritarian abuse and to require a political community to think with more sensitivity about the interests and needs of all its members.

However, the challenge with all the arguments above is that they act as critiques of each other. The critique of supranationalism tells us that the European Union cannot be built on crude majoritarianism where law-makers can do what 51 per cent of its citizens want. By contrast, critiques of national majoritarianism provide a reason for a European Union but they do not establish a measure of democracy of it. A number of authors have tried to find a way to mediate between these two positions to provide a benchmark for when the Union would have democratic authority.

They point, in particular, to three building blocks.

First, the Union institutionalises a principle of 'constitutional tolerance'.[176] It leads nationals to accept and acknowledge a shared destiny with foreigners and to accept the value of foreignness. A British citizen is required to recognise and respect interests, needs and aspirations of a French citizen and acknowledge that she brings something different, but equally valuable, to the Union political community of which the British citizen is part. This ethos of tolerance is something which can be applied to any traditionally underrepresented group. Recent writing has, moreover, tried to develop it in two directions. Some authors observe that it governs not just treatment of other individuals but other political communities. The Union is based on multiple political communities (*demoi*). The central structures of these different political communities should not just be respected by other political communities, such as nation-states, but also by the Union.[177] Other authors argue for a level of mutual respect which extends beyond mere tolerance. They argue that the Union is born out of two deep-seated ideas: liberal democracy and a memory of the destructiveness of conflict. This embeds a culture where only claims which accept the value of the difference of others are politically acceptable, and that the virtue of the Union should be its enabling of this difference.[178]

The second Union building block is the creation of common institutions to realise shared projects (e.g. the single market, the Area of Freedom, Security and Justice, a common environmental policy). These institutions have an elevating effect, it is argued, as they require citizens to come together to realise common goods; to act and negotiate in the public interest recognising each other's needs and arguments rather than acting in a self-interested manner. They require citizens to act in a public rather than a private manner.[179]

Thirdly, the institutional settlements of the Union prevent concentrations of power and foster pluralism.[180] Power is not centred in any one set of institutions, but is spread across

---

[176] J. Weiler, *The Constitution of Europe* (Cambridge, Cambridge University Press, 1999) especially 332–48; M. Poiares Maduro, *We, the Court: The European Court of Justice and the European Economic Constitution* (Oxford, Hart, 1998) 166–74.

[177] K. Nicolaidis, 'European Demoicracy and its Crisis' (2013) 51 *JCMS* 351; R. Bellamy, 'An Ever Closer Union Among the Peoples of Europe: Republican Intergovernmentalism and Demoicratic Representation within the EU' (2013) 35 *JEI* 499.

[178] J.-W. Müller, 'A European Constitutional Patriotism? The Case Restated' (2008) 14 *ELJ* 542, 554.

[179] On the ethic of participation see R. Bellamy and R. Warleigh, 'From an Ethics of Integration to an Ethics of Participation' (1998) 27 *Millennium* 447; P. Magnette, 'European Governance and Civic Participation: Beyond Elitist Citizenship?' (2003) 51 *Political Studies* 1.

[180] N. McCormick, 'Democracy, Subsidiarity and Citizenship in the European Commonwealth' (1997) 16 *Law and Philosophy* 331; K. Nicolaidis, 'Conclusion: The Federal Vision Beyond the Federal State' in K. Nicolaidis and R. Howse (eds.), *The Federal Vision: Legitimacy and Levels of Governance in the United States and the European Union* (Oxford, Oxford University Press, 2001).

the supranational institutions and national governments. Each has its own constituencies and each represents different interests. This allows a voice to be given to a variety of identities and interests.

These three elements – constitutional tolerance, creation of common goods and decentralisation of power – are, it has been argued, institutionalised within the EU law-making settlement through the three institutions representing different interests and working together to realise common projects.

A. Héritier, 'Elements of Democratic Legitimation in Europe: An Alternative Perspective' (1999) 6 *Journal of European Public Policy* 269, 274–6

2.2.1 Mutual horizontal control and 'distrust'
At each step of the European policy process, from the first tentative drafts to the formal decision-making process, policy-making is characterized by a distrustful and circumspect observation of the mutual policy proposals made by the involved actors. The participants controlling each other are generally experts and/or decision-makers from the different Member States, responding to each other's policy proposals with counterproposals backed up by expertise. The mutual distrust signifies an enormous potential for control and a chance to hold actors accountable for individual policy moves which need to be defended in substantive terms. This is the virtuous side of the slowness, and indeed potential deadlock, inherent in the European decisional process. This phenomenon is so widespread, permeating virtually the entire fabric of the decision making process across issue areas, that individual policy examples are superfluous. ...

The dark side of mutual control and distrust is – considering that European decision-making does not usually rely on the majority principle – of course stalemate, where a decisional process is stalled because the participants are exclusively engaged in controlling and fending-off policy initiatives presented by other actors involved. 'Distrust leads to foregone opportunities' unless it is overcome by constructive bargaining.

2.2.2 Bargaining democracy
Fortunately, bargaining constitutes the complementary side of mutual horizontal control and distrust. It is present in all aspects of European policy-making, given the presence of actors with diverse interests and a concrete need for consensual decision-making. Consensus is achieved through negotiating in the course of which compromises are formulated, compensation payments made, and package deals struck.

Actors negotiating may be representatives from territorial units or delegates from functional organizations, such as associations. Thus, in negotiating sectoral questions, such as in regional and social policy under the 'partnership principle', delegates from functional organizations are predominantly involved. During the input phase bargaining mostly takes place at the supranational level. If legislative details need to be specified during the output phase they occur at the national/subnational level as well. Bargaining democracy creates input-legitimation since it prevents individual interests from being outvoted and thereby forces actors to take multiple interests into account. This is reflected in the more equitable outcomes of bargaining processes. By virtue of precisely this fact it also constitutes a source of output-legitimation. The underlying process mechanism is consensus-building with the help of compromises, compensation payments, and package deals.

2.2.3 Pluralistic authorities in a 'composite polity'

The multiple political and jurisdictional authorities which exist in the European Union at the vertical and horizontal level have generated more opportunities for individual citizens and corporate actors to address an authority and voice their concern in the case of a specific policy issue. In practice, this means the opportunity to exit from a specific avenue of decision-making which has proved less than promising and to test prospects in another arena. Thus, a citizen or corporate actor may address his or her representative in parliament at the national or European level, the national or the European Ombudsman, and the national courts or the European Court of Justice. These increased opportunities at the European Union level – as compared with their nation state counterparts – create leverage to press for political action.

These arguments tell us little about how EU law-making fares versus competing national democratic claims. Even if it gives the Union some democratic authority, what happens when its laws come into conflict with laws democratically enacted through national procedures? More broadly, the strength of this model is left unspoken. It is not clear that these elements grant the Union a democratic authority to legislate generally. Other authors have noted that as the Union acquires powers to do ever more tasks, this model works increasingly less well. The reasons are that these tasks touch on issues where there is more polarisation between citizens and which are traditionally characterised by mass (i.e. electoral) democracy.[181] Even strong advocates of European integration have noted that this model allows for too little political competition. There is no possibility to vote the government out or for citizens to choose between competing world views.[182]

There is, also, the question of how well the Union institutionalises this ideal. The Union may require nationals to recognise the rights and identities of foreigners, but there is the question of which foreigners are most valued. Concerns have been expressed about the Union being a cartel of elites, which combine to disenfranchise other subjects within their respective territories.[183] The dominant players, after all, are national governments and the Commission. Similarly, the argument that the European Union diffuses power and encourages pluralism can be turned on its head. The different institutional setting within the Union – the Commission, MEPs, national governments – empower those actors who can arbitrage best between these different institutional settings. These are likely to be well-resourced, well-connected, transnational actors. Only these will have a strong sense of what takes place, for example, in a trilogue. These different settings also allow vested interests to attempt to dominate one of these settings in order to persuade it to act as a veto-player to further their own narrow interests. A unanimity vote in the Council, for example, can lead to one sectoral interest persuading a Member State to block a measure which a much wider array of interests see as beneficial. It can thus act to concentrate power.[184]

---

[181] P. de Wilde and M. Zürn, 'Can the Politicization of European Integration be Reversed?' (2012) 50 (S1) *JCMS* 137.

[182] S. Hix, *What's Wrong with the European Union and How to Fix It* (Oxford, Polity, 2008) ch. 5.

[183] P. Taylor, *International Organization in the Modern World: The Regional and the Global Process* (London, Pinter, 1993) ch. 1.

[184] J. de Areilza, *Enhanced Cooperation in the Treaty of Amsterdam: Some Critical Remarks*, Jean Monnet Working Paper 13/98.

FURTHER READING

G. Brandsma, *Controlling Comitology: Accountability in a Multi-Level System* (Basingstoke, Palgrave, 2013)

F. Cheneval and F. Schimmelfennig, 'The Case for Demoicracy in the European Union' (2013) 51 *Journal of Common Market Studies* 334

S. Hix, *What's Wrong with the European Union and How to Fix it* (Oxford, Polity, 2008)

R. Kardasheva, 'The Power to Delay: The European Parliament's Influence in the Consultation Procedure' (2009) 47 *Journal of Common Market Studies* 385

B. Kohler Koch and B. Rittberger (eds.), *Debating the Democratic Legitimacy of the European Union* (Lanham, MD, Rowman & Littefield, 2007)

C. Reh *et al.*, 'The Informal Politics of Legislation: Explaining Secluded Decision Making in the European Union' (2013) 46 *Comparative Political Studies* 1112

R. de Ruiter, 'Under the Radar? National Parliaments and the Ordinary Legislative Procedure in the European Union' (2013) 20 *Journal of European Public Policy* 1196

L. Senden, *Soft Law in European Community Law* (Oxford/Portland, OR, Hart, 2004)

C. Sprungk, 'A New Type of Representative Democracy? Reconsidering the Role of National Parliaments in the European Union' (2013) 35 *Journal of European Integration* 547

P. de Wilde and M. Zürn, 'Can the Politicization of European Integration be Reversed?' (2012) 50 (S1) *Journal of Common Market Studies* 137

4

The EU Judicial Order

CONTENTS

1 INTRODUCTION

This chapter considers the judicial order of the European Union: the Court of Justice and the institutional relations between it and national courts and tribunals.

Section 2 considers the Court of Justice of the European Union. The institution comprises three courts: the Court of Justice, the General Court and the European Union Civil Service Tribunal. The Court is to ensure that in the interpretation and application of the Treaties the law is observed. It has full jurisdiction over the Treaties other than over the Common Foreign and Security Policy, the validity of operations of police or other law-enforcement services, and the substantive grounds on which a Member State may be expelled from the Union. Its jurisdiction is, however, restricted by the procedures through which a case may come before it. The main one described in this chapter is the preliminary reference procedure in Article 267 TFEU which allows national courts to seek references from the Court of Justice on points of EU law necessary to decide the dispute in front of them.

Section 3 considers the architecture of the preliminary reference procedure. The Court of Justice rules on points of EU law which bind the national referring court. National courts have a monopoly over the adjudication of disputes, and thus questions of fact and national law. The only subjects of this procedure are courts. Institutional relations are not governed by a system of appeal by individuals but a reference from a national court to the Court of Justice on a point of EU law. The Court of Justice has sought to expand the subjects of this judicial order by allowing bodies, which would be considered regulatory or administrative bodies rather than courts under national law, to refer. It has also granted all of these an unfettered and immediate right to refer. This has created a direct relationship between it and every court in the Union which establishes the basis for a pan-Union judicial order. A question mark about this judicial order has been posed with the anticipated establishment of a new Unified Patent Court. This proposes a supranational judicial order dispersed across the Union to which individuals have direct access, and which does not rely for its functioning on a division of duties with the national courts in the same way as Article 267 TFEU.

Section 4 looks at the functions played by this judicial order and the preliminary reference procedure within it. It argues these are, first, the development of EU law with national courts referring new contexts in which EU law is to be applied and pointing to coherencies and incoherencies in the EU legal order. Secondly, it is the central form of judicial review of EU measures. Actors challenge implementation of an EU measure before a national court which then questions the legality of the EU measure in a reference. Thirdly, it is central to preserving the uniformity of EU law. The Court of Justice claims an exclusive responsibility to declare EU measures invalid and to provide authoritative interpretations of EU law which bind courts and other administrative actors across the Union. Finally, it helps national courts to resolve disputes which involve EU law through the provision of an interpretation of EU law, which they may be hesitant, otherwise, to give.

Section 5 looks at how relations between the courts are managed to realise these functions. This is done, first, through setting out the circumstances when national courts must refer. This will be the case where national courts are a court against whose decision there is no judicial remedy in national law unless a materially identical question has already been decided by the Court (*acte éclairé*) or there is no reasonable doubt as to the interpretation of the provision of EU law (*acte clair*). It will also be the case if the national court thinks the EU measure is illegal. Secondly, relations are managed through the Court holding that its judgments bind all authorities in the Union, not just the referring court. Finally, the positions of parties during the reference period are protected either through the prioritisation of certain cases (expedited and urgent procedures) or by allowing national courts to grant interim measures.

2 COURT OF JUSTICE OF THE EUROPEAN UNION

The Court of Justice is to ensure that the law is observed in the interpretation and application of the Treaties. It comprises three courts: the Court of Justice, the General Court and the European Civil Service Tribunal.

> ### Article 19 TEU
>
> 1. The Court of Justice of the European Union shall include the Court of Justice, the General Court and specialised courts. It shall ensure that in the interpretation and application of the Treaties the law is observed.
>
>   Member States shall provide remedies sufficient to ensure effective legal protection in the fields covered by Union law.
> 2. The Court of Justice shall consist of one judge from each Member State. It shall be assisted by Advocates General.
>
>   The General Court shall include at least one judge per Member State.
>
>   The Judges and the Advocates General of the Court of Justice and the Judges of the General Court shall be chosen from persons whose independence is beyond doubt and who satisfy the conditions set out in Articles 253 and 254 TFEU. They shall be appointed by common accord of the governments of the Member States for six years. Retiring Judges and Advocates General may be reappointed.
> 3. The Court of Justice of the European Union shall, in accordance with the Treaties:
>   (a) rule on actions brought by a Member State, an institution or a natural or legal person;
>   (b) give preliminary rulings, at the request of courts or tribunals of the Member States, on the interpretation of Union law or the validity of acts adopted by the institutions;
>   (c) rule in other cases provided for in the Treaties.

Article 19 TEU provides a very bald description of these courts, and the scope and the nature of their powers. We will turn, first, to who they are before examining what they do.

(i) Court of Justice

The Court of Justice is made up of twenty-eight judges, one from each Member State. These are appointed for a renewable period of six years and are required to be persons whose independence is beyond doubt and who are either suitable for the highest judicial office in their respective countries or 'jurisconsults of recognised competence'.[1] The judges elect the President from amongst themselves for a three-year term.[2] His central responsibility is to determine the case list and allocate cases to different Chambers.[3] Both new judges and judges seeking renewal of their term are nominated by individual governments and then appointed by the 'common accord' of the national governments.[4] To prevent a perception of over-politicisation of the process and to ensure that any candidate has the requisite expertise, a panel comprising members of the Court of Justice and members of national supreme courts is consulted beforehand.[5]

The panel has indicated that it will look at the legal expertise of any candidate; their professional experience with, controversially, candidates with less than twenty years' experience

---

[1] See also Article 253 TFEU. This is done on a three-yearly cycle, so that every three years half the Court is replaced.
[2] Article 253(3) TFEU. The current President is Greek, Judge Skouris.
[3] The President also chairs the Grand Chamber and is responsible for interim measures.
[4] Article 19(2) TEU.
[5] Article 255 TFEU. This does not address issues of representativeness or diversity, however. I. Solanke, 'Diversity and Independence in the European Court of Justice' (2009) 15 *CJEL* 89.

unlikely to be favourably viewed for the position of judge at the Court of Justice; their language skills; and their ability to make an effective contribution quickly.[6] The authority of the members of this panel results in a negative opinion given by the panel acting as a de facto veto. Up until the end of 2012, it had given forty-three opinions of which five were negative, with none of these five candidates being appointed.[7] Although the panel gives reasons for its opinions, its deliberations are confidential, and it is not clear why it believes that it, rather than the legislature or the national governments, should determine the general criteria to be a judge. That said, it has led to a welcome formalisation of the procedure with national governments, keen not to be embarrassed, engaging in far more open selection procedures before making a nomination.

The Court works under the principle of collegiality, in which a single judgment is given. This has been criticised on the grounds that the consequent compromises affect the quality of legal reasoning, with the Court often seeming neither to counter a point nor consider a question.[8] However, it does prevent Member States pointing to sympathetic dissenting opinions of their national judge to undermine the authority of a judgment. Members of the Court also argue that it allows for a considerable exchange of views and differing national legal traditions to filter through to the judgment.[9]

The Court is assisted by nine Advocates General. This will increase to eleven in October 2015.[10] The same procedure and conditions of appointment apply to these as to judges of the Court of Justice. The role of the Advocate General is to make, in open court, impartial and independent submissions on any case brought before the Court.[11] She acts not as a legal representative of one of the parties, but as a legal representative of the public interest. These Opinions are adopted in advance of the judgment to allow the Court sufficient time to consider them. They often provide a more detailed analysis of the context and the argument than is found in the judgment of the Court itself. However, they are not binding on the Court, although they are often referred to by the Court of Justice in its judgments. Furthermore, even when the conclusions reached are similar, it is difficult to know whether the reasoning is the same, given that the Opinion is often discursive in nature, whilst the judgment itself is very terse.

For reasons of workload, cases are rarely decided by the full Court. Indeed, it is only to sit in full session in cases of 'exceptional importance' or where it is to rule on a senior EU official being deprived of office for not meeting the requisite conditions.[12] Between 2008 and 2012, out of 2,058 judgments, only two judgments were given by the full Court. In practice, the greatest number of judges involved with a judgment is likely to be when a Grand Chamber of fifteen

---

[6] *Ibid.* 11–12.

[7] EU Council, *Second Activity Report of the Panel Provided for by Article 255 TEU*, Council Doc. 5091/13, 6.

[8] W. Bishop, 'Price Discrimination under Article 86: Political Economy in the European Court' (1981) 44 *MLR* 282, 294–5.

[9] E.g. F. Jacobs, 'Advocates General and Judges in the European Court of Justice: Some Personal Reflections' in D. O'Keeffe and A. Bavasso (eds.), *Judicial Review in European Union Law: Liber Amicorum Lord Slynn* (The Hague/Boston/London, Kluwer Law International, 2000) vol. 1.

[10] Article 252 TFEU. Decision 2013/336/EU increasing the number of Advocates General of the Court of Justice of the European Union [2013] OJ 2013 L179/92. On the Advocates General see N. Burrows and R. Greaves, *The Advocate General and EC Law* (Oxford, Oxford University Press, 2007); I. Solanke, 'The Advocate General: Assisting the CJEU of Article 13 TEU to Secure Trust and Democracy' (2012) 14 *CYEL* 697.

[11] Article 252 TFEU.

[12] The rules on the full Court and the Grand Chamber are set out in Article 251 TFEU and Consolidated Version of the Statute of the Court of Justice of the European Union, Article 16, http://curia.europa.eu/jcms/upload/docs/application/pdf/2012–10/staut_cons_en.pdf.

judges hears it. This will be when a Member State or EU institution party to the proceedings requests this. This happened in 286 judgments during this period. The majority of cases are heard by Chambers of either three or five judges. The former decided 391 judgments and the latter 1,379 judgments.[13]

Whilst Article 19(1) TEU suggests a general jurisdiction for the Court of Justice over both Treaties, this is subject to three forms of exclusion:

- It has no jurisdiction in the field of the Common Foreign and Security Policy.[14]
- In judicial cooperation in criminal matters and police cooperation, it has no jurisdiction to review the validity or proportionality of operations carried out by the police or other law-enforcement services of a Member State or the exercise of the responsibilities incumbent upon Member States with regard to the maintenance of law and order and the safeguarding of internal security.[15]
- If measures are taken to expel a Member State, the Court of Justice can rule on the procedure but not the substance of the grounds for expulsion.[16]

The Court's jurisdiction is further restricted by the rules on *locus standi* which determine the circumstances in which parties can bring actions before it. Matters can come before it in a variety of ways:

- preliminary references from national courts: national courts may, or in some cases must, refer a point of EU law to the Court of Justice if it is necessary to decide the dispute; the Court of Justice will give judgment on the point of EU law, which the national judge will apply to the dispute in hand;[17]
- enforcement actions brought by the Commission or Member States against other Member States: the Commission, or in rare cases another Member State, can bring a Member State before the Court of Justice for a declaration that the latter is in breach of EU law;[18]
- sanctions for failure to comply with Court judgments: if a Member State fails to comply with a Court of Justice judgment, the Commission can bring it back before the Court in order to have it fined for its behaviour;[19]
- judicial review of EU institutions by other EU institutions and judicial review of the Parliament or Council by Member States;[20]
- Opinions on the conclusion of international agreements: the Council, Parliament, Commission or any Member State can ask for an Opinion of the Court as to whether the Union has lawfully concluded a draft treaty; if the Court rules that the international agreement is illegal, it can only enter into force if the treaty is first amended;[21]

---

[13] *Annual Report of the Court of Justice 2012* (Luxembourg, Publications Office of the European Union, 2013) 96. For evidence that these Chambers behave in very different ways see M. Malecki, 'Do ECJ Judges All Speak with the Same Voice? Evidence of Divergent Preferences from the Judgments of Chambers' (2012) 19 *JEPP* 59.

[14] Article 24(1) TEU, Article 275 TFEU. It can, however, rule on the limits relative to other parts of the Treaties, Article 40 TEU.

[15] Article 276 TFEU.   [16] Article 269 TFEU.   [17] Article 267 TFEU.

[18] Articles 258 and 259 TFEU.   [19] Article 260 TFEU.

[20] Articles 263(2) and 265(1) TFEU; Consolidated Version of the Statute of the Court of Justice of the European Union, Article 51. There are limited exceptions for national actions against Council exercise of delegated powers, Council measures authorising state aids and Council measures defining the common commercial policy. These go to the General Court.

[21] Article 218(11) TFEU.

- appeals from the General Court on points of law;[22]
- the Council may confer jurisdiction on the Court with regard to disputes concerning the application of European intellectual property rights.[23]

These procedures are discussed in more detail in subsequent chapters. Combined, they make a substantial docket. In 2012, the Court of Justice disposed of 523 cases and gave 406 judgments.[24]

(ii) General Court

Unlike the Court of Justice, the General Court is not confined to a single judge from each Member State, but must comprise at least one judge from each Member State.[25] At the moment, however, it comprises twenty-eight judges. The General Court can sit in full court if it considers the circumstances require or because of the legal difficulty or importance of the case.[26] Otherwise, it sits in Chambers of three or five judges, with the overwhelming proportion of cases heard by Chambers of three judges.[27] One of the judges will act as Advocate General. A single judge can give judgments in actions brought by private parties, but the circumstances in which this can occur are extremely restricted. The case must raise only questions already clarified by established case law and must not cover certain fields, notably state aids, competition, mergers, agriculture and trade with non-EU states.[28]

The General Court's jurisdiction covers the following:

- judicial review by individuals of actions or illegal action by EU institutions and agencies or action for non-contractual damages against the EU institutions;[29]
- actions by Member States against the Commission, the European Central Bank and the European Council;[30]
- matters referred to the Court of Justice under an arbitration clause;[31]
- appeals from decisions of the Office for Harmonisation in the Internal Market;[32] this agency is responsible for the grant of the Community trade mark and anybody adversely affected by its decisions can appeal these to the General Court;
- appeals from decisions of the European Civil Service Tribunal.[33]

Jurisdiction over these matters results in the General Court being the central administrative court. It has thus become the key actor in the development of administrative principles of due process. As much competition, intellectual property and external trade law develops through

---

[22] Article 256(1) TFEU.   [23] Article 262 TFEU.
[24] *Annual Report*, n. 13 above, 96.   [25] Article 19(2) TEU.
[26] Rules of Procedure of the General Court, article 14(1). Available at http://curia.europa.eu/jcms/upload/docs/ application/pdf/2008-09/txt7_2008-09-25_14-08-6_431.pdf.
[27] 86.05 per cent of cases in 2012 were heard by Chambers of three judges. *Annual Report*, n. 13 above, 188.
[28] Rules of Procedure of the Court of First Instance, article 14(2).
[29] Articles 263(4), 265(3), 268 and 340(2) TFEU.
[30] Articles 263 and 265 TFEU. Protocol on the Statute of the Court of Justice, article 51. There is a limited exception for challenges against Commission authorisation of enhanced cooperation. These go to the Court of Justice.
[31] Article 272 TFEU.
[32] Regulation 40/94/EC on the Community trade mark [2004] OJ L70/1, article 63.
[33] Article 256(2) TFEU.

challenges by private parties adversely affected by EU measures, it is also the central judicial institution in these fields.

In 2012, actions against EU institutions accounted for 45.7 per cent of cases and trade mark cases for 38.6 per cent.[34] The General Court is struggling to keep up with its docket. At the end of 2012, 1,237 cases were pending and the duration of proceedings was, depending on the type of action, between 20.3 and 48.4 months.[35] These delays are so serious that they have led to decisions being overturned on the grounds that they violated the applicant's fundamental right to have the case heard within a reasonable period of time.[36] Notwithstanding this, there is also provision for the General Court to receive preliminary rulings in fields to be specified,[37] albeit that no field has yet been transferred under this heading.

There is a right to appeal from the General Court to the Court of Justice within two months of notification of the decision. The appeal must be on points of law.[38] This right to appeal exists not just for parties to the dispute but also for Member States and EU institutions where they intervened and the decision directly affects them.[39] Even if the Court of Justice finds that the General Court has misapplied EU law, it will only uphold an appeal if the mistake of law relates to the operative part of the judgment. Even if EU law is misapplied there, the appeal will still not be successful if the operative part is shown to be well-founded for other legal reasons.[40] In 2012, the Court of Justice considered 128 appeals, dismissing 98 of these.[41] These statistics tell only part of the story, as differences on significant and controversial areas of law have emerged between the two courts.[42]

If the Court of Justice finds the appeal to be well-founded, it will quash the decision of the General Court. It then has the discretion to give the final judgment or to refer the matter back to the General Court. If it adopts the latter course of action, the General Court is bound by the Court of Justice's decision on the point of law.[43] The General Court takes the view that it is only bound by the judgments of the Court where its decision has been quashed by the Court of Justice and the matter is referred back, or where the principle of *res judicata* operates, namely, a dispute involving the same parties, subject matter and cause of action as one already decided by the Court of Justice.[44] Nevertheless, the circumstances in which the General Court will not follow judgments of the Court of Justice will be rare. In *Kadi*, the Court of Justice had struck down EU measures implementing UN sanctions against individuals suspected of links

---

[34] *Annual Report*, n. 13 above, 183.   [35] *Ibid.* 189–90.

[36] Case C-185/95P *Baustahlgewerbe* v *Commission* [1998] ECR I-8417; Case C-385/07P *Grüne Punkt DSD* v *Commission* [2009] ECR I-6155. There is a duty on the General Court to hear the case within a reasonable period of time. Any judgment will only be set aside, however, if it can be shown that the delay would have affected the outcome. The parties can, however, sue the General Court for loss caused by the delay. Case C-460/09P *Inalca – Industria Alimentari Carni* v *Commission*, Judgment of 28 February 2013.

[37] Article 256(3) TFEU.   [38] Article 256(1) TFEU.

[39] Consolidated Statute of the Court of Justice of the European Union, article 56.

[40] Case C-221/10 P *Artegodan* v *Commission*, Judgment of 19 April 2012.

[41] *Annual Report*, n. 13 above, 197.

[42] There have been strong differences, for example, over the rules on *locus standi* of private parties to challenge EU acts and the levels of information which should be made available to those wishing to defend themselves against EU sanctions: Case T-177/01 *Jégo-Quéré* v *Commission* [2002] ECR II-2365; Case C-263/02P *Commission* v *Jégo-Quéré* [2004] ECR I-3425; Case T-85/09 *Kadi* v *Commission* [2010] ECR II-5177; Joined Cases C-584/10P, C-593/10P and C-595/10P *Commission and United Kingdom* v *Kadi*, Judgment of 18 July 2013.

[43] Protocol on the Statute of the Court of Justice, article 61.

[44] Case T-162/94 *NMB France* v *Commission* [1996] ECR II-427.

with terrorist organisations on the grounds that these individuals had no right to challenge the decision of the UN Committee which had put them on a sanctions list or even know the information on which these sanctions were based.[45] This was criticised on the grounds that it placed EU law above international law. New sanctions were adopted, once again naming Kadi. When they were challenged before the General Court, it had this to say about these criticisms of the Court of Justice's earlier judgment.

Case T–85/09 *Kadi* v *Commission* [2010] ECR II–5177

121. The General Court acknowledges that those criticisms are not entirely without foundation. However, with regard to their relevance, it takes the view that, in circumstances such as those of the present case – which concerns a measure adopted by the Commission to replace an earlier measure annulled by the Court of Justice in an appeal against the judgment of this Court dismissing an action for annulment of the earlier measure – the appellate principle itself and the hierarchical judicial structure which is its corollary generally advise against the General Court revisiting points of law which have been decided by the Court of Justice. That is *a fortiori* the case when, as here, the Court of Justice was sitting in Grand Chamber formation and clearly intended to deliver a judgment establishing certain principles. Accordingly, if an answer is to be given to the questions raised by the institutions, Member States and interested legal quarters following the judgment of the Court of Justice in *Kadi*, it is for the Court of Justice itself to provide that answer in the context of future cases before it.

Whilst the General Court is not formally bound by a decision of the Court of Justice and may disagree with it, it is, consequently, unlikely to overrule it. The only circumstances where it might do so is where the disagreement is severe and the decision was made by a small Chamber, probably of three judges. That said, the General Court reserved for itself the right to criticise prior judgments of the Court of Justice publicly. This might be seen as something which both acts as a curb on Court of Justice power and a vehicle for greater debate. It could also be seen as something undermining of the authority of the Court of Justice.

(iii) European Union Civil Service Tribunal

There is provision for work of the General Court to be transferred to specialised courts. The rules on the organisation for each court are likely to be different, as they will be governed by the legislation establishing it. In all cases, members must be independent and fit for judicial office. There must also be the possibility of appeal to the General Court.[46] To date, only one has been established, the European Union Civil Service Tribunal, which hears disputes between employees of the EU institutions and the institutions themselves.[47]

---

[45] Joined Cases C-402/05P and C-415/05P *Kadi and Al Barakaat International Foundation* v *Council and Commission* [2008] ECR I-6351.

[46] Article 257 TFEU.

[47] Decision 2004/752/EC, EURATOM establishing the European Union Civil Service Tribunal [2004] OJ L333/7. At the end of 2012, 235 cases were pending with a mean duration of 15.9 months, *Annual Report*, n. 13 above, 234–5.

3 ARCHITECTURE OF THE EU JUDICIAL ORDER

The activities of the three Union courts described above are important but, as we will see in more detail later,[48] individuals can invoke EU law before national courts in certain circumstances with a corollary host of duties imposed on national courts. Indeed, Article 19(1) TEU alludes to this by stating that Member States must provide remedies sufficient to ensure effective legal protection in the fields covered by EU law. The EU judicial order must thus be seen as a system of administration of justice which comprises not only Union courts but also national courts, which are more numerous, have greater resources and are more accessible to individual litigants.[49] Combined, these all have a shared responsibility for the application and development of EU law. Into this mix must now be added a third type of court, the Unified Patent Court. Established by international agreement in February 2013,[50] as a single court to cover all EU Member States other than Poland, Croatia and Spain, it is likely to start work in 2015.[51] It is neither a national court nor a Union court but is expected to apply EU law[52] and be bound by the judgments of the Court of Justice.[53] Its relationship to the latter is slightly different from that enjoyed by national courts. If it is probably best consequently to see it as part of the EU judicial order, it also poses some questions about the future structure of that order.

(i) Judicial cooperation and competition within the EU judicial order

There are two provisions governing the division of duties between national courts and the Court of Justice. The first is Article 274 TFEU. This grants the Court of Justice exclusive jurisdiction where the Treaties provide for the Union to be a party to the proceedings.

> **Article 274 TFEU**
>
> Save where jurisdiction is conferred on the Court of Justice of the European Union by the Treaties, disputes to which the Union is a party shall not on that ground be excluded from the jurisdiction of the courts or tribunals of the Member States.

The Union will be a party to the proceedings where:

- judicial review or damages is being sought against an act or omission of one of the EU institutions or agencies;
- one EU institution is seeking judicial review against the action or inaction of another institution(s);
- the Commission is bringing enforcement actions or an action for damages against a Member State for non-compliance with EU law.

---

[48] See Chapter 7.
[49] I. Maher, 'National Courts as European Community Courts' (1994) 14 *Legal Studies* 226.
[50] [2013] OJ C175/1.
[51] The Court is established by international agreement entering into effect on 1 January 2014 or when the thirteenth state has ratified it, whichever is later, Article 89 UPC.
[52] Article 20 UPC.   [53] Article 21 UPC.

If national courts cannot rule in these scenarios, Article 267 TFEU sets out their relationship with the Court of Justice in the contexts where they can adjudicate.

Article 267 TFEU

The Court of Justice of the European Union shall have jurisdiction to give preliminary rulings concerning:

(a) the interpretation of the Treaties;

(b) the validity and interpretation of acts of the institutions, bodies, offices or agencies of the Union.

Where any such question is raised in a case pending before a court or tribunal of a Member State against whose decisions there is no judicial remedy under national law, that court or tribunal shall bring the matter before the Court.

Where such a question is raised before any court or tribunal of a Member State, that court or tribunal may, if it considers that a decision on the question is necessary to enable it to give judgment, request the Court to give a ruling thereon.

If such a question is raised in a case pending before a court or tribunal of a Member State with regard to a person in custody, the Court of Justice of the European Union shall act with the minimum of delay.

Two features of the procedure are striking.

First, subject to Article 274 TFEU, national courts have a monopoly of adjudication over disputes that come before them which involve EU law. If Article 267 TFEU sets out circumstances when national courts refer points of EU law to the Court of Justice and the consequences of its judgments for them, it is they who decide the dispute. They decide not only pertinent points of national law but, even more centrally, they decide the facts to the dispute and, on the basis of this, they decide how to apply EU law to the dispute.[54] The Court of Justice will not look behind the facts presented to it by them. In *WWF*, a challenge was made to the transformation of the military airport in Bolzano, Italy into a commercial airport because there had been a failure to carry out an environmental impact assessment.[55] The airport authorities argued that the facts presented by the national court were inaccurate and that, under Italian law, it had exceeded its jurisdiction by considering these questions of fact as it was confined to considering questions of law. The Court dismissed these arguments. It noted that it was for the national court, not itself, to ascertain the facts and that it was not its role to examine whether the reference had been made in accordance with national laws on court jurisdiction and procedure.

Secondly, Article 267 TFEU is a court to court procedure, with national courts acting as gate-keepers to the Court.[56] Private parties have no direct access to the Court of Justice, nor can they appeal decisions of the national courts to the Court of Justice. The Court has thus characterised the procedure as:

---

[54] Case 104/79 *Foglia* v *Novello* [1980] ECR 745.

[55] Case C-435/97 *WWF* v *Autonome Provinz Bozen* [1999] ECR I-5613.

[56] Private parties not allowed to appear before the national court will not, therefore, be allowed to intervene before the Court of Justice, Case C-181/95 *Biogen* v *Smithkline Beecham* [1996] ECR I-717.

a non-contentious procedure excluding any initiative of the parties who are merely invited to be heard in the course of this procedure.[57]

The role of the parties is confined to generating the dispute before the national court which triggers the reference and submitting observations to the Court of Justice.[58] However, it is for the national court to decide whether to refer. It can do this of its own motion, and irrespective of the wishes of the parties.[59] Furthermore, these cannot change the tenor of the question referred by the national court.[60] The reference takes the form of a question or number of questions about EU law, set out within a statement detailing the factual and legal context to the dispute.

Recommendations to national courts and tribunals in relation to the initiation of preliminary ruling proceedings[61]

20. The decision by which a court or tribunal of a Member State refers one or more questions to the Court of Justice for a preliminary ruling may be in any form allowed by national law as regards procedural steps. However, it must be borne in mind that it is that document which will serve as the basis of the proceedings before the Court and that it must therefore contain such information as will enable the Court to give a reply which is of assistance to the referring court or tribunal. Moreover, it is only the request for a preliminary ruling which is notified to the parties to the main proceedings and to the other interested persons ... in order to obtain any written observations. ...

22. About 10 pages is often sufficient to set out in a proper manner the context of a request for a preliminary ruling. That request must be succinct but sufficiently complete and must contain all the relevant information to give the Court and the interested persons entitled to submit observations a clear understanding of the factual and legal context of the main proceedings ... the request for a preliminary ruling must contain, in addition to the text of the questions referred to the Court for a preliminary ruling:
    • a summary of the subject-matter of the dispute and the relevant findings of fact as determined by the referring court or tribunal, or, at least, an account of the facts on which the questions referred are based;
    • the tenor of any national provisions applicable in the case and, where appropriate, the relevant national case-law;
    • a statement of the reasons which prompted the referring court or tribunal to inquire about the interpretation or validity of certain provisions of European Union law, and the relationship between those provisions and the national legislation applicable to the main proceedings.

23. The European Union law provisions relevant to the case should be identified as accurately as possible in the request for a preliminary ruling, which should include, if need be, a brief summary of the relevant arguments of the parties to the main proceedings.

---

[57] Case C-364/92 *Fluggesellschaft* v *Eurocontrol* [1994] ECR I-43.
[58] Rules of Procedure of the Court of Justice, article 96 [2012] OJ L265/1.
[59] Case C-251/11 *Huet*, Judgment of 8 March 2012.
[60] Joined Cases C-42/10, C-45/10 and C-57/10 *Vlaamse Dierenartsenvereniging and Janssens* [2011] ECR I-2975.
[61] [2012] OJ C338/1.

This statement frames the dispute. The Court of Justice cannot look behind it and will, indeed, sometimes look to it, rather than the explicit questions set out by the national court in providing its judgment.[62]

Beyond this, the wording of Article 267 TFEU is thin, saying little about the relations and duties surrounding it. This has allowed the Court of Justice to craft its own vision of an EU judicial order onto it. This vision is that EU law is an autonomous legal order. For that autonomy to be protected, all national courts have to be able to interpret and apply EU law in an unimpeded manner. This requires that they enjoy a direct relationship with the Court via Article 267 TFEU, which allows them to be able to refer questions of EU law to it, irrespective of any domestic processes or hierarchies.

This issue has arisen in two contexts.

The first goes to whether rulings by superior national courts bind lower courts in such a way that they cannot refer.[63] If a higher court has given a ruling on a point of EU law, can a lower court ignore it and refer the matter to the Court of Justice? In *Križan*, the Slovakian Supreme Court (Najvyšší súd Slovenskej republiky) suspended a permit for the construction of a landfill site in the Slovakian town of Pezinok on the grounds that a proper environmental impact assessment had not been carried out as required (in its view) by EU law. The matter went to the Slovakian Constitutional Court (Ústavný súd Slovenskej republiky) which held that the Supreme Court's decision was wrong and, indeed, violated the Slovakian Constitution insofar as it breached the operator's constitutional right to enjoyment of his property. It set the decision aside and sent it back to the Supreme Court to give a new ruling. The latter, instead referred the matter to the Court of Justice on the point of EU law.

Case C–416/10 *Križan* v *Slovenská inšpekcia životného prostredia*, Judgment of 15 January 2013

66. A reference for a preliminary ruling is based on a dialogue between one court and another, the initiation of which depends entirely on the national court's assessment as to whether that reference is appropriate and necessary ...

67. Moreover, the existence of a national procedural rule cannot call into question the discretion of national courts to make a reference to the Court of Justice for a preliminary ruling where they have doubts, as in the case of the main proceedings, as to the interpretation of European Union law ...

68. A rule of national law, pursuant to which legal rulings of a higher court bind another national court, cannot take away from the latter court the discretion to refer to the Court of Justice questions of interpretation of the points of European Union law concerned by such legal rulings. That court must be free, if it considers that a higher court's legal ruling could lead it to deliver a judgment contrary to European Union law, to refer to the Court of Justice questions which concern it ...

---

[62] Case C-365/02 *Lindfors* [2004] ECR I-7183. T. Tridimas, 'Knocking on Heaven's Door: Fragmentation, Efficiency and Defiance in the Preliminary Reference Procedure' (2003) 40 *CMLRev.* 9, 21–6.

[63] For an early example see Case 166/73 *Rheinmühlen-Düsseldorf* v *Einfuhr- und Vorratstelle für Getreide* [1974] ECR 33.

69. At this stage, it must be noted that the national court, having exercised the discretion conferred on it by Article 267 TFEU, is bound, for the purposes of the decision to be given in the main proceedings, by the interpretation of the provisions at issue given by the Court of Justice and must, if necessary, disregard the rulings of the higher court if it considers, in the light of that interpretation, that they are not consistent with European Union law ...

70. The principles set out in the previous paragraphs apply in the same way to the referring court with regard to the legal position expressed, in the present case in the main proceedings, by the constitutional court of the Member State concerned insofar as it follows from well-established case-law that rules of national law, even of a constitutional order, cannot be allowed to undermine the unity and effectiveness of European Union law ... Moreover, the Court of Justice has already established that those principles apply to relations between a constitutional court and all other national courts ...

71. The national rule which obliges the Najvyšší súd Slovenskej republiky to follow the legal position of the Ústavný súd Slovenskej republiky cannot therefore prevent the referring court from submitting a request for a preliminary ruling to the Court of Justice at any point in the proceedings which it judges appropriate, and to set aside, if necessary, the assessments made by the Ústavný súd Slovenskej republiky which might prove to be contrary to European Union law.

72. Finally, as a supreme court, the Najvyšší súd Slovenskej republiky is even required to submit a request for a preliminary ruling to the Court of Justice when it finds that the substance of the dispute concerns a question to be resolved which comes within the scope of the first paragraph of Article 267 TFEU. The possibility of bringing, before the constitutional court of the Member State concerned, an action against the decisions of a national court, limited to an examination of a potential infringement of the rights and freedoms guaranteed by the national constitution or by an international agreement, cannot allow the view to be taken that that national court cannot be classified as a court against whose decisions there is no judicial remedy under national law within the meaning of the third paragraph of Article 267 TFEU.

The second issue concerns the timing of the reference. It might be felt that, as national courts are creations of the domestic legal order, resort should first be had to domestic processes to determine the validity of a measure under domestic law, before a reference is made under Article 267 TFEU.[64] In *Melki*, two Algerians were stopped at a police check in France 20 kilometres from the Belgian border. They were detained and issued with a deportation order. They argued, unsuccessfully, that the initial check was illegal as it breached the principle that the European Union should be an area without internal frontiers. Before that, the Court of Justice had to rule on the *question prioritaire de constitutionnalité*, a 2010 constitutional reform, which required any question about the constitutionality of a French statute to be referred, in the first place, to the French Conseil Constitutionnel. This had complications for Article 267 TFEU as a violation of EU law was treated in France as a violation of the Constitution. The reform suggested, therefore, that the Conseil Constitutionnel should rule on these matters before the Court of Justice.

---

[64] For an argument that deference should now be had to national hierarchies see Opinion of Advocate General Villalón in Case C-173/09 *Elchinov* [2010] ECR I-8889, paras. 25–37.

Joined Cases C–188/10 and C–189/10 *Melki and Abdeli* [2010] ECR I–5667

52. According to the settled case law of the Court, in order to ensure the primacy of EU law, the functioning of that system of cooperation requires the national court to be free to refer to the Court of Justice for a preliminary ruling any question that it considers necessary, at whatever stage of the proceedings it considers appropriate, even at the end of an interlocutory procedure for the review of constitutionality.

53. Insofar as national law lays down an obligation to initiate an interlocutory procedure for the review of constitutionality, which would prevent the national court from immediately disapplying a national legislative provision which it considers to be contrary to EU law, the functioning of the system established by Article 267 TFEU nevertheless requires that that court be free, first, to adopt any measure necessary to ensure the provisional judicial protection of the rights conferred under the European Union's legal order and, second, to disapply, at the end of such an interlocutory procedure, that national legislative provision if that court holds it to be contrary to EU law.

54. It should also be observed that the priority nature of an interlocutory procedure for the review of the constitutionality of a national law, the content of which merely transposes the mandatory provisions of a European Union directive, cannot undermine the jurisdiction of the Court of Justice alone to declare an act of the European Union invalid, and in particular a directive, the purpose of that jurisdiction being to guarantee legal certainty by ensuring that EU law is applied uniformly ...

55. To the extent that the priority nature of an interlocutory procedure for the review of constitutionality leads to the repeal of a national law – which merely transposes the mandatory provisions of a European Union directive – on the basis that that law is contrary to the national constitution, the Court could, in practice, be denied the possibility, at the request of the courts ruling on the substance of cases in the Member State concerned, of reviewing the validity of that directive in relation to the same grounds relating to the requirements of primary law, and in particular the rights recognised by the Charter of Fundamental Rights of the European Union, to which Article 6 TEU accords the same legal value as that accorded to the Treaties.

56. Before the interlocutory review of the constitutionality of a law – the content of which merely transposes the mandatory provisions of a European Union directive – can be carried out in relation to the same grounds which cast doubt on the validity of the directive, national courts against whose decisions there is no judicial remedy under national law are, as a rule, required – under the third paragraph of Article 267 TFEU – to refer to the Court of Justice a question on the validity of that directive and, thereafter, to draw the appropriate conclusions resulting from the preliminary ruling given by the Court, unless the court which initiates the interlocutory review of constitutionality has itself referred that question to the Court pursuant to the second paragraph of Article 267 TFEU. In the case of a national implementing law with such content, the question of whether the directive is valid takes priority, in the light of the obligation to transpose that directive. In addition, imposing a strict time-limit on the examination by the national courts cannot prevent the reference for a preliminary ruling on the validity of the directive in question.

If domestic courts choose to make a reference, they are bound neither by decisions of higher national courts[65] nor by any domestic procedure which impedes it. This allows lower courts, in particular, to break free from national judicial hierarchies. They are part of a new judicial order, the Union one, to which they can grant precedence over the domestic one. The court

---

[65] They can even continue with a reference if their decision has been overturned on appeal, Case C-210/06 *Cartesio* [2008] ECR I-9641.

structure of the EU judicial order is a flat one. All national courts are granted equal possibilities to make a reference to the Court of Justice and no national court can disenfranchise another national court. However, above them all, with the power to make binding judgments sits the Court of Justice. For lower courts scornful of higher courts or feeling unduly constrained by national judicial hierarchies, the EU judicial order is one which offers them many opportunities.

K. Alter, 'The European Court's Political Power' (1996) 19 *West European Politics* 458, 466–7

While EC law supremacy posed a threat to the influence and authority of high courts and implied a significant compromise of national sovereignty, lower courts found few costs and numerous benefits in making their own referrals to the ECJ and in applying EC law. Being courts of first instance, lower-court judges were used to having another court hierarchically above them, and to having their judgments re-written by courts above. They also did not have to worry about how their individual actions might upset legal certainty or the smooth functioning of the legal system. Thus, they were more open to sending to the ECJ broad and provocative legal questions about the reach and effects of European law in the national legal order. There were also many benefits for lower courts in taking advantage of the ECJ and in invoking EC law. It allowed lower courts to circumvent the restrictive jurisprudence of higher courts, and to re-open legal debates which had been closed, and thus to try for legal outcomes of their preference for policy or legal reasons. For example, recourse to EC law allowed pro-women industrial tribunals to circumvent the Employment Appeals Tribunal and the Conservative government, to get legal outcomes which helped them to promote equal pay for men and women. Having an ECJ decision also magnified the influence of the lower-court decisions in the legal process, as the decision became part of established legal precedence, and it sometimes led to journal articles on decisions which otherwise would not have been publicly reported, but which were able to decisively contribute to the development of national law. Having an ECJ decision behind a lower-court decision also made its reversal by a higher court less likely. Thus, it actually bolstered the legal power and influence of the lower courts. For a lower court, the ECJ was akin to a second parent where parental approval wards off sanction. When a lower court did not like what it thought one parent (a higher national court) would say, or it did not agree with what one parent said, it would ask the other parent (the ECJ). Having the other parent's approval decreased the likelihood of sanctions for challenging legal precedence or government policy. If the lower court, however, did not think that it would like what that other parent might say, it could follow the 'don't ask and the ECJ can't tell' policy and not make a referral.

The different strategic calculations of national courts vis-à-vis the ECJ created a competition-between-courts dynamic of legal integration; this fed the process of legal integration and came to shift the national legal context from under high courts. The limitations on interpretation of national law created by high courts provoked lower courts to make referrals to the ECJ. This enabled lower courts to deviate from established jurisprudence or to obtain preferred new legal outcomes. In so using EC law and the ECJ to achieve outcomes, lower courts created opportunities for the ECJ to expand its jurisdiction and jurisprudence, and, in some cases they actually goaded the ECJ to expand the legal authority of EC law even further. In this respect, one can say that lower courts were the motors of EC legal integration into the national order, and legal expansion through their referrals to the ECJ.

(ii) Subjects of the EU judicial order

Within the framework of Article 267 TFEU, it is everything to be a court or tribunal. National courts and tribunals become gate-keepers for those seeking access to the Court of Justice and independent actors in their own right with new powers to ask questions of the Court of Justice and influence the contours of EU law across the Union. However, throughout the Union, a variety of professional, regulatory and arbitral bodies, not formally designated as courts under national law, adjudicate upon EU law. It would be a problem if a body recognised in one Member State as a court could make a reference, but a functionally identical body in another Member State was unable to do so because it was not recognised as a court there.

In *Broeckmeulen*, the Court of Justice ruled that the uniformity of EU law required that a Union definition be provided for what constituted a court or tribunal for the purposes of Article 267 TFEU.[66] This should be a broad definition, which should include many bodies that were not formally courts within the national legal system. Thus, the Court held that an appeal committee within the Dutch professional body, regulating entry of doctors to the profession, constituted a court because it determined individual rights under EU law, acted under governmental legal supervision and employed quasi-legal procedures.

Over the years, the Court has refined the qualities necessary for a body to be a court. Bodies must be independent, be established by law, have a compulsory jurisdiction, and be taking a decision of a judicial nature.[67]

The criterion of independence means that the body must stand as a third party in relation to the actor which took the decision. It neither took the decision nor was it the subject of the decision.[68] It must have no organisational links with any of the parties appearing before it and no interest in the outcome of the proceedings before it.[69] There must also be more general safeguards protecting the body from external pressure liable to jeopardise the independent judgement of its members as regards the proceedings before them. In *Gabalfrisa*, the Court of Justice considered the Tribunales Ecónomico-Administrativos, which review decisions of the tax authorities in Spain, to be courts.[70] Although members of these bodies were appointed and dismissed by the minister, there was considered to be a clear separation of functions between them and the tax authority. However, this may have to be reviewed in the light of *Syfait*, where the Court did not consider the Greek competition authority to be a court even though it was formally independent, as there were insufficient guarantees against dismissal of its members by the Minister for Economic Development.[71] Similarly, in *Häupl*, an Austrian patent body which heard appeals against decisions of the Austrian patent office was held to be a court because the independence of its members was protected by a five-year term of office which could only be terminated for 'exceptional and well-defined reasons'.[72]

---

[66] Case 246/80 *Broeckmeulen v Huisarts Registratie Commissie* [1981] ECR 2311.

[67] See recently, Case C-363/11 *Epitropos tou Elegktikou Sinedriou sto Ipourgio Politismou kai Tourismou v Ipourgio Politismou kai Tourismou – Ipiresia Dimosionomikou Elenchou*, Judgment of 19 December 2012.

[68] Case C-506/04 *Wilson v Ordre des avocats du barreau de Luxembourg* [2006] ECR I-8613.

[69] Case C-24/92 *Corbiau v Administration des Contributions* [1993] ECR I-1277; Case C-516/99 *Schmid* [2002] ECR I-4573.

[70] Joined Cases C-110/98–C-147/98 *Gabalfrisa* [2000] ECR I-1577.

[71] Case C-53/03 *Syfait v Glaxo Smith Kline* [2005] ECR I-4609.

[72] Case C-246/05 *Häupl v Lidl* [2007] ECR I-4673, para. 18.

Secondly, the body must have a compulsory jurisdiction over the activities in question. Arbitration panels cannot, therefore, be a court for the purposes of Article 267 TFEU as parties opt in to such arrangements.[73]

Finally, the body must take decisions of a judicial nature. This goes to the nature of the activity being carried out rather than the status of the body, so it is perfectly possible for a court not to be able to refer if it is carrying out non-judicial activity. Decisions of a judicial nature are contrasted with those of an administrative nature. Courts allocating the surname to a child,[74] or registering a company[75] have been held to be administrative activities which cannot give rise to a reference. Similarly, regulatory bodies which can hear equal opportunities cases and even impose fines were held to be administrative in nature as challenges to their decisions took the form of a review before the court in which they were the defendant and they could also bring public interest litigation in their own right.[76] By contrast, if a court hears an appeal against such a decision, its decision will be considered to be of a judicial nature.[77]

The consequence is that a number of public bodies have been found to be courts, notwithstanding that they are not part of the formal judiciaries of their Member States. They include immigration adjudicators,[78] professional disciplinary bodies,[79] bodies established to review public contracts[80] or planning decisions,[81] and tax adjudicators.[82] It is not always easy to determine which bodies may refer and the Court has been attacked on two fronts.

First, it is argued that the definition is too narrow. Any body which decides on EU law rights should be able to refer. Otherwise, it is argued, individuals will have to challenge the decision of that body before another body in order to have the possibility of a reference. This adds expense and time and provides a disincentive for parties to seek a referral. Such a view would allow private bodies to refer and would probably not be too worried about whether the decision is of a judicial nature, as all that matters is a denial of rights.[83] Such a critique is, however, open to a floodgates argument as it would allow an extensive array of poorly trained bodies to overload the Court of Justice's docket by sending large numbers of references.

The other criticism is that the current definition is too wide.[84] Advocate General Colomer has argued that the development of EU law is to take place through a judicial dialogue within the framework of Article 267 TFEU. Administrative and regulatory agencies should not be part of that conversation. Colomer also notes many practical consequences of a wide definition.

---

[73] Case 102/81 *Nordsee Deutsche Hochseefischerei* v *Reederei Mond Hochseefischerei* [1982] ECR 1095; Case C-125/04 *Denuit* [2005] ECR I-923.

[74] Case C-96/04 *Standesamt Stadt Niebüll* [2006] ECR I-3561.

[75] Case C-182/00 *Lutz* [2002] ECR I-547.

[76] Case C-394/11 *Belov*, Judgment of 31 January 2013.

[77] Case C-14/08 *Roda Golf and Beach Resort* [2009] ECR I-5439.

[78] Case C-416/96 *El Yassini* v *Secretary of State for the Home Department* [1999] ECR I-1209.

[79] Case C-118/09 *Koller* [2010] ECR I-13629.

[80] Case C-54/96 *Dorsch* v *Bundesbaugesellschaft Berlin* [1997] ECR I-4961; Case C-92/00 *HI* v *Stadt Wien* [2002] ECR I-5553.

[81] Case C-205/08 *Umweltanwalt von Kärnten* v *Kärntner Landesregierung* [2009] ECR I-11525.

[82] Case C-17/00 *De Coster* [2001] ECR I-9445.

[83] G. Bebr, 'Arbitration Tribunals and Article 177 of the EEC Treaty' (1985) 22 *CMLRev.* 489.

[84] See his Opinions in Case C-17/00 *De Coster* [2001] ECR I-9445; Case C-205/08 *Umweltanwalt von Kärnten* v *Kärntner Landesregierung* [2009] ECR I-11525.

It allows bodies with no legal training to formulate references and statements. It has led to unclear restrictions being placed on referrals by courts, notably the test of whether they are doing something of a judicial nature. Most crucially, he argues, it allows administrative actors to disrupt stable domestic judicial hierarchies and systems of judicial precedent by making a reference if they do not agree with these hierarchies or judgments.

(iii) Unified Patent Court as a challenge to the EU judicial order

The European Patent Convention, a 1973 international agreement currently ratified by thirty-eight states, allows for the grant and registration of European patents at the European Patent Office, in Munich. These European patents do not have unitary effects. Instead, they offer protection through the patent laws of each Member State, with the scope of protection varying according to that offered by the national law in question. Twenty-five EU Member States agreed to rectify this by granting unitary effects within their territories to European patents which were registered with the European Patent Office. These patents will have uniform protection and equal effect in all participating states. To secure this, twenty-five EU Member States (all the Member States other than Croatia, Poland and Spain) signed an international agreement establishing a Unified Patent Court (UPC).[85] This court forms part of the EU judicial order set out by Article 267 TFEU but also offers an alternative pattern of judicial cooperation.

The court is, in the first place, specialised. Almost all civil litigation surrounding the patent with unitary effects is to be handled by it.[86] By contrast, the Court of Justice is a general court, with its remit covering the whole of EU law. It also has no monopoly over adjudication of disputes involving EU law.

Secondly, unlike Article 267 TFEU, it comprises a genuine supranational judicial system. The Unified Patent Court, thus, comprises a Court of First Instance, a Court of Appeal and a Registry.[87] All cases are heard, in the first place, by the Court of First Instance.[88] This will have a central division, which is predominantly based in Paris but has specialised subsections in London and Munich.[89] It can also have local divisions set up in a single contracting state, with each state allowed to have up to four divisions within it,[90] and regional divisions which comprise divisions set up for two or more states.[91] Conflicts of law provisions allocate jurisdiction between the divisions.[92] Parties unsuccessful at the Court of First Instance may appeal within two months to the Court of Appeal based at Luxembourg.[93]

Thirdly, if these divisions go to creating a significant supranational judiciary dispersed across the Union, the composition of these divisions is also supranational. Court of First Instance judgments, whether at central, regional or local levels, will be given by panels of three judges, with any panel having a multinational composition.[94]

Fourthly, unlike the Court of Justice, the Unified Patent Court, in making its judgments, can interpret national law in addition to EU and international law.

---

[85] Agreement on a Unified Patent Court [2013] OJ C175/01 (UPC).
[86] Article 32 UPC.   [87] Article 6(1) UPC.   [88] Article 33(1) UPC.
[89] Article 7(2) and Annex II UPC.   [90] Article 7(3) and (4) UPC.   [91] Article 7(5) UPC.
[92] Article 33 UPC.   [93] Article 73(1) UPC.
[94] Article 8(1) UPC. The Court of Appeal must also comprise nationals of different states, Article 9(1) UPC.

Article 24(1) UPC

1. In full compliance with Article 20, when hearing a case brought before it under this Agreement, the Court shall base its decisions on:
   (a) Union law, including Regulation (EU) No. 1257/2012 and Regulation (EU) No. 1260/2012;
   (b) this Agreement;
   (c) the European Patent Convention;
   (d) other international agreements applicable to patents and binding on all the Contracting Member States; and
   (e) national law.

However, for all this, the Unified Patent Court still has to be seen as part of the EU judicial order. EU law is, thus, granted a special status amongst these different sources of law.

Article 20 UPC

The Court shall apply Union law in its entirety and shall respect its primacy.
   Consequently, the Unified Patent Court may make references to the Court of Justice, and the judgments of the latter are binding on it.

Article 21 UPC

As a court common to the Contracting Member States and as part of their judicial system, the Court shall cooperate with the Court of Justice of the European Union to ensure the correct application and uniform interpretation of Union law, as any national court, in accordance with Article 267 TFEU in particular. Decisions of the Court of Justice of the European Union shall be binding on the Court.

If the Unified Patent Court forms part of the EU judicial order, it also acts as a counterpoint to the rest of that order setting out an alternative model of division of judicial responsibilities.

4 FUNCTIONS OF THE PRELIMINARY REFERENCE PROCEDURE

(i) Development of EU law

The reference procedure is significant quantitatively and qualitatively. Of the 632 new cases in 2012, 404 (about 64 per cent)[95] were preliminary references. Almost all the Court of Justice's significant rulings, other than those concerning the remit of the powers of the EU institutions, have come via the preliminary reference procedure. This is no surprise. The procedure sets out numerous decentralised laboratories for the testing and exploration of EU law, in the form of national courts and tribunals, which are, by and large, accessible to private parties. When these find something interesting or complex, they will refer the

---

[95] *Annual Report*, n. 13 above, 90.

matter to the Court of Justice, and, as we have seen, there are incentives particularly for lower courts to make such a reference. It is, thus, through the preliminary reference procedure that the Court of Justice has been able to open up and widen the horizons of EU law through the establishment of new doctrines and principles; systematise EU law through bringing disparate cases under unifying schema and categories; and revisit case law in the light of experience in national arenas.

This places the Court of Justice in an extremely powerful position. A single institution has close to a monopoly over the development of a legal order for half a billion people. It raises the question as to how effectively it is equipped to develop that legal order. In its early years, the Court justified its role by virtue of its greater expertise. In *Rheinmühlen* it stated that Article 267 TFEU made 'available to the national judge a means of eliminating difficulties which may be occasioned by the requirement of giving Community law its full effect'.[96] In other words, it could help national judges struggling to make sense of a new legal system. To be sure, the development of EU law has been facilitated by the presence of a dominant authoritative voice.

Nevertheless, over the years, a number of concerns have emerged.

The first is that the Court of Justice has engaged in judicial activism. The phrase is a polemical and elusive one but seems to have two charges hidden within it. One charge is of judicial legislation. The Court is giving judgments on matters which should be left either to the EU legislature or the Treaty framers. The allegation is that it is no longer engaging in bona fide interpretation of an EU legal text, but is going beyond that. Typically, the claim will, therefore, be that the judgment of the Court is *contra legem*. It goes against any conventional understandings of the text.[97] Although studies show that where two or more national governments make observations before the Court it is likely to follow the same path,[98] there is still a perception that it is not receptive to their concerns about legislative limits. It may be that national government concerns are prompted by its being difficult to amend a disliked Court of Justice ruling. Interpretations of the Treaties will require a Treaty amendment whilst those of EU legislation will require new legislation, which will typically involve a qualified majority or all Member States voting for it. There is an argument, because of this, for greater judicial sensitivity. In 2013, therefore, the Dutch Government indicated that situations where the Court of Justice interpreted EU legislation in a manner unanticipated by the legislature should be avoided, and proactive behaviour should be taken by the legislature to correct such judgments.[99]

The more common allegation is that judgments invariably push towards greater integration, and take insufficient account of other interests. The basis for these allegations lies, in part, in the growth of a Euro-law industry, comprising EU law academics, legal officials of the EU institutions and EU law practitioners who have an interest in the growth of EU law. These will bring test cases, develop new legal doctrines, write articles suggesting new developments and,

---

[96] Case 166/73 *Rheinmühlen-Düsseldorf* v *Einfuhr- und Vorratstelle für Getreide* [1974] ECR 33.

[97] On such a controversy see S. Garben, 'Sky-High Controversy and High-Flying Claims? The *Sturgeon* Case Law in Light of Judicial Activism, Euroscepticism and Eurolegalism' (2013) 50 *CMLRev.* 15.

[98] M. P. Granger, 'When Governments go to Luxembourg ...: The Influence of Governments on the European Court of Justice' (2004) 29 *ELRev.* 1; C. Carubba *et al.*, 'Judicial Behavior under Political Constraints: Evidence from the European Court of Justice' (2008) 102 *APSR* 435.

[99] See www.government.nl/documents-and-publications/notes/2013/06/21/testing-european-legislation-for-subsidiarity-and-proportionality-dutch-list-of-points-for-action.html.

in the case of the EU institutions, institute new legal practice right at the edge of EU law.[100] It is argued that this industry has been more vocal in the preliminary reference procedure than other actors. There are thus far more references arguing for EU legal provisions to cover activities not previously anticipated as being covered by them than for curtailment of these provisions. Insofar as the Court accedes to this, it can lead to a tilt.

The other support for this criticism lies in the style of reasoning deployed by the Court. The use of teleological reasoning is particularly present in the judgments of the Court of Justice.[101] The legal provision will be interpreted in the light of some *telos*, a broader objective (i.e. free movement of goods, effective protection of individual rights or equal treatment)[102] or overall scheme[103] to which the provision is claimed to give effect.

G. Conway, *The Limits of Legal Reasoning and the European Court of Justice* (Cambridge, Cambridge University Press, 2012) 274–5

Teleological interpretation writ large presents several fundamental problems. First, the telos or ends can be understood in varying ways. Without some further control or definition, uncertainty and unpredictability become prominent. The level of generality of ends or teloi, especially, can be altered freely within the method of the ECJ. This is problematic because not every level of generality is equally valid or legitimate. The approach of the ECJ to identify the highest level of generality, ever-increasing integration, ignores the contestability of the extent of legal integration. This approach conceives of legitimacy on the basis of a simple linear narrative of integration ... The extent to which integration should proceed is fundamentally a matter for the constituent power in the EU, which is the Member States, rather than for EU institutional practice to determine autonomously of the Member States. This understanding of the authority of the Member States is inherent in the principle of conferral.

Teleological interpretation as practised by the ECJ results in a strange epistemological asymmetry in how law is interpreted, by opening up a sharp cleavage between the interpretation of participants in the legal system and the judiciary ... Ordinary citizens do not engage in meta-teleological interpretation in adhering to the law on an everyday basis; they look to the most specific, relevant legal provisions, i.e. they adhere to *lex specialis*. This is inevitable, since in the absence of *lex specialis* as a controlling factor, every time a citizen was confronted with a choice of whether to obey the law or not, he or she would have to engage in an overall assessment of the legal system.

If this style of reasoning has its critics,[104] it also has supporters. These argue that interpretation is not a valueless process but must have reference to common collective values, which

---

[100] H. Schepel and R. Wesseling, 'The Legal Community: Judges, Lawyers, Officials and Clerks in the Writing of Europe' (1997) 3 *ELJ* 165; S. Lee Mudge and A. Vauchez, 'Building Europe on a Weak Field: Law, Economics and Scholarly Avatars in Transnational Politics' (2012) 118 *American Journal of Sociology* 449.

[101] The most careful analysis of this reasoning is J. Bengoetxea, *The Legal Reasoning of the European Court of Justice* (Oxford, Oxford University Press, 1993).

[102] In some cases, this is implicit. EU citizenship provisions are, thus, interpreted in light of the intent of EU citizenship which is 'to be the fundamental status of nationals of the Member States'. Joined Cases C-356/11 and C-357/11 *O and S v Maahanmuuttovirasto*, Judgment of 6 December 2012, para. 44.

[103] E.g. Case C-488/11 *Brusse v Jahani*, Judgment of 30 May 2013.

[104] For similar criticism see H. Rasmussen, *On Law and Policy of the European Court of Justice* (Dordrecht, Martijnus Nijhoff, 1986); M. Dawson, 'The Political Face of Judicial Activism: Europe's Law-Politics Balance' in M. Dawson et al., *Judicial Activism at the Court of Justice* (Cheltenham, Edward Elgar, 2013) 11, 21–2.

must, as EU values, necessarily be pan-Union in nature and scale.[105] Insofar as the judiciary is to act independently from other arms of government, these values must have an autonomous quality.[106] In addition, it is claimed, criticisms of teleological reasoning ignore the Court of Justice's institutional role, which is to secure a functioning legal order. This necessarily requires it to engage in significant elaboration of legal provisions to relate them to other parts of EU law, some general sense of coherence, and enable operability where, otherwise, there would be none.[107] This might all be the case but there is a feeling that the two sides of the debate run past each other. Even if these reasons justified teleological reasoning, they would not rob it of its slipperiness and unpredictability as a form of reasoning. In this, Article 24 UPC offers a possible counter-balance, as it offers a variety of sources of law in addition to EU law which comprise international treaties, that treaty and national law. As these sources have equal weight, the Unified Patent Court will not be able to interpret the law exclusively in the light of EU objectives. Instead, it will have to adopt a more plural approach which *balances* the claims of the different legal instruments and different legal orders.

The second criticism made of the Court is that it lacks expertise. Its remit covers a wide array of activities. A typical week can include cases on competition, asylum law, anti-dumping and environmental law. These fields of law will often involve reference to specialised fields of knowledge which inform them, but are not legal in nature. This might be industrial economics in competition law; natural science in environmental or patent law; or accountancy in anti-dumping law. The benefits of a single court are that it can ensure general principles still act to govern all these fields of activity, thereby ensuring coherence and the generality of important EU legal values whilst preventing any field of EU law becoming too ghettoised. However, there is a greater danger of mistake as the Court lacks the detailed knowledge to appreciate the nuances of different fields of law. For some time, therefore, it has been suggested that specialised courts be used for complex, fact-intensive areas of EU law.[108] The General Court is a step in that direction, as much of its work focuses on external trade law, competition law and trade mark law. The Unified Patent Court is a further step in this direction in relation to patent law. It is an ongoing question whether the balance between specialised jurisdictions and a general one is the optimal one.

(ii) Judicial review of EU institutions

Article 267 TFEU allows the Court of Justice to rule on the validity of EU legislation and administrative acts of the EU institutions.[109] Typically, a national measure implementing the EU act will be challenged before a national court, which will then ask whether the EU measure

---

[105] A. Arnull, 'Judicial Activism and the European Court of Justice: How Should Academics Respond?' in M. Dawson *et al.*, *Judicial Activism at the Court of Justice* (Cheltenham, Edward Elgar, 2013).

[106] J. Weiler, 'The Court of Justice on Trial' (1987) 24 *CMLRev.* 555; J. Bengoetxea *et al.*, 'Integration and Integrity in the Legal Reasoning of the European Court of Justice' in G. de Búrca and J. Weiler (eds.), *The European Court of Justice* (Oxford, Oxford University Press, 2001).

[107] T. Horsley, 'Reflections on the Role of the Court of Justice as the "Motor" of European Integration: Legal Limits to Judicial Lawmaking' (2013) 50 *CMLRev.* 931.

[108] P. Kapteyn, 'The Court of Justice of the European Communities after the Year 2000' in D. Curtin and T. Heukels (eds.), *Institutional Dynamics of European Integration: Liber Amicorum Schermers* (Dordrecht, Martijnus Nijhoff, 1994) vol. I, 135, 141–5.

[109] Joined Cases 133–136/85 *Rau* v *Bundesanstalt für Landwirtschaftliche Marktordnung* [1987] ECR 2289.

which provides the legal basis for the national measure is lawful or not. This generates complications, however, about its relationship to those procedures which allow individuals to go directly to the Court of Justice to seek judicial review of acts of the EU institutions.[110] It must, in particular, navigate a course between two positions. One sees a danger of forum-shopping where parties could circumvent the restrictions imposed by one procedure by going through the other. The other sees each procedure acting to correct flaws in the other by allowing parties wrongly deprived of the possibility of seeking review under the latter the possibility of another avenue.

In *Jégo-Quéré*, a French company, fishing for whitebait (a very small fish), wished to challenge a Commission Regulation which set minimum mesh sizes for nets. These were so big that the whitebait could pass through the nets. It could not challenge the measure before a national court, as the Commission Regulation provided for no implementing measures, so there was no national law to challenge. It sought to challenge the Regulation directly before the Court of Justice under Article 263(4) TFEU, the provision allowing individuals to seek direct judicial review of acts of the EU institutions.[111] The Court held that there was no standing under that provision. However, the absence of standing imposed corollary duties on national authorities to allow individuals to challenge measures before national courts, who could then refer the matter.

Case C-263/02P *Jégo-Quéré* v *Commission* [2004] ECR I-3425

29. It should be noted that individuals are entitled to effective judicial protection of the rights they derive from the Community legal order, and the right to such protection is one of the general principles of law stemming from the constitutional traditions common to the Member States. That right has also been enshrined in Articles 6 and 13 of the ECHR ...

30. By Articles [263 and 268 TFEU] ... on the one hand, and by Article [267 TFEU], on the other, the Treaty has established a complete system of legal remedies and procedures designed to ensure review of the legality of acts of the institutions, and has entrusted such review to the Community Courts. Under that system, where natural or legal persons cannot, by reason of the conditions for admissibility laid down in the fourth paragraph of Article [263 TFEU], directly challenge Community measures of general application, they are able, depending on the case, either indirectly to plead the invalidity of such acts before the Community Courts under Article [268 TFEU] or to do so before the national courts and ask them, since they have no jurisdiction themselves to declare those measures invalid, to make a reference to the Court of Justice for a preliminary ruling on validity ...

31. Thus it is for the Member States to establish a system of legal remedies and procedures which ensure respect for the right to effective judicial protection ...

32. In that context, in accordance with the principle of sincere cooperation laid down in Article [4 TEU], national courts are required, so far as possible, to interpret and apply national procedural rules governing the exercise of rights of action in a way that enables natural and legal persons to challenge before the courts the legality of any decision or other national measure relative to the application to them of a Community act of general application, by pleading the invalidity of such an act ...

The duty on national courts to allow challenges to the legality of EU acts before them, which can, or in some cases, must be referred makes the preliminary reference procedure a central

---

[110] On these see pp. 444–64.   [111] See pp. 444–52.

instrument for judicial review of EU acts.[112] Private parties are not required to meet restrictive *locus standi* requirements to bring the matter before their local court. By contrast, the standing requirements for direct access to the Court of Justice are highly restrictive.[113] However, the preliminary reference procedure cannot be used to review an EU measure if a party had *locus standi* to challenge a measure directly before the Court of Justice but failed to bring the action within the necessary time limits. In *TWD*, a German textile company sought to challenge a 1985 Commission Decision declaring a German subsidy to it to be incompatible with the EU law on state aids by asking for a preliminary reference from a German court in 1992.[114] The applicant was only barred from bringing a direct action as the time limits for such an action, under Article 263(5) TFEU, are within two months of the Decision becoming known to it. The Court refused, stating that once the time limit had expired legal certainty required that the national court be bound by the Commission Decision and could not, therefore, raise the question of its validity.[115]

In many cases, it might not be clear whether parties have *locus standi* or not, and two months is a short period in which to decide which avenue to pursue. The Court has, therefore, stated that references will only be barred where parties 'undoubtedly' have standing under one of the procedures which allow direct judicial review.[116] The meaning of this is unclear, with the Court sometimes just determining that a party does not have *locus standi* under these procedures, and a reference can therefore be made.[117] In a couple of cases, the Court has been a little clearer, indicating that the party must be one of a determinate number of parties identified in an EU measure to trigger such a bar.[118]

(iii) Preserving the unity of EU law

The unity of the EU legal system and the uniform application of EU law has repeatedly been held by the Court of Justice to require that EU law 'normally be given an autonomous and uniform interpretation throughout the European Union'.[119] This autonomy and uniformity of interpretation can be undermined in at least two ways. It could happen if national courts took divergent interpretations of the same provision of EU law or if a national court in one Member State considered an EU measure valid whilst a court in another Member State considered it invalid. The requirement of uniformity, thus, grants the Court of Justice a privileged position as it is seen as the only court which can provide authoritative guidance on the interpretation and validity of EU law, which will be accepted across the Union.[120]

---

[112] Case 314/85 *Firma Fotofrost* v *Hauptzollamt Lübeck-Ost* [1987] ECR 4199.
[113] See pp. 451–2.
[114] Case C-188/92 *TWD Textilwerke Deggendorf* v *Germany* [1994] ECR I-833.
[115] D. Wyatt, 'The Relationship between Actions for Annulment and References on Validity after TWD Deggendorf' in J. Lonbay and A. Biondi (eds.), *Remedies for Breach of EC Law* (Chichester, John Wiley, 1997).
[116] Case C-239/99 *Nachi Europe* v *Hauptzollamt Krefeld* [2001] ECR I-1197.
[117] Case C-343/07 *Bavaria and Bavaria Italia* v *Bayerischer Brauerbund* [2009] ECR I-5491.
[118] Joined Cases C-346/03 and C-529/03 *Atzeni et al.* v *Regione autonoma della Sardegna* [2006] ECR I-1875; Case C-550/09 *E and F* [2010] ECR I-6123.
[119] Case C-281/09 *Commission* v *Spain*, Judgment of 24 November 2011, para. 42.
[120] For its views see European Court of Justice, *The Future of the Judicial System of the European Union* (Luxembourg, 1999) 17.

There are two elements to this role: the Court's position with regard to the interpretation of EU law and its privileges in relation to the validity of EU instruments.

If the Court is to give authoritative rulings on EU law, this begs the question as to what EU law is. The first principle which guides the Court here is that there should be uniform application of EU law. Although Article 267 TFEU, thus, only talks of the Court giving rulings on the Treaties and acts of the EU institutions, the Court has, consequently, interpreted it more broadly to include anything which forms part of the wider EU legal order. This includes international agreements concluded prior to the establishment of the European Communities to which the Union has succeeded the Member States[121] and general principles of law and fundamental rights.[122] These generate various kinds of binding effect in EU law, as we shall see, but international agreements and fundamental rights transcend it in that they extend to activities not governed by EU law. The Court has held that it will still rule on their provisions, notwithstanding that they apply to situations governed by both domestic and EU law, and will be invoked more frequently in the former context. In *Hermès*, the Court considered a provision of the WTO Agreement on Trade Related Intellectual Property Rights which concerned enforcement of intellectual property rights. This largely fell within national competence.[123] The Court nevertheless held that insofar as the provision could potentially cover situations which fell within the scope of EU law, most notably where intellectual property rights generated by EU law were infringed, the provision required uniform interpretation, and could be subject to a reference.

The Court has been concerned to secure not just uniformity of application of EU law but also an interpretive unity. EU law, wherever it arises, should be interpreted in the same way.[124] This has led it to accept references on matters that do not fall within EU legal competences but where there is, nevertheless, a reference to EU law. The Court will, thus, give rulings wherever national law refers to the contents of provisions of EU law or reproduces the wording of EU provisions.[125] In *Dzodzi*, a Togolese woman challenged a decision by the Belgian authorities refusing her a residence permit following the death of her Belgian husband: a situation governed exclusively by Belgian law.[126] The Belgian law stated, however, that the spouses of Belgian nationals should be treated in the same way as spouses of other EU nationals, whose treatment was governed by EU law. In other words, the standard for Belgian law was to be that set in EU law. The Court ruled it to be in the EU legal interest that it give a ruling, on the grounds that every EU provision should be given a uniform interpretation, irrespective of the circumstances in which it is to be applied, in order to forestall future differences in interpretation.[127]

---

[121] Joined Cases 267–269/81 *Amministrazione delle Finanze dello Stato* v *SPI* [1983] ECR 801.

[122] E.g. Case 11/70 *Internationale Handelsgesellschaft* v *Einfuhr und Vorratsstelle Getreide* [1970] ECR 1125.

[123] Case C-53/96 *Hermès International* v *FHT* [1998] ECR I-3603; Joined Cases C-300/98 and C-302/98 *Parfums Christian Dior* v *Tuk Consultancy* [2000] ECR I-11307; Case C-431/05 *Merck Genéricos – Produtos Farmacêuticos* v *Merck* [2007] ECR I-7001.

[124] Case C-32/11 *Allianz Hungária Biztosító*, Judgment of 14 March 2013, para. 20.

[125] In recent times see Case C-352/08 *Modehuis A. Zwijnenburg* [2010] ECR I-4303; Case C-603/10 *Pelati*, Judgment of 18 October 2012. For discussion, see S. Lefevre, 'The Interpretation of Community Law by the Court of Justice in Areas of National Competence' (2004) 29 *ELRev.* 501.

[126] Joined Cases C-297/88 and C-197/89 *Dzodzi* v *Belgium* [1990] ECR I-3673.

[127] Similar reasoning has been deployed to allow the Court to accept references on contracts that incorporate terms of EU law, Case C-88/91 *Federconsorzi* v *AIMA* [1992] ECR I-4035.

This concern to secure uniform interpretation raises the question of how explicit the reference to EU law must be to generate jurisdiction for the Court of Justice. In *Les Vergers du Vieux Tauves*, the Belgian Government had transposed a Directive which restricted the taxes parent companies paid on dividends made by subsidiaries in other Member States.[128] The Belgian law replicated, in parts, the language of the Directive, but the substance was wider and the Belgian law did not refer to it explicitly. It also applied more generally to relations between Belgian parents and their subsidiaries, something that fell completely outside the Directive. The Court was asked to give an interpretation on the Belgian law in a case that involved only a Belgian parent company and its subsidiary. Notwithstanding the domestic nature of the case and the absence of an explicit reference, the Court considered it sufficient that the Belgian law was intended to transpose the Directive and there was some replication of the language. This is a very weak nexus. It loses sight of the initial rationale for intervention in such cases, namely, unity of interpretation of EU law. As the Court acknowledged, the Belgian court need have only partial regard to its judgment in interpreting the provision as it would also have to look at the Belgian domestic legal context. There would be no guarantee, therefore, that its interpretation of Belgian law would be the same as interpretations of identically worded provisions in other Member States.

The unity of EU law has led to stronger demands being made by the Court of Justice in relation to the validity of EU measures. In *Fotofrost*, a Commission Decision requiring import duties to be paid on binoculars imported from the eastern part of Germany was challenged before a Hamburg court on the grounds it conflicted with the 1957 Protocol on German Internal Trade, which allowed free trade between the two divided parts of Germany. The Hamburg court asked the Court of Justice whether it could declare the Commission Decision invalid.

Case 314/85 *Firma Fotofrost v Hauptzollamt Lübeck-Ost* [1987] ECR 4199

13. In enabling national courts, against those decisions where there is a judicial remedy under national law, to refer to the Court for a preliminary ruling questions on interpretation or validity, [Article 267 TFEU] did not settle the question whether those courts themselves may declare that acts of Community institutions are invalid.

14. Those courts may consider the validity of a Community act and, if they consider that the grounds put forward before them by the parties in support of invalidity are unfounded, they may reject them, concluding that the measure is completely valid. By taking that action they are not calling into question the existence of the Community measure.

15. On the other hand, those courts do not have the power to declare acts of the Community institutions invalid. As the Court emphasized ... in Case 66/80 *International Chemical Corporation* v *Amministrazione delle Finanze* [1981] ECR 1191, the main purpose of the powers accorded to the Court by Article [267 TFEU] is to ensure that Community law is applied uniformly by national courts. That requirement of uniformity is particularly imperative when the validity of a Community act is in question. Divergences between courts in the Member States as to the validity of Community acts would be liable to place in jeopardy the very unity of the Community legal order and detract from the fundamental requirement of legal certainty.

---

[128] Case C-48/07 *Les Vergers du Vieux Tauves* [2008] ECR I-10627.

16. The same conclusion is dictated by consideration of the necessary coherence of the system of judicial protection established by the Treaty. In that regard it must be observed that requests for preliminary rulings, like actions for annulment, constitute means for reviewing the legality of acts of the Community institutions. As the Court pointed out ... in Case 294/83 *Parti Ecologiste 'Les Verts'* v *European Parliament* [1986] ECR 1339, 'in Articles [263 and 268], on the one hand, and in Article [267 TFEU], on the other, the Treaty established a complete system of legal remedies and procedures designed to permit the Court of Justice to review the legality of measures adopted by the institutions'.

17. Since Article [263 TFEU] gives the Court exclusive jurisdiction to declare void an act of a Community institution, the coherence of the system requires that where the validity of a Community act is challenged before a national court the power to declare the act invalid must also be reserved to the Court of Justice.

18. It must also be emphasized that the Court of Justice is in the best position to decide on the validity of Community acts. Under Article 20 of the Protocol on the Statute of the Court of Justice of the EEC, Community Institutions whose acts are challenged are entitled to participate in the proceedings in order to defend the validity of the acts in question. Furthermore, under the second paragraph of Article 21 of that Protocol the Court may require the Member States and institutions which are not participating in the proceedings to supply all information which it considers necessary for the purposes of the case before it.

19. It should be added that the rule that national courts may not themselves declare Community acts invalid may have to be qualified in certain circumstances in the case of proceedings relating to an application for interim measures; however, that case is not referred to in the national court's question.

The view that only the Court of Justice can declare EU measures illegal is, as we shall see, not uncontested by national courts.[129] The Court has, nevertheless, been unwavering on it. In *Schul*, a Dutch court of last resort asked whether it could strike down an EU instrument when an analogous instrument based on identical principles had already been struck down.[130] The case in question concerned a charge levied on Brazilian sugar imported into the Netherlands on the basis of a Commission Regulation. An identical pricing structure was used as for a measure in the poultry sector ruled illegal by the Court of Justice, namely, the Council had suggested one pricing structure (the representative price) and the Commission had exceeded its delegated power by using a different one (cif price). The Court of Justice stated that the uniformity of EU law and its procedural rules, in which all Member States and EU institutions have the right to make observations, entailed that only it could declare Union acts invalid. This was the case even where an analogous measure had already been struck down. Analogies could be misleading in that the factual and legal context surrounding each measure would necessarily be different.

However, a simple challenge to the validity of an EU measure is not sufficient to require a national court to refer. In *IATA*, IATA, the central association representing airlines, challenged Regulation 261/2004, which provided for compensation and assistance to passengers in the event of being denied boarding and of cancellation or long delay to long-haul flights.[131] The

---

[129] See pp. 222–45.
[130] Case C-461/03 *Schul* v *Minister van Landbouw, Natuur en Voedselkwaliteit* [2005] ECR I-10513.
[131] Case C-344/04 *R ex parte IATA* v *Department for Transport* [2006] ECR I-403.

English court was sceptical of the challenge and, indeed, the challenge was eventually unsuccessful. It therefore asked for the threshold at which it must refer to the Court of Justice. The latter stated it was not required to refer simply because one party challenged the validity of a measure. It should only refer if it considers an argument as to the invalidity of a measure, brought up either by itself or one of the parties, to be well founded.

(iv) Dispute resolution

A monopoly on adjudication is granted to the national court by Article 267 TFEU. It rules on questions of facts, national law and, thus, ultimately who wins the case. The Court of Justice rules on points of EU law. It leads to the process being longer than it otherwise would and to a point of tension. For Article 267(2) TFEU stipulates that the national court refer a question of EU law 'if it considers that a decision on the question is necessary to enable it to give judgment'. This has been interpreted to mean that a reference should only take place when that point of EU law meaningfully contributes to the resolution of the dispute. In *Foglia*, Foglia had contracted to sell Italian liqueur wine to Novello in France with the proviso that Novello would reimburse any taxes Foglia incurred, unless these were levied contrary to EU law. Novello subsequently refused to reimburse a small amount of French tax levied on Foglia, equivalent to about €70, on the grounds that it was contrary to EU law. The matter was brought before an Italian court which was asked to rule on the compatibility of the French taxes with EU law. The case had all the hallmarks of a test case. Both Foglia and Novello argued that the taxes were illegal, the amount of tax paid was derisory and Foglia indicated that he was litigating on behalf of Italian traders of this wine. The Court of Justice refused to give judgment to the initial reference on the grounds that there was no genuine dispute.[132] The Italian court re-referred the matter, asking what the roles of the national court and Court of Justice were in such matters.

Case 244/80 *Foglia* v *Novello (No. 2)* [1981] ECR 3045

14. With regard to the first question it should be recalled, as the Court has had occasion to emphasize in very varied contexts, that [Article 267 TFEU] is based on cooperation which entails a division of duties between the national courts and the Court of Justice in the interest of the proper application and uniform interpretation of Community law throughout all the Member States.

15. With this in view it is for the national court – by reason of the fact that it is seized of the substance of the dispute and that it must bear the responsibility for the decision to be taken – to assess, having regard to the facts of the case, the need to obtain a preliminary ruling to enable it to give judgment.

16. In exercising that power of appraisal the national court, in collaboration with the Court of Justice, fulfils a duty entrusted to them both of ensuring that in the interpretation and application of the Treaty the law is observed. Accordingly the problems which may be entailed in the exercise of its power of appraisal by the national court and the relations which it maintains within the framework of [Article 267 TFEU] with the Court of Justice are governed exclusively by the provisions of Community law.

---

[132] Case 104/79 *Foglia* v *Novello* [1980] ECR 745.

17. In order that the Court of Justice may perform its task in accordance with the Treaty it is essential for national courts to explain, when the reasons do not emerge beyond any doubt from the file, why they consider that a reply to their questions is necessary to enable them to give judgment.

18. It must in fact be emphasized that the duty assigned to the Court by [Article 267 TFEU] is not that of delivering advisory opinions on general or hypothetical questions but of assisting in the administration of justice in the Member States. It accordingly does not have jurisdiction to reply to questions of interpretation which are submitted to it within the framework of procedural devices arranged by the parties in order to induce the Court to give its views on certain problems of Community law which do not correspond to an objective requirement inherent in the resolution of a dispute. A declaration by the Court that it has no jurisdiction in such circumstances does not in any way trespass upon the prerogatives of the national court but makes it possible to prevent the application of the procedure under [Article 267 TFEU] for purposes other than those appropriate for it.

19. Furthermore, it should be pointed out that, whilst the Court of Justice must be able to place as much reliance as possible upon the assessment by the national court of the extent to which the questions submitted are essential, it must be in a position to make any assessment inherent in the performance of its own duties in particular in order to check, as all courts must, whether it has jurisdiction. Thus the Court, taking into account the repercussions of its decisions in this matter, must have regard, in exercising the jurisdiction conferred upon it by [Article 267 TFEU], not only to the interests of the parties to the proceedings but also to those of the Community and of the Member States. Accordingly it cannot, without disregarding the duties assigned to it, remain indifferent to the assessments made by the courts of the Member States in the exceptional cases in which such assessments may affect the proper working of the procedure laid down by [Article 267 TFEU].

Foglia was extremely contentious. The power to refuse a reference established a hierarchical element between the Court of Justice and the national court, as it allowed the Court of Justice to review the national court's decision to refer and examine the factual background to the dispute. There was consequently debate about whether this violated the cooperative spirit of Article 267 TFEU or transgressed unduly on the national court's monopoly over fact-finding.[133] Whatever its merits, there were severe practical difficulties in applying *Foglia*.[134] Without its own fact-finding powers, however, the Court has little capacity to second-guess national courts.

Within this context, the Court of Justice has accepted test cases. In *Leclerc Siplec* v *TF1 Publicité*, Leclerc Siplec challenged a refusal by TF1, one of the major French television broadcasters, to televise an advertisement which sought to persuade viewers to purchase petrol from the forecourts of Leclerc's chain of supermarkets.[135] The reason for the refusal was a French law prohibiting television advertising of the distribution sector. Both parties to the dispute

[133] For differing views see A. Barav, 'Preliminary Censorship? The Judgment of the European Court in *Foglia v Novello*' (1980) 5 *ELRev.* 443, 451–4; H. Rasmussen, *On Law and Policy in the European Court of Justice* (Dordrecht, Martijnus Nijhoff, 1986) 465–97; D. Wyatt, '*Foglia (No. 2)*: The Court Denies it has Jurisdiction to Give Advisory Opinions' (1982) 7 *ELRev.* 186; C. Gray, 'Advisory Opinions and the Court of Justice' (1983) 8 *ELRev.* 24.

[134] G. Bebr, 'The Existence of a Genuine Dispute: An Indispensable Precondition for the Jurisdiction of the Court under Article 177 EC?' (1980) 17 *CMLRev.* 525, 532.

[135] Case C-412/93 *Leclerc Siplec* v *TF1 Publicité* [1995] ECR I-179. M. O'Neill, 'Article 177 and Limits to the Right to Refer: An End to the Confusion?' (1996) 2 *European Public Law* 375.

were in agreement about the domestic legal situation and the need for a reference. The Court accepted the reference. It noted that what was being sought was a declaration from the national court that the French law did not comply with EU law. The parties' agreement did not make the need for that declaration any less pressing or the dispute any less real. Whilst resolution of test cases is an important part of the judicial function, it is very difficult to distinguish them from hypothetical cases. In both, there is little conflict between the immediate parties to the dispute.

The Court has also accepted cases where the national law of one Member State is challenged in the courts of another. In *Eau de Cologne*, Eau de Cologne, a cosmetics company, agreed to supply cosmetics to an Italian company, Provide.[136] The contract contained a warranty that the cosmetics would comply with Italian law. Provide repudiated the contract on the grounds that the cosmetics did not comply with Italian labelling laws. Eau de Cologne argued that they complied with the Directive regulating the matter. Under a choice of forum provision in the agreement, the matter was brought before a German court which referred a question on the interpretation of the Directive. The Court accepted the genuineness of the dispute despite a number of factors, notably the seemingly trivial nature of the breach and the choice of forum which allowed a German court to adjudicate upon the compatibility of Italian legislation with EU law.

The *Foglia* line of reasoning survives, but in an attenuated form. In *Stichting Zuid-Hollandse Milieufederatie* the Court stated that it will only refuse to give a reference where it is 'quite obvious' that the alleged dispute is hypothetical or the point of law referred bears no relationship to the dispute in question.[137] This 'quite obvious' requirement is interpreted loosely, however. In that instance, the Court accepted a question from a Dutch court about Directive 98/8/EC on Biocides, notwithstanding that the litigation concerned legislation on another Directive, Directive 91/414/EEC on Plant Protection, on the grounds that the two Directives were closely related and governed by similar principles. The other legacy of *Foglia* is to ensure that sufficient information is provided by the national court to allow the Court of Justice to give a ruling and other parties who wish to intervene to do so effectively.[138] A template is provided on the Court of Justice website of the information provided, but once again this condition has been interpreted generously. In *Varzim Sol*, a casino concession in Portugal required its owner to engage in additional tourism promotion activities for the area.[139] A dispute arose over whether VAT could be levied by the Portuguese authorities on these activities. In its reference, the Portuguese court simply asked whether the relevant Portuguese provision complied with the EU Directive on the matter. The Portuguese government claimed the reference was inadmissible as it did not set out the content of the provision, and was doing no more than looking for a general opinion. The Court stated sufficient information would be provided if either the factual and legislative context to the questions asked had been defined – this had not happened here – or the national court had explained the factual circumstances. This was the case here as the Portuguese court had set out the amount of VAT levied, and the reason why the tax authority believed the activity not to be exempt from tax.

---

[136] Case C-150/88 *Eau de Cologne* v *Provide* [1989] ECR 3891.
[137] Case C-138/05 *Stichting Zuid-Hollandse Milieufederatie* v *Minister van Landbouw* [2006] ECR I-8339.
[138] T. Kennedy, 'First Steps Towards a European Certiorari' (1993) 18 *ELRev.* 121; D. Anderson, 'The Admissibility of Preliminary References' (1994) 14 *YBEL* 179, 186–8.
[139] Case C-25/11 *Varzim Sol*, Judgment of 16 February 2012.

5 MANAGEMENT OF THE EU JUDICIAL ORDER

If the preliminary reference procedure establishes an EU judicial order deployed to realise a series of functions, there remains the question of the processes through which this is managed and how well this is managed. The procedure relies on three features in particular: identifying the circumstances under which a reference can or should be made; granting legal authority to judgments of the Court of Justice; and the protection of the litigants' positions pending final resolution of the dispute.

(i) Managing the circumstances in which national courts refer

There are two circumstances when a national court must refer the point of EU law to the Court of Justice. The first is if it considers an EU measure may be invalid, as only the Court of Justice has the power to declare a Union measure invalid.[140] The second is if it falls within Article 267(3) TFEU, which states that courts against whose decision there is no judicial remedy in national law are obliged to refer, where the point of EU law is necessary to decide the dispute in hand. Article 267(3) TFEU covers not just the highest courts in the land but also any court where the party has been denied the possibility to take the matter further because they have been denied leave to appeal to a higher court. In *Lyckeskog*, Lyckeskog was prosecuted for importing 500 kg rice into Sweden without paying customs duties as he claimed it was for personal use. He appealed to the West Swedish Court of Appeal (Hovrätt för Västra Sverige), arguing that the relevant EU Regulation allowed this where the rice was for personal use. The Swedish Court of Appeal, whose decisions could be appealed to the Swedish Supreme Court (Högsta domstol), referred the question as to whether it fell within Article 267(3) TFEU if it refused Lyckeskog leave to appeal.

Case C-99/00 *Lyckeskog* [2002] ECR I-4839

14. The obligation on national courts against whose decisions there is no judicial remedy to refer a question to the Court for a preliminary ruling has its basis in the cooperation established, in order to ensure the proper application and uniform interpretation of Community law in all the Member States, between national courts, as courts responsible for applying Community law, and the Court. That obligation is in particular designed to prevent a body of national case-law that is not in accordance with the rules of Community law from coming into existence in any Member State.

15. That objective is secured when, subject to the limits accepted by the Court of Justice ... supreme courts are bound by this obligation to refer ... as is any other national court or tribunal against whose decisions there is no judicial remedy under national law ...

16. Decisions of a national appellate court which can be challenged by the parties before a supreme court are not decisions of a 'court or tribunal of a Member State against whose decisions there is no judicial remedy under national law' within the meaning of Article [267 TFEU]. The fact that examination of the merits of such appeals is subject to a prior declaration of admissibility by the supreme court does not have the effect of depriving the parties of a judicial remedy.

---

[140] Case 314/85 *Firma Fotofrost v Hauptzollamt Lübeck-Ost* [1987] ECR 4199.

17. That is so under the Swedish system. The parties always have the right to appeal to the Högsta domstol against the judgment of a hovrätt, which cannot therefore be classified as a court delivering a decision against which there is no judicial remedy. Under Paragraph 10 of Chapter 54 of the Rättegångsbalk [Swedish Code of Procedure] the Högsta domstol may issue a declaration of admissibility if it is important for guidance as to the application of the law that the appeal be examined by that court. Thus, uncertainty as to the interpretation of the law applicable, including Community law, may give rise to review, at last instance, by the supreme court.

18. If a question arises as to the interpretation or validity of a rule of Community law, the supreme court will be under an obligation, pursuant to the third paragraph of Article [267 TFEU], to refer a question to the Court of Justice for a preliminary ruling either at the stage of the examination of admissibility or at a later stage.

Lyckeskog secures the universal jurisdiction of the Court of Justice. In principle, in every case, there should be a point at which individuals are able to demand a reference from a national court because there will be a moment where either leave to appeal is refused or the case is decided by the highest court in the land, and that court falls within Article 267(3) TFEU.

The duty to refer was reinforced by *Köbler*.[141] Köbler was an Austrian professor who lost bonuses, to which he would otherwise have been entitled for his length of service, because he had spent some years working outside Austria at a German university.[142] The Austrian Administrative Court, a court of last resort, wrongly ruled that this did not breach EU law and that it was not, therefore, obliged to refer. The Court ruled that an action for damages against the state would be available where it was manifestly apparent that a court had failed to comply with its obligations to refer. In this instance, the Court ruled it was not obviously apparent, as the Austrian court had mistakenly, but in good faith, thought that the matter was covered by a previous ruling of the Court, which had held that the treatment was lawful.

This action for damages against a judicial failure to refer when required might only be a paper one.[143] The redress is against the state not the court. It is not clear, short of legislation, what the other arms of government could do to redress a decision of a senior court. The incentives do not, therefore, fall directly on the court in question. Such an action would also require a court of first instance to rule negatively on the actions of the senior court. It seems implausible that many lower courts would do this. *Köbler* is, therefore, more important for what it symbolises. For some, it is securing a comprehensive system for the administration of justice which has the Court of Justice at its apex. Others see it as emasculating the contribution of national judiciaries.[144] This has been described by Davies:

---

[141] Case C-224/01 *Köbler* v. *Austria* [2003] ECR I-10239.

[142] This case is dealt with in more detail in Chapter 7. On the principles of State liability see pp. 333–5.

[143] J. Komárek, 'Federal Elements in the Community Judicial System: Building Coherence in the Community Legal System' (2005) 42 *CMLRev.* 9, 12–18.

[144] P. Allott, 'Preliminary Rulings: Another Infant Disease' (2000) *ELRev.* 538, 542; H. Rasmussen, 'Remedying the Crumbling EC Judicial System' (2000) 37 *CMLRev.* 1071, 1092.

Thus national court interpretations of Community law, while sometimes creative and purposive, take place in a grey area of semi-legitimacy, a sort of tolerated but not approved practice, where the assumption seems to be that ultimately any point of law will in fact make its way to the Court of Justice. Moreover, national final courts will have no interpretive competence at all.[145]

Much, therefore, rests on when national judges enjoy merely *discretion* to make a reference. This will be the case when they fall within Article 267(2) TFEU: they are a court against whose decision there is a judicial remedy. When that is the case, they still form part of this system of universal jurisdiction as their decision is subject to appeal.

There is one exception to this system of universal jurisdiction. National courts against whose decision there is no judicial remedy are not compelled to refer if either the doctrine of *acte éclairé* or that of *acte clair* applies. The former is where a materially identical matter has already been decided by the Court of Justice. The latter is where the EU law provision in question is so clear that there is no reasonable doubt about its interpretation. In *CILFIT*, a group of textile firms challenged levies imposed by the Italian Ministry of Health on wool imported by them from outside the Union. The case centred on whether wool was an animal product, as a Regulation prohibited levies imposed on 'animal products'. The dispute went up to the Italian Court of Cassation, the highest civil court in Italy. The Italian Ministry of Health argued that there was no need to make a reference to the Court of Justice as the question of law, namely, whether wool is an animal product, was obvious.

Case 283/81 *CILFIT* v *Ministry of Health* [1982] ECR 341

13. It must be remembered in this connection that ... in Joined Cases 28 to 30/62 *Da Costa* v *Nederlandse Belastingadministratie* [1963] ECR 31 the Court ruled that: 'Although the third paragraph of [Article 267 TFEU] unreservedly requires courts or tribunals of a Member State against whose decision there is no judicial remedy under national law ... to refer to the Court every question of interpretation raised before them, the authority of an interpretation under [Article 267 TFEU] already given by the Court may deprive the obligation of its purpose and thus empty it of its substance. Such is the case especially when the question raised is materially identical with a question which has already been the subject of a preliminary ruling in a similar case.'

14. The same effect, as regards the limits set to the obligation laid down by the third paragraph of [Article 267 TFEU], may be produced where previous decisions of the Court have already dealt with the point of law in question, irrespective of the nature of the proceedings which led to those decisions, even though the questions at issue are not strictly identical.

15. However, it must not be forgotten that in all such circumstances national courts and tribunals, including those referred to in paragraph (3) of [Article 267 TFEU], remain entirely at liberty to bring a matter before the Court of Justice if they consider it appropriate to do so.

16. Finally, the correct application of Community law may be so obvious as to leave no scope for any reasonable doubt as to the manner in which the question raised is to be resolved. Before it comes to the conclusion that such is the case, the national court or tribunal must be convinced that the matter

---

[145] G. Davies, 'The Division of Powers between the European Court of Justice and National Courts' *ConWeb No.3/2004*, 19.

is equally obvious to the courts of the other Member States and to the Court of Justice. Only if those conditions are satisfied may the national court or tribunal refrain from submitting the question to the Court of Justice and take upon itself the responsibility for resolving it.

17. However, the existence of such a possibility must be assessed on the basis of the characteristic feature of Community law and the particular difficulties to which its interpretation gives rise.

18. To begin with, it must be borne in mind that Community legislation is drafted in several languages and that the different language versions are equally authentic. An interpretation of a provision of Community law thus involves a comparison of the different language versions.

19. It must also be borne in mind, even where the different language versions are entirely in accord with one another, that Community law uses terminology which is peculiar to it. Furthermore, it must be emphasised that legal concepts do not necessarily have the same meaning in Community law and in the law of the various Member States.

20. Finally, every provision of Community law must be placed in its context and interpreted in the light of the provisions of Community law as a whole, regard being had to the objectives thereof and to its state of evolution at the date on which the provision in question is to be applied.

Read literally, the exception is so narrow as to be meaningless.[146] Even the Court of Justice, with all the back-up of its translating services, has struggled to come to terms with the interpretive difficulties posed by the authenticity of all the different language versions of EU law.[147] However, to concentrate on the formal limits of *CILFIT* is to miss its significance. *CILFIT* goes to whether there should be a system of universal jurisdiction or not. It suggests that there are circumstances when this should not be the case, and national courts should decide EU law themselves. To some, this creates a lacuna in judicial protection by providing circumstances where individuals will not have access to the Court of Justice.[148] To others, the doctrine of *acte clair* acts as a valve, defusing potential conflict between the higher national courts and the Court of Justice, by allowing the former to decide matters exclusively by themselves without engaging in any overt act of judicial rebellion.[149]

There is evidence to suggest, therefore, that national courts do not interpret *CILFIT* literally. A study found that between 1978 and 2001, the French Conseil d'État applied the *acte clair* doctrine 191 times whilst only making eighteen references, whilst the Austrian Constitutional Court only made a reference in about half the cases in which EU law was invoked before it.[150] This appears to be the tip of the iceberg. Polish, Slovak and Maltese Constitutional Courts, as well as the Czech Supreme Court, have never made a reference,

---

[146] H. Rasmussen, 'The European Court's *Acte Clair* Strategy in CILFIT' (1984) 9 *ELRev.* 242; F. Mancini and D. Keeling, 'From CILFIT to ERT: The Constitutional Challenge Facing the European Court' (1991) 11 *YBEL* 1, 4. For an argument that the exception should therefore be expanded, see M. Broberg, '*Acte Clair* Revisited: Adapting the Demands of *Acte Clair* to the Demands of the Times' (2008) 45 *CMLRev.* 1383.

[147] For difficulties with the different language versions of EU legislation, see Case C-72/95 *Aanemersbedrijf P. K. Kraaijeveld v Gedeputeerde Staten van Zuid-Hooland* [1996] ECR I-5403.

[148] A. Arnull, 'Reflections on Judicial Attitudes at the European Court' (1985) 34 *ICLQ* 168, 172; A. Arnull, 'The Use and Abuse of Article 177 EEC' (1989) 52 *MLR* 622, 626.

[149] J. Golub, 'The Politics of Judicial Discretion: Rethinking the Interaction between National Courts and the European Court of Justice' (1996) 19 *WEP* 360, 376–7.

[150] N. Fenger and M. Broberg, 'Finding Light in the Darkness: On the Actual Application of the *Acte Clair* Doctrine' (2011) 30 *YBEL* 180, 188.

whilst the Italian Constitutional Court has only made one and the Portuguese Supreme Court only three references.[151]

This leeway is granted, however, in a highly distorted manner. It requires the highest national court to hide behind semantic grounds: the matter has already been decided or the provision is so clear that it does not require interpretation. As a consequence, national courts still make referrals on points of little need. This is evidenced by, first, the use of the simplified procedure which allows for reasoned orders instead of judgments to be given where there is no reasonable doubt about the law.[152] This was used twenty-six times in 2012. In addition, there is provision for the Court to dispense with the opinion of the Advocate General if the case raises no new point of law.[153] It did this in 53 per cent of its judgments in 2012.[154]

Secondly, there is also little evidence that the presence of Article 267(3) TFEU patterns references in a strong way. Broberg and Fenger looked at the variables which might affect references by national courts by comparing references from different territories against a number of indicators.[155] They found that structural elements, such as population size, the relative litigiousness of societies and national government propensity to obey EU law, exercised a powerful effect on the levels of references from different Member States. They were not determinative, however, with judicial whim also being central.

A number of proposals have, therefore, been suggested to temper the rigour of the duty to refer.

The first is a 'green light' procedure. National courts would submit draft answers with their references. The Court would take a preliminary look at the draft. If it considered it unproblematic, the Court would state that it did not object to the suggested interpretation. By contrast, if it were problematic or raised significant issues, the Court would make a ruling itself.[156] This is a 'reform-lite'. It builds on the current simplified procedure by allowing national interpretations where they fit comfortably with the existing case law of the Court of Justice or raise no significant issues. However, it introduces a hierarchical element into the procedure in that the Court is reserving to itself the role of telling the national court that it got the interpretation of EU law wrong. National courts are, in effect, submitting draft judgments for approval. It is not clear why this is necessary, particularly as there will still be all the delays associated with the making of the reference.

A second reform, therefore, suggests that *acte clair* should be broadened and there should be wider circumstances in which national courts against whose decisions there is no judicial remedy should retain a discretion to refer. Broberg has argued, in particular, as follows.

---

[151] *Annual Report*, n. 13 above, 114.

[152] Rules of Procedure of the Court of Justice, article 99.

[153] Statute of the Court of Justice, article 20.

[154] On this and use of the simplified procedure, see *Annual Report*, n. 13 above, 11.

[155] M. Broberg and N. Fenger, 'Variations in Member States' Preliminary References to the Court of Justice: Are Structural Factors (Part of) the Explanation?' (2013) 19 *ELJ* 488.

[156] S. Strasser, *The Development of a Strategy of Docket Control for the European Court of Justice and the Question of Preliminary References*, Jean Monnet Working Paper No. 95/3 (1995); F. Jacobs, 'The Court of Justice in the Twenty First Century: Challenges Ahead for the Judicial System?' in Court of Justice of the European Union (ed.), *The Court of Justice and the Construction of Europe: Analyses and Perspectives on Sixty Years of Case-law* (The Hague, Asser, 2013).

M. Broberg, 'Acte Clair Revisited: Adapting the Acte Clair Criteria to the Demands of the Times' (2008) 45 *Common Market Law Review* 1383, 1397

... the question is not simply whether or not to refer. Rather, the need is to have all the important matters referred to the Court of Justice whereas the less important ones should not be referred. Therefore, to better achieve the purpose underlying [Article 267(3)], an adjustment of the *CILFIT* criteria is required so that national courts of last instance will only be obliged to refer questions where there is a genuine need for a uniform interpretation and where the questions go beyond the main action. Hence, the *CILFIT* criteria should be adjusted so that a national court of last instance is not obliged to make a preliminary reference where the correct application of Community law does not leave any reasonable doubt as to the manner in which the question raised is to be resolved.

The *CILFIT* criteria thus adjusted do not make it possible for the national courts of last instance to attribute any weight to the wishes of the parties in the main action when deciding whether or not to refer a question to the European Court of Justice. Likewise the adjusted criteria only lay down when a national court of last instance must refer a question for a preliminary ruling; they do not affect when such a court may refer. In order to ensure an effective and uniform application of the adjusted *CILFIT* criteria it is suggested that the adjustment is accompanied by two further initiatives. Thus, it is proposed that national courts of last instance shall be required to give reasons whenever they invoke the adjusted *CILFIT* criteria in support of not referring a question to the European Court of Justice. Moreover, it is proposed that the national courts of last instance shall be given access to sophisticated advice when they have to determine whether or not a question of Community law meets the adjusted *CILFIT* criteria.

Broberg's observation is that if the Court of Justice's concern is with the uniformity and development of EU law, then it should only concern itself with those cases which go significantly to that question. This would alleviate its workload and also allow more space for the national judicial experience to inform EU law. This seems right. Nevertheless, he still shares the perspective that the Court has access to some wisdom which is not possessed by senior national courts and these need to be policed. It is not clear that either is necessarily the case. It has, therefore, been suggested that a replacement for much of what the Court does through the preliminary reference procedure would be a database where national courts could access the decisions of other national courts on analogous points of EU law.

D. Chalmers, 'The European Court of Justice is now little more than a rubber stamp for the EU. It should be replaced with better alternative arrangements for central judicial guidance' *LSE EUROPP*, 8 March 2012

The referral procedure is ... skewed by a long backlog, which biases the docket. Parties wishing to enlarge EU law through a Court ruling win not only the case in hand but they secure a more general change of the law within their jurisdiction, because domestic law has to be adapted to the new settlement. As a result many parties to cases are happy to accept the delay. By contrast, there are no such incentives for parties who wish to secure a retrenchment of EU law. It is rare that the

Court will reverse its previous rulings, so a better path is to seek domestic legal resistance by asking for interpretations of domestic law that only just comply with EU law. The consequence of this asymmetry is that almost all the legal questions referred to the European Court of Justice ask for it to extend rather than to retract EU legal obligations. There is no pluralist process before the Court, but simply a relentless one-way traffic.

The final sin of the current system is that it supplants and thereby neglects Europe's rich legal resources. By investing the final word in a single isolated institution, it overlooks the twenty-seven legal jurisdictions out there with years of diverse experimentation, creativity and experience behind them. In this linked up world, judges struggling with a thorny dispute or wishing to build a common European legal heritage should turn their eyes in the direction of Europe's accumulated wealth of legal ideas, which lies there ready to help.

So here's a thought. Replace the current 'preliminary reference procedure' for going to the ECJ for a ruling with a database. All the appellate courts within the European Union interpreting a point of EU law in each of the twenty-seven Member States would be required to submit their judgments to that database. Translators would then make the judgments available in the different languages of the European Union. Courts from states outside the European Union interpreting EU law (it happens more than you think!) would also be invited to submit their judgments to the database, if they so wish. Judges in the EU countries interpreting EU law would then be required to consider rulings in the database on the provision in question – but they could also give reasons why it would not be suitable for their jurisdiction, bearing in mind the obligations of EU membership.

This database would provide quicker justice than a reference to the European Court of Justice. It would almost certainly generate more legal certainty and uniformity, simply by dint of more judgments being available to the local judge to guide her. It would cultivate Europe's legal riches rather than seek to replace them with an inauthentic legal currency of its own. Lastly, it would possibly be cheaper because it would allow the Court's size to be reduced considerably.

(ii) Binding effects of Court of Justice judgments

A judgment given by the Court of Justice binds the referring national court.[157] However, it is free to refer the question back to the Court of Justice if it is either dissatisfied with the ruling or is unclear about the meaning of the ruling. In such circumstances, in a form of judicial ping-pong, the Court has tended to simply reiterate or extrapolate on its prior judgment.[158] National compliance is high. A cross-country study found implementation of the Court's rulings in 96.3 per cent of the cases studied.[159] Challenges to the authority of the Court were rarely in the form of direct non-observance but rather in less direct ways. A study of Austrian courts found that a variety of devices were used to evade rulings of the Court of Justice that were unpopular with the local court. These included narrow constructions of EU legal norms; arguing that EU law does not apply to the facts; weak remedies; *a contrario* reasoning; and

---

[157] Case 52/76 *Benedetti* v *Munari* [1977] ECR 163.

[158] Joined Cases 28–30/62 *Da Costa* [1963] ECR 37; Case 244/80 *Foglia* v *Novello (No. 2)* [1981] ECR 3045.

[159] S. Nyikos, 'The Preliminary Reference Process: National Court Implementation, Changing Opportunity Structures and Litigant Desistment' (2003) 4 *EUP* 397, 410.

application of domestic, rather than EU, legal norms if it would lead to the same result.[160] The Court of Justice has tried to circumvent this in some instances by sending back rulings which are so detailed that they leave national courts little room for discretion in how they decide the dispute in hand. By contrast, in other cases, they have sought to diffuse conflict by sending back rulings sufficiently vague to allow the national court considerable discretion in deciding how to resolve the dispute.[161]

There remains the question of the effects of the Court of Justice's judgments on the wider EU judicial community. The doctrines of *stare decisis* and precedent do not formally exist in EU law. Judgments of the Court only declare the pre-existing state of the law.[162] However, judgments having no broader effects would be highly unsatisfactory for the development of the EU legal order. It was felt to be particularly problematic where the Court declared an EU measure illegal. If the judgment only bound the parties concerned, it would lead to the instrument being invalid for them but binding upon everybody else, albeit open to challenge by everybody else. In *ICC*, therefore, the Court ruled that a judgment declaring an EU measure illegal bound all courts and authorities in the Union.[163] The binding force of Court judgments interpreting EU law, by contrast, was unclear for some time.[164]

In *Kühne*, the Court resolved this by holding that its interpretations of EU law bound all courts and administrative authorities in the Union. Kühne exported chicken legs, with part of the chicken's back still attached, to states outside the EU. In a previous judgment involving other parties, the Court of Justice had ruled these were to be classified as 'chicken legs' for the purposes of customs classification.[165] Kühne then sought reimbursement from the Dutch authorities who had previously placed its goods in a customs classification on which higher customs duties were levied. The Dutch authorities observed that the matter had previously been decided by a Dutch court, which had decided against Kühne, and could not, therefore, be reopened. Kühne argued that they were bound to reconsider the matter in the light of the earlier Court of Justice judgment.

Case C–453/00 *Kühne and Heitz v Productschap voor Pluimvee en Eieren* [2004] ECR I–837

21. The interpretation which, in the exercise of the jurisdiction conferred on it by Article [267 TFEU], the Court gives to a rule of Community law clarifies and defines, where necessary, the meaning and scope of

---

[160] B. Bepuly, *The Application of EC Law in Austria*, IWE Working Paper No. 39 (2003), available at http://eif. univie.ac.at/workingpapers-en/iwearchiv.php.

[161] For different views on this see J. Snell, 'European Courts and Intellectual Property: A Tale of Zeus, Hercules and Cyclops' (2004) 29 *ELRev.* 178; T. Tridimas, 'Constitutional Review of Member State Action: The Virtues and Vices of an Incomplete Jurisdiction' (2011) 9 *I-CON* 737; G. Davies, 'Activism Relocated: The Self-restraint of the European Court of Justice in its National Context' (2012) 19 *JEPP* 76.

[162] Case 61/79 *Denkavit Italiana* [1980] ECR 1205; Joined Cases C-89/10 and C-96/10 *Q-Beef* v *Belgische Staat, Bosschaert* v *Belgische Staat,* Judgment of 8 September 2011; T. Koopmans, 'Stare Decisis in European Law' in D. O' Keeffe and H. Schermers (eds.), *Essays in European Law and Integration* (Deventer, Kluwer, 1982); A. Arnull, 'Owning up to Fallibility: Precedent and the Court of Justice' (1993) 30 *CMLRev.* 247.

[163] Case 66/80 *International Chemical Corp.* v *Amministrazione Finanze* [1981] ECR 1191; Case 314/85 *Firma Fotofrost* v *HZ Lübeck-Ost* [1987] ECR 4199.

[164] For contrasting views of the Advocates General, see Advocate General Darmon in Case 338/85 *Pardini* v *Ministerio del Commercio con L'Estero* [1988] ECR 204; Advocate General Van Gerven in Case 145/88 *Torfaen BC* v *B & Q* [1989] ECR 765; Advocate General Lenz in Case 103/88 *Fratelli Constanzo* v *Milano* [1989] ECR 1839.

[165] Case C-151/93 *Voogd Vleesimport en -export* [1994] ECR I-4915.

that rule as it must be or ought to have been understood and applied from the time of its coming into force ...

22. It follows that a rule of Community law interpreted in this way must be applied by an administrative body within the sphere of its competence even to legal relationships which arose or were formed before the Court gave its ruling on the question on interpretation.

23. The main proceedings raise the question whether the abovementioned obligation must be complied with notwithstanding that a decision has become final before the application for review of that decision in order to take account of a preliminary ruling by the Court on a question of interpretation has been lodged.

24. Legal certainty is one of a number of general principles recognised by Community law. Finality of an administrative decision, which is acquired upon expiry of the reasonable time-limits for legal remedies or by exhaustion of those remedies, contributes to such legal certainty and it follows that Community law does not require that administrative bodies be placed under an obligation, in principle, to reopen an administrative decision which has become final in that way.

25. However, the national court stated that, under Netherlands law, administrative bodies always have the power to reopen a final administrative decision, provided that the interests of third parties are not adversely affected, and that, in certain circumstances, the existence of such a power may imply an obligation to withdraw such a decision even if Netherlands law does not require that the competent body reopen final decisions as a matter of course in order to comply with judicial decisions given subsequent to the decision. The aim of the national court's question is to ascertain whether, in circumstances such as those of the main case, there is an obligation to reopen a final administrative decision under Community law.

26. As is clear from the case-file, the circumstances of the main case are the following. First, national law confers on the administrative body competence to reopen the decision in question, which has become final. Second, the administrative decision became final only as a result of a judgment of a national court against whose decisions there is no judicial remedy. Third, that judgment was based on an interpretation of Community law which, in the light of a subsequent judgment of the Court, was incorrect and which was adopted without a question being referred to the Court for a preliminary ruling in accordance with the conditions provided for in Article [267 TFEU]. Fourth, the person concerned complained to the administrative body immediately after becoming aware of that judgment of the Court.

27. In such circumstances, the administrative body concerned is, in accordance with the principle of cooperation arising from Article [4 TEU], under an obligation to review that decision in order to take account of the interpretation of the relevant provision of Community law given in the meantime by the Court. The administrative body will have to determine on the basis of the outcome of that review to what extent it is under an obligation to reopen, without adversely affecting the interests of third parties, the decision in question.

Although *Kühne* only refers to the Court's judgment binding national administrative authorities, this has been interpreted as applying to other national authorities, such as judges.[166] They are required to change national law as soon as possible after the judgment, making sure that they give full effect to individual rights under EU law.[167] Care has to be had when describing the binding effects of the judgments. As they are assumed to be declaring pre-existing

---

[166] Case C-212/04 *Adeneler* [2006] ECR I-6057.   [167] Case C-231/06 *NPO* v *Jonkman* [2007] ECR I-5149.

law, their binding force applies to all relationships governed by the legal instrument since it entered into force. This poses, as *Kühne* acknowledges, real challenges for legal certainty. In most instances, this will be resolved by national limitation periods which will prevent disputes of a certain vintage being reopened. More challenging is the situation where a court or administrative authority has just given a decision which conflicts with a subsequent Court judgment. In *Kempter*, the Court ruled that legal certainty should, in general, prevent the matter being reopened even if the earlier decision breached EU law.[168] There is no general obligation on courts to reopen cases simply because they conflict with subsequent Court judgments.[169] It did note, however, there is a duty on administrations to review their activities in the light of EU law. This would place an administrative body under an obligation to reopen the matter if four criteria were met:

- it had the power to reopen the decision;
- the decision had become final as a result of a national judgment at final instance;[170]
- that judgment was based on a misinterpretation of EU law and the court failed to refer;
- the party concerned complained to the administrative body immediately after becoming aware of that decision of the court.

These conditions are restrictive, and they will rarely be met. More common is the circumstance where a national judicial decision is binding but its effects either continue after the judgment of the Court of Justice or have a more general lingering effect. In either case, there is an obligation on national authorities to review. In the first instance, a decision of an Italian tax court had *res judicata* effects, and so bound actors, not just for that tax year but the following tax year. The Court held that whilst matters could not be reopened in relation to the earlier tax year, they could in relation to the subsequent one which occurred after its judgment.[171] A more challenging case was *Byankov*. In 2007, a bailiff's order had been placed on a Bulgarian citizen for non-payment of debts which prevented him leaving the country or being issued with a passport until he had paid the debts. It was clear, in the light of a 2008 judgment of the Court of Justice, that this violated EU citizenship law.[172] The Court of Justice ruled that the principle of legal certainty would not apply, first because it violated Byankov's citizenship rights and, secondly, because the absence of any possibility for review in Bulgarian law prevented Bulgarian authorities over a period from responding to case law of the Court which confirmed that their behaviour was illegal. The lingering nature of the illegality, the impossibility of review and the importance of the right asserted, all combined to create this exception. Its ambit is, consequently, unclear, in particular whether it imposes a duty on all administrative authority to review all measures which have effects over time in the light of EU law developments.

(iii) Protection of the parties' positions

Delay is an endemic problem of the preliminary reference procedure. In 2012, the period between the moment of reference by the national court and the judgment of the Court of Justice

---

[168] Case C-2/06 *Kempter* [2008] ECR I-411.
[169] Case C-234/04 *Kapferer* v *Schlank and Schlick* [2006] ECR I-2585.
[170] Joined Cases Case C-392/04 and C-422/04 *i-21 Germany* v *Bundesrepublik Deutschland* [2006] ECR I-8559.
[171] Case C-2/08 *Fallimento Olimpiclub* [2009] ECR I-7501.
[172] Case C-249/11 *Byankov*, Judgment of 4 October 2012.

was an average of 15.7 months.[173] If this period of delay has not increased in recent years, it is still shamefully long. The wait before the national court both prior to making the reference and after receiving it must be added to this period. Furthermore, it is likely that it will increase. The number of references pending has increased from 395 in 2008 to 537 in 2012.[174] This delay has many effects. It puts pressure on the Court of Justice. Deadlines become tight, translation services stretched and time for judicial debate and reflection limited.[175] It alters the balance of power between litigants. For some, the redress arrives too late to be of much use, whilst, for others, the delay can be used as litigation strategy to exert undue pressure on the other side.[176]

To meet these challenges, certain cases are prioritised. The *expedited procedure* allows a national court to request from the President of the Court that the matter be put to the Court as a matter of exceptional urgency. In such circumstances, the case will be prioritised and the time limits for observations restricted to not less than fifteen days.[177] In addition, Article 267(4) TFEU provides that when a reference is made with regard to a person in custody, the Court shall act with the minimum of delay. This is the *urgent procedure* which can either be requested by the national court or decided by the Court of its own motion.[178] It is even more truncated than the accelerated procedure as no minimum time limits for submissions are set.

The use of these procedures is rare. Between 2008 and 2012, the expedited procedure was used eleven times and the urgent procedure sixteen times.[179] For other references, the problem of delay is managed through the use of interim measures. The remedy of interim relief operates in different ways depending on whether the compatibility of an autonomous provision of national with EU law is being contested, or a national law implementing an EU law where the validity of the EU measure is being contested.

With the former, the Court has ruled that the national court must do everything to secure the effectiveness of the Court's judgment. In *Factortame*, a challenge was made by a number of Spanish fishermen to the United Kingdom's Merchant Shipping Act 1988.[180] This Act made it very difficult for non-British boats to fish in British waters by imposing, most notably, a series of residence requirements as a precondition. The national court referred the matter to the Court of Justice. In the meantime, the House of Lords found that the applicants would suffer irreparable damage if interim relief was not granted as many fishermen would go bankrupt before judgment was delivered. As English courts had no jurisdiction to suspend the Act at that time, it referred the question whether national law should be set aside where its application would deprive a party of the enjoyment of rights derived from EU law. The Court of Justice ruled that it should. National courts are under a duty to secure the full effectiveness of EU law. This required that they had to ensure the full effectiveness of any Court judgment on those rights. If the national court considers that the effectiveness of the final judgment might be otherwise undermined, it must grant interim relief. This works to the benefit of applicants

---

[173] *Annual Report*, n. 13 above, 104. On this House of Lords European Union Committee, *Workload of the Court of Justice* (14th Report, TSO, London, 2010–11).

[174] *Ibid.* 105.

[175] J. Weiler, 'Epilogue: The Judicial *après* Nice' in G. de Búrca and J. Weiler (eds.), *The European Court of Justice* (Oxford, Oxford University Press, 2001).

[176] R Rawlings, 'The Eurolaw Game: Some Deductions from a Saga' (1993) 20 *Journal of Law and Society* 309.

[177] Court's Rules of Procedure, article 105.   [178] Court's Rules of Procedure, article 107.

[179] *Annual Report*, n. 13 above, 107.

[180] Case C-213/89 *R v Secretary of State for Transport ex parte Factortame Ltd* [1990] ECR I-2433.

claiming possible entitlements under EU law. They merely have to show that they would not be able to claim those rights if they won to make a strong case for interim relief.

The conditions for interim relief are much more restrictive where a reference is being sought which challenges the validity of an EU measure. The Court has ruled that, in principle, these should be analogous to those where an EU measure is challenged directly before the Court. It has stated that there are four, which are cumulative:

- the national court must have serious doubts as to the validity of the EU measure;
- the relief is urgent and necessary to avoid serious and irreparable damage to the party seeking it;[181]
- account must be taken of the damage to the Union as a whole, particularly from the cumulative effect of such measures being taken by a number of operators;
- if interim relief poses a financial risk for the Union, the national court must be in a position to ask for financial guarantees from the applicant.[182]

The different tests for interim relief result in applicants whose interests are prejudiced in very similar ways being treated very differently. This injustice results because the Court of Justice is giving priority to different systemic concerns: the effectiveness of EU law, in one case, and the cumulative effect of interim relief and the financial risks for the Union, in the other. This priority on systemic interests can obscure the individual needs in particular cases, especially where EU measures are being challenged.

FURTHER READING

K. Alter, *The European Court's Political Power* (Oxford, Oxford University Press, 2009)

D. Anderson and M. Demetriou, *References to the European Court* (London, Sweet & Maxwell, 2002)

M. Broberg and N. Fenger, 'Variations in Member States' Preliminary References to the Court of Justice: Are Structural Factors (Part of) the Explanation?' (2013) 19 *European Law Journal* 488

G. de Búrca and J. Weiler (eds.), *The European Court of Justice* (Oxford, Oxford University Press, 2001)

R. Cichowski, *The European Court and Civil Society: Litigation, Mobilization and Governance* (Cambridge, Cambridge University Press, 2007)

G. Conway, *The Limits of Legal Reasoning and the European Court of Justice* (Cambridge, Cambridge University Press, 2012)

Court of Justice of the European Union (ed.), *The Court of Justice and the Construction of Europe: Analyses and Perspectives on Sixty Years of Case-law* (The Hague, Asser, 2013)

M. Dawson *et al.*, *Judicial Activism at the Court of Justice* (Cheltenham, Edward Elgar, 2013)

N. Fenger and M. Broberg, 'Finding Light in the Darkness: On the Actual Application of the *acte clair* Doctrine' (2011) 30 *Yearbook of European Law* 180

D. Kelemen and S. Schmidt, 'Special Issue: Perpetual Momentum? Reconsidering the Power of the European Court of Justice' (2012) 19(1) *Journal of European Public Policy* 1

J. Komárek, 'In the Court(s) We Trust? On the Need for Hierarchy and Differentiation in the Preliminary Ruling Procedure' (2007) 32 *European Law Review* 467

---

[181] On these see Case C-465/93 *Atlanta Fruchthandelsgesellschaft and others (No. 1)* [1995] ECR I-3761.

[182] On these last two conditions see Joined Cases C-453/03, C-11/04, C-12/04 and C-194/04 *Martini v Ministero delle Politiche Agricole e Forestali* [2005] ECR I-10423.

H. Rasmussen, 'Remedying the Crumbling EC Judicial System' (2000) 37 *Common Market Law Review* 1071

R. Rawlings, 'The Eurolaw Game: Some Deductions from a Saga' (1993) 20 *Journal of Law and Society* 309

T. Tridimas, 'Knocking on Heaven's Door: Fragmentation, Efficiency and Defiance in the Preliminary Reference Procedure' (2003) 40 *Common Market Law Review* 9

5

The Authority of EU Law

CONTENTS

1 INTRODUCTION

This chapter considers the authority of EU law. It is organised as follows.

Section 2 considers the claims made in *Van Gend en Loos* (*VGL*) and *Costa* v *ENEL* that EU law is an autonomous legal order which limits national sovereignty. According to these judgments, EU law is to take precedence over national law and give rise to rights which can be directly invoked in national courts. A feature of national judicial reaction is that if national courts have generally been willing to accept the authority of EU law emanating from these cases, they have been resistant to its implications where EU law encroaches on activities of particular national sensitivity. This tension has become more intense as EU law has intruded into ever more salient fields of activity.

Section 3 examines the different doctrines deployed to establish a system of authority for EU law. The autonomy of EU law requires that EU law alone decides which activities it regulates and that its central principles and institutional features cannot be compromised by other legal orders. The primacy of EU law requires that where a conflict is identified by EU law between it and national law, primacy should be given to EU law. The doctrine of pre-emption determines that it should be EU law which decides when and whether there is a conflict between EU law and national law. The fidelity principle, set out in Article 4(3) TEU, imposes institutional duties on both EU and national authorities to ensure that the EU legal system functions effectively.

Section 4 considers the foundations underpinning the authority of EU law. Its authority relies on the pedigree of those recognising it. Historically, this was largely confined to national courts. This granted EU law formal validity, but its authority had limited resonance. This was altered by a Declaration to the Lisbon Treaty which recognised the primacy of EU law. The use of a Declaration suggested that if a political consensus supported this authority, it was still only half-hearted support which did not extend to granting that authority a formal recognition within the main provisions of the Treaty.

This section also looks at the wider grounds for granting EU law authority over national law. It notes that each legal order can provide values, types of relationship and sensibility which cannot be provided by the other. Increasingly, the question is less *whether* one should have *a priori* authority over the other, but rather, *when* each should have authority. The constitutional pluralist school argues that this question should be answered by reference to shared constitutional principles and values. The pluralist school argues, by contrast, against any overarching principles. It argues, instead, for an incremental process where each legal system commits itself to be open to the claims of others without necessarily conceding them.

Section 5 considers how these different arguments have played out in the conditioning of the authority of EU law by national constitutional courts. Many will not grant authority to EU law where it violates fundamental rights in their national constitutions, albeit that some will give EU law leeway here so long as it has fundamental rights mechanisms of its own in place to prevent and rectify abuses. Even these legal systems require national authorities implementing EU law to comply fully with national fundamental rights standards. The next source of review is ultra vires review. The Union must not exceed its competences. Once again, some leeway is granted by the *Honeywell* judgment in Germany. EU law will only not be granted authority if the exceeding of competences was manifest and significant, and the Court of Justice had an opportunity to rectify it and failed to do so. A much stricter standard was applied in the *Slovak Pensions* judgment in the Czech Republic, where simply acting ultra vires with a failure to consider the views of appropriate national institutions was sufficient to deny an EU measure authority.

The most wide-ranging limit on EU legal authority is where it is considered not to have democratic authority. The first circumstance, identity review, is where the EU acts in certain fields which are so central to a state's democratic identity that, lacking the necessary democratic credentials, it is felt that the Union lacks authority to act here. The other concerns provisions of EU law whose open-ended nature renders EU law-making problematic if there is no national parliamentary agreement. These lines of reasoning were brought together in the *ESM* judgment of the German Constitutional Court which held that in both these fields EU law would only have authority if the national parliament had agreed to it and been given sufficient information to discharge its responsibilities.

2 GENESIS OF EU LEGAL AUTHORITY

In the 1950s, it was widely assumed that the traditional model of international law, marked by state sovereignty, would apply to the European Union. Under this model, it is the Member States which are masters of the Treaties. Collectively, they could change the Union's powers and interpret the meaning of the Treaties if they so desired.[1] Furthermore, it was for states, as sovereigns, to determine the domestic legal effects of EU law as an international treaty, in particular whether it can be invoked in national courts and the relationship between it and national laws within the domestic jurisdiction. However, the period also marked a time when many EU Member States were reconsidering their approach to international law. The horrors of the Second World War had led to a belief in a much stronger authority and role for international organisations and international law. The German Basic Law, therefore, provided for the transfer of sovereign rights to international organisations.[2] Furthermore, Germany was not alone. Luxembourg amended its Constitution in 1956 to allow legislative, judicial and executive power to be vested in international organisations,[3] whilst the Dutch amended their Constitution in 1953 to allow treaties to prevail over all laws, including the national constitution.[4]

It was against this context that the Court of Justice adopted two judgments in the early 1960s which have shaped how we conceive the authority of EU law. First, the Court ruled in *Van Gend en Loos* that the Treaty did not merely regulate mutual obligations between Member States, but established what the Court called a 'new legal order of international law for the benefit of which the states have limited their sovereign rights'.[5] This was taken further in *Costa* v *ENEL*. An Italian law sought to nationalise the electricity production and distribution industries. Costa, a shareholder of Edison Volta, a company affected by the nationalisation, claimed that the law breached EU law. The Italian Government claimed that the matter was one of Italian law as the Italian legislation post-dated the EC Treaty and, for that reason, should be held to be the applicable law.

Case 6/64 *Costa* v *ENEL* [1964] ECR 585

By contrast with ordinary international treaties, the EEC Treaty has created its own legal system which, on the entry into force of the Treaty, became an integral part of the legal systems of the Member States and which their courts are bound to apply.

By creating a Community of unlimited duration, having its own institutions, its own personality, its own legal capacity and capacity of representation on the international plane and, more particularly, real powers stemming from a limitation of sovereignty or a transfer of powers from the States to the Community, the Member States have limited their sovereign rights, albeit within limited fields, and have thus created a body of law which binds both their nationals and themselves.

The integration into the laws of each Member State of provisions which derive from the Community, and more generally the terms and the spirit of the Treaty, make it impossible for the States, as a corollary, to accord precedence to a unilateral and subsequent measure over a legal system accepted by them on a basis of reciprocity. Such a measure cannot therefore be inconsistent with that legal system. The executive force of Community law cannot vary from one State to another in deference to

---

[1] J. Weiler and U. Haltern, 'The Autonomy of the Community Legal Order: Through the Looking Glass' (1996) 37 *Harvard Int. LJ* 411, 417–19.

[2] Basic Law, art. 24.   [3] Luxembourg Constitution, art. 49*bis*.

[4] At the time, this was Netherlands Constitution, art. 66. It is now art. 94. On these developments see G. Bebr, 'Relation of the European Coal and Steel Community Law to the Law of the Member States: A Peculiar Legal Symbiosis' (1958) 58 *Columbia Law Review* 767, 777*et seq.*

[5] Case 26/62 *Van Gend en Loos* v *Nederlandse Administratie der Belastingen* [1963] ECR 1. This is considered in more detail in Chapters 1 and 7. See pp. 16–18 and 293–4.

subsequent domestic laws, without jeopardizing the attainment of the objectives of the Treaty set out in Article [4(3) TEU] and giving rise to the discrimination prohibited by Article [18 TFEU].

The obligations undertaken under the Treaty establishing the Community would not be unconditional, but merely contingent, if they could be called in question by subsequent legislative acts of the signatories. Wherever the Treaty grants the States the right to act unilaterally, it does this by clear and precise provisions...Applications, by Member States for authority to derogate from the Treaty are subject to a special authorization procedure...which would lose their purpose if the Member States could renounce their obligations by means of an ordinary law.

The precedence of Community law is confirmed by Article [288 TFEU], whereby a regulation 'shall be binding' and 'directly applicable in all Member States'. This provision, which is subject to no reservation, would be quite meaningless if a state could unilaterally nullify its effects by means of a legislative measure which could prevail over Community law.

It follows from all these observations that the law stemming from the Treaty, an independent source of law, could not, because of its special and original nature, be overridden by domestic legal provisions, however framed, without being deprived of its character as Community law and without the legal basis of the Community itself being called into question.

The transfer by the Member States from their domestic legal system to the Community legal system of the rights and obligations arising under the Treaty carries with it a permanent limitation of their sovereign rights, against which a subsequent unilateral act incompatible with the concept of the Community cannot prevail.

Van Gend en Loos and *Costa* curb Member State power, and not in a small way. EU law is to limit its most absolute expression, national sovereignty. A feature of the years following these judgments was, consequently, a mixed response. Formally, all national legal systems committed themselves to accepting the primacy of EU law over national law.[6] However, many were unwilling to accept its authority on issues of strong sensitivity. Issues of fundamental rights, national security and taxation were at some time all ruled off limits.[7] Insofar as EU law rarely touched on these sensitive issues in the first years, however, conflicts were only occasional.[8]

As EU legal activities expanded, the tension between this formal commitment to primacy and concerns about the encroachment by EU law onto ever more sensitive activities became ever more difficult to avoid.[9] In *Melloni*, an Italian was charged with fraud. He skipped bail, and, in his absence, was convicted in Italy to ten years' imprisonment. Eleven years later, he

[6] On this see B. de Witte, 'Direct Effect, Supremacy, and the Nature of the Legal Order' in P. Craig and G. de Búrca (eds.), *The Evolution of EU Law* (Oxford, Oxford University Press, 1999) 196–8.

[7] *Frontini v Ministero delle Finanze* [1974] 2 CMLR 372 (Italy, fundamental rights); *Internationale Handelsgesellschaft v Einfuhr und Vorratsstelle für Getreide und Futtermittel* [1974] 2 CMLR 540 (fundamental rights, Germany); *Cohn-Bendit* [1980] 1 CMLR 543 (public security, France); *Re Value Added Tax Directives* [1982] 1 CMLR 427 (tax, Germany). On the reaction in Germany see B. Davies, *Resisting the European Court of Justice: West Germany's Confrontation with European Law, 1949–1979* (Cambridge, Cambridge University Press, 2012) 88 et seq.

[8] D. Chalmers, 'European Restatements of Sovereignty' in R. Rawlings *et al.* (eds.), *Sovereignty and the Law* (Oxford, Oxford University Press, 2013).

[9] The primacy of EU law over national constitutions is not new. See Case 11/70 *Internationale Handelsgesellschaft v Einfuhr und Vorratstelle für Getreide und Futtermittel* [1970] ECR 1125. See also Case C-409/06 *Winner Wetten v Bürgermeisterin der Stadt Bergheim* [2010] ECR I-8015.

was arrested in Spain. He opposed his surrender back to Italy under a European Arrest Warrant, Framework Decision 2002/584/EU, on the grounds that he had been deprived of the right to a fair trial by being convicted *in absentia*. The Framework Decision provided that trial *in absentia* was not a valid reason to refuse surrender. The matter went to the Tribunal Constitucional, the Spanish Constitutional Court, who thought the right to a fair trial, as protected by the Spanish Constitution, might be prejudiced. The matter concerned, therefore, a fundamental right, a constitutional text and the highest court in the land. Its import was shown by nine governments, the Council and the Commission intervening in the case. The Spanish court asked whether Article 53 of the European Union Charter of Fundamental Rights meant that EU law should allow national constitutions with a higher protection of fundamental rights to prevail. Article 53 states: 'Nothing in this Charter shall be interpreted as restricting or adversely affecting human rights and fundamental freedoms as recognised, in their respective fields of application, by Union law and by the Member States' constitutions.'

Case C-399/11 *Melloni*, Judgment of 26 February 2013

56. The interpretation envisaged by the national court at the outset is that Article 53 of the Charter gives general authorisation to a Member State to apply the standard of protection of fundamental rights guaranteed by its constitution when that standard is higher than that deriving from the Charter and, where necessary, to give it priority over the application of provisions of EU law. Such an interpretation would, in particular, allow a Member State to make the execution of a European arrest warrant issued for the purposes of executing a sentence rendered *in absentia* subject to conditions intended to avoid an interpretation which restricts or adversely affects fundamental rights recognised by its constitution, even though the application of such conditions is not allowed under Article 4a(1) of Framework Decision 2002/584.

57. Such an interpretation of Article 53 of the Charter cannot be accepted.

58. That interpretation of Article 53 of the Charter would undermine the principle of the primacy of EU law inasmuch as it would allow a Member State to disapply EU legal rules which are fully in compliance with the Charter where they infringe the fundamental rights guaranteed by that State's constitution.

59. It is settled case-law that, by virtue of the principle of primacy of EU law, which is an essential feature of the EU legal order…rules of national law, even of a constitutional order, cannot be allowed to undermine the effectiveness of EU law on the territory of that State…

60. It is true that Article 53 of the Charter confirms that, where an EU legal act calls for national implementing measures, national authorities and courts remain free to apply national standards of protection of fundamental rights, provided that the level of protection provided for by the Charter, as interpreted by the Court, and the primacy, unity and effectiveness of EU law are not thereby compromised.

61. However…Article 4a(1) of Framework Decision 2002/584 does not allow Member States to refuse to execute a European arrest warrant when the person concerned is in one of the situations provided for therein.

In *Melloni*, the line of reasoning started by *VGL* and *Costa* now requires a constitutional court to disapply a constitutional provision if it conflicts with EU law. Such reasoning is audacious not simply in terms of its politics. It requires a mechanism within the national legal settlement to give effect to the authority of EU law.

B. de Witte, 'Direct Effect, Primacy, and the Nature of the Legal Order' in P. Craig and G. de Búrca (eds.), *The Evolution of EU Law* (2nd edn, Oxford, Oxford University Press, 2011) 323, 350–1

A benign interpretation is that national courts must necessarily find a way to recognise those principles and to achieve the result imposed by the European Court on them. A stronger interpretation would be that national courts have no choice and that they simply cannot resist the authority of EU law. The latter reading implies that national courts, when acting on the duties imposed on them by the European Court, are exercising a jurisdiction attributed to them directly by Union law, and not a jurisdiction given to them by their own constitutions. This view was adopted by many European Community law scholars, particularly those of France and the BENELUX countries, but there is hardly any evidence of national courts adopting this radical approach. National courts see themselves as organs of their state, and try to fit their European mandate within the framework of the powers attributed to them by their national legal system. For them (and, indeed, for most constitutional law scholars throughout Europe) the idea that EU law can claim its primacy within the national legal system on the basis of its own authority seems as implausible as Baron von Munchhausen's claim that he had lifted himself from the sand by pulling on his bootstraps. The national courts (with the possible exception of those of the Netherlands) see EU law as rooted in their constitution, and seek a foundation for the primacy and direct effect of EU law in that constitution.

This is often not an easy task, as most national constitutions fail to deal explicitly with the internal effect of EU law (or international law in general). In the absence of such explicit provisions, recourse may be had to the constitutional clauses allowing for EU membership or, more generally, allowing for the attribution of state powers to organisations like the European Union. Such provisions *do* occur in all the written constitutions of the Member States, except that of Finland; although their wording is different, they serve broadly the same purpose of enabling membership of advanced international organisations such as the European Union. In some countries they have been given an additional significance as the basis for the domestic effect of EU law.

3 CLAIMS OF EU LEGAL AUTHORITY

Costa, *VGL* and these constitutional mechanisms were all necessary to put in place a system of EU legal authority. However, they were not sufficient. For the authority of EU law is about more than simply requiring EU law to be obeyed over national law. A number of claims have to be made by EU law (and met) for it to have its own system of legal authority. Over time, each has crystallised into a doctrine of EU law with its own features. The first demand is that it is for EU law alone to determine which activities are governed by it (*autonomy of EU law*). Secondly, EU law takes precedence over other law unless it expressly says otherwise (*primacy of EU law*). Thirdly, it determines when there is a conflict between it and national law, and the consequences of such a conflict (*pre-emption*). Finally, institutions, in particular national ones, are under a series of duties to secure the functioning of EU law (*fidelity principle*).

(i) Autonomy of EU law

Legal autonomy entails, first, that it is the legal order which determines which activities are governed by it and, secondly, that it determines which particular laws are to apply to these activities and how these laws are to be administered. The assertion that EU law, and no other legal order, determines which activities are governed by it is implicit in *Costa*. The dispute revolved around whether Italian law or EU law was to govern activities that fell within the aegis of the EU Treaties. In asserting that it was to be EU law, the Court of Justice was not merely seeking to resolve the conflict between Italian law and EU law but also claiming a monopoly for EU law to determine the activities governed by it, and which EU law provisions were to apply.

International law poses particular challenges here. The Union is bound by international agreements which are either concluded by it or to which it has succeeded the Member States.[10] Insofar as these then form part of EU law, it could be argued that activities regulated by them are regulated by EU law. However, this is contrived when the content of these agreements clashes with other provisions of EU law. At such moments, it is really international law not EU law which determines the remit of EU legal authority. The Court has squared this circle by stating that the autonomy of EU law allows international agreements to prevail over secondary legislation but not over fundamental principles of the Treaty. In *Kadi*,[11] a challenge was made to two EU measures which implemented United Nations Security Council Resolutions. These provided for sanctions to be applied against individuals named by a United Nations Sanctions Committee as involved in terrorist activities. It was (successfully) argued by Kadi that this process violated EU law, in particular his fundamental rights of defence as he had neither been able to see the inculpatory evidence nor to make a case as to his innocence.[12] This claim, however, begged the question as to whether his status was regulated by international law or EU law.

Joined Cases C–402/05 P and C–415/05 P *Kadi and Al Barakaat International Foundation* v *Council and Commission* [2008] ECR I–6351

281. In this connection it is to be borne in mind that the Community is based on the rule of law, inasmuch as neither its Member States nor its institutions can avoid review of the conformity of their acts with the basic constitutional charter, the EC Treaty, which established a complete system of legal remedies and procedures designed to enable the Court of Justice to review the legality of acts of the institutions...

282. It is also to be recalled that an international agreement cannot affect the allocation of powers fixed by the Treaties or, consequently, the autonomy of the Community legal system, observance of which is ensured by the Court by virtue of the exclusive jurisdiction...that the Court has, moreover, already held to form part of the very foundations of the Community...

283. In addition, according to settled case-law, fundamental rights form an integral part of the general principles of law whose observance the Court ensures. For that purpose, the Court draws

---

[10] See, respectively, Article 216(2) TFEU and Joined Cases 21/72–24/72 *International Fruit* v *Prudktschap voor Groenten en Fruit* [1972] ECR 1219.

[11] The judgment is described in more detail at pp. 433–6.

[12] Procedures were amended requiring the Sanctions Committee to provide reasons, and for the named parties to be able to make a case to the Commission prior to EU implementing measures. These were found not to violate Kadi's rights to defence. However, the sanctions were still declared illegal as insufficient reasons were produced to justify their imposition. Joined Cases C–584/10P, C–593/10P and C–595/10 *European Commission and others* v *Kadi*, Judgment of 18 July 2013.

inspiration from the constitutional traditions common to the Member States and from the guidelines supplied by international instruments for the protection of human rights on which the Member States have collaborated or to which they are signatories. In that regard, the ECHR has special significance...

284. It is also clear from the case-law that respect for human rights is a condition of the lawfulness of Community acts...and that measures incompatible with respect for human rights are not acceptable in the Community...

285. It follows from all those considerations that the obligations imposed by an international agreement cannot have the effect of prejudicing the constitutional principles of the EC Treaty, which include the principle that all Community acts must respect fundamental rights, that respect constituting a condition of their lawfulness which it is for the Court to review in the framework of the complete system of legal remedies established by the Treaty.

286. In this regard it must be emphasised that, in circumstances such as those of these cases, the review of lawfulness thus to be ensured by the Community judicature applies to the Community act intended to give effect to the international agreement at issue, and not to the latter as such.

287. With more particular regard to a Community act which, like the contested regulation, is intended to give effect to a resolution adopted by the Security Council under Chapter VII of the Charter of the United Nations, it is not, therefore, for the Community judicature, under the exclusive jurisdiction provided for by Article 220 EC, to review the lawfulness of such a resolution adopted by an international body, even if that review were to be limited to examination of the compatibility of that resolution with jus cogens.

288. However, any judgment given by the Community judicature deciding that a Community measure intended to give effect to such a resolution is contrary to a higher rule of law in the Community legal order would not entail any challenge to the primacy of that resolution in international law.

Similar reasoning has also been applied with regard to the second dimension of legal autonomy, namely, that EU law is responsible for determining which particular law regulates the activities in question. This could be compromised where the Union accedes to a treaty with its own law-making or judicial institutions, which elaborate norms of international law which displace EU law.[13] Such institutions can be established, putting in measures which become part of EU law,[14] but they must not have such powers that they can alter the essential character of EU law. A good example is *Opinion 1/09*, which concerned the original agreement for a Unified Patent Court.[15] As with the current agreement, the agreement provided for a new court, the Patent Court (PC) to have exclusive jurisdiction over, inter alia, infringements, revocations and damages concerning this unified patent. Only it could make references to the Court of Justice, and there was little recourse if it did not follow these judgments. Unlike its successor, the original agreement provided for the Union to be a member.

[13] J. Czuczai, 'The Autonomy of the EU Legal Order and the Law-making Activities of International Organizations: Some Examples regarding the Council's Most Recent Practice' (2012) 31 *YBEL* 452.

[14] On the decisions made by the EU-Turkey Association Council see Case C-372/06 *Asda* v *Commissioners of Her Majesty's Revenue and Customs* [2007] ECR I-11223.

[15] With international treaties, an Opinion can be sought from the Court after agreement but prior to ratification by a Member State, the Council, Commission or Parliament, Article 218(11) TFEU.

Opinion 1/09 on a European and Community Patents Court [2011] ECR I-1137

71. As regards the characteristics of the PC, it must first be observed that that court is outside the institutional and judicial framework of the European Union. It is not part of the judicial system provided for in Article 19(1) TEU. The PC is an organisation with a distinct legal personality under international law…

74. As regards an international agreement providing for the creation of a court responsible for the interpretation of its provisions, the Court has, it is true, held that such an agreement is not, in principle, incompatible with European Union law. The competence of the European Union in the field of international relations and its capacity to conclude international agreements necessarily entail the power to submit itself to the decisions of a court which is created or designated by such agreements as regards the interpretation and application of their provisions…

75. Moreover, the Court has stated that an international agreement concluded with third countries may confer new judicial powers on the Court provided that in so doing it does not change the essential character of the function of the Court as conceived in the EU and FEU Treaties…

76. The Court has also declared that an international agreement may affect its own powers provided that the indispensable conditions for safeguarding the essential character of those powers are satisfied and, consequently, there is no adverse effect on the autonomy of the European Union legal order…

78. … the international court envisaged in this draft agreement is to be called upon to interpret and apply not only the provisions of that agreement but also the future regulation on the Community patent and other instruments of European Union law, in particular regulations and directives in conjunction with which that regulation would, when necessary, have to be read, namely provisions relating to other bodies of rules on intellectual property, and rules of the FEU Treaty concerning the internal market and competition law. Likewise, the PC may be called upon to determine a dispute pending before it in the light of the fundamental rights and general principles of European Union law, or even to examine the validity of an act of the European Union.

79. As regards the draft agreement submitted for the Court's consideration, it must be observed that the PC:
    - takes the place of national courts and tribunals, in the field of its exclusive jurisdiction described in Article 15 of that draft agreement,
    - deprives, therefore, those courts and tribunals of the power to request preliminary rulings from the Court in that field,
    - becomes, in the field of its exclusive jurisdiction, the sole court able to communicate with the Court by means of a reference for a preliminary ruling concerning the interpretation and application of European Union law and
    - has the duty, within that jurisdiction, in accordance with Article 14a of that draft agreement, to interpret and apply European Union law…

81. The draft agreement provides for a preliminary ruling mechanism which reserves, within the scope of that agreement, the power to refer questions for a preliminary ruling to the PC while removing that power from the national courts.…

84. The system set up by Article 267 TFEU…establishes between the Court of Justice and the national courts direct cooperation as part of which the latter are closely involved in the correct application and uniform interpretation of European Union law and also in the protection of individual rights conferred by that legal order.

85. … the tasks attributed to the national courts and to the Court of Justice respectively are indispensable to the preservation of the very nature of the law established by the Treaties.…

89. Consequently, the envisaged agreement, by conferring on an international court which is outside the institutional and judicial framework of the European Union an exclusive jurisdiction to hear a significant

number of actions brought by individuals in the field of the Community patent and to interpret and apply European Union law in that field, would deprive courts of Member States of their powers in relation to the interpretation and application of European Union law and the Court of its powers to reply, by preliminary ruling, to questions referred by those courts and, consequently, would alter the essential character of the powers which the Treaties confer on the institutions of the European Union and on the Member States and which are indispensable to the preservation of the very nature of European Union law.

The central criticism of both *Kadi* and *Opinion 1/09* is that they privilege EU law at the expense of the autonomy of other legal orders. There is insensitivity, in particular, to the consequences on the international legal order. If every state privileged its legal order in the manner done in *Kadi*, the international legal system would break down. It has been suggested that there is a lack of openness to the perspective of other legal systems.[16] Only EU laws were thus invoked. A better case might have been made if the Court of Justice had considered international law sources, and the validity of the UN Security Council Resolutions in the light of these. Others, by contrast, have commended the Court for standing up for matters of particular significance, such as fundamental rights or the structure of the EU judicial order.[17] In reality, the arguments may not be far apart. Few dispute that valuable elements integral to EU law should be protected. The issue goes to the manner in which this is done and the thought given to the consequences of this for other legal orders.

(ii) Primacy of EU law

The primacy of EU law is in a sense the most straightforward of all the doctrines. It states that when EU law has identified a conflict between it and national law, it should take precedence over national law, as in *Costa* and *Melloni*. The principle also has a jurisdictional dimension. It is not open to national law to determine which courts can hear conflicts. The primacy of EU law applies whenever a conflict appears before any court or body which is competent to take a legal decision. In *Simmenthal*, an Italian system of fees for veterinary inspections of beef imports had already been held by the Court of Justice to breach EU law. An Italian magistrate asked the Court whether he was required to disapply the relevant Italian law. This was a power which at that time was enjoyed only by the Italian Constitutional Court as only it had the power of legislative review.

Case 106/77 *Amministrazione delle Finanze dello Stato* v *Simmenthal* [1978] ECR 629

17. ... in accordance with the principle of the precedence of Community law, the relationship between provisions of the Treaty and directly applicable measures of the institutions on the one hand and the national law of the Member States on the other is such that those provisions and measures not only by their entry into force render automatically inapplicable any conflicting provision of current national law but – in so far as they are an integral part of, and take precedence in, the legal order

---

[16] G. de Búrca, 'The EU, the European Court of Justice and the International Legal Order after Kadi' (2010) 51 *Harvard International Law Journal* 1.
[17] N. Türküler Isiksel, 'Fundamental Rights in the EU after *Kadi and Al Barakaat*' [2010] 16 *ELJ* 551.

applicable in the territory of each of the Member States – also preclude the valid adoption of new national legislative measures to the extent to which they would be incompatible with community provisions.

18. Indeed any recognition that national legislative measures which encroach upon the field within which the Community exercises its legislative power or which are otherwise incompatible with the provisions of Community law had any legal effect would amount to a corresponding denial of the effectiveness of obligations undertaken unconditionally and irrevocably by Member States pursuant to the Treaty and would thus imperil the very foundations of the Community....

21. ... every national court must, in a case within its jurisdiction, apply Community law in its entirety and protect rights which the latter confers on individuals and must accordingly set aside any provision of national law which may conflict with it, whether prior or subsequent to the Community rule.

22. Accordingly any provision of a national legal system and any legislative, administrative or judicial practice which might impair the effectiveness of Community law by withholding from the national court having jurisdiction to apply such law the power to do everything necessary at the moment of its application to set aside national legislative provisions which might prevent Community rules from having full force and effect are incompatible with those requirements which are the very essence of Community law.

The primacy of EU law expands, therefore, the scope of judicial review. If, in some jurisdictions, many courts do not have the power to disapply administrative acts or engage in legislative review because they are considered too junior or there are insufficient procedural safeguards, this is not the case when it comes to EU law. Any court can engage in administrative or legislative review if the measure breaches some EU law. Primacy of EU law, thus, increases judicial power significantly. It also disperses power within the judiciary so that what in many jurisdictions was a very confined power is now a universal power.[18]

(iii) Pre-emption

The doctrine of pre-emption governs the question of when there is a conflict and the consequences of such a conflict for EU and national law.[19] There are three forms of pre-emption.

- *Field pre-emption*: EU law is considered to have a jurisdictional monopoly over a field. National laws, irrespective of whether they conflict with EU measures, can only be enacted with the authorisation of EU law.
- *Rule pre-emption*: There is shared jurisdiction over a policy field. National measures can be adopted but will be set aside if they conflict with an EU law.
- *Obstacle pre-emption*: Member States are free to adopt national measures but must not adopt measures which obstruct the effectiveness of EU policies.[20]

---

[18] All courts also have an unfettered discretion to refer the matter to the Court of Justice, Case C–416/10 *Križan v Slovenská inšpekcia životného prostredia*, Judgment of 15 January 2013. See pp. 146–7.

[19] R. Schütze, 'Supremacy without Pre-emption? The Very Slowly Emergent Doctrine of Pre-emption' [2006] 43 *CMLRev.* 1023, 1033.

[20] This categorisation is taken from Schütze, *Ibid.* 1038.

The Treaties do not follow this categorisation directly. Instead, to set the terms for when there is legal conflict, they make a distinction between two forms of government: one in which the Union has exclusive competence and the other in which there are shared competences between the Union and the Member States.[21]

Article 2 TFEU

1. When the Treaties confer on the Union exclusive competence in a specific area, only the Union may legislate and adopt legally binding acts, the Member States being able to do so themselves only if so empowered by the Union or for the implementation of acts of the Union.
2. When the Treaties confer on the Union a competence shared with the Member States in a specific area, the Union and the Member States may legislate and adopt legally binding acts in that area. The Member States shall exercise their competence to the extent that the Union has not exercised its competence. The Member States shall exercise their competence again to the extent that the Union has decided to cease exercising its competence.

The model of integration in fields of exclusive competence is one of dual federalism. The Union and Member States are co-equals. There is a division of power into mutually exclusive spheres with the Union governing some and Member States others.[22] In fields of exclusive competence, therefore, only the Union may legislate, with Member States being able to legislate only if authorised by the Union or to implement EU measures. From a national perspective, this is the most draconian of competences as it involves a complete surrender of jurisdiction to the Union. There is *a priori* field pre-emption by the Union in these fields. For that reason, the fields of exclusive competence are rather limited. They comprise: the customs union; the competition rules necessary for the functioning of the internal market; monetary policy for the euro area state; the conservation of marine biological resources under the common fisheries policy; and the common commercial policy.[23]

There is also a tension within this model. Its practical consequence goes to when there is no EU legislation in place. In such circumstances, national legislation is not permitted without EU authorisation. It is worth considering why we would wish this. One argument is that the competence simply does not exist unless there is an exclusive competence. There can be no customs union, therefore, without a single external tariff, or single monetary policy without a single currency. Another argument is that exclusivity is necessary for the policy to function optimally. Exclusivity may be necessary for the common commercial policy as different trade policies would compromise defence of a common Union interest.[24] The challenge with both arguments is that they go to the Union having a single policy once it has legislated. Neither argument goes to what to do when there is no EU legislation at all. In such circumstances, the

---

[21] Article 2 TFEU mentions other forms of Union competence: coordination of economic and employment policies; Common Foreign and Security Policy; and measures to support, coordinate or supplement national action. EU law does not claim precedence in these fields.

[22] R. Schütze, 'Dual Federalism Constitutionalised: The Emergence of Exclusive Competences in the EC Legal Order' [2007] 32 *ELRev.* 3.

[23] Article 3 TFEU.

[24] *Opinion 1/75 Re Understanding on a Local Costs Standard* [1975] ECR 1355.

policy is not compromised by national difference as there is no Union policy at all. In such circumstances, the Union has granted wide authorisations to allow Member States to legislate. This has resulted in a softening of exclusive competences, as a *modus vivendi* emerges where competence is effectively shared between EU and national law, with many national regimes still in place in fields such as fisheries and the common commercial policy, albeit placed under a duty to justify themselves to the Union.[25]

The model of integration in fields of shared competence is one of cooperative federalism. A shared responsibility is granted to both the Union and the Member State to realise a common policy. There is no fixed division as they work together to realise this common goal with the balance of responsibilities determined by the terms, limits and presence of EU legislation.[26] This model of integration applies to: the internal market; social policy; cohesion policy; agriculture and fisheries, excluding the conservation of marine biological resources; environment; consumer protection; transport; trans-European networks; energy; freedom, security and justice; and common safety concerns in public health matters.[27]

As there is no fixed division in the sharing of responsibilities, one finds all three forms of pre-emption, described earlier, in areas of shared competences.

Field pre-emption occurs in certain areas, notably the single market and agriculture, where a piece of EU legislation has been adopted. This is deemed to occupy the field of activity and Member States are pre-empted from legislating on the activity in question. This is different from exclusive competence as field pre-emption is not *a priori* here but relies on the enactment of this legislation. An example is *Commission* v *United Kingdom*. The Commission brought an action against a British requirement that cars could only be driven on British roads if they were equipped with dim-dip lights.[28] The relevant Directive on motor vehicle lighting did not impose this requirement and, furthermore, provided that any car which met its stipulations should be able to be driven on the roads. The Court of Justice found the British requirement to be illegal. It stated that the intention of the Directive was to regulate exhaustively the conditions for lighting devices on cars. As this was now exhaustively regulated by EU law, Member States were prohibited from imposing additional requirements on motor vehicle lighting.

This relationship makes sense where there is a need for uniformity. Within the context of the single market, the maintenance of differing national regimes can lead to distortions of competition and trade restrictions, with the consequence that the harmonisation process would be robbed of much of its effect. Even there, it creates a regime which is both monolithic and inflexible. It is impossible to maintain national provisions that impose higher standards, and the only way of adapting legislation to new risks and technologies is through amending the EU legislation in question.[29]

In spheres of activity where this need for uniformity is perceived as less pressing, field pre-emption is less common. Instead, a form of rule pre-emption takes place. Provision is made by

---

[25] For example, national export restrictions have been allowed to be maintained in the field of the common commercial policy on such wide grounds as public policy, Case C-70/94 *Werner* [1995] ECR I-3189.

[26] R. Schütze, 'Co-operative Federalism Constitutionalised: The Emergence of Complementary Competences in the EC Legal Order' [2006] 31 *ELRev.* 167, 168–9.

[27] Article 4(2) TFEU.

[28] Case 60/86 *Commission* v *United Kingdom* [1988] ECR 3921.

[29] S. Weatherill, 'Beyond Preemption? Shared Competence and Constitutional Change in the European Community' in D. O'Keeffe and P. Twomey (eds.), *Legal Issues of the Maastricht Treaty* (London, Chancery, 1994) 13, 18–19.

the Treaties for minimum harmonisation in certain fields.[30] Member States are not prevented from enacting more protective provisions. However, EU law establishes a floor of legal protections below which national legislation must not go. If it does, it violates EU law (rule preemption). The idea of legislation being more or less protective is, of course, a charged notion. Litigation has, thus, focused on when this is the case. In *Deponiezweckverband Eiterköpfe*, a landfill operator was refused permission to fill two sites with waste as it exceeded German limits on the proportion of organic waste that could be disposed of in landfill sites.[31] By contrast, the Directive (on which the German law was based) set limits only for biodegradable organic waste. The operator argued that the national legislation was, therefore, unlawful. The Court of Justice disagreed. It stated that the German legislation pursued the same objective as the Directive, namely, the limitation of waste going into landfill. Insofar as it set limits for a wider range of waste, it was more stringent than the EU Directive and was, therefore, permissible.

Minimum harmonisation can also take place in fields where there is no provision for it in the Treaties but the relevant EU law provides for it. The impact of an EU measure on an important domestic public interest can be overlooked by such legislation. The Court has, thus, on occasion, interpreted EU legislation narrowly, so that it is not deemed to regulate the field covered by national law, thereby allowing the national legislation to remain in place.[32] If this is not possible, in extreme circumstances, the Court will refuse to disapply the national legislation. *Commission v Germany* is an example.[33] Member States were required by Directive 79/409/EEC to designate the most suitable habitats in their territory for certain species of wild bird. Once designated, these habitats were to be preserved and appropriate steps taken to prevent their deterioration. The Directive envisaged no circumstances in which measures could be taken to reduce the size of the special protection areas and there was no provision for minimum harmonisation, as the Directive was based on Article 352 TFEU, the flexibility provision. Germany wished to build a dyke across one of its designated areas in the Leybucht region. It argued this was necessary for good ecological reasons. The coast would be washed away otherwise. Despite there being no provision, the Court held that it could reduce the size of the special protection area. It could do this, the Court ruled, because, exceptionally, there was in this case a general interest (protection of the coastline), which was superior to that represented in the Directive. The Court ruled the dyke could therefore be built but must involve the smallest disruption possible to the protection area that was necessary to secure the coastline.

The final form of pre-emption which takes part in areas of shared competence is in fields where the exercise of EU competence is not 'to prevent Member States from exercising theirs'.[34] Such fields comprise research and development, space, development and humanitarian aid. The Union and Member States exercise parallel competences here. A form of obstacle pre-emption takes place. Member States are, in principle, free to develop their own policy, but there is a

---

[30] Notably criminal justice (Article 82(2) TFEU); social policy (Article 153(2)(b) TFEU); public health legislation on organs and blood (Article 168(4)(a) TFEU); consumer protection (Article 169 TFEU); environment (Article 193 TFEU).

[31] Case C-6/03 *Deponiezweckverband Eiterköpfe* [2005] ECR I-2753.

[32] Examples of this include Case C-11/92 *R v Secretary of State for Health, ex parte Gallaher Ltd* [1993] ECR I-3545.

[33] Case C-57/89 *Commission v Germany* [1991] ECR I-883.   [34] Article 4(3) and (4) TFEU.

commitment not to take any measure which will obstruct the realisation of Union objectives, most notably through disrupting exercise of its competences in these fields.[35]

(iv) Fidelity principle

All legal systems confer responsibilities upon public bodies to ensure that the law is clear, generally applied, policed and that there are sufficient remedies for breach of the law. Known in the United States as the 'fidelity principle', the requirement is that 'each level and unit of government must act to ensure the proper functioning of the system of governance as a whole'.[36] In EU law, the principle is set out in Article 4(3) TEU.

Article 4(3) TEU

3. Pursuant to the principle of sincere cooperation, the Union and the Member States shall, in full mutual respect, assist each other in carrying out tasks which flow from the Treaties.

   The Member States shall take any appropriate measure, general or particular, to ensure fulfilment of the obligations arising out of the Treaties or resulting from the acts of the institutions of the Union.

   The Member States shall facilitate the achievement of the Union's tasks and refrain from any measure which could jeopardise the attainment of the Union's objectives.

Article 4(3) TEU has been described as 'drawing all relevant institutions into the job of effectively sustaining [Union] policy'.[37] It applies not only to the Member States, but also to the EU institutions, which must cooperate with national bodies to secure the full effectiveness of EU law.[38] The cooperation takes place on the basis of 'mutual respect'. This suggests a countervailing principle, under which each institution must not just assist each other but must not transgress upon the prerogatives of the other. This would imply, for example, that if the duty of cooperation currently imposes a responsibility on national courts not to assess a potentially anti-competitive practice being considered by the Commission[39] or to give judgments which run counter to its decisions,[40] there may be a corollary obligation on the Commission to leave to national authorities assessment of practices more appropriately considered by them.[41]

The fidelity provision carries both negative and positive obligations for Member States.

The central negative obligation is that once EU institutions have indicated a point of departure for common action, Member States are under a duty to abstain from any measure which could frustrate realisation of its objectives. In the field of external relations, if the Commission

---

[35] Case C-246/07 *Commission v Sweden* [2010] ECR I-3317; Opinion of Advocate General Mengozzi in Case C-132/09 *Commission v Belgium* [2010] ECR I-8695.

[36] D. Halberstam, 'The Political Morality of Federal Systems' (2004) 90 *Virginia L Rev.* 101, 104.

[37] S. Weatherill, 'Beyond Preemption? Shared Competence and Constitutional Change in the European Community' in D. O'Keeffe and P. Twomey (eds.), *Legal Issues of the Maastricht Treaty* (Chichester, Chancery Law Publishing, 1994) 31.

[38] Case 2/88 *Zwartveld* [1990] ECR I-3365.

[39] Case C-344/98 *Masterfoods v HB Ice Cream* [2000] ECR I-11369.

[40] Case C-199/11 *Otis*, Judgment of 6 November 2012.

[41] This is already established by the Commission Notice on Cooperation within the network of competition authorities [2004] OJ C101/43, para. 8.

has been authorised to conclude an international agreement, therefore, Member States cannot enter independent bilateral agreements of their own on the subject in hand with the non-EU state concerned unless this is done with the cooperation of the EU institutions.[42] Internally, this duty applies with most force to Directives, which have been adopted but whose deadline for transposition has not yet expired. Whilst national authorities have until the deadline to adopt implementing legislation, they are under a duty prior to that to abstain from any measure which would compromise the objectives of the Directive. The national legislature cannot pass legislation that would conflict with the Directive, and national courts, where this choice is open to them under national law, are not free to adopt interpretations that would conflict with it.[43]

The positive obligations are multiple. First, national institutions are required to secure legal certainty for EU law. The Court of Justice has stated that Member States must implement their obligations 'with unquestionable binding force and with the specificity, precision and clarity necessary to satisfy that principle'.[44] Mere administrative practice will not be enough to meet a Member State's obligations. Measures must be in place which, whilst not necessarily legislation, are sufficiently binding that they cannot be changed at will. Such measures must be public so that citizens are able to identify the source of their rights.[45] This entails a duty to publish not only the national measure but also the EU measure which gave rise to it.[46]

Secondly, Member States must actively police EU law. In *Commission* v *France*, French farmers launched a violent campaign targeting the importation of Spanish strawberries.[47] Their action involved threatening shops, burning lorries carrying the goods and blockading roads. The French Government took almost no action either to stop these protests or to prosecute offences committed as a result of them. While the acts stopping the import of Spanish strawberries were performed by *private* actors – the farmers – and while the relevant provision of EU law, Article 34 TFEU, imposed obligations only on *states* not to prevent the free movement of goods, the Court ruled that France had breached EU law. The Member State was required to adopt all appropriate measures to guarantee the full scope and effect of EU law. In taking measures that were manifestly inadequate, France had failed to do this. The requirement to police EU law, however, is not an absolute one: a Member State does not have to police EU law if this would result in public disorder which it could not contain. Similarly, it must not police EU law in such a way that it violates fundamental rights and civil liberties.[48]

Thirdly, Member States are under a duty to notify the Commission if they have any problems applying or enforcing EU law. In this regard, they cannot use Commission reservations, conditions or objections as a basis for derogating from EU law.[49]

Finally, Member States must penalise infringements of EU law under conditions which are, both procedurally and substantively, analogous to those applicable to infringements of

---

[42] Case C-266/03 *Commission* v *Luxembourg* [2005] ECR I-4805.
[43] Case C-212/04 *Adeneler and others* v *ELOG* [2006] ECR I-6057; Joined Cases C-165–167/09 *Stichting Natuur en Milieu* v *College van Gedeputeerde Staten van Groningen* [2011] ECR I-4599.
[44] Case C-159/99 *Commission* v *Italy* [2001] ECR I-4007.
[45] Case C-313/99 *Mulgan and others* [2002] ECR I-5719. The principle of legal certainty also requires that if Member States amend a law to comply with EU law, the amendment must have the same legal force as the original measure, Case C-33/03 *Commission* v *United Kingdom* [2005] ECR I-1865.
[46] Case C-146/11 *Pimix*, Judgment of 12 July 2012.
[47] Case C-265/95 *Commission* v *France* [1997] ECR I-6959.
[48] Case C-112/00 *Schmidberger* v *Republic of Austria* [2003] ECR I-5659.
[49] Case C-105/02 *Commission* v *Germany* [2006] ECR I-9659.

national law of a similar nature and importance.[50] In addition, national courts must ensure that, irrespective of how breaches of national law are handled, penalties for breach of EU law are effective, proportionate and dissuasive.[51] In *Berlusconi*,[52] Advocate General Kokott set out what these criteria mean.

Joined Cases C–387/02, C–391/02 and C–403/02 *Berlusconi et al.* [2005] ECR I-3565

88. Rules laying down penalties are *effective* where they are framed in such a way that they do not make it practically impossible or excessively difficult to impose the penalty provided for and, therefore, to attain the objectives pursued by Community law.

89. A penalty is *dissuasive* where it prevents an individual from infringing the objectives pursued and rules laid down by Community law. What is decisive in this regard is not only the nature and level of the penalty but also the likelihood of its being imposed. Anyone who commits an infringement must fear that the penalty will in fact be imposed on him. There is an overlap here between the criterion of dissuasiveness and that of effectiveness.

90. A penalty is *proportionate* where it is appropriate (that is to say, in particular, *effective* and *dissuasive*) for attaining the legitimate objectives pursued by it, and also necessary. Where there is a choice between several (equally) appropriate penalties, recourse must be had to the least onerous. Moreover, the effects of the penalty on the person concerned must be proportionate to the aims pursued.

---

4 FOUNDATIONS OF EU LEGAL AUTHORITY

The 'elephant in the room' for EU legal authority is that it was all very well its being developed, but there was still the question of whether it would or should be accorded that authority. In relation to the first question of whether it would be granted such authority, the pedigree of the actors recognising its authority was central. If they are too insubstantial or unknown, EU law will either not have authority or it will have only a formal validity which will not resonate strongly with the wider citizenry.

(i) Pedigree of EU legal authority

At one level, *Costa* required only the support of national judges for EU law to enjoy validity. If national courts applied EU law over national law, the commitment to the rule of law in the different Member States entailed that other administrative actors would observe EU law insofar as they felt bound by the judgments of their judiciary.

As we shall see later in this chapter, this is what by and large happened, albeit that the initial ad hoc resistance on matters of particular sensitivity crystallised into a series

---

[50] Case C-180/95 *Draehmpaehl* [1997] ECR I-2195. They must also penalise them in an equivalent manner to breaches of other EU law provisions of a similar importance. Case C-460/06 *Paquay v Société d'architectes Hoet & Minne* [2007] ECR I-8511.

[51] Case 68/88 *Commission v Greece* [1989] ECR 2965; Case C-326/88 *Hansen* [1990] ECR I-2911; Case C-167/01 *Inspire Art* [2003] ECR I-10155.

[52] Joined Cases C-387/02, C-391/02 and C-403/02 *Berlusconi and others* [2005] ECR I-3565.

of doctrines to qualify EU legal authority as EU legal competence has expanded.[53] However, it resulted in the authority of EU law becoming a form of legalese – something known, discussed and contested between judges and those who appeared before judges, but otherwise largely unknown and, therefore, with no great reservoir of legitimacy.

Attempts to secure wider assent for the authority of EU law were made under the Draft Constitutional Treaty (DCT). Article I-13 DCT provided that within the competences conferred upon the Union, EU law would have primacy over the laws of the Member States. Following the failure of the Constitutional Treaty, this provision was seen as expressing too much political enthusiasm for the principle. At Lisbon, a Declaration was attached to the Treaties.[54]

Declaration 17

The Conference recalls that, in accordance with well settled case law of the Court of Justice of the European Union, the Treaties and the law adopted by the Union on the basis of the Treaties have primacy over the law of Member States, under the conditions laid down by the said case law.

An Opinion of the Council Legal Service was also attached, which provides only sparse information.

Opinion of the Council Legal Service, EU Council Doc. 11197/07, 22 June 2007

It results from the case-law of the Court of Justice that primacy of EC law is a cornerstone principle of Community law. According to the Court, this principle is inherent to the specific nature of the European Community. At the time of the first judgment of this established case-law (*Costa/ENEL*, 15 July 1964, Case 6/64) there was no mention of primacy in the treaty. It is still the case today. The fact that the principle of primacy will not be included in the future treaty shall not in any way change the existence of the principle and the existing case-law of the Court of Justice.

The Declaration is the first explicit endorsement of the *Costa* case law by all Member States. It elevates its pedigree by stating that primacy now has the support of all the national governments which negotiated the Lisbon Treaty and the parliaments which ratified it. However, a Declaration is not an instrument which bellows out EU law's authority. Furthermore, it raises questions about who can found this authority. If national governments can provide an interpretation alongside the Treaty, in this Declaration, as to the quality of its authority, this implies that they could also come back to reinterpret the authority of the Treaty not through a formal amendment – which everybody accepts – but through a collective statement as to its effects.

[53] On national judicial responses see M. Claes, *The National Courts' Mandate in the European Constitution* (Oxford/Portland, Hart, 2005); A. Albi, *EU Enlargement and the Constitutions of Central and Eastern Europe* (Cambridge, Cambridge University Press, 2005).

[54] On the Declaration see L. Rossi, 'How Fundamental are Fundamental Principles? Primacy and Fundamental Rights after Lisbon' (2008) 28 *YBEL* 65, 74–7.

(ii) Reasons for EU legal authority

Whatever the pedigree of the messenger proclaiming EU legal authority, there is the bigger question as to why EU law should be granted authority. The advantages promised by *VGL* and *Costa* are, broadly speaking, threefold.

The first is that individuals are granted rights, benefits and freedoms by the EU Treaties which they are not granted in national law. At its most mundane, in *VGL*, it was the right to import goods tariff free from other Member States. At its most ambitious, it has been argued that the European Union can allow individuals to do things which are otherwise not possible.[55] This might be individual liberties, such as the freedom to trade abroad, to move abroad, to meet foreigners at home, or it might be collective goods, such as better environmental protection or financial regulation, which might be more easily secured by pan-Union than national regulation.

Secondly, EU law can facilitate new types of relationship and awareness.[56] The supranational qualities of EU law require citizens to recognise the interests of citizens (foreigners) in other Member States, be it for reasons of interdependence[57] or interests and values which are more shared than historically admitted.[58] In *Melloni*, therefore, the Spanish authorities were asked to consider the interests of Italians defrauded by *Melloni*. This capacity to enlarge awareness and empathy may be something which can justify intervention not just to establish new mutually beneficial relations with foreigners but for interests traditionally marginalised or ignored within a domestic society, but which EU law calls on it to reconsider. EU law has been deployed to protect a series of groups and interests – women, people with disabilities, LGBT groups, ethnic, religious and racial minorities, consumer and ecological interests – historically weakly protected within nation-states.[59]

The third advantage of EU law is its civilising of state power. The phrase 'limitation of national sovereignty' implies the curbing of a raw, brutal power.[60] In *Costa*, therefore, the applicant was pleading (unsuccessfully) for EU law to protect his property from what he perceived as unnecessary and arbitrary nationalisation. Abuses may simply be abuse of administrative power, but they can also reside in the excesses of nationalism, which can lead to polarisation, racism or fascism.

These might all be reasons for obeying EU law. However, its authority must be set against a countervailing authority, that of national law. National law offers things which cannot be easily offered by EU law. Neil Walker has pointed, in particular, to the presence of common goods.

---

[55] J. Kristeva, 'Europhilia, Europhoria' (1998) 3 *Constellations* 321.

[56] On the latter see, in particular, J. Weiler, 'In Defence of the Status Quo: Europe's Constitutional Sonderweg' in J. Weiler and M. Wind (eds.), *European Constitutionalism Beyond the State* (Cambridge, Cambridge University Press, 2003).

[57] E. Balibar 'Europe: Vanishing Mediator' (2003) 10 *Constellations* 314; A. Sangiovanni, 'Solidarity in the European Union' (2013) 33 *OJLS* 213.

[58] J.-P. Müller, 'A European Constitutional Patriotism? The Case Restated' (2008) 14 *ELJ* 542.

[59] J. Weiler, *The Constitution of Europe* (Cambridge, Cambridge University Press, 1999) especially 332–48; M. Poiares Maduro, *We, the Court: The European Court of Justice and the European Economic Constitution* (Oxford, Hart, 1998) 166–74.

[60] J.-W. Müller, *Contesting Democracy: Political Ideas in Twentieth-century Europe* (New Haven, CT, Yale University Press, 2011) 147–9.

N. Walker, 'The Place of European Law' in G. de Búrca and J. Weiler (eds.), *The Worlds of European Constitutionalism* (Cambridge, Cambridge University Press, 2012) 57, 67

... there are other collective goods whose quality as such is bound up with the fact that they are constructed and achieved in common. These common goods, in turn, can be both implicit and explicit. Implicit common goods refer to those benefits inherent in the very idea of living together in a stable community. These include the value of national (or other collective) solidarity – of an accomplished framework of mutual concern and support – and the sense of social, economic and spiritual or 'ontological security' such security brings to those who share in it. They also include a more general value associated with the development and preservation of a national (or other collective) culture, as well as the sense of belonging, of dignity, of posterity, and of distinctiveness or 'originality', such a culture brings to those who share it. Moreover, in addition to such implicit common goods, and indeed, building on the platform of capacities for common action provided by such implicit goods, communities may also determine and pursue certain other explicit common goods, such as economic egalitarianism (through redistribution), or an educated society, or a health society.

EU law may enable Europeans to realise what their different political systems, welfare systems or values have in common. However, common goods are deeper than this. They go, as Walker indicates, to what individuals are seen as enjoying in common through an idea of living together and the mutual narratives and commitments generated by this. There is no strong common pan-Union sense of living together or narratives or commitments which follow from it. Few believe that we will see a common European health system, sense of culture or solidarity as resonant as national ones in the next ten years precisely because few see anything, such as a European living together, to sustain them. They, consequently, look contrived. This does not mean that EU law cannot have authority. It is simply that both EU law and national law can realise things which cannot be realised by the other. EU law holds out possibilities, sensibilities and protection from abuse currently not offered by national law. National law, by contrast, offers common goods which cannot be equally offered by EU law. Furthermore, if each has the potential to realise certain things, it does not follow that either manages this. The freedoms granted by EU law have been criticised for being too insubstantial[61] and economically liberal.[62] The sensibilities promoted by it are equally criticised as too thin to generate strong solidarity.[63] Equally, it is all very well to talk about the solidarity or common sense of belonging generated by the nation-state. However, it is not always easy to see how it is manifested in particular laws, and it is too easy for it to slip into undifferentiated nationalism which is intolerant not just of foreigners but also of difference within the national community.

---

[61] This point is first made strongly in J. Weiler and J. Trachtman, 'European Constitutionalism and Its Discontents' (1997) 17 *Northwestern Journal of International Law and Business* 354, 376–7.

[62] A. Somek, *Individualism: An Essay on the Authority of the European Union* (Oxford, Oxford University Press, 2008) especially ch. 13.

[63] A. Somek, *Engineering Equality: An Essay on European Anti-Discrimination Law* (Oxford, Oxford University Press, 2011) ch. 8.

If there are some who argue that the unity of EU law requires that it should prevail over national law all the time[64] or that, as EU law was authorised by national constitutions, national law prevails over EU law,[65] the consequence of the preceding discussion is that these are increasingly few. An absolutist position, either way, is unattractive. It dismisses the goods and values instituted by the other legal order. It fails also to appreciate that any law may only realise these goods and values in highly imperfect ways, and may itself be an instrument of abuse or neglect. It also paints a poor explanation of the case law, as this has responded to these concerns. Accounts insisting on the primacy of EU law cannot explain why other actors, notably national courts, have not (as we shall see) unquestioningly accepted the depiction of EU legal authority put forward by the Court of Justice. Equally, accounts insisting on the primacy of national law struggle to explain the enduring authority of EU law.

The question is, therefore, rather *when* EU law should enjoy authority over national law. How does one weigh up the benefits provided and the costs extracted by the different legal orders? There are two dominant models: the constitutional pluralist model and the pluralist one.

The constitutional pluralist model argues that conflicts should be mediated by a common language of constitutionalism. As constitutionalism provides a basis for the formation and exercise of public authority, it appears, first, to be a good tie-breaker. Constitutional demands set thresholds for why laws can exert obedience over individuals. If one law better meets these demands than others, this, correspondingly, provides a reason why it should prevail. Secondly, as all EU Member States have constitutional traditions, reference to the language of constitutionalism provides common reference points by which to gauge each law's merits.[66] Indicators of what these may be have been set out by Kumm.

> **M. Kumm, 'The Jurisprudence of Constitutional Conflict: Constitutional Supremacy in Europe Before and After the Constitutional Treaty' (2005) 11 *European Law Journal* 262, 299–300**
>
> The *first* principle is formal and is connected to the *idea of legality*. According to the principle of the effective and uniform enforcement of EU law, further strengthened by the recent explicit commitment by Member States to the primacy of EU law, national courts should start with a strong presumption that they are required to enforce EU law, national constitutional provisions notwithstanding. *The presumption for applying EU law can be rebutted, however, if, and to the extent that, countervailing principles have greater weight.* Here there are three principles to be considered. The first is *substantive*, and focuses on the effective *protection of fundamental rights of citizens*. If, and to the extent that, fundamental rights protection against acts of the EU is lacking in important respects, than that is

---

[64] J. Baquero Cruz, 'The Legacy of the Maastricht-Urteil and the Pluralist Movement' (2008) 14 *ELJ* 389; R. Barents, 'The Fallacy of European Multilevel Constitutionalism' in M. Avebelj and J. Komárek (eds.), *Constitutional Pluralism in the European Union and Beyond* (Oxford, Hart, 2012); G. Letsas, 'Harmonic Law: The Case Against Pluralism' in J. Dickson and P. Eleftheriadis (eds.), *Philosophical Foundations of European Union Law* (Oxford, Oxford University Press, 2012).

[65] T. Schilling, 'The Autonomy of the Community Legal Order: An Analysis of Possible Foundations' (1996) 37 *Harvard Int. LJ* 389; D. Phelan, *Revolt or Revolution: At the Constitutional Boundaries of the European Community* (Dublin, Round Hall Sweet & Maxwell, 1997); T. Hartley, 'The Constitutional Foundations of the European Union' (2001) 117 *LQR* 225.

[66] D. Halberstam, 'Local, Global and Plural Constitutionalism: Europe Meets the World' in G. de Búrca and J. Weiler (eds.), *The Worlds of European Constitutionalism* (Cambridge, Cambridge University Press, 2012) 150, 170–5.

a ground to insist on subjecting EU law to national constitutional rights review. If, however, the guarantees afforded by the EU amount to structurally equivalent protections, then there is no more space for national courts to substitute the EU's judgment on the rights issue with their own. Arguably the EU, and specifically the Court of Justice, has long developed substantially equivalent protections against violations of fundamental rights. At the very least the Constitutional Treaty, with its elaborate Charter of Fundamental Rights should finally put an end to this issue. Even if some doubt that the Court of Justice can be trusted as an institution to take rights seriously, if the Charter of Fundamental Rights becomes the law of the land after ratification the guarantees it provides may not fall below the guarantees provided by the European Convention of Human Rights as interpreted by the ECHR. The second of the counter-principles is *jurisdictional*. It protects national communities against unjustified usurpations of competencies by the European Union and undermines the legitimate scope of self government by national communities. Call this principle the principle of *subsidiarity*. Here the question is whether there are sufficient and effective guarantees against usurpation of power by EU institutions. Much will depend on how the procedural and technical safeguards of the Constitutional Treaty will work in practice once the Treaty has been ratified. If the structural safeguards will succeed in establishing a culture of subsidiarity carefully watched over by the Court of Justice, then there are no more grounds for national courts to review whether or not the EU has remained within the boundaries established by the EU's constitutional charter. Lastly, there is the *procedural* principle of *democratic legitimacy*, the third counter-principle. Given the persistence of the democratic deficit on the European level – the absence of directly representative institutions as the central agenda-setters of the European political process, the lack of a European public sphere, and a sufficiently thick European identity even if the Constitutional Treaty will be ratified – national courts continue to have good reasons to set aside EU Law *when it violates clear and specific constitutional norms that reflect essential commitments of the national community.*

The charges levied against the constitutional pluralist case are twofold. The first is that its criteria are too generic.[67] Values such as fundamental rights or democracy either do not help resolve disputes about which law is to be deployed[68] or, when they are used, are turned into overarching principles with a single meaning, which invariably push for centralisation.[69] The second is that many constitutional pluralist accounts are too orthodox as their principles are taken from federal constitutional states.[70] They pay little heed to the features of the Union:

---

[67] There is a rich literature which uses a number of different principles. Noted contributions include N. Walker, 'The Idea of Constitutional Pluralism' (2002) 65 *MLR* 317; M. Poiares Maduro 'Contrapunctual Law: Europe's Constitutional Pluralism in Action' in Neil Walker (ed.), *Sovereignty in Transition* (Oxford, Oxford University Press, 2003); I. Pernice, 'The Treaty of Lisbon: Multilevel Constitutionalism in Action' (2009) 15 *CJEL* 349; A. v. Bogdandy and S. Schill, 'Overcoming Absolute Primacy: Respect for National Identity under the Lisbon Treaty' (2011) 48 *CMLRev.* 1417; D. Halberstam, 'Systems Pluralism and Institutional Pluralism in Constitutional Law: National, Supranational and Global Governance' in M. Avbelj and J. Komárek (eds.), *Constitutional Pluralism in the European Union and Beyond* (Oxford, Hart, 2012).

[68] J. Weiler, 'Dialogical Epilogue' in G. de Búrca and J. Weiler (eds.), *The Worlds of European Constitutionalism* (Cambridge, Cambridge University Press, 2012) 262, 291–7.

[69] N. Krisch, 'The Case for Pluralism in Postnational Law' in G. de Búrca and J. Weiler (eds.), *The Worlds of European Constitutionalism* (Cambridge, Cambridge University Press, 2012) 203, 210–19.

[70] This is not true of all versions, see e.g., Walker, 'The Idea of Constitutional Pluralism', n. 67 above; C. Sabel and O. Gerstenberg 'Constitutionalising an Overlapping Consensus: The ECJ and the Emergence of a Coordinate Constitutional Order' (2010) 16 *ELJ* 511.

The choice for state constitutionalism as the EU form of power relies on a strong normative assumption: it is believed that the combination of fundamental rights protection, broad legislative powers and representative democracy devices provides the most effective and, probably, the only framework for ensuring the republican ideals of political inclusion, economic prosperity and social cohesion. In this respect, conversion narratives may be regarded not only as proofs of faith on the virtues of constitutionalism and state constitutions, but also as defences of a clear political strategy intended to preserve the European *modus vivendi*.[71]

Dani observes that constitutional pluralism, thus, mistakes the nature of European integration. On the one hand, the Union was established to deal with the consequences of state failure, namely, that domestic constitutions failed to provide or could not provide certain goods to their citizens. On the other hand, this image of state constitutionalism assumes all players are pulling in a similar direction. It might be that a value of the Union is the tension from EU policies and national policies having different dynamics. Dani gives the example of industrial policy where EU policy is about realising market integration, and liberalising industrial sectors, whereas national policy is about addressing market failure and nurturing industrial sectors. He argues therefore that mediation must be built around two functions: addressing state abuse when it occurs, even when it takes place within the domestic constitution, and allowing for structural dissonance, namely, the possibility for significant difference in policy directions.

The pluralist position, therefore, argues for few overarching principles. Each legal system takes its own position on questions of primacy, central values and the parameters of EU legal authority.[72] This may be because of the weight of different legal traditions or acknowledgement that there are no universal answers where deeply held beliefs differ or where there will be significant numbers of winners and losers. There is, however, a commitment to pluralism. Each legal order commits itself to considering the claims of others whilst holding on to its own beliefs and values. In this way, cooperation develops incrementally, over time and through gradual mutual adjustment.

N. Krisch, 'Who is Afraid of Radical Pluralism? Legal Order and Political Stability in the Postnational Space' (2011) 24 *Ratio Juris* 386, 407

Under conditions of strong fluidity and contestation, conflict rules face serious problems of adaptation to a changing environment, and they face challenges from those they place at a disadvantage. Because they cannot rest on a societal consensus on the scope of the relevant polity and the procedures for decision-making, they are unlikely to be able to truly settle conflicts – they might remain ineffectual or even enflame conflicts further. In such a situation, we find certain advantages in a truly, 'radically' pluralist structure in which fundamental questions – about the scope of the polity, ultimate supremacy norms, key values – are bracketed and worked around. Such a pluralism favours pragmatic, incremental processes of mutual accommodation and potential convergence, without overstretching the authority of the norms and institutions that form the regime. Because it allows the different layers of law to

---

[71] M. Dani, 'Constitutionalism and Dissonances: Has Europe Paid Off Its Debt to Functionalism?' (2009) 15 *ELJ* 324, 343.

[72] For a range of pluralist writing see N. MacCormick, 'The Maastricht Urteil: Sovereignty Now' (1995) 1 *ELJ* 259; M. la Torre, 'Legal Pluralism as an Evolutionary Achievement of Community Law' (1999) 12 *Ratio Juris* 182; N. Barber, 'Legal Pluralism and the European Union' (2006) 12 *ELJ* 306.

maintain their own fundamental, supreme norms, it also allows for meaningful signals about the limits of cooperation, thus anticipating political challenges. For the creation and consolidation of European and global political and legal institutions, this may be more beneficial than the existence of an overarching framework which will often antagonise actors and fail to match its social environment. Radical pluralism will not eliminate conflict and friction, but in the rugged, contested terrain of the postnational, no institutional structure would. Unitary, constitutionalist models may seem to hold out hope for a more reasoned, more civilised political order beyond the state..., but in the non-ideal world of European and global politics they may well backfire. Here, more unconventional, irregular structures may well be more appropriate.

The advantages of pluralism lie in its modesty and respect for difference. However, herein may lay its greatest challenge. There may be certain commitments – human rights, the central provisions and instruments of EU law – which are seen as so fundamental that they cannot be subject to national dallying. If a state cannot commit itself to these, then it has to be asked whether it is really committed to Union membership. Pluralist approaches can also struggle to explain the stability and reach of EU law. If EU law is only what national legal systems concede, this would suggest a very unstable, limited legal order. The reality is that it prevails most of the time over a wide array of activities. It would not be so contentious otherwise.

5 CONDITIONAL AUTHORITY OF EU LAW

The debate in the previous section about whether the European Union should be a constitutional pluralist legal order or simply a pluralist one indicates a problem of characterisation. Twenty-eight legal orders had to respond to the claims to authority of EU law, and each could respond in a different way. Initial responses fell into three broad categories. A number of Member States, notably Austria and the BENELUX states,[73] accepted the authority of EU law pretty much on the terms set out by the Court of Justice in *VGL* and *Costa*. Conversely, there was one Member State, Poland, which refused to accept the Treaties as different in nature from any other international treaty.[74] Most States, however, accepted the authority of EU law, albeit neither on the terms set out by the Court nor over their constitutions, and subject to some qualifications.[75] Over the years, a convergence has taken place, with the position of the two

---

[73] *Connect Austria*, VfSlg 15.427/1999 (Austria); *Orfinger v Belgium* [2000] 1 CMLR 612 (Belgium); Constitution of the Kingdom of the Netherlands 2002, arts. 91–93. On Luxembourg case law, see M. Claes, *The National Courts' Mandate in the European Constitution* (Oxford, Hart, 2006) 53–4.

[74] K 18/04 *Polish Membership of the European Union (Accession Treaty)*, Polish Constitutional Tribunal, Judgment of 11 May 2005.

[75] *Crotty v An Taoiseach* [1987] IR 713 (Ireland); *Carlsen v Rasmussen* [1999] 3 CMLR 854 (Denmark); *Brunner v European Union* [1994] 1 CMLR 57 (Germany); *Re EU Constitutional Treaty and the Spanish Constitution* [2005] 1 CMLR 981; *Admenta and others v Federfarma* [2006] 2 CMLR 47 (Italy); *Re Ratification of the Lisbon Treaty* [2010] 2 CMLR 26 (France); U-1-113/04 *Rules on the Quality Labelling and Packaging of Feeding Stuffs*, Slovenian Constitutional Court, Judgment of 7 February 2007 (Slovenia); *Re Czech Sugar Quotas* [2006] 3 CMLR 15; *Ratification of the Lisbon Treaty* [2010] 1 CMLR 42 (Latvian Constitutional Court); European Union Act 2011, s. 18 and Explanatory Notes paras. 118–24 (United Kingdom); Case 3-4-1-6-12 *Request of the Chancellor of Justice to Declare Article 4(4) of the Treaty Establishing the European Stability Mechanism in Conflict with the Constitution*, Judgment of 12 July 2012 (Estonia). On Lithuania see P. Ravluševiius, 'The Enforcement of the Primacy of European Union Law: Legal Doctrine and Practice' (2011) 18 *Jurisprudencija* 1369.

outlier groups softening, and moving to this position of qualified authority for EU law. Member States willing to grant full authority to EU law were not necessarily willing to grant full authority to Court of Justice judgments, separating out the institution from the legal order.[76] At the other end of the spectrum, even if EU law was seen as a form of international law in Poland, it was nevertheless granted as much authority as those Member States in the middle category.[77]

Whilst different Member States use a variety of constitutional doctrines to characterise the status of EU law within their territories, the dominant stance is that expressed by the German Constitutional Court in its response to a challenge to the compatibility of the Lisbon Treaty with the German constitutional document, the Basic Law. Article 23 provides, inter alia, that the German Federation will consent to such limitations upon its sovereign powers as will bring about and secure a peaceful and lasting order in Europe.[78] It was argued that this was subject to other provisions, in particular those on the right to self-determination. These were violated by excessive powers being transferred to the Union from the Bundestag, the German Parliament.

---

2 BvE 2/08 *Treaty of Lisbon*, Judgment of 30 June 2009

225. The constitutional mandate to realise a united Europe, which follows from Article 23.1 of the Basic Law and its Preamble...means in particular for the German constitutional bodies that it is not left to their political discretion whether or not they participate in European integration. The Basic Law wants European integration and an international peaceful order. Therefore not only the principle of openness towards international law, but also the principle of openness towards European law applies.

226. It is true that the Basic Law grants the legislature powers to engage in a far-reaching transfer of sovereign powers to the European Union. However, the powers are granted under the condition that the sovereign statehood of a constitutional state is maintained on the basis of an integration programme according to the principle of conferral and respecting the Member States' constitutional identity, and that at the same time the Member States do not lose their ability to politically and socially shape the living conditions on their own responsibility...

228. Integration requires the willingness to joint action and the acceptance of autonomous common opinion-forming. However, integration into a free community neither requires submission removed from constitutional limitation and control nor the forgoing one's own identity. The Basic Law does not grant powers to bodies acting on behalf of Germany to abandon the right to self-determination of the German people in the form of Germany's sovereignty under international law by joining a federal state. Due to the irrevocable transfer of sovereignty to a new subject of legitimation that goes with it, this step is reserved to the directly declared will of the German people alone....

---

[76] On this within Belgium and the Netherlands see P. Popelier, 'Judicial Conversations in Multilevel Constitutionalism: The Belgian Case' in M. Claes *et al.* (eds.), *Constitutional Conversations in Europe: Actors, Topics and Procedures* (Cambridge, Intersentia, 2012) 73, 83–4; S. Garben, 'The *Sturgeon* Case Law in Light of Judicial Activism, Euroscepticism and Eurolegalism' (2013) 50 *CMLRev.* 15.

[77] K 32/09 *Treaty of Lisbon*, Polish Constitutional Tribunal, Judgment of 24 November 2010.

[78] The literature on the judgment is enormous. See C. Schonberger, 'Lisbon in Karlsruhe: Maastricht's Epigones at Sea' (2010) 10 *German Law Journal* 1201; D. Thym, 'In the Name of Sovereign Statehood: A Critical Introduction to the Lisbon Judgment of the German Constitutional Court' (2009) 46 *CMLRev.* 1795; D. Jan i, 'Caveats from Karlsruhe and Berlin: Whither Democracy after Lisbon' (2009) 16 *CJEL* 337; P. Kuiver, 'The Lisbon Judgment of the German Constitutional Court: A Court-Ordered Strengthening of the National Legislature in the EU' (2010) 16 *ELJ* 578.

231. The empowerment to transfer sovereign powers to the European Union or other intergovernmental institution permits a shift of political rule to international organisations. The empowerment to exercise supranational powers, however, comes from the Member States of such an institution. They therefore permanently remain the masters of the Treaties. In a functional sense, the source of Community authority, and of the European constitution that constitutes it, are the peoples of Europe with democratic constitutions in their states. The 'Constitution of Europe', international treaty law or primary law, remains a derived fundamental order. It establishes a supranational autonomy which undoubtedly makes considerable inroads into everyday political life but is always limited factually. Here, autonomy can only be understood – as is usual regarding the law of self-government – as an autonomy to rule which is independent but derived, i.e. is granted by other legal entities. In contrast, sovereignty under international law and public law requires independence from an external will precisely for its constitutional foundations…It is not decisive here whether an international organisation has legal personality, i.e. whether it for its part can enter into binding acts as a subject in international legal relations. What is decisive is how the fundamental legal relationship between the international organisation and the Member States and Contracting States which have created it and have vested it with legal personality is elaborated.

232. In accordance with the powers granted with a view to European integration under Article 23.1…there can be no independent subject of legitimation for the authority of the European Union which would constitute itself, so to speak, on a higher level, without being derived from an external will, and thus of its own right.

233. The Basic Law does not grant the German state bodies powers to transfer sovereign powers in such a way that their exercise can independently establish other competences for the European Union. It prohibits the transfer of competence to decide on its own competence (*Kompetenz-Kompetenz*)…Also a far-reaching process of independence of political rule for the European Union brought about by granting it steadily increased competences and by gradually overcoming existing unanimity requirements or rules of state equality that have been decisive so far can, from the perspective of German constitutional law, only take place as a result of the freedom of action of the self-determined people. According to the constitution, such steps of integration must be factually limited by the act of transfer and must, in principle, be revocable. For this reason, withdrawal from the European union of integration…may, regardless of a commitment for an unlimited period under an agreement, not be prevented by other Member States or the autonomous authority of the Union…

339. The primacy of application of European law remains, even with the entry into force of the Treaty of Lisbon, a concept conferred under an international treaty, i.e. a derived concept which will have legal effect in Germany only with the order to apply the law given by the Act Approving the Treaty of Lisbon. This derivative connection is not altered by the fact that the concept of primacy of application is not explicitly provided for in the treaties but was developed in the early phase of European integration in the case law of the Court of Justice by means of interpretation. It is a consequence of the continuing sovereignty of the Member States that in any case in the clear absence of a constitutive order to apply the law, the inapplicability of such a legal instrument to Germany is established by the Federal Constitutional Court. Such determination must also be made if, within or outside the sovereign powers conferred, these powers are exercised with the consequent effect on Germany of a violation of its constitutional identity, which is inviolable under Article 79.3 of the Basic Law and is also respected by European treaty law, namely Article 4.2 first sentence Lisbon TEU.

340. The Basic Law strives to integrate Germany into the legal community of peaceful and free states, but does not waive the sovereignty contained in the last instance in the German constitution as a right of

the people to take constitutive decisions concerning fundamental questions as its own identity. There is therefore no contradiction to the aim of openness to international law if the legislature, exceptionally, does not comply with international treaty law – accepting, however, corresponding consequences in international relations – provided this is the only way in which a violation of fundamental principles of the constitution can be averted...The Court of Justice of the European Communities based its decision of 3 September 2008 in the *Kadi* case on a similar view according to which an objection to the claim of validity of a United Nations Security Council Resolution may be expressed citing fundamental legal principles of the Community...The Court of Justice has thus, in a borderline case, placed the assertion of its own identity as a legal community above the commitment that it otherwise respects. Such a legal construct is not only familiar in international legal relations as a reference to the *ordre public* as the boundary of a treaty commitment; it also corresponds, if used constructively, to the idea of contexts of political order which are not structured according to a strict hierarchy. It does not in any case factually contradict the objective of openness towards European law, i.e. to the participation of the Federal Republic of Germany in the building of a united Europe (Preamble, Article 23.1 first sentence of the Basic Law), if exceptionally, and under special and narrow conditions, the Federal Constitutional Court declares European Union law inapplicable in Germany.

The judgment states that EU law cannot found its own authority. Sovereignty rests in the national constitution and it is ultimately for the national constitutional court to determine the relative legal authority of EU law in accordance with national constitutional principles. The judgment is not, however, a bald restatement of national constitutional sovereignty. It rather sets this up against a constitutional commitment to European integration. The importance of this counterweighing argument should not be understated. In particular, the commitment to an 'openness to EU law' mentioned in paragraph 340 indicates that EU law will be granted precedence over German law other than in exceptional circumstances. In the remainder of this section, we go through the different elements which comprise these circumstances, and have been invoked not just by German but other national courts. In considering this resistance, it is important to be aware that the authority of EU law relies on all the doctrines described earlier in the chapter: the autonomy of EU law, primacy of EU law, pre-emption and the fidelity principle. Challenges to any of these, not simply whether national or EU law prevails in a particular conflict, qualify EU legal authority, as without these doctrines the EU legal order cannot function in the way anticipated.

(i) EU law and national fundamental rights

A central challenge is whether EU law should still have authority when it does bad things. The most evident example of this is where an EU measure violates fundamental rights. It would be odd, indeed, if the ideal of European integration was so treasured that it took precedence over these freedoms regarded as most central to democracy and the good life within national systems. This challenge confronted both the Italian and German Constitutional Court in the mid-1970s where challenges were made to EU measures on the grounds that these violated fundamental rights in their respective constitutions.[79] Both courts held

---

[79] *Frontini v Ministero delle Finanze* [1974] 2 CMLR 372 (Italy); *IHT v Einfuhr und Vorratsstelle für Getreide und Futtermittel* [1974] 2 CMLR 540.

that EU law could not prevail over fundamental rights protected in their national constitutions. There was a tension in the reasoning of both courts which has pervaded national approaches since. On the one hand, it was felt to be wrong to allow fundamental rights to be violated. On the other, there was resistance for jurisdictional reasons. In *Frontini*, the Italian Constitutional Court stated that EU law was to be confined to economic relations with its being difficult to imagine that it could 'have effect in civil, ethno-social or political relations through which provisions can conflict with the Constitution'.[80] It was argued not simply that EU law should not violate national fundamental values but these were something over which it had no competence. These were central matters which were to be reserved to the national constitutional settlements.

This has led to a split in how national courts have treated issues of fundamental rights. For some, it is sufficient that EU law does not violate fundamental rights.[81] If it can develop mechanisms to prevent this, even better. In 1986, the German Constitutional Court, in response to a challenge that an EU Regulation limiting imports of mushrooms into Germany from Taiwan violated the fundamental right to trade, stated that it would not strike down EU law as long as (*so lange* in German) EU law had sufficient fundamental rights checks of its own – something it was deemed to have.

Wünsche Handelsgesellschaft [Solange II] [1987] 3 CMLR 225

The provision does not confer a power to surrender by way of ceding sovereign rights to international institutions the identity of the prevailing constitutional order of the Federal Republic by breaking into its basic framework, that is, into its very structure. That applies in particular to legislative instruments of the international institution which, perhaps as a result of a corresponding interpretation or development of the underlying treaty law, would undermine essential, structural parts of the Basic Law. An essential part which cannot be dispensed with and belongs to the basic framework of the constitutional order in force is constituted in any event by the legal principles underlying the provisions of the Basic Law on fundamental rights...Article 24(1) of the Basic Law, subject to conditions, allows these legal principles to be treated according to context.[82] In so far as sovereign power is accorded to an international institution within the meaning of Article 24(1) which is in a position within the sovereign sphere of the Federal Republic to encroach on the essential content of the fundamental rights recognized by the Basic Law, it is necessary, if that entails the removal of legal protection existing under the terms of the Basic Law, that instead, there should be a guarantee of the application of fundamental rights which in substance and effectiveness is essentially similar to the protection of fundamental rights required unconditionally by the Basic Law. As a general rule this will require a system of protection of individual rights by independent courts which are given adequate jurisdiction and, in particular, power to review and decide on factual and legal questions appropriate to the relevant claim to

---

[80] *Ibid.* para. 21.

[81] For other states where this appears to be the case see *Decision 17/04 regarding Agricultural Surpluses*, Hungarian Constitutional Court, Judgment of 25 May 2004; Pl. ÚS 50/04 *Sugar Quotas III*, Czech Constitutional Court, Judgment of 3 March 2008; *Ratification of the Lisbon Treaty* [2010] 2 CMLR 26 (French Constitutional Council).

[82] This provision allows for sovereign powers to be transferred to international organisations. It was the provision governing transfer of powers to the EU at the time.

protection of rights, and by courts which reach their decisions on the basis of a proper procedure allowing the right to a legal hearing and providing for means of attack or defence appropriate to the subject matter of the dispute and for the availability of freely chosen expert assistance, and the decisions of which, if necessary, contain adequate and effective sanctions for the infringement of a fundamental right.

This Court explained in [*IHT*] that, having regard to the state of integration which had been reached at that time, the standard of fundamental rights under Community law, generally binding within the European Communities, did not yet show the level of legal certainty for the Court to conclude that that standard would permanently satisfy the fundamental rights standards of the Basic Law...It said that the Community still lacked a parliament legitimized by direct democratic means and established by general suffrage, which possessed legislative powers and to which the Community institutions competent to issue legislation were politically fully responsible; in particular, the Community still lacked a codified catalogue of fundamental rights; European Court case law, as it then stood, did not by itself guarantee necessary legal certainty. So far as that legal certainty remained unachieved in the course of subsequent integration, the reservation...remained in force. This Court accordingly held in the above mentioned judgment: as long as the integration process has not progressed so far that Community law also receives a catalogue of fundamental rights decided on by a parliament and of settled validity which is adequate in comparison with the catalogue of fundamental rights contained in the Basic Law, a reference by a court in the Federal Republic of Germany to the Federal Constitutional Court in judicial review proceedings after obtaining a ruling of the European Court under Article [267 TFEU] is admissible and necessary if the German court regards that rule of Community law which is relevant to its decision in the interpretation given by the European Court to be inapplicable in the interpretation given by the European Court because and in so far as it conflicts with one of the fundamental rights in the Basic Law...

In the judgment of this Chamber a measure of protection of fundamental rights has been established in the meantime within the sovereign jurisdiction of the European Communities which in its conception, substance and manner of implementation is essentially comparable with the standards of fundamental rights provided for in the Basic Law. All the main institutions of the Community have since acknowledged in a legally significant manner that in the exercise of their powers and the pursuit of the objectives of the Community they will be guided as a legal duty by respect for fundamental rights, in particular as established by the constitutions of Member States and by the European Convention on Human Rights. There are no decisive factors to lead one to conclude that the standard of fundamental rights which has been achieved under Community law is not adequately consolidated and is only of a transitory nature.

This standard of fundamental rights has in the meantime, particularly through the decisions of the European Court, been formulated in content, consolidated and adequately guaranteed...

In view of those developments it must be held that, so long as the European Communities, in particular European Court case law, generally ensure effective protection of fundamental rights as against the sovereign powers of the Communities which is to be regarded as substantially similar to the protection of fundamental rights required unconditionally by the Basic Law, and in so far as they generally safeguard the essential content of fundamental rights, the Federal Constitutional Court will no longer exercise its jurisdiction to decide on the applicability of secondary Community legislation cited as the legal basis for any acts of German courts or authorities within the sovereign jurisdiction of the Federal Republic of Germany, and it will no longer review such legislation by the standard of the fundamental rights contained in the Basic Law.

On a charitable interpretation, the space granted to EU law to develop its own safeguards can lead to a dialogue between national courts and the Court of Justice on fundamental rights. Each responds to interpretations made by the other, leading to a cycle of continual improvement and mutual learning.[83] A less benign view is that this space grants excessive deference to EU law over these matters. As long as it has formal mechanisms in place, there will be insufficient verification by national courts of whether the fundamental rights of individuals have been protected.

Other courts take the position that fundamental rights are a matter for final settlement by national constitutional law alone as they are so central to national constitutional identities. The Court of Justice can rule on whether an EU measure violates fundamental rights, but the national constitutional court will look at the issue independently from that.[84] The central exemplar of this is the Polish Constitutional Tribunal in its judgment on whether the Treaty of Lisbon was compatible with the Polish Constitution.[85]

K 32/09 *Treaty of Lisbon*, Judgment of 24 September 2010 (Polish Constitutional Tribunal)

Article 4 of the Constitution stipulates that supreme power in the Republic of Poland 'shall be vested in the Nation', which excludes the possibility of conferring it to another entity. Within the meaning of Article 5 of the Constitution, the Republic of Poland safeguards the independence and integrity of its territory, and ensures the freedoms and rights of persons and citizens. The provisions of Articles 4 and 5 of the Constitution in conjunction with the Preamble set the fundamental relation between sovereignty and the guarantee of the constitutional status of the individual, and at the same time exclude the possibility of surrendering sovereignty, the regaining of which the Constitution regards as the premise of the Nation's independence to determine its own fate.

The Constitutional Tribunal shares the view expressed in the doctrine that the competences, under the prohibition of conferral, manifest about a constitutional identity, and thus they reflect the values the Constitution is based on…Therefore, constitutional identity is a concept which determines the scope of 'excluding – from the competence to confer competences – the matters which constitute…"the heart of the matter", i.e. are fundamental to the basis of the political system of a given state'…the conferral of which would not be possible pursuant to Article 90 of the Constitution. Regardless of the difficulties related to setting a detailed catalogue of inalienable competences, the following should be included among the matters under the complete prohibition of conferral: decisions specifying the fundamental principles of the Constitution and decisions concerning the rights of the individual which determine the identity of the state, including, in particular, the requirement of protection of human dignity and constitutional rights, the principle of statehood, the principle of democratic governance, the principle of a state ruled by law, the principle of social justice, the principle of subsidiarity, as well as the requirement of ensuring better implementation of constitutional values and the prohibition to confer the power to amend the Constitution and the competence to determine competences.

---

[83] For an argument to this effect see A. Torres Pérez, *Conflicts of Rights in the European Union: A Theory of Supranational Adjudication* (Oxford, Oxford University Press, 2009) ch. 5.

[84] SK 45/09 *Regulation 44/2001 on Jurisdiction and the Recognition and Enforcement of Judgments*, Polish Constitutional Tribunal, Judgment of 16 November 2011.

[85] For similar positions see *Admenta and others* v *Federfarma* [2006] 2 CMLR 47 (Italian Constitutional Council). Furthermore, on selected rights see Protocol on the Concerns of the Irish People on the Treaty of Lisbon, Article 1 [2013] OJ L60/131; Protocol No. 7 Act of Accession of Malta to the European Union 2003.

If the German position seems to be one of constructive engagement, whilst the Polish appears more 'hands off', the two come together in relation to the fidelity principle, and the national implementation of EU duties which may violate fundamental rights. In *European Arrest Warrant*, the German Constitutional Court considered the constitutionality of the German law which faithfully implemented the European Arrest Warrant.[86] This required the surrender of somebody accused of committing certain crimes in another Member State, irrespective of their nationality and largely irrespective of the quality of justice they would receive in that state. It was argued, in particular, that this violated article 16 of the Basic Law which allowed extradition of German nationals to another European state only if the rule of law was observed. The German Constitutional Court agreed. It stated, inter alia, that surrender of a German national to another Member State could only take place, and her fundamental rights be safeguarded, if the requesting state had equivalent legal structures to those in Germany for the conduct of the trial. The rights of defence of the accused had, in other words, to enjoy a similar level of protection. As there was no provision for this in the implementing measure, it was unconstitutional. Unlike *Wünsche*, the German court was not bothered about the fundamental rights guarantees in EU law. It simply reviewed the national measure against national constitutional norms, and, where it violated these, held it illegal, notwithstanding the presence of the fidelity principle in EU law. Even in Germany, there is a national constitutional monopoly over the review of national implementing measures and, without these, much EU law cannot have any effect.

(ii) Ultra vires review

The second source of constraint is where EU institutions are believed to act outside the powers formally given to them. This ultra vires review is extremely formal in nature. It does not go to whether the competences in question are too broad or not, but simply to whether EU institutions have acted within the mandate granted by the Treaties. It was most explicitly described in the *Lisbon Treaty* judgment of the German Constitutional Court.

---

2 BvE 2/08 *Treaty of Lisbon*, Judgment of 30 June 2009

240. … it must be possible within the German jurisdiction to assert the responsibility for integration if obvious transgressions of the boundaries occur when the European Union claims competences…The Federal Constitutional Court has already opened up the way of the *ultra vires* review for this, which applies where Community and Union institutions transgress the boundaries of their competences. If legal protection cannot be obtained at the Union level, the Federal Constitutional Court examines whether legal instruments of the European institutions and bodies keep within the boundaries of the sovereign powers accorded to them by way of conferral…whilst adhering to the principle of subsidiarity under Community and Union law…

241. The *ultra vires* review…may result in Community law or, in future, Union law being declared inapplicable in Germany. To preserve the viability of the legal order of the Community, taking into

---

[86] *Re Constitutionality of German Law Implementing the Framework Decision on a European Arrest Warrant* [2006] 1 CMLR 16. On this see J. Komárek, 'European Constitutionalism and the European Arrest Warrant: In Search of the Limits of "Contrapunctual Principles"' (2007) 44 *CMLRev.* 9.

account the legal concept expressed in Article 100.1 of the Basic Law, an application of constitutional law that is open to European law requires that the *ultra vires* review as well as the finding of a violation of constitutional identity is incumbent on the Federal Constitutional Court alone.

The challenges with ultra vires review are alluded to above. Simply put, whenever a national court disagrees with a Court of Justice judgment or an EU law, it could assert that the EU institution exceeded its power. Extensive use of ultra vires review could pose a systemic threat to the authority of EU law. However, the converse is also true. Awareness of this could parallelise national courts with the consequence they do not really patrol the limits of EU competences. In *Honeywell*, a challenge was made to a 2002 German law which allowed employees older than 52 years of age to be granted fixed-term contracts, whilst these could not be granted for those below that age.[87] Between February 2003 and March 2004, Honeywell, a supplier of cars, employed thirteen new employees over 52 years of age on such contracts. Such contracts were challenged before the Court of Justice and found in *Mangold* to be an illegal form of age discrimination under the Framework Directive, even though the deadline for transposition for that Directive was December 2006.[88] It was argued that the decision that a Directive could be invoked against a private company before the deadline for transposition was ultra vires. The German Constitutional Court found nothing awry with the reasoning of the Court of Justice. It added a few words on ultra vires review.

2 BvR 2661/06 *Honeywell*, Judgment of 6 July 2010

58. *Ultra vires* review may only be exercised in a manner which is open towards European law…

59. The Union understands itself as a legal community; it is in particular bound by the principle of conferral and by the fundamental rights, and it respects the constitutional identity of the Member States (see in detail Article 4.2 sentence 1, Article 5.1 sentence 1 and Article 5.2 sentence 1, as well as Article 6.1 sentence 1 and Article 6.3 TEU). According to the legal system of the Federal Republic of Germany, the primacy of application of Union law is to be recognised and it is to be guaranteed that the control powers which are constitutionally reserved for the Federal Constitutional Court are only exercised in a manner that is reserved and open towards European law.

60. This means for the *ultra vires* review at hand that the Federal Constitutional Court must comply with the rulings of the Court of Justice in principle as a binding interpretation of Union law. Prior to the acceptance of an *ultra vires* act on the part of the European bodies and institutions, the Court of Justice is therefore to be afforded the opportunity to interpret the Treaties, as well as to rule on the validity and interpretation of the legal acts in question, in the context of preliminary ruling proceedings according to Article 267 TFEU. As long as the Court of Justice did not have an opportunity to rule on the questions of Union law which have arisen, the Federal Constitutional Court may not find any inapplicability of Union law for Germany…

---

[87] M. Payandeh, 'Constitutional Review of EU Law after *Honeywell*: Contextualizing the Relationship between the German Constitutional Court and the EU Court of Justice' (2011) 48 *CMLRev.* 9; C. Möllers, 'German Federal Constitutional Court: Constitutional *Ultra Vires* Review of European Acts Only Under Exceptional Circumstances' (2011) 7 *European Constitutional Law Review* 161.

[88] Case C-144/05 *Mangold* v *Helm* [2005] ECR I-9981.

61. *Ultra vires* review by the Federal Constitutional Court can moreover only be considered if it is manifest that acts of the European bodies and institutions have taken place outside the transferred competences…A breach of the principle of conferral is only manifest if the European bodies and institutions have transgressed the boundaries of their competences in a manner specifically violating the principle of conferral (Article 23.1 of the Basic Law), the breach of competences is in other words sufficiently qualified (see on the wording 'sufficiently qualified' as an element in Union liability law for instance ECJ Case C-472/00 P *Fresh Marine* [2003] ECR I-7541 paras. 26–27). This means that the act of the authority of the European Union must be manifestly in violation of competences and that the impugned act is highly significant in the structure of competences between the Member States and the Union with regard to the principle of conferral and to the binding nature of the statute under the rule of law…

66. If the supranational integration principle is not to be endangered, *ultra vires* review must be exercised reservedly by the Federal Constitutional Court. Since it also has to find on a legal view of the Court of Justice in each case of an *ultra vires* complaint, the task and status of the independent suprastate case-law must be safeguarded. This means, on the one hand, respect for the Union's own methods of justice to which the Court of Justice considers itself to be bound and which do justice to the 'uniqueness' of the Treaties and goals that are inherent to them (see ECJ Opinion 1/91 *EEA Treaty* [1991] ECR I-6079 para. 51). Secondly, the Court of Justice has a right to tolerance of error. It is hence not a matter for the Federal Constitutional Court in questions of the interpretation of Union law which with a methodical interpretation of the statute can lead to different outcomes in the usual legal science discussion framework, to supplant the interpretation of the Court of Justice with an interpretation of its own. Interpretations of the bases of the Treaties are also to be tolerated which, without a considerable shift in the structure of competences, constitute a restriction to individual cases and either do not permit impacts on fundamental rights to arise which constitute a burden or do not oppose domestic compensation for such burdens.

There is a deep reticence in this judgment about going against EU law. It is not enough, therefore, for the Union to act ultra vires. There are two further tests to be met before the German Constitutional Court will intervene. There is, first, a substantive test. The breach must be manifest and significant. There is, then, a procedural test. The Court of Justice must have had a prior opportunity to review the offending measure. This reluctance is, undoubtedly, in part because of the difficulties posed for EU law by ultra vires review. However, it also creates challenges for the domestic legal system. In this instance, if parties were told there was a fair chance that EU law stood and fixed-term contracts could not be offered for certain age groups, and there was also a fair chance that German law stood and they *could* be offered, there would be chaos for both legal systems. Consequently, national courts had historically threatened that EU measures might be ultra vires but not actually declared any measure to be so.[89]

An indication of the threshold for this test has now been provided in the *ESM/ECB* judgment of the German Constitutional Court. The thrust of the judgment concerned a challenge to the Decision of the European Central Bank (ECB) establishing the Outright Monetary Transactions (OMT) programme. The programme committed the ECB to unlimited purchase of bonds of

---

[89] See *R* v *MAFF, ex parte First City Trading* [1997] 1 CMLR 250 (United Kingdom); 1 BvR 1215/07 *Counter-Terrorism Database*, German Constitutional Court, Judgment of 24 April 2013.

those euro area States which were unable to sell these on the capital markets. Such purchases allowed these States to raise capital and therefore secure their public finances when it would otherwise have been impossible. The German court found two legal objections to this. The first was that the ECB was granted no powers by the Treaty to engage in such wide-ranging purchases. The second was that Article 123 TFEU prohibited the ECB to purchase bonds directly from national governments (the prohibition on monetary financing). The question arose whether these were sufficiently manifest and significant for the Decision to be overturned. The German Constitutional Court held that they might be, and referred the matter to the European Court of Justice.

2 BvR 2728/13 *ESM/ECB*, Judgment of 14 January 2014

37. A sufficiently qualified violation of the integration programme requires that the violation is manifest and that the challenged act entails a structurally significant shift in the allocation of powers to the detriment of the Member States…Transgressions of the mandate are structurally significant especially (but not only) if they cover areas that are part of the constitutional identity of the Federal Republic of Germany…or if they particularly affect the democratic discourse in the Member States…

38. It would have to be considered a manifest and structurally significant transgression of its mandate if the European Central Bank acted beyond its monetary policy mandate, or if the prohibition of monetary financing of the budget was violated by the OMT programme.

39. If the European Central Bank exceeded its monetary policy mandate with the OMT Decision, it would thus interfere with the responsibility of the Member States for economic policy. According to [TFEU]… the responsibility for economic policy lies clearly with the Member States. In this field of economic policy, the European Union is…essentially limited to a coordination of Member States' economic policies…The European Central Bank may only support the general economic policies of the Member States…It is not authorised to pursue its own economic policy. If one assumes – subject to the interpretation by the Court of Justice – that the OMT Decision is to be qualified as an independent act of economic policy, it manifestly violates this distribution of powers.

40. Such an act would also be structurally significant. This derives in particular from the fact that the OMT Decision – functionally equivalent in this regard – could be superimposed onto assistance measures which are part of the "Euro rescue policy" and which, due to their significant financial scope and general political implications, belong to the core aspects of the Member States' economic policy responsibilities…Decisions on the choice of instruments for the stabilisation of the monetary union or on the composition of the euro currency area substantially depend on the democratic process in the Member States. In addition, actions by the European Central Bank in this area could make diverging decisions by the Member States politically no longer feasible or sensible.

41. Acts of the kind that were announced in the OMT Decision are structurally significant especially because they lead to a considerable redistribution between the budgets and the taxpayers of the Member States, and can thus gain effects of a system of fiscal redistribution, which is not entailed in the integration programme of the European Treaties. On the contrary, independence of the national budgets, which opposes the direct or indirect common liability of the Member States for government debts, is constituent for the design of the monetary union…

42. Should the OMT Decision violate the prohibition of monetary financing of the budget, this, too, would have to be considered a manifest and structurally significant transgression of powers.

43. The violation would be manifest because the TFEU stipulates an explicit prohibition of monetary financing of the budget and the Treaty thus unequivocally excludes such powers of the European Central Bank (cf. Art. 123 sec. 1 TFEU). The violation would also be structurally significant. The current integration programme designs the monetary union as a "community of stability". As the Federal Constitutional Court has repeatedly emphasised....this is the basis for the participation of the Federal Republic of Germany in the monetary union. The prohibition of monetary financing of the budget is one of the fundamental rules that guarantee the design of the monetary union as a "community of stability". Apart from this, it safeguards the overall budgetary responsibility of the German *Bundestag*...

The test is, thus, a twofold one. The requirement that a breach be *manifest* goes to there having to be a clear breach of EU law. Alone, this is not enough. The requirement that the breach be *structurally significant* entails that it must redistribute power between the Union and Member States in a marked way and in a way which undermines national democracy by either touching on an area marked out as falling within the constitutional identity of that State or if it 'particularly affects the democratic discourse' of that State (para. 37).

It will only be in the most occasional circumstances that this threshold is met. A more aggressive stance was taken in the judgment of the Czech Constitutional Court in *Slovak Pensions*. Under article 20 of the Agreement dissolving Czechoslovakia, pension entitlements were determined by the state of residence of the employer at the time of dissolution. Czechs working in Slovakia would thus receive Slovak entitlements and vice versa. However, the Slovak pension was very low relative to Czech living costs. For that reason, all Czechs resident in the Czech Republic (at the time of claiming their pension) were entitled to a supplement which levelled up this pension to the same level as if they had been working in the Czech Republic. This had been upheld by the Czech Constitutional Court as a constitutional right, namely, that all Czechs should have the right to material security without discrimination. This was not available to Slovaks and was declared illegal in the *Landtóva* case by the Court of Justice insofar as it violated Regulation 1408/71 which provided for equality of treatment in social security for EU migrant workers.[90] Subsequent cases were then brought before the Czech Constitutional Court asking it to revisit its case law. It refused.

Pl. ÚS 5/12: *Slovak Pensions*, **Judgment of 31 January 2012 (Czech Constitutional Court)**

... if European bodies interpreted or developed EU law in a manner that would jeopardize the foundations of materially understood constitutionality and the essential requirements of a democratic, law-based state that are, under the Constitution of the Czech Republic, seen as inviolable...such legal acts could not be binding in the Czech Republic...

---

[90] Case C-399/09 *Landtóva* [2011] ECR I-5573.

This entire issue is not comparable to evaluating entitlements for social security in view of the inclusion of periods served in various countries; it is an issue of the consequences of the dissolution of Czechoslovakia and evaluating the entitlements of citizens of the Czech Republic with regard to the allocation of expenses for social security between the successor countries (as the secondary party also says in its statement). Insofar as, as previously stated, Art. 2 par. 1 of the Regulation states that it shall apply to persons (in particular employed persons or self-employed persons and students) who are or were subject to the legislation of one or more Member States and who are nationals of one of the Member States, then within the indicated case law of the Constitutional Court, in the case of citizens of the Czech Republic all the effects arising from their social security until 31 December 1992 must be considered to be subject to the legal regulation of the state of which they are citizens. Failure to distinguish the legal relationships arising from the dissolution of a state with a uniform social security system from the legal relationships arising for social security from the free movement of persons in the European Communities, or the European Union, is a failure to respect European history, it is comparing things that are not comparable.

Due to the foregoing, European law, i.e. Regulation (EEC) No. 1408/71 of the Council of 14 June 1971 on the application of social security schemes to employed persons, self-employed persons, and members of their families moving within the Community, cannot be applied to entitlements of citizens of the Czech Republic arising from social security until 31 December 1992; and...we cannot do otherwise than state, in connection with the effects of [*Landtóva*] on analogous cases, that in that case there were excesses on the part of a European Union body, that a situation occurred in which an act by a European body exceeded the powers that the Czech Republic transferred to the European Union under Art. 10a of the Constitution; this exceeded the scope of the transferred powers, and was ultra vires.

Moreover, the Constitutional Court also points to deficiencies concerning the safeguards of a fair trial in the proceeding [in *Landtóva*]. Although the Constitutional Court, as the judicial body for protection of the constitutionality of the Czech Republic, was not a party to the proceeding on the preliminary question before the ECJ, and although it was not even asked by the ECJ to submit a statement, it did provide supplementary information and arguments for the proceeding in [*Landtóva*]. It submitted its statement of 8 March 2011 file no. P. 31/11 with the knowledge that the Czech government, as a party to the proceeding on the preliminary question, unprecedentedly stated in its statement that the case law of the Constitutional Court violates European Union law...

In the submission of 25 March 2011 the head of the judicial office of the ECJ, based on an instruction from the chairperson of the fourth chamber of the ECJ returned the statement in question to the Constitutional Court with the justification that 'pursuant to established customs, members of the ECJ do not correspond with third persons regarding cases that have been submitted to the ECJ'.

In this regard, the Constitutional Court notes that the ECJ regularly makes use of the institution of amici curiae in proceedings on preliminary questions, especially in relation to the European Commission. In a situation where the ECJ was aware that the Czech Republic, as a party to the proceeding, in whose name the government acted, expressed in its statement a negative position on the legal opinion of the Constitutional Court, which was the subject matter for evaluation, the ECJ's statement that the Constitutional Court was a 'third party' in the case at hand cannot be seen otherwise than as abandoning the principle audiatur et altera pars.

The judgment has been criticised on the grounds that it was less about constitutional principle and more about the Czech Constitutional Court protecting its prerogatives.[91] Be that as it may, the judgment need not be read as so disruptive of EU law. On the substance, the matter was a highly sensitive one. For the Czech state to grant full pensions not merely to Czechs but also Slovaks who chose to retire, there would be imposed – given the possible numbers – significant demands on its pension system which would lead to a reduction in the size of individual pensions. The converse, as the judgment states, was to discriminate between many Czechs, based on where they had worked in the old Czechoslovakia. The EU Regulation, drawn up well before the dissolution of that state, had clearly not anticipated the consequences. Procedurally, the court was irritated by the refusal to consider its views. This procedural irritation suggests a possible way forward, namely, if national courts are wary about EU acts overstepping their competences, they should be allowed to make submissions to that effect. The EU institutions can ignore their submission, albeit in the knowledge that the measure might be declared ultra vires. Equally, if a national institution made a frivolous submission, it would be there in front of twenty-eight governments for all to see, and would consequently lack credibility.

(iii) EU law and protection of democratic authority

The requirements that EU law not violate fundamental rights and EU institutions not act ultra vires are weak constraints. They only require that the Union does not do really bad things and keeps vaguely to its tasks. They do not address the broader question of the remit of Union authority, and whether there is a point where its remit is excessive and encroaches too far on things of domestic value. In this, the Lisbon Treaty introduced a new provision, the 'identity' provision.[92]

Article 4(2) TEU

2. The Union shall respect the equality of Member States before the Treaties as well as their national identities, inherent in their fundamental structures, political and constitutional, inclusive of regional and local self-government. It shall respect their essential State functions, including ensuring the territorial integrity of the State, maintaining law and order and safeguarding national security. In particular, national security remains the sole responsibility of each Member State.

The provision is not a simple restatement of the importance of national identity. The fundamental 'constitutional' and 'political' structures constituting this identity must also be respected. If the former, self-evidently, requires that domestic constitutional identities be respected,[93] the latter requires that domestic democratic identities be respected. For it is impossible, within liberal democracies, to argue that a state's democracy is not central to its political identity. The other feature of note about the article is the idea of 'respect'. Respect conveys an idea of esteem for things as they are which means that these identities cannot be seen as exceptions to EU law,

---

[91] J. Komárek, 'Playing with Matches: The Czech Constitutional Court Declares a Judgment of the Court of Justice of the EU *Ultra Vires*' (2012) 8 *European Constitutional Law Review* 323; R. Zbíral, 'A Legal Revolution or Negligible Episode? Court of Justice Decision Proclaimed Ultra Vires' (2012) 49 *CMLRev.* 1475.

[92] On the provision see M. Claes, 'Negotiating Constitutional Identity or Whose Identity is it Anyway?' in M. Claes *et al.* (eds.), *Constitutional Conversations in Europe: Actors, Topics and Procedures* (Cambridge, Intersentia, 2012).

[93] On whether this requires national courts to disapply EU law where it violates nationals constitutions see v. Bogdandy and Schill, n. 67 above.

which must be interpreted, correspondingly, in a narrow manner.[94] Instead, they act to limit the authority of EU law, and must be given equal weight to it.[95] The German Constitutional Court turned to this question in its *Lisbon Treaty* judgment, where, alongside ultra vires review, it set out identity review as a further form of refusing EU law authority. In the judgment, the Court found that the European Union did not meet the conditions for being a representative democracy, as Union citizens were not equally represented either through the allocation of seats in the European Parliament or the allocation of votes within the Council. It, consequently, considered whether this limited the fields in which EU law could have authority.[96] Of particular concern was article 1 of the Basic Law, which set out the right to human dignity, and article 20(2) which stated that all state authority is derived from the people, and shall be exercised by the people through elections. Article 79(3), the eternity clause, states that this provision, as one of the first twenty provisions of the Basic Law, is so central that it cannot be amended.

2 BvE 2/08 *Treaty of Lisbon*, Judgment of 30 June 2009

216. The principle of democracy may not be balanced against other legal interests; it is inviolable…The constituent power of the Germans which gave itself the Basic Law wanted to set an insurmountable boundary to any future political development. Amendments to the Basic Law affecting the principles laid down in Article 1 and Article 20 of the Basic Law shall be inadmissible (Article 79.3 of the Basic Law). The so-called eternity guarantee even prevents a constitution-amending legislature from disposing of the identity of the free constitutional order. The Basic Law thus not only presumes sovereign statehood for Germany but guarantees it.

217. … Within the order of the Basic Law, the structural principles of the state laid down in Article 20 of the Basic Law, i.e. democracy, the rule of law, the principle of the social state, the republic, the federal state, as well as the substance of elementary fundamental rights indispensable for the respect of human dignity are, in any case, not amenable to any amendment because of their fundamental quality…

240. … Furthermore, the Federal Constitutional Court reviews whether the inviolable core content of the constitutional identity of the Basic Law…is respected…The exercise of this review power, which is rooted in constitutional law, follows the principle of the Basic Law's openness towards European Law (*Europarechtsfreundlichkeit*), and it therefore also does not contradict the principle of sincere cooperation (Article 4.3 Lisbon TEU); otherwise, with progressing integration, the fundamental political and constitutional structures of sovereign Member States, which are recognised by Article 4.2 first sentence Lisbon TEU, cannot be safeguarded in any other way. In this respect, the guarantee of national constitutional identity under constitutional and under Union law goes hand in hand in the European legal area. The identity review makes it possible to examine whether due to the action of European institutions, the principles under Article 1 and Article 20 of the Basic Law, declared inviolable in Article 79.3 of the Basic Law, have been violated. This ensures that the primacy of application of Union law only applies by virtue and in the context of the constitutional empowerment that continues in effect….

[94] Cf. the case law of the Court of Justice which has interpreted it as an exception, Case C-208/09 *Sayn-Wittgenstein* [2010] ECR I-1369; Case C-51/08 *Commission* v *Luxembourg*, Judgment of 4 May 2011; Case C-391/09. *Runevi-Vardyn*, Judgment of 12 May 2011.
[95] B. Guastaferro, 'Beyond the Exceptionalism of Constitutional Conflicts: The Ordinary Functions of the Identity Clause' (2012) 31 *YBEL* 263, 271–85.
[96] See paras. 280–94 of the judgment.

244. The shape of the European Union must comply with democratic principles as regards the nature and the extent of the transfer of sovereign powers as well as with regard to the organisational and procedural elaboration of the Union authority acting autonomously...European integration may neither result in the system of democratic rule in Germany being undermined nor may the supranational public authority as such fail to comply with fundamental democratic requirements.

245. A permanent responsibility for integration is incumbent upon the German constitutional bodies. In the transfer of sovereign powers and the elaboration of the European decision-making procedures, it is aimed at ensuring that, seen overall, the political system of the Federal Republic of Germany as well as that of the European Union comply with democratic principles within the meaning of Article 20.1 and 20.2 in conjunction with Article 79.3 of the Basic Law.

246. The election of the Members of the German Bundestag by the people fulfils its central role in the system of the federal and supranational intertwining of power only if the German Bundestag, which represents the people, and the Federal Government sustained by it, retain a formative influence on the political development in Germany. This is the case if the German Bundestag retains own responsibilities and competences of substantial political importance or if the Federal Government, which is answerable to it politically, is in a position to exert a decisive influence on European decision-making procedures...

247. Inward federalisation and outward supranationalisation can open up new possibilities of civic participation. An increased cohesion of smaller or larger units and better opportunities for a peaceful balancing of interests between regions and states grow from them. Federal or supranational intertwining creates possibilities of action which otherwise would encounter practical or territorial limits, and facilitates the peaceful balancing of interests. At the same time, it makes it more difficult to create a will of the majority that can be asserted and that directly derives from the people...The assignment of decisions to specific responsible actors becomes less transparent, with the result that citizens have difficulty in having their vote guided by tangible contexts of responsibility. The principle of democracy therefore sets content-related limits to the transfer of sovereign powers, limits which do not already result from the inalienability of the constituent power and of state sovereignty.

248. The safeguarding of sovereignty, demanded by the principle of democracy in the valid constitutional system prescribed by the Basic Law in a manner that is open to integration and to international law, does not mean that a pre-determined number or certain types of sovereign rights should remain in the hands of the state. The participation of Germany in the development of the European Union, which is permitted by Article 23.1 first sentence of the Basic Law, also comprises a political union, in addition to the creation of an economic and monetary union. Political union means the joint exercise of public authority, including legislative authority, even reaching into the traditional core areas of the state's area of competence. This is rooted in the European idea of peace and unification especially when dealing with the coordination of cross-border aspects of life and when guaranteeing a single economic area and area of justice in which citizens of the Union can freely develop.

249. European unification on the basis of a treaty union of sovereign states may, however, not be achieved in such a way that not sufficient space is left to the Member States for the political formation of the economic, cultural and social living conditions. This applies in particular to areas which shape the citizens' living conditions, in particular the private sphere of their own responsibility and of political and social security, protected by fundamental rights, as well as to political decisions that rely especially on cultural, historical and linguistic perceptions and which

develop in public discourse in the party political and parliamentary sphere of public politics. Essential areas of democratic formative action comprise, inter alia, citizenship, the civil and the military monopoly on the use of force, revenue and expenditure including external financing and all elements of encroachment that are decisive for the realisation of fundamental rights, above all in major encroachments on fundamental rights such as deprivation of liberty in the administration of criminal law or placement in an institution. These important areas also include cultural issues such as the disposition of language, the shaping of circumstances concerning the family and education, the ordering of the freedom of opinion, press and of association and the dealing with the profession of faith or ideology.

250. Democracy not only means respecting formal principles of organisation…and not just a cooperative involvement of interest groups. Democracy first and foremost lives on, and in, a viable public opinion that concentrates on central acts of determination of political direction and the periodic allocation of highest-ranking political offices in the competition of government and opposition. Only this public opinion shows the alternatives for elections and other votes and continually calls them to mind also in decisions relating to individual issues in order that they may remain continuously present and effective in the political opinion-formation of the people via the parties, which are open to participation for all citizens, and in the public information area. To this extent, Article 38 and Article 20.1 and 20.2 of the Basic Law also protect the connection between political decisions on facts and the will of the majority constituted by elections, and the resulting dualism between government and opposition in a system of a multiplicity of competing parties and of observing and controlling formation of public opinion.

251. Even if due to the great successes of European integration, a common European polity that engages in issue-related cooperation in the relevant areas of their respective states is visibly growing…it cannot be overlooked, however, that the public perception of factual issues and of political leaders remains connected to a considerable extent to patterns of identification related to the nation-state, language, history and culture. The principle of democracy as well as the principle of subsidiarity…therefore require factually to restrict the transfer and exercise of sovereign powers to the European Union in a predictable manner, particularly in central political areas of the space of personal development and the shaping of living conditions by social policy. In these areas, it is particularly necessary to draw the limit where the coordination of cross-border situations is factually required.

252. Particularly sensitive for the ability of a constitutional state to democratically shape itself are decisions on substantive and formal criminal law, on the disposition of the monopoly on the use of force by the police within the state and by the military towards the exterior, fundamental fiscal decisions on public revenue and public expenditure, the latter being particularly motivated, inter alia, by social policy considerations, decisions on the shaping of living conditions in a social state and decisions of particular cultural importance, for example on family law, the school and education system and on dealing with religious communities.

The limited democratic qualities of the Union mean, according to the German Constitutional Court, that, by itself it does not have authority to adopt laws which go, in the words of paragraph 249, to 'the political formation of the economic, cultural and social living conditions'. These include the central features of criminal law, deployment of the use of force, central budgetary issues, the central issues of social policy and culturally important fields, in particular religion, education and family life. In principle, Member States must have the possibility to govern these fields through their domestic parliaments if democracy is to be respected. Furthermore, according to the court, by virtue of Article 4(2) TEU, this is also a requirement of EU law. If this 'democratic identity' limit on the authority of EU law is set out at most length in the judgment above, similar positions have also been taken in Poland,[97] the Czech Republic,[98] Portugal,[99] France[100] and Estonia.[101]

This approach has been criticised for centring itself too much around the idea of 'identity', with the latter's corollary polarising associations of 'Them' (Europeans) and 'Us' (nationals).[102] It also has been argued that it gives Member States a free pass in these protected fields, and looks insufficiently at the quality of democracy which takes place there.[103] The identification of certain fields of activity as more central to democratic life than others has, finally, been seen as arbitrary.[104] All these criticisms have some force. However, to focus on these is to miss the importance of the judgment. It emphasises that EU law must have democratic authority, and that, where this is not the case, care is needed as to what effect should be given to it. In particular, there is scepticism about granting it authority in fields of activity which are either wide-ranging or culturally or politically sensitive. To argue that national democracies have faults does not counter this 'Achilles heel' of EU legal authority.

The point is more acutely made in another part of the judgment, which did not go to identity review, but, instead, noted that the doctrine of conferred powers required Union powers to be limited in nature.[105] In areas where the Union enjoyed ill-defined powers, EU law could only enjoy authority if it also had national parliamentary assent.

---

2 BvE 2/08 *Treaty of Lisbon*, Judgment of 30 June 2009

238. Under the constitution, however, faith in the constructive force of the mechanism of integration cannot be unlimited. If in the process of European integration primary law is amended, or expansively interpreted by institutions, a constitutionally important tension will arise with the principle of conferral and with the individual Member State's constitutional responsibility for integration. If legislative or administrative competences are only transferred in an unspecified manner or with a view to further dynamic development, or if the institutions are permitted to re-define expansively, fill lacunae or factually extend competences, they risk transgressing the predetermined integration programme and acting beyond the powers granted to them. They are moving on a road at the end of which there is

---

[97] K 32/09 *Treaty of Lisbon*, Polish Constitutional Tribunal, Judgment of 24 November 2010.

[98] *Re Constitutionality of Framework Decision on the European Arrest Warrant* [2007] 3 CMLR 24 (Czech Constitutional Court).

[99] Portuguese Constitution (2005, 7th revision), art. 8(4).

[100] Decision 2012–653 *Treaty on Stability, Coordination and Governance in the Economic and Monetary Union*, French Constitutional Council, Judgment of 9 August 2012, para. 10.

[101] Case 3–4–1–6–12 *Article 4(4) ESM Treaty*, Estonian Supreme Court, Judgment of 12 July 2012, para. 134 *et seq.*

[102] K. Nicolaidis, 'Germany as Europe: How the Constitutional Court Unwittingly Embraced EU Demoi-cracy' (2011) 9 *I-CON* 786.

[103] F. Mayer, 'Rashomon in Karlsruhe: A Reflection on Democracy and Identity in the European Union' (2011) 9 *I-CON* 757.

[104] D. Halberstam and C. Möllers, 'The German Constitutional Court Says *"Ja zu Deutschland!"*' (2009) 10 *German Law Journal* No. 8.

[105] On concern with the ill-defined powers of the Lisbon Treaty see Pl ÚS 19/08 *Treaty of Lisbon*, Czech Constitutional Court, Judgment of 26 November 2008, paras. 184–6.

the power of disposition of their foundations laid down in the treaties, i.e. the competence of freely disposing of their competences. There is a risk of transgression of the constitutive principle of conferral and of the conceptual responsibility for integration incumbent upon Member States if institutions of the European Union can decide without restriction, without any outside control, however restrained and exceptional, how treaty law is to be interpreted.

239. It is therefore constitutionally required not to agree dynamic treaty provisions with a blanket character or if they can still be interpreted in a manner that respects the national responsibility for integration, to establish, at any rate, suitable national safeguards for the effective exercise of such responsibility. Accordingly, the Act approving an international agreement and the national accompanying laws must therefore be capable of permitting European integration continuing to take place according to the principle of conferral without the possibility for the European Union of taking possession of *Kompetenz-Kompetenz* or to violate the Member States' constitutional identity, which is not open to integration, in this case, that of the Basic Law. For borderline cases of what is still constitutionally admissible, the German legislature must, where necessary, take precautions in its legislation accompanying approval to ensure that the responsibility for integration of the legislative bodies can sufficiently develop.

The Court ruled that there were a number of 'dynamic' Treaty provisions within the TEU and TFEU.[106] Proposals adopted under these measures would only be lawful, and enjoy legal authority, if the German Parliament had, first, approved these. The most prominent of these provisions was Article 352 TFEU, the flexibility provision.

Article 352(1) TFEU

1. If action by the Union should prove necessary, within the framework of the policies defined by the Treaties, to attain one of the objectives set out in the Treaties, and the Treaties have not provided the necessary powers, the Council, acting unanimously on a proposal from the European Commission and after obtaining the consent of the European Parliament, shall adopt the appropriate measures. Where the measures in question are adopted by the Council in accordance with a special legislative procedure, it shall also act unanimously on a proposal from the Commission and after obtaining the consent of the European Parliament.

This provision is particularly controversial as it grants the Union legislative power where none is provided elsewhere in the Treaty if this is necessary to realise broadly defined Union objectives.[107] In Germany, concern about its predecessor had been raised by the German Länder

[106] On this see D. Jan i, 'Caveats from Karlsruhe and Berlin: Whither Democracy after Lisbon' (2009) 16 *CJEL* 337, 362–4. The other provisions are the passerelle provisions which allow measures decided by unanimity to be decided by qualified majority voting (QMV): both general (Article 48(7) TEU) and specific (Article 31(2) TEU, 81(3)(2)(3), 153(2)(4), 192(2), 312(2) and 33(1) and (2) TFEU); the emergency brake provisions which allow measures touching on fundamental aspects of a Member State's social security or criminal justice system to be referred to the European Council (Articles 48(2), 82(3) and 83(3) TFEU); extension of the list of criminal offences which may be harmonised and of the powers of the European public prosecutor (Articles 83(1)(3) and 86(4) TFEU); amendment of the Statute of the European Investment Bank, Article 308 TFEU.

[107] Declaration 41 to the Lisbon Treaty states that the objectives which serve as the basis for action under Article 352 TFEU are those set out in Article 3(2)(3) and (5). On the remit of Article 352 TFEU see T. Konstadinides, 'Drawing the Line between Circumvention and Gap-Filling: An Exploration of the Conceptual Limits around the Scope of Article 352 TFEU' (2012) 31 *YBEL* 1.

who saw it as so broad that it allowed the Union to legislate in fields where not even the central German authorities could legislate.[108]

---

2 BvE 2/08 *Treaty of Lisbon*, Judgment of 30 June 2009

326. Article 352 TFEU not only establishes a competence for action for the European Union but at the same time relaxes the principle of conferral. Because action by the European Union in areas set out in the treaties is intended to be possible if the treaties have not provided the necessary specific competence but action by the European Union is required in order to attain the objectives set out in the treaties…

327. … The amendments made by the Treaty of Lisbon must lead to a new assessment of the provision. Article 352 TFEU is no longer confined to the attainment of objectives in the context of the Common Market but makes reference to 'the policies defined in the Treaties' (Article 352.1 TFEU) with the exception of the Common Foreign and Security Policy (Article 352.4 TFEU). The provision can thus serve to create a competence which makes action on the European level possible in almost the entire area of application of the primary law. This extension of the area of application is partly compensated by procedural safeguards. The use of the flexibility clause continues to require a unanimous decision by the Council on a proposal from the Commission which now requires the consent of the European Parliament (Article 352.1 first sentence TFEU). Moreover, the Commission is obliged to inform national parliaments of corresponding lawmaking proposals in the context of the procedure for monitoring compliance with the subsidiarity principle (Article 352.2 TFEU). Furthermore, such a lawmaking proposal shall not entail harmonisation of Member States' laws or regulations in cases where the treaties otherwise exclude such harmonisation (Article 352.3 TFEU). The approval by the Member States in accordance with their respective constitutional requirements is not a requirement for the decision to enter into force.

328. The provision meets with constitutional objections with regard to the ban on transferring blanket empowerments or on transferring *Kompetenz-Kompetenz*, because the newly worded provision makes it possible substantially to amend treaty foundations of the European Union without the constitutive participation of legislative bodies in addition to the Member States' executive powers…The duty to inform the national parliaments set out in Article 352.2 TFEU does not alter this; for the Commission only needs to draw the national parliaments' attention to a corresponding lawmaking proposal. Because of the indefinite nature of future application of the flexibility clause, its use constitutionally requires ratification by the German Bundestag and the Bundesrat…The German representative in the Council may not express formal approval on behalf of the Federal Republic of Germany of a corresponding lawmaking proposal of the Commission as long as these constitutionally required preconditions are not met.

The terms of trade are, therefore, changed. In this field, EU law will only have authority if it has certain democratic pedigree, namely, that it has both been approved by the EU legislature and the national parliament. The balance of power within the EU legislative process has been altered, with national parliaments being granted (in Article 352 TFEU at least) an enhanced role. This approach has been copied in the United Kingdom.

---

[108] '*Forderungen der Länder zur Regierungskonferenz* 1996', Drucksache 667/95 (Beschluß), 15 December 1995, 12–21.

European Union Act 2011, section 8

(1) A Minister of the Crown may not vote in favour of or otherwise support an Article 352 decision unless one of subsections (3) to (5) is complied with in relation to the draft decision...

(3) This subsection is complied with if a draft decision is approved by Act of Parliament.

(4) This subsection is complied with if:

  (a) in each House of Parliament a Minister of the Crown moves a motion that the House approves Her Majesty's Government's intention to support a specified draft decision and is of the opinion that the measure to which it relates is required as a matter of urgency, and

  (b) each House agrees to the motion without amendment.

(5) This subsection is complied with if a Minister of the Crown has laid before Parliament a statement specifying a draft decision and stating that in the opinion of the Minister the decision relates only to one or more exempt purposes.

(6) The exempt purposes are:

  (a) to make provision equivalent to that made by a measure previously adopted under Article 352 of TFEU, other than an excepted measure;

  (b) to prolong or renew a measure previously adopted under that Article, other than an excepted measure;

  (c) to extend a measure previously adopted under that Article to another Member State or other country;

  (d) to repeal existing measures adopted under that Article;

  (e) to consolidate existing measures adopted under that Article without any change of substance.

This requirement acts as a brake on EU law-making. There is a further hurdle to be met, the agreement of the national parliament, before a law can be adopted. However, it also allows EU measures to be adopted in fields where it might otherwise be precluded on grounds of identity review. If it can be said that, in these fields, domestic parliaments were engaged in the process of EU decision-making, the objections against EU involvement in these fields, namely, the undemocratic quality of decision-making, disappears. This matter came to a head in the *ESM* judgment. The judgment involved a challenge to the European Stability Mechanism Treaty which consolidated the different forms of financial assistance granted to euro area Member States experiencing difficulties in their public finances into a single instrument, the European Stability Mechanism (ESM). This Treaty established a fund of €700 billion with Germany financially liable for just over €190 billion of it. A company in Luxembourg administered the fund, with its Board of Governors (comprising the Finance Ministers of the euro area states) being responsible for the central decisions: making calls for more capital, guaranteeing loans to euro area states and setting out the conditions for these loans. Almost all decisions were taken by unanimity. In Germany, two laws were adopted which required further legislation if the capital stock was to be increased; parliamentary approval for guarantees of any loans; involvement of the parliamentary budgetary committee in the management of the ESM; and comprehensive and continuous updating of the Bundestag.

2 BvR 1390/12 *ESM Treaty (Temporary Injunctions),* Judgment of 12 September 2012 (German Constitutional Court)

209. The Basic Law not only prohibits the transfer of competence to decide on its own competence (*Kompetenz-Kompetenz*) to the European Union or to institutions created in connection with the European Union...Blanket empowerments for the exercise of public authority may also not be granted by the German constitutional bodies...It is therefore constitutionally required not to agree dynamic treaty provisions with a blanket character, or if they can still be interpreted in a manner that respects the responsibility for integration, to establish, at any rate, suitable safeguards for the effective exercise of such responsibility. Accordingly, the Act of assent and the national accompanying laws must therefore be capable of permitting European integration continuing to take place according to the principle of conferral without the possibility for the European Union, or for institutions created in connection with the European Union, of taking possession of *Kompetenz-Kompetenz* or of otherwise violating the Basic Law's constitutional identity, which is not open to integration. For borderline cases of what is still constitutionally admissible, the German legislature must, where necessary, make effective arrangements in its legislation accompanying the Act of assent to ensure that the responsibility for integration of the legislative bodies can sufficiently develop...

210. There is a violation of Article 38(1) of the Basic Law in particular if the German Bundestag relinquishes its parliamentary budget responsibility with the effect that it or a future Bundestag can no longer exercise the right to decide on the budget on its own responsibility...The decision on public revenue and public expenditure is a fundamental part of the ability of a constitutional state to democratically shape itself...The German Bundestag must therefore make decisions on revenue and expenditure with responsibility to the people. In this connection, the right to decide on the budget is a central element of the democratic development of informed opinion...

211. As representatives of the people, the elected Members of the German Bundestag must retain control of fundamental budgetary decisions even in a system of intergovernmental governing. In its openness to international cooperation, systems of collective security and European integration, the Federal Republic of Germany binds itself not only legally, but also with regard to fiscal policy. Even if such commitments assume a substantial size, parliament's right to decide on the budget is not necessarily infringed in a way that could be challenged with reference to Article 38(1) of the Basic Law. Rather, the relevant factor for adherence to the principles of democracy is whether the German Bundestag remains the place in which autonomous decisions on revenue and expenditure are made, including those with regard to international and European liabilities...If essential budget questions relating to revenue and expenditure were decided without the mandatory approval of the German Bundestag, or if supranational legal obligations were created without a corresponding decision by free will of the Bundestag, parliament would find itself in the role of mere subsequent enforcement and could no longer exercise its overall budgetary responsibility as part of its right to decide on the budget...

212. In its judgment of 7 September 2011 (BVerfGE 129, 124) the Senate stated in detail that the German Bundestag may not transfer its budgetary responsibility to other entities by means of imprecise budgetary authorisations. The larger the financial amount of the commitments to accept liability or of commitment appropriations is, the more effectively must the German Bundestag's rights to approve and to refuse and its right of monitoring be elaborated. In particular, the German Bundestag

may not deliver itself up to any mechanisms with financial effect which – whether by reason of their overall conception or by reason of an overall evaluation of the individual measures – may result in incalculable burdens with budget significance without prior mandatory consent, whether these are expenses or losses of revenue. This prohibition of the relinquishment of budgetary responsibility does not impermissibly restrict the budgetary competence of the legislature, but is specifically aimed at preserving it...

213. A necessary condition for the safeguarding of political latitude in the sense of the core of identity of the constitution (Article 20(1) and (2), Article 79(3) of the Basic Law) is that the budget legislature makes its decisions on revenue and expenditure free of other-directedness on the part of the bodies and of other Member States of the European Union and remains permanently 'the master of its decisions'...Admittedly, it is primarily the duty of the Bundestag itself to decide, while weighing current needs against the risks of medium- and long-term guarantees, in what maximum amount guarantee sums are responsible...But it follows from the democratic basis of budget autonomy that the Bundestag may not consent to an intergovernmentally or supranationally agreed automatic guarantee or performance which is not subject to strict requirements and whose effects are not limited, which – once it has been set in motion – is removed from the Bundestag's control and influence...

214. Moreover, no permanent mechanisms may be created under international treaties which are tantamount to accepting liability for decisions by free will of other states, above all if they entail consequences which are hard to calculate. The Bundestag must individually approve every large-scale federal aid measure on the international or European Union level made in solidarity resulting in expenditure. Insofar as supranational agreements are entered into which by reason of their scale may be of structural significance for parliament's right to decide on the budget, for example by giving guarantees the honouring of which may endanger budget autonomy, or by participation in equivalent financial safeguarding systems, not only every individual disposal requires the consent of the Bundestag; in addition it must be ensured that sufficient parliamentary influence shall continue to be made on the manner of dealing with the funds provided...

215. The German Bundestag cannot exercise its overall budgetary responsibility without receiving sufficient information concerning the decisions with budgetary implications for which it is accountable. The principle of democracy under Article 20(1) and (2) of the Basic Law therefore requires that the German Bundestag is able to have access to the information which it needs to assess the fundamental bases and consequences of its decision...The core of the right of parliament to be informed is therefore also entrenched in Article 79(3) of the Basic Law. Sufficient information of parliament by the government is therefore a necessary precondition of an effective preparation of parliament's decisions and of the exercise of its monitoring function...This principle not only applies in national budget law...but also in matters concerning the European Union...

The *ESM* judgment brings the 'identity review' line of reasoning and the 'dynamic treaty provision' line of reasoning together.[109] Budgetary policy is one of the fields central to democratic identity, and so falls within the former. The treaty is sufficiently general and

---

[109] On the judgment see M. Wendel, 'Judicial Restraint and the Return to Openness: The Decision of the German Federal Constitutional Court on the ESM and the Fiscal Treaty of 12 September 2012' (2013) 14 *German Law Journal* 21.

open-ended to fall within the latter. In both instances, what matters is the quality of national parliamentary engagement. Furthermore, mere formal involvement is insufficient. The involvement must be of a nature to allow the parliament to discharge its 'budgetary responsibilities' in this field. It was, therefore, not enough that it be able to veto any guarantee; it must be granted sufficient information to monitor what is taking place. In short, it must be an active player in the policy-making process, and be given the tools necessary to allow it discharge this.

A dichotomy is emerging, therefore. In fields perceived as confined, EU law has authority subject to the ultra vires doctrine and to its not violating fundamental rights. In other fields, where it is seen as exercising more wide-ranging competences or intruding on more sensitive issues, a new test of relative democratic authority is emerging. An EU law will only enjoy authority if it has been approved by national parliaments: something which should only happen if these perceive that the overall gains by it exceed anything which could be secured through alternative measures and that these gains exceed any domestic costs. Invariably, there will be questions about how well equipped national parliaments are to discharge this role. However, it provides an important counter-weight to the executive dominance of the EU legislative processes, as well as emphasising the point that the authority of EU law cannot be seen as something separate from the democratic authority of the European Union. However, it begs one final question, which is the rationale for this dichotomy. It is not at all clear why national parliaments should have this role in only some fields of EU law rather than all fields of EU law, as the issue of democratic authority touches on all its activities.[110]

FURTHER READING

M. Avbelj and J. Komárek (eds.), *Constitutional Pluralism in the European Union and Beyond* (Oxford, Hart, 2012)

G. de Búrca and J. Weiler (eds.), *The Worlds of European Constitutionalism* (Cambridge, Cambridge University Press, 2012)

A. v. Bogdandy and S. Schill, 'Overcoming Absolute Primacy: Respect for National Identity under the Lisbon Treaty' (2011) 48 *Common Market Law Review* 1417

D. Chalmers, 'European Restatements of Sovereignty' in R. Rawlings *et al.* (eds.), *Sovereignty and the Law* (Oxford, Oxford University Press, 2013)

M. Claes, *The National Courts' Mandate in the European Constitution* (Oxford/Portland, Hart, 2005)

M. Claes *et al.* (eds.), *Constitutional Conversations in Europe: Actors, Topics and Procedures* (Cambridge, Intersentia, 2012)

M. Dani, 'Constitutionalism and Dissonances: Has Europe Paid Off Its Debt to Functionalism?' (2009) 15 *European Law Journal* 324

G. Davies, 'Democracy and Legitimacy in the Shadow of Purposive Competence' (2014) 20 *European Law Journal* (forthcoming)

B. Guastaferro, 'Beyond the Exceptionalism of Constitutional Conflicts: The Ordinary Functions of the Identity Clause' (2012) 31 *Yearbook of European Law* 263

---

[110] D. Chalmers, *Democratic Self-Government in Europe* (London, Policy Network, 2013).

D. Jančić, 'Caveats from Karlsruhe and Berlin: Whither Democracy after Lisbon' (2009) 16 *Columbia Journal of European Law* 337

J. Komárek, 'European Constitutionalism and the European Arrest Warrant: In Search of the Limits of "Contrapunctual Principles"' (2007) 44 *Common Market Law Review* 9

R. Schütze, *From Dual to Cooperative Federalism: The Changing Structure of European Law* (Oxford, Oxford University Press, 2009)

N. Walker (ed.), *Sovereignty in Transition* (Oxford/Portland, Hart, 2003)

6

Fundamental Rights

CONTENTS

1 INTRODUCTION

This chapter considers EU fundamental rights law. It is organised as follows.

Section 2 considers the salient features of EU fundamental rights law mapped out in Article 6 TEU. First, there is no single EU Bill of Rights. Instead, EU fundamental rights law has three sources: general principles of law as guaranteed by national constitutional traditions and the European Convention for the Protection of Human Rights and Freedoms (ECHR); the ECHR itself; and the European Union Charter of Fundamental Rights (EUCFR). Secondly, Article 6 TEU states that the EUCFR is not to enlarge Union competences, marking EU fundamental rights law as a field beset by institutional sensitivity. Finally, it provides for the Union to accede to the ECHR. This places the Union more firmly within a more general European human rights order but raises the question if it is acceding simply because the ECHR acts as a valuable check against Union power or because the Union is becoming a powerful allocator of values in its own right.

Section 3 considers the rights provided by EU fundamental rights law. It traces, first, the development of general principles of law which have emerged, non-codified, out of the case law of the Court of Justice. Since the Treaty of Lisbon, these have been largely submerged within the EUCFR, with the exception of a number of rights which have no equivalent there, notably those on non-discrimination, proportionality, legitimate expectations and non-retroactivity. The EUCFR contains six types of right: rights to human dignity, freedoms, equality rights, solidarity rights, rights to justice and citizenship rights. A wide array of rights is, thus, recognised. To sustain this ambition, the EUCFR makes a distinction between rights and principles, with the latter being judicially enforceable only in relation to legislation implementing them. It is unclear, however, which entitlements are rights and which are principles. Furthermore, a number of important rights, such as the right to nationality, decent pay, housing and work are not included in the EUCFR.

Section 4 considers the standard of protection offered by EU fundamental rights law. Reference must, first, be had to the Explanations of the Secretariat which drafted the EUCFR, national constitutional traditions and the ECHR. In practice, it is only the last of these which has had a significant hold on interpretations of EU fundamental rights in recent years. This raises questions about why there is so much deference to the ECHR and why regard for national constitutional traditions, in particular, is not greater. Interpretation of EU fundamental rights is also powerfully guided by the objectives and tasks of European integration: be this realisation of the single market, the Area of Freedom, Security and Justice or the other projects set out in Article 3 TEU. This raises questions about whether these objectives and tasks are granted too great a weight in relation to the protection offered to the individual. The interpretation of fundamental rights in their light also leads to interpretations which differ markedly from those traditionally given in national contexts.

Section 5 considers the institutions bound by EU fundamental rights law. EU fundamental rights are used to review the administrative practice of EU institutions quite extensively. It is rare, by contrast, for EU laws to be struck down for violating EU fundamental rights. The significance of EU fundamental rights lies rather in how they are considered in the EU law-making process and how EU laws are interpreted in the light of them. Member States are only bound by EU fundamental rights law where they implement Union measures. Historically, this was where they either transposed EU Directives or measures breached an EU law but fell within an exception recognised by EU law. A third circumstance has emerged following *Fransson*. This is where national measures fall within the scope of EU law. This will be the case where an EU law governs some part of the activity in question. This is controversial because it extends the remit of EU fundamental rights law considerably and has been challenged by the German Constitutional Court in its *Counterterrorism Database* judgment.

Section 6 considers the accession of the Union to the ECHR. A draft agreement was concluded in June 2013. It sought to address a number of issues associated with EU accession. These included how accession would affect the autonomy of EU law; how different national obligations under the ECHR would be respected; and how accession would not be used to extend EU competences. The draft Agreement tries to address these by making Member States responsible under the ECHR whenever they apply, enforce or administer EU law, with EU institutions only responsible for measures that require no national involvement.

2 FUNDAMENTAL RIGHTS AND THE SCHEMA OF THE TREATIES

Article 2 TEU states that respect for human dignity, freedom, equality and human rights are the values on which the Union is founded. Notwithstanding this, references to fundamental rights are scarce and oblique in the Treaties. The central provision is Article 6 TEU.

Article 6 TEU

1. The Union recognises the rights, freedoms and principles set out in the Charter of Fundamental Rights of the European Union of 7 December 2000, as adapted at Strasbourg, on 12 December 2007, which shall have the same legal value as the Treaties.

   The provisions of the Charter shall not extend in any way the competences of the Union as defined in the Treaties.

   The rights, freedoms and principles in the Charter shall be interpreted in accordance with the general provisions in Title VII of the Charter governing its interpretation and application and with due regard to the explanations referred to in the Charter, that set out the sources of those provisions.
2. The Union shall accede to the European Convention for the Protection of Human Rights and Fundamental Freedoms. Such accession shall not affect the Union's competences as defined in the Treaties.
3. Fundamental rights, as guaranteed by the European Convention for the Protection of Human Rights and Fundamental Freedoms and as they result from the constitutional traditions common to the Member States, shall constitute general principles of the Union's law.

Article 6 TEU must be understood as, above all, a provision which maps out the contours of EU fundamental rights law. To be sure, Article 6(2) TEU provides for Union accession to the ECHR but the other provisions were described by Advocate General Sharpston in *Radu* as:

> a 'codification' of the pre-existing position. They encapsulate, to put it another way, a political desire that the provisions they seek to enshrine and to protect should be more visible in their expression. They do not represent a sea change of any kind.[1]

This consolidation sets out three striking features which both characterise EU fundamental rights law and reflect its tensions.

First, there is no single European Union bill of rights. Instead, Article 6 refers to three sources of rights:

- the European Union Charter of Fundamental Rights (EUCFR) (Article 6(1) TEU);
- the European Convention for the Protection of Human Rights and Fundamental Freedoms (ECHR) (Article 6(2) TEU);
- general principles of law as guaranteed by the ECHR and constitutional traditions common to the Member States (Article 6(3) TEU).

---

[1] Case C-396/11 *Radu*, Judgment of 29 January 2013, Opinion of Advocate General Sharpston, para. 51.

The position is further complicated by significant overlap in content between each of these instruments. The EUCFR is so broad that it encompasses almost all rights in the other two headings. On top of this, the EUCFR and general principles of law both identify the ECHR as a source of law for them. To confuse matters a little bit more, none of these instruments are seen as constitutive of the fundamental rights in EU law. Although Article 6(1) TEU states that the EUCFR has the same status as the Treaty, it, the ECHR and general principle of law only 'recognise', 'guarantee' or 'set out' these rights.[2] These recognised rights are seen as having an independent existence in EU law. Freedom of expression may, for example, be recognised in the EUCFR, the ECHR and general principles of law but these merely confirm the presence of such a right in EU law, which, as an EU legal right, will be understood as such.

This multiplicity of overlapping sources of uncertain force has been criticised for generating unnecessary complexity and obscurity about the content of EU fundamental rights.[3] This complexity may well be there but it may also be seen as a hallmark of EU law which could provide it with a normative richness. There is no single instrument which provides an authoritative narrative about what values are fundamental in EU law. Instead, these result from interplay between different instruments, which act to inform and interrogate each other with the content of fundamental rights remaining an open-ended process.[4]

Secondly, EU fundamental rights law raises institutional sensitivities. Assertions of the fundamental qualities of certain rights by central courts are not just statements about the value of these but also a claim to a central competence to regulate them. There is therefore a particular sensitivity to judicial activism here. Article 6(1) TEU, therefore, states that the EUCFR shall not extend in any way the competences of the Union.

Thirdly, the accession of the Union to the ECHR raises questions about the Union's mission in the field of fundamental rights. It could be that this is just an additional constraint to ensure EU institutions do no wrong. However, historically states acceded to the ECHR not only because they can easily violate fundamental rights, but also because they allocate values. They set out a stall of what is right and wrong within a society. Allowing the Union to accede to the ECHR is therefore a double admission. It is a body whose measures increasingly affect human rights, but it is also a body that is increasingly involved in setting out visions of what is right and wrong for EU citizens.

3 SUBSTANCE OF EU FUNDAMENTAL RIGHTS LAW

Although the EUCFR is first mentioned in Article 6 TEU, the provision builds on a legacy of fundamental rights which first began with national constitutional traditions and the ECHR.

---

[2] On the status of the ECHR pending Union accession see Case C-503/11P *Schindler Holdings v Commission*, Judgment of 18 July 2013.
[3] R. Schütze, 'Three "Bills of Rights" for the European Union' (2011) 30 *YBEL* 1.
[4] On this see S. Douglas Scott, 'A Tale of Two Courts: Luxembourg, Strasbourg and the Growing European Human Rights Acquis' (2006) 43 *CMLRev.* 619; G. Harpaz, 'The European Court of Justice and Its Relations with the European Court of Human Rights: The Quest for Enhanced Reliance, Coherence and Legitimacy' (2009) 46 *CMLRev.* 105.

(i) National constitutional traditions and the ECHR in EU fundamental rights law

The original Treaties contained no system of fundamental rights protection. Their scope also provided limited opportunities for possible conflicts.[5] If these did arise, Member States expected their national constitutions to be the best guarantee of protection of fundamental rights. The early case law of the European Court of Justice reflected this line of thinking as it refused to countenance arguments that the EU institutions had violated some right protected in national constitutions.[6]

The advent of the primacy of EU law challenged these assumptions. It threatened to undermine safeguards in national constitutions.[7] This created not only a lacuna in protection of fundamental rights, but begged questions about EU law's authority. The benefits of the single market did not legitimate the Treaties to such a degree that it should exercise constitutional authority.[8] Human rights, by contrast, were a much more powerful instrument of polity legitimation. They not only offered assurances about the conduct of the Union and an attractive array of values as its vision. They also represented something archetypically European: a common heritage with the Union, as a self-styled European organisation, as the guardian of that heritage.[9] The development of fundamental rights within the EU had a double value. It offered, first, a reassurance about EU conduct and EU laws by offering a check against egregious behaviour. Secondly, it offered a new reason for European integration which had much more resonance than that of market integration.

The Court's case law softened towards the end of the 1960s. In *Van Eick*, the Court stated that EU institution staff disciplinary procedures were 'bound in the exercise of [their] powers to observe the fundamental principles of the law of procedure'.[10] In *Stauder*, faced with two possible interpretations of a Commission Decision, the Court stated that the interpretation would be chosen which would not prejudice the 'fundamental human rights enshrined in the general principles of [EU] law and protected by the Court'.[11] In other words, the Court would interpret EU measures in the light of fundamental rights instruments. However, fundamental rights still occupied no more than a second-order status. They could not be used as a basis for steering the actions of EU authorities and as a ground for judicial review. National courts were still left with a choice between refusing to apply EU law or neglecting fundamental liberties enshrined in their national constitutions.[12]

The matter came to a head in *Internationale Handelsgesellschaft*. An EU Regulation awarded a German trader a licence to export maize on condition that it set down a deposit which would

---

[5] On the discussions prior to the Treaty of Rome about fundamental rights and this early silence see G. de Búrca, 'The Evolution of EU Human Rights Law' in P. Craig and G. de Búrca (eds.), *The Evolution of EU Law* (2nd edn, Oxford, Oxford University Press, 2011) 465–77.

[6] Case 1/58 *Stork* v *High Authority* [1959] ECR 17; Joined Cases 36, 37, 38 and 40/59 *Geitling* v *High Authority* [1960] ECR 423; Case 40/64 *Sgarlata* v *Commission* [1965] ECR 215.

[7] See pp. 202–3 and 225–8.

[8] A. Williams, *EU Human Rights Policies: A Study in Irony* (Oxford, Oxford University Press, 2004) 139.

[9] *Ibid.* 133–4. Less sceptically see J. Habermas, *The Divided West* (Cambridge, Polity, 2006) 75–81; J.-W. Müller, 'A European Constitutional Patriotism? The Case Restated' (2008) 14 *ELJ* 542; S. Smijsmans, 'The European Union's Fundamental Rights Myth' (2010) 48 *JCMS* 45.

[10] Case 35/67 *Van Eick* v *Commission* [1968] ECR 329.

[11] Case 29/69 *Stauder* v *City of Ulm* [1969] ECR 419.

[12] U. Scheuner, 'Fundamental Rights in European Community Law and in National Constitutional Law' (1975) 12 *CMLRev.* 171, 173–4.

be forfeited if it failed to export the maize within the time stipulated in the licence. When this happened, the Regulation was challenged before the administrative court in Frankfurt which held that the Regulation violated the Basic Law right to freedom to trade. It therefore asked the Court of Justice whether the Regulation was valid.

Case 11/70 *Internationale Handelsgesellschaft v. Einfuhr und Vorratstelle für Getreide und Futtermittel* [1970] ECR 1125

3. Recourse to the legal rules or concepts of national law in order to judge the validity of measures adopted by the institutions of the [Union] would have an adverse effect on the uniformity and efficacy of [EU] law. The validity of such measures can only be judged in the light of Community law. In fact, the law stemming from the Treaty, an independent source of law, cannot because of its very nature be overridden by rules of national law, however framed, without being deprived of its character as [EU] law and without the legal basis of the [Union] itself being called in question. Therefore the validity of [an EU] measure or its effect within a Member State cannot be affected by allegations that it runs counter to either fundamental rights as formulated by the constitution of that State or the principles of a national constitutional structure.

4. However, an examination should be made as to whether or not any analogous guarantee inherent in [EU] law has been disregarded. In fact, respect for fundamental rights forms an integral part of the general principles of law protected by the Court of Justice. The protection of such rights, whilst inspired by the constitutional traditions common to the Member States, must be ensured within the framework of the structure and objectives of the [Union] …

The judgment establishes that fundamental rights form an integral part of EU law although the Court went on to rule that there had been no violation of the fundamental right to trade in this instance. Having offered this protection in EU law, the Court stated that EU law takes precedence even over national constitutional provisions.[13] The birth of EU fundamental rights law could not be easily separated, therefore, from its twin: securing the primacy of EU law. If the Court offered a further assurance that the source for EU fundamental rights will be national constitutional traditions, as we have seen, this did not placate, initially at least, either the German or Italian Constitutional Courts.[14] It set in play a particular dynamic. The implication was that if EU law developed a sufficiently rigorous fundamental rights doctrine of its own, there would be little reason for national constitutional courts not to accept its authority.[15] The threat to national fundamental rights would be averted by EU law putting in place its own checks so that a conflict should – in theory at least – never happen. This led to a cynicism, which has never fully disappeared, that the motivations for the development of EU fundamental rights law were highly instrumental.[16] It also required, however, a high threshold to be offered by EU fundamental rights law.

---

[13] See p. 202.   [14] See pp. 225–6.

[15] See Case 7/76 *IRCA* [1976] ECR 1213, 1237, Opinion of Advocate General Warner.

[16] See the debate between J. Coppell and A. O' Neill, 'The European Court of Justice: Taking Rights Seriously' (1992) 29 *CMLRev.* 669; J. Weiler and N. Lockhart, '"Taking Rights Seriously" Seriously: The European Court and Fundamental Rights Jurisprudence – Part I' (1995) 32 *CMLRev.* 51; J. Weiler and N. Lockhart, '"Taking Rights Seriously" Seriously: The European Court and Fundamental Rights Jurisprudence – Part II' (1995) 32 *CMLRev.* 579.

This had to meet any concern about fundamental rights provided by any national constitutional court if the threat to the primacy of EU law was to be averted.[17]

The Court of Justice next began to look at sources other than national constitutions to inspire the content of EU fundamental rights law. In *Nold*, the Court stated that international human rights treaties were another source of fundamental rights in EU law.[18] Following *Nold*, the Court has recognised a number of human rights treaties as sources. Most importantly, in *Rutili*, it referred to the ECHR.[19] Whilst the Court has indicated that the ECHR has a particular status,[20] it has also looked to incorporate other international human rights treaties as sources of fundamental rights: the International Covenant on Civil and Political Rights,[21] the UN Convention on the Rights of the Child,[22] the Community Charter of Fundamental Social Rights of Workers and the European Social Charter.[23]

Relying on national constitutional traditions and international human rights treaties, the Court recognised a number of categories of different rights.

Civil rights: these include the right to respect for family and private life;[24] protection of the child;[25] freedom of religion;[26] freedom of trade union activity;[27] freedom of expression;[28] protection of personal data;[29] access to basic data held about oneself;[30] equality;[31] protection from discrimination on grounds of sexual orientation;[32] the right to choose one's place of residence;[33] the right to free and informed consent before any medical procedure and the right to human dignity;[34] and freedom from torture or subjection to inhuman and degrading treatment.[35]

Economic rights: normally subject to provisos which may be placed in the public interest and which restrict their exercise, these include the right to trade;[36] the right to own property;[37] and the right to carry out an economic activity.[38]

---

[17] Debate focused, therefore, on whether EU law could or should adopt some maximalist standard of fundamental rights. J. Weiler, 'Fundamental Rights and Fundamental Boundaries: On Standards and Values in the Protection of Human Rights' in N. Neuwahl and A. Rosas (eds.), *The European Union and Human Rights* (The Hague, Martijnus Nijhoff, 1995); L. Besselink, 'Entrapped by the Maximum Standard: On Fundamental Rights, Pluralism and Subsidiarity in the European Union' (1998) 35 *CMLRev.* 629.

[18] Case 4/73 *Nold* v *Commission* [1974] ECR 491.

[19] Case 36/75 *Rutili* v *Ministre de l'Intérieur* [1975] ECR 1219.

[20] Case C-299/95 *Kremzow* v *Austria* [1997] ECR I-2629.   [21] Case 374/87 *Orkem* [1989] ECR 3283.

[22] Case C-540/03 *Parliament* v *Council* [2006] ECR I-5769.

[23] Case 24/86 *Blaizot* v *Belgium* [1988] ECR 379; Case 149/77 *Defrenne II* [1978] ECR 1365.

[24] Case 136/79 *National Panasonic* [1980] ECR 2033; Case C-249/86 *Commission* v *Germany* [1989] ECR 1263.

[25] Case C-540/03 *Parliament* v *Council* [2006] ECR I-5769; Case C-244/06 *Dynamic Medien Vertriebs* v *Avides Media* [2008] ECR I-505.

[26] Case 130/75 *Prais* [1976] ECR 1589.   [27] Case 175/73 *Union Syndicale* [1974] ECR 917.

[28] Case C-260/89 *ERT* v *DEP* [1991] ECR I-2925; Case C-250/06 *United Pan-Europe Communications Belgium and others* [2007] ECR I-11135.

[29] Case C-101/01 *Lindqvist* [2003] ECR-12971; Joined Cases C-465/00, C-138/01 and C-139/01 *Österreichisches Rundfunk* [2003] ECR I-4919.

[30] Case C-553/07 *College van Burgemeester en Wethouders van Rotterdam* v *Rijkeboer* [2009] ECR I-3889.

[31] Case C-43/75 *Defrenne* v *Sabena* [1976] ECR 455.

[32] Case C-117/01 *KB* v *National Health Service Pensions Agency* [2004] ECR I-541.

[33] Case C-370/05 *Festersen* [2007] ECR I-1129.

[34] Case C-377/98 *Netherlands* v *Parliament and Council* [2001] ECR I-7079.

[35] Case C-475/07 *Elgafaji* v *Staatssecretaris van Justitie* [2009] ECR I-19.

[36] Case 240/83 *ADBHU* [1985] ECR 531.   [37] Case 44/79 *Hauer* [1979] ECR 3727.

[38] Case 230/78 *Eridania* [1979] ECR 2749.

Rights of defence: these include the right to an effective judicial remedy;[39] the presumption of innocence;[40] the right to be informed in a criminal trial of the nature and cause of accusation against one;[41] the right to legal assistance and the right to all lawyer-client communications prepared for the purpose of defending oneself to be confidential;[42] the right to be heard in one's own defence before any measure is imposed;[43] and protection from self-incrimination.[44]

General principles of law: these include the principles of non-discrimination;[45] proportionality;[46] legitimate expectations;[47] and non-retroactivity.[48]

All the rights in the first three categories above can be found in the EUCFR. Following ratification of the Lisbon Treaty, they have been subsumed within the interpretation of its provisions.[49] This has not been the case with the last category, general principles of law, which finds no correspondence within the EUCFR. The principles therein continue to be developed predominantly through the case law of the Court of Justice.[50] This led to a concern that this might lead to these rights being reduced to canonical interpretations of particular provisions of the Charter, with the open-ended texture of the process and multiplicity of sources being lost.[51] This concern persists with regard to constitutional traditions, which are only explicitly referenced by the Court of Justice in relation to one or two provisions of the EUCFR.[52]

(ii) European Union Charter of Fundamental Rights

The Charter emerged out of a twofold impetus at the end of the 1990s. There was a desire to give social rights the same status as other rights, notably civil liberties.[53] There was also agreement that EU fundamental rights law should not be hidden away in the case law of the Court of Justice but should be more visible. In 1999, at the Cologne European Council, it was agreed, therefore, that a charter of fundamental rights should be established. It should include the rights contained in the ECHR and the constitutional traditions common to the Member States. It should also include the rights set out in the EU citizenship provisions and economic and social rights as contained in the European Social Charter and the Community Charter of the Fundamental Social Rights of Workers.

---

[39] Case 222/84 *Johnston* v *RUC* [1986] ECR 1651.   [40] Case C-344/08 *Rubach* [2009] ECR I-7033.

[41] Case C-14/07 *Weiss* v *Industrie- und Handelskammer Berlin* [2008] ECR I-3367.

[42] Case 155/79 *AM & S* [1982] ECR 1575.   [43] Case 17/74 *Transocean Marine Paint* [1974] ECR 1063.

[44] Joined Cases 374/87 and 27/88 *Orkem SA and Solvay* [1989] ECR 3283.

[45] Case C-144/04 *Mangold* [2005] ECR I-9981.

[46] Case 11/70 *Internationale Handelsgesellschaft* v *Einfuhr und Vorratsstelle Getreide* [1970] ECR 1125.

[47] Joined Cases C-37/02 and C-38/02 *Di Lenardo and Dilexport* [2004] ECR I-6911.

[48] Case 63/83 *Kirk* [1984] ECR 2689.

[49] This is indeed required, see Case C-70/10 *Scarlet Extended*, Judgment of 24 November 2011, Opinion of Advocate General Cruz Villalón, para. 30. For an argument, however, as to their autonomous force see H. Hofmann and C. Mihaescu, 'The Relation between the Charter's Fundamental Rights and the Unwritten General Principles of EU Law: Good Administration as the Test Case' (2013) 9 *EuConst* 73.

[50] See e.g. Case C-59/11 *Association Kokopelli* v *Baumaux*, Judgment of 12 July 2012; Case C-401/11 *Soukupová*, Judgment of 11 April 2013; Case C-643/11 *LVK*, Judgment of 31 January 2013.

[51] J. Weiler, 'Editorial: Does the European Union Truly Need a Charter of Rights?' (2000) 6 *ELJ* 95.

[52] The central provision in which reference to constitutional traditions regularly takes place is Article 47 EUCFR, on the right to effective judicial protection, i.e. Case C-279/09 *DEB* [2010] ECR I-13849; Case C-93/12 *ET Agrokonsulting-04-Velko Stoyanov*, Judgment of 27 June 2013.

[53] Report of the Expert Group on Fundamental Rights, *Affirming Fundamental Rights in the European Union: Time to Act* (Brussels, EU Commission, 1999) (Simitis Report).

This Charter was drafted by a Convention comprised of representatives from national governments, the Commission, the European Parliament and national parliaments. Other EU institutions were to be given observer status. Human rights groups, regional bodies, trade unions and wider civil society were invited to make contributions.[54] The draft of the Charter was adopted by the Convention in October 2000. At the Nice European Council in December 2000, agreement on its legal status and consequences could not, however, be reached. Instead, it was 'proclaimed' by the Council, the Commission and the Parliament, with its final status to be resolved by the Constitutional Treaty. Notwithstanding this, the Charter came increasingly to be seen as both an authoritative statement of the rights considered to be fundamental in the Union,[55] and as a document which informed understandings of fundamental rights more generally.[56] At the Constitutional Treaty, it was inserted in Part II of the Treaty, which detailed its provisions while also constraining its remit and meaning.[57] Part II was felt to be one of the 'constitutionalising elements' which had to be removed if the Lisbon Treaty was to be distinguished as a reform treaty rather than a constitutional treaty. The Charter was re-proclaimed by the three EU institutions following the signing of the Lisbon Treaty.[58] Article 6 TEU, as can be seen above,[59] now only provides for a reference to it in the main Treaties, albeit that the reference indicates that the EUCFR 'shall have the same legal value as the Treaties'.

If one of the purposes of the EUCFR is to make fundamental rights more visible in EU law, hiding away its text in this manner is unlikely to achieve this. Its equal status to the Treaties is, furthermore, belied by the subsequent sentence in Article 6 TEU which states that nothing in the EUCFR shall affect the competences of the Union as defined in the Treaties. It takes effect, therefore, subject to division of the powers set out by the Treaties.

The EUCFR rights are taken from three sources: the EU Treaty, constitutions of the Member States, and international human rights treaties concluded by the Member States.[60] It sets out its rights and principles under six headings, of which the central ones are set out below.

Rights to human dignity: right to life; integrity of the person; prohibition of torture or inhuman and degrading treatment; prohibition of slavery or forced labour; prohibition on cloning or eugenics (Articles 1–5).

Freedoms: right to liberty and security; respect for private and family life; protection of personal data; right to marry and found a family; freedom of thought, conscience and religion; freedom of expression and information; freedom of assembly; freedom of the arts and sciences; right to education; freedom to choose an occupation and right to engage in work; freedom to conduct a business; right to asylum; right to property (Articles 6–19).

Equality: equality before the law; non-discrimination on sex, race, colour, ethnic or social origin, genetic features, language, religion or belief or political opinion, disability, sexual orientation, birth; cultural, religious and linguistic diversity; equality between men and women; rights of the elderly, integration of persons with disabilities (Articles 20–26).

---

[54] For discussion see G. de Búrca, 'The Drafting of the EU Charter of Fundamental Rights' (2001) 26 *ELRev.* 126: O. de Schutter, 'Europe in Search of its Civil Society' (2002) 8 *ELJ* 198, 206–12.

[55] On these years see S. Sánchez, 'The Court and the Charter: The Impact of the Entry into Force of the Lisbon Treaty on the ECJ's Approach to Fundamental Rights' (2012) 49 *CMLRev.* 1565, 1569–73.

[56] The European Court of Human Rights, thus, referred to it in Case 28957/95 *Goodwin* v *United Kingdom* [2002] ECHR 588.

[57] The limits on the remit of the EUCFR were similar to those now in the Lisbon Treaty.

[58] The full text of the Charter can be found at [2007] OJ C303/1.

[59] See p. 249.   [60] CHARTER 4473/00, 11 October 2000.

Solidarity: workers' right to information and consultation; right of collective bargaining; protection in the event of unfair dismissal; right to placement services; fair and just working conditions; prohibition on child labour; right to social security; right to health care; protection of the family; high level of environmental and consumer protection; access to services of general economic interest (Articles 27–38).

Citizens' rights: right to vote and stand in municipal and European Parliament elections; right to good administration; right of access to documents; right to refer matters to the European Parliament and to petition the Ombudsman; freedom of movement and residence; right to diplomatic protection (Articles 39–46).

Justice: right to an effective remedy and a fair trial; presumption of innocence; right not to be tried or punished twice for same office; principle of legality and proportionality of criminal offences (Articles 47–50).

Most of these rights are conditioned by limitations and exceptions. Article 52(1) EUCFR sets out limits on how these exceptions may be invoked.

Article 52(1)

1. Any limitation on the exercise of the rights and freedoms recognised by this Charter must be provided for by law and respect the essence of those rights and freedoms. Subject to the principle of proportionality, limitations may be made only if they are necessary and genuinely meet objectives of general interest recognised by the Union or the need to protect the rights and freedoms of others.

The requirement that there must be a legal framework setting out these limitations and exceptions is not only a formal requirement but also has a substantive dimension.[61] This has been addressed at length by the European Court of Human Rights. In *Scarlet Extended*,[62] Advocate General Cruz Villalón set out the implications for EU law.

Case C–70/10 *Scarlet Extended* v *SABAM*, Judgment of 24 November 2011

94. The European Court of Human Rights has repeatedly held that the provisions of the ECHR making interference in the exercise of a right or the restriction on the exercise of a freedom which it guarantees subject to the condition that it is 'provided for by law' means not only that the measure is founded on a legal basis as such, has 'a basis in domestic law', but also imposes requirements relating, to use the expression which it has enshrined, to 'the quality of the law in question'. That 'law' must, in effect, be 'adequately accessible and foreseeable, that is, formulated with sufficient precision to enable the individual – if need be with appropriate advice – to regulate his conduct', to 'foresee its consequences for him', 'to foresee, to a degree that is reasonable in the circumstances, the consequences which a given action may entail'.

95. The 'law' must therefore be sufficiently clear and foreseeable as to the meaning and nature of the applicable measures, and must define with sufficient clarity the scope and manner of exercise of the power of interference in the exercise of the rights guaranteed by the ECHR. A law which confers a

---

[61] On the need for this legal framework see Case C-407/08P *Rauf* v *Commission* [2010] ECR I-6375, para. 91.
[62] Case C-70/10 *Scarlet Extended* v *SABAM*, Judgment of 24 November 2011.

discretion is not in itself inconsistent with that requirement, provided that the scope of the discretion and the manner of its exercise are indicated with sufficient clarity, having regard to the legitimate aim in question, to give the individual adequate protection against arbitrary interference. A law which confers a discretion must also establish the scope of that discretion.

96. A limitation is therefore acceptable only if it is founded on a legal basis in domestic law, a legal basis which must be accessible, clear, foreseeable, conditions which all stem from the idea of the supremacy of the law. From that requirement of the supremacy of the law stems the need for the law to be accessible and foreseeable to the person concerned ...

98. ... the scope of the concept of foreseeability and accessibility depends to a considerable degree on the content of the instrument in issue, the field it covers and the number and status of those to whom it is addressed. A law may still satisfy the requirement of foreseeability even if the person concerned has to take appropriate legal advice to assess, to a degree that is reasonable in the circumstances, the consequences which a given action may entail. This is particularly true in the case of persons engaged in a professional activity, who are used to having to proceed with a high degree of caution when pursuing their occupation.

There are a number of further general noteworthy features about the EUCFR.

First, it incorporates a wider array of rights and freedoms than possibly any other human rights treaty. There are, thus, not just civil, political, economic and social rights, but protection of cultural and ecological interests as well. This can therefore be seen as ambitious and nuanced in what it regards humans as needing for a good life. The centrality of socio-economic rights to aspiration and justice has been raised in contexts outside the European Union, with these being seen as no less important than civil liberties.[63] The counter-argument is a risk of an inflation of the language of rights. The right of free access to a placement service is worthwhile (Article 29) but can hardly be seen as central to human dignity as the prohibition on slavery (Article 5). Treating everything as fundamental, it is argued, leads in the end to nothing being special with a dilution in the value of those entitlements which were once held in the highest regard. It can also lead to the trumping effects of the language of rights having an overbearing effect on complex dilemmas where the myriad of interests and values to be gauged and balanced is both considerable and fluid.

Secondly, certain important rights are missing.[64] The right to nationality, the right to decent pay, the right to work and the right to housing are all not included.[65] Certain other rights (for example, the right to marry, the right to collective bargaining, the right of workers to information and consultation, the right to protection against unfair dismissal, the right to social security and health care) are to be recognised only in accordance with the rules laid down by national or EU laws. National laws are to determine the content of these rights so that instead of acting as a basis for review of EU and national practices, these are turned around to justify even egregious practices.[66]

---

[63] Joint Committee of Houses of Parliament, *A Bill of Rights for the United Kingdom?* (29th Report, Session 2007–08, London, SO) vol. 1, para. 191.

[64] J. Kenner, 'Economic and Social Rights in the EU Legal Order: The Mirage of Indivisibility' in T. Hervey and J. Kenner (eds.), *Economic and Social Rights under the EU Charter of Fundamental Rights* (Oxford, Hart, 2003) 1, 16–18.

[65] Albeit that the right to 'housing assistance' is provided for in Article 34(3) (II-94(3) CT).

[66] D. Ashiagbor, 'Economic and Social Rights in the European Charter of Fundamental Rights' (2004) 1 *European Human Rights Law Review* 62.

Thirdly, the EUCFR suggests the indivisibility of these rights. Social, civil, political and environmental rights should all be treated equally as fundamental rights. To enable this, it introduces a distinction between rights and principles.

Article 52(5) EUCFR

5. The provisions of this Charter which contain principles may be implemented by legislative and executive acts taken by Institutions, bodies, offices and agencies of the Union and by acts of Member States when they are implementing Union law, in the exercise of their respective powers. They shall be judicially cognisable only in the interpretation of such acts and in the ruling on their legality.

Some provisions will, thus, be protected more absolutely than others. All institutional behaviour falling within the aegis of the Charter can be judicially reviewed against rights. By contrast, courts will only be able to look at principles in cases where institutions are implementing these principles rather than at activities that cut across them. The justification is that the sheer breadth of the Charter prevents a 'one size fits all' approach to protection. Courts are arguably not well-suited to determining the substance of wide-ranging socio-economic or environmental rights, for example, when a right to sustainable development warrants protection, or when the level of health provision is so low that it violates the right to access to health care. More partial judicial control might be a price worth paying for having these recognised.

However, the question of which provisions articulate rights and which articulate principles is unaddressed. There are only three provisions which explicitly use the word 'principle': those on the principle of equality between men and women (Article 23), sustainable development (Article 37) and the need for legality and proportionality of criminal offences (Article 49). Of these, only the provision on sustainable development would seem in any way to generate problems with judicial enforcement. Reliance cannot be had therefore to the terminology of the EUCFR. Instead, it may be that provisions whose content is dependent upon their realisation by national or EU law would be considered to be principles.[67] Yet, many of the provisions to be implemented by national law describe themselves as 'rights'.[68] There are also provisions where the Union commits itself to respect certain values in its policies, such as a high level of environmental protection or consumer protection or respect for services of a general economic interest.[69] Further ambiguity is provided by the Explanations of the Secretariat. These state that the provisions on rights of the elderly, integration of people with disabilities and protection of the environment are examples of principles. By contrast, those on equality between men and women, protection of the family, and the right to social security benefits and social services are examples of provisions which 'contain both elements of a right and of a principle'.[70]

---

[67] E.g. the right to marry (Article 9); the right to found educational establishments (Article 14(3)); workers' right to information and consultation within their undertaking (Article 27); the right to collective bargaining (Article 28); social and housing assistance (Article 34); the right to protection in the event of unjustified dismissal (Article 30); the right to health care (Article 35).

[68] All the provisions mentioned in n. 67 above (e.g. the right to marry), with the exception of Article 34 on the right to housing assistance, do this.

[69] Articles 37 and 38, respectively.

[70] Explanations to the Charter of Fundamental Rights [2007] OJ C303/17, 35.

4 STANDARD OF PROTECTION OF FUNDAMENTAL RIGHTS

It is all very well the Union developing a plethora of rights but this means little if these are just paper rights which offer individuals little protection. The EUCFR holds itself out here as occupying a position of virtue. Its rights are not to be interpreted restrictively,[71] and it is not to undermine any right granted in EU law, international law or national constitutions.

Article 53 EUCFR

Nothing in this Charter shall be interpreted as restricting or adversely affecting human rights and freedoms as recognised, in their respective fields of application by Union law and international law and by international agreements to which the Union or all the Member States are party, including the European Convention on Human Rights and Fundamental Freedoms, and by the Member States constitutions.

It is not clear what this means. Rights often contain choices between values. Laws about press reporting of politicians have to balance rights of freedom of expression against those on protection of privacy and family life. Similarly, copyright protection has to balance freedom of expression against the property rights of the right-holder. In some instances, most obviously abortion, certain Member States will recognise as fundamental rights for the unborn which are to be asserted against the rights of the mother. These will simply not be granted such a status elsewhere. It is not simply that these rights are different but that they frame scenarios in such different ways that there are also very different understandings of what is taking place. The right to life of the unborn, thus, portrays the mother and the foetus as having separate and conflicting interests which are to be equal in status. A denial of that right is also a denial of the presence of that separation, conflict and equality. Rights inevitably are informed by visions of political morality, which cannot easily be calibrated along a sliding scale. In *Melloni*, it will be remembered, a challenge was made by an Italian to his being surrendered back to Italy by the Spanish authorities.[72] This was required by the European Arrest Warrant after his having been convicted there, in his absence, of fraud. He argued, unsuccessfully, that his absence compromised his rights to a fair trial, which was indeed the position under the Spanish Constitution. The Court stated that Article 53 could not be used to elevate national constitutional rights above EU law.[73] In addition, Advocate General Bot set out the principles which should guide interpretation of EU fundamental rights law.

Case C–399/11 *Melloni*, Judgment of 26 February 2013, Opinion of Advocate General Bot

106. Although it is true that the interpretation of the rights protected by the Charter must tend towards a high level of protection, as may be inferred from Article 52(3) of the Charter and from the explanatory remarks concerning Article 52(4) of the Charter, it is nevertheless important to state that this must be a level of protection which accords with European Union law, as is stated, moreover, in those same explanatory remarks.

---

[71] Joined Cases C-229/11 and C-230/11 *Heimann v Kaiser*, Judgment of 8 November 2012.

[72] See pp. 202–3.

[73] On the early debates surrounding this see J. Liisberg, 'Does the EU Charter of Fundamental Rights Threaten the Supremacy of Community Law' (2001) 38 *CMLRev.* 1171.

107. That is a reminder of a principle that has long guided the interpretation of fundamental rights within the European Union, namely that the protection of fundamental rights within the European Union must be ensured within the framework of the structure and objectives of the European Union. In that regard, it is not irrelevant that the preamble to the Charter refers to the main objectives of the European Union, including the creation of an area of freedom, security and justice.

108. It is therefore not possible to reason only in terms of a higher or lower level of protection of human rights without taking into account the requirements linked to the action of the European Union and the specific nature of European Union law.

109. The fundamental rights to be protected and the level of protection to be afforded to them reflect the choices of a society as regards the proper balance to be achieved between the interests of individuals and those of the community to which they belong. That determination is closely linked to assessments which are specific to the legal order concerned, relating particularly to the social, cultural and historical context of that order, and cannot therefore be transposed automatically to other contexts.

110. To interpret Article 53 of the Charter as allowing Member States to apply, in the field of application of European Union law, their constitutional rule guaranteeing a higher level of protection for the fundamental right in question, would therefore be tantamount to disregarding the fact that the exercise of determining the level of protection for fundamental rights to be achieved cannot be separated from the context in which it is carried out.

111. Accordingly, even though the objective is to tend towards a high level of protection for fundamental rights, the specific nature of European Union law means that the level of protection deriving from the interpretation of a national constitution cannot be automatically transposed to the European Union level nor can it be relied upon as an argument in the context of the application of European Union law.

112. As regards the assessment of the level of protection for fundamental rights which must be guaranteed within the legal order of the European Union, the specific interests which motivate the action of the European Union must be taken into account. The same applies, inter alia, to the necessary uniformity of application of European Union law and to the requirements linked to the construction of an area of freedom, security and justice. Those specific interests cause the level of protection for fundamental rights to be adjusted depending on the different interests at stake....

131. The drafters of the Charter could not have been unaware of the existence of a plurality of sources of protection for fundamental rights binding the Member States and therefore had to provide a way for the Charter to coexist with them. That is the main objective of Title VII of the Charter, which contains the general provisions governing its interpretation and application. From that point of view, Article 53 of the Charter supplements the principles stated in Articles 51 and 52 thereof, by pointing out that, in a system in which the pluralism of sources of protection of fundamental rights prevails, the Charter is not intended to become the exclusive instrument for protecting those rights and, also, that it cannot have the effect, on its own, of adversely affecting or reducing the level of protection resulting from those different sources in their respective fields of application.

132. The Charter is not an isolated instrument, unconnected with the other sources of protection of fundamental rights. The Charter itself provides that its provisions must be interpreted taking due account of other legal sources, whether national or international. Accordingly, Article 52(3) of the Charter makes the ECHR a minimum standard below which European Union law cannot fall and Article 52(4) of the Charter provides that, insofar as the Charter recognises fundamental rights as they result from the constitutional traditions common to the Member States, those rights must be interpreted in harmony with those traditions.

Advocate General Bot suggests, therefore, that EU fundamental rights law is to be interpreted through two types of lens. There are a series of sources, international treaties, notably the ECHR and national constitutional traditions which act as indicators or more of what it should do. Alongside these formal parameters, he indicates (most strongly in paragraph 109) that interpretations of fundamental rights will also be informed by a vision of a particular way of life which the EU legal order is dedicated to realise. This vision is particular to EU law, will involve social choices and will be informed by the social, cultural and historical contexts surrounding the EU legal order. There is, of course, a tension between these two lenses of interpretation. The first is formalistic and looks to external legal sources, whilst the second looks far more explicitly beyond legal provisions to objectives particular to the European Union. This tension may play out differently and unpredictably, with some judgments referring more to external legal sources and others to objectives of EU law. Its implications are worth exploring a little further.

(i) Formal parameters of interpretation

There are three formal constraints on how EU fundamental rights law is to be interpreted.

First, regard is to be had to the Explanations drawn up by the Secretariat to the Convention on the EUCFR in interpreting particular provisions.[74]

Article 52(7) EUCFR

7. The explanations drawn up as a way of providing guidance in the interpretation of the Charter of Fundamental Rights shall be given due regard by the courts of the Union and the Member States.

The purpose of this is to restrict unanticipated interpretations with far-reaching consequences by setting out a doctrine of original intent. However, this is undercut by the Secretariat's Explanations being silent on the scope and content of each right as they do no more than state its source (e.g. a particular international human rights treaty). However, it does encourage backward-looking interpretations. The Explanations locate individual articles as simply the culmination of prior case law of the Court of Justice or existing international treaties. Over time there would thus be a danger that undue prominence be given to dated interpretations, rather than to interpretations which meet the demands of an evolving society. This has been countered by the Court not stating that it will give the Explanations 'due regard' but merely that it will take them into account.[75] This suggests less weight for these Explanations, which are simply one amongst many factors to which the Court will look. Typically, it uses the Explanations to confirm an interpretation rather than as a tie-breaker between interpretations.[76]

---

[74] These are found at [2007] OJ C303/17.

[75] Case C-279/09 *DEB* [2010] ECR I-13849; Case C-283/11 *Sky Österreich v Österreichischer Rundfunk*, Judgment of 22 January 2013; Case C-426/11 *Alemo-Herron v Parkwood Leisure*, Judgment of 18 July 2013.

[76] See e.g. Case C-648/11 *R v Secretary of State for the Home Department ex parte MA*, Judgment of 6 June 2013; Case C-233/12 *Gardella v INPSS*, Judgment of 4 July 2013.

The second principle is more significant. This requires interpretations of the EUCFR to be aligned with those of the ECHR where they concern rights laid down in the ECHR.

Article 52(3) EUCFR

3. Insofar as this Charter contains rights which correspond to rights guaranteed by the Convention for the Protection of Human Rights and Fundamental Freedoms, the meaning and scope of those rights shall be the same as those laid down by the said Convention. This provision shall not prevent Union law providing more extensive protection.

This provision places a lot of faith in the ECHR.[77] It has been argued that this is necessary for an integrated system of law in which EU law and the ECHR share jurisdiction over a wide array of activities.[78] However, even if this is so, it is unclear why this would justify such deference rather than some other form of coordination. The ECHR covers forty-seven states parties. It is committed to a less intense form of political integration and governs a more diverse array of situations than the European Union. It is not clear that the judgments of a court, such as the European Court of Human Rights, operating in that context, should be accepted almost unquestioningly. A preferable arrangement would be one of mutual justification. Union courts treat any judgment given by the European Court of Human Rights as a persuasive suggestion. If the latter's judgment is not considered to protect the individual freedom or collective interest in question, they can depart from it, but must give reasons for their choice.[79]

The Court of Justice allows itself the formal possibility to depart from ECHR case law where it believes this does not protect individual liberties sufficiently, but follows this case law pretty uncritically.[80] The central case is *McB*. A British-Irish couple had lived together for ten years, and had three children during that time. The relationship was a tumultuous one, and the British mother left Ireland abruptly with the children to go back to Britain. The Irish father sought an order under the relevant EU Regulation 2201/2003, that she had wrongly removed the children and they should be returned to Ireland. The Regulation stated that wrongful removal would be determined by whether there had been a violation of custody rights in the state where the child was habitually resident: in this case Ireland. Under Irish law, unmarried fathers had no automatic right to custody, but had to apply for a court order to secure it. The Irish father had failed to do this, largely because the mother's departure to the United Kingdom had taken him by surprise, albeit that she claimed that it had been precipitated by his repeated aggressive

---

[77] For a persuasive critique see S. Greer and A. Williams, 'Human Rights in the Council of Europe and the EU: Towards "Individual", "Constitutional" or "Institutional" Justice?' (2009) 15 *ELJ* 462, 466–70.

[78] P. Eeckhout, 'Human Rights and the Autonomy of EU Law: Pluralism or Integration?' (2013) 66 *Current Legal Problems* 169, 176 *et seq.*

[79] N. Krisch, 'The Open Architecture of European Human Rights Law' (2008) 71 *MLR* 183; D. Halberstam and E. Stein, 'The United Nations, the European Union, and the King of Sweden: Economic Sanctions and Individual Rights in a Plural World Order' (2009) 46 *CMLRev.* 13. A variation on this is a commitment to certain common principles governing interpretation of the different provisions which would still allow the possibility for some disagreement. G. Itzcovich, 'Legal Order, Legal Pluralism, Fundamental Principles: Europe and its Law in Three Concepts' (2012) 18 *ELJ* 358, 375 *et seq.*

[80] This was astutely first spotted in M. Bronckers, 'The Relationship of the EC Courts with Other International Tribunals: Non-Committal, Respectful or Submissive?' (2007) 44 *CMLRev.* 601.

behaviour. The father argued that this violated his right to respect for family life, protected by Article 7 EUCFR and Article 8 ECHR.

Case C–400/10 PPU *McB* v *LE* [2010] ECR I–8965

53. ... it follows from Article 52(3) of the Charter that, in so far as the Charter contains rights which correspond to rights guaranteed by the ECHR, their meaning and scope are to be the same as those laid down by the ECHR. However, that provision does not preclude the grant of wider protection by European Union law. Under Article 7 of the Charter, '[e]veryone has the right to respect for his or her private and family life, home and communications'. The wording of Article 8(1) of the ECHR is identical to that of the said Article 7, except that it uses the expression 'correspondence' instead of 'communications'. That being so, it is clear that the said Article 7 contains rights corresponding to those guaranteed by Article 8(1) of the ECHR. Article 7 of the Charter must therefore be given the same meaning and the same scope as Article 8(1) of the ECHR, as interpreted by the case-law of the European Court of Human Rights ...

54. The European Court of Human Rights has already considered a case in which the facts were comparable to those of the case in the main proceedings, where the child of an unmarried couple was taken to another State by its mother, who was the only person with parental responsibility for that child. In that regard, that court ruled, in essence, that national legislation granting, by operation of law, parental responsibility for such a child solely to the child's mother is not contrary to Article 8 of the ECHR, interpreted in the light of the 1980 Hague Convention, provided that it permits the child's father, not vested with parental responsibility, to ask the national court with jurisdiction to vary the award of that responsibility ...

55. It follows that, for the purposes of applying Regulation No 2201/2003 in order to determine whether the removal of a child, taken to another Member State by its mother, is lawful, that child's natural father must have the right to apply to the national court with jurisdiction, before the removal, in order to request that rights of custody in respect of his child be awarded to him, which, in such a context, constitutes the very essence of the right of a natural father to a private and family life.

56. The European Court of Human Rights has also ruled that national legislation which does not allow the natural father any possibility of obtaining rights of custody in respect of his child in the absence of the mother's agreement constitutes unjustified discrimination against the father and is therefore a breach of Article 14 of the ECHR, taken together with Article 8 of the ECHR ...

57. On the other hand, the fact that, unlike the mother, the natural father is not a person who automatically possesses rights of custody in respect of his child within the meaning of Article 2 of Regulation No 2201/2003 does not affect the essence of his right to private and family life, provided that the right described in paragraph 55 of this judgment is safeguarded.

58. That finding is not invalidated by the fact that, if steps are not taken by such a father in good time to obtain rights of custody, he finds himself unable, if the child is removed to another Member State by its mother, to obtain the return of that child to the Member State where the child previously had its habitual residence. Such a removal represents the legitimate exercise, by the mother with custody of the child, of her own right of freedom of movement, established in Article 20(2)(a) TFEU and Article 21(1) TFEU, and of her right to determine the child's place of residence, and that does not deprive the natural father of the possibility of exercising his right to submit an application to obtain rights of custody thereafter in respect of that child or rights of access to that child....

60. It must also be borne in mind that Article 7 of the Charter, mentioned by the referring court in its question, must be read in a way which respects the obligation to take into consideration the child's best interests, recognised in Article 24(2) of that Charter, and taking into account the fundamental right of a child to maintain on a regular basis personal relationships and direct contact with both of his or her parents, stated in Article 24(3) ... Moreover, it is apparent from recital 33 in the preamble to Regulation No 2201/2003 that that regulation recognises the fundamental rights and observes the principles of the Charter, while, in particular, seeking to ensure respect for the fundamental rights of the child as set out in Article 24 of the Charter. Accordingly, the provisions of that regulation cannot be interpreted in such a way that they disregard that fundamental right of the child, the respect for which undeniably merges into the best interests of the child ...

61. In those circumstances, it remains to be determined whether Article 24 of the Charter, respect for which is ensured by the Court, precludes the interpretation of Regulation No 2201/2003 which is set out in paragraph 44 of this judgment.

62. It is necessary to take into account, in this regard, the great variety of extra-marital relationships and consequent parent-child relationships, a variety referred to by the referring court in its order for reference, which is reflected in the variation among Member States of the extent of parental responsibilities and their attribution. Accordingly, Article 24 of the Charter must be interpreted as not precluding a situation where, for the purposes of applying Regulation No 2201/2003, rights of custody are granted, as a general rule, exclusively to the mother and a natural father possesses rights of custody only as the result of a court judgment. Such a requirement enables the national court with jurisdiction to take a decision on custody of the child, and on rights of access to that child, while taking into account all the relevant facts, such as those mentioned by the referring court, and in particular the circumstances surrounding the birth of the child, the nature of the parents' relationship, the relationship of the child with each parent, and the capacity of each parent to take the responsibility of caring for the child. The taking into account of those facts is apt to protect the child's best interests, in accordance with Article 24(2) of the Charter.

63. It follows from the foregoing that Articles 7 and 24 of the Charter do not preclude the interpretation of the regulation set out in paragraph 44 of this judgment.

Despite stating that it will look beyond the ECHR, the judgment is a peculiarly unsatisfying one. There is a 'cut out and paste' of ECHR dicta with no engagement with the substance of the right to respect for family life. A distinction between families with married and unmarried parents is, thus, accepted unquestioningly. In this instance, if the father had been married and the relationship had been one year old, he would have had greater custody rights than in this ten-year relationship. There is, alongside this, a failure to distinguish properly between the contexts considered by the ECHR and those generated by EU law. The ECHR states that it is important for the father to have the possibility to assert custody. However, this was not possible here because he was ambushed by EU law free movement rights which allowed the mother to leave Ireland without his being able to raise this. Finally, and perhaps most importantly, the excessive reliance on ECHR precedent sidelines other rights, most notably those of the children. There was no possibility in this instance, because of the mother's departure, for a court to consider the needs and interests of the children. It may be that these would have been best served by the exclusive custody of the mother or by some joint custody arrangement. There was no hearing to examine this, however, and the assertion that there could have been if the father had anticipated the mother's departure is not a substitute.

The third principle of interpretation is that EU fundamental rights law be interpreted in harmony with national constitutional traditions.

Article 52(4) EUCFR

4. Insofar as this Charter recognises fundamental rights as they result from the constitutional traditions common to the Member States, those rights shall be interpreted in harmony with those traditions.

The circumstance in which EU law confronts a national constitution has to be distinguished from that in which national constitutional traditions act more generally as a source of inspiration for the interpretation of EU fundamental rights.

In the former, as we have seen, the Court of Justice has no hesitation in asserting the primacy of EU law. According to it at least, albeit not according to many national constitutional courts, EU law prevails over national constitutional rights.[81] However, there is one exception to this. This is where EU law allows an exception to a prohibition, which is also recognised by the national constitution, and the question emerges how that exception should be interpreted. Should it be given the interpretation provided by the national constitution or a different one by EU law? In such circumstances, EU law has been highly deferential to the national constitution.

In *Omega*, the authorities in Bonn, Germany, prohibited a game whereby competitors attempted to shoot each other with laser guns.[82] Sensory tags worn by competitors picked up whether they had been shot and 'killed' under the rules of the game. The game was prohibited on the grounds that it simulated murder, and therefore, violated the right to human dignity under section 1(1) of the German Basic Law. This was argued to breach Article 56 TFEU, the provision on the freedom to provide services, as the game had been franchised out in Germany from a British company. EU law allowed exceptions to this freedom to provide services to be maintained on grounds of public policy, and it was argued that this protection of the right to human dignity fell within this. This was not unproblematic, as, in Germany, human dignity is seen as an independent right whilst in other states it is seen as an umbrella concept which justifies all rights but has no independent existence beyond that. Nevertheless, the Court held that not only did the right to human dignity justify this public policy exception being invoked, but that the German tradition was compatible with EU law. It was immaterial that other states did not grant human dignity the status of an independent right. Furthermore, the Court chose not to resolve the question whether EU law protection of human dignity created independent rights. This respect for constitutional autonomy can, of course, be applauded, but it does mean that the substance of the EU law vision on human dignity is completely empty. The Court, by unquestioningly accepting the values of one state, may be accepting values as fundamental which other states find egregious.[83]

---

[81] Case C-409/06 *Winner Wetten v Bürgermeisterin der Stadt Bergheim* [2010] ECR I-8015; Case C-399/11 *Melloni*, Judgment of 26 February 2013. On the reaction of national constitutional courts see pp. 225–9.

[82] Case C-36/02 *Omega Spielhallen- und Automatenaufstellungs v Oberbürgermeisterin der Bundesstadt Bonn* [2004] ECR I-9609.

[83] Sánchez, n. 55 above, 1605–6.

The other circumstance is when national constitutions guide interpretation of EU fundamental rights more generally. These traditions are not codified into a single legal instrument, have different value priorities and, in some cases, conflict.[84] This has both made them less accessible than the ECHR as a tool of interpretation, and also given the Court more 'wiggle' room. The Court rarely engages in detailed comparative analysis of these constitutional traditions.[85] One does find such analysis, however, in some of the Opinions of the Advocates General.[86] Through these Opinions, these traditions might inform the thinking of the Court. The relationship is, however, an opaque one, and the proportion of Opinions which engage in such analysis is disappointingly small: possibly because Advocates General are under tight time constraints to deliver these Opinions and such analysis is highly time-consuming. This is a pity, as national constitutional traditions offer a wider variety of expertise, experience and panoramas than any international court or tribunal can provide.

(ii) Development of fundamental rights in the light of EU objectives

Following parameters set out by other instruments provides no reason why EU law should have a strong fundamental rights presence. Adoption of such a presence involves a claim to what is known in US law as authoritative settlement.[87] The legal order is claiming the power to set authoritative narratives of right and wrong which set out not only the basis for institutional action but also inform citizens' ideas of right and wrong and provide powerful reasons for why we should believe in and obey that legal system. If a legal system looks elsewhere for these, it is eschewing that role. It is, therefore, important as Advocate General Bot indicated in *Melloni* that EU law develop a model of fundamental rights which has its own independent conception of right and wrong.[88]

However, what should inform such a vision? Commentary focuses on elements identified with the ideas and ideals of Europe. It has been argued this includes a greater insistence on social rights and more scepticism of 'market rights' than in the United States.[89] Others have suggested that Europe's painful history, most notably the Holocaust, imposes particularly strong imperatives to rectify suffering and pain and remedy injustices.[90] A final view is a more cynical one. It bemoans the lack of vision behind EU fundamental rights and sees it beset by a

---

[84] R. García, 'The General Provisions of the Charter of Fundamental Rights of the European Union' (2002) 8 *ELJ* 492, 508.

[85] For an example see Case C-619/10 *Trade Agency* v *Seramico Investments*, Judgment of 6 September 2012.

[86] Case C-279/09 *DEB* [2010] ECR I-13849, Opinion of Advocate Mengozzi; Case C-120/10 *European Air Transport* v *Collège d'Environnement de la Région de Bruxelles-Capitale and Région de Bruxelles-Capitale* [2011] ECR I-7865, Opinion of Advocate General Cruz Villalón; Case C-163/10 *Patriciello* [2011] ECR I-7565, Opinion of Advocate General Jääskinen; Case C-282/10 *Dominguez* v *Centre informatique du Centre Ouest Atlantique and Préfet de la Région Centre*, Judgment of 24 January 2012, Opinion of Advocate General Trstenjak.

[87] On this within the United States see L. Alexander and E. Sherwin, *The Rule of Rules: Morality, Rules and the Dilemmas of Law* (Chapel Hill, NC, Duke University Press, 2001) chs. 1–4.

[88] For powerful earlier statements on this see J. Weiler, 'Fundamental Rights and Fundamental Boundaries: On Standards and Values in the Protection of Human Rights' in N. Neuwahl and A. Rosas, *The European Union and Human Rights* (The Hague, Martijnus Nijhoff, 1995) 51, 52–3; M. Avbelj, *The European Court of Justice and the Question of Value Choices*, Jean Monnet Working Paper 6/04 (2004).

[89] C. Leben, 'Is there a European Approach to Human Rights?' in P. Alston (ed.), *The EU and Human Rights* (Oxford, Oxford University Press, 1999).

[90] K. Günther, 'The Legacies of Injustice and Fear: A European Approach to Human Rights and their Effects on Political Culture' in P. Alston (ed.), *The EU and Human Rights* (Oxford, Oxford University Press, 1999).

lack of substance and intellectual vacuity, with the language of fundamental rights deployed to protect the Union from more stinging criticism.[91]

None of these criticisms are fully persuasive. Casting EU fundamental rights law in terms of wider aspirations about European ideals is simply that: aspirational and speculative. It does not indicate what is particular to this organisation rather than any other organisation or political community which enables it to be the authoritative interlocutor of these ideals, nor does it set out how the tasks performed by the European Union relate to these ideals. Conversely, to argue for the lack of ethical content of EU law belies the fact that EU law must deal with issues with a strong ethical dimension. Arguments will be presented about these ethics by the different protagonists, and judges and legislatures will consider these arguments before making or interpreting a law. This process of ethical reflection is inevitably institutionalised within its norms.

The vision informing EU fundamental rights law is a more prosaic one. It is realisation of the objectives of the European Union. These include the policies and aims set out in Article 3 TEU, in particular. This includes policies such as realisation of the single market, economic and monetary union, an Area of Freedom, Security and Justice, but it also includes more diffuse aims such as a social market economy, sustainable development, combating social exclusion. The vision informing EU fundamental rights is a way of life structured by the interplay between these aims and policies. They will, for example, be informed by the need to realise the single market but this single market will be one which must contribute to a social market economy. This vision is one beset with ambiguity, which both allows plenty of room for conflict and for particular institutions to put their own imprint on it.

The best example of how this works is, perhaps, *Brüstle*. Brüstle filed for a patent in Germany for a biotechnological invention under the German law which implemented Directive 98/44/EC, which allows patenting of these. The process isolated stem cells taken from a human embryo. These were used to treat a range of neural conditions, most notably Parkinson's disease. Embryo stem cells were particularly valuable for such treatment because of their capacity to divide and differentiate into any form of body cell. This possibility for division and differentiation only exists at the early stage of a body's development. Greenpeace, the environmental NGO, sought to have the patent annulled on the grounds that article 6 of the Directive prohibited the patenting of inventions whose commercial exploitation would be contrary to public morality. Article 6(2)(c) stated that human embryos were not to be used for commercial purposes.

Case C–34/10 *Brüstle* v *Greenpeace* [2011] ECR I-9821

25. ... the need for a uniform application of European Union law and the principle of equality require that the terms of a provision of European Union law which makes no express reference to the law of the Member States for the purpose of determining its meaning and scope must normally be given an independent and uniform interpretation throughout the European Union ...

---

[91] I. Ward, 'Making Sense of Integration: A Philosophy of Law for the European Community' (1993) 17 *Journal of European Integration* 101, 128–9 and 132–3; A. Williams, *EU Human Rights Policies: A Study in Irony* (Oxford, Oxford University Press, 2004) 159–60.

26. Although the text of the Directive does not define human embryo, nor does it contain any reference to national laws as regards the meaning to be applied to those terms. It therefore follows that it must be regarded, for the purposes of application of the Directive, as designating an autonomous concept of European Union law which must be interpreted in a uniform manner throughout the territory of the Union.

27. That conclusion is supported by the object and the aim of the Directive. It follows from recitals 3 and 5 to 7 in the preamble to the Directive that it seeks, by a harmonisation of the rules for the legal protection of biotechnological inventions, to remove obstacles to trade and to the smooth functioning of the internal market that are brought about by differences in national legislation and case-law between the Member States, and thus, to encourage industrial research and development in the field of genetic engineering …

28. The lack of a uniform definition of the concept of human embryo would create a risk of the authors of certain biotechnological inventions being tempted to seek their patentability in the Member States which have the narrowest concept of human embryo and are accordingly the most liberal as regards possible patentability, because those inventions would not be patentable in the other Member States. Such a situation would adversely affect the smooth functioning of the internal market which is the aim of the Directive.…

30. As regards the meaning to be given to the concept of 'human embryo' set out in Article 6(2) (c) of the Directive, it should be pointed out that, although, the definition of human embryo is a very sensitive social issue in many Member States, marked by their multiple traditions and value systems, the Court is not called upon, by the present order for reference, to broach questions of a medical or ethical nature, but must restrict itself to a legal interpretation of the relevant provisions of the Directive …

31. It must be borne in mind, further, that the meaning and scope of terms for which European Union law provides no definition must be determined by considering, inter alia, the context in which they occur and the purposes of the rules of which they form part …

32. In that regard, the preamble to the Directive states that although it seeks to promote investment in the field of biotechnology, use of biological material originating from humans must be consistent with regard for fundamental rights and, in particular, the dignity of the person. Recital 16 in the preamble to the Directive, in particular, emphasises that 'patent law must be applied so as to respect the fundamental principles safeguarding the dignity and integrity of the person'.

33. To that effect … Article 5(1) of the Directive provides that the human body at the various stages of its formation and development cannot constitute a patentable invention. Additional security is offered by Article 6 of the Directive, which lists as contrary to *ordre public* or morality, and therefore excluded from patentability, processes for cloning human beings, processes for modifying the germ line genetic identity of human beings and uses of human embryos for industrial or commercial purposes. Recital 38 in the preamble to the Directive states that this list is not exhaustive and that all processes the use of which offends against human dignity are also excluded from patentability …

34. The context and aim of the Directive thus show that the European Union legislature intended to exclude any possibility of patentability where respect for human dignity could thereby be affected. It follows that the concept of 'human embryo' within the meaning of Article 6(2)(c) of the Directive must be understood in a wide sense.

35. Accordingly, any human ovum must, as soon as fertilised, be regarded as a 'human embryo' within the meaning and for the purposes of the application of Article 6(2)(c) of the Directive, since that fertilisation is such as to commence the process of development of a human being.

36. That classification must also apply to a non-fertilised human ovum into which the cell nucleus from a mature human cell has been transplanted and a non-fertilised human ovum whose division and further development have been stimulated by parthenogenesis. Although those organisms have not, strictly speaking, been the object of fertilisation, due to the effect of the technique used to obtain them they are, as is apparent from the written observations presented to the Court, capable of commencing the process of development of a human being just as an embryo created by fertilisation of an ovum can do so.

37. As regards stem cells obtained from a human embryo at the blastocyst stage,[92] it is for the referring court to ascertain, in the light of scientific developments, whether they are capable of commencing the process of development of a human being and, therefore, are included within the concept of 'human embryo' within the meaning and for the purposes of the application of Article 6(2)(c) of the Directive....

47. By its third question, the referring court asks the Court, in essence, whether an invention is unpatentable even though its purpose is not the use of human embryos, where it concerns a product whose production necessitates the prior destruction of human embryos or a process which requires a base material obtained by destruction of human embryos.

48. It is raised in a case concerning the patentability of an invention involving the production of neural precursor cells, which presupposes the use of stem cells obtained from a human embryo at the blastocyst stage. It is apparent from the observations presented to the Court that the removal of a stem cell from a human embryo at the blastocyst stage entails the destruction of that embryo.

49. Accordingly, on the same grounds as those set out in paragraphs 32 to 35 above, an invention must be regarded as unpatentable, even if the claims of the patent do not concern the use of human embryos, where the implementation of the invention requires the destruction of human embryos. In that case too, the view must be taken that there is use of human embryos within the meaning of Article 6(2)(c) of the Directive. The fact that destruction may occur at a stage long before the implementation of the invention, as in the case of the production of embryonic stem cells from a lineage of stem cells the mere production of which implied the destruction of human embryos is, in that regard, irrelevant.

This judgment took place against a context where, within the European Union, a variety of approaches were taken to research involving embryos.[93] Particular concerns focused on the destruction of the embryo, the therapeutic benefits of the research and whether the research was exploited largely for this or for narrower commercial reasons. The first step of the Court of Justice's reasoning is to eschew this pluralism. The needs of market integration require, in its view, a single approach. Moreover, these demands are to funnel this approach. It, thus, states that it will confine itself to a 'legal interpretation' and not broach the wider medical or ethical contexts (paragraph 30). If its judgment has profound implications for both these contexts, the intent of this statement is to indicate that the Court will not consider these contexts too explicitly. The Court uses fundamental rights in the second stage of its reasoning, notably the right to human dignity and integrity of the person, to allow this uniform definition to embrace a very wide interpretation of the embryo to include even (in certain circumstances) non-fertilised eggs. It is to include processes

---

92 This is the period five days after fertilisation of the egg.
93 R. Isasi and B. Knoppers, 'Mind the Gap: Policy Approaches to Embryonic Stem Cells and Cloning Research in 50 Countries' (2006) 13 *European Journal of Health Law* 9. On the wider cleavages see G. Gaskell *et al.*, 'How Europe's Ethical Divide Looms over Biotech Law and Patents' (2012) 30 *Nature Biotechnology* 392.

'capable of commencing the process of development of a human being'. There is, of course, a slippage here. Debates about the human qualities of embryos and the processes leading up to them go to much of the controversy. This wide definition of human life is a particular preference of this Court. This allows it, in turn, to reach the final step of its reasoning, which goes to patents which involve either no destruction of the embryo or rely on historic research which involved destruction of the embryo but whose own innovation engaged in no such destruction. For the Court, the fact that no actual destruction of the embryo has taken place in the research in question is irrelevant. For it is concerned with the protection of human dignity and integrity: in this case, in its view, that of the embryo. This can be affected by processes which do not involve its destruction or which, albeit indirectly, subsequently benefit from its destruction, but which throw its status into question.

The judgment, thus, engages in an interpretation of human dignity, which clearly extends beyond the context of the single market.[94] It has implications, thus, for when we think life begins. However, this interpretation is shaped by the context of the single market and the Preamble to the Directive, which allowed certain considerations to be backgrounded and others to be foregrounded, and which pushed for a uniform definition.

The divisiveness of such an approach is best illustrated by an analysis of a 2010 survey carried out by Eurobarometer, the arm of the European Commission which analyses public opinion, of 15,000 people resident in the current European Union, Turkey, Norway, Switzerland and Iceland. This survey asked for views on a variety of questions related to research on human embryos. These views were collated around two ethical principles: the duty to care and heal and respect for human dignity and the sanctity of life. The analysis below emphasises that not only did the judgment invoke fundamental rights to assert a different ethical perspective from that of most Europeans but the very search for a uniform perspective, which would allow a single market to flourish, was problematic.

> ### G. Gaskell, S. Stares and A. Pottage, 'How Europe's Ethical Divide Looms over Biotech Law and Patents' (2012) 30 *Nature Biotechnology* 392
>
> Comparing the strong supporters ... 13 countries have a majority in favor of the principle of duty of care and 13 for the principle of the sanctity of life, with 6 having roughly equal percentages of the two. Combining the strong and moderate supporters, 18 countries (including France, Italy and the UK) have a majority for the principle of duty of care, whereas 10 (including Austria, Germany and Poland) have a majority for the principle of the sanctity of life; four countries are roughly split between the two. Overall, Europe leans toward the principle of duty of care, but clearly both ethical principles find support in all countries.
>
> Do the different ethical orientations merely reflect religious denomination? The answer is no.... strong support for 'sanctity of life' predominates among Muslims, whereas strong support for the 'duty of care' is more frequent among the nonreligious. By a small majority, both Catholics and Protestants support 'duty of care'. In a further analysis, we find that the more religiously committed

---

[94] On the debates see M. Varju and J. Sandor, 'Patenting Stem Cells in Europe: The Challenge of Multiplicity in European Union Law' (2012) 49 *CMLRev.* 1007; E. Bonadio, 'Biotech Patents and Morality after Brüstle' (2012) 7 *EIPR* 433.

an individual is, as assessed by the frequency of attendance of services, the more likely he or she is to be a strong supporter of the sanctity of life ethic.

This diversity of views, and more especially the basic tension between dignity and care, is likely to trouble the European patent system for some time to come.

Indeed, by emphasizing the EU's policy of harmonization in the field of patent law, the CJEU is likely to intensify political and ethical opposition. In the process of turning Europe into a competitive market for biotech research, it may flatten the moral debate entirely and so offend those on both sides of the tension between 'dignity' and 'care'. So the decision by the CJEU is likely to be followed by others in which tribunals respond, not necessarily with a single voice, to challenges from both sides of Europe's ethical divide.

A further challenge with the objectives of European integration informing EU fundamental rights law is that, at times, these objectives may appear to be granted priority over protection of the individual. In *NS*, an Afghan had initially entered the European Union via Greece, where he had not claimed asylum. The Greek authorities deported him to Turkey, where he claimed he was detained in appalling conditions. He escaped and fled to the United Kingdom where he claimed asylum. Regulation 343/2003 sets out the procedures for determining which Member State considers asylum claims. In a case like this it should be the state of first entry, which was Greece. The British authorities sought to deport him to Greece. He protested on the grounds that this would violate his fundamental rights. He claimed, in particular, a violation of Article 4 EUCFR, the prohibition on torture and inhuman and degrading treatment as there was widespread evidence of asylum seekers being kept in dreadful conditions in Greece or forced out destitute on to the streets. He also claimed a breach of Article 18 EUCFR, which set out the right to asylum and the commitment to respect the 1967 Geneva Convention on Refugees as the number of successful asylum and refugee claims in Greece was very low.

Joined Cases C–411/10 and C–493/10 *NS* v *Secretary of State for the Home Department*, Judgment of 21 December 2011

75. The Common European Asylum System is based on the full and inclusive application of the Geneva Convention and the guarantee that nobody will be sent back to a place where they again risk being persecuted. Article 18 of the Charter and Article 78 TFEU provide that the rules of the Geneva Convention and the 1967 Protocol are to be respected …

78. Consideration of the texts which constitute the Common European Asylum System shows that it was conceived in a context making it possible to assume that all the participating States, whether Member States or third States, observe fundamental rights, including the rights based on the Geneva Convention and the 1967 Protocol, and on the ECHR, and that the Member States can have confidence in each other in that regard.

79. It is precisely because of that principle of mutual confidence that the European Union legislature adopted Regulation No 343/2003 … in order to rationalise the treatment of asylum claims and to avoid blockages in the system as a result of the obligation on State authorities to examine multiple claims by the same applicant, and in order to increase legal certainty with regard to the determination of the State responsible for examining the asylum claim and thus to avoid forum shopping, it being the

principal objective of all these measures to speed up the handling of claims in the interests both of asylum seekers and the participating Member States.

80. In those circumstances, it must be assumed that the treatment of asylum seekers in all Member States complies with the requirements of the Charter, the Geneva Convention and the ECHR.

81. It is not however inconceivable that that system may, in practice, experience major operational problems in a given Member State, meaning that there is a substantial risk that asylum seekers may, when transferred to that Member State, be treated in a manner incompatible with their fundamental rights.

82. Nevertheless, it cannot be concluded from the above that any infringement of a fundamental right by the Member State responsible will affect the obligations of the other Member States to comply with the provisions of Regulation No 343/2003.

83. At issue here is the raison d'être of the European Union and the creation of an area of freedom, security and justice and, in particular, the Common European Asylum System, based on mutual confidence and a presumption of compliance, by other Member States, with European Union law and, in particular, fundamental rights....

86. By contrast, if there are substantial grounds for believing that there are systemic flaws in the asylum procedure and reception conditions for asylum applicants in the Member State responsible, resulting in inhuman or degrading treatment, within the meaning of Article 4 of the Charter, of asylum seekers transferred to the territory of that Member State, the transfer would be incompatible with that provision....

88. In a situation similar to those at issue in the cases in the main proceedings, that is to say the transfer, in June 2009, of an asylum seeker to Greece, the Member State responsible within the meaning of Regulation No 343/2003, the European Court of Human Rights held, inter alia, that the Kingdom of Belgium had infringed Article 3 of the ECHR, first, by exposing the applicant to the risks arising from the deficiencies in the asylum procedure in Greece, since the Belgian authorities knew or ought to have known that he had no guarantee that his asylum application would be seriously examined by the Greek authorities and, second, by knowingly exposing him to conditions of detention and living conditions that amounted to degrading treatment ...

89. The extent of the infringement of fundamental rights described in that judgment shows that there existed in Greece, at the time of the transfer ... a systemic deficiency in the asylum procedure and in the reception conditions of asylum seekers.

90. In finding that the risks to which the applicant was exposed were proved, the European Court of Human Rights took into account the regular and unanimous reports of international non-governmental organisations bearing witness to the practical difficulties in the implementation of the Common European Asylum System in Greece, the correspondence sent by the United Nations High Commissioner for Refugees (UNHCR) to the Belgian minister responsible, and also the Commission reports on the evaluation of the Dublin system and the proposals for recasting Regulation No 343/2003 in order to improve the efficiency of the system and the effective protection of fundamental rights ...

94. It follows from the foregoing that in situations such as that at issue in the cases in the main proceedings, to ensure compliance by the European Union and its Member States with their obligations concerning the protection of the fundamental rights of asylum seekers, the Member States, including the national courts, may not transfer an asylum seeker to the 'Member State responsible' within the meaning of Regulation No 343/2003 where they cannot be unaware that systemic deficiencies in the asylum procedure and in the reception conditions of asylum seekers in that Member State amount to substantial grounds for believing that the asylum seeker would face a real risk of being subjected to inhuman or degrading treatment within the meaning of Article 4 of the Charter.

As the violations of fundamental rights were so widespread and systemic in Greece, the Court ruled that NS could not be transferred back to Greece. Of greater concern are its comments in relation to fundamental rights abuses which are not systemic. The Court states that the EU legislation creates a presumption that Member States are observing fundamental rights. There is, of course, no reason why that should be the case. Indeed, a reason for fundamental rights guarantees is precisely that other laws do not always secure that observance. More troubling still is the ethical compass shown by the Court of Justice. It states that the Common European Asylum System creates a policy of real value: that of asylum seekers only being able to make one claim within the Union and not being able to shop around for the most sympathetic state. The value of this policy, a collective good, is such that it can override violations of fundamental rights. Action will only be taken against those which are systemic in nature. This is troubling at a number of levels. It is a nebulous threshold so it is not clear when abuses are so bad that protection will be triggered. It is also troubling because the idea of a fundamental right is that it inheres to the individual. When one moves to a system where abuses need to be totted up before action is taken, this rationale for fundamental rights, namely, protection of what is special in each of us, is undermined.

The final concern is that EU fundamental rights might be interpreted in the light of Union objectives to grant them a meaning different from that traditionally associated with such rights. In *Mesopotamia*, two Danish companies broadcast television programmes throughout Europe supportive of the PKK, a group classified as a terrorist organisation by the European Union. The question went to the contentious issue of the relationship between hate speech and political expression within the European Union. It was regulated by article 22 of the Audiovisual Services Directive which required Member States to ensure that broadcasts did not contain any incitement to hatred on grounds of race, sex, religion or nationality. Following a complaint from the Turkish Government, the German government sought to stop broadcasts into Germany, albeit that the programmes could still be rebroadcast from Germany to other states and the Danish authorities had found that there was no incitement to racial hatred and the broadcasts were largely facts and opinion. When this was challenged, the German administrative court found that the broadcasts did amount to incitement to racial hatred as they justified the activities of the PKK and portrayed those carrying out violent acts as heroes.

Joined Cases C–244/10 and C–245/10 *Mesopotamia Broadcast and Roj TV* [2011] ECR I-8777

33. ... it is clear from recital 8 in the preamble to [the Directive] that the law applied to the broadcasting and distribution of television services is also a specific manifestation of a more general principle, namely the freedom of expression as enshrined in Article 10(1) of the Convention for the Protection of Human Rights and Fundamental Freedoms, signed in Rome on 4 November 1950. Furthermore, it follows from the wording of recital 15 in the preamble to [the Directive] that, Article F(2) of the EU Treaty (now Article 6(2) EU) that the European Union is to respect the rights, freedoms and principles laid down in the Charter of Fundamental Rights of the European Union, so that any measure aimed at restricting the reception and/or suspending the retransmission of television broadcasts must be compatible with the abovementioned principles....

38. ... it must be observed, first, that the Directive does not contain any definition of the terms referred to in Article 22a thereof.

39. Furthermore, ... the drafting history ... does not contain any relevant information relating to the scope of the concept of 'incitement to hatred', and confirms that the European legislature intended to lay down, in Article 22a of the Directive, a ground for prohibition based on public order considerations which would be distinct from the grounds relating particularly to the protection of minors.

40. It follows that the scope of Article 22a of the Directive must be determined by considering the usual meaning in everyday language of the terms used in that article, while also taking into account the context in which they occur and the purposes of the rules of which they are part ...

41. As regards the words 'incitation' and 'hatred', it must be observed that they refer, first, to an action intended to direct specific behaviour and, second, a feeling of animosity or rejection with regard to a group of persons.

42. Thus, the Directive, by using the concept 'incitement to hatred', is designed to forestall any ideology which fails to respect human values, in particular initiatives which attempt to justify violence by terrorist acts against a particular group of persons.

43. As regards the infringement of the principles of international understanding, as stated in paragraph 25 of the present judgment, Mesopotamia Broadcast and Roj TV, according to the referring court, play a role in stirring up violent confrontations between persons of Turkish and Kurdish origin in Turkey and in exacerbating the tensions between Turks and Kurds living in Germany, thereby infringing the principles of international understanding.

44. Consequently, it must be held that such behaviour is covered by the concept of 'incitement to hatred'.

The Court of Justice sees the EU legislation as institutional realisation of the right to freedom of expression rather than as something which must be assessed against this right. Fundamental rights become, in this manner, above all something which justifies EU law-making rather than something to guide, check or question it. There is, thus, no evaluation of the Directive against independent standards of freedom of expression or non-discrimination on grounds of race. This allows the Court to reduce this question of 'hate speech' to one of interpretation of the Directive. It is to be assessed in the light of the purpose of the Directive, a single market in broadcasting. As a consequence, it draws the balance between autonomy of expression and respect for other members of the community differently from many constitutional jurisdictions. In some of these, autonomy is so valued that expression is only to be illegal where it incites violence. In others, expression is not allowed if it violates the dignity of others. A third position sees it in terms of whether the expression is understood by the target group as denigrating it and by other groups as desensitivising them to abuse of that group.[95] The interpretation in *Mesopotamia* refers back to none of these. It states that incitement to hatred involves action intended to direct specific behaviour and a feeling of animosity or rejection towards a group of persons. It is empty on the element of race, gender, religion or nationality which must be present, and which provides meaning to these elements. The question of how the expression is thus understood is left unanswered. Finally, the prohibition is cast in very general terms. The

[95] M. Rosenfeld, 'Hate Speech in Constitutional Jurisprudence: A Comparative Analysis' (2002) 24 *Cardozo Law Review* 1523; E. Bleich, *The Freedom to Be Racist?: How the United States and Europe Struggle to Preserve Freedom and Combat Racism* (Oxford, Oxford University Press, 2011) 17–84.

animus requires only a feeling of rejection, so that it would allow restrictions of broadcasts supportive of the ANC during the apartheid period, the Free Syrian Army, regional boycotts of services or goods. A case can, of course, be made for a broad definition of hate speech but, given the importance of political expression within a democracy, one would expect a greater level of justification for this which relates it more clearly to democratic concerns.

5 FUNDAMENTAL RIGHTS AND THE INSTITUTIONAL SCHEME OF THE EUROPEAN UNION

A central concern of Article 6 TEU is that the EUCFR should not extend in any way the competences of the Union. This concern is also expressed in the EUCFR.

Article 51(2) EUCFR

2. This Charter does not extend the field of application of Union law beyond the powers of the Union or establish any new power or task for the Union, or modify powers and tasks in the other Parts of the Constitution.

The most obvious concern was that the Court of Justice might use the EUCFR to found new powers of judicial review for itself over activities that were thought to fall outside the Treaties or to interpret EU legislative competencies in the light of the EUCFR to extend Union powers.

(i) Fundamental rights and the EU institutions

Fundamental rights are most obviously used to review the behaviour of EU institutions. Whilst the Union courts are quite willing to strike down administrative acts by either the Commission or Council for breaching EU fundamental rights law,[96] it is another matter when it comes to EU legislative acts. Here the Court of Justice is pusillanimous.[97] There is, for example, only one instance of a Directive being struck down for failure to comply with fundamental rights, and this concerned discrimination against men over the sale of car insurance.[98]

A more central role is the use of fundamental rights to orient and interpret that legislation. With regard to the orientation of EU legislation, in a 2010 Communication on a *Strategy for the Effective Implementation of the Charter of Fundamental Rights by the European Union*, the Commission argued that the EUCFR should act as the 'compass for the Union's policies'.[99] To that end, a culture of fundamental rights should inform EU law-making. This would involve at least four stages. In initial consultation with stakeholders prior to any legislative proposal,

---

[96] For examples involving both courts see Case T-187/11 *Trabelsi* v *Council*, Judgment of 28 May 2013; Joined Cases T-147/09 and T-148/09 *Trelleborg Industry* v *Commission*, Judgment of 15 May 2013; Case C-110/10P *Solvay* v *Commission* [2011] ECR I-11439.

[97] Particularly noteworthy examples of judicial feebleness are Case C-540/03 *Parliament* v *Council* [2006] ECR I-5769; Case C-303/05 *Advocaten voor de Wereld* [2007] ECR I-3633; Case C-396/11 *Radu*, Judgment of 29 January 2013.

[98] Case C-236/09 *Association Belge des Consommateurs Test-Achats* v *Conseil des ministres* [2011] ECR I-773.

[99] COM(2010)573, 4.

the Commission would, first, highlight any potentially sensitive fundamental rights issues. Secondly, in carrying out its impact assessments on any proposal, the Commission would also consider impacts of fundamental rights. Thirdly, in the drafting of any legislation, the Commission would indicate how the legislation complies with specific rights in the recitals in the Preamble, as well as expanding on this at more length in the Explanatory Memorandum accompanying the legislation. Fourthly, the Commission must verify that amendments by the other institutions comply with fundamental rights. These institutions are committed to not proposing such amendments and the Commission is committed to opposing them if they are made.[100]

There is a thin line between verifying that EU law-making does not violate fundamental rights and moving to a human rights policy in which EU institutions see EU goals as increasingly about realisation of the rights and principles in the EUCFR rather than other more discrete tasks. Whilst a case can be made for the former,[101] it sets a more ambitious agenda for the Union with a wider remit. Beyond this debate, few would oppose the idea that legislative proposals be verified for their impact on fundamental rights. However, there remains the question of the rigour of this process. If it is simply box-ticking, fundamental rights become a rhetorical instrument to justify EU law-making.[102] In that regard, it is a pity that the Court of Justice has not yet had the opportunity to rule on whether a procedural failure to engage sufficiently with fundamental rights in the legislative process is, by itself, a violation of fundamental rights insofar as it shows inadequate care for these.

The interpretation of EU legislation in light of EU fundamental rights can have a significant impact on EU powers. A good example is *Jaeger*. Directive 93/104/EC on the organisation of working time required a minimum daily rest period of eleven consecutive hours per twenty-four hour period.[103] Jaeger was a doctor who worked in a hospital in the German town of Kiel. For about three-quarters of his working time, he was on call. This required him to be present in the hospital to be available when needed. It was agreed that he performed services about 49 per cent of the time he was on call. The hospital considered that the time on call counted as a rest period for the purposes of the Directive, and limited his rest periods outside of this accordingly. Jaeger believed it was work. The Court of Justice agreed with him.

Case C-151/02 *Jaeger* [2003] ECR I-8389

45. ... it should be stated at the outset ... that the purpose of the directive is to lay down minimum requirements intended to improve the living and working conditions of workers through approximation of national provisions concerning, in particular, the duration of working time ...

46. ... such harmonisation at Community level in relation to the organisation of working time is intended to guarantee better protection of the safety and health of workers by ensuring that they are entitled to minimum rest periods – particularly daily and weekly – and adequate breaks and by providing for a ceiling on the duration of the working week ...

---

[100] *Ibid.* 4–10.

[101] P. Alston and J. Weiler, 'An "Ever Closer Union" in Need of a Human Rights Policy' (1998) 9 *EJIL* 658.

[102] On its effects on EU legislative proposals see I. de Jesus Butler, 'Ensuring Compliance with the Charter of Fundamental Rights in Legislative Drafting: The Practice of the European Commission' (2012) 37 *ELRev.* 397.

[103] This has now been replaced by Directive 2003/88/EC concerning certain aspects of the organisation of working time [2003] OJ L299/9. This makes similar provision for rest periods.

47. In that context it is clear from the Community Charter of the Fundamental Social Rights of Workers, adopted at the meeting of the European Council held at Strasbourg on 9 December 1989, and in particular points 8 and 19, first subparagraph, thereof, which are referred to in the fourth recital in the preamble to Directive 93/104, that every worker in the European Community must enjoy satisfactory health and safety conditions in his working environment and must have a right, inter alia, to a weekly rest period, the duration of which in the Member States must be progressively harmonised in accordance with national practices.

48. With regard more specifically to the concept of 'working time' for the purposes of Directive 93/104, it is important to point out that at paragraph 47 of the judgment in *Simap*,[104] the Court noted that the directive defines that concept as any period during which the worker is working, at the employer's disposal and carrying out his activity or duties, in accordance with national laws and/or practices, and that that concept is placed in opposition to rest periods, the two being mutually exclusive.

49. At paragraph 48 of the judgment in *Simap* the Court held that the characteristic features of working time are present in the case of time spent on call by doctors in primary care teams in Valencia (Spain) where their presence at the health centre is required. The Court found, in the case which resulted in that judgment, that it was not disputed that during periods of duty on call under those rules, the first two conditions set out in the definition of the concept of working time were fulfilled and, further, that, even if the activity actually performed varied according to the circumstances, the fact that such doctors were obliged to be present and available at the workplace with a view to providing their professional services had to be regarded as coming within the ambit of the performance of their duties.

The Community Charter of Fundamental Social Rights was, thus, used to allow a wide interpretation of what constitutes work for the purposes of this Directive. This broadened EU competences as it allowed the Union to verify what constituted 'rest' in securing work-life balances. It also recalibrated not simply what employers could ask of employees more broadly, as the Directive put in place a general limit of forty-eight hours work per week. The judgments, therefore, had dramatic implications for the cost base of many organisations that had previously taken on call not to count as work. This was particularly so in national health services. The excerpt below relates the views of the different British stakeholders, but the experience was not confined to the United Kingdom.

House of Lords European Union Committee, *The Working Time Directive: A Response to the European Commission's Review* (Session 2003–4, 9th Report, London, SO)

3.27. The Royal College of Nursing also expressed concern about the potential impact of the *SiMAP* and *Jaeger* judgments. The College called for clarification of the definition of compensatory rest and how it should be applied. It drew attention to the particular difficulty in calculating working time where 24 hour nursing care was provided by agency nurses living in patients' homes....

3.31. The NHS Confederation agreed that 'sizeable numbers' of hospitals in the United Kingdom could not comply with the Directive by 1 August 2004 because of these judgments.

---

[104] Case C-303/98 *Simap* [2000] ECR I-7963.

3.32. The BMA claimed that if the *Jaeger* ruling remained unchanged the effect would be tantamount to losing the equivalent of 3,700 junior doctors by August 2004 and between 4,300 and 9,900 junior doctors by 2009 when the full 48 hour limit would come into effect. One BMA witness commented that the United Kingdom would be in 'real trouble'....

3.38. The Health Minister explained the implications of the *Jaeger* ruling for the NHS: 'To require compensatory rest to be taken immediately would potentially have a massively destructive effect across the NHS and might mean that doctors could not work the following shift on rota that they were required to do. This would have knock-on consequences right across the hospital. At the end of the day, the only people who would be negatively affected would be the patients and that is a ridiculous result'.

3.39. The NHS Confederation put it in equally strong terms: '*Jaeger* makes no sense at all in terms of how you run NHS organisations'. The BMA described how it might work in practice and commented 'This is nonsense'.

Reactions in other Member States

3.40. The *Jaeger* judgment poses problems for other health sectors in the EU. In its Communication, the Commission cites Germany as saying that if both *SiMAP* and *Jaeger* were left unamended it would have to increase its doctors by 24% with costs running to €1.75 billion. It also reports that the Netherlands estimated the extra cost of both judgments to be €400 million to fund recruitment of 10,000 new staff.

3.41. In order to avoid the full implications of these judgments for hospitals, the Commission reports that France and Spain have chosen to apply the individual opt-out for use in the health sector.[105] Austria, Germany and the Netherlands are planning to do so. Of the countries that will join the EU on 1 May 2004, Slovenia has already applied the opt-out to the health sector. Estonia, Hungary, Latvia and Lithuania may also apply the opt-out to the health sector alone.

The use of fundamental rights as an interpretive tool is also deployed to limit the circumstances in which EU legislation is reviewed. The Court of Justice will seek a benign interpretation wherever possible. It is only in the rare circumstances where this is not available that it will strike down the measure. In *Family Reunification*, Directive 2003/86/EC on family reunification set out the conditions under which family members of non-EU nationals resident in the Union could join them. In principle, children who were minors under the law of the state of reception had a right to family reunification (article 4(1) of the Directive). However, article 4(6) stated that:

> By way of derogation, Member States may request that the applications concerning family reunification of minor children have to be submitted before the age of 15, as provided for by its existing legislation on the date of the implementation of this Directive. If the application is submitted after the age of 15, the Member States which decide to apply this derogation shall authorise the entry and residence of such children on grounds other than family reunification.

This was one of the elements in the Directive challenged by the European Parliament as violating the right to respect for family life.

---

105 Member States can opt workers out of the requirement of the forty-eight hour week, subject to a large number of conditions. *Ibid.* article 22. This is what many states did for the health sector as a response to *Jaeger*.

Case C–540/03 *Parliament v Council (Family Reunification)* [2006] ECR I–5769

84. In the present action, the review conducted by the Court concerns whether the contested provision, in itself, respects fundamental rights and, in particular, the right to respect for family life, the obligation to have regard to the best interests of children and the principle of non-discrimination on grounds of age. It must be determined in particular whether Article 4(6) of the Directive expressly or impliedly authorises the Member States not to observe those fundamental principles in that it allows them, in derogation from the other provisions of Article 4 of the Directive, to formulate a requirement by reference to the age of a minor child for whom application is made for entry into, and residence in, national territory in the context of family reunification.

85. It does not appear that the contested provision infringes the right to respect for family life set out in Article 8 of the ECHR as interpreted by the European Court of Human Rights. Article 4(6) of the Directive does give the Member States the option of applying the conditions for family reunification which are prescribed by the Directive only to applications submitted before children have reached 15 years of age. This provision cannot, however, be interpreted as prohibiting the Member States from taking account of an application relating to a child over 15 years of age or as authorising them not to do so.

86. It does not matter that the final sentence of the contested provision provides that the Member States which decide to apply the derogation are to authorise the entry and residence of children in respect of whom an application is submitted after they have reached 15 years of age 'on grounds other than family reunification'. The term 'family reunification' must be interpreted in the context of the Directive as referring to family reunification in the cases where family reunification is required by the Directive. It cannot be interpreted as prohibiting a Member State which has applied the derogation from authorising the entry and residence of a child in order to enable the child to join his or her parents.

87. Article 4(6) of the Directive must, moreover, be read in the light of the principles set out in Article 5(5) thereof, which requires the Member States to have due regard to the best interests of minor children, and in Article 17, which requires them to take account of a number of factors, one of which is the person's family relationships.

88. It follows that, while Article 4(6) of the Directive has the effect of authorising a Member State not to apply the general conditions of Article 4(1) of the Directive to applications submitted by minor children over 15 years of age, the Member State is still obliged to examine the application in the interests of the child and with a view to promoting family life.

This use of the ECHR gave rise not only to a more liberal interpretation of the Directive but also a more contrived one. The interpretation given by the Court of Justice was that the provision required Member States to admit children under fifteen whilst granting them discretion to do this when children were older. This looks odd when the Directive expressly prohibits the latter being admitted on grounds of family reunification. A more honest interpretation would have been to strike this provision down. It also leads to an awkward reallocation of risks between EU institutions and Member States. It is the national implementation of the Directive which shoulders the burden for avoidance of breaches of fundamental rights even where the Directive makes it difficult to observe these. In this instance, therefore, article 4(6) prohibits Member States from admitting children over 15 years of age on grounds of family reunification whilst the judgment states, by contrast, that in considering their applications, Member States are to take account of the interests of the child and their existing family relations. There is clearly an incongruity between formal compliance with the Directive and observance of EU fundamental rights law which leaves national administrations exposed and, more importantly, the migration status of children vulnerable.

(ii) Fundamental rights and the Member States

Requiring EU institutions to comply with fundamental rights carries less sensitivity than review of national laws or administrations against EU fundamental rights law. In the latter case, a claim is being made that EU law not only has an authority to state what is right and wrong on matters of such significance to our societies that they are described as 'fundamental' but that it can do so at the expense of national institutions which have traditionally had that role. The EUCFR grants EU fundamental rights law, therefore, only a limited role.

Article 51(1) EUCFR

1. The provisions of this Charter are addressed to the institutions, bodies, offices and agencies of the Union with due regard for the principle of subsidiarity and to the Member States only when they are implementing Union law.

National measures are to be reviewed only when they are 'implementing' EU law. This term is less clear than it might appear. Some language versions use the word 'apply' instead,[106] and the Explanations to Article 51 refer to measures 'acting in the context' of EU law. They cite judgments with very different parameters for when national measures fall to be reviewed by EU fundamental rights law.[107]

Explanations relating to the Charter of Fundamental Rights (Article 51)

As regards the Member States, it follows unambiguously from the case law of the Court of Justice that the requirement to respect fundamental rights defined in a Union context is only binding on the Member States when they act in the context of Community law (judgment of 13 July 1989, Case 5/88 *Wachauf* [1989] ECR 2609; judgment of 18 June 1991, Case C-260/89 *ERT* [1991] ECR I-2925; judgment of 18 December 1997, Case C-309/96 *Annibaldi* [1997] ECR I-7493).

In *Wachauf*, national measures were found to be subject to EU fundamental rights where they were transposing a Directive.[108] This left the range of national activities caught by EU

---

[106] A. Rosas, 'When is the EU Charter of Fundamental Rights Applicable at National Level?' (2012) 19 *Jurisprudencija* 1269, 1277.
[107] For a discussion see G. de Búrca, 'The Drafting of the EU Charter of Fundamental Rights' (2001) 26 *ELRev.* 126, 136–7.
[108] Case 5/88 *Wachauf* v *Germany* [1989] ECR 2609.

fundamental rights law very circumscribed. This was altered by the subsequent *ERT* judgment. ERT, a Greek radio and television company enjoying exclusive broadcasting rights under Greek law, sought an injunction against another company, DEP, and Mr Kouvelas, the Mayor of Thessaloniki, who had set up a rival television station. The respondents argued that ERT's exclusive rights infringed, inter alia, the right to free provision of services. The Greek Government invoked Articles 52 and 62 TFEU, which allow it to impose restrictions for reasons of public policy. DEP counter-argued that these could not be invoked as the restriction violated Article 10 ECHR relating to freedom of expression.

Case C–260/89 *Elliniki Radiophonia Tileorassi (ERT) v Dimitiki (DEP)* [1991] ECR I–2925

42. As the Court has held …, it has no power to examine the compatibility with the ECHR of national rules which do not fall within the scope of Community law. On the other hand, where such rules do fall within the scope of Community law, and reference is made to the Court for a preliminary ruling, it must provide all the criteria of interpretation needed by the national court to determine whether those rules are compatible with the fundamental rights the observance of which the Court ensures and which derive in particular from the ECHR.

43. In particular, where a Member State relies on the combined provisions of [Articles 52 and 62 TFEU] in order to justify rules which are likely to obstruct the exercise of the freedom to provide services, such justification, provided for by Community law, must be interpreted in the light of the general principles of law and in particular of fundamental rights. Thus the national rules in question can fall under the exceptions provided for by the combined provisions of [Articles 52 and 62 TFEU] only if they are compatible with the fundamental rights the observance of which is ensured by the Court.

44. It follows that in such a case it is for the national court, and if necessary, the Court of Justice to appraise the application of those provisions having regard to all the rules of Community law, including freedom of expression, as embodied in Article 10 ECHR, as a general principle of law the observance of which is ensured by the Court.

ERT expanded the reach of EU fundamental rights law significantly. It provided that wherever a Member State invoked an exception to EU law, that exception would only be lawful if it complied with EU fundamental rights law. Its greatest practical significance lay in relation to the economic freedoms, which all allow a range of public interest exceptions to free movement of goods, persons, capital and services otherwise required by them. These exceptions must now respect fundamental rights. Broadcasting laws, pornography laws, banning orders on hooligans or laws restricting individuals going abroad for assisted suicide all fell for assessment for their compliance with fundamental rights, insofar as they had the potential to restrict free movement.[109]

To compound matters, a number of commentators and academics argue that the Union is now more oriented towards realisation and respect for fundamental rights than at the time of

---

[109] Sánchez, n. 55 above, 1588–92; K. Lenaerts, 'Exploring the Limits of the EU Charter of Fundamental Rights' (2012) 8 *EuConst* 375, 376–87.

Wachauf and *ERT*. They point to the presence of Article 6 TEU, which can trace its origins back to the Treaty of Amsterdam, and the introduction of Article 2 TEU by the Treaty of Lisbon, which, as stated at the beginning of this chapter, founds the Union on respect for human rights. It is argued that this new orientation changes the rules of the game.[110] At its most adventurous, a case has been made that the Union should be able to intervene to prevent serious and persistent human rights violations even when these involve activities that fall outside the Union competences.[111] Others have argued that it calls for all national activities which fall within the Union competences, whether or not it has acted, to be assessed against EU fundamental rights law.[112]

The matter came to a head in *Fransson*. Fransson was found to have falsified his value added tax (VAT) returns. The Swedish administrative court had already imposed financial penalties on him for doing this. He was then taken before the criminal courts, who sought to impose further financial penalties. Fransson argued that this violated his fundamental right to *ne bis in idem*, the right not to be tried twice for the same offence. VAT is a system of taxation established by EU law with considerable discretion left for the Member States. There were duties in both the relevant Directive and as a consequence of Article 4(3) TEU for all national authorities to ensure collection of the tax and to prevent tax evasion. Furthermore, a proportion of VAT goes to the EU Budget, and Article 325 TFEU, consequently, requires Member States to combat budget fraud. It was very difficult, however, to argue that the Swedish Government was transposing the Directive in the case in hand.

Case C-617/10 Åklagaren v *Fransson*, Judgment of 26 February 2013

17. It is to be recalled in respect of those submissions that the Charter's field of application so far as concerns action of the Member States is defined in Article 51(1) thereof, according to which the provisions of the Charter are addressed to the Member States only when they are implementing European Union law.

18. That article of the Charter thus confirms the Court's case-law relating to the extent to which actions of the Member States must comply with the requirements flowing from the fundamental rights guaranteed in the legal order of the European Union.

19. The Court's settled case-law indeed states, in essence, that the fundamental rights guaranteed in the legal order of the European Union are applicable in all situations governed by European Union law, but not outside such situations. In this respect the Court has already observed that it has no power to examine the compatibility with the Charter of national legislation lying outside the scope of European Union law. On the other hand, if such legislation falls within the scope of European Union law, the Court, when requested to give a preliminary ruling, must provide all the guidance as to interpretation

---

[110] More cautious interpretations can be found in Rosas, n. 106 above, 1280–1; Case C-617/10 *Åklagaren* v *Fransson*, Judgment of 26 February 2013, Opinion of Advocate General Cruz Villalón.

[111] Case C-380/05 *Centro Europa 7* v *Ministero delle Comunicazioni* [2008] ECR I-349, Opinion of Advocate General Poiares Maduro; A. v. Bogdandy *et al.*, 'Reverse *Solange*: Protecting the Essence of Fundamental Rights against EU Member States' (2012) 49 *CMLRev.* 489.

[112] Case C-34/09 *Zambrano* [2011] ECR I-1177, Opinion of Advocate General Sharpston.

needed in order for the national court to determine whether that legislation is compatible with the fundamental rights the observance of which the Court ensures ...

20. That definition of the field of application of the fundamental rights of the European Union is borne out by the explanations relating to Article 51 of the Charter, which, in accordance with the third subparagraph of Article 6(1) TEU and Article 52(7) of the Charter, have to be taken into consideration for the purpose of interpreting it ... According to those explanations, 'the requirement to respect fundamental rights defined in the context of the Union is only binding on the Member States when they act in the scope of Union law'.

21. Since the fundamental rights guaranteed by the Charter must therefore be complied with where national legislation falls within the scope of European Union law, situations cannot exist which are covered in that way by European Union law without those fundamental rights being applicable. The applicability of European Union law entails applicability of the fundamental rights guaranteed by the Charter.

22. Where, on the other hand, a legal situation does not come within the scope of European Union law, the Court does not have jurisdiction to rule on it and any provisions of the Charter relied upon cannot, of themselves, form the basis for such jurisdiction ...

23. These considerations correspond to those underlying Article 6(1) TEU, according to which the provisions of the Charter are not to extend in any way the competences of the European Union as defined in the Treaties. Likewise, the Charter, pursuant to Article 51(2) thereof, does not extend the field of application of European Union law beyond the powers of the European Union or establish any new power or task for the European Union, or modify powers and tasks as defined in the Treaties ...

24. In the case in point, it is to be noted at the outset that the tax penalties and criminal proceedings to which Mr Åkerberg Fransson has been or is subject are connected in part to breaches of his obligations to declare VAT.

25. In relation to VAT, it follows, first, from Articles 2, 250(1) and 273 of Council Directive 2006/112/EC ... on the common system of value added tax ... and second, from Article 4(3) TEU that every Member State is under an obligation to take all legislative and administrative measures appropriate for ensuring collection of all the VAT due on its territory and for preventing evasion ...

26. Furthermore, Article 325 TFEU obliges the Member States to counter illegal activities affecting the financial interests of the European Union through effective deterrent measures and, in particular, obliges them to take the same measures to counter fraud affecting the financial interests of the European Union as they take to counter fraud affecting their own interests ... Given that the European Union's own resources include ... revenue from application of a uniform rate to the harmonised VAT assessment bases determined according to European Union rules, there is thus a direct link between the collection of VAT revenue in compliance with the European Union law applicable and the availability to the European Union budget of the corresponding VAT resources, since any lacuna in the collection of the first potentially causes a reduction in the second ...

27. It follows that tax penalties and criminal proceedings for tax evasion, such as those to which the defendant in the main proceedings has been or is subject because the information concerning VAT that was provided was false, constitute implementation of Articles 2, 250(1) and 273 of Directive 2006/112 ... and of Article 325 TFEU and, therefore, of European Union law, for the purposes of Article 51(1) of the Charter.

Fransson states that any national measures which fall within the scope of EU law are governed by EU fundamental rights law. However, it does not state *when* something falls within the scope of EU law. It appears that this will not be where the Union has competences but has failed to act. It will be when the measure is governed by EU law. That is to say that there is some EU legal norm which regulates the activities in question, albeit, as was the case in *Fransson*, quite generally.

In *Texdata*, an Austrian law was challenged which imposed automatic periodic penalties on companies which failed to register their accounts.[113] The automaticity of these periodic penalties was argued to violate companies' fundamental rights because it allowed them little opportunity to make a case that they did not need to register their accounts or to present any other kind of defence. The Court of Justice found that the Austrian law was subject to EU fundamental rights law as Directive 89/666/EEC, the Eleventh Company Law Directive, requires Member States to impose appropriate penalties for failure to disclose accounting documents. There was thus an EU instrument which stood over the activity in question, and it fell within the scope of EU law. By contrast, in *Hadj Ahmed*, an Algerian woman had acquired residence rights in Belgium by virtue of her living there when she had a French partner.[114] They separated and she remained in Belgium with her Algerian child. She claimed a family allowance for her daughter on the grounds that it would have been granted to an EU citizen with analogous residence rights and to a non-EU national who was the parent of a child with EU citizenship. It was held that, by virtue of her being a non-EU national, she did not fall within the scope of EU legislation. She then invoked the right to respect for family life. In addition to the analogous family situations already described, if she had still been with her French partner, she could have claimed EU rights. Nevertheless, the Court stated that as she fell outside the scope of the legislation, she could not assert any fundamental right, even though it was this very curtailing of EU legislation which seemed to deprive her of her fundamental rights.

The broadening of the range of national activities caught by EU fundamental rights law does not remedy the problems generated by coverage still only being partial.[115] This partiality results in inconsistency, as there will be analogous situations where one person is offered protection by EU fundamental rights law and another is not; in legal uncertainty, as there will always be some doubt as to which activities are covered by EU fundamental rights law; and in possibilities for arbitrage where parties engineer situations so that these fall to be governed by EU law in order to obtain its fundamental rights protection.

The most celebrated example of these issues is *SPUC* v *Grogan*. In 1986, the Irish Supreme Court ruled that it was against the Irish Constitution to help Irish women to have abortions by informing them of the identity and location of abortion clinics abroad. A number of Irish student unions provided the details of abortion clinics in the United Kingdom. This information was provided for free. The Society for the Protection of the Unborn Child (SPUC) sought an undertaking that the student unions would cease to do this. The students invoked EU law arguing their right to freedom of expression had been violated. SPUC countered, arguing that the measure fell outside the field of EU law, as it did not constitute a restriction on the freedom to provide services under what is now Article 56 TFEU.

---

[113] Case C-418/11 *Texdata Software*, Judgment of 26 September 2013.
[114] Case C-45/12 *Hadj Ahmed*, Judgment of 13 June 2013.
[115] For strong criticism see P. Huber, 'The Unitary Effect of the Community's Fundamental Rights: The *ERT* Doctrine Needs to be Reviewed' (2008) 14 *EPL* 323.

> **Case C-159/90 *Society for the Protection of the Unborn Child (SPUC)* v *Grogan* [1991] ECR I-4685**
>
> 22. ... the national court seeks essentially to establish whether it is contrary to Community law for a Member State in which medical termination of pregnancy is forbidden to prohibit students associations from distributing information about the identity and location of clinics in another Member State where medical termination of pregnancy is lawfully carried out and the means of communicating with those clinics, where the clinics in question have no involvement in the distribution of the said information....
>
> 24. As regards, first, the provisions of [Article 56 TFEU], which prohibit any restriction on the freedom to supply services, it is apparent from the facts of the case that the link between the activity of the students associations of which Mr Grogan and the other defendants are officers and medical terminations of pregnancies carried out in clinics in another Member State is too tenuous for the prohibition on the distribution of information to be capable of being regarded as a restriction within the meaning of [Article 56 TFEU]....
>
> 26. The information to which the national court's questions refer is not distributed on behalf of an economic operator established in another Member State. On the contrary, the information constitutes a manifestation of freedom of expression and of the freedom to impart and receive information which is independent of the economic activity carried on by clinics established in another Member State.
>
> 27. It follows that, in any event, a prohibition on the distribution of information in circumstances such as those which are the subject of the main proceedings cannot be regarded as a restriction within the meaning of [Article 56 TFEU]....
>
> 30. It was important to bear in mind that when national legislation fell within the field of application of Community law the Court, when requested to give a preliminary ruling, must provide the national court with all the elements of interpretation necessary in order to enable it to assess the compatibility of that legislation with the fundamental rights – as laid down in particular in the ECHR – the observance of which the Court ensures. However, the Court had no such jurisdiction with regard to national legislation lying outside the scope of Community law.

Fundamental rights are treated in a paradoxical manner.[116] On the one hand, they are seen as so valuable that they must be protected against all institutional activity, be it EU or national. On the other, they only have partial existence, whereby their presence and bite is governed by the scope of EU law, which is, of course, determined by that institutional activity against which they are to be protected. This paradox leads to perverse incentives. The clear message in *Grogan*, for example, was that the students should offer to advertise, for a nominal fee, on behalf of the British abortion clinics, in order to bring themselves within the field of EU law.

This paradox reflects the tension between universalism and particularism which lies at the heart of many debates about fundamental rights. This tension is particularly exposed where there is a conflict between a more local law, the national one, and a more general one, the European Union, over fundamental rights. It is described below by a distinguished academic who is now a judge on the Italian Constitutional Court.

---

[116] P. Eeckhout, 'The EU Charter of Fundamental Rights and the Federal Question' (2002) 39 *CMLRev.* 945, 957–8; G. de Búrca, 'Fundamental Rights and the Reach of EC Law' (1993) 13 *OJLS* 283.

M. Cartabia, 'Europe and Rights: Taking Dialogue Seriously' (2009) 5 *European Constitutional Law Review* 5, 20–1

We must not, however, forget the ambivalent nature of fundamental rights. In the struggle for fundamental rights there is a longing for *universality* that justifies the need to go beyond the boundaries of the national legal systems; but there is also a *historical dimension* in which the traditions and deepest conscience of each people is reflected, of which the national constitutional charters are one of the salient expressions. Rooted in the value of human dignity, the idea of fundamental rights necessarily contains a *universal dimension*. Embedded in the historical, religious, moral, linguistic and political peculiarities of each people, such rights are fed by particularity and pluralism.

The attraction to a European protection of human rights risks sacrificing the national historical and cultural traditions that characterise the pluralistic nature of Europe. Even more serious: what happens if one of the fundamental rights protected at the European and international level belongs only to one or some specific traditions or cultures and does not reflect any common shared value? Who will guarantee that the European and the international institutions will stick to the protection of the common fundamental rights and are not tempted to impose a particular interpretation of them as if it were universal?

The position of the Court of Justice is crucial and extremely delicate. Its pronouncements on the subject of fundamental rights tend to establish *the* standard that must be respected throughout the 27 countries of the Union. Once a fundamental right enters the jurisdiction of the Court of Justice it becomes a European fundamental right. The decisions taken by the Court of Justice are binding in all the Member States even if the case originated in a particular legal system.

Herein lies the risk of 'judicial colonialism' in the field of fundamental rights. As history has shown us, colonialism often claims to promote progress and civilisation, but on more than one occasion pre-existing cultural and historical patrimonies have been sacrificed in the name of a specific culture, although more progressive. Fostering fundamental rights is indeed a clear sign of progress and civilization. But, what about the native cultures and traditions of the European peoples? And how can a society be able to welcome and respect the cultures of immigrant peoples if it proves to be unable to take care of its own historical patrimony and diversity?

As has been highlighted, the very nature of the European Union is that of a pluralistic, tolerant, multiple, 'contra-punctual' legal order, where a plurality of voices tends to harmonisation. Should the European Union move towards a uniform standard in the field of fundamental rights, trampling on the plurality of national constitutional traditions, then it would betray its own ontological structure.

In *Fransson* there is some recognition of this tension. The Court of Justice seemed to imply that EU fundamental rights law was to act as no more than a base-line with Member States free to adopt a higher level of protection if they desired:

29. ... where a court of a Member State is called upon to review whether fundamental rights are complied with by a national provision or measure which, in a situation where action of the Member States is not entirely determined by European Union law, implements the latter for the purposes of Article 51(1) of the Charter, national authorities and courts remain free to apply national standards of protection of fundamental rights, provided that the level of protection provided for by the Charter, as interpreted by the Court, and the primacy, unity and effectiveness of European Union law are not thereby compromised.

This was insufficient to assuage national concerns. Already, *Fransson* has been explicitly challenged by the German Constitutional Court in its *Counterterrorism Database* judgment.[117] A challenge was made to a new German counterterrorism database, in particular the grounds on which individuals could be added to that database. The measure was, in part, governed by Directive 95/46/EC, which sets out the conditions under which States can process personal data and by Decision 2005/671/JHA which sets out a framework for the exchange of information between national authorities about terrorist offences. The question was, therefore, raised whether, following *Fransson*, the measure was governed by EU fundamental rights law. The Constitutional Court stated that *Fransson* could not be granted an interpretation which would result in an ultra vires act by the Court of Justice. It had to be confined to its facts, namely, the particular characteristics of the tax field.[118] The legislation had domestic goals and EU fundamental rights law could not be used to review measures which affected EU law only indirectly, as was the case here. The EUCFR was not to extend the competence of EU institutions.[119]

If *Counterterrorism Database* suggests a resistance to the scope of EU fundamental rights review, two other forms of resistance have emerged. The first is resistance to EU law derecognising rights seen as fundamental by the state concerned but not by other states. Malta secured protection of its abortion laws from EU law.[120] Ireland obtained protection not only for these, but also for its family and education law.[121] In like vein, Poland obtained a Declaration at the Lisbon Treaty that the Charter does not affect in any way the right of Member States to legislate in the spheres of public morality, family law, protection of human dignity or respect for human physical and moral integrity.[122]

The second is resistance to wide-ranging interpretations of the rights in the EUCFR. Poland and the United Kingdom secured a Protocol on the Application of the Charter to Poland and the United Kingdom.[123] The first provision states as follows.

Protocol on the Application of the Charter to Poland and the United Kingdom, Article 1(1)

1. The Charter does not extend the ability of the Court of Justice of the European Union, or any court or tribunal of Poland or of the United Kingdom, to find that the laws, regulations or administrative provisions, practices or actions of Poland or of the United Kingdom are inconsistent with the fundamental rights, freedoms and principles that it reaffirms.

---

[117] 1 BvR 1215/07 *Counterterrorism Database*, Judgment of 24 April 2013, paras. 88–91.

[118] This injunction was, of course, ignored in Case C-418/11 *Texdata Software*, Judgment of 26 September 2013.

[119] This position should not be seen as exclusive to Germany. The Czech Government appended a Declaration to the Lisbon Treaty stating that the EUCFR only applied to states implementing EU law and not when they adopted measures independently from EU law: Declaration 53 of the Czech Republic on the Charter of the Fundamental Rights of the European Union.

[120] Protocol No. 7 Act of Accession 2003.

[121] Protocol on the Concerns of the Irish People on the Treaty of Lisbon [2013] OJ L60/131, Article 1.

[122] Declaration 61 to the Treaty of Lisbon by the Republic of Poland on the Charter of Fundamental Rights of the European Union.

[123] It is also intended that the Czech Government accede to this Protocol. Although not concluded in the original negotiations on the Treaty of Lisbon, it was a condition of Czech ratification. It was agreed that a Protocol to this effect would be added at the next accession, that of Croatia. This has happened but the European Parliament has, for the moment, refused to ratify that Protocol. European Parliament, *Report on the Draft Protocol on the Application of the Charter of Fundamental Rights of the European Union to the Czech Republic* (A7–0174/2013, Report of 15 May 2013).

The formal effects of this provision are unclear. The Protocol does not give these two states an 'opt-out', and the Court of Justice has stated that the EUCFR applies to these like any other Member State.[124] Focus on these formal effects obscures the broader chilling effect which is intended. The expectation is that there should only be conservative interpretations of the EUCFR. In this regard, there were two particular areas of concern for those states. The first was the 'solidarity' rights in Title IV of the Charter. These are largely concerned with labour protection, but also include wider social rights such as the right to health care and social assistance, as well as Union policies committing themselves to a high level of environmental and consumer protection. The Member States insisted that the EUCFR could not transform these into justiciable rights.

Protocol on the Application of the Charter to Poland and the United Kingdom, Article 1(2)

2. In particular, and for the avoidance of doubt, nothing in Title IV of the Charter creates justiciable rights applicable to Poland or the United Kingdom except in so far as Poland or the United Kingdom has provided for such rights in its national law.

Secondly, a large number of provisions in the Charter state that they are only to be recognised in accordance with the rules laid down by national laws.[125] There was a concern that 'national laws' would be understood as national laws across the Union rather than the law in Poland or the United Kingdom. A provision was, therefore, added emphasising that it was the latter.[126]

6 EUROPEAN UNION ACCESSION TO THE EUROPEAN CONVENTION FOR THE PROTECTION OF HUMAN RIGHTS

Although there had been discussion since the 1970s, it was only with the Treaty of Lisbon, in Article 6(2) TEU, that provision was made for Union accession to the ECHR.[127] The matter raised a number of issues of ECHR law. The EU was not a state, and the Convention only provided for accession of states. There were issues of co-respondency: namely, whom did third states or individuals sue, the Union or Member States? There were also questions of membership rights, in terms of voting and participation rights within the Council of Europe and whether an EU judge should sit on the European Court of Human Rights, and membership responsibilities in terms of budgetary commitments. Negotiations, therefore, took three years with a draft agreement only being reached in June 2013.[128]

---

[124] Joined Cases C-411/10 and C-493/10 *NS* v *Secretary of State for the Home Department*, Judgment of 21 December 2011.
[125] See p. 257.
[126] Protocol on the Application of the Charter to the United Kingdom and Poland, Article 2.
[127] On the background of EU accession to the ECHR and the issues see J.-P. Jacqué, 'The Accession of the European Union to the European Convention on Human Rights and Fundamental Freedoms' (2011) 48 *CMLRev.* 995; T. Lock, 'Walking on a Tightrope: The Draft Accession Agreement and the Autonomy of the EU Legal Order' (2011) 48 *CMLRev.* 1025; C. Eckes, 'EU Accession to the ECHR: Between Autonomy and Adaptation' (2013) 76 *MLR* 254.
[128] See www.coe.int/t/dghl/standardsetting/cddh/cddh-documents/47_1(2013)008rev2_EN.pdf.

The agreement is still only a draft because it has been referred to the Court of Justice to see whether the Union can lawfully ratify it.[129] This is because accession also raised a number of legal issues within EU law. A Protocol was attached to the Treaties setting in place three safeguards.[130] First, accession should not affect the competences of the Union or the powers of its institutions.[131] Secondly, the arrangements for Union participation in the ECHR and ensuring that proceedings by non-Member States and individual applications are correctly addressed to Member States and/or the Union must not affect the special characteristics of EU law, in particular its autonomy. Thirdly, the situation of individual Member States, particularly in relation to individual derogations from the Convention or choices of accession to particular Protocols of the ECHR, should not be affected.[132]

These concerns are addressed by Articles 1 and 3 of the draft Agreement on Accession.

Draft Revised Agreement on the Accession of the European Union to the Convention for the Protection of Human Rights and Fundamental Freedoms, Article 1(3), (4)

3. Accession to the Convention and the protocols thereto shall impose on the European Union obligations with regard only to acts, measures or omissions of its institutions, bodies, offices or agencies, or of persons acting on their behalf. Nothing in the Convention or the protocols thereto shall require the European Union to perform an act or adopt a measure for which it has no competence under European Union law.

4. For the purposes of the Convention, of the protocols thereto and of this Agreement, an act, measure or omission of organs of a Member State of the European Union or of persons acting on its behalf shall be attributed to that State, even if such act, measure or omission occurs when the State implements the law of the European Union ... This shall not preclude the European Union from being responsible as a co-respondent for a violation resulting from such an act, measure or omission ...

The central division of powers set out by this article is that the Union is responsible under the ECHR only for acts carried out by EU institutions (i.e. decisions by the Commission in the field of competition law or agency decisions) where there is no subsequent involvement by national institutions. Insofar as EU law is implemented, applied or enforced by national authorities, actions are to be brought against the Member State concerned.

It is anticipated that this will protect against the danger of competence creep. The Union cannot argue for new powers to meet responsibilities under the ECHR insofar as most of these will be met by the national authorities. It is hoped it might also protect the autonomy of EU law insofar as if national application of EU law is found to violate the ECHR, technically it is the Member State not EU law which is at fault. Finally, it protects national derogations and non-accession to particular Protocols as these national safeguards against ECHR intrusion remain intact whether or not that state is applying EU law.

There is, of course, a danger that EU institutions could be sidelined in all this. A challenge is made against the use of EU law in a domestic court or by a national administration. It is

[129] *Opinion 2/13 on Accession to the European Convention on Human Rights* [2013] OJ C260/19.
[130] Protocol relating to Article 6(2) TEU on the Accession of the Union to the ECHR.
[131] This is also contained in Article 6(2) TEU.
[132] Not all ECHR Protocols are signed by all the Member States. Article 15(1) ECHR also allows states to make derogations from particular provisions in times of war or public emergency.

taken up against the state concerned. The matter becomes simply one of that state protecting its position within the ECHR system. To that end, Article 3 provides for a system of voluntary co-respondence. Either a Member State or the European Union can be joined as a co-respondent where the other is a party if it is plausible that a violation of the ECHR could have been avoided only by either of these disregarding an obligation under EU law. In this way, if EU institutions are worried about the EU position not being articulated fully or Member States are worried about these being too easily absolved of responsibility, they can participate in the case, albeit at the expense of the Union being held responsible.

If the agreement enters into force, there remains the question of what standard of ECHR protection should apply. In *Bosphorus*, the European Court of Human Rights held that as EU law offered a standard of protection at least equivalent to that offered by the ECHR, Member States implementing EU law would only be found to be in breach of the ECHR if the protection of rights was 'manifestly deficient':[133] a far lower threshold than that which applies to states acting outside the scope of EU law. The rationale for this was that the ECHR encouraged international cooperation, and therefore granted a margin of tolerance to other international organisations for the sake of international comity. Always questionable, as it prioritises the workings of international organisations over protection of the rights of individuals, this rationale has even less force with EU accession to the ECHR. It has now made a commitment to observe the norms of that organisation which should afford it no difference in treatment from the other parties to the ECHR.

FURTHER READING

C. Eckes, 'EU Accession to the ECHR: Between Autonomy and Adaptation' (2013) 76 *Modern Law Review* 254

S. Greer and A. Williams, 'Human Rights in the Council of Europe and the EU: Towards "Individual", "Constitutional" or "Institutional" Justice?' (2009) 15 *European Law Journal* 462

N. Krisch, 'The Open Architecture of European Human Rights Law' (2008) 71 *Modern Law Review* 183

B. Kunoy and A. Dawes, 'Plate Tectonics in Luxembourg: The *Ménage à Trois* between EC Law, International Law and the European Convention on Human Rights following the UN Sanctions Cases' (2009) 46 *Common Market Law Review* 73

K. Lenaerts, 'Exploring the Limits of the EU Charter of Fundamental Rights' (2012) 8 *European Constitutional Law Review* 375

S. Peers and A. Ward (eds.), *The EU Charter of Fundamental Rights* (Oxford, Hart, 2004)

A. Rosas, 'When is the EU Charter of Fundamental Rights Applicable at National Level?' (2012) 19 *Jurisprudencija* 1269

S. Sánchez, 'The Court and the Charter: The Impact of the Entry into Force of the Lisbon Treaty on the ECJ's Approach to Fundamental Rights' (2012) 49 *Common Market Law Review* 1565

R. Schütze, 'Three "Bills of Rights" for the European Union' (2011) 30 *Yearbook of European Law* 1

M. Varju and J. Sandor, 'Patenting Stem Cells in Europe: The Challenge of Multiplicity in European Union Law' (2012) 49 *Common Market Law Review* 1007

A. Williams, *EU Human Rights Policies: A Study in Irony* (Oxford, Oxford University Press, 2004)

---

[133] *Bosphorus Airways* v *Ireland* ECHR Appl. No. 45036/98 (2005).

7

Rights and Remedies in National Courts

1 INTRODUCTION

This chapter considers the rights and remedies that EU law allows to be invoked in national courts. It is organised as follows.

Section 2 looks at the emergence of direct effect, the doctrine which provides for EU law to be invoked in national courts. Initially, direct effect was confined to a narrow range of provisions and seemed to offer limited entitlements to individuals. It imposed no positive duty on national administrations to secure individual rights or on other actors not to infringe them.

Section 3 looks at how, over time, direct effect was reconceptualised to provide rights which generate a full set of entitlements against all parties and impose a duty on administrations and courts to protect and realise these entitlements for individuals. This led to EU Treaty provisions being capable of being invoked both against the Member State (vertical direct effect) and against private parties (horizontal direct effect).

Section 4 considers what remedies and procedures are available to individuals where an EU provision is invoked in a domestic court. As a general rule, these are a matter for domestic law. This autonomy is subject to two constraints. The remedies and procedures for infringement of EU law rights should be, first, no less favourable than those for similar domestic claims and, secondly, should not make it practically impossible to exercise EU rights. However, there is a right to EU remedies in four circumstances: a right to restitution for illegally levied taxes; a right to interim relief pending a preliminary reference to the Court of Justice; a right to claim damages or force repayment of illegal subsidies in the field of EU competition law; and, finally, a right to sue the Member State for damages where a serious breach of EU law by it has led to loss for the individual.

Section 5 considers the direct effect of secondary legislation. Direct effect is granted to all binding instruments of EU law: Treaty provisions, Regulations, international agreements, Directives and Decisions. The first three sets of instruments are capable of both vertical and horizontal direct effect. Directives and Decisions are only capable of being invoked against the Member State. However, these can generate incidental direct effects for third parties. Incidental direct effect can occur where the individual invokes a directly effective provision of a Directive against the Member State and this imposes burdens on private parties. More controversially, it also occurs where a Directive grants a private actor the right for certain activities to be protected from Member State interference. This, in turn, allows that actor to use the Directive to protect it from other private actors who invoke national laws to prevent or impede those activities.

Section 6 considers indirect effect. This requires national courts to interpret all national law, insofar as this is possible, in light of all EU law. The extent of this duty is considerable as it requires national courts to give effect to Directives if this is, in any way, interpretively possible. It does not require, however, *contra legem* interpretations and is not to be used to aggravate possible criminal liabilities. Two separate but related doctrines have emerged alongside. National courts are required to disapply laws which conflict with Directives which provide the framework for or elaborate either a fundamental right or a general principle of law even in disputes between private parties. Additionally, during the transposition period, national courts are required to disapply any measure which compromises the objectives of the Directives. Both these additional doctrines are controversial, however, with the consequence that their use has been unsteady.

Section 7 considers the doctrine of Member State liability. This requires Member States to compensate individuals where a breach of EU law by the Member State has led to loss for the individual and the provision breached creates rights for the individual. State liability covers illegal conduct by all governmental institutions, including the judiciary. There are two further conditions to be met to attract liability. The breach of EU law must cause the loss and it must be sufficiently serious. Typically, there are four circumstances when the latter is considered to be the case: a failure to transpose a Directive; breach of a clear provision of EU law; a failure to comply with settled case law; and failure to comply with an order of the Court of Justice.

2 DIRECT EFFECT AND THE IDEA OF AN EU RIGHT

We already considered *Van Gend en Loos* in Chapters 1 and 5. There are two central elements to that judgment.

The first concerns claims made about the quality of EU law. The Court of Justice claimed that EU law did not fall within traditional categories of international law but rather formed a new legal order with its own powerful authority. The consequences of this were addressed in Chapter 5. The second is the establishment of a system of individual rights through the doctrine of direct effect. This element has different dynamics. The language of rights calls for us to rethink EU law in terms of the benefits it grants individuals. It also requires consistency in the interpretation of the Treaty. Provisions appearing to grant individuals benefits cannot be interpreted differently simply because the consequences for the relationship between EU law and national law are too extravagant. If these elements have distinct rationales, in *Van Gend en Loos*, they inform one another. If the justification for the establishment of these rights is the presence of a new legal order, the vehicle for the expression of this order is the development of a system of judicially protected rights.

The facts of *Van Gend en Loos* were discussed earlier.[1] The central bone of contention was whether the provision, now Article 28 TFEU, prohibiting the imposition of customs duties or charges having equivalent effect on imports from other Member States, could be invoked as a matter of EU law in the Dutch court where it had been asserted.

Case 26/62 *Van Gend en Loos* v *Nederlandse Administratie der Belastingen* [1963] ECR 1

The first question ... is whether Article [28 TFEU] has direct application in national law in the sense that nationals of Member States may on the basis of this article lay claim to rights which the national court must protect.

To ascertain whether the provisions of an international treaty extend so far in their effects it is necessary to consider the spirit, the general scheme and the wording of those provisions ...

... The Community constitutes a new legal order of international law for the benefit of which the States have limited their sovereign rights, albeit within limited fields, and the subjects of which comprise not only Member States but also their nationals. Independently of the legislation of Member States, Community law therefore not only imposes obligations on individuals but is also intended to confer upon them rights which become part of their legal heritage. These rights arise not only where they are expressly granted by the Treaty, but also by reason of obligations which the Treaty imposes in a clearly defined way upon individuals as well as upon the Member States and the Institutions of the Community.

With regard to the general scheme of the Treaty as it relates to customs duties and charges having equivalent effect it must be emphasized that ... [basing] the Community upon a customs union, includes as an essential provision the prohibition of these customs duties and charges. This provision is found at the beginning of the part of the Treaty which defines the 'foundations of the Community'. It is applied and explained by Article [28 TFEU].

The wording of Article [28 TFEU] contains a clear and unconditional prohibition which is not a positive but a negative obligation. This obligation, moreover, is not qualified by any reservation on the

---

[1] See p. 16.

part of states which would make its implementation conditional upon a positive legislative measure enacted under national law. The very nature of this prohibition makes it ideally adapted to produce direct effects in the legal relationship between Member States and their subjects.

The implementation of Article [28 TFEU] does not require any legislative intervention on the part of the states. The fact that under this article it is the Member States who are made the subject of the negative obligation does not imply that their nationals cannot benefit from this obligation.

It follows from the foregoing considerations that according to the spirit, the general scheme and the wording of the Treaty, Article [28 TFEU] must be interpreted as producing direct effects and creating individual rights which national courts must protect.

If ground-breaking in its development of the EU legal order, the judgment is narrow in terms of its elaboration of an EU system of rights.

First, the judgment does not state that all Treaty provisions can be invoked by individuals in national courts. It only holds that some provisions, which meet certain criteria – namely, that they are clear, unconditional, negatively phrased and require no legislative intervention – can be invoked by individuals. Moreover, the judgment only indicated with certainty that one provision met this: the arcane Article 28 TFEU prohibiting customs duties and charges having equivalent effect. This is undoubtedly why the judgment did not provoke more controversy at the time.

Secondly, the judgment is narrow in its understanding of a right.[2] It is vague about the extent and nature of the obligations owed to the right-holder by others. At its narrowest EU law may only grant certain rights vis-à-vis the Member State: a duty for it not to violate certain interests. Such rights are little more than immunity from national law in which the right-holder can do things that others cannot (e.g. withhold taxes). A broader conception allows the right-holder to call on all parties to respect, protect and make good the interests that lie at the heart of the right. Such a right can be asserted against anybody and calls for full redress of the interests infringed. The wording of *Van Gend en Loos* suggests that it was concerned with the narrower type of protection.[3] The stipulation that provisions be negatively phrased meant that national administrations can only be called upon to refrain from doing things but cannot be called upon to take positive action to protect individuals. It is a duty not to violate addressed only to the national administration. Equally, the proviso that provisions be unconditional suggested courts could not be called upon to weigh individual entitlements against other public interests if these are recognised by EU law. If the language of rights pushes for full protection of an individual's entitlements by all parties, it was only used hesitantly in *Van Gend en Loos*. There is, in particular, a countervailing reserve about the duties to be imposed on other parties. As we shall see in the rest of this chapter, the case law of the Court of Justice is marked by a push and pull between these two elements.

---

[2] For a useful discussion see T. Downes and C. Hilson, 'Making Sense of Rights: Community Rights in E.C. Law' (1999) 24 *ELRev.* 121. This has led some to say that direct effect is not about rights but merely about individuals invoking EU law before national courts. S. Prechal, 'Member State Liability and Direct Effect: What's the Difference After All?' (2006) 17 *European Business Law Review* 299.

[3] On this early period see T. Eilmansberger, 'The Relationship between Rights and Remedies in EC Law: In Search of the Missing Link' (2004) 41 *CMLRev.* 1199, 1202–6.

3 DIRECT EFFECT AND DEVELOPMENT OF INDIVIDUAL RIGHTS

(i) Relaxing the criteria: towards a test of justiciability

In the 1960s the Court of Justice applied the doctrine of direct effect only to a limited number of provisions.[4] It also did not elaborate further on the implications of the doctrine. In part, this was because most Treaty provisions only entered fully into force with the end of the transitional period in 1970. In the 1970s the Court relaxed the criteria for when a Treaty provision may be directly effective.[5] The issue came up most acutely in *Defrenne (No. 2)*. Under Belgian law female air stewards were required to retire at the age of forty, unlike their male counterparts. Defrenne, forced to retire on this ground, brought an action claiming that the lower pension payments generated by this breached Article 157(1) TFEU. This required that 'each Member State shall ensure and maintain the principle that men and women should receive equal pay for work of equal value'. It was argued that the provision was not directly effective. First, the provision set out only general principles about the treatment of men and women rather than conferring individual rights or entitlements, and, secondly, it was programmatic in nature requiring further measures for its implementation.

Case 43/75 *Defrenne* v *Sabena (No. 2)* [1976] ECR 455

18. For the purposes of the implementation of these provisions a distinction must be drawn within the whole area of application of Article [157 TFEU] between, first, direct and overt discrimination which may be identified solely with the aid of the criteria based on equal work and equal pay referred to by the Article in question and, secondly, indirect and disguised discrimination which can only be identified by reference to more explicit implementing provisions of a Community or national character.

19. It is impossible not to recognise that the complete implementation of the aim pursued by Article [157 TFEU], by means of the elimination of all discrimination, direct or indirect, between men and women workers, not only as regards individual undertakings but also entire branches of industry and even of the economic system as a whole, may in certain cases involve the elaboration of criteria whose implementation necessitates the taking of appropriate measures at Community and national level ...

21. Among the forms of direct discrimination which may be identified solely by reference to the criteria laid down by Article [157 TFEU] must be included in particular those which have their origin in legislative provisions or in collective labour agreements and which may be detected on the basis of a purely legal analysis of the situation.

22. This applies even more in cases where men and women receive unequal pay for equal work carried out in the same establishment or service, whether public or private.

23. As is shown by the very findings of the judgment making the reference, in such a situation the court is in a position to establish all the facts which enable it to decide whether a woman worker is receiving lower pay than a male worker performing the same tasks.

24. In such situation, at least, Article [157 TFEU] is directly [effective] and may thus give rise to individual rights which the courts must protect.

---

[4] Case 57/65 *Lütticke* v *HZA Sarrelouis* [1966] ECR 205; Case 27/67 *Firma Fink-Frucht GmbH* v *Hauptzollamt München-Landsbergerstrasse* [1968] ECR 327; Case 13/68 *Salgoil* v *Italian Foreign Trade Ministry* [1968] ECR 453.

[5] On the early developments see A. Dashwood, 'The Principle of Direct Effect in European Community Law' (1978) 16 *JCMS* 229; P. Craig, 'Once Upon a Time in the West: Direct Effect and the Federalization of EEC Law' (1992) 12 *OJLS* 453, 460–70.

The Court of Justice gave the provision a double meaning to enable the finding of direct effect. On the one hand, it had a programmatic, wide-ranging, ambitious purpose, namely, to secure equality between men and women within the economic system as a whole. On the other hand, the prohibition prohibited overt pay discrimination between men and women in individual workplaces. This was considered sufficiently precise to be invoked in national courts. This relaxed the requirement for legal clarity as it is not possible to suggest that a provision which has a double meaning is clear.

Since *Defrenne (No. 2)*, the criteria set out in *Van Gend en Loos* are not deployed. Instead, the test is whether the content of a provision is sufficiently precise and unconditional.[6] In the eyes of one judge, the invocability of Treaty provisions is a simple question of justiciability.[7] The Court of Justice will not look at whether the provision is qualified by other provisions or constraints, but simply at whether the provision is 'unequivocal'.[8] This suggests that a provision must set out some entitlements which are clearly for the benefit of individuals and impose direct duties on national administrations to protect these entitlements. That these may have some discretion about how to protect the entitlements is not important.[9]

(ii) Member State's duty to protect individual rights and emergence of horizontal direct effect

Defrenne (No. 2) is important for a second reason. It was the first case to address the institutional implications of holding a positively phrased obligation to be directly effective.[10] The Belgian Government argued that the discrimination was not perpetrated by it but by Sabena, a commercial operator. It therefore could not be held liable for this. By contrast, it argued that Sabena could not be liable for obligations under Article 157 TFEU as the latter explicitly addressed these to the Member States, and only the administration was therefore bound.

Case 43/75 Defrenne v Sabena (No. 2) [1976] ECR 455

30. It is … impossible to put forward arguments based on the fact that Article [157] only refers expressly to 'Member States'.

31. Indeed, as the Court has already found in other contexts, the fact that certain provisions of the Treaty are formally addressed to the Member States does not prevent rights from being conferred at the same time on any individual who has an interest in the performance of the duties thus laid down.

32. The very wording of Article [157 TFEU] shows that it imposes on States a duty to bring about a specific result to be mandatorily achieved within a fixed period.

33. The effectiveness of this provision cannot be affected by the fact that the duty imposed by the Treaty has not been discharged by certain Member States and that the joint institutions have not reacted sufficiently energetically against this failure to act.

---

[6] More recently, see Case C-203/10 *Auto Nikolovi* [2011] ECR I-1083; Joined Cases C-621/10 and C-129/11 *Balkan and Sea Properties* and *Provadinvest*, Judgment of 26 April 2012.

[7] P. Pescatore, 'The Doctrine of "Direct Effect": An Infant Disease of Community Law' (1983) 8 *ELRev.* 155, 176–7.

[8] Case C-138/07 *Belgische Staat* v *Cobelfret* [2009] ECR I-731, para. 64.

[9] Case C-226/07 *Flughafen Köln/Bonn* [2008] ECR I-5999.

[10] This had been done earlier in Case 2/74 *Reyners* v *Belgium* [1974] ECR 631.

34. To accept the contrary view would be to risk raising the violation of the right to the status of a principle of interpretation, a position the adoption of which would not be consistent with the task assigned to the Court by Article [19(1) TEU].

35. Finally, in its reference to 'Member States', Article [157 TFEU] is alluding to those States in the exercise of all those of their functions which may usefully contribute to the implementation of the principle of equal pay.

36. Thus, contrary to the statements made in the course of the proceedings this provision is far from merely referring the matter to the powers of the national legislative authorities.

37. Therefore, the reference to 'Member States' in Article [157 TFEU] cannot be interpreted as excluding the intervention of the courts in direct application of the Treaty.

38. Furthermore it is not possible to sustain any objection that the application by national courts of the principle of equal pay would amount to modifying independent agreements concluded privately or in the sphere of industrial relations such as individual contracts and collective labour agreements.

39. In fact, since Article [157 TFEU] is mandatory in nature, the prohibition on discrimination between men and women applies not only to the action of public authorities, but also extends to all agreements which are intended to regulate paid labour collectively, as well as to contracts between individuals.

Direct effect is not therefore just about protecting individuals from Member States violating their duties. It also imposes duties upon the Member State to secure the protection of these individual rights. In this regard, *Defrenne (No. 2)* makes two particularly important findings. First, it reminds national courts that they are part of the Member State and that this duty to protect falls particularly strongly on them. Secondly, as a consequence of this institutional duty, Treaty provisions can be invoked against private parties, who, correspondingly, have a duty to respect EU law. It therefore established two forms of direct effect which have been referred to in the academic literature in the following manner:

- vertical direct effect: this is where a party invokes a provision of EU law in a national court against a Member State;
- horizontal direct effect: this is where a party invokes a provision of EU law in a national court against a private party. A corollary of this right is that private parties have responsibilities in EU law for which they can be held liable in national courts if they fail to discharge them.

In terms of developing individual EU rights, this judgment can be viewed very positively. In a market economy, most violations of legal actors' rights are committed not by the Member State but by other private parties. Discrimination on grounds of gender is a case in point. It is both egregious and a long-standing problem in workplaces, the majority of which are in the private sector. At the beginning of this chapter, however, we noted that the story of direct effect was not just one about rights but also about the reorganisation of legal power. Private litigation allows EU law to be deployed in a much wider array of disputes, and, in turn, this provides more opportunities for private parties to challenge national law as they can now do this not only formally seeking judicial review but by saying it does not govern the legal dispute between them and another private party.

This was all too much for the British and Irish Governments. They argued, shamefully, that to allow the principle of equal pay for men and women for work of equal value to be invoked in national courts would lead to an unmanageable disruption of economic life. The Irish Government argued that the costs of compliance would exceed Irish receipts from the European Regional Development Fund for the period 1975–77 and the British Government argued that it would add 3.5 per cent to labour costs: a considerable admission!

Case 43/75 *Defrenne v Sabena (No. 2)* [1976] ECR 455

69. The Governments of Ireland and the United Kingdom have drawn the Court's attention to the possible economic consequences of attributing direct effect to the provisions of Article [157 TFEU], on the ground that such a decision might, in many branches of economic life, result in the introduction of claims dating back to the time at which such effect came into existence.

70. In view of the large number of people concerned such claims, which undertakings could not have foreseen, might seriously affect the financial situation of such undertakings and even drive some of them to bankruptcy.

71. Although the practical consequences of any judicial decision must be carefully taken into account, it would be impossible to go so far as to diminish the objectivity of the law and compromise its future application on the ground of the possible repercussions which might result, as regards the past, from such a judicial decision.

72. However, in the light of the conduct of several of the Member States … it is appropriate to take exceptionally into account the fact that, over a prolonged period, the parties concerned have been led to continue with practices which were contrary to Article [157 TFEU], although not yet prohibited under their national law …

74. In these circumstances, it is appropriate to determine that, as the general level at which pay would have been fixed cannot be known, important considerations of legal certainty affecting all the interests involved, both public and private, make it impossible in principle to reopen the question as regards the past.

75. Therefore, the direct effect of Article [157 TFEU] cannot be relied on in order to support claims concerning pay periods prior to the date of this judgment, except as regards those workers who have already brought legal proceedings or made an equivalent claim.

The Court of Justice gave here what is known as a prospective ruling. To manage the consequences of departing so far from Member State expectations, it had to grant Article 157 TFEU two meanings. For discrimination occurring prior to the date of the judgment, the provision is interpreted as not being directly effective. The opposite is true for discrimination which occurs after the date of the judgment. The symbolism of this is considerable. As Rasmussen has observed, these two interpretations destroy the illusion that the Court is engaging in a neutral exercise of merely giving life to the text. It is impossible 'to maintain this myth while ruling that Article [157] was deprived of direct effects until the day of pronouncement of the Court's decision; only to produce such effects from that day onwards'.[11]

4 DIRECT EFFECT AND THE DEVELOPMENT OF EU REMEDIES AND PROCEDURES

Although direct effect refers only to the right to invoke a provision in a national court, this would be less meaningful if remedies did not follow from its successful invocation. Indeed, the ethos of the Lisbon Treaty was that EU rights should give rise to sufficient remedies to secure protection of those rights.

---

[11] H. Rasmussen, *On Law and Policy in the European Court of Justice* (Dordrecht, Martinus Nijhoff, 1986) 441.

Article 19(1) TEU

1. Member States shall provide remedies sufficient to ensure effective legal protection in the fields covered by Union law.

However, how would such a system of remedies be instigated? Full protection of EU rights, taken to its conclusion, might require a system of pan-Union remedies, procedures and pan-Union enforcement machinery to secure such protection. In short, the Union would have to establish its own system of administrative justice. This is not only impracticable but would draw EU law into difficult and sensitive questions about the scale and type of interest to be protected and compensated, which might include how long a claim can stand open, the types of loss which can be compensated, the level of responsibility for open-ended losses and the types of non-pecuniary remedy which could be required. These raise difficult distributive questions which are addressed differently across the Union.

This tension between the need to secure effective legal protection and the impossibility of constructing a comprehensive pan-Union machinery of redress was broached first in *Rewe*. Rewe, a trader, claimed a refund for charges unlawfully levied by the German authorities for health inspections on fruit and vegetables. The German authorities argued that the limitation period had passed and Rewe would not have been able to claim a refund if the measure had breached an equivalent domestic law.

Case 33/76 *Rewe–Zentralfinanz and others* v *Landwirtschaftskammer für das Saarland* [1976] ECR 1989

5. The prohibition(s) ... have a direct effect and confer on citizens rights which the national courts are required to protect.

   Applying the principle of cooperation laid down in Article [4(3) TEU], it is the national courts which are entrusted with ensuring the legal protection which citizens derive from the direct effect of the provisions of Community law.

   Accordingly, in the absence of Community rules on this subject, it is for the domestic legal system of each Member State to designate the courts having jurisdiction and to determine the procedural conditions governing actions at law intended to ensure the protection of the rights which citizens have from the direct effect of Community law, it being understood that such conditions cannot be less favourable than those relating to similar actions of a domestic nature.

   Where necessary ... the Treaty enable[s] appropriate measures to be taken to remedy differences between the provisions laid down by law, regulation or administrative action in Member States if they are likely to distort or harm the functioning of the common market.

   In the absence of such measures of harmonization the right conferred by Community law must be exercised before the national courts in accordance with the conditions laid down by national rules.

   The position would be different only if the conditions and time-limits made it impossible in practice to exercise the rights which the national courts are obliged to protect. This is not the case where reasonable periods of limitation of actions are fixed. The laying down of such time-limits with regard to actions of a fiscal nature is an application of the fundamental principle of legal certainty protecting both the tax-payer and the administration concerned.

On the one hand, *Rewe* argues for national procedural autonomy by stating that the question of remedies for violation of directly effective rights is one for the national legal system subject to these being no less favourable than for those relating to equivalent domestic claims. On the other hand, the requirement that national procedures and remedies should not make it practically impossible to exercise EU rights pushes for the development of a Union system of remedies even where it is not available in other domestic cases. It sets a minimum standard of protection which all domestic systems must meet, and, therefore, provides for some harmonisation of domestic remedies and procedures.

This tension has led to a differentiated approach in EU law. In some fields, indeed most, EU law leaves it almost entirely for national law to determine the remedies and procedures for the protection of direct effective provisions subject to some loose constraints and oversight. On some issues, EU law provides its own pan-Union remedies and procedures.

(i) Union oversight of local remedies in domestic courts

The default position for remedies and procedures surrounding the invocation of EU law rights before domestic courts is that these should 'not be less favourable than those governing similar domestic situations (principle of equivalence) and... not render impossible in practice or excessively difficult the exercise of rights'.[12] The equivalence principle is the less contentious of these two principles. The question of whether a domestic measure is equivalent to an EU measure is one for the national court, which must look to the purpose and essential characteristics of each law to see if this is the case.[13] If the measures are equivalent, a remedy or procedure available for the domestic law must also be available for the EU law equivalent. However, if there is a particularly strong public interest protected by EU law, a particular remedy or procedure can be required for its breach whereas it is optional for the equivalent domestic law. In *Brusse and Garabito* v *Jahani*, action was taken under a contract against two residential tenants for €13,897, of which only €5,366 was unpaid rent.[14] Under Dutch law a court can consider of its own motion, if it so wishes, whether a contractual term is unduly onerous. Directive 93/13/EEC on unfair terms in contracts states that such terms are not binding on consumers (which the tenants were in this case). The Court of Justice noted the importance of this consumer protection. As a consequence, it ruled, the Dutch court had not merely a discretion, but a duty to consider of its own motion whether the contract term was unfair.

The question of when domestic processes or remedies render exercise of EU rights impossible or excessively difficult is more intricate. Since the Treaty of Lisbon, this has been increasingly interpreted through the prism of Article 47 of the European Union Charter of Fundamental Rights (EUCFR).

---

[12] Case C-603/10 *Pelati*, Judgment of 18 October 2012.
[13] Case C-261/95 *Palmisani* v *INPS* [1997] ECR I-4025; Case C-329/96 *Levez* v *Jennings* [1998] ECR I-7835; Case C-246/09 *Bulicke* v *Deutsche Büro Service* [2010] ECR I-7003.
[14] Case C-488/11 *Brusse and Garabito* v *Jahani*, Judgment of 30 May 2013.

Article 47 EUCFR

Everyone whose rights and freedoms guaranteed by the law of the Union are violated has the right to an effective remedy before a tribunal in compliance with the conditions laid down in this Article.

Everyone is entitled to a fair and public hearing within a reasonable time by an independent and impartial tribunal previously established by law. Everyone shall have the possibility of being advised, defended and represented.

Legal aid shall be made available to those who lack sufficient resources in so far as such aid is necessary to ensure effective access to justice.

This Article extends EU legal scrutiny of national courts beyond questions of protection of rights and reparation to wider issues of due process and administration of justice. These play out differently with regard to remedies, procedural rules and limitation periods.

On remedies, the Court has said very little except where a Member State limits the level or type of compensation in an *a priori* way. National measures which cap compensation at very low levels are illegal,[15] as are those which provide for only nominal compensation with no regard to the damage sustained.[16] Similarly, Member States are not allowed to prevent compensation for certain types of damage, notably economic loss.[17]

It has been more extensive on procedures. Relying on the principle of effective judicial protection, the Court of Justice has insisted that Member States cannot screen off certain sectors, such as the military, from judicial review if their activities give rise to EU law rights.[18] Alongside this, there are positive duties on Member States to ensure that any professional, regulatory or administrative body which takes decisions affecting EU law rights is subject to judicial review. Furthermore, reasons for its decision must be accessible to enable both the person concerned to defend their rights with full knowledge of the relevant facts and effective judicial review of the lawfulness of the decision.[19] More broadly, although the modalities are a matter for the domestic legal standing, it must afford parties standing wherever directly effective rights have been infringed. In *Unibet*, Swedish authorities obtained injunctions and initiated criminal proceedings against parties providing advertising space to Unibet, a British Internet gambling company, whose activities contravened Swedish law. No action was brought against Unibet itself. Unibet, therefore, brought an action for a declaration that the Swedish law violated Article 56 TFEU, which provides for the right to provide services in another Member State. In Swedish law, no possibility exists for a self-standing action for a declaration that a Swedish statute is illegal. Swedish law did provide for the possibility for Unibet to sue the authorities for damages and to seek an exception from the authorities from the gambling restrictions. It could, in turn, challenge a refusal to grant such an exception before a Swedish court. The Swedish court asked whether these were sufficient for effective judicial protection of EU rights or whether a new independent action needed to be created.

---

[15] Case C-271/91 *Marshall* v *Southampton and South-West Hampshire AHA (No. 2)* [1993] ECR I-4367.

[16] Case 14/83 *Von Colson and Kamann* v *Land Nordrhein-Westfalen* [1984] ECR 1891.

[17] Joined Cases C-46/93 and C-48/93 *Brasserie du Pêcheur* v *Germany* and *R* v *Secretary of State for Transport ex parte Factortame (No. 3)* [1996] ECR I-1029.

[18] Case 222/84 *Johnston* v *Chief Constable of the Royal Ulster Constabulary* [1986] ECR 1651.

[19] Joined Cases C-372/09 and C-373/09 *Peñarroja Fa* [2011] ECR I-1785; Case C-300/11 *ZZ* v *Secretary of State for the Home Department*, Judgment of 4 June 2013.

Case C–432/05 *Unibet* v *Justitiekanslern* [2007] ECR I–2271

37. It is to be noted at the outset that, according to settled case-law, the principle of effective judicial protection is a general principle of Community law stemming from the constitutional traditions common to the Member States, which has been enshrined in Articles 6 and 13 of the European Convention for the Protection of Human Rights and Fundamental Freedoms ... and which has also been reaffirmed by Article 47 of the Charter of Fundamental Rights of the European Union ...

40. Although the EC Treaty has made it possible in a number of instances for private persons to bring a direct action, where appropriate, before the Community Court, it was not intended to create new remedies in the national courts to ensure the observance of Community law other than those already laid down by national law ...

41. It would be otherwise only if it were apparent from the overall scheme of the national legal system in question that no legal remedy existed which made it possible to ensure, even indirectly, respect for an individual's rights under Community law ...

42. Thus, while it is, in principle, for national law to determine an individual's standing and legal interest in bringing proceedings, Community law nevertheless requires that the national legislation does not undermine the right to effective judicial protection ...

54. In that regard, each case which raises the question whether a national procedural provision renders the application of Community law impossible or excessively difficult must be analysed by reference to the role of that provision in the procedure, its progress and its special features, viewed as a whole, before the various national instances ...

55. It is apparent from the order for reference that Swedish law does not prevent a person, such as Unibet, from disputing the compatibility of national legislation, such as the Law on Lotteries, with Community law but that, on the contrary, there exist various indirect legal remedies for that purpose.

56. Thus, firstly, the Högsta domstolen states that Unibet may obtain an examination of whether the Law on Lotteries is compatible with Community law in the context of a claim for damages before the ordinary courts.

57. It is also clear from the order for reference that Unibet brought such a claim and that the Högsta domstolen found it to be admissible.

58. Consequently, where an examination of the compatibility of the Law on Lotteries with Community law takes place in the context of the determination of a claim for damages, that action constitutes a remedy which enables Unibet to ensure effective protection of the rights conferred on it by Community law.

59. It is for the Högsta domstolen to ensure that the examination of the compatibility of that law with Community law takes place irrespective of the assessment of the merits of the case with regard to the requirements for damage and a causal link in the claim for damages.

60. Secondly, the Högsta domstolen adds that, if Unibet applied to the Swedish Government for an exception to the prohibition on the promotion of its services in Sweden, any decision rejecting that application could be the subject of judicial review proceedings before the Regeringsrätten, in which Unibet would be able to argue that the provisions of the Law on Lotteries are incompatible with Community law. Where appropriate, the competent court would be required to disapply the provisions of that law that were considered to be in conflict with Community law.

61. It is to be noted that such judicial review proceedings, which would enable Unibet to obtain a judicial decision that those provisions are incompatible with Community law, constitute a legal remedy securing effective judicial protection of its rights under Community law ...

62. Moreover, the Högsta domstolen states that if Unibet disregarded the provisions of the Law on Lotteries and administrative action or criminal proceedings were brought against it by the competent national authorities, it would have the opportunity, in proceedings brought before the administrative court or an ordinary court, to dispute the compatibility of those provisions with Community law. Where appropriate, the competent court would be required to disapply the provisions of that law that were considered to be in conflict with Community law. ...

64. In any event, it is clear from paragraphs 56 to 61 above that Unibet must be regarded as having available to it legal remedies which ensure effective judicial protection of its rights under Community law. If, on the contrary, as mentioned at paragraph 62 above, it was forced to be subject to administrative or criminal proceedings and to any penalties that may result as the sole form of legal remedy for disputing the compatibility of the national provision at issue with Community law, that would not be sufficient to secure for it such effective judicial protection.

The right to effective judicial protection is not concerned solely with the possibility of securing a party's presence in court. In *Unibet*, the possibility of this as a consequence of prosecution was not sufficient to establish effective judicial protection (paragraphs 62 and 64). Its meaning is more substantial. Right-holders must have the possibility to bring matters before the court themselves. This entitles them to bring their action before a single court for a single claim rather than to bring different elements of it before different courts.[20] Once there, the court must also allow them full due process in the pleading of their EU law rights. Parties must be given a genuine opportunity to raise pleas based on EU law before national courts;[21] sufficient opportunity to enable them to comment effectively on any evidence[22] or any point raised by the court of its own motion;[23] sufficient time to prepare their defence, and protection from abusive use of the litigation process by their adversaries.[24]

Access to a court will be impossible if individuals cannot afford the costs of litigation. In this regard, the last sentence of Article 47 EUCFR requires that legal aid be made available for those who wish to litigate their EU rights. The extent of this duty was considered in *DEB*. A Germany company sued the German Government for late transposition of Directive 98/30/EC on securing the single market in gas, which prevented it from bidding for access to the German gas network. It claimed as a result that it had foregone profits of over €3 billion. DEB, however, was a paper company. It had no employees, assets or liabilities. To bring the action, it was asked to make an advance on court costs of over €274,000. It did not have the money for this. It was refused legal aid on the grounds that this was not offered to companies and there was insufficient public interest in the litigation. It claimed that this violated the principle of effective judicial protection.

---

[20] Case C-268/06 *Impact* v *MAFF* [2008] ECR I-2483.

[21] Joined Cases C-222–225/05 *Van der Weerd* v *Minister van Landbouw, Natuur en Voedselkwaliteit* [2007] ECR I-4233.

[22] Case C-276/01 *Steffenson* [2003] ECR I-3735.

[23] Case C-472/11 *Banif Plus Bank* v *Csipai*, Judgment of 21 February 2013.

[24] Case C-443/03 *Leffler* v *Berlin Chemie* [2005] ECR I-9611.

Case C-279/09 *DEB* [2010] ECR I-13849

59. ... the principle of effective judicial protection, as enshrined in Article 47 of the Charter, must be interpreted as meaning that it is not impossible for legal persons to rely on that principle and that aid granted pursuant to that principle may cover, inter alia, dispensation from advance payment of the costs of proceedings and/or the assistance of a lawyer.

60. In that connection, it is for the national court to ascertain whether the conditions for granting legal aid constitute a limitation on the right of access to the courts which undermines the very core of that right; whether they pursue a legitimate aim; and whether there is a reasonable relationship of proportionality between the means employed and the legitimate aim which it is sought to achieve.

61. In making that assessment, the national court must take into consideration the subject-matter of the litigation; whether the applicant has a reasonable prospect of success; the importance of what is at stake for the applicant in the proceedings; the complexity of the applicable law and procedure; and the applicant's capacity to represent himself effectively. In order to assess the proportionality, the national court may also take account of the amount of the costs of the proceedings in respect of which advance payment must be made and whether or not those costs might represent an insurmountable obstacle to access to the courts.

62. With regard more specifically to legal persons, the national court may take account of their situation. The court may therefore take into consideration, inter alia, the form of the legal person in question and whether it is profit-making or non-profit-making; the financial capacity of the partners or shareholders; and the ability of those partners or shareholders to obtain the sums necessary to institute legal proceedings.

DEB indicates the challenges of securing protection of EU rights. It can also involve charged assessments of which litigation may be privileged and which will not. In *DEB*, therefore, the Court of Justice required Member States to hold out the possibility of legal aid for companies: something controversial in many societies where many poor individuals do not even get that opportunity. Furthermore, if one looks at the factors to be taken account in granting legal aid in paragraph 61, only a few go directly to whether the litigant would otherwise be able to bring the case but most go rather to other questions, such as the complexity and importance of the case and the nature of the subject matter of the litigation. These issues, in turn, determine which EU rights should receive support at the expense of other rights: a necessarily contentious question.[25]

Limitation periods and other forms of temporal restriction bar a litigant from pursuing their rights if the matter is not brought within a stipulated period of time. If they deny pursuit of these rights, they are also a perennial feature of legal systems by dint of the need to secure legal certainty, and to protect people from continually worrying about historic claims.

Reasonable limitation periods may be set.[26] The Court of Justice's understanding of what is 'reasonable' grants, however, considerable leeway to national systems. Sixty days to bring civil proceedings before a court has been held not to be too short.[27] Indeed, it seems even shorter

---

[25] These criteria have been reaffirmed in Case C-260/11 *R* v *Environment Agency ex parte Edwards and Pallikaropoulos*, Judgment of 11 April 2013.

[26] Case C-261/95 *Palmisani* v *INPS* [1997] ECR I-4025.

[27] Case C-40/08 *Asturcom Telecomunicaciones* v *Rodríguez Nogueira* [2009] ECR I-9579.

periods may not be deemed to be unreasonable. A thirty-day period to claim a tax advantage from the Slovenian tax authorities was considered fine, albeit that the limitation applied to bringing the matter before the administration rather than the judiciary.[28] The most draconian example, however, was *Samba Diouf*, in which the Court held that a period of only fifteen days for asylum seekers to appeal to court against an administrative decision refusing asylum was not a denial of justice.[29] As a mistake may go to whether that person may be killed on their return or not, this appears very short indeed. Equally important to the Court's decision is whether the individual was in a position to ascertain their rights from the moment from which the limitation period begins to run.[30] Limitation periods beginning from the day on which an anti-competitive practice is adopted might be unreasonable.[31] Similarly, in the case of people employed on a series of short-term contracts, the limitation period must begin from the end of the relationship and not from the end of each of these contracts.[32] Related to this, the Court will also look at whether individuals did not bring a claim within the required time because of unconscionable behaviour by the defendant,[33] or the Member State,[34] which induced them to defer their action.

Requirements may also be made of claimants to mitigate or exercise due diligence to avoid the loss.[35] This stipulation of due diligence requires parties to use all legal remedies available to them before claiming for loss unless it would be excessively difficult or it would not be reasonable to ask this of them.[36] An example of when this might be the case occurred in *Fuß*.[37] Fuß worked for the Halle town fire service in Germany. In December 2006, he requested that he not be required to work longer than forty hours per week as this breached EU law. He was transferred to another department shortly afterwards. He claimed for the longer hours that he had worked prior to December 2006. Under German law, there was a requirement of good faith which only allowed such a claim if the claimant had first approached the employer. The Court of Justice observed that this was unreasonable here. Employees were weaker parties in an employment relationship who were well aware that such an approach might result in negative treatment by the employer, as appeared to be the case here.

(ii) EU law procedures and remedies in national courts

There are four circumstances when EU law requires particular remedies to be provided in national courts:

---

[28] Case C-603/10 *Pelati*, Judgment of 18 October 2012.

[29] Case C-69/10 *Samba Diouf* v *Ministre du Travail, de l'Emploi et de l'Immigration* [2011] ECR I-7151.

[30] If the law is very unclear, this might affect when a limitation period starts. It is not necessary that there be a prior judgment clarifying the situation. Case C-452/09 *Iaia and others* v *Ministero dell'Istruzione* [2011] ECR I-4043.

[31] Joined Cases C-295/04–298/04 *Manfredi* v *Lloyd Adriatico Assicurazioni* [2006] ECR I-6619.

[32] Case C-78/98 *Preston* v *Wolverhampton Health Care Trust* [2000] ECR I-3201.

[33] In *Levez*, an employer led a female employee to believe the disparity in pay between her and a male counterpart was less than it was leading her to abstain from action, Case C-326/96 *Levez* v *Jennings* [1998] ECR I-7835. The unconscionable behaviour can be a failure to act such as an illegal failure to tell consumers about their contractual rights, Case C-481/99 *Heininger* [2001] ECR I-9945.

[34] Case C-327/00 *Santex* v *Unità Socio Sanitaria Locale no. 42 di Pavia* [2003] ECR I-1877; Case C-241/06 *Lämmerzahl* [2007] ECR I-8415.

[35] Joined Cases C-46/93 and C-48/93 *Brasserie du Pêcheur* v *Germany* [1996] ECR I-1029; Joined Cases C-95/07 and C-96/07 *Ecotrade* v *Agenzia delle Entrate – Ufficio di Genova 3* [2008] ECR I-3457.

[36] Case C-445/06 *Danske Slagterier* v *Germany* [2009] ECR I-2119.

[37] Case C-429/09 *Fuß* v *Stadt Halle* [2010] ECR I-12167.

- the principle of Member State liability which allows individuals, under certain circumstances, to sue Member States for loss suffered as a result of the latter's breach of EU law;
- repayment of charges or taxes levied in breach of directly effective EU law;
- damages and repayment for breaches of EU competition law;
- interim relief where a national court wishes to make a preliminary reference to the Court of Justice.[38]

Member State liability is a self-standing procedure, conceptually distinct from direct effect, which is dealt with later in the chapter.[39] The second and third types of remedy are restitutionary in nature. At their heart lies the idea that a party should not be enriched as a result of illegal behaviour, and that to allow this would be a denial of other parties' directly effective rights. Interim relief emerged out of a concern to secure the effective operation of the preliminary reference procedure.

Repayment of charges or taxes levied contrary to EU law was considered in *San Giorgio*.[40] The Italian State had levied charges for health inspections contrary to EU law. Under Italian law, no repayment of illegal tax occurred where the sums involved had been passed on to other persons, typically through higher pricing. Although the facts were similar to those in *Rewe*, the Court of Justice used different reasoning. It found the entitlement to repayment of charges levied contrary to EU law was 'a consequence of, and an adjunct to, the rights' conferred by EU law. Whilst the Court created some leeway for the national system by providing that it was for it to determine when taxes have been passed on, a concrete remedy, namely, the right to restitution of illegally levied taxes, had been put in place. In subsequent years, the Court has extended this remedy.[41] It applies not just to taxes levied by the Member State, but to taxes and charges levied by public bodies,[42] illegal requirements to pay tax in advance[43] and levying of guarantees in breach of EU law.[44] The conditions for non-repayment have also become highly circumscribed. If charges or taxes have only been partially passed on to other persons, the national authority can only refuse to repay that part which has not been passed on.[45] To determine the amount, national courts must engage in economic analysis, as the degree of enrichment will be affected not just by the increase in price but also by possible declines in volumes of sales as a result of that increase.[46] Finally, the Court has touched on the level of compensation that may be levied. It has ruled that complainants are entitled not only to repayment of the tax, but also to compensation for any losses which accrued as a result of not having this revenue available to them.[47] As a consequence, Member States are also obliged to pay interest on these losses.[48]

---

[38] This last remedy is explored in more detail at pp. 196–7.   [39] See pp. 325–35.

[40] Case 199/82 *Amministrazione delle Finanze dello Stato* v *San Giorgio* [1983] ECR 3595.

[41] P. Wattel, 'National Procedural Autonomy and the Effectiveness of EC Law: Challenge the Charge, File for Restitution, Sue for Damages?' (2008) 35/2 *LIEI* 109.

[42] Case C-242/95 *GT-Link* v *DSB* [1997] ECR I-4449.

[43] Joined Cases C-397/98 and C-410/98 *Metallgesellschaft* v *IRC* [2001] ECR I-1727. Case C-446/04 *Test Claimants in the FII Group Litigation* v *Commissioners of Inland Revenue* [2006] ECR I-11753.

[44] Case C-470/04 *N* v *Inspecteur van de Belastingdienst Oost/kantoor Almelo* [2006] ECR I-7409.

[45] Joined Cases C-192/95–218/95 *Comateb and others* [1997] ECR I-165.

[46] Case C-147/01 *Weber's Wine World and others* [2003] ECR I-11365; Case C-309/06 *Marks & Spencer* v *CCE* [2008] ECR I-2283.

[47] Joined Cases C-397/98 and C-410/98 *Metallgesellschaft* v *IRC* [2001] ECR I-1727; Case C-446/04 *Test Claimants in the FII Group Litigation* v *Commissioners of Inland Revenue* [2006] ECR I-11753.

[48] Case C-565/11 *Irimie* v *Administraia Finan elor Publice Sibiu*, Judgment of 18 April 2013.

In the case of remedies in the field of competition, the Court of Justice has ruled that contracts which breach Article 101 TFEU, the provision prohibiting anti-competitive conduct by two or more parties, allow individuals to claim damages where they can show that there is a direct causal link between the harm suffered and the illegal conduct or contract.[49] Similar reasoning operates in the field of state aids. If a national court finds that unlawful aid has been paid to an undertaking by a national authority, it must order repayment of that aid as it is under a duty to provide protection to individuals against illegal state aids.[50] This reasoning follows a parallel reasoning to that in cases concerning illegally levied taxes. In addition to wishing to secure the full effect of the provisions, the Court does not wish to see the unjust enrichment of those who have benefited from illegal conduct.[51]

The final remedy is the grant of interim relief. In *Factortame*, the Court of Justice stated that interim relief had to be granted where this was necessary to secure the full effectiveness of judgments on EU law.[52] In *Factortame*, the interim relief was sought pending a preliminary reference to the Court. It was required, partly, to secure its own prerogatives. There is, however, now a duty on national courts to grant interim relief even in cases which involve no reference, where a failure to do otherwise would imperil the full effectiveness of the final decision. In *Aziz*,[53] a Spanish bank started enforcement proceedings to secure title on Mr Aziz's family home as a result of his failure to meet his mortgage payments. He subsequently claimed that a number of terms in the mortgage contract were unfair under the Unfair Contract Terms Directive, and therefore void. The Spanish court at the initial hearing did not have the power to stay the mortgage proceedings if this was the case, however. Once title had reverted to the vendors, moreover, it could not easily be transferred back to Mr Aziz. The Court of Justice held that interim relief had to be available in such a case as the Spanish court had to be able to secure the full effect of its final decision, which might, in this case, involve holding the mortgage term to be unfair and, therefore, upholding Mr Aziz's right to remain there.

Both *Factortame* and *Aziz* are vague about when interim relief should be granted, suggesting that it should happen whenever the effectiveness of EU law is being undermined. A different set of principles apply when relief is sought against a national law implementing an EU measure.[54] In such circumstances, the challenge is seen as being, in reality, against the EU measure. Relief will only be granted if there is serious and irreparable damage to the applicant and this must be weighed against other considerations such as the damage to the EU legal order and its financial interests. From the perspective of two litigants, whose interests have been damaged equally, this difference seems perverse.[55]

---

[49] Case C-453/99 *Courage v Crehan* [2001] ECR I-6297; Joined Cases C-295/04–298/04 *Manfredi v Lloyd Adriatico Assicurazioni* [2006] ECR I-6619. However, information may be withheld from a litigant where it was obtained as part of a leniency programme whereby a cartel participant blew the whistle on a cartel in exchange for immunity. The interests involved must be weighed up on a case-by-case basis, Case C-360/09 *Pfleiderer v Bundeskartellamt* [2011] ECR I-5161; Case C-536/11 *Bundeswettbewerbsbehörde v Donau Chemie*, Judgment of 6 June 2013.

[50] Case C-39/94 *SFEI* [1996] ECR I-3547; Case C-71/04 *Xunta de Galicia* [2005] ECR I-7419.

[51] Case C-354/90 *FNCE* [1991] ECR I-5505.

[52] Case C-213/89 *R v Secretary of State for Transport ex parte Factortame Ltd* [1990] ECR I-2433.

[53] Case C-415/11 *Aziz v Catalunyacaixa*, Judgment of 14 March 2013.

[54] Joined Cases 143/88 and C-92/89 *Zuckerfabrik Süderdithmarschen and Zuckerfabrik Soest* [1991] ECR I-415; Case C-465/93 *Atlanta Fruchthandelsgesellschaft and others (No. 1)* [1995] ECR I-3761; Case C-68/95 *T. Port* [1996] ECR I-6065; Joined Cases C-453/03, C-11/04, C-12/04 and C-194/04 *Martini v Ministero delle Politiche Agricole e Forestali* [2005] ECR I-10423.

[55] This is particularly the case where EU law gives national authorities a choice and the arguments about uniformity do not seem to apply.

After *Factortame*, it looked for a while as if the Court of Justice might be moving to developing a fully-fledged system of EU remedies on the grounds that this was necessary to secure the full effect of EU law.[56] This has not happened in recent years. The four sets of pan-Union remedies granted remain quite confined. The moment of truth was, in many ways, *Unibet*. The Court was offered the possibility to develop a pan-Union remedy or to stick with the elaborate procedures provided by the national system. It chose the latter. With the exception of the limited instances described above, EU law accepts that the development of remedies and procedures to secure EU rights direct effect is overwhelmingly for the national legal system. The Union will intervene only if there has been a severe failure of protection by the domestic system or a sense that individuals with EU law rights are not receiving the same treatment as those with domestic law rights.

5 DIRECT EFFECT AND EU SECONDARY LEGISLATION

The vast bulk of EU law is secondary legislation.[57] It was not surprising, therefore, that, after the end of the transitional period, the question arose as to whether the different types of secondary legislation were capable of direct effect. The most straightforward case was that of Regulations. Deemed to have general application, be binding and directly applicable in all Member States, Regulations are the closest thing the Union has to domestic statutes.[58] They were therefore held to be capable of direct effect in the same way as Treaty provisions in the early 1970s.[59] International agreements with non-EU states have also been held to be capable of direct effect. This will not be the case with all international agreements, however. The test is a two-tier one.[60] First, the wording, nature and purpose of the agreement is compared, with some international agreements considered incapable of generating direct effect simply by virtue of their overall framework being too flexible and open-ended. Secondly, the specific provision is considered in the light of this. Only if it is sufficiently precise and unconditional will it be directly effective.

(i) Direct effect of Directives

Directives are arguably the legislative instrument used most often for politically significant and controversial issues. This is reflected in their only being binding upon Member States as to the result to be achieved but leaving discretion to these over how to realise this. This feature

---

[56] On the debates see D. Curtin and K. Mortelmans, 'Application and Enforcement of Community Law by the Member States: Actors in Search of a Third Generation Script' in D. Curtin and T. Heukels (eds.), *Institutional Dynamics of European Integration* (The Hague, Martijnus Nijhoff, 1994); T. Tridimas, 'Black, White and Shades of Grey: Horizontality of Directives Revisited' (2002) 21 *YBEL* 327; K. Lenaerts and T. Corthaut, 'Of Birds and Hedges: The Role of Primacy in Invoking Norms of EU Law' (2006) 31 *ELRev.* 287; M. Dougan, 'When Worlds Collide: Competing Visions of the Relationship Between Direct Effect and Supremacy' (2007) 44 *CMLRev.* 931.

[57] The different types of secondary legislation have been considered in Chapter 3. See pp. 111–12.

[58] J. Winter, 'Direct Effect and Direct Applicability: Two Distinct and Different Concepts in Community Law' (1972) 9 *CMLRev.* 425.

[59] Case 93/71 *Leonesio* v *Italian Ministry of Agriculture* [1972] ECR 293; Case 39/72 *Commission* v *Italy* [1973] ECR 101. Regulations will come into effect twenty days after publication in the Official Journal or on the date stipulated in the Regulation, Article 297 TFEU.

[60] Case 104/81 *Hauptzollamt Mainz* v *Kupferberg* [1982] ECR 3641; Case 12/86 *Demirel* v *Stadt Schwäbisch* [1987] ECR 2719.

has complicated debates about whether they should generate individual rights. A number of objections could be made against their being capable of direct effect:

- The discretion granted to Member States to implement Directives should result in individuals being able to derive rights only from the acts of national authorities themselves, and not from the Directives themselves.
- To grant direct effect to Directives would blur the distinction between Directives and Regulations, a distinction clearly spelt out in Article 288 TFEU, as both would have similar legal effects.
- In numerous fields, the Union enjoys a competence to adopt Directives but not Regulations and granting full direct effect to Directives would allow the Union to generate legal obligations through the backdoor in fields that the Treaty had not permitted through the front.[61]

Notwithstanding these arguments, the Court of Justice ruled in *Van Duyn* that Directives could generate direct effect.[62] Van Duyn was refused leave to enter the United Kingdom in order to take up an offer of a secretarial post at the Church of Scientology, as the UK Government had imposed a ban on foreign scientologists entering the United Kingdom. She challenged the ban on the grounds, inter alia, that it breached Directive 64/221/EEC, which required that any ban be based upon the personal conduct of the individual. The Court of Justice considered that her association with the Church of Scientology met the requirements of the Directive. However, prior to that, it considered whether the Directive was capable of direct effect.

Case 41/74 *Van Duyn* v *Home Office* [1974] ECR 1337

12. ... It would be incompatible with the binding effect attributed to a Directive by Article [288 TFEU] to exclude, in principle, the possibility that the obligation which it imposes may be invoked by those concerned. In particular, where the Community authorities have, by Directive, imposed on Member States the obligation to pursue a particular course of conduct, the useful effect of such an act would be weakened if individuals were prevented from relying on it before their national courts and if the latter were prevented from taking it into consideration as an element of Community law. Article [267 TFEU], which empowers national courts to refer to the Court questions concerning the validity and interpretation of all acts of the Community institutions, without distinction, implies furthermore that these acts may be invoked by individuals in the national courts. It is necessary to examine, in every case, whether the nature, general scheme and wording of the provisions in question are capable of having direct effects on the relations between Member States and individuals.

This reasoning is remarkably weak. It starts from an *a contrario* position as to whether there is any good reason why Directives should not have direct effect. The arguments that their binding nature and their effectiveness require that they be invoked in national courts are simply *non sequiturs*. Put simply, neither of these qualities prescribes the types

---

[61] On this debate see S. Prechal, *Directives in European Community Law: A Study of Directives and their Enforcement in National Courts* (2nd edn, Oxford, Oxford University Press, 2005) 216–20.

[62] Decisions have also been held, on similar grounds, to be capable of bearing direct effect: see Case 9/70 *Grad* v *Finanzamt Traustein* [1970] ECR 838.

of effects Directives should have in a domestic legal system. Indeed, no less a figure than Federico Mancini, a former judge at the Court of Justice, has admitted that 'this judgment goes beyond the letter of Article [288 TFEU]', the provision that sets out the central characteristics of Regulations and Directives.[63] More significantly, the ruling provoked a strong counter-reaction from both French and German courts. The French Conseil d'État, the highest administrative law court in France, and the Bundesfinanzhof, the highest tax court in Germany, both refused to accord Directives direct effect when provisions were invoked before them.[64]

The Court of Justice resorted, therefore, to a new justification for Directives, which distinguished both the reasons for their having direct effect and the quality of that direct effect from other EU legal instruments. This was the estoppel argument. The estoppel argument reasons that, as Member States have a duty to secure the legal regime set out in the Directive by a certain date, it would be wrong for these to gain advantage through their failure to carry this out. They are thus estopped from denying the direct effect of Directives once the time limit for their implementation into national law has expired. In *Ratti*,[65] a trader was prosecuted for not labelling his solvents in accordance with Italian law. He sought to rely upon two Directives. While the transitional period for one of these had expired, it had not for the other. The Court held that he could rely only upon the first Directive. The Member State was estopped by its failure to take the necessary implementing measures from denying this Directive's direct effect. The other Directive was not directly effective, however, as the Member State was still within its period of grace. Directives will be directly effective, therefore, only from the end of the transposition period and, even then, will be capable of direct effect only if the Member State has failed to implement them or has not implemented them correctly. Where Directives are correctly implemented, individual rights flow from the national implementing provisions and not from the Directives themselves.

The estoppel argument has an important implication. As the direct effect of Directives is predicated on the 'fault' of the Member State, parties may invoke Directives against the Member State. It does not follow that parties may invoke Directives in national legal proceedings against other private parties as these have no duties to transpose the Directive into national law, and, thus, are not at 'fault' if this does not take place. In other words, the estoppel argument may be used to justify the vertical direct effect of Directives, but not their horizontal direct effect. This limitation was set out in *Marshall*. Marshall, a dietician employed by a British health authority, was dismissed at the age of 62 on the ground that she had passed the pensionable age, which was, at that time, 60 years for women. A man would not have been dismissed at that age, but Marshall had no redress as British law excluded contractual conditions relating to death and retirement from equal opportunities law. She claimed a breach of article 5 of the Equal Treatment Directive 76/207/EEC, which provides for equal treatment for men and women concerning *all* terms and conditions of dismissal, including when this occurred because an employee had reached pensionable age.

---

[63] G. Mancini and D. Keeling, 'Language, Culture and Politics in the Life of the European Court of Justice' (1995) 1 *CJEL* 397, 401.

[64] *Minister of the Interior* v *Cohn-Bendit* [1980] 1 CMLR 543; *Re Value Added Tax Directives* [1982] 1 CMLR 527.

[65] Case 148/78 *Ratti* [1979] ECR 1629. See also Case 8/81 *Becker* v *Finanzamt Münster-Innenstadt* [1982] ECR 53.

Case 152/84 *Marshall* v *Southampton and South-West Hampshire Area Health Authority* [1986] ECR 723

48. With regard to the argument that a Directive may not be relied upon against an individual, it must be emphasised that according to Article [288 TFEU], the binding nature of a Directive, which constitutes the basis for the possibility of relying on the Directive before a national court, exists only in relation to 'each Member State to which it is addressed'. It follows that a Directive may not of itself impose obligations on an individual and that a provision of a Directive may not be relied upon as such against such a person.

49. In that respect it must be pointed out that where a person involved in legal proceedings is able to rely on a Directive as against the State he may do so regardless of the capacity in which the latter is acting, whether employer or public authority. In either case it is necessary to prevent the State from taking advantage of its own failure to comply with Community law ...

51. The argument submitted by the United Kingdom that the possibility of relying on provisions of the Directive against the respondent *qua* organ of the State would give rise to an arbitrary and unfair distinction between the rights of State employees and those of private employees does not justify any other conclusion. Such a distinction may easily be avoided if the Member State concerned has correctly implemented the Directive in national law.

Marshall created a distinction between Regulations and Directives by holding that only the former were capable of horizontal direct effect. This addressed some of the initial concerns about the direct effect of Directives but created problems of its own. For one thing, it generated uncertainty as to which bodies formed part of the state and could consequently be sued. Defining the state can, to be sure, be something of a challenge. The multiple legal structures that form part of the state are frequently a consequence of historical happenstance, on the one hand, and recurring reinvention of the place of public intervention, on the other.[66]

The question was addressed most clearly in *Foster* v *British Gas*. Like Marshall, Foster was forced to retire at 60, whereas men could continue working until 65. She and four other women invoked the Equal Treatment Directive against her former employer, British Gas. The latter was at the time a nationalised industry. Its board members were appointed by a British minister who could also issue to the board various directions and instruments. In addition, the board was required to submit periodic reports to the Secretary of State.

Case C-188/89 *Foster* v *British Gas* [1990] ECR I-3313

17. The Court further held in ... *Marshall* that where a person is able to rely on a Directive as against the State he may do so regardless of the capacity in which the latter is acting, whether as employer or as public authority. In either case it is necessary to prevent the State from taking advantage of its own failure to comply with Community law.

18. On the basis of those considerations, the Court has held in a series of cases that unconditional and sufficiently precise provisions of a Directive could be relied on against organisations or bodies which

---

[66] D. Curtin, 'The Province of Government: Delimiting the Direct Effect of Directives in the Common Law Context' (1990) 15 *ELRev.* 195, 198–9.

19. The Court has accordingly held that provisions of a directive could be relied on against tax authorities ..., local or regional authorities ..., constitutionally independent authorities responsible for the maintenance of public order and safety ..., and public authorities providing public health services ...

20. It follows ... that a body, whatever its legal form, which has been made responsible, pursuant to a measure adopted by the State, for providing a public service under the control of the State and has for that purpose special powers beyond those which result from the normal rules applicable in relations between individuals, is included ... among the bodies against which the provisions of a Directive capable of having direct effect may be relied upon.

The test of whether a body is part of the state is a dual one. A body may be deemed to be part of the state on functional grounds: an entity is carrying out a public service and, for that reason, has special powers. Its legal form and the presence of state control is not determinative there. In *Vassallo* the Court of Justice held, therefore, that a Directive could be invoked against an Italian hospital which, although it received public funding, was not run by the Italian state but was an autonomous establishment with its own directors. In that instance, it was crucial for the Court that the hospital, notwithstanding this, was still seen by the national court as part of the public sector and performing a public service.[67]

In other cases, the Court will look at the degree of state control. It has thus held that any entity which forms part of or is subject to the control of a public authority forms part of the state, and can be sued. In *Rohrbach*, two Austrian companies which were owned by a public authority and carried out laundrette and gardening activities were held to be part of the state.[68] This was held on the grounds that they carried out a social function – their mission was to employ people with disabilities – but purely by virtue of the local authority ownership.

The difficulties of definition of the state were not the only problems generated by *Marshall*. Its style of analysis sits uncomfortably with *Defrenne* v *Sabena*.[69] The latter holds that obligations addressed to Member States lead, by virtue of their binding nature, to horizontal direct effect as they require courts, as part of the Member State's obligation under EU law, to apply EU law in cases before them. In *Marshall* the opposite is stated. More practically, *Marshall* creates incongruous outcomes. Marshall could rely on the Directive because she was employed by a public authority, a part of the state. Had she been employed by a private hospital she would not have been able to rely on the Directive. A two-tier legal system was created in which parties had greater protection against public bodies than against private ones, notwithstanding the fact that their functional relationship with the two may be the same. Finally, *Marshall* rests on a false assumption. It is difficult to see how the estoppel argument can justify reliance on a Directive against a public health authority. For sure, the state is responsible for implementing Directives and public health authorities are a part of the state, but there is no sense in which public health authorities are responsible for transposing the terms of equal pay Directives into national law.

[67] Case C-180/04 *Vassallo v Azienda Ospedaliera Ospedale San Martino di Genova e Cliniche Universitarie Convenzionate* [2006] ECR I-7251.
[68] Case C-297/03 *Sozialhilfeverband Rohrbach v Arbeiterkammer Oberösterreich* [2005] ECR I-4305.
[69] Case 43/75 *Defrenne v Sabena (No. 2)* [1976] ECR 455.

(ii) Incidental direct effect

As a consequence, *Marshall* came under withering attack, from academic commentators[70] and Advocates General.[71] This provided the context for some of the doctrines which subsequently developed granting Directives effects within national courts.[72] Yet, notwithstanding this, the Court of Justice has resolutely stated that Directives are not capable of horizontal direct effect as they cannot impose direct obligations on individuals.[73] The full force of this has been belied by the phenomenon of 'triangular situations' or 'incidental direct effects'. A triangular situation is a dispute between two parties which affects the legal rights or imposes a financial burden on a third party. This creates a dilemma when the defendant is a state, as defined by *Foster*, but the third party is a private actor. For *Marshall* says, on the one hand, that an individual can sue the state, but, on the other, that the Directive may not impose obligations on a private party.[74]

The Court of Justice has ruled that repercussions for another private party are not sufficient to deprive a litigant of their right to sue the Member State under a Directive. This was set out at greatest length in *Arcor*.[75] A telephone service provider challenged a decision by the German regulatory authority to allow Deutsche Telekom, the owner of the telephone network in Germany, to charge for use of that network, as two Directives precluded this charge where the network was run by a market dominant business and the fee was unrelated to the costs of connection. Whilst the case was brought against the German regulators, its central target was, of course, Deutsche Telekom, a private company.

Joined Cases C-152/07–154/07 *Arcor v Germany* [2008] ECR I-5959

35. ... according to settled case-law, a directive cannot of itself impose obligations on an individual, but can only confer rights. Consequently, an individual may not rely on a directive against a Member State where it is a matter of a State obligation directly linked to the performance of another obligation falling, pursuant to that directive, on a third party ...

36. On the other hand, mere adverse repercussions on the rights of third parties, even if the repercussions are certain, do not justify preventing an individual from relying on the provisions of a directive against the Member State concerned ...

---

[70] D. Curtin, 'The Effectiveness of Judicial Protection of Individual Rights' (1990) 27 *CMLRev.* 709; S. Prechal, 'Remedies after Marshall' (1990) 27 *CMLRev.* 451; J. Coppell, 'Rights, Duties and the End of *Marshall*' (1994) 57 *MLR* 859; T. Tridimas, 'Horizontal Effect of Directives: A Missed Opportunity?' (1994) 19 *ELRev.* 621.

[71] Advocate General Van Gerven in Case C-271/91 *Marshall II* [1993] ECR I-4367, Advocate General Jacobs in Case C-316/93 *Vaneetveld* v *Le Foyer* [1994] ECR I-763 and Advocate General Lenz in Case C-91/92 *Faccini Dori* v *Recreb* [1994] ECR I-3325.

[72] For reasons why the estoppel argument has been maintained see J. Dickson, 'Directives in European Union Legal Systems: Whose Norms are They Anyway?' (2011) 17 *ELJ* 190.

[73] For a recent example see Case C-476/11 *HK Danmark* v *Experian*, Judgment of 26 September 2013.

[74] On incidental direct effect see H. Nyssens and K. Lackhoff, 'Direct Effect of Directives in Triangular Situations' (1998) 23 *ELRev.* 397; D. Colgan, 'Triangular Situations: The Coup de Grâce for the Denial of Horizontal Direct Effect of Community Directives' (2002) 8 *EPL* 545; F. Becker and A. Campbell, 'The Direct Effect of European Directives: Towards the Final Act?' (2007) 13 *CJEL* 401.

[75] It was established earlier in Case C-201/02 *R* v *Secretary of State for Transport, Local Government and the Regions ex parte Wells* [2004] ECR I-723.

37. In the main proceedings ... the actions before the referring court have been brought by private persons against the Member State concerned, represented by the national regulatory authority which made the contested decision and has sole competence to set the rates of both the connection charge at issue in the main proceedings and the interconnection charge to which the former is added.

38. It is clear that Deutsche Telekom is a third party in relation to the dispute before the referring court and is capable only of suffering adverse repercussions because it levied the connection charge at issue in the main proceedings and because, if that charge were removed, it would have to increase its own subscribers' rates. Such a removal of benefits cannot be regarded as an obligation falling on a third party pursuant to the directives relied on before the referring court by the appellants in the main proceedings.

This raises the question as to when individuals can impose burdens on private third parties. Nyssens and Lackhoff suggest that there are three circumstances.[76] The first is when a Directive entitles an individual to require the Member State to do something which places a burden on another party. This is uncontroversial. It happens when individuals invoke Directives requiring local authorities to set things out properly for public tender. Such tenders require significant information from other companies and are costly.[77] The second is where Directives require Member States to impose a burden on private parties. Another party cannot require that they impose these burdens. Nevertheless, the latter can invoke the provisions of a Directive where a decision is taken which affects their rights asking it to be reviewed. And the review might impose burdens. This was the situation in *Arcor*. The applicant had no ex ante right to compel a decision to be taken but once one was taken in breach of the Directive which affected their interests they were able to challenge it. The third is the most controversial. A Directive grants a party a legal right to engage in certain activities protected from the Member State. In violation of this, the Member State allows private third parties to stop these activities. Incidental direct effect allows the party a right to protect itself from claims made by these third parties.

In *CIA*, Signalson and Securitel sought to restrain CIA Security from marketing an alarm system on the grounds that it had not received authorisation as required by Belgian law. They argued, therefore, that by marketing an illegal good, CIA was engaging in unfair competition. This requirement of prior authorisation breached EU law, however, as, under Directive 83/189/EC, it should have been notified to the European Commission. This had not happened and CIA therefore argued that the national law was inapplicable.

Case C-194/94 CIA Security International v Signalson and Securitel [1996] ECR I-2201

44. That view cannot be adopted. Articles 8 and 9 of Directive 83/189 lay down a precise obligation on Member States to notify draft technical regulations to the Commission before they are adopted. Being, accordingly, unconditional and sufficiently precise in terms of their content, those articles may be relied on by individuals before national courts.

---

[76] Nyssens and Lackhoff, n. 74 above, 401–2.

[77] This was the case in *Wells*, where a neighbour to a quarry challenged a failure to carry out an environmental impact assessment, as required by an EU Directive, Case C-201/02 *R* v *Secretary of State for Transport, Local Government and the Regions ex parte Wells* [2004] ECR I-723.

45. It remains to examine the legal consequences to be drawn from a breach by Member States of their obligation to notify and, more precisely, whether Directive 83/189 is to be interpreted as meaning that a breach of the obligation to notify, constituting a procedural defect in the adoption of the technical regulations concerned, renders such technical regulations inapplicable so that they may not be enforced against individuals.

46. The German and Netherlands Governments and the United Kingdom consider that Directive 83/189 is solely concerned with relations between the Member States and the Commission, that it merely creates procedural obligations which the Member States must observe when adopting technical regulations, their competence to adopt the regulations in question after expiry of the suspension period being, however, unaffected, and, finally, that it contains no express provision relating to any effects attaching to non-compliance with those procedural obligations.

47. The Court observes first of all in this context that none of those factors prevents non-compliance with Directive 83/189 from rendering the technical regulations in question inapplicable.

48. For such a consequence to arise from a breach of the obligations laid down by Directive 83/189, an express provision to this effect is not required. As pointed out above, it is undisputed that the aim of the directive is to protect freedom of movement for goods by means of preventive control and that the obligation to notify is essential for achieving such Community control. The effectiveness of Community control will be that much greater if the directive is interpreted as meaning that breach of the obligation to notify constitutes a substantial procedural defect such as to render the technical regulations in question inapplicable to individuals.

The Directive, therefore, grants CIA a right to free movement of goods, in this case importing burglar alarms from other Member States, if there is a failure by the Belgian authorities to notify new technical regulations to the Commission or they implement these before the Commission has had a chance to consider them. CIA was, therefore, entitled to protection from the Belgian authorities. Insofar as its competitors were seeking to remove that protection through the back-door by enforcing Belgian law through a private action, it was entitled to protection from them.

This was taken a step further in *Unilever*.[78] Unilever had delivered some Italian olive oil to Central Food under a contract which required that oil to be labelled in accordance with Italian law. Central Food refused to accept the oil as it did not comply with an Italian law which stated that olive oil could not be termed 'Italian' unless the entire cycle of harvesting, production, processing and packaging had taken place in Italy. This law had been implemented in breach of the same Directive as in *CIA*. The circumstance was different from *CIA* in that the law did not prevent but rather *hindered* its being sold. It could be sold but not using the word 'Italian'. This diminished the value of the good. The Court of Justice stated that the law was, consequently, unenforceable against individuals, even in private actions, because it hindered the marketing or use of a product. The individual had the right to protection by the Directive for full free movement of goods. This protection required not merely that their good not be

---

[78] Case C-443/98 *Unilever v Central Food* [2000] ECR I-7535. Similar reasoning to *Unilever* can be found in *Bernáldez* which held exclusions in motor insurance contracts based on an illegal Spanish statute to be void insofar as they limited free movement of vehicles which was the purpose of the relevant Directive, Case C-129/94 *Bernáldez* [1996] ECR I-1829.

precluded from the market but also that it not be placed at a disadvantage on that market by that legislation.

Incidental direct effect, as it is about protecting a party's position, only allows Directives to be used as a shield from litigation by other parties.[79] It does not grant parties the right to use Directives as a cause of action. This distinction is not a happy one, however. It still allows individuals to impose burdens on a wide array of other parties. The fact that these are not described as legal duties is not important. In *Unilever*, therefore, the effect of the Directive was to allow olive oil to be marketed whose provenance was not known to Italian consumers or, in-sofar as it claimed to be Italian when arguably it was not, to mislead them.[80] If there is a belief that Directives should impose obligations on private parties, it would be more straightforward to grant them horizontal direct effect.

The other feature of incidental direct effect is that it can lead to contrived interpretations of EU legislation. In *CIA* and *Unilever*, the Court, therefore, argued that the purpose of the Directive was to secure free movement of goods. This purpose justified the grant of incidental direct effect.[81] However, whilst this is the context for the Directive, it is not mentioned in any of its provisions. This style of interpretation, consequently, generates a lot of uncertainty as it looks for a legislative intent which is not explicit. As a consequence, incidental direct effect has not been deployed by the Court since *Unilever*. It is a doctrine which is invariably confined to interpretations of a select number of instruments, and is unsteady as an autonomous doctrine in its own right.

6 INDIRECT EFFECT

(i) Evolution of indirect effect

Direct effect has, in the last twenty years, become merely one route amongst others through which individuals may invoke EU law in national courts. It is arguably no longer even the predominant doctrine. This may be the doctrine of indirect effect.[82] As the development of direct effect has faltered, this has expanded. Back in 1998 an empirical study found that it was deployed more widely in British courts than direct effect.[83] Despite the greater academic attention often given to direct effect, it has therefore been argued persuasively that indirect effect 'is currently the main form of ensuring effect of Directives whether correctly, incorrectly or not transposed at all'.[84]

Indirect effect has evolved in three stages.

The first began inauspiciously in *Von Colson*. It required national legislation implementing a Directive to be interpreted in the light of the latter where the national legislation was ambigu-ous and an interpretation could be taken which complied with the Directive. In *Von Colson*

---

[79] J. Jans, 'The Effect in National Legal Systems of the Prohibition of Discrimination on Grounds of Age as a General Principle of Community Law' (2007) 34 *LIEI* 53, 61–2.

[80] S. Weatherill, 'Breach of Directives and Breach of Contract' (2001) 26 *ELRev.* 177, 182–3.

[81] Compare the interpretation of *CIA* given above with that provided in Nyssens and Lackhoff, n. 74 above, at 403.

[82] For analysis, see S. Drake, 'Twenty Years after *Von Colson*: The Impact of "Indirect Effect" on the Protection of the Individual's Community Rights' (2005) 30 *ELRev.* 329.

[83] D. Chalmers, 'The Positioning of EU Judicial Politics within the United Kingdom' (2000) 23 *WEP* 169, 190.

[84] G. Betlem, 'The Doctrine of Consistent Interpretation: Managing Legal Uncertainty' (2002) 22 *OJLS* 397, 399.

two social workers were refused employment in a German prison because they were women.[85] Under the German law implementing Directive 76/207/EEC, the Directive on equal treatment for men and women in the workplace, loss could be claimed as 'a result of his [sic] reliance on the expectation that the establishment of the employment relationship would not be precluded by such a breach'. This had been interpreted by German courts to mean that individuals could only be compensated for the losses incurred in coming to the interview. In *Von Colson*, there were travel expenses, which were about €3 in one case. The Court of Justice interpreted the Directive to require Member States to give real and effective judicial protection to victims of discrimination. Such protection involved imposing sanctions which would have a deterrent effect on employers who illegally discriminated. The provision in question was, however, insufficiently clear and unconditional to be directly effective. The Court of Justice, nevertheless, required that Article 4(3) TEU, the fidelity provision, required national courts to interpret national law in the light of the wording and purpose of the Directive. Insofar as national law could be given an interpretation consistent with that, it should be given that interpretation.

Von Colson offered two possibilities for litigants unprotected by direct effect. It allowed individuals to invoke Directives even where the provision was not sufficiently justiciable to be direct effect. It could also be used in cases against private actors. However, the doctrine was limited to very confined circumstances. It only applied where national laws were implementing Directives and a national provision was highly ambiguous.

The second stage in the evolution of indirect effect changed all that. In *Marleasing*,[86] an action was brought against a company to have its articles of association declared void on the grounds it had been created for the sole purpose of defrauding and evading creditors. The Spanish Civil Code stated that contracts (the company was established by a contract) made with 'lack of cause' were void. Directive 68/151/EEC contained an exhaustive list of reasons under which companies could be declared void. Avoidance of creditors was not on that list. To interpret the Code, which predated the Directive, involved interpreting a provision of contract law in the light of an EU company law provision so that setting up a company to avoid creditors was a sufficiently good cause to found a contract in Spanish law. The Court of Justice held that this is what should happen. The national court was required to interpret the Code 'as far as possible, in the light of the wording and the purpose of the Directive in order to achieve the result pursued by the latter'.

Marleasing thereby expanded indirect effect in two ways. First, it expanded its scope as it required *all* national legislation to be interpreted in the light of EU law, irrespective of whether it is implementing legislation or not and irrespective of whether it was enacted prior or subsequent to the provision of EU law in question. Secondly, it strengthened the national courts' interpretive duty. As Docksey and Fitzpatrick observed, 'it is no longer sufficient for a national court to turn to Community law only if the national provision is "ambiguous". Its priority must be to establish the meaning of the Union obligation and only then to conclude whether it is possible to achieve the necessary reconciliation with the national law'.[87] In short, in the absence of an explicit contradiction, national courts were to read EU law provisions into national laws.

---

[85] Case 14/83 *Von Colson and Kamann* v *Land Nordrhein-Westfalen* [1984] ECR 1891; Case 79/83 *Harz* v *Deutsche Tradax* [1984] ECR 192.

[86] Case C-106/89 *Marleasing SA* v *La Comercial Internacionale de Alimentacion* [1990] ECR I-4135.

[87] C. Docksey and B. Fitzpatrick, 'The Duty of National Courts to Interpret Provisions of National Law in accordance with Community Law' (1991) 20 *ILJ* 113, 119.

The third stage, a refinement of *Marleasing*, occurred in *Pfeiffer*. This stated that it was not simply individual laws which had to be interpreted in the light of EU law but the legal system as a whole.[88] These also included rules which went to whether a national law should apply to a particular dispute. In a case where two national laws governed a dispute, one compliant with EU law and the other not, the Court of Justice ruled that national courts should look, within the discretion allowed to them by national law, at whether it was possible just to apply the law which was compliant with EU law by interpreting the other as not applying to the dispute.[89] In this manner, indirect effect sets out an internal hierarchy of norms within national law. National laws compliant with EU law will take precedence over other national laws insofar as the latter are presumed not to apply to disputes where this would involve a breach of EU law.

The current situation on indirect effect is most elaborately set out in *Dominguez*. Dominguez had an accident on her way to work as a result of which she was unable to work for fourteen months. She subsequently claimed for twenty-two days annual paid leave. Her employer refused to grant it, as a condition under the French law (article L.223–2 Code du travail) was that the employee had actually worked for at least a month. This restriction did not apply where the absence was twelve months or less and due to a work-related illness (article L.223–4 Code du Travail). Article 7 of Directive 2003/88, on the organisation of working time, granted the right to twenty working days annual leave per year. It had been interpreted by the Court to mean that Member States could not stipulate a minimum amount of time be worked before a pro rata amount of leave be claimed.

Case C-282/10 *Dominguez v CICOA*, Judgment of 24 January 2012

24. ... when national courts apply domestic law they are bound to interpret it, so far as possible, in the light of the wording and the purpose of the directive concerned in order to achieve the result sought by the directive and consequently comply with the third paragraph of Article 288 TFEU. This obligation to interpret national law in conformity with European Union law is inherent in the system of the Treaty on the Functioning of the European Union, since it permits national courts, for the matters within their jurisdiction, to ensure the full effectiveness of European Union law when they determine the disputes before them ...

25. It is true that this principle of interpreting national law in conformity with European Union law has certain limitations. Thus the obligation on a national court to refer to the content of a directive when interpreting and applying the relevant rules of domestic law is limited by general principles of law and it cannot serve as the basis for an interpretation of national law contra legem ...

26. In the dispute in the main proceedings, the national court states that it has encountered such a limitation. According to that court, the first paragraph of Article L.223–2 of the Code du travail, which makes entitlement to paid annual leave conditional on a minimum of one month's actual work during the reference period, is not amenable to an interpretation that is compatible with Article 7 of Directive 2003/88.

---

[88] Joined Cases C-397/01–403/01 *Pfeiffer and others* [2004] ECR I-8835.
[89] On this power of set-aside see Case C-124/12 *AES-3C Maritza East 1*, Judgment of 18 July 2013.

27. In that regard, it should be noted that the principle that national law must be interpreted in conformity with European Union law also requires national courts to do whatever lies within their jurisdiction, taking the whole body of domestic law into consideration and applying the interpretative methods recognised by domestic law, with a view to ensuring that the directive in question is fully effective and achieving an outcome consistent with the objective pursued by it ...

28. In the dispute in the main proceedings, Article L.223–4 of the Code du travail, which provides an exemption from the requirement of actual work during the reference period in respect of certain periods of absence from work, is an integral part of the domestic law to be taken into consideration by the French courts.

29. If Article L.223–4 of the Code du travail were to be interpreted by the national court as meaning that a period of absence due to an accident on the journey to or from work must be treated as being equivalent to a period of absence due to an accident at work in order to give full effect to Article 7 of Directive 2003/88, that court would not encounter the limitation, referred to in paragraph 26 above, as regards interpreting Article L.223–2 of the Code du travail in accordance with European Union law.

30. In that regard, it should be pointed out that Article 7 of Directive 2003/88 does not make any distinction between workers who are absent on sick leave during the reference period and those who have actually worked in the course of that period (see paragraph 20 above). It follows that the right to paid annual leave of a worker who is absent from work on health grounds during the reference period cannot be made subject by a Member State to a condition concerning the obligation actually to have worked during that period. Thus, according to Article 7 of Directive 2003/88, any worker, whether he be on sick leave during the reference period as a result of an accident at his place of work or elsewhere, or as the result of sickness of whatever nature or origin, cannot have his entitlement to at least four weeks' paid annual leave affected.

31. It is clear from the foregoing that it is for the national court to determine, taking the whole body of domestic law into consideration, in particular Article L.223–4 of the Code du travail, and applying the interpretative methods recognised by domestic law with a view to ensuring that Directive 2003/88 is fully effective and achieving an outcome consistent with the objective pursued by it, whether it can find an interpretation of that law that allows the absence of the worker due to an accident on the journey to or from work to be treated as being equivalent to one of the situations covered by that article of the Code du travail.

The expansion of indirect effect in this manner has closed to a considerable degree the lacunae created in *Marshall*, which did not allow Directives to be invoked against private parties. With indirect effect, as long as there is a relevant national law and the national legal system allows some room for interpretation, Directives govern the substance of disputes between private parties. In *Marleasing* and, arguably, *Dominguez*, the dispute was between two private parties with the substantively determinative provisions being those of the Directive, albeit that the formal vehicle governing the parties' rights was national law. It has been argued, therefore, that indirect effect creates a new form of 'inter-legality', in which a mix of national and EU law regulates a dispute. The EU element opens up adjudication to wider norms and concerns, whilst the national law element ensures that the local traditions and contexts surrounding the dispute are not overlooked.

M. Amstutz, 'In-between Worlds: *Marleasing* and the Emergence of Interlegality in Legal Reasoning' (2005) 11 *European Law Journal* 766, 781–2

The internal culture-specific 'constraints' on national adjudication remain unaffected by the requirement for interpretation in conformity with Directives; local specificities of the various legal discourses are not pushed aside, say, by rational arguments that in the end are always weaker than the constraints of organically grown legal cultures. For ultimately it is the legal policies present in the private law of the individual Member States that act as 'regulators' in the process of incorporating Community private-law positions into the national legal discourses. They are ensuring that two separate sets of norms do not emerge in Member States' civil legal systems – one deriving from the historical trajectory of the State concerned, the other dictated by the Community. They alone can offer guarantees for a Community private law integrated into the national legal culture, and this fact immediately makes it clear how they ensure the evolutionary capacity of national law in the biotope of the European Community: by on the one hand – as artful combinations of 'flexible' and 'fixed' control parameters – blocking the propagation of the 'perturbations' from European law throughout the national private law, without on the other losing the national law's responsiveness to EC law.

If indirect effect creates a new form of hybrid law, with some sensitivity to both national and EU concerns, this hybrid law generates a number of concerns of its own. The pre-eminent one is legal uncertainty.[90] The central source of this uncertainty is the quality of interpretation asked of the national judge. *Dominguez* is a case in point. In principle, no restrictions on the right to annual leave are allowed in EU law. The French regime clearly contained some restrictions. The Court of Justice seeks to reconcile this through asking the French court to interpret opportunistically in the case in hand. It is to interpret the exception for work-related accidents as including those which occur on the way to work. This still leaves the source of the conflict intact. It is a contrived interpretation, so it is not clear whether it now generates new employer responsibilities for all journeys on the way to work, as these are now 'work-related'. It raises further uncertainties about what is a journey to work. Does it include a detour to leave children at school, for example?

The contrived nature of this raises the question at what point a court is no longer engaging in interpretation, and indirect effect cannot bite. A number of constraints have, therefore, been placed on the duty of interpretation. First, it does not require *contra legem* interpretations of national law, which require a provision of national law to be given a meaning that contradicts its 'ordinary' meaning.[91] There will, of course, be uncertainty about when an interpretation moves to the point that it is *contra legem*. Secondly, because indirect effect is asking parties to look at two sources of law, EU and national, with its being completely unclear about which is the governing norm, the Court of Justice has been wary about using it in the field of criminal law. In principle, indirect effect cannot be used to determine or aggravate the criminal liability

---

[90] G. de Búrca, 'Giving Effect to European Community Directives' (1992) 55 *MLR* 215.
[91] Most notably, Case C-334/92 *Wagner-Miret* v *Fondo de Garantia Salarial* [1993] ECR I-6911.

of private actors.[92] However, even this is unclear because it beggars belief that where a national law transposes a Directive and is completely ambiguous, some reference cannot be had to the Directive. If that is the case, there is the question of the level of weight allowed to it. Furthermore, in *Dominguez*, the Court makes a general reference here to the duty of interpretation being confined by general principles of law. If that is so, the concerns particularly salient in criminal law, namely, those of civil liberties and legal certainty, might also have force in other fields where individuals are exposed to significant liabilities by EU law. Finally, although indirect effect was developed in the context of Directives, it can also be used with other binding legal instruments (i.e. Regulations, Decisions and international agreements). In *Grimaldi*,[93] the Court stated that national courts were also to take account of legally non-binding recommendations in interpreting national law. In that instance, it concerned ambiguous national law implementing the Recommendation. There remains the question whether soft law imposes the same expansive and demanding duty of interpretation as so-called hard law.

(ii) Duty to disapply and fundamental rights

There are two circumstances where indirect effect will not come to the rescue of individuals granted entitlements by Directives. One is where there is no national measure to interpret and the other is where the national legislation contradicts the Directive. These cases represent, however, the most flagrant violations of EU law by Member States. This lack of protection is particularly exposed in the case of fundamental rights, where Member States are violating the human dignity of somebody whilst refusing to meet the terms of a Directive. The response of EU law to this is not traditionally conceived in terms of indirect effect. There is little reference to the fidelity principle, therefore, in Article 4(3) TEU. However, like indirect effect, its focus has concentrated on the institutional duties of courts in such circumstances. It therefore makes sense to consider it within this context.

In *Mangold*,[94] an eight-month fixed-term employment contract between Mangold, a 56-year-old, and Helm, a German lawyer was challenged on the grounds that it contravened Directive 2000/78/EC which prohibited discrimination on grounds of age. The context was a 2002 German law which allowed fixed-term contacts for workers who were 52 years or older but these were generally prohibited for employees younger than this. It was impossible, therefore, for this law to be reconciled with the Directive through interpretation as it clearly discriminated on grounds of age. It was, furthermore, a dispute between private parties so direct effect could not come into play. The Court of Justice, therefore, came up with a new form of reasoning. It stated that the Directive did not establish the principle of equal treatment. This already existed as a general principle of law. The Directive rather did no more than establish a framework for its application. In such circumstances, the national court should set aside the national law which conflicted with the Directive and apply the prohibition on age discrimination.

The judgment seemed to say that where a Directive gave expression to a general principle of law – here prohibition of age discrimination – it could be invoked between private parties.

---

[92] Case C-168/95 *Arcaro* [1996] ECR I-4705; Case C-321/05 *Kofeod* v *Skatteministeriet* [2007] ECR I-5795. On this see P. Craig, 'The Legal Effects of Directives: Policy, Rules and Exceptions' (2009) 34 *ELRev.* 349, 360–4.
[93] Case 322/88 *Grimaldi* v *Fonds des Maladies Professionelles* [1989] ECR 4407.
[94] Case C-144/04 *Mangold* v *Helm* [2005] ECR I-9981.

However, the judgment was mired in obscurity.[95] It was not clear, in particular, whether it was the general principle of law which was granting rights independently of the Directive or a combination of the Directive and the general principle of law, where the former was to be interpreted in the light of the latter to grant rights in this instance.[96] The question was addressed more directly in *Kücükdeveci*. Kücükdeveci had been employed by Swedex for ten years. This would normally have entitled her to four months' notice before being dismissed. She was given less than six weeks' notice, as a German law allowed employment prior to somebody's twenty-fifth birthday not to be included in calculating how long they had been employed, which, in turn, determined the length of notice which had to be given. She claimed that this was age discrimination by virtue of Directive 2000/78/EC. Once again, the case involved a private dispute in which the law could not be reconciled with the Directive.

Case C-555/07 *Kücükdeveci v Swedex* [2010] ECR I-365

20. ... the Court has held that that [Directive 2000/78/EC] does not itself lay down the principle of equal treatment in the field of employment and occupation, which derives from various international instruments and from the constitutional traditions common to the Member States, but has the sole purpose of laying down, in that field, a general framework for combating discrimination on various grounds including age (see *Mangold*, paragraph 74).

21. In that context, the Court has acknowledged the existence of a principle of non-discrimination on grounds of age which must be regarded as a general principle of European Union law (see, to that effect, *Mangold*, paragraph 75). Directive 2000/78 gives specific expression to that principle.

22. It should also be noted that Article 6(1) TEU provides that the Charter of Fundamental Rights of the European Union is to have the same legal value as the Treaties. Under Article 21(1) of the Charter, '[a]ny discrimination based on ... age ... shall be prohibited'.

23. For the principle of non-discrimination on grounds of age to apply in a case such as that at issue in the main proceedings, that case must fall within the scope of European Union law. ...

50. It must be recalled here that, as stated in paragraph 20 above, Directive 2000/78 merely gives expression to, but does not lay down, the principle of equal treatment in employment and occupation, and that the principle of non-discrimination on grounds of age is a general principle of European Union law in that it constitutes a specific application of the general principle of equal treatment ...

51. In those circumstances, it is for the national court, hearing a dispute involving the principle of non-discrimination on grounds of age as given expression in Directive 2000/78, to provide, within the limits of its jurisdiction, the legal protection which individuals derive from European Union law and to ensure the full effectiveness of that law, disapplying if need be any provision of national legislation contrary to that principle ...

If a Directive gives expression to a fundamental right or general principle of law, it can therefore be invoked between individuals, and the national law must be disapplied. There will, therefore, be the question as to when a Directive will be considered to do this. In *Azienda*

---

[95] For different views see A. Dashwood, 'From *Van Duyn* to *Mangold* via *Marshall*: Reducing Direct Effect to Absurdity?' (2006–7) 9 *CYELS* 81; C. Tobler, 'Putting *Mangold* in Perspective: In Response to *Editorial Comments*, Horizontal Direct Effect – A Law of Diminishing Coherence?' (2007) 44 *CMLRev.* 1177.

[96] C. Semmelmann, 'General Principles in EU Law Between a Compensatory Role and an Intrinsic Value' (2013) 19 *ELJ* 457, 476–7.

Agro-Zootecnica Franchini,[97] a challenge was made to a refusal by the region of Puglia in Italy to authorise the erection of wind turbines in a national park. It was argued that an Italian law prohibiting the use of wind turbines in national parks rather than allowing these after an environmental impact assessment violated a provision of a Directive on the promotion of renewable energy sources which required rules on these to be objective, transparent and non-discriminatory, as some other industrial activities were allowed in these parks. Whilst the Court of Justice was unclear whether any unjustified discrimination had taken place here, it nevertheless held that this provision was also an expression of the principle of equality set out in Article 6(1) TEU. It used the same language for this Directive, therefore, as for the Equal Treatment Directive. It is hard to believe, however, that a right for an industry to be subject to the same authorisation procedures as other industries is seen as integral to human dignity in the same way as the prohibition of discrimination on grounds of race, sexual orientation, age, gender, disability or religion.

For that reason, the Court has been reluctant to use this line of reasoning since *Kücükdeveci*. The opportunity came up in the *Dominguez* case, cited earlier.[98] The Directive in question implemented the right to annual leave, which is set out in Article 31 EUCFR. However, the Court does not mention this provision in its reasoning. As a consequence, it provided no possibility for the national law to be disapplied if it could not be interpreted in line with EU law. This raises doubts about the resilience of this line of reasoning.[99] It is, of course, possible that it has been abandoned. An alternative, and possibly preferable approach, is that it is reserved for those issues which are seen as going to the core of human dignity, the rights in questions are seen as very justiciable and clear expression is given by an implementing Directive.[100] It would thus apply to issues of non-discrimination on grounds of age, race, gender, and so on but not, possibly, to social rights such as the right to annual leave.

(iii) Duty to refrain from compromising EU law

Direct effect and indirect effect only bite from the date of transposition set out in the Directive.[101] However, unlike Regulations, this date will usually be several years after the date of publication in the Official Journal. There is the issue of whether this period of interregnum generates any legal effects of its own or whether Member States are free to do as they wish during this period. In *Adeneler*, eighteen employees were, from May 2001, employed on a variety of successive fixed-term contracts with the Greek milk board which came to an end between June and September 2003. They claimed that the contracts were in reality a single contract, and that they should be compensated accordingly. Directive 1999/70/EC on fixed-term work provided that successive fixed-term contracts were only permitted if there were objective reasons for this. It was due to be transposed by 10 July 2001, but a state could ask for an extension (which Greece did) of a further one year. The original 1994 Greek legislation did not comply with this requirement of 'objective reasons' in the Directive. Greece brought in

---

[97] Case C-2/10 *Azienda Agro-Zootecnica Franchini* v *Regione Puglia* [2011] ECR I-6561.
[98] Case C-282/10 *Dominguez* v *CICOA*, Judgment of 24 January 2012.
[99] There has been criticism on these grounds, therefore in Semmelmann, n. 96 above, 482–4.
[100] On this and the debates surrounding the judgments see E. Muir, 'Of Ages in – and Edges of – EU Law' (2011) 48 *CMLRev.* 39, 54–60.
[101] Joined Cases C-457/11–460/11 *VG Wort* v *Kyocera*, Judgment of 27 June 2013.

further legislation in 2004, which breached the Directive and was designed to exclude employees such as the ones in this case from the Directive's protection. The question arose whether
the employees could claim for compensation for the period prior to July 2002, the formal date
of Greek transposition.

Case C–212/04 *Adeneler and others* v *ELOG* [2006] ECR I–6057

121. ... it follows from [Article 4(3) TEU] in conjunction with the third paragraph of Article [288 TFEU]
and the directive in question itself that, during the period prescribed for transposition of a directive,
the Member States to which it is addressed must refrain from taking any measures liable seriously to
compromise the attainment of the result prescribed by it ... In this connection it is immaterial whether
or not the provision of national law at issue which has been adopted after the directive in question
entered into force is concerned with the transposition of the directive ...

122. Given that all the authorities of the Member States are subject to the obligation to ensure that
provisions of Community law take full effect ... the obligation to refrain from taking measures, as set
out in the previous paragraph, applies just as much to national courts.

123. It follows that, from the date upon which a directive has entered into force, the courts of the Member
States must refrain as far as possible from interpreting domestic law in a manner which might seriously
compromise, after the period for transposition has expired, attainment of the objective pursued by that
directive.

There is, thus, a duty on Member States from the date of publication not to take measures
which would compromise realisation of a Directive's objectives. The meaning of this obligation
is very unclear. It is clearly not direct or indirect effect, and relies on the introduction of some
national measure to trigger it. In *Mangold*, the age discrimination emerged in the two years
following a law adopted in 2002. This was after the adoption of the Equal Treatment Directive
prohibiting it, which was adopted in 2000, but before the date for transposition, which, in the
case of Germany, was in 2006.[102] The national court was nevertheless required to disapply
the German law, in large measure because the Directive was seen as the expression of a more
general fundamental right, namely, the prohibition of discrimination.

However, the Court of Justice has rowed back in two subsequent cases.[103] In *Römer*,[104] the
Court had to consider a case on discrimination on grounds of sexual orientation in which a
same-sex civil partner was refused a survivor's pension that would have been available to a
spouse. The Court ruled that this was illegal discrimination under the Equal Treatment Directive but that it fell outside the scope of EU law insofar as it occurred before the date for transposition. However, the case only fell outside the aegis of EU law in the same way as *Mangold*,
namely, that before the Equal Treatment Directive neither age discrimination nor discrimination on grounds of sexual orientation were prohibited by EU law.

---

[102] Case C-144/04 *Mangold* v *Helm* [2005] ECR I-9981.

[103] This may, in part, have been because of a furious reaction to *Mangold*, where it was felt that granting Directives
effects before the transposition date was according them legal effects they clearly should not have. R. Herzog
and L. Gerken, 'Stop the European Court of Justice', *Frankfurter Allgemeine Zeitung*, 8 September 2008. An
English translation can be found at http://euobserver.com/opinion/26714.

[104] Case C-147/08 *Römer* v *Freie und Hansestadt Hamburg* [2011] ECR I-3591. For criticism see L. Pech, 'Between
Judicial Minimalism and Avoidance: The Court of Justice's Sidestepping of Fundamental Constitutional Issues in
Römer and *Dominguez*' (2012) 49 *CMLRev.* 1841, 1857–63.

A similar reticence was shown in *Stichting Natuur en Milieu*.[105] A 2001 Directive required Member States to put in place national emission ceilings for sulphur dioxide and nitrogen dioxide. Three Dutch environmental NGOs challenged three decisions by the Dutch authorities in 2007 and 2008 to authorise the construction of three new power stations. It was estimated that these power stations would, combined, increase the national emissions of sulphur dioxide by just under 6 per cent and nitrogen dioxide by just under 1 per cent. The Dutch Environment Agency noted, however, that the Netherlands was not going to meet its 2010 ceilings. These power stations made (from an ecological perspective) a bad situation worse. However, the Court ruled that the Dutch were free to construct them. It noted that a single measure (or here three measures!) could not by itself seriously compromise annual Dutch targets, particularly as the stations did not come online until 2012. This may be true but, particularly with regard to sulphur dioxide ceilings, it made a mockery of these targets. It is very unclear why there was a less signification violation here than in *Mangold*. The sense is that the Court took a pragmatic decision not to get involved in something that went to the heart of Dutch energy and industrial policy. However, the effect is not greater national leeway during the transposition period but further legal uncertainty, with its consequent chilling effects on administrative and private behaviour.

7 STATE LIABILITY

(i) Arrival and challenges of Member State liability

The limits of indirect effect and direct effect in the case of Directives emerged well before *Mangold*.[106] Already by the early 1990s, it was clear that these doctrines would not protect against flagrant violations of EU law by Member States where these either passed no legislation to transpose a Directive or had legislation in place which explicitly contradicted it. In *Francovich*, Italy had persistently failed to implement Directive 80/987/EC, which granted employees privileged claims vis-à-vis other creditors in the event of the insolvency of their employer for unpaid wages. In 1987 the Commission brought a successful enforcement action against the Italian Government.[107] Even after the judgment, there was still no transposition. *Francovich* concerned an action by thirty-four employees, owed back-pay by bankrupt employers, against the Italian state for the losses suffered as a consequence of its failure to transpose the Directive.

Joined Cases C-6/90 and C-9/90 *Francovich and Bonifaci* v *Italy* [1991] ECR I-5357

31. It should be borne in mind at the outset that the EEC Treaty has created its own legal system, which is integrated into the legal systems of the Member States and which their courts are bound to apply. The subjects of that legal system are not only the Member States but also their nationals. Just as it imposes burdens on individuals, Community law is also intended to give rise to rights which become part of their legal patrimony. Those rights arise not only where they are expressly granted by the Treaty but also by

---

[105] Joined Cases C-165/09–167/09 *Stichting Natuur en Milieu and others* v *College van Gedeputeerde Staten van Groningen and others* [2011] ECR I-4599.
[106] Case C-144/04 *Mangold* v *Helm* [2005] ECR I-9981.
[107] Case 22/87 *Commission* v *Italy* [1989] ECR 143.

virtue of obligations which the Treaty imposes in a clearly defined manner both on individuals and on the Member States and the Community institutions ...

32. Furthermore, it has been consistently held that the national courts whose task it is to apply the provisions of Community law in areas within their jurisdiction must ensure that those rules take full effect and must protect the rights which they confer on individuals ...

33. The full effectiveness of Community rules would be impaired and the protection of the rights which they grant would be weakened if individuals were unable to obtain redress when their rights are infringed by a breach of Community law for which a Member State can be held responsible.

34. The possibility of obtaining redress from the Member State is particularly indispensable where, as in this case, the full effectiveness of Community rules is subject to prior action on the part of the State and where, consequently, in the absence of such action, individuals cannot enforce before the national courts the rights conferred upon them by Community law.

35. It follows that the principle whereby a State must be liable for loss and damage caused to individuals as a result of breaches of Community law for which the State can be held responsible is inherent in the system of the Treaty.

36. A further basis for the obligation of Member States to make good such loss and damage is to be found in Article [4(3) TEU], under which the Member States are required to take all appropriate measures, whether general or particular, to ensure fulfilment of their obligations under Community law. Among these is the obligation to nullify the unlawful consequences of a breach of Community law ...

37. It follows from all the foregoing that it is a principle of Community law that the Member States are obliged to make good loss and damage caused to individuals by breaches of Community law for which they can be held responsible.

38. Although State liability is thus required by Community law, the conditions under which that liability gives rise to a right to reparation depend on the nature of the breach of Community law giving rise to the loss and damage.

39. Where, as in this case, a Member State fails to fulfil its obligation under the third paragraph of Article [288 TFEU] to take all the measures necessary to achieve the result prescribed by a Directive, the full effectiveness of that rule of Community law requires that there should be a right to reparation provided that three conditions are fulfilled.

40. The first of those conditions is that the result prescribed by the Directive should entail the grant of rights to individuals. The second condition is that it should be possible to identify the content of those rights on the basis of the provisions of the Directive. Finally, the third condition is the existence of a causal link between the breach of the State's obligation and the loss and damage suffered by the injured parties.

41. Those conditions are sufficient to give rise to a right on the part of individuals to obtain reparation, a right founded directly on Community law.

42. Subject to that reservation, it is on the basis of the rules of national law on liability that the State must make reparation for the consequences of the loss and damage caused. In the absence of Community legislation, it is for the internal legal order of each Member State to designate the competent courts and lay down the detailed procedural rules for legal proceedings intended fully to safeguard the rights which individuals derive from Community law ...

43. Further, the substantive and procedural conditions for reparation of loss and damage laid down by the national law of the Member States must not be less favourable than those relating to similar domestic claims and must not be so framed as to make it virtually impossible or excessively difficult to obtain reparation ...

Francovich was seen as a seminal judgment.[108] At that time, most Member States did not provide a system of governmental liability for equivalent breaches of national law, and, in the negotiations leading up to Maastricht, drew the line at the notion that national courts should be able to award damages against the state for breach of EU law.[109] Notwithstanding this, most academic commentators welcomed the decision on the grounds that it would lead to better enforcement of EU law[110] and greater citizen empowerment.[111]

There was concern that this might lead to resistance from national administrations.[112] The most wide-ranging study found this to be unfounded.[113] All Member States had adopted the principle, normally by adapting their tort laws,[114] and national courts have not been hesitant to award substantial damages.[115] The only qualification was in cases of legislative liability, where a parliament has passed a law contradicting EU law. In such circumstances, there was widespread evasion with decisions by courts in Belgium, Greece, France and Italy all giving cause for concern.[116]

If national administrations and legal systems were largely quiescent, it does not follow that *Francovich* is necessarily a desirable or effective instrument. Many of the actions involved group actions or actions by large undertakings and this begged the question as to who is empowered by *Francovich*. One of the most powerful critiques of *Francovich* was offered by Harlow who observed that little thought had been given to who paid and who benefited from state liability.

C. Harlow, '*Francovich* and the Problem of the Disobedient State' (1996) 2 *European Law Journal* 199, 204

At the outset we should dismiss the vision of a squad of citizen policemen engaged in law enforcement. There are, of course, actions fought by individuals or groups of individuals. *Marshall* falls into this category; *Francovich* … and *Faccini Dori* may. In the field of environmental law, we find a developing pattern derived from human rights law, where a number of specialist organisations (NGOs) dedicated to the enforcement of human rights through courts operate; in Article [288] cases, their place has largely

---

[108] The academic literature is voluminous. P. Craig, '*Francovich*, Remedies and the Scope of Damages Liability' (1993) 109 *LQR* 595; R. Caranta, 'Governmental Liability after *Francovich*' (1993) *CLJ* 272 and M. Ross, 'Beyond *Francovich*' (1993) 56 *MLR* 55; E. Szyszczak, 'Making Europe More Relevant to its Citizens' (1996) 21 *ELRev*. 35; J. Steiner, 'From Direct Effects to *Francovich*: More Effective Means of Enforcement of Community Law' (1993) 18 *ELRev*. 3; R. Caranta, 'Judicial Protection Against Member States: A New *jus commune* Takes Shape' (1995) 32 *CMLRev*. 703.

[109] J. Tallberg, 'Supranational Influence in EU Enforcement: The ECJ and the Principle of State Liability' (2000) 7 *JEPP* 104, 114–16.

[110] Caranta, n. 108 above, 710.

[111] See e.g. Szyszczak, n. 108 above; Steiner, n. 108 above.

[112] Tallberg, n. 109 above, 110–11.

[113] M.-P. Granger, '*Francovich* and the Construction of a European Administrative *ius commune*' (2007) 32 *ELRev*. 157.

[114] On differences in approach in Germany and the United Kingdom see M. Künnecke, 'Divergence and the *Francovich* Remedy in German and English Courts' in S. Prechal and B. van Roermund (eds.), *The Coherence of EU Law: The Search for Unity in Divergent Concepts* (Oxford, Oxford University Press, 2008).

[115] The most widely reported was a fine of €26.4 million imposed by the Spanish Supreme Court in 2003 for failure to comply with EU broadcasting law, *Canal Satelite Digital* v *State Attorney* [2005] 5 *EuroCL* 33, Tribunal Supremo, 12 June 2003. S. Lage and H. Brokelmann, 'The Liability of the Spanish State for Breach of EC Law: The Landmark Ruling of the Spanish Tribunal Supremo in the Canal Satelite Digital Case' (2004) 24 *ELRev*. 530.

[116] *Ibid* 163–7.

been assumed by State-funded agencies. Whether or not these groups and agencies can be said to represent 'citizens' is a moot point but they do embody the private enforcement machinery to which the ECJ apparently aspires. This is not to imply, however, that the model of 'politics through law' espoused by the ECJ is best pursued through the medium of the action for damages; ... there is much to be said in favour of judicial review as the standard procedure, with annulment or declaratory orders as the standard remedy, in this type of citizen enforcement. In other areas, citizen enforcement is in any event a fantasy... [A]n overwhelming majority of actions against the Community are brought by corporations... [in litigation that] typically involves licences and other economic interests ...

This was particular apposite, she argued, because systems of government liability locked courts into tragic choices. Awarding compensation was never simply granting compensation to a plaintiff from some limitless budget. Instead, as Member States invariably never increased taxes to pay for liability claims, claims awarded to plaintiffs were awarded at the expense of other public goods – typically, as welfare spending is the highest proportion of national budgets, money intended for the old, the sick and the poor. She wondered whether such a distributive exercise was best done through the happenstance of individual litigation.[117]

Other work challenges the idea that systems of state liability give rise to a widespread practice of law enforcement through litigation. A series of case studies of litigation in relation to nature protection Directives in the Netherlands, France and Germany found that litigation was conditioned by a series of features, which were rarely all in place at the same time.[118] These included the organisational capacity of groups to litigate; effective access of parties to courts, unimpeded by standing rules or financial restrictions; the willingness by courts to give full interpretations; and the propensity of the administration to implement court rulings fully and quickly. Analysis of patterns of state liability and litigation in Germany and the United Kingdom, thus, found both very low levels of litigation and low levels of success. A total of sixty-two cases had been brought in these two large Member States in twenty years, of which seventeen had been successful: less than one per year for Germany and the United Kingdom combined.[119]

(ii) Conditions of liability

Francovich left open the question as to when a Member State would be held liable for breaching EU law. This was addressed in the joined cases of *Brasserie du Pêcheur* and *Factortame III*. Brasserie du Pêcheur, a French firm, had been forced to discontinue exports of beer to Germany in 1981 by virtue of a 'purity law' which prohibited the marketing of beers in Germany if they contained additives. In 1987, this law was found to restrict free movement of goods illegally.[120] Brasserie du Pêcheur sought compensation for the loss of sales between 1981 and 1987. In *Factortame*, a British law imposing a number of requirements on those wishing to fish in its waters, notably a requirement on other EU citizens to have a base and be resident in the

---

[117] *Ibid.* 210–12.
[118] R. Slepcevic, 'The Judicial Enforcement of EU Law Through National Courts: Possibilities and Limits' (2009) 16 *JEPP* 378.
[119] T. Lock, 'Is Private Enforcement of EU Law Through State Liability a Myth? An Assessment 20 Years after *Francovich*' (2012) 49 *CMLRev.* 1675, 1685.
[120] Case 178/84 *Commission* v *Germany* [1987] ECR 1227.

United Kingdom, had been declared illegal in 1991 on the grounds that it restricted freedom of establishment.[121] A number of Spanish fishermen subsequently claimed for loss suffered as a result of their illegal exclusion from British waters.

Joined Cases C–46 and C–48/93 *Brasserie du Pêcheur v Germany* and *R v Secretary of State for Transport ex parte Factortame (No. 3)* [1996] ECR I–1029

38. Although Community law imposes State liability, the conditions under which that liability gives rise to a right to reparation depend on the nature of the breach of Community law giving rise to the loss and damage ...

39. In order to determine those conditions, account should first be taken of the principles inherent in the Community legal order which form the basis for State liability, namely first, the full effectiveness of Community rules and the effective protection of the rights which they confer and, second, the obligation to cooperate imposed on Member States by Article [4(3) TEU] ...

40. In addition ... it is pertinent to refer to the Court's case law on non-contractual liability on the part of the Community.

41. First, ... Article [340 TFEU] refers as regards the non-contractual liability of the Community, to the general principles common to the laws of the Member States, from which, in the absence of written rules, the Court also draws inspiration in other areas of Community law.

42. Second, the conditions under which the State may incur liability for damage caused to individuals by a breach of Community law cannot, in the absence of particular justification, differ from those governing the liability of the Community in like circumstances. The protection of the rights which individuals derive from Community law cannot vary depending on whether a national authority or a Community authority is responsible for the damage.

43. The system of rules which the Court has worked out with regard to Article [340 TFEU], particularly in relation to liability for legislative measures, takes into account, inter alia, the complexity of the situations to be regulated, difficulties in the application or interpretation of the texts and, more particularly, the margin of discretion available to the author of the act in question.

44. Thus, in developing its case law on the non-contractual liability of the Community, in particular as regards legislative measures involving choices of economic policy, the Court has had regard to the wide discretion available to the institutions in implementing Community policies.

45. The strict approach taken towards the liability of the Community in the exercise of its legislative activities is due to two considerations. First, even where the legality of measures is subject to judicial review, exercise of the legislative function must not be hindered by the prospect of actions for damages whenever the general interest of the Community requires legislative measures to be adopted which may adversely affect individual interests. Second, in a legislative context characterised by the exercise of a wide discretion, which is essential for implementing a Community policy, the Community cannot incur liability unless the institution concerned has manifestly and gravely disregarded the limits on the exercise of its powers ...

46. That said, the national legislature – like the Community institutions – does not systematically have a wide discretion when it acts in a field governed by Community law. Community law may impose upon it obligations to achieve a particular result or obligations to act or refrain from acting which reduce its margin of discretion, sometimes to a considerable degree. This is so, for instance, where, as in the circumstances to which the judgment in *Francovich* relates, Article [288 TFEU] places the Member State

---

[121] Case C–221/89 *R v Secretary of State for Transport ex parte Factortame* [1991] ECR I–3905.

under an obligation to take, within a given period, all the measures needed in order to achieve the result required by a directive. In such a case, the fact that it is for the national legislature to take the necessary measures has no bearing on the Member State's liability for failing to transpose the directive.

47. In contrast, where a Member State acts in a field where it has a wide discretion, comparable to that of the Community institutions in implementing Community policies, the conditions under which it may incur liability must, in principle, be the same as those under which the Community institutions incur liability in a comparable situation.

48. In the case which gave rise to the reference in Case C-46/93, the German legislature had legislated in the field of foodstuffs, specifically beer. In the absence of Community harmonization, the national legislature had a wide discretion in that sphere in laying down rules on the quality of beer put on the market.

49. As regards the facts of Case C-48/93, the United Kingdom legislature also had a wide discretion. The legislation at issue was concerned, first, with the registration of vessels, a field which, in view of the state of development of Community law, falls within the jurisdiction of the Member States and, secondly, with regulating fishing, a sector in which implementation of the common fisheries policy leaves a margin of discretion to the Member States.

50. Consequently, in each case the German and United Kingdom legislatures were faced with situations involving choices comparable to those made by the Community institutions when they adopt legislative measures pursuant to a Community policy.

51. In such circumstances, Community law confers a right to reparation where three conditions are met: the rule of law infringed must be intended to confer rights on individuals; the breach must be sufficiently serious; and there must be a direct causal link between the breach of the obligation resting on the State and the damage sustained by the injured parties ...

54. The first condition is manifestly satisfied in the case of Article [34 TFEU], the relevant provision in Case C-46/93, and in the case of Article [49 TFEU], the relevant provision in Case C-48/93 ...

55. As to the second condition, as regards both Community liability under Article [340 TFEU] and Member State liability for breaches of Community law, the decisive test for finding that a breach of Community law is sufficiently serious is whether the Member State or the Community institution concerned manifestly and gravely disregarded the limits of its discretion.

56. The factors which the competent court may take into consideration include the clarity and precision of the rule breached, the measure of discretion left by that rule to the national or Community authorities, whether the infringement and the damage caused was intentional or involuntary, whether any error of law was excusable or inexcusable, the fact that the position taken by a Community institution may have contributed towards the omission, and the adoption or retention of national measures or practices contrary to Community law.

57. On any view, a breach of Community law will clearly be sufficiently serious if it has persisted despite a judgment finding the infringement in question to be established, or a preliminary ruling or settled case-law of the Court on the matter from which it is clear that the conduct in question constituted an infringement ...

65. As for the third condition, it is for the national courts to determine whether there is a direct causal link between the breach of the obligation borne by the State and the damage sustained by the injured parties. ...

67. As appears from ... *Francovich*, subject to the right to reparation which flows directly from Community law where the conditions referred to in the preceding paragraph are satisfied, the State must make reparation for the consequences of the loss and damage caused in accordance with the domestic rules

on liability, provided that the conditions for reparation of loss and damage laid down by national law must not be less favourable than those relating to similar domestic claims and must not be such as in practice to make it impossible or excessively difficult to obtain reparation ...

82. Reparation for loss or damage caused to individuals as a result of breaches of Community law must be commensurate with the loss or damage sustained so as to ensure the effective protection for their rights.

83. In the absence of relevant Community provisions, it is for the domestic legal system of each Member State to set the criteria for determining the extent of reparation. However, those criteria must not be less favourable than those applying to similar claims based on domestic law and must not be such as in practice to make it impossible or excessively difficult to obtain reparation.

Following *Brasserie du Pêcheur*, the Court of Justice moved towards a simple threefold test for establishing liability:

- the rule of EU law infringed must be intended to confer rights on the individual litigants;
- the breach of that rule must be sufficiently serious;
- there must be a direct causal link between the breach and the loss or damage sustained by the individuals.[122]

With regard to the requirement that the provision must be intended to confer rights on the individuals concerned, the test is the same as for direct effect. The provision must generate entitlements which are sufficiently identifiable, precise and unconditional to establish justiciable rights.[123]

The second part of the test has proved to be more complex. The criteria for determining when a breach is sufficiently serious to incur liability are set out in paragraph 56 of *Brasserie du Pêcheur*. In some instances, where the national authority enjoys no discretion under EU law, simple breach of EU law is sufficiently serious to incur liability. In areas where the Court of Justice believes that there is some margin for discretion, illegality is insufficient. The Member State must, as paragraph 55 above indicates, manifestly and gravely disregard the limits of this discretion. However, as no national authority enjoys discretion to disregard its limits in this way, the tests boil down to the same thing. A breach will be sufficiently serious if a Member State breaches an EU law which unequivocally prohibits such conduct. Breaches of EU law will be sufficiently serious to incur liability therefore where there is:

- a failure to transpose a Directive[124] or a clearly incorrect transposition of a Directive;[125]
- breach of an order of the Court of Justice;[126]

---

[122] Case C-118/08 *Transportes Urbanos y Servicios Generales* [2010] ECR I-635; Case C-568/08 *Combinatie Spijker Infrabouw-De Jonge Konstruktie and others* [2010] ECR I-12655; Case C-94/10 *Danfoss and Sauer-Danfoss v Skatteministeriet* [2011] ECR I-9963.

[123] Joined Cases C-178/94, C-179/94 and C-188/94–190/94 *Dillenkofer and others v Bundesrepublik Deutschland* [1996] ECR I-4845.

[124] *Ibid.*

[125] Case C-278/05 *Robins v Secretary of State for Work and Pensions* [2007] ECR I-1053; Case C-445/06 *Danske Slagterier v Bundesrepublik Deutschland* [2009] ECR I-2119.

[126] There was an allegation that the British Government had done this in Joined Cases C-46 and C-48/93 *Brasserie du Pêcheur v Germany* and *R v Secretary of State for Transport ex parte Factortame (No. 3)* [1996] ECR I-1029.

- breach of settled case law;[127]
- breach of a provision of EU law whose interpretation leaves no room for reasonable doubt.[128]

When these conditions are not met, liability will not be incurred.[129] If provisions are reasonably capable of bearing the meaning understood by the Member State[130] or the case law is unsettled or extremely recent, then no liability will be found.[131] State liability is thus a backstop measure. Its focus is sanctioning egregious or highly neglectful behaviour rather than securing redress for litigants. It has proved the highest hurdle for litigants to surmount when claiming loss from illegal state behaviour,[132] and leaves them exposed when the provision is neither clear nor can be interpreted to comply with EU law. This, in turn, raises an important further question, namely, whether it should be for the Court of Justice to attach punitive measures to the Treaties not to secure individual protection but rather national compliance with EU law.

The third condition, that of causation, has also proved challenging in recent years. Whilst, in principle, it is for the national court to establish that the illegal behaviour has led to loss, there are two circumstances which can limit the establishment of that loss. First, it must be shown that, if the Member State had not carried out the illegal behaviour, the claimant would not have suffered a loss. A failure to observe a particular procedural requirement is therefore unlikely to lead to liability. In *Leth*, therefore, a claimant was unable to claim for a loss of value in her home which occurred as a result of the extension of an airport in Vienna.[133] This extension had been carried out illegally as no environmental impact assessment had been carried out. However, the Court of Justice noted that this procedural failure did not of itself generate liability, as the requirement to carry out an assessment involved no substantive requirements to balance ecological versus other needs which would necessarily have led to the extension not taking place. Alongside this, if no direct burden is imposed by the Member State on the claimant, only exceptionally will loss be found to have been caused. In *Danfoss*, oil companies passed an excise duty on oil illegally levied on them by Denmark on to Danfoss, when it bought the oil from them.[134] Danfoss sued the Danish state which claimed that it should have sued the oil companies for the loss and not it. The Court agreed. It stated that if this was virtually impossible or excessively difficult under national law, then Danfoss should be able to sue the Danish government. Only in those circumstances, where the absence of a legal regime and the imposition of the illegal tax combined to cause the loss, would causation be found to be present.

---

[127] Case C-429/09 *Fuß* v *Stadt Halle* [2010] ECR I-12167.

[128] Case C-150/99 *Stockholm Lindöpark* [2001] ECR I-493; Case C-118/00 *Larsy* v *INASTI* [2001] ECR I-5063; Case C-470/03 *AGM-COS.MET* [2007] ECR I-2749; Case C-452/06 *R* v *Licensing Authority of the Department of Health ex parte Synthon* [2008] ECR I-7681. This was also the case in *ex parte Factortame (No. 3)* where the British restriction was seen as breaching a very clear EU law prohibition.

[129] For a discussion of the early case law see T. Tridimas, 'Liability for Breach of Community Law: Growing Up and Mellowing Down?' (2001) 38 *CMLRev.* 301, 310 *et seq.*

[130] Case C-392/93 *R* v *HM Treasury ex parte British Telecommunications* [1996] ECR I-1631.

[131] Case C-470/04 *N* v *Inspecteur van de Belastingdienst Oost/kantoor Almelo* [2006] ECR I-7409. Likewise in *Brasserie du Pêcheur*, the case law of the Court of Justice on when Member States could restrict the marketing of additives was considered to be unclear.

[132] Lock, n. 119 above, 1688–97.

[133] Case C-420/11 *Leth* v *Republik Österreich*, Judgment of 14 March 2013.

[134] Case C-94/10 *Danfoss and Sauer-Danfoss* v *Skatteministeriet* [2011] ECR I-9963.

(iii) Liability of judicial institutions

Arguably the most interesting and certainly the most challenging dimension to Member State liability concerns liability for rulings by national courts. This arose in *Köbler* v *Austria*.[135] Köbler, an Austrian university professor, had part of his salary calculated on his length of university service. Periods of employment in universities in other Member States, however, did not count. The Austrian Administrative Court initially decided to refer the matter to the Court of Justice, but then withdrew the reference on the grounds that the matter had already been decided by the Court, which had ruled such a practice to be lawful.[136] Köbler argued that the Member State was liable for this judicial failure to refer and misinterpretation of the Court of Justice's case law. The Court agreed that a misinterpretation had taken place. It considered whether this gave grounds for liability.

Case C–224/01 *Köbler* v *Austria* [2003] ECR I–239

33. In the light of the essential role played by the judiciary in the protection of the rights derived by individuals from Community rules, the full effectiveness of those rules would be called in question and the protection of those rights would be weakened if individuals were precluded from being able, under certain conditions, to obtain reparation when their rights are affected by an infringement of Community law attributable to a decision of a court of a Member State adjudicating at last instance.

34. It must be stressed, in that context, that a court adjudicating at last instance is by definition the last judicial body before which individuals may assert the rights conferred on them by Community law. Since an infringement of those rights by a final decision of such a court cannot thereafter normally be corrected, individuals cannot be deprived of the possibility of rendering the State liable in order in that way to obtain legal protection of their rights.

35. Moreover, it is, in particular, in order to prevent rights conferred on individuals by Community law from being infringed that under the third paragraph of Article [267 TFEU] a court against whose decisions there is no judicial remedy under national law is required to make a reference to the Court of Justice.

36. Consequently, it follows from the requirements inherent in the protection of the rights of individuals relying on Community law that they must have the possibility of obtaining redress in the national courts for the damage caused by the infringement of those rights owing to a decision of a court adjudicating at last instance ...

51. As to the conditions to be satisfied for a Member State to be required to make reparation for loss and damage caused to individuals as a result of breaches of Community law for which the State is responsible, the Court has held that these are threefold: the rule of law infringed must be intended to confer rights on individuals; the breach must be sufficiently serious; and there must be a direct causal link between the breach of the obligation incumbent on the State and the loss or damage sustained by the injured parties ...

52. State liability for loss or damage caused by a decision of a national court adjudicating at last instance which infringes a rule of Community law is governed by the same conditions.

53. With regard more particularly to the second of those conditions and its application with a view to establishing possible State liability owing to a decision of a national court adjudicating at last instance, regard must be had to the specific nature of the judicial function and to the legitimate requirements of

---

[135] P. Wattel, '*Köbler*, *CILFIT* and *Welthgrove*: We Can't Go on Meeting Like This' (2004) 41 *CMLRev.* 177.

[136] The Austrian court sought to rely on the Court of Justice's ruling in Case C-15/96 *Schöning-Kougebetopoulou* [1998] ECR I-47.

legal certainty, as the Member States which submitted observations in this case have also contended. State liability for an infringement of Community law by a decision of a national court adjudicating at last instance can be incurred only in the exceptional case where the court has manifestly infringed the applicable law.

54. In order to determine whether that condition is satisfied, the national court hearing a claim for reparation must take account of all the factors which characterise the situation put before it.

55. Those factors include, in particular, the degree of clarity and precision of the rule infringed, whether the infringement was intentional, whether the error of law was excusable or inexcusable, the position taken, where applicable, by a Community institution and non-compliance by the court in question with its obligation to make a reference for a preliminary ruling under [Article 267(3) TFEU].

56. In any event, an infringement of Community law will be sufficiently serious where the decision concerned was made in manifest breach of the case-law of the Court in the matter ...

At the time only Spain and Austria had systems of liability for judicial decisions in place. As the extract below illustrates, the judgment raised questions about legal certainty and traditional judicial hierarchies.

H. Scott and N. Barber, 'State Liability under *Francovich* for Decisions of National Courts' (2004) 120 *Law Quarterly Review* 403, 404–5

The extension of *Francovich* liability to courts of final decision has profound implications for the domestic legal hierarchy. After *Köbler* the English High Court could find itself compelled to pass judgment on a decision of the English House of Lords. A litigant disappointed by the House of Lords' decision could start a fresh action against the United Kingdom. The High Court, a few months later, would then be called on to assess whether the House of Lords had made an error of law that was sufficiently serious to warrant damages. The High Court would, almost certainly, refer the question to the ECJ under Article [267 TFEU] if it thought there was any doubt as to the correctness of the Lords' ruling. In response to such a reference the ECJ would give a ruling on the content of European law ...

This prospect raises a number of problems for domestic legal systems. First, and most superficially, it reduces legal certainty. This is not, as some in *Köbler* tried to argue, because it allows the reopening of concluded cases. Once the State's highest court has ruled, the judgment is definitive between the parties and cannot be challenged; the principle of *res judicata* is not affected. The *Francovich* action is a separate legal right and is directed against the State; a body which, ordinarily, would not have been a party to the original action. However, *Köbler* does have the effect of allowing litigants a second chance to raise the legal question apparently resolved in the primary action: frustrated in the House of Lords, the litigant could re-start the process through *Francovich* in the High Court. Secondly, the decision upsets the domestic legal hierarchy. The High Court would be obliged to question the correctness of a decision of the House of Lords made a few months earlier: it would have to decide whether there was a sufficient chance of error to warrant a reference to the ECJ, and, when this ruling was returned, how severe the error had been. Further problems might arise as this secondary action progressed up the legal order, perhaps ending with one group of Law Lords ruling on the judgment of their colleagues. Thirdly, the decision has the potential to create serious constitutional conflict within the domestic legal order. The German Constitutional Court has ruled that in exceptional cases it might refuse to accept rulings of the ECJ (see *Brunner* [1994] 1 CMLR 57). If such a decision was then challenged under *Francovich*, a first instance judge might be forced to choose between loyalty to the final court of appeal and to the ECJ.

However, for all this, *Köbler* hints that judicial liability will be found in only the most exceptional circumstances. The national ruling must manifestly infringe EU law, and this will be found in only the most exceptional case.[137] This was reaffirmed in *Traghetti*, where an Italian law on judicial liability confined this to cases of intentional fault and serious misconduct on the part of the court. With regard to this, it stated that judicial liability would only 'be incurred in the exceptional case where that court manifestly infringed the applicable law'.[138] It has been questioned, therefore, in which circumstances the Court of Justice would insist on judicial liability being applied, particularly as the Union judicial order relies on cooperation between national courts and the Court of Justice. Even occasional invocation of national judicial liability would destroy the ethos behind this cooperation.[139]

This last point might give the game away as to when judicial liability is to be imposed. In both *Köbler* and *Traghetti*, the Court stated that manifestly ignoring its case law or failing to make reference as required by Article 267(3) TFEU would lead to judicial liability. This is likely to occur not in cases of widespread violation of individual rights but where a senior national court is deeply unhappy with either the development of a line of reasoning by the Court of Justice or believes the latter has overstepped its authority. As we have seen in Chapter 5,[140] this dissatisfaction is quite widespread. It is furthermore not a bad thing, as it acts as a check on the Court of Justice and provides alternative sources of legal ideas. Judicial liability gets the lower courts in a national jurisdiction to do the Court of Justice's dirty work for it. If a senior court challenges the Court, there is now the possibility that litigants can take the matter before a junior court for damages, and to arbitrate between the Court of Justice and the senior national court. This cannot be a good thing.

FURTHER READING

G. Betlem, 'The Doctrine of Consistent Interpretation: Managing Legal Uncertainty' (2002) 22 *Oxford Journal of Legal Studies* 397

B. Beutler, 'State Liability for Breaches of Community Law by National Courts: Is the Requirement of a Manifest Infringement of the Applicable Law an Insurmountable Obstacle?' (2009) 46 *Common Market Law Review* 773

P. Craig, 'The Legal Effects of Directives: Policy Rules and Exceptions' (2009) 34 *European Law Review* 349

A. Dashwood, 'From *Van Duyn* to *Mangold* via *Marshall*: Reducing Direct Effect to Absurdity?' (2006–7) 9 *Cambridge Yearbook of European Legal Studies* 81

M. Dougan, *National Remedies Before the Court of Justice* (Oxford, Hart, 2005)
'When Worlds Collide: Competing Visions of the Relationship Between Direct Effect and Supremacy' (2007) 44 *Common Market Law Review* 931

S. Drake, 'Twenty Years after *Von Colson*: The Impact of "Indirect Effect" on the Protection of the Individual's Community Rights' (2005) 30 *European Law Review* 329

---

[137] B. Beutler, 'State Liability for Breaches of Community Law by National Courts: Is the Requirement of a Manifest Infringement of the Applicable Law an Insurmountable Obstacle?' (2009) 46 *CMLRev.* 773.

[138] Case C-173/03 *Traghetti del Mediterraneo* v *Italian Republic* [2006] ECR I- 5177.

[139] A. Davies, 'State Liability for Judicial Decisions in European Union and International Law' (2012) 61 *ICLQ* 585, 604–7.

[140] See pp. 223–45.

T. Eilmansberger, 'The Relationship Between Rights and Remedies in EC Law: in Search of the Missing Link' (2004) 41 *Common Market Law Review* 1199

M.-P. Granger, '*Francovich* and the Construction of a European Administrative *ius commune*' (2007) 32 *European Law Review* 157

K. Lenaerts and T. Corthaut, 'Of Birds and Hedges: The Role of Primacy in Invoking Norms of EU Law' (2006) 31 *European Law Review* 287

T. Lock, 'Is Private Enforcement of EU Law through State Liability a Myth? An Assessment 20 Years after Francovich' (2012) 49 *Common Market Law Review* 1675

E. Muir, 'Of Ages in – and Edges of – EU Law' (2011) 48 *Common Market Law Review* 39

L. Pech, 'Between Judicial Minimalism and Avoidance: The Court of Justice's Sidestepping of Fundamental Constitutional Issues in *Römer* and *Dominguez*' (2012) 49 *Common Market Law Review* 1841

C. Semmelmann, 'General Principles in EU Law Between a Compensatory Role and an Intrinsic Value' (2013) 19 *European Law Journal* 457

8

The Infringement Proceedings

CONTENTS

1 INTRODUCTION

This chapter considers the infringement and sanctions proceedings that the European Commission may bring before the Court of Justice against Member States for failure to comply with EU law. It is organised as follows.

Section 2 considers the main features of the infringement proceedings set out in Articles 258–260 TFEU. The central provision is Article 258 TFEU which allows the Commission to take the Member State to the Court of Justice and to obtain a ruling that it has failed to comply with EU law. The roles of the proceedings are threefold: to secure compliance with EU law; to serve as an instrument which contributes to the effective functioning of EU policies; and to be a public law arena, in which the different interests of the EU institutions, Member States, complainants and EU citizens can be mediated. All three roles are important and there is a danger in over-emphasising any one.

Section 3 considers the scope of Member State responsibilities under Article 258 TFEU. Actions can be brought only against the Member State, but they can be brought for the failure of any state agency, including courts and local and regional government, even if it is constitutionally independent of the central government which is, in practice, the body against whom the action is taken. The Member State is also responsible not just for legal instruments that conflict with EU law but also administrative practices that conflict with EU law. These usually have to be general and consistent in nature to attract liability. The Member State is finally under a duty to secure and police the effective functioning of EU law, and will be held liable for a failure to do so.

Section 4 considers the stages of the Article 258 TFEU procedure. These will be instigated following a Commission investigation or complaint by a third party. After an initial screening to check if there is a case to answer, the Commission starts the process through placing the dossier within EU Pilot, an online procedure whereby Member States have seventy days to set out their position and the Commission the same time to consider their response. The overwhelming majority of cases are settled at this stage. If there is no resolution, the Commission begins formal proceedings through a letter of formal notice setting out the complaint on which the Member State gives its observations. If there is still no resolution, a Reasoned Opinion is given by the Commission setting out the details of the complaint and a deadline for compliance. Following this deadline the matter is referred by the Commission to the Court of Justice.

Section 5 considers the management of the process by the Commission. It has complete freedom to decide whether to start the proceedings or to cease them. This has raised concerns about the transparency of the process and the accountability of the Commission for what takes place. Complainants, in particular, are granted only modest procedural guarantees. Centrally, there is a commitment to keep the complainant informed about the process and to reach a decision about whether to close a file or to instigate proceedings within twelve months. The secrecy of the process has come under increasing criticism from both the European Ombudsman and the European Parliament with the former stating that there are no good general reasons for it and the latter pushing for a Regulation to structure the process and make it more transparent.

Section 6 considers the sanctions that may be imposed. The Court of Justice may impose a fine on the Member State at the same time as it gives a judgment for non-compliance with EU law where the proceedings concern a failure by the Member State to notify transposition of a Directive. For all other infringements, a further proceeding under Article 260(2) TFEU must be instigated. This follows a similar process to that under Article 258 TFEU except that the Reasoned Opinion may be dispensed with. The Court of Justice may impose two types of sanction. The lump sum penalises the Member State for its failure to comply with EU law whereas the penalty payment acts to deter the Member State from continuing non-compliance. The central principles governing the size of the sanction are the seriousness of the breach, the duration of the breach and the ability of the Member State to pay the sanction, calculated by reference to its GDP and voting weight within the Council.

2 DIFFERENT DIMENSIONS TO THE INFRINGEMENT PROCEEDINGS

The enforcement of EU law through the assertion of individual rights before national courts is an important and distinctive feature of EU law. However, it relies on the EU law in question giving rise to individual rights and there will be many circumstances where it does not do this.[1] Furthermore, even when this is the case, the primary focus of litigation is to secure individual redress. Questions of compliance with EU law are tailored around this so that the judgment might address only some features of the illegal behaviour that is taking place, and not extend to other activities that fall outside the scope of the litigation.

The centralised procedures for the enforcement of EU law against the Member States are, thus, particularly important. They cover the full range of EU law for which the Court of Justice has jurisdiction. They can be framed so that they cover all the behaviour which breaches a particular EU law provision, and, finally, they go against the bodies with the most extensive responsibilities for the administration of EU law in the Union: the Member States. The central procedure is Article 258 TFEU.

Article 258 TFEU

If the Commission considers that a Member State has failed to fulfil an obligation under the Treaties, it shall deliver a reasoned opinion on the matter after giving the State concerned the opportunity to submit its observations.

If the State concerned does not comply with the opinion within the period laid down by the Commission, the latter may bring the matter before the Court of Justice of the European Union.

There are a number of other provisions which allow legal proceedings to be brought against Member States. Article 259 TFEU allows Member States to take other Member States before the Court of Justice for failure to comply with EU law. Its use is rare. Member States prefer to leave it to the Commission to take action rather than to institute legal proceedings themselves.[2] Article 108(2) TFEU allows legal proceedings to be brought against Member States for breach of the EU law provisions on state aids. However, it is Article 258 TFEU which plays the central role. It is used extensively: 1,775 infringement proceedings were open at the end of 2011.[3] Proceedings were open against all Member States, with Latvia subject to the lowest number of proceedings, 23, and Italy the highest, 135. The proceedings stretched, furthermore, across all the significant fields of EU law.[4]

If the use of Article 258 TFEU is wide-ranging and significant, it is less easy to sum up its central mission. Indeed, there are a number of ways of looking at what it does and should do. Each of these characterises the proceeding in a different way in terms of what it is to do and which elements of it are most significant and, correspondingly, each provides a different prism through which to evaluate the success and limits of the procedure.

---

[1] See pp. 295–6 in particular.

[2] Examples are rare. See Case 141/78 *France* v *United Kingdom* [1979] ECR 2923; Case C-388/95 *Belgium* v *Spain* [2000] ECR I-3123; Case C-145/04 *Spain* v *United Kingdom* [2006] ECR I-7917; Case C-364/10 *Hungary* v *Slovakia*, Judgment of 16 October 2012.

[3] *Ibid.* European Commission, *Twenty-ninth Annual Report on Monitoring the Application of EU Law*, COM(2012)714, 9.

[4] *Ibid.* 9–10.

(i) Policing compliance with EU law

The first view of Article 258 TFEU is that it is a policing procedure to secure the rule of EU law within the Union. This is the view expressed in much legal scholarship.[5] It is also expressed in the case law of the Court of Justice.[6] In *Commission* v *Germany*, the government of Lower Saxony concluded a contract for the collection of waste water which broke EU law on public procurement. The German Government admitted it violated EU law but stated that the contract could not be terminated without payment of substantial compensation to the contractor. The Commission brought the infringement before the Court of Justice. The German Government argued that it was inadmissible as there was no good reason for the Commission's action. It had admitted its guilt and the payment of compensation was disproportionately large when put next to the benefits of securing the EU law in question.

Joined Cases C-20/01 and C-28/01 *Commission* v *Germany* [2003] ECR I-3609

219. ...in exercising its powers under Article [258 TFEU] the Commission does not have to show that there is a specific interest in bringing an action. The provision is not intended to protect the Commission's own rights. The Commission's function, in the general interest of the Community, is to ensure that the Member States give effect to the Treaty and the provisions adopted by the institutions thereunder and to obtain a declaration of any failure to fulfil the obligations deriving there from with a view to bringing it to an end.

30. Given its role as guardian of the Treaty, the Commission alone is therefore competent to decide whether it is appropriate to bring proceedings against a Member State for failure to fulfil its obligations and to determine the conduct or omission attributable to the Member State concerned on the basis of which those proceedings should be brought. It may therefore ask the Court to find that, in not having achieved, in a specific case, the result intended by the directive, a Member State has failed to fulfil its obligations...

41. The Court has already held that it is responsible for determining whether or not the alleged breach of obligations exists, even if the State concerned no longer denies the breach and recognises that any individuals who have suffered damage because of it have a right to compensation...

42. Since the finding of failure by a Member State to fulfil its obligations is not bound up with a finding as to the damage flowing therefrom... the Federal Republic of Germany may not rely on the fact that no third party has suffered damage...

44. In the light of the foregoing, the actions brought by the Commission must be held to be admissible.

Securing compliance with EU law is important. As stated earlier, Article 258 TFEU is the only procedure which enables this in many fields of EU law. The procedure is also egalitarian. The Commission, not private parties, bears the cost of litigation. It can therefore act for those who do not have resources or do not have standing and also in cases where particularly large

---

[5] A. Dashwood and R. White, 'Enforcement Actions under Article 169 and 170 EEC' (1989) 14 *ELRev.* 388; L. Prete and B. Smulders, 'The Coming of Age of Infringement Proceedings' (2010) 47 *CMLRev.* 9. For a differentiated account that still falls within this school see A. Gil Ibañez, *The Administrative Supervision and Enforcement of EC Law, Powers, Procedures and Limits* (Oxford/Portland, Hart, 1999) esp. 26–35.

[6] For similar reasoning see Case C-76/08 *Commission* v *Malta* [2009] ECR I-8213; Case C-456/08 *Commission* v *Ireland* [2010] ECR I-859.

numbers of legal interests are adversely affected. There are, however, reservations to adopting such a view wholeheartedly.

First, conceiving the procedure in these terms can be excessively doctrinaire in individual cases. *Commission* v *Germany* is an example. The German Government argued that there was no practical way to rescind the contracts. It would violate individual property rights, disrupt construction of the waste water system as everything would have to be restarted, and lead to the public authorities having to pay large amounts of compensation. The German Government did not implement the judgment. It was then successfully prosecuted by the Commission under Article 260 TFEU and, finally, rescinded the contracts.[7] The problems remained, however.

There is a second danger. Compliance with EU law is valuable but not exclusively so. There are other values that may sometimes have to be weighed against it, particularly as in most cases we are not talking about 'law' or 'no law' but rather 'EU law' or 'national law'. This is not just an ethical question but also one of mischaracterising the procedure. As *Commission* v *Germany* indicates, the Commission has discretion whether or not to prosecute. The presence of that discretion indicates that other values and considerations can be taken into account by the Commission. As Börzel has noted, the mission of Article 258 TFEU is to consider *whether* 'the observed level of non-compliance is considered as a serious problem for a community'.[8] There may be circumstances where breaches of EU law cross that threshold but there may be other circumstances where a view can be taken that the level of illegality can be lived with because there are other more important issues at stake.

Thirdly, the analysis misdescribes the law. Article 258 TFEU does not permit the Commission to seek to secure full compliance with EU law 100 per cent of the time. The breach must be of a certain gravity before proceedings can be launched. Cases can always be brought against a Member State where a domestic law violates EU law. The position is more complex in respect of administrative practices. The Commission may, in certain circumstances, initiate proceedings against a Member State for violation of EU law through a single administrative act. These cases are rare and have all concerned residence or expulsion of non-nationals[9] or public procurement.[10] More often, the Court of Justice will find that the Commission may only bring an action if either the national law conflicts with EU law or if there is a general and consistent administrative practice breaching EU law.

In *Commission* v *Greece*, the Commission brought an action against Greece on the grounds that its hospitals in their tendering procedures for medical devices were excluding devices that met EU legal standards. The Greek Government claimed that it had transposed the relevant Directives into EU law and that it had sent a circular to Greek hospitals reminding them of their obligations under EU law. The Court of Justice nevertheless found a breach of EU law.[11]

---

[7] Case C-503/04 *Commission* v *Germany* [2007] ECR I-6153.

[8] T. Börzel, 'Non Compliance in the European Union: Pathology or Statistical Artefact' (2001) 8 *JEPP* 803, 818.

[9] Case C-441/02 *Commission* v *Germany* [2006] ECR I-3449; Case C-157/03 *Commission* v *Spain* [2005] ECR I-2911; Case C-503/03 *Commission* v *Spain* [2006] ECR I-1097.

[10] Joined Cases C-20/01 and C-28/01 *Commission* v *Germany* [2003] ECR I-3609; Case C-456/08 *Commission* v *Ireland* [2010] ECR I-859.

[11] In like vein see Case C-160/08 *Commission* v *Germany* [2010] ECR I-3713.

Case C-489/06 *Commission* v *Greece* [2009] ECR I-1797

46. ...even if the applicable national legislation itself complies with Community law, a failure to fulfil obligations may arise due to the existence of an administrative practice which infringes that law...

48. In order for a failure to fulfil obligations to be found on the basis of the administrative practice followed in a Member State, the Court has held that the failure to fulfil obligations can be established only by means of sufficiently documented and detailed proof of the alleged practice; that administrative practice must be, to some degree, of a consistent and general nature; and, in order to find that there has been a general and consistent practice, the Commission may not rely on any presumption...

49. It must be pointed out that, according to the information in the file before the Court, the products in question are products fulfilling the requirements of the European Pharmacopoeia technical standard and must, by their very nature, be purchased repeatedly and regularly by hospitals and, consequently, with an established degree of regularity.

50. None the less, at least 16 hospital contracting authorities rejected the medical devices in question, during tendering procedures, including the hospitals of Komotiní, Messolonghi, Agios Nikolaos of Crete, Venizeleio-Pananeio of Heraklion, Attica, Agios Savvas, Elpis, Argos, Korgialenio-Benakio, Geniko Nosokomio of Kalamata, Nauplie, P. & A. Kyriakou, Sparta, Panakardiko of Tripoli, Elena Venizelou and Asklipiio Voula.

51. The list of the hospitals mentioned by the Commission shows a variety in the size of the establishments, since some of the largest Greek hospitals such as Agios Savvas, Kyriakou and Asklipiio Voula are referred to, as well as medium-sized hospitals such as Argos, Agios Nikolaos of Crete or Sparta.

52. Moreover, that list refers to establishments with a geographical coverage encompassing the entire country with, in particular, hospitals in Athens, in the Peloponnese and on Crete, but concerns also a wide field of competence, including general hospitals, a children's hospital, a hospital treating cancer-related illnesses and a maternity hospital.

53. Therefore, it can be deduced that the administrative practice of the contracting authorities in question... demonstrates a certain degree of consistency and generality.

The approach taken, therefore, is more of a regulatory one. Concern is with the level of general performance of the Member State with a certain threshold being required before an infringement proceeding can be brought before the Court of Justice. This threshold will vary according to the case in hand. The instances where an isolated illegal act was sufficient involved either civil liberties concerns or significant public purchases where the particularity of each tender would always make it difficult to identify a general practice. Furthermore, it cannot be said that particular thresholds are identified with certain sectors. Public procurement is a field where isolated acts have led to successful infringement proceedings,[12] but it is also the sector which involved the *Commission* v *Greece* judgment above. Instead, there is a spectrum. In general, regard will be had to the duration, geographical spread and the number of illegal acts in determining whether infringement proceedings can be pursued against administrative practices.[13]

---

[12] See n.10 above.

[13] P. Wennerås, 'A New Dawn for Commission Enforcement under Articles 226 and 228: General and Persistent (GAP) Infringements, Lump Sums and Penalty Payments' (2006) 43 *CMLRev.* 31, 38.

(ii) An instrument for securing satisfactory performance of Union policies

This regard to the quality of legal performance of Member States suggests a second function to Article 258 TFEU: namely, that of being a public policy tool. Such a conception sees its dominant role as being to secure the effective functioning of EU policies. Compliance with EU law forms part of this but only insofar as it is instrumental to bringing about a successful policy.[14] Such a view explains the gradated approach to enforcement. If a Member State's laws fail to comply formally with EU law, then there is no hope of realising the policy as not even the formal norms are in place to bring it into being. Beyond this, in fields such as human rights, prosecution may be desirable for individual breaches as these are not measured simply in terms of general compliance but individual violations are seen as, per se, egregious. For other matters, prosecution only takes place where the alleged illegal behaviour seriously impedes the functioning of the policy. The Commission set out such a prioritisation in 2002.

European Commission, *Better Monitoring of the Application of Community Law,* COM(2002)725 final/4, 11–12

The Commission, in its White Paper on Governance,[15] announced that it would conduct surveillance and bring proceedings against infringements effectively and fairly by applying priority criteria reflecting the seriousness of the potential or known failure to comply with the legislation. Filling in the framework sketched out by the White Paper, the criteria are based on accumulated experience. They rank the following infringements as serious:

(a) Infringements that undermine the foundations of the rule of law
- Breaches of the principles of the primacy and uniform application of Community law (systemic infringements that impede the procedure for preliminary rulings by the Court of Justice or prevent the national courts from acknowledging the primacy of Community law, or provide for no redress procedures in national law: examples include the failure to apply the redress procedures in a Member State and national court rulings that conflict with Community law as interpreted by the Court of Justice).
- Violations of the human rights or fundamental freedoms enshrined in substantive Community law (e.g. interference with the exercise by European citizens of their right to vote, refusal of access to employment or social welfare rights conferred by Community law, threats to human health and damage to the environment with implications for human health).
- Serious damage to the Community's financial interests (fraud with implications for the Community budget, or violation of Community law in relation to a project receiving financial support from the Community budget).
(b) Infringements that undermine the smooth functioning of the Community legal system
- Action in violation of an exclusive European Union power in an area such as the common commercial policy; serious obstruction of the implementation of a common policy.

---

[14] M. Mendrinou, 'Non-compliance and the Commission's Role in Integration' (1996) 3 *JEPP* 1; M. Smith, *Centralised Enforcement, Legitimacy and Good Governance in the EU* (Abingdon, Routledge, 2009) 10–15 and 114–17.

[15] On this see pp. 381–8.

- Repetition of an infringement in the same Member State within a given period or in relation to the same piece of Community legislation; these are mainly cases of systematic incorrect application detected by a series of separate complaints by individuals.
- Cross-border infringements, where this aspect makes it more complicated for European citizens to assert their rights.
- Failure to comply with a judgment given by the Court of Justice against a Member State on an application from the Commission for failure to comply with Community law.

(c) Infringements consisting in the failure to transpose or the incorrect transposal of directives which can in reality deprive large segments of the public of access to Community law and actually are a common source of infringements.

The above criteria will help the Commission to make the best use of the various mechanisms designed to restore a situation in line with the Treaties as rapidly as possible, bearing in mind that the Commission's purpose in monitoring the application of Community law and bringing proceedings against infringements is not to 'punish' a Member State, but to ensure that Community law is applied correctly.

In practice, where it is found that an infringement meets these priority criteria, infringement proceedings will be commenced immediately unless the situation can be remedied more rapidly by some other means. Other cases – of lower priority – will be handled on the basis of complementary mechanisms [16]... which does not rule out the possibility of bringing proceedings for failure to fulfil an obligation. This approach will meet a concern for efficiency – more rapid and effective intervention including where proceedings for failure to fulfil an obligation would not be the most appropriate mechanism – while ensuring equal treatment for the Member States and for the different channels for identifying presumed infringements (complaints, cases identified by the Commission itself, cases referred by the European Parliament or the European Ombudsman).

These criteria indicate a willingness to prioritise cases according to policy needs.[17] Indeed, in 2012, in a Communication on *Better Governance for the Single Market*, the Commission promised to enforce compliance with EU law 'with utmost vigour' in this sector (thereby implying a less vigorous approach in other sectors!), and, to that end, even set out a list of legislation which it considered of particular importance and on whose correct application it would focus.[18] This prioritisation casts Article 258 TFEU as a less even-handed instrument than one simply concerned with securing the operation of the law. It is used to realise certain political preferences at the expense of others. Insofar as this will disadvantage certain Member States and social groups relative to others, it begs questions about whether there should be unstinting deference to the process.

However, this prioritisation is not a steady one. As we shall, the Commission is required to consider complaints about breaches of EU law raised by private and other actors. Insofar as

---

[16] See pp. 357–9.

[17] There is a prioritisation of pursuing certain styles of breach. These will be non-transposition of Directives, breaches with a particularly 'negative impact' on EU citizens and non-compliance with Court of Justice judgments. European Commission, *A Europe of Results: Applying Community Law*, COM (2007)502, 9.

[18] European Commission, *Better Governance for the Single Market*, COM (2012)259, 3 and 13–23. On discussion see Editorial Comments, 'A Revival of the Commission's Role as Guardian of the Treaties?' (2012) 49 *CMLRev.* 1553, 1555–6.

these shape its work, the procedure cannot be seen simply as a vehicle for its policy preferences. Furthermore, the extent to which it carries through on its statements is unclear. Protection of the environment and public health were mentioned as top priorities in the 2002 Communication above. However, this was not strictly followed. In the years following the Communication, environment was the sector in which the Commission examined most cases, followed by internal market, energy, tax and employment.[19] The case of the single market communication on enforcement is to be awaited. In the prior year, it made up 15 per cent of all infringement proceedings, behind both transport and environment.[20]

If Article 258 TFEU is used to secure a level of legal performance which allows policies to operate effectively, this raises questions about how receptive the process should be to national capacities. It is not possible in any Member State to realise perfect application of EU law on the ground on a day-to-day basis as this relies on many things, not least administrative resources and the general law-abidingness of the society.[21] Public policy specialists have therefore noted that the capacity of Member States to implement EU law falls into a number of categories.[22]

G. Falkner and O. Treib, 'Three Worlds of Compliance or Four? The EU-15 Compared to New Member States' (2008) 46 *Journal of Common Market Studies* 293, 296–7 and 308–9

In the *world of law observance*, the compliance goal typically overrides domestic concerns. Even if there are conflicting national policy styles, interests or ideologies, transposition of EU Directives is usually both in time and correct. This is supported by a 'compliance culture' in the sense of an issue-specific 'shared interpretive scheme'… a 'set of cognitive rules and recipes'… Application and enforcement of the national implementation laws is also characteristically successful, as the transposition laws tend to be well considered and well adapted to the specific circumstances and enforcement agencies as well as court systems are generally well-organized and equipped with sufficient resources to fulfil their tasks. Non-compliance, by contrast, typically occurs only rarely and not without fundamental domestic traditions or basic regulatory philosophies being at stake. In addition, instances of non-compliance tend to be remedied rather quickly…

Obeying EU rules is at best one goal among many in the *world of domestic politics*. Domestic concerns frequently prevail if there is a conflict of interests, and each single act of transposing an EU Directive tends to happen on the basis of a fresh cost-benefit analysis. Transposition is likely to be timely and correct where no domestic concerns dominate over the fragile aspiration to comply. In cases of a manifest clash between EU requirements and domestic interest politics, non-compliance is the likely outcome. While in the countries belonging to the world of law observance breaking EU law would not be a socially acceptable state of affairs, it is much less of a problem in one of the countries in this second category. At times, their politicians or major interest groups even openly call for disobedience with European duties – an appeal that is not met with much serious condemnation in these countries.

---

[19] Smith, n. 14 above, 123–31.

[20] European Commission, *Twenty-ninth Annual Report*, n. 3 above, 10.

[21] For a case study of British, German, Spanish and Dutch application (or non-application!) of Directive 91/155/EC, the Safety Data Sheets Directive, see E. Versluis, 'Even Rules, Uneven Practices: Opening the "Black Box" of EU Law in Action' (2007) 30 *WEP* 50.

[22] Most extensively see G. Falkner *et al.*, *Complying with Europe: EU Harmonisation and Soft Law in the Member States* (Cambridge, Cambridge University Press, 2005).

Since administrations and judiciaries generally work effectively, application and enforcement of transposition laws are not a major problem in this world – the main obstacle to compliance is political resistance at the transposition stage...

In the countries forming the *world of transposition neglect*, compliance with EU law is not a goal in itself. Those domestic actors who call for more obedience thus have even less of a sound cultural basis for doing so than in the world of domestic politics. At least as long as there is no powerful action by supranational actors, transposition obligations are often not recognized at all in these 'neglecting' countries. A posture of 'national arrogance' (in the sense that indigenous standards are typically expected to be superior) may support this, as may administrative inefficiency. In these cases, the typical reaction to an EU-related implementation duty is inactivity. After an intervention by the European Commission, the transposition process may finally be initiated and may even proceed rather swiftly. The result, however, is often correct only on the surface. Where literal translation of EU Directives takes place at the expense of careful adaptation to domestic conditions, for example, shortcomings in enforcement and application are a frequent phenomenon. Potential deficiencies of this type, however, do not belong to the defining characteristics of the world of transposition neglect...

...we suggest a fourth category: the 'world of dead letters'. Countries belonging to this cluster of our typology may transpose EU Directives in a compliant manner, depending on the prevalent political constellation among domestic actors, but then there is non-compliance at the later stage of monitoring and enforcement. In this group of countries, what is written on the statute books simply does not become effective in practice. Shortcomings in the court systems, the labour inspections and finally also in civil society systems are among the detrimental factors accounting for this.

Such analyses of Article 258 TFEU would have it be sensitive to these domestic environments, mindful that it can only stimulate limited change and that use in the wrong circumstances could be counter-productive.[23] However, if there is a case for responsiveness, there is also a danger of perverse consequences. The lesson from the extract from Falkner and Treib would be to punish the law-abiding Member States hard as these respond well to proceedings, and to be fatalistic about those where law is a dead letter as the latter will show limited responsiveness. Yet it is not clear that Article 258 TFEU is there to reinforce a world in which states are categorised into those seeking perfection, on the one hand, and those damned by their lack of resources, on the other.

Alongside this, there is the question of anticipating how Member States will respond to infringement proceedings: a different question from how they apply EU law. Börzel, Hofmann and Panke carried out a large quantitative study in which they looked at how Member States responded to infringement actions. They looked, in particular, for three types of responses. *Enforcement responses* were where Member States responded to the sanctions which, as we shall see, can be imposed. Compliance in such cases would be determined by national sensitivity to sanction. In this regard, they argued that wealthier, more politically powerful states can bear the economic costs of infringement proceedings most easily (power of recalcitrance). This

---

[23] A study of environmental and social policy case studies in Germany found that enforcement proceedings could stimulate compliance by shaming the national administration and mobilising social groups in favour of change. It was not always effective and could stimulate a backlash, however. D. Panke, 'The European Court of Justice as an Agent of Europeanization? Restoring Compliance with EU Law' (2007) 14 *JEPP* 847.

might in turn deter the Commission from pursuing these as aggressively, with the result that the more drawn out litigation would fall on the other states (power of deterrence). *Managerial responses* went to government possibilities to implement EU law. They noticed two challenges here. One is that of government autonomy, where there are a number of different actors within the Member State who can veto action (i.e. weak coalitions, powerful local governments) and the other is government capacity to impose its will on the domestic society. The third were what they called *legitimacy responses*, where government responses were conditioned by their commitment to EU law or support for the policy or measure at stake. Their study found little evidence that legitimacy issues affected Member State compliance with infringement proceedings. Nor did they find evidence of the Commission backing off from more powerful states. There was significant evidence of other factors coming into play, however.

> T. Börzel, T. Hofmann and D. Panke, 'Caving in or Sitting Out? Longitudinal Patterns of Non-compliance in the European Union' (2012) 19 *Journal of European Public Policy* 454, 467
>
> …we find strong empirical support for the effect of bureaucratic efficiency and a low number of domestic veto players on the ability to overcome violations of EU law. At the same time, the power of recalcitrance allows Member States to sit out long and escalating infringement proceedings. The power of deterrence, in contrast, cannot explain why countries such as Portugal, Denmark and the UK tend to settle cases early, while Italy, France, Greece and Belgium wait until the later stages. Finally, legitimacy does not seem to influence the persistence of non-compliance at all.
>
> Our study highlights that some of the major findings of the literature on the occurrence of non-compliance travel to the persistence of non-compliance. Unlike legitimacy, management and enforcement variables do have an impact on the persistence of non-compliance across the different stages and, to a lesser extent, on the duration of the infringement proceedings. Power and veto players keep infringement cases alive, while capacities increase the likelihood of early settlement. The findings show that states combining high capacities with low power, such as Denmark, tend to be the better compliers, whereas countries that lack government capacity and autonomy, but have political influence (e.g. Italy), are the biggest compliance laggards. However, our findings also hint at what the Commission and the ECJ can do to foster compliance and keep infringement proceedings from escalating. While changing Member States' political system and influence might be out of reach, capacity building through the transfer of financial resources and managerial know-how has long been a priority of the European Commission. Our findings suggest that this might actually be a feasible way to substantially reduce the persistence of non-compliance with the stages of the infringement proceedings.

This extract illustrates both the limits and possibilities of infringement proceedings. On the one hand, it is formally difficult for the type of incentives and support to be offered through the infringement proceeding that the authors suggest is necessary for compliance. As a regulatory instrument, they are quite limited. The only formal consequence of their instigation is a declaration that the Member State has breached EU law and a fine. On the other, infringements proceedings cast a shadow in which negotiations can and do take place, with the majority of infringement proceedings not going to court. The article above is a plea for imaginative solutions to the issue of national compliance which look beyond simple issues of enforcement to questions of capacity, know-how and domestic politics.

(iii) A public law framework to structure domestic negotiation of EU law

Concerns about the dogmatism of the first approach and the instrumentalism of the second approach have led to a third conception of the Article 258 TFEU procedure. In this, Article 258 TFEU is characterised not 'simply as single-faceted legal provision, but also a unique space of interaction for a multitude of actors'.[24] The procedure involves not just national governments and the Commission, but also other EU institutions, notably the Ombudsman, and EU citizens, be these complainants or those affected by national compliance or non-compliance with EU law. If the procedure serves as a forum enabling interaction between all these actors, it also involves the exercise of considerable administrative power. Successful Commission proceedings can change the quality of people's lives significantly.[25]

There is, consequently, a politics to infringement proceedings. Research suggests that if questions such as capacity go to Member State compliance with EU law once infringement proceedings have started, straightforward disagreement with the measure is a reason why many do not comply with the measure in the first place. Rates of non-compliance are, therefore, higher amongst Member States who voted against the measure when it is adopted.[26] The infringement proceedings represent, in part, a continuation of the political struggle within the EU legislative process. There is also another form of political struggle which takes place. By the nature of things, only certain domestic interests will be represented in the EU legislative process. The domestic application or transposition of EU law represents a moment when these other interests have an opportunity to exercise a voice in forums which may be more receptive to that voice. The infringement proceedings, therefore, represent the moment in this process when the Commission and other interests react to this domestic politics.

This vision of the infringement proceedings as a forum in which a variety of political interests are interested and a variety of politics takes place calls for a public law framework to structure and regulate all this, as clearly some of this politics might be desirable and other parts of it less so.

This framework would, first, focus on issues of participation, representation and accountability within the infringement proceedings themselves. It would look at whether different interests can participate sufficiently and whether they are sufficiently represented. These interests may be those of different private actors, domestic institutions or supranational institutions. It would also look at how accountable the Commission is to these different interests for its action or inaction during the infringement proceedings.[27] This is discussed in more detail when we examine the responsibilities of the Commission under the procedures themselves.

---

[24] Smith, n. 14 above, 17.   [25] *Ibid.* 15–20 and ch. 7.

[26] T. König and B. Luetgert, 'Troubles with Transposition? Explaining Trends in Member State Notification and the Delayed Transposition of EU Directives' (2009) 39 *BJPS* 163; B. Steunenberg and D. Toshkov, 'Comparing Transposition in the 27 Member States of the EU: The Impact of Discretion and Legal Fit' (2009) 16 *JEPP* 951.

[27] The starting point for such an analysis is R. Rawlings, 'Engaged Elites: Citizen Action and Institutional Attitudes in Commission Enforcement' (2000) 6 *ELJ* 4.

The framework might act, secondly, to constrain the expansion of EU law. In the United States, debates on 'anti-commandeering', whereby the federal legislature, Congress, cannot require states to enact or enforce federal programmes,[28] or 'uncooperative federalism',[29] whereby state administration of federal programmes (which is constitutionally allowed) is used by states to subvert these programmes where the latter are seen as unconstitutional or undemocratic, are not seen as evidence of a collapse of the system of law in the United States. They are rather seen as healthy constraints on central actors by local actors which not only act to curb central power but also to foster local innovation and debate. If the United States can allow this diversity and level of local challenge to central rule-making, it might be thought that the European Union should as well. There is a further reason. In the United States, a key ingredient in protecting states against central power is the extreme difficulty in passing federal law. Obtaining the agreement of the President and of sufficient numbers of Senators and Congressmen is, most of the time, far from straightforward. This difficulty is not present in the Union. In the Union the most effective check on excessive law-making may well lie in the fact that the vast bulk of European law is administered, not by a pan-Union executive but by national and regional authorities within Member States.[30]

On such a view, the infringement procedure is Janus-faced. It can be conceived as a threat to local democracy by being the remorseless, insensitive instrument through which EU law is enforced. Alternatively, it is a political arena where the implications of an EU law for a Member State are considered in the light of the domestic implications that have come to the fore. In this, it is one of the few places where national democracy can meet Union democracy, namely, that German or Slovenian citizens can talk about how an EU measure affects Germany or Slovenia, respectively. To be sure, this also takes place when a Member State transposes a Directive. The infringement proceeding debate is different. It is about how to mitigate the rigour of those norms, which cause most difficulties. The other feature of a debate at this stage is that it is a debate *ex post facto*, where the implications of an EU law on the ground are now more imminent and local concerns more focused.

This role for Article 258 TFEU is not formalised. However, the question of whether the rigour of EU law could be mitigated for non-legal reasons was addressed in *Commission v Poland*. The Commission brought an action against a Polish law, the Law on Seeds, which, in effect, prohibited the marketing of genetically modified seeds in Poland. This violated Directive 2001/18 on the deliberate release into the environment of genetically modified organisms, which allowed the marketing of these where they had been authorised by EU authorities. The Polish Government justified its non-compliance by challenging both the ethics of genetically modified food and by arguing that their release violated important tenets of Catholic thought.

---

[28] For a very useful comparison see D. Halberstam, K. Nicolaidis and R. Howse (eds.), *The Federal Vision: Legitimacy and Levels of Government in the United States of America and the European Union* (Oxford, Oxford University Press, 2001).

[29] J. Bulman-Pozen and H. Gerken, 'Uncooperative Federalism' (2009) 118 *Yale LJ* 1256.

[30] E. Young, 'Protecting Member State Autonomy in the European Union: Some Cautionary Tales from American Federalism' (2002) 77 *NYULRev.* 1612, 1708 *et seq.*; G. Bermann, 'Taking Subsidiarity Seriously: Federalism in the European Community and the United States' (1994) 94 *Colum. L Rev.* 331, 399.

Case C-165/08 *Commission* v *Poland* [2009] ECR I-6843

49. In its defence and its rejoinder, the Republic of Poland concentrated its arguments wholly on the ethical or religious considerations on which the contested national provisions are based...

56. However, a Member State cannot rely in that manner on the views of a section of public opinion in order unilaterally to challenge a harmonising measure adopted by the Community institutions... As the Court observed in a case specifically concerning Directive 2001/18, a Member State may not plead difficulties of implementation which emerge at the stage when a Community measure is put into effect, such as difficulties relating to opposition on the part of certain individuals, to justify a failure to comply with obligations and time-limits laid down by Community law...

57. Secondly, and as regards the more specifically religious or ethical arguments put forward by the Republic of Poland for the first time in the defence and rejoinder submitted to the Court, it must be held that that Member State has failed to establish that the contested national provisions were in fact adopted on the basis of such considerations.

58. The Republic of Poland essentially referred to a sort of general presumption according to which it can come as no surprise that such provisions were adopted in the present case. First, the Republic of Poland relies on the fact that it is well known that Polish society attaches great importance to Christian and Roman Catholic values. Secondly, it states that the political parties with a majority in the Polish Parliament at the time when the contested national provisions were adopted specifically called for adherence to such values. In those circumstances, according to that Member State, it is reasonable to take the view that the Members of Parliament, who do not, as a general rule, have scientific training, are more likely to be influenced by the religious or ethical ideas which inspire their political actions, rather than by other considerations, in particular, those linked to the complex scientific assessments relating to the protection of the environment or of human health.

59. However, such considerations are not sufficient to establish that the adoption of the contested national provisions was in fact inspired by the ethical and religious considerations described in the defence and the rejoinder, especially since the Republic of Poland had, in the pre-litigation procedure, based its defence mainly on the shortcomings allegedly affecting Directive 2001/18, regard being had to the precautionary principle and to the risks posed by that directive to both the environment and human health.

Whilst the Court holds that a Member State cannot defy EU law for populist reasons, it leaves open the question whether a state can do so for ethical or religious reasons. If such a defence does exist, it must be argued from the start and the law or administrative practice in question must be justified on those grounds. Leaving open the possibility of such a defence is not the same thing as suggesting that there *is* such a defence. The Court of Justice has not returned to this question since this judgment. A tentative opening remains, therefore, for public deliberation at a domestic level where, if a state actor comes to a view that an EU law poses insurmountable ethical or religious difficulties for its domestic law, this might not be incompatible with EU law.

There is a danger of focusing too exclusively on the infringement proceeding through this prism. To do so would fail to acknowledge the other elements of the process, namely, its concerns to secure compliance with EU law and to contribute to the effective functioning of EU policies. There is obviously a tension between these different dimensions to the proceedings, which might play out differently in particular instances, with concerns to emphasise compliance more prevalent in some cases and local concerns or policy needs more evident in other cases. It is a challenge to know how to mediate between these tensions other than to suggest somewhat vaguely and unsatisfactorily that these pressures will play out differently on a case-by-case basis.

3 SCOPE OF MEMBER STATE RESPONSIBILITIES

Infringement proceedings may only be instigated against Member States. Although actions are formally brought against the Member State, in practice, proceedings are taken against the central government. This prompts two related questions: first, what is considered to be state action for these purposes; and secondly, what capacities and responsibilities are to be assumed of the state, in particular whether it should be accountable for everything that happens within its territory.

(i) Acts and omissions of all state agencies

Two related doctrines have emerged from the notion that it is the Member State, and not the government, which is responsible for any illegality.[31] First, it is the acts and omissions of state agencies, and only these acts and omissions, which attract liability. Secondly, the Member State is responsible for these agencies even if these are constitutionally independent.

A state agency is considered to comprise any institution from any tier of government: be it national, regional or local.[32] It also comprises certain bodies that are not formally part of the state but which are subject to particular public controls.[33] Private companies will be held to be a state agency if the government exercises considerable influence over them. In *CMA*, a public body financed by a levy on the German food and agriculture sector, the Fund, was set up to promote German agriculture. A private company, the CMA, was further established to realise the objectives of the Fund. It had to observe the latter's guidelines and was financed by it. The CMA adopted a quality label certifying the qualities of produce from Germany. The Commission argued this label violated the EU provisions on free movement, as it was only available to German produce. The German Government argued, to no avail, that the CMA was a private body and, it, therefore, was not responsible.

Case C-325/00 *Commission v Germany (CMA)* [2002] ECR I-9977

17. In that regard, it must be recalled that the CMA, although set up as a private company is:
    - established on the basis of a law ... is characterised by that law as a central economic body and has, among the objects assigned to it by that law, the promotion, at central level, of the marketing and exploitation of German agricultural and food products;
    - is bound, according to its Articles of Association, originally approved by the competent federal minister, to observe the rules of the Fund, itself a public body, and additionally to be guided, in particular in relation to the commitment of its financial resources, by the general interest of the German agricultural and food sector;
    - is financed, according to the rules laid down by the AFG, by a compulsory contribution by all the undertakings in the sectors concerned.

---

[31] Case 77/69 *Commission v Belgium* [1970] ECR 237.   [32] Case 199/85 *Commission v Italy* [1987] ECR 1039.
[33] Case 249/81 *Commission v Ireland* [1982] ECR 4005; Case 222/82 *Apple and Pear Development Council* [1983] ECR 4083; Opinion of Advocate General Trstenjak in Case C-171/11 *Fra.bo* v *DVGW*, Judgment of 12 July 2012.

18. Such a body, which is set up by a national law of a Member State and which is financed by a contribution imposed on producers, cannot, under Community law, enjoy the same freedom as regards the promotion of national production as that enjoyed by producers themselves or producers' associations of a voluntary character... Thus it is obliged to respect the basic rules of the Treaty on the free movement of goods when it sets up a scheme, open to all undertakings of the sectors concerned, which can have effects on intra-Community trade similar to those arising under the scheme adopted by the public authorities.

19. Furthermore, it must be observed that:
   - the Fund is a public law body;
   - the CMA is required to respect the Fund's guidelines;
   - the financing of the CMA's activities, under legislation, comes from resources which are granted to it through the Fund, and
   - the Fund supervises the CMA's activities and the proper management of the finances which are granted to it by the Fund.

20. In those circumstances, it must be held that the Commission could rightly take the view that the contested scheme is ascribable to the State.

21. Thus it follows that the contested scheme must be considered to be a public measure... ascribable to the State.

There remains the question as to whether a similar definition of what constitutes a state body should be taken for infringement proceedings, as that taken for the direct effect of Directives.[34] In addition to the cases above, a body will be considered a state agency even if not subject to particular public controls if it is performing a public service and, for that reason, has special powers.[35] To adopt the case law on the direct of Directive would not only lead to more coherence but also prevent Member States escaping responsibility for EU law by simply contracting out their responsibilities.

The second dimension to the doctrine of state responsibility, that the government be responsible for the actions of constitutionally independent units, is more controversial. It has led to governments being accountable when they were unable, despite their best intentions, to get legislation through parliament.[36] It also has led to central governments being responsible for the actions of regional authorities even when the former do not have the power under their constitutions to compel action by the latter.[37] The most controversial application of this doctrine is holding Member States accountable for the actions of national courts. In *Commission* v *Italy*, infringement proceedings were brought against a series of decisions by the Italian Court of Cassation, the highest Italian civil court, in which the latter had consistently interpreted Italian law on customs duties in a way that conflicted with EU law.

---

[34] See pp. 311–12.
[35] Case C-180/04 *Vassallo* v *Azienda Ospedaliera Ospedale San Martino di Genova e Cliniche Universitarie Convenzionate* [2006] ECR I-7251.
[36] Case 77/69 *Commission* v *Belgium* [1970] ECR 237.
[37] Case 1/86 *Commission* v *Belgium* [1987] ECR 2797.

> **Case C-129/00 *Commission* v *Italy* [2003] ECR I-14637**
>
> 29. A Member State's failure to fulfil obligations may, in principle, be established under Article [258 TFEU] whatever the agency of that State whose action or inaction is the cause of the failure to fulfil its obligations, even in the case of a constitutionally independent institution...
> 30. The scope of national laws, regulations or administrative provisions must be assessed in the light of the interpretation given to them by national courts...
> 31. In this case what is at issue is Article 29(2) of Law No. 428/1990 which provides that duties and charges levied under national provisions incompatible with Community legislation are to be repaid, unless the amount thereof has been passed on to others. Such a provision is in itself neutral in respect of Community law in relation both to the burden of proof that the charge has been passed on to other persons and to the evidence which is admissible to prove it. Its effect must be determined in the light of the construction which the national courts give it.
> 32. In that regard, isolated or numerically insignificant judicial decisions in the context of case-law taking a different direction, or still more a construction disowned by the national supreme court, cannot be taken into account. That is not true of a widely-held judicial construction which has not been disowned by the supreme court, but rather confirmed by it.
> 33. Where national legislation has been the subject of different relevant judicial constructions, some leading to the application of that legislation in compliance with Community law, others leading to the opposite application, it must be held that, at the very least, such legislation is not sufficiently clear to ensure its application in compliance with Community law.

If the issue was framed as one of poor Italian legislation rather than one of judicial practice, it was the Italian Court of Cassation's interpretation of these laws which generated the problem. This slightly evasive reasoning was probably used to minimise the risk of directly confronting national courts. Holding national courts in breach of EU law can pose difficulties for judicial independence and *res judicata* as it can require the national government to suspend the effects of judgments and cast doubt on their binding effects.[38] Notwithstanding this, in subsequent dicta, both the Court of Justice and Advocates General have been much more explicit. The judiciary, including the highest courts in the land, are to be treated like any other state actor. The Member State is liable for them, and can be held liable for judgments which breach EU law.[39] These issues came back to haunt the Court of Justice in *Commission* v *Slovak Republic*. A Slovak court approved an arrangement between a bankrupt Slovak company, Frucona, and its creditors where these would receive only 35 per cent of the money owed to them. As compensation, they would receive a tax write-off for the money received. The Commission subsequently found that this tax write-off was an illegal state aid, and issued a Decision requiring Slovakia to recover the tax. The Slovak authorities claimed this was impossible because they were bound by the initial Slovak judgment authorising the deal, which acquired the force of *res judicata*. The Commission then took Slovakia before the Court of Justice.[40]

---

[38] Compare Case C-224/01 *Köbler* v *Austria* [2003] ECR I-239, discussed at pp. 333–5.

[39] In the case see Case C-154/08 *Commission* v *Spain* [2009] ECR I-187. Also see Opinion of Advocate General Mazák Case C-489/06 *Commission* v *Greece* [2009] ECR I-1797; Opinion of Advocate General Bot in Case C-42/07 *Liga Portuguesa de Futebol Profissional* v *Departamento de Jogos da Santa Casa da Misericórdia de Lisboa* [2009] ECR I-7633; Opinion of Advocate General Mengozzi in Case C-423/07 *Commission* v *Spain* [2010] ECR I-3429.

[40] The action was brought under the special powers for state aids in Article 108(2) TFEU rather than under Article 258 TFEU. The issues are the same, however.

Case C-507/08 *Commission v Slovak Republic* [2010] ECR I-13489

57. In the present case, the court judgment possessed of the force of *res judicata* relied on by the Slovak Republic precedes the decision whereby the Commission requires the recovery of the aid at issue....

59. ... attention should be drawn to the importance, both in the European Union legal order and in the national legal orders, of the principle of *res judicata*. In order to ensure stability of the law and legal relations, as well as the sound administration of justice, it is important that judicial decisions which have become definitive after all rights of appeal have been exhausted or after expiry of the time-limits provided to exercise those rights can no longer be called into question...

60. Accordingly, European Union law does not in all circumstances require a national court to disapply domestic rules of procedure conferring the force of *res judicata* on a judgment, even if to do so would make it possible to remedy an infringement of European Union law by the judgment in question...

61. As stated by the Advocate General in his Opinion, it is clear both from the documents before the Court and from the observations made at the hearing by the Slovak Republic that under national law there were available to the national authorities resources which, if diligently used, could have ensured that the Slovak Republic was able to recover the aid at issue.

62. Nonetheless, the Slovak Government has not provided any precise information on the circumstances in which it used the resources which were available to it.

63. In particular, the Slovak Republic has not clearly explained what action was taken in response to the request by the tax office that an extraordinary appeal be brought against the contested judgment.

64. The Court can therefore do no other than hold that, standing the Commission's specific criticism, the information provided by the Slovak Republic is insufficient to allow the conclusion that it took, within the prescribed period, all the measures which it could have employed in order to obtain the repayment of the aid at issue.

65. In the light of the foregoing, it must be held that, by failing to take within the prescribed period all the measures necessary to recover from the beneficiary the aid... the Slovak Republic has failed to fulfil its obligations...

In instances where the judgment precedes the Commission action, Member States will not be required, therefore, to compromise the principle of *res judicata*. They will be required to take all other means necessary to secure compliance with EU law, which, if the court is not a court of last resort, will mean exhausting the appeal process.[41]

If the challenge is most intense for breaches by the judiciary, it exists in relation to all constitutionally independent arms of government. Central authorities are enjoined to trespass beyond their constitutional limits to secure compliance with EU law. The problem arises from the fiction of the unitary state. In domestic law, individuals rarely sue the state but rather the agency which they allege is harming their interests. Litigation against the state in these instances causes a lot of problems. Whilst it puts duties on central authorities to uphold the rule of law, the constitutional independence of other actors may prevent effective measures by central government. They can only uphold the rule of law by violating domestic constitutional arrangements, thereby creating difficulties for the domestic rule of law. In public policy

---

[41] On the issues see M. Taboroski, 'Infringement Proceedings and Non-Compliant National Courts' (2012) 49 *CMLRev.* 1881.

terms, a system of perverse incentives is established. As other governmental actors will not be litigated against, there is simply no reason for them to take measures to comply with EU law, as they know that central government (with whom they are often in competition) will 'take the rap'.[42] Finally, this can hardly be good for local democracy. Powers of enforcement are used to justify central intervention at the domestic level to secure compliance, thereby curbing local self-government.

(ii) Accountability of state actors

The Member State will be responsible for any measure that formally conflicts with EU law: be it a law, statutory instrument or judgment. It is for the Commission to prove that the national law conflicts with EU law.[43] It is insufficient that it is ambiguous. The Court of Justice will therefore often insist that there be interpretations by national courts of the measure which conflict with EU law before holding that there is a violation.[44]

The Member State is also responsible for administrative practices conflicting with EU law. As we have seen, in some cases, a specific act must be sufficient whilst in others the Court of Justice will look for a generalised practice.[45] These practices can also consist of omissions and failures to act as state agencies are also under positive duties to secure the effective functioning of EU law. These duties have been developed through the interpretation of the fidelity principle, Article 4(3) TEU, and they have been explored in more detail in Chapter 5.[46] To recap, briefly, Member States can be subject to infringement proceedings for:

- a failure to secure legal certainty for EU law;[47]
- a failure to police EU law actively;[48]
- the duty to penalise infringements of EU law under analogous conditions applicable to infringements of national law of a similar nature and importance[49] and to ensure that penalties for breach of EU law are effective, proportionate and dissuasive;[50]
- the duty to notify the Commission of any problems applying or enforcing EU law.[51]

These are general duties reflecting assumptions about Member State capacity and good faith in EU law. They apply with particular force in the case of enforcement proceedings, as it is here, in the context of an alleged failure by the state, that they are explored at most length. There is, however, one particular duty which is specific to the infringement procedure itself

---

[42] In Belgium, for example, administrative coordination was so difficult and there was so much mistrust the Wallonian regional government actually took the Flemish regional government to the Court of Justice through the preliminary reference procedure for its failure to observe the free movement provisions. Case C-212/06 *Government of the French Community and Walloon Government* v *Flemish Government* [2008] ECR I-1683.

[43] See e.g. Case C-369/11 *Commission* v *Italy*, Judgment of 3 October 2013.

[44] Case C-300/95 *Commission* v *United Kingdom* [1997] ECR I-2649; Case C-418/04 *Commission* v *Ireland* [2007] ECR I-10947.

[45] See pp. 340–2.   [46] See pp. 213–15.

[47] Case C-159/99 *Commission* v *Italy* [2001] ECR I-4007; Case C-441/02 *Commission* v *Germany* [2006] ECR I-3449.

[48] Case C-265/95 *Commission* v *France* [1997] ECR I-6959.

[49] Case C-180/95 *Draehmpaehl* [1997] ECR I-2195.

[50] Case 68/88 *Commission* v *Greece* [1989] ECR 2965; Case C-81/12 *Asociatia ACCEPT* v *Consiliul National pentru Combaterea Discriminarii*, Judgment of 25 April 2013.

[51] Case C-105/02 *Commission* v *Germany* [2006] ECR I-9659.

and relates to the question of the burden of proof. If the Commission notifies the Member State of a possible breach of EU law and provides sufficient evidence of that breach, the duty is on the Member State to investigate that breach in order to prove otherwise. In *Commission* v *Ireland*, the Commission received twelve complaints of illegal dumping of waste or operating unlicensed waste dumps across Ireland in breach of EU environmental law. It wrote to the Irish Government but received only limited replies. The Irish Government argued that the Commission had failed to provide sufficient proof of any infringement.

Case C-494/01 *Commission v Ireland* [2005] ECR I-3331

41. ... in proceedings under Article [258 TFEU] for failure to fulfil obligations it is incumbent upon the Commission to prove the allegation that the obligation has not been fulfilled. It is the Commission's responsibility to place before the Court the information needed to enable the Court to establish that the obligation has not been fulfilled, and in so doing the Commission may not rely on any presumption...

42. However, the Member States are required, under Article [4(3) TEU], to facilitate the achievement of the Commission's tasks, which consist in particular, pursuant to Article [17(1) TEU], in ensuring that the provisions of the Treaty and the measures taken by the institutions pursuant thereto are applied...

43. In this context, account should be taken of the fact that, where it is a question of checking that the national provisions intended to ensure effective implementation of the directive are applied correctly in practice, the Commission which... does not have investigative powers of its own in the matter, is largely reliant on the information provided by any complainants and by the Member State concerned.

44. It follows in particular that, where the Commission has adduced sufficient evidence of certain matters in the territory of the defendant Member State, it is incumbent on the latter to challenge in substance and in detail the information produced and the consequences flowing therefrom...

45. In such circumstances, it is indeed primarily for the national authorities to conduct the necessary on-the-spot investigations, in a spirit of genuine cooperation and mindful of each Member State's duty, recalled in paragraph 42 of the present judgment, to facilitate the general task of the Commission...

46. Thus, where the Commission relies on detailed complaints revealing repeated failures to comply with the provisions of the directive, it is incumbent on the Member State to contest specifically the facts alleged in those complaints...

47. Likewise, where the Commission has adduced sufficient evidence to show that a Member State's authorities have developed a repeated and persistent practice which is contrary to the provisions of a directive, it is incumbent on that Member State to challenge in substance and in detail the information produced and the consequences flowing therefrom.

The onus on the Commission, in the case of administrative failure to comply with EU law, is to make no more than a prima facie case. It must provide sufficient evidence for it to be plausible that there has been non-compliance. Whilst this question appears just to be an evidentiary one, its consequence is to impose some investigatory duties on the Member States, which stems from the duty of cooperation in Article 4(3) TEU.[52] They must know what is going on in their

---

[52] See also Case C-135/05 *Commission v Italy* [2007] ECR I-3475.

backyard. If they do not, they are responsible for the consequences. A lower threshold of proof will be adduced to show non-compliance.

4 DIFFERENT STAGES OF ARTICLE 258 TFEU PROCEEDINGS

The description of the infringement proceedings set out in Article 258 TFEU is brief. It has been elaborated over the years by case law, and the proceedings are best seen as a series of stages which, extrapolated out, are:

- an initial screening by the Commission;
- the launch of EU Pilot except in urgent cases;
- a letter of formal notice by the Commission to the Member State that it is in breach of EU law;
- the submission of observations by the Member State;
- the issuing of a Reasoned Opinion by the Commission setting out the breach of EU law;
- a period for the Member State to comply with the Reasoned Opinion and submit observations;
- lodging of the case with the Court by the Commission;
- judgment by the Court.

The process is arduous and time-consuming. However, there are three central points in the process. These are the deployment of EU Pilot; the letter of formal notice setting out the breach and the Member State's observations on this; and the issue of a Reasoned Opinion by the Commission with possible referral to the Court if the Member State does not comply with that opinion.

(i) EU Pilot

There are two triggers to the procedure. The Commission will launch its own investigations ('own initiative') or it will receive a complaint of an infringement from a third party. Complaints from third parties will be recorded and acknowledged in all but a few exceptional circumstances.[53] Both triggers are numerous. In 2011, the Commission launched 1,271 investigations of its own and received 3,115 complaints.[54] The Commission will then carry out an initial assessment. The majority of third party complaints and about half of its own investigations fall at this hurdle.[55] If the Commission believes that a Member State has a case to answer, in cases of urgency it issues a letter of formal notice.[56] More commonly, it deploys EU Pilot. This is a process whereby, in return for responding relatively quickly to concerns, the relevant government is offered the possibility of informal settlement.[57] Its operation has been fine-tuned since first use in 2008 and is best described below.

---

[53] These will be if no grievance is alleged; it is against a private party; the complaint is made anonymously or it does not specify a Member State: European Commission, *Updating the Handling of Relations with the Complainant in respect of the Application of Union Law*, COM (2012)154, 4–5.

[54] European Commission, *Twenty-ninth Annual Report*, n. 3 above, 6–7.

[55] In 2011, the Commission opened 1,201 EU Pilot files of which 510 were based on complaints and 691 on its own investigation. European Commission, *Twenty-ninth Annual Report*, n. 3 above, 8.

[56] This is rare. In 2011, it occurred in only two disputes, albeit that one concerned twenty Member States. *Ibid.* 7.

[57] European Commission, *A Europe of Results: Applying Community Law*, COM(2007)502, 7–8. On the early process see M. Smith, 'Enforcement, Monitoring, Verification, Outsourcing: The Decline and Decline of the Infringement Process' (2008) 33 *ELRev.* 777.

European Commission, *Second Evaluation Report on EU Pilot,* SEC(2011)1629/2, 3–4

Wherever there might be recourse to the infringement proceeding, as a general rule EU Pilot is used before the first step in such a proceeding under Article 258 TFEU is taken by the Commission. This replaces the previous regular practice whereby the Commission sent administrative letters for this purpose. However, where urgency or another overriding interest requires the immediate launching of an infringement procedure under Article 258 TFEU, exceptions may be authorised and infringement procedures can be launched without previous contacts through EU Pilot. In such exceptional situations, the Commission can immediately respond to an alleged infringement by a Member State and urge that Member State to act in conformity with EU law. The system manages enquiries and complaints received from citizens and businesses as well as own-initiative cases. These include issues raised with the Commission in the European Parliament Petitions' Committee or via a letter from a Member of the European Parliament.

The database is built in English. However, several Member States have maintained their right to correspond in their official language. The need for translations is met by the Commission as necessary.

Individual files, including a description and questions about a particular issue, are then submitted to the Member State concerned via the EU Pilot application, giving ten weeks for the national authorities to reply to the questions raised as exhaustively as possible and propose a solution to the identified problems that is compatible with EU law. The Member States may likewise justify the need for an extension of the ten week period, thereby indicating to the Commission that they need more time to work on their response. It is decided on a case-by-case basis whether or not to accept the request for an extension of the general timeframe. In exceptional cases a timeframe shorter than ten weeks may be set. The reasons for a shorter timeframe are explained to the Member State.

Within a further ten weeks benchmark, the replies received from the Member State, if required, after being translated, are examined and an assessment of the Member State's response is uploaded into the EU Pilot database. If no solution compatible with EU law is found, an infringement proceeding under Article 258 TFEU may be launched. In the event of a complaint, a response will also be prepared to inform the complainant of the outcome of the enquiry into her/his complaint. If needed, the Member State authorities may be asked to provide additional information.

The assumption is that during the initial seventy days, national governments negotiate settlements with claimants. These are then assessed within the next seventy days by the Commission for their compliance with EU law. This assumption is not more than that, however. There is no requirement for the complainant to be involved and the second stage, the Commission assessment, involves simply it and the national government.[58] In 2013, all Member States, other than France, Spain and Belgium, met or were close to meeting the seventy-day time limit for submitting observations on the concern to EU Pilot. Even the most unresponsive state, France, took only ninety-three days.[59] The system is thus central to speeding up the infringement proceedings. The average time in the period 1999–2006 between the Commission opening a file on the matter and it being referred to the Court of Justice was twenty-three months.[60] There is now a target in relation to complaints by third parties for this not to be

[58] For criticism of this see *European Parliament Report on the 28th Annual Report from the Commission on Monitoring the Application of EU Law (2012)*, A7–0330/2012 (2012) para. 10.

[59] See http://ec.europa.eu/internal_market/scoreboard/performance_by_governance_tool/eu_pilot/index_en.htm%23;maincontentSec5.

[60] European Commission, *25th Annual Report on Monitoring the Application of Community Law*, COM(2008)777, 2.

more than twelve months.[61] However, if this has quickened national responses, it has led to the Commission being overloaded. Between 1 June 2012 and 26 March 2013, it opened 1,251 EU Pilot files but was only able to evaluate 378 files.[62]

At the moment, about 75 per cent of the files which pass through EU Pilot are resolved there. This might sound high but is not. In the period above, therefore, the Commission opened 1,251 files but was only able to resolve 237 files, a far less impressive 18.9 per cent.[63] The quality of the settlement is also of concern. There is no general access to the EU Pilot database to see what was offered by the Member State concerned. It is not required to set out within EU Pilot which, if any, stakeholders it engaged with, and whether they only came from its territory. Equally, the general public is not allowed to see the Commission's assessment of the legal and factual situation, nor is it even clear whether it is even required to submit all the evidence which informs its view onto EU Pilot. As a consequence, it is not possible for anybody, even other governments, national parliaments or the European Parliament, to make a submission on what is taking place. It is a closed system of negotiation at its most unaccountable and most opaque.

(ii) Letter of formal notice and Member State observations

The formal process only begins with the Commission issuing a letter of formal notice. The reason for this formal notice is that Article 258 TFEU only allows the Commission to issue a Reasoned Opinion once the Member State concerned has had the opportunity to submit observations. For the latter to be able to do this, there must be a letter of formal notice upon which they can submit observations. As the letter of formal notice is central to safeguarding the rights of defence of the Member State, it is also seen as framing the dispute. The Commission can only take a Member State to court for complaints that are specifically set out in the letter of formal notice.[64] A sense of its role is set out in *Commission v Denmark*. The Commission brought an action against the Danish Government for failing to transpose Directive 76/891/EC on electrical energy meters into Danish law. The Danish Government claimed that the letter of formal notice was insufficient as it had merely noted Denmark's failure to act and not set out what positive steps the Danish Government needed to take to remedy the breach.

Case 211/81 *Commission v Denmark* [1982] ECR 4547

8. It follows from the purpose assigned to the pre-contentious stage of the proceedings for failure of a state to fulfil its obligations that a letter giving formal notice is intended to delimit the subject matter of the dispute and to indicate to the Member State which is invited to submit its observations the factors enabling it to prepare its defence.

9. ... the opportunity for the Member State concerned to submit its observations constitutes an essential guarantee required by the Treaty and, even if the Member State does not consider it necessary to avail itself thereof, observance of that guarantee is an essential formal requirement of the procedure under Article [258 TFEU].

---

[61] European Commission, *Updating the Handling of Relations with the Complainant*, n. 53 above, 6.
[62] See n. 59 above. [63] *Ibid.* [64] Case C-522/09 *Commission v Romania* [2011] ECR I-2963.

10. It appears from the documents before the Court that by a letter dated 23 May 1979 giving formal notice the Commission merely asserted that in its view the Danish Government had not put into force the measures necessary to transpose Directive 76/891 into national law but refrained from specifying the obligations which, in its view, were imposed on that State by virtue of the directive and which had been disregarded.

11. In the present case, however, that fact did not have the effect of depriving the Danish Government of the opportunity of submitting its observations to good effect. On 7 June 1978 the Commission had addressed to the Danish Government a letter setting out the precise reasons which led it to conclude that the Kingdom of Denmark had failed to fulfil one of the obligations imposed on it by Directive 76/891. It was by reference to the position adopted by the Commission in that letter of 7 June 1978 that the Danish Government submitted its observations on 22 August 1979.

Whilst the Commission does not have to set out what Member States need to do to comply with EU law, it must set out all legal complaints in the letter of formal notice. Anything not mentioned there will be deemed inadmissible.[65] However, the Commission can subsequently bring in new evidence to clarify the grounds on which it is making the complaint on condition that this does not alter the subject matter of the dispute.[66]

(iii) Reasoned Opinion and period for national compliance

If, after the Member State has submitted its observations on the letter of formal notice, agreement is still not reached, the Commission will issue a Reasoned Opinion. As the subject matter of the dispute is delimited by the formal letter of notice, the Reasoned Opinion cannot modify this by introducing new claims.[67] However, account can be taken of changes in circumstances. In *Commission v Belgium*, the Commission challenged, in its letter of formal notice, a 1987 broadcasting law set up by the Flemish Communities.[68] The 1987 law was then replaced by a 1994 law. This latter law was challenged in the Reasoned Opinion. The Court of Justice rejected a Belgian claim that this amendment compromised the latter's rights of defence, noting that the national provisions mentioned need not be identical if the change in legislation resulted in the system as a whole not being altered.

The Commission must be much more direct in the Reasoned Opinion than the letter of formal notice. Whilst the latter need do no more than give a summary of the complaints, the Reasoned Opinion must give a coherent and detailed statement of the reasons that led the Commission to believe that the Member State has breached EU law, and which is sufficiently precise to enable the Court of Justice to determine whether a breach has taken place as alleged.[69] This should include a detailed statement of the legal and factual context to the dispute and take account

---

[65] Case C-371/04 *Commission v Italy* [2006] ECR I-10257.
[66] Case C-494/01 *Commission v Ireland* [2005] ECR I-3331.
[67] Case 278/85 *Commission v Denmark* [1987] ECR 4065.
[68] Case C-11/95 *Commission v Belgium* [1996] ECR I-4115. See also Case C-32/05 *Commission v Luxembourg* [2006] ECR I-11323.
[69] Case C-365/10 *Commission v Slovenia* [2011] ECR I-40; Case C-34/11 *Commission v Portugal*, Judgment of 15 November 2012.

of any resolutions submitted by the Member State.[70] Finally, and importantly, the Reasoned Opinion must also set out a reasonable period for compliance by the Member State. The following extract summarises the current position.

Case C–350/02 *Commission v Netherlands* [2004] ECR I–6213

18. In... an action for failure to fulfil obligations the purpose of the pre-litigation procedure is to give the Member State concerned an opportunity, on the one hand, to comply with its obligations under Community law and, on the other, to avail itself of its right to defend itself against the charges formulated by the Commission...

19. The proper conduct of that procedure constitutes an essential guarantee required by the Treaty not only in order to protect the rights of the Member State concerned, but also so as to ensure that any contentious procedure will have a clearly defined dispute as its subject-matter...

20. It follows that the subject-matter of proceedings under Article [258 TFEU] is delimited by the pre-litigation procedure governed by that provision. The Commission's reasoned opinion and the application must be based on the same grounds and pleas, with the result that the Court cannot examine a ground of complaint which was not formulated in the reasoned opinion... which for its part must contain a cogent and detailed exposition of the reasons which led the Commission to the conclusion that the Member State concerned had failed to fulfil one of its obligations under the Treaty...

21. It should also be emphasised that, whilst the formal letter of notice which comprises an initial succinct résumé of the alleged infringement, may be useful in construing the reasoned opinion, the Commission is none the less obliged to specify precisely in that opinion the grounds of complaint which it already raised more generally in the letter of formal notice and alleges against the Member State concerned, after taking cognizance of any observations submitted by it under the first paragraph of Article [258 TFEU]. That requirement is essential in order to delimit the subject-matter of the dispute prior to any initiation of the contentious procedure provided for in the second paragraph of Article [258 TFEU] and in order to ensure that the Member State in question is accurately apprised of the grounds of complaint maintained against it by the Commission and can thus bring an end to the alleged infringements or put forward its arguments in defence prior to any application to the Court by the Commission.

Once the Reasoned Opinion has been issued, the Commission must afford Member States both sufficient time to respond to its views and sufficient time to comply with the Opinion.[71] The minimum length laid down will depend upon a number of factors. These include the urgency of the matter and when the matter was first brought to the attention of the Member State by the Commission.[72] Perhaps the starkest example of what circumstances might be taken into account is *Commission v Belgium*. Under a 1985 law, Belgian universities were authorised to charge a supplementary fee (a 'minerval') on nationals from other Member States who enrolled with them. The Commission considered such action to be illegal following the *Gravier* judgment, given on 13 February 1985.[73] It had an informal meeting with Belgian officials on

---

[70] Case C-266/94 *Commission* v *Spain* [1995] ECR I-1975.

[71] See e.g. Case 211/81 *Commission* v *Denmark* [1982] ECR 4547.

[72] In determining this, account is taken not of when the letter of formal notice was sent but when informal contacts were first made. Case C-56/90 *Commission* v *United Kingdom* [1993] ECR I-4109; Case C-473/93 *Commission* v *Luxembourg* [1996] ECR I-3207.

[73] Case 293/83 *Gravier* v *City of Liège* [1985] ECR 593.

25 June 1985, where it expressed that view but also stated that it was still considering the effects of the judgment. On 17 July 1985 it issued a letter of formal notice stating that, in view of the onset of the new academic year, the Belgian Government should submit its observations within eight days. The Belgian authorities asked for more time. On 23 August 1985 the Commission issued a Reasoned Opinion, with the Belgian Government being given fifteen days to comply. The Belgians claimed that the action was inadmissible given the limited periods offered for compliance.

Case 293/85 *Commission v Belgium* [1988] ECR 305

13. It should be pointed out first that the purpose of the pre-litigation procedure is to give the Member State concerned an opportunity, on the one hand, to comply with its obligations under Community law and, on the other, to avail itself of its right to defend itself against the complaints made by the Commission.

14. In view of that dual purpose the Commission must allow Member States a reasonable period to reply to the letter of formal notice and to comply with a reasoned opinion, or, where appropriate, to prepare their defence. In order to determine whether the period allowed is reasonable, account must be taken of all the circumstances of the case. Thus, very short periods may be justified in particular circumstances, especially where there is an urgent need to remedy a breach or where the Member State concerned is fully aware of the Commission's views long before the procedure starts.

15. It is therefore necessary to examine whether the shortness of the periods set by the Commission was justified in view of the particular circumstances of this case...

16. .... the imminent start of the 1985 academic year may indeed be regarded as a special circumstance justifying a short time limit. However, the Commission could have taken action long before the start of the academic year because the major part of the Belgian provisions were already part of its legislation before the law of 21 June 1985. They were therefore known to the Commission at the latest when the judgment of 13 February 1985 was delivered, which was six months before the start of the 1985 academic year. Furthermore, it should be noted that at the time the Commission had not made any criticism of the minerval and had even given the impression, prior to the entry into force of the law in question, that it accepted that the minerval was compatible with Community law. In those circumstances the Commission cannot rely on urgency which it itself created by failing to take action earlier.

17. As for the Commission's alternative argument that the time limits laid down were not absolute and that consequently replies given after their expiry would have been accepted, it should be remarked that that factor is not relevant. A Member State to which a measure subject to a time limit is addressed cannot know in advance whether, and to what extent, the Commission will if necessary grant it an extension of that time limit. In this case, moreover, the Commission did not reply to the Kingdom of Belgium's request for an extension of time.

18. As regards the question whether the Kingdom of Belgium was aware sufficiently in advance of the Commission's views, it is common ground that although the Commission had expressed its views to the competent officials of the Belgian ministries of national education on 25 June 1985, at a meeting of the education committee of 27 and 28 June 1985 it stated that it was still considering the effects of the judgments of the Court in the field of university education. It follows that the Kingdom of Belgium was not fully informed of the definitive views of the Commission before these proceedings were brought against it.

It is only if compliance with the Reasoned Opinion does not occur that the matter may be brought before the Court of Justice. Indeed, once the period set out in the Reasoned Opinion has elapsed there is nothing a Member State can do to prevent the matter being heard by the Court. The Court will consider the position at the end of the period laid down in the Reasoned Opinion, and will not take account of subsequent changes.[74] Compliance by the Member State with the Reasoned Opinion after the deadline set out in the latter but before judgment will not therefore prevent the Court's declaring that the Member State has acted illegally.[75] The reasons for this are that the unwieldy nature of the procedure would, otherwise, be unable to capture breaches of a relatively short duration,[76] and that Member States could, otherwise, manipulate the procedures by simply bringing their conduct to an end shortly before judgment was given.[77]

5 ADMINISTRATION OF THE INFRINGEMENT PROCEEDINGS

(i) Commission's discretion over the management of the proceedings

There are a number of striking features about the Article 258 TFEU process. The first is how few actions reach court. In 2011, the Court of Justice had to give only sixty-two judgments under Article 258 TFEU.[78] A small fraction of the cases initially screened or which even go through EU Pilot are, thus, referred to the Court. Settlements may be made between the Commission and the Member State all the way up until the point of referral. The heart of the infringement procedure is thus an administrative process, with judicial proceedings predominantly acting as a backdrop to structure the negotiations between the Commission and the Member States. Secondly, the Commission wins the overwhelming majority of cases that reach court. In 2011, for example, 85 per cent of Commission actions were successful.[79] This is a reduction on historical averages, with the Commission typically winning over 90 per cent of the cases arriving before the Court of Justice: a staggeringly high proportion when it is remembered that the case can be dismissed not just on substantive but also on procedural grounds.[80] The third feature is that the instigation and cessation of proceedings is entirely a matter of Commission discretion.[81] Its motives for starting or stopping proceedings cannot be challenged[82] and neither can protracted administrative delays in instigating proceedings unless they are so extreme that they would infringe the Member State's procedural rights by making it more difficult for the Member State concerned to refute the Commission's arguments.[83]

---

[74] See e.g. Case C-200/88 *Commission* v *Greece* [1990] ECR I-4299; Case C-133/94 *Commission* v *Belgium* [1996] ECR I-2323.

[75] See e.g. Case C-446/01 *Commission* v *Spain* [2003] ECR I-6053.

[76] Advocate General Lenz in Case 240/86 *Commission* v *Greece* [1988] ECR 1835.

[77] Advocate General Lagrange in Case 7/61 *Commission* v *Italy* [1961] ECR 317.

[78] European Commission, *Twenty-ninth Annual Report*, n. 3 above, 10. It is a little misleading to compare this figure with the other figures for 2011, as these cases arrived at the Commission in earlier years.

[79] *Ibid.*

[80] D. Chalmers, 'Judicial Authority and the Constitutional Treaty' (2005) 4 *ICON* 448, 452–3.

[81] Case 48/65 *Lütticke* v *Commission* [1965] ECR 19. More recently see Case C-205/98 *Commission* v *Austria* [2000] ECR I-7367.

[82] Case 416/84 *Commission* v *United Kingdom* [1988] ECR 3127.

[83] Case C-96/89 *Commission* v *Netherlands* [1991] ECR I-2461.

These three features raise a number of concerns.[84] There is a concern about Commission leniency as the statistics suggest that it may well cease proceedings when national compliance is still far from perfect. Indeed, in 2006, the European Parliament deployed strong words in its assessment of the Commission's exercise of its discretion. In its report on the Commission's 2004 and 2005 Annual Reports it stated that the European Parliament:

> Calls on the Commission to place the principle of the rule of law and citizens' experience above purely economic criteria and evaluations; urges the Commission to monitor carefully the respect of the fundamental freedoms and general principles of the Treaty as well as the respect of regulations and framework directives; invites the Commission to use secondary legislation as a criterion for determining whether there has been an infringement of fundamental freedoms; [and]
>
> Calls on the Commission seriously to reassess its indulgence of Member States when it comes to the deadlines for submitting requested information to the Commission, adopting and communicating national implementing measures and correctly applying Community legislation at national, regional and local levels.[85]

Whilst this is something of an isolated condemnation, the European Parliament has noted in a subsequent report that it has been petitioned repeatedly by citizens who believed settlements did not fully protect their legal rights.[86] There has also been occasional abuse of the process with one celebrated instance in which a Greek Commission official publicly involved with the governing Greek political party chose not to take action against the Greek Government.[87]

There is also a concern about what checks and balances are in place to ensure that the Commission acts in a coherent and systematic manner in this field. In principle, the Commission prioritises certain proceedings,[88] but, as Smith has observed, enforcement policy owes as much to the organisational structures and politics of the organisation as anything else.

M. Smith, *Centralised Enforcement, Legitimacy and Good Governance in the EU* (Abingdon, Routledge, 2009) 136–7

When assessing the statistical information produced by the Commission, it must be acknowledged that there does seem to be a coherent output of the enforcement policy, although not one that necessarily matches the stated policy criteria. Whatever the stated approach to the enforcement policy, the result appears to guarantee that the environment sector always produces the greatest number of investigation and referrals to the ECJ. This sector is followed by cases on the internal market and/or energy and transport, although neither of these sectors are mentioned in the priority criteria at all. This of course may not be a result of the policy on enforcement, but rather the particular organisation of the Commission and the way in which each DG mobilises its resources to combat infringements.

---

[84] For academic commentary see R. Mastroianni, 'The Enforcement Procedure under Article 169 of the EC Treaty and the Powers of the European Commission: *Quis Custodiet Custodes?*' (1995) 1 *EPL* 535; I. Harden, 'What Future for the Centralised Enforcement of Community Law?' (2002) 55 *CLP* 495.

[85] *European Parliament Report on the Commission's 21st and 22nd Annual Reports on Monitoring the Application of Community Law (2003 and 2004)*, A6–0089/2006, paras. 13 and 15.

[86] *European Parliament Report on the 28th Annual Report from the Commission on Monitoring the Application of EU Law (2012)*, A7–0330/2012, para. 14.

[87] For analysis see Smith, n. 14 above, 175–83.   [88] See pp. 343–4.

For instance, DG Environment is one of the few DGs that contain a unit specifically responsible for dealing with infringements, as opposed to (say) DG Justice, Freedom and Security, which has no such department and generates very few infringement cases. It may be that the type of legislation produced by DG Environment (predominantly directives) is particularly prone to generating infractions (which appears to be confirmed by the Commission's Annual Reports), or it may be that the subject matter is particularly unpopular with Member States. It could be that DG Environment is particularly focused upon enforcement more than other DGs.

The final concern is that the process is unconstrained by the usual public law disciplines of participation, accountability and transparency. The Commission publishes the issuing of a letter of formal notice or Reasoned Opinion on its website.[89] However, no information is provided beyond the EU measure breached and the identity of the Member State concerned. The General Court has held that Member States are entitled to expect that all documents relating to active investigative procedures as well as the Reasoned Opinion remain confidential.[90] The argument is that this facilitates amicable resolution. This has now come under strong attack from both the European Ombudsman and the European Parliament.

The issues were addressed at most length in a Decision by the Ombudsman that concerned a complaint from Danish citizens about a change of practice by the Environment Directorate General in the Commission. In the period 2006–2007 it adopted a more open policy where it made available its letters of formal notices, in these cases concerning infringement proceedings against Denmark for breaching various nature conservation Directives. It discontinued that practice and refused to disclose to the complainants a supplementary letter that it had sent to the Commission. These then took the Commission before the Ombudsman, arguing that this failure constituted maladministration.

Draft Recommendations of the European Ombudsman in his Inquiry into Complaint 2207/2010/PB Against the European Commission, Decision of 26 September 2013

47. The European Ombudsman is not aware of any detailed empirical research into the benefits or drawbacks, for the Rule of Law and for compliance with EU law, of either an open or a secretive enforcement policy. It is, however, well known that EU Member States which generally have a more transparent public administration also tend to enjoy a high degree of Rule of Law and of compliance with EU law. It is also noteworthy that the internationally recognised transparency organisation *Transparency International* is financially supported by both public and private actors of very different kinds. The idea that transparency constitutes a means for better ensuring the Rule of Law appears to be broadly shared by very different societal actors, including powerful commercial organisations.

48. The European Commission has a long and profound experience in enforcing EU law. The Ombudsman naturally takes very seriously the preoccupations that this Institution may have with regard to risks associated with an increased level of openness in relation to its Treaty-based task of guarding the Treaties and the law flowing from them. If it is indeed the case that the Rule of Law in the EU would

---

[89] See http://ec.europa.eu/eu_law/infringements/infringements_decisions_en.htm.
[90] Case T-191/99 *Petrie* v *Commission* [2001] ECR II-3677. It is, however, possible to request documents about past infringement proceedings which are now closed. T-59/09 *Germany* v *Commission*, Judgment of 14 February 2012.

suffer detriment because of greater transparency in the Commission's enforcement approach, it would only be natural for the Commission to opt for secrecy.

49. The Ombudsman notes that the European Commission, and the tasks it fulfils, have evolved over time. For a long period, the Commission was very much 'on its own' in ensuring Member States' respect for EU (or EEC) law. Its main co-actor, the Court of Justice, was, and remains, a body that by its very nature can only act in response to cases brought before it. In such a context, the presumption that secrecy – some would in the earlier context broadly refer to diplomacy – would better serve the Commission's enforcement tasks, may indeed be entirely plausible.

50. The institutional and societal environment has changed however. The EU now has a strong and mature European Parliament. It also has a well-established civil society operating across the various sectors and issues covered by Union policy making. Other slightly less visible or well-known developments have taken place too, such as, to mention but one, the creation of a European network of ombudsmen who apply EU law.

51. In the Ombudsman's view, it is a plausible assumption that the overwhelming majority of such (historically) recent EU actors share, notwithstanding their sometimes diverging orientations, the above-mentioned common desire to contribute to a strong Rule of Law in the EU. It appears to be an equally plausible assumption that they are better able to support that aim if they have more ample knowledge of ongoing EU law enforcement issues.

52. When he opened the present inquiry, the Ombudsman asked the Commission a number of questions concerning its approach to public access to documents relating to infringement cases. He was prompted to do so by the content of the correspondence that the Commission had exchanged with the complainants. In its opinion, the Commission replied to those questions, essentially outlining the various approaches and arguments on which it intends to rely to prevent public disclosure of documents relating to ongoing infringement cases. The Ombudsman considers that the present inquiry presents an appropriate opportunity to address some of the key issues relating to public access to documents in relation to ongoing infringement cases....

54. The starting point is a general presumption of non-disclosure....

63. In the present inquiry, the Commission used a formulation that it appears to wish to adopt as a standard explanation [for non-disclosure]... It is that disclosure would be likely to cause 'undue external pressure'....

65. The Ombudsman is... concerned that, when left undefined, the notion of 'undue external pressure' can give the general public the impression that the Commission essentially wishes to refer to attempts by members of civil society, or even public policy makers, to bring forward, during the infringement investigation, their points of view regarding the issues that are the subject of the infringement investigation in question....

71. With regard to the Commission's view that disclosure of documents relating to ongoing infringement investigations may harm court proceedings because the administrative phase of the infringement procedure may give rise to a court case, the Ombudsman can only note that the Commission did not explain this point of view in any detail. The Ombudsman is not aware of any principles, rules, or case-law that clearly lend the argument credibility. He is therefore unable to engage with the Commission's point of view, but can only remind the Commission that, if it wishes to invoke the said argument in response to particular applications for public access to documents, the case-law requires it to explain in concrete and non-hypothetical terms why the argument is valid.

On the basis of his inquiries into this complaint, the Ombudsman makes the following draft recommendations to the European Commission:

The Commission should, when it receives applications for public access to documents relating to ongoing infringement cases, systematically consult the Member State concerned in order to obtain its view, notably, on whether it wishes to insist on its right to confidentiality referred to in the case-law on that issue. The written correspondence on the consultation should, as a rule, be public.

The Commission should, whenever a Member State consults it about possible public disclosure of documents relating to ongoing infringement investigations, and in case of a negative opinion, produce a reply that complies with the standards now required of Member States when they recommend the non-disclosure of a document by the Commission.[91] Relatedly, the Ombudsman recommends that, as a rule, the Commission's reply be classified as public.

The Commission should, in the present case and, generally, when handling applications for access, explain to applicants what it means by the expression 'undue external pressure' used to invoke the protection of the purpose of investigations as a basis for non-disclosure of documents relating to ongoing infringement investigations. Specifically, the Commission should explain what kind of potential external actors it wishes to refer to, and what it means by 'undue' and 'pressure'.

Moreover, the Commission should examine, when preparing its response to the present draft recommendations, whether it possesses concrete information on specific examples of intended or accidental disclosure of documents relating to ongoing infringement investigations which clearly resulted in harm to the purpose of the investigations in question… It should give such information in its response, and it should provide copies of any relevant documentation.

The Decision is a damning critique of existing practice. The Recommendations do not require full disclosure, but rather set a high burden which must be met for disclosure not to be granted. Although the Ombudsman refers to the Court of Justice's case law which allows both national and Commission refusal to disclose on grounds that this may comprise investigative and judicial process, he suggests that the reasons for this refusal are generally unconvincing. If his Recommendations are followed, the Commission would have to show why this was so in the case in hand, and if the national government refused disclosure[92] there is a suggestion that it must shame the national government by publishing its letter.

The Decision above must be seen within a context where the European Parliament is pushing for an EU Regulation to structure this discretion and make it more accountable. The European Parliament made an initial call in 2011, but returned with more gusto to the point in 2012.

European Parliament Report on the 28th Annual Report from the Commission on Monitoring the Application of EU Law (2012), A7–0330/2012

[The European Parliament:]

13. Reiterates its view that the discretionary power conferred by the Treaties upon the Commission in dealing with the infringement procedure must respect the rule of law, the principle of legal clarity, the

---

[91] Member States can only refuse access to a document if its disclosure risks a protected interest, which is here most likely to be protection of the judicial and investigative processes, in a specific and reasonably foreseeable way.

[92] On this see pp. 421–2.

requirements of transparency and openness and the principle of proportionality, and that nothing must under any circumstances jeopardise the basic purpose of that power, which is to guarantee the timely and correct application of Union law;...

17. Deplores the absence of any follow-up to Parliament's above-mentioned resolution on the 27th annual report, and in particular its call for a procedural law in the form of a regulation... setting out the various aspects of the infringement procedure and the pre-infringement procedure, including notifications, binding time-limits, the right to be heard, the obligation to state reasons, and the right for every person to have access to her or his file, in order to reinforce citizens' rights and guarantee transparency;

18. Calls therefore once again on the Commission to propose a 'procedural law' in the form of a regulation;...

19. Notes in this context the Commission's reply to Parliament's request for a procedural law, in which it expresses doubts regarding the possibility of adopting any future regulation... because of the discretionary power conferred by the Treaties on the Commission 'to organise the way in which it manages infringement proceedings and related work to ensure the correct application of EU law'; is convinced that such a procedural law would not in any way limit the discretionary power of the Commission, but would only guarantee that when exercising its power the Commission would respect the principles of an 'open, efficient and independent European administration' as referred to in Article 298 TFEU and the right to good administration referred to in Article 41 of the Charter of Fundamental Rights of the European Union;

Any such Regulation would require the agreement of the Commission and a qualified majority of Member States. As there is likely to be reluctance not only from the Commission but a number of these, it is doubtful whether it will be enacted in the short-term. However, the Resolution and the Ombudsman's Decision may have greater influence in how they inform the Court of Justice's interpretation of the Transparency Regulation 1049/2001 which sets out the terms on which access to documents may be obtained.[93] They suggest a climate where the historic reasons provided for non-disclosure are now seen as unconvincing, and this may, in turn, persuade the Court of Justice that the public should have access to these materials.

(ii) Complainants and Article 258 TFEU

Notwithstanding the key role they play, complainants are frozen out of the procedure. They have no right to require the Commission to commence proceedings or for them to be involved in the dispute. In *Star Fruit*, a Belgian banana trader alleged that it had been prejudiced by the organisation of the French banana market, which it believed was contrary to EU law. It complained to the Commission but the latter did not commence proceedings against France. Star Fruit sought to take the Commission before the Court of Justice for failure to act. The Court ruled that the action was inadmissible.

---

93 On this more generally see pp. 412–22.

Case 247/87 Star Fruit v Commission [1989] ECR 291

11. ... it is clear from the scheme of Article [258 TFEU] that the Commission is not bound to commence the proceedings provided for in that provision but in this regard has a discretion which excludes the right for individuals to require that institution to adopt a specific position.

12. It is only if it considers that the Member State in question has failed to fulfil one of its obligations that the Commission delivers a reasoned opinion. Furthermore, in the event that the State does not comply with the opinion within the period allowed, the institution has in any event the right, but not the duty, to apply to the Court of Justice for a declaration that the alleged breach of obligations has occurred.

13. It must also be observed that in requesting the Commission to commence proceedings pursuant to Article [258 TFEU] the applicant is in fact seeking the adoption of acts which are not of direct and individual concern to it within the meaning of the second paragraph of Article [263(4) TFEU] and which it could not therefore challenge by means of an action for annulment in any event.[94]

14. Consequently, the applicant cannot be entitled to raise the objection that the Commission failed to commence proceedings against the French Republic pursuant to Article [258 TFEU].

This freezing out is controversial even within the EU judiciary. It excludes parties who triggered the infringement proceedings and those suffering significant adversity because of illegal acts by national governments. In *max.mobil* the General Court held that the 'principle of sound administration' required complainants to be able to seek judicial review of Commission decisions not to take action against Member States under Article 106(3) TFEU, the provision that allows the Commission to require Member States to bring public undertakings into line with EU law.[95] Even though it distinguished this provision from Article 258 TFEU by suggesting that this duty does not apply to the latter, the General Court was clearly paving the way for it to do so as the principle of sound administration is a general principle of EU law. The Court of Justice was, however, having none of it and overturned the judgments. It held that the Commission was not required to bring proceedings and that individuals could require the Commission to take a position on a specific issue.[96]

This exclusion led in the 1990s to a large number of parties turning to the European Ombudsman to complain about the Commission's handling of their complaint.[97] In a 1997 report the Ombudsman observed:

[T]he Ombudsman has received many complaints concerning the administrative procedures used by the Commission in dealing with complaints lodged by private citizens concerning Member States' failure to fulfil their Community law obligations. The object of these complaints was... the administrative process which takes place before judicial proceedings may begin. The allegations... concerned, in particular, excessive time taken to process complaints, lack of information about the ongoing treatment of the complaints and not receiving any reasoning as to how the Commission had reached a conclusion that there was no infringement.[98]

---

94 There are the *locus standi* requirements for challenging EU acts. They are discussed at pp. 444–52.
95 Case T-54/99 *max.mobil v Commission* [2002] ECR II-313.
96 Case C-141/02P *Commission v max.mobil* [2005] ECR I-1283.
97 On these early years see Rawlings, n. 27 above.
98 European Ombudsman, *Own-Initiative Inquiry into the Commission's Administrative Procedures for Dealing with Complaints under Article [258]*, EO Annual Report 1997, 270.

Matters reached a nadir in 2001 with the *Macedonian Metro* Decision. This concerned a complaint that the Greek authorities had violated EU public procurement law in a tender for construction of a metro in Thessaloniki. The Ombudsman found that the Commission had lied to the complainant by telling him that it was closing the file because there was no breach of EU law when in fact the file was closed as an act of political discretion.[99] Secondly, the Commission had violated the complainant's right to be heard as it had sent its provisional views to the complainant eight days before closing the file and at the beginning of the summer holidays. This clearly gave the latter insufficient time to comment on these.[100] As a consequence, in 2002, the Commission set out certain procedural entitlements for complainants.[101] These have been updated and now involve the following principles:

- anybody may bring a complaint free of charge without having to prove an interest;
- all correspondence shall be recorded. The Commission shall acknowledge receipt within 15 days. It shall not be investigable if it is anonymous, fails to refer to a Member State, denounces private parties unless public authorities are involved or fail to act; fails to set out a grievance or sets out a grievance on which the Commission has adopted a clear, public, consistent position, or it concerns something which falls outside EU law. In such circumstances, the Commission shall inform the complainant and also inform them of other possible avenues, such as national courts or the Ombudsman;
- the Commission Departments will communicate with the complainant and inform them after each Commission decision of the steps taken in response to the complaint;
- the Commission will endeavour to close the case or issue a formal notice within one year from registering the complaint;
- if infringement proceedings are launched, the complainant will be informed of each procedural step adopted (formal notice, reasoned opinion, referral to the Court or closure);
- if the Commission closes the case, unless there are exceptional circumstances justifying urgent measures, the Commission shall give the complainant four weeks to submit comments having set out the reasons for its decision.[102]

Whilst this brings some structure to the processes, the Commission retains complete discretion over initiation and management of the proceedings. It also leaves a number of procedural matters unaddressed. Citizen involvement is left until very late in the day – four weeks before the closing of the file – and this rarely allows for effective input. Furthermore, there is no requirement to do more than provide ex post notifications of what took place to the complainant once a letter of formal notice has been issued.[103] More generally, there are few overarching norms governing the process, such as a commitment to fairness and non-discrimination in the investigation and follow-up of the complaint.[104]

---

[99] Decision of the European Ombudsman on Complaint 995/98/OV against the European Commission, 31 January 2001, paras. 3.1–3.7.
[100] *Ibid.* paras. 4.1–4.6.
[101] European Commission, *On Relations with the Complainant in respect of Infringements of Community Law*, COM(2002)141.
[102] European Commission, *Updating the Handling of Relations with the Complainant in respect of the Application of Union Law*, COM (2012) 154, 4–7.
[103] On these see Rawlings, n. 27 above, 18.   [104] Smith, above n. 14, 191–4.

6 SANCTIONS AND ARTICLE 260 TFEU

(i) Article 260 TFEU and two routes to sanctions

Prior to the Lisbon Treaty, the procedure in Article 258 TFEU could result merely in a declaration by the Court of Justice that the Member State concerned had breached EU law. Compliance with these judgments was uncertain.[105] Research found that, in 2002, for example, Member States failed to comply with 37.33 per cent of the judgments within twelve months.[106] The procedure for sanctioning Member States, introduced at Maastricht, was, therefore, amended and is now contained in Article 260 TFEU.[107]

Article 260 TFEU

1. If the Court of Justice of the European Union finds that a Member State has failed to fulfil an obligation under the Treaties, the State shall be required to take the necessary measures to comply with the judgment of the Court.

2. If the Commission considers that the Member State concerned has not taken the necessary measures to comply with the judgment of the Court, it may bring the case before the Court after giving that State the opportunity to submit its observations. It shall specify the amount of the lump sum or penalty payment to be paid by the Member State concerned which it considers appropriate in the circumstances.

   If the Court finds that the Member State concerned has not complied with its judgment it may impose a lump sum or penalty payment on it.

   This procedure shall be without prejudice to Article 259.

3. When the Commission brings a case before the Court pursuant to Article 258 on the grounds that the Member State concerned has failed to fulfil its obligation to notify measures transposing a directive adopted under a legislative procedure, it may, when it deems appropriate, specify the amount of the lump sum or penalty payment to be paid by the Member State concerned which it considers appropriate in the circumstances.

   If the Court finds that there is an infringement it may impose a lump sum or penalty payment on the Member State concerned not exceeding the amount specified by the Commission. The payment obligation shall take effect on the date set by the Court in its judgment.

The provision sets in place a dual track system of sanction, set out in Article 260(2) and (3) TFEU, respectively. As the latter is more straightforward, it makes sense to address it first.

There was felt at the Future of Europe Convention to be a particular problem with Member State failure to transpose Directives. It is seen by the Commission as widespread. It opened

---

[105] This was in large part due to limited use of the procedures by the Commission. In the period between the entry into force of the Maastricht Treaty and that of the Lisbon Treaty, only fourteen cases were brought before the Court. P. Wennerås, 'Sanctions against Member States under Article 260 TFEU: Alive but not Kicking?' (2012) 49 *CMLRev.* 145.

[106] Chalmers, n. 80 above, 453.

[107] For a detailed analysis of the provision see S. Peers, 'Sanctions for Infringement of EU Law after the Treaty of Lisbon' (2012) 18 *EPL* 33.

1,185 files on late transposition in 2011 and 763 cases were open at the end of that year.[108] It also presents a particular problem in that, as the Member State concerned has already had typically two to three years to transpose a Directive, a failure to transpose can mean that a Directive is still inoperative several years after its publication. To that end, Article 260(3) TFEU provides that in the case of infringement proceedings brought for failure to notify measures transposing a Directive, the Court of Justice can impose a sanction at the same time that it rules against the Member State under Article 258 TFEU. The procedure is discretionary. It relies on the Commission asking for a sanction to be applied, which it can choose not to do. The Commission has indicated, in this respect, that it 'should be used as a matter of principle in all cases of failure to fulfil an obligation covered by this provision'.[109] Notwithstanding this, it is only towards the end of 2011 that the Commission began referring cases to the Court with a recommendation for this sanction to be applied.

As there is no case law yet on Article 260(3) TFEU, its operation is marked by some uncertainty. One issue likely to arise will be the remit of the provision. In a 2010 Communication, the Commission observed that it believed that the procedure can be used not simply for a total failure to notify any measures to transpose a Directive but also in cases of partial notification, such as where the measures do not cover the whole of the national territory. It cannot be used for inadequate transpositions, however, where the Member State believes that it has met its duties under the Directive but the Commission believes the measures are insufficient. In such circumstances, the Commission will bring an infringement proceeding merely for a declaration to comply with EU law, and nothing more.[110]

Other breaches of EU law are governed by Article 260(2) TFEU. This requires, first, a holding by the Court of Justice that a Member State has breached EU law. Following this, the Commission may issue a letter of formal notice on which the Member State can submit its observations. If there is no resolution at this point, the Commission can refer the case to the Court of Justice for the Member State to be sanctioned. There is no need for the Commission to issue a reasoned opinion.

This raises the question as to whether the letter of formal notice is subject to the same legal constraints as the reasoned opinion in Article 258 TFEU, namely, it must give a statement of the reasons why there is non-compliance which is sufficiently precise to enable the Member State and the Court to identify whether this is the case, and must set out a reasonable period for compliance before the matter can be referred back to the Court. In *Commission* v *Portugal*, the Court of Justice stated that the opportunity for Member States to submit observations was an essential guarantee of both procedures.[111] It would appear, therefore, that the Commission could not subsequently include complaints that were not in the original letter of formal notice and is under a duty both to consider national observations submitted in response to it and to give Member States a date for compliance. This sense was reinforced in *Commission* v *Spain*, where the Court stated that the date for determining whether a Member State had complied

---

[108] European Commission, *Twenty-ninth Annual Report*, n. 3 above , 2–3. Late transposition of Directives is different from other breaches of EU law not simply with respect to the procedure followed, but also because as Member States either fail to notify or notify inadequate transposition, there is no need for a complaint by a third party or a Commission investigation.

[109] European Commission, *Implementation of Article 260(3) of the Treaty*, SEC(2010)1371, para. 17.

[110] *Ibid.* para. 19.

[111] Case C-457/07 *Commission* v *Portugal* [2009] ECR I-8091.

with the ruling was that set out in the letter of formal notice.[112] Compliance after that date does not prevent the Member State from being referred to the Court or absolve it from penalty.[113] The requirement of that date indicates it must be set out in the letter of formal notice.

The greatest challenge with the Article 260(2) TFEU procedure has not been the process itself but rather its limited instigation. There is a strong suspicion that the Commission is indulgent of national non-compliance with Court of Justice judgments. In the instances where Article 260(2) TFEU is instigated, a letter of formal notice is only issued many years after the initial judgment.

B. Jack, 'Article 260(2) TFEU: An Effective Judicial Procedure for the Enforcement of Judgments?' (2013) 19 *European Law Journal* 404, 406–7

In the first three enforcement actions that come before the Court, the Commission waited between 2 and 3 years from the Court's initial judgement before serving a formal notice under Article 260(2). In more recent cases, it has, generally, acted more quickly. In two of the last three cases before the Court, the formal notice was issued within 8 months of the Court's initial judgement, while in three earlier cases it was issued within 3 months of that judgement. However, more than 3 years elapsed in its most recent case. Once the formal notice has been served, the Commission has, since 2007, set an objective of referring cases back to the Court within 12–24 months. Following the abolition of the use of the reasoned opinion, it has revised this objective to between 8 and 18 months. Overall, however, the period between the Court's initial judgement and its judgement under Article 260(2) was still more than 3 years in two of the last three cases that it considered, and over 7 years in the third. The abolition of the use of the reasoned opinion will reduce this period. But, in practice, a period of at least 2–3 years is still likely to remain between the Court's judgements.

There is one other issue which is necessary to address before we look at the levels and types of sanction which are applied. This is the assumption underpinning both procedures that a financial penalty is sufficient to secure compliance and provide restoration for damage. There seems some evidence to support this. Jack looked at the responses where financial sanctions were applied. There were eight at the time of the article. In two instances, it was too early to tell but in the other instances compliance was relatively fast.

B. Jack, 'Article 260(2) TFEU: An Effective Judicial Procedure for the Enforcement of Judgments?' (2013) 19 *European Law Journal* 404, 412–13

The remaining six cases, with one important exception, suggest that penalty payments have, ultimately, been effective in achieving Member State compliance with Court judgments. Greece initially ignored the Court's first penalty payment order, neither addressing the requirement to close the illegal waste site involved nor making the required penalty payments. The European Parliament's Environment Committee, by making the issue a standing item on its agenda, pressurised the Commission and, indirectly, Greece

---

[112] Case C-610/10 *Commission v Spain*, Judgment of 11 December 2012.
[113] Case C-475/08 *Commission v Belgium* [2009] ECR I-11503; Case C-407/09 *Commission v Greece* [2011] ECR I-2467.

to secure compliance. Greece eventually complied with the Court's judgement and discharged the penalty payments due. Their delay transformed the daily €20 000 penalty payment into a total penalty of €4.7 million. This is equivalent to a delay of 235 days. Subsequently, Portugal took 189 days to comply with the Court's judgement, confirming that its national laws infringed EU public procurement law, turning a daily payment of €19 392 into a total penalty of almost €3.7 million. In the remaining cases, however, Member States complied more quickly. In one, a penalty payment was suspended for 1 month to enable Greece to produce evidence establishing the recovery of illegal state aid payments. Greece complied, and consequently no penalty payment fell due. Equally, France was ordered to pay €57 761 250 for each 6-month period in which it continued not to adequately enforce fishery conservation laws. Only one such payment was made before the Commission adjudged compliance had been fully achieved. Finally, France took just 24 days to comply with the Court's judgement, confirming that its national laws failed to fully comply with Directive 85/374 on producer responsibility for defective products. This, therefore, turned a daily penalty payment of €31 650 into a total payment of €759 000. Ultimately, however, compliance was achieved in each case, and the penalty payments levied paid to the Commission.

The relative success of these cases, however, obscures an ongoing failure. In October 2006, the Court held that Greek legislation making the installation and operation of electrical, electromechanical and electronic games illegal contravened the free movement of goods and services and the freedom of establishment. In June 2009, the Court ordered Greece to pay a penalty payment of €31 536 per day until it complied with its initial judgement. Greece has so far paid a total of €23 841 216 in penalty payments to the Commission, but its failure to comply with the Court's initial judgement continues. The Court's financial penalty clearly has not had the intended coercive effect. This highlights the danger that penalty payments may prove ineffective where Member States consider that broader national interests outweigh the economic pressure that they apply.

If financial penalties seem to secure formal compliance, the last point made by Jack raises a wider issue. They do not go to the wider dynamics which led to the breach of EU law. In some cases, these may be simple deviance. Often, however, complying with EU law will be a significant domestic political challenge for the Member State concerned. It may involve an administrative capacity it does not have or imposing significant costs on a recalcitrant population. Infringement proceedings are, thus, year-on-year highest in these fields which are most complex and costly to implement, namely, transport, energy, environment and the single market.[114] These dynamics are not addressed by financial penalties, which, insofar as they impose extra costs on stretched administrations and can fan resentment against unpopular measures, can exacerbate the problems rather than resolve them.

(ii) Level and form of sanctions levied under Article 260 TFEU

Two types of financial sanction, the lump sum and the penalty payment, are mentioned in Article 260 TFEU. The relationship between these was set out most clearly in *Commission* v *France*.[115] In 1991 the Court of Justice found France had failed to comply with EU fisheries

---

[114] M. Smith, 'Inter-Institutional Dialogue and the Establishment of Enforcement Norms: A Decade of Financial Penalties under Article 228 EC (now Article 260 TFEU)' (2010) 16 *EPL* 547, 558.

[115] Case C-64/88 *Commission* v *France* [1991] ECR I-2727.

law between 1984 and 1987 by insufficiently monitoring the mesh size of fishing nets, thereby allowing undersized fish to be caught and sold. Little was done to implement this judgment, and the Commission, therefore, instigated Article 260 TFEU proceedings. It asked for a lump sum sanction to be imposed to punish France for its current and past behaviour and a penalty payment also to be imposed to induce it to comply as quickly as possible.

Case C-304/02 *Commission* v *France* [2005] ECR I-6263

80. The procedure laid down in Article [260 TFEU] has the objective of inducing a defaulting Member State to comply with a judgment establishing a breach of obligations and thereby of ensuring that Community law is in fact applied. The measures provided for by that provision, namely a lump sum and a penalty payment, are both intended to achieve this objective.

81. Application of each of those measures depends on their respective ability to meet the objective pursued according to the circumstances of the case. While the imposition of a penalty payment seems particularly suited to inducing a Member State to put an end as soon as possible to a breach of obligations which, in the absence of such a measure, would tend to persist, the imposition of a lump sum is based more on assessment of the effects on public and private interests of the failure of the Member State concerned to comply with its obligations, in particular where the breach has persisted for a long period since the judgment which initially established it.

82. That being so, recourse to both types of penalty provided for in Article [260(2) TFEU] is not precluded, in particular where the breach of obligations both has continued for a long period and is inclined to persist....

91. ...The procedure provided for in Article [260(2) TFEU] is a special judicial procedure, peculiar to Community law, which cannot be equated with a civil procedure. The order imposing a penalty payment and/or a lump sum is not intended to compensate for damage caused by the Member State concerned, but to place it under economic pressure which induces it to put an end to the breach established. The financial penalties imposed must therefore be decided upon according to the degree of persuasion needed in order for the Member State in question to alter its conduct....

103. As to those submissions, while it is clear that a penalty payment is likely to encourage the defaulting Member State to put an end as soon as possible to the breach that has been established... it should be remembered that the Commission's suggestions cannot bind the Court and are only a useful point of reference... In exercising its discretion, it is for the Court to set the penalty payment so that it is appropriate to the circumstances and proportionate both to the breach that has been established and to the ability to pay of the Member State concerned...

104. In that light... the basic criteria which must be taken into account in order to ensure that penalty payments have coercive force and Community law is applied uniformly and effectively are, in principle, the duration of the infringement, its degree of seriousness and the ability of the Member State to pay. In applying those criteria, regard should be had in particular to the effects of failure to comply on private and public interests and to the urgency of getting the Member State concerned to fulfil its obligations...

113. ... the French Republic should be ordered to pay to the Commission, into the account 'European Community own resources', a penalty payment of 182.5 x EUR 316 500, that is to say of EUR 57 761 250, for each period of six months from delivery of the present judgment at the end of which the judgment in Case C-64/88 *Commission* v *France* has not yet been fully complied with.

114. In a situation such as that which is the subject of the present judgment, in light of the fact that the breach of obligations has persisted for a long period since the judgment which initially established it and of the public and private interests at issue, it is essential to order payment of a lump sum (see paragraph 81 of the present judgment).

115. The specific circumstances of the case are fairly assessed by setting the amount of the lump sum which the French Republic will have to pay at EUR 20 000 000.

The judgment indicates that, possibly contrary to the explicit wording of Article 260(3) TFEU, both a lump sum sanction and penalty payments can be imposed for the same breach. This is because each serves a different function. The lump sum is punitive in nature. It is sanctioning the Member State for the damage caused. By contrast, the periodic penalty has a deterrent objective, namely, to provide incentives for the Member State to comply with EU law by imposing financial penalties until it does. In general, the Commission will press for both.[116] However, by dint of their different functions, there are certain instances where this cannot be the case. As it is to deter future conduct, a penalty payment may not be imposed if the Member State has complied with EU law by the time of judgment.[117] By contrast, a lump sum can still be imposed. The deadline to avoid its sanction is the period set out in the letter of formal notice.[118]

The judgment also sets out the general principles which are to govern the level of sanction applied. These are the duration of the infringement, its seriousness and the ability of the Member State to pay. The Court cannot impose more than that requested by the Commission.[119] Although the Court has indicated that it will do no more than take account of it,[120] this grants an importance to the Commission Communication on the calculation of sanctions.[121] It acts as a ceiling on what will be exacted from a deviant Member State. The Communication acts, therefore, as the starting point for the interpretation of the three principles set out above.

For the penalty payment, the starting point is a flat rate of €630 per day. The clock for this runs from the date of the Article 260 TFEU judgment until Member State compliance with the original judgment (Article 260(2) TFEU) or notification of the full transposition of the Directive (Article 260(3) TFEU). This flat rate is then multiplied by coefficients representing the three principles set out in *Commission* v *France*. The coefficient for duration is set out on a scale of 1–3. It does not begin from the date of the fine but from the date of the Article 258 TFEU judgment (Article 260(2) TFEU) or non-transposition of the Directive. It increases by 0.10 for each month after that time. This is then multiplied by a coefficient for seriousness set out on a scale of 1–20. Seriousness will be judged by the 'importance' of the norm breached. Laws relating to the single market, non-discrimination, fundamental rights or citizenship are

---

[116] European Commission, *Application of Article 228 of the EC Treaty*, SEC(2005)1658, paras. 10.3 and 10.4.

[117] Case C-496/09 *Commission* v *Italy*, Judgment of 17 November 2011; Case C-374/11 *Commission* v *Ireland*, Judgment of 19 December 2012.

[118] Case C-610/10 *Commission* v *Spain*, Judgment of 11 December 2012.   [119] Article 260(3) TFEU.

[120] Case C-241/11 *Commission* v *Czech Republic*, Judgment of 25 June 2013.

[121] Communication, n. 116 above. It has twice been amended to take account of inflation and changes in Member State GDP. European Commission, *Application of 260 TFEU: Up-dating of Data Used to Calculate Lump Sum and Penalty Payments to be Proposed by the Commission to the Court of Justice in Infringement Proceedings*, SEC(2010)923/3; European Commission, *Up-dating of Data Used to Calculate Lump Sum and Penalty Payments to be Proposed by the Commission to the Court of Justice in Infringement Proceedings*, COM(2012)6106.

granted a particular weight.[122] It will then be assessed by the effect of the breach on public and private interests.[123] The former might include things such as effect on public goods such as the environment, impact on the functioning of the Union or on the Union's Budget.[124] Finally, this will be multiplied by an *n* which is calculated on the basis of the capacity of the Member State to pay and its votes in the Council. In 2013, this ranged and ranges from 0.34 for Malta to 21.12 for Germany.

The lump sum differs in its calculation from the penalty payment in three ways. First, there is a minimum sum for each Member State which will be applied. This ranges from €179, 000 for Malta to €11,192,000 for Germany. The Commission, then, applies a system of calculation similar to that for the penalty payment which is a daily rate multiplied by coefficients for duration, seriousness and ability to pay. The second difference is that this only kicks in if it exceeds the minimum sum. The daily rate is, furthermore, lower than for the penalty payment, being €210 per day in 2013, albeit that the other multipliers are identical. The third difference is that the date from when both the fine starts and the calculations begin is that of the Article 258 TFEU judgment. This usually means that by the time of an Article 260(2) TFEU judgment the lump sum owed is already quite substantial. The situation is different with an Article 260(3) TFEU action. In that case, a Member State is sanctioned on the same day as it is found to have acted illegally under Article 258 TFEU. For this reason, the Commission has indicated that it will not normally push for lump sum sanctions under Article 260(3) TFEU.[125] The reason is that, as that penalty serves to punish a Member State for a continuing illegality, it will usually be unfair to punish it for this on the day it discovers it has acted illegally.

Frequently, the Court of Justice will impose less than that requested by the Commission. This is in large part because, in addition to these principles, the sanction must be appropriate to the circumstances and proportionate to the infringement.[126] This constraint overlaps with the principles above but has been used to introduce certain additional factors which may push the sanction down. Examples include whether it is the first time the Member State is being sanctioned under Article 260 TFEU;[127] where a Member State has made progress towards implementation;[128] or where the Member State has taken the measures to comply but it is still unclear whether these have borne the necessary results.[129]

FURTHER READING

T. Börzel, T. Hofmann and D. Panke, 'Caving In or Sitting Out? Longitudinal Patterns of Non-compliance in the European Union' (2012) 19 *Journal of European Public Policy* 454

C. Harlow and R. Rawlings, 'Accountability and Law Enforcement: The Centralised EU Infringement Procedure' (2006) 31 *European Law Review* 447

B. Jack, 'Article 260(2) TFEU: An Effective Judicial Procedure for the Enforcement of Judgments?' (2013) 19 *European Law Journal* 404

---

[122] European Commission, *Application of Article 228 of the EC Treaty*, n. 116 above, para. 16.1.
[123] Case C-270/11 *Commission v Sweden*, Judgment of 30 May 2013.
[124] European Commission, *Application of Article 228 of the EC Treaty*, n. 116 above, para. 16.4.
[125] European Commission, *Implementation of Article 260(3) of the Treaty* [2011] OJ C12/1, para. 21.
[126] Case C-177/04 *Commission v France* [2006] ECR I-2479.
[127] Case C-270/11 *Commission v Sweden*, Judgment of 30 May 2013.
[128] Case C-278/01 *Commission v Spain* [2003] ECR I-14141.
[129] European Commission, n. 125 above, para. 13.4.

S. Peers, 'Sanctions for Infringement of EU Law after the Treaty of Lisbon' (2012) 18 *European Public Law* 33

L. Prete and B. Smulders, 'The Coming of Age of Infringement Proceedings' (2010) 47 *Common Market Law Review* 9

R. Rawlings, 'Engaged Elites: Citizen Action and Institutional Attitudes in Commission Enforcement' (2000) 6 *European Law Journal* 4

M. Smith, *Centralised Enforcement, Legitimacy and Good Governance in the EU* (Abingdon, Routledge, 2009)

B. Steunenberg and D. Toshkov, 'Comparing Transposition in the 27 Member States of the EU: The Impact of Discretion and Legal Fit' (2009) 16 *Journal of European Public Policy* 951

M. Taboroski, 'Infringement Proceedings and Non-Compliant National Courts' (2012) 49 *Common Market Law Review* 1881

E. Versluis, 'Even Rules, Uneven Practices: Opening the "Black Box" of EU Law in Action' (2007) 30 *West European Politics* 50

P. Wennerås, 'Sanctions Against Member States under Article 260 TFEU: Alive but not Kicking?' (2012) 49 *Common Market Law Review* 145

9

Governance

CONTENTS

1 INTRODUCTION

This chapter considers EU governance. It is organised as follows.

Section 2 considers the EU Governance agenda in the round. Established in the 2001 Commission White Paper, the Governance agenda comprises, in the first place, a series of norms guiding the exercise of Union power. These are openness, participation, accountability, effectiveness, coherence, subsidiarity and proportionality. The Governance agenda in the White Paper also sets out to characterise the style of Union decision-making. Its central mission is to solve problems that cannot be resolved by the Member States unilaterally. There is flexibility about the legal instruments to be deployed, as what matters is that the problem be resolved. Finally, the commitment to openness and participation has led to an engagement by the Union with the idea of a pan-European civil society.

Section 3 considers the duty on EU institutions to include non-institutional actors more extensively and more actively in the decision-making process. The most radical application of this is the European Citizens' Initiative set out in Regulation 211/2011/EC. This requires the European Commission to consider petitions which have at least 1 million statements of support from at least one-quarter of the Member States and have a minimum number of statements of support from at least one-quarter of the Member States. There are a number of procedural steps that must also be met, which go to the organisation of the initiative before statements of support can be collected and to the certification of the statements of support once they have been collected within the deadline of one year. The conditions have, to date, proved demanding with only one initiative meeting the conditions. Evidence from petitions to the EU institutions prior to the European Citizens' Initiative is that such procedures engage a much wider array of actors in Union decision-making and lead to much more contentious politics.

Section 4 examines the principles of subsidiarity and proportionality. Subsidiarity sets out when, acting within its powers, the Union should adopt a measure. It is based around two logics. One states that the Union should only act when the objectives of a measure cannot be realised through unilateral domestic action. This is concerned with protecting domestic identities from Union intrusion. The other, based on comparative efficiency, looks at whether a measure can, by reason of its scale and effects, be better realised at EU rather than national level. The two logics are difficult to reconcile and the Court of Justice has yet to strike down a Union measure for violating the principle. The proportionality principle states that Union measures shall not exceed what is necessary to realise the objectives of the Treaties. In practice, Union courts will only intervene when the Union measure is manifestly inappropriate. This has resulted in the central importance of the proportionality principle being its reshaping of the Union legislative culture. It has led to a commitment to consider non-legislative instruments wherever these would be equally effective. In recent years, the two principles guide the Smart Regulation agenda. This agenda requires, inter alia, a reduction in the administrative burdens imposed on private actors by EU law; ex post evaluation of the effectiveness of all EU legislation and assessments of the economic, social, fundamental rights and environmental impacts of all Union legislative proposals.

Section 5 considers the duty on the EU institutions to consult widely before taking any legislative action. There is a commitment that such consultation should involve dialogue, be transparent and be plural. Whilst there is a duty to give reasons for any measure, this duty is a weak one, which allows EU institutions to give reasons in very general terms and does not require them to respond to particular observations. This has limited the requirement on them to engage in active dialogue rather than merely take views. The commitment to transparent consultation is expressed in a Register of lobbyists, all of whom must observe a Code of Conduct. Whilst the EU institutions commit themselves to inclusive consultation, a central challenge is that consultation on specific issues has led to actors represented in Brussels who benefit most from the activity in question being predominant in the consultation.

Section 6 considers the transparency principle. Its central expression is Regulation 1049/2001/EC. This allows actors to seek access from EU bodies for documents in their possession. The central justifications for refusing access are the exceptions set out in article 4 of the Regulation. These fall into three categories. First, there are exceptions where the institution must refuse access to a document. Here, Union courts will look merely to see whether there has been a manifest error of assessment and whether accurate reasons have been given. Secondly, there are exceptions where EU institutions must grant access if disclosure is in the overriding public interest. Courts will engage in much stronger review here, often looking at the strength of interest which is claimed to be protected. Finally, there are documents originating from third parties and Member States. The former must be consulted before disclosure takes place. Member States can refuse to consent to a document being released if it falls within one of the categories justifying non-release of documents by the EU institutions but they must also provide reasons.

2 GOVERNANCE AGENDA

The term 'governance' came to the fore in the Union as a consequence of the biggest administrative scandal to hit the European Union. In 1998, a series of allegations about fraud and financial mismanagement by the Santer Commission were made to the European Parliament. The subsequent report by the Parliament's Committee of Independent Experts established to examine the allegations was damning.[1] On its publication, the entire College of Commissioners resigned.[2] To counter the damage, the incoming Commission published a series of Codes of Conduct and consultation papers on Commission reform and accountability which culminated in the *White Paper on European Governance*.[3] The document sets out a series of principles which guide how EU decision-making is to take place:[4]

> The White Paper on European Governance concerns the way in which the Union uses the powers given by its citizens. Reform must be started now, so that people see changes well before further modification of the EU Treaties.
>
> The White Paper proposes opening up the policy-making process to get more people and organisations involved in shaping and delivering EU policy. It promotes greater openness, accountability and responsibility for all those involved. This should help people to see how Member States, by acting together within the Union, are able to tackle their concerns more effectively.[5]

To this end, the White Paper understands governance as:

> the rules, processes and behaviour that affect the way in which powers are exercised at European level, particularly as regards openness, participation, accountability, effectiveness and coherence.

Although terse, this definition hints at two dimensions to the governance agenda. First, it is about setting norms that justify and guide EU decision-making. Criteria are set for acceptable

---

[1] Committee of Independent Experts, *First Report on Allegations regarding Fraud, Mismanagement and Nepotism in the European Commission* (15 March 1999) para. 9.4.25. Both this report and the committee's second report (see below) are available at www.europarl.eu/experts/.

[2] A. Tomkins, 'Responsibility and Resignation in the European Commission' (1999) 62 *MLR* 744; P. Craig, 'The Fall and Renewal of the Commission: Accountability, Contract and Administrative Organisation' (2000) 6 *ELJ* 98; V. Mehde, 'Responsibility and Accountability in the European Commission' (2003) 40 *CMLRev.* 423.

[3] European Commission, *European Governance: A White Paper*, COM(2001)428.

[4] For criticism see L. Metcalfe, 'Reforming the European Governance: Old Problems or New Principles?' (2001) 67 *International Review of Administrative Sciences* 415; F. Scharpf, 'European Governance: Common Concerns vs. The Challenge of Diversity' in C. Joerges *et al.* (eds.), *Mountain or Molehill: Critical Appraisal of the Commission White Paper on Governance*, Jean Monnet Working Paper 6/01 (New York, New York University, 2001).

[5] At n. 3 above, 3.

behaviour and legal standards and procedures established on the basis of them. Secondly, governance is also a description of how the Union is to go about its decision-making. To that end, it sets out a number of features which are to characterise EU decision-making. We shall now consider each of these in further detail.

(i) Norms of governance

The White Paper sets out seven principles of governance which are to guide Union decision-making and are elaborated below.

European Commission, *European Governance: A White Paper*, COM(2001)428, 10–11

Openness. The Institutions should work in a more open manner. Together with the Member States, they should actively communicate about what the EU does and the decisions it takes. They should use language that is accessible and understandable for the general public. This is of particular importance in order to improve the confidence in complex institutions.

Participation. The quality, relevance and effectiveness of EU policies depend on ensuring wide participation throughout the policy chain – from conception to implementation. Improved participation is likely to create more confidence in the end result and in the Institutions which deliver policies. Participation crucially depends on central governments following an inclusive approach when developing and implementing EU policies.

Accountability. Roles in the legislative and executive processes need to be clearer. Each of the EU Institutions must explain and take responsibility for what it does in Europe. But there is also a need for greater clarity and responsibility from Member States and all those involved in developing and implementing EU policy at whatever level.

Effectiveness. Policies must be effective and timely, delivering what is needed on the basis of clear objectives, an evaluation of future impact and, where available, of past experience. Effectiveness also depends on implementing EU policies in a proportionate manner and on taking decisions at the most appropriate level.

Coherence. Policies and action must be coherent and easily understood. The need for coherence in the Union is increasing: the range of tasks has grown; enlargement will increase diversity; challenges such as climate and demographic change cross the boundaries of the sectoral policies on which the Union has been built; regional and local authorities are increasingly involved in EU policies. Coherence requires political leadership and a strong responsibility on the part of the Institutions to ensure a consistent approach within a complex system....

Proportionality and subsidiarity. From the conception of policy to its implementation, the choice of the level at which action is taken (from EU to local) and the selection of the instruments used must be in proportion to the objectives pursued. This means that before launching an initiative, it is essential to check systematically (a) if public action is really necessary, (b) if the European level is the most appropriate one, and (c) if the measures chosen are proportionate to those objectives.

Union decision-making must respect these principles. However, they also formulate a vision for Union decision-making by prescribing goals it must realise. That is to say it must be as accountable, open, coherent, and so on, as possible. A further feature of the Governance agenda is its informality. These principles are not legally binding norms but rather general principles to be realised in a number of ways. The devil lies, thus, in the detail and how they are institutionalised: be it through legal norms, new procedures or new institutions. Only through consideration of these will it be possible to see if these principles are met and the consequences of the Governance agenda.

(ii) Features of governance

The White Paper also describes how the Union is to govern. Its decision-making is to be marked by a number of features.

First, Union decision-making is characterised as being about problem-solving. The central objectives for the Union are how to solve an identified problem in a way that meets the governance criteria. It is a test that conceives the measure of Union performance as whether it is fit for purpose in terms of the problems it has been set up to resolve. Weiler has described this in the following way:

> The refocusing of the Commission's tasks proposed here takes on board the vision of a Union concentrating on the realisation of a few major projects with widespread appeal. It is by rallying support for such projects rather than seeking to replace national allegiances by a wider collective identity that we will encourage the people of the Union – in existing Member States and applicant countries alike – to see themselves as Europeans. Taking this line of thinking a step further, the political purpose of the Union is not to supplant the existing States with a new super-State, but to establish a system of shared legislative powers in order to carry through common projects.[6]

He then lambasts this.

J. Weiler 'The Commission as Euro-Skeptic: A Task Oriented Commission for a Project-Based Union, a Comment on the First Version of the White Paper' in C. Joerges et al. (eds.), *Symposium: Mountain or Molehill? A Critical Appraisal of the Commission White Paper on Governance*, Jean Monnet Working Paper 6/01 (EUI–NYU, 2002)

11. I can understand the temptation of packaging Europe as consisting of some well defined 'appealing' projects and the Commission as simply a friendly, attentive and responsive body concerned with the task of effectively realizing these projects. It can produce some important and immediate political capital. Who can, after all, object to appealing projects and such a minimalist conception of the Commission?

12. But it comes with some notable longer term dangers and costs. And in part it also leads to some naïve positions which will not be taken seriously by large constituencies. Let me explain.

13. There have always been two principal strands in the European debate which has taken place from time to time (and in some national quarters endlessly). In some Member States the debate has mostly followed functionalist premises: Whether or not Europe serves the national interest. 'What's-in-it-for-us?' Where that has been the premise of the debate (and it is not necessary to mention Member States by name) the legitimacy of the very European construct has remained contingent, subject to a continuous assessment and re-assessment of the 'appeal' of Europe and the extent that it continued to serve interests. Under this conception a failure of the Commission, like the Santer Commission, calls

---

[6] European Commission, *Draft Memorandum to the Commission: Approaches to European Governance for Democratic European Governance*, 10 March 2001, para. 2.4.

into question the very legitimacy of Europe itself. Europe under this form of discourse is analogous to a politician in power whose policies and efficiency in implementing these policies are subject to contingent acceptance and rejection. Europe becomes a continuous experiment not fully integrated into the political culture in the same way that some German historians claimed that in Post War Germany, democracy itself was treated as a contingent proposition, the approval of which was dependent on its success.

This position is the hall mark of classical Euro-Skepticism.

14. The other strand, and this is the one that (inadvertently) has been sacrificed in the Draft, does not regard Europe only in functionalist terms. Under this strand Europe is not, for sure, considered as a proto-state or a would-be state nor is European identity conceived with a vocabulary associated with national identity and allegiance. But Europe is much more than project oriented. It is process oriented and above all it is a Community of Values the principal one of which is an historical commitment to a different, more civil, process of inter-statal intercourse, to a different, more civil, method of drawing boundaries between states and nations to a different, more civil, way of managing certain domains of the public sphere. To be European, under this conception, is a commitment to 'doing things' (hence process) in a different, European, way – *whatever the current major appealing project happens to be*. To be European is essentially about the way we do things, rather than what we do.

Secondly, the Union's success in realising these tasks is measured by whether a notional external observer would consider that the Union measure in question resolves the problem whilst meeting the seven principles set out earlier.[7] This leads to considerable faith being placed in what are perceived as external sources of truth and validation, namely, expertise and feedback.[8]

Thirdly, the Governance agenda is relatively agnostic about the institutions or forms of legal norm deployed to realise its goals, as what matters is simply meeting its goals and principles. The institutions deployed to realise these can be public or private, and the norms may be legally binding instruments, soft law, technical standards and codes drawn up by private actors, or a mix of all the above.

European Commission, *European Governance: A White Paper*, COM(2001)428, 20–2

The European Union will rightly continue to be judged by the impact of its regulation on the ground. It must pay constant attention to *improving the quality, effectiveness and simplicity of regulatory acts.* Effective decision-making also requires the combination of different policy instruments (various forms of legislation, programmes, guidelines, use of structural funding, etc.) to meet Treaty objectives...

... *legislation is often only part of a broader solution* combining formal rules with other non-binding tools such as recommendations, guidelines, or even self-regulation within a commonly agreed framework. This highlights the need for close coherence between the use of different policy instruments and for more thought to be given to their selection.

---

[7] C. Möllers, 'European Governance: Meaning and Value of a Concept' (2006) 43 *CMLRev.* 313, 315–18.
[8] European Commission, *European Governance: A White Paper*, COM (2001)428, 18–22.

...the *right type of instrument* must be used whenever legislation is needed to achieve the Union's objectives:

- The *use of regulations* should be considered in cases with a need for uniform application and legal certainty across the Union. This can be particularly important for the completion of the internal market and has the advantage of avoiding the delays associated with transposition of directives into national legislation.
- So-called *'framework directives'* should be used more often. Such texts are less heavy-handed, offer greater flexibility as to their implementation, and tend to be agreed more quickly by Council and the European Parliament.

Whichever form of legislative instrument is chosen, *more use should be made of 'primary' legislation* limited to essential elements (basic rights and obligations, conditions to implement them), leaving the executive to fill in the technical detail via implementing 'secondary' rules.

...under certain conditions, implementing measures may be prepared within the *framework of co-regulation*. Co-regulation combines binding legislative and regulatory action with actions taken by the actors most concerned, drawing on their practical expertise. The result is wider ownership of the policies in question by involving those most affected by implementing rules in their preparation and enforcement. This often achieves better compliance, even where the detailed rules are non-binding.

- It has already been used, for example, in areas such as the internal market (agreeing product standards under the so-called 'New Approach' directives)[9] and the environment sector (reducing car emissions).
- The exact shape of co-regulation, the way in which legal and non-legal instruments are combined and who launches the initiative – stakeholders or the Commission – will vary from sector to sector...

A perusal of any field of EU policy finds, therefore, that, typically an Action Plan or programme has been agreed which sets out the instruments needed to realise its goals.[10] These instruments will usually include Regulations and Directives, but also soft law instruments, such as Recommendations, benchmarks or Codes of Conduct[11] and standards set up by private or professional bodies.[12] To many, this adaptability, flexibility and responsiveness are highly desirable. EU law is no longer simply about telling people what they do. Instead, it acquires a more enabling role. The formal norms provide a backdrop against which informal, collective arrangements are put in place – be it through soft law or other informal instruments – bringing actors together both to maximise their resources and to develop shared commitments to resolving common problems on the basis of shared criteria.[13]

[9] See pp. 687–92.
[10] On the single market see European Commission, *Single Market Act II: Together for New Growth*, COM(2012)573.
[11] See pp. 114–16.
[12] On the variety of these see D. Chalmers, 'Private Power and Public Authority in European Union Law' (2005–6) 8 *CYELS* 59; D. Schiek, 'Private Rule-making and European Governance: Issues of Legitimacy' (2007) 32 *ELRev.* 443.
[13] In addition see J. Scott and D. Trubek, 'Mind the Gap: Law and New Approaches to Governance in the European Union' (2002) 8 *ELJ* 1; G. de Búrca and J. Scott (eds.), *Law and New Governance in the EU and the US* (Oxford/Portland, Hart, 2006); C. Sabel and J. Zeitlin (eds.), *Experimentalist Governance in the European Union Towards a New Architecture* (Oxford, Oxford University Press, 2010).

C. Sabel and J. Zeitlin, 'Learning from Difference: The New Architecture of Experimentalist Governance in the EU' (2008) 14 *European Law Journal* 271, 307–8

This 'shadow of hierarchy' view extends to EU governance a trope originally developed to explain collective bargaining and neo-corporatist concertation between the state, labour and capital. The core idea is that the state or public hierarchy more generally is limited – perhaps because of the volatility of the situation in which it acts – in its ability to secure the outcomes that it prefers, or would prefer if it could identify them in advance. Given this limitation, the state enlists non-state actors who do command the necessary capacities in its problem solving by proposing an exchange: in return for their promise to bargain with one another fairly and in a public-regarding way, the relevant parties are endowed with a semi-constitutional authority to speak on behalf of their members and the assurance that their agreements will be backed by the authority of the state, provided only that they respect the conditions of the founding bargain itself. Parties to such agreements are thus reasonably said to be 'bargaining in the shadow of the state' and acting in some sense as its authorised agents or deputies in reaching solutions not directly available to the authorities themselves. Seen this way, the new architecture that we describe might be thought to be simply a capacity-increasing extension of the EU's formal hierarchical decision-making apparatus rather than a networked, deliberative alternative to it. At the limit, this argument simply applies to governance an idea familiar from organisational sociology, in which the capacities of a rigid formal organisation are rendered flexible by connecting it to an informal network over which the official hierarchy maintains control.

This view, however, is not uncontroversial and others have pointed to the dangers of too much informality.[14]

C. Joerges, 'Integration Through De-legalisation?' (2008) 33 *European Law Review* 291, 310

Iterative benchmarking of national practices, the management of national states to agree upon guidelines and the mutual learning thereby stimulated are seen as genuinely democratic processes through which a problem-related *demos* articulates itself. These are fascinating and highly conditioned perspectives which provoke sceptical questions: How can transnational criteria that enable and legitimate a benchmarking of national experience, national history and national expectations be found? Why can we reliably expect that confrontation with the experience of others will change national perceptions and practices so as to lead to coordinated policies? And if indeed learning occurs in some quarters, how is its successful implementation conceivable if we are confronted not only with extremely complex fields of social policy but also with vested interests? There are no valid reasons which could be put forward against transnational exchanges of ideas among bureaucracies and expert communities. What seems risky however, is the delegation of quasi-regulatory tasks to such networks. This sort of governance would be considered 'soft' to the extent that it is no longer dependent on binding law. But it might be considered 'strong' because its informality permits its evasion of risks of being tied down and controlled by the regular political process including the constraints of the rule of law.

[14] See also I. Chiu, 'On the Identification of an EU Legal Norm' (2007) 26 *YBEL* 193.

The final feature of governance is a commitment to what the White Paper calls better involvement. This includes, inter alia, greater consultation, transparency and a stronger mobilisation of civil society.[15]

European Commission, *European Governance: A White Paper*, COM(2001)428, 14–16

Democracy depends on people being able to take part in public debate. To do this, they must have access to reliable information on European issues and be able to scrutinise the policy process in its various stages...

Providing more information and more effective communication are a pre-condition for generating a sense of belonging to Europe. The aim should be to create a trans-national 'space' where citizens from different countries can discuss what they perceive as being the important challenges for the Union. This should help policy makers to stay in touch with European public opinion, and could guide them in identifying European projects which mobilise public support...

Involving civil society...

Civil society plays an important role in giving voice to the concerns of citizens and delivering services that meet people's needs. Churches and religious communities have a particular contribution to make. The organisations which make up civil society mobilise people and support, for instance, those suffering from exclusion or discrimination...

Trade unions and employers' organisations have a particular role and influence. The EC Treaty requires the Commission to consult management and labour in preparing proposals, in particular in the social policy field. Under certain conditions, they can reach binding agreements that are subsequently turned into Community law (within the social dialogue). The social partners should be further encouraged to use the powers given under the Treaty to conclude voluntary agreements.

Civil society increasingly sees Europe as offering a good platform to change policy orientations and society. This offers a real potential to broaden the debate on Europe's role. It is a chance to get citizens more actively involved in achieving the Union's objectives and to offer them a structured channel for feedback, criticism and protest.

With better involvement comes greater responsibility. Civil society must itself follow the principles of good governance, which include accountability and openness. The Commission intends to establish, before the end of this year, a comprehensive on-line database with details of civil society organisations active at European level, which should act as a catalyst to improve their internal organisation.

What is needed is a *reinforced culture of consultation and dialogue*; a culture which is adopted by all European Institutions and which associates particularly the European Parliament in the consultative process, given its role in representing the citizen. The European Parliament should play a prominent role, for instance, by reinforcing its use of public hearings. European political parties are an important factor in European integration and contribute to European awareness and voicing the concerns of citizens.

---

[15] On civil society and Union more generally see C. Ruzza, *Europe and Civil Society* (Manchester, Manchester University Press, 2004); J. Greenwood, 'Organized Civil Society and Democratic Legitimacy in the European Union' (2007) 37 *BJPS* 333; B. Kohler-Koch and C. Quittkat, *De-Mystification of Participatory Democracy: EU-Governance and Civil Society* (Oxford, Oxford University Press, 2013).

This seems all highly desirable but begs the question as to who actually takes part. This can give rise to uneasy questions.[16] The excerpt below surveyed the empirical literature. It found that as the Union only engages in a limited number of activities, it particularly attracts those who benefit most from these activities. The only way to counter this has been through the funding of other groups, which, in turn, throws into question the independence of the latter.

S. Saurugger, 'Interest Groups and Democracy in the European Union' (2008) 31 *West European Politics* 1276, 1283–4

As the European integration process was initially based on economic integration, most of the European associations are still economic interest groups, that is trade associations or firms, even if the strengthened social regulation has brought about an increase of associations representing general interests… Even if one observes considerable differences among the various economic interest groups, they do not only differ by number from groups representing general interests. Their strong presence shows that they possess a greater organisational potential. Generally, they are financially stronger, employ more staff and possess more access points to the Commission than to the European Parliament. They also enjoy better access to litigation strategies through the European Court of Justice. A final and important characteristic is their strong economic legitimacy. The legitimacy of producer groups is linked to their properties as representative organisations as well as to their ability to aggregate member opinions. As the member companies of the European associations perform indispensable functions in the EU market economy, European institutions must take into account possible fatal effects on companies stemming from European regulation.

Faced with this inequality, a number of authors have shown how European institutions and, in particular, the European Commission strengthen the capacities of general interest groups by co-financing a certain number of European associations while offering them privileged access to the public arena, i.e. consultative committees. According to Commission figures, diffuse interest groups such as the European Network Against Racism and the European Social Platform receive 80 to 90 per cent of their funding from the EU political institutions. This allows so-called outsider groups critical of EU politics and policies to be drawn into the decision-making process. Thus… political institutions can wield strong influence through direct subsidies, payments, grants and other financial incentives.

Having looked at the general features of the Governance agenda, it is now time to turn our attention to the individual principles and their interpretation and application.

3 PARTICIPATORY DEMOCRACY AND THE EUROPEAN CITIZENS' INITIATIVE

The *White Paper on European Governance* talked of the need for increased participation by non-institutional actors to secure the 'quality, relevance and effectiveness of EU policies'. It saw participation as having instrumental value insofar as it enabled better policies by increasing the knowledge base for these policies. This would be realised through wider and more

---

[16] See also S. Smismans, 'European Civil Society: Shaped by Discourses and Institutional Interests' (2003) 9 *ELJ* 473; S. Smismans, *Law, Legitimacy, and European Governance: Functional Participation in Social Regulation* (Oxford, Oxford University Press, 2004).

structured consultation processes. The challenge with this, as the Saurugger piece suggests, is that such consultation has historically attracted issue-specific organisations working day-in and day-out in the Brussels sphere. At the Future of Europe Convention, this was seen as too narrow by a network of NGOs, Democracy International, who campaigned for direct democracy, as it does not include wider social movements wishing to articulate, in possibly more spontaneous and less structured ways, broader public concerns.[17] As a consequence of Democracy International's efforts, provision was made in the Constitutional Treaty for a European Citizens' Initiative (ECI). This was replicated in the Lisbon Treaty and is contained in Article 11(4) TEU.

Article 11(4) TEU

4. Not less than one million citizens who are nationals of a significant number of Member States may take the initiative of inviting the European Commission, within the framework of its powers, to submit any appropriate proposal on matters where citizens consider that a legal act of the Union is required for the purpose of implementing the Treaties.

   The procedures and conditions required for such a citizens' initiative shall be determined in accordance with Article 24(1) TFEU.

As the last sentence indicates, Article 11(4) TEU merely sets out a framework for the ECI. Its detail and modalities are established by Regulation 211/2011/EC.[18] The Regulation breaks the process up into four stages: the organisation and registration of the ECI; the collection of signatures; the certification of the ECI by the national authorities; and its examination by the Commission.

> *The organisation and registration of the ECI*: An ECI will only be eligible for consideration by the Commission if it is registered with it prior to the collection of signatures.[19] There are procedural and substantive requirements to be met for this registration. Procedurally, an organising committee must be established which comprises EU citizens from at least seven different Member States, who are eligible to vote for the European Parliament but are not MEPs.[20] The organising committee must provide information to the Commission which, inter alia, sets out the title, subject matter and objectives of the ECI, and the Treaty Articles under which it is proposed Union action be taken.[21] Within two months, the Commission must check whether the proposed ECI is eligible. This will be the case unless the organising committee does not meet the criteria set out above; or the ECI is manifestly abusive, vexatious or frivolous; falls outside EU competences; or contradicts the fundamental rights and values set out in Article 2 TEU.[22] By October 2013, twelve ECIs had been refused registration.[23] Sixteen, by contrast, had been registered.[24]

---

[17] See, on this, in particular, J. de Clerck-Sachsse, 'Civil Society and Democracy in the European Union: The Paradox of the European Citizens' Initiative' (2012) 13 *Perspectives on European Politics and Society* 299. On evidence of this split within the Union see B. Kohler-Koch and C. Quittkat, 'What is Civil Society and Who Represents Civil Society in the EU? Results of an Online Survey among Civil Society Experts' (2009) 28 *Policy and Society* 11.

[18] Regulation 211/2011/EC on the citizens' initiative [2011] OJ L65/1.   [19] *Ibid.* article 4(1).

[20] *Ibid.* article 3(1) and (2).   [21] *Ibid.* Annex II.   [22] *Ibid.* article 4(2).

[23] See http://ec.europa.eu/citizens-initiative/public/initiatives/non-registered.

[24] See http://ec.europa.eu/citizens-initiative/public/initiatives/non-registered.

The collection of statements of support: The heart of the ECI is the collection of statements of support. These may be provided electronically or on paper.[25] Like the organising committee, signatories must be EU citizens eligible to vote for the European Parliament. The organising committee has twelve months from registration to meet three thresholds:

- at least one million statements of support;[26]
- these must come from at least one-quarter of the Member States;
- there must be a minimum number of statements of support from each of at least one-quarter of the Member States. This will equate to the number of MEPs of that Member State multiplied by 750.

Comparative analyses show that, proportionate to overall population, the requirement of one million signatories is less onerous than citizens' initiatives used in other jurisdictions.[27] It has still proved a demanding threshold. In the first sixteen months of operation, only one initiative, that on water sanitation being a basic human right, met the first threshold.[28] These thresholds also possibly affect the quality of those initiatives arriving before the Commission. Only a highly organised movement institutionally entrenched across a large part of the Union will be capable, in practice, of meeting its demands. Many spontaneous movements or ones expressing matters of particular regional interest are unlikely to be successful.

Certification of the ECI: After collecting the necessary statements of support, the organising committee must submit the ECI to the national authorities of the signatories for verification and certification. The procedure for determining which national authority is to verify which signatory is a complex one.[29] For some Member States it will be determined by who is resident in their territory.[30] For others it comprises residents and their nationals who are resident abroad.[31] Others take a similar position except that non-resident nationals, to be eligible, must have informed the national authorities.[32] Finally, there is a fourth category of Member States who issue a personal identification number, or the citizen must submit the number of a designated document such as residence permit, ID card or passport to be a signatory.[33] Almost certainly, there will be problems of overlap and coordination between authorities.[34] Be that as it may, within three months the authorities must provide a certificate setting out the valid number of statements of support. If, on the basis of these certificates, the ECI meets the criteria of eligibility, it can proceed to the next stage.

Examination of the ECI by the Commission: Article 11(4) TEU provides nothing further than that an ECI be submitted to the Commission. No provision was made for what should

---

[25] Regulation 211/2011, article 5(2).   [26] Article 11(4) TEU.

[27] V. Cuesta-López, 'A Comparative Approach to the Regulation on the European Citizens' Initiative' (2012) 13 *Perspectives on European Politics and Society* 257, 261.

[28] It had over 1.8 million signatories in October 2013. See www.right2water.eu/.

[29] The basic division is set out in Regulation 211/2011, article 8(1) with the details for each State in Part C of Annex III.

[30] Ireland, Netherlands and the United Kingdom.   [31] Estonia, Slovakia and Finland.

[32] Belgium, Germany and Denmark.

[33] Bulgaria, Cyprus, Italy, Latvia, Lithuania, Luxembourg, Hungary, Malta, Austria, Poland, Portugal, Slovenia, Sweden, Romania, Spain, Czech Republic, France and Greece.

[34] For criticism see M. Dougan, 'What are We to Make of the Citizens' Initiative' (2011) 48 *CMLRev.* 1807, 1825–8.

happen subsequently. Further duties strengthening the position of the organising committee were imposed by the Regulation, which not only granted the right to a hearing and imposed a duty on the Commission to provide reasons for its position within three months, but also established a public hearing, which will bring other institutional actors, notably the European Parliament, into the process.

Regulation 211/2011/EC, articles 10, 11

Article 10
1. Where the Commission receives a citizens' initiative in accordance with Article 9 it shall:
   (a) publish the citizens' initiative without delay in the register;
   (b) receive the organisers at an appropriate level to allow them to explain in detail the matters raised by the citizens' initiative;
   (c) within three months, set out in a communication its legal and political conclusions on the citizens' initiative, the action it intends to take, if any, and its reasons for taking or not taking that action.
2. The communication referred to in paragraph 1(c) shall be notified to the organisers as well as to the European Parliament and the Council and shall be made public.

Article 11

Where the conditions of Article 10(1)(a) and (b) are fulfilled, and within the deadline laid down in Article 10(1)(c), the organisers shall be given the opportunity to present the citizens' initiative at a public hearing. The Commission and the European Parliament shall ensure that this hearing is organised at the European Parliament, if appropriate together with such other institutions and bodies of the Union as may wish to participate, and that the Commission is represented at an appropriate level.

The Commission is still not required to make a proposal after this process, and, even if does, there is no guarantee that it will be adopted by the other EU institutions. As the ECI only began in April 2011, it is still too early to evaluate what initiatives have been attracted by it and what success these will have before the EU institutions. In this context, the most interesting work is that which looks at the signature campaigns and petitions which were presented on matters of European politics prior to the instigation of the ECI. There were twenty-one of these. The piece below suggests that they have some possibility to pluralise the political process and include new actors as well as to introduce greater political contestation. If this is the case, it will be interesting to see how the EU institutions respond. It may lead to ECIs having little prospect of legislative success as they will not obtain the requisite legislative majorities. Alternately, it might provoke increased scrutiny and public engagement with the EU institutions which will require these to be more responsive than they might otherwise have been.

L. García, 'New Rules, New Players? The ECI as a Source of Competition and Contention in the European Public Sphere' (2012) 13 *Perspectives on European Politics and Society* **337, 339 and 342–3**

...the ECI may have two important effects on the field of European civil society relations. The first is that it may attract so far weakly involved organisations such as national groups or those less strongly institutionalised in Brussels. Since the ECI requires the support of one million citizens, it may empower organisations more able to mobilise citizens than to participate in institutionalized consultations. In this sense it could introduce competition for the attention of EU institutions between different kinds of organisations using different collective action mechanisms.

This evolution may contribute to make the recourse to 'outside lobbying' more frequent and to advance a policy style more likely to interest the public by promoting more cleaved political debates. The second possible effect is a change of style and register in EU institutions – civil society relations. Whereas these relations have been characteristically consensus-prone, the emergence of new actors and issues could contribute to increased contention in the field of civil society EU relations.

The analysis of these initiatives focuses on understanding whether regularities can be found regarding the implication of different types of actors and sectors. It is very difficult to obtain complete data on the number of signatures and on whether the campaigns would be acceptable in terms of the Regulation...In this sense, only five out of 21 initiatives (Oneseat, 1million4disability, GMO Initiatives I and II and the ELIANT initiative) collected one million or more signatures. Very significant failures are those of two large EU associations (European Trade Union Confederation (ETUC) and Friends of the Earth) to reach one million signatures on issues at the core of their policy goals, such as the protection of public services and a ban on nuclear energy. On the other hand, Greenpeace has been able to collect one million signatures twice on different initiatives calling for a ban on genetically modified crops. More surprisingly, a relatively specialised issue such as the ELIANT initiative on applied anthroposophy is also capable of collecting one million signatures. This is a strong suggestion that the size of the organisation and the salience of the topic are not the only relevant variables to consider when assessing the usage of the ECI.

By contrast it is possible to proceed to a more complete analysis on the types of promoters and subject matter. Each of the initiatives launched has been coded according to its subject and the type of promoter. The result is a list of 25 subjects as some initiatives address more than one subject. For instance, proposals on genetically modified organisms (GMOs) are both on health and environment matters. The promoters have been classified according to the type of organisation. The result is the classification of the 21 promoters into four broad categories: EU CSOs; national CSOs; commercial organisations and political representatives and officials such as MEPs or MPs.

European-level organisations are the promoters of more than half of the initiatives (12 out of 21). This seems contradictory with the previous finding that EU organisations were weakly involved in the previous discussions on the ECI. A more qualitative analysis reveals, however, that this finding is indeed highly aligned with expectations. In this sense European organisations can be divided into two clearly different groups. The first includes well-established European organisations (European Association for the Defence of Human Rights (AEDH), European Disability Forum (EDF or ETUC)) that have used signature-collection campaigns to promote a particular policy. The European Emergency Number Association (EENA) seems to have used their signature collection campaign similarly: the campaign served to consolidate the organisation around a very specific policy proposal. A second type of promoter includes European organisations that either specifically aim to grant citizens a bigger say in EU politics – such as European Federalist associations and foundations like King Baudoin or Madariaga – or have a strong contestation potential – such as Greenpeace and Friends of the Earth.

4 SUBSIDIARITY AND PROPORTIONALITY

(i) An outline of the subsidiarity and proportionality principles

The central elements of the subsidiarity and proportionality principles are set out in Article 5 TEU.

Article 5(3), (4) TEU

3. Under the principle of subsidiarity, in areas which do not fall within its exclusive competence, the Union shall act only if and insofar as the objectives of the proposed action cannot be sufficiently achieved by the Member States, either at central level or at regional and local level, but can rather, by reason of the scale or effects of the proposed action, be better achieved at Union level.

   The institutions of the Union shall apply the principle of subsidiarity as laid down in the Protocol on the application of the principles of subsidiarity and proportionality. National Parliaments ensure compliance with the principle of subsidiarity in accordance with the procedure set out in that Protocol.

4. Under the principle of proportionality, the content and form of Union action shall not exceed what is necessary to achieve the objectives of the Treaties.

On their face, the principles do two very different things.

The subsidiarity principle goes to when the Union should intervene. It expresses the political philosophy of self-government.[35] Local decisions are, in principle, better than regional ones and national decisions are, likewise, better than international ones.[36] The proportionality principle goes, by contrast, not to when to intervene, but to the quality of that intervention. It is concerned with the density and intrusiveness of EU law. Its philosophy is a presumption in favour of private autonomy and that state intrusion on that should always be justified.[37] The measure must, thus, be suitable for realising the objectives set by the administration, and, of several equally suitable measures, the one chosen should be the one which imposes the fewest constraints on individuals.

As they seek different goals, the subsidiarity and proportionality principles have to be treated separately. Yet, they have been conflated by the Governance agenda. This conflation is present in the central provision in the Protocol on the Application of the Principles of Subsidiarity and Proportionality (PASP).

---

[35] A. Follesdal, 'Subsidiarity' (1998) 6 *Journal of Political Philosophy* 190; Y. Soudan, 'Subsidiarity and Community in Europe' (1998) 5 *Ethical Perspectives* 177; N. Barber, 'The Limited Modesty of Subsidiarity' (2005) 11 *ELJ* 308.

[36] In its consultations on any legislative proposal, the Commission is required, where appropriate, to take into account the regional and local dimension of the action envisaged, Protocol on the Application of the Principles of Subsidiarity and Proportionality, Article 2.

[37] J. Schwarze, *European Administrative Law* (London, Sweet & Maxwell, 1992) 685.

Protocol on the Application of the Principles of Subsidiarity and Proportionality, Article 5

Draft legislative acts shall be justified with regard to the principles of subsidiarity and proportionality. Any draft legislative act should contain a detailed statement making it possible to appraise compliance with the principles of subsidiarity and proportionality. This statement should contain some assessment of the proposal's financial impact and, in the case of a directive, of its implications for the rules to be put in place by Member States, including, where necessary, the regional legislation. The reasons for concluding that an objective of the Union can be better achieved at the level of the Union shall be substantiated by qualitative and, wherever possible, quantitative indicators. Draft legislative acts shall take account of the need for any burden, whether financial or administrative, falling upon the Union, national governments, regional or local authorities, economic operators and citizens, to be minimised and commensurate with the objective to be achieved.

There are two strands in the provision. On the one hand, the Union has to justify the relative efficacy of EU legislation vis-à-vis its national or regional alternatives. On the other, there is a concern with the regulatory weight of EU legislation. Its financial and administrative impacts should be minimised and attention should be addressed to the legislative disturbance that it will cause. If these strands are distinct, views on one inevitably inform views about the other.

(ii) Subsidiarity

Two logics sit at the heart of the subsidiarity principle.

The first expresses a concern that the Union should not intrude on national, regional and local political and cultural identities. It is directed at limiting the reach of EU legislation. Although the idea goes back to the mid-1970s,[38] the first general incorporation of subsidiarity into the Treaty provision was a reflection of this concern prompted by the explosive growth in the quantity of EU legislation from just under 400 binding acts adopted in 1984 to nearly 2,500 in 1992.[39] There has been a concern ever since about the amount of EU legislation produced by the Union. In 2010, the British House of Commons estimated that between 1997 and 2009 6.8 per cent of statutes and 14.1 per cent of Statutory Instruments 'had a role' in implementing EU obligations.[40] Similar estimates have been produced for Denmark, where it was estimated that about 9.6 per cent of Danish law was strongly informed by EU law. For Member States without opt-outs the figures are higher. Dutch studies have estimated about 12–18 per cent of Dutch law is governed by the Union; French studies suggest just under 20 per cent in France; and the most robust of the German studies about 15 per cent of laws there. If these figures suggest that the amount of EU law is slightly more confined than the scaremongers would try to have us believe, it is still a significant number. Furthermore, these figures do not take

---

[38] *Tindemans Report on European Union*, Supplement 1/76, Bull. EC.

[39] N. Fligstein and J. McNichol, 'The Institutional Terrain of the European Union' in W. Sandholtz and A. Stone Sweet (eds.), *European Integration and Supranational Governance* (Oxford, Oxford University Press, 1998) 76.

[40] House of Commons Library, *How Much Legislation Comes from Europe?*, House of Commons Research Paper 10/62 (London, 2010) 1. The studies on other Member States are cited at 24–41 of the Report.

account of the clustering of EU law, so the same British study estimates that about 50 per cent of UK legislation with a significant economic impact is derived from the Union. Nor do they take account of the relative resonance, controversy or impact of different pieces of legislation. If some EU legislation is uncontroversial, limited and largely unnoticed, other legislative acts can have huge impact and generate significant divisions.

This concern is reflected in the first part of the test in Article 5(3) TEU: namely, that the Union only should act if *the objectives of the proposed action cannot be sufficiently achieved by the Member States.* This part of the test is not based on whether EU or national laws would be more effective, but rather goes to the Member State's sense of self-government, and what it believes it can do itself. This goes to wider issues than legal effectiveness such as how far a measure forms part of a wider valued tradition. The British decision to drive on the left-hand side of the road is thus an expression of quirky Britishness. It is chosen over the right not because it is safer but because that is the tradition within the United Kingdom and this tradition asserts British distinctiveness.

The second logic is a federal one. All federal systems have a principle mediating the relationship between federal and local government, and when it is appropriate for the central federal authorities to intervene and when it is not. A good example is article 72(2) of the German Basic Law.

German Basic Law, article 72(2)

In this field the [federal authorities] will have the right to legislate if federal legal regulation is needed:

(1) because a matter could not be settled effectively by the legislation of the various Länder [regions], or

(2) because the regulation of a matter by the law of a Land [region] could affect the interests of other or all Länder, or

(3) to safeguard the legal or economic unity, and in particular, to safeguard the homogeneity of the living conditions beyond the territory of a Land.

This logic is different. Everybody is part of a unitary order with the question being one of comparative efficiency. The question goes to whether the measure could be more effectively resolved by central rather than local legislation or vice versa. Article 72(2) therefore sets out three types of circumstance where the former is the case. However, it does not cover the sort of issue raised by the first test. No regional authority in Germany would claim therefore to require drivers to drive on the left when in the rest of Germany they drive on the right. It would prevent an integrated road system, a national car industry and concerns would be expressed about the effect on road safety if drivers suddenly had to swap from one side to the other.

This federal logic, adopted in the second part of Article 5(3) TEU and the indicators set out in Article 5 PASP, goes to whether the object of a measure can, by reason of its scale or effects, be better achieved at EU level. The test is whether one central measure would be more effective than twenty-eight different ones. A central parameter, the success of the policy, is used to gauge whether this is the case, with indicators or values that do not go to the success of the policy not being considered. It is, thus, a much centralising test.

The logic of each test slides past the other. One is about expression of collective identity and the other about effective realisation of common Union action.[41] Interpretation of the subsidiarity principle would require, therefore, a further balancing to take place which provides for some mutual accommodation between these two logics. A consequence of this balancing would be that any final decision by the Court of Justice would not look coherent when viewed through the perspective of either of these logics. Adjudicating subsidiarity is, therefore, a difficult task for any court. The Union context is further complicated by the Court of Justice, if it finds a breach of the principle, having to come to a different conclusion about the need for a measure after all three political institutions had indicated their support for it.[42]

The Court of Justice has, however, side-stepped this challenge in two ways. In the first place, there is no evidence of its directing itself to the first test. The question of whether an activity could be realised satisfactorily through domestic processes has never been mentioned in any of the judgments of the Court. In the second place, the comparative efficiency is not deployed to assess whether an EU measure would bring advantages for the regulated activity that a national measure could not bring but rather whether it helps to realise a general objective set by EU law: such as the single market, a common environment policy, etc. As the piece below indicates, this is a hopelessly tilted test as national measures never can realise such a policy whereas EU measures always can.

G. Davies, 'Subsidiarity: The Wrong Idea, in the Wrong Place, at the Wrong Time' (2006) 43 *Common Market Law Review* 63, 72–4

The fact that the Community's competences tend to be defined in terms of objectives to be achieved, rather than areas of activity to be regulated, is at the heart of the mismatch…Whereas the Member States often look at a measure in terms of its effects on an area of activity – which corresponds to the degree to which it invades their powers – the Community, and the Court, assess it primarily in terms of the degree to which it achieves Community goals. There is a failure to agree on the subject of conversation.

In the cases in which subsidiarity has come before the Court of Justice – which concerned attempts to annul Community measures – this is clearly visible. In these cases the Court rejects the claim that there is a violation of subsidiarity. The argument seems to follow a repetitive pattern. First, the complainant states that the measure regulates an area, such as health and safety at work, public health, or food safety, which is primarily a Member State competence. They then claim that the ways in which safety or health are advanced by the measure could have been just as well – perhaps better – achieved by the Member States acting alone. Therefore, they conclude, subsidiarity should prevent the Community action.

Yet the substantive argument would fail anyway, as it failed in the annulment cases. The reason is that it asks the wrong question. The goal of the measures or provisions being challenged or interpreted was not exclusively, generally not even primarily, that of regulating the substantive area of law in question. The measures or judgments were not aiming to regulate health, civil procedure, or language

---

[41] F. Scharpf, 'Community and Autonomy: Multi-level Policy Making in the European Union' (1994) 1 *JEPP* 219, 225–6.

[42] It has thus been argued that subsidiarity is necessarily a centralising notion. G. Davies, 'Subsidiarity: The Wrong Idea, in the Wrong Place, at the Wrong Time' (2006) 43 *CMLRev.* 63.

as such, not making any claim that these were matters that belonged to the centre. Rather they were pursuing one of the Community's functional competences – in most cases the aim of removing obstacles to movement or distortions of competition.

In the annulment cases, the aim by which the measures were defined was that of harmonization as such; the removal of the particular problems which may arise through differences between national laws, or national laws restrictive of movement. Of course, health and safety and so on are important, and so the harmonization was done in a way ensuring a high level of protection of this. Such measures therefore look like health and safety measures.

However, defining them in terms of health and safety objectives, as the subsidiarity arguments of the Member States do, is incomplete. Hence the subsidiarity arguments were rebuffed. The Court points out that the Community objective being pursued by the measures was that of harmonization, which is necessary in order to prevent differences between national laws causing obstacles to movement or distortions of competition. Since it is manifestly the case that Member States acting alone cannot harmonize, there is no subsidiarity criticism to be made.

An illustration of both this reasoning and its terseness is the judgment below which concerns Directive 98/44/EC, which requires Member States to protect biotechnological inventions by patents.[43] The Dutch Government challenged this on the grounds that the Directive provided few reasons why its objectives were better realised at EU level and in the light of Article 345 TFEU, which stipulates that nothing in the Treaties should prejudice national rules governing the system of property ownership.[44]

Case C-377/98 *Netherlands* v *European Parliament and Council* [2001] ECR I-7079

2. The Directive was adopted on the basis of Article [114 TFEU], and its purpose is to require the Member States, through their patent laws, to protect biotechnological inventions, whilst complying with their international obligations.

3. To that end the Directive determines inter alia which inventions involving plants, animals or the human body may or may not be patented...

30. The applicant submits that the Directive breaches the principle of subsidiarity...and, in the alternative, that it does not state sufficient reasons to establish that this requirement was taken into account...

32. The objective pursued by the Directive, to ensure smooth operation of the internal market by preventing or eliminating differences between the legislation and practice of the various Member States in the area of the protection of biotechnological inventions, could not be achieved by action taken by the Member States alone. As the scope of that protection has immediate effects on trade, and, accordingly, on intra-Community trade, it is clear that, given the scale and effects of the proposed action, the objective in question could be better achieved by the Community.

---

[43] See to similar effect Case C-84/94 *United Kingdom* v *Council* [1996] ECR I-5755; Case C-491/01 *British American Tobacco* [2002] ECR I-11453; Joined Cases C-154/04 and C-155/04 *R* v *Secretary of State for Health ex parte Alliance for Natural Health* [2005] ECR I-6451.

[44] The situation has been changed in this regard by the Lisbon Treaty which explicitly provides for the first time for some harmonisation of intellectual property rights, Article 118 TFEU.

33. Compliance with the principle of subsidiarity is necessarily implicit in the fifth, sixth and seventh recitals of the preamble to the Directive, which state that, in the absence of action at Community level, the development of the laws and practices of the different Member States impedes the proper functioning of the internal market. It thus appears that the Directive states sufficient reasons on that point.

Although the principle of subsidiarity has regularly been invoked before the Court of Justice, the Court has yet to annul a measure for breach of the principle. Commentators have, therefore, suggested a variety of institutional innovations to compensate for this.[45] Weiler has argued for the creation of a European Constitutional Court, presided over by the President of the European Court of Justice and comprising judges drawn from the constitutional courts or their equivalents in the various Member States.[46] He considers that only a body comprising the most senior judges in the EU would have the authority and confidence to police the limits of Union powers. Others think the task should not be in the hands of judges. In 1994, the British Commissioner, Leon Brittan, proposed the creation of a chamber of national parliamentarians who would vet the EU's legislative proposals on grounds of subsidiarity before they became law.[47] It is this latter suggestion which was taken up in the Treaty of Lisbon. As was seen earlier,[48] a central function of national parliaments is now to patrol Commission drafts for verification with the principle of subsidiarity. There is evidence that this has been more effective at patrolling the exercise of EU competences, but only at the expense of abandonment of the subsidiarity principle, with national parliaments simply giving opinions on whether they like the EU measure or not.[49]

If it is difficult for the Court of Justice to engage in substantive review, it should be able, at least, to verify that the legislative institutions address the question meaningfully. Article 5 PASP requires that any proposal be 'justified' with regard to those principles.[50] The quality of the justification – whether the reasons given are consistent, properly considered and accurately reflected the legal text – is something that the Court ought to be able to monitor. However, the intensity of review is weak. In the judgment below, Germany challenged Directive 94/19/EC, the Deposit Guarantee Directive, which required all credit institutions to have guarantee schemes for depositors which would provide the latter with some coverage if the institution ran into trouble. The German Government argued that the compulsory nature of the scheme had insufficient regard to established national practices. It was forcing Germany to scrap an effective voluntary scheme. The German Government argued that insufficient reasons were provided in the Directive why a binding Union scheme was necessary. The Court did not accept Germany's arguments and the Directive survived.

---

[45] It has also been argued that a sufficiently strong case has never been made that a measure violates the subsidiarity principle. P. Craig, 'Subsidiarity: A Political and Legal Analysis' (2012) 50 *JCMS* 72, 80–1.

[46] J. Weiler, 'The European Union Belongs to Its Citizens: Three Immodest Proposals' (1997) 22 *ELRev.* 150, 155–6.

[47] L. Brittan, *The Europe We Need* (London, Hamilton, 1994).   [48] See pp. 131–2.

[49] K. Granat and F. Fabbrini, '"Yellow Card, but No Foul": The Role of the National Parliaments under the Subsidiarity Protocol and the Commission Proposal for a Right to Strike' (2013) 50 *CMLRev.* 115.

[50] On this see G. Bermann, 'Taking Subsidiarity Seriously: Federalism in the EC and in the USA' (1994) 94 *Columbia Law Review* 331, 391–5; G. de Búrca, *Reappraising Subsidiarity's Significance after Amsterdam*, Jean Monnet Working Paper 7/99.

Case C–233/94 *Germany* v *European Parliament and Council* [1997] ECR I–2405

22. The German Government claims that the Directive must be annulled because it fails to state the reasons on which it is based...It does not explain how it is compatible with the principle of subsidiarity...

23. As to the precise terms of the obligation to state reasons in the light of the principle of subsidiarity, the German Government states that the Community institutions must give detailed reasons to explain why only the Community, to the exclusion of the Member States, is empowered to act in the area in question. In the present case, the Directive does not indicate in what respect its objectives could not have been sufficiently attained by action at Member State level or the grounds which militated in favour of Community action...

26. In the present case, the Parliament and the Council stated in the second recital in the preamble to the Directive that 'consideration should be given to the situation which might arise if deposits in a credit institution that has branches in other Member States became unavailable' and that it was 'indispensable to ensure a harmonized minimum level of deposit protection wherever deposits are located in the Community'. This shows that, in the Community legislature's view, the aim of its action could, because of the dimensions of the intended action, be best achieved at Community level. The same reasoning appears in the third recital, from which it is clear that the decision regarding the guarantee scheme which is competent in the event of the insolvency of a branch situated in a Member State other than that in which the credit institution has its head office has repercussions which are felt outside the borders of each Member State.

27. Furthermore, in the fifth recital the Parliament and the Council stated that the action taken by the Member States in response to [a] Commission Recommendation has not fully achieved the desired result. The Community legislature therefore found that the objective of its action could not be achieved sufficiently by the Member States.

28. Consequently, it is apparent that, on any view, the Parliament and the Council did explain why they considered that their action was in conformity with the principle of subsidiarity and, accordingly, that they complied with the obligation to give reasons...An express reference to that principle cannot be required.

The judgment suggests that the procedural requirements will be met even where there is no evidence to suppose that the institutions actually considered whether the measure satisfied the principle of subsidiarity and no part of the measure in question specifically refers to it. As Dashwood has concluded, the Court of Justice has shown that 'while the justiciability of the principle cannot any longer be doubted, the case law indicates equally clearly that annulment of a measure on the ground that it offends against subsidiarity is likely to occur only in extreme circumstances'.[51]

(iii) Proportionality

The proportionality principle requires that the content and form of Union action not exceed what is necessary to achieve the objectives of the Treaties.[52] Established by a long line of case

---

[51] A. Dashwood, 'The Relationship between the Member States and the European Union/European Community' (2004) 41 *CMLRev.* 355, 368.

[52] For detailed analysis and commentary, see E. Ellis (ed.), *The Principle of Proportionality in the Laws of Europe* (Oxford, Oxford University Press, 1999); G. de Búrca, 'The Principle of Proportionality and its Application in EC Law' (1993) 13 *YEL* 105.

law,[53] its current formulation is set out in *Fedesa*. This concerned a challenge to Directive 88/146/EEC, which prohibited the use of five hormonal substances in livestock farming. This was argued, inter alia, to be disproportionate for the reasons set out in paragraph 12.

Case C-331/88 *R* v *Minister of Agriculture, Fisheries and Food* ex parte *Fedesa* [1990] ECR I-4023

12. It was argued that the directive at issue infringes the principle of proportionality in three respects. In the first place, the outright prohibition on the administration of the five hormones in question is inappropriate in order to attain the declared objectives, since it is impossible to apply in practice and leads to the creation of a dangerous black market. In the second place, outright prohibition is not necessary because consumer anxieties can be allayed simply by the dissemination of information and advice. Finally, the prohibition in question entails excessive disadvantages, in particular considerable financial losses on the part of the traders concerned, in relation to the alleged benefits accruing to the general interest.

13. The Court has consistently held that the principle of proportionality is one of the general principles of Community law. By virtue of that principle, the lawfulness of the prohibition of an economic activity is subject to the condition that the prohibitory measures are appropriate and necessary in order to achieve the objectives legitimately pursued by the legislation in question; when there is a choice between several appropriate measures recourse must be had to the least onerous, and the disadvantages caused must not be disproportionate to the aims pursued.

Proportionality has, thus, been conflated into two balancing processes. The first goes to whether there is an appropriate balance between the ends sought and means used, and whether the latter are *suitable* for the former. Judgment about this is a matter of degree. It is when is the hammer too big to be used to crack the nut. The other form of balancing, frequently expressed as the *necessity* of the measure, goes to whether the effect of the measure on other interests and values is excessive.[54] This balancing is seen by some as one of the elements which confers value on proportionality as it serves to secure both value pluralism and coherence between otherwise conflicting legal values and principles.[55] Critics have pointed, however, to a rule of thumb feel to it, which allows unconstrained and unprincipled choices between different values and interests.[56]

Entering into this debate is beyond the scope of this book. The debate illustrates, however, the *possibility* of a very wide-ranging review of legislative and administration action offered

---

[53] The principle was stated to be a general principle of law in Case 11/70 *Internationale Handelsgesellschaft* v *Einfuhr- und Vorratsstelle Getreide* [1970] ECR 1125.

[54] On the history and evolution of these two elements of balancing within proportionality see M. Cohen-Eliya and I. Porat, *Proportionality and Constitutional Culture* (Cambridge, Cambridge University Press, 2013) 10–24 and 32–43. Within EU law see T. Tridimas, *The General Principles of EU Law* (2nd edn, Oxford, Oxford University Press, 2006) 139–40; A. Portuese, 'Principle of Proportionality as a Principle of Economic Efficiency' (2013) 19 *ELJ* 612.

[55] Most famously R. Alexy, 'On Balancing and Subsumption: A Structural Comparison' (2003) 16 *Ratio Juris* 433. More recently in a modified form see M. Klatt and M. Meister, *The Constitutional Structure of Proportionality* (Oxford, Oxford University Press, 2012) especially chs. 4 and 5.

[56] J. Habermas, *Between Facts and Norms* (Polity, Cambridge, 1997) 244 *et seq.*; G. Webber, 'Proportionality, Balancing, and the Cult of Constitutional Rights Scholarship' (2010) 23 *Canadian Journal of Law and Jurisprudence* 179.

by the proportionality principle. Its scope allows judges the possibility to address the merits of the measure as they can always hold it is either not suitable to the ends or is excessive. It also goes to the range of arguments they can consider. The test of suitability goes to the relationship between the measure, the wider policy of which it forms part and the broader ethos and rationale behind the political system which gives rise to it. The test of necessity allows all manner of interests and values to be balanced against each other. The extent to which this possibility is taken up, Cohen-Eliya and Porat observe, is highly dependent on the legal culture within which it arises. It might be affected by the values cherished by that tradition, its sense of institutional balance, and the styles of interpretation developed by the judiciary. They point, in particular, to two ideal-types.[57]

One is a culture of justification. Within this culture, every administrative and legislative action is required to justify itself. Broad conceptions of rights tend to reinforce this culture of justification as they provide additional grounds for judicial intervention as well as greater possibilities of conflict which the judiciary must resolve. In EU law, such a culture of rights exists in relation to action by national authorities. There is a wealth of rights in the Treaty and secondary legislation which individuals can invoke against these. Proportionality has been interpreted to allow a wide-ranging and intensive review in which a national measure restricting a right granted by EU law will be prohibited unless the Member State can establish that it is necessary to achieve a legitimate aim and that no less restrictive alternative exists.[58]

The other is a culture of authority. Proportionality exists not to probe the merits of the measures but rather to check that the institution is the appropriate body to be taking the decision in question, and is acting within the sphere of authorisation granted to it. Once that is determined, this sphere is treated as a black box in which the institution has discretion over what measure to take. This culture of authority is deployed by the Court of Justice in relation to measures by the EU institutions.

Case C–331/88 R v Minister of Agriculture, Fisheries and Food ex parte Fedesa [1990] ECR I–4023

14. …with regard to judicial review…it must be stated that in matters concerning the common agricultural policy the Community legislature has a discretionary power which corresponds to the political responsibilities given to it by…the Treaty. Consequently, the legality of a measure adopted in that sphere can be affected only if the measure is manifestly inappropriate having regard to the objective which the competent institution is seeking to pursue…

15. On the question whether or not the prohibition is appropriate in the present case, it should first be stated that even if the presence of natural hormones in all meat prevents detection of the presence of prohibited hormones by tests on animals or on meat, other control methods may be used and indeed were imposed on the Member States by [other legislation]. It is not obvious that the authorization of only those hormones described as 'natural' would be likely to prevent the emergence of a black market for dangerous but less expensive substances. Moreover, according to the Council, which was not contradicted on that point, any system of partial authorization would require costly control measures

---

[57] M. Cohen-Eliya and I. Porat, n. 54 above, 111–29.   [58] See pp. 789–95.

whose effectiveness would not be guaranteed. It follows that the prohibition at issue cannot be regarded as a manifestly inappropriate measure.

16. As regards the arguments which have been advanced in support of the claim that the prohibition in question is not necessary, those arguments are in fact based on the premise that the contested measure is inappropriate for attaining objectives other than that of allaying consumer anxieties which are said to be unfounded. Since the Council committed no manifest error in that respect, it was also entitled to take the view that, regard being had to the requirements of health protection, the removal of barriers to trade and distortions of competition could not be achieved by means of less onerous measures such as the dissemination of information to consumers and the labelling of meat.

17. Finally, it must be stated that the importance of the objectives pursued is such as to justify even substantial negative financial consequences for certain traders.

18. Consequently, the principle of proportionality has not been infringed.

The test that EU measures will only be disproportionate if the action is 'manifestly inappropriate' is a weak one.[59] One reason might be that the Court of Justice places a great premium on the value of European integration. In instances, where the Union legislature, in particular, has taken measures to realise the objectives of this integration, the Court sees that as sufficient to intervene only exceptionally.[60] If this is so, it is damning as it is difficult to see how simply realising a system, independent of anything else, is necessarily valuable.

The impact of the proportionality principle may be felt not so much through the intervention of judicial review.[61] It may, instead, be the change in legislative culture brought about through it, whereby EU institutions commit themselves to consider more carefully the relationship between the ends sought and the means deployed to realise these ends. In 2003, the EU institutions moved away from a process of law-making to a process of regulation in which the instrument deployed would no longer necessarily be legislation but other instruments which were more suited (in the institutions' view) to realising a task and would, in so doing, impose less intrusive effects on private parties.[62] These other instruments may be co-regulation (the delegation to private parties to agree norms according to EU set criteria) or self-regulation (the possibility for any area to be regulated entirely by private operators).

[59] The test is routinely used. Case C-380/03 *Germany* v *Parliament and Council* [2006] ECR I-11573. Case C-343/07 *Bavaria and Bavaria Italia* v *Bayerischer Brauerbund* [2009] ECR I-5491; Joined Cases C-379/08 and C-380/08 *ERG and others* v *Ministero dello Sviluppo Economico* [2010] ECR I-2007; Case C-15/10 *Etimine* v *Secretary of State for Work and Pensions* [2011] ECR I-6681. For detailed discussion see H. Hofmann *et al.*, *Administrative Law and Policy of the European Union* (Oxford, Oxford University Press, 2011) 129–34.

[60] T.-I. Harbo, 'The Function of the Proportionality Principle in EU Law' (2010) 16 *ELJ* 158, 172–3. For a rare example of where an EU measure was found disproportionate see Case C-310/04 *Spain* v *Council* [2006] ECR I-7285.

[61] It has been argued that the principle calls for this as a measure might be manifestly inappropriate if the legislature has failed to show that it has considered different options and their consequences. There is, as yet, no case, however, where a measure has been struck down for this reason cf. K. Lenaerts, 'The European Court of Justice and Process-Oriented Review' (2012) 31 *YBEL* 3.

[62] On the shift to this, see A. Héritier, 'New Modes of Governance in Europe: Policy-Making without Legislating' in A. Héritier (ed.), *Common Goods: Reinventing European and International Governance* (Lanham, MD, Rowan & Littlefield, 2002); J. Caporaso and J. Wittenbrink, 'The New Modes of Governance and Political Authority in Europe' (2006) 13 *JEPP* 471.

Inter-institutional Agreement on Better Law-Making [2003] OJ C321/01

16. The three Institutions recall the Community's obligation to legislate only where it is necessary, in accordance with the Protocol on the application of the principles of subsidiarity and proportionality. They recognise the need to use, in suitable cases or where the Treaty does not specifically require the use of a legal instrument, alternative regulation mechanisms.

17. The Commission will ensure that any use of co-regulation or self-regulation is always consistent with Community law and that it meets the criteria of transparency (in particular the publicising of agreements) and representativeness of the parties involved. It must also represent added value for the general interest. These mechanisms will not be applicable where fundamental rights or important political options are at stake or in situations where the rules must be applied in a uniform fashion in all Member States. They must ensure swift and flexible regulation which does not affect the principles of competition or the unity of the internal market.

Co-regulation

18. Co-regulation means the mechanism whereby a Community legislative act entrusts the attainment of the objectives defined by the legislative authority to parties which are recognised in the field (such as economic operators, the social partners, non-governmental organisations, or associations). This mechanism may be used on the basis of criteria defined in the legislative act so as to enable the legislation to be adapted to the problems and sectors concerned, to reduce the legislative burden by concentrating on essential aspects and to draw on the experience of the parties concerned...

20. In the context defined by the basic legislative act, the parties affected by that act may conclude voluntary agreements for the purpose of determining practical arrangements. The draft agreements will be forwarded by the Commission to the legislative authority. In accordance with its responsibilities, the Commission will verify whether or not those draft agreements comply with Community law (and, in particular, with the basic legislative act).

    At the request of inter alia the European Parliament or of the Council, on a case-by-case basis and depending on the subject, the basic legislative act may include a provision for a two-month period of grace following notification of a draft agreement to the European Parliament and the Council. During that period, each Institution may either suggest amendments, if it is considered that the draft agreement does not meet the objectives laid down by the legislative authority, or object to the entry into force of that agreement and, possibly, ask the Commission to submit a proposal for a legislative act.

21. A legislative act which serves as the basis for a co-regulation mechanism will indicate the possible extent of co-regulation in the area concerned. The competent legislative authority will define in the act the relevant measures to be taken in order to follow up its application, in the event of non-compliance by one or more parties or if the agreement fails. These measures may provide, for example, for the regular supply of information by the Commission to the legislative authority on follow-up to application or for a revision clause under which the Commission will report at the end of a specific period and, where necessary, propose an amendment to the legislative act or any other appropriate legislative measure.

Self-regulation

22. Self-regulation is defined as the possibility for economic operators, the social partners, non-governmental organisations or associations to adopt amongst themselves and for themselves common guidelines at European level (particularly codes of practice or sectoral agreements). As a general rule,

this type of voluntary initiative does not imply that the Institutions have adopted any particular stance, in particular where such initiatives are undertaken in areas which are not covered by the Treaties or in which the Union has not hitherto legislated. As one of its responsibilities, the Commission will scrutinise self-regulation practices in order to verify that they comply with the provisions of the EC Treaty.

The use of co-regulation, in particular, is widespread with private standards deployed as a substitute for legislation across wide swathes of Union activity. They are prevalent in the fields of the internal market, employment and social policy, protection of the environment, financial services, information and communications technology, fighting crime and consumer protection.[63] The justification is that these enable market participants to decide the level and form of regulation in a manner suitable for them and in a way that minimises adjustment and financial costs. Yet such arrangements bring a host of unanswered questions: in particular there is a concern that many checks and balances are lost.[64]

D. Chalmers, 'Private Power and Public Authority in European Union Law' (2005–6) 8 *Cambridge Yearbook of European Legal Studies* 59, 79

[These] regimes consequently generate a number of possible difficulties. The first is with the protection of public goods, such as protection of the environment, administration of justice or an effective financial system. They are set up to protect these public goods, but, invariably, the questions arise as to how effectively they do it and whether they are ambitious enough in their reach. The second is the protection of so called 'credential goods'. Credential goods deal with problems of asymmetries of information. Professional regimes are, for example, typically justified on the ground that consumers will know little about the quality of services provided by professionals, and it is, therefore, important to have a professional regime to regulate them. Yet all problem-solving regimes surround the individual with a bewildering array of semi-formal structures, which open up some possibilities, whilst closing off others. The forms of advertising she sees; her Internet provision; the quality and price of the goods and services she buys; access to professional help; and much of her natural environment: all are governed by this twilight zone of EU private law making. An individual goes to replace a part in her car, but can no longer obtain it because a manufacturer has discontinued it to meet its CO_2 obligations under the Union agreements, and she is, therefore, unable to drive any more. She has no redress, no sense of transparency, and no sense of identifying who is responsible for this significant change in her life. Moreover, in contrast to parliamentary statutes or case law, the opacity of her entitlements undermines her ability to feel comfortable about and trust her surrounding environment, and her sense of social status, self-esteem and confidence to make choices. The final difficulty is distributive asymmetries. Problem-solving regimes may benefit some participants at the expense of others, and the entitlements they provide for third parties may benefit some more than others or actually disadvantage some parties by withdrawing entitlements they might otherwise have had.

---

[63] For a survey see D. Chalmers, 'Private Power and Public Authority in European Union Law' (2005–6) 8 *CYELS* 59, 64–73.

[64] See also L. Senden, 'Soft Law, Self-regulation and Co-regulation in European Law: Where do they Meet?' (2005) 9 *Electronic Journal of Comparative Law* No. 1; A. Héritier and S. Eckert, 'New Modes of Governance in the Shadow of Hierarchy: Self-regulation by Industry in Europe' (2008) 28 *Journal of Public Policy* 113; P. Verbruggen, 'Does Co-regulation Strengthen EU Legitimacy?' (2009) 15 *ELJ* 425; N. Meyer, 'Political Contestation of Self-regulation in the Shadow of Hierarchy' (2013) 20 *JEPP* 760; Hofmann *et al.*, n. 59 above, 588–605.

(iv) Subsidiarity, proportionality and 'Smart Regulation'

Concern with the impact of EU legislation on the competitiveness of enterprises in the Union led the Commission to establish a programme in 2005 simplifying the regulatory environment. This brought together the subsidiarity and proportionality principles.[65] Its central ethos was the following:

> the EU should only regulate if a proposed action can be better achieved at EU level. Any such action should not go beyond what is necessary to achieve the policy objectives pursued. It needs to be cost efficient and take the lightest form of regulation called for. In this respect simplification intends to make legislation at both Community and national level less burdensome, easier to apply and thereby more effective in achieving their goals.[66]

The commitment to EU regulation only where it is necessary, simple and effective led the Commission to propose a strategy whose five central points were the following:

- Repeal of all legislative acts that are irrelevant or obsolete. The Commission will introduce review clauses to all legislation to ensure that new legislation is reviewed within a particular time frame (typically three to five years).
- Codification of existing EU legislation into more readable, coherent texts.
- Recasting of legislation. This is different from codification as it involves the merging of legal texts so as to increase consistency and minimise overlaps.
- Modification of the regulatory approach to make more use of co-regulation.
- Greater use of Regulations rather than Directives as the former have immediate application, and subject all actors to the same rules at the same time.[67]

In the wake of the euro area crisis, the simplification programme was not seen as sufficiently radical. It was supplanted by a 'Smart Regulation' initiative, which integrated elements of the simplification agenda whilst imposing further demands of its own. The Smart Regulation agenda has the following central elements:

- A programme of reducing the administrative burdens imposed on private actors by EU law either through simplifying EU legislation or, in some cases, repealing it. Between 2007 and 2012, 120 measures were taken, which, when all have been finally adopted, will, according to the Commission, reduce the total administrative burden of EU law by 30.5 per cent or about €37.6 billion.[68]
- Ex post evaluation of the effectiveness of all EU legislation. In addition, 'fitness checks' take place assessing whether regulatory frameworks for whole policy areas are fit for purpose or whether they should be changed.[69]

---

[65] European Commission, *Better Regulation for Growth and Jobs*, COM(2005)97.
[66] European Commission, *Implementing the Community Lisbon Programme: A Strategy for the Simplification of the Regulatory Environment*, COM(2005)535, 2.
[67] *Ibid.* 6–9.
[68] European Commission, *Action Programme for Reducing Administrative Burdens in the EU Final Report*, SWD(2012)423, 7.
[69] European Commission, *Smart Regulation in the European Union*, COM(2010)583, 4.

- Assessments of the economic, social, fundamental rights and environmental impacts of all legislative proposals. These impact assessments are then evaluated by an independent Impact Assessment Board for their quality.[70]
- Improving the implementation of EU legislation, most notably by requiring Member States to be more transparent about how they transpose EU law.[71]

This was taken further in the Regulatory Fitness programme, which, in addition to the above, involves a mapping exercise looking for the regulatory areas and pieces of legislation with greatest potential for simplification and reduction of regulatory costs for businesses.[72] This screening exercise was carried out with stakeholders, most notably small and medium-size enterprises.[73]

Subsidiarity and proportionality are thus recasting the EU legislative landscape in dramatic and wide-ranging ways. In this, they have acquired a strong deregulatory bias. To be sure, the dismantling of unnecessary legislation is not to be decried. However, there is a worrying lack of transparency about the process. The repeal and recasting of EU legislation is characterised by a process which is far less structured and pluralist than the enactment of that legislation. The basis for declaring measures ineffective or inefficient is, furthermore, unclear. Simple disuse as a criterion is too vague and invites selective enforcement. Whilst some laws may be obsolete it may be that, with others, they are 'dormant' because they are widely accepted and rarely violated.[74]

5 CONSULTATION

(i) General standards and the minimum principles for consultation

A central concern of the Governance agenda is that EU institutions should consult widely before taking any legislative action.[75] Article 11 TEU sets out three underlying principles – dialogue, transparency and pluralism – that must inform such consultations.

Article 11 TEU

1. The institutions shall, by appropriate means, give citizens and representative associations the opportunity to make known and publicly exchange their views in all areas of Union action.
2. The institutions shall maintain an open, transparent and regular dialogue with representative associations and civil society.
3. The European Commission shall carry out broad consultations with parties concerned in order to ensure that the Union's actions are coherent and transparent.

---

[70] European Commission, *Impact Assessment Guidelines*, SEC(2009)92.
[71] European Commission, *Smart Regulation in the European Union*, COM(2010)583, 7–8.
[72] European Commission, *EU Regulatory Fitness*, COM(2012)476, 4.
[73] European Commission, *Regulatory Fitness and Performance (REFIT): Results and Next Steps*, COM(2013)685, 5.
[74] On this see J. Wiener, 'Better Regulation in Europe' (2006) 59 *CLP* 447, 503.
[75] On the evolution of the Commission's and Court's approaches to consultation see F. Bignami, 'Three Generations of Participation Rights before the Commission' (2004) 68 *Law and Contemporary Problems* 61.

These principles are detailed in the 2002 Commission Communication on General Standards and Minimum Principles for Consultation:[76]

> *The content of consultation is to be clear*: The Commission should set out a summary of the context, scope and objectives of consultation, including a description of the specific issues open for discussion or questions with particular importance for the Commission. It should make available details of any hearings, meetings or conferences, as well as contact details and information on deadlines. It should provide explanation of the Commission processes for dealing with contributions, what feedback to expect, and details of the next stages involved in the development of the policy.
>
> *Relevant parties should have an opportunity to express their opinions*: In its consultations, the Commission should ensure adequate coverage of those affected by the policy, those who will be involved in implementation of the policy, or bodies that have stated objectives giving them a direct interest in the policy. In determining the relevant parties for consultation, it should take into account the impact of the policy on other policy areas, the need for specific experience, expertise or technical knowledge, the need to involve non-organised interests. It should consider the track record of participants in previous consultations as well as the need for a proper balance between representatives of social and economic bodies, large and small organisations or companies, wider constituencies (such as churches and religious communities) and specific target groups (for example women, the elderly, the unemployed, or ethnic minorities).
>
> *The Commission should publish consultations widely*: This is via the web portal, 'Your Voice in Europe',[77] which is the Commission's single access point for consultation.
>
> *Participants are to be given sufficient time to respond*: The Commission should allow at least eight weeks for reception of responses to written public consultations and twenty working days' notice for meetings.
>
> *Acknowledgement and adequate feedback is to be provided*: Receipt of contributions should be acknowledged and the results displayed on websites. Explanatory memoranda accompanying legislative proposals following a consultation process must include the results of these consultations, an explanation as to how these were conducted and how the results were taken into account in the proposal.

Like any procedure, there is a danger that this consultation is no more than a formal hoop to climb through for the EU institutions. To assess its bite, it is necessary to consider whether it gives rise to the dialogue, transparency and pluralism alluded to in Article 11 TEU.

(ii) Dialogue within the consultation process

Dialogue, to be meaningful, has to be more than merely talk, as talk does not necessarily have any bearing on the subsequent legislation. To be significant, dialogue has to be similar to the

---

[76] European Commission, *General Principles and Minimum Standards for Consultation of Interested Parties by the Commission*, COM(2002)704. See D. Obradovic and J. Alonso, 'Good Governance Requirements Concerning the Participation of Interest Groups in EU Consultations' (2006) 43 *CMLRev.* 1049.

[77] See http://ec.europa.eu/yourvoice/index_en.htm.

notion of accountability used by Bovens in which 'the actor has an obligation to explain and justify his or her conduct, the forum can pose questions and pass judgment and the actor may face consequences'.[78] The duty on EU institutions to give reasons is central to such a dialogue. It imposes duties on them to justify themselves, to be questioned and to be held to account for the reasons they present. The duty is set out in Article 296 TFEU.

Article 296(2) TFEU

2. Legal acts shall state the reasons on which they are based and shall refer to any proposals, initiatives, recommendations, requests or opinions required by the Treaties.

The duty is not a strong one. The reasons given can be quite general and they do not have to respond to points made by those consulted. A good example is *Commission v Spain*.[79] Aid had been granted to farmers in Extremadura, one of the poorest areas of Spain. The aid to each farmer was for relatively small amounts and applied to just nine products with the aid paid, in the case of most of the vegetables, only if they were to be used for processing. The Commission argued that, in light of the significant trade in vegetables between Spain and the other Member States, the aid could distort competition and affect trade between Member States by virtue of the subsidy to production costs for Spanish undertakings. It declared the aid illegal. The Spanish Government stated that the reasons were inadequate on a number of grounds. First, the decision looked at the market for all green vegetables rather than the nine vegetables in question. Secondly, it did not look at the share of Extremaduran produce in the national market and its contribution to trade within the Union. Finally, there was no explanation of the relationship between the total volume of trade between Spain and the other Member States and the quantity of aid in question, in particular it was not shown how the latter affected the former. These points had previously been made to the Commission by the Spanish Government, and the latter's failure to address them was quite an indictment. The Court nevertheless held that the Commission's reasoning was sufficient.

Case C–113/00 *Spain v Commission* [2002] ECR I–7601

47. It should first of all be observed that the obligation to provide a statement of reasons laid down in Article [296(2) TFEU] is an essential procedural requirement, as distinct from the question whether the reasons given are correct, which goes to the substantive legality of the contested measure. Accordingly, the statement of reasons required by Article [296(2) TFEU] must be appropriate to the act at issue and must disclose in a clear and unequivocal fashion the reasoning followed by the institution which adopted the measure in question in such a way as to enable the persons concerned to ascertain the reasons for the measure and to enable the competent court to exercise its power of review.

---

[78] M. Bovens, 'Analysing and Assessing Accountability: A Conceptual Framework' (2007) 13 *ELJ* 447, 450.
[79] In like vein see Joined Cases C-346/03 and C-529/03 *Atzeni and others* v *Regione autonoma della Sardegna* [2006] ECR I-1875; Case T-335/08 *BNP Paribas* v *Commission* [2010] ECR II-3323; Case C-221/09 *AJD Tuna* v *Commission* [2011] ECR I-1655.

48. Furthermore, that requirement must be appraised by reference to the circumstances of each case, in particular the content of the measure, the nature of the reasons given and the interest which the addressees of the measure, or other parties to whom it is of direct and individual concern, may have in obtaining explanations. It is not necessary for the reasoning to go into all the relevant facts and points of law, since the question whether the statement of reasons meets the requirements of Article [296(2) TFEU] must be assessed with regard not only to its wording but also to its context and to all the legal rules governing the matter in question.

49. In the light of that case-law, it does not appear that the Commission failed in this case to fulfil its obligation to provide an adequate statement of reasons in the contested decision for the finding that the aid in question affects trade between Member States.

50. First of all…the Commission provides figures on the total quantity of vegetables produced in Spain and on the volume of trade in vegetables between Spain and the other Member States in 1998. It is clear from this information that a sizeable portion of Spanish horticultural goods is exported to other Member States. Whilst the Commission did not provide detailed figures on exports of those vegetables to which the aid scheme in question applies, it nonetheless noted that the overall context in which the scheme operates is one of a high level of trade between Member States of products in the horticultural sector.

51. Next…the Commission refers to the direct and immediate effect of the aid measures on the production costs of undertakings producing and processing fruit and vegetables in Spain, and to the economic advantage that they confer on such undertakings over those that do not have access to comparable aid in other Member States.

52. …the Commission also refers explicitly to Regulation No. 2200/96 which established a common organisation of the market in the fruit and vegetable sector. The Spanish Government could therefore not be unaware that the Commission's assessment of the aid scheme in question, including its finding that trade between Member States was affected by it, necessarily had to be viewed in the context of the rules on the common organisation of the markets.

53. In that connection it must be pointed out that the regime under Regulation No. 2200/96, which contains a set of uniform rules on production, marketing and competition between the economic operators concerned, benefits both trade in the fruit and vegetable sector and the development and maintenance of effective competition at Community level.

54. Finally, whilst it is common ground that in the statement of reasons for its decision the Commission is bound to refer at least to the circumstances in which aid has been granted where those circumstances show that the aid is such as to affect trade between Member States…it is not bound to demonstrate the real effect of aid already granted…

The Commission is let off with scant engagement with the issues raised by the Spanish Government because the duty to give reasons does not require EU institutions to enter into dialogue with and justify themselves to interested parties. Instead, as paragraph 47 sets out, it is merely there to enable the Court of Justice to orient the decision by providing a rationale for the measure which enables judicial review.

The consequence is that there is a very light onus on EU institutions to be responsive to the consultation. This is reflected in how the Commission treats the results of its consultations. Typically, a synthesis is brought together of all the central views. This synthesis will set out the views but will rarely express a Commission opinion. It is entirely descriptive in nature. The question of how these views inform any subsequent Commission proposal is left completely opaque. The Commission is also of the view that it is under no legal obligation to consult an individual party or to respond or give individual feedback to a particular view.[80]

(iii) Transparency of the consultation process

To be consulted may involve being heard but it does not follow that one is listened to. Influence, it appears, rests on supplying a combination of things to the EU institutions: information, citizen support and economic buy-in.[81] The identity of those with the ear of the EU institution is, thus, important. The 2002 Communication required representative institutions to set out which interests they represent and how inclusive that representation is.[82] A failure to do so would result in their submission being treated as an individual submission and given less weight. The thinness of these responsibilities was perceived as a central weakness in the lobbying system.[83] A further weakness was that both the Parliament and the Commission had separate registers. In 2011, a combined register, the European Transparency Register, was established.[84] The register covers all activities carried out with the objective of directly or indirectly influencing policy formulation or EU decision-making. It includes, therefore, not merely lobbying of EU institutions but also national governments and also those who might, themselves, lobby EU institutions.[85] Its heart comprises a Code of Conduct, under which the central obligations of the lobbyist include:

- to identify themselves by name and the entity they work for or represent;
- not to misrepresent themselves so as to mislead third parties and/or EU staff;
- to declare the interests, and where applicable the clients or the members, which they represent;
- to ensure that, to the best of their knowledge, information which they provide is unbiased, complete, up-to-date and not misleading;
- not to obtain or try to obtain information, or any decision, dishonestly;
- not to claim any formal relationship with the EU or its institutions in their dealings with third parties or sell third parties EU documents;
- not to induce EU staff to contravene rules and standards of behaviour applicable to them;
- if employing former EU staff, to respect their obligation to abide by the rules and confidentiality requirements which apply to them.[86]

---

[80] For a description of the evolution of Commission views see Obradovic and Alonso, n. 76 above, 1059–61.

[81] H. Klüver, 'Lobbying as a Collective Enterprise: Winners and Losers of Policy Formulation in the European Union' (2013) 20 *JEPP* 59.

[82] European Commission, *General Principles and Minimum Standards*, n. 76 above, 17.

[83] European Commission, *Follow-up to the Green Paper 'European Transparency Initiative'*, COM(2007)127, 3–4.

[84] Agreement between the European Parliament and the European Commission on the establishment of a transparency register for organisations and self-employed individuals engaged in EU policy-making and policy implementation [2011] OJ L191/29. On the background to this see M. Cini, 'EU Decision-Making on Inter-Institutional Agreements: Defining (Common) Rules of Conduct for European Lobbyists and Public Servants' (2013) 36 *WEP* 1143, 1146–9.

[85] *Ibid.* principle 8. Certain activities are excluded such as legal and professional advice relating to the rights of the defence, the activities of the social partners and responses to individual requests by the EU institutions. In addition, certain actors are not expected to register. These include churches and other religious actors, political parties and local, regional and municipal authorities. *Ibid.* principles 10–13.

[86] *Ibid.* Annex III.

Membership is voluntary. Nevertheless, there is a sense that if one is not registered, one will not be consulted. The Register, thus, has more than 5,900 registrants.[87] That said, there are questions about how well the register is policed and the Code of Conduct observed. Checks by the Secretariat established to administer the register found that in over half of the instances checked there was either non-compliance with the Code of Conduct or inadequate information provided.[88]

(iv) Inclusiveness of EU consultation

It is clearly undesirable if EU institutions only listen to a limited number of groups, possibly promoting policies too closely aligned to the interests of these groups. There is a further problem of credibility if EU institutions are perceived not to act in the wider public interest. In its Communication, the Commission stated that it wished to be as inclusive as possible, but there were practical limits.

European Commission, General Principles and Minimum Standards for Consultation of Interested Parties by the Commission, COM(2002)704, 11–12

The Commission wishes to stress that it will maintain an inclusive approach in line with the principle of open governance: every individual citizen, enterprise or association will continue to be able to provide the Commission with input. In other words, the Commission does not intend to create new bureaucratic hurdles in order to restrict the number of those that can participate in consultation processes.

However, two additional considerations must be taken into account in this context. First, best practice requires that the target group should be clearly defined prior to the launch of a consultation process. In other words, the Commission should actively seek input from relevant interested parties, so these will have to be targeted on the basis of sound criteria. Second, clear selection criteria are also necessary where access to consultation is limited for practical reasons. This is especially the case for the participation of interested parties in advisory bodies or at hearings.

The Commission would like to underline the importance it attaches to input from representative European organisations. However, the issue of representativeness at European level should not be used as the only criterion when assessing the relevance or quality of comments. The Commission will avoid consultation processes which could give the impression that 'Brussels is only talking to Brussels', as one person put it. In many cases, national and regional viewpoints can be equally important in taking into account the diversity of situations in the Member States. Moreover, minority views can also form an essential dimension of open discourse on policies. On the other hand, it is important for the Commission to consider how representative views are when taking a political decision following a consultation process.

Although over 90 per cent of consultations are open, engagement is uneven.[89] The most wide-ranging study of participation in the consultation process found that there were imbalances in territorial representation. Actors from larger, older Member States, such as France, Germany or

---

[87] See http://ec.europa.eu/transparencyregister/public/consultation/statistics.do?locale=en&action=prepareView.

[88] Joint Transparency Register Secretariat, *Annual Report on the Operations of the Transparency Register 2012*, 9–10. This is available at http://ec.europa.eu/transparencyregister/info/about-register/reportsAndPublications.do?locale=en.

[89] C. Quittkat, 'The European Commission's Online Consultations: A Success Story?' (2011) 49 *JCMS* 653, 659–60.

the United Kingdom were much more likely to be engaged than those from other Member States. It also found an imbalance in the interests represented. Notwithstanding that commercial interests make up only about 50 per cent of the interests now represented in Brussels,[90] it found that these dominated the consultations, particularly where these focused on narrow sectoral questions.[91]

6 TRANSPARENCY

The principle of transparency is set out in Article 15(3) TFEU.[92]

Article 15(3) TFEU

3. Any citizen of the Union, and any natural or legal person residing or having its registered office in a Member State, shall have a right of access to documents of the Union institutions, bodies, offices and agencies, whatever their medium, subject to the principles and the conditions to be defined in accordance with this paragraph.

   General principles and limits on grounds of public or private interest governing this right of access to documents shall be determined by the European Parliament and the Council, acting by means of regulations in accordance with the ordinary legislative procedure.

   Each institution, body, office or agency shall ensure that its proceedings are transparent and shall elaborate in its own Rules of Procedure specific provisions regarding access to its documents, in accordance with the regulations referred to in the second subparagraph.

Article 15(3) TFEU is a framework provision. It sets out a right of access to EU documents but the modalities are set out in secondary legislation. The central instrument is Regulation 1049/2001/EC.[93]

(i) Scope of the right of access to documents

The central entitlement is set out in article 2 of the Regulation:

Regulation 1049/2001/EC, article 2

1. Any citizen of the Union, and any natural or legal person residing or having its registered office in a Member State, has a right of access to documents of the institutions, subject to the principles, conditions and limits defined in this Regulation.
2. The institutions may, subject to the same principles, conditions and limits, grant access to documents to any natural or legal person not residing or not having its registered office in a Member State.
3. This Regulation shall apply to all documents held by an institution, that is to say, documents drawn up or received by it and in its possession, in all areas of activity of the European Union.

---

[90] See http://ec.europa.eu/transparencyregister/public/consultation/statistics.do?action=prepareView&locale=en#en.
[91] Quittkat, n. 89 above, 666–70.
[92] On the early development of the principle in EU law see A. Tomkins, 'Transparency and the Emergence of a European Administrative Law' (1999) 19 *YBEL* 217. The right is also contained in Article 42 EUCFR.
[93] Regulation 1049/2001/EC regarding public access to European Parliament, Council and Commission documents [2001] OJ L145/43. See M. De Leeuw, 'The Regulation on Public Access to European Parliament,

The right of access to documents is a demand which may be made of EU institutions. Although article 2(1) of the Regulation only refers to institutions, Article 15(3) TFEU refers to this right also being applied against EU bodies, offices and agencies. Actions have been allowed against these other entities as well.[94] The demand can ask, furthermore, by virtue of article 2(3), not just for documents drawn up by the EU institutions but also for those documents which fall into their possession. This widens the scope of available information considerably as the Commission, in particular, acts very much as a clearing house, receiving documentation from private parties, other EU institutions and, above all, national governments. Alongside this, the right is a right of access to the information in the document itself. As a consequence, the institution has to consider whether to give partial access to a document, namely, it must give access to all information that does not fall within an exception.[95]

Access is provided in two ways. First, all EU institutions are required to keep electronic up-to-date registers of documents to which the public should have access.[96] Secondly, parties can request access to particular information. The number of requests per annum floats around 6,000.[97] These numbers are small for a polity of close to half a billion people. The composition of requests is also skewed. In 2012, the two largest groups requesting documents were academics (22.7 per cent) and lawyers (13.58 per cent), with other EU institutions(!) being the fourth largest group (7.64 per cent).[98] The territorial breakdown indicates that access to information is something of most interest to those already strongly engaged with the Brussels policy-making sphere. The highest number of requests came from Belgium (21.85 per cent) with the next highest being Germany (14.04 per cent).[99]

Any request must be made in writing and be sufficiently precise to enable the institution to identify the document.[100] There is no duty to state the reason for the application.[101] If the application is not sufficiently precise, the institution must ask the applicant to clarify the application and provide assistance to enable her to do so.[102] A corollary of this is that it cannot say that a document does not exist. It must indicate documents which are similar or which are likely to contain some or all of the information sought.[103] Institutions must acknowledge receipt of any application and, within fifteen days, either provide access to the documents or give reasons for refusing access.[104] Furthermore, individuals may make requests for documents to which they were previously denied access. Denial of access is only allowed on the grounds considered later. As these may only justify denial of access for a limited period of time, institutions are required to consider new demands and see if either the legal and factual context has changed so that access should be granted.[105]

Council and Commission Documents in the European Union: Are Citizens Better Off?' (2003) 28 *ELRev.* 324. Amendments have been on the table for some time, with little success. European Commission, *Proposal for a Regulation regarding Public Access to European Parliament, Council and Commission Documents*, COM(2008)229. For discussion see I. Harden, 'The Revision of Regulation 1049/2001 on Public Access to Documents' (2009) 15 *EPL* 239.

[94] Case T-339/10 *COSEPURI v EFSA*, Judgment of 29 January 2013.

[95] Case C-353/99P *Hautala v Council* [2001] ECR I-9565.   [96] Regulation 1049/2001, article 11.

[97] They were 6,361 in 2010, 6,477 in 2011 and 6,014 in 2012. European Commission, *Report on the Application in 2012 of Regulation 1049/2001*, COM(2013)515, Annex.

[98] *Ibid.* 11.   [99] *Ibid.* 11–12.   [100] Regulation 1049/2001, article 6(1).

[101] Case C-362/08P *Internationaler Hilfsfonds v Commission* [2010] ECR I-669.

[102] Regulation 1049/2001, article 6(2).   [103] T-436/09 *Dufour v ECB* [2011] ECR II-7727.

[104] Regulation 1049/2001, article 7.

[105] Case C-362/08P *Internationaler Hilfsfonds v Commission* [2010] ECR I-669.

If the application is for a very long document or a very large number of documents, the institution may confer with the applicant informally to find a fair solution about what should be supplied.[106] If agreement cannot be reached, this can, in certain circumstances, lead to access being refused. The General Court has held that the right of access must be balanced against that of good administration. If providing the documents would involve a manifestly unreasonable amount of work, regard can be had to whether the applicant could have tailored their request to be less exacting in a way that secures their interests. This reason for refusal will be allowed, however, only in the most exceptional circumstances and the burden of proof lies with the institution.[107] The courts are largely unreceptive to institutional arguments, and it seems denial can only be made for the most vexatious requests where the applicant has made little compromise. In *Williams*, a doctoral student asked for all the internal documentation within the Commission on six pieces of legislation which constituted the heart of the Union's regime on genetically modified organisms.[108] She met with the Commission and agreed to split her request into six separate requests with a priority being made between the six. In relation to the first request, the Commission still refused access to twenty-three documents on the grounds that the request was so wide-ranging that it was difficult to calculate the number of documents requested by the applicant. This was rejected by the General Court. It noted that the splitting of the request into six requests had made the process more manageable and the fact that the exact number of documents was not known could affect how long it took the Commission to supply the documents. It could not provide a reason for denial of access.

(ii) Exceptions to the right of access to information

Most litigation has focused on the exceptions which allow access to information to be denied. Set out in article 4, these exceptions cover whole fields of EU governmental or legislative activity. They demarcate, thereby, which political and legal activity is to be secret and what citizens are allowed to know about, and therefore hold institutions to account.

Regulation 1049/2001/EC, article 4

1. The institutions shall refuse access to a document where disclosure would undermine the protection of:
   (a) the public interest as regards:
      - public security,
      - defence and military matters,
      - international relations,
      - the financial, monetary or economic policy of the Community or a Member State;
   (b) privacy and the integrity of the individual, in particular in accordance with Community legislation regarding the protection of personal data.

---

[106] Regulation 1049/2001, article 6(3).
[107] Case T-2/03 *Verein für Konsumenteninformation* v *Commission* [2005] ECR II-1121.
[108] Case T-42/05 *Williams* v *Commission* [2008] ECR II-156.

2. The institutions shall refuse access to a document where disclosure would undermine the protection of:
   - commercial interests of a natural or legal person, including intellectual property,
   - court proceedings and legal advice,
   - the purpose of inspections, investigations and audits,

   unless there is an overriding public interest in disclosure.

3. Access to a document, drawn up by an institution for internal use or received by an institution, which relates to a matter where the decision has not been taken by the institution, shall be refused if disclosure of the document would seriously undermine the institution's decision-making process, unless there is an overriding public interest in disclosure.

   Access to a document containing opinions for internal use as part of deliberations and preliminary consultations within the institution concerned shall be refused even after the decision has been taken if disclosure of the document would seriously undermine the institution's decision-making process, unless there is an overriding public interest in disclosure.

4. As regards third-party documents, the institution shall consult the third party with a view to assessing whether an exception in paragraph 1 or 2 is applicable, unless it is clear that the document shall or shall not be disclosed.

5. A Member State may request the institution not to disclose a document originating from that Member State without its prior agreement.

6. If only parts of the requested document are covered by any of the exceptions, the remaining parts of the document shall be released.

The ethos of the Union courts in relation to this was expressed most clearly in an appeal by the Swedish Government and MyTravel, a package holiday company, against a General Court decision allowing the Commission to refuse the latter access to a report and preparatory papers of a working group established to consider whether the Commission should appeal against an earlier judgment of the General Court which allowed two of this company's competitors to merge. The Court of Justice allowed the appeal. Before that, it set out its overall philosophy.

Case C-506/08P *Sweden and MyTravel Group* v *Commission* [2011] ECR I-6237

72. As a preliminary observation, it should be noted that, in accordance with the first recital of Regulation 1049/2001, that regulation reflects the intention expressed in the second paragraph of Article 1 EU – inserted by the Treaty of Amsterdam – of marking a new stage in the process of creating an ever closer union among the peoples of Europe, in which decisions are taken as openly as possible and as closely as possible to the citizen. As is stated in recital 2 in the preamble to Regulation 1049/2001, the right of public access to documents of the institutions is related to the democratic nature of those institutions…

73. To that end, Regulation 1049/2001 is intended, as is apparent from recital 4 in its preamble and from Article 1, to give the fullest possible effect to the right of public access to documents of the institutions…

74. However, that right is none the less subject to certain limitations based on grounds of public or private interest. More specifically, and in reflection of recital 11 in the preamble thereto, Article 4 of Regulation No. 1049/2001 provides that the institutions are to refuse access to a document where its disclosure would undermine the protection of one of the interests protected by that provision…

75. However, since they derogate from the principle of the widest possible public access to documents, those exceptions must be interpreted and applied strictly...

76. Thus, if the institution concerned decides to refuse access to a document which it has been asked to disclose, it must, in principle, explain how disclosure of that document could specifically and effectively undermine the interest protected by the exception – among those provided for in Article 4 of Regulation No. 1049/2001 – upon which it is relying...Moreover, the risk of that undermining must be reasonably foreseeable and not purely hypothetical...

For all that the Court of Justice states that they should be interpreted narrowly, the exceptions are very wide-ranging. They are furthermore, frequently invoked by the EU institutions. In 2012, 16.91 per cent of requests were refused completely, and a further 8.61 per cent were granted only partial access to the information sought.[109] There has been extensive case law on article 4, and only some of the more salient issues will be addressed here.[110] The exceptions can be grouped into three categories.

• The first category, set out in article 4(1), *requires* the institution to refuse access to the document if it falls within that category.
• The second category, set out in article 4(2) and (3), creates an 'overriding public interest' reason which requires an institution to grant access to a document if, notwithstanding that it falls within one of the protected headings, there is an overriding public interest.
• The third category, set out in article 4(4) and (5), relates to documents provided by parties other than the EU institutions. Certain procedural requirements are imposed there. There is a requirement of consultation before release in the case of third parties and, subject to the constraints discussed below, Member States may request that documents not be disclosed without their prior agreement.

The Regulation, thus, sets out three tests of review. This is not uncontroversial. It is hard to see why, for example, the overriding public interest defence can never exist in relation to the first heading. There may, for example, be 'security' documents whose disclosure makes the decision-maker uncomfortable, but nevertheless in which there is a strong interest in public debate. A good example is the controversy surrounding the Anti-Counterfeiting Trade Agreement (ACTA), an agreement signed by the European Union in 2012, which involved nine non-EU states. The treaty was controversial because of its wide understanding of counterfeiting, raising concerns that marketing of many generic goods would be criminalised; the increased level of surveillance of the Internet it required in order to curb counterfeiting; and weak controls over data protection. In 2012, the agreement fell because a huge majority in the European Parliament rejected it.[111] Subsequent requests

---

[109] European Commission, *Report on the Application*, n. 97 above, 8. Care must be had in reading these figures. Some might be repeat refusals against campaigners for complete open government. On other side, the extent of the exceptions might have a stifling effect deterring many requests for information.

[110] For more extensive treatment see B. Driessen, *Transparency in EU Institutional Law* (2nd edn, Alphen aan den Rijn, Kluwer Law International, 2012) chs. 2–4.

[111] The concerns are also set out at www.europarl.europa.eu/sides/getDoc.do?type=REPORT&reference=A7–2012–0204&language=EN.

for documents were denied, however, because they fell within the first category heading of undermining international relations. The General Court held, therefore, that no wider public interest could be invoked to justify their disclosure if it was believed that this might risk harming relations with other states.[112]

The other challenge of these tests of review is that they have been given an almost exclusively substantive interpretation. Regard is had exclusively to whether there is a reasonably foreseeable risk to the interest protected by article 4. There is little examination of the quality of the internal processes within each EU institution which led to the classification of a document in a particular way, such as the seniority of the official doing this, the internal checks and balances, or the level of reasoning provided.[113] The failure to engage in this by the Union courts is regrettable.

With regard to the first category, a test of marginal review is applied. Union courts will not substitute their judgment for that of the institution but confine themselves to seeing whether accurate reasons have been given for the refusal and whether there was a manifest error of assessment. An example is *WWF European Policy Programme*. The WWF, an environmental NGO, asked for documents concerning international trade negotiations taking place within the World Trade Organization. These documents set out other states' positions as well as the Union in the negotiations as well as the minutes of the meetings. The Council refused under article 4(1)(a), arguing that this undermined the Union's commercial interests and would be prejudicial to its relations with other states.

Case T-264/04 *WWF European Policy Programme* v *Council* [2007] ECR II-911

40. ...the institutions enjoy a wide discretion when considering whether access to a document may undermine the public interest and, consequently, that the Court's review of the legality of the institutions' decisions refusing access to documents on the basis of the mandatory exceptions relating to the public interest must be limited to verifying whether the procedural rules and the duty to state reasons have been complied with, the facts have been accurately stated, and whether there has been a manifest error of assessment of the facts or a misuse of powers...

41. As to whether there was a manifest error of assessment of the facts, as the applicant essentially submits is the case, it must be noted that the Council refused to grant access to the note so as not to risk upsetting the negotiations that were taking place at that time in a sensitive context, which was characterised by resistance on the part of both the developing and the developed countries and the difficulty in reaching an agreement, as illustrated by the breakdown of negotiations at the WTO Ministerial Conference in Cancun in September 2003. Thus, in considering that disclosure of that note could have undermined relations with the third countries which are referred to in the note and the room for negotiation needed by the Community and its Member States to bring those negotiations to a conclusion, the Council did not commit a manifest error of assessment and was right to consider that disclosure of the note would have entailed the risk of undermining the public interest as regards international relations and the Community's financial, monetary and economic policy, which was reasonably foreseeable and not purely hypothetical.

---

[112] Case T-301/10 *In't Veld* v *Commission*, Judgment of 19 March 2013.
[113] On the haphazard nature of these processes and the large number of EU and national officials who can classify documents see D. Curtin, 'Official Secrets and the Negotiation of International Agreements: Is the EU Executive Unbound?' (2013) 50 *CMLRev.* 423.

This review is thin. The General Court defers to the Council's assessment in paragraph 41 that providing the information will upset negotiation. However, it has not been consistent and, in some instances, the review of whether there has been a manifest error of assessment will be quite exacting. In *Kuijer*, a university lecturer challenged a decision by the Council to refuse him access to human rights reports on a number of countries which had been prepared for CIREA, a Union body that compiled documentation and exchanged information on questions of asylum.[114] As some of these were quite damning, the Council refused on the grounds that this would damage relations with these countries. The General Court did not agree with this characterisation and overturned the Council's decision. It held that refusal had to be made by reference to the specific content and context of each human rights report. These reports contained general information on the protection of human rights which had already been made public and did not involve any politically sensitive appraisal of the Member State by the Council itself. The Court held therefore that neither the content nor the nature of the reports justified a refusal to grant access.

In relation to this category, in particular, the courts will also look at whether partial access should have been granted to the documents. If only parts of the documents are covered by the exceptions, *pace* article 4(6), the remainder must be released. Furthermore, if documents can be redacted so that sensitive passages can be blanked out, this should also take place. This possibility of partial access, in addition, imposes a procedural requirement on EU institutions, namely, to consider whether it is possible to grant partial access to the documents. A failure to consider this will make the refusal illegal.[115]

In relation to the second category, documents must be released if there is an overriding public interest which justifies disclosure. The strongest example of the demands of this latter test is *Turco*. Turco, an MEP, sought access to advice the Council had received from its legal services on a proposed Directive laying down minimum standards for the reception of asylum seekers. This was refused under the exception in article 4(2) which allows protection of legal advice. This denial of access was upheld by the General Court. Turco and the Swedish Government appealed to the Court of Justice. Having found that the advice constituted legal advice for the purposes of article 4(2), the Court considered whether there was an overriding public interest justifying disclosure.

Joined Cases C–39/05 and C–52/05 *Sweden and Turco* v *Council* **[2008] ECR I–4723**

45. ...it is for the Council to balance the particular interest to be protected by non-disclosure of the document concerned against, inter alia, the public interest in the document being made accessible in the light of the advantages stemming, as noted in recital 2 of the preamble to Regulation No. 1049/2001, from increased openness, in that this enables citizens to participate more closely in the decision-making process and guarantees that the administration enjoys greater legitimacy and is more effective and more accountable to the citizen in a democratic system.

46. Those considerations are clearly of particular relevance where the Council is acting in its legislative capacity, as is apparent from recital 6 of the preamble to Regulation No. 1049/2001, according to

---

[114] Case T-211/00 *Kuijer* v *Council* [2002] ECR II-485.
[115] On both the procedural requirement and the duty to redact see Case T-529/09 *In't Veld* v *Commission*, Judgment of 4 May 2012.

which wider access must be granted to documents in precisely such cases. Openness in that respect contributes to strengthening democracy by allowing citizens to scrutinize all the information which has formed the basis of a legislative act. The possibility for citizens to find out the considerations underpinning legislative action is a precondition for the effective exercise of their democratic rights.

47. It is also worth noting that, under [Article 16(8) TEU], the Council is required to define the cases in which it is to be regarded as acting in its legislative capacity, with a view to allowing greater access to documents in such cases. Similarly, Article 12(2) of Regulation No. 1049/2001 acknowledges the specific nature of the legislative process by providing that documents drawn up or received in the course of procedures for the adoption of acts which are legally binding in or for the Member States should be made directly accessible....

67. In any event, in so far as the interest in protecting the independence of the Council's legal service could be undermined by that disclosure, that risk would have to be weighed up against the overriding public interests which underlie Regulation No. 1049/2001. As was pointed out in paragraphs 45 to 47 of this judgment, such an overriding public interest is constituted by the fact that disclosure of documents containing the advice of an institution's legal service on legal questions arising when legislative initiatives are being debated increases the transparency and openness of the legislative process and strengthens the democratic right of European citizens to scrutinize the information which has formed the basis of a legislative act, as referred to, in particular, in recitals 2 and 6 of the preamble to Regulation No. 1049/2001.

The case is unusual. Typically, the balancing required leads to regard being had to the strength of the protected interest in determining whether there should be disclosure. It is easier to make a case that there is an overriding public interest where the case for denial is weak. Cases examining the presence of an overriding public interest are rare. Instead, focus has shifted increasingly to whether it is democratically desirable to deny access to protect the interest asserted in the case in hand.

The best example of this relates to possibly the most wide-ranging ground for denial of access, article 4(3), which allows access to be denied if it would seriously undermine the institution's decision-making process. In *Access Info Europe*, a Spanish NGO asked for a Report from a Working Group of Member State representatives established to consider amendments to Regulation 1049/2001/EC. It was granted only partial access with the names of the Member States redacted. It was argued by the Council that, as the issues were sensitive and at a delicate moment, granting access to the information would undermine decision-making as it might make national delegations wary about setting out negotiating positions for which they might be criticized. In reasoning that was upheld by the Court of Justice,[116] the General Court was dismissive of such arguments.

Case T–233/09 *Access Info Europe v Council* [2011] ECR II–1073

55. In view of the objectives pursued by Regulation No. 1049/2001 and especially the fact, noted in recital 2 in the preamble thereto, that the public right of access to the documents of the institutions is connected with the democratic nature of those institutions and the fact that, as

---

[116] Case C-280/11P *Council v Access Info Europe*, Judgment of 17 October 2013.

stated in recital 4 and in Article 1, the purpose of the regulation is to give the public the widest possible right of access, the exceptions to that right set out in Article 4 of the regulation must be interpreted and applied strictly...

56. Giving the public the widest possible right of access entails, therefore, that the public must have a right to full disclosure of the requested documents, the only means of limiting that right being the strict application of the exceptions provided for in Regulation No. 1049/2001. If only one part of a requested document is covered by an exception, the other parts of the document are to be disclosed. In those circumstances, openness makes it possible for citizens to participate more closely in the decision-making process and for the administration to enjoy greater legitimacy and to be more effective and more accountable to the citizen in a democratic system.

57. As the Court has held, those considerations are clearly of particular relevance where the Council is acting in its legislative capacity, a fact reflected in recital 6 to Regulation No. 1049/2001, which states that wider access must be granted to documents in precisely such cases. Openness in that respect contributes to strengthening democracy by enabling citizens to scrutinise all the information which has formed the basis for a legislative act. The possibility for citizens to find out the considerations underpinning legislative action is a precondition for the effective exercise of their democratic rights...

58. It should also be noted that, under the second subparagraph of Article 207(3) EC, the Council is required to define the cases in which it is to be regarded as acting in its legislative capacity, with a view to allowing greater access to documents in such cases...

60. In the present case, it is for the Council to weigh the specific interest which must be protected through non-disclosure of part of the requested document – that is to say, the identity of those who put forward the proposals – against the general interest in the entire document being made accessible, given the advantages of a more open legislative procedure. It is common ground that the requested document was drawn up in the context of the Council's legislative activity. The first paragraph of Article 7 of the Rules of Procedure states that 'the Council acts in its legislative capacity within the meaning of the second subparagraph of Article 207(3)...EC...when it adopts rules which are legally binding in or for the Member States, by means of regulations, directives, framework decisions or decisions, on the basis of the relevant provisions of the Treaties, with the exception of discussions leading to the adoption of internal measures, administrative or budgetary acts, acts concerning interinstitutional or international relations or non-binding acts (such as conclusions, recommendations or resolutions)'....

67. As regards the arguments put forward by the Council in support of its contention alleging that the ongoing legislative process has been seriously undermined because the delegations' room for manœuvre would thereby be reduced, it should be noted that those arguments do not establish that there is a sufficiently serious and reasonably foreseeable risk justifying the application of the exception provided for in the first subparagraph of Article 4(3) of Regulation No. 1049/2001.

68. In general, the Council contends that the identification, at a time when it has not yet taken a decision, of the delegations which put forward proposals for amendment or re-drafting would cause the positions of those delegations to become entrenched, since they would lose some of their ability to modify their positions in the course of discussions and to justify before their public a solution which may differ from their initial position...In its answer to the first question put by the Court, the Council even alleges that, as a consequence of the disclosure by the organisation Statewatch of the names of the delegations which made the proposals in the requested document, those delegations, or others, which may wish to make proposals for restricting or reducing openness would no longer do so for fear of the pressure likely to be exerted on them by public opinion...In other words, the pressure which the

public could exert would be such that it would no longer be possible for a delegation to the Council to submit a proposal tending towards the restriction of openness.

69. Those arguments are not sufficiently substantiated to justify, in themselves, the refusal to disclose the identity of those responsible for the various proposals, who must, in a system based on the principle of democratic legitimacy, be publicly accountable for their actions. In that regard, it should be noted that public access to the entire content of Council documents – including, in the present case, the identity of those who made the various proposals – constitutes the principle, above all in the context of a procedure in which the institutions act in a legislative capacity, and the exceptions must be interpreted and applied strictly (see paragraphs 55 to 57 above). If citizens are to be able to exercise their democratic rights, they must be in a position to follow in detail the decision-making process within the institutions taking part in the legislative procedures and to have access to all relevant information. The identification of the Member State delegations which submit proposals at the stage of the initial discussions does not appear liable to prevent those delegations from being able to take those discussions into consideration so as to present new proposals if their initial proposals no longer reflect their positions. By its nature, a proposal is designed to be discussed, whether it be anonymous or not, not to remain unchanged following that discussion if the identity of its author is known. Public opinion is perfectly capable of understanding that the author of a proposal is likely to amend its content subsequently.

The practical consequences of the judgment are immense. Prior to it, there was no general right of access to Council documents in the trilogue, the crucible of EU law-making.[117] The reason was that it might compromise national negotiating positions. This is no longer the case. This must be as open to scrutiny as all other parts of the law-making process. The reasoning is also significant. Its central thread is the characterisation of the decision-making process, namely, whether it comprises diplomatic negotiations between Member States or a legislative process. The Court of Justice characterises it as the latter because it sees an overriding public interest, namely, the quality of EU democracy, in characterising it in this way. This allows it to say that the process is not compromised by disclosure as the nature of a legislative process is that it should be accountable and involve public debate.

The final category, set out in article 4(4) and (5), involves documents where the EU institutions are not the authors but nevertheless have possession of these documents. There are additional procedural concerns which must be met here. Third parties must be consulted and Member States must grant their consent. The latter was particularly significant, as it could mean that there was little access to information about what was taking place in infringement proceedings as these invariably involve information provided by the state being proceeded against. The traditional view was that the Member State concerned had an unqualified veto over disclosure.[118]

This changed in *Sweden* v *Commission*.[119] IFAW, a nature conservation NGO, sought disclosure of documents relating to the reclaiming of part of an estuary for the construction of a runway in Germany. The General Court upheld the German veto over denial of access to the documents for the traditional reasons mentioned above. The Court of Justice upheld the

---

[117] On the trilogue see pp. 120–3.   [118] Case T-76/02 *Messina* v *Commission* [2003] ECR II-3203.
[119] Case C-64/05P *Sweden* v *Commission* [2007] ECR I-11389.

appeal. It held that such an unqualified veto would be incompatible with the purpose of the Regulation, which is to grant the widest possible access to documents by allowing that right to be frustrated without any objective reason. It would also introduce arbitrary distinctions whereby documents of a similar kind held by the EU institutions would have different rules applying to them depending on the origin of the document. If an EU institution received a request for a national document, it was required to open a dialogue with the Member State, which could only refuse disclosure if it provided reasons why the document fell within one of the exceptions set out in article 4(1)–(3).

The judgment widens considerably the documents which will be accessible to the public. The different national governments produce much more information than any of the EU institutions, and, insofar as it passes through any of the latter, a claim can now be made against it. In this regard, the judgment indicates that the same principles concerning disclosure should apply whatever the provenance of the document. This is the case, but the body making the assessment is different. For documents originating from a Member State, it is the Member State which makes the assessment of whether they should be disclosed under the framework set out in Regulation 1049/2001/EC. This assessment cannot be challenged by the EU institution, who can do no more than pass on the reasons to the applicant. If the latter disagrees with the assessment, its only remedy is to ask the EU institution to proceed against the Member State. It has no recourse of its own.

FURTHER READING

D. Curtin, 'Official Secrets and the Negotiation of International Agreements: Is the EU Executive Unbound?' (2013) 50 *Common Market Law Review* 423

G. Davies, 'Subsidiarity: The Wrong Idea, in the Wrong Place, at the Wrong Time' (2006) 43 *Common Market Law Review* 63

M. Dougan, 'What are We to Make of the Citizens' Initiative' (2011) 48 *Common Market Law Review* 1807

T.-I. Harbo, 'The Function of the Proportionality Principle in EU Law' (2010) 16 *European Law Journal* 158

H. Hoffmann, G. Rowe and A. Türk, *Administrative Law and Policy of the European Union* (Oxford, Oxford University Press, 2011) chs. 6 and 17

C. Joerges, Y. Mény and J. Weiler (eds.), *Mountain or Molehill? A Critical Appraisal of the Commission White Paper on Governance*, EUI-NYU (2002), available at www.jeanmonnetprogram.org/papers/01/010601.html

C. Möllers, 'European Governance: Meaning and Value of a Concept' (2006) 43 *Common Market Law Review* 313

D. Obradovic and J. Alonso, 'Good Governance Requirements Concerning the Participation of Interest Groups in EU Consultations' (2006) 43 *Common Market Law Review* 1049

C. Quittkat, 'The European Commission's Online Consultations: A Success Story?' (2011) 49 *Journal of Common Market Studies* 653

J. Scott and D. Trubek, 'Mind the Gap: Law and New Approaches to Governance in the European Union' (2002) 8 *European Law Journal* 1

J. Wiener, 'Better Regulation in Europe' (2006) 59 *Current Legal Problems* 447

10

Judicial Review

CONTENTS

1 INTRODUCTION

This chapter considers judicial review by the Court of Justice. It is organised as follows.

Section 2 considers the scope of Article 263 TFEU, the central provision governing direct actions for judicial review of Union measures. It can be invoked against all EU institutions, agencies, offices and bodies. The measures susceptible to review include not just formal legal acts but any measure intended to produce legal effects. The latter will be any measure which is definitive, the culmination of an institutional process, and produces a change in the applicant's legal situation.

Section 3 considers the grounds for review. A measure will be annulled, first, if the EU institution does not have the formal competence to adopt it. Review is possible, secondly, if the institution misuses its power. This may be an abuse of power where a power is used for purposes other than that for which it was granted. More common is a manifest error of assessment. This requires Union measures to be substantiated by the evidence provided, and for that evidence to be accurate, reliable, consistent and sufficiently complete. The third heading of review involves rights of process. These include rights to defence where EU measures will lead to sanction; the right to a hearing where one's interests are adversely restricted by a Union measure; and finally, the right to administration of one's affairs with due care by the EU institutions. The final heading of review is infringement of the Treaties or any rule of law relating to its application. This includes breach of any substantive provision of EU law and violation of fundamental rights. It also encompasses EU legal principles developed by the Court of Justice, namely, non-discrimination, proportionality, legal certainty and protection of legitimate expectations.

Section 4 considers the standing requirements for bringing an action under Article 263 TFEU. Privileged applicants – the Member States, Parliament, the Commission and Council – have unlimited standing to challenge a measure subject to their observance of the time limits. Semi-privileged applicants – the Court of Auditors, European Central Bank (ECB) and Committee of the Regions – may bring an action to protect their institutional prerogatives. All other parties have standing to bring an action against measures addressed to them, a regulatory act if it is of direct concern to them and entails no implementing measures, and against other measures of direct and individual concern to them. Regulatory acts are non-legislative measures which are general in nature. Direct concern will be established where the Union measure directly affects a legal entitlement of the applicant without any significant intermediation by another party. For regulatory acts, the measure must, furthermore, lead to no implementing measure, and be by a EU institution or Member State. Individual concern is governed by the *Plaumann* formula. This requires the interest affected belong to a fixed, ascertainable and limited group of interests which is not capable, even hypothetically, of being added to. This is a highly restrictive test and has been criticised for making economically arbitrary distinctions and for favouring private interests over public ones.

Section 5 considers Article 265 TFEU and the failure to act. This allows parties to challenge omissions by EU institutions where these are under a duty to act. The standing requirements are similar to Article 263 TFEU as it complements this provision. However, an action under Article 265 TFEU can, first, only be commenced against an EU institution if it is under a duty to perform a task. Secondly, an institution, if called upon to act, avoids any further action if it defines its position within two months. Finally, the institution must be called upon to act by the applicant before any action can be commenced.

Section 6 considers the plea of illegality set out in Article 277 TFEU. This is not an independent action but, in an action against a measure brought under another provision (e.g. Article 263 TFEU), it allows challenge of a parent measure. It is subject to two constraints. It cannot be brought where the measure is being challenged before a court elsewhere by the parties. It also cannot be brought by parties who have already had the opportunity to challenge the measure but did not take up that opportunity.

Section 7 considers the action for non-contractual liability under Article 340(2) TFEU. Parties can sue EU institutions for damages where three conditions are met: first, the institution has infringed a rule of law intended to confer rights on individuals; secondly, the breach is sufficiently serious; and finally, that there is a direct causal link between the breach and the loss sustained. In fields where EU institutions enjoy no discretion, a simple breach of EU law or failure to exercise reasonable care will be sufficient to establish liability. In fields where they enjoy some discretion or the issues are complex, liability will only exist if they manifestly and gravely disregard the limits of their discretion and the EU legal norm has a certain weight, such as being a fundamental right or general principle of law.

Section 8 considers the consequences of a finding of annulment. Such a ruling is binding on all institutional actors within the Union. In only the most grave cases of illegality will measures be declared void and to have produced no legal effect. Usually, a measure is deemed to produce legal effects until it is annulled. At the moment of annulment, the Court of Justice has a wide discretion with respect to the legal effects a measure will have after it is annulled. Part of the measure may continue in force or temporal limitations may be established allowing it to continue in force for a period.

2 SCOPE OF JUDICIAL REVIEW AND ARTICLE 263 TFEU

The starting point for considering judicial review of EU institutions' behaviour is Article 263 TFEU.

Article 263 TFEU

The Court of Justice of the European Union shall review the legality of legislative acts, of acts of the Council, of the Commission and of the European Central Bank, other than recommendations and opinions, and of acts of the European Parliament and of the European Council intended to produce legal effects vis-à-vis third parties. It shall also review the legality of acts of bodies, offices or agencies of the Union intended to produce legal effects vis-à-vis third parties.

It shall for this purpose have jurisdiction in actions brought by a Member State, the European Parliament, the Council or the Commission on grounds of lack of competence, infringement of an essential procedural requirement, infringement of the Treaties or of any rule of law relating to their application, or misuse of powers.

The Court shall have jurisdiction under the same conditions in actions brought by the Court of Auditors, by the European Central Bank and by the Committee of the Regions for the purpose of protecting their prerogatives.

Any natural or legal person may, under the conditions referred to in the first and second subparagraphs, institute proceedings against an act addressed to that person or which is of direct and individual concern to them, and against a regulatory act which is of direct concern to them and does not entail implementing measures.

Acts setting up bodies, offices and agencies of the Union may lay down specific conditions and arrangements concerning actions brought by natural or legal persons against acts of these bodies, offices or agencies intended to produce legal effects in relation to them.

The provision can be invoked against a wide range of actors. These include not only all EU institutions, but also all EU agencies, offices and other bodies. The inclusion of the European Council is the most intriguing element here, as subjecting the decisions of twenty-eight Heads of Government to judicial challenge is unprecedented in human history and illustrates the symbolic importance attached to the rule of law in the European Union. This range of actors raises challenging questions about the types of measure subject to review. The European Council cannot adopt legislative measures and very few agencies have the power to adopt legally binding decisions.[1] However, European Council guidelines are intended to inform legal changes. Equally, EU institutions invariably not only follow the expert opinions of agencies in setting out legal norms, but are also obliged to do so unless they can find a substitute expert body and provide reasons for following the opinion of the latter.[2] There are, therefore, strong arguments for subjecting these activities to review.

In this regard, Article 263(1) TFEU deploys a formula first used in the *ERTA* judgment for determining when a measure is subject to review.[3] A measure will be reviewable not merely when it is a formal legal act but also, whatever its form, when it is intended to produce legal effects. The meaning of this was set out in *IBM*. A Commission Decision indicating that it had initiated proceedings against IBM to determine whether there had been a breach of EU competition law was challenged. The Commission argued that the decision to open proceedings was not a formal act in any way and not, therefore, reviewable.

Case 60/81 *IBM v Commission* [1981] ECR 2639

8. According to Article [263 TFEU] proceedings may be brought for a declaration that acts of the Council and the Commission other than recommendations or opinions are void. That remedy is available in order to ensure, as required by Article [19(1) TEU], that in the interpretation and application of the Treaty the law is observed, and it would be inconsistent with that objective to interpret restrictively the conditions under which the action is admissible by limiting its scope merely to the categories of measures referred to in Article [288 TFEU].

9. In order to ascertain whether the measures in question are acts within the meaning of Article [263] it is necessary, therefore, to look to their substance…any measure the legal effects of which are binding on, and capable of affecting the interests of, the applicant by bringing about a distinct change in his legal position is an act or decision which may be the subject of an action under Article [263] for a declaration that it is void. However, the form in which such acts or decisions are cast is, in principle, immaterial as regards the question whether they are open to challenge under that Article.

10. In the case of acts or decisions adopted by a procedure involving several stages, in particular where they are the culmination of an internal procedure, it is clear from the case-law that in principle an act is open to review only if it is a measure definitively laying down the position of the Commission or the Council on the conclusion of that procedure, and not a provisional measure intended to pave the way for the final decision.

11. It would be otherwise only if acts or decisions adopted in the course of the preparatory proceedings not only bore all the legal characteristics referred to above but in addition were themselves the culmination of a special procedure distinct from that intended to permit the Commission or the Council to take a decision on the substance of the case.

---

[1] Article 15(1) TEU.   [2] Case T-13/99 *Pfizer Animal Health* v *Council* [2002] ECR II-3305.
[3] Case 22/70 *Commission* v *Council (ERTA)* [1971] ECR 263.

The measure will therefore be reviewable if the EU institution sets out a definitive position which brings about a change in the applicant's legal situation. In *IBM*, the Court of Justice found that no such position had been taken as the decision to initiate proceedings was just a preparatory measure. Whilst IBM's situation had changed, as it was now under investigation, the Commission had not yet taken a definitive view on whether there had been a breach.

To be reviewable, the definitive position must, furthermore, be the culmination of an administrative process rather than a position which begins such a process.[4] However, if there is a process discrete from that which goes to the substance of a case, there can be a review of the measure which constitutes the culmination of that process. In *Österreichische Postsparkasse*, an Austrian political party, the Freedom Party, had asked the Commission to investigate an alleged Austrian banking cartel.[5] In subsequent investigations, the Commission obtained information from the banks, which, it informed the banks, was not covered by its duty of confidentiality, and which it would thus disclose to the Freedom Party. The General Court held that the banks could challenge this disclosure as the question of whether to disclose or not was quite separate from whether they had engaged in anti-competitive conduct.

A definitive position, and reviewable act, will invariably be found if the EU institution states that it requires action from another party.[6] The position is more complicated where that is not the case. Regard will be had in those circumstances to whether the institution has altered its position in a concrete way which has legal consequences for a third party. To ascertain this, the Court of Justice will look at the content of the measure, the context, and the intention of the institution.[7] Restating an existing position is not reviewable.[8] Similarly, indicating no more than an intention to follow a particular line of conduct will not be reviewable.[9] There must be some stronger reorientation. Identification of an activity or product exposing a party to additional requirements under EU law is a reviewable measure.[10] Similarly, if an EU institution refuses to instigate, brings to an end or suspends some decision-making procedure in the field of EU competition or state aids law, this will be a reviewable measure as it indicates that the activity in question will not be sanctioned.[11]

It is often difficult to predict, however, when a definitive position is taken. In *Commission v Council*,[12] the Commission reported both France and Germany to the Council for running excessive budgetary deficits. The Council did two things. First, it decided not to follow the Commission's recommendations to impose sanctions on France and Germany. Secondly, it stated that the procedure would be held in abeyance as Germany and France had made certain commitments about bringing their deficits into line. If these were not met, the procedure could be continued. The Commission sought judicial review of both measures. On the first measure, the Court of Justice ruled that there had simply been no decision. In its view, nothing had taken

---

[4] Case C-521/06P *Athinaïki Techniki* v *Commission* [2008] ECR I-5829; Case C-322/09P *NDSHT* v *Commission* [2010] ECR I-11911.

[5] Joined Cases T-213/01 and T-214/01 *Österreichische Postsparkasse and Bank für Arbeit und Wirtschaft* v *Commission* [2006] ECR II-1601.

[6] Joined Cases C-463/10P and C-475/10P *Deutsche Post* v *Commission* [2011] ECR I-9639.

[7] Case T-369/08 *ERWIA* v *Commission* [2010] ECR II-6283.

[8] Case T-351/02 *Deutsche Bahn* v *Commission* [2006] ECR II-1047.

[9] Case T-185/05 *Italy* v *Commission*, Judgment of 20 November 2008.

[10] Case T-96/10 *Rütgers Germany* v *ECHA*, Judgment of 7 March 2013.

[11] Case C-39/93P *SFEI* v *Commission* [1994] ECR I-2681; Case T-3/93 *Air France* v *Commission* [1994] ECR II-121. R. Greaves, 'The Nature and Binding Effect of Decisions under Article 189 EC' (1996) 21 *ELRev.* 3, 9–10.

[12] Case C-27/04 *Commission* v *Council* [2004] ECR I-6649.

place. There was thus nothing to review. It came to a different view on the second measure. It noted that this was not merely confirming the existing position but making it conditional on Germany and France meeting certain commitments. It was altering a defined position, and it was intended to change the legal responsibilities of those two Member States. The measure was therefore reviewable.

The law is confusing and arbitrary distinctions emerge. The two measures in *Commission v Council* were, in practice, part and parcel of the same thing, and it makes no sense to look at one but not the other. The initial refusal to take a decision could be argued to have legal consequences for France and Germany, namely, they were protected from sanctions, in a parallel manner to the request of commitments. Similarly, the distinction between decisions to start (non-reviewable) and not to start (reviewable) competition investigations is economic nonsense. However, in part, these fine distinctions emerge because regard is had to the surrounding context in deciding whether to review. In this, there is a suspicion that the context to a measure is not just deployed to determine the concreteness of the measure, but also as a policy background which goes to whether the measure *ought* to be reviewed. In the case of competition proceedings, the Court of Justice was unwilling to allow every undertaking against which proceedings were instigated to try and bully the Commission by threatening litigation from the onset. Decisions to start competition proceedings were, therefore, not reviewable. By contrast, if no proceedings were started, the only remedy for competitors or consumers groups, if there was evidence of illegal behaviour, was often to challenge the failure to proceed. Similarly, in *Commission v Council*, the Court probably did not want to be at the heart of endless challenges over whether the Council had policed the sanction procedures for monetary union sufficiently. By contrast, when the Council did something outside these procedures, in the form of seeking commitments from Germany and France, there was a case for its intervening to safeguard the integrity of the process. If this policy context makes some sense, it gives rise to a legally confusing case law about the material scope of judicial review.

3 GROUNDS OF REVIEW

Four grounds of review are listed in Article 263 TFEU: lack of competence; infringement of an essential procedural requirement; infringement of the Treaty or of any rule of law relating to its application; and misuse of power. These can be recategorised in the following way. First, the EU institution in question must not exceed the power granted to it. Secondly, it must not abuse the discretion granted to it by a manifest error of assessment or an abuse of power. Thirdly, there must not be a breach of process. Finally, there must be no breach of the substantive obligations imposed by EU law. This comprises not just explicit provisions of EU law, but also fundamental rights and general principles of law such as legal certainty, non-discrimination and proportionality.

(i) Lack of competence

It will be rare that EU institutions will be found to have exceeded the powers granted to the Union. The Union has very broad powers, most notably in Article 352 TFEU, the flexibility provision, which allows it to take action necessary to realise the objectives of the Union where no other legislative procedure is available.[13] There has only been one instance, therefore, of an EU institution being found to have taken action which was not available to the Union.[14] More common are two circumstances where an EU institution is found to have exceeded powers granted to it particularly. These are where it has taken action that should have been taken by other EU institutions or it has exceeded powers granted to it.

The first goes to institutional balance, preserving both the institutional checks and balances within the Treaties and protecting the prerogatives of the different institutions. This is addressed in part through the case law on whether legislation has been adopted under the appropriate legal base.[15] In institutional terms, this case law is about whether the legislative powers of the different institutions have been respected. Occasionally, however, an institution adopts a unilateral measure which should have been adopted by another. In *Safe Countries of Origin*,[16] under the legal regime at the time, EU legislation on the granting or withdrawal of refugee status had to be based on the ordinary legislative procedure if there were already common rules in force. In Directive 2005/85/EC setting out principles for the grant and withdrawal of refugee status, provision was made for safe countries of origin with persons coming from these presumed not to be entitled to refugee status. The Directive stated that the Council would draw up a list of these countries having consulted the Parliament. The Parliament challenged this procedure. It argued that as EU legislation was now in force, further rules on what was a safe country of origin could only be drawn up through the ordinary legislative procedure. The Court of Justice agreed. It held that the rules regarding the manner in which EU institutions made decisions were set by the Treaty alone and were not at the disposal of the institutions or Member States. To allow the Council to set new procedures would undermine the institutional balance in the Treaty and the Council did not have the competence to do this.

The second context is where the Commission is granted certain powers and acts outside these powers. In *Boyle*, EU funding was made available to national governments within the context of the common fisheries policy on condition that, inter alia, it did not increase overall national fishing capacity.[17] To this end, the Commission was delegated powers to determine when funding for modernisation of fishing vessels was appropriate. The applicants, a group of Irish fishermen, successfully challenged a Commission Decision which introduced new criteria for funding which were not in the parent instrument. These were that the boat be registered, be at least five years old and the works concern a particular part of the boat. It was argued successfully that nothing in the original legislation gave the Commission the power to introduce additional criteria, and these were therefore illegal.

(ii) Manifest error of assessment and abuse of power

There are only a scattering of cases where a lack of competence has been found. More common is the finding of an abuse of institutional discretion. This will happen in two circumstances:

---

[13] On concerns about its scope see pp. 240–2.

[14] *Opinion 2/94 Accession to the European Convention on Human Rights* [1996] ECR I-1759.

[15] See pp. 109–11.

[16] Case C-133/06 *Parliament v Council* [2008] ECR I-3189. See also Case C-355/10 *Parliament v Council*, Judgment of 5 December 2012. See pp. 240–2.

[17] Joined Cases T-218–240/03 *Boyle v Commission* [2006] ECR II-1699. See also T-263/07 *Estonia v Commission* [2009] ECR II-3463. The latter was upheld in Case C-505/09P *Commission v Estonia*, Judgment of 29 March 2012.

where there has been a manifest error of assessment and where there has been an abuse of power.

The central judgment on manifest error of assessment is *Tetra Laval*. The case concerned a merger ('concentration') between Tetra Laval, the world-leader for carton packaging, and Sidel, a company specialising in PET packaging, a form of packaging comprised of a resin through which oxygen and light can pass. The Commission disallowed the merger on the grounds that Tetra Laval would leverage its dominant position on the market for cartons to persuade its customers to use Sidel's PET packaging, thereby eliminating competition in that market. The General Court found that the Commission had committed a manifest error of assessment in that it had used reports which overestimated the possibility for leveraging and the possibility for growth in the PET market. The Commission appealed to the Court of Justice.

Case C–12/03P *Commission* v *Tetra Laval* [2005] ECR I–987

39. Whilst the Court recognises that the Commission has a margin of discretion with regard to economic matters, that does not mean that the Community Courts must refrain from reviewing the Commission's interpretation of information of an economic nature. Not only must the Community Courts, inter alia, establish whether the evidence relied on is factually accurate, reliable and consistent but also whether that evidence contains all the information which must be taken into account in order to assess a complex situation and whether it is capable of substantiating the conclusions drawn from it...

41. Although the [General Court] stated...that proof of anti-competitive conglomerate effects of a merger of the kind notified calls for a precise examination, supported by convincing evidence, of the circumstances which allegedly produce those effects, it by no means added a condition relating to the requisite standard of proof but merely drew attention to the essential function of evidence, which is to establish convincingly the merits of an argument or, as in the present case, of a decision on a merger....

44. The analysis of a 'conglomerate-type' concentration is a prospective analysis in which, first, the consideration of a lengthy period of time in the future and, secondly, the leveraging necessary to give rise to a significant impediment to effective competition mean that the chains of cause and effect are dimly discernible, uncertain and difficult to establish. That being so, the quality of the evidence produced by the Commission in order to establish that it is necessary to adopt a decision declaring the concentration incompatible with the common market is particularly important, since that evidence must support the Commission's conclusion that, if such a decision were not adopted, the economic development envisaged by it would be plausible....

46. With respect to the particular case of judicial review exercised by the [General Court] in the judgment under appeal, it is not apparent from the example given by the Commission, which relates to the growth in the use of PET packaging for sensitive products, that the [General Court] exceeded the limits applicable to the review of an administrative decision by the Community Courts. Contrary to what the Commission claims,...the judgment under appeal merely restates more concisely, in the form of a finding by the [General Court], the admission made by the Commission at the hearing...that its forecast in the contested decision with regard to the increase in the use of PET for packaging UHT milk was exaggerated...the [General Court] gave the reasons for its finding that the evidence produced by the Commission was unfounded by stating that, of the three independent reports cited by the Commission, only the PCI report contained information on the use of PET for milk packaging. It went on, in that paragraph, to show that the evidence produced by the Commission was unconvincing by pointing out that the increase forecast in the PCI report was of little significance and that the Commission's forecast

was inconsistent with the undisputed figures...contained in the other reports. In...the judgment under appeal, the [General Court] merely stated that the Commission's analysis was incomplete, which made it impossible to confirm its forecasts, given the differences between those forecasts and the forecasts made in the other reports....

48. It follows from these examples that the [General Court] carried out its review in the manner required of it, as set out in paragraph 39 of this judgment. It explained and set out the reasons why the Commission's conclusions seemed to it to be inaccurate in that they were based on insufficient, incomplete, insignificant and inconsistent evidence.

Formally, the Court of Justice will not substitute its assessment for that of the EU institutions but will simply check that any measure is sufficiently substantiated by the evidence provided, and that the evidence deployed is accurate, reliable, consistent and sufficiently complete. A distinction is therefore drawn between the assessment of the institution (not reviewable) and the grounds for the assessment (reviewable). However, as the excerpt below illustrates, the distinction is slippery, with even judges disagreeing about the intensity of review required.

A. Fritzsche, 'Discretion, Scope of Judicial Balance and Institutional Review in European Law' (2010) 47 *Common Market Law Review* 361, 399–400 and 401–2

Bo Vesterdorf (the former President of the Court of First Instance) speaking extra-judicially has suggested his understanding of the appropriate standard of review, that it should be 'intense and effective'.[18] It is for the General Court to check whether the Commission has 'clearly overlooked, underestimated, or exaggerated the relevant economic data, drawn unconvincing, in the sense of implausible, direct inferences from primary material facts or adopted an erroneous approach to assessing the material facts'.[19] In the absence of such errors, the Court should uphold the decision, 'even if it would not itself have subscribed to the Commission's economic assessment'.[20] However, this standard is far-reaching. There is no discretion if the General Court double-checked the inferences drawn from primary facts, as any deviating evaluation may be attributed to overlooking, underestimating, or exaggerating primary data. The same is true if the Court substitutes judgment on the approach adopted to assess material facts. Economic assessments require many methodological choices and a preselection and weighing of material to be taken into account. According to this standard, the court could intervene at any stage and it seems hardly conceivable that an economic assessment not shared by the court could be upheld. Under these circumstances, to invoke the Commission's discretion in economic matters is close to paying lip-service, as has occasionally been done in the *Tetra Laval* case.

More latitude in assessing economic facts and circumstances would follow from the proposal of former Judge Hubert Legal.[21] For him, the discretion lies within the freedom of choice of the economic

---

[18] B. Vesterdorf, 'Standard of Proof in Merger Cases: Reflections in the Light of Recent Case Law of the Community Courts' (2005) 1 *Eur. Comp. Journal* 3, 32.
[19] *Ibid.*   [20] *Ibid.*
[21] H. Legal, 'Standards of Proof and Standards of Judicial Review in EU Competition Law' in B. Hawk (ed.), *Annual Proceedings of the Fordham Corporate Law Institute, International Antitrust Law and Policy 1999* (New York, Juris Publishing, 2000).

methodology to be applied and in the global determination reached on the basis of this methodology; the latter applies as long as it is not contradicted by facts and not obviously contrary to accepted methods of economic reasoning. Yet, Legal wants inferences drawn from primary facts to be subjected to full control. These inferences are made on the basis of the methodological choice for which, according to Legal, the Commission is to enjoy some latitude....

In *Tetra Laval*, the ECJ held that for prospective analyses (but this also true for retrospective assessments) it is necessary to 'envisage various chains of cause and effect with a view to ascertaining which of them are the most likely'. It has to be added that the choice of the most likely chain of cause and effect is within the Commission's power. The General Court only checks whether various likely chains of cause were addressed and excluded for logical and consistent reasons and whether state of the art forensic social science methods were applied. The complainants have to devote their efforts not to establishing alternative assessments, but to finding methodological errors in the analyses conducted by the Commission – which, if the parties have cooperated in the administrative proceedings, should be the result of a joint effort.

To be able to exercise meaningful judicial review, quality standards of forensic social science methodology have to be set. Those standards are already available. The courts should – if necessary, i.e. the complainant substantiates it – use their power to consult experts to check the observance of these standards. In order to make such review possible, transparency is the paramount postulate. Studies must be comprehensible to and replicable by other scientists. Regardless of whether qualitative or quantitative techniques are employed, there are some points that have to be addressed in any study: study design (object of investigation, goals, period of time), data acquisition or sources, and the methods of analysis used, including a discussion of potential errors.

As Fritzsche observes, a premium is placed on scientific methodology. It acquires an elevated normative status, as if the EU institution can show it has deployed a robust methodology, it is less likely to be successfully reviewed. However, even this does not prevent applicants chancing their arm. The obscurity about the quality of reasoning which must be provided by EU institutions has, thus, been a fertile source of litigation.[22]

In contrast to the doctrine of manifest error of assessment, the doctrine of misuse of powers can be mentioned almost as a postscript. It arises if it appears:

on the basis of objective, relevant and consistent indications to have been adopted to achieve purposes other than those for which it was intended.[23]

The principle has rarely brought joy to applicants. First, the test is one of bad faith, namely, whether the EU institution intentionally used a power for a purpose for which it should not be used. This bad faith has proved difficult for applicants to prove. Secondly, the threshold is further raised by the requirement that the decision challenged must have been guided exclusively

[22] A study of challenges to Commission Decisions punishing cartels between 1995 and 2004 found that they were only fully successful in 6 per cent of cases. They were partially successful in securing a reduction of the fine in 122 cases (61 per cent). The predominant ground was manifest error of assessment. The Union courts were, thus, finding in these cases that the Commission erred in some of its reasoning but not in all of it: a very woolly scenario. C. Harding and A. Gibbs, 'Why Go to Court in Europe? An Analysis of Cartel Appeals 1995–2004' (2005) 30 *ELRev.* 349, 365–7.
[23] Case C-323/88 *Sermes* v *Directeur de Service des Douanes de Strasbourg* [1990] ECR I-3027.

or predominantly by this motivation to use the power for purposes other than those for which they were conferred.[24] This is difficult to prove and, outside two staff cases,[25] the principle has only been successfully invoked once.[26]

(iii) Rights of process

Procedural guarantees are set out throughout the Treaties and EU secondary legislation in relation to specific activities. There are, however, more general rights of process which exist, in the absence of these, across all fields of EU law. These can be categorised into three: rights of defence, the right to a hearing and the right to good administration of one's affairs.

(a) Rights of defence

Both natural and legal persons have rights of defence whenever EU institutions are to impose some penalty on them. These rights of defence exist not merely in relation to the proceedings which impose the penalty but in relation to all proceedings, no matter how preparatory, which lead up to these.[27] These rights of defence fall under two discrete but related headings. There are those rights which must be observed by the EU institution imposing the penalty. In addition, there is a right to effective judicial protection: those rights which allow an actor to seek judicial review of any penalty imposed.

The relationship between the two was explored at most length in *Kadi*.[28] EU Regulations implementing UN sanctions restricted financial and material resources allowed to individuals who were on a list of people suspected of associating with al-Qaeda. This list was compiled by a Sanctions Committee set up by the United Nations. Kadi was placed on this list. He was neither provided with the reasons for this nor given a chance to challenge this. In 2008, the Court held that this failure of due process rendered the EU Regulations illegal. As a response, the UN Sanctions Committee set out a statement of reasons which the Commission communicated to Kadi. This stated that he had set up a foundation, which had operated under the umbrella of Al Qaeda and its predecessors. This foundation had hired people who worked with Bin Laden and were associated with radical Islamic Tunisian organisations, and had funded terrorist activities in Bosnia Herzegovina. It was also claimed that Albanian organisations owned by Kadi were funding these terrorist activities. Kadi disputed this. After hearing him, the Commission, nevertheless, adopted a new Regulation restating the restrictions. Kadi went back to the Union courts to challenge these new restrictions. The Court of Justice went on to find for Kadi, as it found insufficient evidence had been provided to substantiate the claims against him. It stated the following on the rights of defence.

---

[24] Case C-48/96P *Windpark Groothusen* v *Commission* [1998] ECR I-2873; Case C-407/04P *Dalmine* v *Commission* [2007] ECR I-829.

[25] Joined Cases 18/65 and 35/65 *Gutmann* v *Commission* [1966] ECR 103; Case 105/75 *Giuffrida* v *Council* [1976] ECR 1395.

[26] Joined Cases 351/85 and 360/85 *Fabrique de Fer de Charleroi* v *Commission* [1987] ECR 3639.

[27] They cover all proceedings that lead up to this sanction, no matter how preparatory, Case 46/87 *Hoechst* v *Commission* [1989] ECR 2859.

[28] For a detailed discussion of the issues surrounding EU policy here see C. Eckes, *EU Counter-Terrorist Policies and Fundamental Rights: The Case of Individual Sanctions* (Oxford, Oxford University Press, 2009); I. Cameron (ed.), *EU Sanctions: Law and Policy Issues concerning Restrictive Measures* (Cambridge, Intersentia, 2013).

Joined Cases C–584/10 P, C–593/10 P and C–595/10 P *Commission* v *Kadi*, Judgment of 18 July 2013

98. …fundamental rights include, inter alia, respect for the rights of the defence and the right to effective judicial protection.

99. The first of those rights, which is affirmed in Article 41(2) EUCFR includes the right to be heard and the right to have access to the file, subject to legitimate interests in maintaining confidentiality.

100. The second of those fundamental rights, which is affirmed in Article 47 of the Charter, requires that the person concerned must be able to ascertain the reasons upon which the decision taken in relation to him is based, either by reading the decision itself or by requesting and obtaining disclosure of those reasons, without prejudice to the power of the court having jurisdiction to require the authority concerned to disclose that information, so as to make it possible for him to defend his rights in the best possible conditions and to decide, with full knowledge of the relevant facts, whether there is any point in his applying to the court having jurisdiction, and in order to put the latter fully in a position to review the lawfulness of the decision in question.

101. Article 52(1) of the Charter nevertheless allows limitations on the exercise of the rights enshrined in the Charter, subject to the conditions that the limitation concerned respects the essence of the fundamental right in question and, subject to the principle of proportionality, that it is necessary and genuinely meets objectives of general interest recognised by the European Union.

102. Further, the question whether there is an infringement of the rights of the defence and of the right to effective judicial protection must be examined in relation to the specific circumstances of each particular case…including, the nature of the act at issue, the context of its adoption and the legal rules governing the matter in question…

111. …respect for the rights of the defence and the right to effective judicial protection requires that the competent Union authority disclose to the individual concerned the evidence against that person available to that authority and relied on as the basis of its decision, that is to say, at the very least, the summary of reasons provided by the Sanctions Committee…so that that individual is in a position to defend his rights in the best possible conditions and to decide, with full knowledge of the relevant facts, whether there is any point in bringing an action before the Courts of the European Union.

112. When that disclosure takes place, the competent Union authority must ensure that that individual is placed in a position in which he may effectively make known his views on the grounds advanced against him…

114. When comments are made by the individual concerned on the summary of reasons, the competent European Union authority is under an obligation to examine, carefully and impartially, whether the alleged reasons are well founded, in the light of those comments and any exculpatory evidence provided with those comments…

116. Lastly, without going so far as to require a detailed response to the comments made by the individual concerned…the obligation to state reasons laid down in Article 296 TFEU entails in all circumstances, not least when the reasons stated for the European Union measure represent reasons stated by an international body, that that statement of reasons identifies the individual, specific and concrete reasons why the competent authorities consider that the individual concerned must be subject to restrictive measures.

117. As regards court proceedings, in the event that the person concerned challenges the lawfulness of the decision to list or maintain the listing of his name…the review by the Courts of the European Union must extend to whether rules as to procedure and rules as to competence, including whether or not the legal basis is adequate, are observed.

Kadi indicates that the rights of defence will include, at the very least, a right to be heard. This right to be heard imposes a duty on the authority to disclose sufficient evidence and reasons for the penalty and for the accused to defend his case in the best conditions possible;[29] an opportunity for the accused to comment on this; a duty on the authority to examine the case carefully and impartially in the light of these comments; and a duty to provide reasons for the imposition of penalties. This right to be heard only goes, however, to those matters which form the basis for the measure but not to the final position adopted.[30] The institution is thus not obliged to hear an applicant with regard to the final factual assessment which forms part of its decision.[31]

The rights of defence extend beyond the right to be heard to include a number of other rights. These include prosecution only for clearly and unambiguously defined criminal or administrative penalties;[32] the presumption of innocence;[33] the right not to be tried twice for the same facts;[34] the right to legal assistance and for lawyer-client communications prepared for the purpose of defence to be privileged;[35] and protection from self-incrimination.[36] As *Kadi* indicates, these rights of defence also include the right to effective judicial protection. This right to seek judicial review exists even where the measure no longer exists, as the applicant can argue it is necessary to restore her to her original position, to induce suitable behaviour in the future or to deter future illegal behaviour.[37] This right includes not merely the formal possibility of review but also a right to a certain level of substantive scrutiny.

> **Joined Cases C–584/10P, C–593/10P and C–595/10P *Commission* v *Kadi*, Judgment of 18 July 2013**
>
> 118. The Courts of the European Union must, further, determine whether the competent European Union authority has complied with the procedural safeguards set out…and the obligation to state reasons laid down in Article 296 TFEU…and, in particular, whether the reasons relied on are sufficiently detailed and specific.
>
> 119. The effectiveness of the judicial review guaranteed by Article 47 of the Charter also requires that, as part of the review of the lawfulness of the grounds which are the basis of the decision to list or to maintain the listing of a given person…is taken on a sufficiently solid factual basis…That entails a

---

[29] This will usually involve access to the file setting out the obligation. This is subject to restrictions for reasons of security and confidentiality, Case C-300/11 *ZZ* v *Secretary of State for the Home Department*, Judgment of 4 June 2013. Only failure to disclose inculpatory information will render a measure automatically illegal. Failure to disclose exculpatory information will only render any measure illegal if it effectively hinders the applicant's rights of defence, Case T-30/91 *Solvay* v *Commission* [1995] ECR II-1775; Case T-240/07 *Heineken Netherland* v *Commission* [2011] ECR II-3355.

[30] Case T-16/02 *Audi* v *OHIM (TDI)* [2003] ECR II-5167.

[31] Case T-458/05 *Tegometall International* v *OHIM – Wuppermann (TEK)* [2007] ECR II-4721.

[32] Case C-303/05 *Advocaten voor de Wereld* v *Leden van de Ministerraad* [2007] ECR I-3633.

[33] Case C-344/08 *Rubach* [2009] ECR I-7033.

[34] Case C-469/03 *Miraglia* [2005] ECR I-2009.

[35] Case 155/79 *AM & S Europe* v *Commission* [1982] ECR 1575; Joined Cases T-125/03 and T-253/03 *Akzo Nobel Chemicals* v *Commission* [2007] ECR II-3523.

[36] Case 374/87 *ORKEM* v *Commission* [1989] ECR 3283; Case T-352/09 *Novácke chemické závody* v *Commission*, Judgment of 12 December 2012.

[37] Case C-239/12P *Abdulrahim* v *Council and Commission*, Judgment of 28 May 2013.

verification of the allegations factored in the summary of reasons underpinning that decision…with the consequence that judicial review cannot be restricted to an assessment of the cogency in the abstract of the reasons relied on, but must concern whether those reasons, or, at the very least, one of those reasons, deemed sufficient in itself to support that decision, is substantiated.

120. To that end, it is for the Courts of the European Union, in order to carry out that examination, to request the competent European Union authority, when necessary, to produce information or evidence, confidential or not, relevant to such an examination…

121. That is because it is the task of the competent European Union authority to establish, in the event of challenge, that the reasons relied on against the person concerned are well founded, and not the task of that person to adduce evidence of the negative, that those reasons are not well founded.

122. For that purpose, there is no requirement that that authority produce before the Courts of the European Union all the information and evidence underlying the reasons alleged in the summary provided by the Sanctions Committee. It is however necessary that the information or evidence produced should support the reasons relied on against the person concerned.

123. If the competent European Union authority finds itself unable to comply with the request by the Courts of the European Union, it is then the duty of those Courts to base their decision solely on the material which has been disclosed to them…If that material is insufficient to allow a finding that a reason is well founded, the Courts of the European Union shall disregard that reason as a possible basis for the contested decision.

Kadi, however, raised a final issue about the rights of defence. It was to what extent security concerns could limit the duty of the administration to provide information to both the accused and the court. The Court of Justice stated that a balance had to be struck between security and the disclosure of information to the accused. There could, therefore, be no disclosure or partial disclosure on grounds of security. The excerpt above, however (paragraphs 122–3), indicates that a failure to disclose might harm the case of the EU institution. Furthermore, the Court has to be given the opportunity to see if these security grounds justify non-disclosure. If they do not, then the EU authority has to be given the opportunity to disclose the information to the accused. By contrast, if disclosure is justified, the EU institution is still not absolved. Alternative possibilities have to be considered, such as providing summaries of the information or evidence.[38]

The rights of defence are extensive and there is a judicial scepticism about institutional justifications for limiting them. *Kadi* must be seen, therefore, as a highly liberal judgment. It is also a judgment which generated huge national resistance. Twenty Member States intervened against *Kadi* in the case. At the time of writing, it will be interesting to see the national reaction against it. There is a counter-balance to this liberalism. Violation of the rights of defence will only result in annulment of the measure, if, but for the violation, the result might have been different. There are many circumstances, therefore, where a finding of a violation has little more than declaratory value.[39]

[38] Similar reasoning was applied in Case C-300/11 *ZZ* v *Secretary of State for the Home Department*, Judgment of 4 June 2013.

[39] Case C-288/96 *Germany* v *Commission* [2000] ECR I-8237; Case C-383/13PPU *MG* v *Staatssecretaris van Veiligheid en Justitie*, Judgment of 10 September 2013.

(b) Right to a hearing

The second situation is where a party has a right to a hearing even though the situation does not give to any rights of the defence. This right to a hearing will give rise to the rights stated earlier. It will exist whenever proceedings take place which culminate in a measure adversely affecting that person.[40] This is broader than the penalty mentioned earlier, as it can include denial of a benefit, such as the grant of humanitarian protection to asylum seekers.[41] In the absence of such proceedings, a general measure which adversely affects a party's interests is insufficient to grant them a right to a hearing.[42] However, if a party is named or addressed in a Union measure and their interests are significantly affected, they do acquire that right.[43] If an individual is not named in a measure but nevertheless has *locus standi* to challenge it before the Union courts, this will also grant them a right to a hearing[44] unless they acquired this standing by dint of making a complaint to an EU institution.[45] The reason for this last qualification is, according to the Court of Justice, that they are doing no more than providing information, and this is insufficient to justify a hearing.[46]

(c) Right to good administration

A third broader right has emerged in recent years, which subsumes the rights of defence and the rights to a hearing, but imposes further institutional duties. It is set out in Article 41 of the European Union Charter of Fundamental Rights (EUCFR).[47]

Article 41 EUCFR

1. Every person has the right to have his or her affairs handled impartially, fairly and within a reasonable time by the institutions and bodies of the Union.
2. This right includes:
   - the right of every person to be heard, before any individual measure which would affect him or her adversely is taken;
   - the right of every person to have access to his or her file, while respecting the legitimate interests of confidentiality and of professional and business secrecy;
   - the obligation of the administration to give reasons for its decisions.
3. Every person has the right to have the Community make good any damage caused by its institutions or by its servants in the performance of their duties, in accordance with the general principles common to the laws of the Member States.
4. Every person may write to the institutions of the Union in one of the languages of the Treaties and must have an answer in the same language.

---

[40] Case C-349/07 *Sopropé* [2008] ECR I-10369.
[41] Case C-277/11 *MM* v *Minister for Justice, Equality and Law Reform*, Judgment of 22 November 2012.
[42] Case T-37/92 *BEUC and NCC* v *Commission* [1994] ECR II-285.
[43] Case C-32/95P *Commission* v *Lisrestal and others* [1996] ECR I-5373; Case C-141/08P *Foshan Shunde Yongjian Housewares & Hardware Co.* v *Commission* [2009] ECR I-9147.
[44] Case C-49/88 *Al-Jubail* v *Council* [1991] ECR I-3187.   [45] On when this grants standing see p. 451.
[46] Case T-198/01 *Technische Glaswerke Ilmenau* v *Commission* [2004] ECR II-2717.
[47] On the evolution of this right see H.-P. Nehl, *Principles of Administrative Procedure in EC Law* (Oxford/Portland, Hart, 1999) 127–49; J. Wakefield, *The Right to Good Administration* (The Hague, Kluwer, 2007).

This right, first, imposes a duty of care on the EU institutions. They must act in good faith[48] and give due consideration and attention to all the arguments presented[49] and to the task in hand.[50] This duty of consideration requires them to provide reasons for the measure, which must be coherent, take account of the evidence provided and form the basis for the measure itself.[51] It also requires them to be proactive in gathering information. There is, in particular, a duty to fill in gaps in information through seeking it from parties who have a right to a hearing.[52] In addition, there is a requirement of impartiality. No member of the institution concerned responsible for the matter may show bias or personal prejudice, and there must, also, be sufficient guarantees to exclude any legitimate doubt as to bias on the part of the institution concerned.[53]

Secondly, EU institutions cannot impose unreasonable demands on parties subject to proceedings, in the form of unreasonable requests for information.[54] Thirdly, EU institutions must exercise their powers within a reasonable period of time.[55] The delay must not be such as to compromise the rights of defence.[56] The reasonableness of the time taken will be assessed in relation to the particular circumstances of each case: its background, complexity, the procedural stages followed and its importance for the parties involved.[57] These conditions can be read separately, so the complexity of a case alone may justify a lengthy investigation.[58] If the case is uncomplicated, twenty-six months has been ruled excessive.[59] In other cases where the applicant has contributed to the delay or the matter has had to go through the domestic courts, they have not found seven or twelve years unduly long.[60]

The right to good administration grants additional rights to parties who already possess certain rights of process: be it rights of defence, a right to a hearing or a right to complain granted by specific legislation. It does not give rights to other parties.[61] This raises a question about whether a distinction is made between privileged parties who have significant protection and access to the EU institutions and other parties who are excluded. Mendes has, in particular, argued that the narrow range of parties granted rights of process, typically in relation to administrative acts seen as harming them rather than general acts, excludes the possibility for a more wide-ranging participatory democracy in which those whose interests are affected by EU measures, whatever their form or remit, would have a right to more active engagement with EU institutions. She argues for a reform that would require hearings to be granted to two types of actor.

---

[48] For a failure here see Case T-410/03 *Hoechst v Commission* [2008] ECR II-881.
[49] Case 210/81 *Demo-Studio Schmidt v Commission* [1983] ECR 3045.
[50] Case C-16/90 *Nölle v Hauptzollamt Bremen-Freihafen* [1991] ECR I-5163.
[51] Case T-263/07 *Estonia v Commission* [2009] ECR I-3463. This was upheld in Case C-505/09P *Commission v Estonia*, Judgment of 29 March 2012.
[52] Case T-420/05 *Vischim v Commission* [2009] ECR II-3841.
[53] Case C-439/11 *Ziegler v Commission*, Judgment of 11 July 2013.
[54] Case T-6/12 *Godrej Industries v Council*, Judgment of 6 September 2013.
[55] Joined Cases C-74/00P and C-75/00P *Falck and Acciaierie di Bolzano v Commission* [2002] ECR I-7869; Joined Cases C-346/03 and C-529/03 *Atzeni and others* [2006] ECR I-1875.
[56] Joined Cases C-238/99P, C-244/99P, C-245/99P, C-247/99P, C-250/99P –252/99P and C-254/99P *Limburgse Vinyl Maatschappij and others v Commission* [2003] ECR I-8375.
[57] Case T-73/95 *Oliveira v Commission* [1997] ECR II-381.
[58] Joined Cases C-322/07P, C-327/07P and C-338/07P *Papierfabrik August Koehler v Commission* [2009] ECR I-7191.
[59] Case 223/85 *RSV v Commission* [1987] ECR 4617.
[60] Joined Cases T-30/01–32/01 and T-86/02–88/02 *Diputación Foral de Álava v Commission*, Judgment of 9 September 2009; Case T-347/03 *Branco v Commission* [2005] ECR II-2555.
[61] Case C-367/95P *Commission v Sytraval* [1998] ECR I-1719.

> **J. Mendes, *Participation in EU Rule-Making: A Rights-Based Approach* (Oxford, Oxford University Press, 2011) 463**
>
> ...it is possible to distinguish two categories of persons concerned: holders of subjective rights and holders of legally protected interests affected by the final decision. The former are persons who, in the light of the applicable norms, may aim to acquire a certain good or advantage through the decision that is being adopted or prevent an effect that this decision is intended to produce in their legal sphere. The latter, while being sufficiently connected to the material situation under examination, voice 'objectivized interests' the fulfilment of which is, at the same time, one of the goals of the legal system and should therefore be considered in the exercise of the decisional function. Holders of legally protected interests cannot aspire to having their personal situation considered as such by the decision-maker, since their intervention is legally valued on the basis of their contribution to the procedure. Provided that they have a substantive link to the material situation, their capacity as persons concerned...derives from the fact that they defend legally protected interests which may be adversely affected by the decision and which ought to be considered by the decision-maker as part of the overall assessment that forms the basis of the decision. On the contrary, holders of subjective rights who might be adversely affected by the decision have a qualified subjective entitlement vis-à-vis the decision-maker. The latter needs to consider their subjective position as such while assessing the material situation that is being regulated.

(iv) Infringement of the Treaties or of any rule of law relating to their application

The final grounds of review relate to infringement of the Treaties or of any rule of law relating to their application. This 'rule of law' can be a breach of a substantive piece of EU law: be it a provision of the Treaties or a piece of binding secondary legislation.[62] It can also be a breach of a number of other legal norms: These include fundamental rights; proportionality; non-discrimination; legal certainty; and legitimate expectations. As the first two of these have been addressed in detail elsewhere, this section will focus on the latter three norms: non-discrimination, legal certainty and legitimate expectations.

(a) Non-discrimination

EU law protects against parties being disadvantaged by virtue of their gender, ethnicity, race, age, disability, religion, belief or sexual orientation. These are set out in Articles 10 and 19 TFEU, and are discussed in Chapter 13. Beyond these, there is a general principle that like cases be treated alike.[63] The seminal case is *Ruckdeschel*. Identical subsidies were historically granted to starch and quellmehl producers by the EU institutions as the two products were seen as economically substitutable. The quellmehl subsidy was withdrawn. Ruckdeschel, a

---

[62] There is one exception to this. No judicial review for non-compliance with the WTO Agreement is possible on the grounds that the agreement is not such as to generate rights for individuals. Case C-377/02 *Van Parys v BIRB* [2005] ECR I-1465.

[63] For a more recent example of this reasoning see Case C-550/07P *Akzo Nobel Chemicals v Commission* [2010] ECR I-8301.

quellmehl producer, challenged this, arguing that this discriminated between it and starch producers. The Court of Justice agreed.

Joined Cases 117/76 and 16/77 *Ruckdeschel v Council* [1977] ECR 1753

7. The second subparagraph of [Article 40(2) TFEU] provides that the common organization of agricultural markets 'shall exclude any discrimination between producers or consumers within the [Union]'.

   Whilst this wording undoubtedly prohibits any discrimination between producers of the same product it does not refer in such clear terms to the relationship between different industrial or trade sectors in the sphere of processed agricultural products.

   This does not alter the fact that the prohibition of discrimination laid down in the aforesaid provision is merely a specific enunciation of the general principle of equality which is one of the fundamental principles of Community law.

   This principle requires that similar situations shall not be treated differently unless differentiation is objectively justified.

8. It must therefore be ascertained whether quellmehl and starch are in a comparable situation, in particular in the sense that starch can be substituted for quellmehl in the specific use to which the latter product is traditionally put.

   In this connexion it must first be noted that the Community Regulations were, until 1974, based on the assertion that such substitution was possible...

   While the Council and the Commission have given detailed information on the manufacture and sale of the products in question, they have produced no new technical or economic data which appreciably change the previous assessment of the position.

   It has not therefore been established that, so far as the Community system of production refunds is concerned, quellmehl and starch are no longer in comparable situations.

   Consequently, these products must be treated in the same manner unless differentiation is objectively justified.

The prohibition on discrimination will prohibit not just like cases being treated differently but also different cases being treated in a like manner.[64] In practice, however, it is rare that there will be a finding of discrimination. Often, where there is differential treatment the Court of Justice will simply state that the cases are not alike. This will always be the case where the EU institution can justify the differential treatment (e.g. there is a different basis for the treatment of each).[65] In *Melli Bank*, for example, an Iranian bank pleaded discrimination on the grounds that EU sanctions had targeted it but not other British subsidiaries of Iranian banks.[66] The General Court had little difficulty in finding that there was no discrimination. It noted that the Regulation in question implemented a UN Security Council Resolution which targeted financial institutions engaged in assisting nuclear proliferation. This rationale provided a basis for the differential treatment of Iranian owned banks. This identification of a reason for differentiation entails that the Court is

---

[64] Joined Cases T-222/99, T-327/99 and T-329/99 *Martinez and others* v *Parliament* [2001] ECR II-2823.

[65] On why the EU legislature has more authority to do this than the EU judiciary see J. Croon, 'Comparative Institutional Analysis, the European Court of Justice and the General Principle of Non-Discrimination, or Alternative Tales on Equality Reasoning' (2013) 19 *ELJ* 153.

[66] Joined Cases T-246/08 and T-332/08 *Melli Bank* v *Council* [2009] ECR II-2629. This was upheld in Case C-380/09P *Council* v *Melli Bank*, Judgment of 13 March 2012.

largely looking at the reasonableness of the Union measure in such cases. There is, correspondingly, less intense review where EU institutions enjoy a margin of discretion. Discrimination will only be found if the conduct borders on the 'arbitrary'.[67] In these circumstances the non-discrimination principle seems to add little to the proportionality principle.[68]

(b) Legal certainty

The principle of legal certainty was stated in *Heinrich* as requiring that:

> [Union] rules enable those concerned to know precisely the extent of the obligations which are imposed on them. Individuals must be able to ascertain unequivocally what their rights and obligations are and take steps accordingly.[69]

The first dimension to this is a prohibition against retroactivity. A measure must not take effect prior to its publication.[70] It will not be retroactive if it regulates the future effects of situations which arose prior to publication but only if it applies to events which have already been concluded.[71] The principle is absolute in relation to penal measures.[72] The Court of Justice has also indicated that it should be observed strictly where the rules are liable to have financial consequences.[73] Other measures may exceptionally take effect before publication where the purpose to be achieved so demands and the legitimate concerns of those concerned are respected. In *Fedesa*, following the annulment of a Directive outlawing the use of certain hormones, the subsequent Directive, which was published on 7 March 1988, stipulated that it was to take effect from the beginning of 1988.[74] The reason was to prevent the market being unregulated for that earlier period as a consequence of the annulment of the earlier Directive. The Court considered there to be no breach of the legal certainty principle in light of the short time-span between the annulment of the first Directive and the publication of the second. It did not believe that during this time traders had been led to believe that the EU institutions had changed their stance on regulation of the matter.

The second dimension to legal certainty is that of clarity: enabling EU law's subjects to know their rights and obligations. At the very least, this means that the EU law in question must be published. In *Heinrich*, an unpublished Annex to a Regulation which prohibited tennis rackets from being taken on civil aircraft was found to be void because it had not been published.[75] Alongside this, the Court of Justice has repeatedly stated that EU legislation must be clear and its application foreseeable.[76] This would suggest that if an EU measure is too obscure it could be struck down. However, this is yet to happen.

---

[67] Case 245/81 *Edeka* v *Commission* [1982] ECR 2745; Case C-479/93 *Francovich* v *Italian Republic* [1995] ECR I-3843.

[68] M. Herdegen, 'The Equation Between the Principles of Equality and Proportionality' (1985) 22 *CMLRev.* 683.

[69] Case C-345/06 *Heinrich* [2009] ECR I-1659, para. 44. The principle was first set out in Joined Cases 42/59 and 49/59 *SNUPAT* v *High Authority* [1961] ECR 109.

[70] Case 84/78 *Tomadini* v *Amminstrazione delle Finanze dello Stato* [1979] ECR 1801; Case T-509/10 *Manufacturing Support and Procurement Kala Naft* v *Council*, Judgment of 25 April 2012.

[71] Case 63/83 *R* v *Kirk* [1984] ECR 2689.

[72] Case C-331/88 *R* v *MAFF ex parte FEDESA* [1990] ECR I-4023.

[73] Case C-94/05 *Emsland-Stärke* [2006] ECR I-2619.

[74] Case C-331/88 *R* v *MAFF ex parte FEDESA* [1990] ECR I-4023.

[75] Case C-345/06 *Heinrich* [2009] ECR I-1659. See also Case T-115/94 *Opel Austria* v *Council* [1997] ECR II-39.

[76] Case 325/85 *Ireland* v *Commission* [1987] ECR 5041; Case C-301/97 *Netherlands* v *Council* [2001] ECR I-8853.

(c) Legitimate expectations

The roots of the principle of legitimate expectations lie in the concept of good faith and require that having induced an operator to take one course of action, the administration should not renege so that the individual suffers loss.[77] An example of the reasoning deployed is *Branco*. Branco was awarded funding under the European Social Fund for the training of young adults. The training was certified by the Portuguese ministry who sent a request to the Commission for payment. As the ministry subsequently found irregularities in the performance of the contract, the Commission refused to make the final payment and sought repayment of the funds already granted. Branco claimed a violation of the principle of legitimate expectations in that the work had been certified by the Portuguese ministry in question. The General Court made the following observation:

> Three conditions must be satisfied in order to claim entitlement to the protection of legitimate expectations. First, precise, unconditional and consistent assurances originating from authorised and reliable sources must have been given to the person concerned by the Community authorities. Second, those assurances must be such as to give rise to a legitimate expectation on the part of the person to whom they are addressed. Third, the assurances given must comply with the applicable rules.[78]

In *Branco*, the General Court found that the action failed on the first condition. It noted that the decision to authorise payment was one for the Commission and not the Portuguese authorities, and it had given no assurances here. Even if assurances are made, they must create an expectation on the part of the applicant. This is not simply a subjective test. The expectation must be legitimate and the Court will look to whether an ordinary, prudent trader would have relied on it on the basis of the institution's representation.[79] Finally, the Union measure in question must not be illegal. If it is, it will not generate any protected expectation.[80]

Branco refers to the grant of a precise, unconditional and consistent assurance as the first condition to be met. This assurance can take any form. In *Mulder*, farmers were paid by the Union to take land out of milk production to reduce milk surpluses. Mulder took his land out of production under the scheme but when he sought to resume milk production without paying a levy, he was refused on the ground that this possibility was only available to those who had produced milk in the preceding year. He argued that he had been encouraged to take his land out of production by the Union offering him premiums. This had led him to believe that there would be no penalties for his action. The Court of Justice agreed, ruling that 'where a producer...has been encouraged by a [Union] measure to suspend marketing for a limited period in the general interest...he may legitimately expect not to be subject, upon the expiry of his undertaking, to restrictions which specifically affect him precisely because he availed himself of the possibilities offered by the [Union] provisions'.[81]

---

[77] See generally, S. Schonberg, *Legitimate Expectations in Administrative Law* (Oxford, Oxford University Press, 2000).

[78] Case T-347/03 *Branco* v *Commission* [2005] ECR II-255, para. 102.

[79] Case 265/85 *Van den Bergh en Jurgens* v *Commission* [1987] ECR 1155. On this see E. Sharpston, 'Legitimate Expectations and Economic Reality' (1990) 15 *ELRev.* 103, 108–15.

[80] Case T-336/94 *Efisol* v *Commission* [1996] ECR II-1343.

[81] Case 120/86 *Mulder* v *Minister van Landbouw en Visserij* [1988] ECR 2321.

If the assurance is made to an individual, an ambiguous or general statement about future conduct is insufficient. It must be more concrete: akin to a promise about a specific course of action.[82] The assurance also does not have to be individualised. The adoption of Codes of Conduct is seen as generating legitimate expectations insofar as their publication indicates to third parties the practices that an institution will follow. It can only depart from these in particular cases if it can provide good reasons for this.[83]

This raises the question whether a simple reversal of policy could violate legitimate expectations.[84] The steady view of the Court of Justice is that it depends on whether this could be anticipated by a prudent trader. As there is a presumption of a freedom to legislate, the Court almost always considers that prudent traders ought to be able to anticipate this possibility.[85] However, in exceptional circumstances a reversal in policy can give rise to a successful claim in legitimate expectations. In *CNTA* the Commission suddenly stopped granting subsidies in the colza and rape seed sectors to protect traders against losses from currency fluctuations.[86] This reversal of policy was unusual in that it was a sudden withdrawal of a subsidy. The financial effects were immediate and unexpected. The Court found that whilst the subsidies could not be considered a guarantee against risks on the exchange rate, nevertheless, they meant, in practice, that a prudent trader might not insure himself against the risk. In the absence of an overriding public interest, the Court considered that the immediate withdrawal of the subsidies with no provision for transitional measures breached the principle of legitimate expectations.

4 STANDING UNDER ARTICLE 263 TFEU

(i) Privileged and semi-privileged applicants

So-called privileged applicants – the Member States, the Commission, the Council and the European Parliament – have a general power to seek judicial review of acts of the EU institutions by virtue of Article 263(1) TFEU. The only constraint is the observance of the time limits set out in the final paragraph of Article 263 TFEU. The justification for this is that each represents an important public interest that must be legally protected: the Member States represent individual national interests, the Council collective national interests, the European Parliament a pan-Union democratic voice and the Commission the pan-Union public interest.

The actors in Article 263(2) TFEU – the European Central Bank, the Court of Auditors and the Committee of the Regions – are semi-privileged applicants. The justification for their interest in litigation is different. It is to protect their institutional prerogatives: a defensive power to ensure that other EU institutions do not trespass on their legal entitlements. Infringement of these can occur in three ways. First, an institution may fail to observe a procedure at the expense of another institution.[87] Secondly, an institution may use one procedure when it should

---

[82] Case T-387/09 *Applied Microengineering* v *Commission*, Judgment of 27 September 2012.
[83] Joined Cases C-189/02P–202/02P, C-205/02P–208/02P and C-213/02P *Dansk Rørindustri and others* v *Commission* [2005] ECR I-5425; Case T-93/11 *Stichting Corporate Europe Observatory* v *Commission*, Judgment of 7 June 2013.
[84] For an argument that occasionally it should, see P. Craig, 'Substantive Legitimate Expectations in Domestic and Community Law' (1996) 55 *CLJ* 289, 299.
[85] Case 52/81 *Faust* v *Commission* [1982] ECR 3745.
[86] Case 74/74 *CNTA* v *Commission* [1975] ECR 533.
[87] Case C-65/90 *Parliament* v *Council* [1992] ECR I-4593.

have used another procedure which gives another institution greater entitlements.[88] The final circumstance is when the institutional balance is shifted through the grant of broad powers to the Commission at the expense of the primary legislative procedures. As this pre-empts other institutions' entitlements, they can challenge this grant.

(ii) Non-privileged applicants

(a) Regulatory acts and legislative acts

Historically, most debate has centred around the circumstances under which private parties, so-called non-privileged applicants, can seek judicial review of acts of EU institutions. This is set out in Article 263(4) TFEU. This provision makes a threefold distinction for the purposes of standing between:

- acts addressed to the person concerned;
- acts of direct and individual concern to the person concerned;
- regulatory acts of direct concern to the person concerned which do not entail implementing measures.

The first category is self-explanatory. However, the central distinction, introduced by the Lisbon Treaty, is between regulatory acts, for which individuals need only establish direct concern and no implementing measures to acquire standing, and other acts for which they must establish individual concern. However, no definition is provided of regulatory acts. The matter was addressed at some length in *Inuit Tapiriit Kanatami*. A Canadian Inuit organisation challenged a 2009 Regulation adopted under the ordinary legislative procedure which banned the marketing of seal products within the European Union. The Regulation provided for a number of limited exceptions, one of which was to allow the marketing of seal products which resulted from hunts traditionally conducted by Inuit and contributed to their subsistence. These were seen by the applicants as too limited. They claimed that the Regulation was a 'regulatory act' for the purposes of Article 263(4) TFEU, and therefore they had standing. The General Court disagreed. It held that regulatory acts were general acts, which were not legislative acts.[89] The applicants appealed to the Court of Justice, which upheld both the conclusions and the reasoning of the General Court.

Case C–583/11P *Inuit Tapiriit Kanatami* v *Council*, Judgment of 3 October 2013

58. As regards the concept of 'regulatory act', it is apparent from the third limb of the fourth paragraph of Article 263 TFEU that its scope is more restricted than that of the concept of 'acts' used in the first and second limbs of the fourth paragraph of Article 263 TFEU, in respect of the characterisation of the other types of measures which natural and legal persons may seek to have annulled. The former concept cannot, as the General Court held correctly in paragraph 43 of the order under appeal, refer to all acts of general application but relates to a more restricted category of such acts. To adopt an interpretation

---

[88] Case C-70/88 *Parliament* v *Council* [1990] ECR 2041.
[89] Case T-18/11 *Inuit Tapiriit Kanatami* v *European Parliament and Council* [2011] ECR II-5599.

to the contrary would amount to nullifying the distinction made between the term 'acts' and 'regulatory acts' by the second and third limbs of the fourth paragraph of Article 263 TFEU.

59. Further, it must be observed that the fourth paragraph of Article 263 TFEU reproduced in identical terms the content of Article III-365(4) of the proposed treaty establishing a Constitution for Europe. It is clear from the *travaux préparatoires* relating to that provision that while the alteration of the fourth paragraph of Article 230 EC was intended to extend the conditions of admissibility of actions for annulment in respect of natural and legal persons, the conditions of admissibility laid down in the fourth paragraph of Article 230 EC relating to legislative acts were not however to be altered. Accordingly, the use of the term 'regulatory act' in the draft amendment of that provision made it possible to identify the category of acts which might thereafter be the subject of an action for annulment under conditions less stringent than previously, while maintaining 'a restrictive approach in relation to actions by individuals against legislative acts (for which the "of direct and individual concern" condition remains applicable)'...

60. In those circumstances, it must be held that that the purpose of the alteration to the right of natural and legal persons to institute legal proceedings, laid down in the fourth paragraph of Article 230 EC, was to enable those persons to bring, under less stringent conditions, actions for annulment of acts of general application other than legislative acts.

Inuit Tapiriit Kanatami held, therefore, that a regulatory act was a general act which was not a legislative act. Identifying measures as legislative acts is relatively easy, following the Lisbon Treaty, as these are acts adopted by the legislative procedures set out in the Treaty.[90] Regulatory acts will, therefore, be delegated and implementing measures, as well as powers enjoyed by the Commission directly under the Treaty which are general in nature.[91] In *Microban*, the General Court considered when a measure will be sufficiently general in nature to be a regulatory act. The Commission, acting under powers delegated to it by a Directive, banned an additive, triclosan. A manufacturer challenged this ban even though it was not individually concerned as it argued the measure was a regulatory act. The Commission challenged this, noting that the measure was formally a Decision. The General Court ruled against the Commission. It held that any non-legislative measure is a regulatory act, notwithstanding its formal designation, if it:

applies to objectively determined situations and it produces legal effects with respect to categories of persons envisaged in general and in the abstract.[92]

The Decision was a regulatory act, therefore, even though the measure banned an individual additive. Insofar as this additive could be produced by anybody and particular parties were not identified, it fell within the definition. The scope of regulatory acts is, therefore, a wide one. It covers all measures which do not identify particular actors or are not addressed to particular actors.

These judgments have been criticised as subjecting legislative acts to restrictive conditions for standing which are not applied to other acts. It has been argued that this weakens judicial

---

[90] Article 289(3) TFEU.
[91] These exist in the fields of competition, public undertakings and state aids.
[92] Case T-262/10 *Microban* v *Commission* [2011] ECR II-7697, para. 23.

protection in the Union and results in the legislature often being unaccountable to private actors, at least via the judiciary.[93] However, legislative acts involve representative institutions and allow for public participation. Historically, a reason for restricting judicial review of legislation is that the judiciary is not a representative institution and affording parties the possibility to litigate cannot be seen as public participation as it prioritises the involvement of litigants over other members of the public.[94] Too relaxed standing rules would, thereby, allow policy-making by litigation. These considerations do not apply with the same force in the case of administrative rule-making. The Commission, typically the defendant in these cases, is not a representative institution, and the possibility for public participation might have been less. There is, thus, a stronger case for judicial oversight as the democratic credentials of these administrative processes are weaker.

(b) Direct concern and implementing measures

There are two dimensions to direct concern. The first involves causation. There must be a direct link between the act of the EU institution and the damage inflicted on the application. The second involves the nature of the interest affected by the Union measure, which must be the legal position of the applicant.

Turning to the first of these, the Union measure must affect the applicant's legal position directly:

> The contested measure must directly produce effects on the legal situation of the person concerned and its implementation must be purely automatic and follow solely from the [Union] rules, without the application of other intermediate measures.[95]

The central question is whether the Union measure allows national authorities discretion as whether to implement or not.[96] If it does, the chain of causation is broken as the national measure not the Union one will be deemed responsible for the change in the applicant's legal situation by virtue of the choice available to the national authorities. However, in determining whether there is discretion, the Court will look not merely at the leeway granted to national authorities but also at whether in practice they will exercise that discretion. In *Piraiki-Pitraiki*, Greek cotton exporters challenged a restriction on exporting to other parts of the Union applied during the transitional period for Greek membership of the Union.[97] The background was that the French Government applied a pre-existing regime and came to the Commission to ask for authorisation to continue it. This was granted. When the exporters challenged this authorisation, the Commission argued that, as the authorisation did not compel the French authorities to do anything, the applicants were not directly concerned by it. The Court of Justice rejected this argument. It noted the pre-existing French regime, and stated that there was no more than

---

[93] S. Peers and M. Costa, 'Judicial Review of EU Acts after the Treaty of Lisbon' (2012) 8 *European Constitutional Law Review* 82; A. Albors Llorens, 'Remedies Against the EU Institutions after Lisbon: An Era of Opportunity?' (2012) 71 *CLJ* 507, 526–7.

[94] On this last point see A. Türk, 'Oversight of Administrative Rulemaking: Judicial Review' (2013) 19 *ELJ* 126, 141.

[95] Joined Cases C-445/07P and C-455/07P *Commission v Ente per le Ville Vesuviane* and *Ente per le Ville Vesuviane v Commission* [2009] ECR I-7993. For an early ruling on this see Case 69/69 *Alcan v Commission* [1970] ECR 385.

[96] Case T-262/10 *Microban v Commission* [2011] ECR II-7697.

[97] Case 11/82 *Piraiki-Pitraiki v Commission* [1985] ECR 207.

a theoretical possibility that the French would not continue it. The Commission authorisation, therefore, directly concerned the applicants by legalising a national regime.[98]

As a test of causation, this stance is not uncontroversial. Direct concern is only established where EU institutions have exclusive responsibility for the measure as national authorities are deemed to have no discretion. This is a high threshold. In many cases where the latter has some discretion there is, arguably, a shared responsibility as national authorities would not have taken the action but for the Union measure. In such circumstances, it would seem more appropriate, as both parties are responsible, that action should lie against both of them.

Secondly, the measure must adversely affect the applicant's legal position. This will only be the case where the measure affects an entitlement granted by EU law. In *Front National*, a number of MEPs from the far right party, the Front National, sought to establish a political grouping within the European Parliament. When this was refused on the grounds that it did not meet the Parliament's criteria, the Front National challenged the European Parliament decision. The matter was sent up through the EU judiciary to the Court of Justice, which ruled that the Front National was not directly concerned by the European Parliament decision.

Case C-486/01P *Front National v European Parliament* [2004] ECR I-6289

35. In this instance there is no question that the contested act – to the extent to which it deprived the Members…the opportunity of forming…a political group…– affected those Members directly. As the [General Court] rightly pointed out…those Members were in fact prevented, solely because of the contested act, from forming themselves into a political group and were henceforth deemed to be non-attached Members…; as a result, they were afforded more limited parliamentary rights and lesser material and financial advantages than those they would have enjoyed had they been members of a political group…

36. Such a conclusion cannot be drawn, however, in relation to a national political party such as the Front National.…[A]lthough it is natural for a national political party which puts up candidates in the European elections to want its candidates, once elected, to exercise their mandate under the same conditions as the other Members of the Parliament, that aspiration does not confer on it any right for its elected representatives to form their own group or to become members of one of the groups being formed within the Parliament.…

39. …the [General Court] admittedly found that, since the contested act deprived the Members concerned, particularly those elected from the Front National's list, of the opportunity to organise themselves into a political group, it directly impinged on the promotion of the ideas and projects of the party which they represented in the European Parliament and, hence, on the attainment of that political party's stipulated object at European level, the reason why the Front National was directly affected by the act.

40. Such effects, however, cannot be regarded as directly caused by the contested act.

The Front National was held not to be directly concerned because, although it was affected by the measure, it had no legal entitlement to create a political grouping within the European

---

[98] That said, it will only be in exceptional circumstances that the Court will be willing to make inferences about behaviour by national authorities. It will normally therefore assume that if they have been granted a discretion, they will exercise it. Joined Cases C-445/07P and C-455/07P *Commission v Ente per le Ville Vesuviane*, Judgment of 10 September 2009.

Parliament. It was only MEPs who had that right. The presence of a legal entitlement is, however, not always clear. In *Regione Siciliana*, the General Court and the Court of Justice disagreed about when this would be so. The Commission had cancelled regional assistance for the construction of a dam in Sicily. The Region of Sicily, named in the document as the authority to administer the assistance, challenged this. The General Court stated that the measure directly concerned the region by depriving it of assistance it would have otherwise received and requiring it to repay money already received.[99] The sums combined came to over €48 million. The Court of Justice overturned this. It stated that the region had no right in EU law to the assistance as, although it was noted as the administering authority, it was the Italian Republic which had made the application.[100] As the region had no legal entitlement to the assistance, in the Court of Justice's view, notwithstanding the financial impact, it could not be said to be directly concerned.

To establish *locus standi* for regulatory acts, there is a further condition. The measure must not entail implementing measures. In *Eurofer*, a trade association representing the steel industry challenged Commission implementation of the trading scheme in greenhouse gases.[101] Directive 2003/87/EC granted the Commission the power to set benchmarks for greenhouse gas emissions for different industrial sectors. Emissions exceeding these had to be purchased. The Commission's Decision was challenged on the grounds that it did not grant sufficient allowances to the steel industry. The General Court held that the challenge was inadmissible, inter alia, because this Decision required a number of further implementing measures from both the Member States and the Commission to determine the allowances granted to individual installations, such as determination of the installations in question and the greenhouse gases emitted by other sectors. It was irrelevant in this regard that Member States had no discretion about whether to take these implementing measures, as this test was different from that for direct concern. The need for implementing measures blocks standing, therefore, for regulatory acts. However, *Eurofer* leaves open the question of the absoluteness of this requirement. In that instance, the implementing measures were considerable. It is not clear whether simple transposition, application or enforcement of EU regulatory acts by national authorities would be sufficient where these were required to do this by the regulatory act in question.

(c) Individual concern and *Plaumann*

For measures which are not regulatory acts and not addressed to the applicant, the other requirement for standing is the presence of individual concern. The seminal ruling on individual concern is *Plaumann*. The German authorities wished to suspend customs duty on importation of clementines. They needed, under EU law, authorisation from the Commission, which was refused. The applicant, an importer of clementines, sought judicial review of the Commission Decision. He had to show individual concern as the Decision had been addressed to the German authorities and not to him. The Court of Justice ruled that the applicant lacked standing.

---

[99] Case T-60/03 *Regione Siciliana* v *Commission* [2005] ECR II-4139.
[100] Case C-15/06P *Regione Siciliana* v *Commission* [2007] ECR I-2591.
[101] Case T-381/11 *Eurofer* v *Commission*, Judgment of 4 June 2012.

> ### Case 25/62 *Plaumann & Co. v Commission* [1963] ECR 95
>
> Persons other than those to whom a decision is addressed may only claim to be individually concerned if that decision affects them by reason of certain attributes which are peculiar to them or by reason of circumstances in which they are differentiated from all other persons and by virtue of these factors distinguishes them individually just as in the case of the person addressed. In the present case the applicant is affected by the disputed Decision as an importer of clementines, that is to say, by reason of a commercial activity which may at any time be practised by any person and is not therefore such as to distinguish the applicant in relation to the contested Decision as in the case of the addressee.

The test needs dissecting. *Plaumann* states that private parties are individually concerned only if they can distinguish themselves by virtue of certain attributes or circumstances from all other persons. Although not explicitly stated, these attributes or circumstances must be fixed and determinate and distinguish those identified by them from the rest of the world. The test, furthermore, is not whether the group is fixed and determinate at a particular date, such as the date of the decision or commencement of litigation, but rather whether it is irrecoverably fixed and determinate. It has, in other words, to be a closed category which can never be added to.[102]

An example of the operation of this is *Koninklijke Friesland Campina (KFC)*. A Dutch law created a scheme to give tax benefits to Dutch companies providing international financing activities (the GFA scheme). In 2000 KFC applied for authorisation to join the scheme. In 2001 the Commission announced it was investigating the scheme to see if it was illegal state aid. Following this, the Dutch Government announced it would not admit any more undertakings to the scheme, and would not, therefore, admit KFC to the scheme. In 2003, the Commission declared the scheme illegal but stated that all undertakings which were currently members of the scheme could continue to enjoy its benefits. KFC successfully challenged the Commission Decision before the General Court. The Commission successfully appealed this before the Court of Justice. One of the Commission's arguments, which was unsuccessful, was that KFC was not individually concerned.

> ### Case C-519/07P *Commission v Koninklijke Friesland Campina* [2009] ECR I-8495
>
> 52. …natural or legal persons may claim that a contested provision is of individual concern to them only if it affects them by reason of certain attributes which are peculiar to them or by reason of circumstances in which they are differentiated from all other persons…
> 53. An undertaking cannot, in principle, contest a Commission decision prohibiting a sectoral aid scheme if it is concerned by that decision solely by virtue of belonging to the sector in question and being a potential beneficiary of the scheme. Such a decision is, vis-à-vis that undertaking, a measure of general application covering situations which are determined objectively and entails legal effects for a class of persons envisaged in a general and abstract manner…

---

[102] On this very point see Case T-400/11 *Altadis v Commission*, Judgment of 9 September 2013.

54. By contrast, the Court has held that, where a contested measure affects a group of persons who were identified or identifiable when that measure was adopted by reason of criteria specific to the members of the group, those persons might be individually concerned by that measure inasmuch as they form part of a limited class of traders...

55. It is not in dispute, first, that the contested decision had the effect that requests for first GFA authorisation, which were pending on the date of notification of the contested decision, were rejected without being examined and, second, that the undertakings concerned were easily identifiable, owing to the very existence of such a request, at the time when that decision was adopted. In that regard, it should be recalled that KFC was part of a group of, at most, 14 applicants for first GFA authorisation, whose requests were pending at the time of the 11 July 2001 decision, that those requests were suspended following that decision, and that the Netherlands authorities announced on 5 December 2002 that they would be ceasing, with immediate effect, to consider any new requests for the application of the GFA scheme.

56. Thus,...KFC formed part of a closed group of undertakings – and not of an indefinite number of undertakings belonging to the sector concerned – specifically affected by the contested decision.

57. It should be borne in mind that, in order to benefit from the GFA scheme, an undertaking which had made a request for first GFA authorisation must have already taken the necessary measures in order to fulfil the criteria required for that scheme. Furthermore, as the Netherlands authorities did not have any discretion in that regard, they were obliged to grant such an authorisation if those criteria were fulfilled. Thus, the undertakings whose requests for first GFA authorisation were pending must be regarded as being concerned by the contested decision, by reason of attributes which are peculiar to them and by reason of circumstances in which they are differentiated from every other undertaking in that sector which had not lodged a request for first GFA authorisation.

58. It follows that those undertakings have standing to bring an individual action against the contested decision.

A distinction was thus made between companies engaging in international financial activities and the category of undertakings who had already made an application to join the GFA scheme at the time of the Commission Decision. In principle, anybody could engage in the former category. It was, thus, an open category which could not sustain individual concern. The latter was, by contrast, closed in that nobody could join that category of pending applications as once the Decision was taken the category closed definitively. This founded individual concern.

There are a couple of exceptions to this general rule. The first is where EU law requires the EU decision-maker to take account of a closed group of actors, who would otherwise form part of a larger open group. In *Sofrimport*, a Regulation required the Commission, when it imposed restrictions of imports of fruit and vegetables from outside the Union, to take account of the position of goods in transit.[103] The Commission took a Decision banning the import of dessert apples from Chile. Sofrimport had a shipment in transit which was then refused entry into the Union. On the one hand, it formed part of an open category, namely, apple importers. However, the Court of Justice ruled that it had standing as the Regulation required the Commission to

---

[103] Case C-152/88 *Sofrimport* v *Commission* [1990] ECR I-2477. For similar reasoning see Case 11/82 *Piraiki-Patraiki* v *Commission* [1985] ECR 207; Cases T-219/09 and T-326/09 *Albertini* v *European Parliament* [2010] ECR II-5935.

take account of a closed group, importers with goods in transit on the date of the Decision, and it had failed to do this.

The other circumstance is similar. It is where EU legislation grants parties certain procedural safeguards. A closed group of actors, who would otherwise be part of an open category, have exercised these procedural rights by a certain date. These are then considered to be individually concerned. In *Vischim*, EU legislation provided for the phasing out of certain plant protection products.[104] During a transitional period, manufacturers of these were invited by the legislation to present dossiers setting out the qualities of these products. Vischim was one of sixteen who presented dossiers in relation to a product which was duly prohibited by a subsequent Directive. The General Court held that as Vischim was provided procedural safeguards by the original legislation and it was part of a small group who could not be added to after the date of the subsequent Directive, it was individually concerned.

Two justifications are provided for *Plaumann*. The first is set out below.[105]

A. Arnull, 'Private Applicants and the Action for Annulment under Article 173 of the EC Treaty' (1995) 32 *Common Market Law Review* 7, 46

One other consideration seems worth mentioning. This is that a proliferation of direct challenges to Community acts by natural and legal persons, perhaps accompanied by applications for interim measures, could have seriously disrupted the proper functioning of the Community system…The most progressive of the Court's decisions have been concerned principally with making the Community work. Where, as in cases on direct effect, this has meant protecting the rights of the individual under Community law against encroachment by national authorities, the Court has not hesitated to uphold the rights of the individual. Where the conflict was between the rights of the individual and those of the Community's still immature institutions, however, the Court initially tended to give precedence to the latter.

This may be an argument for restrictive rules of standing but it does not explain the arbitrariness of the current test and the obscure difference between open and closed categories. The Court of Justice has ruled that a party is not individually concerned by a Union measure where it is the only party affected on the grounds that it belongs to an open category which others could potentially join.[106] If the measure was concerned solely with restricting applicants, it would look at those actually affected by a measure – and confine it to a very limited group – and not those affected speculatively.

The second justification is that it protects the status of the Court of Justice. It has been argued that restrictive *locus standi* requirements have been used to channel applicants to challenge Union measures before national courts in the first resort. These then act as a filter for

---

[104] Case T-420/05 *Vischim* v *Council* [2009] ECR II-3911. See also Case T-13/99 *Pfizer Animal Health* v *Council* [2002] ECR II-3305.

[105] See also C. Harding, 'The Private Interest in Challenging Community Action' (1980) 5 *ELRev*. 354. It should be noted that Arnull is very critical of this argument. For excellent coverage of the different arguments see A. Arnull, *The European Union and Its Court of Justice* (2nd edn, Oxford, Oxford University Press, 2006) 91–4.

[106] Case 231/82 *Spijker* v *Commission* [1983] ECR 2559.

the Court of Justice.[107] The Court has thus frequently made the point, when refusing standing, that parties should try their luck before the national courts.[108] This begs the question whether national courts are effective filters. In principle, following the *Fotofrost* doctrine, they should refer any Union measure carrying a whiff of illegality, as they are not allowed to declare a Union measure invalid.[109] It could therefore become a free-for-all with the only question being whether the applicant has standing domestically. In some instances, this may be very liberal whereas in others there may not even be a domestic measure which can be the subject of a challenge. There is, moreover, an institutional contradiction, as the procedures send the applicant to different courts. An action under Article 263(4) TFEU is brought before the General Court whilst a reference goes to the Court of Justice.[110] It would be absurd if the clear Treaty preference for individual administrative challenges to be the main concern of the General Court was undermined in this way.

The bulk of academic literature has thus been highly critical of *Plaumann*. It is viewed as highly restrictive, denying applicants adversely affected by Union measures any effective judicial redress. There is also a sense that it is textually unjustified.[111] Nothing in the Treaty implies that the phrase 'direct and individual concern' should be interpreted as narrowly as the Court of Justice chose to do in *Plaumann*. The relaxation of standing rules can, however, open the door to other concerns. These include disruption of the legislative process by courts, with the latter substituting their views for those of the legislature, and the capture of courts by minority interests who bombard the courts with actions as a strategy to secure objectives they cannot achieve elsewhere. The argumentative force of both sides of debate will, in reality, depend upon the context of the case. In some instances, restrictive rules will lead to a denial of justice, whereas, in others, relaxation might lead to some hijacking. Perhaps the greatest criticism of *Plaumann*, therefore, may be that it gives no regard to the context so that a more nuanced approach to judicial review could be realised.

(d) Standing and interest groups

A sense of this blindness to context is present in the criticism that the test of 'individual concern' is easier to meet for those who can point to some individual financial or material interest that has been prejudiced. It thus benefits trading interests over groups representing public interests such as the environment, the regions or the consumer. This is particularly problematic if judicial review is seen as allowing different social groups to challenge legislative or administrative abuse. It cannot be right if this is only available to some interests and not to others.

---

[107] See, critically, H. Rasmussen, 'Why is Article 173 Interpreted Against Private Plaintiffs?' (1980) 5 *ELRev.* 112. For a defence of this argument see J. Usher, 'Direct and Individual Concern: An Effective Remedy or a Conventional Solution?' (2003) 28 *ELRev.* 575.

[108] Joined Cases T-443/08 and T-455/08 *Freistaat Sachsen* v *Commission* [2011] ECR II-1311; Case T-221/10 *Iberdrola* v *Commission*, Judgment of 8 March 2012.

[109] Case 314/85 *Foto-Frost* v *Hauptzollamt Lübeck-Ost* [1987] ECR 4199.

[110] Article 256(1) TFEU.

[111] A. Barav, 'Direct and Individual Concern: An Almost Insurmountable Barrier to the Admissibility of Individual Appeal to the EEC Court' (1974) 11 *CMLRev.* 191; A. Arnull, 'Private Applicants and the Action for Annulment since *Codorníu*' (2001) 38 *CMLRev.* 7; K. Lenaerts and T. Corthaut, 'Judicial Review as a Contribution to the Development of European Constitutionalism' (2003) 22 *YBEL* 1.

The standing of interest groups is, thus, an important question in its own right. These will have standing where they have been granted certain procedural rights or privileges either by EU law or through the practice of the EU institutions. The argument is that this recognition by the political process confers a parallel entitlement to protection of this recognition by the courts. The position was set out most cogently in *Associazione Nazionale Bieticoltori*. In this instance, a trade association representing Italian sugar beet producers brought an action against a Regulation that granted aid to their Portuguese counterparts whilst reducing aid for the Italian growers. It was found to lack standing.

Case T–38/98 *Associazione Nazionale Bieticoltori (ANB)* v Council [1998] ECR II–4191

25. It should be pointed out, second, that an application for annulment lodged by an association may be admissible in three types of situation, namely:

   (a) where a legislative provision expressly confers a range of procedural powers on trade associations...
   (b) where the association represents the interests of undertakings having locus standi to seek the annulment of the provision in question...
   (c) where the association is distinguished because its own interests as an association are affected, in particular because its position as a negotiator has been affected by the measure whose annulment is sought...

26. In those three types of situation the Court of Justice and the [General Court] have also taken into account the participation of the associations in question in the procedure...

27. As regards the first type of situation, mentioned above, it is sufficient to point out that the regulations on the common organisation of the markets in the sugar sector do not recognise that associations have any right of a procedural nature.

28. As regards the second of the abovementioned types of situation, it should be observed that the fact that the contested provision will affect sugar beet producers whose interests are represented by the Associazione Nazionale Bieticoltori is not such as to differentiate those producers from all other persons, since they are in a situation which is comparable to that of any other operator who may enter the same market...

29. As regards, last, the third type of situation referred to above, it should be pointed out that, according to a consistent line of decisions, an association formed to promote the collective interests of a category of persons cannot be regarded as individually concerned by a measure affecting the general interests of that category, and is therefore not entitled to bring an action for annulment where its members may not do so individually...Nonetheless, the existence of particular circumstances, such as the role played by an association in a procedure leading to the adoption of an act within the meaning of Article [263 TFEU], may justify admitting an action brought by an association whose members are not directly and individually concerned by the act at issue, particularly when its position as negotiator is affected by it.

Such procedural entitlements will be rare, and will often only be given to 'insider' groups who have good relationships with the EU institutions. These are likely to be the last people who wish to challenge a measure as their privileged position in negotiations or consultations is likely to have already secured some influence for them. More interesting, therefore, is whether other interest groups with a strong stake in a measure can challenge it. In *Greenpeace*, three environmental campaigning groups and several individuals resident on the Canary Islands challenged the legality of a series of Commission decisions granting aid from the European Regional Development Fund (ERDF) to assist with the construction of two power stations, one on Gran Canaria and the other on Tenerife. The General Court ruled that neither the associations nor the individuals had standing.[112]

Case T-585/93 *Greenpeace and others* v *Commission* [1995] ECR II-2205

32. The applicants ask the Court to adopt a liberal approach on this issue and recognize that, in the present case, their *locus standi* can depend not on a purely economic interest but on their interest in the protection of the environment...

39. In the alternative, the applicants submit that the representative environmental organizations should be considered to be individually concerned by reason of the particularly important role they have to play in the process of legal control by representing the general interests shared by a number of individuals in a focused and coordinated manner....

56. Nor can the fact that [certain of the] applicants have submitted a complaint to the Commission constitute a special circumstance distinguishing them individually from all other persons and thereby giving them *locus standi* to bring an action under Article [263]. No specific procedures are provided for whereby individuals may be associated with the adoption, implementation and monitoring of decisions taken in the field of financial assistance granted by the ERDF. Merely submitting a complaint and subsequently exchanging correspondence with the Commission cannot therefore give a complainant *locus standi* to bring an action under Article [263]...

59. ...[S]pecial circumstances such as the role played by an association in a procedure which led to the adoption of an act within the meaning of Article [263] may justify holding admissible an action brought by an association whose members are not directly and individually concerned by the contested measure...

60. The three applicant associations...claim that they represent the general interest, in the matter of environmental protection, of people residing on Gran Canaria and Tenerife and that their members are affected by the contested decision; they do not, however, adduce any special circumstances to demonstrate the individual interest of their members as opposed to any other person residing in those areas. The possible effect on the legal position of the members of the applicant associations cannot, therefore, be any different from that alleged here by the applicants who are private individuals. Consequently, in so far as the applicants in the present case who are private individuals cannot, as the Court has held, be considered to be individually concerned by the contested decision, nor can the members of the applicant associations, as local residents of Gran Canaria and Tenerife...

62. In the present case...the Commission did not, prior to the adoption of the contested decision, initiate any procedure in which Greenpeace participated; nor was Greenpeace in any way the interlocutor of the Commission with regard to the adoption of the...decision. Greenpeace cannot, therefore, claim to have any specific interest distinct from that of its members to justify its *locus standi*.

Public interest associations will therefore only be individually concerned if they are granted specific procedural privileges or safeguards within the legislative process; their members are individually concerned; or in negotiations they are recognised by the EU institutions as the

---

[112] The judgment was affirmed on appeal. Case C-321/95P *Greenpeace and others* v *Commission* [1998] ECR I-1651.

central interlocutor of particular interests. It will be rare that any of these will be met. Since *Greenpeace*, the Court of Justice has consistently refused to relax standing requirements for public interest litigation.[113] EU law has therefore been criticised as resulting in diffuse public interests being less well protected than private interests.[114]

Whilst apparently attractive, this argument must be treated cautiously. There are dangers with substituting judicial review for political accountability. Take the *Greenpeace* case, for example: why should it be characterised as being a *legal* concern to decide whether European funds should be allocated to the environmentally controversial construction of a new power station? To accept this might be lead to a 'dilution of the objectivity and neutrality of the law'.[115] Harlow suggests therefore that a better way might be to give public interest groups wider rights of intervention in proceedings – something that has not yet happened.

C. Harlow, 'Towards a Theory of Access for the European Court of Justice' (1992) 12 *Yearbook of European Law* 213, 247–8

The most economical way to increase interest representation without overloading the Court is, however, undoubtedly through intervention procedure. Many modern courts feel able to allow intervention freely and interventions by interest groups are particularly a feature of constitutional courts. In the Court of Justice, in sharp contrast, group interventions are rare and Articles 37 and 20[[116]] of the Statute are largely the preserve of the privileged applicants.

The Court's distinctive inquisitorial procedures could be used to design an appropriate intervention procedure without adding to burdens on applicants in the shape of greater expense or delay. Strict time-limits can already be imposed for interventions with limited rights of contradiction and oral observations already require the Court's permission. Submissions could be limited as to length. Increased use could be made of the *juge rapporteur* if orality were thought necessary; alternatively, they could be collected and evaluated by the Advocate General, forming part of his Opinion.

---

5 ARTICLE 265 TFEU AND THE FAILURE TO ACT

In certain circumstances positive duties are placed by EU law upon the EU institutions to act. They are under a duty to realise some Treaty objectives[117] and secondary legislation often places duties upon them.[118] The conditions for bringing an action if an institution fails to act in such circumstances are set out in Article 265 TFEU.

---

[113] Case T-461/93 *An Taisce* v *Commission* [1994] ECR II-733; Case T-219/95R *Danielsson* v *Commission* [1995] ECR II-3051.

[114] M. Führ *et al.*, 'Access to Justice: Legal Standing for Environmental Associations in the European Union' in D. Robinson and J. Dunkley (eds.), *Public Interest Perspectives in Environmental Law* (Chichester, Chancery, 1995); L. Krämer, 'Public Interest Litigation in Environmental Matters before European Courts' (1996) 8 *JEL* 1; N. Gerard, 'Access to Justice on Environmental Matters: A Case of Double Standards?' (1996) 8 *JEL* 139.

[115] C. Harlow, 'Public Law and Popular Justice' (2002) 65 *MLR* 1, 13.

[116] The right to intervene is now set out in article 40 of the Statute of the Court of Justice. Private actors may intervene if they can show an interest and the dispute is not between Member States, EU institutions or between a Member State and an EU institution.

[117] On the common transport policy see Case 13/83 *Parliament* v *Council* [1985] ECR 1513.

[118] E.g. the Commission is required to examine the factual and legal particulars of any complaint about a breach of EU competition law which is made by a person with a legitimate interest, Case T-24/90 *Automec* v *Commission* [1992] ECR II-2223.

Article 265 TFEU

Should the European Parliament, the European Council, the Council, the Commission or the European Central Bank, in infringement of the Treaties, fail to act, the Member States and the other institutions of the Union may bring an action before the Court of Justice to have the infringement established. This Article shall apply, under the same conditions, to bodies, offices and agencies of the Union which fail to act.

The action shall be admissible only if the institution, body, office or agency concerned has first been called upon to act. If, within two months of being so called upon, the institution, body, office or agency concerned has not defined its position, the action may be brought within a further period of two months.

Any natural or legal person may, under the conditions laid down in the preceding paragraphs, complain to the Court that an institution, body, office or agency of the Union has failed to address to that person any act other than a recommendation or an opinion.

Privileged applicants comprise a wider group under Article 265 TFEU than under Article 263 TFEU as all EU institutions and Member States are granted that status. It, thus, grants a privileged status to the European Council, the European Central Bank and (hypothetically) the Court of Justice not granted by the latter. Beyond this, Articles 263 and 265 TFEU were described in an early judgment as prescribing 'one and the same method of recourse'.[119] The reason is, as one author put it, that:

> the system of remedies…would be incomplete if [Union] institutions were subject to judicial control only in respect of their positive actions while they could evade the obligations imposed upon them by simply failing to act.[120]

The provisions are, therefore, interpreted in parallel manners. Non-privileged applicants can only invoke Article 265 TFEU if they are directly concerned by a regulatory act or directly and individually concerned by a non-regulatory act which should have been adopted.[121]

However, there are some distinctive features to Article 265 TFEU.

First, an action under Article 265 TFEU can only be commenced against an EU institution if it is under a duty to perform a task. If there is only a discretion, no remedy exists.[122] The establishment of a matter as one of discretion rather than obligation has been controversial as it creates a gap in protection. We saw earlier how the discretion enjoyed by the Commission over the launch of infringement proceedings against a Member State led to private parties being largely excluded from this important process.[123] Secondly, an institution, if called upon to act,[124] avoids any further action if it defines its position within two months. This definition of position is an act which is reviewable under Article 263 TFEU.[125] It takes the form of the

---

[119] Case 15/70 *Chevalley* v *Commission* [1970] ECR 979.

[120] A. Toth, 'The Law as It Stands on the Appeal for Failure to Act' (1975/2) *LIEI* 65.

[121] Case T-395/04 *Air One* v *Commission* [2006] ECR II-1343; Case T-167/04 *Asklepios Kliniken* v *Commission* [2007] ECR II-2379.

[122] Case T-423/07 *Ryan Air* v *Commission* [2011] ECR II-2397.

[123] Case 247/87 *Star Fruit* v *Commission* [1989] ECR 291. See pp. 368–70.

[124] Joined Cases T-30/01–32/01 and T-86/02–88/02 *Diputación Foral de Álava* v *Commission* [2009] ECR II-2919.

[125] Case T-3/02 *Schlüsselverlag JS Moser* v *Commission* [2002] ECR II-1473. The one qualification to this is where it leads to an act which is reviewable. In such circumstances, it is the latter which is reviewable. Case T-34/05R *Makhteshim-Agan Holding BV and others* v *Commission* [2005] ECR II-1465.

institution acting in the way called for; acting in a different way from that called for;[126] or refusing to act at all.[127] Finally, the institution must be called upon to act by the applicant. If this does not happen, there will be no action.[128] The call to act need not take any form but must be sufficiently clear and precise to enable the institution to ascertain the specific content of the measure it is being asked to adopt, and it must make clear that its purpose is to compel the institution to state its position.[129]

6 PLEA OF ILLEGALITY

Particularly in the field of delegated or implementing powers, parties face a problem if they want to challenge a measure on the basis that the parent measure is illegal. The time limits for challenging the parent instrument may have passed, or they may not satisfy the *locus standi* requirements. The plea of illegality addresses this by allowing a party in proceedings against a measure to plead the illegality of its parent measure.

> **Article 277 TFEU**
>
> Notwithstanding the expiry of the period laid down in Article 263, fifth paragraph, any party may, in proceedings in which an act of general application adopted by an institution, body, office or agency of the Union is at issue, plead the grounds specified in Article 263, second paragraph, in order to invoke before the Court of Justice of the European Union the inapplicability of that act.

The plea of illegality is, thus, a parasitic procedure. It cannot be brought as an independent action but can only be invoked in the context of proceedings brought under some other procedure, whose *locus standi* requirements and time limits have been observed.[130] A challenge to a Decision on the grounds that the enabling Regulation was illegal would, for example, have to show that it had *locus standi* under Article 263 TFEU to challenge the Decision, and that it observed the time limits of challenging the Decision within two months of its publication.[131]

A concern with the plea of illegality is that it should not be used to subvert other procedures. This has led to two refinements.

First, a plea of illegality may not be invoked where a matter is pending before another court or in another action before the same court (*lis pendens*).[132] This will happen if three conditions are met. The action must be between the same parties, must seek the

---

[126] Case C-25/91 *Pesqueras Echebastar v Commission* [1993] ECR I-1719; Case T-420/05 *Vischim v Council* [2009] ECR I-3841.

[127] Case T-12/12 *Laboratoires CTRS v Commission*, Judgment of 4 July 2012.

[128] Joined Cases T-30/01–32/01 and T-86/02–88/02 *Diputación Foral de Álava v Commission*, Judgment of 9 September 2009.

[129] Joined Cases 81/85 and 119/85 *Usinor v Commission* [1986] ECR 1777; Case T-12/12 *Laboratoires CTRS v Commission*, Judgment of 4 July 2012.

[130] Joined Cases 31/62 and 33/62 *Wöhrmann v Commission* [1962] ECR 506.

[131] The use of Article 277 TFEU is rare but for a (procedurally) successful example see Case T-526/10 *Inuit Tapiriit Kanatami v Commission*, Judgment of 25 April 2013.

[132] Joined Cases T-246/08 and T-332/08 *Melli Bank v Council* [2009] ECR I-2629.

same object and must do so on the basis of the same submissions. This will very rarely be the case. Even if the substance of the dispute is similar, the litigation before the courts may look at different dimensions, and parties will, in any case, often use different arguments.

Secondly, a party who had an earlier opportunity to challenge the parent measure cannot subsequently raise the plea of illegality.[133] The most obvious example is privileged parties under Article 263 TFEU who had unlimited standing to challenge the parent measure at the time of adoption. If they could subsequently raise a plea of illegality, this would allow them to evade the time limits in that procedure and generate uncertainty. In *Spain* v *Commission*, the Court of Justice refused to allow a Spanish challenge to a 1993 Commission Decision extending the regime on subsidies to the motor vehicle industry.[134] The basis of the Spanish challenge was that the initial 1990 regime on which the Decision was based was illegal. The Court ruled that as Spain had not challenged the regime at the time, it could not subsequently raise a plea of illegality.

However, the principle also applies to non-privileged parties. In *TWD (No. 2)*, a 1986 Commission Decision that a subsidy from the German Land of Bavaria to the applicant, a textile company, was illegal was not challenged.[135] A new subsidy was authorised by a second Commission Decision on condition that the initial subsidy granted to the applicant be repaid. The applicant challenged the 1986 Decision, under a plea of illegality, claiming that its economic effects only became apparent following the second Decision. The General Court deemed this inadmissible, noting that, as the applicant could have challenged the first Decision using Article 263 TFEU, it was debarred now from bringing a challenge under Article 277 TFEU.[136]

7 NON-CONTRACTUAL LIABILITY

The final head of action under which Union measures can be reviewed is that of non-contractual liability. In such circumstances, the applicant will not merely be seeking annulment of the measure but also damages from the EU institution. This is governed by Article 340(2) TFEU.

> **Article 340(2) TFEU**
>
> In the case of non-contractual liability, the Union shall, in accordance with the general principles common to the laws of the Member States, make good any damage caused by its institutions or by its servants in the performance of their duties.

Although an equivalent Treaty provision has been present since the Treaty of Rome in the 1950s, the law on the non-contractual liability of EU institutions was reshaped by the *Brasserie du Pêcheur* judgment. This judgment, it will be remembered, set out the circumstances

---

[133] On the early debate surrounding this see G. Bebr, 'Judicial Remedy of Private Parties Against Normative Acts of the European Communities: The Role of the Exception of Illegality' (1966) 4 *CMLRev.* 7; A Barav, 'The Exception of Illegality in Community Law: A Critical Analysis' (1974) 11 *CMLRev.* 366.

[134] Case C-135/93 *Spain* v *Commission* [1995] ECR I-1651.

[135] Joined Cases T-244/93 and T-486/93 *TWD Textilwerke Deggendorf* v *Commission* [1995] ECR I-2265.

[136] This will also be the case where the possibility to make such a challenge still exists, Case T-15/11 *Sina Bank* v *Council*, Judgment of 11 December 2012.

when Member States could be liable for individual loss that arose from their failure to comply with EU law. Aware of the inconsistencies that might otherwise arise, the Court of Justice stated that the same criteria set out in that case delimiting Member State liability should also govern the liability of EU institutions under Article 340(2) TFEU.[137] To be sure, it has proved difficult for the Court to apply these parallels too formulaically but it has tried to reason from similar principles for both.

(i) Quality of the breach of EU law

The leading case is *Bergaderm*. A Commission Decision banned the use of a chemical, bergap-ten, in sun oil on the ground that it was carcinogenic. Bergaderm was the only company that produced sun oil using this chemical. Following the Decision, it went into liquidation. It sued the Commission, claiming that the latter had misinterpreted the scientific evidence. The application failed, but the Court of Justice set out new parameters for Article 340(2) TFEU.

Case C-352/98P *Laboratoires Pharmaceutiques Bergaderm v Commission* [2000] ECR I-5291

40. The system of rules which the Court has worked out with regard to [Article 340(2) TFEU] takes into account, inter alia, the complexity of the situations to be regulated, difficulties in the application or interpretation of the texts and, more particularly, the margin of discretion available to the author of the act in question...

41. The Court has stated that the conditions under which the State may incur liability for damage caused to individuals by a breach of Community law cannot, in the absence of particular justification, differ from those governing the liability of the Community in like circumstances. The protection of the rights which individuals derive from Community law cannot vary depending on whether a national authority or a Community authority is responsible for the damage...

42. As regards Member State liability for damage caused to individuals, the Court has held that Community law confers a right to reparation where three conditions are met: the rule of law infringed must be intended to confer rights on individuals; the breach must be sufficiently serious; and there must be a direct causal link between the breach of the obligation resting on the State and the damage sustained by the injured parties...

43. As to the second condition, as regards both Community liability under Article [288(2) – the predecessor to 340(2) TFEU] of the Treaty and Member State liability for breaches of Community law, the decisive test for finding that a breach of Community law is sufficiently serious is whether the Member State or the Community institution concerned manifestly and gravely disregarded the limits on its discretion...

44. Where the Member State or the institution in question has only considerably reduced, or even no, discretion, the mere infringement of Community law may be sufficient to establish the existence of a sufficiently serious breach...

46. In that regard, the Court finds that the general or individual nature of a measure taken by an institution is not a decisive criterion for identifying the limits of the discretion enjoyed by the institution in question.

---

[137] Joined Cases C-46/93 and C-48/93 *Brasserie du Pêcheur v Germany* [1996] ECR I-1029, paras. 42–5. On these criteria see pp. 329–32. See also T. Tridimas, 'Liability for Breach of Community Law: Growing Up and Mellowing Down?' (2001) 38 *CMLRev.* 301.

Three conditions must, thus, be met for the institution to incur liability (paragraph 42):

- the conduct of the EU institution must infringe a rule of law intended to confer rights on individuals;
- the breach of EU law must be sufficiently serious;
- there must be a direct causal link between the breach by the EU institution and the damage sustained by applicant.

Bergaderm sets out a spectrum of cases ranging from situations where EU institutions are faced with complex choices and enjoy considerable discretion, to scenarios where they have little or no discretion or the choices before them are straightforward. On the latter, it is sufficient that an EU law has been breached which grants rights for individuals. Breach of an instrument, such as the WTO Agreement which does not do this, will, thus, not lead to liability.[138] Beyond that, any breach of any EU legal obligation, be it substantive or procedural, will be sufficient.[139] A failure to exercise due diligence will also incur liability,[140] as will a failure to respect business secrets or confidentiality.[141]

The situation is different where EU institutions enjoy a measure of discretion or the measure is complex.[142] Not all breaches of EU law lead to liability. General principles of EU law, fundamental rights and the doctrine of misuse of powers have been held to be norms that will lead to liability.[143] The duty to give reasons, on the other hand, is not regarded as having that status, so a failure to give reasons cannot give rise to an action under Article 340(2) TFEU.[144] Similarly a failure of due diligence – be it in the form of an error of assessment, a failure to consider evidence that should have been considered – will not be sufficient to incur liability.[145] A simple breach of EU law by an EU institution will, furthermore, not be sufficient to incur liability. The breach must be sufficiently serious and that would involve the EU institution 'manifestly and gravely' exceeding the limits on its discretion (paragraph 43).

The meaning of this was addressed in most detail in *Schneider*. Schneider and Legrand were two companies specialising in electrical distribution and low voltage installations who merged into a single company. The Commission declared the merger illegal and ordered a break-up of the company. In 2002, the General Court found the Commission decision to be illegal on two grounds.[146] First, there were errors in its economic analysis of all the national markets other than the French market. Notwithstanding this, the General Court held that the competition effects on the French market were sufficient for the merger to be declared incompatible with the single market. Secondly, in its initial statement of objections, the Commission had failed to tell

---

[138] Joined Cases C-120/06 and C-121/06 *FIAMM* v *Council* [2008] ECR I-6513.

[139] Case T-351/03 *Schneider* v *Commission* [2007] ECR II-2237. The most extensive list of grounds can be found in Case T- 48/05 *Franchet and Byk* v *Commission* [2008] ECR II-1585.

[140] Case T-178/98 *Fresh Marine* v *Commission* [2000] ECR II-3331.

[141] Case T-88/09 *Idromacchine* v *Commission* [2011] ECR II-7833.

[142] Either complexity or discretion can lead to this more demanding threshold for liability, Case T-341/07 *Sison* v *Council* [2011] ECR II-7915.

[143] For a summary of the position, see Joined Cases T-481/93 and T-484/93 *Vereniging van Exporteurs in Levende Varkens* v *Commission* [1995] ECR II-2941.

[144] See e.g. Case C-76/01P *Eurocoton* v *Council* [2003] ECR I-10091, para. 98 and the case law cited therein.

[145] Case T-212/03 *MyTravel* v *Commission* [2008] ECR II-1967.

[146] Case T-310/01 *Schneider* v *Commission* [2002] ECR II-4071.

Schneider in sufficiently clear terms what measures it needed to take to avoid the merger being declared illegal. Schneider then sued under Article 340(2) TFEU.[147]

Case T-351/03 *Schneider* v *Commission* [2007] ECR II-2237

121. ...the Commission contends that, if it were to incur financial liability in circumstances such as those of this case, its capacity fully to function as a regulator of competition, a task entrusted to it by the EC Treaty, would be compromised as a result of the possible inhibiting effect that the risk of having to bear damages alleged by the undertakings concerned might have on the control of concentrations.

122. It must be conceded that such an effect, contrary to the general Community interest, might arise if the concept of a serious breach of Community law were construed as comprising all errors or mistakes which, even if of some gravity, are not by their nature or extent alien to the normal conduct of an institution entrusted with the task of overseeing the application of competition rules, which are complex, delicate and subject to a considerable degree of discretion.

123. Therefore, a sufficiently serious breach of Community law, for the purposes of establishing the non-contractual liability of the Community, cannot be constituted by failure to fulfil a legal obligation, which, regrettable though it may be, can be explained by the objective constraints to which the institution and its officials are subject as a result of the provisions governing the control of concentrations.

124. On the other hand, the right to compensation for damage resulting from the conduct of the institution becomes available where such conduct takes the form of action manifestly contrary to the rule of law and seriously detrimental to the interests of persons outside the institution and cannot be justified or accounted for by the particular constraint to which the staff of the institution, operating normally, is objectively subject.

125. Such a definition of the threshold for the establishment of non-contractual liability of the Community is conducive to protection of the room for manoeuvre and freedom of assessment which must, in the general interest, be enjoyed by the Community regulator of competition, both in its discretionary decisions and in its interpretation and application of the relevant provisions of primary and secondary Community law, without thereby leaving third parties to bear the consequences of flagrant and inexcusable misconduct...

129. In principle, the possibility cannot be ruled out that manifest and serious defects affecting the economic analysis underlying competition policy decisions may constitute sufficiently serious breaches of a rule of law to cause the Community to incur non-contractual liability.

130. However, for such a finding to be made it is first necessary to verify that the rule infringed by the incorrect analysis is intended to confer rights on individuals. Whilst certain principles and certain rules which must be observed in any competitive analysis are indeed rules intended to confer rights on individuals, not all norms, whether of primary or secondary law or deriving from case-law, which the Commission must observe in its economic assessments can be automatically held to be rules of that kind.

131. Next, it must be noted that the economic analyses necessary for the classification, under competition law, of a given situation or transaction are generally, as regards both the facts and the reasoning based on the account of the facts, complex and difficult intellectual formulas, which may inadvertently contain certain inadequacies, such as approximations, inconsistencies, or indeed certain omissions,

---

[147] The decision of the General Court on when this test for liability is met was upheld on appeal. Case C-440/07P *Commission* v *Schneider Electric* [2009] ECR I-6413.

in view of the time constraints to which the institution is subject. That is even more so where, as in the case of the control of concentrations, the analysis has a prospective element. The gravity of a documentary or logical inadequacy, in such circumstances, may not always constitute a sufficient circumstance to cause the Community to incur liability.

132. Last, it must be borne in mind that the Commission enjoys discretion in maintaining control over Community competition policy, which means that rigorously consistent and invariable practice in implementing the relevant rules cannot be expected of it, and, as a corollary, that it enjoys a degree of latitude regarding the choice of the econometric instruments available to it and the choice of the appropriate approach to the study of any matter (see, for example, regarding the definition of the relevant market…) provided that those choices are not manifestly contrary to the accepted rules of economic discipline and are applied consistently.

The Court of Justice could have used a risk-based test. This would have involved deciding, when there are conditions of uncertainty, whether EU institutions or private parties would be better equipped to bear responsibility for the costs of things going wrong. Misbehaviour by EU institutions would be irrelevant to this test. The Court has left open the possibility that such a test may be applied in the future, but, as yet, has only applied a fault-based test.[148] The institution is liable solely because of the egregiousness of its behaviour. The virtues of such a test are that it carries with it a duty of care on the part of EU institutions to those affected by their actions. This test is not, however, without its own challenges. With regard to substantive obligations, only the most flagrant violations of clear obligations or arbitrary conduct will incur liability: a very narrow fault test indeed. As regards matters of process, the situation is reversed, with relatively small failures to observe due process or rights of defence being likely to lead to liability. Incentives are provided, therefore, for EU institutions to focus on process in their activities at the expense of substance.

(ii) Presence of loss caused by the Union

The final condition for liability is the presence of a direct causal link between the breach of EU law and the loss. The range of loss that may be recovered is to be determined in line with national laws on non-contractual liability. It can include not merely financial compensation but also compensation in kind.[149] The principles are most clearly set out by Advocate General Capotorti in *Ireks-Arkady*:

the legal concept of 'damage' covers both a material loss *stricto senso*, that is to say, a reduction in the person's assets and also the loss of an increase in those assets which would have occurred if the harmful act had not taken place (these two alternatives are known respectively as *damnum emergens* and *lucrum cessans*)…The object of compensation is to

---

[148] Ambiguous language is therefore used in Case C-414/08P *Sviluppo Italia Basilicata v Commission* [2010] ECR I-2559, paras. 139–42. On this see K. Gutmann, 'The Evolution of the Action for Damages against the European Union and its Place in the System of Judicial Protection' (2011) 48 *CMLRev.* 695, 740–7.

[149] Case T-279/03 *Galileo International Technology and others v Commission* [2006] ECR II-1291; Case T-88/09 *Idromacchine v Commission* [2011] ECR II-7833.

restore the assets of the victim to the condition in which they would have been apart from the unlawful act, or at least to the condition closest to that which would have been produced if the unlawful act had not taken place: the hypothetical nature of that restoration often entails a certain degree of approximation.[150]

Recoverable losses can include any incidental loss, such as penalties the applicant had to pay as a result of having to repudiate a contract[151] or bank interest as a result of loans taken out to pay money wrongfully levied.[152] The Court has also been ready to award compensation for non-pecuniary loss such as anxiety, hurt feelings[153] and slurs on professional reputation.[154] The 'expectation interest' will also be protected. Compensation will be awarded for loss of profits.[155] Finally, interest can be recovered on the period between the date of the infringement and the date of judgment at a rate of 2 per cent above the ECB base rate.[156]

If the range of recoverable losses is considerable, two hurdles often prevent applicants securing reparation.

The first is the issue of joint or concurrent liability: situations where both an EU institution and a Member State may be liable.[157] This may arise where a national authority implements or administers an unlawful Union measure or where a decision is taken jointly by a Member State and an institution, such as in the field of external trade, where Member States are permitted to restrict imports of third country goods with the permission of the Commission.[158] The most equitable solution would be to establish a system of joint and several liability. The applicant could choose whom to sue, with unsuccessful defendants recovering contributions from each other afterwards. Such a scheme, however, has not been established in EU law. Instead, the Court presumes that parties should first exhaust remedies in domestic courts,[159] although the presumption is rebuttable where it would be impossible for an applicant to obtain a remedy in a national court.[160] This has resulted in unsatisfactory and needless complexity, requiring, in some instances, that applicants simultaneously commence actions in both the domestic courts and the Court of Justice.[161]

Secondly, the burden of proof is upon applicants to show a direct causal link between the loss and the illegal act.[162] The chain of causation can be severed by acts of third parties, such as those of a Member State.[163] It is, furthermore, insufficient to prove that the loss would not

---

[150] Case 238/78 *Ireks-Arkady* v *Council and Commission* [1979] ECR 2955, 2998–9.

[151] Case 74/74 *CNTA* v *Commission* [1975] ECR 533.

[152] Case T-167/94 *Nölle* v *Commission and Council* [1995] ECR II-2589.

[153] Case 110/63 *Willame* v *Commission* [1965] ECR 649.

[154] Case T-48/05 *Franchet and Byk* v *Commission* [2008] ECR I-1585.

[155] Joined Cases 56/74–60/74 *Kampffmeyer* v *Commission and Council* [1976] ECR 711; Joined Cases C-104/89 and C-37/90 *Mulder* v *Council and Commission* [1992] ECR I-3061.

[156] Case T-88/09 *Idromacchine* v *Commission* [2011] ECR II-7833.

[157] For detailed critique see A. Ward, *Judicial Review and the Rights of Private Parties in EU Law* (2nd edn, Oxford, Oxford University Press, 2007) 375–90.

[158] W. Wils, 'Concurrent Liability of the Community and a Member State' (1992) 17 *ELRev.* 191, 194–8.

[159] Case 96/71 *Haegeman* v *Commission* [1972] ECR 1005.

[160] Case 281/82 *Unifrex* v *Commission and Council* [1984] ECR 1969.

[161] Case T-167/94 *Nölle* v *Council and Commission* [1995] ECR II-2589.

[162] Case T-168/94 *Blackspur DIY* v *Council and Commission* [1995] ECR II-2627. On this see A. Toth, 'The Concepts of Damage and Causality as Elements of Non-Contractual Liability' in H. Schermers *et al.* (eds.), *Non-Contractual Liability of the European Communities* (Dordrecht, Martijnus Nijhoff, 1988).

[163] Case 132/77 *Société pour l'Exportation des Sucres SA* v *Commission* [1978] ECR 1061.

have occurred but for the illegal act.[164] There must be sufficient proximity between the illegal act and the loss suffered.[165] In practice, this has made it very difficult for applicants to claim for loss of profits as these will often be too remote or speculative, with the Court of Justice only compensating loss that is actual and certain,[166] with hypothetical or indeterminate damage irrecoverable.[167] Even where a causal link is established, the applicant might still not recover full compensation. This may be, first, as a result of the doctrine of contributory negligence, where the applicant is considered to have contributed to the damage as a result of a failure to take due care.[168] Secondly, the applicant is under a duty to mitigate any loss suffered. A failure to do so will result in compensation being reduced.[169] Finally, compensation will be reduced if there is evidence that the applicant has, or could have, passed the loss on to somebody else.[170]

8 CONSEQUENCES OF ANNULMENT

The consequences of a finding of illegality are set out in Article 264 TFEU.

Article 264 TFEU

If the action is well founded, the Court of Justice shall declare the act concerned to be void.

In the case of a regulation, however, the Court of Justice shall, if it considers this necessary, state which of the effects of the regulation which it has declared void shall be considered as definitive.

A finding of invalidity can be made not just on the basis of Article 263 TFEU and under the plea of illegality, but also under a claim brought for damages.[171] This finding has *erga omnes* effects, binding all national courts in the EU.[172] In *BASF*, the Court of Justice ruled that 'acts of the [Union] institutions are in principle presumed to be lawful and accordingly produce legal effects, even if they are tainted by irregularities, until such time as they are annulled or withdrawn'.[173] The Court went on to add the following rider:

> by way of exception to that principle, acts tainted by an irregularity whose gravity is so obvious that it cannot be tolerated by the [Union] legal order must be treated as having no legal effect, even provisional, that is to say that they must be regarded as legally non-existent. The purpose of this exception is to maintain a balance between two fundamental, but sometimes conflicting, requirements with which a legal order must comply, namely stability of legal relations and respect for legality.[174]

---

[164] Case T-478/93 *Wafer Zoo* v *Commission* [1995] ECR II-1479.
[165] Joined Cases 64/76, 113/76, 167/78, 239/78, 27/79, 28/79, 45/79 *Dumortier Frères* v *Council* [1979] ECR 3091.
[166] Joined Cases T-3/00 and T-337/04 *Pitsiorlas* v *Council and ECB* [2007] ECR I-4779.
[167] Case T-436/09 *Dufour* v *ECB* [2011] ECR II-7727.
[168] Case 145/83 *Adams* v *Commission* [1985] ECR 3539.
[169] Joined Cases C-104/89 and C-37/90 *Mulder* v *Council and Commission* [1992] ECR I-3061.
[170] Case 238/78 *Ireks-Arkady* v *Council and Commission* [1979] ECR 2955.
[171] Joined Cases 5/66, 7/66, 13–24/66 *Kampfmeyer* v *Commission* [1967] ECR 245.
[172] Case 66/80 *International Chemical Corporation* v *Amministrazione delle Finanze* [1981] ECR 1191.
[173] See Case C-137/92P *Commission* v *BASF* [1994] ECR I-2555.
[174] *Ibid.* para. 49.

In principle, therefore, in the absence of such irregularities, parties are bound by Union measures until a finding of invalidity. Whilst a ruling under Article 264(1) TFEU has the effect of releasing all parties from any obligation to which they might otherwise have been subject under the measure, considerable discretion is given to the Court of Justice by Article 264(2) TFEU to determine the effects of a ruling. Accordingly, the Court may declare that only part of a measure is void, maintaining in place other aspects. Temporal limitations may also be placed upon an annulment, meaning that the legislation will remain in force until new legislation is passed to replace it.[175]

FURTHER READING

A. Albors Llorens, 'Remedies Against the EU Institutions after Lisbon: An Era of Opportunity?' (2012) 71 *Cambridge Law Journal* 507

A. Arnull, 'Private Applicants and the Action for Annulment since Codorníu' (2001) 38 *Common Market Law Review* 7

P. Craig, *EU Administrative Law* (2nd edn, Oxford, Oxford University Press, 2012) chs. 17, 18 and 22

A. Fritzsche, 'Discretion, Scope of Judicial Balance and Institutional Review in European Law' (2010) 47 *Common Market Law Review* 361

K. Gutmann, 'The Evolution of the Action for Damages Against the European Union and its Place in the System of Judicial Protection' (2011) 48 *Common Market Law Review* 695

H. Hoffmann, G. Rowe and A. Türk, *Administrative Law and Policy of the European Union* (Oxford, Oxford University Press, 2011) chs. 7, 18 and 25

J. Mendes, *Participation in EU Rule-Making: A Rights-Based Approach* (Oxford, Oxford University Press, 2011)

T. Tridimas, *The General Principles of EU Law* (2nd edn, Oxford, Oxford University Press, 2006)

A. Türk, 'Oversight of Administrative Rulemaking: Judicial Review' (2013) 19 *European Law Journal* 126

M. Vogt, 'Indirect Judicial Protection in EC Law: The Case of the Plea of Illegality' (2006) 31 *European Law Review* 364

A. Ward, *Judicial Review and the Rights of Private Parties in EU Law* (2nd edn, Oxford, Oxford University Press, 2007) chs. 6 and 8

---

[175] See e.g. Case C-392/95 *Parliament v Council* [1997] ECR I-3213.

11

Citizenship of the Union

CONTENTS

1 INTRODUCTION

This chapter considers the ideas and rights associated with European Union citizenship. This is granted by the Treaty to all those who are citizens of one of the Member States of the European Union. The chapter is organised as follows.

Sections 2 and 3 discuss ideas of citizenship.

(a) Modern citizenship evolved in the period of the industrial revolution, following the American and French revolutions. Society became less feudal and more democratic and individuals acquired more rights and possibilities. The core elements of the resulting notion of citizenship were legally enforceable rights, loyalty, a sense of belonging to the national community and participation in political decision-making.

(b) One view of European Union citizenship is that it follows this tradition. On this view, citizenship is a limited success. Rights are primarily for those who migrate and who are economically active or independent. The sense of a community of Europeans is but a pale shadow of that found in nation-states and citizens do not have political rights to participate in some of the most important elections.

(c) Others would like to see Union citizenship break with nationality and include all those living within the European Union, even if they have the nationality of a non-EU state. This would make Union citizenship more open, accessible and a true challenge to nationalism, arguably in the original spirit of the Union.

(d) An alternative view of Union citizenship is that its value is not as a free-standing institution at all, but as a mechanism for changing what national citizenship means. It works to transform national societies, requiring them to redefine and reconstitute their own structures of membership, and it should be judged against this measure.

Section 4 considers the right of Union citizens to move and reside throughout the Union.

(a) This right is found in Articles 20 and 21 TFEU. It is complemented by Article 18 TFEU, the prohibition on nationality discrimination. The rights in these Articles are expressed in more detail in Directive 2004/38/EC (Citizenship Directive).

(b) The right to free movement and residence is subject to conditions: citizens must either be economically active, or they must be economically independent of the state in which they live. Those who are not economically active must also show that they have sickness insurance covering their costs in the host state, which may be difficult for some to obtain. This exclusion of the disadvantaged from migration rights inspires the criticism that Union citizenship is still a quasi-economic policy as opposed to a proper constitutional citizenship embodying solidarity, equality and universality.

(c) Lawfully present migrant citizens and their families enjoy a right to equal treatment with nationals in their host state. A particularly sensitive issue concerns equal access to public benefits and support. Member States sometimes make these conditional upon a period of prior residence, or some degree of integration into society. Such requirements can come close to nationality discrimination, but the Court of Justice finds that they are acceptable if they are justified and proportionate in the particular circumstances.

(d) As a corollary of their own free movement rights, Union citizens who migrate may bring their family to live with them, even if these family members are not Union citizens. The Court of Justice has extended this right to citizens returning home with family members from a period living in another Member State, and even, where the citizen is sufficiently dependent that their own residence in the EU requires the presence of family members, to citizens who have never migrated at all.[1]

(e) Union citizens and their family members can only be excluded from a Member State under very serious circumstances. Mere criminality is not enough. They must represent a current and serious threat to one of the fundamental interests of society. In general, if a migrant citizen misbehaves, the host state should punish or prosecute him just as they would their own citizens. Expulsion is the exception.

Section 5 concerns the political rights of citizens. The most important of these is that Union citizens may vote for the European Parliament in whichever state they live and may vote in

---

[1] Case C-34/09 *Gerardo Ruiz Zambrano* v *ONEm* [2011] ECR I-1177.

local elections in the state where they live. However, if they are in a host state EU law gives them no right to vote in national elections.

2 EVOLUTION OF MODERN CITIZENSHIP

Contemporary national citizenship is the product of modernity. Economic, social and political change in the eighteenth and nineteenth centuries transformed the state, the national community and the position of the individual in that community.[2]

R. Bellamy, 'Introduction: The Making of Modern Citizenship' in R. Bellamy et al. (eds.), *Lineages of European Citizenship: Rights, Belonging and Participation in Eleven Nation States* (Basingstoke, Palgrave Macmillan, 2004) 1, 6–7

[The American and French Revolutions] provided the basis for a distinctly modern conception of citizenship. First, it gave rise to the new political context of the nation-state. Rather than being the fiefdoms of monarchs, these new political units found legitimacy through being the territorial expression of a given culture and people. The political apparatus no longer referred simply to the administration of the monarch's domain and subjects, but likewise had a popular justification. Second, this development was linked in its turn to the emergence of commercial and increasingly industrial market economies. These required regular forms of government and justice that, in various ways facilitated the free movement and exchange of goods, capital, labour and services. Thus, states had to uphold the rule of law, particularly freedom of contract and the protection of property rights. Nation-building and a state education system that promoted a common language and guaranteed standards of numeracy and literacy helped create a mobile workforce capable of acquiring the generic skills needed for industry. Nation-states could also provide the infrastructural public goods required by market economies, such as a unified transport system, a single currency and a standardized system of weights and measures. Third, markets broke down traditional social hierarchies and systems of ascribed status, thereby fostering equality of opportunity. This feature was also associated with demands for equal political as well as legal rights by hitherto politically excluded sections of the nation. The national people gradually transformed into a demos, who sought to ensure that the state governed in their interest.

   These three interrelated developments associated with the rise of national industrial states promoted the three key components of modern citizenship. First, they fostered an emphasis on individual rights. Lack of ascribed status led individuals to being treated as equals possessing certain rights simply by virtue of their humanity – including the right to be treated equally before the law. Their involvement as actors in markets also gave them equal rights to pursue their interests by buying and selling goods, services and labour. Meanwhile, they looked to the state to provide social and economic rights, as part of its regulatory function and demanded political rights to secure equal access and recognition within its policies, decision-making and organizational structures. Second, citizenship became closely associated with belonging to the national community. National identity shaped a common civic

[2] On the broader evolution of the term 'citizenship', see R. Bendix, *Nation-Building and Citizenship* (New York, Wiley, 1964); W. Brubaker, *Citizenship and Nationhood in France and Germany* (Cambridge, MA, Harvard University Press, 1992); P. Riesenberg, *Citizenship in the Western Tradition: Plato to Rousseau* (Chapel Hill, NC, University of North Carolina Press, 1992).

consciousness and allegiance to the state and one's fellow citizens. It encouraged reciprocity and solidarity in both politics and economics. National systems of education created a public political language and inducted citizens into a certain civic culture and set of values. Third, as a mark of citizenship was the capacity and right to participate as a full and equal member within the economy and the polity, the right to vote was often obligatory and in any case tied to the payment of taxes, military service, and the undertaking of such public duties as sitting on juries. Similarly, social and economic rights were linked to the duty and ability to work and to contribute to national schemes of social insurance. Those deemed socially irresponsible, a label that at various times and places has been applied to lunatics, children, criminals, women, the propertyless and the indigent, either forfeited or were ineligible for most citizenship rights.

As the state was transformed from a personal fiefdom into a rational and efficient socio-economic machine, the subject was transformed into a citizen. The marks of this citizenship were rights, a sense of belonging and political participation. All three enhanced the position of the individual, protecting them from arbitrariness and extending their influence over the society around them. Yet, they also served the national interest, helping to create a cohesive and loyal population, better able to work and live together and act responsibly. Citizenship was part of a pragmatic and multifaceted social contract.

The specific content of citizenship has varied from state to state and over time. The Cambridge historian T. H. Marshall observed that the growth of the welfare state and its importance in contemporary understandings of justice following the Second World War led to a greater emphasis on social rights, as increasingly it was felt that equal membership of the political community entailed a right to participate in the wealth and welfare provided by that community.[3] More recently, the sociologist Bryn Turner has observed that politics has concerned itself with the protection of the individual against risk.[4] These risks might be environmental risks, such as that posed by floods or pollution, uncertainty generated by terrorism, or risks associated with financial markets, such as losing one's savings or pension. In such a world, he has argued, equal membership within a political community entails equal protection against risk. He speaks of the emergence of a new citizenship right, a 'right to security', which would give all citizens minimum assurances against certain types of risks.

Another event to transform understandings of citizenship was the migration into Western Europe since the Second World War. From being less than or around 1 per cent in most Western European states in 1960, the foreign population grew, by 1990, to between 3 and 9 per cent of the general population.[5] An important feature of this foreign population is its permanence. Many migrants who came to Europe did not return to their home states, something for which the states hosting them were ill-prepared.

---

[3] This division was first made, most famously, in T. Marshall, *Citizenship and Social Class* (T. Bottomore (ed.), London, Pluto, 1992). This model was first applied to the European Union in J. Shaw, 'The Interpretation of Union Citizenship' (1998) 61 *MLR* 293.

[4] B. Turner, 'The Erosion of Citizenship' (2001) 52 *British Journal of Sociology* 189.

[5] Y. Soysal, *Limits of Citizenship: Migrants and Postnational Membership in Europe* (Chicago, IL, University of Chicago Press, 1994) 23. These figures do not include migrants who subsequently became naturalised and thereby citizens of the nation-states in which they were resident.

This non-native population challenged the existing notion of citizenship. Although Shaw has argued that the decoupling of rights and identity is an important post-war phenomenon, as long as citizenship remained a significant vehicle for rights its link to nationality was problematic.[6] This tie turned citizenship into an exclusionary device. When citizens are just a sub-set of those living and participating in the nation, then citizenship takes on a less universalistic and idealistic flavour and tribal and ethnic undertones emerge. Is it about recognition of the dignity and rights of the individual or about closure against the outsider?

Scholars have sought to resolve the resulting tensions in different ways, with many arguing that citizenship should become more open. This can either occur by making nationality more accessible (it has traditionally been very hard to acquire the nationality of some EU Member States, even after decades of residence), or by decoupling citizenship from nationality. Balibar is the leading proponent of a citizenship based on factual presence rather than the accident of birth, although he is more concerned to expose the contradictions of national citizenship – to deconstruct it – than to lobby for concrete change.[7] His view of citizenship seems less exclusionary, as it opens up membership of a community to anyone who chooses to participate and to all those who do participate. Yet concerns have been raised that mere practical participation may not suffice to generate commitment of citizens to each other and to society, without which shared projects may not be achievable.[8] Participation may also not provide a shared identity, without which the community may not be a satisfying or enriching context for individuals to live in. This commitment and identity may be more likely to materialise in communities of fate – those where membership is not a choice, but is ascribed on the basis of factors outside individual control such as family origin or place of birth.[9] Commitment to such communities is arguably more profound because the individual enjoys unconditional membership. This also gives the community a certain tolerance, as people of opposing political views can seek to impose their own interpretation of the community without calling membership as such into question. An identity is maintained despite such political diversity through the use of myths and symbols, such as those surrounding the nation-state.

Habermas is the best known of those who seek a middle way between these extremes. He has suggested that a commitment to the values of a community, such as democracy and human rights, should be a condition for citizenship. This requirement, combined with participatory political practices, would offer a foundation for a citizenship lying between the mystical and closed, but tough, community of fate and the possibly shallow and unstable community of participation.[10] His view of citizenship has been particularly prominent in the debate on Union citizenship and he places his arguments in the context of Europe.

---

[6] J. Shaw, *Citizenship of the Union: Towards Post-national Membership?*, Jean Monnet Working Paper 97/6, available at www.jeanmonnetprogram.org/archive/papers/97/97-06-.html.

[7] E. Balibar, *We the Peoples of Europe: Reflections on Transnational Citizenship* (Princeton, NJ, Princeton University Press, 2004). See also D. Schnapper, 'The European Debate on Citizenship' (1997) 126 *Daedalus* 199; L. Bosniak, 'Citizenship Denationalised' (2000) 7 *Indiana Journal of Global Law Studies* 447.

[8] D. Miller, *Citizenship and National Identity* (Oxford, Polity, 2000) ch. 2. See also R. Bellamy, 'Evaluating Union Citizenship: Belonging, Rights and Participation within the EU' (2008) 12 *Citizenship Studies* 597.

[9] *Ibid.*

[10] J. Habermas, 'Citizenship and National Identity: Some Reflections on the Future of Europe' (1992) 12 *Praxis International* 1. See also the thinking of Hannah Arendt on citizenship, presented in P. Hansen, *Hannah Arendt: Politics, History and Citizenship* (Stanford, CA, Stanford University Press, 1993).

Like many other contemporary and recent scholars, Habermas is trying to reconcile closure with humanity. As Bosniak puts it, citizenship is inherently about membership and can never be fully open; a 'purely inclusionary inside' is a fantasy.[11] The task, in their view, is not to eliminate the bounded community, but to keep trying to make it more decent and fair. This is, rather like Kostakopoulou suggests in the next section, citizenship at least partly as process.

3 NATURE OF UNION CITIZENSHIP

There was no mention of citizenship in the initial EC Treaty. Indeed, there was no discussion of the term until the 1970s. First use of the term was made in the Tindemans Report in 1975, which contained a chapter entitled 'Towards a Europe for Citizens'. The thrust of this was a number of proposals aimed at integrating Member State nationals resident in other Member States more fully into their host states. It was, therefore, proposed that they should be given a bundle of civil, political and social rights, which would place them on an equal footing with that state's own nationals. Throughout the 1970s and 1980s, the Commission and Parliament brought forward a series of proposals to try and flesh out and implement the ideas in this Report, but to little avail.[12] The breakthrough moment was the Intergovernmental Conference on Political Union that preceded the adoption of the Treaty on European Union at Maastricht. In September 1990, the Spanish Government submitted a proposal entitled 'The Road to European Citizenship'. The Spanish Government indicated in this paper that the move to political and economic union meant that it was no longer sufficient for EU nationals to be treated as 'privileged aliens' in other Member States. A European Union citizenship should be established. This was defined as:

> The personal and indivisible status of nationals of the Member States, whose membership of the Union means that they have special rights and duties that are specific to the nature of the Union and are exercised and safeguarded specifically within its boundaries.[13]

This proposal attracted support from both the Commission and the Parliament and from a number of Member States. The resulting citizenship provisions are now found in Part 2 of the TFEU. The rights of citizens are stated in full detail in Articles 21–4 of this Part. However, Article 20 is the central article. It establishes citizenship of the Union and summarises the associated rights.

Article 20 TFEU

1. Citizenship of the Union is hereby established. Every person holding the nationality of a Member State shall be a citizen of the Union. Citizenship of the Union shall be additional to and not replace national citizenship.

[11] L. Bosniak, *The Citizen and the Alien* (Princeton, NJ, Princeton University Press, 2006) 139.
[12] On the history of European Union citizenship, see A. Wiener, *'European' Citizenship Practice: Building Institutions of a Non-state* (Boulder, CO, Westview, 1998); S. O'Leary, *The Evolving Concept of Community Citizenship: From the Free Movement of Persons to Union Citizenship* (The Hague, Kluwer, 1996) 18–30.
[13] C. Dc SN/3940, 24 September 1990 in F. Laursen and S. van Hoonacker (eds.), *The Intergovernmental Conference on Political Union: Institutional Reforms, New Policies and International Identity of the European Community* (Dordrecht, Martinus Nijhoff, 1992).

2. Citizens of the Union shall enjoy the rights and be subject to the duties provided for in the Treaties. They shall have, inter alia:

   (a) the right to move and reside freely within the territory of the Member States;

   (b) the right to vote and to stand as candidates in elections to the European Parliament and in municipal election in their Member State of residence, under the same conditions as nationals of that State;

   (c) the right to enjoy, in the territory of a third country in which the Member State of which they are nationals is not represented, the protection of the diplomatic and consular authorities of any Member State on the same conditions as the nationals of that State;

   (d) the right to petition the European Parliament, to apply to the European Ombudsman, and to address the institutions and advisory bodies of the Union in any of the Treaty languages and to obtain a reply in the same language.

   These rights shall be exercised in accordance with the conditions and limits defined by the Treaties and by the measures adopted hereunder.

Article 20(1) TFEU ties Union citizenship to national citizenship. A person is a citizen of the Union if and only if she is a citizen of a Member State. The idea of replacing national citizenship is explicitly rejected. This has conceptual and practical consequences. Martiniello has said of Union citizenship:

> It stimulates a European political identity which is largely linked to a prior communitarian belonging: one can be a European citizen only if one is previously a French, a Belgian or a German citizen, for example. In its present shape, the citizenship of the European Union is thus a complementary set of rights which confirms the existence of the cultural and political identities corresponding to the Member States.[14]

On the one hand, Article 20(1) gives Member States the power to control access to Union citizenship, since it is they who determine who is a national citizen. However, as ever where national measures may influence EU rights, this link cuts both ways, and means that national citizenship laws may be subject to EU law constraints. Mr Rottmann was initially an Austrian citizen who gave up this citizenship to become a German. When the German authorities later discovered that he had fraudulently concealed information about an Austrian criminal prosecution on his application for German nationality they revoked his German citizenship retroactively. This meant that under German law Mr Rottmann would not be, nor ever have been, a German. However, this would leave him stateless, and also deprive him of Union citizenship, reason enough for the German court to refer a question to the Court of Justice.

Case C–135/08 *Janko Rottmann* v *Freistaat Bayern* [2010] ECR I–1449

39. It is to be borne in mind here that, according to established case-law, it is for each Member State, having due regard to Community law, to lay down the conditions for the acquisition and loss of nationality.

[14] M. Martiniello, 'The Development of European Union Citizenship' in M. Roche and R. van Berkel (eds.), *European Citizenship and Social Exclusion* (Aldershot, Ashgate, 1998) 35, 37–8.

[The Court then refers to declaration 2, annexed to the TEU, which provides that 'the question whether an individual possesses the nationality of a Member State shall be settled solely by reference to the national law of the Member State concerned'.]

41. Nevertheless, the fact that a matter falls within the competence of the Member States does not alter the fact that, in situations covered by European Union law, the national rules concerned must have due regard to the latter.

42. It is clear that the situation of a citizen of the Union who, like the applicant in the main proceedings, is faced with a decision withdrawing his naturalisation, adopted by the authorities of one Member State, and placing him, after he has lost the nationality of another Member State that he originally possessed, in a position capable of causing him to lose the status conferred by Article [20 TFEU] and the rights attaching thereto falls, by reason of its nature and its consequences, within the ambit of European Union law.

43. As the Court has several times stated, citizenship of the Union is intended to be the fundamental status of nationals of the Member States....

48. The proviso that due regard must be had to European Union law does not compromise the principle of international law previously recognised by the Court, and mentioned in paragraph 39 above, that the Member States have the power to lay down the conditions for the acquisition and loss of nationality, but rather enshrines the principle that, in respect of citizens of the Union, the exercise of that power, in so far as it affects the rights conferred and protected by the legal order of the Union, as is in particular the case of a decision withdrawing naturalisation such as that at issue in the main proceedings, is amenable to judicial review carried out in the light of European Union law.

49. Unlike the applicant in the case giving rise to the judgment in *Kaur* who, not meeting the definition of a national of the United Kingdom of Great Britain and Northern Ireland, could not be deprived of the rights deriving from the status of citizen of the Union, Dr Rottmann has unquestionably held Austrian and then German nationality and has, in consequence, enjoyed that status and the rights attaching thereto.

50. Nevertheless, as several of the governments having submitted observations to the Court have argued, if a decision withdrawing naturalisation such as that at issue in the main proceedings is based on the deception practised by the person concerned in connection with the procedure for acquisition of the nationality in question, such a decision could be compatible with European Union law.

51. A decision withdrawing naturalisation because of deception corresponds to a reason relating to the public interest. In this regard, it is legitimate for a Member State to wish to protect the special relationship of solidarity and good faith between it and its nationals and also the reciprocity of rights and duties, which form the bedrock of the bond of nationality....

55. In such a case, it is, however, for the national court to ascertain whether the withdrawal decision at issue in the main proceedings observes the principle of proportionality so far as concerns the consequences it entails for the situation of the person concerned in the light of European Union law, in addition, where appropriate, to examination of the proportionality of the decision in the light of national law.

56. Having regard to the importance which primary law attaches to the status of citizen of the Union, when examining a decision withdrawing naturalisation it is necessary, therefore, to take into account the consequences that the decision entails for the person concerned and, if relevant, for the members of his family with regard to the loss of the rights enjoyed by every citizen of the Union. In this respect it is necessary to establish, in particular, whether that loss is justified in relation to the gravity of the offence committed by that person, to the lapse of time between the

naturalisation decision and the withdrawal decision and to whether it is possible for that person to recover his original nationality....

59. Having regard to the foregoing, the answer to the first question and to the first part of the second question must be that it is not contrary to European Union law, in particular to Article [20 TFEU], for a Member State to withdraw from a citizen of the Union the nationality of that State acquired by naturalisation when that nationality has been obtained by deception, on condition that the decision to withdraw observes the principle of proportionality.

The substantive rule, formulated in the later paragraphs, appears to be that any decision resulting in the loss of Union citizenship must be proportionate, in the sense of representing a fair balance of interests. By contrast, where a person has never been a Union citizen the Court suggests, by reference to *Kaur* (which concerned an application for British citizenship by someone who was not already a Union citizen), that EU law will not necessarily apply.

This distinction is more troublesome than may appear. Where a person obtains the nationality of a state this is sometimes conditional upon good behaviour for a certain number of years, and if crimes are committed nationality is often revoked with retroactive effect, so that as a matter of national law that person has never in fact been a citizen. Would this be like *Kaur* or like *Rottmann*? It is suggested that once a state recognises a person as a national, and therefore a Union citizen, any decision to stop doing so is likely to be treated as subject to EU law.

First, this is arguably the more principled approach: it is not the fact that Union citizenship rights have already been vested that should engage EU law, but the fact that their scope is affected. This is equally true of a refusal to grant citizenship and a later removal of it. Secondly, there is some acknowledgment of this in the judgment. It is notable that in paragraph 48 the Court suggests that 'the conditions for the acquisition and loss of nationality' are subject to EU law wherever they affect EU law rights – not just the loss. The Court also refers to Mr Rottmann having been 'unquestionably' German, even though this nationality had already been retroactively withdrawn.[15] Thirdly, and most forcefully, an over-reliance on the nuances of national administrative law would result in arbitrary differences between the extent of application of *Rottmann* in different Member States, according to whether they denaturalised retrospectively or not, and would offer Member States an easy path to avoid its substantive application.[16]

Rottmann therefore opens the door to a reversal of the traditional relationship between nationality and Union citizenship. Prior to the case it was conventional to refer to Union citizenship as derivative or dependent, and to emphasise the gate-keeping role of Member States. Now it seems that tying Union citizenship to national citizenship was not just an act of legal dependency, but also one of legal colonialism, allowing the Court of Justice to engage and supervise yet another field of national law.[17]

Its hard-wiring to national citizenship has meant that Union citizenship sometimes seems to lack substance. It has not escaped the nation-state to become a truly new, open and voluntary

---

[15] He had, however, been Austrian before, so his prior Union citizenship was incontestable.

[16] See Case C-369/90 *Micheletti* v *Delegación del Gobierno Cantabria* [1992] ECR I-4239.

[17] G. Davies and K. Rostek, 'The Impact of Union Citizenship on National Citizenship Policies' (2006) 10 *European Integration Online Papers* no. 5; D. Kochenov, *Rounding up the Circle: The Mutation of Member States' Nationalities under Pressure from EU Citizenship*, EUI RSCAS Working Paper 2010/23.

form of community, for example by including all residents of Europe, as Kochenov has argued it should.[18] Yet sticking close to nationality has not given it richness: by the standards of traditional modern citizenship it offers a weak and shallow identity and it has inspired nothing close to the loyalty or sense of belonging that attach to nation-states.

Kostakopoulou has argued that this is an incomplete analysis of what Union citizenship is and what it does. It should not be judged solely on its contents, but also on its effects. She argues that the value of Union citizenship is partly that it transforms national communities. These are vulnerable to insularity, but the imposition of Union citizenship on top of its national counterparts inserts a globalising element into the nation. That fact that to be French is also to be a Union citizen changes what it means to be French, and that change is in the direction of the more open and cosmopolitan perspective that is necessary for states to thrive in the contemporary world. Thus, Union citizenship is not to be understood as a free-standing entity, but as something that penetrates national citizenship and changes it.[19]

D. Kostakopoulou, 'European Union Citizenship: Writing the Future' (2007) 13(5) *European Law Journal* 623

But the reduction of European citizenship to a transnational citizenship downplays both the resourcefulness of Union citizenship and the supranational character of EU law…Above all, it conceals the extent to which European citizenship penetrates and subverts national citizenship, thereby triggering off tensions, institutional displacement and the incremental transformation of domestic structures and practices in ways that had not been anticipated…

I would suggest that the novelty, and in many respects the challenge, of the European citizenship design does not lie simply in the emergence of 'nested' citizenships (supranational, national, subnational citizenships) and institutional pluralism. More significant is the interaction between 'old' (national) and 'new' (European) citizenships and the ensuing process of incremental, transformative change. European legal and political dynamics subvert the fundamental premises of the nationality model of citizenship and change the organisational logic and practices of national citizenship.

This transformative view of Union citizenship resonates upon reading the case law. A recurring theme in this chapter is the way in which the institution of Union citizenship requires Member States to redefine and reconstitute their own structures of membership.

4 RIGHT TO MOVE AND RESIDE WITHIN THE UNION

The most useful right for Union citizens, and the one demanding most adaptation from national authorities, is the right to move and reside throughout the Union. This right is conceptually very similar to the free movement rights relating to goods, economically active persons, services and capital, discussed in later chapters in this book.[20] Many of the abstract themes, such as the notions of discrimination, of the proportionality of national measures and of

---

[18] D. Kochenov, 'Ius Tractum of Many Faces: European Citizenship and the Difficult Relationship between Status and Rights' (2009) 15(2) *Columbia Journal of European Law* 169.

[19] Bellamy, n. 8 above; P. Magnette, 'How Can One be European? Reflections on the Pillars of European Civic Identity' (2007) 13(5) *European Law Journal* 664.

[20] See Chapters 15–20.

wholly internal situations, will recur in those chapters, which provide a useful complement to this one. However, the citizenship right also has its own nuances. The constitutional tone of citizenship, and the fact that citizens are not just factors of production, but human beings, with correspondingly broad needs and concerns, has generated a diverse and purposive body of law that is increasingly self-contained.

This right to move and reside within the Union is first stated in Article 20(2)(a) TFEU and then repeated in Article 21.

Article 21(1) TFEU

1. Every citizen of the Union shall have the right to move and reside freely within the territory of the Member States, subject to the limitations and conditions laid down in the Treaties and by the measures adopted to give them effect.

This is elaborated in the Citizenship Directive.[21] This Directive consolidates previous Directives applying to different categories of persons and now provides the framework for almost all legal issues concerning the free movement of persons. It sets out the rights of citizens to move and reside in other Member States, bring their families to live with them and participate in socio-economic life without experiencing discrimination.

Its provisions on movement and residence fall naturally into three categories.

(1) *Right to movement and short-term residence*: Articles 4 to 6 of the Directive provide that citizens may move throughout the territory of the Union and live in any state for up to three months, without any formalities other than the possession of a valid identity card or passport.

The only condition imposed is that the citizen not be an unreasonable burden on the social assistance system of the host state.[22] This is probably of limited impact, since the Directive provides later that migrants in this first period of residence have no right to social assistance anyway.[23] It is therefore unlikely that they will be an unreasonable burden. Citizens who are employed or self-employed, or looking for work and able to show that they have a genuine chance of finding it, may in any case not be expelled.[24] They are effectively exempted from the 'unreasonable burden' condition.[25]

(2) *Residence in another Member State for periods of more than three months*: For periods greater than three months, the conditions are more restrictive.

Citizenship Directive, article 7(1)

1. All Union citizens shall have the right of residence on the territory of another Member State for a period of longer than three months if they:
   (a) are workers or self-employed persons in the host Member State; or
   (b) have sufficient resources for themselves and their family members not to become a burden on the social assistance system of the host Member State during their period of residence and have comprehensive sickness insurance cover in the host Member State;

---

[21] Directive 2004/38/EC on the right of citizens of the Union and their family members to move and reside freely within the territory of the Member States [2004] OJ L158/77 ('Citizenship Directive').
[22] *Ibid.* article 14(1).   [23] *Ibid.* article 24(2).   [24] *Ibid.* article 14(4).   [25] *Ibid.* article 14(4).

(c) are enrolled at a private or public establishment, accredited or financed by the host Member State on the basis of its legislation or administrative practice, for the principal purpose of following a course of study, including vocational training; and have comprehensive sickness insurance cover in the host Member State and assure the relevant national authority, by means of a declaration or by such equivalent means as they may choose, that they have sufficient resources for themselves and their family members not to become a burden on the social assistance system of the host Member State during their period of residence.

To fall into the first category, the citizen must be employed or self-employed within the definitions in the Court of Justice's case law on Articles 45 and 49 TFEU, respectively.[26] They can retain this status and its associated residence rights if they subsequently cease to fulfil these definitions. The general position is that the person who loses their job involuntarily, is temporarily unable to work because of ill health, or makes a choice to stop working in order to do further training, continues to enjoy the status of worker or self-employed person for the purposes of residence.[27]

(3) *Permanent residence*: Citizens who have resided legally in another Member State for five years acquire the right of permanent residence.[28] This brings certain benefits, notably exemption from conditions concerning sufficient resources.[29] Once acquired, the status is only lost after two consecutive years of absence.[30]

The requirement to reside 'legally' is satisfied when the residence complies with the substantive conditions of article 7(1).[31] The possession of a residence document is entirely irrelevant,[32] as is even whether the person was a Union citizen for the entire period – some cases have involved citizens of the Eastern Member States who successfully argued that residence in another Member State prior to the accession of their own Member State should still count towards the five years.[33] Several Member States argued that the residence prior accession had been clearly outside the scope of EU law, and so to take account of it was giving a form of retroactive effect to the Citizenship Directive. The Court of Justice rejected this with the slightly cryptic statement that 'the Court has held that the provisions on citizenship of the European Union are applicable as soon as they enter into force and must therefore be applied to the present effects of situations arising previously'.[34] Permanent resident status cannot be acquired prior to accession, but integration into the host society may occur, and can then be recognised as soon as the migrant becomes a Union citizen.

On the other hand, residence that was lawful under national law, but not in compliance with the Directive's conditions, will not count, and if occurring after permanent residence is acquired, for more than two years, could even undermine it.[35] Permanent residence is a reward

---

[26] See Chapter 19.   [27] Citizenship Directive, article 7(3).   [28] *Ibid.* article 16.
[29] *Ibid.* article 16(1).   [30] *Ibid.* article 16(4).
[31] Case C-262/09 *Lassal* [2010] ECR I-9217; Joined Cases C-147/11 and C-148/11 *Czop and Punakova*, Judgments of 6 September 2012.
[32] Case C-325/09 *Dias* [2011] ECR I-6387.
[33] Joined Cases C-424/10 and C-425/10 *Ziolkowski and Szeja* v *Land Berlin*, Judgment of 21 December 2011; *Czop and Punakova*, n. 31 above.
[34] *Ziolkowski and Szeja*, n. 33 above, para. 58.   [35] *Ibid.*; *Dias*, n. 32 above.

for those whose integration into their host state is based on sustained economic activity or self-sufficiency. In the view of the Court this approach reflects the status of permanent residence as 'a key element in promoting social cohesion' which works to 'strengthen the feeling of Union citizenship'.[36]

Nevertheless, some people can acquire permanent residence status in less than five years. In general, this applies to persons who move to another state, work there and then, as a result of retirement or permanent ill health, stop working before five years is up. For these persons, shorter time limits are provided in article 17 of the Citizenship Directive. The purpose of this is to prevent these citizens, who are no longer economically active but cannot reasonably be expected to be, from having their rights of residence threatened by the article 7(1)(b) condition of 'sufficient resources'.

(i) Conditions of residence

The fear of Member States has traditionally been that citizens would use their free movement rights to move to states with high levels of public assistance, where they would live as parasites, enjoying benefits without contributing to society. In order to ease this fear, EU law has always imposed conditions of self-sufficiency on free movement, requiring certain categories of migrants to have sickness insurance and sufficient resources to live from. On the one hand, these conditions make free movement viable: Member States do not yet feel enough mutual solidarity to accept a free movement regime which permits migration purely for the purposes of claiming benefits. More practically, national communities are the primary locus of taxation and spending. In the absence of mechanisms for redistribution between states (as for example exist in a federal state such as Germany or the United States), benefit tourism is easily portrayed as inequitable.

Yet the practical effect of these conditions is that 'expensive' members of society do not enjoy free movement rights. Those dependent upon state support or suffering medical conditions which are expensive to treat or difficult to insure are excluded from the Europe without borders. Union citizenship is a citizenship for all Europeans who are not poor or sick. This goes to the justice of citizenship, but also to the question of whether it deserves its name.[37] Are not equality and solidarity a part of what citizenship entails? The cases below suggest that the Court of Justice's answer is 'to some extent'.

A caveat is that these conditions do not apply to economically active persons. It may be the case, therefore, that a worker or self-employed citizen earns little from their activity and so is entitled to social assistance, perhaps even significant social assistance. Yet, this has no consequences for their residence rights.[38] This softens the conditions a little in practice, since the threshold for economic activity is relatively low and may often be met by just a 'small number' of hours of work per week.[39] Yet, it also highlights the economic roots of free movement and suggests that despite its constitutional tone, citizenship has not fully transformed the law on free movement of persons from an economic policy tool to a dignified and socially cohesive institution.

---

[36] Citizenship Directive, recital 17; *Lassal*, n. 31 above, at para. 32; See annotation of *Ziolkowski* by M. Jesse at (2012) 49 *CMLRev.* 2003. See also Case C-378/12 *Onuekwere*, Judgment of 16 January 2014.

[37] Kochenov, n. 18 above.

[38] Citizenship Directive, article 7; see also Case 139/85 *Kempf* [1986] ECR 1741.

[39] Case C-46/12 *LN* v *Styrelsen for Videregående Uddannelser og Uddannelsesstøtte*, Judgment of 21 February 2013, para. 41; Case 53/81 *Levin* v *Staatssecretaris van Justitie* [1982] ECR 1035.

For the non-economically active citizen, however, residence for more than three months in a host state is conditional upon possessing 'sufficient resources... not to become a burden' as well as 'comprehensive sickness insurance'.[40] This sounds strict. However, national interpretations of these conditions will be subject to the principle of proportionality. In *Baumbast*, the UK Government objected to the fact that a German citizen and his family had sickness insurance which did not cover all of the costs which they might incur (although had not incurred) in the United Kingdom.[41] This looked like a fairly straightforward breach of the Directive then in force, which was similarly worded to the Citizenship Directive. However, the family had been in the United Kingdom for some time, had never been a burden on the state in the past and it seemed harsh to deny them further residence for a breach which had not actually cost the United Kingdom any money and was, it seemed, fairly minor.

Case C-413/99 *Baumbast v Secretary of State for the Home Department* [2002] ECR I-7091

90. In any event, the limitations and conditions which are referred to in Article [21 TFEU] and laid down by Directive 90/364 are based on the idea that the exercise of the right of residence of citizens of the Union can be subordinated to the legitimate interests of the Member States. In that regard, according to the fourth recital in the preamble to Directive 90/364 beneficiaries of the right of residence must not become an 'unreasonable' burden on the public finances of the host Member State.

91. However, those limitations and conditions must be applied in compliance with the limits imposed by Community law and in accordance with the general principles of that law, in particular the principle of proportionality. That means that national measures adopted on that subject must be necessary and appropriate to attain the objective pursued...

93. Under those circumstances, to refuse to allow Mr Baumbast to exercise the right of residence which is conferred on him by Article [21(1) TFEU] by virtue of the application of the provisions of Directive 90/364 on the ground that his sickness insurance does not cover the emergency treatment given in the host Member State would amount to a disproportionate interference with the exercise of that right.

Proportionality is an open-textured concept and it will often be open to dispute whether a denial of residence rights on the basis of an application for social assistance or a defect in sickness insurance is proportionate or not.[42] It is important to bear in mind that the aim of preventing migrants from draining public resources needs to be balanced against the openness and solidarity inherent in the idea of Union citizenship. In *Grzelczyk*, the Court of Justice pointed out that EU law 'accepts a certain degree of financial solidarity between nationals of a host Member State and nationals of other Member States, particularly if the difficulties which a beneficiary of the right of residence encounters are temporary'.[43] It is unreasonable for a migrant to ask too much, but equally unreasonable for a state to accept only those who need nothing at all.

---

[40] Citizenship Directive, article 7(1)(b).

[41] Case C-413/99 *Baumbast* v *Secretary of State for the Home Department* [2002] ECR I-7091.

[42] G. De Búrca, 'The Principle of Proportionality and its Application in EC Law' (1993) 13 *YBEL* 105; G. Davies, 'Abstractness and Concreteness in the Preliminary Reference Procedure' in N. Nic Shuibhne (ed.), *Regulating the Internal Market* (Cheltenham, Edward Elgar Publishing, 2006); E. Spaventa, 'Seeing the Wood Despite the Trees? On the Scope of Union Citizenship and its Constitutional Effects' (2008) 45 *CMLRev.* 13.

[43] Case C-184/99 *Grzelczyk* [2001] ECR I-6193; see also Citizenship Directive, recital 16.

Moreover, the determination of a sufficient level of resources is to be decided with reference to the particular circumstances of the individual. A state may use rules of thumb, but inflexible rules are prohibited.

Citizenship Directive, article 8(4)

4. Member States may not lay down a fixed amount which they regard as 'sufficient resources' but they must take into account the personal situation of the person concerned. In all cases this amount shall not be higher than the threshold below which nationals of the host Member State become eligible for social assistance, or where this criterion is not applicable, higher than the minimum social security pension paid by the host Member State.

Some interpretation of 'the personal situation of the person concerned' is provided by recital 16 to the Directive, which refers to the length of time which the citizen has already been resident and the amount of public assistance they have needed, as well as other 'personal circumstances'. Where a denial of residence would have consequences for family life, Article 8 ECHR may also be relevant.[44]

This citizen-centred approach to resources makes it difficult to know exactly what a Member State may demand. In *Commission v Netherlands*, the Court of Justice found that a state could not require demonstrable resources sufficient for a year of residence before recognising the residence right.[45] This was, again, disproportionate. Furthermore, the citizen does not need to personally possess any resources at all provided there is someone covering their costs. In *Chen*, a baby was able to establish residence because her non-EU mother had sufficient resources to care for her,[46] while in *Commission v Belgium*, the Court found that there was no need for the provider of resources to be either a family member or someone with a legal relationship with the citizen.[47]

Moreover, the sufficient resources condition will be, for most citizens, a one-time test. Once they have received their residence document they should not generally be subject to continuing checks on their resources, as long as they do not in fact behave in a way raising a legitimate doubt about their self-sufficiency. If they get by without public assistance there is no reason why the state should revisit the issue.

Citizenship Directive, article 14(2)

2. Union citizens and their family members shall have the right of residence provided for in Articles 7, 12 and 13, as long as they meet the conditions set out therein. In specific cases where there is a reasonable doubt as to whether a Union citizen or his/her family member satisfies the conditions set out in Articles 7, 12 and 13, Member States may verify if these conditions are fulfilled. This verification shall not be carried out systematically.

---

[44] See Chapter 6.   [45] Case C-398/06 *Commission v Netherlands* [2008] ECR I-56.
[46] Case C-200/02 *Zhu and Chen* [2004] ECR I-9925.
[47] Case C-408/03 *Commission v Belgium* [2006] ECR I-2647.

Even if a citizen does subsequently make an application for public assistance this does not necessarily lead to a loss of residence rights. Article 14(3) provides that 'An expulsion measure shall not be the automatic consequence of a Union citizen's or his or her family member's recourse to the social assistance system of the host Member State'. By contrast, expulsion can only follow a decision-making process in which the citizen enjoys the protection of procedural safeguards.[48]

(ii) Overcoming obstacles to migration

(a) Prohibition of discrimination

For the migrant who has gained entry to a host state, the most useful additional legal tool is usually the prohibition on nationality discrimination. This enables her to participate in work and society on equal terms with nationals. The primary rule is found in Article 18 TFEU.

Article 18 TFEU

Within the scope of application of the Treaties, and without prejudice to any special provisions contained therein, any discrimination on grounds of nationality shall be prohibited.

Article 24(1) of the Citizenship Directive extends and refines this slightly.

Citizenship Directive, article 24(1)

1. Subject to such specific provisions as are expressly provided for in the Treaty and secondary law, all Union citizens residing on the basis of this Directive in the territory of the host Member State shall enjoy equal treatment with the nationals of that Member State within the scope of the Treaty. The benefit of this right shall be extended to family members who are not nationals of a Member State and who have the right of residence or permanent residence.

The Directive chooses to speak of equal treatment rather than discrimination, and extends the right to non-EU family members. This extension is important and not yet fully reflected in the practices of national institutions and national laws. One often sees job vacancies, for example, that are 'open to Union citizens', which should, correctly, be 'open to Union citizens and their family members'.

Discrimination is often defined by the Court of Justice in these classical words: 'the principle of non-discrimination requires that comparable situations must not be treated differently and that different situations must not be treated in the same way'.[49] This elegant formulation is not always the most transparent or practical. It does not reveal how to determine what is comparable and what is different, which is really the essence of the matter. A less compressed approach, which amounts to the same in substance and is also reflected in case law, is to ask two questions. First, does a measure tend to advantage or disadvantage one group or another?

---

[48] See Citizenship Directive, articles 15, 30, 31.
[49] Case C-148/02 *Garcia Avello* [2003] ECR I-11613, para. 31.

Secondly, if so, is it sufficiently justified: does it serve a legitimate goal, is it based on objective and legitimate criteria and is it proportionate? This approach originated in older cases on free movement of workers, *Sotgiu* and *O'Flynn*, but is still relied on by the Court of Justice.[50] It reflects the understanding of discrimination that is also used in other areas of EU law, such as employment regulation.[51] The more explicit the distinction between nationalities – the greater the discriminatory effect – the harder it will usually be to justify it. A rule providing free museum entry only to national citizens would have to have truly exceptional justifications to survive, but a municipal rule providing free entry to local school-children, while it might tend to relatively disadvantage foreign tourists, would probably be easier to justify.[52]

(b) Scope of the prohibition

The prohibition applies 'within the scope of the Treaty'. In the context of citizenship, the Court of Justice has repeatedly found that where a national measure affects a migrant citizen exercising her Treaty rights to move and reside, this is in itself enough to bring the measure within the Treaty. As a result, the non-discrimination rule may affect all areas of national law. Even if these are primarily national and not EU competences, if they discriminate against migrants the rule will bite. Thus, Article 18 has been applied to compensation for victims of crime in France and criminal procedure in Italy, motorway toll reductions for disabled people, as well as to national laws implementing the European Arrest Warrant, among other matters.[53] Some of the cases involve discrimination against mere movers, those transiting a state or on holiday there.[54] However, the majority involve discrimination against migrant residents.

In *Garcia Avello*, it was the Belgian law on surnames that was in issue.[55] A Spanish citizen resident in Belgium was unable to persuade the Belgian authorities to register his children with a Spanish style surname, consisting of the father's surname followed by the mother's surname. The children were Spanish/Belgian dual nationals.

Case C-148/02 *Garcia Avello* [2003] ECR I-11613

20. It is first of all necessary to examine whether, contrary to the view expressed by the Belgian State and by the Danish and Netherlands Governments, the situation in issue in the main proceedings comes within the scope of Community law and, in particular, of the Treaty provisions on citizenship of the Union.

21. Article [20 TFEU] confers the status of citizen of the Union on every person holding the nationality of a Member State. Since Mr Garcia Avello's children possess the nationality of two Member States, they also enjoy that status.

---

[50] Case 152/73 *Sotgiu v Deutsche Bundespost* [1974] ECR 153; Case C-237/94 *O'Flynn v Adjudication Officer* [1996] ECR I-2617. See G. Davies, *Nationality Discrimination in the European Internal Market* (The Hague, Kluwer Law International, 2003).

[51] See generally C. Costello and E. Barry (eds.), *Equality in Diversity: The New Equality Directives* (Dublin, Irish Centre for European Law, 2003).

[52] See Case C-388/01 *Commission v Italy* [2001] ECR I-721; Case C-45/93 *Commission v Spain* [1994] ECR I-911.

[53] Case C-164/07 *Wood* [2008] ECR I-4143; Case C-274/96 *Bickel and Franz* [1998] ECR I-7637; see also Case 186/87 *Cowan v Trésor Public* [1989] ECR 195; Case C-103/08 *Gottwald v Bezirkshauptmannschaft Bregenz* [2009] ECR I-9117; Case C-123/08 *Wolzenburg v London Borough of Ealing and Secretary of State for Education and Skills* [2009] ECR I-9621.

[54] See e.g. *Gottwald*, n. 53 above; Case C-388/01 *Commission v Italy* [2001] ECR I-721.

[55] See also Case C-96/04 *Standesamt Stadt Niebüll* [2006] ECR I-3561.

22. As the Court has ruled on several occasions, citizenship of the Union is destined to be the fundamental status of nationals of the Member States.

23. That status enables nationals of the Member States who find themselves in the same situation to enjoy within the scope *ratione materiae* of the EC Treaty the same treatment in law irrespective of their nationality, subject to such exceptions as are expressly provided for.

24. The situations falling within the scope *ratione materiae* of Community law include those involving the exercise of the fundamental freedoms guaranteed by the Treaty, in particular those involving the freedom to move and reside within the territory of the Member States, as conferred by Article [21 TFEU].

25. Although, as Community law stands at present, the rules governing a person's surname are matters coming within the competence of the Member States, the latter must none the less, when exercising that competence, comply with Community law, in particular the Treaty provisions on the freedom of every citizen of the Union to move and reside in the territory of the Member States.

This is the reply to national authorities who claim that a certain matter is 'a Member State competence outside EU law'.[56] Belgium went on to lose the case, since it could not show an adequate justification for its refusal to take account of the Garcia Avello family's particular situation and the problems that the law caused for them. A similar result was achieved in the later *Grunkin and Paul*, where Germany refused to recognise a hyphenated surname that had already been officially registered in Denmark.[57]

A. Iliopoulou Penot, 'The Transnational Character of Union Citizenship' in M. Dougan, N. Nic Shuibhne and E. Spaventa (eds.), *Empowerment and Disempowerment of the European Citizen* (Oxford, Hart, 2012) 19–20

Interestingly, in *Garcia Avello*, the Belgian Government argued that its practice could be justified by the objective of promoting *integration* (and equality) into Belgian society of nationals from other Member States. The Court rejects this argument in view of the fact that migration within the Union has already lead to the co-existence in Member States of different systems for the attribution of surnames applicable to residents. As a result of this migration, the situation of the children in the *Garcia Avello* case, as well as in the *Grunkin Paul* case, cannot be assessed by reference to the framework of only one society. Instead, it has to be repositioned within a wider social context, recomposed at the European level. The legal bond of EU citizenship reflects a certain social reality resulting from migration and membership in European society conceived as a 'society of societies'. This status protects against the risk, somehow inherent to migration, that original identity will be changed or even erased against the will of the individual. Therefore, new identity elements can only be chosen by the migrant (as in *Grunkin Paul*); they cannot be imposed on him or her. It is certain that integration into the host society is desirable. But integration does not mean assimilation. Instead, it can sometimes be achieved by recognition of the migrant's difference. In other words, when in Rome, you do not (necessarily) have to do as the Romans do.

---

[56] See also Case C-524/06 *Huber* v *Bundesrepublik Deutschland* [2008] ECR I-9705.
[57] Case C-353/06 *Grunkin and Paul* [2008] ECR I-7639.

The case law under examination also illustrates the changing conception of the State. Member States can no longer be represented as bounded worlds which correspond to closed and isolated entities. Instead, they belong to a wider area where movement is continuous and where diversity is accepted, preserved, and even encouraged as a source of richness. As parts of a larger organism, Member States have to consider the potential impact of their choices on transnational situations. Interests beyond the confines of the national polity have to be taken into account within the policy- and decision-making system. Judicial review on grounds of Union citizenship seeks to ensure precisely this. Therefore, Union citizenship enhances a phenomenon already taking place because of the internal market where Member States are 'forced to confront and internalize the externalities that they cause for one another'.[58] This phenomenon is now extended as a result of Union citizenship to new areas such as personal and family status.

(c) Restrictions on movement

As well as the right to equal treatment, or non-discrimination, the Treaty also provides a directly effective right to free movement.[59] This enables citizens to rely on the right to move and reside against their own state, in circumstances where an analysis in terms of nationality discrimination would often be artificial or even impossible.[60]

D'Hoop concerned a Belgian allowance, available to job-seeking school-leavers if they had been to school in Belgium. Ms D'Hoop had been to school in France and was therefore refused the benefit. However, she was a Belgian citizen, making it impossible for her to argue nationality discrimination. She therefore simply claimed that the rule deterred interstate movement.

Case C-224/98 *D'Hoop* [2002] ECR I-6191

27. Article 8 of the Treaty confers the status of citizen of the Union on every person holding the nationality of a Member State. Since she possesses the nationality of a Member State, Ms D'Hoop enjoys that status.

28. Union citizenship is destined to be the fundamental status of nationals of the Member States, enabling those who find themselves in the same situation to enjoy within the scope *ratione materiae* of the Treaty the same treatment in law irrespective of their nationality, subject to such exceptions as are expressly provided for.

29. The situations falling within the scope of Community law include those involving the exercise of the fundamental freedoms guaranteed by the Treaty, in particular those involving the freedom to move and reside within the territory of the Member States, as conferred by Article [21 TFEU].

---

[58] A. Somek, 'The Argument from Transnational Effects: Representing Outsiders through Freedom of Movement' (2010) 16 *ELJ* 315.

[59] Case C-224/98 *D'Hoop* [2002] ECR I-6191; Case C-224/02 *Pusa* [2004] ECR I-5763; Case C-76/05 *Schwarz and Gootjes-Schwarz v Finanzamt Bergisch Gladbach* [2007] ECR I-6849; Case C-192/05 *Tas-Hagen and Tas v Raadskamer WUBO van de Pensioen- en Uitkeringsraad* [2006] ECR I-10451; Case C-11/06 *Morgan v Bezirksregierung Köln* [2007] ECR I-9161; Case C-221/07 *Zablocka*, Judgment of 4 December 2008; Case C-499/06 *Nerkowska* [2008] ECR I-3993; Case C-403/03 *Schempp* [2005] ECR I-6421.

[60] M. Cousins, 'Citizenship, Residence and Social Security' (2007) 32 *ELRev.* 386.

30. In that a citizen of the Union must be granted in all Member States the same treatment in law as that accorded to the nationals of those Member States who find themselves in the same situation, it would be incompatible with the right of freedom of movement were a citizen, in the Member State of which he is a national, to receive treatment less favourable than he would enjoy if he had not availed himself of the opportunities offered by the Treaty in relation to freedom of movement.

31. Those opportunities could not be fully effective if a national of a Member State could be deterred from availing himself of them by obstacles raised on his return to his country of origin by legislation penalising the fact that he has used them....

33. In situations such as that in the main proceedings, national legislation introduces a difference in treatment between Belgian nationals who have had all their secondary education in Belgium and those who, having availed themselves of their freedom to move, have obtained their diploma of completion of secondary education in another Member State.

34. By linking the grant of tideover allowances to the condition of having obtained the required diploma in Belgium, the national legislation thus places at a disadvantage certain of its nationals simply because they have exercised their freedom to move in order to pursue education in another Member State.

35. Such inequality of treatment is contrary to the principles which underpin the status of citizen of the Union, that is, the guarantee of the same treatment in law in the exercise of the citizen's freedom to move.

36. The condition at issue could be justified only if it were based on objective considerations independent of the nationality of the persons concerned and were proportionate to the legitimate aim of the national provisions.

Another example of this type of reasoning is found in *Grunkin and Paul*, where German parents gave their child, born in Denmark, the surname Grunkin-Paul.[61] Although this was on the Danish birth certificate, the German authorities refused to recognise it, because Germany did not allow such composite surnames. The Court of Justice found this to violate Article 21 because it disadvantaged migration. The interest of the case lies in the fact that the parents were not obliged to choose a hyphenated surname in Denmark, but freely chose to. Clearly, if a migrant makes use of wider rights and opportunities available in a host state, their home state must respect and take account of these choices when the migrant returns.

The same free-movement-based approach was applied to a host state in *Rüffler*.[62] Mr Rüffler, a German citizen, lived in Poland but received a pension from Germany, where he had worked. Polish tax calculations did not take account of insurance premiums deducted from that pension in Germany before it was paid to Mr Ruffler, but they would have taken account of equivalent deductions made in Poland. The judgment is similarly reasoned to *D'Hoop*, but by contrast to paragraph 31 above, the Court of Justice in *Ruffler* said:

> it would be incompatible with the right to freedom of movement were a citizen to receive, *in the host Member State*, treatment less favourable than that which he would enjoy if he had not availed himself of the opportunities offered by the Treaty in relation to freedom of movement. (emphasis added)

[61] Case C-353/06 *Grunkin and Paul* [2008] ECR I-7639.
[62] Case C-544/07 *Rüffler* [2009] ECR I-3389.

By contrast, Mr Radziejewski, a Swedish citizen, was penalised for leaving Sweden by Swedish rules which granted him post-bankruptcy debt relief but only on the condition that he continued to live in Sweden.[63] Exit would therefore lead to Swedish debtors rushing to claim money from him. The Court found the rule to be an unjustified deterrent to emigration.

Another case in which a home state hindered exit is *Sayn-Wittgenstein*. In this case, Ilonka Kerekes, an Austrian, was adopted by Lothar, Prince of Sayn-Wittgenstein, a German.[64] Her new name was entered on both German and Austrian official documents as Ilonka, Princess (Fürstin) of Sayn-Wittgenstein. However, after a period of some fifteen years, the Austrian authorities realised that this was contrary to an Austrian law which prohibited the use of aristocratic titles, and they took steps to amend her name in the Austrian register, and ultimately in her passport, to Ilonka Sayn-Wittgenstein. She challenged this decision on the grounds that it would lead to practical problems in Germany, where people might doubt her identity or the authenticity of her title as her Austrian and German documents showed different names. It might also hinder her in her business, which was selling castles. The Court of Justice accepted that such discrepancies could cause problems which might be seen as a hindrance to free movement, but found that in this case the Austrian rule could be justified, as the rejection of aristocratic titles reflected genuine and fundamental Austrian constitutional values, notably equality.

What these cases create is a new kind of non-discrimination rule, not between citizens of different nationalities, but between citizens who exercise their EU rights and those who do not.[65] Where cross-border activities are treated less advantageously than domestic ones, or where migration is made more difficult than staying at home or leads to disadvantages under national rules, Article 21 TFEU applies.

The limits to this free movement right begin to emerge from *Runevič-Vardyn and Wardyn*.[66] Ms Runevič, a Lithuanian, had married Mr Wardyn, a Pole, in Poland, and her name was entered on the Polish marriage certificate as Runiewicz-Wardyn, the Polish way of spelling and writing it. However, the Lithuanian authorities, when registering her marriage, entered her husband's name in the Polish way, as Wardyn, but refused to do so for her, because she was a Lithuanian citizen and obliged to use Lithuanian spelling and script on official documents. Her married name was thus recorded as Runevič-Vardyn. She demanded that this, and indeed her name on her birth certificate, be changed to the Polish style, claiming that if her name was spelt differently from that of her husband and her future children, then this would create difficulties for them in Belgium, where they now lived. The case is far more politically sensitive than may first appear, as Ms Runevič-Vardyn was a member of the Polish minority in Lithuania, and her case was symbolic of wider disputes about identities, languages and minorities in the Baltic states. Perhaps for this reason, or perhaps because they were fed up with the increasingly obscure stream of naming cases, or perhaps simply because they did not believe that there would really be any problems, the Court of Justice did not find that movement had been obstructed.

---

[63] Case C-461/11 *Radziejewski*, Judgment of 8 November 2012.
[64] Case C-208/08 *Ilonka Sayn-Wittgenstein* v *Landeshauptmann von Wien* [2010] ECR I-13693.
[65] N. Bernard, 'Discrimination and Free Movement' (1996) 45 *ICLQ* 82, 85–6. See e.g. Case C-11/06 *Morgan* v *Bezirksregierung Köln* [2007] ECR I-9161.
[66] H. van Eijken, annotation of *Runevič-Vardyn* (2012) 49 *CMLRev.* 809.

Case C-391/01 *Runevič–Vardyn and Wardyn* [2011] ECR I-3787

74. ... it cannot be excluded that the fact that, on the marriage certificate, her husband's surname is added to her maiden name in a form which does not correspond to the husband's surname as registered in his Member State of origin or, moreover, as it is entered, for the second applicant in the main proceedings, on the same marriage certificate, might be liable to cause inconvenience for those concerned.

75. Such inconvenience might arise from the discrepancy in the forms in which the same surname is entered for two persons constituting the same married couple.

76. However, according to the Court's case-law, in order to constitute a restriction on the freedoms recognised by Article 21 TFEU, the refusal to amend the joint surname of the applicants in the main proceedings under the national rules at issue must be liable to cause 'serious inconvenience' to those concerned at administrative, professional and private levels.

77. It is therefore for the national court to decide whether there is a real risk, for a family such as that of the applicants in the main proceedings, because of the refusal on the part of the competent authorities to change the letter 'V' into a 'W' in the spelling of the surname of one of the members of that family, that family members will be obliged to dispel doubts as to their identity and the authenticity of the documents which they submit. If, in the circumstances of the case in the main proceedings, that refusal involves the possibility that the truthfulness of the information contained in those documents will be called into question and the identity of that family and the relationship which exists between its members placed in doubt, that might have significant consequences as regards, among other things, the exercise of the right of residence conferred directly by Article 21 TFEU.

While even minor instances of nationality discrimination are prohibited,[67] non-discriminatory measures claimed to hinder free movement will probably not be recognised as restrictions within Article 21 if their practical consequences for movement are minimal, and the inconvenience they cause is less than 'serious'.

(d) Citizenship and social assistance

Workers will rarely require social assistance, but if they do, because they earn little, then they enjoy full equal treatment with nationals of their host state, both on the basis of the Citizenship Directive, Article 18 TFEU, and article 7 of Regulation 492/211, which provides that workers have equal rights to 'social advantages'.[68] They are well-protected, reflecting the fact that work is seen as indicating a deep form of integration into society.[69]

Those residing on the basis of article 7(1)(a) or (b) of the Citizenship Directive are, by contrast, in a somewhat paradoxical situation. On the one hand, the Court of Justice has emphasised, first in *Martínez Sala* and later in *Grzelczyk*, that if lawfully resident they enjoy the right to equal treatment, including where social assistance is concerned.[70] On the other hand, the Court found, also in *Grzelczyk*, that if an application for social assistance was made then it

---

[67] Case C-524/06 *Huber v Bundesrepublik Deutschland* [2008] ECR I-9705.

[68] Previously article 7 of Regulation 1612/68, now replaced by Regulation 492/211 on freedom of movement for workers.

[69] Case C379/11 *Caves Krier*, Judgment of 13 December 2012.

[70] *Grzelczyk*, n. 43 above; Case C-85/96 *Martínez Sala v Freistaat Bayern* [1998] ECR I-2691. See annotation by S. O'Leary, 'Flesh on the Bones of European Citizenship' (1999) 24 *ELRev.* 68.

was open to a state to conclude that the conditions of article 7 were no longer satisfied, and so residence was no longer lawful, provided this conclusion was proportionate in the light of the particular circumstances.[71]

Work-seekers are in an intermediate position. Their right to enter a host state and stay there while looking for work is long-established, being necessary to make the free movement of workers a meaningful policy. It was developed in case law, and is now contained in article 14(4)(b) of the Directive, which provides that the residence right continues as long as they have a 'genuine chance' of finding work. However, Member States have always been reluctant to grant work-seekers benefits: it is an easy status to claim, a hard one to disprove, and a right to benefits might be seen as a way of undermining the 'sufficient resources' requirement for the non-economically active.

Nevertheless, the Court of Justice in *Collins* took a different approach, based on primary law. This Irish work-seeker in the United Kingdom wanted job-seekers' allowance, but was refused it. The Court said that:

> In view of the establishment of citizenship of the Union and the interpretation in the case-law of the right to equal treatment enjoyed by citizens of the Union, it is no longer possible to exclude from the scope of Article [45] of the Treaty – which expresses the fundamental principle of equal treatment, guaranteed by Article [18] of the Treaty – a benefit of a financial nature intended to facilitate access to employment in the labour market of a Member State.

Shortly after *Collins*, the Citizenship Directive came into force, containing article 24(2).

Citizenship Directive, article 24(2)

2. By way of derogation from paragraph 1, the host Member State shall not be obliged to confer entitlement to social assistance during the first three months of residence or, where appropriate, the longer period provided for in Article 14(4)(b), nor shall it be obliged, prior to acquisition of the right of permanent residence, to grant maintenance aid for studies, including vocational training, consisting in student grants or student loans to persons other than workers, self-employed persons, persons who retain such status and members of their families.

In explicitly denying work-seekers (those residing on the basis of article 14(4)(b)) a right to social assistance, in derogation from the general equal treatment rule, this would seem to flatly contradict *Collins*. However, reconciliation is provided in *Vatsouras*, where the Court of Justice found that benefits 'intended to facilitate access to the employment market' are not in fact social assistance, and therefore not covered by article 24(2). It chose not to provide reasons for this finding,[72] which is probably not at all what the Member States intended by article 24, but it can be justified: if the consistent policy of free movement law is to help those who try to help themselves, while excluding those who will not, or cannot, help themselves, then benefits which help migrants find work are importantly different from benefits which merely help them live.

---

[71] *Grzelczyk*, n. 43 above, para. 42.
[72] Case C-22/08 *Vatsouras* v *Arbeitsgemeinschaft Nürnberg* [2009] ECR I-4585. Although see the Advocate General's opinion for greater explanation.

Vatsouras raises the question of how these two classes of benefits are to be distinguished, and it is notable that in the judgment the Court of Justice suggests that the mere fact that a benefit was only awarded to those 'capable of earning a living' might be enough to show it was intended to help recipients find work. This is broad, and suggests that, for example, if a benefit is conditional upon an obligation to apply for jobs then this would be enough to take it outside of article 24(2) and make it available to migrant job-seekers on equal terms. Since, in many Member States, an obligation to seek work is almost a default condition of benefit receipt, the exclusion of social assistance for work-seekers is greatly reduced in scope.

(e) Real links and integration

Even if a work-seeker, or other migrant, has a right to equal treatment in social benefits, the defence mechanisms of the state are not exhausted. A trend of recent years is to make all kinds of social assistance and benefits only available to those who are to some extent integrated in that state's society.[73] Typical clauses make benefits only available to those who have been resident for a certain period, or who have been schooled in that state, or who have family or other links with the state which demonstrate a genuine bond. Such rules are not directly discriminatory, but of course do tend to favour nationals over migrants, and must therefore be justified by some policy need, and proportionate. Older case law tended to find residence clauses unlawful, the Court of Justice clearly seeing them as unmeritorious and smacking of nationalism.[74] However, there appears to be an increasing recognition in the Court, as among policy-makers, that a restriction of some benefits to those who are in some sense 'members' of society, is not only legitimate but perhaps even necessary to ensure the stability and sustainability of benefit systems.[75]

Ioannidis concerned a Belgian allowance available to those seeking their first job, but only if they had completed their secondary schooling in Belgium – the same allowance as in *D'Hoop*. Mr Ioannidis, a Greek citizen, had been to school in Greece, but was now seeking work in Belgium.

Case C-258/04 *Ioannidis* [2005] ECR I-8275

30. As the Court has already held, it is legitimate for the national legislature to wish to ensure that there is a real link between the applicant for that allowance and the geographic employment market concerned.

31. However, a single condition concerning the place where the diploma of completion of secondary education was obtained is too general and exclusive in nature. It unduly favours an element which is not necessarily representative of the real and effective degree of connection between the applicant for the tideover allowance and the geographic employment market, to the exclusion of all other representative elements. It therefore goes beyond what is necessary to attain the objective pursued.

---

[73] See C. O'Brien, 'Real Links, Abstract Rights and False Alarms: The Relationship Between the ECJ's "Real Link" Case Law and National Solidarity' (2008) 33 *ELRev*. 643.
[74] Case 152/73 *Sotgiu* v *Deutsche Bundespost* [1974] ECR 153.   [75] See O'Brien, n. 73 above.

If a requirement to have completed school in Belgium is too strict, this begs the question of what kind of requirements can legitimately be imposed. In *Prete*, with almost identical facts, the Court of Justice suggested that having married a national of the host state, moved there, and then having sought work in the state for a 'reasonable time' might all be factors providing evidence of a 'real link'.[76] In *Bidar*, concerning a student applying for a subsidised loan in their host state, the Court suggested that integration might be demonstrated by having 'resided in the host Member State for a certain length of time'.[77] Yet that is not to say that prior residence is always a legitimate requirement. Where a citizen, or in the case of a student their parents, work in the host Member State this is usually enough evidence of integration, and a further residence requirement will be disproportionate.[78]

It is clear that there are no simple rules, rather a general principle of proportionality which may lead to different conclusions in different cases. In *Commission* v *Austria*, a case on discounted transport for students (something that is neither a grant, which would be excluded by article 24(2), nor social assistance which might threaten compliance with article 7(1)), the Court of Justice remarked that:

> the genuine link required between the student claiming a benefit and the host Member State need not be fixed in a uniform manner for all benefits, but should be established according to the constitutive elements of the benefit in question, including to its nature and purpose or purposes. The objective of the benefit must be analysed according to its results and not according to its formal structure.[79]

This suggests that the particular nature of each benefit must be taken account of in determining appropriate conditions. *Gottwald* applies a similar particularist philosophy to the recipient, suggesting that it is legally desirable for national rules to have flexibility, so that they can take account of the various forms of connection with a society that applicants may have.[80] In that case, an Austrian rule exempting disabled drivers from motorway tolls was only available to the ordinarily resident, but the Court noted, in finding the Austrian rule to be justified, that the 'conditions are interpreted widely, so that other connecting factors allow a sufficiently close connection to Austrian society to be established for the purposes of grant of the free toll disc'.[81]

This concern not to apply over-rigid exclusionary rules to migrants is consistent with other free movement case law, but nevertheless fits a little uncomfortably with the assertion, also in the judgment in *Gottwald*, that:

> with regard to the degree of connection of the recipient of a benefit with the society of the Member State concerned ... Member States enjoy a wide margin of appreciation in deciding which criteria are to be used when assessing the degree of connection to society.

---

[76] Case C-367/11 *Prete*, Judgment of 25 October 2012.

[77] Case C-209/03 *Bidar* [2005] ECR I-2119. This was prior to the implementation of the Citizenship Directive, which addresses financial aid for studies in article 24.

[78] *Caves Krier*, n. 69 above; Case C-542/09 *Commission* v *Netherlands*, Judgment of 14 June 2012.

[79] Case C-75/11 *Commission* v *Austria*, Judgment of 4 October 2012, para. 59.

[80] See on this flexibility O'Brien, n. 73 above; E. Spaventa, 'Seeing the Wood Despite the Trees? On the Scope of Union Citizenship and its Constitutional Effects' (2008) 45(1) *CMLRev.* 13.

[81] Case C-103/08 *Gottwald* v *Bezirkshauptmannschaft Bregenz* [2009] ECR I-9117. See also Case C-542/09 *Commission* v *Netherlands*, Judgment of 14 June 2012; Case C-503/09 *Stewart* [2011] ECR I-6497; Case C-11/06 *Morgan* v *Bezirksregierung Köln* [2007] ECR I-9161; Case C-220/12 *Thiele Meneses*, Judgment of 24 October 2013.

Nevertheless, not all the cases have emphasised the need to adapt to migrants. *Förster* provides a powerful counter-example, whose wider implications remain uncertain.[82] The Netherlands required foreign students to be resident for five years before having a right to finance support for study, but did not apply this rule to Dutch students – even if they had never lived in the Netherlands. This follows the wording of article 24(2), but nevertheless the referring court asked whether that article, and the Dutch measure, were not both in conflict with the Treaty principle of non-discrimination. A prior residence rule might be reasonable, but why did it need to be directly discriminatory? However, the Court of Justice framed the issue differently:

> Since that requirement concerning the duration of residence is not applicable to students of Netherlands nationality, the issue is raised of what restrictions may be imposed on the right of students who are nationals of other Member States to a maintenance grant without the different treatment of those students in comparison to national students which may result in being considered discriminatory and, consequently, prohibited under the first paragraph of Article [18 TFEU].

The question, in the view of the Court, is how much different treatment on the basis of nationality a state can apply before it becomes discriminatory. Quite a lot, it would seem, at least where students are concerned: the five-year residence requirement in question did not violate the principle of non-discrimination.

The Court of Justice finds, in substance, that nationality itself is a 'real link' with a state, so that preferential treatment for nationals is not always discrimination, but may be a justified distinction reflecting the real difference between nationals and foreigners. In the context of EU law, that is a radical statement, but it is doubtful whether it will be extended to matters to which article 24(2) does not apply.[83] It does reflect a certain policy realism: if states are entitled to reserve their support to members, then there is a risk that the itinerant citizen falls between safety nets, not sufficiently integrated in a new state of residence, but no longer entitled to support from an old one. The idea that the state of nationality should be a permanent refuge – a home – in which the citizen is always seen as integrated, as belonging, is not just nationalism, but can also be viewed as safeguarding the European commitment to a socially inclusive and protective society.

(f) Internal situation and reverse discrimination

In *Uecker and Jacquet*, two German citizens attempted to rely on EU family rights to bring their partners to Germany.[84] They failed to establish a case because '[i]t has consistently been held that the Treaty rules governing freedom of movement and regulations adopted to implement them cannot be applied to cases which have no factor linking them with any of the situations

---

[82] Case C-158/07 *Förster v Hoofddirectie van de Informatie Beheer Groep* [2008] ECR I-8507. See S. O'Leary, 'Equal Treatment and EU Citizens: A New Chapter on Cross-Border Educational Mobility and Access to Student Financial Assistance' (2009) 34 *ELRev.* 612.

[83] See Case 186/87 *Cowan v Trésor Public* [1989] ECR 195; Case C-22/08 *Vatsouras*, Judgment of 4 June 2009; Case C-123/08 *Wolzenburg v London Borough of Ealing and Secretary of State for Education and Skills* [2009] ECR I-9621.

[84] Joined Cases C-64/96 and C-65/96 *Uecker and Jacquet* [1997] ECR I-3171; see also Joined Cases 35/82 and 36/82 *Morson and Jhanjan v Netherlands* [1982] ECR 3723.

governed by Community law and all elements of which are purely internal to a single Member State'. Since Uecker and Jacquet had not exercised EU movement rights, there was no such linking factor and the Treaty simply did not apply. Their situation under the Citizenship Directive would be the same today – it too applies only to citizens in states other than their own.[85]

The core objection of the parties in *Uecker* was that they were worse off than a foreign Union citizen in Germany would have been. They experienced so-called reverse discrimination: discrimination against home nationals, in favour of EU migrants. It has been argued that this is just as objectionable as discrimination against foreigners; it is still nationality discrimination and therefore the Court of Justice should not have allowed it.[86] However, the Court's response was that the non-discrimination rule only applies within the scope of the Treaty and the whole point is that situations with no cross-border aspect are not within that scope. It could be argued that citizenship supports a broad and constitutional approach to equality, which can balance these technical legal arguments,[87] but the Court disagreed: 'citizenship of the Union is not intended to extend the material scope of the Treaty to internal situations which have no link with Community law'. Jurisdiction is prior to substance.

Since the matter was not within the Treaty, any discrimination was the result of German law, not EU law and so not the Court's concern. If Germany wanted to solve the problem by granting its nationals the same rights as migrants, it was free to do so. Some states do in fact take this approach, granting their own nationals rights equivalent to migrant citizens.[88]

The Court of Justice's answer is not fully satisfying. It remains the case that EU law played a central role in creating the inequality and that within a state, EU law does distinguish between nationals and foreigners, which is prima facie at odds with Article 18 TFEU. Nor is it necessary to read the citizenship provisions of the Treaty as only applying to cross-border situations: the Article 20 TFEU right to 'move and reside freely within the territory of the Member States' reads quite naturally in a way including internal movement too. Nevertheless, for the Court to adopt such a reading would extend the scope of the Treaty significantly, which was certainly not intended by the authors of the Treaty. For this reason it has maintained the line that wholly internal situations are outside the scope of EU law.

Nevertheless, the law has developed through refinements of what an internal situation actually is. A number of cases have extended the ways in which a connection can be made to cross-border movement, so that EU law can be engaged. The most important single case is *Singh*.[89] This concerned a British woman who went to work in Germany, where she lived with her Indian husband on the basis of EU law. After a few years she wanted to return to the United Kingdom, but was told that her husband would not be granted a right of residence. The United Kingdom considered that if she was in the United Kingdom, then as a British citizen she would be in an internal situation, outside the scope of EU law and so only national immigration rules would apply, to the disadvantage of Mr Singh.

---

[85] Citizenship Directive, article 3; Case C-456/12 *O and B*, Judgment of 12 March 2014; Case C-457/12 *S and G*, Judgment of 12 March 2014; Case C-434/09 *McCarthy* [2011] ECR I-3375. See A. Tryfonidou, 'Reverse Discrimination in Purely Internal Situations: An Incongruity in a Citizens' Europe' (2008) 35 *LIEI* 43.
[86] *Ibid.*   [87] *Ibid.*   [88] See e.g. Case C-448/98 *Guimont* [2000] ECR I-10663.
[89] Case C-370/90 *Singh* [1992] ECR I-4265. See also Case C-212/06 *Government of the French Community and Walloon Government v Flemish Government (Flemish Insurance Case)* [2008] ECR I-1683. See C. Dautricourt and S. Thomas, 'Reverse Discrimination and the Free Movement of Persons under Community Law: All for Ulysses, Nothing for Penelope?' (2009) 34 *ELRev.* 433.

The Court of Justice took a different view. It argued that to take away Ms Singh's EU rights upon her return would be a deterrent to movement: had she known this would happen it would have made it less attractive for her to go to Germany in the first place. This remark must be understood in the context of Ms Singh's family situation – her husband would not want to lose his UK residence status, as would happen if he moved to Germany, unless he could be sure of getting it back when he returned. However, the principle is broader: when an individual returns to their home state after exercising EU rights, they do not return to an internal situation. On the contrary, the status of migrant 'sticks' and they can rely on EU rights against their home state to challenge any measures making their return more difficult, or 'punishing' them for having been away.[90] Movement to the home state is still, it might be commented, cross-border movement.

A case that caused some surprise is *Carpenter*.[91] Here, the Court of Justice found that EU law on the free movement of services could be applied by a British citizen resident in the United Kingdom, against the UK Government, simply because he often travelled on the continent to provide services and therefore was engaged in cross-border service provision. Measures which made it harder for him to go abroad on business trips – in this case the deportation of his non-European wife, leaving no one to look after his children – were thus restrictions on his movement. There is nothing unorthodox about the reasoning as such, but it does show a willingness to find even a relatively marginal cross-border connection sufficient to invoke EU law. This is also evident in *Garcia Avello*, discussed above.[92] The children in that case were born in Belgium, of a Spanish and a Belgian parent. They obtained both nationalities. When they challenged Belgian rules on family names, the Belgian state claimed that the situation was internal: these were Belgians who had never been abroad, let alone exercised EU cross-border rights. On the contrary, the mere fact that they had Spanish nationality was sufficient to engage EU law. They were lawfully resident citizens of another Member State.

These cases, in combination with *D'Hoop*, *Ruffler* and the other cases in that line,[93] highlight that the important distinction within Union citizenship is less and less between different nationalities and more between migrants and stay-at-homes. This distinction can be more precisely drawn out as between those whose life is connected to more than one state and those whose life is encompassed by one state. The former can draw on Union citizenship rights, whether against their own state or another state to which they move, while the latter remain exclusively subject to domestic law. EU law has created a privileged and cosmopolitan client group to whom it affords protection wherever they are in the European Union. Given that Union citizenship was introduced to connect the European Union with the national citizen, it is perhaps an irony that it becomes most real precisely when it liberates the citizen from national law.

That conclusion, while still generally true, must now, however, be seen in the light of *Ruiz Zambrano*. In this case, whose consequences for family rights will be discussed below,[94] the Court of Justice found that Article 20 TFEU prevented Belgium from expelling the Colombian parents of Belgian children. The reason was that the children, who as minors would have to

---

[90] *D'Hoop*, n. 59 above. See also *O and B*, n. 85 above.
[91] Case C-60/00 *Carpenter* [2002] ECR I-6279. See now *S and G*, n. 85 above.
[92] Case C-148/02 *Garcia Avello* [2003] ECR I-11613. See pp. 482–4.
[93] See nn. 59, 62 above.   [94] *Ruiz Zambrano*, n. 1 above.

go with their parents, would then be effectively forced to leave the territory of the Union, and that to force a citizen to leave the Union was to deprive them of the 'genuine enjoyment of the substance' of their citizenship rights, and therefore contrary to the Treaty.

Since the children were minors their right to vote cannot have been in issue, so there are only two plausible ways of understanding *Zambrano*. One is that expulsion from the Union is a direct violation of the Article 20 right to reside in the territory of the Member States. This would be very conventional – it is an accepted principle of international law that citizens have the right to live in the territory of which they are a citizen. The alternative reading is that Article 20 is violated because if a citizen is prevented from being in the Union then she can hardly exercise her rights of free movement, notably her right to move to other Member States. While true, this is a little artificial, and the first reading is much tidier and more logical.

Nevertheless, later cases appear to emphasise the hindrance to free movement that results from expulsion to the other side of the world, although they do so unclearly, and it remains uncertain what precisely the Court of Justice's reasoning is.[95] However, it probably does not matter. De facto there is a right to live in the Union which can be exercised even against one's home state, whether that right is free-standing or merely necessary to make interstate migration possible.

While significant, this does not mean the abolition of the internal situation doctrine.[96] Neither reading provides support for the view that reverse discrimination is now prevented by EU law, nor for the view that there is a right to move from London to Birmingham. On the contrary, it continues to be necessary in every case to show some connection with an EU law right before EU law can be engaged. *Ruiz Zambrano* shows how in some domestic situations such a connection can be found. That does not mean it can always be found. In fact, the only innovation of the case regarding the law on internal situations is that it is clearly not necessary to show that the citizen actually intends to or wishes to cross a border within the EU. The mere fact that a state measure prevents this from happening is sufficient to engage the Treaty. The potential consequences of a measure are, as with the economic freedoms, also within the scope of EU law.[97]

(iii) Family rights

Family members of the Union citizen, whether or not they are themselves Union citizens, have a series of parallel rights to those of the Union citizen:

---

[95] See Case C-526/11 *Dereci*, Judgment of 15 November 2011; Case C-40/11 *Iida*, Judgment of 8 November 2012; Joined Cases C-356/11 and C-357/11 *O and S v Maahanmuuttovirasto and Maahanmuuttovirasto v L*, Judgment of 6 December 2012; Case C-87/12 *Ymeraga*, Judgment of 8 May 2013. Case C-434/09 *McCarthy* [2011] ECR I-3375 is commonly included in this line, but in fact concerns an entirely different issue, and the question of expulsion of family members was not referred, nor addressed by the Court. See G. Davies, *The Family Rights of European Children: Expulsion of Non-European Parents*, EUI Working Paper RSCAS 2012/04; C. O'Brien, 'I Trade Therefore I Am: Legal Personhood in the European Union' (2014) 50 *CMLRev.* 1643; L. Azoulai, '"Euro-Bonds": The Ruiz Zambrano Judgment or the Real Invention of EU Citizenship' (2011) 3(2) *Perspectives on Federalism* 31; D. Kochenov, 'The Essence of EU Citizenship Emerging from the Last Ten Years of Academic Debate: Beyond the Cherry Blossoms and the Moon?' (2013) 62(1) *ICLQ* 97; N. Nic Shuibhne, '(Some of) the Kids are All Right: Comment on *McCarthy* and *Dereci*' (2012) 49(1) *CMLRev.* 349; A. Wiesbrock, 'Union Citizenship and the Redefinition of the "Internal Situations" Rule: The Implications of Zambrano' (2012) 12 *GLJ* 2077.

[96] Wiesbrock, *ibid.*

[97] See Case 8/74 *Dassonville* [1974] ECR 837; cf. *Iida*, n. 95 above; Case C299/95 *Kremzow* [1997] ECR I-2629.

- the same right of entry and exit between Member States as the citizen;[98]
- the right to reside up to three months in the host state provided that they are accompanying or joining the citizen;[99]
- the right to reside for longer than three months provided the Union citizen to whom they are related satisfies the conditions for residence and the family members are accompanying or joining the citizen;[100]
- family members enjoying the right of residence or permanent residence have the right to take up employment or self-employment in the host state,[101] and the right to equal treatment with nationals of that state;[102]
- the right to permanent residence when they have legally resided in the host state with the Union citizen for a continuous period of five years.[103]

(a) The EU idea of the family

The family members acquiring these rights are set out in article 2(2) of the Citizenship Directive:

(a) the spouse;

(b) the partner with whom the Union citizen has contracted a registered partnership, on the basis of the legislation of a Member State, if the legislation of the host Member State treats registered partnerships as equivalent to marriage and in accordance with the conditions laid down in the relevant legislation of the host Member State;

(c) the direct descendants who are under the age of twenty-one or are dependants and those of the spouse or partner as defined in point (b);

(d) the dependent direct relatives in the ascending line and those of the spouse or partner as defined in point (b).

In addition, a second group of family members enjoy more conditional rights.

Citizenship Directive, article 3(2)

2. Without prejudice to any right to free movement and residence the persons concerned may have in their own right, the host Member State shall, in accordance with its national legislation, facilitate entry and residence for the following persons:

(a) any other family members, irrespective of their nationality, not falling under the definition in point 2 of Article 2 who, in the country from which they have come, are dependants or members of the household of the Union citizen having the primary right of residence, or where serious health grounds strictly require the personal care of the family member by the Union citizen;

(b) the partner with whom the Union citizen has a durable relationship, duly attested.

The host Member State shall undertake an extensive examination of the personal circumstances and shall justify any denial of entry or residence to these people.

---

[98] Citizenship Directive, articles 4(1) and 5(2). [99] *Ibid.* article 6(2). [100] *Ibid.* article 7(1) and (2).
[101] *Ibid.* article 23. [102] *Ibid.* article 24(1). [103] *Ibid.* article 16(2).

The notion of a 'dependant' was defined in *Jia*, a case in which the mother-in-law of a German resident in Sweden sought entry to Sweden from China on the basis of the legislation then in force that was equivalent to article 2(2)(d). A family member qualifies as a dependant, the Court of Justice found, when 'having regard to their financial and social conditions they are not in a position to support themselves. The need for material support must exist in the State of origin of those relatives or the state whence they came at the time when they apply to join the Community national'.[104] The Court went on to consider how dependency could be proved and rejected the Swedish Government's claim that only an official document from the Chinese authorities could suffice. The Court found that 'evidence could be adduced by any appropriate means'.

An important element of this definition is that a dependant is a relative who depends upon the Union citizen in the country where she (the dependant) is coming from. Dependency must exist prior to reunification: it is a reason for reunification, not a result of it. This is particularly important for parents from relatively poor countries, who may be able to support themselves in their home state, but would become dependent if living in an expensive EU country where they do not speak the language. They would not, following *Jia*, be dependants within the sense of the Directive.

In *Rahman* the Court of Justice explained what it means to 'facilitate entry'.

Case C-83/11 *Secretary of State for the Home Department* v *Rahman*, Judgment of 5 September 2012

21. Whilst it is therefore apparent that Article 3(2) of Directive 2004/38 does not oblige the Member States to accord a right of entry and residence to persons who are family members, in the broad sense, dependent on a Union citizen, the fact remains, as is clear from the use of the words 'shall facilitate' in Article 3(2), that that provision imposes an obligation on the Member States to confer a certain advantage, compared with applications for entry and residence of other nationals of third States, on applications submitted by persons who have a relationship of particular dependence with a Union citizen.

22. In order to meet that obligation, the Member States must, in accordance with the second subparagraph of Article 3(2) of Directive 2004/38, make it possible for persons envisaged in the first subparagraph of Article 3(2) to obtain a decision on their application that is founded on an extensive examination of their personal circumstances and, in the event of refusal, is justified by reasons.

23. As is clear from recital 6 in the preamble to Directive 2004/38, it is incumbent upon the competent authority, when undertaking that examination of the applicant's personal circumstances, to take account of the various factors that may be relevant in the particular case, such as the extent of economic or physical dependence and the degree of relationship between the family member and the Union citizen whom he wishes to accompany or join.

Although their right of entry may be weaker, if article 3 family members are in fact admitted then it seems probable that they fall within the scope of 'family members' as used elsewhere in the Directive and as such enjoy the same rights to employment and equality as article 2 family members.

---

[104] Case C-1/05 *Jia* v *Migrationsverket* [2007] ECR I-1. See also Case C-432/12 *Reyes*, Judgment of 16 January 2014.

An issue which the Directive does not resolve clearly and is therefore likely to engage the Court of Justice soon is same-sex marriage.[105] At the time the Directive was adopted, no states had instituted this, but now several have.[106] The right to bring a spouse is unconditional in article 2(2)(a), and it remains to be seen whether the Court will permit conservative states to refuse recognition to same-sex spouses by reliance on a public policy derogation.

(b) Separation, death and divorce

If family members lose their link with the migrant citizen, either through his or her death or the break-up of the relationship, their own rights of residence may become threatened. The Directive provides a degree of protection.

For EU family members, their right of residence continues after divorce or the death of the partner.[107] For non-EU family members, it continues under a number of conditions: that they had lived together in the state for at least a year before the death or divorce, and in the case of divorce had also been married for at least three years.[108] The stricter approach partly reflects a fear of marriages of convenience, and partly a view that non-EU family members who have only been present for a short period have less right to remain. Non-EU family members also maintain their right of residence after a divorce if they have custody of the Union citizen's children or a right of access to them, or if particular circumstances such as domestic violence warrant more generosity.[109]

For both EU and non-EU partners, the post-relationship right of residence is subject to conditions. EU family members are subject to the same article 7 conditions as any other citizen, while non-EU family members must be either economically active or have resources and sickness insurance.[110] However, these conditions do not apply to the children of the dead or departed Union citizen if they are in school in the host state, nor to the parent who has custody of them.[111] Irrespective of nationality or resources, these retain their right of residence at least until school-leaving age has been reached. If children have come to a host state to join a migrant worker, who has subsequently departed the family for whatever reason, or lost the status of worker, those children and their carer enjoy an additional right of residence on the basis of article 10 of Regulation 492/211. This right is not dependent on resources, and extends until education is completed and care is no longer necessary, even potentially well into adulthood.[112]

In reality, family life may encompass more options than married cohabitation and divorce. For various reasons, partners may live apart while still having a legal bond to each other. In *Diatta* and *Baumbast*, the Court maintained that (i) until a marriage was finally dissolved, it

---

[105] See generally H. Toner, *Partnership Rights, Free Movement and EU Law* (Oxford/Portland, Hart, 2004); M. Bell, 'Holding Back the Tide? Cross-border Recognition of Same Sex Partnerships within the European Union' (2004) 5 *ERPL* 613.

[106] As of 2014 eight Member States allow same-sex marriage (see http://en.wikipedia.org/wiki/Recognition_of_same-sex_unions_in_Europe); fifteen allow registered partnerships with rights similar to marriage, although note that the Directive treats these differently: see article 2.

[107] Citizenship Directive, articles 12–13.

[108] *Ibid.*   [109] *Ibid.* article 13(2).   [110] *Ibid.* articles 12 and 13.

[111] Citizenship Directive, article 12(3).

[112] Case C-310/08 *Ibrahim* [2010] ECR I-1065; Case C-480/08 *Teixeira* [2010] ECR I-1107; Case C-529/11 *Alarape*, Judgment of 8 May 2013, applying article 12 of Regulation 1612/68, which has now been replaced by the identically worded article 10 of Regulation 492/211.

was to be considered as existing,[113] and so a divorce in progress did not affect residence rights; and (ii) cohabitation was not as such a condition for residence rights for a family member.

(c) Rights of children and carers

As mentioned above, children of school age enjoy protection of their residence rights in the event of family breakdown, as does the parent with custody of them. Children who are Union citizens also enjoy an independent right of free movement and residence; they are citizens just as much as adults are.[114] Baby Catherine Zhu had Irish nationality and to the dismay of the Irish and UK Governments, her mother, Mrs Chen, who was Chinese, asserted a right for them both to live in the United Kingdom. They had sufficient resources and sickness insurance.[115]

Case C-200/02 Zhu and Chen [2004] ECR I-9925

20. Moreover, contrary to the Irish Government's contention, a young child can take advantage of the rights of free movement and residence guaranteed by Community law. The capacity of a national of a Member State to be the holder of rights guaranteed by the Treaty and by secondary law on the free movement of persons cannot be made conditional upon the attainment by the person concerned of the age prescribed for the acquisition of legal capacity to exercise those rights personally....

45. On the other hand, a refusal to allow the parent, whether a national of a Member State or a national of a non-member country, who is the carer of a child to whom Article [21 TFEU] and Directive 90/364 grant a right of residence, to reside with that child in the host Member State would deprive the child's right of residence of any useful effect. It is clear that enjoyment by a young child of a right of residence necessarily implies that the child is entitled to be accompanied by the person who is his or her primary carer and accordingly that the carer must be in a position to reside with the child in the host Member State for the duration of such residence.

46. For that reason alone, where, as in the main proceedings, Article [21 TFEU] and Directive 90/364 grant a right to reside for an indefinite period in the host Member State to a young minor who is a national of another Member State, those same provisions allow a parent who is that minor's primary carer to reside with the child in the host Member State.

The Court of Justice here adds a new category of family member to those in the Directive. Where EU children exercise their EU movement and residence rights, the person primarily responsible for their care is granted parallel rights of movement and residence, irrespective of the carer's nationality. It does not even appear from the judgment that the carer must necessarily be a parent or even a family member, simply 'the person who is his or her primary carer'. Following the cases on carers in other contexts, one may expect this dependent right to continue until education is completed[116] Since, in most cases, by this time the family will have been present in the state for a number of years, it is then less likely that it will be possible to remove the carer, for reasons of human rights. It is also arguable that as family members assimilated

---

[113] See Case C-267/83 *Diatta v Land Berlin* [1985] ECR 567; Case C-413/99 *Baumbast v Secretary of State for the Home Department* [2002] ECR I-7091; *Iida*, n. 95 above.
[114] See H. Stalford and E. Drywood, 'Coming of Age: Children's Rights in the EU' (2009) 46 *CMLRev.* 143.
[115] See Case C-86/12 *Alokpa*, Judgment of 10 October 2013.   [116] See p. 497.

to those covered by the Directive, carers should have a parallel right to acquire permanent resident status after five years.[117] Helen Stalford has commented that the child is in a sense an 'anchor' for her carer in their host state, a phenomenon which she traces through the different lines of case law about children, not just *Chen*, but also the situations of family break-up discussed above, and *Ruiz Zambrano*, discussed below.[118]

H. Stalford, *Children and the European Union: Rights, Welfare and Accountability* (Oxford, Oxford University Press, 2012) 48–9

Historically, children's status as EU citizens has been regarded as rather vacuous and incidental: given that children do not, for the most part, migrate independently, they only benefit from the rights associated with free movement as a consequence of their parents' decision to live and work in another Member State. More recent case law, however, has seen the Court of Justice heightening the currency of children's status as EU citizens in their own right. Indeed, this has occurred to such a degree that the tables have turned: while children have traditionally derived their citizenship entitlement from their parents it is becoming increasingly common for parents to derive valuable entry and residence rights within the EU from their children. This is particularly decisive, for instance, for adults of third country nationality who, having lived and perhaps even worked for a period in the host state with their family, no longer qualify for ongoing residence under national immigration law. In such cases, the Court of Justice has willingly extended the residence rights of third country national parents who have children of EU nationality. This is in acknowledgment of the fact that the entitlement accruing to their children by virtue of their EU citizenship status – notably their right to pursue education in the host state – can only be exercised if their primary carers (usually the parents) are allowed to remain with them.

This development in the case law is significant in that it establishes, first and foremost, that EU citizenship yields tangible and direct entitlement for individuals regardless of their age or level of dependency. Furthermore, it explicitly acknowledges the important social, emotional and material interdependence between family members. On the one hand, the application of EU citizenship is a key illustration of how children's rights are operable largely by virtue of the support and assistance of their parents. The very existence of that dependency, on the other hand, can 'anchor' their parents to the host state too. The conceptualization provides a useful illustration of the distinction between child autonomy and self-sufficiency that pervades children's rights and citizenship literature more broadly: children have an autonomous right to reside in a Member State founded on their status as EU citizens but are not expected to exercise that right without appropriate parental support, even if recognition of this might serve to undermine domestic immigration law, and even, it seems, if it implies an additional burden on the host state's welfare system.

Ruiz Zambrano applied *Chen*-style reasoning to a citizen in their home Member State.[119] Having found that a child citizen has a right to live in the territory of the Union, the Court of Justice went on to conclude that this prevented the expulsion of their parents, non-Europeans, from the Union, since the children would be compelled to accompany them. It began by excluding the application of the Citizenship Directive, since the children were Belgian citizens living in Belgium, and then turned to the direct application of Article 20 TFEU.

---

[117] See *Alarape*, n. 112 above.   [118] See pp. 499–503.   [119] *Ruiz Zambrano*, n. 1 above.

> **Case C-34/09 *Ruiz Zambrano* v *Office national de l'emploi (ONEm)* [2011] ECR I-1177**
>
> 41. As the Court has stated several times, citizenship of the Union is intended to be the fundamental status of nationals of the Member States.
>
> 42. In those circumstances, Article 20 TFEU precludes national measures which have the effect of depriving citizens of the Union of the genuine enjoyment of the substance of the rights conferred by virtue of their status as citizens of the Union.
>
> 43. A refusal to grant a right of residence to a third country national with dependent minor children in the Member State where those children are nationals and reside, and also a refusal to grant such a person a work permit, has such an effect.
>
> 44. It must be assumed that such a refusal would lead to a situation where those children, citizens of the Union, would have to leave the territory of the Union in order to accompany their parents. Similarly, if a work permit were not granted to such a person, he would risk not having sufficient resources to provide for himself and his family, which would also result in the children, citizens of the Union, having to leave the territory of the Union. In those circumstances, those citizens of the Union would, in fact, be unable to exercise the substance of the rights conferred on them by virtue of their status as citizens of the Union.

The fact that the conditions of 'sufficient resources' do not apply in one's home state might seem to mean that the child at home is better off than the child migrant, who must rely on the Directive for their initial residence right.[120] There are also many more children in their home states than living as migrants, which suggests a significant broadening of the scope of EU law. However, later cases have confirmed that the *Zambrano* test is strict, so that in practice the consequences may not be so large, and the number of beneficiaries may be low. It will take time and more references for this to become clear.

The first expansion, and explanation, of the principles of *Zambrano* occurred in *Dereci*, a reference which concerned a number of different family situations in which one family member was a European citizen and another was a non-European threatened with expulsion from the EU. Might *Ruiz Zambrano* apply? Could expelling an adult son mean that his aged mother had to leave the Union? Could expelling the partner of a citizen mean that this partner was effectively forced to leave?

> **Case C-256/11 *Dereci*, Judgment of 15 November 2011**
>
> 66. ... the criterion relating to the denial of the genuine enjoyment of the substance of the rights conferred by virtue of European Union citizen status refers to situations in which the Union citizen has, in fact, to leave not only the territory of the State of which he is a national but also the territory of the Union as a whole.
>
> 67. That criterion is specific in character inasmuch as it relates to situations in which, although subordinate legislation on the right of residence of third country nationals is not applicable, a right of residence may not, exceptionally, be refused to a third country national, who is a family member of a Member State national, as the effectiveness of Union citizenship enjoyed by that national would otherwise be undermined.

---

[120] *Alokpa*, n. 115 above.

68. Consequently, the mere fact that it might appear desirable to a national of a Member State, for economic reasons or in order to keep his family together in the territory of the Union, for the members of his family who do not have the nationality of a Member State to be able to reside with him in the territory of the Union, is not sufficient in itself to support the view that the Union citizen will be forced to leave Union territory if such a right is not granted.

On the one hand, the Court of Justice makes clear that the test is a strict one; the mere desirability of being with a family member is not enough. It has to be the case that a citizen is in fact forced to leave the Union. Yet on the other hand, the case also shows that this is a question of fact, to be considered in each case. The Court does not preclude, in principle, the application of the *Zambrano* rule to other forms of family relationship, and ultimately it left it to the national court to decide whether the expulsion of the family member complied with Article 20 TFEU or not. *Dereci* therefore leaves room for a great deal of discretion and variability in the application of the law.

This is important, because the test is in fact an impossible one to carry out, and full of logical loopholes. Contrary to the reasoning in *Zambrano*, it is quite possible that in some circumstances parents would leave their children behind if expelled. Consider the Afghan parents of teenage girls, brought up in a European state where they have other family members and friends. Is it unthinkable that the parents would, however sadly, come to the conclusion that it is better for the children to remain than to accompany them back to Afghanistan? Yet how is a court to know what parents will do in such a situation? Should it deport the parents, see if the children follow, and if so conclude that they all might have stayed? Whereas if the children remain, then this proves the expulsion was lawful? This transforms the case into a modern witchcraft test.[121] These arguments apply *a fortiori* where other family relations are involved. They also become particularly important where only one parent is a non-European. Some immigration authorities have taken the view that if mother and children are European citizens, then there is no obstacle to expelling the father since the children can stay with the mother. Splitting a family may be sad, but *Dereci* makes clear that this is not sufficient to engage EU law. However, such logic would have the bizarre consequence that as soon as Mr Ruiz Zambrano won his case, and earned a right to remain, his wife might have become vulnerable to expulsion.

In reality a test of whether a citizen is actually forced to leave the Union is meaningless: Belgium is a wealthy social democratic state that would have provided for the needs of the Ruiz Zambrano children if they were left behind. No Union citizen is ever forced to leave, if taken literally. The real question is whether they can stay behind without their family members at a personal cost that EU law finds acceptable. This begins to emerge in the judgment in *O and S*, a Finnish reference in which the children were Finnish, the mothers were non-EU nationals with residence permits for Finland, but the husbands of the mothers, also not Union citizens, had been refused residence permits and faced expulsion. Having reiterated the general principles of *Ruiz Zambrano* and *Dereci* the Court of Justice went into more detail on how these are to be applied.

---

[121] 'Ordeal by water' was a medieval test for witchcraft; when dunked in water, those who floated were proven to be witches, while those who drowned were shown to have been innocent.

Joined Cases C–356/11 and C–357/11 *O and S v Maahanmuuttovirasto and Maahanmuuttovirasto v L*, **Judgment of 6 December 2012**

53. …the referring court…must examine all the circumstances of the case in order to determine whether, in fact, the decisions refusing residence permits at issue in the main proceedings are liable to undermine the effectiveness of the Union citizenship enjoyed by the Union citizens concerned.

54. Whether the person for whom a right of residence is sought on the basis of family reunification lives together with the sponsor and the other family members is not decisive in that assessment, since it cannot be ruled out that some family members who are the subject of an application for family reunification may arrive in the Member State concerned separately from the rest of the family.

55. It should also be noted that, contrary to the submissions of the German and Italian Governments, while the principles stated in the *Ruiz Zambrano* judgment apply only in exceptional circumstances, it does not follow from the Court's case-law that their application is confined to situations in which there is a blood relationship between the third country national for whom a right of residence is sought and the Union citizen who is a minor from whom that right of residence might be derived.

56. On the other hand, both the permanent right of residence of the mothers of the Union citizens concerned who are minors and the fact that the third country nationals for whom a right of residence is sought are not persons on whom those citizens are legally, financially or emotionally dependent must be taken into consideration when examining the question whether, as a result of the refusal of a right of residence, those citizens would be unable to exercise the substance of the rights conferred by their status. As the Advocate General observes in point 44 of his Opinion, it is the relationship of dependency between the Union citizen who is a minor and the third country national who is refused a right of residence that is liable to jeopardise the effectiveness of Union citizenship, since it is that dependency that would lead to the Union citizen being obliged, in fact, to leave not only the territory of the Member State of which he is a national but also that of the European Union as a whole, as a consequence of such a refusal.

Once again, there is emphasis on the strictness of the rule, and the Court of Justice went on to suggest that in this case the expulsion of the men would probably be acceptable – they were in fact neither the fathers nor the carers of the children.[122] However, the judgment also emphasises the importance of the circumstances of the case, and suggests that the heart of the national court's task is to establish the degree of legal, financial and emotional dependence of the child to its parent – and by extrapolation to a *Dereci*-type situation, between two other family members, or theoretically even a non-family carer. If such dependence is sufficient, it will prevent expulsion.

In opening the door to emotional – human – considerations the Court of Justice takes this law in a new direction. In reality, where children are concerned, economic dependency is irrelevant, because children will always be taken care of by the state. Their need to be with their parents is primarily emotional. Thus *O and S* moves away from the clumsy 'what will the citizen do if we deport his family – will he go or will he stay?' test of *Ruiz Zambrano*, and towards an assessment of the human consequences of splitting family members. This is an assessment in which

---

[122] Any dependency which existed was apparently between the mothers of the children and the men. The judgment appears to condone the idea that such indirect dependency could also in some conditions fall within *Zambrano*, since if the mothers were compelled to leave they would take the children with them.

human rights and Article 8 ECHR may be expected to play a role as helpful legal guides to a judge seeking to determine when the degree of dependency is sufficient. Thus, it is possible that *Zambrano* will, in substance, amount to a rule that family members may not be expelled from the Union if separation of the citizen from those family members would violate Article 8 ECHR.

It may go further than this. In *Carpenter*, an older case, the Court of Justice had to consider the expulsion of a third-country family member from the Union, and the argument again was that this would impact on the conditions under which her partner was able to enjoy his free movement rights within the EU.[123] Having acknowledged the importance to states of enforcing their immigration rules, which were claimed to be vital to public order, the Court continued:

> 43. A decision to deport Mrs Carpenter, taken in circumstances such as those in the main proceedings, does not strike a fair balance between the competing interests, that is, on the one hand, the right of Mr Carpenter to respect for his family life, and, on the other hand, the maintenance of public order and public safety....
>
> 45. In those circumstances, the decision to deport Mrs Carpenter constitutes an infringement which is not proportionate to the objective pursued.

In *Carpenter* the harm threatened was that the family was to be split. In *Ruiz Zambrano* the harm was precisely that it would not be – so the children would leave the EU. That means the law is engaged in different ways: in *Carpenter* by a loss of quality of free movement and in *Ruiz Zambrano* by a loss of any possibility of it. *O and S* does not transform *Ruiz Zambrano* into *Carpenter*, but in putting dependency central it does take a step towards uniting the two.

A question which *Chen* and *Ruiz Zambrano* raise is when a carer's rights begin. It seems clear following these cases that a parent arriving from outside the Union with a baby in their arms which they can demonstrate to be a Union citizen will consequently have a right to remain. However, suppose that they cannot prove that the baby is a Union citizen, but they have a plausible claim that he has a right to such citizenship – perhaps it is the fruit of a holiday romance with an EU tourist? Arguably, the Member State where they are present should grant them a period, for example, to make contact with the father and take legal steps to establish paternity.[124] This may seem far-fetched but the alternative is that a Member State risks deporting a Union citizen from the Union, possibly to deeply disadvantageous socio-economic circumstances, which is entirely at odds with the perspective expressed in *Chen* and *Ruiz Zambrano*. One might even extrapolate to the position of a pregnant woman arriving at Heathrow airport from a non-EU state and claiming she carries a baby which will be entitled to citizenship of a Member State upon its birth, say a few months away. Would it be in the spirit of the law to turn her away and let the little proto-European be born in possibly dangerous conditions outside the European Union?

(d) Family members arriving from outside the Union

That migrant citizens can take their family from one Member State to another is a logical corollary of their own right of free movement. In practice, if people cannot take their family they will not move. However, it is less obvious that the migrant should have the right to

---

[123] Expulsion of a family member which 'discourages' cross-border work is now prohibited: *S and G*, n. 85 above.
[124] See Case C-135/08 *Janko Rottmann v Freistaat Bayern* [2010] ECR I-1449, para. 58.

bring family members into the Union for the first time. It is certainly true that the quality of migration will be enhanced if it is possible to bring distant family members to the host state. However, if this is not the case the migrant will be no worse off in the host state than at home, so it is not clear that there is any deterrent to free movement. It may perhaps be argued that the position of a migrant in a host state is particularly lonely and difficult and therefore the presence of family members is a necessary accompaniment, whether or not they were with the Union citizen prior to her migration. The Directive seems to reflect this latter view, providing for a right of residence for family members 'accompanying or joining' the citizen, without any condition that they join from within the European Union.

In *Akrich*, the Court of Justice wrote such a condition into the Directive, saying that it only applied to family members already lawfully present in an EU Member State.[125] However, this innovation was short-lived and has been reversed in *Metock*.[126] The latter case concerned asylum seekers in Ireland, who had married UK citizens resident in Ireland and thereby become the spouses of migrant citizens. The judgment was complex, but set out a number of important points:

- The right of a family member to live with the Union citizen is simply dependent upon compliance with the definitions and conditions in the Directive. A state may impose no other conditions (such as previous lawful residence in another Member State).
- It does not matter that the citizen met and married their partner in the host state, as in *Metock*. This still counts as family 'joining' the citizen.[127]
- It does not matter if the partner previously entered the country illegally, or prior to the marriage was illegally present.
- Becoming a family member in the Directive sense has the effect of wiping the slate almost clean. The slate is only wiped 'almost' clean because the state may still impose proportionate sanctions upon the family member for any previous violations of immigration law, but these must not go so far as to deter free movement – one should think of a fine, but not of a denial of residence.[128]

The policy reasons for the *Metock* decision are diverse. An important one put forward by the Court of Justice is that Directives concerning non-EU nationals who are long-term residents in an EU Member State give them the right to bring their family into the European Union.[129] It would be odd if migrant Union citizens then had lesser rights. This is not entirely logical. Such a comparison would suggest that Union citizens should be able to bring their family members into the Union if they were previously resident together in the non-EU country (avoiding family break-up) but not necessarily otherwise, where migration does not change the family circumstances. However, this approach would have entailed a rather complex judicial rewriting of the Directive, which is perhaps one reason why the Court chose to simply accept the wording of the Directive at face value, over the protests of several Member States about the effect on immigration.

---

[125] Case C-109/01 *Secretary of State for the Home Department v Akrich* [2003] ECR I-9607.

[126] Case C-127/08 *Metock* [2008] ECR I-6241. See C. Costello, '*Metock*: Free Movement and "Normal Family Life" in the Union' (2009) 46 *CMLRev.* 587; S. Currie, 'Accelerated Justice or a Step Too Far? Residence Rights of Non-EU Family Members and the Court's Ruling in *Metock*' (2009) 34 *ELRev.* 310.

[127] See also Case C-551/07 *Sahin* [2008] ECR I-1043.   [128] See pp. 507–8.

[129] *Metock*, n. 126 above, para. 69; see Directive 2003/86/EC.

The judgment has huge implications. In a time where many Member States make it difficult for their own nationals to bring family members in from outside the Union, EU migrants have a significant legal advantage. The Danish citizen struggling to bring his Angolan wife to Denmark because of Danish immigration law may move to Sweden, whereupon both he and she can rely on the Directive rights. A small but growing number of Union citizens now engage in such migration for the purposes of family reunification, to the concern of some national authorities.

The effect of *Metock* is greatly enhanced by *Singh*:[130] where a citizen returns to her home state after spending a period exercising EU rights in another Member State, she continues to fall within the scope of EU law and continues to enjoy the EU rights that she had while she was abroad. Combining the two allows a citizen to go abroad, bring their family member to the EU – or bring them out of illegality by marrying them – and then take them home.

This has since been clarified and confirmed in *Eind*.[131] In this case, a Dutch citizen working in the United Kingdom brought his daughter to live with him in Britain from outside the Union. When he returned to the Netherlands, the Dutch authorities claimed that the situation was internal and governed by Dutch immigration law, which did not permit the daughter's residence. Mr Eind, by contrast, claimed that he could continue to rely on EU rights as a returning migrant. The Court of Justice agreed with him.

Case C-291/05 *Minister voor Vreemdelingenzaken en Integratie* v *Eind* [2004] ECR I-10719

35. A national of a Member State could be deterred from leaving that Member State in order to pursue gainful employment in the territory of another Member State if he does not have the certainty of being able to return to his Member State of origin, irrespective of whether he is going to engage in economic activity in the latter State.

36. That deterrent effect would also derive simply from the prospect, for that same national, of not being able, on returning to his Member State of origin, to continue living together with close relatives, a way of life which may have come into being in the host Member State as a result of marriage or family reunification.

37. Barriers to family reunification are therefore liable to undermine the right to free movement which the nationals of the Member States have under Community law, as the right of a Community worker to return to the Member State of which he is a national cannot be considered to be a purely internal matter.

38. It follows that, in circumstances such as those in the case before the referring court, Miss Eind has the right to install herself with her father, Mr Eind, in the Netherlands, even if the latter is not economically active.

Returning migrants therefore continue to enjoy the family rights that they have exercised for the first time while abroad. The Dane who has brought his Angolan wife to Sweden and lived there for a while may then return to Denmark and rely on EU law against his own state to enforce her right to live with him. This U-turn construction is becoming increasingly popular.

---

[130] Case C-370/90 *Singh* [1992] ECR I-4265; see pp. 492–3 above. See also A. Tryfonidou, 'Family Reunification Right of (Migrant) Union Citizens: Towards a More Liberal Approach' (2009) 15 *ELJ* 634.

[131] Case C-291/05 *Minister voor Vreemdelingenzaken en Integratie* v *Eind* [2004] ECR I-10719.

In *O and B*, the Court found that U-turn rights exist to protect family life which was created or strengthened abroad. Thus they do not arise after very brief residence, or where a citizen merely brings a family member over for weekends. However, the Court found that when the family resides on the basis of article 7 of the Directive, evidencing an intention to stay for at least three months, this should normally suffice. That is, it may be noted, a low hurdle.[132] Attempts to bring family rights home when there was no substantive exercise of family life and rights abroad will amount to abuse, the Court found. However, the mere fact that the migration was for the purpose of acquiring family rights will not make it abusive, as long as those rights were genuinely exercised in the host state to a sufficient degree.[133]

The effect of these cases is that migrants' rights become vested and can be applied against their home state. This raises a number of difficult questions, notably whether there are financial conditions or limits to the time that such rights continue at home. In *Eind*, the Dutch Government argued that any such returnee rights should only continue as long as the returnee was economically active in his home state. It may be noted that in *Singh*, the Court of Justice referred to a worker who returns to take up economic activity in their home state. However, the introduction of citizenship and of broader residence rights changes the position and the Court rejected the Dutch Government's argument. It pointed out that citizens have an unconditional right of residence in their home state, so reference to conditions for residence, which might be applied to non-nationals, was not appropriate. This suggests that not only do returnees not need to work to maintain their EU rights, but they do not need to comply with the conditions on resources and sickness insurance. Family rights brought home may well be permanent and unconditional in practice.

National immigration law is made increasingly untenable by these developments, with all those having the initiative and capacity to find some kind of work abroad now able to bring themselves within the more family-friendly EU legal regime and opt out of national immigration law. The judgment in *Metock* contained an extensive discussion of the relative competences of the Member States and the Union and it is most likely that future years will see increasing harmonisation in this area.

(iv) Administrative formalities

Member States are entitled to ask EU migrants and their families to comply with a number of administrative formalities. For entry to a state, a valid passport or identity card may be demanded from Union citizens, whereas non-EU family members may also have to have a visa under certain circumstances, at least until they have obtained a residence card, whereupon this and their passport are sufficient for travel.[134]

For short-term residence, up to three months, no conditions or formalities may be imposed other than the requirement that the citizen and family members report their presence to the police within a reasonable and non-discriminatory time.[135]

For longer residence, Member States may require that citizens and their families register with the authorities.[136] To do so they may be required to present valid identity documents and evidence that they comply with the substantive conditions for residence. Thus, citizens may be

---

[132] See *O and B*, n. 85 above.
[133] *O and B*, ibid. para 58; Case C-109/01 *Akrich* [2003] ECR I-9607; Case 53/81 *Levin* [1982] ECR I-1035.
[134] Citizenship Directive, article 5(2).   [135] *Ibid.* article 5(5).   [136] *Ibid.* article 8(1).

required to show that they are economically active, or that they have resources and sickness insurance. Students do not have to show evidence of resources, but can simply sign a declaration that they have them.[137] Family members have to show evidence of their relationship with the migrant citizen. Those falling within the 'extra' family members whose entry is to be facilitated under article 3 of the Citizenship Directive are required to produce evidence that they are indeed dependants or family members.[138]

Despite the sometimes forbidding sound of all these requirements, a number of factors mitigate them so that they should (in principle) rarely be a cause of problems for migrants.

First, it has long been established that the residence documents issued by states upon registration are merely evidentiary and not constitutive of the rights of the citizen, and *Oulane* confirms that this remains the case after the Directive.[139] In this case, a French citizen had neither a residence card, nor even a valid passport. The Dutch authorities claimed he was therefore illegally present in the Netherlands. On the contrary, the Court of Justice took the view that he had a Treaty right as a result of being a Union citizen and such documents (including the residence card) were simply evidence of this, but not necessary evidence.

Case C–215/03 *Oulane v Minister voor Vreemdelingenzaken en Integratie* [2005] ECR I–1215

17. …the right of nationals of a Member State to enter the territory of another Member State and reside there for the purposes intended by the Treaty is a right conferred directly by the Treaty or, as the case may be, by the provisions adopted for its implementation.…

18. It follows that issuance of a residence permit to a national of a Member State is to be regarded not as a measure giving rise to rights but as a measure by a Member State serving to prove the individual position of a national of another Member State with regard to provisions of Community law.

The citizen or family member who fails to comply is therefore not in any sense illegally present in the host state and cannot be expelled. In fact, the Directive goes further than this.

Citizenship Directive, article 25(1)

1. Possession of a residence certificate as referred to in Article 8, of a document certifying permanent residence, of a certificate attesting submission of an application for a family member residence card, of a residence card or of a permanent residence card, may under no circumstances be made a precondition for the exercise of a right or the completion of an administrative formality, as entitlement to rights may be attested by any other means of proof.

A failure to register should therefore have no consequences for functioning in the host state. Work, education, access to benefits and other aspects of life should be unaffected. The registration procedure and documents are not to be conditions for access to host state life, but merely

---

[137] *Ibid.* article 8(3); C–424/98 *Commission v Italy* [2000] ECR I–4001.   [138] *Ibid.* article 8(5).
[139] See also *Dias*, n. 32 above, para. 54. Cf. Case C–456/02 *Trojani* [2004] ECR I–7573, para. 46.

a mechanism for states to gather information and establish those present on their territory. In practice, obtaining the registration documents tends to make life in the host state much easier, as they comprise evidence that the state has recognised the right of residence. Despite article 25, it is common for public authorities to want to see these documents before granting access to other rights and benefits.

Since article 25 prohibits registration being a condition for the exercise of other rights, states who wish to enforce the registration requirement have to hunt for and punish non-registered migrants and their families. However, the Directive limits any sanctions to those that are proportionate and non-discriminatory.[140] Sanctions of such a severity that they seriously impair the very right of residence are disproportionate.[141] A proper approach to determining appropriate sanctions is to consider how comparable infringements by nationals are punished; for example, violations of an obligation to inform the authorities of a new address when moving house.

The importance of formalities and documentary requirements is further diminished by the Court of Justice's approach to evidence, which is highly pragmatic and non-formalistic. In *Oulane*, it went so far as to find that possession of a valid passport or identity card is not a condition for lawful residence, since nationality may be proved in other ways:

> If the person concerned is able to provide unequivocal proof of his nationality by means other than a valid identity card or passport, the host Member State may not refuse to recognise his right of residence on the sole ground that he has not presented one of those documents.[142]

This approach was continued in *MRAX*, where the Court of Justice considered Belgian practice on third-country partners of Union citizens.[143] The Belgian state took the view that if these were not in possession of a valid identity document and visa, as the Directives in force required, they were not entitled to a residence card and could be deported. In a long but important judgment, the Court affirmed that just as with Union citizens, the right of the third-country partner stems directly from the Treaty and a failure to comply with formalities does not remove it. If they have no documents, they may have difficulty proving their identity and family relationship, but if they can somehow do this (the Court noted that an expired passport may still be evidence of identity), then the responsibility of the state is to assist them in obtaining the necessary documents in the host state, as quickly as possible, while any sanctions imposed must be no more than are proportionate.

(v) Grounds for exclusion

In tandem with other provisions on movement of EU nationals, the Citizenship Directive sets out certain circumstances in which Union citizens can be expelled from or refused entry to another Member State, even though they would otherwise meet the requirements for residence.[144]

---

[140] See also Case C-230/97 *Awoyemi* [1998] ECR I-6781.
[141] Case 118/75 *Watson and Belmann* [1976] ECR 1185.
[142] Case C-215/03 *Oulane* v *Minister voor Vreemdelingenzaken en Integratie* [2005] ECR I-1215.
[143] Case C-459/99 *MRAX* [2002] ECR I-6591.
[144] See generally N. Nic Shuibhne, 'Derogating from the Free Movement of Persons: When Can Union Citizens be Deported?' (2006) 8 *Cambridge Yearbook of European Legal Studies* 187; D. Kostakopoulou and N. Ferreira, 'Testing Liberal Norms: The Public Policy and Public Security Derogations and the Cracks in European Citizenship' (2014) 20(2) *Columbia Journal of European Law* (forthcoming); D. Kochenov and B. Pirker, 'Deporting EU Citizens: A Counter-Intuitive Trend' (2013) 19 *Columbia Journal of European Law* 369.

The rules in article 27 also apply to national measures restricting a migrant to a particular part of the national territory, or excluding him from one part of it.[145]

Citizenship Directive, article 27

1. Subject to the provisions of this Chapter, Member States may restrict the freedom of movement and residence of Union citizens and their family members, irrespective of nationality, on grounds of public policy, public security or public health. These grounds shall not be invoked to serve economic ends.
2. Measures taken on grounds of public policy or public security shall comply with the principle of proportionality and shall be based exclusively on the personal conduct of the individual concerned. Previous criminal convictions shall not in themselves constitute grounds for taking such measures. The personal conduct of the individual concerned must represent a genuine, present and sufficiently serious threat affecting one of the fundamental interests of society. Justifications that are isolated from the particulars of the case or that rely on considerations of general prevention shall not be accepted.

In any case where a decision is made to deport an individual, the person must be notified in writing of the decision. They must be told the reasons for exclusion, precisely and in full, unless this is contrary to the interests of state security.[146] All persons must have access to judicial and administrative redress procedures to appeal against or seek review of any decision taken against them.[147] These procedures will consider the legality and proportionality of the decision, as well as the facts and circumstances on which the decision was based.[148] Individuals must be told in the initial decision by the relevant court or administrative authority where they may lodge an appeal, the time limits for the appeal and the time allowed to leave the territory.[149]

These procedural guarantees apply to all migrant citizens, not just those lawfully present in the Member State.[150] To impose a condition of lawfulness on the procedural protections would be to some extent to pre-empt precisely the issue that the procedures in question are to determine.

The most commonly used grounds for exclusion are public policy and public security. Although these are two separate criteria, article 27(2) provides that they both turn on the question whether the individual's conduct poses a genuine, present and sufficiently serious threat to the fundamental interests of society. States have some discretion in determining the threshold here, since norms may vary. However, the derogations are EU law concepts, subject to the jurisdiction of the Court of Justice, which interprets them restrictively, since they are derogations from the fundamental freedom to move. The Court is particularly vigilant in asking whether a consistent approach is being taken to nationals and foreigners.[151] In *Adoui*,[152] Belgium wished

---

[145] Case C-100/01 *Ministre de l'Intérieur* v *Olazabal* [2002] ECR I-10981.
[146] Citizenship Directive, article 30(1) and (2). See now Case C-300/11 *ZZ*, Judgment of 4 June 2013.
[147] *Ibid.* article 31(1).   [148] *Ibid.* article 31(3).   [149] *Ibid.* article 30(3).
[150] Case C-459/99 *MRAX* [2002] ECR I-6591; Case C-50/06 *Commission* v *Netherlands* [2007] ECR I-4383; Case C-136/03 *Dörr and Ünal* [2005] ECR I-4759.
[151] Case 41/74 *Van Duyn* v *Home Office* [1974] ECR 1337; Joined Cases C-65/95 and C-111/95 *R* v *Secretary of State for the Home Department ex parte Shingara and ex parte Radiom* [1997] ECR I-03343; Case 121/85 *Conegate* v *Customs and Excise Commissioners* [1986] ECR 1007; Case 34/79 *R* v *Henn and Darby* [1979] ECR 3795. Cf. Case C-364/10 *Hungary* v *Slovak Republic*, Judgment of 16 October 2012.
[152] Joined Cases 115/81 and 116/81 *Adoui and Cornuaille* v *Belgian State and City of Liège* [1982] ECR 1665.

to deport some French women who were 'waitresses in a bar which was suspect from the point of view of morals'.[153]

Joined Cases 115/81 and 116/81 *Adoui and Cornuaille* v *Belgian State and City of Liège* [1982] ECR 1665

8. Although Community law does not impose upon the Member States a uniform scale of values as regards the assessment of conduct which may be considered as contrary to public policy, it should nevertheless be stated that conduct may not be considered as being of a sufficiently serious nature to justify restrictions on the admission to or residence within the territory of a Member State of a national of another Member State in a case where the former Member State does not adopt, with respect to the same conduct on the part of its own nationals, repressive measures or other genuine and effective measures intended to combat such conduct.

The deportation of foreign prostitutes was conditional upon adequately harsh repression of national ones.

The threat to society which the individual represents must, moreover, be a present one. However bad their behaviour has been in the past, if there is no reason to believe that they will re-offend, then there are no grounds for deportation. This demands that each case be looked at on its facts and rules which provide for automatic deportation after committal of certain offences will inevitably contravene the Directive. In *Orfanopoulos*, a Greek and an Italian drug addict had each been convicted of multiple drugs-related offences, as well as for violent offences and for theft. Germany had a law that any foreigner sentenced to a custodial sentence of two years or more for drugs-related offences would be automatically deported. The German court asked whether the automatic nature of the deportation was disproportionate.

Joined Cases C-482/01 and C-493/01 *Orfanopoulos* v *Land Baden-Württemberg* [2004] ECR I-5257

65. ... a particularly restrictive interpretation of the derogations from that freedom is required by virtue of a person's status as a citizen of the Union....

67. While it is true that a Member State may consider that the use of drugs constitutes a danger for society such as to justify special measures against foreign nationals who contravene its laws on drugs, the public policy exception must, however, be interpreted restrictively, with the result that the existence of a previous criminal conviction can justify an expulsion only insofar as the circumstances which gave rise to that conviction are evidence of personal conduct constituting a present threat to the requirements of public policy.

68. ... Community law precludes the deportation of a national of a Member State based on reasons of a general preventive nature, that is one which has been ordered for the purpose of deterring other aliens, in particular where such measure automatically follows a criminal conviction, without any account being taken of the personal conduct of the offender or of the danger which that person represents for the requirements of public policy.

---

[153] *Ibid.* para. 2. They were accused of prostitution.

69. The question asked by the national court refers to national legislation which requires the expulsion of nationals of other Member States who have received certain sentences for specific offences.

70. It must be held that, in such circumstances, the expulsion automatically follows a criminal conviction, without any account being taken of the personal conduct of the offender or of the danger which that person represents for the requirements of public policy.

71. In the light of the foregoing, the answer to the first question must be that [EU law] preclude[s] national legislation which requires national authorities to expel nationals of other Member States who have been finally sentenced to a term of youth custody of at least two years or to a custodial sentence for an intentional offence against the Law on narcotics, where the sentence has not been suspended.

A similar automatism was present in *Commission* v *Spain*, which addressed a Spanish practice of denying entry to those against whose name an alert had been entered in the Schengen Information System.[154] Although the System is part of EU law, and exists precisely to prevent the free movement of dangerous persons within the EU, nevertheless the Court of Justice found that Spain had an obligation to make its own independent assessment of the degree of threat, and could only give the alert 'due consideration'.

The requirement that the threat must be present has further consequences. If an expulsion order is enforced more than two years after it was issued (as will often be the case where the citizen has to serve a lengthy prison sentence before deportation), the Member State must consider whether, at the moment of enforcement, the individual is still a current and genuine threat to public policy or security.[155] In addition, if a citizen has been deported, she can submit an application for a lifting of the exclusion order after a reasonable period and, in any event, after three years, on the basis that there has been a material change to circumstances.[156]

There is also a scale of seriousness which determines whether exclusion can take place. Residents, or those applying for residency, can be excluded for conduct which would not justify exclusion if they were permanent residents, for the latter may only be expelled on 'serious grounds' of public policy or security.[157] Moreover, if a citizen has been resident in another state for the previous ten years or is a minor, she may not be expelled except for 'imperative' grounds of public security, (public policy is not a sufficient reason to expel these groups), or, in the case of the minor, if it is in the best interests of the child.[158] In *Tsakouridis*, the Court of Justice found that being part of an organised drugs gang could be sufficient to engage 'imperative grounds' of public security, while in *PI* it found that sexual crimes against children might meet this standard too, if the crimes had 'particularly serious characteristics'. Controversially, the Court took account not just of the consequences for victims, but also of the possible impact on the 'calm and physical security of the population'.[159] Kostakopoulou and Ferreira have commented that the Court does not seem to be really assessing the degree of threat to the state, more the general seriousness of the crime, the behaviour of the individual, and its circumstances, moving from what they call the 'security threat' to the 'security constellation'.

---

[154] Case C-503/03 *Commission* v *Spain* [2006] ECR I-1097. See also Case C-348/96 *Calfa* [1999] ECR I-11.

[155] Citizenship Directive, article 33(2). See also Joined Cases C-482/01 and C-493/01 *Orfanopoulos* v *Land Baden-Württemberg* [2004] ECR I-5257.

[156] Citizenship Directive, article 32(1).   [157] *Ibid.* article 28(2).

[158] *Ibid.* article 28(3). See also Case C-400/12 *M.G.*, judgment of 16 January 2014.

[159] Case C-145/09 *Tsakouridis* [2010] ECR I-11979; Case C-348/09 *PI*, Judgment of 22 May 2012. See Kostakopoulou and Ferreira, n. 144 above.

D. Kostakopoulou and N. Ferreira, 'Testing Liberal Norms: The Public Policy and Public Security Derogations and the Cracks in European Citizenship' (2014) 20(2) *Columbia Journal of European Law*

While the 'everydayness' or 'normalization' of the public security derogation will please Member States which remain free to categorize conduct as contrary to public security 'according to the particular values of their legal order', it is deeply problematic and worrying from the point of view of EU law. The phrase 'threat to the calm and physical security of the population' constitutes an interpretational innovation (*Tsakouridis* referred to the economic and social danger for society) which undermines the rationale of the Citizenship Directive and its objectives of promoting security of residence for long-term resident EU citizens and enhancing their citizenship status. Similarly, the reference to the referring court's assessment of conduct leading to expulsion in the light of 'the particular values of the legal order of the Member State' (paragraph 29) is so ambiguous that it is bound to lead to legal uncertainty and the unequal treatment of Union citizens throughout the European Union. The Grand Chamber's deference to the Member States' 'interpretational freedom' may be attuned to the present rise in Euro-scepticism in several countries, but it is certainly at odds with its traditional attestation of the strict interpretation of the derogations.

The exceptions also apply to restrictions on exit. In *Jipa*, the Romanian Government imposed an order on one of its own citizens that he not travel to Belgium for three years.[160] This was because he had earlier been expelled from Belgium. The order had as its background a cooperation agreement between these states relating to 'illegal' Romanians in Belgium. The Court of Justice accepted that such an order could, in principle, be legitimate. It seems reasonable that if one state legitimately expels a Union citizen, there should be little objection to other states helping to make this expulsion effective. However, the judgment shows suspicion of whether the measure was actually disproportionate, with the Court emphasising that such measures, given their fundamental conflict with free movement, should not go beyond what was strictly necessary. A part of the doubt was whether the Belgian order had in fact been legitimate. This was something the national judge should examine.

Even if the citizen's conduct poses a sufficient threat to public policy or public security, it will still not automatically follow that she can be excluded. Article 28(1) of the Citizenship Directive lists a whole host of factors which must be taken into account before making an exclusion order. To these may be added fundamental rights, as reflected in the Charter of Fundamental Rights and the ECHR.

Citizenship Directive, article 28(1)

1. Before taking an expulsion decision on grounds of public policy or public security, the host Member State shall take account of considerations such as how long the individual concerned has resided on its territory, his/her age, state of health, family and economic situation, social and cultural integration into the host Member State and the extent of his/her links with the country of origin.

---

[160] Case C-33/07 *Jipa* [2008] ECR I-5157. See also Case C-434/10 *Aladzhov*, Judgment of 17 November 2011.

Public policy and public security are not trump cards, but rather factors to be weighed in the balance against the interests and circumstances of the individual in question and those close to them.

5 POLITICAL RIGHTS OF UNION CITIZENS

At the heart of modern citizenship is the right to engage fully and equally in the common affairs of the political community. This is usually translated into a series of political rights: the right to vote, to hold office and to hold office holders accountable.[161] For Union citizens residing in a Member State not their own, Article 22 TFEU (and Article 20(2)(b) TFEU) grant them the right to vote and stand in municipal and European elections on the same conditions as nationals of that state. The procedure is regulated by two Directives, which also provide for limited exceptions and conditions in municipalities where there are particularly high levels of non-national Union citizens. Only Luxembourg and Belgium have made use of these.[162] However, the most important cases to date have concerned issues which are less to do with migrating citizens, and more to do with the very nature of the European political community.

Spain v *United Kingdom* raised the question whether only Union citizens can vote for the European Parliament.[163] Spain challenged the United Kingdom's grant of voting rights to some commonwealth citizens resident in Gibraltar. Qualified commonwealth citizens are also entitled to vote in elections, including European Parliament elections, in mainland United Kingdom, although Spain was less upset about this. The Spanish Government made both textual and purposive arguments that the right to vote for the European Parliament was an essential privilege of Union citizens, that it was regulated by EU law and therefore a matter within the sphere of EU law. Hence, Spain argued, a single Member State could not unilaterally extend the franchise to others. The Commission, by contrast, argued that '[a] link does not exist, in all Member States, between the legitimacy of public power and nationality. It is appropriate to take account of different approaches, such as that resulting from the constitutional tradition of the United Kingdom'. The Court of Justice appeared to adopt this latter view, finding that the Treaty simply required that citizens could vote on equal terms with nationals, but did not anywhere suggest that only Union citizens could vote. Indeed, it noted that '[n]o clear conclusion can be drawn in that regard from Article [14 TFEU] relating to the European Parliament, which state[s] that it is to consist of representatives of the peoples of the Member States, since the term "peoples", which is not defined, may have different meanings in the Member States and languages of the Union'. The Court also made repeated references to the ways in which EU law grants and acknowledges rights for non-Union citizens within the Union. The judgment is symbolically important for setting out a vision in which non-Union citizens are still part of the community of Europe.[164] Citizens may be the first clients of the Union, but they are not the only

---

[161] See J. Shaw, *The Transformation of Citizenship in the European Union* (Cambridge, Cambridge University Press, 2007); H. Lardy, 'The Political Rights of Union Citizenship' (1997) *EPL* 611; D. Kostakopoulou, 'Ideas, Norms and European Citizenship: Explaining Institutional Change' (2005) 68 *MLR* 233, 239–40.

[162] Directive 94/80/EC, article 12 [1994] OJ L368/38; Directive 93/109/EC, article 14 [1993] OJ L329/34; European Commission, *Report on the Right to Vote and to Stand as a Candidate in Elections to the European Parliament*, COM(2007)846 final; European Commission, *Report on the Right to Vote and Stand as a Candidate in Municipal Elections*, COM(2005)382 final.

[163] Case C-145/04 *Spain* v *United Kingdom* [2006] ECR I-7917.

[164] Cf. M. Bell, 'Civic Citizenship and Migrant Integration' (2007) 13 *EPL* 311; Kochenov, n. 18 above.

ones. It remains to be seen whether this judgment still stands in the light of Article 14(2) TEU, which now provides that 'The European Parliament shall be comprised of representatives of the Union's citizens'. While this undermines the textual argument in *Spain* v *United Kingdom*, it is suggested that the underlying policy approach may still prevail.

The Court of Justice intervened in national electoral procedure for the European Parliament in a more critical way in *Eman and Sevinger*, a judgment delivered on the same day as *Spain* v *United Kingdom*.[165] These two Dutch citizens complained that they were not allowed to vote in European elections because they lived in Aruba, an overseas territory of the Netherlands to which EU law, in general, does not apply. Moreover, to rub salt in the wound, Dutch citizens resident in a third country (the United States, or Australia, for example) could vote for the European Parliament. It was only those in the overseas territories that were excluded.

The Court did not object to states having territorial requirements for voting 'best adapted to their constitutional structure'. However, it found that any such rules had to comply with the principle of equality, which is a general principle of EU law and therefore applied to European Parliament elections. This prevented arbitrary distinctions of any kind and the Court was not convinced that the distinction between Dutch citizens in Aruba and those in third countries had any coherent reasoning behind it. In fact it does, but that reasoning is of a highly political and historical nature and reflects the complex ex-colonial relationship between the Netherlands and Aruba. The Dutch Government was, however, unable to explain the distinction in a way that made it seem constitutionally rational.[166]

Despite this fairly high-powered litigation, Union citizenship has not been a great success as a political citizenship. Turn-out in European Parliament elections is generally low, presenting a challenge to the idea of a European political community and to the idea that by stimulating public participation in the political process, Union citizenship can add to Union legitimacy.[167] Similarly, the rate of participation by migrant citizens in local elections in their host states has also been low.[168] Clearly, many non-national citizens do not feel sufficient attachment to their place of residence to wish to participate in the management of its affairs. This may be because their political horizons hark back to their state of origin, because there are no transnational political parties reflecting their interests, or because they conceive of themselves only as temporary residents of their host state.[169]

A factor limiting the impact of EU political rights is that they do not extend to participation in core national political decision-making processes. First, migrant citizens do not acquire a right to participate in national elections, either as voters or candidates.[170] Even in federal states such as Spain, Belgium and Germany, these remain the most high-profile and most significant elections in every state in the European Union. Secondly, Union citizenship also does not give

---

[165] Case C-300/04 *Eman and Sevinger* [2006] ECR I-8055.

[166] See annotations of *Spain* v *United Kingdom* and *Eman and Sevinger* by J. Shaw in (2008) 4 *ELRev.* 162; L. Besselink in (2008) 45 *CMLRev.* 787.

[167] Bellamy, n. 8 above.

[168] European Commission, *Report to the European Parliament and Council on the Application of Directive 94/80/EC on the Right to Vote and Stand as a Candidate in Municipal Elections*, COM(2002)260 final. See also Bellamy, n. 8 above.

[169] H. Schmitt, 'The European Parliament Elections of June 2004: Still Second-Order?' (2005) 28 *West European Politics* 650; S. Hix and M. Marsh, 'Punishment or Protest? Understanding European.Parliament Elections' (2007) 69 *Journal of Politics* 495.

[170] See R. Bauböck, P. Cayla and C. Seth (eds.), *Should EU Citizens Living in Other Member States Vote There in National Elections?*, EUI Working Paper RSCAS 2012/32.

citizens any right to hold high office or exercise any duties which require them regularly to safeguard the interests of the state. Two provisions of EU law set out these latter exclusions, Articles 45(4) and 51 TFEU. The first provides that the free movement of workers shall not apply to 'employment in the public service', while the second provides that the free movement of services gives no right to provide services connected 'even occasionally, with the exercise of official authority'. While these Articles are not formally part of the provisions on citizenship,[171] the idea that they embody is very much a limit on what Union citizenship is.

The Articles, which are interpreted in parallel, suggest that while foreigners may participate in economic life, that participation may justifiably be limited to matters outside the heart of the state and of public authority. They have been interpreted strictly. 'Public service' does not mean, in the eyes of the Court of Justice, any state employment, but only the more sensitive public positions. The Court has said that citizens of other states may legitimately be excluded only from functions which 'presume on the part of those occupying them the existence of a special relationship of allegiance to the state and reciprocity of rights and duties which form the foundation of the bond of nationality'.[172] Advocate General Mancini referred to those who 'don full battle dress' in the service of the state.[173] Jobs as postal workers,[174] teachers,[175] notaries,[176] nurses or railway drivers[177] may therefore not be reserved for nationals, even where these are public posts. On the other hand, most functions in the armed forces or police, the higher parts of the civil service or the judiciary, or other functions involving coercion on behalf of the state,[178] probably do fall within the exception.[179] While the scope of the exception may therefore be limited, it does reveal starkly the limits of Union citizenship. There is an inner core of national membership to which the migrant is not admitted. Fundamentally, she cannot be trusted, because she is foreign.

FURTHER READING

N. Barber, 'Citizenship, Nationalism and the European Union' (2002) 27 *European Law Review* 241

L. Bosniak, *The Citizen and the Alien* (Princeton, NJ, Princeton University Press, 2006)

M. Dougan, N. Nic Shuibhne and E. Spaventa (eds.), *Empowerment and Disempowerment of the European Citizen* (Oxford, Hart Publishing, 2012)

D. Kochenov, 'Ius Tractum of Many Faces: European Citizenship and the Difficult Relationship between Status and Rights' (2009) 15 *Columbia Journal of European Law* 169

---

[171] They are discussed in more detail in Chapter 20.

[172] Case C-405/01 *Colegio de Oficiales de la Marina Mercante Española* v *Administración del Estado* [2003] ECR I-10391.

[173] Case 307/84 *Commission* v *France* [1986] ECR 1725, para. 5 of the Opinion.

[174] Case 152/73 *Sotgiu* v *Deutsche Bundespost* [1974] ECR 153.

[175] Case 33/88 *Allue* v *Università degli Studi di Venezia* [1989] ECR 1591; Case 4/91 *Bleis* v *Ministère de l'Education Nationale* [1991] ECR I-5627.

[176] See e.g. Case C-54/08 *Commission* v *Germany* [2011] ECR I-4355.

[177] Case 149/79 *Commission* v *Belgium (No. 2)* [1982] ECR 1845.

[178] Case C-160/08 *Commission* v *Germany* [2010] ECR I-3713, para. 79.

[179] European Commission, *Free Movement of Workers: Achieving the Full Benefits and Potential*, COM(2002)694, 18–19. See also J. Handoll, 'Article 48(4) EEC and Non-national Access to Public Employment' (1988) 13 *ELRev.* 223; D. O'Keeffe, 'Judicial Interpretation of the Public Service Exception to the Free Movement of Workers' in D. Curtin and D. O'Keeffe (eds.), *Constitutional Adjudication in European Community and National Law: Essays for the Hon. Mr. Justice O'Higgins* (Dublin, Butterworths, 1992).

D. Kochenov 'The Essence of EU Citizenship Emerging from the Last Ten Years of Academic Debate: Beyond the Cherry Blossoms and the Moon?' (2013) 62(1) *ICLQ* 97

D. Kostakopoulou, 'European Union Citizenship: Writing the Future' (2007) 13 (5) *European Law Journal* 623

D. Kostakopoulou and N. Ferreira 'Testing Liberal Norms: The Public Policy and Public Security Derogations and the Cracks in European Citizenship' (2014) 20 (2) *Columbia Journal of European Law* (forthcoming)

P. Magnette, 'How Can One be European? Reflections on the Pillars of European Civic Identity' (2007) 13 (5) *European Law Journal* 664

C. O' Brien, 'I Trade Therefore I Am: Legal Personhood in the European Union' (2014) 50 *Common Market Law Review* 1643

J. Shaw, *The Transformation of Citizenship in the European Union* (Cambridge, Cambridge University Press, 2007)

A. Somek, 'Solidarity Decomposed: Being and Time in European Citizenship' (2007) 32 (6) *European Law Review* 818

E. Spaventa, 'Seeing the Wood Despite the Trees? On the Scope of Union Citizenship and its Constitutional Effects' (2008) 45 (1) *Common Market Law Review* 13

12

EU Law and Non-EU Nationals

CONTENTS

1 INTRODUCTION

This chapter considers the treatment of non-EU nationals by EU law.[1] It is organised as follows.

Section 2 looks at the central Union competences, Articles 77–79 TFEU, which provide for EU law to be adopted in the fields of border checks, asylum and immigration, respectively.

---

[1] It does not consider the situation where non-EU nationals acquire rights by virtue of a relationship with an EU citizen. This is addressed in Chapter 11. See pp. 495–506.

Although subject, since the Lisbon Treaty, to the legislative and judicial procedures associated with others TFEU competences, this field is marked strongly by differentiated integration. The Protocol on United Kingdom and Ireland gives these states the right to decide whether to participate in the legislation. A Protocol on Denmark provides that any measure adopted in this field will only bind it as a matter of international law. The Protocols, however, compete with the Protocol on the Schengen Acquis. This allows the Union to adopt EU law developing the acquis implementing the 1985 and 1990 Schengen Conventions, which provide for common external frontiers, visa, immigration and asylum policies. This Protocol prevails over the other Protocol. Ireland and the United Kingdom are not signatories to these Conventions and can only participate in the development of such measures when all other members agree. There is a lack of clarity as to when EU law develops the Schengen Acquis, with only border control and visa policy so far being held to do this.

Section 3 considers the central themes governing this field. EU law on non-EU nationals forms part of the Area of Freedom, Security and Justice. This Area is seen as contributing to a wider European way of life, with Union measures on non-EU nationals regulating the latter's perceived contribution and threat to this way of life. This has led to a number of competing themes governing this field. The first is economic mercantilism which treats non-EU nationals as a human resource whose benefits and costs are to be assessed in terms of their impact on labour markets, welfare systems and EU competitiveness. The second is the protection of national security. Non-EU nationals are considered in terms of their perceived cultural, political and social risks. This has led to a strong emphasis on policing of non-EU nationals and territorial control with visa policy increasingly being used to enable the latter. The third is humanitarianism. The idea that the Union should shelter those in need is the basis for those policies which go to international protection, most subsidiary protection and refugee policies. EU law is also subject to significant human rights constraints in this field. The final theme is that of European solidarity. Member States should share the costs of policy in this field. There is limited provision for distribution of financial costs. The central instrument in this field is the Dublin Regulation, Regulation 604/2013. This provides that those seeking international protection should only be allowed a single application, a hierarchy of criteria for determining which Member State is to consider it, and a system of transfer to enable the applicant to be considered by that state.

Section 4 considers the Returns Directive, Directive 2008/115/EC. This requires Member States to return non-EU nationals who have irregularly entered or remained on their territory unless there are strong compassionate reasons. In principle, the return should be voluntary. This will not be the case if the non-EU national does not leave within the term set or, inter alia, there is a risk of her absconding. In such circumstances, there will be a forced return. There is also provision for a ban on her re-entering the Union and the possibility of detention.

Section 5 considers non-EU nationals who have worker resident and long-term resident status. The right to work within the Union (worker resident status) is largely governed by national law, although a system of Union preference operates where a vacancy should only be offered to a non-EU national if there is no EEA citizen or permanent resident non-EU national that is suitable for it. Long-term resident status is provided to those who can show lawful residence in a Member State for five years and sufficient resources to support themselves and their families. Worker residents are entitled to freedom from discrimination in the marketplace and equal treatment with regard to a number of social entitlements, notably education and housing. Long-term residents are entitled to the same socio-economic entitlements as a Member State's own nationals, albeit that Member States can limit these to those core social benefits which go to realisation of the resident's rights under the European Union Charter of Fundamental Rights. There is also a right to family reunification where a non-EU national has been lawfully resident in a Member State for more than one year and has reasonable prospects of permanent residence. Family members 12 years or older can be required, however, to undergo integration tests before reunification and Member States can require that the non-EU national be lawfully resident for two years before her family is able to join her.

Section 6 considers the entitlements granted to those applying for international protection. International protection is where the non-EU national is granted either refugee status or subsidiary protection. There is an entitlement to remain on the territory of the Member State pending consideration of their case and to individual consideration of their application unless there is a safe third country to which it would be reasonable for the applicant to go or the applicant has arrived in the Union via a safe European country. Member States must provide material reception conditions for applications. These include housing, food, health care and education for minors. Applicants also have a right to access to the labour market within nine months of their application provided a final decision has not been taken and they have not contributed to the delay. All these benefits are contingent on, inter alia, applicants complying with the reporting and accommodation requirements set by Member States. They can also be withdrawn if the application is not made as soon as reasonably practicable on entering the Member State.

Section 7 considers EU law on refugees and those seeking subsidiary protection. Refugee status is granted to those who have a well-founded fear of being persecuted for reasons of race, religion, nationality, political opinion or membership of a particular social group. The acts of persecution must be sufficiently serious to constitute a severe violation of human rights. Subsidiary protection is granted to those for whom there are substantial grounds for believing that they run a real risk of serious harm if they return to their state of origin. This harm consists of death, torture or a serious and individual threat to a civilian's life from indiscriminate violence. Both groups are granted family, education and housing rights as well as the right to free movement. Refugees are also given full socio-economic rights, whilst those acquiring subsidiary protection status are only granted core benefits.

2 UNION COMPETENCES ON BORDER CHECKS, ASYLUM AND IMMIGRATION

(i) Central competences

The history of Union competences on immigration and asylum is convoluted. Introduced at Maastricht, these were governed on a largely intergovernmental basis under the third pillar of the TEU and separate international treaties. These competences were then made a central part of the newly established Area of Freedom, Security and Justice by the Treaty of Amsterdam. Inserted into the EC Treaty, unanimity voting in the Council was the rule, however, and there were only limited possibilities for national courts to refer questions of EU law to the Court of Justice. The Treaty of Lisbon has made things a lot easier. The policies on border checks, asylum and immigration, as they are now known, are set out in Articles 77–79 TFEU. They are subject to the preliminary reference procedure in the same way as the rest of the TFEU. They are, with two limited exceptions,[2] to be governed by the ordinary legislative procedure.

Article 77(1) TFEU

1. The Union shall develop a policy with a view to:
    (a) ensuring the absence of any controls on persons, whatever their nationality, when crossing internal borders;
    (b) carrying out checks on persons and efficient monitoring of the crossing of external borders;
    (c) the gradual introduction of an integrated management system for external borders.

Article 78(1) TFEU

1. The Union shall develop a common policy on asylum, subsidiary protection and temporary protection with a view to offering appropriate status to any third-country national requiring international protection and ensuring compliance with the principle of non-refoulement. This policy must be in accordance with the Geneva Convention of 28 July 1951 and the Protocol of 31 January 1967 relating to the status of refugees, and other relevant treaties.

Article 79(1) TFEU

1. The Union shall develop a common immigration policy aimed at ensuring, at all stages, the efficient management of migration flows, fair treatment of third-country nationals residing legally in Member States, and the prevention of, and enhanced measures to combat, illegal immigration and trafficking in human beings.

The history of this field has resulted in these competences not being established against a blank canvas. Their establishment has only been possible through differentiated integration. This differentiated integration takes two forms: Protocols for particular Member States and the Protocol integrating the Schengen Acquis.

(ii) Differentiated integration and EU border control, asylum and immigration policy

The relationship of the United Kingdom and Ireland to Union border checks, asylum and immigration policy is governed, in the first place, by two Protocols which address their position directly.

The first Protocol provides that nothing in EU law affects the rights of the United Kingdom and Ireland to exercise frontier controls on persons entering from other parts of the European

---

[2] Rights of non-EU national family members derived from EU citizens moving and residing in another Member State and emergency measures to deal with a sudden inflow of non-EU nationals into one Member State are governed by the consultation procedure, Articles 77(3) and 78(3) TFEU, respectively.

Union or elsewhere.[3] As a quid pro quo, the other Member States may impose border checks on persons coming from the United Kingdom and Ireland.[4]

The second Protocol provides that, inter alia, no measures adopted under Articles 77–79 TFEU and no court judgment interpreting these competences or any measure adopted under these competences shall bind the United Kingdom and Ireland.[5] There is, however, provision for their participation, should they so desire, in individual measures. Article 3(1) of the Protocol allows the United Kingdom and Ireland, within three months of the Commission's publication of a proposal, to 'opt in' and participate in the adoption and application of any proposed measures. However, the Council may adopt the measure without either participating if 'after a reasonable period of time a measure…cannot be adopted with the United Kingdom or Ireland taking part'. Each may also subsequently adopt a measure by notifying the Council and Commission of its intention to do so.[6] The Commission must, within three months, give its opinion to the Council on such a notification and on what arrangements it deems necessary to be taken by either Member State to comply with the measure.

Although Denmark did not want its immigration and asylum policies to be governed by EU law, it is bound by international law commitments to the other Member States, as it is a signatory to the Schengen Conventions. A Protocol was agreed, therefore, which provides that Denmark will not be bound by or participate in the adoption of any measures in this field.[7] Nor is there any possibility for it to participate, should it so desire, unlike Ireland or the United Kingdom. Denmark's obligations under the Schengen Conventions mean, however, that if the Council decides to build upon the Schengen Acquis, Denmark has six months to decide whether it will implement the decision.[8] If it chooses to do so, the decision will create an obligation under international law between Denmark and those Member States who participated in the measure. If Denmark decides against implementation, the other Member States and Denmark are to consider what appropriate measures should be taken.[9]

The other form of differentiated integration which takes place is set out in the Protocol on the Schengen Acquis.

The Schengen Conventions of 1985 and 1990 were international agreements concluded between thirteen of the EU-15 Member States, Norway and Iceland.[10] Switzerland and Liechtenstein subsequently acceded to the Conventions in 2008 and 2011, respectively, and all

---

[3] Protocol on the Application of Certain Aspects of Article 26 TFEU, Article 1. The position is a little complicated with regard to Ireland. This entitlement exists only for so long as it forms a common travel area allowing for free movement between it and the United Kingdom, Article 2.

[4] *Ibid.* Article 3.

[5] Protocol on the Position of the United Kingdom and Ireland in respect of the Area of Freedom, Security and Justice, Articles 1 and 2. This Protocol applies to all competences covered by the Area of Freedom, Security and Justice. It, thus, also includes judicial cooperation in civil and criminal matters and police cooperation and some anti-terrorism measures. In relation to EU criminal law see p. 636.

[6] *Ibid.* Article 4.

[7] Protocol on Position of Denmark, Articles 1 and 2. It also applies all measures taken in the Area of Freedom, Security and Justice.

[8] *Ibid.* Article 4(1).

[9] *Ibid.* Article 4(2).

[10] See also pp. 29 and 139. The central Convention is the Schengen Implementing Convention agreed in 1990 (CISA). The text is at [2000] OJ L239/19. For critical comment see J. Schutte, 'Schengen: Its Meaning for the Free Movement of Persons in Europe' (1991) 28 *CMLRev.* 549; H. Meijers *et al.* (eds.), *Schengen: Internationalisation of Central Chapters of the Law of Aliens, Refugees, Privacy, Security and Police* (2nd rev. edn, Leiden, Stichting NJM-Boekerij, 1992); D. O' Keeffe, 'The Schengen Convention: A Suitable Model for European Integration?' (1992) 12 *YBEL* 185.

Member States are currently parties to them except Ireland and the United Kingdom. However, before any party can secure the full benefits of the Conventions, it must demonstrate that it can meet the commitments demanded by the Conventions and the body of measures built up under them. This is not considered possible in Cyprus because of the dispute within the island which means that no common external frontier can be established for the island. In the case of Bulgaria, Romania and Croatia, other parties have raised concerns that they are not yet in a position to meet their commitments. These four states thus currently only have the status of candidate states.

The Conventions require the abolition of internal frontier checks[11] and a common external frontier.[12] There is also provision for a common visa,[13] asylum[14] and immigration policy.[15] To this end, a number of implementing measures, known as the Schengen Acquis, were adopted by an Executive Committee set up by those states to further those policies. At the Treaty of Amsterdam, it was agreed to incorporate this acquis into the TEU framework. In 1999 a Decision was taken granting EU legal status to all individual measures comprising the Schengen Acquis.[16] Furthermore, a Protocol was agreed, the Protocol on the Schengen Acquis, which allows the Schengen states to continue to take measures to build on the Schengen Acquis, albeit that these are now measures of EU law.

Protocol on the *Schengen Acquis* Integrated into the Framework of the European Union

Article 1

[All Member States other than Ireland and the United Kingdom] shall be authorised to implement closer cooperation among themselves in areas covered by provisions defined by the Council which constitute the Schengen acquis. This cooperation shall be conducted within the institutional and legal framework of the European Union and with respect for the relevant provisions of the Treaties.

Article 5(1)

1. Proposals and initiatives to build upon the Schengen acquis shall be subject to the relevant provisions of the Treaties.

Non-participating states can request to participate in any measure that is already part of the acquis or builds upon it. They will only be allowed to participate if the other Member States agree to the request by unanimity.[17] The consequence is that there are two parallel sets of decision-making procedures governing differentiation in this field: those on the position of the United Kingdom and Ireland and those set out in the Protocol on the Schengen Acquis. Under the former, Ireland and the United Kingdom have a right to participate in a measure should they wish, whereas the latter allows any Schengen state to veto their participation.

---

[11] *Ibid.* Article 2.　[12] *Ibid.* Articles 3–8.　[13] *Ibid.* Articles 9–18.
[14] *Ibid.* Articles 28–39.　[15] *Ibid.* Articles 19–27.
[16] Decision 1999/436/EC determining the legal basis for each of the provisions or decisions which constitute the Schengen Acquis [1999] OJ L 176/19. On these measures see P. Kuijper, 'Some Legal Problems Associated with the Communitarization of Policy on Visas, Asylum and Immigration under the Amsterdam Treaty and Incorporation of the Schengen Acquis' (2000) 37 *CMLRev.* 345; D. Thym, 'The Schengen Law: A Challenge for Legal Accountability in the European Union' (2002) 8 *ELJ* 218, 235.
[17] Protocol on the Schengen Acquis Integrated into the Framework of the European Union, Article 4.

The question of which should prevail was addressed in the British challenge to the establishment of the European Frontiers Agency (FRONTEX) under the Protocol on the Schengen Acquis. In that judgment, the Court of Justice stated that if a measure is built upon the Schengen Acquis, it should be governed by that Protocol.[18] Other states would have a veto on British and Irish participation. This raised the question of which fields are covered by the Protocol on the Schengen Acquis. Article 5 refers, in this regard, to anything which *builds* upon the Schengen Acquis. The meaning of this was raised in a British challenge to Regulation 2252/2004, which set standards for security features in passports, and in which British participation was refused. The United Kingdom argued that measures building upon the acquis included only measures integral to the acquis which amended existing measures. It did not include measures which complemented existing measures and pursued similar objectives. The Court of Justice rejected this argument.

Case C-137/05 *United Kingdom* v *Council* [2007] ECR I-11593

56. …by analogy with what applies in relation to the choice of the legal basis of a Community act, it must be concluded that in a situation such as that at issue in the present case the classification of a Community act as a proposal or initiative to build upon the Schengen acquis within the meaning of the first subparagraph of Article 5(1) of the Schengen Protocol must rest on objective factors which are amenable to judicial review, including in particular the aim and the content of the act…

58. As to the purpose of Regulation No. 2252/2004, it is apparent from recitals 2 and 3 in the preamble and from Article 4(3) that it was intended to combat falsification and fraudulent use of passports and other travel documents issued by the Member States.

59. To achieve that objective, Regulation No. 2252/2004, as is apparent from Articles 1 and 2, harmonises and improves the minimum security standards with which passports and travel documents issued by the Member States must comply, and provides for a number of biometric features relating to the holders of such documents to be inserted in those documents.

60. In that connection, it should be recalled that, as the Court held in…Case C-77/05 *United Kingdom* v. *Council*, checks on persons at the external borders of the Member States and consequently the effective implementation of the common rules on standards and procedures for those checks must be regarded as constituting elements of the Schengen acquis.…

65. In so far as the verification of the authenticity of passports and other travel documents thus constitutes the main element of checks on persons at external borders, measures which make it possible to establish that authenticity and the identity of the holder of the document in question more easily and more reliably must be regarded as capable of guaranteeing and improving the effectiveness of those checks and thereby of the integrated management of external borders established by the Schengen acquis.

The Court of Justice will look therefore to the 'constituting elements' of the Schengen Conventions to see which measures are governed by the Protocol on the Schengen Acquis (paragraph 60). If the aim and content of a measure fall within these, it is covered by that Protocol. This phrase is, however, a vague one. It is clear from the judgment above that external border

---

[18] Case C-77/05 *United Kingdom* v *Council* [2007] ECR I-11459. The full reasoning of the judgment is set out in Chapter 3 at pp. 140–1.

checks are one such element. Visa policy has been held to be another.[19] Beyond this, institutional practice is uncertain. The Directive on the return of irregular migrants, part of immigration policy, is seen as developing the Schengen Acquis.[20] By contrast, EU legislation on which Member States are responsible for processing asylum application makes no reference to the acquis,[21] notwithstanding that the Schengen Conventions provide for common rules on this.[22]

3 NON-EU NATIONALS AND THE AREA OF FREEDOM, SECURITY AND JUSTICE

Union competences on border checks, asylum and immigration form part of the Area of Freedom, Security and Justice. They are consequently bound by its general principles and procedures.[23] The Area is conceived, on the one hand, as a series of policies. These are summarised in Article 67 TFEU.

Article 67 TFEU

1. The Union shall constitute an area of freedom, security and justice with respect for fundamental rights and the different legal systems and traditions of the Member States.
2. It shall ensure the absence of internal border controls for persons and shall frame a common policy on asylum, immigration and external border control, based on solidarity between Member States, which is fair towards third-country nationals. For the purpose of this Title, stateless persons shall be treated as third-country nationals.
3. The Union shall endeavour to ensure a high level of security through measures to prevent and combat crime, racism and xenophobia, and through measures for coordination and cooperation between police and judicial authorities and other competent authorities, as well as through the mutual recognition of judgments in criminal matters and, if necessary, through the approximation of criminal laws.
4. The Union shall facilitate access to justice, in particular through the principle of mutual recognition of judicial and extrajudicial decisions in civil matters.

The policies comprising the Area are not, therefore, just external border controls, asylum and immigration. They also include removal of internal border controls, access to justice, judicial cooperation in civil and criminal matters; police cooperation; and combating racism and xenophobia. Bringing these policies together subjects them not merely to certain common norms and procedures but suggests that they should be developed in a complementary manner and should inform one another.

Yet what are the norms which inform and align these policies? Whilst Article 67(1) TFEU talks of respect for fundamental rights, other documents use broader terms. The Commission

---

[19] Case C-482/08 *United Kingdom* v *Council* [2010] ECR I-10413.
[20] Directive 2008/115/EC on common standards and procedures in Member States for returning illegally staying third-country nationals [2008] OJ L348/98.
[21] Regulation 604/2013 establishing the criteria and mechanisms for determining the Member State responsible for examining an application for international protection lodged in one of the Member States by a third-country national or a stateless person [2013] OJ L180/31.
[22] CISA 1990, Articles 28–38.
[23] These principles perform a similar role for EU criminal law which also forms part of this Title.

has talked of freedom, security and justice as 'an integral part of the European model of society'.[24] The Working Group on Freedom, Security and Justice at the Future of Europe Convention leading to the Constitutional Treaty used similar language. It argued that the Area should lead to citizens feeling that a 'proper sense of "European public order" has taken shape and is actually visible in their daily lives'.[25] These views see the policies set out in Article 67 TFEU as contributing to a wider European way of life. Within such a vision, the Area of Freedom, Security and Justice comprises not just the Union policies but also all the institutions, procedures and norms – be they Union, national, regional or local – which contribute to a particular European way of life.

If EU law on non-EU nationals is conceived as central to the establishment of the Area of Freedom, Security and Justice, and this field is understood as a Union contribution to sustaining a particular way of life for its citizens, EU border control, immigration and asylum law can only be understood, in turn, through consideration of how immigration and asylum is identified as affecting this way of life. In this, there is a paradox. Migration is seen both as contributing to and sustaining this way of life, and as threatening it. In 2012, 20.5 million non-EU nationals lawfully resided in the EU, about 4.1 per cent of its total population.[26] Between 2002 and 2006, levels increased by between 1.5 and 2 million a year, so that it was the main element in EU population growth.[27] If, since the crisis, net levels of migration to the European Union have slowed, it was still 900,000 in 2011. Alongside this, 71,580 asylum seekers were given some form of humanitarian protection in 2012, about 27 per cent of total applicants. However, alongside this, the official rhetoric and the policing measures taken against non-EU nationals are extremely harsh. 427,195 individuals were apprehended in 2012 for being irregular migrants and 186,630 were returned to their state of nationality.[28] These figures do not take account, furthermore, of the deprivation and abuse suffered by these within the Union, and that many enter and live in the Union under the most precarious of circumstances.

To understand these tensions and how EU law has been shaped by it, it is necessary to consider four central pressures which underpin this regime and each of which have left a legal imprint. The first, economic mercantilism, is concerned to manage migration in a way that advantages national economies and does not impose burdens on welfare states. It conceives migrants in terms of the economic benefits and costs they bring to EU societies. The second theme concerns the perceived risks posed by non-EU nationals, be these as potential sources of crime, political threats or threats to local public services or labour market. As these risks are conceived, often in highly racist terms, as a threat to *national* security, this has led to corollary concerns with protecting national territory and national sovereignty. The third theme embodies concerns of a humanitarian nature. It is the idea that the European way of life requires hospitality to be offered to the stranger, particularly those in most need. This has led to EU law treating some categories, such as family members and asylum seekers, more favourably than others, and a commitment to respect a whole series of fundamental rights in this field. The

---

[24] European Commission, *An Area of Freedom, Security and Justice Serving the Citizen*, COM(2009)262, 2.
[25] European Convention, *Final Report of Working Group X 'Freedom, Security and Justice'*, CONV 426/02, 2.
[26] European Commission, *Fourth Annual Report on Migration and Integration*, COM(2013)422, 3.
[27] European Commission, *Third Annual Report on Migration and Integration*, COM(2007)512, 3.
[28] These figures are all taken from European Commission, *Fourth Annual Report on Migration and Integration*, n. 26 above, 3–4.

final theme is that of solidarity towards protecting a shared European way of life. There is a responsibility both to manage migration and to share that responsibility and the costs amongst the Member States of the Union.

(i) Economic mercantilism

Policy towards non-EU nationals has been strongly framed by the economic benefits or costs these are perceived to bring. Attitudes on this depend as much on the economic circumstances of the time as on the skills of the individual. The 1950s was a period of labour market shortages across Europe, with workers being actively recruited from outside Europe to fill posts. This was reflected in the EU law of the time. It was initially envisaged that the right to move freely to work within the Union was available to all.[29] By the end of the 1960s, the European Union was moving from a period of labour shortages to one of unemployment. In 1968, legislation confining the right to work within the Union to EU nationals was enacted.[30] Increasingly, non-EU nationals were seen as threats to national labour markets and Member States developed restrictive immigration laws throughout the 1980s and 1990s to foreclose economic migration by non-EU nationals.[31] By the beginning of the millennium, there were signs that the pendulum was swinging back towards the opening of labour markets. A Commission Communication in 2000 suggested that economic migration could be a means of coping with falling populations within the Union, skills shortages and the lack of a sufficient workforce to pay for the increased cost of pensions.[32] The consequence has been a shift away from *restricting* economic migration to *managing* it, with the Union trying to cherry-pick those non-EU nationals who will benefit its economy, whilst preventing others from entering its markets.[33]

Treatment of non-EU nationals has, thus, become, in part, a human resource strategy. In case of international protection where the law has to accommodate other concerns, most notably humanitarian ones, this is done through EU legislation finding ways to manage the welfare and reception costs of those applying for it.[34] In the case of economic migration, there is a tiered response.

The question is treated in the first place as one of national political economy. That is to say, Member States have the entitlement to do what they perceive as generally right for their labour markets, economies and welfare costs. Responsibility for overall levels of migration is therefore treated as a matter of exclusively domestic concern.

---

[29] See Articles 52 and 48 EC Treaty, respectively.
[30] Directive 68/360/EEC, article 1 [1968] OJ Spec. Ed. L257/13. See the debates in W. Böhning, *The Migration of Workers in Britain and the EC* (Oxford, Oxford University Press/Institute for Race Relations, 1972); P. Oliver, 'Non-Community Nationals and the Treaty of Rome' (1985) 5 *YBEL* 57.
[31] On the evolution of immigration policies within the Member States see C. Joppke, *The Challenge to the Nation State: Immigration in Western Europe and the United States* (Oxford, Oxford University Press, 1998); A. Geddes, *The Politics of Migration and Immigration in Europe* (London, Sage, 2003); A. Messina, *The Logics and Politics of Post-WW II Migration to Western Europe* (Cambridge, Cambridge University Press, 2007).
[32] European Commission, *On a Community Immigration Policy*, COM(2000)757.
[33] European Commission, *Communication on Migration*, COM(2011)248, 12. For recent examples see the Commission's suggestion to use non-EU migrants to address Union skill shortages or foster entrepreneurship. European Commission, *Towards a Job-Rich Recovery*, COM(2012)173, 18; European Commission, *Entrepreneurship 2020 Action Plan*, COM(2012)795, 24–5.
[34] See pp. 557–62.

> ### Article 79(5) TFEU
>
> 5. This Article shall not affect the right of Member States to determine volumes of admission of third-country nationals coming from third countries to their territory in order to seek work, whether employed or self-employed.

If overall levels of migration are seen as a national matter, the skills-set of the migrant labour force is seen as an EU matter. There is a concern that Member States do not secure cheap labour or highly sought after skills in a way that undercuts other states. With regard to the former, a 1996 Council Resolution was agreed setting out the 'Union preference' principle whereby:

> Member States will consider requests for admission to their territories for the purpose of employment only where vacancies in a Member State cannot be filled by national and Community manpower or by non-Community manpower lawfully resident on a permanent basis in that Member State and already forming part of the Member State's regular labour market.[35]

With regard to highly qualified workers, the opposite approach is taken. In 2009, the Union introduced a 'Blue Card' scheme. This grants access to the Union labour market for non-EU nationals who hold higher education qualifications or at least five years of equivalent professional experience and have been offered a contract of employment of at least one year's length by an EU employer.[36] The salary must be one and a half times the national average, and the employee must show that that they have sickness insurance to cover any normal health risks.[37] Furthermore, the 'Blue Card' card scheme is a malleable scheme. It allows for such non-EU nationals to be offered work in the Union but does not give them and their employers a right to make such contracts. The scheme is without prejudice to national quotas on levels of non-EU national migrants[38] and a 'Blue Card' might still be refused if a Member State believes that the vacancy should have been filled by the existing EU workforce.[39]

There is thus a dual track system. For so-called low-skills workers, a policy of Fortress Europe is adopted. It is all but impossible to secure economic migration. The opposite is the case for those seen as high-skills. For these the intention is to make the Union as attractive a place as possible to come.[40]

---

[35] Council Resolution on limitation on admission of third-country nationals to the territory of the Member States for employment [1996] OJ C 274/3.

[36] Directive 2009/50/EC on the conditions of entry and residence of third-country nationals for the purposes of highly qualified employment [2009] OJ L155/17. Ireland and the United Kingdom do not participate in this Directive. On the Directive see Y. Gümüs, 'EU Blue Card Scheme: The Right Step in the Right Direction?' (2010) 12 *European Journal of Migration and Law* 435; L. Cerna, 'The EU Blue Card: Preferences, Policies, and Negotiations Between Member States' (2014) 2 *Migration Studies* (forthcoming).

[37] The salary can be 1.2 times the national average for professionals if the Member State elects. The conditions are set out in article 5 of the Directive.

[38] *Ibid.* article 6.   [39] *Ibid.* article 8(2).

[40] European Commission, *Fourth Annual Report on Migration and Integration* n. 26 above, 5–6.

(ii) National security and national sovereignty

If there has been a long-standing concern about foreigners engaged in crime, this 'securitisation' of migration and asylum is also concerned with the threat these are seen to pose to perceived ideas of societal identity and integrity.[41] The image of threat, in both cases, is to an idea of security that is national in nature and which has, consequently to be regulated by the Member States.

Article 72 TFEU

This Title shall not affect the exercise of the responsibilities incumbent upon Member States with regard to the maintenance of law and order and the safeguarding of internal security.

Yet, other than as a claim to non-interference by the Union, how does this securitisation shape Union competences in respect of non-EU nationals?

(a) Frontiers as national markers

Borders are seen as important cultural markets of sovereignty, so there is provision that the geographical demarcation of national borders not be affected by EU immigration policy.[42] They are also seen as important policing points. This is most explicit in the case of the United Kingdom and Ireland for whom a Protocol has been adopted allowing them to retain frontier controls.[43] Yet even for the other states who claim to have abolished internal border controls, police powers can be exercised around the frontier. The regulation of this is set out in the Schengen Borders Code.[44]

Schengen Borders Code, article 21

The abolition of border control at internal borders shall not affect:

(a) the exercise of police powers by the competent authorities of the Member States under national law, insofar as the exercise of those powers does not have an effect equivalent to border checks; that shall also apply in border areas. Within the meaning of the first sentence, the exercise of police powers may not, in particular, be considered equivalent to the exercise of border checks when the police measures:
   (i) do not have border control as an objective,
   (ii) are based on general police information and experience regarding possible threats to public security and aim, in particular, to combat cross-border crime,

---

[41] M. Heisler and Z. Layton-Henry, 'Migration and the Links Between Social and Societal Security' in O. Waever (ed.), *Identity, Migration and the New Security Agenda* (London, Pinter, 1993); J. Huysmans, 'The European Union and the Securitization of Migration' (2000) 38 *JCMS* 751; A. Triandafyllidou, *Immigrants and National Identity in Europe* (London, Routledge, 2001).

[42] Article 77(4) TFEU.   [43] See n. 3 above.

[44] Regulation 562/2006 establishing a Community Code on the rules governing the movement of persons across borders (Schengen Borders Code) [2006] OJ L105/1.

(iii) are devised and executed in a manner clearly distinct from systematic checks on persons at the external borders,

(iv) are carried out on the basis of spot-checks;

(b) security checks on persons carried out at ports and airports by the competent authorities under the law of each Member State, by port or airport officials or carriers, provided that such checks are also carried out on persons travelling within a Member State;

(c) the possibility for a Member State to provide by law for an obligation to hold or carry papers and documents.

Frontier policing is, thus, allowed provided it is not equivalent to border checks. This phrase is a little cryptic, to say the least. It was addressed in *Melki*. Two Algerian irregular migrants were apprehended under a French law, article 78 of the Code of Criminal Procedure, which allowed police officers special powers to ask for identity papers 20 kilometres or less from a border.[45] In principle, this check could only be made to prevent the commission of offences, disruption to public order, or to seek the perpetrators of an offence. That none of these subsequently transpired to be the case would, however, not affect the legality of the check. It was argued that, in reality, these checks were border checks and, therefore, illegal.

Joined Cases C-188/10 and C-189/10 *Melki and Abdeli* [2010] ECR I-05667

69. Article 21(a) of Regulation No. 562/2006 provides that the abolition of border control at internal borders is not to affect the exercise of police powers by the competent authorities of the Member States under national law, in so far as the exercise of those powers does not have an effect equivalent to border checks; that is also to apply in border areas. It follows that controls within the territory of a Member State are, pursuant to Article 21(a), prohibited only where they have an effect equivalent to border checks.

70. The exercise of police powers may not, under the second sentence of that provision, in particular, be considered equivalent to the exercise of border checks when the police measures do not have border control as an objective; are based on general police information and experience regarding possible threats to public security and aim, in particular, to combat cross-border crime; are devised and executed in a manner clearly distinct from systematic checks on persons at the external borders; and, lastly, are carried out on the basis of spot-checks.

71. In relation to the question whether the exercise of the control powers granted by Article 78-2, fourth paragraph, of the Code of Criminal Procedure has an effect equivalent to border checks, it must be held, first, that the objective of the control under that provision is not the same as that of border control within the meaning of Regulation No. 562/2006. The objective of that border control, according to Article 2, points 9 to 11, of that regulation, is, first, to ensure that persons may be authorised to enter the territory of the Member State or authorised to leave it and, second, to prevent persons from circumventing border checks. By contrast, the national provision in question relates to checking whether the obligations laid down by law to hold, carry and produce papers and documents are fulfilled. The possibility for a Member State to provide for such obligations in its national law is not, pursuant to Article 21(c) of Regulation No. 562/2006, affected by the abolition of border control at internal borders.

---

[45] See also pp. 168–70.

72. Second, the fact that the territorial scope of the power granted by the national provision at issue in the main proceedings is limited to a border area does not suffice, in itself, to find that the exercise of that power has an equivalent effect within the meaning of Article 21(a) of Regulation No. 562/2006, in view of the wording and objective of Article 21. However, as regards controls on board an international train or on a toll motorway, the national provision at issue in the main proceedings lays down specific rules regarding its territorial scope, a factor which might constitute evidence of the existence of such an equivalent effect.

73. Furthermore, Article 78-2, fourth paragraph, of the Code of Criminal Procedure, which authorises controls irrespective of the behaviour of the person concerned and of specific circumstances giving rise to a risk of breach of public order, contains neither further details nor limitations on the power thus conferred – in particular in relation to the intensity and frequency of the controls which may be carried out on that legal basis – for the purposes of preventing the practical application of that power, by the competent authorities, from leading to controls with an effect equivalent to border checks within the meaning of Article 21(a) of Regulation No. 562/2006.

74. In order to comply with Articles 20 and 21(a) of Regulation No. 562/2006, interpreted in the light of the requirement of legal certainty, national legislation granting a power to police authorities to carry out identity checks – a power which, first, is restricted to the border area of the Member State with other Member States and, second, does not depend upon the behaviour of the person checked or on specific circumstances giving rise to a risk of breach of public order – must provide the necessary framework for the power granted to those authorities in order, inter alia, to guide the discretion which those authorities enjoy in the practical application of that power. That framework must guarantee that the practical exercise of that power, consisting in carrying out identity controls, cannot have an effect equivalent to border checks, as evidenced by, in particular, the circumstances listed in the second sentence of Article 21(a) of Regulation No. 562/2006.

If *Melki* suggests Schengen area states are limited in what they can do at their actual frontiers, it replaces these limits with a more amorphous form of borderlands in which there can be special policing of non-EU nationals.[46] These borderlands may be physically near a frontier, as was the case in that judgment. However, they may also exist more metaphorically. Member States may introduce special measures to control migration and police the behaviour and presence of non-EU nationals, which are distinct from those used for EU citizens and their own nationals. The judgment suggests only that this policing must be subject to some legal framework but beyond that is unspecific. This, of course, raises the question what is it about non-EU nationals that requires these special policing regimes which *Melki* observes are quite distinct in their operation and purpose from migration controls.

---

[46] A similar regime operating in the Netherlands allowing identity checks 20 kilometres from the frontier to combat illegal residence was declared to be a policing power not a border check as this was, in the view of the Court, concerned with securing public order and public security rather than border control, Case C-278/12 PPU *Adil*, Judgment of 19 July 2012. This relationship between internal borders and internal security has been reinforced by amendments which allow the reintroduction of temporary controls for thirty days for internal security reasons: Regulation 562/2006 as amended by Regulation 1051/2013/EU in order to provide for common rules on the temporary reintroduction of border control at internal borders in exceptional circumstances, articles 23–6 [2013] OJ L 295/1.

(b) Criminalisation of migration

This special policing of migration requires, for its justification, a criminalisation of migration. Migration must become something associated with criminal activities or be a crime itself. Once this becomes the case, it is then a matter for police intervention. As the extract below indicates, there is nothing inevitable about this criminalisation. Migration can be seen in terms of the opportunity for all human beings, regardless of background, to make a decent life for themselves or as responding to human rights needs of those seeking protection. Indeed, up until the middle of the twentieth century, these were powerful narratives. Since then, criminalisation has emerged as the culmination of seeing migration in terms of national security.

J. Valluy, 'The Metamorphosis of Asylum in Europe: From the Origins of "Fake Refugees" to their Internment' in S. Palidda (ed.), *Racial Criminalization of Migrants in the 21st Century* (Farnham, Ashgate, 2011) 107, 113–14

This swing [towards criminalisation] resulted primarily from the endogenous growth of national-securitarian forces (the precocious conversion of the high-level civil servant to the idea of migration as a 'problem', starting with the 1960s; the administrative closing of borders and intensification of policies against migration from which the reversal of asylum stems, in the 1970s; the emergence of a nationalist far-right in the political arena during the 1980s). Nonetheless, the shift was also an effect of less visible aspects which tended towards the weakening of humanist-asylum supporting forces, a weakening whose origins must be sought in the transformation of associative, academic and political forces that had explicitly embraced the value of humanitarian and social action.

During the 1980s when far-right parties emerged in Europe and took over the issue of arrival of foreigners as a reason to criticize government policies…governments had been discrediting exiles for ten years already, relentlessly raising asylum application rejection rates and producing justifications for such restrictions in the public sphere: the stigmatization of exiles as 'economic refugees' attracted by our wealth which took advantage of the Geneva Convention on Refugees. Its electoral use by political forces and government actors alike, merely amplified this public stigmatization and increased the political significance of rejection rates.

From this perspective, the internment of immigrants became a crucial element of policies to counter immigration with two important collateral effects: it strengthened the social perception of the social dangerousness of immigrants, whilst simultaneously trumpeting the authorities' mobilization against this threat. Massive research about the strong increase in the imprisonment of foreigners has led to converging conclusions: since the 1980s, the figures on foreign detainees have grown as a result of breaches of immigration legislation (irregular residence, refusal to comply with expulsion…), offences that are directly linked to being forced to live underground (forgery and use of false documents, contravening employment laws…) and preventive imprisonment, which was even more frequent because foreigners do not offer the guarantees (stability and lawfulness of residence, a home address, family situation, employment, schooling etc) that are required to benefit from alternative measures to preventive imprisonment. Beyond these aspects, the over-representation of foreigners is not linked to their national origins, but rather, to their statistical distribution on the basis of other variables: age, gender and socioeconomic condition.

This criminalisation is evidenced most explicitly in the Treaties by the presence of an internal security committee, which is to consider issues of immigration and asylum alongside issues of policing and cooperation in criminal justice.

Article 71 TFEU

A standing committee shall be set up within the Council in order to ensure that operational cooperation on internal security is promoted and strengthened within the Union. Without prejudice to Article 240[47], it shall facilitate coordination of the action of Member States' competent authorities. Representatives of the bodies, offices and agencies of the Union concerned may be involved in the proceedings of this committee. The European Parliament and national Parliaments shall be kept informed of the proceedings.

The criminalisation of the migrant takes many forms. It is particularly acute in the field of international protection and non-EU nationals entering or staying irregularly in the Union.[48] Its most pervasive machinery is the development of large information databases on non-EU nationals.[49]

The longest established is EURODAC.[50] Established to prevent asylum seekers making multiple applications under different identities, Member States must fingerprint all those who are 14 years or over and entering the Union to seek international humanitarian protection,[51] as well as all irregular migrants who are apprehended and over 14 years and who are neither turned back nor held in custody.[52] They must transfer this data to a central system, which will carry out a comparison with these fingerprints within twenty-four hours or, in urgent cases within one hour, which (in cases of a match) are verified by the receiving state.[53] In 2011, 412,303 'successful transactions' were made in which this data was entered into the central system searching for comparisons.[54] In relation to asylum applications, it showed about 22.4 per cent of applications were multiple applications.[55]

Reforms in 2013 allow this data to be made available to law-enforcement and policing agencies responsible for the investigation, detection and prevention of terrorist offences and other serious crime and Europol.[56] This can make a request for fingerprint comparison when these have searched other fingerprint databases; the comparison is necessary in a specific case for the investigation, detection or prevention of such offences; it has proportionate and reasonable grounds to consider that it will substantially contribute to the investigation, and so on.[57] These reforms turn this database into a more general policing tool. In most national systems, fingerprints of nationals are only kept, if at all, of those who have committed significant criminal acts. With non-EU nationals, it is sufficient to fall into certain immigration or asylum categories.

---

[47] Article 240 TFEU provides for the establishment of COREPER. See pp. 86–8.

[48] See pp. 544–6.

[49] On these see M. Besters and F. Brom, '"Greedy" Information Technology: The Digitalization of the European Migration Policy' (2010) 12 *EJML* 455; M. den Boer and J. van Buuren, 'Security Clouds: Towards an Ethical Governance of Surveillance in Europe' (2012) 5 *Journal of Cultural Economy* 85.

[50] This was initially established in Regulation 2725/2000 concerning the establishment of 'EURODAC' for the comparison of fingerprints for the effective application of the Dublin Convention [2000] OJ L316/1. This was replaced and repealed by Regulation 603/2013 on the establishment of 'EURODAC' [2013] OJ L180/1. The United Kingdom is participating in this. Ireland is not.

[51] *Ibid.* article 9(1).   [52] *Ibid.* article 14(1).

[53] *Ibid.* article 25(2) and (4). This system is located in Brussels within the Commission.

[54] European Commission, *Annual Report on the Activities of the EURODAC Central Unit*, COM(2012)533, 5.

[55] *Ibid.* 7.

[56] Regulation 603/2013, articles 5(1) and 7(2). These offences are set out in article 2(j) and (k).

[57] *Ibid.* article 20.

It is a measure of how things have developed that the EURODAC model is increasingly being generalised for non-EU nationals. A criminalisation of the migrant does, therefore, take place.[58] Furthermore, EURODAC has been criticised on data protection grounds insofar as it violates the usual requirement that data can only be stored on an individual if it is for specified, explicit and legitimate purposes and the data retained is not excessive in relation to the purposes for which it is collected.[59]

More wide-ranging is the Schengen Information System (SIS). This is a databank established under the Schengen Convention of people and objects who may pose a threat to security.[60] It includes details of all non-EU nationals refused entry or deported from the Union or who are considered to be a security risk.[61] In April 2013, the data was extended to include biometric data (for example, data identifying the physical features of individuals, such as photographs, fingerprints, DNA profiles or retina scans).[62] For such persons an 'alert' is entered on the system notifying other Member States. Individuals for whom an alert has been issued will normally be refused a visa or entry to the Union. A wide number of authorities can access this database. They include border control authorities, police, judicial and custom authorities, as well as those responsible for visas and residence permits and those responsible for public prosecutions.[63] Once again, policing and migration control are brought together. This criminalisation of migration is further accentuated by the same Information System being used for those who are sought on a European Arrest Warrant, namely, individuals suspected of committing a significant criminal offence in one of the Member States.[64] The database is huge, capable of holding up to 100 million alerts. In January 2013, it had over 46 million entries. The overwhelming majority were in relation to forged documents or stolen vehicles. However, over 1 million individuals or aliases were also registered on the database.[65]

The move to generalised databases for non-EU nationals was taken further with the establishment of the Visa Information System. This contains fingerprints, digital photographs, travel document details and photographs for all persons who are 12 years of age or over, and who have applied for a short-term visa to enter the Union. It also contains details of refusal or revocation of a visa.[66] This database will dwarf the other two. Over 14 million short-term visas are issued annually by the Schengen zone.[67] The terms for access to the SIS are similar to

---

[58] E. Brouwer, 'Eurodac: Its Limitations and Temptations' (2002) 4 *EJML* 231.

[59] Directive 95/46/EC on the protection of individuals with regard to the processing of personal data and on the free movement of such data [1995] OJ L281/31, article 6(1).

[60] CISA 1990, Articles 92–119. United Kingdom and Ireland participate in the system. Decision 2000/365/EC concerning the request of the United Kingdom to take part in some of the provisions of the Schengen Acquis [2000] OJ L131/43; Decision 2002/192/EC concerning Ireland's request to take part in some of the provisions of the Schengen Acquis [2002] OJ L64/20.

[61] CISA 1990, Article 96.

[62] Regulation 1987/2006 on the establishment, operation and use of the second generation Schengen Information System (SIS II) [2006] OJ L381/4. Ireland and the United Kingdom do not participate in this second-generation system.

[63] *Ibid.* article 27.

[64] Decision 2007/533/JHA on the establishment, operation and use of the second generation Schengen Information System (SIS II) [2007] OJ L205/63. Ireland and the United Kingdom do participate in this Decision. It is not clear how their authorities will be restricted to searches for those wanted for criminal offences.

[65] EU Council, *SIS Database Statistics 01/01/2013*, Council Doc. 7389/13, 13 March 2013.

[66] Regulation 767/2008 concerning the Visa Information System (VIS) and the exchange of data between Member States on short-stay visas (VIS Regulation) [2008] OJ L218/60. Ireland and the United Kingdom cannot participate in this.

[67] See http://ec.europa.eu/dgs/home-affairs/what-we-do/policies/borders-and-visas/visa-policy/.

EURODAC. Law-enforcement agencies may have access to individual data if there are reasonable grounds to consider that this will substantially contribute to the prevention, detection or investigation of terrorist offences and of other serious criminal offences.[68]

(c) External frontier

The third expression of this concern with national security lies in the idea that the relaxing of internal frontier controls must be compensated through the strengthening of the external Union frontier. The central legal instrument regulating this is the Schengen Borders Code.[69] This imposes duties on states only to let entry into their territories through designated external border points,[70] to carry out border checks at those points,[71] and to stamp systematically the entry and exit of non-EU nationals from their territories.[72] They are also under duties to carry out border surveillance and to put aside appropriate resources for this.[73] The central provision is article 5. Nominally for short-stay visitors, it covers all non-EU nationals who do not otherwise have a recognised status. In principle, anybody not meeting the conditions below should be refused entry.[74]

Schengen Borders Code, article 5(1)

1. For intended stays on the territory of the Member States of a duration of no more than 90 days in any 180-day period, which entails considering the 180-day period preceding each day of stay, the entry conditions for third-country nationals shall be the following:
   (a) they are in possession of a valid travel document entitling the holder to cross the border satisfying the following criteria:
      (i) its validity shall extend at least three months after the intended date of departure from the territory of the Member States. In a justified case of emergency, this obligation may be waived;
      (ii) it shall have been issued within the previous 10 years;
   (b) they are in possession of a valid visa, if required…except where they hold a valid residence permit;
   (c) they justify the purpose and conditions of the intended stay, and they have sufficient means of subsistence, both for the duration of the intended stay and for the return to their country of origin or transit to a third country into which they are certain to be admitted, or are in a position to acquire such means lawfully;

---

[68] Regulation 767/2008, article 3(1). Decision 2008/633/JHA concerning access for consultation of the Visa Information System (VIS) by designated authorities of Member States and by Europol for the purposes of the prevention, detection and investigation of terrorist offences and of other serious criminal offences [2008] OJ L218/129, article 5.

[69] Regulation 562/2006 establishing a Community Code on the rules governing the movement of persons across borders (Schengen Borders Code) [2006] OJ L105/1 as amended by Regulation 610/2013 [2013] OJ L182/1. Ireland and the United Kingdom do not participate in this Regulation.

[70] *Ibid.* article 4. This is subject to a very limited number of exceptions in article 4(2).

[71] *Ibid.* article 7.

[72] *Ibid.* article 10. Limited exception is provided for those for whom such a stamp may cause serious difficulties for the person concerned. A record must still be kept and statistics of the number of such cases, *ibid.* article 10(3).

[73] *Ibid.* articles 12 and 14. There is a Union agency, Frontex, to assist with this and coordinate it. Regulation 1168/2011 amending Council Regulation 2007/2004 establishing a European Agency for the Management of Operational Cooperation at the External Borders of the Member States of the European Union [2011] OJ L304/1.

[74] Schengen Borders Code, article 13. There are a few limited exceptions in article 5(4) for transit, humanitarian reasons or where visas may be issued at a border.

(d) they are not persons for whom an alert has been issued in the SIS for the purposes of refusing entry;

(e) they are not considered to be a threat to public policy, internal security, public health or the international relations of any of the Member States, in particular where no alert has been issued in Member States' national databases for the purposes of refusing entry on the same grounds.

Non-EU nationals arriving at the border should be treated with dignity.[75] Written reasons must be given for any refusal of entry in a standard form.[76] They are also to have a right of appeal against any refusal of entry to either a court or administrative body which has the same function and offers the same guarantees.[77] However, this right is tempered by this appeal not having suspensive effect. The non-EU national cannot remain on the EU territory pending the appeal. Furthermore, it is vitiated by arguably the most significant feature of article 5, the seemingly arcane point in article 5(1)(b) that the non-EU national have a valid visa. The Union has a list of states whose nationals require short-term visas to enter the Union and the list is considerable.[78] It includes all states who are seen as a significant source of economic migration, irregular migration, political radicalism and asylum seekers.[79] For non-EU nationals falling within this category, article 5(1)(b) transfers decision-making over entry away from the physical Union frontier to two other points, both usually within the non-EU national's state of origin.[80]

The first is the EU Member State consular office in the state where the non-EU national applies for the visa. It is there that her case for entering the Union is considered in most depth at the time of deciding whether to grant her a visa. The test is set out in article 21 of the Community Visas Code.[81]

Community Visas Code, article 21(1)

1. In the examination of an application for a uniform visa, it shall be ascertained whether the applicant fulfils the entry conditions set out in article 5(1)(a), (c), (d) and (e) of the Schengen Borders Code, and particular consideration shall be given to assessing whether the applicant presents a risk of illegal immigration or a risk to the security of the Member States and whether the applicant intends to leave the territory of the Member States before the expiry of the visa applied for.

This test is significantly different from that in article 5 of the Borders Code in that it calls for a much wider consideration of the security risk or the risk of irregular migration. It thus allows the application of more severe criteria away from the frontiers to states whose nationals

[75] *Ibid.* article 6; Case C-23/12 *Zakaria*, Judgment of 17 January 2013.

[76] *Ibid.* article 13(2).   [77] *Ibid.* article 13(3).

[78] Regulation 539/2001 listing the third countries whose nationals must be in possession of visas when crossing the external borders and those whose nationals are exempt from that requirement [2001] OJ L 81/1. This has been amended a number of times, most recently by Regulation 1932/2006 [2006] OJ L405/23.

[79] The Regulation refers to criteria including 'illegal immigration, public policy and security, and to the European Union's external relations with third countries'. *Ibid.* Preamble, para. 5.

[80] More broadly see A. Meloni, 'The Community Code on Visas: Harmonisation at Last?' (2009) 34 *ELRev.* 671.

[81] Regulation 810/2009 establishing a Community Code on Visas [2009] OJ L243/1. Ireland and the United Kingdom do not participate in this.

are seen as a particular threat. It also applies a different threshold. Whilst the border officer must consider whether the migrant threatens security, the consular officer must only consider whether she presents a risk to security or of irregular migration. The risk does not need to be quantified and can only be marginal.

If the central decision for entry for visa holders is applied away from the frontiers using different parameters, it is policed by private bodies. This is because of the Carriers Sanctions Directive.[82] This imposes sanctions on carriers for bringing people to Union frontiers without proper travel documents. Penalties are a minimum of €3,000 for each case.[83] There is also an obligation on the carrier to take responsibility for the migrant if they are refused entry, notwithstanding that they may have the right travel documents. In such circumstances, the carrier is responsible for the costs of return and for returning the migrant as soon as possible, if necessary with another carrier.[84] This leads to carriers engaging in two tasks before they will admit a migrant on board their vessel. They will, first, check that these have the necessary travel documents and visas. Secondly, they will carry out their own assessment as to the risk of refusal of entry. The policing role of the carrier as a long arm of the immigration authorities is completed by its having to communicate information about passengers, their names, travel documents and dates of birth to the latter before the end of check-in in the state of departure.[85] The carrier's decision on whether to admit a migrant to their vessel is likely to be highly cautious as the carrier will not want the risks of having to bear the costs of return. There is, of course, no accountability for this as the terms of the contract between the carrier and migrant is that of a private transaction between two parties in a non-EU state.[86]

(iii) Humanitarianism

Competing against the attitudes above is a powerful discourse of fundamental rights. This emphasises the universalism of the human condition and the arbitrariness of distinguishing between individuals on grounds of nationality.[87] It presses for lenient immigration policies and more extensive rights for non-EU nationals once they are on the territory of the Union. Despite its being reported in a less strident manner than opposing views, this perspective has surprising force with policy-makers, possibly because its advocates, NGOs and big business, tend to be forces capable of organising themselves well within the political decision-making and judicial processes,[88] but also because policy-makers may be wary about the danger of populism in reactions to migrants and this discourse acts as a constraint on that.[89]

---

[82] Directive 2001/51/EC supplementing the provisions of Article 26 of the Convention implementing the Schengen Agreement of 14 June 1985 [2001] OJ L187/45. Ireland and the United Kingdom do participate in this Directive.

[83] *Ibid.* article 4.   [84] *Ibid.* articles 2 and 3.

[85] Directive 2004/82/EC on the obligation of carriers to communicate passenger data, article 3 [2004] OJ L261/24. Ireland and the United Kingdom do participate in the Directive.

[86] N. El-Enany, 'Who is the New European Refugee?' (2008) 33 *ELRev.* 313.

[87] For a variety of arguments see V. Bader, 'The Ethics of Immigration' (2005) 12 *Constellations* 331; L. Ypi, 'Justice in Migration: A Closed Borders Utopia?' (2008) 16 *Journal of Political Philosophy* 391; A. Shachar, *The Birthright Lottery: Citizenship and Global Inequality* (Cambridge, MA, Harvard University Press, 2009) chs. 2 and 3; C. Offe, 'From Migration in Geographic Space to Migration in Biographic Time: Views from Europe' (2011) 19 *Journal of Political Philosophy* 333.

[88] G. Freeman, 'Modes of Immigration Politics in Liberal States' (1995) 29 *International Migration Review* 881; G. Sasse, 'Securitization or Securing Rights? Exploring the Conceptual Foundations of Policies Towards Minorities and Migrants in Europe' (2005) 43 *JCMS* 673.

[89] C. Joppke, 'Why Liberal States Accept Unwanted Immigration' (1998) 50 *World Politics* 266.

This humanitarian impulse is set out most strongly in Article 67(1) TFEU which states that the Area of Freedom, Security and Justice must respect fundamental rights. There are many fundamental rights of relevance in this field, but possibly the most germane is that of non-refoulement. Article 78(1) TFEU states that the Union's asylum and refugee policy must comply with this principle. It is set out in Article 33(1) of the 1951 Geneva Convention on Refugees:

> No Contracting State shall expel or return ('refouler') a refugee in any manner whatsoever to the frontiers of territories where his life or freedom would be threatened on account of his race, religion, nationality, membership of a particular social group or political opinion.

Although the provision only refers to refugees, it also applies to asylum seekers, who, until a decision has been taken on their status, are to be regarded as potential refugees.[90] The right is assumed to have, at least, three elements.[91] First, as it applies to anybody claiming to have a well-founded fear that they will be subject to persecution in their country of origin, Member States are not permitted to turn people away from their territory without assessing the veracity of the claim. Secondly, Member States must carry out an individual assessment of each case, observing requirements of due process.[92] Finally, the individual may neither be transferred to unsafe territories nor to any state which may subsequently return her to a territory in which she may be at risk. It is not available, however, to anybody for whom there are reasonable grounds for regarding as a danger to the security of the host country.[93]

Humanitarian norms inform EU law-making in three fields, in particular. First, they form the basis for granting protection to those suffering persecution and harm in their country of origin. EU law has thus developed a gamut of different types of law to address these needs. These include legislation on asylum, refugee protection, temporary protection and subsidiary protection. To be sure, these laws can be subject to much criticism but their very presence can only be explained by a concern about human need. Secondly, there is a concern with family rights: whether these be non-EU relatives of EU citizens residing in other states,[94] families of Turkish nationals exercising their rights under the EU-Turkey Association Agreement[95] or family members of non-EU nationals lawfully resident in the Union.[96] The third field in which this humanitarian impulse is felt concerns non-EU nationals lawfully resident in the Union. Union policy is to claim to seek to integrate these into Union society as much as possible and, in the case of long-term residents, to approximate their rights to those of Union citizens.[97]

---

[90] It is thus set out as a right to asylum in Article 18 EUCFR. It is also acknowledged in Directive 2005/85/EC on minimum standards on procedures in Member States for granting and withdrawing refugee status, article 20(2) [2005] OJ L326/13.

[91] E. Lauterpacht and D. Bethlehem, 'The Scope and Content of the Principle of Non-Refoulement' in E. Feller *et al.* (eds.), *Refugee Protection in International Law: UNHCR's Global Consultations on International Protection* (Cambridge, Cambridge University Press, 2003) 78–177.

[92] Although see p. 556.

[93] This is set out in Article 33(2) of the 1951 Geneva Convention. It has also been accepted in EU law in Joined Cases C-57/09 and C-101/09 *B and D* [2010] ECR I-10979.

[94] Directive 2004/38/EC on the right of citizens of the Union and their family members to move and reside freely within the territory of the Member States [2004] OJ L158/77. This is discussed at pp. 475–91.

[95] Decision 1/80 of the EC-Turkey Association Council, articles 7 and 9. This can be found in EU Council, *EEC-Turkey Association Agreement and Protocols and Other Basic Texts* (Luxembourg, Office for Official Publications of the European Communities, 1992).

[96] See pp. 552–4.   [97] See pp. 550–2.

The influence of humanitarian norms will probably be felt most keenly within the judiciary. These norms will grant individual entitlements that will allow Union and national measures to be struck down if they are violated.[98] They also provide principles which can be used to guide the interpretation of individual pieces of EU legislation. Much will depend therefore, in the first place, on how the Court of Justice and national courts interpret these principles. An indication of the ebb and flow of the reasoning here is provided by the case of *X, Y and Z*. These were asylum seekers from Sierra Leone, Uganda and Senegal, respectively, who sought refugee status in the Netherlands as they were gay, and homosexuality was a criminal offence in these African states, with the possibility of prison terms up to life imprisonment in the first two, and five years in Senegal. The Dutch authorities refused refugee status on the grounds that possible criminalisation was not sufficient to justify the well-founded fear of persecution necessary to claim such status. The relevant EU legislation indicated that this persecution would only be present if there was severe violation of basic human rights.[99] It was argued by the men's lawyers that there was a violation of the right to respect for private life (Article 7 EUCFR) and the right to non-discrimination (Article 21 EUCFR) here.

Joined Cases C-199/12, C-200/12 and C-201/12 *X, Y and Z*, Judgment of 7 November 2013

53. …for a violation of fundamental rights to constitute persecution within the meaning…of the Geneva Convention, it must be sufficiently serious. Therefore, not all violations of fundamental rights suffered by a homosexual asylum seeker will necessarily reach that level of seriousness.

54. In that connection, it must be stated at the outset that the fundamental rights specifically linked to the sexual orientation concerned in each of the cases in the main proceedings, such as the right to respect for private and family life, which is protected by Article 8 of the ECHR, to which Article 7 of the Charter corresponds, read together, where necessary, with Article 14 ECHR, on which Article 21(1) of the Charter is based, is not among the fundamental human rights from which no derogation is possible.

55. In those circumstances, the mere existence of legislation criminalising homosexual acts cannot be regarded as an act affecting the applicant in a manner so significant that it reaches the level of seriousness necessary for a finding that it constitutes persecution…

56. However, the term of imprisonment which accompanies a legislative provision which, like those at issue in the main proceedings, punishes homosexual acts is capable, in itself of constituting an act of persecution within the meaning of Article 9(1) of the Directive, provided that it is actually applied in the country of origin which adopted such legislation.

57. Such a sanction infringes Article 8 ECHR, to which Article 7 of the Charter corresponds, and constitutes punishment which is disproportionate or discriminatory.

Although the Court of Justice found for the men, there is wavering in the judgment. Criminalisation alone is found not to be sufficient to be a violation of their fundamental rights, as it does not appear to be deemed sufficiently serious. However, if the criminalisation is actually enforced and the penalties are 'disproportionate' or discriminatory, there is a violation of

---

[98] On the scope of national and EU institution fundamental rights and responsibilities see pp. 275–88.

[99] Directive 2004/83/EC on minimum standards for the qualification and status of third country nationals or stateless persons as refugees, article 9(1)(a) [2004] OJ L304/12.

fundamental rights. The Court, thus, seems to tie itself up in knots. It is impossible to conceive of a criminal penalty applied by dint of a person's sexual orientation not being discriminatory and the idea that there are proportionate penalties in this field is a curious notion indeed! In other words, the Court finds a violation of fundamental rights without giving any clear reasoning as to why these rights are violated or as to how other cases in this field are to be approached.

This equivocation is possibly because the adoption of liberal judgments can lead to powerful political reactions. In *Metock*, the Court of Justice held that EU citizens residing in another Member State had a right to marry non-EU nationals granted asylum there.[100] The Danish Government responded by asking for an amendment to the EU legislation in question and by seeking to impose a new criterion before non-Danish EU citizens could marry non-EU nationals in Denmark, namely, that the former had to show genuine and effective residence in Denmark.[101] These measures were intended not just to counter the judgment but also as a shot across the bows of the Court of Justice not to develop that case law further in that field.

(iv) European solidarity

The final theme is that of burden-sharing. Member States should share the costs of managing this policy and support should be offered to those states who struggle to find the resources to meet their obligations in this field.

Article 80(1) TFEU

1. The policies of the Union set out in this Chapter and their implementation shall be governed by the principle of solidarity and fair sharing of responsibility, including its financial implications, between the Member States. Whenever necessary, the acts of the Union adopted pursuant to this Chapter shall contain appropriate measures to give effect to this principle.

This principle has led to the establishment of a number of common funds to help Member States manage the costs of receiving refugees, returning non-EU nationals and policing their external frontiers.[102] Beyond this, EU law has been more concerned with administrative managerialism, with a concern above all to channel and limit the number of applications and attempts a non-EU national can make to enter the Union. This policy is particularly apparent in two policy fields: visas and international protection.

In the field of visas, the Community Code for Visas establishes the idea of a uniform visa. If a non-EU national is granted a visa the presumption is that this is valid for all the Schengen states.[103] The attractiveness of this for the non-EU national is offset by, in principle, an

---

[100] Case C-127/08 *Metock* [2008] ECR I-6241.

[101] On this saga see M. Wind, 'When Parliament Comes First: The Danish Concept of Democracy Meets the European Union' (2009) 27 *Nordisk Tidsskrift For Menneskerettigheter* 272.

[102] Decision 573/2007 establishing the European Refugee Fund [2007] OJ L144/1; Decision 574/2007/EC establishing the External Borders Fund [2007] OJ L144/22; Decision 575/2007 establishing a European Return Fund [2007] OJ L144/45; Decision 2007/435 establishing the European Fund for the Integration of Third-country Nationals [2007] OJ L168/16.

[103] Regulation 810/2009, articles 2(2)(3) and 25.

entitlement to only a single state considering her application. The state competent for considering her application is determined by article 5 of the Code.

Community Code for Visas, article 5(1)

1. The Member State competent for examining and deciding on an application for a uniform visa shall be:
   (a) the Member State whose territory constitutes the sole destination of the visit(s);
   (b) if the visit includes more than one destination, the Member State whose territory constitutes the main destination of the visit(s) in terms of the length or purpose of stay; or
   (c) if no main destination can be determined, the Member State whose external border the applicant intends to cross in order to enter the territory of the Member States.

The principle – that of destination or entry – for allocating which Member State should consider the application is uncontroversial. More arguable is the implicit principle of negative mutual recognition in the Code. Any refusal is entered on the Visa Information System.[104] Other authorities may look at it and use it as a basis for refusal where there are subsequent applications. There is thus a danger of a snowball effect whereby a non-EU national's subsequent application is refused on the basis of a (possibly mistaken?) earlier assessment. A further application is then refused on the grounds that she has been refused twice and so on.

The system follows the trajectory established for international protection governed by the so-called Dublin Regulation, Regulation 604/2013.[105] Under this, the European Union has set up a one-stop-shop whereby anybody seeking international protection within the Union can make only a single application.[106]

Dublin Regulation 604/2013, article 3

1. Member States shall examine any application for international protection by a third-country national or a stateless person who applies on the territory of any one of them, including at the border or in the transit zones. The application shall be examined by a single Member State, which shall be the one which the criteria set out in Chapter III indicate is responsible.
2. Where no Member State responsible can be designated on the basis of the criteria listed in this Regulation, the first Member State in which the application for international protection was lodged shall be responsible for examining it...
   Where the transfer cannot be made pursuant to this paragraph to any Member State designated on the basis of the criteria set out in Chapter III or to the first Member State with which the application was lodged, the determining Member State shall become the Member State responsible.

---

[104] *Ibid.* article 32(5).

[105] Regulation 343/2003/EC establishing the criteria and mechanisms for determining the Member State responsible for examining an application for international protection lodged in one of the Member States by a third-country national or a stateless person [2013] OJ L180/31. Both Ireland and the United Kingdom participate in this Regulation. The 2013 Regulation replaces a 2003 Regulation which in turned replaced a 1990 Convention.

[106] International protection is the main form of protection offered to those seeking a safe haven. It is where a person is making an application for either refugee status or subsidiary protection, Directive 2011/95/EU on standards for the qualification of third-country nationals or stateless persons as beneficiaries of international protection, for a uniform status for refugees or for persons eligible for subsidiary protection, and for the content of the protection granted, article 2(h) [2011] OJ L337/9.

Chapter III sets out the hierarchy of criteria for the allocation of responsibilities. The hierarchy is bedevilled by exceptions but, broadly speaking, its formal (most important first) hierarchy of priority is:

- for unaccompanied minors, the state where a family member is present provided it is in the best interests of the child;[107]
- the state of any family member who has received or is seeking international protection provided that the parties have expressed their desire for that in writing;
- in the case of multiple applications by family members which are close enough in time to be considered together, the state in which the largest number are present or, failing that, the state where the oldest is present;
- the state which issued a valid residence permit or visa for the applicant;
- the state by which the applicant irregularly entered into the Union;
- the state which allowed the applicant to enter the Union by waiving his visa requirement;
- if the application was made in an international transit area, the state where the application was made.[108]

If the applicant will not fall within one of the categories above, the Member State where the applicant first lodged the application is responsible for considering it.[109] In all such cases, other states can transfer the applicant to the relevant state which is now responsible for his or her application. A 2013 study found that this last ground (of first entry) is the most common reason for transfer to another state, accounting for 53 per cent of cases.[110] Burdens are not shared equitably, therefore, as some Member States receive many more applications than others. In 2012–13 Sweden had over sixty times the number of asylum applications per capita of population as Denmark, and Malta and Hungary both had over eighty times the number of applications as Portugal (and fifty times that of Denmark).[111] Furthermore, whilst evidence is dated, it appears that the number of transfers under these criteria is, as a proportion of the total number of applications to the Union, trivial.[112] Moreover, in the vast majority of cases, even where a request for transfer was accepted, it was not executed.[113]

If the process has failed as a system of equitable burden-sharing, its operation shows how the logic of burden-sharing can run contrary to other values.

There is, first, the question of the humanity of the transfer itself. *MA* considered the distressing case of three unaccompanied children, two from Eritrea and one from Iraq, who sought asylum in the United Kingdom.[114] None had any family in the European Union. The Eritreans had made prior applications in Italy and the Iraqi in the Netherlands. The British authorities

---

[107] If there is more than one family member, the Member State where the application was made is to consider what is in the best interests of the child. *Ibid.* article 8(3).

[108] *Ibid.* articles 7–15.   [109] *Ibid.* article 3(2).

[110] ECRE, *Dublin II Regulation: Lives on Hold* (Brussels, ECRE, 2013) 131.

[111] Eurostat, *Asylum Applicants Q2 2012–2013*, available at http://epp.eurostat.ec.europa.eu/cache/ITY_OFFPUB/KS-QA-13-012/EN/KS-QA-13-012-EN.PDF.

[112] The Commission found that by mid-2006 only 16,842 transfers had been made out of just over 657,000 asylum applications. European Commission, *Report on the Evaluation of the Dublin System*, COM(2007)299, 4.

[113] It was executed in only 34.86 per cent of cases. ECRE, n. 110 above, 21.

[114] Case C-648/11 *R v Secretary of State for the Home Department ex parte MA*, Judgment of 6 June 2013. The reasoning of this judgment was incorporated in the 2013 amendments which state that in such cases it shall be in the Member State where the child has lodged his or her application provided it is in the best interests of the child, Regulation 603/2013, article 8(4).

sought to return them to those states on the grounds that these were the states where the children had made their first applications. This was challenged on the basis that the subsequent delay violated Article 24 EUCFR, which requires all public action to have primary regard to the best interests of the child. The Court of Justice agreed. It found that the Dublin Regulation had to be read in the light of Article 24 EUCFR. It stated that this required that the procedure not be prolonged unnecessarily. This would, of course, happen with the transfer. It therefore stated that for unaccompanied minors with no family present in the Union, the Member State in which the minor was present should consider the application. If the judgment exposed, rightly, the lack of humanity in the process with regard to a particularly vulnerable group, it raised questions, in turn, about its use vis-à-vis other groups. The system of transfer acts to keep people who have often been subjected to highly traumatic experiences in a state of limbo.

The other troubling aspect of the Dublin Regulation is that of negative mutual recognition. Whilst Member States are not bound to recognise positive decisions by other Member State authorities granting international protection, the 'one-stop-shop' principle in article 3(1) means that they are required to recognise decisions by other national authorities denying that status. When they make transfers, they consequently recognise the capacity of other Member States to consider the claims of international protection in an equivalent manner and to offer applicants a decent quality of life whilst their case is being considered.[115]

This assumption was thrown into doubt by the *NS* judgment. Five asylum seekers had entered Greece irregularly, and then made their way to the United Kingdom and Ireland, respectively. They resisted transfer back to Greece. The central grounds, documented in a large number of NGO reports, were that Greece was expelling many asylum seekers back to their states of origin without any consideration of their case, providing little or no reception facilities for them to stay, and there were many allegations both of ill-treatment by officials and of a failure to police abuse against asylum seekers. The European Court of Human Rights had, therefore, ruled in 2011 that a transfer of asylum seekers back to Greece violated their fundamental rights, in particular not to be subject to inhuman and degrading treatment.

Joined Cases C-411/10 and C-493/10 *NS* v *Secretary of State for the Home Department*; *ME* v *Refugee Applications Commissioner*, Judgment of 21 December 2011

80. ...it must be assumed that the treatment of asylum seekers in all Member States complies with the requirements of the Charter, the Geneva Convention and the ECHR.

81. It is not however inconceivable that that system may, in practice, experience major operational problems in a given Member State, meaning that there is a substantial risk that asylum seekers may, when transferred to that Member State, be treated in a manner incompatible with their fundamental rights.

82. Nevertheless, it cannot be concluded from the above that any infringement of a fundamental right by the Member State responsible will affect the obligations of the other Member States to comply with the provisions of Regulation [603/2013].

83. At issue here is the *raison d'être* of the European Union and the creation of an area of freedom, security and justice and, in particular, the Common European Asylum System, based on mutual confidence and

[115] For long-standing criticism see A. Hurwitz, 'The 1990 Dublin Convention: A Comprehensive Assessment' (1999) 11 *IJRL* 646; R. Marx, 'Adjusting the Dublin Convention: New Approaches to Member State Responsibility for Asylum Applications' (2001) 3 *EJML* 7; G. Noll, 'Formalism v Empiricism. Some Reflections on the Dublin Convention on the Occasion of Recent European Case Law' (2001) 70 *NJIL* 161.

a presumption of compliance, by other Member States, with European Union law and, in particular, fundamental rights....

86. By contrast, if there are substantial grounds for believing that there are systemic flaws in the asylum procedure and reception conditions for asylum applicants in the Member State responsible, resulting in inhuman or degrading treatment, within the meaning of Article 4 of the Charter, of asylum seekers transferred to the territory of that Member State, the transfer would be incompatible with that provision....

88. In a situation similar to those at issue in the cases in the main proceedings, that is to say the transfer, in June 2009, of an asylum seeker to Greece, the Member State responsible within the meaning of Regulation [603/213], the European Court of Human Rights held, inter alia, that the Kingdom of Belgium had infringed Article 3 of the ECHR, first, by exposing the applicant to the risks arising from the deficiencies in the asylum procedure in Greece, since the Belgian authorities knew or ought to have known that he had no guarantee that his asylum application would be seriously examined by the Greek authorities and, second, by knowingly exposing him to conditions of detention and living conditions that amounted to degrading treatment (European Court of Human Rights, *MSS* v. *Belgium and Greece*, § 358, 360 and 367, judgment of 21 January 2011, not yet published in the *Reports of Judgments and Decisions*).

89. The extent of the infringement of fundamental rights described in that judgment shows that there existed in Greece, at the time of the transfer of the applicant MSS, a systemic deficiency in the asylum procedure and in the reception conditions of asylum seekers....

94. It follows from the foregoing that in situations such as that at issue in the cases in the main proceedings, to ensure compliance by the European Union and its Member States with their obligations concerning the protection of the fundamental rights of asylum seekers, the Member States, including the national courts, may not transfer an asylum seeker to the 'Member State responsible' within the meaning of Regulation [603/2013] where they cannot be unaware that systemic deficiencies in the asylum procedure and in the reception conditions of asylum seekers in that Member State amount to substantial grounds for believing that the asylum seeker would face a real risk of being subjected to inhuman or degrading treatment within the meaning of Article 4 of the Charter.

95. With regard to the question whether the Member State which cannot carry out the transfer of the asylum seeker to the Member State identified as 'responsible' in accordance with Regulation No. 343/2003 is obliged to examine the application itself, it should be recalled that Chapter III of that Regulation refers to a number of criteria and that...those criteria apply in the order in which they are set out in that chapter.

The judgment was incorporated into the 2013 amendments to the Dublin Regulation.

Dublin Regulation 604/2013, article 3(2)

2. Where it is impossible to transfer an applicant to the Member State primarily designated as responsible because there are substantial grounds for believing that there are systemic flaws in the asylum procedure and in the reception conditions for applicants in that Member State, resulting in a risk of inhuman or degrading treatment within the meaning of Article 4 EUCFR, the determining Member State shall continue to examine the criteria set out in Chapter III in order to establish whether another Member State can be designated as responsible.

Once again there is a sting in the tail. To be sure, the claims of the asylum seekers in that instance are vindicated. It is, however, only because there were 'systemic flaws' in the fundamental rights protection in Greece. This is a high threshold to be met, and indicates that transfers can still be made, notwithstanding that there is little reason to believe the fundamental rights in a particular instance will be observed. Indeed, at paragraph 83, the Court of Justice indicated that authorities are not to observe in every case whether fundamental rights are protected. This is highly disturbing as these cases can go to questions of life and death. It also throws into question the individual nature of fundamental rights, as it suggests that they are not properties of every individual but rather group rights whose collective violation must reach a certain level before transfer becomes legally problematic.

4 'UNWELCOME FOREIGNERS': RETURNS DIRECTIVE

The presence and residence of many non-EU nationals within the European Union is dependent on their meeting certain conditions. It might be that they do not work or engage in criminal activity; that they retain a certain status, such as being a student; have sickness insurance; or that they leave the Union within a certain time. The consequences of not meeting those conditions are set out by the Returns Directive, Directive 2008/115/EC.[116] Such persons are deemed to be staying illegally within the Union.

> **Returns Directive 2008/115/EC, article 3(2)**
>
> 2. 'Illegal stay' means the presence on the territory of a Member State, of a third-country national who does not fulfil, or no longer fulfils the conditions of entry as set out in Article 5 of the Schengen Borders Code or other conditions for entry, stay or residence in that Member State.

In addition to breach of the conditions of entry, the central conditions set out in article 5 of the Schengen Borders Code which may result in the non-EU national being deemed to be staying illegally within the Union are those of no longer having a valid travel document or visa or sufficient means; or being a threat to public policy, public health or public security. Falling ill, being robbed or civil disobedience could, thus, all be reasons for return.[117]

A non-EU national staying illegally on Union territory is required to be returned to his state of origin or, failing that, to a state of transit with whom the Union has an agreement, or any other state to which he is willing to return and which will accept him.[118]

---

[116] Directive 2008/115/EC on common standards and procedures in Member States for returning illegally staying third-country nationals [2008] OJ L348/98. Ireland and the United Kingdom are not participating in this Directive. The Directive does not apply to non-EU nationals who enjoy more favourable status by virtue of rights given to them in some other EU law, article 4(1) and (2).

[117] Member States may decide not to apply the Directive to those refused entry or subject to a criminal sanction, *Ibid.* article 2(2). In addition family members of EU citizens or those covered by an agreement between the EU and a non-EU state which grants them rights of free movement are excluded from the Directive, *Ibid.* article 2(3).

[118] *Ibid.* article 3(3).

> **Returns Directive 2008/115/EC, article 6(1)**
>
> 1. Member States shall issue a return decision to any third-country national staying illegally on their territory, without prejudice to the exceptions referred to in paragraphs 2 to 5.

The obligation on the Member States to issue a return decision is new, as previously states enjoyed discretion over whether to require return.[119] It was intended to stop large-scale amnesties to irregular migrants as a way of integrating them into the host society. There is only one significant exception. Member States may offer authorisation to stay for 'compassionate, humanitarian or other reasons'.[120] However, there is no requirement to be compassionate.[121] The Directive still allows for Member States to split up families and to send back very sick people to poor medical facilities. The only obligation is to respect the principle of non-refoulement and to 'take due account' of the best interests of any children, family life or the state of health of the non-EU national.[122]

A return decision should usually provide for the possibility of voluntary departure within typically between seven and thirty days.[123] This is to make the issue as consensual as possible. There are thus possibilities for extension because of schooling issues or family reasons.[124] There are also certain procedural guarantees. The non-EU national is granted the right of appeal and review against the decision before an independent judicial or administrative body.[125] She should also be provided with legal advice and linguistic help.[126]

Forced return will take place where the non-EU national does not voluntarily return within the period granted.[127] It can also happen as a matter of first resort where there is a risk of the non-EU national absconding; she poses a risk to public policy or national security; or her application to stay is manifestly fraudulent or unfounded.[128]

In the case of forced removal two sanctions kick in.

The first is an automatic ban on re-entry into the Union.[129] Provision is made for this to be up to five years and longer where there is a risk to public policy or public security.[130] This automatic ban is to incentivise voluntary return. However, Member States still have discretion to impose a re-entry ban even in cases of voluntary return.[131] If this discretion is habitually exercised, the consequences will, in practice, be the same for the non-EU national. More generally,

---

[119] On this being mandatory see Joined Cases C-261/08 and C-348/08 *Zurita García* v *Delegado del Gobierno en la Región de Murcia* [2009] ECR I-10143.

[120] Directive 2008/115, article 6(4). Other exceptions are limited. These include where the non-EU national has a right to reside in another Member State in which case she should go to the latter state unless there is a security risk, *Ibid.* article 6(2); or where she is the subject of a pending decision renewing her authorisation to stay in which case there is a discretion not to refer, *Ibid.* article 6(5). The other provision mentioned, article 6(3), allows the non-EU national to be transferred to another Member State if there is a bilateral agreement between these states on this matter which existed prior to the Directive. In such circumstances, the latter is responsible for returning the non-EU national.

[121] If somebody detained under the Returns Directive subsequently claims international protection, they cannot be returned whilst their case is being considered and must enjoy the entitlements of that regime, Case C-534/11 *Arslan*, Judgment of 30 May 2013.

[122] Directive 2008/115, article 5.   [123] *Ibid.* article 7(1).   [124] *Ibid.* article 7(2).

[125] *Ibid.* article 13(1).   [126] *Ibid.* article 13(3).   [127] *Ibid.* article 8(1).   [128] *Ibid.* article 7(4).

[129] *Ibid.* article 11(1).   [130] *Ibid.* article 11(2).   [131] *Ibid.* article 11(1).

a re-entry ban provides incentives for determined non-EU nationals to seek irregular entry, possibly through being trafficked or other hazardous means.[132]

The second sanction is that of detention.

Returns Directive 2008/115/EC, article 15(1)

1. Unless other sufficient but less coercive measures can be applied effectively in a specific case, Member States may only keep in detention a third-country national who is the subject of return procedures in order to prepare the return and/or carry out the removal process, in particular when:
   (a) there is a risk of absconding, or
   (b) the third-country national concerned avoids or hampers the preparation of return or the removal process.
   Any detention shall be for as short a period as possible and only maintained as long as removal arrangements are in progress and executed with due diligence.

Detention is a matter of last resort and one of discretion. Furthermore, it should only be used to prepare the return. This possibility of detention still raises the question of the criminalisation of the irregular migrant, whereby her stay is not just deemed illegal but she is also deemed to be a criminal by virtue of it.[133] This was addressed at most length in *Achughbabian*.[134] An Armenian was charged under a French law which provided for his imprisonment solely by virtue of his irregular presence in France. The Court of Justice found such a law to violate the Returns Directive. It made such a finding not on civil liberties grounds but on the basis that any detention must contribute to the removal of the non-EU national. Imprisonment did not do that and thwarted the objective of removal insofar as it could delay it.

Detention should thus only be used as a matter of last resort if there is a risk of absconding or the return is being hampered. It must be reviewed regularly and should not be for an initial period of more than six months.[135] However, it can be extended by a further twelve months if the non-EU national is uncooperative or there are delays securing documentation from third countries.[136] Notwithstanding this, eighteen months is a long period of incarceration, and suggests that the possibility remains, therefore, for the pseudo-criminalisation of the irregular migrant.[137]

5 'DESIRABLE FOREIGNERS': WORKER RESIDENTS AND LONG-TERM RESIDENTS

If irregular migrants sit at one end of the spectrum, non-EU nationals lawfully working in the Union or who are long-term residents occupy the other end. These enjoy favourable rights

---

[132] A. Baldaccini, 'The Return and Removal of Irregular Migrants under EU Law: An Analysis of the Returns Directive' (2009) 11 *EJML* 1, 9–10.

[133] R. Rafaelli, 'Criminalizing Irregular Immigration and the Returns Directive: An Analysis of the *El Dridi* Case' (2011) 13 *EJML* 467.

[134] Case C-329/11 *Achughbabian*, Judgment of 6 December 2011. In like vein see Case C-61/11PPU *El Dridi* [2011] ECR I-3015.

[135] Directive 2008/115, article 15(3) and (5).   [136] *Ibid.* article 15(6).

[137] On the motives for the use of detention see A. Leerkes and D. Broeders, 'A Case of Mixed Motives? Formal and Informal Functions of Administrative Immigration Detention' (2010) 50 *British Journal of Criminology* 830. On

under two Directives: Directive 2011/98/EU which, inter alia, grants a common set of rights to third-country workers legally resident in a Member State,[138] and Directive 2003/109/EC which governs the rights of long-term resident non-EU nationals.[139]

Two philosophies underpin this regime. On the one hand, there is a concern to grant these individuals significant membership rights within the communities within which they live. At the Tampere European Council in 1999, the European Council committed itself to integrating long-term residents within host societies and granting rights analogous to those of Union citizenship. This was reaffirmed by the Stockholm Programme in 2010 and extended to all those legally resident within the Union.[140] On the other, there is a philosophy of 'managed migration'. This takes an instrumental view of non-EU nationals. It grants rights almost exclusively to those who bring skills to the Union in which there is a shortage of supply, and, even there, holds that there are certain thresholds to levels of migration, provision of welfare or tolerance of belief, which must not be exceeded if national economies, welfare states and cultural traditions are not to be endangered. These notional thresholds are sometimes used in invidious ways to deny these non-EU nationals key membership rights in the societies of their host Member States.

(i) Acquisition of employment and long-term residence status

The two Directives establish two types of status for non-EU nationals, respectively: the resident worker and the long-term resident. These grant comparable but different sets of rights and responsibilities.

Resident worker status is granted by Directive 2011/98 on the following basis.

Directive 2011/98/EU, article 3(b), (c)

3. ...

(b) third-country nationals who have been admitted to a Member State for purposes other than work in accordance with Union or national law, who are allowed to work and who hold a residence permit in accordance with Regulation 1030/2002[[141]]; and

(c) third-country nationals who have been admitted to a Member State for the purpose of work in accordance with Union or national law.

---

the wider civil liberties concerns with detention see H. Askola, '"Illegal Migrants", Gender and Vulnerability: The Case of the EU's Returns Directive' (2010) 18 *Feminist Legal Studies* 159.

[138] Directive 2011/98/EU on a single application procedure for a single permit for third-country nationals to reside and work in the territory of a Member State and on a common set of rights for third-country workers legally residing in a Member State [2011] OJ L343/1. Ireland and the United Kingdom do not participate in this Directive.

[139] Directive 2003/109/EC concerning the status of third-country nationals who are long-term residents [2003] OJ L16/44, as amended by Directive 2011/51/EU [2011] OJ L132/1. The United Kingdom and Ireland are not participating in the Directive. See E. Guild, *The Legal Elements of European Identity* (Dordrecht, Kluwer, 2004) ch. 12; L. Halleskov, 'The Long-Term Residents Directive: A Fulfilment of the Tampere Objective of Near Equality' (2005) 7 *EJML* 181; K. Groenendijk and E. Guild, 'Converging Criteria: Creating an Area of Security of Residence for Europe's Third Country Nationals' (2001) 3 *EJML* 37.

[140] The Stockholm Programme sets out the programme of Union action to be taken between 2010 and 2014 in the Area of Freedom, Security and Justice [2010] OJ C115/1. This point is at para. 6.1.4.

[141] This merely sets out the format for the resident permit these must possess. Regulation 1030/2002 laying down a uniform format for residence permits for third-country nationals [2002] OJ L157/1.

Non-EU nationals meeting these conditions will be issued with a 'single permit' which sets out the permission to work granted to them.[142] Whilst there are certain Union requirements which must be met, notably that of Union preference, before this permit can be granted, access to this status is largely governed by national law. EU law governs more extensively the acquisition of long-term resident status. Individuals must apply to the competent national authority, providing documentary evidence showing that they satisfy three conditions.[143]

The first is that they have lawfully and continuously resided for a period of five years in the Member State in question.[144] The question of what constitutes lawful residence is a matter for national law.[145] However, many forms of lawful residence will not be considered sufficient to entitle the non-EU national to acquire long-term residence status. These include residence as students, those who have applied for international protection, seasonal workers, au pairs and diplomats.[146]

The second and third conditions are set out in Directive 2011/98, article 5.

Directive 2011/98/EU, article 5

1. Member States shall require third-country nationals to provide evidence that they have, for themselves and for dependent family members:
   (a) stable and regular resources which are sufficient to maintain himself/herself and the members of his/her family, without recourse to the social assistance system of the Member State concerned. Member States shall evaluate these resources by reference to their nature and regularity and may take into account the level of minimum wages and pensions prior to the application for long-term resident status;
   (b) sickness insurance in respect of all risks normally covered for his/her own nationals in the Member State concerned.
2. Member States may require third-country nationals to comply with integration conditions, in accordance with national law.

There is something pernicious about asking individuals to provide sufficient resources for themselves and their families after they have already lawfully resided for five years in a society, and contributed to that society.[147] Of equal concern is the requirement that Member States can require individuals to comply with integration conditions: typically tests to show their knowledge of local culture, language or history. Such tests are traditionally reserved for the granting of citizenship status where the individual is seeking full membership rights and to identify herself with her host society. Kofman has observed, in this, a shift to a limited cultural tolerance of migrants in which these have to show that they fit in before they be granted important entitlements.

---

[142] *Ibid.* article 6.   [143] Directive 2003/109, article 7(1).   [144] *Ibid.* article 4(1).
[145] Case C-40/11 *Iida* v *Stadt Ulm*, Judgment of 8 November 2012.
[146] Directive 2003/109, article 3(2).
[147] Long-term resident status can also be refused if an individual poses a threat to public policy or public security, *Ibid.* article 6(1).

E. Kofman, 'Citizenship, Migration and the Reassertion of National Identity' (2005) 9 *Citizenship Studies* 453, 461–2

Though the values to which migrants are increasingly required to subscribe are in fact general liberal values such as human rights, the rule of law, tolerance for others, and so on, they are also presented with a certain view of national identity re-inscribing these liberal values within a national framework. Amongst these values, tolerance by the majority is seen to have been stretched to a breaking point, and…tolerance is clearly showing its limits. In critiquing the acceptance of tolerance as a quality of European societies, Essed suggests that the dominated is dependent on the goodwill of the dominant who have the power to be tolerant and what, in effect, is a form of cultural control.[148] The identity of the dominant group or 'us' is formulated around its tolerance and adherence to human rights compared to the intolerant other. In the latest Dutch integration measures, it is stipulated that people must integrate into and understand the norms and values of a broadly tolerant Dutch community.

In the UK, David Blunkett, the Home Secretary, was to announce on the eve of the publication of the Cantle Report on the disturbances, 'We have norms of acceptability and those who come into our home – for that is what it is – should accept these norms'. As he had already stated in the White Paper, newcomers would have to 'develop a sense of belonging, an identity and shared mutual understanding which can be passed from one generation to another'. The White Paper also noted problematic practices, such as arranged marriages, especially where these involved bringing in partners from countries of origin.

Demands for conformity to an unchanging and homogeneous cultural norm have advanced furthest in Denmark. We hear echoes of the earlier British rhetoric of the 1970s of the swamping of the settled population by newcomers. A conservative Danish politician expounded the view that: Denmark is a country that is built around one people.…Danish Christianity, history, culture, view on democracy and our thoughts about freedom must continue to be the foundation that Denmark rests on.…We don't want a Denmark where the Danish become a temporary ethnic minority and where our freedom is pulled away.

Long-term resident status may be lost if there is subsequent evidence that it was fraudulently acquired or the non-EU national poses a threat to public policy and is expelled as a consequence.[149] Perhaps more draconian is the possibility for loss if a non-EU national spends more than twelve consecutive months outside the Union.[150] Whilst this is a matter of discretion for the Member States, it is difficult to believe that such a short period indicates any kind of loss of attachment, particularly in light of the length of time required for a person to acquire the status of long-term resident.

(ii) Rights acquired against the host state

Worker resident and long-term resident status secure three sets of rights: rights of entry and residence; rights to equal treatment and the right to family reunion.

Worker resident status grants the non-EU national the right to enter and reside in the territory and have free access to the entire territory of the state. These rights exist, however, only

---

[148] P. Essed, *Understanding Everyday Racism: An Interdisciplinary Theory* (London, Sage, 1991) 210.
[149] Directive 2003/109, article 9(1)(a) and (b).   [150] *Ibid.* article 9(1)(c).

for the period of the permit. Furthermore, national law may limit the territory to which there is access.[151] By contrast, long-term resident status grants the non-EU national the right to reside permanently in the Member State in question.[152] The only circumstance in which she may be expelled is where she constitutes an actual and sufficiently serious threat to public policy or security.[153] However, there is some protection for long-term residents even where it is determined that they do pose such a threat. Before expulsion, Member States must have regard to the duration of residence on the territory, the individual's age, the consequences for her and her family and the relative links she has with both her country of residence and country of origin.[154] She must also have the possibility to seek judicial review of any such decision.[155]

Secondly, both worker residents and long-term residents have the right to equal treatment with a Member State's own nationals with regard to a number of socio-economic entitlements. The differences granted to each reflect, maybe crudely, perceptions about their relative contributions to the host society.

Worker residents are granted equal treatment, first, with regard to a number of economic benefits, most notably working conditions and freedom of association and recognition of diplomas and other professional qualifications.[156] They are, secondly, granted equal treatment to a number of social advantages. These include education and vocational training, social security branches, and access to goods and services, including those made available to the public such as housing, and employment advice services.[157] This does not include all social advantages but a much more limited list. It is also subject to a number of exclusions. Equal access to education and vocational training can be limited to those in employment, can exclude non-EU nationals who entered as students and can exclude maintenance grants and loans.[158] Access to social security branches can be limited to those who have been in work for more than six months.[159] Finally, access to housing can be restricted if a Member State chooses.[160] The third form of advantage to which worker residents have a right to equal treatment are tax advantages[161] and accrued pension rights, with the latter to be offered on the same basis as those offered to a Member State's own nationals when they reside in a third country.[162] Once again, there is a limitation in that Member States can refuse to grant tax benefits to family members not resident in their territory.[163]

Long-term residents secure equal access with regard to a wider array of entitlements.

Directive 2011/98/EU, article 11(1)

1. Long-term residents shall enjoy equal treatment with nationals as regards:
   (a) access to employment and self-employed activity, provided such activities do not entail even occasional involvement in the exercise of public authority, and conditions of employment and working conditions, including conditions regarding dismissal and remuneration;
   (b) education and vocational training, including study grants in accordance with national law;

---

[151] Directive 2011/98, article 11(a)–(c).
[152] Directive 2003/109, article 8. On national practice see E. Guild and P. Minderhood (eds.), *Security of Residence and Expulsion: Protection of Aliens in Europe* (The Hague/London/Boston, Kluwer, 2001).
[153] Directive 2003/109, article 12(1).   [154] *Ibid.* article 12(3).   [155] *Ibid.* article 12(4).
[156] Directive 2011/98, article 12(1)(a), (b) and (d).   [157] *Ibid.* article 12(1) (c), (e), (g) and (h).
[158] *Ibid.* article 12(2)(a).   [159] *Ibid.* article 12(2)(b).   [160] *Ibid.* article 12(2)(d).
[161] *Ibid.* article 12(1)(f).   [162] *Ibid.* article 12(4).   [163] *Ibid.* article 12(2)(c).

(c) recognition of professional diplomas, certificates and other qualifications, in accordance with the relevant national procedures;

(d) social security, social assistance and social protection as defined by national law;

(e) tax benefits;

(f) access to goods and services and the supply of goods and services made available to the public and to procedures for obtaining housing;

(g) freedom of association and affiliation and membership of an organisation representing workers or employers or of any organisation whose members are engaged in a specific occupation, including the benefits conferred by such organisations, without prejudice to the national provisions on public policy and public security;

(h) free access to the entire territory of the Member State concerned, within the limits provided for by the national legislation for reasons of security.

Member States may choose to grant additional benefits.[164] Notwithstanding this, the provision is less generous than it might appear due to a series of limitations.[165] The most significant exclusion is in article 11(4):

> Member States may limit equal treatment in respect of social assistance and social protection to core benefits.

The Preamble to the Directive states that the notion of 'core benefits' is one for national law, but must cover at least minimum income support, assistance in case of illness, pregnancy, parental assistance and long-term care.[166]

The breadth of this exception was addressed in *Kamberaj*. An Albanian who enjoyed permanent resident status in Italy and had lived there for fifteen years was refused social housing in 2009 by the municipality of Bolzano as the fund allocating for housing for non-EU nationals had been exhausted. The authorities argued that article 11(4) allowed Member States to determine the core benefits to which non-EU nationals had access, and, in this case, the Italian authorities had decided housing was not a core benefit. The Court of Justice rejected this argument.

Case C-571/10 *Kamberaj* v *IPES*, Judgment of 24 April 2012

84. It is apparent from recital 13 in the preamble to that directive that the concept of core benefits covers at least minimum income support, assistance in case of illness, pregnancy, parental assistance and long-term care. The modalities for granting such benefits are to be determined, in accordance with that recital, by national law.

85. It must, first, be observed that the list set out in recital 13 which illustrates the concept of 'core benefits' stated in Article 11(4) of Directive 2003/109 is not exhaustive, as is clear from the use of the wording 'at least'. The fact that no express reference is made in that recital to housing benefits does not therefore mean that they do not constitute core benefits to which the principle of equal treatment must in any event be applied.

---

[164] Directive 2003/109, article 11(5).

[165] They can be excluded from public sector employment and activities like EU citizens. *Ibid.* article 11(2) and (3).

[166] *Ibid.* para. 13.

86. Second, it must be noted that, since the integration of third-country nationals who are long-term residents in the Member States and the right of those nationals to equal treatment in the sectors listed in Article 11(1) of Directive 2003/109 is the general rule, the derogation provided for in Article 11(4) thereof must be interpreted strictly...

87. In that regard, it should be held that a public authority, at national, regional or local level, can rely on the derogation provided for in Article 11(4) of Directive 2003/109 only if the bodies in the Member State concerned responsible for the implementation of that directive have stated clearly that they intended to rely on that derogation.

88. It is not apparent from the file before the Court that the Italian Republic stated that it intended to rely on the derogation from the principle of equal treatment provided for under Article 11(4) of Directive 2003/109.

89. Finally, it must be noted that the reference to national law in recital 13 in the preamble to Directive 2003/109 is limited to the modalities of the grant of the benefits in question, that is the laying down of the conditions of access and of the level of such benefits and of the procedures relating thereto.

90. The meaning and scope of the concept of 'core benefits' in Article 11(4) of Directive 2003/109 must therefore be sought taking into account the context of that article and the objective pursued by that directive, namely the integration of third-country nationals who have resided legally and continuously in the Member States.

91. Article 11(4) of Directive 2003/109 must be understood as allowing Member States to limit the equal treatment enjoyed by holders of the status conferred by Directive 2003/109, with the exception of social assistance or social protection benefits granted by the public authorities, at national, regional or local level, which enable individuals to meet their basic needs such as food, accommodation and health.

92. In that regard, it should be recalled that, according to Article 34 of the Charter, the Union recognises and respects the right to social and housing assistance so as to ensure a decent existence for all those who lack sufficient resources. It follows that, in so far as the benefit in question in the main proceedings fulfils the purpose set out in that article of the Charter, it cannot be considered, under European Union law, as not being part of core benefits within the meaning of Article 11(4) of Directive 2003/109. It is for the referring court to reach the necessary findings, taking into consideration the objective of that benefit, its amount, the conditions subject to which it is awarded and the place of that benefit in the Italian system of social assistance.

The third form of right is that of the right to family reunion. This right is granted in the main by Directive 2003/86/EC on the right to family reunification.[167] Its relationship with these two Directives is an awkward one.

Directive 2003/86/EC, article 3(1)

1. This Directive shall apply where the sponsor is holding a residence permit issued by a Member State for a period of validity of one year or more who has reasonable prospects of obtaining the right of permanent residence, if the members of his or her family are third country nationals of whatever status.[168]

---

[167] [2003] OJ L251/12. Ireland and the United Kingdom are not participating in this Directive. A more liberal regime for family reunification is provided for those with a Blue Card, Directive 2009/50, article 15.

[168] The Directive also applies where national measures grant a right to permanent residence independently of the Directive. Refugees benefit from the Directive, *ibid.* articles 9–12 but not those seeking international protection, *ibid.* article 3(2).

The right is thus granted to many residents who are far away from long-term resident status. On the other hand, not all worker residents secure it as the permit must be for one year or more and there must be a reasonable prospect of permanent residence. If the exclusion of many worker residents from the right to family reunion is harsh, most notably where they have a long contract of employment but no prospect of permanent residence, the Directive also sets out a very narrow conception of the family. Member States are only required to admit the spouse of the sponsor and minor children (including those adopted) over which the sponsor or spouse has exclusive custody.[169]

The right to family reunification is also a contingent one. Any family member may be refused entry for reasons of public policy, public health or public security.[170] Member States may also require that the sponsor demonstrate she has sufficient resources to support herself and her family without recourse to social assistance; sickness insurance for all the family; and can provide family accommodation that is regarded as normal for the region and complies with health and safety requirements.[171] This requirement was qualified in *Chakroun* where a Dutch requirement that a sponsor earn 120 per cent of the minimum income was found to be illegal.[172] The Court of Justice found that the sponsor need only show stable and regular resources sufficient to maintain himself and the members of his family in the absence of specific needs, which would, in this instance, be the minimum wage. Recourse to the social assistance system for specific needs such as tax refunds or local authority schemes to supplement his income would not deny him the right to family reunification.

There are two more controversial requirements. First, Member States are permitted to require the sponsor to have lawfully resided for two years in the territory before her family can join her: a period of separation which seems draconian.[173] Secondly, Member States can require family members to comply with 'integration' measures, such as language assessments and tests on the culture, politics and history of the host state.[174] Particularly contentious is the possibility for these tests to be applied to children as young as 12 years old where they arrive independently of the rest of the family.[175] This was challenged by the Parliament as violating the right to respect for family life under Article 8 ECHR in *Parliament* v *Council*. The Court of Justice's reasoning was unconvincing. It noted that the Directive only granted discretion to prevent a 12-year-old entering the Union. In exercising that discretion Member States would have to observe the right to respect for family life and the interests of the child. The principle that children take these tests, and, therefore, the possibility that they be kept apart from their families if they failed them was not held to be illegal, however.[176] There is an air of disingenuousness in this as it is impossible to conceive of circumstances where separating a 12-year-old child from their family because they fail an integration test has regard either to the interests of the child or respects family life.

Family members are granted a limited number of rights once they have entered the European Union.

---

[169] *Ibid.* article 4(2).   [170] *Ibid.* article 6.   [171] *Ibid.* article 7(1).
[172] Case C-578/08 *Chakroun* v *Minister van Buitenlandse Zaken* [2010] ECR I-1839.
[173] Directive 2003/86, article 8(1).   [174] *Ibid.* article 7(2).   [175] *Ibid.* article 4(1).
[176] Case C-540/03 *Parliament* v *Council* [2006] ECR I-5769, paras. 52–76.

Directive 2003/86/EC, article 13

1. The sponsor's family members shall be entitled, in the same way as the sponsor, to:
   (a) access to education;
   (b) access to employment and self-employed activity;
   (c) access to vocational guidance, initial and further training and retraining.
2. Member States may decide according to national law the conditions under which family members shall exercise an employed or self-employed activity. These conditions shall set a time limit which shall in no case exceed 12 months, during which Member States may examine the situation of their labour market before authorising family members to exercise an employed or self-employed activity.
3. Member States may restrict access to employment or self employed activity by first-degree relatives in the direct ascending line or adult unmarried children...

Whilst this provision suggests that family members acquire a right to employment or to self-employment after twelve months, significant entitlements are lacking, namely, social assistance and social security. The implication is that the resident must not only have sufficient resources to support her family on first arrival in the Member State but also for the first twelve months of residence, and to assume any risks to their health or economic self-sufficiency thereafter.

6 'SUSPICIOUS FOREIGNERS': EU REGIME ON INTERNATIONAL PROTECTION

Until the mid-1980s, Member States were content to offer quite liberal regimes to asylum seekers. This was aided by flows of asylum seekers vis-à-vis other forms of migrants being quite limited. However, asylum applications to the Union tripled from 200,000 in 1980 to 700,000 per annum in 1990.[177] The cost of administering asylum increased in major industrialised states from US$500 million per annum to US$7 billion per annum.[178] This led to increasingly draconian measures being taken to deny asylum seekers many welfare benefits.[179] In 1986, Denmark introduced a law whereby it would not hear an asylum seeker's claim if she could have applied for protection in a safe third country, i.e. one she had passed through on route to its territory. This law marked the beginning of a swathe of restrictive national legislation being enacted across the Union, with the most high-profile being the German amendment to the unconditional right to asylum in its Constitution in 1993.[180] These measures led to a fall-off in the number of asylum applications since 2002, even if these still remain higher than the early 1980s, with 383,575 asylum applications to the Union in the year up to June 2013.[181]

---

[177] For trends see ECRE, *Asylum Trends in 35 Industrialised Countries 1982–2002* (Brussels, ECRE, 2004).

[178] UNHCR, *The State of the World's Refugees: In Search of Solutions* (Oxford, Oxford University Press, 1995) 199.

[179] See pp. 557–9.

[180] On the recent history of asylum law in 1980s and 1990s Europe see I. Boccardi, *Europe and Refugees: Towards an EU Asylum Policy* (The Hague, Kluwer, 2002); R. Byrne *et al.*, 'Understanding Refugee Law in an Enlarged European Union' (2004) 15 *EJIL* 355. On the relationship between the practice of states and the wider ethical issues see M. Gibney, *The Ethics and Politics of Asylum: Liberal Democracy and the Response to Refugees* (Cambridge, Cambridge University Press, 2004).

[181] Care must be taken with these figures as the Union has enlarged since 1980. See http://epp.eurostat.ec.europa.eu/portal/page/portal/product_details/publication?p_product_code=KS-QA-13–012.

Tensions have materialised most acutely over the entitlements offered to those applying for international protection once they arrive in the Union. Until an applicant's need of protection has been established as bona fide, there is institutional suspicion over whether she is merely engaged in economic migration or welfare tourism.

(i) Right to remain pending examination of the application and to individual examination of the application

The right of asylum has become submerged within a more generalised right: the right to seek international protection. International protection is the grant one of two statuses: refugee status or subsidiary protection.[182] A refugee is:

> a third-country national who, owing to a well-founded fear of being persecuted for reasons of race, religion, nationality, political opinion or membership of a particular social group, is outside the country of nationality and is unable or, owing to such fear, is unwilling to avail himself or herself of the protection of that country, or a stateless person, who, being outside of the country of former habitual residence for the same reasons as mentioned above, is unable or, owing to such fear, unwilling to return to it.[183]

Subsidiary protection is a more diffuse notion. It is provided when:

> a third-country national or a stateless person who does not qualify as a refugee but in respect of whom substantial grounds have been shown for believing that the person concerned, if returned to his or her country of origin, or in the case of a stateless person, to his or her country of former habitual residence, would face a real risk of suffering serious harm as defined in Article 15…and is unable, or, owing to such risk, unwilling to avail himself or herself of the protection of that country.[184]

The serious harm identified in article 15 of Directive 2011/95/EU is set out in the following terms.

Directive 2011/95/EU, article 15

Serious harm consists of:
(a) death penalty or execution; or
(b) torture or inhuman or degrading treatment or punishment of an applicant in the country of origin; or
(c) serious and individual threat to a civilian's life or person by reason of indiscriminate violence in situations of international or internal armed conflict.

Those applying for international protection acquire a number of rights not granted to many other non-EU nationals such as economic migrants or migrants fleeing from starvation.[185]

---

[182] Directive 2011/95, article 2(a). Ireland and the United Kingdom do not participate in this Directive.
[183] *Ibid.* article 2(d).   [184] *Ibid.* article 2(f).
[185] J. Hathaway, 'A Reconsideration of the Underlying Premises of Refugee Law' (1990) 31 *Harvard International Law Journal* 129.

However, the rights granted are so full of caveats and exceptions that, from a civil liberties perspective, many are deeply problematic. As we shall see, almost all are conditional on their meeting certain obligations which enables the applicant both to be heavily policed and to be segregated from the society of their host state.

The central entitlement, set out in Article 9 of Directive 2013/32/EU, is a right to remain whilst the application for protection is being considered.[186]

Directive 2013/32/EU, article 9(1)

Applicants shall be allowed to remain in the Member State, for the sole purpose of the procedure, until the determining authority has made a decision in accordance with the procedures [set out]…This right to remain shall not constitute an entitlement to a residence permit.

The right is subject to one significant exception. It does not apply where there is a 'safe third country'[187] to which it would be 'reasonable' for the applicant to go.[188] Each Member State draws up its own list of these states, basing this list on a methodology set out in national law.[189] Such states are typically neighbouring states to the state of origin or states through which the applicant has transited. The consequence is that the applicant will often have to show that there was no safe state more accessible for her than the European Union before she will be provided protection. There are a number of other conditions which must be met for a third country to be considered safe.[190]

Directive 2013/32/EU, article 38(1)

1. Member States may apply the safe third country concept only where the competent authorities are satisfied that a person seeking asylum will be treated in accordance with the following principles in the third country concerned:
   (a) life and liberty are not threatened on account of race, religion, nationality, membership of a particular social group or political opinion;
   (b) there is no risk of serious harm as defined in Directive 2011/95/EU;
   (c) the principle of non-refoulement in accordance with the Geneva Convention is respected;
   (d) the prohibition of removal, in violation of the right to freedom from torture and cruel, inhuman or degrading treatment as laid down in international law, is respected;
   and
   (e) the possibility exists to request refugee status and, if found to be a refugee, to receive protection in accordance with the Geneva Convention.

---

[186] Directive 2013/32/EU on common procedures for granting and withdrawing international protection [2013] OJ L180/60. The United Kingdom and Ireland do not participate in this Directive. This Directive is not to be transposed until 20 July 2015. Until then, this right is provided by Directive 2005/85/EC on minimum standards on procedures in Member States for granting and withdrawing refugee status [2005] OJ L326/13, article 7.

[187] Directive 2013/32, article 33(2)(c); Directive 2005/85/EC, article 25(2)(c). All EU Member States are considered safe states, Protocol on Asylum for Nationals of Member States of the European Union.

[188] Directive 2013/32, article 38(2)(a); Directive 2005/85, article 27(2)(a).

[189] Directive 2013/32, article 38(2)(b); Directive 2005/85, article 27(2)(b).

[190] The equivalent provision is Directive 2005/85, article 27(1).

These criteria are troublingly vague. The civil liberties organisation, Statewatch, noted that when the issue was initially discussed in the Council, there was substantial disagreement about at least nine states. It also noted that the criteria seemed to be applied in ways that gave misgivings. Senegal had, in 2001, about 10,000 refugees living in neighbouring states but was considered safe in thirteen out of seventeen responses.[191] Equally troubling is the lack of clear safeguards to verify that these states will not send back applicants to their state of origin.

The onus is on the applicant to furnish proof of all the elements necessary to substantiate her case.[192] She satisfies this if she makes a genuine effort to substantiate the application, has submitted all the elements at her disposal, applied at the earliest possible time and her general credibility has been established.[193] Member States are then required to assess each case individually, taking account of all the relevant circumstances.[194] They are in principle, required to examine each case within six months.[195] This examination must involve interviewing the applicant, and providing free legal assistance and interpreter services to her.[196] The applicant is entitled to a decision in writing setting out the reasons for the decision.[197] They are also entitled to appeal this decision before a court or tribunal and to an effective remedy where this appeal is successful.[198]

There are two circumstances where this right to individual examination is qualified. The first is where the applicant is entering the Union from a 'safe European country'. Such a country will be a European state, which has ratified the ECHR and the Geneva Convention on Refugees, and has its own asylum procedures in place.[199] In such a circumstance, a Member State may choose to carry out no examination. The assumption – and it is an assumption – is that the applicant should have sought international protection there. The second is where the applicant is considered to come from a 'safe country of origin'. This will typically be her state of nationality. Member States may designate certain states safe, and this designation leads to a much less thorough examination. In such circumstances, there is a presumption that there is no case for international protection unless the applicant can provide evidence to show that there are serious grounds for not considering the country to be safe in her particular circumstances.[200]

(ii) Provision of material reception conditions

Member States must provide material reception conditions adequate for the health and subsistence of those seeking international protection. These conditions are set out in Directive 2013/33/EU.[201] The central principle is that in Article 13(2).[202]

---

[191] See www.statewatch.org/analyses/no-38-safe-countries.pdf.
[192] Directive 2011/95, article 4(1).   [193] *Ibid.* article 4(5).   [194] *Ibid.* article 4(3).
[195] Directive 2013/32, article 31; Directive 2005/85, article 23.
[196] Directive 2013/32, articles 14, 19 and 12(1)(b), respectively.
[197] Directive 2013/32, article 11(1); Directive 2005/85, article 9(1).
[198] Directive 2013/32, article 46; Directive 2005/85, article 39.
[199] Directive 2013/32, article 39.
[200] Directive 2013/32, article 36; Directive 2005/85, article 31.
[201] Directive 2013/33/EU laying down the standards for the reception of applicants for international protection [2013] OJ L180/96. This does not come into force until 20 July 2015. In the meantime, Directive 2003/9/EC laying down minimum standards for the reception of asylum seekers [2003] OJ L31/18, applies. Ireland and the United Kingdom are participating in Directive 2013/33.
[202] The equivalent provision is Directive 2003/9, article 13(1) and (2).

> ## Directive 2013/33/EU, article 17(1)
>
> 1. Member States shall ensure that material reception conditions are available to applicants when they make their application for international protection.
> 2. Member States shall ensure that material reception conditions provide an adequate standard of living for applicants, which guarantees their subsistence and protects their physical and mental health.

Material reception conditions include housing, food and clothing. However, these can be provided in a way that separates out and identifies the applicant. In the case of food and clothing, provision may take the form of vouchers or a daily expense allowance.[203] Housing 'in kind' can include housing used specifically for asylum seekers (for example, accommodation centres).[204] In such cases, Member States must ensure that the housing protects the family life; they have the possibility of communicating with relatives, legal advisers and UNHCR representatives, and that these and family members have access to the accommodation unless security grounds justify limits.[205] Alongside these material reception conditions, Member States shall ensure that applicants receive necessary health care which, at the least, shall include emergency care and essential treatment of illness.[206] However, Member States are permitted to grant benefits on the basis of a means test. This allows them to require the applicant to cover the cost of material reception conditions and health care if she is deemed to have sufficient resources.[207]

In addition to the entitlements above, a number of family and economic rights are granted.

Applicants do not have a right to respect for their family life. Member States must only take appropriate measures as far as possible to secure family unity.[208] The best interests of the child are to be a primary consideration for Member States.[209] These are weak provisions which allow for families to be split up for administrative or economic reasons. Although this must be done with the applicant's agreement,[210] it will be difficult for an individual, aware that the decision to award her refugee status or subsidiary protection is a matter of discretion, to refuse to cooperate with the authorities. Member States should grant access to the education system to minor asylum seekers under *similar* conditions as for their own nationals. These are not the same conditions, however. Member States can therefore provide for the ghettoisation of these children by requiring them to be educated in accommodation centres.[211]

Finally, applicants have certain employment rights. They must have access to the labour market no later than nine months from the date when the application for international protection was lodged if a first instance decision by the competent authority has not been taken and the delay cannot be attributed to the applicant.[212] Conditions on access are to be determined by national law but must allow effective access to the market. Preference on that market, for

---

[203] Directive 2013/33, article 2(g); Directive 2003/9, article 2(j).
[204] Directive 2013/33, article 18(1); Directive 2003/9, article 14(1).
[205] Directive 2013/33, article 18(2); Directive 2003/9, article 14(2).
[206] Directive 2013/33, article 19; Directive 2003/9, article 15.
[207] Directive 2013/33, article 17(3) and (4); Directive 2003/9, article 13(3) and (4).
[208] Directive 2013/33, article 12; Directive 2003/9, article 8.
[209] Directive 2013/33, article 23(1); Directive 2003/9, article 18(1).
[210] Directive 2013/33, article 12; Directive 2003/9, article 8.
[211] Directive 2013/33, article 14(1); Directive 2003/9, article 10(1).
[212] Directive 2013/33, article 15(1).

reasons of labour market policy, may, however, be granted to EU citizens, EEA nationals and non-EU nationals lawfully resident in the Union.[213]

(iii) Policing of applicants through welfare

The applicant must meet a series of conditions and behave in particular ways set out by Directive 2013/33/EU if almost all the benefits on offer are not to be subject to withdrawal.[214]

Directive 2013/33/EU, article 20

1. Member States may reduce or, in exceptional and duly justified cases, withdraw material reception conditions where an applicant:
   (a) abandons the place of residence determined by the competent authority without informing it or, if requested, without permission; or
   (b) does not comply with reporting duties or with requests to provide information or to appear for personal interviews concerning the asylum procedure during a reasonable period laid down in national law; or
   (c) has lodged a subsequent application as defined in Article 2(q) of Directive 2013/32/EU.[215]

   In relation to cases (a) and (b), when the applicant is traced or voluntarily reports to the competent authority, a duly motivated decision, based on the reasons for the disappearance, shall be taken on the reinstallation of the grant of some or all of the material reception conditions withdrawn or reduced.

2. Member States may also reduce material reception conditions when they can establish that the applicant, for no justifiable reason, has not lodged an application for international protection as soon as reasonably practicable after arrival in that Member State.
3. Member States may reduce or withdraw material reception conditions where an applicant has concealed financial resources, and has therefore unduly benefited from material reception conditions.
4. Member States may determine sanctions applicable to serious breaches of the rules of the accommodation centres as well as to seriously violent behaviour.
5. Decisions for reduction or withdrawal of material reception conditions or sanctions referred to in paragraphs 1, 2, 3 and 4 of this Article shall be taken individually, objectively and impartially and reasons shall be given. Decisions shall be based on the particular situation of the person concerned, especially with regard to persons covered by Article 21, taking into account the principle of proportionality. Member States shall under all circumstances ensure access to health care in accordance with Article 19 and shall ensure a dignified standard of living for all applicants.
6. Member States shall ensure that material reception conditions are not withdrawn or reduced before a decision is taken in accordance with paragraph 5.

These sanctions seek to ensure that the applicant is traceable (the reporting and residence requirements); not disruptive (violent behaviour and breach of rules of the accommodation centre) and frank about her financial circumstances. Perhaps the most draconian is the

---

[213] Directive 2013/33, article 15(2).   [214] The equivalent provision in Directive 2003/9 is article 16.
[215] This is where an applicant makes a further application for international protection after a final decision on the initial application has been made.

possibility for the withdrawal of material reception conditions if the application is not made as soon as reasonably practical after arrival. This condition was criticised in particular by the United Nations High Commission for Refugees (UNHCR) when it was introduced in the 2003 Directive.[216]

E. Guild, 'Seeking Asylum: Storm Clouds between International Commitments and Legislative Measures' (2004) 29 *European Law Review* 198, 216–17

By the draft of April 2002, agreement had been reached in the Council that withdrawal of reception conditions would apply where: the asylum applicant abandons the place of residence allocated without permission; fails to comply with report duties; has already lodged an application in the same Member State; where the individual has sufficient resources of his or her own; or for serious breaches of the rules on places of accommodation or violent behaviour. The ground proposed by the Commission of withdrawal for war crimes and national security had been removed.[217] It was believed that political agreement on the Directive had been reached in April 2002, indeed UNHCR prepared a press release regarding the proposal, referring to the achievement of political agreement. However, this was not the case.

By September 2002 new demands for changes to the text were put forward by the UK Government which had decided to introduce draconian national legislation to exclude asylum seekers who failed to apply for asylum at the port of entry from any benefits. Apparently the Council could not agree the new insertion at the Justice and Home Affairs Council meeting of October 2002. It is believed that the Swedish delegation refused to accede to the UK demand. However, by the December 2002 JHA meeting the issue was resolved in favour of the UK. A change to the 'almost' agreed text was made to Article 16(2) that 'a Member State may refuse conditions in cases where an asylum seeker has failed to demonstrate that the asylum claim was made as soon as reasonably practicable after arrival in that Member State'. UNHCR reserved its strongest criticism of the Directive for this provision in general and Article 16(2) in particular. It considered that if Member States identify real abuse in their asylum systems these should be dealt with in the procedures themselves not be used as an excuse to starve asylum seekers or leave them homeless. It noted that 'the core content of human rights applies to everyone in all situations'. As regards Article 16(2) UNHCR stated 'this provision may constitute an obstacle for asylum-seekers to have access to fair asylum procedures. Asylum-seekers may lack basic information on the asylum procedure and be unable to state their claims formally or intelligibly without adequate guidance…These difficulties would be exacerbated where asylum-seekers arrive with insufficient means and are denied assistance through the rigid application of the "reasonably practicable" criteria'.

Alongside the withdrawal of benefits, the 2003 Directive allowed, furthermore, Member States, in accordance with their national law to detain applicants for legal reasons or reasons of public order.[218] The discretion to do this was broad and the provision did not require the applicant to have broken the law. Its breadth caused concern.

[216] *R* v *Secretary of State for the Home Department ex parte Adam* [2006] 1 AC 396.
[217] Council Document 8351/02 of 29 April 2002: Outcome of Proceedings of Council on 25 April 2002.
[218] Directive 2003/9, article 7(3).

E. Guild, 'Seeking Asylum: Storm Clouds Between International Commitments and Legislative Measures' (2004) 29 *European Law Review* 198, 214

...detention is not prescribed, however, it is set out to be the exception to the norm and it must be justified on the grounds permitted in the Directive. In the original proposal of the Commission, this provision was much stronger in favour of the asylum applicant. Specifically Article 7(2) required that 'Member States shall not hold applicants for asylum in detention for the sole reason that their applications for asylum need to be examined'. This part of the provision was removed completely. UNHCR, concerned about the width of the detention powers, recommended that national legislation take into account a number of factors for determining the area of location where applicants could be required to reside: the presence of NGOs, legal aid providers, language training facilities and, where possible, an established community of the asylum-seekers' national or ethnic group; the possibilities for harmonious relations between asylum-seekers and the surrounding communities; the need for supplementary financial support to cover the cost which the asylum-seekers will incur when they have to travel to the assigned area.[219]

This was heeded in the 2013 amendments in Directive 2013/33/EU which restrict the use of detention to a narrow range of circumstances.

Directive 2013/33/EU, article 8(1)

1. Member States shall not hold a person in detention for the sole reason that he or she is an applicant in accordance with Directive 2013/32/EU...
2. When it proves necessary and on the basis of an individual assessment of each case, Member States may detain an applicant, if other less coercive alternative measures cannot be applied effectively.
3. An applicant may be detained only:
    (a) in order to determine or verify his or her identity or nationality;
    (b) in order to determine those elements on which the application for international protection is based which could not be obtained in the absence of detention, in particular when there is a risk of absconding of the applicant;
    (c) in order to decide, in the context of a procedure, on the applicant's right to enter the territory;
    (d) when he or she is detained subject to a return procedure under Directive 2008/115/EC...in order to prepare the return and/or carry out the removal process, and the Member State concerned can substantiate on the basis of objective criteria, including that he or she already had the opportunity to access the asylum procedure, that there are reasonable grounds to believe that he or she is making the application for international protection merely in order to delay or frustrate the enforcement of the return decision;
    (e) when protection of national security or public order so requires;
    (f) in accordance with Article 28 of Regulation 604/2013...
    The grounds for detention shall be laid down in national law.
4. Member States shall ensure that the rules concerning alternatives to detention, such as regular reporting to the authorities, the deposit of a financial guarantee, or an obligation to stay at an assigned place, are laid down in national law.

---

[219] UNHCR annotated comments on Council Directive 2003/9 of 27 January 2003.

Detention, therefore, cannot be used in a blanket way. The central ground for which it is likely to be used is that in article 8(3)(b), namely, to limit risk of absconding. In the absence of further evidence, it will always be easy for the national authorities to make a case that there is such a risk. Applicants have, after all, often sacrificed much and taken considerable risks to reach the European Union. Much will hang, therefore, on how courts interpret article 8(4), and the duties these place on national authorities to find alternatives.

7 'POOR FOREIGNERS': REFUGEES AND SUBSIDIARY PROTECTION

The treatment of applicants for international protection should not disguise that the motive behind international protection is a humanitarian one. International protection exists, after all, to offer safe haven to those at risk from persecution or serious harm. This humanitarian ethos guides many of the concepts which determine whether an applicant should receive protection, and leads to a strong contrast between their entitlements prior to a decision on their status and their entitlements in the event of a successful application.

As a preface to the discussion on each of these categories, it is worth noting that there are certain features common to the definitions of both refugee status and subsidiary protection.

First, the fear of harm or persecution may stem not just from events which took place when the applicant was in the country of origin but also from events occurring after the applicant has left the country of origin or from acts committed outside the country of origin.[220] Secondly, a liberal interpretation has been taken of which actors may be considered perpetrators of the harm or persecution which gives rise to the status. These include not just the state and parties or organisations controlling the state or a substantial part of its territory, but also non-state actors if the state or these parties and organisations are unable or unwilling to provide protection against persecution or serious harm.[221] Thirdly, protection in the country of origin will generally be considered to have been provided if the state (or these other parties and organisations) has taken reasonable steps to prevent the persecution or harm by operating an effective legal system for the detection and punishment of the acts causing it[222] or there is a part of the country within which the applicant may be protected and she could reasonably be expected to stay.[223]

Fourthly, refugee status or subsidiary protection will not be offered to those for whom there are serious reasons to believe that she has committed crimes against humanity; has committed serious crimes; is guilty of acts contrary to the purposes and principles of the United Nations;[224] or there are reasonable grounds for regarding the applicant as a danger to the security of the Member State from which they are seeking protection.[225]

Fifthly, Member States may revoke or refuse to renew refugee status or subsidiarity protection if the applicant has misrepresented or omitted decisive facts in her application.[226] Finally, she will cease to have international protection if the circumstances which gave rise to the risk of persecution or harm have ceased.[227]

---

[220] Directive 2011/95, article 5.   [221] *Ibid.* article 6.   [222] *Ibid.* article 7(2).   [223] *Ibid.* article 8.

[224] *Ibid.* articles 12(2) and 17(1)(a)–(c). In the case of refugees, the crime must be of a non-political nature. Subsidiary protection also cannot be sought where the act is an imprisonable offence in the Member State of sanctuary and the applicant is fleeing merely to avoid sanction, article 17(3).

[225] *Ibid.* articles 14(4)–(5) and 17(1)(d).   [226] *Ibid.* articles 14(3)(b) and 17(3)(b).

[227] *Ibid.* articles 11(1)(e) and 16(1).

(i) Acquisition of refugee status

As stated earlier, an individual acquires refugee status if she has a well-founded fear of an act or acts of persecution and the persecution must be for reasons of race, religion, nationality, political opinion or membership of a particular social group. Directive 2011/95 sets out in more detail the reasons for persecution.

Directive 2011/95/EU, article 10(1)

1. Member States shall take the following elements into account when assessing the reasons for persecution:
   (a) the concept of race shall, in particular, include considerations of colour, descent, or membership of a particular ethnic group;
   (b) the concept of religion shall in particular include the holding of theistic, non-theistic and atheistic beliefs, the participation in, or abstention from, formal worship in private or in public, either alone or in community with others, other religious acts or expressions of view, or forms of personal or communal conduct based on or mandated by any religious belief;
   (c) the concept of nationality shall not be confined to citizenship or lack thereof but shall, in particular, include membership of a group determined by its cultural, ethnic, or linguistic identity, common geographical or political origins or its relationship with the population of another State;
   (d) a group shall be considered to form a particular social group where in particular:
      • members of that group share an innate characteristic, or a common background that cannot be changed, or share a characteristic or belief that is so fundamental to identity or conscience that a person should not be forced to renounce it, and
      • that group has a distinct identity in the relevant country, because it is perceived as being different by the surrounding society.
   Depending on the circumstances in the country of origin, a particular social group might include a group based on a common characteristic of sexual orientation. Sexual orientation cannot be understood to include acts considered to be criminal in accordance with national law of the Member States. Gender related aspects, including gender identity, shall be given due consideration for the purposes of determining membership of a particular social group or identifying a characteristic of such a group;
   (e) the concept of political opinion shall, in particular, include the holding of an opinion, thought or belief on a matter related to the potential actors of persecution...and to their policies or methods, whether or not that opinion, thought or belief has been acted upon by the applicant.
2. When assessing if an applicant has a well-founded fear of being persecuted it is immaterial whether the applicant actually possesses the racial, religious, national, social or political characteristic which attracts the persecution, provided that such a characteristic is attributed to the applicant by the actor of persecution.

This list includes many forms of persecution which go beyond traditional state oppression. Furthermore, it includes grounds of persecution, such as sexual orientation, atheism and gender, which were not recognised in the 1951 Geneva Convention in the manner they are today. Combined with the possibility for persecution by non-state actors to generate refugee status, the scope for attaining that status has been considerably widened. Grounds now include forced female circumcision, child slavery or failure to protect expression of sexual orientation. The central concern has moved to the dignity of the individual rather than the nature of the oppression. From a humanitarian perspective this is to be welcomed, but it has been argued that, by increasing the number of individuals entitled to refugee status, it has led to an increased reluctance on the part of Member States to accept refugees, including those who have been subject to traditional protection.[228]

This tension is reflected in the threshold of persecution to be met for refugee status to be granted. The acts of persecution must be sufficiently serious to constitute a severe violation of human rights or, alternately, be sufficiently serious to 'affect an individual in a similar manner'.[229] The question of when this would be the case arose in *Y and Z*. This concerned the rejection by the German authorities of applications for refugee status by two members of the Ahmadiyya community in Pakistan, which is an Islamic reformist movement. Under Pakistani law, it is a criminal offence, punishable by up to three years' imprisonment, for members of this community to claim to be Muslims or to propagate their faith to others. Y had been beaten up at his home because of his beliefs, stoned in the streets and had death threats issued against him. Z had been imprisoned because of his beliefs. The German authorities argued that this constituted no violation of their religious beliefs, as protected by Article 10 EUCFR, as they could still practise these in private, and they would not be at risk of persecution if they did this.

Joined Cases C–71/11 and C–99/11 *Y and Z*, Judgment of 5 September 2012

59. …it is apparent from the wording…of the Directive that there must be a 'severe violation' of religious freedom having a significant effect on the person concerned in order for it to be possible for the acts in question to be regarded as acts of persecution.…

62. For the purpose of determining, specifically, which acts may be regarded as constituting persecution within the meaning of…the Directive, it is unnecessary to distinguish acts that interfere with the 'core areas' ('forum internum') of the basic right to freedom of religion, which do not include religious activities in public ('forum externum'), from acts which do not affect those purported 'core areas'.

63. Such a distinction is incompatible with the broad definition of 'religion' given by…the Directive, which encompasses all its constituent components, be they public or private, collective or individual. Acts which may constitute a 'severe violation' within the meaning of…the Directive include serious acts which interfere with the applicant's freedom not only to practise his faith in private circles but also to live that faith publicly.

64. That interpretation is likely to ensure that…the Directive is applied in such a manner as to enable the competent authorities to assess all kinds of acts which interfere with the basic right of freedom of religion in order to determine whether, by their nature or repetition, they are sufficiently severe as to be regarded as amounting to persecution.

65. It follows that acts which, on account of their intrinsic severity as well as the severity of their consequences for the person concerned, may be regarded as constituting persecution must be identified, not on the basis of the particular aspect of religious freedom that is being interfered with but on the basis of the nature of the repression inflicted on the individual and its consequences…

66. It is therefore the severity of the measures and sanctions adopted or liable to be adopted against the person concerned which will determine whether a violation of the right guaranteed by Article 10(1) of the Charter constitutes persecution…

---

[228] A. Fabbricotti, 'The Concept of Inhuman and Degrading Treatment in Asylum Cases' (1998) 10 *IJRL* 637.
[229] Directive 2011/95, article 9.

67. Accordingly, a violation of the right to freedom of religion may constitute persecution within the meaning of…the Directive where an applicant for asylum, as a result of exercising that freedom in his country of origin, runs a genuine risk of, inter alia, being prosecuted or subject to inhuman or degrading treatment or punishment by one of the actors referred to in Article 6 of the Directive….

70. In assessing such a risk, the competent authorities must take account of a number of factors, both objective and subjective. The subjective circumstance that the observance of a certain religious practice in public, which is subject to the restrictions at issue, is of particular importance to the person concerned in order to preserve his religious identity is a relevant factor to be taken into account in determining the level of risk to which the applicant will be exposed in his country of origin on account of his religion, even if the observance of such a religious practice does not constitute a core element of faith for the religious community concerned.

Y and Z suggests that regard has to be had to two elements in determining whether there is sufficient persecution to warrant refugee status. The first goes to the severity of the consequences for the individual, in particular whether it leads to imprisonment or inhuman and degrading treatment. The second goes to the 'intrinsic severity' of the measure, namely, whether it prevents the individual engaging in something really significant, here exercising her religion. If prevention of the latter makes the persecution more egregious, there is, nevertheless, a danger in focusing too much on it. Refugee status is often granted to individuals not because of the value of what they do but rather simply because of the severity of the persecution imposed on them. It is not clear, therefore, why it was important that Y and Z were practising a religious belief. Persecution for any belief should have been sufficient.

(ii) Subsidiary protection

Subsidiary protection is a complementary category which applies only when the individual is not eligible for refugee status but is still in need of international protection. The probative threshold is higher than for refugees as applicants have to show that there are substantial grounds for believing that they run a real risk of serious harm if they return to their state of origin rather than simply a well-founded fear of serious harm.[230] Serious harm, it will be remembered, was defined in article 15 of Directive 2011/95 as including the death penalty or inhuman and degrading treatment. The most wide-ranging category of harm was set out in article 15(c), namely, that there must be a 'serious and individual threat to a civilian's life or person by reason of indiscriminate violence in situations of international or internal armed conflict'. This was considered in *Elgafaji*. Elgafaji, an Iraqi, had worked for a British security firm there during the occupation following the removal of Saddam Hussein. His uncle, employed by the same firm, had been killed by militia and a letter had been pinned on Elgafaji's home door threatening 'death to collaborators'. His request for subsidiary protection in the Netherlands was refused by the Dutch authorities who thought that there was no serious risk of his being executed or tortured, and argued that article 15(c) did not establish a separate category of protection.

---

[230] *Ibid.* article 2(f).

Case C-465/07 *Elgafaji* v *Staatssecretaris van Justititie* [2009] ECR I-921

33. ... the harm defined in Article 15(c) of the Directive as consisting of a 'serious and individual threat to [the applicant's] life or person' covers a more general risk of harm.

34. Reference is made, more generally, to a 'threat ... to a civilian's life or person' rather than to specific acts of violence. Furthermore, that threat is inherent in a general situation of 'international or internal armed conflict'. Lastly, the violence in question which gives rise to that threat is described as 'indiscriminate', a term which implies that it may extend to people irrespective of their personal circumstances.

35. In that context, the word 'individual' must be understood as covering harm to civilians irrespective of their identity, where the degree of indiscriminate violence characterising the armed conflict taking place – assessed by the competent national authorities before which an application for subsidiary protection is made, or by the courts of a Member State to which a decision refusing such an application is referred – reaches such a high level that substantial grounds are shown for believing that a civilian, returned to the relevant country or, as the case may be, to the relevant region, would, solely on account of his presence on the territory of that country or region, face a real risk of being subject to the serious threat referred to in Article 15(c) of the Directive.

36. That interpretation, which is likely to ensure that Article 15(c) of the Directive has its own field of application, is not invalidated by the wording of recital 26 in the preamble to the Directive, according to which '[r]isks to which a population of a country or a section of the population is generally exposed do normally not create in themselves an individual threat which would qualify as serious harm'.

37. While that recital implies that the objective finding alone of a risk linked to the general situation in a country is not, as a rule, sufficient to establish that the conditions set out in Article 15(c) of the Directive have been met in respect of a specific person, its wording nevertheless allows – by the use of the word 'normally' – for the possibility of an exceptional situation which would be characterised by such a high degree of risk that substantial grounds would be shown for believing that that person would be subject individually to the risk in question.

38. The exceptional nature of that situation is also confirmed by the fact that the relevant protection is subsidiary, and by the broad logic of Article 15 of the Directive, as the harm defined in paragraphs (a) and (b) of that article requires a clear degree of individualisation. While it is admittedly true that collective factors play a significant role in the application of Article 15(c) of the Directive, in that the person concerned belongs, like other people, to a circle of potential victims of indiscriminate violence in situations of international or internal armed conflict, it is nevertheless the case that that provision must be subject to a coherent interpretation in relation to the other two situations referred to in Article 15 of the Directive and must, therefore, be interpreted by close reference to that individualisation.

39. In that regard, the more the applicant is able to show that he is specifically affected by reason of factors particular to his personal circumstances, the lower the level of indiscriminate violence required for him to be eligible for subsidiary protection.

Subsidiary protection must be offered wherever a region becomes so dangerous that simple presence places an individual at risk of death. This opens the way for protection for individuals wherever there is a conflict zone without their having to show that they have some trait that places them at risk. The Court of Justice makes clear that a sliding scale operates here. If the violence in a region is intense that will be sufficient. If it is of a lesser scale, the Court will look to the level of individual threat in the case of the applicant.

(iii) Benefits of international protection

Beneficiaries of international protection are entitled to five categories of rights.

Security of residence and movement: Unless there are compelling reasons of public order and national security, beneficiaries should be given a renewable residence permit for at least three years in the case of refugees[231] and one year in the case of beneficiaries of subsidiary protection,[232] and travel documents which allow them to travel outside the territory.[233] They should also be granted free movement within the national territory on the same basis as for other non-EU nationals legally resident there.[234]

Right to family unity: Member States are to ensure that family unity can be maintained.[235] Family members include spouses or unmarried partners in a stable relationship where these are treated by national law as equivalent to spouses. They also include minor children who are unmarried and dependent. In all cases, these are only granted rights if they are present in the same Member State where the application is made.[236] There is, therefore, no requirement for Member States to accept family members from other Member States. These family members enjoy a more vulnerable status than the beneficiary of international protection. Residence permits of less than three years may be offered.[237] Furthermore, where these are not entitled to international protection in their own name, they are only to be offered benefits in accordance with national legal procedures.[238] Benefits can also be restricted for public order or national security reasons.[239] The invidiousness of this is seen in relation to education. Full access to the education system shall be granted to all minors granted international protection.[240] If they do not enjoy that status, there is more discretion for Member States as to what education they offer such children.

Economic rights: Beneficiaries of international protection should be allowed to work or be self-employed, albeit there is no requirement that they be protected from discrimination.[241] However, they should have access to vocational training and employment related educational opportunities on the same terms as a Member State's own nationals.[242] There should also be equal treatment with regard to the procedures for certifying recognition of diplomas and qualifications.[243]

Social rights: Adult beneficiaries of international protections should have access to a Member State's education system[244] and accommodation on the same basis as other non-EU nationals lawfully resident there.[245] They must also be granted health care on the same terms as a Member State's own nationals.[246] In the case of beneficiaries with special needs, be this people with disabilities, torture victims or pregnant women, there is a stronger duty to provide adequate health care on the same basis as for that Member State's own nationals.[247] Beyond these specific duties, there are more general duties of social provision. Access to integration programmes taking account of the special needs of beneficiaries must be provided.[248] Most wide-ranging, however, is the duty to provide social assistance on the same terms as to a Member State's own nationals.[249] In the case of beneficiaries of subsidiarity protection, this may be

---

[231] *Ibid.* article 24(1).
[232] *Ibid.* article 24(2). When this is renewed, it should be for a minimum of two years.
[233] *Ibid.* article 25.   [234] *Ibid.* article 33.   [235] *Ibid.* article 23(1).   [236] *Ibid.* article 2(j).   [237] *Ibid.* article 24(1).
[238] *Ibid.* article 23(2).   [239] *Ibid.* article 23(4).   [240] *Ibid.* article 27(1).   [241] *Ibid.* article 26(1).
[242] *Ibid.* article 26(2).   [243] *Ibid.* article 28(1).   [244] *Ibid.* article 27(2).   [245] *Ibid.* article 32(1).
[246] *Ibid.* article 30(1).   [247] *Ibid.* article 30(2).   [248] *Ibid.* article 34.   [249] *Ibid.* article 29(1).

limited to 'core benefits'.[250] This limitation must be read in the light of the *Kamberaj* judgment which interpreted a parallel limitation for long-term residents as requiring Member States to set this out legally in advance and not to exclude any benefit securing realisation of the rights in the EUCFR, be this housing, education or meeting of basic needs.[251]

Right to non-refoulement and repatriation assistance: In the case of refugees, a Member State must respect the principle of non-refoulement unless there are reasonable grounds for considering that person a danger to national security or she has been convicted of a particularly serious offence and constitutes a danger to the community.[252] By contrast, assistance is to be given to those who wish to repatriate.[253]

Combined, the rights granted to beneficiaries of international protection are similar to those granted to long-term residents. They have significant membership rights in their new societies. However, if the intention is to provide them with the support to start a new life in the Member State of sanctuary, this is limited by the more restricted and contingent entitlements granted to members or their family members. Indeed, it is somewhat invidious to divide a family between those members protected by international protection and those who are not, with all the uncertainty and anxiety provided. It is also unrealistic. If a significant parental figure benefits from international protection, it beggars belief to assume that the events which gave rise to this have not marked the whole family unit. The weaker entitlements offered to family members act as an indirect lever on the beneficiary of international protection to consider return as they prevent her family from integrating into the host society as easily as she can herself.

FURTHER READING

A. Baldaccini, 'The Return and Removal of Irregular Migrants under EU Law: An Analysis of the Returns Directive' (2009) 11 *European Journal of Migration and Law* 1

M. Besters and F. Brom, '"Greedy" Information Technology: The Digitalization of the European Migration Policy' (2010) 12 *European Journal of Migration and Law* 455

I. Boccardi, *Europe and Refugees: Towards an EU Asylum Policy* (The Hague/London/Boston, Kluwer, 2002)

E. Guild, 'The Europeanisation of Europe's Asylum Policy' (2006) 18 *International Journal of Refugee Law* 630

Y. Gümüs, 'EU Blue Card Scheme: The Right Step in the Right Direction?' (2010) 12 *European Journal of Migration and Law* 435

L. Halleskov, 'The Long-Term Residents Directive: A Fulfilment of the Tampere Objective of Near Equality' (2005) 7 *European Journal of Migration and Law* 181

A. Meloni, 'The Community Code on Visas: Harmonisation at Last?' (2009) 34 *European Law Review* 671

C. Offe, 'From Migration in Geographic Space to Migration in Biographic Time: Views from Europe' (2011) 19 *Journal of Political Philosophy* 333

S. Peers, *EU Justice and Home Affairs Law* (3rd edn, Oxford, Oxford University Press, 2012) chs. 3–7

D. Thym, 'EU Migration Policy and Its Constitutional Rationale: A Cosmopolitan Outlook' (2013) 50 *Common Market Law Review* 709

N. Walker (ed.), *Europe's Area of Freedom, Security and Justice* (Oxford, Oxford University Press, 2004)

---

[250] *Ibid.* article 29(2).
[251] Case C-571/10 *Kamberaj* v *IPES*, Judgment of 24 April 2012. See pp. 551–2.
[252] *Ibid.* article 21(1) and (2).   [253] *Ibid.* article 35.

13

Equal Opportunities Law and Policy

1 INTRODUCTION

EU law today regulates discrimination on grounds of sex, gender, race, ethnic origin, religion or belief, sexual orientation, age and disability. In this chapter we examine the key legislative provisions, the motivation for the EU to intervene, and the evolution of the EU's equal opportunities policy.

Section 2 explores four issues to place the law in a wider context. First we ask why the EU needs an equal opportunities policy. On the one hand, banning discrimination is a necessary complement to the economic project of creating an internal market: discrimination reduces economic welfare and so must be prohibited. On the other hand, the tasks of the EU are wider: to enhance the rights of its citizens, irrespective of economic considerations. Secondly, and related, we look to the various sources of law that may be utilised to protect victims of discrimination. In addition to the Directives, we note that there is an as yet undefined role for other sources: EU fundamental rights, the EU Charter of Fundamental Rights and the European Convention of Human Rights. Thirdly, we consider what kind of anti-discrimination policy the European Union is developing. One model sees discrimination law as promoting equality of opportunities, and the other suggests that discrimination laws can be successful only if they yield equality of results. Fourthly, we outline the common core of EU equal opportunities law, which is found in the field of labour law, where a rights-based model operates and has been utilised successfully in the past forty years by victims of sex discrimination.[1]

Section 3 considers the grounds upon which discrimination is forbidden. In tracing the way the EU has come to protect certain groups, a number of common themes emerge. First, the claims of each group have been supported by non-governmental organisations (NGOs) which have 'framed' discrimination in an economic manner, noting how discrimination against that group (for example, homosexuals or ethnic minorities) hampers the achievement of the internal market. Secondly, NGOs have used test cases as a means of asserting the rights of protected groups. Thirdly, EU institutions have responded in different ways: the European Parliament has for a long time been most receptive to demands to develop EU-wide discrimination laws, but its legislative powers are limited.[2] Recently, the Commission has also supported the development of equal opportunities law but its scope for activity is limited to drafting soft law measures in the form of recommendations or codes of practice. Yet, these have proven to be effective in anticipating future legislation.[3] The Council's legislative intervention has been hampered by the resistance of Member States, thus legislation tends to follow a pattern of lobbying, cajoling by the Parliament and Commission, rulings of the Court of Justice, and external political events that precipitate action, as in the case of race discrimination.

In Section 4 we examine the common core of EU equal opportunities law more fully by considering the three main grounds upon which an employee may assert her rights (direct discrimination, indirect discrimination and harassment); what justifications might be offered by employers to escape liability; and the remedies available to the employee.

In Section 5 we consider the limitations of the rights-based policy discussed in section 4 and discuss four novel ways through which EU equal opportunities law is evolving. First, the policy is extended to areas beyond the workplace, for example protecting victims who

---

[1] It is beyond the scope of this chapter to examine this field exhaustively. See C. Barnard, *EU Employment Law* (4th edn, Oxford, Oxford University Press, 2012).

[2] See further Chapter 2.

[3] S. Sciarra, 'European Social Policy and Labour Law: Challenges and Perspectives' (1995) IV *Collected Courses of the Academy of European Law* 301, 340.

experience discrimination in education or the provision of services; secondly, inviting Member States to experiment with affirmative action programmes; thirdly, promoting various forms of dialogue to entrench existing rights; finally, utilising 'mainstreaming' as a means of integrating equality rights within the framework of EU law.

2 DEVELOPMENT OF EU EQUAL OPPORTUNITIES LAW

(i) Economic versus non-economic visions of EU law

The beginnings of equal opportunities law were humble, limited to guaranteeing equal pay between men and women, and only a more limited version of the first two paragraphs of what is now Article 157 TFEU was in place.[4]

Article 157 TFEU

1. Each Member State shall ensure that the principle of equal pay for male and female workers for equal work or work of equal value is applied.
2. For the purpose of this Article, 'pay' means the ordinary basic or minimum wage or salary and any other consideration, whether in cash or in kind, which the worker receives directly or indirectly, in respect of his employment, from his employer.
    Equal pay without discrimination based on sex means:
    (a) that pay for the same work at piece rates shall be calculated on the basis of the same unit of measurement;
    (b) that pay for work at time rates shall be the same for the same job.
3. The European Parliament and the Council, acting in accordance with the ordinary legislative procedure, and after consulting the Economic and Social Committee, shall adopt measures to ensure the application of the principle of equal opportunities and equal treatment of men and women in matters of employment and occupation, including the principle of equal pay for equal work or work of equal value.
4. With a view to ensuring full equality in practice between men and women in working life, the principle of equal treatment shall not prevent any Member State from maintaining or adopting measures providing for specific advantages in order to make it easier for the underrepresented sex to pursue a vocational activity or to prevent or compensate for disadvantages in professional careers.

The reason for including this provision was a concern of the French Government that it would be at a competitive disadvantage because its laws guaranteed equal pay for men

---

[4] For a helpful account of the development of equality law, see M. Bell, 'The Principle of Equal Treatment: Widening and Deepening' in P. Craig and G. de Búrca (eds.), *The Evolution of EU Law* (2nd edn, Oxford, Oxford University Press, 2011) and M. Bell, *Anti-Discrimination Law and the European Union* (Oxford, Oxford University Press, 2002).

and women while the laws of other states did not.[5] This suggests that one rationale for EU discrimination law is economic: it prevents Member States who do not safeguard equality at work from exploiting lower labour costs thereby gaining an advantage. Discrimination is harmful because it means that human resources are not used to their full capacity: if an employer has a policy of not hiring women, he may lose out by not hiring the best candidate for the job. This can stifle economic progress and undermine the EU's desire to develop a competitive single market.[6] From an economic perspective then, harmonised discrimination legislation complements the internal market rules and enhances competitiveness.[7]

An alternative justification for equal opportunities is that the EU is gradually recognising the political aspect to European integration whereby discrimination law forms a fundamental plank in the protection of EU citizens.[8] Those who support this argument draw upon the underlying intentions of the Treaties, the development, especially since the late 1980s by the then President of the Commission, Jacques Delors, of a 'social' dimension to accompany economic integration, resulting in the Community Charter of Basic Social Rights for Workers,[9] and the Court of Justice's recognition that the principle of equal treatment set out in Article 157 TFEU enshrines a fundamental right:[10]

> the economic aim pursued by Article [157 TFEU], namely the elimination of distortions of competition between undertakings established in different Member States, is secondary to the social aim pursued by the same provision, which constitutes the expression of a fundamental human right.[11]

This judicial pronouncement is reflected in the enlargement of Community competence in the field of social policy in the Amsterdam Treaty,[12] the evolution of the concept of citizenship (noted in Chapter 11), and the increased role of fundamental rights in the European Union (discussed in Chapter 6).[13]

Today, the EU's equal opportunities policy is largely based upon Article 19 TFEU, first included in the Treaty of Amsterdam.[14]

---

[5] B. Ohlin, 'Social Aspects of European Economic Co-operation: Report by a Group of Experts' (1956) 102 *International Labour Review* 99; C. Barnard, 'The Economic Objectives of Article 119' in T. Hervey and D. O'Keefe (eds.), *Sex Equality Law of the European Union* (Chichester, Wiley, 1996).

[6] See Recital 9 of Directive 2000/43/EC implementing the principle of equal treatment between persons irrespective of racial or ethnic origin [2000] OJ L180/22 (Race Directive).

[7] *Green Paper on Equality and Non-Discrimination in an Enlarged European Union*, COM(04)379 final, 15–16.

[8] For a helpful account, see D. Scheik, 'Broadening the Scope and the Norms of EU Gender Equality Law: Towards a Multidimensional Conception of Equality Law' (2005) 12 *MJ* 427.

[9] Declaration by Council of the Community Charter of Basic Social Rights for Workers, COM(89)568 final.

[10] Case 43/75 *Defrenne(No 2)* v *Sabena* [1976] ECR 455; Case C-13/94 *P* v *S and Cornwall County Council* [1996] ECR I-2143, para 18.

[11] Case C-50/96 *Deutsche Telekom AG* v *Lilli Schröder* [2000] ECR I-743, para 57.

[12] Article 153 TFEU (ex Article 137 EC). See C. Barnard, 'The United Kingdom, the "Social Chapter" and the Amsterdam Treaty' (1997) 26 *ILJ* 275.

[13] See e.g. E. Spaventa, 'From *Gebhard* to *Carpenter*: Towards a (Non) Economic Constitution' (2004) 41 *CML Rev.* 743.

[14] M. Bell and L. Waddington, 'The 1996 Intergovernmental Conference and the Prospects of a Non-Discrimination Treaty Article' (1996) 25 *ILJ* 320; L. Waddington, 'Article 13 EC: Mere Rhetoric or a Harbinger of Change?' (1998) 1 *CYELS* 175.

Article 19 TFEU

1. Without prejudice to the other provisions of the Treaties and within the limits of the powers conferred by them upon the Union, the Council, acting unanimously in accordance with a special legislative procedure and after obtaining the consent of the European Parliament, may take appropriate action to combat discrimination based on sex, racial or ethnic origin, religion or belief, disability, age or sexual orientation.

2. By way of derogation from paragraph 1, the European Parliament and the Council, acting in accordance with the ordinary legislative procedure, may adopt the basic principles of Union incentive measures, excluding any harmonisation of the laws and regulations of the Member States, to support action taken by the Member States in order to contribute to the achievement of the objectives referred to in paragraph 1.

Article 19(1) TFEU grants the EU legislative competence to safeguard the rights of a range of groups, and it is not confined to prohibiting discrimination in the workplace. This breadth was achieved with certain limitations: the Article does not have direct effect, the European Parliament (the institution which had most assiduously pursued the cause of discrimination law) is given a relatively limited role in the law-making process,[15] and the requirement for unanimity creates a risk that the legislation imposes only low standards, or results in tests that are so ambiguous that they can be watered down by national implementation measures. During the negotiations leading to the Treaty of Nice there were attempts to make it easier for the EU to legislate. The result was Article 19(2) TFEU, but this only applies for measures designed to help Member States in giving effect to the legislation enacted in Article 19(1).[16]

The Preambles to the discrimination Directives based on Article 19 TFEU lend support to the non-economic vision by their reference to the importance of creating an ever closer Union among the peoples of Europe; the principles of liberty, democracy, human rights and fundamental freedoms that underpin the EU; and the universality of the right to equality, recognised in several international instruments.[17] Nevertheless, it should be noted that when new equality measures are proposed, an attempt is made to emphasise the economic dimension so as to persuade recalcitrant Member States that the measure in question contributes to the traditional economic aims of the Treaties.[18]

(ii) Sources of equal opportunities law

Having sketched the economic and rights-based approaches to EU equal opportunities law, we turn to observe that there are four alternate or overlapping frameworks for EU discrimination law.[19]

---

[15] But Article 19 TFEU enhances it. Under Article 13 EC it merely had the right to be consulted.

[16] An alternative (but more limited) legal basis would be Article 153 TFEU (ex Article 137 EC).

[17] Race Directive, recitals 1–3; Directive 2000/78 establishing a general framework for equal treatment in employment and occupation, recitals 1, 3 and 4 [2000] OJ L303/16 (Framework Directive); Directive 2006/54/EC on the implementation of the principle of equal opportunities and equal treatment of men and women in matters of employment and occupation (recast), recitals 2 and 4 [2006] OJ L204/23 (Recast Equal Treatment Directive).

[18] M. A. Pollack and E. Hafner-Burton, 'Mainstreaming Gender in the European Union' (2000) 7 *JEPP* 432, 441–2.

[19] This draws on C. Kilpatrick, 'The Court of Justice and Labour Law in 2010: A New EU Discrimination Law Architecture' (2011) 40(3) *Industrial Law Journal* 280, 300–1.

First, are the various equality Directives. These have a haphazard (and unequal) coverage. Sex discrimination is addressed in one set of instruments (for example, a Directive that consolidates previous disparate Directives on equal pay and equal treatment,[20] a Directive relating to equal treatment in the access to and supply of goods and services,[21] and a Directive extending non-discrimination in the field of social security);[22] race and ethnic origin discrimination is covered by the Race Directive 2000/43/EC; while religion, belief, disability, age and sexual orientation discrimination are regulated by a single Directive (the Framework Directive 2000/78/EC).[23] There are small and not so small divergences between the scope of protection offered to different victims of discrimination, depending on which Directive applies.[24] For instance, the Framework Directive only applies to discrimination in the workplace, while the Race Directive also applies to prohibit discrimination outside of the workplace. This contradicts the Council's position that the 'different forms of discrimination cannot be ranked: all are equally intolerable'.[25] The lack of consolidated protection for discriminated groups is not a problem that besets EU law exclusively: differentiated political willingness to address all forms of discrimination equally is deeply embedded in national politics.[26]

Secondly, the Court of Justice has discovered that the principle of non-discrimination on grounds of age is a general principle of EU law.[27] These rulings are discussed in Chapter 7 for their significance with respect to EU constitutional law. For present purposes, what matters is the impact that this general principle has on supplementing the protection afforded by the equality Directives. The circumstances surrounding the *Mangold* case help explain this. In 2003 Mangold (at the time 56 years old) entered into a fixed-term employment contract with Helm. The terms specified that the duration was fixed in accordance with German law at the time, which was designed to make it easier to enter into fixed-term contracts with older workers (defined as workers aged 52 and above), while restricting the freedom to enter into fixed-term contracts with younger workers. Mangold argued that his contract was in breach of the Framework Directive and constituted discrimination based on age. At that time the Directive had not yet been transposed into German law; it appears that the parties to the litigation had designed the employment contract as a means of launching a challenge to test the legality of the German legislation against the forthcoming EU standards. The Court of Justice found that the Directive applied even though it had not yet been transposed into German law. This was based on the Court discovering a general principle in EU law prohibiting age discrimination.

---

[20] Recast Equal Treatment Directive. N. Burrows and M. Robinson, 'An Assessment of the Recast of Community Equality Laws' (2006) 13 *ELJ* 186.

[21] Council Directive 2004/113/EC of 13 December 2004 implementing the principle of equal treatment between men and women in the access to and supply of goods and services.

[22] Council Directive 79/7/EC [1979] OJ L6/24 (Social Security Directive).

[23] See n. 17 above.

[24] L. Waddington and M. Bell, 'More Equal than Others: Distinguishing European Union Equality Directives' (2001) 38 *CML Rev.* 587.

[25] Council Decision 2000/750 establishing a Community Action Programme to combat discrimination, recital 5 [2000] OJ L303/23.

[26] At the time of writing this is best exemplified by controversies in some Member States with regard to laws recognising same-sex relationships.

[27] Case C-144/04 *Werner Mangold v Rüdiger Helm* [2005] ECR I-9981; Case C-555/07 *Seda Kücükdeveci v Swedex GmbH & Co. KG* [2010] ECR I-365.

Case C-144/04 *Werner Mangold* v *Rüdiger Helm* [2005] ECR I-9981

75. The principle of non-discrimination on grounds of age must thus be regarded as a general principle of Community law. Where national rules fall within the scope of Community law, which is the case with [the German law in question], as being a measure implementing Directive 1999/70, and reference is made to the Court for a preliminary ruling, the Court must provide all the criteria of interpretation needed by the national court to determine whether those rules are compatible with such a principle.

76. Consequently, observance of the general principle of equal treatment, in particular in respect of age, cannot as such be conditional upon the expiry of the period allowed the Member States for the transposition of a directive intended to lay down a general framework for combating discrimination on the grounds of age, in particular so far as the organisation of appropriate legal remedies, the burden of proof, protection against victimisation, social dialogue, affirmative action and other specific measures to implement such a directive are concerned.

77. In those circumstances it is the responsibility of the national court, hearing a dispute involving the principle of non-discrimination in respect of age, to provide, in a case within its jurisdiction, the legal protection which individuals derive from the rules of Community law and to ensure that those rules are fully effective, setting aside any provision of national law which may conflict with that law.

This means that provided the action complained of is linked to the implementation of EU law, then Member States have a general obligation not to discriminate on grounds of age.[28] Professor Schiek thought the judgment constituted 'a first step in what will hopefully lead towards judicial development of a coherent framework for equal treatment of persons from a less than satisfactory legislative package'.[29] On the other hand, critics have noted that supplementing the equality Directives in this way is unwise because it shatters the delicate political balance that the Member States had reached in negotiating the secondary legislation.[30] As we will see below, equality law has a major impact on the design of national economic policy, and a general principle risks undermining this. The Court of Justice's use of this general principle has been uneven: in a number of cases, the Court declined to apply the general principle it set out and ruled in a more restrictive manner.[31] Moreover, while the general principle was used to find the source of the rights to be protected in *Mangold*, the Court then returned to the structure of the Directive to test how far the law in question complied with equality principles, so the Court did not see it as necessary to develop a parallel case law-based equality law: the principle discovered in *Mangold* only supplements the equality Directives.

---

[28] For support, see Kilpatrick, n. 19 above, 285–7, but see also the critical reflections in E. Muir, 'Enhancing the Effects of Community Law on National Employment Policies: The *Mangold* Case' (2006) 31 *EL Rev.* 879.

[29] D. Schiek, 'The ECJ Decision in *Mangold*: A Further Twist on Effects of Directives and Constitutional Relevance of Community Equality Legislation' (2006) 35 *ILJ* 329.

[30] Case C-13/05 *Sonia Chacón Navas* v *Eurest Colectividades SA* [2006] ECR I-6467, Opinion of Advocate General Geelhoed, paras. 50–5.

[31] For example, in three cases on age discrimination. In Case C-427/06 *Birgit Bartsch* v *Bosch und Siemens Hausgeräte* [2008] ECR I-7245, the Court found that the national rules did not fall within the scope of EU law; in Case C-411/05 *Palacios* [2007] ECR I-8531, the Court applied the relevant Directive; in C-227/04P *Lindorfer* [2007] ECR I-6767 (a mixed age and sex discrimination case) the Court decided on grounds of sex discrimination. In Case C-394/11 *Valeri Hariev Belov* v *ChEZ Elektro BalgariaAD and others*, Judgment of 31 January 2013. Advocate General Kokott took the view that there was also a principle against race discrimination, but the case was dismissed for procedural reasons.

Thirdly, the EU Charter of Fundamental Rights (EUCFR) may serve as a basis for testing national and EU law. The most striking illustration is the Court of Justice's approach in *Test-Achats*. In 2004 the EU adopted a Directive to protect discrimination based on sex in the provision of goods and services.[32] The car insurance industry lobbied extensively for an exemption. Their argument was that insurance premiums are fixed having regard to actuarial data and this necessarily results in women paying lower premiums than men because they are less likely to cause accidents. The Directive accommodated this building in a transitional period for the insurance sector to adjust.[33] This was challenged by a Belgian consumer association. The Court held (relying on Articles 21 and 23 of the EUCFR) that the Directive was contrary to EU law because it created a risk that insurers would be able to retain discrimination based on gender indefinitely.[34] As with *Mangold*, one must be careful not to read too much into this approach. The Court has not always found it necessary to rely on the EUCFR, even when asked to do so by the applicant, when the equality Directives appear to offer an appropriate answer instead.[35] It appears that, just as in the *Mangold* line of cases, the Court of Justice is probably not constructing a parallel set of discrimination rules, but is using the EUCFR as a basis for invalidating certain provisions of national or EU law when the equality Directives leave a gap. Of course, using the EUCFR in this way leads to the criticism that the jurisprudence evolves in a casuistic way. It remains to be noted that the EUCFR contains a wider range of equality grounds than Article 19 TFEU (for example, ethnic or social origin, genetic features, language, and political or any other opinion are covered by Article 21 and cultural, religious and linguistic diversity are covered by Article 22). In the implementation of EU law one will have to ensure that these rights are safeguarded,[36] but it is not likely that a person would be able to make a claim simply on the basis that they suffered discrimination because of their social origin, absent a link to the implementation of EU law.

The fourth source that is relevant is the European Convention on Human Rights (ECHR). Even before accession, the principles developed by the European Court of Human Rights (ECtHR) may prove a source of law for interpreting EU equality law. Moreover, there have been some litigants who, dissatisfied with the degree of protection afforded by the EU Directives, have explored whether the ECHR offers more protection. An example of this is *Eweida* v *United Kingdom*. There, the applicant challenged the employer's decision to ban the wearing of crucifixes on the basis of religious discrimination. Her claim based on discrimination was unsuccessful, but she had more success in the ECtHR in establishing that her right to manifest her religious belief (under Article 9 ECHR) had been infringed.[37] The ECHR thus provides an alternative basis for securing one's rights. Further, as we see below, it also serves as a basis for interpreting EU law.

From this account, two lessons should be drawn. The first is that there are multiple sources that protect the same (or similar) rights, each of these having a different origin and framework.

---

[32] Directive 2004/113 implementing the principle of equal treatment between men and women in the access to and supply of goods and services [2004] OJ L373/37. This is discussed more fully below pp. 613–614.

[33] *Ibid.* article 5(2).

[34] Case C-236/09 *Association belge des Consommateurs Test-Achats ASBL and others* v *Conseil des ministres* [2011] ECR I-773, para. 32.

[35] Case C-132/11 *Tyrolean Airways* v *Betriebsrat Bord*, Judgment of 7 June 2012; Case C-152/11 *Odar* v *Baxter*, Judgment of 6 December 2012.

[36] See e.g. Case C-202/11 *Las* v *PSA Antwerp NV*, Judgment of 16 April 2013, para. 26.

[37] *Eweida and others* v *United Kingdom* [2013] ECHR 37, Judgment of 15 January 2013, paras. 89–95. See also *Horváth and Kiss* v *Hungary*, no. 11146/11, 29 January 2013 (discrimination against Roma children in public education).

For practical purposes, it means that litigants may have to test more than one legal basis in trying to receive protection. The second lesson is that neither the EUCFR, nor the general principle established in *Mangold,* create a general, overarching basis for equality laws, even if there are some who support this more expansive approach.[38] The scope of *Mangold* and the EUCFR remains uncertain, but those two sources of law appear to add to, rather than replace the scope of rights agreed by the Member States in the various equality Directives.

(iii) Equal opportunities versus substantive equality

It is beyond the scope of this chapter to explore all the theories that have been deployed to justify discrimination legislation.[39] However, in order to be able to evaluate the efforts of the EU, we need to have an idea of what discrimination law might be used to achieve. We therefore sketch two contrasting approaches: one focusing on equality of opportunity, the other on equality of results. The first view provides that like should be treated alike. When an employer hires someone, race, religion, sex, sexual orientation or age must not play a part in selecting the successful candidates. This approach guarantees 'formal' equality among persons. The competing model favours the use of discrimination law to generate substantive equality. From this perspective, discrimination laws are successful if the result is that more underrepresented groups have access to employment, education and other opportunities. This may entail discriminating in favour of an excluded group, for example by determining that a certain percentage of the workforce should consist of women or ethnic minorities. This model provides equality of results but is incompatible with the liberal, formal equality model.[40]

There are three main differences between the formal and the substantive approach to equality. First, formal equality does not guarantee equality of results and does not address the causes of inequality. Secondly, the formal equality model is concerned with individual rights, while the substantive equality model is concerned to promote the rights of persons who have been systemically discriminated against. The primary means of enforcement of the formal equality model is litigation by the person who is wronged; for the substantive equality model, regulatory means of achieving equality and which support group rights are preferred. A third and wider difference between the two models is that the formal equality model requires everyone to act like the privileged group, thus it does not recognise the legitimacy of differences between groups, whereas supporters of substantive equality argue that merely promoting the participation of traditionally underrepresented persons is meaningless if we demand that they comply with a white, male culture.[41] Substantive equality models entail a respect for differences and the integration and celebration of differences within society.

---

[38] See Advocate General Kokott in *Test-Achats,* n. 34 above, and in *Belov,* n. 31 above. Contrast Case C-363/11 *Elegktiko Sinedrio* v *Ipourgeio Politismou kai Tourismou,* Judgment of 19 December 2012, Opinion of Advocate General Sharpston, para. 80.

[39] See S. Fredman, *Discrimination Law* (Oxford, Oxford University Press, 2002) ch. 1; N. Bamforth, 'Conceptions of Anti-discrimination Law' (2004) 24 *OJLS* 693.

[40] For an attempted justification of reverse discrimination, see M. Rosenfeld, *Affirmative Action and Justice: A Philosophical and Constitutional Inquiry* (New Haven, CT, Yale University Press, 1991); L. Jacobs, *Pursuing Equal Opportunities* (Cambridge, Cambridge University Press, 2004) ch. 5.

[41] For this critique, see S. Fredman, *Women and the Law* (Oxford, Oxford University Press, 1997) chs. 1 and 4.

(iv) Common core of EU equal opportunities: the labour market

As we will see, there are differences in the level of protection offered to different underrepresented groups, with the majority opinion being that those discriminated against because of sex, race and ethnic origin are best protected, and those suffering from age discrimination having the least rights. However, there is a floor of protection that EU law guarantees to each group, and in this section we set out what this comprises. The legislation provides the plaintiff with a right she can exercise against private or public bodies when she faces discrimination in the following fields.

Framework Directive, article 3(1)

1. Within the limits of the areas of competence conferred on the Community, this Directive shall apply to all persons, as regards both the public and private sectors, including public bodies, in relation to:
   (a) conditions for access to employment, to self-employment or to occupation, including selection criteria and recruitment conditions, whatever the branch of activity and at all levels of the professional hierarchy, including promotion;
   (b) access to all types and to all levels of vocational guidance, vocational training, advanced vocational training and retraining, including practical work experience;
   (c) employment and working conditions, including dismissals and pay;
   (d) membership of, and involvement in, an organisation of workers or employers, or any organisation whose members carry on a particular profession, including the benefits provided for by such organisations.

The rights listed above are also available for victims of discrimination on grounds of race and sex, but are based on different Directives.[42] The right is to be free from four forms of discrimination: direct discrimination (which is aimed at an individual because of, for example, her race or religion); indirect discrimination (when an apparently neutral job requirement is more easily satisfied by one sex or racial group than another, for example, if a job is only available to people who are clean-shaven this indirectly excludes Sikhs); harassment and victimisation (that is, adverse treatment directed at a person who has made a discrimination claim against an employer). Direct and indirect discrimination are justified in certain circumstances: for example, all Directives provide for the defendant to claim that discrimination was on the basis of a genuine occupational requirement (thus, for example, a Buddhist cannot be eligible to work as a priest in a Roman Catholic church).[43] If discrimination is unjustified, the plaintiff has a right to a remedy, and Member States have an obligation to provide an enforcement mechanism, as well as to grant effective remedies to the plaintiff (including financial compensation).

---

[42] Race Directive, article 3(1)(a)–(d); Article 157 TFEU, and Recast Equal Treatment Directive. In the main text in this chapter we only extract the provision from the Framework Directive unless specific differences arise.
[43] Recast Equal Treatment Directive, article 14(2); Race Directive, article 4; Framework Directive, article 4.

Supplementing this common core of rights have been the decisions of the Court of Justice. It will be recalled that the Court's early case law established that EU law had supremacy over national law, and that certain provisions of EU law (including Article 157 TFEU) have direct effect.[44] In the sphere of sex discrimination, these principles have had a profound impact because they have allowed the Court of Justice to challenge national sex equality law. Supremacy meant that a national court would be required to disapply national law which conflicts with EU law. For example, in *Macarthys Ltd* v *Smith*, a woman made a claim for equal pay based on the fact that her predecessor (a man) had been paid more for doing the same work as her. At that time it was not clear whether her claim was admissible under the British Equal Pay Act 1970, but the Court of Justice held that Article 157 TFEU did cover this dispute,[45] and therefore the national court was required to disapply national law in order to afford the plaintiff her EU law rights.[46] In the 1980s, the UK's Equal Opportunities Commission devised a highly successful litigation strategy bringing test cases like this one to challenge national sex equality laws based on their infringement of EU equality law.[47]

The limitations of the Court of Justice's contribution to EU equal opportunities policy can be explored with a case study: a judgment which challenged the lack of protection afforded by UK sex discrimination law when employers contract out work. The plaintiff, Ms Allonby, had been employed part-time by a teaching college. The college found that part-time employees were too expensive because the law required that they be entitled to statutory benefits equal to those of full-time teachers and she, along with other part-timers, was made redundant. She was then engaged by a new company, ELS, who supplied her as a self-employed teacher to the same college that had made her redundant. This arrangement was cheaper for the college because they had no obligations to provide her with the same benefits as when she was a part-time employee, and Ms Allonby received less pay than before. Moreover, because she was classified as self-employed, she lost her right to be a member of the teachers' pension scheme. Her claim for unequal pay against ELS was based on the fact that men employed directly by the college were paid more. This was not successful because she could only compare her rate of pay with people that had the same employer as herself (and she was engaged by ELS, not the college).[48] The policy consideration that led the Court to refuse comparing Ms Allonby's pay to that of men doing the same work for other employers is practical, as it is near to impossible for employers to monitor what the pay is in other institutions.[49]

Her second claim was against the state (represented by the Department for Education and Employment), where she claimed that she suffered discrimination because the law made it impossible for her to join the pension scheme merely because she was classified as self-employed. As a preliminary matter, the Court of Justice had no hesitation in finding the denial of access to an occupational pension scheme as an unequal pay claim. This reflects the breadth of the meaning

---

[44] See Chapter 7 and note that many of the key cases on direct effect are based upon sex discrimination.

[45] Case 129/79 *Macarthys Ltd* v *Smith* [1980] ECR 1275.

[46] *Macarthys Ltd* v *Smith* [1980] ICR 672, 693–4.

[47] K. J. Alter and J. Vargas, 'Explaining Variation in the Use of European Litigation Strategies: European Community Law and British Gender Equality Policy' (2000) 33 *Comparative Political Studies* 452; C. Kilpatrick, 'Gender Equality: A Fundamental Dialogue' in S. Sciarra (eds.), *Labour Law in the Courts* (Oxford, Hart Publishing, 2001).

[48] The Court of Justice followed Case C-320/00 *Lawrence and others* v *Regent Office Care Ltd and others* [2002] ECR I-7325.

[49] *Macarthys Ltd* v *Smith* [1980] ICR 672.

of the concept of 'pay' developed by the Court.[50] Throughout the 1980s and early 1990s the Court of Justice expanded the concept of pay to include a range of benefits, for example occupational pension schemes,[51] travel concessions,[52] redundancy pay,[53] maternity leave pay,[54] unfair dismissal compensation[55] and statutory sick pay.[56] The test set out by the Court is that any consideration that the worker receives directly or indirectly in respect of employment from her employer is to be considered pay.[57] The Court held that the fact that she was not an 'employee' under national law did not mean that she was not a worker for the purposes of Article 157 TFEU, and went on to explore the meaning of the term 'worker'.

Case C–256/01 *Allonby v Accrington and Rossendale College* [2004] ECR I–873

66. …the term 'worker' used in Article [157(1) TFEU] cannot be defined by reference to the legislation of the Member States but has a Community meaning. Moreover, it cannot be interpreted restrictively.

67. For the purposes of that provision, there must be considered as a worker a person who, for a certain period of time, performs services for and under the direction of another person in return for which he receives remuneration.

68. Pursuant to the first paragraph of Article [157(2) TFEU], for the purpose of that article, 'pay' means the ordinary basic or minimum wage or salary and any other consideration, whether in cash or in kind, which the worker receives directly or indirectly, in respect of his employment, from his employer. It is clear from that definition that the authors of the Treaty did not intend that the term 'worker', within the meaning of Article [157(1) TFEU], should include independent providers of services who are not in a relationship of subordination with the person who receives the services.

69. The question whether such a relationship exists must be answered in each particular case having regard to all the factors and circumstances by which the relationship between the parties is characterised.

70. Provided that a person is a worker within the meaning of Article [157(1) TFEU], the nature of his legal relationship with the other party to the employment relationship is of no consequence in regard to the application of that article.

71. The formal classification of a self-employed person under national law does not exclude the possibility that a person must be classified as a worker within the meaning of Article [157(1) TFEU] if his independence is merely notional, thereby disguising an employment relationship within the meaning of that article.

72. In the case of teachers who are, vis-à-vis an intermediary undertaking, under an obligation to undertake an assignment at a college, it is necessary in particular to consider the extent of any limitation on their freedom to choose their timetable, and the place and content of their work. The fact that no obligation is imposed on them to accept an assignment is of no consequence in that context.

---

[50] It is beyond the scope of this chapter to examine in detail the meaning of 'pay'. See E. Ellis and P. Watson, *EU Anti-Discrimination Law* (2nd edn, Oxford, Oxford University Press, 2012) ch. 4.

[51] Case 170/84 *Bilka-Kaufhaus GmbH v Karin Weber von Hartz* [1986] ECR 1607.

[52] Case 12/81 *Garland v British Rail Engineering* [1982] ECR 359.

[53] Case 262/88 *Barber v Guardian Royal Exchange Assurance Group* [1990] ECR I-1889.

[54] Case C-342/93 *Gillespie v Northern Health and Social Services Board* [1996] ECR I-457.

[55] Case C-167/97 *R v Secretary of State for Employment ex parte Seymour-Smith and Perez* [1999] ECR I-623.

[56] Case 171/88 *Rinner-Kühn v FWW Spezial-Gebäudereinigung GmbH & Co. KG* [1989] ECR 2743.

[57] Case C-167/97 *R v Secretary of State for Employment ex parte Seymour-Smith and Perez* [1999] ECR I-623, para. 23.

The effect of this ruling is to widen the meaning of 'workers' so that Member States are unable to reclassify persons as 'self-employed' merely to avoid obligations under Article 157 TFEU. For Ms Allonby, this meant that the national court might now classify her as a worker by considering the nature of her work. Assuming she was a worker, she would have a remedy if it was proven that the exclusion of self-employed teachers from the scheme adversely affected more women than men.[58]

Thus, the judgment was good news for the plaintiff in that it means she might be entitled to join the relevant pension scheme, but bad news for her in that her complaint about her lower salary was not accepted.[59] It is interesting to note that the reason why Ms Allonby was in the predicament she was in was, paradoxically, because of Article 157 TFEU. In earlier cases, the Court of Justice had moved to protect part-time workers (who are predominantly female) using sex discrimination rules, thus guaranteeing that their remuneration was comparable to full-time workers.[60] The employer in this dispute was responding to the implications of one such ruling, which compelled employers to grant equivalent rights to part-time workers.[61] It sought to evade the costs placed upon him by contracting her services out so she was no longer their part-time worker. The irony was not lost on Advocate General Geelhoed:

> [a] legal device has been used precisely ... in order to evade the consequences of the principle of equal treatment laid down in Article [157 TFEU]. A change in the legal form of the relationship between Ms Allonby and her original employer, the College, thus results in the loss of the protection conferred by Article [157 TFEU] on Ms Allonby as a female employee.[62]

However, he felt that a solution to this loophole required legislative action rather than judicial creativity. In recasting the equality Directives in 2006 the Commission wished to overrule the first ground in *Allonby* but was persuaded to drop this, because the process of recasting only allows for legislation to be consolidated and clarified.[63]

3 EQUALITY GROUNDS

Discrimination is wrong where a person is treated differently because of a 'morally irrelevant' characteristic,[64] or where she is treated with unwarranted contempt,[65] for example, refusing to hire a person because she is black or has blonde hair. However, refusing to hire a person as a doctor because she has no qualifications for the job is a legitimate basis for discrimination. More blurred is the refusal to hire a Sikh who wears a turban because he is unable to wear a protective helmet, or preventing a female pupil from wearing her traditional religious dress at school on the basis that this conflicts with the school's policy of requiring a school uniform.

---

[58] Thus, it is a claim for indirect discrimination, a concept explored in detail at p. 597.

[59] S. Fredman, 'Marginalising Equal Pay Laws' (2004) 33 *ILJ* 281.

[60] See Directive 97/81/EC on part-time work [1998] OJ L14/9, which broadly codifies the case law.

[61] Employment Protection (Part-time Employees) Regulations 1995, SI 1995/31, which were the result of *R* v *Secretary of State for Employment ex parte EOC* [1994] 1 All ER 910, where the House of Lords held that inferior rights for part-time workers were contrary to EU law.

[62] Case C-256/01 *Allonby* v *Accrington and Rossendale College* [2004] ECR I-873, para. 43.

[63] J. Shaw, J. Hunt and C. Wallace, *Economic and Social Law of the European Union* (Basingstoke, Palgrave McMillan, 2007) 372–3.

[64] D. Feldman, *Civil Liberties and Human Rights in England and Wales* (2nd edn, Oxford, Oxford University Press, 2002) 135–6.

[65] M. Cavanagh, *Against Equality of Opportunity* (Oxford, Clarendon Press, 2002) ch. 4.

It is not clear why law prohibits discrimination on the basis of religion but not on the basis of political opinion, and there is a difficult question here as to what grounds of discrimination are legally irrelevant. As we will see in the sections that follow, the EU has identified certain personal attributes that make discrimination unlawful, but has excluded others. Furthermore, one important omission in the discrimination Directives is any definition of the protected group. This gives Member States discretion on setting out a definition, but it also means that the Court of Justice will have a determinative role in shaping the meaning of concepts like race, ethnicity and religion. The disadvantages of legal uncertainty and diversity among the Member States can be balanced by the potential for the definitions to evolve organically in response to changing social conditions.

A preliminary remark is important: the Directives protect a person who is a member of a protected group, but they also safeguard the rights of a person who does not belong to a protected group but suffers discrimination on the grounds of, for example, sex or race.[66] This means that if a person is discriminated against because he is caring for an elderly relative, or because he has homosexual friends, he is discriminated against on grounds of age or sexual orientation.[67] The Court of Justice confirmed this in *Coleman*, where the plaintiff was the primary carer of a disabled child and claimed she was harassed and discriminated against on the grounds of her child's disability when she sought flexible working arrangements to care for him.

Case C-303/06 S. Coleman v Attridge Law and Steve Law [2008] ECR I-5603

38. ... the purpose of the directive, as regards employment and occupation, is to combat all forms of discrimination on grounds of disability. The principle of equal treatment enshrined in the directive in that area applies not to a particular category of person but by reference to the grounds mentioned in Article 1. That interpretation is supported by the wording of Article [19 TFEU], which constitutes the legal basis of Directive 2000/78, and which confers on the Community the competence to take appropriate action to combat discrimination based, inter alia, on disability. ...

50. Although, in a situation such as that in the present case, the person who is subject to direct discrimination on grounds of disability is not herself disabled, the fact remains that it is the disability which, according to Ms Coleman, is the ground for the less favourable treatment which she claims to have suffered. As is apparent from paragraph 38 of this judgment, Directive 2000/78, which seeks to combat all forms of discrimination on grounds of disability in the field of employment and occupation, applies not to a particular category of person but by reference to the grounds mentioned in Article 1.

51. Where it is established that an employee in a situation such as that in the present case suffers direct discrimination on grounds of disability, an interpretation of Directive 2000/78 limiting its application only to people who are themselves disabled is liable to deprive that directive of an important element of its effectiveness and to reduce the protection which it is intended to guarantee.

It remains to be seen how close the bond between the victim of discrimination and the person with whom she is associated must be. Here the plaintiff was the primary carer, but what if the bond was looser, say a white person is discriminated against because he has friends of other ethnicities? Moreover, while a victim is entitled to damages, it is not clear how far the

---

[66] Recast Equal Treatment Directive, article 2(1); Race Directive, article 1; Framework Directive, article 2(1).
[67] R. Whittle, 'The Framework Directive for Equal Treatment in Employment and Occupation: An Analysis from a Disability Rights Perspective' (2002) 27 *EL Rev*. 303, 321–2.

employer has a duty to accommodate the employee who cares for a disabled person, because the Court of Justice considered that the duties imposed in the Directive to make reasonable accommodation for the disabled were specifically designed to integrate the disabled person in the workplace and not for the protection of persons like the claimant in this case.[68]

(i) Sex/gender

The early development sex discrimination laws owes much to a French civil servant, Jacqueline Nonon, who pressed for the adoption of equal rights policies in the 1970s.[69] There are now several bodies that coordinate and promote gender equality, including the Advisory Committee on Equal Opportunities for Women and Men,[70] and in 2007 the European Institute for Gender Equality was established, with a budget of €52.5 million for 2007–2013.[71] The Court of Justice's heavy involvement in sex discrimination is the result of a concerted effort by one Belgian lawyer, Eliane Vogel-Polsky, who in the 1970s tested the legality of Belgian law with Article 157 TFEU by taking up a complaint from Gabrielle Defrenne, an air hostess who had been awarded a pension inferior to that of her male colleagues. In *Defrenne* v *Sabena*, the Court of Justice held that the equal pay provision, Article 157 TFEU had direct effect,[72] and this led to increased litigation testing the compatibility of national law with EU law, especially emanating from the United Kingdom and the Netherlands.[73] The pace of sex equality legislation stalled in the 1980s and 1990s, in part because of the reluctance of Member States to take equality further. The Commission responded to this hiatus by drafting a range of soft law measures to encourage Member State action.[74] It has been suggested that the increased legislative output in the mid-1990s was in part motivated by the need for the EU to show that it was not merely about achieving economic goals (at the time the establishment of a single currency).[75]

As we have indicated, the Court of Justice has played a significant role in shaping and extending the scope of sex equality legislation, and some of the principles established in the judgments were later translated into legislation.[76] Moreover, the Court extended the scope of sex equality to discrimination against transsexuals. In *P* v *S and Cornwall County Council*, P was dismissed by her employer after informing him of her decision to undergo male-to-female gender reassignment, a medical procedure designed to allow her to have a more integrated

---

[68] Case C-303/06 *S. Coleman* v *Attridge Law and Steve Law* [2008] ECR I-5603, para. 42.

[69] C. Harlow and R. Rawlings, *Pressure Through Law* (London, Routledge, 1992) 282.

[70] Decision 82/43/EEC relating to the setting up of an Advisory Committee on Equal Opportunities for Women and Men [1982] OJ L20/35.

[71] Regulation 1922/2006 of the European Parliament and of the Council of 20 December 2006 on establishing a European Institute for Gender Equality [2006] OJ L403/9.

[72] Case 43/75 *Defrenne* v *Sabena* [1976] ECR 455.

[73] Harlow and Rawlings, n. 69 above, 283–4; C. Kilpatrick, 'Community or Communities of Courts in European Integration? Sex Equality Dialogues Between UK Courts and the ECJ' (1998) 4 *ELJ* 121.

[74] See e.g. Recommendation 84/635 on the promotion of positive action for women [1984] OJ L331/34; Directive 92/85/EC of 19 October 1992 on the introduction of measures to encourage improvements in the safety and health at work of pregnant workers and workers who have recently given birth or are breastfeeding [1992] OJ L348/1.

[75] Bell, n. 4 above, 47–8.

[76] See e.g. Case 109/88 *Handels-og Kontorfunktionærernes Forbund I Danmark* v *Dansk Arbejdsgiverforening, acting on behalf of Danforss* [1989] ECR 3199 and Case C-127/92 *Enderby* v *Frenchay Health Authority and Secretary of State for Health* [1993] ECR I-5535, leading to Directive 97/80/EC on the burden of proof in cases of discrimination based on sex [1998] OJ L14/6.

identity. The Court found that this constituted discrimination on the basis of sex in breach of the Equal Treatment Directive in force at that time (Directive 76/207/EEC [1976] OJ L39/40).

Case C–13/94 *P* v *S and Cornwall County Council* [1996] ECR I–2143

20. ...[t]he scope of the Directive cannot be confined simply to discrimination based on the fact that a person is of one or other sex. In view of its purpose and the nature of the rights which it seeks to safeguard, the scope of the Directive is also such as to apply to discrimination arising, as in this case, from the gender reassignment of the person concerned.

21. Such discrimination is based, essentially if not exclusively, on the sex of the person concerned. Where a person is dismissed on the ground that he or she intends to undergo, or has undergone, gender reassignment, he or she is treated unfavourably by comparison with persons of the sex to which he or she was deemed to belong before undergoing gender reassignment.

22. To tolerate such discrimination would be tantamount, as regards such a person, to a failure to respect the dignity and freedom to which he or she is entitled, and which the Court has a duty to safeguard.

This was widely welcomed because the Court moved away from a narrow emphasis on sex discrimination towards an appreciation of gender identities.[77] It was affirmed in *KB* v *National Health Service Pensions Agency*, where a female employee wished to assign her survivor's pension rights to R, a female-to-male transsexual, but was unable to do so because at the time UK law did not allow R's sex change to be legally recognised, and so KB and R were unable to marry.[78] As a result KB was unable to nominate R as the person entitled to receive KB's pension should she die before R. The Court of Justice held that while there was no discrimination in the law restricting the right to the survivor's pensions to married spouses,[79] UK law de facto prevented R from qualifying by denying her the right to marry. Having noted that the ECtHR had earlier ruled that UK law was incompatible with the ECHR's right to marry,[80] the fact that R was unable to qualify to obtain the survivor's pension was in breach of Article 157 TFEU.[81] However, the Court of Justice left it to the national court to determine whether KB could rely on Article 157 to gain recognition of her right to nominate R as beneficiary.[82] It is not clear why the national court has any discretion in the matter, given the Court's firm stance that R's inability to qualify constituted a breach of EU law. One answer is that the Court implicitly refuses to challenge the Member State's choices about which persons can marry, and does not provide clear answers to other types of cases, for example, in relation to those who choose not to undergo gender reassignment and yet consider themselves as belonging to the other sex (transgender).[83]

---

[77] It was applied to retirement pensions for transsexuals in Case C-423/04 *Richards* v *Secretary of State for Work and Pensions*, Judgment of 27 April 2006.

[78] Case C-117/01 *KB* [2004] ECR I-541. For a critique, see M. Bell, 'A Hazy Concept of Equality' (2004) 12 *Feminist Legal Studies* 223.

[79] *KB*, n. 78 above, paras. 28–9.

[80] *Goodwin* v *United Kingdom* (2002) 35 EHRR 18 and *I* v *United Kingdom* [2002] ECHR 592. See now the Gender Recognition Act 2004.

[81] *KB*, n. 78 above, para. 34.   [82] *KB*, n. 78 above, para. 35.

[83] Bell, n. 78 above, 223. But see Case C-423/04 *Richards* v *Secretary of State for Work and Pensions*, Opinion of Advocate General Jacobs, 15 December 2005, para. 45.

Judicial reluctance to engage with the complexities of gender identity is matched by the legislature's timid revision of the Equal Treatment Directive.[84]

(ii) Racial or ethnic origin

The need for EU legislation in this field has been discussed since the 1980s. However, there was little action, in part because there was no certain legal basis for legislation.[85] Increased immigration brought racism to the attention of legislators in the 1990s and was accompanied by more effective lobbying, in particular the 'Starting Line Group' (a coalition of 200 NGOs established in 1989).[86] It proposed a Race Directive in 1992, and this gained wide support.[87] At the same time, the EU institutions were becoming increasingly concerned about racism, although there were differences among Member States preventing legislative action.[88] The European Year Against Racism in 1997 was designed to raise awareness, and the European Monitoring Centre on Racism and Xenophobia was established that year to gather further information on these social problems and aid in the formulation of policy.[89] Once Article 19 TFEU was introduced, however, it only took six months for the Commission's proposed Race Directive to be adopted by the Council.[90] The main reason for this urgency was the election of a far-right government in Austria in 2000 and the wish of the EU to assert a set of values to underscore its commitment to racial equality.[91] A second factor was the forthcoming enlargement of the European Union. Incorporating non-discrimination in the Community acquis was not only a means of sending a strong message against racial intolerance to new Member States, but also of addressing concerns expressed about manifestations of racism in the older Member States, for example France and the United Kingdom.[92]

The central difficulty in applying the Race Directive in practice is that there is no definition of race or ethnic origin, and there is no uniform practice in this context that can be drawn upon.[93] The Preamble to the Race Directive states that the European Union 'rejects theories which attempt to determine the existence of separate human races'.[94] This reflects the practice

---

[84] Recast Equal Treatment Directive, recital 3 merely provides that it also applies to discrimination arising from the gender reassignment of a person.

[85] See e.g. Joint Declaration of the Institutions against Racism and Xenophobia, [1986] OJ C158/1; European Parliament, Resolution on racism and xenophobia and anti-semitism and further steps to combat further racial discrimination, [1999] OJ C98/488.

[86] On the origins of this group, see P. Iganski, 'Legislating Morality and Competing Rights: Legal Instruments against Racism and Anti-semitism in the European Union' (1999) 25 *Journal of Ethnic and Migration Studies* 509; I. Chopin, 'The Starting Line Group: A Harmonised Approach to Fighting Racism and to Promote Equal Treatment' (1999) 1 *European Journal of Migration and Law* 111.

[87] A. Dummett, 'The Starting Line: A Proposal for a Draft Community Directive concerning the Elimination of Racial Discrimination' (1994) 20 *New Community* 530. On their impact on the Directive, see A. Tyson, 'The Negotiation of the European Community Directive on Racial Discrimination' (2001) 3 *European Journal of Migration and Law* 199.

[88] Bell, n. 4 above, 70–1.   [89] Regulation 1035/97 [1997] OJ L151/1.

[90] European Commission, *Proposal for a Council Directive Implementing the Principle of Equal Treatment between Persons Irrespective of Racial or Ethnic Origin*, COM(1999)566.

[91] See G. de Búrca, 'The Drafting of the European Union Charter of Fundamental Rights' (2001) 26 *EL Rev.* 126, 136.

[92] For background, see C. Brown, 'The Race Directive: Towards Equality for *All* Peoples of Europe?' (2002) *YEL* 195, 196–204.

[93] E. Guild, 'The EC Directive on Race Discrimination: Surprises, Possibilities and Limitations' (2000) 24 *ILJ* 416.

[94] Race Directive, recital 6.

in the United States, where the Supreme Court has taken a wide, purposive approach to identifying race.[95] It recognises that a person's race is a social construct based upon certain attributes, for example skin colour, language, culture or religion. One criticism of the Directive is its failure to suggest that 'observable characteristics' like skin colour can be the basis for defining race, as this would have facilitated the implementation of effective laws.[96] Ethnicity is an even more complex term to define. In UK law, the House of Lords identified two essential conditions for the existence of an ethnic group: first, a long shared history as a separate group and, secondly, a cultural tradition, including family and social customs.[97] Other features indicative of ethnicity are a common geographical origin, common language, literature or religion, and being a separate group within a larger community. On this basis, Sikhs, Jews and gypsies form distinct ethnic groups, while Rastafarians do not because they lack a sufficiently long shared history.[98] This creates a complex borderline between discrimination on the grounds of race and religion.

Difficulties in providing definitions of race and ethnic origin might be surmounted by eschewing a literal approach in favour of a purposive interpretation which explores the social and historical context of racism. If this might lead to divergent definitions of race and ethnicity among the Member States, this should be welcomed, for it allows each state to develop the law in a manner consistent with the origins of racism within each state.[99] To date the Court of Justice has not been called upon to decide any significant cases to interpret the notion of race.

(iii) Religion or belief

Forbidding discrimination on grounds of religion is particularly significant because while some religious groups would be able to secure protection on the basis of the Race Directive, others might fall outside it. In the context of the United Kingdom, for example, Muslims found it difficult to make a claim for race discrimination.[100] The Directive is likely to cover Buddhists as 'believers' in a specific way of life,[101] but it is uncertain whether pacifists or vegetarians are protected, even though they hold a set of beliefs that informs their life choices.[102] In implementing the Framework Directive, the United Kingdom has taken the view that the Directive only prohibits discrimination on the grounds of 'any religion, religious belief or *similar* philosophical belief'.[103] Following the approach taken by the ECtHR, it means the belief in question

---

[95] *St Francis College* v *Al-Khazraji* 481 U.S. 604 (1987).
[96] F. Brennan, 'The Race Directive: Recycling Racial Inequality' (2002–03) 5 *CYELS* 311, 320–1.
[97] *Mandla* v *Lee* [1983] 2 AC 548.
[98] See, respectively, *Deide* v *Gillette* [1980] IRLR 427 (Jews); *CRE* v *Dutton* [1989] QB 783 (gypsies); *Dawkins* v *Department of the Environment* [1993] ICR 517 (Rastafarians).
[99] See J. Rex, 'Multiculturalism in Europe and America' (1995) 1 *Nations and Nationalism* 243, who notes that it would be difficult to transplant the United Kingdom's race relations laws to France.
[100] B. Hepple and T. Choudhury, *Tackling Religious Discrimination: Practical Implications for Policy-Makers and Legislators*, Home Office Research Study 221 (London, Home Office, 2001) 12; S. Poulter, 'Muslim Headscarves in School: Contrasting Approaches in England and France' (1997) *OJLS* 43.
[101] Ellis and Watson, n. 50 above, 33.
[102] Under Article 9 ECHR (which safeguards 'freedom of thought, conscience and religion'), the ECtHR extended its scope to atheism and agnosticism (*Kokkinakis* v *Greece* (1994) 17 EHRR 397), and the European Commission on Human Rights had included pacifism (*Arrowsmith* v *United Kingdom* (1978) 19 DR 5) and veganism (*H* v *United Kingdom* (1993) 16 EHRR CD 44).
[103] Employment Equality (Religion or Belief) Regulations 2003, SI 2003/1660, reg. 2(1).

must be coherent and serious, and must be one which merits respect in a democratic society.[104] Atheism and humanism fall within this definition, but the support of a political party or a football team do not. Absence of belief is also protected, so a religious employer may not refuse a job to a non-believer.[105]

(iv) Disability

Before the Framework Directive, the EU had devoted some energies to address the difficulties faced by disabled persons via action programmes. The first was designed to exchange information and notes on good practice in education and employment of disabled persons.[106] But the EU was unsuccessful in implementing legislation conferring rights on disabled persons; for example, it failed to obtain agreement on legislation obliging employers to adopt quotas to promote employment of disabled people.[107] Nevertheless, as of the mid-1990s, the Council was resolved to legislate to provide equality of opportunity for disabled people,[108] and the European Parliament's Disability Intergroup pressed for the inclusion of discrimination in Article 19 TFEU.[109]

More recently, by Decision 2010/48, the European Union has approved the UN Convention on the Rights of Persons with Disabilities (UNCRPD).[110] The provisions of that Convention are henceforth an integral part of the EU legal order. This is helpful because that Convention goes some way in providing a definition of discrimination, and this has proven helpful in aiding the Court of Justice in drawing a line between disability and illness.

The leading case was brought by a Danish trade union on behalf of two of its members. One suffered from constant lumbar pain which could not be treated, the other suffered the effects of a whiplash injury: both were unable to work full time but both remained capable of working reduced working hours, and the trade union argued that the Directive imposed a duty on their employers to offer them this arrangement.

> **Joined Cases C–335/11 and C–337/11 *HK Danmark, acting on behalf of Jette Ring* v *Dansk almennyttigt Boligselskab* and *HK Danmark, acting on behalf of Lone Skouboe Werge* v *Dansk Arbejdsgiverforening acting on behalf of Pro Display A/S*, Judgment of 11 April 2013**
>
> 37. The UN Convention, which was ratified by the European Union ... acknowledges in recital (e) that 'disability is an evolving concept and that disability results from the interaction between persons with impairments and attitudinal and environmental barriers that hinder their full and effective participation in society on an equal basis with others'. Thus the second paragraph of Article 1 of the

---

[104] *Campbell and Cosans* v *United Kingdom* (1982) 4 EHRR 293, at 304.

[105] *Kokkanikis* v *Greece* (1994) 17 EHRR 397, at 418.

[106] Community Social Action Programme on the Social Integration of Handicapped People, 1983–88 [1981] OJ C347/1.

[107] D. Mabbett, 'The Development of Rights-based Social Policy in the European Union: The Example of Disability Rights' (2005) 43 *JCMS* 97, 107.

[108] Draft Resolution of the Council and of Representatives of the Governments of the Member States on equality of opportunity for people with disabilities, COM(96)406.

[109] See www.disabilityintergroup.eu.

[110] Council Decision 2010/48/EC of 26 November 2009 [2010] OJ L23/35.

38. ...the concept of 'disability' must be understood as referring to a limitation which results in particular from physical, mental or psychological impairments which in interaction with various barriers may hinder the full and effective participation of the person concerned in professional life on an equal basis with other workers.

39. In addition, it follows from the second paragraph of Article 1 of the UN Convention that the physical, mental or psychological impairments must be 'long-term'.

40. It may be added that, as the Advocate General observes in point 32 of her Opinion, it does not appear that Directive 2000/78 is intended to cover only disabilities that are congenital or result from accidents, to the exclusion of those caused by illness. It would run counter to the very aim of the directive, which is to implement equal treatment, to define its scope by reference to the origin of the disability.

41. It must therefore be concluded that if a curable or incurable illness entails a limitation which results in particular from physical, mental or psychological impairments which in interaction with various barriers may hinder the full and effective participation of the person concerned in professional life on an equal basis with other workers, and the limitation is a long-term one, such an illness can be covered by the concept of 'disability' within the meaning of Directive 2000/78.

42. On the other hand, an illness not entailing such a limitation is not covered by the concept of 'discrimination' within the meaning of Directive 2000/78. Illness as such cannot be regarded as a ground in addition to those in relation to which Directive 2000/78 prohibits discrimination.

43. The circumstance that the person concerned can work only to a limited extent is not an obstacle to that person's state of health being covered by the concept of 'disability'. Contrary to the submissions of DAB and Pro Display, a disability does not necessarily imply complete exclusion from work or professional life.

This ruling qualifies the narrower position the Court of Justice had taken earlier.[111] It is to be welcomed insofar as it allows those who experience long-term illness to be brought within the scope of the Directive. Moreover, reliance on the UNCRPD also leads the courts away from a medical model to a social model.[112] The latter gives protection to a wider range of persons (for example, those who have a facial disfigurement).[113]

The Directive also recognises that disability is the result of barriers in the workplace;[114] and that it is socially constructed.[115] Therefore special duties are imposed on the employer.

---

[111] Case C-13/05 *Sonia Chacón Navas* v *Eurest Colectividades SA* [2006] ECR I-6467, para. 43.

[112] M. Perlin, *International Human Rights and Mental Disability Law: When the Silenced are Heard* (Oxford, Oxford University Press, 2011) ch. 7; G. Quinn, 'The United Nations Convention on the Rights of Persons with Disabilities: Towards a New International Politics of Disability' (2009) *Texas Journal on Civil Liberties and Civil Rights*15, 33–50.

[113] D. L. Hosking 'A High Bar for EU Disability Rights' (2007) 36 *ILJ* 228. See further M. Oliver and C. Barnes, *Disabled People and Social Policy: From Exclusion to Inclusion* (Harlow, Longman, 1998).

[114] K. Wells, 'The Impact of the Framework Employment Directive on UK Disability Discrimination Law' (2003) 32 *ILJ* 253.

[115] See generally, C. Barnes, 'A Working Social Model? Disability, Work and Disability Politics in the 21st Century' (2000) 20 *Critical Social Policy* 441.

> **Framework Directive, article 5**
>
> In order to guarantee compliance with the principle of equal treatment in relation to persons with disabilities, reasonable accommodation shall be provided. This means that employers shall take appropriate measures, where needed in a particular case, to enable a person with a disability to have access to, participate in, or advance in employment, or to undergo training, unless such measures would impose a disproportionate burden on the employer. This burden shall not be disproportionate when it is sufficiently remedied by measures existing within the framework of the disability policy of the Member State concerned.

The practical significance of this policy can be illustrated by returning to the seminal judgment above. It will be recalled that the two claimants felt that they would have been able to continue work if their work hours were reduced. The employers claimed that this was not the sort of accommodation that Article 5 had in mind, but the Court of Justice disagreed.

> **Joined Cases C-335/11 and C-337/11** *HK Danmark, acting on behalf of Jette Ring* v *Dansk almennyttigt Boligselskab* and *HK Danmark, acting on behalf of Lone Skouboe Werge* v *Dansk Arbejdsgiverforening acting on behalf of Pro Display A/S*, Judgment of 11 April 2013
>
> 53. In accordance with the second paragraph of Article 2 of the UN Convention, 'reasonable accommodation' is 'necessary and appropriate modification and adjustments not imposing a disproportionate or undue burden, where needed in a particular case, to ensure to persons with disabilities the enjoyment or exercise on an equal basis with others of all human rights and fundamental freedoms'. It follows that that provision prescribes a broad definition of the concept of 'reasonable accommodation'.
>
> 54. Thus, with respect to Directive 2000/78, that concept must be understood as referring to the elimination of the various barriers that hinder the full and effective participation of persons with disabilities in professional life on an equal basis with other workers.
>
> 55. As recital 20 in the preamble to Directive 2000/78 and the second paragraph of Article 2 of the UN Convention envisage not only material but also organisational measures, and the term 'pattern' of working time must be understood as the rhythm or speed at which the work is done, it cannot be ruled out that a reduction in working hours may constitute one of the accommodation measures referred to in Article 5 of that directive.
>
> 56. It should be observed, moreover, that the list of appropriate measures to adapt the workplace to the disability in recital 20 in the preamble to Directive 2000/78 is not exhaustive and, consequently, even if it were not covered by the concept of 'pattern of working time ', a reduction in working hours could be regarded as an accommodation measure referred to in Article 5 of the directive, in a case in which reduced working hours make it possible for the worker to continue employment, in accordance with the objective of that article.
>
> 57. It must be recalled, however, that, as stated in recital 17 in the preamble, Directive 2000/78 does not require the recruitment, promotion or maintenance in employment of a person who is not competent, capable and available to perform the essential functions of the post concerned, without prejudice to the obligation to provide reasonable accommodation for people with disabilities, which includes a possible reduction in their hours of work.

58. Moreover, in accordance with Article 5 of that directive, the accommodation persons with disabilities are entitled to must be reasonable, in that it must not constitute a disproportionate burden on the employer.

59. In the disputes in the main proceedings, it is therefore for the national court to assess whether a reduction in working hours, as an accommodation measure, represents a disproportionate burden on the employers.

60. As follows from recital 21 in the preamble to Directive 2000/78, account must be taken in particular of the financial and other costs entailed by such a measure, the scale and financial resources of the undertaking, and the possibility of obtaining public funding or any other assistance. ...

62. It may be of relevance for the purposes of that assessment that, as noted by the referring court, immediately after the dismissal of Ms Ring, DAB advertised a position for an office worker to work part-time, 22 hours a week, in its regional office in Lyngby. There is nothing in the documents before the Court to show that Ms Ring was not capable of occupying that part-time post or to explain why it was not offered to her. Moreover, the referring court stated that soon after her dismissal Ms Ring started a new job as a receptionist with another company and her actual working time was 20 hours a week.

63. In addition, as the Danish Government pointed out at the hearing, Danish law makes it possible to grant public assistance to undertakings for accommodation measures whose purpose is to facilitate the access to the labour market of persons with disabilities, including initiatives aimed at encouraging employers to recruit and maintain in employment persons with disabilities.

The judgment has been welcomed by the European Disability Forum, and one may wonder whether the obligations found in article 5 may not be worth considering for other disability grounds, because positive obligations to integrate previously excluded groups can be vital to develop a sound equality policy. While the approach taken here is grounded in common sense (the case seems to have been brought more to test the limits of the law rather than to establish a controversial point of law), one might wonder whether the state's support for an employer making adjustments to the workplace should be relevant: it may make it too easy for employers to escape from having to modify their workplace when such funds are unavailable. Moreover, if the government makes such funds available, it may be more effective to create incentives for employers to take advantage of these funds than to use strategic litigation to force an allocation of these resources.

(v) Age

Before Article 19 TFEU, the major legal step that had an impact on older workers was the *Barber* ruling, where the Court of Justice held that it was unlawful to have different retirement ages for men and women insofar as occupational pension schemes were concerned.[116] The effect is that most Member States have implemented a common retirement age of 65, increasing the participation of women in the marketplace.[117] On a legislative plane, by contrast, there was reluctance amongst Member States to give the European Union competence in developing

---

[116] Case C-262/88 *Barber* v *Guardian Royal Exchange Assurance Group* [1990] ECR I-1889.

[117] F. McDonald and M. Potton, 'The Nascent European Policy Towards Older Workers: Can the European Union Help the Older Worker?' (1997) 26 *Personnel Review* 293, 299–300.

policy towards the aged.[118] The inclusion of age discrimination in the Framework Directive is probably the result of Europe's large ageing population.[119] Having encouraged early retirement for some decades, states find themselves with a pensions crisis whereby it is unlikely that sufficient funds are available for retired persons. Moreover, persons are living longer. These patterns have stimulated the demand for legislation aimed at lengthening the time people are able to work, and promoting the continued employment of older workers. As Sandra Fredman notes, '[t]he new emphasis on combating age discrimination is not…a result of a sudden appreciation of the need for fairness, but gains its chief impetus from business and macro-economic imperatives'.[120]

However, the Framework Directive is not limited to discrimination against the elderly. Discrimination against young employees is also forbidden.[121] This is in contrast to American law where comparable legislation is directed at persons aged 40 or over.[122] Given that workers of all ages require protection, it may be suggested that the aim of age discrimination law should be to promote age diversity among the working population. This aspiration is reflected in the Commission's *Green Paper on Demographic Change,* which suggests that EU policy should develop to ensure solidarity across generations by granting opportunities and benefits to all age groups.[123] However, there are two limits to what the Framework Directive can achieve in this context: first, discrimination is not the sole cause of the current social problems, and it must be seen as part of a wider range of social policy measures. Secondly, an empirical study of the American statute outlawing discrimination of older workers suggests that it has mainly benefited white men.[124] Taken together, these observations indicate the inherent limitations of a legal framework premised upon a formal equality model.

(vi) Sexual orientation

In common with other protected groups, a combination of factors led to the progressive incorporation of sexual orientation in the EU's discourse.[125] In the 1990s, NGOs, in particular the UK-based organisation Stonewall and the International Lesbian and Gay Association, began to lobby, focusing upon the barriers to the internal market resulting from national laws. Then, in the 1990s, Member States began to draw up legislation to protect persons from discrimination on the grounds of sexual orientation, which facilitated the development of soft law at Union level,[126] and led to increased support from the European Parliament, whose role in the final stages was crucial.[127]

---

[118] *Ibid.* 302.   [119] Framework Directive, recital 6.   [120] Fredman, n. 39 above, 62.

[121] Young workers are also protected by Directive 94/33/EC of 22 June 1994 on the protection of young people at work [1994] OJ L216/12, establishing a minimum age for work and several protective measures for young workers.

[122] Age Discrimination in Employment Act 1967, 29 USC 621–34.

[123] *Green Paper on Confronting Demographic Change: A New Solidarity Between the Generations,* COM(2005)94 final.

[124] G. Rutherglen, 'From Race to Age: The Expanding Scope of Employment Discrimination Law' (1995) 24 *Journal of Legal Studies* 491.

[125] This paragraph draws on Bell, n. 4 above, 91–7.

[126] See e.g. the reference to sexual orientation in para. 5 of the Code of Practice on Harassment [1992] OJ L49/1.

[127] Resolution on Equal Rights for Homosexuals and Lesbians in the EC [1994] OJ C61/40. See M. Mos, 'Of Gay Rights and Christmas Ornaments: The Political History of Sexual Orientation Non-discrimination in the Treaty of Amsterdam' (2013) *JCMS* 1.

Discrimination on grounds of sexual orientation operates at two levels: first, there is discrimination against those who are open about their sexuality, but secondly (and perhaps distinct from other grounds of discrimination) some choose to keep their sexual orientation a secret for fear of discrimination. The Framework Directive addresses the first type of discrimination, but the second requires a societal shift in attitudes. Nevertheless, a potentially helpful dimension for those who do not wish to disclose their sexuality is that discrimination arises if an *assumption* is made about their sexual orientation. This seems to be the position in the Directive, and according to some, this might help encourage litigation.[128]

While the Framework Directive might be seen to provide an effective means for guaranteeing the rights of the homosexual employee, it excludes any interference with the design of national law insofar as family rights are concerned. Recital 22 of the Framework Directive provides that '[t]his Directive is without prejudice to national laws on marital status and the benefits dependent thereon'. However, this recital was read narrowly by the Court of Justice in *Tadao Maruko*. The claimant was in a same-sex registered partnership (a 'life partnership' under German law) and was denied a widower's pension on his partner's death because the rules of the association managing that pension made no provision for same-sex partners. After finding that the pension constituted 'pay' so that the dispute fell within the Framework Directive, the Court noted that the conditions for life partnerships were increasingly aligned with those of marriage. It followed that if the national court should decide that surviving spouses and surviving life partners are in a comparable situation, then the denial of a widower's pension to the latter would constitute direct discrimination.[129] This leaves national courts with the task of determining if married couples and registered partners are in a comparable situation having regard to the issue at stake. On the facts, the German law gave life partners increasingly similar rights to married couples, allowing a successful claim. However, in Member States where the rights of registered partners are not similar to those of married couples, claimants will have to rest their arguments on indirect discrimination, which may prove more arduous.

The approach of the Court of Justice in this and a similar case is problematic from two different perspectives.[130] First, it requires the same-sex couple to assimilate their relationship to that of marriage. In this view the law does not so much recognise homosexual partnerships as it forces them into the framework for heterosexual ones: if you get close enough, you can claim equality rights, if you don't then no rights accrue.[131] This is more oppressive than emancipatory. The second line of criticism starts from a different premise: the law requires a Member State that has designed a legal form whereby homosexuals can secure recognition of their union to extend a wide range of benefits to the couple. However, in so doing the Court ignores the reasons why benefits are paid to married couples. For example, the survivor's pension in *Maruko* was probably based on the assumption that there was a spouse bearing the child care obligations who would receive help from the pension. It does not then follow that a childless couple should be entitled to similar levels of support.[132] However, this raises an even wider issue about how

---

[128] H. Oliver, 'Sexual Orientation Discrimination: Perceptions, Definitions and Genuine Occupational Requirements' (2004) 33 *ILJ* 1. But some have expressed caution: Bell, n. 4 above, 115.

[129] Case C-267/06 *Tadao Maruko* v *Versorgungsanstalt der deutschen Bühnen* [2008] ECR I-1757, para. 72.

[130] The other judgment is Case C-147/08 *Römer* [2011] ECR I-3591, where the claim was for higher levels of supplementary pension entitlements, but is reasoned in the same way as *Maruko*.

[131] J. Mulder, 'Some More Equal than Others? Matrimonial Benefits and the CJEU's Case Law on Discrimination on the Grounds of Sexual Orientation' (2012) 19(4) *MJ* 505.

[132] J. Cornides, 'Three Case Studies on "Anti-discrimination"' (2012) 32(2) *EJIL* 517, 523–6. Obviously homosexual couples may have children just as much as heterosexual couples could be childless.

to design pension rights appropriately: limiting them to married couples is discriminatory, but extending them to registered partners is also invidious, for it leaves out those whose lifestyle choices do not conform to the registered partnership model designed by the state. But focusing on categories at all makes one lose sight of a wider issue: how best to design the welfare state. Thus EU law, under the guise of equality, has a profound impact on national welfare policies where the EU ostensibly lacks competence. It may be preferable to tackle these head on rather than through the lens of discrimination law, by reformulating the way benefits are paid out.

Finally, it is worth noting that in this round of litigation the Court of Justice preferred to base itself upon finding direct discrimination. However, it seems as if the problem raised is one of indirect discrimination: the national laws all use one seemingly neutral criterion (marriage) to determine entitlements to pay, which affects a wide range of persons who, by virtue of the legal framework, are unable to qualify. This approach would then have led the Member State to articulate reasons why this form of discrimination is justified and would thus have allowed for one to consider the appropriate design of widowers' pension entitlements by considering expressly the policy objectives pursued by such benefits.[133]

(vii) Excluded groups

In view of the universality of the right to equality, and the recognition that discrimination against foreigners was likely in the face of increased migration into the EU, the Council's expert committee on racism (the Kahn Commission) recommended that Article 19 TFEU should prohibit discrimination against EU and non-EU citizens. However, there is no reference to citizenship in Article 19,[134] and the Directives expressly exclude from their coverage discrimination on the basis of nationality.

Framework Directive and Race Directive, article 3(2)

2. This Directive does not cover differences of treatment based on nationality and is without prejudice to provisions and conditions relating to the entry into and residence of third-country nationals and stateless persons in the territory of Member States, and to any treatment which arises from the legal status of the third-country nationals and stateless persons concerned.

While EU nationals have little to worry about, since they remain protected by Article 18 TFEU (which we discussed in Chapter 11), third-country nationals are open to discrimination on the basis of nationality. In some Member States, discrimination on the grounds of nationality is covered by race discrimination legislation,[135] but in other Member States the exclusion of nationality can lead to the risk that nationality discrimination is used as a way of concealing race discrimination. Moreover, article 3(2) of the Framework Directive and Race Directive means that discrimination against nationalities like the Welsh or the Catalans is not covered, thus a

---

[133] See Mulder, n. 131 above, for this approach.

[134] European Council Consultative Commission on Racism and Xenophobia, *Final Report*, 6906/1/95 Rev. 1 Limite RAXEN 24 (General Secretariat of the Council of the European Union, 1995).

[135] Race Relations Act 1976, s. 3(1).

sign excluding Scots from a bar would not fall foul of the Directive. The text of article 3(2) was heavily influenced by Member States who were keen to keep immigration controls outside the scope of the Race Directive. Thus, third-country nationals who are discriminated against because of their race or ethnicity by immigration officials when their entry into the country is concerned, gain no protection from the Directive.

The major criticism to be levelled at this provision is that it threatens to undermine the EU's equality policy and in particular its race equality policy, by maintaining discrimination against immigrants.[136]

B. Hepple, 'Race and Law in Fortress Europe' (2004) 67 *Modern Law Review* 1, 7

The effects of this exclusion are felt disproportionately by ethnic minorities, who make up the majority of third country nationals (TCNs). Their inferior legal status has serious repercussions on the perception of ethnic minorities generally, and on their integration. Any policy that aims to promote integration needs to take account of the interrelationship between human rights, citizenship and the labour market. The recent history of European immigration shows that migrants are often seen simply as a means of filling temporary needs in the labour market. This means that little attention is paid to citizenship or human rights. It is an illusion to believe that the forces of the labour market, generated by globalisation, can be halted by limiting the rights of TCNs to those of temporary 'guest workers' or by withholding citizenship rights. The political rhetoric of 'Fortress Europe' and restrictions on migrant workers and other legal residents, undermines the civil and social rights which belong to all human beings. Inhumane restrictions on welfare benefits, harsh policies against family reunification, and marginalization in the labour market prevent the realisation of the principle of equality which must be the foundation of all integration policies.

This undermines the commitment to race equality, although of course a third-country national living in the European Union has every right to claim on the basis of race, sex or other forms of discrimination.[137] In addition, there are other grounds of discrimination which have been omitted. Article 21 EUCFR, for example, has a wider list of discrimination grounds.

Article 21 EUCFR

1. Any discrimination based on any ground such as sex, race, colour, ethnic or social origin, genetic features, language, religion or belief, political or any other opinion, membership of a national minority, property, birth, disability, age or sexual orientation shall be prohibited.
2. Within the scope of application of the Treaty establishing the European Community and of the Treaty on European Union, and without prejudice to the special provisions of those Treaties, any discrimination on grounds of nationality shall be prohibited.

---

[136] See also J. Weiler, 'Thou Shalt Not Oppress a Stranger: On the Judicial Protection of the Human Rights of Non-EC Nationals: a Critique' (1992) 3 *EJIL* 65; Lord Lester, 'New European Equality Measures' (2000) *PL* 562; Brown, n. 92 above, 212.

[137] Race Directive, recital 13; Framework Directive, recital 12.

As we have seen, the grounds provided in the EU are the result of political compromise and lobbying, but the incomplete coverage of EU law calls into question the idealism displayed in the Preambles to the Framework Directive and Race Directive, which hail the EU's wish to safeguard human rights.

The Directives also fail to take into consideration the phenomenon of 'intersectional discrimination', first raised by American scholars.

K. Crenshaw, 'Demarginalizing the Intersection of Race and Sex: A Black Feminist Critique of Antidiscrimination Doctrine, Feminist Theory and Antiracist Politics' (1989) *University of Chicago Legal Forum* **139, 149–50**

Black women can experience discrimination in ways that are both similar to and different from those experienced by white women and Black men. Black women sometimes experience discrimination in ways similar to white women's experiences; sometimes they share very similar experiences with Black men. Yet often they experience double-discrimination – the combined effects of practices which discriminate on the basis of race, and on the basis of sex. And sometimes, they experience discrimination as Black women – not the sum of race and sex discrimination, but as Black women. Black women's experiences are much broader than the general categories that discrimination discourse provides. Yet the continued insistence that Black women's demands and needs be filtered through categorical analyses that completely obscure their experiences guarantees that their needs will seldom be addressed.

For example, a black woman may be passed over for promotion but fail in a claim for sex discrimination if there is evidence that the employer promotes white women, and may fail on grounds of racial discrimination because the employer promotes black men. The employer discriminates against 'black women' but there is no such legal category.[138] The Framework Directive and Race Directive allude to this problem by exhorting Member States, when implementing the principle of equal treatment, to 'promote equality between men and women, especially since women are often victims of multiple discrimination' but provide no concrete means for addressing the issue.[139] The issue becomes particularly poignant when the degree of protection afforded differs depending how the case is brought. In *Rosenbladt* (which we discuss more fully below) the claimant was a part-time cleaner who faced compulsory retirement: she pleaded that this constituted discrimination based on age but was not successful because a specific provision allows for age discrimination to be justified with relative ease.[140] However, it has been argued that she may well also have been the victim of indirect sex discrimination: it is not unusual for women to wish to work beyond retirement age because of lower wages (and so a lower pension) they tend to receive, as was the case here. It may well be that such a claim could have been more successful.[141]

---

[138] For examples in the UK and US courts that show the salience of this issue, see S. Hannett, 'Equality at the Intersections: The Legislative and Judicial Failure to Tackle Multiple Discrimination' (2003) 23 *OJLS* 65.

[139] Framework Directive, recital 3; Race Directive, recital 14. S. Fredman, 'Equality: A New Generation?' (2001) 30 *ILJ* 145, 159.

[140] Case C-45/09 *Rosenbladt v Oellerking Gebäudereinigungsges mbH* [2010] ECR I-9391.

[141] This example is from D. Sheick, 'Age Discrimination Before the ECJ: Conceptual and Theoretical Issues' (2011) 48 *CML Rev.* 777, 795–6.

4 DISCRIMINATION: MEANING, DEFENCES AND REMEDIES

(i) Direct discrimination

The discrimination Directives use a common formula in defining direct discrimination:

> direct discrimination shall be taken to occur where one person is treated less favourably than another is, has been or would be treated in a comparable situation on grounds of [sex, race, ethnic origin, religion, belief, age, disability, sexual orientation].[142]

There is no need to show that the employer intended to discriminate, nor that he was negligent. Direct discrimination is found when 'but for' the relevant 'ground' (for example, sex or race), the employer would not have discriminated. To show the causal link between the relevant ground and the less favourable treatment, the plaintiff must compare her treatment with that of others. The Equal Treatment Directive allows her to show less favourable treatment in three ways: that there *is* a difference between her treatment and that of others; that there *has been* a difference (by reference to former employees); or that other employees *would be* treated differently. The ability to rely on a hypothetical comparison is likely to be helpful where, because of certain stereotypes, all actual comparators are of the same group as the plaintiff. For example, if all cleaners are black women, they may be unable to compare their less favourable treatment with a white, male cleaner but they may be able to show that such a person would be treated differently because of a general practice to discriminate against black women.

Normally, claims of direct discrimination are brought by an individual who suffers a disadvantage, but a recent judgment indicates the possibilities of using direct discrimination in a wider context. The Centre for Equal Opportunities and Opposition to Racism, a body charged with the promotion of equal treatment in Belgium, took action against an employer who had stated publicly that he was not going to recruit persons of certain races, seeking a declaration that these statements breached the Belgian laws implementing the Race Directive. Significantly, there was no evidence that the employer had in fact rejected a job applicant on the basis of race or ethnicity, so the question arose whether on the facts the defendant had acted illegally.

Case C-54/07 *Centrum voor gelijkheid van kansen en voor racismebestrijding v Firma Feryn NV* [2008] ECR I-5187

22. It is true that ... Article 2(2) of Directive 2000/43 defines direct discrimination as a situation in which one person 'is treated' less favourably than another is, has been or would be treated in a comparable situation on grounds of racial or ethnic origin. Likewise, Article 7 of that directive requires Member States to ensure that judicial procedures are available to 'all persons who consider themselves wronged by failure to apply the principle of equal treatment to them' and to public interest bodies bringing judicial proceedings 'on behalf or in support of the complainant'.

23. Nevertheless, it cannot be inferred from this that the lack of an identifiable complainant leads to the conclusion that there is no direct discrimination within the meaning of Directive 2000/43. The aim of that directive, as stated in recital 8 of its preamble, is 'to foster conditions for a socially inclusive labour market'. For that purpose, Article 3(1)(a) states that the directive covers, inter alia, selection criteria and recruitment conditions.

---

[142] Race Directive, article 2(1); Framework Directive, article 2(2)(a); Recast Equal Treatment Directive, article 2(1)(a).

24. The objective of fostering conditions for a socially inclusive labour market would be hard to achieve if the scope of Directive 2000/43 were to be limited to only those cases in which an unsuccessful candidate for a post, considering himself to be the victim of direct discrimination, brought legal proceedings against the employer.
25. The fact that an employer declares publicly that it will not recruit employees of a certain ethnic or racial origin, something which is clearly likely to strongly dissuade certain candidates from submitting their candidature and, accordingly, to hinder their access to the labour market, constitutes direct discrimination in respect of recruitment within the meaning of Directive 2000/43. The existence of such direct discrimination is not dependent on the identification of a complainant who claims to have been the victim.

While the ruling might be criticised for not explaining that the rights of those discriminated against trump the defendant's freedom of expression, this ruling serves to emphasise the role both of national equality bodies in promoting the rights of victims of discrimination, and of strategic litigation.[143] In a subsequent ruling, the Court of Justice stretched this precedent a little further. The facts involved a shareholder of a football club in Romania, who presented himself as the club's patron. He made a statement suggesting he would not recruit gay players. Asociaţia-ACCEPT (a Romanian lesbian, gay, bisexual and transgender organisation) brought charges to the Romanian anti-discrimination council against the shareholder and the club. The club argued that since the person who made the statement had no role in recruitment (unlike the director in *Feryn*) then there should be no liability attaching to it. The Court disagreed. In its view, in such a situation the club should have publicly distanced itself from the statement. What counted was the perception of the public.[144]

Clearly, this line of cases facilitates strategic public interest litigation by activist organisations: there is no need to find a victim, and it is easy to infer discrimination. Shifting the onus on to the employer forces that person to make visible changes to its policy to remove the perception that it has a discriminatory policy, and such change is beneficial to all.

(ii) Indirect discrimination

(a) Concept of indirect discrimination

Indirect discrimination takes place where, even though the conditions for access to employment appear on their face to be non-discriminatory, they do in fact exclude a particular group. For example, a rule that employees must work all of Friday indirectly discriminates against Muslims who require time off for prayers. Note that by prohibiting indirect discrimination, the law safeguards the interests of an entire group, not just those of the individual plaintiff, because a finding that one person is indirectly discriminated against requires that the employer change the unlawful working practice, which benefits everyone in the underrepresented group. The discrimination Directives provide a uniform definition:

---

[143] According to some, encouraging this kind of litigation was precisely one of the factors behind the design of the Race Directive. See E. Evans Case and T. E. Givens, 'Re-engineering Legal Opportunity Structures in the European Union? The Starting Line Group and the Politics of the Racial Equality Directive' (2010) 48(2) *JCMS* 221.

[144] Case C-81/12 *Asociaţia ACCEPT* v *Consiliul Naţional pentru Combaterea Discriminării*, Judgment of 23 April 2013, paras. 50–1.

indirect discrimination shall be taken to occur where an apparently neutral provision, criterion or practice would put persons of [the protected group] at a particular disadvantage compared with other persons, unless that provision, criterion or practice is objectively justified by a legitimate aim and the means of achieving that aim are appropriate and necessary.[145]

The Court of Justice, in the sex discrimination case law, requires that the plaintiff demonstrate indirect discrimination by way of statistics indicating that a considerably smaller percentage of women than men are able to satisfy the condition.[146] This has raised some questions about what 'considerably smaller' means. The new legislation removes this stumbling block because there is no requirement to show that a practice affects a significantly higher proportion of persons of a particular group. Instead, it is enough to show a disadvantage for the protected group in a statistically significant way. Moreover, it is also sufficient to demonstrate that an apparently neutral provision *would* put a person at a particular disadvantage. This can be particularly valuable in cases where the ethnic minority population is small and there is little statistical information on ethnic minorities. Proof of a particular disadvantage creates a prima facie case of discrimination, and it is for the employer to justify his practices.

It bears emphasising that indirect discrimination is actually the more powerful instrument to protect equality, because it requires employers to change their working methods to accommodate the needs of those belonging to excluded groups. While direct discrimination is an individual wrong requiring a discrete remedy, indirect discrimination requires more from the employer, which, according to Somek, goes to the heart of what discrimination law should protect.

A. Somek *Engineering Equality: An Essay in European Anti-discrimination Law* (Oxford, Oxford University Press, 2011) 181–2

Usually, people experience situations of unequal treatment as situations that they cannot alter. Therefore, they decide to adapt. They may undertake efforts to pass as members of the preferred group (in the twentieth century, for example, by joining a political party) or cover up aspects of themselves which they fear to be stigmatizing (for example, religious beliefs)....Some experience extreme hardship and decide to revolt against the unequal allocation of the pains of adaptation. The question arises then—sometimes as a question concerning 'responsibility'—of who has to come towards whom. Do the structures of social cooperation have to reach out to those left behind or does it fall on the latter to 'improve'? Exemplifications of the problem abound. Women who find themselves relatively disadvantaged when working in part-time jobs or when ineligible for higher termination payments would have had a choice not to procreate and not to assume caregiving responsibilities; alternatively, they could have fitted their lives into the existing organization of full-time employment and delegated much of their maternal labour to nannies and maids; or women could have even tried to improve their performance as both professionals and caregivers. It is understood, of course, by anti-discrimination law that any of these alternatives would ask too much from women because it is reasonable to expect from employers to treat part-time and full-time employees alike...

---

[145] Recast Equal Treatment Directive, article 2(1)(b) Race Directive, article 2(1)(b); Framework Directive, article 2(2)(b) (although note special provisos for disability discrimination, discussed further below).

[146] Case C-167/97 *R* v *Secretary of State for Employment ex parte Nicole Seymour-Smith and Laura Perez* [1999] ECR I-623, para. 60.

These examples, facile as they may seem, demonstrate how protection from discrimination lifts from persons pressures of adaptation. These pressures range from ordinary learning and ducking all the way down to retreating from the scene owing to the denial of opportunities. Whereas in the latter, most drastic, case the threat is one of exclusion, cases that concern passing or hiding involve the damage that market-based inclusion itself inflicts on human life.

Here Somek suggests an alternative and potentially more robust vision for anti-discrimination law. However, implementing this approach within the framework of the EU is near impossible. First, we can note how in *Coleman* (discussed above) the Court of Justice said that the obligation to make accommodation for disability in the Framework Directive is only applicable insofar as it facilitates the recruitment of disabled workers, and the Court said nothing about the duties employees would have on the facts at hand. Furthermore, the defences discussed below pit equality against market objectives.

(b) Legitimate aim defence

A specific defence applies in indirect discrimination cases. The discrimination Directives codify the case law: first, there must be a legitimate aim; secondly, the means to achieve the aim must be appropriate; and thirdly, the means to achieve that end must be necessary.[147] This means that if there is a less discriminatory alternative practice that achieves the same goal, the defence is defeated.[148]

Two questions remain: first, what reasons can be put forward to justify discrimination? And secondly, how much discretion is afforded to the defendant? Many of the decisions where the Court of Justice has had to confront these questions concern provisions which give lesser benefits to part-time workers. These constitute indirect sex discrimination because women are more likely to be part-time workers. It seems that lesser benefits may be justified if they are an incentive for persons to take up full-time employment,[149] or if the employer wishes to ensure that there are staff working at all times and part-time workers tend not to want to work at weekends or evenings.[150] The Court has also insisted that there must be convincing evidence that indirect discrimination is necessary to obtain the results sought and that generalisations about certain types of worker are insufficient.[151] The defence may also be invoked by the Member State to defend indirectly discriminatory legislation, but here the Court of Justice has given Member States greater room to apply the defence, holding that there is a justification when the law meets a necessary aim of a state's social policy and the measures are 'suitable' (not necessary, as in the case of businesses trying to rely on the defence) for attaining the aim.[152]

---

[147] Case 170/84 *Bilka-Kaufhaus GmbH* v *Karin Weber von Hartz* [1986] ECR 1607.

[148] M. Connolly, 'Discrimination Law: Justification, Alternative Measures and Defences Based on Sex' (2001) 30 *ILJ* 311, 318.

[149] Case 96/80 *Jenkins* v *Kingsgate (Clothing Productions) Ltd* [1981] ECR 911.

[150] Case 170/84 *Bilka-Kaufhaus GmbH* v *Karin Weber von Hartz* [1986] ECR 1607.

[151] 6 See e.g. Case 171/88 *Rinner-Kühn* v *FWW Spezial-Gebaudereingung* [1989] ECR 2743; Case C-184/89 *Nimz* v *Freie und Hansestadt Hamburg* [1991] ECR I-297; Case C-167/97 *Seymour-Smith and Perez* [1999] ECR I-00623, para. 75–6.

[152] Case 171/88 *Rinner-Kühn* v *FWW Spezial-Gebaudereingung* [1989] ECR 2743. See also Case C-322/98 *Kachelmann* v *Bankhaus Hermann Lampe KG* [2000] ECR I-7505.

For example, the Court suggested that legislation which exempts small businesses from giving part-time workers certain employment rights could be justified given the economic importance of small firms.[153] Given that the discrimination Directives codify the stricter standard set out in the case law, Member States may in future find it more difficult to benefit from the defence.

(iii) Harassment

There is a broad consensus that harassment is a harmful workplace practice, which can range from unpleasant remarks or physical violence directed at a person to the creation of a work environment that is intimidating or humiliating for a group (for example, displaying pornography in the workplace).[154] The Commission recommended that Member States promote awareness of sexual harassment and implement a code of practice.[155] However, the Commission was dissatisfied with the progress made by Member States,[156] and harassment is now covered in the discrimination Directives. It is not clear why harassment constitutes discrimination, however.[157] In the context of American and UK law, the lack of a specific statute prohibiting discrimination led the courts to extend the meaning of discrimination to encompass sexual harassment.[158] In contrast, in some Member States (for example, Ireland, France, Germany and Sweden) harassment is a discrete wrong.[159] The EU follows the American and UK approach and locates harassment in discrimination legislation, and there are differences between the approach taken by the Framework Directive and Race Directive, on the one hand, and the Recast Equal Treatment Directive, on the other. The former provide:

> Harassment shall be deemed to be a form of discrimination...when unwanted conduct related [to any of the protected grounds except sex] takes place with the purpose or effect of violating the dignity of a person and of creating an intimidating, hostile, degrading, humiliating or offensive environment. In this context, the concept of harassment may be defined in accordance with the national laws and practice of the Member States.[160]

The final sentence is problematic. If it were not there, then we would be able to say that the Directives define harassment in a way that excludes the need to show discrimination. The second sentence, however, adds a complication because it may be read to suggest that the definition of harassment is a matter for Member States, which allows each to water down the

---

[153] Case C-189/91 *Kirsammer-Hack* v *Sidal* [1993] ECR I-6185. See T. Hervey, 'Small Business Exclusion in German Dismissal Law' (1994) 23 *ILJ* 267.

[154] European Commission, *Sexual Harassment at the Workplace in the European Union* (1998).

[155] Commission Recommendation 92/131/EEC of 27 November 1991 on the protection of the dignity of women and men at work, [1992] OJ L49/1.

[156] Communication Initiating the Second-Stage Consultation of Management and Labour on the Prevention of Sexual Harassment at Work, SEC(97)568 final.

[157] J. Dine and B. Watt, 'Sexual Harassment: Moving Away from Discrimination' (1995) 58 *MLR* 343.

[158] *Porcelli* v *Strathclyde Regional Council* [1986] ICR 564; *Meritor Savings Bank* v *Vinston* 477 U.S. 57 (1986). See generally, Fredman, n. 39 above, 320–30.

[159] Irish Employment Act 1998, s. 26; French Labour Code, art. L.122–46; German Act for the Protection of Employees against Sexual Harassment 1994. For comment, see A. C. Saguy, 'French and American Lawyers Define Sexual Harassment' in C. A. MacKinnon and R. B. Siegal (eds.), *Directions in Sexual Harassment Law* (New Haven, CT, Yale University Press, 2004); S. Baer, 'Dignity or Equality? Responses to Workplace Harassment in European, German, and U.S. Law' in C. A. MacKinnon and R. B. Siegal (eds.), *Directions in Sexual Harassment Law* (New Haven, CT, Yale University Press, 2004).

[160] Race Directive, article 2(3); Framework Directive, article 2(3).

meaning of harassment. In practical terms then, a Member State might be able to implement the Directives by legislating that the plaintiff prove that the harassment was because of the plaintiff's attribute (for example, race or religion), allowing an employer to escape liability if he shows that he harassed others of a different race or religion. Under this approach, a wide range of forms of discrimination may not be caught; for example, if an employer displays a poster degrading black persons, this would not constitute discriminatory harassment because all persons would be offended by it. In contrast, article 2 of the Recast Equal Treatment Directive avoids this by providing that harassment is wrongful per se.

H. Samuels, 'A Defining Moment: A Feminist Perspective on the Law of Sexual Harassment in the Workplace in the Light of the Equal Treatment Amendment Directive' (2004) 12 *Feminist Legal Studies* 181, 203–4

One of the most important changes that the [Recast Equal Treatment Directive] makes is to deem sexual harassment as discrimination, which eliminates the need for a comparator of the opposite sex...It also resonates with the approach taken with regard to pregnancy by the European Court of Justice in *Webb* where dismissal of a woman on the grounds of pregnancy was deemed to be discrimination. This is an important development that denies a defence to the 'equal opportunity harasser' who is accused of harassing men and women equally...Despite the fact that the comparator has been removed in sexual harassment cases, the male standard may still prevail if women have to establish that the conduct complained of was not reasonable. The complete elimination of the male comparator will also depend on the way in which the courts are likely to interpret concepts such as reasonableness and unwelcomeness. If men can argue that behaviour that is offensive to women is reasonable then the law on sexual harassment will be ineffective in tackling harassment. These imprecise concepts may well provide opportunities for courts and tribunals to reintroduce sexist ideas on acceptable behaviour in the workplace and women's response to such conduct.

The notion of sexual harassment in the Recast Equal Treatment Directive is drawn from the American case law, which identified as harassment conduct that creates a 'hostile environment'. Unfortunately, the discrimination Directives do not follow the American approach to harassment completely because omitted is a second method of harassment which the American courts have called 'quid pro quo' sexual harassment where the employer demands sexual favours in exchange for granting the victim a better position or other working conditions. Moreover, the Directives leave it for each Member State to determine the question of whether the employer is liable for harassment carried out by an employee or a client against the victim. Reducing the scope for vicarious liability can have a detrimental impact on the victim's right to meaningful compensation.

(iv) Defences

(a) Genuine occupational requirements

It has been argued that there should be no basis for the defendant to justify directly discriminatory practices.[161] However, outside of the equal pay context, the discrimination Directives

---

[161] Ellis and Watson, n. 5044 above, 111–13.

provide that differences in treatment on the basis of sex, race or ethnic origin, age, sexual orientation, religion or belief or disability may be justified:

> where, by reason of the nature of the particular occupational activities concerned or of the context in which they are carried out, such a characteristic constitutes a genuine and determining occupational requirement.[162]

Examples include hiring a male actor for a man's role, or banning men from the profession of midwifery.[163] The Preamble to the Recast Equal Treatment Directive cites the case law of the Court of Justice, which provides that in applying this defence it must be shown that the objective sought was legitimate, and that the discrimination was proportionate to the objective being sought.[164] Arguably, those principles also apply to the other discrimination Directives.

The application of this provision can be explored by considering the Court of Justice's approach to laws restricting women's access to employment in the army. In *Kreil*, German law forbade women from serving in military positions involving the use of arms. It meant women could only be engaged in the medical and military music services. An attempt was made to justify the exclusion on the basis that it was necessary to guarantee public security, but this was rejected on two grounds. First, the Court held that discrimination on the basis of a genuine occupational requirement applied to specific activities and could not exclude women from almost all military positions.[165] Secondly, the Court found that arms training was provided to all army personnel, including for those services to which women had access, thus the restriction was disproportionate.[166] In contrast, the exclusion of women from a segment of the armed forces was upheld in *Sirdar*.[167] The plaintiff wished to work as a chef in the Royal Marines but this regiment had a policy that every member should be able to fight in a commando unit whatever their rank, and used this to justify not hiring women for any position. The Court of Justice held that because of the specific role played by the Royal Marines in the United Kingdom's armed forces (inter alia, that they are a small force and intended to be the first line of attack), it was legitimate to exclude women if this was seen as necessary to maintain the effectiveness of this military unit. The Court in these cases sought to balance the application of EU law with the rights of the Member States to protect their security interests, and while some have considered that the Court has drawn an appropriate balance by banning blanket exclusions of women,[168] it has been criticised because the Court accepted without analysis the claim that women would not be able to join men in commando units.[169] There is a risk, therefore, that the 'genuine occupational requirements' exception can be used to retain gender and other stereotyped roles in employment practices.[170] On the other hand, these two cases addressed a highly sensitive field where national policy clashed with sex equality rights, and the Court may adopt a more demanding stance where a private employer wishes to justify a discriminatory practice (e.g. if

---

[162] Article 14(2) Recast Equal Treatment Directive, Article 4 Race Directive, Article 4(1) Framework Directive.
[163] Case 165/82 *Commission* v *United Kingdom* [1983] ECR 3431.
[164] Recast Equal Treatment Directive, recital 19.
[165] C-285/98 *Kreil* v *Germany* [2000] ECR I-69, paragraph 27.
[166] C-285/98 *Kreil* v *Germany* [2000] ECR I-69, paragraph 28.
[167] Case C-273/97 *Sirdar* v *Army Board and Secretary of State for Defence* [1999] ECR I-7403.
[168] P. Koutrakos, 'EC Law and Equal Treatment in the Armed Forces' (2000) 25 *EL Rev.* 433.
[169] E. Ellis, 'The Recent Jurisprudence of the Court of Justice in the Field of Sex Equality' (2000) 37 *CML Rev.* 1403, 1414–5.
[170] See also Case 222/84 *Johnston* v *Chief Constable of the Royal Ulster Constabulary* [1986] ECR 1651.

the owner of a Chinese restaurant tries to defend a policy of only hiring Oriental waiters in his restaurant to maintain an authentic atmosphere), especially as the Preambles indicate that this defence applies in 'very limited circumstances'.[171] It remains to be seen whether its application in *Wolf* to justify a minimum recruitment age of 30 years for firefighters leads to a more widespread use of the defence. The concern here is that the Court appeared to accept too easily the stereotype that older persons are unable to perform the roles this job entails.[172]

Applying this defence in the disability context means that an employer does not have to hire a person when the disability prevents the person from carrying out an essential part of the job, and where the employer is unable to make any modifications to the workplace to accommodate the disabled person. Sexual orientation may be a genuine occupational requirement that allows an employer to select a person or choose not to select a person on the basis of her sexual orientation. It is likely that this will be invoked only rarely: for example, a centre that offers counselling to gay and lesbian persons might consider it necessary to have as its chair someone who is homosexual.[173] In most other instances (for example, banning gay persons from the army), it is likely that the ban would be disproportionate.[174] Nevertheless, the possibility of establishing a genuine occupational requirement in the context of sexual orientation discrimination raises two difficult issues. The first is that some argue that one's sexuality is not fixed but fluid, as persons may experiment with their sexuality over time. On this view, it may be asked whether a requirement of homosexuality for a position in a centre advising gay and lesbian persons would not be met by a candidate who in the past has had heterosexual relationships.[175] The second problem is that the genuine occupational requirement defence means that the prospective employee has to disclose his sexuality. There is a tension between this and the point noted earlier that a person may be reluctant to disclose her sexuality.

(b) Other defences

The Framework Directive contains an additional set of defences: one of general application and some that are limited to one specific ground.

Framework Directive, article 2(5)

This Directive shall be without prejudice to measures laid down by national law which, in a democratic society, are necessary for public security, for the maintenance of public order and the prevention of criminal offences, for the protection of health and for the protection of the rights and freedoms of others.

---

[171] Recital 18 Race Directive, Recital 23 Framework Directive.

[172] Case C-229/08 *Wolf* ECR [2010] I-1, paragraph 41. For comment, see D. Schiek, 'Age Discrimination Before the ECJ: Conceptual and Theoretical Issues' (2011) 48 *CMLRev.* 777, 791.

[173] A view taken by the United Kingdom's Advisory, Conciliation and Arbitration Service, 'Sexual Orientation and the Workplace: A Guide for Employees and Employers', Appendix 1 available at http://www.acas.org.uk/CHttpHandler.ashx?id=105&tp=0 (visited on 19 December 2013).

[174] In *Smith and Grady* v *United Kingdom* [1999] IRLR 734, the ECtHR held that banning gay persons from the armed forces was disproportionate and infringed the individuals' right to private life. Arguably, the interpretation of the Directive by national courts and the Court of Justice has to have regard to safeguarding fundamental rights, so a similar conclusion is likely in the EU context.

[175] H. Oliver, 'Sexual Orientation Discrimination: Perceptions, Definitions and Genuine Occupational Requirements' (2004) 33 *ILJ* 1, 18–20.

Tolerance of others is the norm in liberal society but the rationale for this defence is that acts which undermine the moral and political values of the state must be suppressed.[176] Seen in this light, the defence is necessary and it may be surprising that a similar provision is not present in other Directives. The defence seems to have been inserted at the insistence of the United Kingdom, which wished to make it clear that measures to 'protect the public from the activities of religious cults or individuals with a disabling illness such as paranoid schizophrenia which could make them a danger to others would not be prohibited under the Directive'.[177] However, the defence might have a greater impact. In *Petersen*, for example, a maximum working age of 68 for dentists was challenged. The Court of Justice was willing to consider two justifications under article 2(5): first, the risks to patient heath if operated on by a dentist over the age of 68; and secondly, the financial balance of the statutory health insurance scheme, which is maintained by forcibly retiring older dentists so that the costs of running dental services is lower than if they were able to remain on the payroll. On the facts, the Court of Justice was not convinced that the risk to patient health was maintained by the legislation, because of the exceptions to the mandatory retirement rule. It left it to the national court to consider the financial balance of the scheme.[178] For present purposes, what matters is that the Court appears to apply the exception beyond the narrow confines for which it had been designed. This is unhelpful because, as we explain below, there is a specific exception for age discrimination, and to find an alternative angle from which this may be justified is not conducive to legal certainty.

The first specific defence applies to religious organisations and was inserted at the request of some Member States, in particular the Irish Government, concerned that the Directive may hamper the employment practices of religious institutions.[179]

Framework Directive, article 4(2)

Member States may maintain national legislation in force at the date of adoption of this Directive or provide for future legislation incorporating national practices existing at the date of adoption of this Directive pursuant to which, in the case of occupational activities within churches and other public or private organisations the ethos of which is based on religion or belief, a difference of treatment based on a person's religion or belief shall not constitute discrimination where, by reason of the nature of these activities or of the context in which they are carried out, a person's religion or belief constitute a genuine, legitimate and justified occupational requirement, having regard to the organisation's ethos. This difference of treatment shall be implemented taking account of Member States' constitutional provisions and principles, as well as the general principles of Community law, and should not justify discrimination on another ground.

Provided that its provisions are otherwise complied with, this Directive shall thus not prejudice the right of churches and other public or private organisations, the ethos of which is based on religion or belief, acting in conformity with national constitutions and laws, to require individuals working for them to act in good faith and with loyalty to the organisation's ethos.

---

[176] S. Mendus, *Toleration and the Limits of Liberalism* (London, Macmillan, 1989) 8–9.
[177] House of Lords Select Committee on the EU, 'The EU Framework Directive on Discrimination', Session 2000–01, 4th Report, HL Paper 13, paragraph 37.
[178] Case C-341/08 *Petersen v Berufungsausschuss für Zahnärzte für den Bezirk Westfalen-Lippe* [2010] ECR I-47.
[179] Bell, above n. 4, 154–5.

The exception is in conformity with the autonomy that states tend to grant to religious organi-sations, although it may be argued that such organisations could be protected by the genuine occupational requirement defence so that article 4 is unnecessary. It has been noted that the article is the result of lobbying by religious groups who wished to have a wider exclusion for religious organisations,[180] but it remains to be seen how far-reaching this provision is. The first paragraph seems intended to justify not hiring a Buddhist as a Catholic priest, but the second paragraph seems to allow Member States considerable flexibility to discriminate against the entire workforce. The US Supreme Court, for example, has shown considerable deference to religious organisations under comparable legislation. In *Amos*, a Mormon Church terminated the employment of a gymnasium building engineer who was not a Mormon and who had failed to obtain a 'Temple recommend' which is issued only to individuals who observe the Church's standards in such matters as regular church attendance, tithing and abstinence from coffee, tea, alcohol and tobacco. While it might be argued that his job was unrelated to the religious activities of his employer, the Supreme Court declined to interfere with the decision of the church, because:

> it is a significant burden on a religious organization to require it, on pain of substantial liability, to predict which of its activities a secular court will consider religious. The line is hardly a bright one, and an organization might understandably be concerned that a judge would not understand its religious tenets and sense of mission. Fear of potential liability might affect the way an organization carried out what it understood to be its religious mission.[181]

Such judicial deference on the part of the Court of Justice would risk excluding religious or-ganisations from their obligations under the Framework Directive altogether.[182]

A second exception provides that the Framework Directive does not apply to discrimination on the grounds of age and disability in the armed forces.[183] This blanket exception contrasts with the approach taken by the Court of Justice when reviewing sex discrimination in the armed forces, where disproportionate sex discrimination was prohibited.

Lastly, the Framework Directive has a special defence in cases of age discrimination de-signed to reflect the link between discrimination law and national employment policies.

Framework Directive, article 6(1)

1. Notwithstanding Article 2(2), Member States may provide that differences of treatment on grounds of age shall not constitute discrimination, if, within the context of national law, they are objectively and reasonably justified by a legitimate aim, including legitimate employment policy, labour market and vocational training objectives, and if the means of achieving that aim are appropriate and necessary.

    Such differences of treatment may include, among others:

    (a) the setting of special conditions on access to employment and vocational training, employment and occupation, including dismissal and remuneration conditions, for young people, older workers and

---

[180] *Ibid.* 117.
[181] *Corporation of the Presiding Bishop of the Church of Jesus Christ of Latter-Day Saints* v *Amos* 483 U.S. 327, 337 (1987).
[182] For a wide-ranging analysis of the difficulties in reconciling the demands of liberal society with religious doctrine, see B. Barry, *Culture and Equality* (London, Polity Press, 2001) Chapter 5.
[183] Article 3(4) Framework Directive.

persons with caring responsibilities in order to promote their vocational integration or ensure their protection;

(b) the fixing of minimum conditions of age, professional experience or seniority in service for access to employment or to certain advantages linked to employment;

(c) the fixing of a maximum age for recruitment which is based on the training requirements of the post in question or the need for a reasonable period of employment before retirement.

The significance of this defence has become increasingly prominent as Member States face significant youth unemployment as a result of the ongoing economic crisis. Member States pursue two kinds of policies that discriminate on the grounds of age: they try and retain older workers at the expense of younger ones, or they may impose compulsory retirement on older workers to facilitate the entry of younger workers (this is often referred to as inter-generational solidarity). At the time of writing the legality of these policies is the issue which has been referred to the Court of Justice most frequently. The case law is not wholly consistent.[184]

In *Mangold*, the Court found that legislation making the conclusion of fixed-term contracts with older workers easier was based on a legitimate objective: 'to promote the vocational integration of unemployed older workers, in so far as they encounter considerable difficulties in finding work'.[185] But the Court ruled that the law went beyond what was necessary to achieve that aim by taking into consideration only age and not the personal circumstances of the individual or the conditions in the labour market.[186] This suggested a strict standard of review. However, when the Court has been faced with schemes of compulsory employment termination for older workers, a less searching kind of scrutiny appears to have been applied. In *Rosenbladt*, for example, the Court of Justice considered a challenge to a scheme (established as a result of collective bargaining between employers and workers) which made retirement compulsory at the age of 65. The Court held that one must test whether the measure in question is appropriate and necessary to meet a legitimate aim.

Case C–45/09 *Gisela Rosenbladt v Oellerking Gebäudereinigungsges mbH* [2010] ECR I–9391

62. The Court has held that clauses on automatic termination of employment contracts of employees who are eligible to receive a retirement pension may be justified in the context of a national policy seeking to promote better access to employment, by means of better distribution of work between the generations and aims of that kind must, in principle, be considered to justify 'objectively and reasonably', 'within the context of national law', as provided in the first subparagraph of Article 6(1) of Directive 2000/78, a difference in treatment on the ground of age prescribed by Member States. It follows that objectives such as those described by the referring court are 'legitimate' within the meaning of that provision....

---

[184] In addition to the cases referred to in the text, see: C-227/04P *Lindorfer* [2007] ECR I-6767, Case C-411/05 *Félix Palacios de la Villa* v *Cortefiel Servicios SA* [2007] ECR I-8531.

[185] Case C-144/04 *Werner Mangold* v *Rüdiger Helm* [2005] ECR I-9981, paragraph 59. P. Skidmore, 'The European Employment Strategy and Labour Law: a German Case Study' (2004) 29 *EL Rev.* 52

[186] Case C-144/04 *Werner Mangold* v *Rüdiger Helm* [2005] ECR I-9981, paragraphs 64–5.

The Court of Justice then considered the appropriateness of this policy.

67. In the light of the assessment made by the referring court, it must be observed that the clause on the automatic termination of employment contracts at issue in the main proceedings is the result of an agreement negotiated between employees' and employers' representatives exercising their right to bargain collectively which is recognised as a fundamental right. The fact that the task of striking a balance between their respective interests is entrusted to the social partners offers considerable flexibility, as each of the parties may, where appropriate, opt not to adopt the agreement.

68. By guaranteeing workers a certain stability of employment and, in the long term, the promise of foreseeable retirement, while offering employers a certain flexibility in the management of their staff, the clause on automatic termination of employment contracts is thus the reflection of a balance between diverging but legitimate interests, against a complex background of employment relationships closely linked to political choices in the area of retirement and employment.

69. Accordingly, in the light of the wide discretion granted to the social partners at national level in choosing not only to pursue a given aim in the area of social policy, but also in defining measures to implement it, it does not appear unreasonable for the social partners to take the view that a measure such as Paragraph 19(8) of the RTV [framework collective agreement for commercial cleaning sector employees] may be appropriate for achieving the aims set out above. ...

Finally, the Court of Justice considered whether the measure was necessary.

73. In order to examine whether the measure at issue in the main proceedings goes beyond what is necessary for achieving its objective and unduly prejudices the interests of workers who reach the age of 65, when they may obtain liquidation of their pension rights, that measure must be viewed against its legislative background and account must be taken both of the hardship it may cause to the persons concerned and of the benefits derived from it by society in general and the individuals who make up society.

74. ...German employment law does not prevent a person who has reached the age at which he is eligible for payment of a pension from continuing to work. Furthermore, according to those explanations, a worker in that position continues to enjoy protection from discrimination on grounds of age under the AGG. The referring court made clear, in that connection, that the AGG [General Law on Equal Treatment] prevents a person in Mrs Rosenbladt's position, after termination of her employment contract on the ground that she has reached retirement age, from being refused employment, either by her former employer or by a third party, on a ground related to her age.

75. Viewed against that background, the termination by operation of law of an employment contract as a result of a measure such as Paragraph 19(8) of the RTV does not have the automatic effect of forcing the persons concerned to withdraw definitively from the labour market. It follows that that provision does not establish a mandatory scheme of automatic retirement... It does not prevent a worker who wishes to do so, for example, for financial reasons, from continuing to work beyond retirement age. It does not deprive employees who have reached retirement age of protection from discrimination on grounds of age where they wish to continue to work and seek a new job.

The Court of Justice is not wholly deferential to national policy; indeed, in some cases it has found that measures that discriminate against older workers may not be justified.[187] However, the approach is not without problems. First, it appears to defer to collective bargaining, which is different from the position taken in sex discrimination (where instead one sees the Court noting the risk that collective agreements may also be discriminatory). It thus substitutes a close look as to whether the measure in question is appropriate with a procedural question. On the facts, the national court had been sceptical as to whether the measure was indeed working to stimulate employment, but the Court deemed this irrelevant. Secondly, when applying the necessity test, the Court does not ask whether the measure is the least restrictive way to achieve the policy objectives at hand, but instead considers if the measure strikes a fair balance between the interests of employers and employees. Again, it is instructive to note that the referring court appeared to be more concerned about whether there were less onerous measures for the welfare of the employees. It is not clear that this approach really safeguards the interests of the claimant, who will not find it easy to secure employment after compulsory termination.[188]

Furthermore, with two different standards of review (a stricter one as in *Mangold*; a looser one as in *Rosenbladt*) there is a risk of inconsistency in how similar policies are assessed by national courts. More generally, it is not even clear how best to resolve the matter: the difficult balance between promoting youth employment and safeguarding an elderly workforce means that Member States are operating in a field where there is no right answer. However, it would be a step too far to conclude that the Court of Justice should just defer to national policies. A closer look as to whether the relevant retirement policy is well designed to achieve the ends it is said to achieve would be desirable.[189]

(v) Remedies

(a) Procedures

Rights are meaningless without remedies, and the discrimination Directives seek to enhance the plaintiffs' prospects for success, especially in the light of evidence that litigation under the sex equality legislation has proven difficult.[190] A common procedure is prescribed in the Directives.[191]

> **Framework Directive, article 9**
>
> 1. Member States shall ensure that judicial and/or administrative procedures, including where they deem it appropriate conciliation procedures, for the enforcement of obligations under this Directive are available to all persons who consider themselves wronged by failure to apply the principle of equal

---

[187] E.g. Case C-499/08 *Ingeniørforeningen i Danmark, acting on behalf of Ole Andersen* v *Region Syddanma* [2010] ECR I-9343.

[188] Kilpatrick, above n.19, 290–8.

[189] See the valuable guidance offered by E. Dewhurst, 'Intergenerational Balance, Mandatory Retirement and Age Discrimination in Europe: How Can the ECJ better support national courts in finding a balance between the generations?' (2013) 50 *CMLRev.*1333.

[190] See J. Blom, B. Fitzpatrick, J. Gregory, R. Knegt and U. O'Hare, *The Utilisation of Sex Equality Litigation in the Member States of the European Community*, V/782/96-EN (Report to the Equal Opportunities Unit of D-G V, 1995).

[191] Article 7 Race Directive, Article 17, 20 Recast Equal Treatment Directive.

2. Member States shall ensure that associations, organisations or other legal entities which have, in accordance with the criteria laid down by their national law, a legitimate interest in ensuring that the provisions of this Directive are complied with, may engage, either on behalf or in support of the complainant, with his or her approval, in any judicial and/or administrative procedure provided for the enforcement of obligations under this Directive.
3. Paragraphs 1 and 2 are without prejudice to national rules relating to time limits for bringing actions as regards the principle of equality of treatment.

The discrimination Directives do not interfere with national procedures regarding the appropriate forum to hear claims (thus the procedure may be judicial and/or administrative) and time limits remain to be set according to national law. The major innovation is article 9(2), which empowers organisations to offer support and advice to the victim, which can be decisive for the success of a claim. These organisations are also able to select and support cases likely to set significant precedents and have repercussions for all employers, benefiting future victims of discrimination.[192] However, these organisations have limited budgets and evidence from the United Kingdom suggests that little of it is spent on assisting claimants.[193] Moreover, the Directives do not require that these organisations should be empowered to bring a claim directly. Finally, Member States may determine which groups have a legitimate interest, which can lead to the exclusion of certain influential groups.

An additional procedural advantage is that first provided by the Burden of Proof Directive,[194] and which is now available for all grounds of discrimination.[195]

Framework Directive, article 10

1. Member States shall take such measures as are necessary, in accordance with their national judicial systems, to ensure that, when persons who consider themselves wronged because the principle of equal treatment has not been applied to them establish, before a court or other competent authority, facts from which it may be presumed that there has been direct or indirect discrimination, it shall be for the respondent to prove that there has been no breach of the principle of equal treatment.
2. Paragraph 1 shall not prevent Member States from introducing rules of evidence which are more favourable to plaintiffs.

If the plaintiff establishes a presumption that there has been direct or indirect discrimination, it is for the defendant to prove that there has been no discrimination. This aids the plaintiff considerably because while the presumption may be rebutted, it is very difficult to prove the non-existence of something. The issue was brought up by a Bulgarian court. Having decided

---

[192] On the use of test cases to advance EU law, see Harlow and Rawlings, above n. 62, 282–5.
[193] H. Collins, K. Ewing and E. McColgan, *Labour Law: Text and Materials* (Oxford, Hart, 2005) 332.
[194] Directive 97/80/EC on the burden of proof in the cases of discrimination based on sex, OJ 1998 L14/6, Article 4 as amended by Directive 98/52/EC, OJ 1998 L205/66.
[195] Article 8(1) Race Directive; Article 19 Recast Equal Treatment Directive.

that the statements of a football club's patron that the club would not recruit gay players could render the club liable, the court then asked whether this placed the club in an impossible position: how could they refute the claim? Surely they would not be able to point to evidence of having recruited gay players in the past as this would breach their privacy. Does the Directive then not put the defendant in a corner? The court said that the club could have publicly distanced itself from the statement or by showing that it had in place a recruitment policy aimed at ensuring compliance with the principle of equal treatment.[196] One has to be naïve to believe that this is meaningful: well-advised companies now have the tools to draft a set of documents that will protect them against similar claims. In this light the views of some that this article would have a deterrent effect seem somewhat optimistic.[197]

The discrimination Directives also extend the scope of protection in two ways: first, the employer's duties extend beyond the period of employment (for example, the employer must provide a past employee a reference).[198] Secondly, the Directives protect plaintiffs from reprisals once they initiate a claim, a significant provision in that many who are successful in discrimination cases experience difficulties in finding employment.[199] The Directives codify the Court of Justice's case law on victimisation.[200]

Framework Directive, article 11[201]

Member States shall introduce into their national legal systems such measures as are necessary to protect employees against dismissal or other adverse treatment by the employer as a reaction to a complaint within the undertaking or to any legal proceedings aimed at enforcing compliance with the principle of equal treatment.

(b) Compensation

The victim of sex discrimination normally has a right to damages. In its case law the Court of Justice has exercised some control over the quantum by indicating that no upper limit may be imposed, except in cases where even without sex discrimination the applicant would not have obtained employment because she is less well qualified than the successful applicant,[202] and that the award must be adequate in relation to the damage suffered.[203] These principles have now been codified in the context of sex discrimination claims.

---

[196] *Asociaţia ACCEPT*, n. 144 above, paras. 57–8.
[197] D. Chalmers, 'The Mistakes of the Good European?' in S. Fredman (ed.), *Discrimination and Human Rights: the Case of Racism* (Oxford, Oxford University Press, 2001) 216–17.
[198] Article 7(1) Race Directive, Article 9(1) Framework Directive, Article 17(1) Recast Equal Treatment Directive.
[199] A. Leonard, *Pyrrhic Victories: Winning Sex Discrimination and Equal Pay Cases in the Industrial Tribunals 1980–1984* (London, HMSO, 1987).
[200] Case C-185/97 *Coote* v *Granada Hospitality* [1998] ECR I-5199; M. Dougan, 'The Equal Treatment Directive: Retaliation, Remedies and Direct Effect' (1999) 24 *EL Rev.* 664.
[201] Article 9 Race Directive, Article 24 Recast Equal Treatment Directive.
[202] Case C-180/95 *Draehmpaehl* v *Urania Immobilienservice* [1997] ECR I-2195.
[203] Case C-271/91 *Marshall* v *Southampton and South-West Hampshire AHA* [1993] ECR I-4367.

Recast Equal Treatment Directive, article 18

Member States shall introduce into their national legal systems such measures as are necessary to ensure real and effective compensation or reparation as the Member States so determine for the loss and damage sustained by a person injured as a result of discrimination on grounds of sex, in a way which is dissuasive and proportionate to the damage suffered. Such compensation or reparation may not be restricted by the fixing of a prior upper limit, except in cases where the employer can prove that the only damage suffered by an applicant as a result of discrimination within the meaning of this Directive is the refusal to take his/her job application into consideration.

In contrast, the Race Directive and Framework Directives are less prescriptive.

Race Directive, article 15; Framework Directive, article 17

Member States shall lay down the rules on sanctions applicable to infringements of the national provisions adopted pursuant to this Directive and shall take all measures necessary to ensure that they are applied. The sanctions, which may comprise the payment of compensation to the victim, must be effective, proportionate and dissuasive.

However, it may well be that, as in the case of sex discrimination, the Court of Justice will bolster the remedies available by removing national limits like caps on remedies. Moreover, it must not be forgotten that the Article 19 TFEU Directives were implemented by unanimity and the weaker remedial structure may have been necessary to gain agreement. Thus, looking at individual Member States reveals some with more progressive remedies. For instance, in Italy a finding of discrimination may lead to a bar on public tenders. In Italy, Spain and Hungary the findings are published in the press; and in some states like France criminal law applies.[204] Particularly weak regimes may be challenged, for example, those that impose purely symbolic penalties (such as, a reprimand to the defendant) which are not adequate to ensure that the enforcement of the Directive has dissuasive effects.[205]

5 WIDENING THE SCOPE OF EU EQUAL OPPORTUNITIES POLICY

For most commentators, the common core of EU equality law reviewed above is disappointing because it rests on an antiquated approach to discrimination.[206] As Professor Hepple has put it in discussing the Race Directive, the EU's approach borrows from the UK Race Relations Act 1976 and reproduces a model for combating racism which is out of date with modern conceptions about how to address discrimination and integrate excluded groups more fully in society.[207] However, this criticism may be countered by noting that the discrimination

---

[204] V. Guiraudon, 'Equality in the making: implementing European non-discrimination law' (2009) 13 *Citizenship Studies* 527, 536–7.
[205] See the Discussion in *Asociaţia ACCEPT*, above n. 144, paragraphs 60–73.
[206] A. Masselot, 'The New Equal Treatment Directive: Plus ça Change…' (2004) 12 *Feminist Legal Studies* 93, 103.
[207] B. Hepple, 'Race and Law in Fortress Europe' (2004) 67 *MLR* 1.

Directives have to be implemented across a diverse range of jurisdictions, not all of which have engaged seriously with discrimination in the workplace.[208] Thus, as the Commission notes, for some states the Directives 'involved the introduction of an entirely new rights-based approach to anti-discrimination legislation and policy'.[209] In this light, they constitute a necessary starting point, equalising the scope of protection across the European Union.

In this section we consider some of the more innovative means by which EU equality law moves beyond protecting rights in the labour market, and towards a model that might secure the fulfilment of the right to equality in a more effective manner.

(i) Beyond the labour market

In addition to safeguarding rights in the labour market, the Race Directive was the first to forbid discrimination in other fields as well. It has been suggested that this indicates a move to a broader conception of European social law.[210] This seems necessary because confining discrimination law to the labour market disenfranchises many by assuming that the central form of citizenship is manifested by participation in the labour market.

Race Directive, article 3(1)

1. Within the limits of the powers conferred upon the Community, this Directive shall apply to all persons, as regards both the public and private sectors, including public bodies, in relation to:...

   (e) social protection, including social security and health care;

   (f) social advantages;

   (g) education;

   (h) access to and supply of goods and services which are available to the public, including housing.

Thus, EU norms regulate matters like university fees, restrictions on the preparation of Halal meat, the allocation of housing by municipal authorities, employer bans on the playing of rap music because of its misogynistic content and bans on wearing the veil at school.[211] However, there is some uncertainty over the scope of these four categories. In article 3(1)(e), it is not clear whether social security embraces the rules set out in the Social Security Directive 79/7/EC, which applies to sex discrimination. It is not clear to what 'social protection' extends, and how far non-discrimination in health care can be regulated given that the Treaty indicates that the delivery of health care is a matter for the Member States.[212] The reference to 'social advantages' in article 3(1)(f) is drawn from the law on free movement of persons.[213] It includes subsidised public transport, free school meals, unemployment benefits and assistance with funeral costs. On the other hand, some have suggested that because the Race Directive is premised upon equality and not merely encouraging the free movement of workers, the phrase 'social

---

[208] For a critique of French discrimination law, see K. Berthou, 'New Hopes for French Anti-Discrimination Law' (2003) 19 *International Journal of Comparative Labour Law and Industrial Relations* 109.

[209] Green Paper, *Equality and Non-Discrimination in an Enlarged European Union* (May 2004) 11.

[210] M. Bell, 'Beyond European Labour Law? Reflections on the EU Racial Equality Directive' (2002) 8 *ELJ* 384, 387.

[211] Chalmers, above n. 195, 215.   [212] Article 168(7) TFEU.

[213] Regulation 1612/68, OJ Spec. Ed. 1968 L257/2, Article 7(2).

advantages' might be read more widely.[214] In the context of education it is not clear whether the Directive is only about access to school for persons of a given race or whether it can also forbid the teaching of subjects that may be discriminatory (for example, a law requiring schools to teach the virtues of colonisation). Services for the public may include the provision of housing, although it is unclear if this also applies to the provision of private services such as banking, hotels and shops. Moreover, it has been argued that the provision of general public services such as policing should also be included, especially in the light of evidence that the police may discriminate by providing less effective investigations in cases involving racial minorities,[215] as graphically illustrated by the findings of 'institutional racism' in the Stephen Lawrence Inquiry.[216] In sum, the potential for the Race Directive to integrate racial and ethnic minorities by preventing such a potentially wide range of discriminatory practices is undermined by the uncertainty as to the scope of the obligations imposed by the Directive and as to the 'constitutional validity' of the Directive when it comes to health care and housing, which seem to fall outside the EU's competences.[217]

The Race Directive pioneered these measures. In the context of sex discrimination, the Council later agreed a Directive establishing the right of equal treatment in the access to and supply of goods and services.[218]

Directive 2004/113/ EC implementing the principle of equal treatment between men and women in the access to and supply of goods and services, article 3

1. Within the limits of the powers conferred upon the Community, this Directive shall apply to all persons who provide goods and services, which are available to the public irrespective of the person concerned as regards both the public and private sectors, including public bodies, and which are offered outside the area of private and family life and the transactions carried out in this context.

2. This Directive does not prejudice the individual's freedom to choose a contractual partner as long as an individual's choice of contractual partner is not based on that person's sex.

3. This Directive shall not apply to the content of media and advertising nor to education.

The scope of this Directive is narrower than the Race Directive because it does not apply to education, but it is potentially wider because it applies to both public and private services, although the Commission insisted that in this respect the scope of the two Directives is the same.[219] Article 3 also shows how the EU's thinking in this sphere has evolved: the Race Directive was criticised in some quarters for infringing the freedom of contract, thus this Directive is careful to stipulate that the obligation not to discriminate in the provision of services affects freedom of contract only insofar as this is necessary to prevent discrimination.

---

[214] E. Ellis, 'Social Advantages: a New Lease of Life?' (2003) 40 *CML Rev.* 639.

[215] C. Brown, 'The Race Directive: Towards Equality for All the Peoples of Europe?' (2002) 21 *YEL* 195, 215.

[216] W. MacPherson, *Stephen Lawrence Inquiry Report* (Cm 4262-I, 1999). Race Relations (Amendment) Act 2000, s. 1.

[217] Brown, above n. 196, 214–5; M. Bell, 'The New Article 13 EC Treaty: a Sound Basis for European Anti-Discrimination Law?' (1999) 6 *MJ* 5.

[218] Directive 2004/113/ EC of 13 December 2004 implementing the principle of equal treatment between men and women in the access to and supply of goods and services, OJ 2004 L373/37.

[219] COM(2003)657, 13.

One of the criticisms of the 2004 Directive was that the evidence base on which the legislation had been implemented was weak, and insufficient attention had been paid to the needs of certain industries.[220] In proposing a similar Directive for other protected groups, the Commission has consulted more broadly, but at the time of writing the proposal has not yet been enacted.[221]

(ii) Positive action

Equality of opportunities does not guarantee equality of results because the problem of discrimination is more deeply rooted in society, which has historically denied rights to certain groups, known as 'systematic' discrimination.[222] One solution to this gap are measures of positive discrimination that tackle the causes of inequality by encouraging the underrepresented group to participate or by going as far as to discriminate in favour of an underrepresented group, for instance by giving a job to a woman in favour of a man because women are underrepresented.[223] EU law does not compel Member States to deploy positive action; rather, the Commission has encouraged Member States to take positive action to promote women in employment as far back as 1984 on the one hand,[224] while the Court of Justice has limited the scope of such programmes when these are incompatible with EU law, on the other.

The new generation of discrimination legislation seeks to give Member States greater freedom to design positive action measures. The principle in Article 157(4) TFEU is replicated in the Race Directive and in the Framework Directive:[225]

> With a view to ensuring full equality in practice, the principle of equal treatment shall not prevent any Member State from maintaining or adopting specific measures to prevent or compensate for disadvantages linked to [race, ethnic origin, sexual orientation, age, religion, or disability].

In practice EU law forbids a measure providing that a percentage of jobs should go to women, and measures whereby if a man and a woman are equally well qualified, the job should go to the woman, also infringe the equality principle.[226]

In contrast, EU law allows a measure which introduces a presumption that the (equally qualified) female should be employed, which is in turn rebuttable by the man on grounds of certain characteristics that entitle him to the post (so-called 'secondary selection criteria'). For example, he could point out that his seniority made him a worthier candidate.[227] These

---

[220] In particular there was criticism from the insurance market. See Paul MacDonnell, 'Equal Treatment Directive Misunderstands Risk and Threatens Insurance Markets' (2005) 25 *Economic Affairs* 48; House of Lords European Union Committee *Sexual Equality in Access to Goods and Services* (27th Report of Session 2003–04, HL Paper 165-I) Chapter 9. As noted earlier, the Court then nullified their lobbying efforts.

[221] Proposal for a Council Directive on implementing the principle of equal treatment between persons irrespective of religion or belief, disability, age or sexual orientation COM(2008) 426 final.

[222] S. Joseph, J. Schultz and M. Castan, *The International Covenant on Civil and Political Rights: Cases, Materials and Commentary* (Oxford, Oxford University Press, 2000) 563–4.

[223] See generally S. Fredman, 'Reversing Discrimination' (1997) 113 *LQR* 575.

[224] Council Recommendation 84/635/EEC of 13 December 1984 on the promotion of positive action for women, OJ 1984 L331/34.

[225] Article 7 Directive 2000/78/EC and Article 5 Directive 2000/43/EC.

[226] Case C-450/93 *Kalanke* v *Freie Hansestadt Bremen* [1995] ECR I-3051.

[227] Case C-409/95 *Hellmut Marschall* v *Land Nordrhein-Westfalen* [1997] ECR I-6363.

schemes satisfy two conditions: they do not give automatic priority to women and allow for an objective evaluation that takes into account the personal situation of each candidate.[228]

Several criticisms were levelled at the Court of Justice's approach.[229] First, the Court narrowed down considerably the ability of Member States to engage in positive discrimination and undermined the potential of such measures. Moreover, positive discrimination policies that are lawful under EU law are easy to evade. For instance, it has been said that it is easy for the employer to claim that the woman is not equally qualified, and the 'secondary selection criteria' cannot be subjected to strict judicial scrutiny, therefore leaving the employer free to favour men instead of women.[230] The upshot is that Member States find it very difficult to implement meaningful positive discrimination measures.

The language of the Framework Directive and Race Directive can also be read as permitting discrimination as a way of promoting an underrepresented group, because all the texts begin with the same prefatory words: 'with a view to achieving full equality in practice'. This suggests that equality of results is now an EU objective, which may open the way for more aggressive positive discrimination schemes, perhaps even allowing for a quota system whereby a given proportion of persons from an underrepresented group must be employed provided this is the least restrictive way of achieving equal participation. Support for this may be drawn from the use of the language in Article 19 TFEU (combating discrimination, not merely preventing it),[231] and from the fact that the Framework Directive tolerates a fairly aggressive form of positive discrimination in one region of the European Union.

Framework Directive, article 15

1. In order to tackle the under-representation of one of the major religious communities in the police service of Northern Ireland, differences in treatment regarding recruitment into that service, including its support staff, shall not constitute discrimination insofar as those differences in treatment are expressly authorised by national legislation.

2. In order to maintain a balance of opportunity in employment for teachers in Northern Ireland while furthering the reconciliation of historical divisions between the major religious communities there, the provisions on religion or belief in this Directive shall not apply to the recruitment of teachers in schools in Northern Ireland insofar as this is expressly authorised by national legislation.

While this provision was included to safeguard a policy of specific interest to a politically troubled region, it represents a sign of increased support for positive discrimination more generally. However, that EU law leaves positive discrimination measures to the Member States

---

[228] It is not clear if the ECJ, in view of the new legal framework in Article 157(4) would adopt a more expansive reading in Case C-407/98 *Abrahamsson and Anderson* v *Fogelqvist* [2000] ECR I-5539. Paragraph 55 may be read to suggest that a scheme that favours the underrepresented candidate may be allowed if it is proportionate, but it is risky to base this conclusion on a single paragraph. In Case C-319/03 *Serge Brihenche* v *Ministre de l'Interieur* [2004] ECR I-8807 the Court also noted that Article 157 TFEU warrants a different interpretation from Art. 2(4), but what this means in practice remains to be specified.

[229] See generally S. Fredman, 'After *Kalanke* and *Marschall*: Affirming Affirmative Action' (1998) 1 *CYELS* 199.

[230] D. Caruso, 'Limits of the Classic Method: Positive Action in the European Union after the New Equality Directives' (2003) 44 *Harvard International Law Journal* 331, 342.

[231] Z. Apostolopoulou, *Equal Treatment of People with Disabilities in the EC: What Does "Equal" Mean?*, Jean Monnet Working Paper 09/04, 10–11.

does not imply that these measures will be put in place. In contrast, the transposition of the Race Directive in the Netherlands led to a limited positive action measure being rescinded; and in Germany and Hungary, where the law was amended to take into account the Court of Justice's case law, there has been no use of positive action measures.[232] At the time of writing the Commission has tried to buck this trend by proposing legislation that would set large publicly listed companies in the EU a target of ensuring that 40 per cent of members of non-executive boards are women by 2020.[233]

Perhaps there is an alternative: to impose positive duties on those best placed to eliminate discrimination. This model has been advocated by Professor Sandra Fredman, making reference to legislation that places statutory duties on public bodies (and sometimes on private actors) to promote equality, which do not give rise to individual rights. In her view this kind of legislation has the following advantages: it spreads the obligation to remedy inequality to those who have the power and capacity to change it; reform is systematic and not dependent upon individual lawsuits; finally the causes of discrimination are addressed collectively, harnessing local actors who know where the barriers lie and are best placed to propose measures to resolve them. By increasing participation among stakeholders, the system gains more legitimacy and is also flexible to adjust as needs change.[234]

(iii) Dialogue

To a limited extent, the discrimination Directives introduce some methods for promoting equality suggested by Fredman by establishing three types of dialogue. First, the Member State has an obligation to inform those concerned of their rights and obligations under the Directives.[235] This is a relatively inexpensive way of bringing employers and other potential defendants up to date on their obligations.

Secondly, Member States are to promote social dialogue between employers and employees. All three Directives impose the following obligations.[236]

Race Directive, article 11

1. Member States shall, in accordance with national traditions and practice, take adequate measures to promote the social dialogue between the two sides of industry with a view to fostering equal treatment, including through the monitoring of workplace practices, collective agreements, codes of conduct, research or exchange of experiences and good practices.

---

[232] V. Guiraudon, 'Equality in the making: implementing European non-discrimination law' (2009) 13 *Citizenship Studies* 527, 538.

[233] Proposal for a Directive on improving the gender balance among non-executive directors of companies listed on stock exchanges and related measures COM (2012) 614 (final). On this issue generally, see C. Fagan, M. González Menèndez and S. Gómez Ansón (eds.), *Women on Corporate Boards and in Top Management: European Trends and Policy* (Basingstoke, Palgrave Macmillan, 2012).

[234] Sandra Fredman, *Human Rights Transformed: Positive Rights and Positive Duties* (Oxford, Oxford University Press, 2008) 190.

[235] Article 10 Race Directive, Article 12 Framework Directive, Article 30 Recast Equal Treatment Directive.

[236] Article 21 Recast Equal Treatment Directive, Article 13 Framework Directive.

> 2. Where consistent with national traditions and practice, Member States shall encourage the two sides of the industry without prejudice to their autonomy to conclude, at the appropriate level, agreements laying down anti-discrimination rules...which fall within the scope of collective bargaining. These agreements shall respect the minimum requirements laid down by this Directive and the relevant national implementing measures.

In addition, the Equal Treatment Directive obliges Member States to encourage employers to promote equal treatment and to provide employees with information on equal treatment, e.g. statistics on the promotion of men and women.[237] Moreover, all the Directives call upon Member States to encourage dialogue with NGOs with a legitimate interest in discrimination.[238]

These forms of dialogue encourage 'reflexive regulation', that is, a kind of self-regulation which encourages the employer to be self-reflective and self-critical about his practices. One potential use of these forms of dialogue is to address the problem of 'intersectional discrimination', which as we noted earlier is not covered by the Directives. An employer employing several Asian women might use social dialogue as a means of understanding and remedying the specific concerns of this group which would remain invisible if he merely sought to avoid sex and race discrimination separately. Given that the Race Directive extends beyond the labour market, it is unfortunate that the provisions for dialogue are restricted to the labour market and are not extended to other points of authority (such as schools or hospitals).[239]

Thirdly, and perhaps most significantly, Member States must set up a regulatory body under the Race Directive and Equal Treatment Directives.[240]

Race Directive, article 13

1. Member States shall designate a body or bodies for the promotion of equal treatment of all persons without discrimination on the grounds of racial or ethnic origin. These bodies may form part of agencies charged at national level with the defence of human rights or the safeguard of individuals' rights.
2. Member States shall ensure that the competences of these bodies include:
   - without prejudice to the right of victims and of associations, organisations or other legal entities...providing independent assistance to victims of discrimination in pursuing their complaints about discrimination,
   - conducting independent surveys concerning discrimination,
   - publishing independent reports and making recommendations on any issue relating to such discrimination.

These organisations can be indispensable in Member States for whom the implementation of discrimination legislation is a novelty, although their success will depend upon the agencies

---

[237] Article 8b, paragraphs 3 and 4 Equal Treatment Directive.
[238] Article 12 Race Directive, Article 14 Framework Directive, Article 8c Equal Treatment Directive.
[239] Chalmers, above n. 195, 238.
[240] Article 8a Equal Treatment Directive. For discussion, see B. De Witte, 'New institutions for promoting equality in Europe: Legal transfers, national bricolage and European Governance' (2012) 60 *AJCL* 49.

being well funded and politically independent. Their success will depend on how much power and how many resources Member States commit, and some have appeared to do as little as necessary.[241] One inherent limitation is that none of these organisations have any independent powers to enforce the law. This has been criticised because many entrenched forms of discrimination cannot be easily resolved through individuals litigating to assert individual rights.[242] However, as suggested above, the litigation model should not be seen as the exclusive means to bring about equality.

(iv) Mainstreaming

Perhaps the most significant commitment to promoting equality outside the framework of the rights-based model is found in the Lisbon Treaty's commitment to 'mainstreaming' equality.

Article 8 TFEU

In all its activities, the Union shall aim to eliminate inequalities, and to promote equality, between men and women.

Article 10 TFEU

In defining and implementing its policies and activities, the Union shall aim to combat discrimination based on sex, racial or ethnic origin, religion or belief, disability, age or sexual orientation.

The separate reference to gender policy probably has to do with lobbying by the European Women's Group for a separate provision on gender equality.[243] According to the Commission, mainstreaming means:

> The systematic integration of the respective situations, priorities and needs of women and men in all policies and with a view to promoting equality between women and men and mobilizing all general policies and measures specifically for the purpose of achieving equality by actively and openly taking into account, at the planning stage, their effects on the respective situation of women and men in implementation, monitoring and evaluation.[244]

The aim is to ensure gender issues (and those of race, disability, and so on) are considered and integrated in all EU actions. Potentially, this is an imaginative way of addressing the systemic

---

[241] V. Guiraudon, 'Equality in the making: implementing European non-discrimination law' (2009) 13 *Citizenship Studies* 527, singling out Italy and Spain as having weak agencies to address racial discrimination.

[242] Mark Bell, 'Beyond European Labour Law? Reflections on the EU Racial Equality Directive' (2002) 8 *ELJ* 384, 397–8.

[243] M. Bell, 'Equality and the European Constitution' (2004) 33 *ILJ* 242, 257–8. A declaration attached to Article 8 TFEU also provides that 'the Union will aim in its different policies to combat all kinds of domestic violence. The Member States should take all necessary measures to prevent and punish these criminal acts and to support and protect the victims.' This may impact the measures adopted under Title V TFEU (Area of Freedom, Security and Justice).

[244] Communication from the Commission, *Incorporating Equal Opportunities for Women and Men into All Community Policies and Activities*, COM(96)67 final, 2.

causes of inequality between men and women. We begin by exploring how this policy emerged in the context of sex equality, and then we look into how it has been implemented to tackle discrimination against all protected groups.

A range of factors brought gender mainstreaming onto the EU's agenda in the mid-1990s, not least the accession of Sweden and Finland (states with a strong tradition of gender equality policies) and the Parliament's opinion on the gender balance of the Santer Commission, which led the Commissioner to commit himself to looking closely at gender equality.[245] The European Women's Lobby was also instrumental in the adoption of gender mainstreaming in the Treaty.[246] Thirdly, the reason why mainstreaming was selected as the keystone of the new equality policy was because it fitted with international political events (it gained prominence during the United Nations' Fourth World Conference in Beijing in 1995) and it was a policy with which the EU was familiar because a similar approach had been taken in the context of developing the EU's environmental policy.

Mainstreaming in this field is not premised upon legislative measures that Member States must implement. Rather, it is designed to create incentives for the EU and Member States to embed gender consideration in their policies. To this end, the EU's role is to facilitate increased action at national level. This role was enhanced by the EU's employment and social solidarity programme, PROGRESS, launched in 2007. It is designed to promote mainstreaming of the principle of non-discrimination and to promote gender equality by commissioning studies on the effect of current legislation, supporting the implementation of EU discrimination law and raising awareness of the key policy issues.[247] Mainstreaming also occurs in the context of the European Employment Strategy.[248] In brief, the strategy provides for the Council to review national employment policies and make recommendations to Member States on, inter alia, the success of national policies in improving the work prospects of women.[249] However, the effectiveness of gender mainstreaming on national employment policies is uneven and one study concludes that, aside from Sweden, there is little sustained effort in mainstreaming in employment policy.[250]

The effect of mainstreaming on EU institutions is mixed. On the one hand, the Commission undertook to increasing the participation of women (the number of women in committees and expert groups has increased somewhat as a result),[251] establishing a Commissioner's Group on

---

[245] This section draws from M. A. Pollack and E. Hafner-Burton, 'Mainstreaming Gender in the European Union' (2000) 7 *JEPP* 432.

[246] S. Mazey, 'Gender Mainstreaming Strategies in the EU: Delivering on an Agenda?' (2002) 10 *Feminist Legal Studies* 227.

[247] Articles 2, 7 and 8 Decision 1672/2006 establishing a Community Programme for Employment and Social Solidarity [2006] OJ L315/1.

[248] F. Beveridge and S. Velluti (eds.), *Gender and the Open Method of Coordination* (Farnham, Ashgate, 2008).

[249] For example, see Council Recommendation on the implementation of Member States' employment policies, OJ 2004 L326/47 where each Member State's employment policy towards women is assessed.

[250] C. Fagan, J. Rubery, D. Grimshaw, M. Smith, G. Hebson and H. Figueiredo, 'Gender Mainstreaming in the Enlarged European Union: Recent Developments in the European Employment Strategy and Social Inclusion Process' (2005) 36 *Industrial Relations Journal* 568, 587. See also L. Mósesdóttir and R. Gerlingsdóttir, 'Spreading the Word Across Europe: Gender Mainstreaming as a Political and Policy Project' (2005) 7 *International Feminist Journal of Politics* 513.

[251] For example, Decision 2000/407/EC of 19 June 2000 relating to gender balance within the committees and expert groups established by it, OJ 2000 L154/34. See European Commission, *Work Programme for 2002 for the Implementation of the Framework Strategy on Gender Equality*, SEC(2001).773 final, 5, noting an increase in women from 13 to 29 per cent from 2000 to 2001.

Equal Opportunities chaired by the President, and training Commission staff on the impact of Community policies on gender equality.[252] However, women remained underrepresented, and mainstreaming was also marginalised in the *White Paper on Governance*,[253] and has had less of an impact on the Council and the Court of Justice.[254]

In terms of Community policies, a test case for implementing mainstreaming is in the field of the EU's Structural Funds. In brief, the EU has four funds (the Regional Fund, the Social Fund, the Fisheries, and the Guidance and Guarantee Fund) from which it provides financial support to reduce the gap in living standards across the EU and to promote economic and social cohesion. The Commission's efforts in this field were to insert gender equality as one criterion to allocate the relevant funds. Thus, in all Regulations setting out the operation of the structural funds we find reference to the promotion of gender equality as a condition for releasing funds.[255] In practical terms, the funds have financed a range of programmes designed to facilitate women's access to jobs that were traditionally reserved for men, or to facilitate working opportunities for women in poor European regions.[256] In addition to supporting programmes directly linked to improving the economic position of women, the release of funds for any other purpose is conditional on applicants indicating how their proposal promotes gender equality, which allows the EU to force Member States to embed gender equality as a condition for Community assistance.[257] But the results are modest: between 2000 and 2006, only 6 per cent of the European Social Fund went to gender-specific actions.[258] A similar approach is presently attempted in the field of public procurement: that is, when Member States and local authorities purchase goods and services to discharge their functions.[259] However, this is also likely to prove difficult to realise in practice. Public procurement law is already quite complex so that to include a provision that favours the supply of goods from firms that, say, employ many disabled workers, is an approach that some purchasers will shy away from because of the legal risks should their tenders be challenged and quashed.[260]

The other concern is that in areas where the impact of policy on a protected group is more remote, mainstreaming has no bite. A provocative example is provided by Heather MacRae. She notes how airline liberalisation increased the number of cheap flights to Estonia and this is linked to an increase in sex tourism in the area, with a concomitant increase in prostitution and sex trade. But while the effects of airline liberalisation on the environment and on employment practices of airlines have been looked at, the impact of liberalisation on the sex trade has not been identified.

---

[252] European Commission, *Work Programme for 2005 for the Implementation of the Framework Strategy on Gender Equality*, SEC(2005)1044, 7.

[253] J. Shaw, 'The European Union and Gender Mainstreaming: Constitutionally Embedded or Comprehensively Marginalised?' (2002) 10 *Feminist Legal Studies* 213, 224–6.

[254] Mazey, above n. 225.

[255] For example, Regulation 1784/1999 on the European Social Fund OJ 1999 L213/5, Article 2.

[256] See http://europa.eu.int/comm/employment_social/esf2000/index-en.htm for an overview.

[257] Mazey, above n. 225, 230.

[258] *Assessment document SEC (2006) 275.*

[259] C. Tobler, 'Encore: Women's Clauses in Public Procurement under Community Law' (2000) 25 *EL Rev.* 618.

[260] T. Uyen Do, 'In the Face of diversity: public procurement to promote social objectives' (2013) 16 *European Anti-discrimination Law Review* 10, identifying the options and the challenges for this strategy.

H. MacRae, 'The EU as a Gender Equal Polity: Myths and Realities' (2010) 48(1) *Journal of Common Market Studies* 155, 170, 171

The equality policies cannot compete against the more powerful narratives of liberalization and competition which have formed the very base of the European project. This contributes to the gap between the policy intentions and the policy outcomes of the EU gender legislation. If certain groups of women are disadvantaged through the neo-liberal policies of the EU, then they are unlikely to recognize the potential benefits of the EU gender policies...Gender mainstreaming has failed to propel the gender myth into the middle of European Union policy-making. It has not been able to influence much of the core of EU policy including the liberalization of the market.

One riposte to this claim may be to question whether we really expect gender issues to play a role even when they are so remotely linked to the main policy issue at hand: if the concern is the sexual exploitation of women in Eastern Europe, then this is an issue that can be tackled more effectively through other means. The counter-argument is that unless all policies are integrated there is a risk that some nullify the effectiveness of others.

Mainstreaming also occurs beyond the sphere of gender.[261] For example, disability-related issues have affected a number of legislative initiatives: a Directive on special provisions for certain vehicles requires that they should be accessible to disabled persons,[262] and the Directive on Universal Services in the field of electronic communication, which is designed to ensure that all citizens have affordable access to telecommunication services, guarantees access to disabled persons by requiring Member States to ensure that disabled users have access 'equivalent to that enjoyed by other end-users'.[263] These measures are supported by the European Parliament's Disability Intergroup and, as their work programme makes clear, the effect of provisions like these is to remove barriers faced by disabled people.[264] This takes us very far away from the traditional vision of discrimination law, which is about granting individuals the right to sue. Rather, the political philosophy that motivates mainstreaming is that of ensuring social inclusion.[265] That said, mainstreaming has yet to achieve significant results.[266] This may be for the reasons suggested by MacRae (mainstreaming fails when it faces the more embedded discourses in EU law, like market opening) or perhaps because it remains limited in ambition: it identifies the harm suffered by a group rather than demanding a more wholesale transformation of society to accommodate the interests of all groups.[267] However, this more ambitious approach may take mainstreaming outside the competence of the EU, or may even be too idealistic to achieve.

---

[261] In the sphere of race, see M. Bell, *Racism and Equality in the European Union* (Oxford, Oxford University Press, 2008).

[262] Directive 2001/85/EC of the European Parliament and of the Council of 20 November 2001 relating to special provisions for vehicles used for the carriage of passengers comprising more than eight seats in addition to the driver's seat, and amending Directives 70/156/EEC and 97/27/EC, OJ 2002 L42/1, Article 3.

[263] Article 7 Directive 2002/22/EC (Universal Service Directive), OJ 2002 L108/51.

[264] <http://www.edf-feph.org/Page_Generale.asp?DocID=18390> (last visited 19 December 2013).

[265] H. Collins, 'Discrimination, Equality and Social Inclusion' (2003) 66 *MLR* 16.

[266] F. Beveridge, 'Bulding Against the Past: The Impact of Mainstreaming on EU Gender Law and Policy' (2007) 32 *European Law Review* 193; Bell above n. 239, 185–8.

[267] J Rubery 'Gender Mainstreaming and Gender Equality in the EU: the Impact of the EU Employment Strategy' (2002) 33 *Industrial Relations Journal*, 500, 503.

FURTHER READING

K. J. Alter and J. Vargas, 'Explaining Variation in the Use of European Litigation Strategies: European Community Law and British Gender Equality Policy' (2000) 33 *Comparative Political Studies* 452

C. Barnard, 'The Changing Scope of the Fundamental Principle of Equality?' (2001) 46 *McGill Law Journal* 955

M. Bell, *Anti-Discrimination Law and the European Union* (Oxford, Oxford University Press, 2002)

C. Brown, 'The Race Directive: Towards Equality for *All* Peoples of Europe?' (2002) *Yearbook of European Law* 195

D. Caruso, 'Limits of the Classic Method: Positive Action in the European Union after the New Equality Directives' (2003) 44 *Harvard International Law Journal* 331

J. Cornides, 'Three Case Studies on "Anti-discrimination"' (2012) 32(2) *European Journal of International Law* 517, 523–6

B. De Witte, 'New Institutions for Promoting Equality in Europe: Legal Transfers, National Bricolage and European Governance' (2012) 60 *American Journal of Comparative Law* 49

E. Dewhurst, 'Intergenerational Balance, Mandatory Retirement and Age Discrimination in Europe: How Can the ECJ Better Support National Courts in Finding a Balance Between the Generations?' (2013) 50 *Common Market Law Review* 1333

E. Ellis and P. Watson, *EU Anti-Discrimination Law* (2nd edn, Oxford, Oxford University Press, 2012)

S. Fredman, *Discrimination Law* (2nd edn, Oxford, Oxford University Press, 2011)

V. Guiraudon, 'Equality in the Making: Implementing European Non-discrimination Law' (2009) 13 *Citizenship Studies* 527

C. Hoskins, *Integrating Gender: Women, Law and Politics in the European Union* (London, Verso, 1996)

E. Howard, 'The European Year of Equal Opportunities for All 2007: Is the EU Moving Away from a Formal Idea of Equality?' (2008) 14 *European Law Journal* 168

H. MacRae, 'The EU as a Gender Equal Polity: Myths and Realities' (2010) 48(1) *Journal of Common Market Studies* 155

H. Oliver, 'Sexual Orientation Discrimination: Perceptions, Definitions and Genuine Occupational Requirements' (2004) 33 *Industrial Law Journal* 1

D. Schiek, 'Broadening the Scope and the Norms of EU Gender Equality Law: Towards a Multidimensional Conception of Equality Law' (2005) 12 *Maastricht Journal of European and Comparative Law* 427

A. Somek, *Engineering Equality: An Essay in European Anti-discrimination Law* (Oxford, Oxford University Press, 2011)

14

EU Criminal Law

CONTENTS

1 INTRODUCTION

This chapter considers EU criminal law. It is organised as follows.

Section 2 considers the central traits of EU criminal law. EU criminal law is subject to particular sensitivities. In the first place, it is constrained by the requirements in Article 4(2) TEU that it respect essential Member State functions maintaining law and order and that national security be the sole responsibility of each Member State. In the second place, prior to the Lisbon Treaty it was subject to arrangements, which were predominantly intergovernmental in nature. This has left a legacy in that it still relies heavily on legal instruments from that period, notably Framework Decisions. Thirdly, a number of additional institutional checks are deployed to patrol it. Member States, when there are one-quarter of them, share the power of initiative with the Commission. 'Emergency brake' procedures allow any Member State to refer a proposal affecting fundamental aspects of its criminal justice system to the European Council. One-quarter of national parliaments (rather than one-third elsewhere) can ask the Commission to reconsider a proposal for failure to comply with the subsidiarity principle. Finally, this field is strongly marked by differentiated integration. Denmark does not participate in measures adopted since the Lisbon Treaty, and the United Kingdom and Ireland can choose whether or not to participate. Notwithstanding this, an EU criminal legal order has emerged, centred on two rationales. The first involves taking collective measures which augment the security of Member States, individually and collectively. The second is a European public order based around certain shared interests and values. These include the development of certain pan-Union crimes, the use of criminal law to secure the regulatory effectiveness of other EU policies, and the establishment of pan-Union rights for the victims of crime.

Section 3 considers judicial cooperation in criminal justice and the principle of mutual recognition of judicial decisions. Mutual recognition requires a judicial decision in one Member State to be given effect in other Member States. It applies in a variety of settings. These include decisions which inculpate the individual; enable him to be tried in the issuing state where he otherwise could not be; sanction the individual; and which exculpate the individual. In the majority of cases, mutual recognition strengthens the power of the Member State issuing the decision to prosecute, put on trial and punish by granting its decision an extra-territorial reach. Alongside this, mutual recognition presupposes a convergence of values between the state issuing the decision and the state executing it, as well as mutual trust in the system of administration of justice of each. Its most prominent instrument is the European Arrest Warrant which requires surrender of a person sought for prosecution or detention by the judicial authority of another Member State. The European Arrest Warrant has generated a number of concerns. These go, first, to the fairness of the trial the individual will have in the executing state. Secondly, for thirty-two offences the European Arrest Warrant abolishes the principle of double criminality whereby the alleged activity must be a criminal one in both the issuing and executing state. This has raised concerns about the type of activities for which the Arrest Warrant is issued, notably whether it is issued for too trivial offences. Finally, the European Arrest Warrant has generated tensions in Member States where there is a constitutional prohibition on the extradition of one's own citizens.

Section 4 considers the harmonisation of criminal offences and sanctions in EU law. Two types of offence are subject to harmonisation. The first are offences which are serious and have a cross-border dimension. These constraints have been weakened over time so that many offences are now subject to some harmonisation. The common feature of many of these is that they involve more than one perpetrator and have some prior infrastructure. Such harmonising measures are often vague, however, and have been used to criminalise activities that were not previously illegal in many Member States. The second type of offence involves EU criminal law being used as a regulatory tool to ensure the effective implementation of a Union policy.

Section 5 considers the rights granted to victims of crime by EU law. The central instrument is Directive 2012/29/EU. The rights provided by it are general ones granted to anybody who has suffered harm as a consequence of a criminal act within the European Union. Victims' rights are, thus, protected by EU law in a more sweeping way than many other rights, including fundamental rights. Three types of right are provided. There are, first, rights of information and support. This includes both a right to understand what is taking place in any criminal process and a right to be understood. Secondly, there is a right to participate in the criminal proceedings. This includes, most centrally, a right to be heard and to give evidence, and a right to review any decision not to prosecute. Finally, there is a right to protection. This includes protection from repeat victimisation, intimidation or retaliation. It also includes a number of protections, depending on the circumstances of the victim, in both the interview process and during the criminal proceedings themselves. Crucially, however, EU law does not give victims a right to compensation. Their central role is rather to patrol the investigative process and criminal proceedings.

2 CHARACTERISING EU CRIMINAL LAW

Prior to the Lisbon Treaty, policing and criminal law were placed in a discrete Treaty title, 'Title VI TEU Provisions on Police and Judicial Cooperation in Criminal Matters'. The supranational features of EU law governed this title in only an attenuated fashion.[1] Decision-making in the Council was by unanimity.[2] The Commission had to share its power of initiative with the Member States.[3] The Parliament only had limited consultative powers.[4] The Court of Justice only had very limited powers with Member States able to choose whether to grant their national courts the powers to refer to it.[5] Finally, the Union had no power to adopt directly effective legislation in the field.[6] At Lisbon, the supranational disciplines associated with other fields of EU law set out in the TFEU were extended, in principle, to criminal law and policing.[7]

Article 67 TFEU

1. The Union shall constitute an area of freedom, security and justice with respect for fundamental rights and the different legal systems and traditions of the Member States....
3. The Union shall endeavour to ensure a high level of security through measures to prevent and combat crime, racism and xenophobia, and through measures for coordination and cooperation between police and judicial authorities and other competent authorities, as well as through the mutual recognition of judgments in criminal matters and, if necessary, through the approximation of criminal laws.

EU criminal law became, thus, in many ways a field like any other. It forms part of the Area of Freedom, Security and Justice (AFSJ), and comprises three central competences: judicial cooperation in criminal matters based on the mutual recognition of judgments;[8] the establishment of minimum rules concerning the definition of criminal offences and sanctions;[9] and police

---

[1] On this trajectory see E. Baker and C. Harding, 'From Past Imperfect to Future Perfect? A Longitudinal Study of the Third Pillar' (2009) 34 *ELRev.* 25; E. Herlin-Karnell, *The Constitutional Dimension of European Criminal Law* (Oxford, Hart, 2012) ch. 2.

[2] Article 34(2) TEU(M). TEU(M) is used to indicate the provision which existed prior to the reforms introduced by the Lisbon Treaty.

[3] Article 34(2) TEU(M).   [4] Article 39 TEU(M).   [5] Article 35(2) TEU(M).   [6] Article 34(2) TEU(M).

[7] S. Peers, 'Finally "Fit for Purpose"? The Treaty of Lisbon and the End of the Third Pillar Legal Order' (2008) 27 *YBEL* 47.

[8] Article 82 TFEU.   [9] Article 83 TFEU.

cooperation.[10] There is provision for qualified majority voting (QMV) in the Council in almost all competences.[11] Parliament acquires rights by virtue of the wide application of the assent[12] and ordinary legislative procedures here.[13] The Court of Justice has full jurisdiction. Regulations and Directives are to be adopted in this field like any other. However, significant caveats need to be placed on this general claim. This field is marked by particular domestic sensitivities which limit its remit, on the one hand, and shape its form of intervention, on the other. Alongside this, it operates in the shadow of a longer legacy of intergovernmental law-making than other TFEU policy. This legacy casts, as we shall see, a powerful legal footprint in that most EU criminal law comes from that intergovernmental period. Finally, possibly because of the deep domestic sensitivities about criminal law, deep divisions between Member States have been exposed about the manner and form of EU intervention in this field.

(i) Member States and internal security

Criminal law institutionalises the monopoly of lawful violence enjoyed by a state over its territory. It has powers of detention, coercion and surveillance not granted to private citizens to allow it to secure order and collective ideas of right. It sets out arguably the most delicate relationship between states and their citizens. The language of national sovereignty and identity correspondingly exercises a powerful influence on EU law in this field. This is reflected in Article 4(2) TEU.[14]

Article 4(2) TEU

2. [The Union] shall respect their essential State functions, including ensuring the territorial integrity of the State, maintaining law and order and safeguarding national security. In particular, national security remains the sole responsibility of each Member State.

The provision imposes a double injunction. The first sentence requires the Union to respect, inter alia, national law and order functions. You do not respect somebody or something by telling them what they are or what they cannot do. Respect involves allowing the object of respect to see out what it is about and giving it the benefit of the doubt in the way it goes about its business. It, thus, suggests that EU law is to allow national institutions to see out what law and order involves for their territory, and for it to intervene in only the most exceptional cases.

---

[10] Article 87 TFEU.

[11] The only competences where unanimity is required involve operational cooperation (Articles 86(3) and 89 TFEU), the establishment of the European Public Prosecutors Office (Article 86(1) TFEU) and the establishment of new crimes for which there should be harmonisation in addition to those mentioned in Article 83 TFEU (Article 83(1) TFEU).

[12] This applies to the rules on specific aspects of criminal procedure (Article 82(2)(d) TFEU); the establishment of new crimes for which there should be harmonisation (Article 83(1) TFEU); and the establishment of the European Public Prosecutors Office and extension of its powers (Article 86(1) and(4) TFEU).

[13] This applies in all other areas other than n. 12 above and measures concerning operational cooperation (Articles 87(3) and 89 TFEU).

[14] A corresponding provision stating that the Area of Freedom, Security and Justice shall not affect the exercise of the responsibilities incumbent upon Member States with regard to the maintenance of law and order and the safeguarding of internal security is set out in the TFEU, Article 72 TFEU.

The second sentence creates a monopoly for the Member States. The protection of national security is for them alone. The meaning of national security shapes the remit and operation of EU criminal law, with national institutions restricting it wherever they believe its activities intrude into matters better categorised as ones of security. The best view is provided by Loader and Walker who argue security has three dimensions. First, security is something that can be externally measured as a safe environment. This is the security referred to in crime statistics. Secondly, security is about a sense of secure belonging. People only feel safe – notwithstanding statistics – if they live in a world of stable relations and stable identities. Thirdly, the realisation of security is central to the creation of a collective feeling of 'We'.[15] The nation-state's ability to bring security brings not only faith in its institutions but contributes to our feeling British, Czech, Polish, and so on. These different dimensions lead to security being vested so heavily in the nation-state. Only it has the symbolic authority and resources to provide the environment and social relations upon which ideas of security depend.[16] As a corollary, security is perceived as threatened when national identities or ideas of political community are seen as being attacked.

National sensitivities about security, manifested in Article 4(2) TEU, cannot, consequently, be confined to a narrow technical range of activities. They also manifest themselves when EU criminal law touches on valued social relations or strong political identities. This was expressed most sharply in the *Lisbon Treaty* judgment of the German Constitutional Court where it indicated that EU laws transgressing too far into these issues would be struck down.[17]

---

2 BvE 2/08 *Treaty of Lisbon*, Judgment of 30 June 2009

253. ... the administration of criminal law depends on cultural processes of previous understanding that are historically grown and also determined by language, and on the alternatives which emerge in the process of deliberation and which move the respective public opinion ... The common characteristics in this regard, but also the differences, between the European nations is shown by the relevant case-law of the European Court of Human Rights concerning the procedural guarantees in criminal proceedings ... The penalisation of social behaviour can, however, only to a limited extent be normatively derived from values and moral premises that are shared Europe-wide. Instead, the decision on punishable behaviour, on the rank of legal interests and the sense and the measure of the threat of punishment, is to a particular extent left to the democratic decision-making process ... In this context, which is of importance as regards fundamental rights, a transfer of sovereign powers beyond intergovernmental cooperation may only under restrictive preconditions lead to harmonisation for certain cross-border circumstances; the Member States must, in principle, retain substantial space of action in this context...

351. ... Particularly the newly conferred competences in the areas of judicial cooperation in criminal ... matters ... can, and must, be exercised by the institutions of the European Union in such a way that on the level of the Member States, tasks of sufficient weight as to their extent as well as their substance remain which legally and practically are the precondition of a living democracy. The

---

[15] I. Loader and N. Walker, *Civilising Security* (Cambridge, Cambridge University Press, 2007) 146–66.

[16] A. Crawford, 'Networked Governance and the Post-regulatory State? Steering, Rowing and Anchoring the Provision of Policing and Security' (2006) 10 *Theoretical Criminology* 449, 459.

[17] See pp. 236–8.

newly established competences are – at any rate with the required interpretation – not 'elements that establish a state', which also in an overall perspective do not infringe the sovereign statehood of the Federal Republic of Germany in a constitutionally relevant manner. For the assessment of the challenge of an unconstitutional depletion of the competences of the German Bundestag, it can remain undecided how many legislative acts in the Member States are already influenced, pre-formed or determined by the European Union … What is decisive for the constitutional assessment of the challenge is not the quantitative relations but whether the Federal Republic of Germany retains substantial national scope of action for central areas of statutory regulation and areas of life....

355. Securing legal peace by the administration of criminal law has always been a central duty of state authority. As regards the task of creating, securing and enforcing a well-ordered social existence by protecting the elementary values of community life on the basis of a legal order, criminal law is an indispensable element to secure the unswervingness of this legal order … Every provision in criminal law contains a social and ethical verdict of unworthiness on the action which it penalises. The specific content of this verdict of unworthiness results from the constituent elements of the criminal offence and the sanction … To what extent and in what areas a polity uses exactly the means of criminal law as an instrument of social control is a fundamental decision. By criminal law, a legal community gives itself a code of conduct that is anchored in its values, whose violation is, according to the shared convictions on law, regarded as so grievous and unacceptable for social existence in the community that it requires punishment...

356. With the decision on punishable conduct, the legislature takes the democratically legitimised responsibility for a form of sovereign action that counts among the most intensive encroachments on individual freedom in a modern constitutional state. The legislature is in principle free concerning the decision of whether it wants to defend a specific legal interest whose protection it regards as essential exactly with the means of criminal law how it wants to do this … Within the boundaries of the commitment to the constitution, it can, additionally decide which sanction it will impose on culpable conduct. The investigation of crimes, the detection of the perpetrator, the establishment of his guilt and his punishment are incumbent on the bodies of administration of criminal law, which for this purpose and under the conditions determined by the law, have to institute and to conduct criminal proceedings and have to execute imposed sanctions …

358. Due to the fact that democratic self-determination is affected in an especially sensitive manner by provisions of criminal law and law of criminal procedure, the corresponding foundations of competence in the Treaties must be interpreted strictly – on no account extensively – and their use requires particular justification. The core content of criminal law does not serve as a technical instrument for effectuating international cooperation but stands for the particularly sensitive democratic decision on the minimum standard according to legal ethics.

The judgment suggests criminal law is central to Germany's constitutional identity as it anchors its social values and, as it is where the state encroaches most strongly on individual freedom, it presents greatest need for democratic controls. The range of criminal law and policing measures which can impinge on these social values or democratic controls is extensive, as the list in paragraph 356 illustrates. The Constitutional Court suggests, therefore, that EU competences in this field should be interpreted strictly and, implicitly, its activities limited.

(ii) Rationales of EU criminal law: augmentation of national security and European Union public order

On its face, the highly restrictive terms of Article 4(2) TEU and the tight controls imposed by the German Constitutional Court leave little scope for the development of EU criminal law. However, the German court still finds the terms of the Lisbon Treaty unproblematic. This begs the question as to what rationales can be provided for EU criminal law, which can justify its presence and guide its operation and development, on the one hand, and navigate domestic sensitivities, on the other. There are two rationales: augmentation of a Member State's own national security and protection of a pan-Union European public order.

The first holds that, by cooperating with other states, a Member State can augment protection of its own internal security. Other states may have information or resources unavailable to it in the fight against crime, be able to take action against threats to it which are located outside its borders, or track down persons or evidence wanted by it in relation to activities on its territories. Viewed in this light, EU law is not about creating a pan-Union criminal law but about augmenting individual Member State security capacity.[18] Undoubtedly, some of EU law can only be understood thus in this way. A committee is established to augment operational capacity precisely for these purposes.

Article 71 TFEU

A standing committee shall be set up within the Council in order to ensure that operational cooperation on internal security is promoted and strengthened within the Union. Without prejudice to Article 240[[19]], it shall facilitate coordination of the action of Member States' competent authorities. Representatives of the bodies, offices and agencies of the Union concerned may be involved in the proceedings of this committee. The European Parliament and national Parliaments shall be kept informed of the proceedings.

Furthermore, as the ethos is about augmenting individual domestic security, Member States are free to organise other arrangements between themselves as they see fit.

Article 73 TFEU

It shall be open to Member States to organise between themselves and under their responsibility such forms of cooperation and coordination as they deem appropriate between the competent departments of their administrations responsible for safeguarding national security.

This narrative has an underside, however: an unattractive vision of law-enforcement agencies increasing each other's powers and resources through European integration unfettered from domestic constraints and checks and balances.

---

[18] B. Bowling, 'Transnational Policing: The Globalization Thesis, a Typology and Research Agenda' (2009) 3 *Policing* 1, 6–7.
[19] This sets out the powers of COREPER. See pp. 84–6.

S. Lavenex and W. Wagner, 'Which European Public Order? Sources of Imbalance in the European Area of Freedom, Security and Justice' (2007) 16 *European Security* 225, 239–40

Reminiscent of the 'new raison d'etat' thesis, we argued that European integration opens up a transgovernmental venue which allows national justice and home affairs officials to pool their respective 'monopolies over the use of violence' while shielding them from the established liberal norms and procedures that limit this monopoly in national constitutions. As Elspeth Guild has put it, this system is incomplete, because 'it is only criminal judgements that have this power to cross the border without risk of further control. The individual's rights in respect of a criminal charge, trial, and sentence remain bound within the territory of each member state'.[20] There are strong parallels with the Single Market, in which goods, services, capital and EU citizens move freely, but where production standards, social policies or pension systems remain nationally bound. As we have argued, these parallels result from the diffusion of market-based mechanisms of integration from the economic to the political field, that is, an emphasis on negative integration and mutual recognition.

The mutual recognition of asylum procedures, criminal laws or warrants, however, presupposes a high level of mutual trust in the member states' judicial systems. As our cases show, even among near neighbours who have a long history of cooperation, this trust cannot be taken for granted. As long as doubts remain about the proper respect for individual rights in other member states, courts are unlikely to accept other states' decisions without further scrutiny and citizens are unlikely to welcome such a Europeanisation of internal security cooperation as an advancement. Thus, there is a strong case for the neofunctionalist notion that European cooperation in criminal law necessitates a common approach to defendants' rights, that European police-cooperation 'spills over' into European level controls of data protection and asylum cooperation needs an integrated asylum system. Legal approximation, as an alternative or complement to mutual recognition, would have the advantage of replicating the fundamental rights and guaranties found in national legal systems at the European level, enforceable through supranational judicial control.

This critique illustrates why the narrative of augmenting domestic security tells only part of the story. Law-enforcement agencies helping each other merely in anticipation of reciprocal behaviour is a very thin basis for explaining and justifying Union action. It cannot explain why EU criminal law is stronger in certain fields of criminal law activity than others; national courts and parliaments would allow it to develop at all; or broader Union legal and democratic controls have emerged. Loader and Walker have therefore suggested a second rationale. Interaction and a sense of shared interests and values lead to the emergence of a common European public order with its own social relations, values and sense of community.

---

[20] E. Guild, 'Crime and the EU's Constitutional Future in an Area of Freedom, Security and Justice' (2004) 10 *ELJ* 218, 220.

> I. Loader and N. Walker, *Civilizing Security* (Cambridge, Cambridge University Press, 2007) 260–1
>
> [F]irst ... the fact that states have a strong self-interest in security means that they are, and will always remain, willing participants in collaborative strategies, notwithstanding the difficulties in stabilizing these strategies in institutional terms. Indeed, the problems of stabilization do not arise from a lack of awareness of their interdependence, but, rather, from an *acute and constant* awareness of interdependence coupled with a sometimes unbridled determination to assert one's own national interest in the light of the factors of interdependence. Secondly, as the content of the internal security imperative of states is in all cases strikingly similar, states may be encouraged nevertheless to think of the global public good as something more than the optimal convergence of presumptively diverse individual state interests ... perhaps more so than in any other policy domain all states adhere to the same broad conception of general order – the same appreciation of (and appreciation of their need to respond to) their populations' desire to live in a state of tranquility and in a context of predictable social relations. Thirdly, and relatedly, states may find common cause in their very understanding of the social quality of the public good of security ... For all that their particular interests may differ, states also have a common understanding of the social and public quality of that which they seek to defend, which in turn allows, however unevenly and intermittently, for a greater imaginative openness to the possibility of *other* sites and levels of social and public 'added value' in the accomplishment of security.

The Commission's early documents on the Area of Freedom, Justice and Security, thus, talked of the mission of EU law in this field being to establish a European public order.[21] However, this idea of a European public order was addressed most directly by Advocate General Bot in *Josemans*. The town of Maastricht in the Netherlands sought to curb drug tourism by requiring coffee shops selling cannabis to allow access only to residents of the town. The coffee shop of Josemans, the 'Easy Going' coffee shop, was closed down for not observing this condition. It was argued that the municipal restriction on non-residents discriminated against other EU citizens, and therefore breached the provisions on freedom to provide services.[22] The (successful) defence was that this was justified on grounds of public policy.

> Case C-137/09 *Joseman v Burgemeister van Maastricht* [2010] ECR I-13019, Advocate General Bot
>
> 116. ... the adoption of the contested measure is necessary under Article 4 TEU and Article 72 TFEU. It should be noted, that under those provisions, the Member States retain responsibility for maintaining public order in their territory and that, according to settled case-law, they retain the freedom to determine

---

[21] European Commission, *Towards an Area of Freedom, Security and Justice*, COM(98)459, 9.
[22] See p. 803.

the measures capable of maintaining public order in accordance with their national needs. Whilst it is established that the notion of public policy must be given a strict interpretation and may be relied upon only in the event of a genuine and sufficiently serious threat to the requirements of public policy affecting one of the fundamental interests of society, there is no doubt that drug tourism, in view of the problems it causes, comes under that notion.

117. However, drug tourism also causes serious problems for European Union public order. This misnomer actually conceals international trafficking in narcotic drugs and fuels organised crime activities which, as the Council recognises in the Stockholm Programme, challenges the European Union's internal security. These repercussions are all the more serious because they have an impact on the effectiveness of more repressive measures adopted by the neighbouring Member States. This phenomenon itself undoubtedly has a European and an international dimension and it is at that level that the Member States have undertaken to combat it....

122. It is undeniable that drug tourism generates and, in any case, encourages the illegal cross-border trafficking of narcotic drugs and also attracts other criminal activity. Consequently, the fight against these phenomena must represent both a major objective pursued by EU law and a common concern for each of the Member States. The EU legislature understood this and the entry into force of the Treaty of Amsterdam followed by that of the Treaty of Lisbon finally gave another dimension to the fight against the illicit trafficking of narcotic drugs and organised crime. Recognising that these are areas of particularly serious crime with a cross-border dimension resulting from the nature or impact of such offences or from a special need to combat them on a common basis, the EU legislature recognises the need to ensure a minimum harmonisation of national laws concerning the definition of criminal offences and sanctions. These provisions have added the illicit trafficking of narcotic drugs to what are now known as 'Eurocrimes' and under the Stockholm Programme such 'Eurocrimes', since they challenge the internal security of the European Union, are 'an urgent challenge which requires a clear and comprehensive response'. For that reason, in my view, the contested measure would be valid even in the absence of internal public order problems, solely on the basis of the obligation to contribute to the maintenance of European public order.

123. In the present case, since this measure represents the expression for the State not only of the right conferred on it to maintain its internal public order, but also its obligation vis-à-vis other Member States to contribute to the maintenance of European public order in accordance with the commitments made, it must therefore be valid under the abovementioned provisions.

It is all very well to talk about a European public order, but there remains the question of its content. Advocate General Bot is very vague on this in *Josemans*. Its strongest elaboration was a Commission Communication on EU Criminal Justice Policy. The Communication stressed that criminal law should be used as a matter of last resort but suggested four rationales for its deployment: Union citizen concerns; better enforcement of other EU policies; facilitating common understandings of Union added value in this field; and securing the fundamental rights of victims.[23]

---

[23] On this see C. Harding and J. Beata Banach-Gutierrez, 'The Emergent EU Criminal Policy: Identifying the Species' (2012) 37 *ELRev.* 758. See also M. Fletcher, 'EU Criminal Justice beyond Lisbon' in C. Eckes and T. Konstadines (eds.), *Crime Within the Area of Freedom, Security and Justice: A European Public Order* (Cambridge, Cambridge University Press, 2012).

European Commission, *Towards an EU Criminal Policy: Ensuring the Effective Implementation of EU Policies Through Criminal Law*, COM(2011)573, 12

- EU criminal law can be an important tool to better fight crime as a response to the concerns of citizens and to ensure the effective implementation of EU policies.
- In fields of EU policy where there is an identified enforcement deficit, the Commission will assess the need for new criminal law measures based on an evaluation of the enforcement practice and in full respect of fundamental Treaty principles such as subsidiarity and proportionality. This concerns notably the protection of the functioning of the financial markets, the protection of the financial interests of the EU, the protection of the euro against counterfeiting, serious infringements of road transport rules, serious breaches of data protection rules, customs offences, environmental protection, fisheries policy and internal market policies to fight illegal practices such as counterfeiting and corruption or undeclared conflict of interests in the context of public procurement.
- There should be a common understanding on the guiding principles underlying EU criminal law legislation, such as the interpretation of basic legal concepts used in EU criminal law; and how criminal law sanctions can provide most added value at EU level.
- Criminal law measures should be firmly grounded in strong EU-wide standards for procedural rights and victims' rights in line with the EU Charter of Fundamental Rights.

A pan-Union agenda is thus set out, with its own demands for supranational EU law and pan-Union democratic controls. However, as with the national security agenda, it raises its own concerns. Baker has observed that similar language, notably focusing on the rights of victims and the *fear* of crime, rather than actual crime itself, was used in the United States as a justification for extending government and a wider criminalisation of activities. She notes a similar trajectory in the European Union.[24]

E. Baker, 'Governing Through Crime: The Case of the European Union' (2010) 7 *European Journal of Criminology* 187, 196

Two further features of this transition are of particular interest ... The first is the recurring emphasis on citizens' (alleged) anxiety about their inability to enjoy the freedoms that the Union has provided 'in conditions of security and justice accessible to all'. This freedom is portrayed as a beacon that inspires third-country nationals to seek entry to the Union's space and as a target for those who indulge in organized crime. Drawing the three strands of the Area together, the document proceeds to suggest that the Union's resulting vulnerability is then compounded by divergences between Member States' criminal justice systems, which perpetrators can exploit to frustrate law enforcement. Although the text does not say so literally, the gist is surely clear: all legitimate occupants of the Union are, at the very least, *potential*

---

[24] The document to which she refers is that of the Tampere European Council in 1999 setting out the first programme for the Area of Freedom, Security and Justice, Conclusions of the European Council on the Creation of the Area of Freedom, Security and Justice, *Bulletin*, 10–1999.

victims of those who would violate the collective benefits (principally, freedom) that it is striving to provide.

Notably, not a shred of evidence is provided to substantiate the implicit claims about the existence or magnitude of violations, nor the allegedly 'frequently expressed concerns of citizens' about them. That is not to say that no such evidence exists, but its absence in the Tampere text means that it is possible to venture further in the direction of one of Simon's observations on the situation in the USA: the hook that is being dangled is the *fear* of crime; not crime itself.[25]

Secondly, there is a further transparent difference between the approach of the Union to the construction of the AFSJ and the earlier phases of its intervention in the criminal sphere. Production of the Tampere Programme, and of the subsequent Hague and Stockholm Programmes, definitely does constitute the agreement and development of *strategy*. Therefore, with the arrival of the AFSJ, the Union has achieved a sufficient state of maturity for it to be feasible to enquire into the uses to which crime may be being put.

(iii) Mediation of domestic and Union security concerns

(a) Retention of pre-Lisbon Treaty normative order

The Lisbon Treaty did not erase the intergovernmental legacy which characterised EU criminal law prior to its ratification but, instead builds upon it. Institutionally, its arrangements only fully kick in from 1 December 2014.[26] Prior to then, there is no possibility for the Commission to launch infringement proceedings against Member States in this field. Furthermore, there is only a limited possibility for the Court of Justice to entertain preliminary references. It can only accept these from courts whose Member State has given a Declaration to that effect.[27] Member States can choose to limit this power to courts against whose decision there is no judicial remedy[28] and to absolve courts from the obligation to make a reference.[29]

Of greater lasting effect is that measures adopted prior to the Lisbon Treaty are not transformed automatically into Regulations and Directives. They continue their pre-Lisbon Treaty existence. That being so, it is necessary to consider the legal instruments, set out in Article 34(2) TEU(M),[30] which could be adopted prior to Lisbon.[31]

---

[25] J. Simon, *Governing Through Crime: How the War on Crime Transformed American Democracy and Created a Culture of Fear* (New York, Oxford University Press, 2007) 21 and 77.

[26] Protocol on Transitional Provisions, Article 10(1) and (3).

[27] Article 35(2)(b) TEU(M). These are Belgium, Czech Republic, Cyprus, Germany, Greece, France, Italy, Latvia, Lithuania, Luxembourg, Hungary, Netherlands, Austria, Portugal, Romania, Slovenia, Finland and Sweden. Notice from the Council [2010] OJ C56/7.

[28] Article 35(2)(a) TEU(M). Only Spain has chosen this option.

[29] Article 35(1) TEU(M). The Member States whose courts are obliged to refer are Belgium, Czech Republic, Germany, Spain, France, Italy, Luxembourg, Netherlands, Austria and Slovenia.

[30] Article 34(2) TEU lists 'common positions' as a measure that can be adopted. These define the approach of the Union to a particular matter, but cannot be considered legislation as it is not clear what legislative effects these have.

[31] See A. Hinarejos, 'On the Legal Effects of Framework Decisions and Decisions: Directly Applicable, Directly Effective, Self-Executing, Supreme?' (2008) 14 *ELJ* 620.

Framework Decisions. These are used for harmonisation of legislation. They are binding upon the Member States as to the result to be achieved, but leave the form and method of implementation to national authorities. Although they are not capable of direct effect, they are capable of indirect effect. National courts are required to interpret national law so far as possible in the light of the wording and purpose of them.[32]

Decisions. These are to be adopted for all purposes other than harmonisation of legislation. A good example is Decision 98/701/JHA on common standards for filling in the residence permit for non-EU nationals.[33] This appears to harmonise procedures for administrative officials on how to fill in residence permits. A Framework Decision was not chosen, however, as the measure was intended to be purely administrative, and was not intended to affect the competence of Member States relating either to the recognition of states or to passports from these states. Decisions are binding, but, like Framework Decisions, they cannot generate direct effect.

Conventions. These are similar to international agreements. They generate commitments between the Member States and the Union, but their effects upon the internal legal order of Member States is unclear. The Union can only recommend to the Member States that they be adopted within a time limit in accordance with national constitutional requirements. They were typically adopted in areas of particular national sensitivity.

(b) National controls over the law-making process

Whilst EU law-making was supranationalised by the Lisbon Treaty, a number of additional controls were placed to distinguish this field from other fields of EU law.

First, the Commission does not have the monopoly of initiative. Instead, it is shared with the Member States, so that, beside the Commission, one-quarter of Member States can make a proposal for a measure in this field.[34]

The second control is the emergency brake procedure. This applies to measures on judicial cooperation in criminal matters,[35] measures harmonising minimum rules on the definition of criminal offences and criminal sanctions and operational cooperation in policing.[36] In the first two instances, if a Member State considers that a measure affects *fundamental aspects* of its criminal justice system it may ask for the matter to be referred to the European Council. With operational cooperation in policing, it is assumed all aspects are sensitive. If it is not possible to secure unanimity within the Council, the matter is automatically referred to the European Council.

Article 83(3) TFEU

3. Where a member of the Council considers that a draft directive … would affect fundamental aspects of its criminal justice system, it may request that the draft directive be referred to the European Council. In that case, the ordinary legislative procedure shall be suspended. After discussion, and in case of a consensus, the European Council shall, within four months of this suspension, refer the draft back to the Council, which shall terminate the suspension of the ordinary legislative procedure.

---

[32] Case C-105/03 *Pupino* [2005] ECR I-5285. See M. Fletcher, 'Extending "Indirect Effect" to the Third Pillar: The Significance of Pupino' (2005) 30 *ELRev.* 862; B. Kuracz and A. Lazowski, 'Two Sides of the Same Coin? Framework Decisions and Directives' (2006) 25 *YBEL* 177; S. Peers, 'Salvation Outside the Church: Judicial Protection in the Third Pillar after the Pupino and Segi Judgments' (2007) 44 *CMLRev.* 883.
[33] [1998] OJ L333/8.   [34] Article 76 TFEU.   [35] Article 82(3) TFEU.   [36] Article 87(3) TFEU.

Although the European Council has four months to reach a decision, a reference is likely to lead to the measure not being adopted. Decisions are reached in the European Council by unanimity and it would need the Head of State to agree to an EU measure which her own government has already stated affects fundamental aspects of the national criminal justice system. This would politically be very difficult to concede and there may also be domestic constraints limiting what the Head of State can agree. The German Constitutional Court in its *Lisbon Treaty* judgment stated that, if the emergency brake procedure is invoked, agreement can only be granted with the assent of the German parliament.[37] There is acknowledgment that national perceptions of the fundamental interests within criminal justice systems are likely to be highly individual. Consequently, if there is no agreement and nine or more Member States still want to proceed they will be deemed to have the necessary authorisation for the purposes of engaging in enhancing cooperation and adopting an EU law between them.[38]

Thirdly, this field allows for more intense patrolling by national parliaments. In addition to the general EU provisions on parliamentary patrolling of the legislative process for compliance with the subsidiarity principle,[39] there is additional provision that national parliaments must ensure that all proposals and legislative initiatives in the field of criminal law comply with that principle.[40] The thresholds for intervention are also different. In all other fields, if one-third of legislative chambers raise concerns over subsidiarity, the Commission is required to review the legislative proposal. In this field, it is only one-quarter: a lower threshold recognising a higher domestic sensitivity to Union intervention.[41]

(c) Differentiated integration

As EU criminal law forms part of the Area of Freedom, Security and Justice, the United Kingdom and Ireland do not participate in legislative procedures and are not bound by EU measures unless either notifies the Council of its intention to participate in the adoption of a measure.[42] Denmark neither takes part in nor is bound by measures adopted here.[43] If the measure builds upon the Schengen Acquis, as Denmark is party to the Schengen Convention, it must decide within six months whether to implement the measure. In such a case, Denmark has a commitment in international law to the other Member States to comply with the measure.[44] If it is not willing to adopt the measure, it must notify the other Member States and all parties should consider what appropriate measures should be taken.[45]

There is a particular twist, however. The Protocol on the Position of Denmark makes clear that Denmark is bound by all measures adopted prior to the Lisbon Treaty.[46] The regime set out above only applies to measures adopted after the Lisbon Treaty came into effect. The position for the United Kingdom and Ireland differs. If pre-existing acts are amended, both states have to decide whether to participate in and be bound by the amended act, albeit that such

---

[37] 2 BvE 2/08 *Treaty of Lisbon*, Judgment of 30 June 2009, para. 365.

[38] Article 83(3) TFEU. On enhanced cooperation see pp. 135–9.

[39] Article 12(b) TEU and Protocol on the Application of the Principles of Subsidiarity and Proportionality, Articles 6–8.

[40] Article 69 TFEU.

[41] Protocol on the Application of the Principles of Subsidiarity and Proportionality, Article 7(2). On the procedure see pp. 131–3.

[42] Protocol on the Position of the United Kingdom and Ireland, Articles 1–4.

[43] Protocol on the Position of Denmark, Article 2.

[44] *Ibid.* Article 4(1).   [45] *Ibid.* Article 4(2).   [46] *Ibid.* Article 2.

post-Lisbon acts will now be adopted as Regulations, Directives, and so on. If they do not, insofar as the original measure is repealed it will not bind them.[47] Insofar as it remains in force, it will continue to bind them. The United Kingdom is also required to notify other Member States by 1 June 2014 whether it wishes to continue to be bound by acts adopted prior to the Lisbon Treaty.[48] However, following this date, the United Kingdom can subsequently notify the Member States that it wishes to participate in a measure which has ceased to apply to it. In such an instance, it can 'opt in' if the other Member States agree unanimously.[49] No such procedures exist for Ireland who will continue to be bound by pre-Lisbon measures in the same way as Denmark.

In September 2012, and then again in July 2013, the British Government announced its intention to exercise this right to 'opt out' of pre-Lisbon measures, of which there were about 130. It would then apply to rejoin thirty-five of these. At the date of writing, it is not clear whether the Council will allow it to rejoin these measures. The central measures in which the British Government wishes to participate are the main instruments governing mutual recognition and victims' rights; the supranational law-enforcement institutions, Europol and Eurojust; and a number of legal instruments governing exchange of information between law-enforcement agencies. The central instruments from which it is withdrawing are those establishing minimum rules concerning the definition of criminal offences and sanctions in the areas of particularly serious crime; EU agreements with non-EU states in this field; and a significant number of measures governing exchange of information between law-enforcement agencies.[50] Furthermore, the British Government had opted into another twenty-one measures, agreed since the coming into force of the Lisbon Treaty, which were not covered by this opt-out.[51] A feature of this division is that the British Government sees most value in those measures which are most demanding in terms of civil liberties or national sovereignty, be they those on mutual recognition, participation in supranational institutions, or the new supranational rules agreed since Lisbon. By contrast, many of the opt-outs were largely for symbolic reasons. The opt-out of minimum rules on criminal offences and sanctions was likely therefore to have little immediate effect as British law went further than the EU laws in question.

In this, the British Government's position indicated that exit from EU law poses as many challenges as its agreement. For a relationship still has to be established between that Member State and EU law. The Committees in the House of Commons and House of Lords disagreed on whether British Government pressure will lead to participation in too many or too few measures in this field.[52] The House of Lords identified inadequate consultation of stakeholders in the process.[53] Both Committees were, furthermore, furious with the lack of timely information provided to it by the Government, notably inadequate explanation of the reasons for both the

---

[47] *Ibid.* Article 4(a).   [48] Protocol on Transitional Provisions, Article 10(4).

[49] *Ibid.* Article 10(5). For criticism see M. Fletcher *et al.*, *EU Criminal Law and Justice* (Cheltenham, Edward Elgar, 2008) 225–6.

[50] On the measures in which the British Government wishes to participate see HM Government, *Decision pursuant to Article 10 of Protocol 36 to The Treaty on the Functioning of the European Union* (Cm 8671, London, SO, 2013).

[51] House of Commons European Scrutiny Committee, *The UK's Block Opt-Out of Pre-Lisbon Criminal Law and Policing Measures* (21st Report 2012–13, London, SO, 2013) Annex.

[52] House of Lords European Union Committee, *EU Police and Criminal Justice Measures: The UK's 2014 Opt-out Decision* (13th Report Session 2012–13, London, SO, 2012) paras. 274–6; House of Commons, n. 51 above, paras. 553–73.

[53] House of Lords, n. 52 above, paras. 57–9.

'opt-ins' and the 'opt-outs' and the lack of impact assessment provided to the British parliament which would allow it to evaluate these.[54]

3 JUDICIAL COOPERATION IN CRIMINAL JUSTICE

(i) Principle of mutual recognition

One of the central principles of EU criminal law is mutual recognition of judicial decisions. The meaning of the principle was set out in a Commission Communication:

> once … a decision taken by a judge in exercising his or her official powers has been taken, that measure – in so far as it has extranational implications – would automatically be accepted in all other Member States, and have the same or at least similar effects there.[55]

The principle has been given effect by Article 82(1) TFEU.

Article 82 TFEU

1. Judicial cooperation in criminal matters in the Union shall be based on the principle of mutual recognition of judgments and judicial decisions and shall include the approximation of the laws and regulations of the Member States in the areas referred to in paragraph 2 and in Article 83.

   The European Parliament and the Council, acting in accordance with the ordinary legislative procedure, shall adopt measures to:
   (a) lay down rules and procedures for ensuring recognition throughout the Union of all forms of judgments and judicial decisions;
   (b) prevent and settle conflicts of jurisdiction between Member States;
   (c) support the training of the judiciary and judicial staff;
   (d) facilitate cooperation between judicial or equivalent authorities of the Member States in relation to proceedings in criminal matters and the enforcement of decisions.

2. To the extent necessary to facilitate mutual recognition of judgments and judicial decisions and police and judicial cooperation in criminal matters having a crossborder dimension, the European Parliament and the Council may, by means of directives adopted in accordance with the ordinary legislative procedure, establish minimum rules. Such rules shall take into account the differences between the legal traditions and systems of the Member States.

   They shall concern:
   (a) mutual admissibility of evidence between Member States;
   (b) the rights of individuals in criminal procedure;
   (c) the rights of victims of crime;
   (d) any other specific aspects of criminal procedure which the Council has identified in advance by a decision; for the adoption of such a decision, the Council shall act unanimously after obtaining the consent of the European Parliament.

   Adoption of the minimum rules referred to in this paragraph shall not prevent Member States from maintaining or introducing a higher level of protection for individuals.

---

[54] House of Commons, n. 51 above, paras. 85–102 and 545–50; House of Lords, n. 52 above, paras. 45–6.
[55] European Commission, *Mutual Recognition of Final Decisions in Criminal Matters*, COM(2000)495, 2.

If mutual recognition is about giving effect to a decision of a court from another Member State in one's own territory, it nevertheless performs a number of different functions.

First, there can be mutual recognition of decisions which inculpate the defendant. The European Evidence Warrant allows a judge in one Member State to ask authorities in other Member States to collect evidence which might be used in the prosecution of an offence.[56]

Secondly, there may be mutual recognition of decisions which allow an individual to be tried. The European Arrest Warrant allows courts to require authorities in other Member States to surrender an individual to be tried for certain punishable acts.[57] Mutual recognition also extends to other processes which allow the proper pursuit of the trial. The European Supervision Order allows one Member State to recognise the supervision order issued by another pending trial.[58] This requires it to supervise an individual in its territory pending the trial of the latter in another Member State and ensure that (s)he does not abscond, intimidate witnesses or do anything which might threaten the trial.

Thirdly, there may be mutual recognition of sanctions. Member States are committed to enforcing a wide variety of non-custodial sanctions against individuals on their territories issued by courts of other Member States. These include probation and other non-custodial sentences,[59] confiscation orders[60] and financial penalties.[61] However, they also relate to custodial sentences. Member States can be required to surrender individuals who have been sentenced for certain offences to the state concerned.[62] Alternately, there is provision for Member States who have sentenced an individual to recognise the conditions of detention in other states and, subject to the prisoner's consent, allow for the prisoner to serve the remainder of his sentence in the state of nationality or prior residence.[63]

Finally, there is mutual recognition of decisions which exculpate the defendant. Known under its Latin title of *ne bis in idem*, a court finding of innocence or no case to answer in one Member State means that an individual cannot be tried in another Member State for a similar offence.[64]

In all cases, other than the last, mutual recognition increases the power of the state over the individual. Its powers of prosecution, trial and punishment are increased by its being

[56] Framework Decision 2008/978/JHA on the European evidence warrant for the purpose of obtaining objects, documents and data for use in proceedings in criminal matters [2008] OJ L350/72.

[57] Framework Decision 2002/584/JHA on the European arrest warrant and the surrender procedures between Member States [2002] OJ L190/1 as amended by Framework Decision 2009/299/JHA [2009] OJ L81/24.

[58] Framework Decision 2009/829/JHA on the application, between Member States of the European Union, of the principle of mutual recognition to decisions on supervision measures as an alternative to provisional detention [2009] OJ L294/20. See also Framework Decision 2003/577/JHA on the execution in the European Union of orders freezing property or evidence [2003] OJ L196/45.

[59] Framework Decision 2008/947/JHA on the application of the principle of mutual recognition to judgments and probation decisions with a view to the supervision of probation measures and alternative sanctions[2008] OJ L337/102, as amended by Framework Decision 2009/299/JHA [2009] OJ L81/24.

[60] Framework Decision 2006/783/JHA on the application of the principle of mutual recognition to confiscation orders [2006] OJ L328/59, as amended by Framework Decision 2009/299/JHA [2009] OJ L81/24.

[61] Framework Decision 2005/214/JHA of 24 February 2005 on the application of the principle of mutual recognition to financial penalties [2005] OJ L76/16, as amended by Framework Decision 2009/299/JHA [2009] OJ L81/24.

[62] Framework Decision 2002/584/JHA on the European arrest warrant and the surrender procedures between Member States [2002] OJ L190/1, as amended by Framework Decision 2009/299/JHA [2009] OJ L81/24.

[63] Framework Decision 2008/909/JHA on the application of the principle of mutual recognition to judgments in criminal matters imposing custodial sentences or measures involving deprivation of liberty for the purpose of their enforcement in the European Union [2008] OJ L327/27, as amended by Framework Decision 2009/299/JHA [2009] OJ L81/24.

[64] See Schengen Implementing Convention, Article 54.

able to coopt another state to supply evidence, surrender individuals, impose penalties and so on. Furthermore, this system relies on mutual trust. The Member State supplying the evidence, for example, assumes that the other state will not use it to violate the fundamental rights of the citizen concerned. Equally, the Member State seeking the individual or the evidence relies on the implementing state to do so in a manner which respects the fundamental rights of the accused. In both cases, there is a leap of faith. The safeguarding of fundamental rights is something presumed rather than something which the legal system sees as its task to be vigilant and protective about. This is particularly worrying in a field (as we have seen) which carries such democratic sensitivities and where, given the possibility of deprivation of liberty, the consequences of miscarriages of justice are so serious. The application of the principle of mutual recognition to this field was thus subject to considerable criticism by both academics[65] and practitioners,[66] particularly insofar as it might apply with any automaticity. As we shall see, a number of constraints have emerged which qualify the operation of the principle. This has led to further difficulties, however, insofar as it has created new privileged categories protected from the principle whilst leaving other categories vulnerable to it.

(ii) European Arrest Warrant

(a) European Arrest Warrant and duties of surrender

The most controversial and high-profile application of the mutual recognition principle is the European Arrest Warrant (EAW) set out in Decision 2002/584/JHA.[67] The EAW is:

> a judicial decision issued by a Member State with a view to the arrest and surrender by another Member State of a requested person, for the purposes of conducting a criminal prosecution or executing a custodial sentence or detention order.[68]

The EAW has a number of distinctive features.

First, the authority issuing the warrant is a judicial authority and the warrant is sent to judicial authorities in the executing state where the person is being sought.[69] It might appear, therefore, that an important safeguard of the process is that the process is an exclusively judicial one. However, a number of Member States allow not just judges but also prosecutors to issue EAWs,[70] and the British Supreme Court has held that the term is sufficiently wide to include both.[71] The second noteworthy feature of the process is its speed. In principle, if

---

[65] For criticism of the early law see S. Alegre and M. Leaf, 'Mutual Recognition and Judicial Co-operation: A Step Too Far Too Soon? Case Study – The European Arrest Warrant' (2004) 10 *ELJ* 200; S. Peers, 'Mutual Recognition and Criminal Law in the European Union: Has the Council Got It Wrong?' (2004) 41 *CMLRev.* 5; V. Mitsilegas, 'The Constitutional Implications of Mutual Recognition in Criminal Matters in the EU' (2006) 43 *CMLRev.* 1277.

[66] E. Simon, 'Running Before We Can Walk? Mutual Recognition at the Expense of Fair Trials in Europe's Area of Freedom, Justice and Security' (2013) 4 *New Journal of European Criminal Law* 82.

[67] Framework Decision 2002/584/JHA, n. 62 above. The literature is significant: see R. Blextoon *et al.* (eds.), *Handbook on the European Arrest Warrant* (The Hague, TMC Asser, 2004); J. Wouters and F. Naert, 'Of Arrest Warrants, Terrorist Offences and Extradition Deals: An Appraisal of the EU's Main Criminal Law Measures against Terrorism after "11 September"' (2004) 41 *CMLRev.* 911.

[68] Framework Decision 2002/584/JHA, article 1(1).

[69] *Ibid.* articles 6 and 9(1).

[70] EU Council, *Final Report on the Fourth Round of Mutual Evaluations*, Council Doc. 8302/1/09 Rev. 1.

[71] *Assange* v *Swedish Prosecution Authority* [2012] UKSC 22, per Lord Philips.

the accused consents to his surrender to the requesting state, the surrender should take place within ten days of consent.[72] If there is no consent, surrender should take place within sixty days of arrest.[73] In all cases, there must be a judicial hearing in the executing state before a decision is made to surrender the person being sought.[74] Furthermore, states can provide for appeals to this hearing with suspensive effects (so the person cannot be surrendered pending appeal) provided that these time limits are still observed.[75] The third noteworthy feature, its most controversial, is the abolition of double criminality for a number of offences (Article 2(2)). For thirty-two offences, the Member State is required to surrender the requested person even if the acts alleged do not constitute an offence within the executing state. For offences where the period of detention is of at least twelve months or a detention order has been given of at least four months, the judicial authority in the executing state can choose to waive the requirement of double criminality (Article 2(4)).

Decision 2002/584/JHA, Article 2

1. A European arrest warrant may be issued for acts punishable by the law of the issuing Member State by a custodial sentence or a detention order for a maximum period of at least 12 months or, where a sentence has been passed or a detention order has been made, for sentences of at least four months.

2. The following offences, if they are punishable in the issuing Member State by a custodial sentence or a detention order for a maximum period of at least three years and as they are defined by the law of the issuing Member State, shall, under the terms of this Framework Decision and without verification of the double criminality of the act, give rise to surrender pursuant to a European arrest warrant:[76] ...

4. For offences other than those covered by paragraph 2, surrender may be subject to the condition that the acts for which the European arrest warrant has been issued constitute an offence under the law of the executing Member State, whatever the constituent elements or however it is described.

This duty to surrender is subject to some exceptions. The executing state is not to surrender the person if the offence is covered by an amnesty in that state; the person sought is below the age of criminal responsibility in that state; or where the person has already been judged and sentenced by another Member State in respect of the same acts.[77]

---

[72] Framework Decision 2002/584/JHA, article 17(2).

[73] *Ibid.* article 17(3). The time limits may be extended by thirty days where it is impossible for the surrendering state to meet the deadlines. In such cases, the surrendering state must notify the judicial authorities in the requesting state and give reasons for its failure to meet the deadlines. *Ibid.* article 17(4).

[74] *Ibid.* article 19.

[75] Case C-168/13 PPU *F* v *Premier Ministre*, Judgment of 30 May 2013.

[76] The Framework Decision then lists the thirty-two offences. They are participation in a criminal organisation, terrorism, trafficking in human beings, sexual exploitation of children and child pornography, illicit trafficking in narcotics and weapons, corruption, fraud, money laundering, counterfeiting and piracy, environmental crime, facilitation of unauthorised entry and residence, murder, grievous bodily injury, illicit trade in hormonal substances, human organs, kidnapping, hostage-taking, racism and xenophobia, organised or armed robbery, illicit trafficking in cultural goods, swindling, racketeering and extortion, forgery, illicit trafficking in radioactive materials, trafficking in stolen vehicles, rape, arson, crimes within the jurisdiction of the International Criminal Court, unlawful seizure of aircraft/ships, and sabotage.

[77] *Ibid.* article 3.

There are a number of exceptions, furthermore, where it may choose not to surrender the person:

- the executing state is prosecuting,[78] has chosen not to prosecute or has passed judgment on the requested person for the same act;[79]
- the prosecution of the requested person falls within the executing state's jurisdiction and is statute-barred;[80]
- the requested person has been judged by a third state in respect of the same acts and, where there has been sentence, the sentence has been or is being served, or may no longer be executed in the sentencing state;[81]
- if the EAW is served for purposes of a detention order, and (a) the requested person is staying in, or is a national or resident of the executing state and (b) that state undertakes to execute the detention in accordance with its own law;[82]
- the offence was committed in whole or in part in the territory of the executing state or was committed outside the territory of the issuing state and the law of the executing state does not allow for prosecution of the offence;[83]
- the person was not present at their trial.[84]

The EAW has prompted more challenges before constitutional courts than any other EU law.[85] It has provoked concerns on three grounds: first, that there are insufficient guarantees that the surrendered person will receive a fair trial back in the issuing state; secondly, the abolition of double criminality requires states to expose individuals to criminal processes and sanctions for activities which are not illegal within their territories; thirdly, many states have traditionally provided that they cannot surrender their citizens for punishment to other states.

(b) European Arrest Warrant and rights of defence

The EAW creates a presumption about the quality of justice present in the issuing state, namely, that due process is observed and the accused will secure or has had a fair trial. This presumption has been challenged most strongly before the German Constitutional Court, which has ruled that German nationals can only be surrendered when 'the rule of law is observed' in the issuing state. This has been interpreted to mean that the state in question must offer corresponding legal structures and protections to the accused to those offered by Germany.[86] It has

---

[78] *Ibid.* article 4(2). The notion of what is the 'same act' as interpreted identically to that in the *ne bis in idem* principle. Acts are the same when 'encompass[ing] a set of concrete circumstances which are inextricably linked together'. Case C-261/09 *Mantello* [2010] ECR I-11477, para. 39.

[79] *Ibid.* article 4(3).   [80] *Ibid.* article 4(4).   [81] *Ibid.* article 4(5).

[82] *Ibid.* article 4(6). This is addressed in more detail later. See pp. 649–51.

[83] *Ibid.* article 4(7).

[84] *Ibid.* article 4a(1). This is subject to a number of exceptions, of which the most notable are that the person was summoned and informed in due time of the date and place of the trial and that a decision may be handed down if she does appear at the trial or that they choose to be represented by a legal counsellor rather than appearing in person.

[85] The literature is enormous. See V. Mitsilegas, *EU Criminal Law* (Oxford/Portland, Hart, 2009) 133–8 which refers to most of the literature. Also helpful are the Special Issues (2008) 6(1) *I-CON* and (2013) 4(1) *New Journal of European Criminal Law*.

[86] Article 16(2) of the German Basic Law imposes this requirement that Germans can only be surrendered to other EU Member States where 'the rule of law is observed'. The judgment is *Re Constitutionality of German Law Implementing the Framework Decision on a European Arrest Warrant* [2006] 1 CMLR 16.

also been considered a number of times by the Court of Justice. In *Radu*, four arrest warrants were issued by the German authorities to the Romanian authorities for the surrender of Radu on charges of robbery. He argued that surrender to Germany would violate his fundamental rights as the Romanian court could not be sure that these would be observed during the German process. The Court of Justice considered whether the German authorities issuing warrants without first giving Radu a right to a hearing violated his fundamental rights.

Case C-396/11 *Radu*, Judgment of 29 January 2013

31. ...the referring court is essentially asking whether Framework Decision 2002/584, read in the light of Articles 47 and 48 of the Charter and of Article 6 of the ECHR, must be interpreted as meaning that the executing judicial authorities can refuse to execute a European arrest warrant issued for the purposes of conducting a criminal prosecution on the ground that the issuing judicial authorities did not hear the requested person before that arrest warrant was issued.

32. In that regard, it must first of all be noted that the right to be heard, which is guaranteed by Article 6 of the ECHR and mentioned by the referring court in its questions, is today laid down in Articles 47 and 48 of the Charter. It is therefore necessary to refer to those provisions of the Charter...

36. As the Court has already held, according to the provisions of Framework Decision 2002/584, the Member States may refuse to execute such a warrant only in the cases of mandatory non-execution provided for in Article 3 thereof and in the cases of optional non-execution listed in Articles 4 and 4a...

38. By contrast, the fact that the European arrest warrant has been issued for the purposes of conducting a criminal prosecution, without the requested person having been heard by the issuing judicial authorities, does not feature among the grounds for non-execution of such a warrant as provided for by the provisions of Framework Decision 2002/584.

39. Contrary to what Mr Radu argues, the observance of Articles 47 and 48 of the Charter does not require that a judicial authority of a Member State should be able to refuse to execute a European arrest warrant issued for the purposes of conducting a criminal prosecution on the ground that the requested person was not heard by the issuing judicial authorities before that arrest warrant was issued.

40. It must be stated that an obligation for the issuing judicial authorities to hear the requested person before such a European arrest warrant is issued would inevitably lead to the failure of the very system of surrender provided for by Framework Decision 2002/584 and, consequently, prevent the achievement of the area of freedom, security and justice, in so far as such an arrest warrant must have a certain element of surprise, in particular in order to stop the person concerned from taking flight.

41. In any event, the European legislature has ensured that the right to be heard will be observed in the executing Member State in such as way as not to compromise the effectiveness of the European arrest warrant system.

42. Thus, it is apparent from Articles 8 and 15 of Framework Decision 2002/584 that, before deciding on the surrender of the requested person for the purposes of prosecution, the executing judicial authority must subject the European arrest warrant to a degree of scrutiny. In addition, Article 13 of that framework decision provides that the requested person has the right to legal counsel in the case where he consents to his surrender and, where appropriate, renounces his entitlement to the speciality rule. Furthermore, under Articles 14 and 19 of Framework Decision 2002/584, the requested person, where he does not consent to his surrender and is the subject of a European arrest warrant issued for the purposes of conducting a criminal prosecution, is entitled to be heard by the executing judicial authority, under the conditions determined by mutual agreement with the issuing judicial authorities.

The Court of Justice indicates that the EAW will be read and interpreted in the light of EU fundamental rights and that individual surrenders must comply with it. However, it also takes a strong view that the EAW expresses and respects fundamental rights guarantees. This position was repeated in *Melloni*. The case, described earlier in this book, concerned an Italian who skipped bail and was sentenced in his absence to ten years in prison for fraud.[87] A request was made to the Spanish authorities to surrender him. Trial *in absentia* was considered a violation of fundamental rights under the Spanish Constitution. The EAW allows surrender where there has been such a trial either where the person waived that right by refusing to attend having been given due notice of the time and place or chooses to be represented by a lawyer.

Case C–399/11 *Melloni*, Judgment of 26 February 2013

49. Regarding the scope of the right to an effective judicial remedy and to a fair trial provided for in Article 47 of the Charter, and the rights of the defence guaranteed by Article 48(2) thereof, it should be observed that, although the right of the accused to appear in person at his trial is an essential component of the right to a fair trial, that right is not absolute … The accused may waive that right of his own free will, either expressly or tacitly, provided that the waiver is established in an unequivocal manner, is attended by minimum safeguards commensurate to its importance and does not run counter to any important public interest. In particular, violation of the right to a fair trial has not been established, even where the accused did not appear in person, if he was informed of the date and place of the trial or was defended by a legal counsellor to whom he had given a mandate to do so.

50. This interpretation of Articles 47 and 48(2) of the Charter is in keeping with the scope that has been recognised for the rights guaranteed by Article 6(1) and (3) of the ECHR by the case-law of the European Court of Human Rights.

51. Furthermore, as indicated by Article 1 of Framework Decision 2009/299, the objective of the harmonisation of the conditions of execution of European arrest warrants issued for the purposes of executing decisions rendered at the end of trials at which the person concerned has not appeared in person, effected by that framework decision, is to enhance the procedural rights of persons subject to criminal proceedings whilst improving mutual recognition of judicial decisions between Member States.

52. Accordingly, Article 4a(1)(a) and (b) of Framework Decision 2002/584 lays down the circumstances in which the person concerned must be deemed to have waived, voluntarily and unambiguously, his right to be present at his trial, with the result that the execution of a European arrest warrant issued for the purposes of executing the sentence of a person convicted *in absentia* cannot be made subject to the condition that that person may claim the benefit of a retrial at which he is present in the issuing Member State. This is so either where, as referred to in Article 4a(1)(a), the person did not appear in person at the trial despite having been summoned in person or officially informed of the scheduled date and place of the trial or, as referred to in Article 4a(1)(b), the person, being aware of the scheduled trial, deliberately chose to be represented by a legal counsellor instead of appearing in person.

Melloni follows *Radu* in finding the fundamental rights guarantees in the EAW to be sufficient. However, it goes further insofar as it states that the EAW takes precedence over fundamental rights set out in national constitutions.[88] This assertion was challenged within two months by the Regional Court in Munich. A Bulgarian had initially been given a probation order for drink-driving. He breached it and was sentenced to ten months in prison. He claimed this latter

[87] See pp. 202–3.   [88] On prior national responses, see pp. 228–9.

sentence violated his fundamental rights as it had been passed *in absentia*. The German court considered this in the light of the German law implementing the EAW which only allows surrender if the principles set out in Article 6 TEU (i.e. respect for fundamental rights) are respected in the case in hand. It found there to be no violation of fundamental rights but stated the following.

General Public Prosecution Office v *K*, Order of 15 May 2013 (Superior Regional Court Munich)[89]

... the ECJ jurisprudence [*Radu* and *Melloni*] does not imply that [the] German Act would be rendered inapplicable by virtue of the primacy of European Union law.

While it is true that national law must be interpreted in conformity with framework decisions ... this does not suggest that domestic law be interpreted clearly *contra legem*. In addition and at least until 1 December 2014, framework decisions have no direct effects [Article 34(2) second sentence lit. b) TEU Amsterdam, Articles 9 and 10(2), (3) Protocol on Transitional Provisions to the Treaty of Lisbon]; even after this date, direct effects seem doubtful to the extent that they limit individual rights.

Further, ECJ judgments must not, as part of a cooperative relationship between the ECJ and national courts, 'be read in a way that would view it as an apparent ultra vires act or as if it endangered the protection and enforcement of the fundamental rights in the Member States in a way that questioned the identity of the constitutional order of the Basic Law' (German Constitutional Court – 1st Senate – 24 April 2013 – 1 BvR 1215/07, para. 91; translation provided for in the official English press release). Accordingly, it must not be presumed that the ECJ intended to make national courts and authorities execute European Arrest Warrants even where they, or the criminal proceedings upon which they are based, evidently violate the fundamental rights and freedoms of the requested person as they are spelt out in the Charter of Fundamental Rights of the European Union or the European Convention for the Protection of Human Rights and Fundamental Liberties. Indeed, states must not lend a willing hand to evident human rights violations by other states; this also and in particular holds true within the European Union, which constitutes an area of freedom, security and justice; and certainly mutual recognition must not be a cloak to mutually recognize human rights violations. If it were otherwise, the Senate would, with a view to Article 6 TEU, ask the ultra vires question and, with a view to Article 23 German Basic Law, the question whether the identity of the German constitutional order be impaired, which would oblige the Senate to refer these questions to the German Constitutional Court.

Even if the EAW is, thus, unlikely to be challenged under EU law, there is a good chance that individual national courts will scrutinise its operation in individual cases certainly against EU human rights norms. Notwithstanding the Court of Justice's judgment in *Melloni*, many national legal systems insist that national constitutional provisions should also prevail over EU law. It may well, therefore, be scrutinised against these as well.[90]

In a bid to bridge this gap, the Union has adopted legislation setting out minimum rights for the accused and those suspected of crimes. Provision is made for a right to interpretation and

---

[89] This translation is taken from J. Vogel, 'Reaction to *Radu* Judgment of the Oberlandesgericht of Munich of 15 May 2013' (2013) 4 *New Journal of European Criminal Law* 310.

[90] This may well be the case in the United Kingdom where the EU police and judicial cooperation in criminal justice provisions were held not to be covered by European Communities Act 1972, s. 2, with the consequence that primacy of EU law does not prevail in these fields. In such instances, the human rights standard is the British Human Rights Act 1998, *Assange* v *Swedish Prosecution Authority* [2012] UKSC 22, per Lord Manse.

translation in criminal proceedings.[91] Persons not speaking or understanding the language of the criminal proceedings are to be granted access to an interpreter before investigative and judicial authorities. This right to an interpreter will exist during all police questioning, all court hearings and any necessary interim hearings,[92] and will also be made available for communication with legal counsel.[93] In addition, all documents essential to preserving the rights of defence and safeguarding the fairness of the proceedings must be translated within a reasonable period of time.[94]

The most extensive set of rights are those, however, in the Directive on the right to information, Directive 2012/13/EU.[95] This sets out two tiers of rights to information.

The first is a series of rights which the accused or suspects must be provided with promptly. These might be communicated orally or in writing, but this must be done in simple and accessible language, taking account of the particular needs of vulnerable suspects or accused.[96]

Directive 2012/13/EU, Article 3(1)

1. Member States shall ensure that suspects or accused persons are provided promptly with information concerning at least the following procedural rights, as they apply under national law, in order to allow for those rights to be exercised effectively:
   (a) the right of access to a lawyer;
   (b) any entitlement to free legal advice and the conditions for obtaining such advice;
   (c) the right to be informed of the accusation, in accordance with Article 6;
   (d) the right to interpretation and translation;
   (e) the right to remain silent.

In addition to these, information must also be provided about the criminal act of which the person is suspected or accused.[97]

The second tier of rights is communicated promptly in a Letter of Rights to those who are arrested or detained.[98] This contains the rights set out above in article 3 and a number of others set out below in article 4(2).

Directive 2012/13/EU, Article 4(2)

2. In addition to the information set out in Article 3, the Letter of Rights referred to in paragraph 1 of this Article shall contain information about the following rights as they apply under national law:
   (a) the right of access to the materials of the case;
   (b) the right to have consular authorities and one person informed;
   (c) the right of access to urgent medical assistance; and
   (d) the maximum number of hours or days suspects or accused persons may be deprived of liberty before being brought before a judicial authority.

---

[91] Directive 2010/64/EU on the right to interpretation and translation in criminal proceedings [2010] OJ L280/1. Ireland and the United Kingdom participate in this Directive.
[92] *Ibid.* article 2(1). [93] *Ibid.* article 2(2). [94] *Ibid.* article 3(1).
[95] Directive 2012/13/EU on the right to information in criminal proceedings [2012] OJ L142/1. Ireland and the United Kingdom participate in this Directive.
[96] *Ibid.* article 3(2). [97] *Ibid.* article 6(1). [98] *Ibid.* article 4(1).

The accused or detained must also be granted access to the file about them unless this poses a serious threat to the fundamental rights of others or refusal is necessary to safeguard an important public interest.[99] They must be provided with the reasons for their arrest or detention, including the criminal act they are suspected or accused of having committed,[100] and, at the latest when the submission is presented before a court, detailed information must be provided on the accusation, including the nature and legal classification of the criminal offence, as well as the nature of participation by the accused person.[101]

Implicit in the provision of information about these rights is the expectation that they will be granted to the suspect or the accused. Welcome as this is, it is doubtful whether this is sufficient. These procedural guarantees do not deal with the risks that arise as a consequence of coordination between legal systems. Long-standing warrants for relatively small offences can remain in the system with the consequent delay leading to real questions about the fairness of any trial. It is not possible for the executing court to ask further questions if there are justified concerns about the accused or suspect being a case of mistaken identity.[102]

Some of these issues were addressed by Directive 2013/48/EU.[103] For those subject to EAW proceedings, this provides for a right of access to a lawyer in both the executing state[104] and the issuing state.[105] This right of access must be granted without undue delay and in such a way that it allows the person to exercise their rights of defence practically and effectively. The right of access to a lawyer exists right up to the conclusion of the case, namely, the final determination of whether the person has committed the offence.[106] Its substance includes the right to communicate in private with one's lawyer, notably prior to questioning; the right for the lawyer to be present during questioning; and the right for the lawyer to attend any investigative actions where such actions are provided for by national law and attendance of the suspect is permitted or required.[107] These rights may be waived where the accused or suspect has been informed clearly about their rights and the consequence of waiver and has, notwithstanding this, waived these rights unequivocally and voluntarily.[108] There is also a right to confidentiality of lawyer-client communications.[109]

(c) European Arrest Warrant and principles of legality and proportionality

The majority of offences subject to the abolition of the principle of double criminality are not harmonised at Union level, and some are not even crimes in every Member State.[110] The consequence is that in some cases a Member State may have to surrender a person for activities which the state itself does not consider illegal. This was challenged in *Advocaten voor de Wereld* by a Belgian non-profit organisation. One of the grounds was that the Framework Decision violated the principle of legality of criminal offences.

---

[99] *Ibid.* article 7(4).   [100] *Ibid.* article 6(2).   [101] *Ibid.* article 6(3).

[102] J. Baker, *A Review of the United Kingdom's Extradition Arrangements* (London, SO, 2011) 119–20.

[103] Directive 2013/48/EU on the right of access to a lawyer in criminal proceedings and in European arrest warrant proceedings, and on the right to have a third party informed upon deprivation of liberty and to communicate with third persons and with consular authorities while deprived of liberty [2013] OJ L294/1. The United Kingdom and Ireland are not participating in this Directive.

[104] *Ibid.* article 10(1).   [105] *Ibid.* article 10(4).   [106] *Ibid.* article 2(1).

[107] *Ibid.* article 3(3). The last of these rights may be derogated from where the geographical remoteness of a suspect makes access to a lawyer impossible without undue delay after deprivation of liberty, *Ibid.* article 3(5).

[108] *Ibid.* article 9.   [109] *Ibid.* article 4.

[110] M. Fichera, 'The European Arrest Warrant and the Sovereign State: A Marriage of Convenience' (2009) 15 *ELJ* 70, 79.

> **Case C–303/05 *Advocaten voor de Wereld* v *Leden van de Ministerraad* [2007] ECR I–3633**
>
> 48. According to Advocaten voor de Wereld, the list of more than 30 offences in respect of which the traditional condition of double criminality is henceforth abandoned if those offences are punishable in the issuing Member State by a custodial sentence or detention order for a maximum period of at last three years is so vague and imprecise that it breaches, or at the very least is capable of breaching, the principle of legality in criminal matters. The offences set out in that list are not accompanied by their legal definition but constitute very vaguely defined categories of undesirable conduct. A person deprived of his liberty on foot of a European arrest warrant without verification of double criminality does not benefit from the guarantee that criminal legislation must satisfy conditions as to precision, clarity and predictability allowing each person to know, at the time when an act is committed, whether that act does or does not constitute an offence, by contrast to those who are deprived of their liberty otherwise than pursuant to a European arrest warrant.
>
> 49. The principle of the legality of criminal offences and penalties (*nullum crimen, nulla poena sine lege*), which is one of the general legal principles underlying the constitutional traditions common to the Member States, has also been enshrined in various international treaties, in particular in Article 7(1) ECHR...
>
> 50. This principle implies that legislation must define clearly offences and the penalties which they attract. That condition is met in the case where the individual concerned is in a position, on the basis of the wording of the relevant provision and with the help of the interpretative assistance given by the courts, to know which acts or omissions will make him criminally liable...
>
> 51. In accordance with Article 2(2) of the Framework Decision, the offences listed in that provision give rise to surrender pursuant to a European arrest warrant, without verification of the double criminality of the act, 'if they are punishable in the issuing Member State by a custodial sentence or a detention order for a maximum period of at least three years and as they are defined by the law of the issuing Member State'.
>
> 52. Consequently, even if the Member States reproduce word-for-word the list of the categories of offences set out in Article 2(2) of the Framework Decision for the purposes of its implementation, the actual definition of those offences and the penalties applicable are those which follow from the law of 'the issuing Member State'. The Framework Decision does not seek to harmonise the criminal offences in question in respect of their constituent elements or of the penalties which they attract.
>
> 53. Accordingly, while Article 2(2) of the Framework Decision dispenses with verification of double criminality for the categories of offences mentioned therein, the definition of those offences and of the penalties applicable continue to be matters determined by the law of the issuing Member State, which, as is, moreover, stated in Article 1(3) of the Framework Decision, must respect fundamental rights and fundamental legal principles as enshrined in Article 6 TEU, and, consequently, the principle of the legality of criminal offences and penalties.
>
> 54. It follows that, in so far as it dispenses with verification of the requirement of double criminality in respect of the offences listed in that provision, Article 2(2) of the Framework Decision is not invalid on the ground that it infringes the principle of the legality of criminal offences and penalties.

The issue of double criminality is a threshold question. It goes to the quality of suspected or alleged behaviour sufficient to justify a Member State surrendering somebody to another state. The EAW indicates that, for thirty-two offences, it is not that of whether the alleged activity is illegal in the executing state and for other offences it need not be. However, it is insufficient that it simply be illegal in the issuing state. *Advocaten voor de Wereld* indicates (at paragraph 53) that the offences in question must respect certain fundamental rights and legal principles, such as being clear and ascertainable.

This is not always sufficient nationally. In Germany, an additional requirement has been introduced by the Higher Regional Court in Stuttgart. The warrant must be proportionate. It, thus, has been reluctant to surrender where either the offence is seen as minor or the penalty as excessive. It, thus, refused to surrender somebody to Lithuania who had no previous criminal record and was wanted for possession of 1.44 grams of methamphetamine, or to make a surrender to Spain where the public prosecutor was seeking a prison term of four years for somebody who sold 0.2 grams of cocaine to an undercover police officer.[111] More broadly, the European Commission has noted two persistent concerns. The warrant is too often used for trivial offences, with bicycle theft being one notorious example. A further concern is that warrants are often used at an early stage to facilitate investigation of the crime rather than apprehension of the accused, with the corollary risk of inappropriate detention of people at too early a stage in the proceedings.[112]

(d) European Arrest Warrant and national citizenship

The concern on which there has been most debate within national constitutional courts is the surrender by a Member State of its own citizens for trial or punishment in another state.[113] A number of national constitutions, notably the Cypriot, Czech, German and Polish, have historically banned extradition on the grounds that this amounts to a de facto stripping of citizenship, as citizenship involves the state giving the citizen a territory of their own which they cannot be forced to leave. This has, in turn, acted as a basis for states prosecuting their citizens for crimes committed abroad.[114]

Some concession to this is made by the EAW. Article 4(6), it will be remembered, allows it not to be served for a national or resident of the executing state where that state undertakes to execute the detention in accordance with its own law. In *Wolzenburg*, a German national had entered the Netherlands from Germany in 2005. A year later an arrest warrant was issued

---

[111] For these examples and analysis see Baker, n. 102 above, 162–77.

[112] European Commission, *On the Implementation since 2007 of the Council Framework Decision of 13 June 2002 on the European Arrest Warrant and the Surrender Procedures Between Member States*, COM(2011)175, 7–8. See also K. Weiss, 'The European Arrest Warrant: A Victim of Its Own Success?' (2011) 2 *New Journal of European Criminal Law* 124. The latter concern has been reduced by the European Supervision Order which allows bail restrictions to be monitored by the executing state with the result that the issuing state does not have to detain people because they are a flight risk or might interfere with the prosecution of the trial. Framework Decision 2009/829/JHA on the application, between Member States of the European Union, of the principle of mutual recognition to decisions on supervision measures as an alternative to provisional detention [2009] OJ L294/20.

[113] *Re Constitutionality of Framework Decision on the European Arrest Warrant* [2007] 3 CMLR 24 (Czech Republic); *Re Constitutionality of German Law Implementing the Framework Decision on a European Arrest Warrant* [2006] 1 CMLR 16; P1/05 *Re Enforcement of a European Arrest Warrant (Polish Constitutional Tribunal)* [2006] 1 CMLR 36; SK 26/08 *Surrender of a Person who is the Subject of the European Arrest Warrant*, Judgment of 5 October 2010 (Polish Constitutional Tribunal); *Attorney General* v *Konstantinou* [2007] 3 CMLR 42 (Cyprus). For concerns in Greece see *Re Enforcement of a European Arrest Warrant against Tzoannos* [2008] 2 CMLR 38 (Greek Court of Appeal). By contrast, special provision for a Member State's own nationals has been declared unconstitutional in Italy, Italian Constitutional Court, Judgment 227 of 24 June 2010 [2010] 12 *Cassazione Penale* 4148.

[114] *Re Constitutionality of German Law Implementing the Framework Decision on a European Arrest Warrant* [2006] 1 CMLR 16, paras. 66 and 67.

by the German authorities for importation of marijuana. The Dutch legislation provided for non-surrender of Dutch nationals and other EU citizens who had been lawfully resident in the Netherlands for five years. Wolzenburg argued that this residence condition of five years unlawfully discriminated against other EU citizens.

Case C–123/08 *Wolzenburg* [2009] ECR I-9621

62. ...it must be emphasised that, although the ground for optional non-execution set out in Article 4(6) of the Framework Decision has ... in particular the objective of enabling the executing judicial authority to give particular weight to the possibility of increasing the requested person's chances of reintegrating into society when the sentence imposed on him expires ... such an objective, while important, cannot prevent the Member States, when implementing that Framework Decision, from limiting, in a manner consistent with the essential rule stated in Article 1(2)[115] thereof, the situations in which it is possible to refuse to surrender a person who falls within the scope of Article 4(6) thereof.

63. Next, with regard to whether a requirement for residence for a continuous period of five years, as laid down in the national legislation at issue in the main proceedings, is contrary to the principle of non-discrimination based on nationality, it must be borne in mind that that principle requires that comparable situations must not be treated differently and that different situations must not be treated in the same way unless such treatment is objectively justified ...

67. It is necessary to point out, as has already been stated in paragraph 62 of the present judgment, that the ground for optional non-execution set out in Article 4(6) of Framework Decision 2002/584 has in particular the objective of enabling the executing judicial authority to give particular weight to the possibility of increasing the requested person's chances of reintegrating into society when the sentence imposed on him expires. The Member State of execution is therefore entitled to pursue such an objective only in respect of persons who have demonstrated a certain degree of integration in the society of that Member State.

68. In the present case, the single condition based on nationality for its own nationals, on the one hand, and the condition of residence of a continuous period of five years for nationals of other Member States, on the other, may be regarded as being such as to ensure that the requested person is sufficiently integrated in the Member State of execution. By contrast, a Community national who does not hold the nationality of the Member State of execution and has not resided in that State for a continuous period of a given length generally has more connection with his Member State of origin than with the society of the Member State of execution.

69. In order to be justified in the light of Community law, the difference in treatment provided for by the Netherlands legislation must also be proportionate to the legitimate objective pursued by the national law. It may not go beyond what is necessary in order to attain that objective ...

70. In that regard, the view may reasonably be taken that the rule that a European arrest warrant may not be executed against nationals of the Member State of execution does not appear to be excessive. Those nationals have a connection with their Member State of origin such as to ensure their social reintegration after the sentence imposed on them has been enforced. Moreover, nor can a condition requiring residence for a continuous period of five years for nationals of other Member States be considered to be excessive, having regard, in particular, to the conditions necessary to satisfy the requirement of integration of non-nationals in the Member State of execution.

---

[115] Framework Decision 2002/584/JHA, article 1(2) sets out the basic principle of mutual recognition.

The protection extends beyond a right to refuse to execute a warrant for a Member State's own nationals or residents. Article 5(3) of the Framework Decision also allows a state to make surrender conditional on the person being returned to serve any custodial sentence or detention order there. The ethos is that set out in *Wolzenburg*, namely, that serving one's sentence there facilitates subsequent social reintegration. Whilst this is clearly desirable, as the piece from Mitsilegas below indicates, it creates a two-tier system of those settled in one Member State, who enjoy significant protection, and a more mobile population exposed to the full vicissitudes of the EAW.

V. Mitsilegas, 'The Limits of Mutual Trust in Europe's Area of Freedom, Security and Justice: From Automatic Inter-State Cooperation to the Slow Emergence of the Individual' (2012) 31 *Yearbook of European Law* 319, 371

… systems of automatic inter-state cooperation based upon a high level of mutual trust founded upon the uncritical acceptance that fundamental rights are respected by all EU Member States in all circumstances have been seriously challenged. There has been a gradual shift from automaticity based on the interests of the State and blind mutual trust to the examination of the impact of cooperative systems on the fundamental rights and the specific situation of the individuals affected. This shift has been reflected in the interventions by both the European judiciary (in rejecting the conclusive presumption that fundamental rights are respected across the EU and establishing the requirement for courts asked to participate in inter-state cooperation systems to examine the situation of the affected individual on a case-by-case basis), and the EU legislator (in accepting the need for the adoption of specific fundamental rights standards in EU secondary law to address the issues arising from inter-state cooperation). The second facet concerns *trust from the perspective of the affected individuals*. Here it is important to distinguish between different categories of individuals affected by inter-state cooperation mechanisms resulting in the enforced intra-EU transfer of individuals. On the one hand, one can discern a privileged category of individuals consisting of EU citizens based in their State of nationality. Elevated protection against transfer has been accepted in favour of this category of citizens in the context of the operation of the European Arrest Warrant in the executing Member State, although in a discriminatory manner this level of protection does not necessarily extend to other EU citizens resident in the same State. On the other hand, one can also discern a category of underprivileged individuals, whose enforced movement within the EU is largely automatic. Unwanted individuals such as foreign prisoners and asylum seekers fall under this category. Not only does the operation of automaticity in this context seriously challenge the protection of fundamental rights of these individuals, but it is also doubtful whether inter-state cooperation in this context serves freedom, security, or justice within the European Union.

(iii) Principle of *ne bis in idem*

As mentioned earlier, the principle of mutual recognition can be applied in an exculpatory manner whereby national authorities recognise prior decisions of other authorities in the Union with regard to allegations of criminal activity.[116] The principle, that of *ne bis in idem*, is set out in Article 54 of the 1990 Schengen Implementing Convention (referred to often by its French acronym, CISA).

---

[116] On the principle see B. van Bockel, *The Ne Bis in Idem Principle in EU Law* (Alphen aan den Rijn, Kluwer Law International, 2010) especially ch. 4.

> **Article 54 CISA**
>
> A person whose trial has been finally disposed of in one Contracting Party may not be prosecuted in another Contracting Party for the same acts provided that, if a penalty has been imposed, it has been enforced, is actually in the process of being enforced or can no longer be enforced under the laws of the sentencing Contracting Party.

On an initial reading, the provision appears narrow. It seems only to cover a person who has already been subject to a judicial trial, and appears only to be a prohibition on a double trial which is furthermore not absolute in that the person could still be tried if the penalty had been waived. This interpretation was rejected in *Gözütok and Brügge*.[117] Gözütok owned a coffee shop in the Netherlands. He was charged with possession of large amounts of marijuana. He did a plea bargain with the Dutch prosecution authorities where, in return for making a financial settlement, charges were dropped. A similar sequence of events occurred with Brügge. Charges of assault and wounding were dropped by the Belgian authorities in return for him paying an out-of-court settlement. Both Gözütok and Brügge subsequently went to Germany where they were charged with the offences. The German authorities argued that they were not bound by Article 54 CISA as the case had not been disposed of by a court but merely dropped by the prosecuting authorities.

> **Joined Cases C-187/01 and C-385/01 *Gözütok and Brügge* [2003] ECR I-1345**
>
> 26. It is clear from the wording of Article 54 of the CISA that a person may not be prosecuted in a Member State for the same acts as those in respect of which his case has been 'finally disposed of' in another Member State.
> 27. A procedure whereby further prosecution is barred, such as those at issue in the main actions, is a procedure by which the prosecuting authority, on which national law confers power for that purpose, decides to discontinue criminal proceedings against an accused once he has fulfilled certain obligations and, in particular, has paid a certain sum of money determined by the prosecuting authority.
> 28. Therefore, it should be noted, first, that in such procedures, the prosecution is discontinued by the decision of an authority required to play a part in the administration of criminal justice in the national legal system concerned.
> 29. Second, a procedure of this kind, whose effects as laid down by the applicable national law are dependent upon the accused's undertaking to perform certain obligations prescribed by the Public Prosecutor, penalises the unlawful conduct which the accused is alleged to have committed.
> 30. In those circumstances, the conclusion must be that, where, following such a procedure, further prosecution is definitively barred, the person concerned must be regarded as someone whose case has been 'finally disposed of' for the purposes of Article 54 of the CISA in relation to the acts which he is alleged to have committed. In addition, once the accused has complied with his obligations, the penalty entailed in the procedure whereby further prosecution is barred must be regarded as having been 'enforced' for the purposes of Article 54.

---

[117] M. Fletcher, 'Some Developments to the *Ne Bis in Idem* Principle in the European Union' (2003) 66 *MLR* 769.

31. The fact that no court is involved in such a procedure and that the decision in which the procedure culminates does not take the form of a judicial decision does not cast doubt on that interpretation, since such matters of procedure and form do not impinge on the effects of the procedure, as described at paragraphs 28 and 29 of this judgment, which, in the absence of an express indication to the contrary in Article 54 of the CISA, must be regarded as sufficient to allow the *ne bis in idem* principle laid down by that provision to apply.

32. Furthermore, it should be pointed out that nowhere … is the application of Article 54 of the CISA made conditional upon harmonisation, or at the least approximation, of the criminal laws of the Member States relating to procedures whereby further prosecution is barred.

33. In those circumstances, whether the *ne bis in idem* principle enshrined in Article 54 of the CISA is applied to procedures whereby further prosecution is barred (regardless of whether a court is involved) or to judicial decisions, there is a necessary implication that the Member States have mutual trust in their criminal justice systems and that each of them recognises the criminal law in force in the other Member States even when the outcome would be different if its own national law were applied.

34. For the same reasons, the application by one Member State of the *ne bis in idem* principle, as set out in Article 54 of the CISA, to procedures whereby further prosecution is barred, which have taken place in another Member State without a court being involved, cannot be made subject to a condition that the first State's legal system does not require such judicial involvement either.

35. The aptness of that interpretation of Article 54 of the CISA is borne out by the fact that it is the only interpretation to give precedence to the object and purpose of the provision rather than to procedural or purely formal matters, which, after all, vary as between the Member States concerned, and to ensure that the principle has proper effect.

36. First,… the European Union set itself the objective of maintaining and developing the Union as an area of freedom, security and justice in which the free movement of persons is assured.

37. Furthermore, as the first paragraph of the preamble to the Protocol shows, the integration of the Schengen acquis (which includes Article 54 of the CISA) into the framework of the European Union is aimed at enhancing European integration and, in particular, at enabling the Union to become more rapidly the area of freedom, security and justice which it is its objective to maintain and develop.

38. Article 54 of the CISA, the objective of which is to ensure that no one is prosecuted on the same facts in several Member States on account of his having exercised his right to freedom of movement, cannot play a useful role in bringing about the full attainment of that objective unless it also applies to decisions definitively discontinuing prosecutions in a Member State, even where such decisions are adopted without the involvement of a court and do not take the form of a judicial decision.

39. Second, national legal systems which provide for procedures whereby further prosecution is barred do so only in certain circumstances or in respect of certain exhaustively listed or defined offences which, as a general rule, are not serious offences and are punishable only with relatively light penalties.

40. In those circumstances, if Article 54 of the CISA were to apply only to decisions discontinuing prosecutions which are taken by a court or take the form of a judicial decision, the consequence would be that the *ne bis in idem* principle laid down in that provision (and, thus, the freedom of movement which the latter seeks to facilitate) would be of benefit only to defendants who were guilty of offences which – on account of their seriousness or the penalties attaching to them – preclude use of a simplified method of disposing of certain criminal cases by a procedure whereby further prosecution is barred, such as the procedures at issue in the main actions.

The *ne bis in idem* principle requires, first, that 'the trial be disposed of'. In *Gözütok and Brügge* this was interpreted as meaning that the *prosecution* be disposed of. The reasons for the disposal are not important. In *Gaspirini*, a Spanish prosecution of the defendant, who had illegally imported olive oil into the Union, was found to violate the principle. This was because a prior prosecution in Portugal had failed as it had not been brought within sufficient time under Portuguese law.[118] In *Bourquain*, a German national had been found guilty *in absentia* by a French military tribunal of a murder committed during the Algerian war of independence, and was sentenced to death.[119] He fled to Eastern Germany. Under French law, penalties not enforced within twenty years lapse, and Bourquain's offence was also covered by an amnesty granted by the French Government. In 2001 the Germany authorities discovered what happened and sought to prosecute him for the murder. It was held that *Bourquain* was protected by the *ne bis in idem* principle as the case had been disposed of both because of the twenty-year rule and because the penalty was unable to be enforced.

There are, however, qualifications to the principle. First, there must be no possibility of further prosecution in the original Member State. In *Turansky*, a decision by the police in Slovakia to suspend prosecution against Turansky for robbery of an Austrian national did not under Slovak law stop them reopening the prosecution if they judged fit.[120] This was held not to bar an Austrian court hearing the case, as it had not been finally disposed of in Slovakia, and it was this idea of final disposition that lay at the heart of *ne bis in idem*. Secondly, an authority will not be held to have disposed of the matter unless it has assessed the facts. In *Miraglia*, the defendant was charged with importing heroin into the European Union by both the Dutch and the Italian authorities.[121] The Dutch authorities brought charges one month before the Italian authorities but dropped them on the basis that Miraglia was in Italy and being tried in Italy. Miraglia argued that as the case had been dropped in the Netherlands, it had been disposed of there and should be dropped in Italy. This was rejected by the Court of Justice. It noted that there had been no assessment of the unlawful conduct by the Dutch authorities, and to consider the dropping of the case because the Italian authorities were prosecuting it as sufficient to dispose of the matter and thus forestall further investigation would run contrary to the ethos of the Area of Freedom, Security and Justice which was to prevent crime.

The *ne bis in idem* principle requires, secondly, that the 'same acts' be disposed of. In *Van Esbroeck*, the Court of Justice had to consider a Belgian who had been convicted in Norway of illegally importing narcotics into Norway.[122] On his return to Belgium, he was charged with illegally exporting narcotics from Belgium. The Court held that one should not look at how acts are classified in national law as national classifications would necessarily vary. Instead, an EU definition was set out of whether the acts were materially identical or not. This would be the case where a set of concrete circumstances 'are inextricably linked together' – something that appeared to be the case here but which the Court of Justice left for the national court to decide. The test is necessarily dependent on the factual context, and has to be somewhat vague for that reason. It does seem, however, that it will cover a range of actions rather than just a single act or transaction. In *Van Straaten*, the accused was convicted in the Netherlands with

---

[118] Case C-467/04 *Gaspirini* [2006] ECR I-9199. [119] Case C-297/07 *Bourquain* [2008] ECR I-9425.
[120] Case C-491/07 *Turansky* [2008] ECR I-11039. [121] Case C-469/03 *Miraglia* [2005] ECR I-2009.
[122] Case C-436/04 *Van Esbroeck* [2006] ECR I-2333. Norway is party to the Schengen Convention so a disposal by it counts in the same way.

one co-accused of importing and possessing heroin on 26 March 1983. He was subsequently convicted in Italy with another co-accused of exporting a far larger amount of heroin to the Netherlands on 27 March 1983.[123] Van Straaten appealed against the Italian conviction, arguing that he was protected by the principle of *ne bis in idem* because of the earlier Dutch conviction notwithstanding that the drugs and the co-accused in each case were different. The Court stated the activities could still be classified as the same acts if the national court considered them to be inextricably linked. This suggests that where prosecution or sentencing is brought against just a part of the activity of the defendant it will still be held to bar a subsequent prosecution or court decision against the activity as a whole. This is a very broad interpretation of what constitutes the 'same acts', and limits were placed in *Kraaijenbrink*.[124] Kraaijenbrink was sentenced in the Netherlands for several offences of drug trafficking committed over a seven-month period. She was subsequently tried for other drugs offences in Belgium that began at the same time but continued for another ten months. She claimed that these were all part of the same activity based on a common intention to deal in drugs. Neither the Dutch nor the Belgian court shared this view, with both believing that the offences were discrete. The Court of Justice agreed. It stated that the fact that there was a common intention behind the offences was insufficient to make them materially identical. For that to happen, the offences needed to be inextricably linked: something that did not appear to be the case in this instance.

The wide interpretation of the *ne bis in idem* principle has led to Member States being required to recognise not merely each other's judicial decisions but also each other's criminal procedure and prosecutorial policy. The principle of mutual recognition is also applied in a fairly absolute way, and this had led to many references, as Mitsilegas has noted, reflecting unease at authorities having to acquiesce to decisions by other authorities within the Union with which they do not agree.[125] In *Bourquain*, other Member States were being asked to recognise the procedures of a military tribunal that were widely seen by all states intervening in the case as esoteric. The judgment offended their sense of when murder cases should be prosecuted, so struck a very deep moral chord. Arguing that these sentiments should be trumped to enable an interpretation that secures free movement seems perverse indeed. The system is also odd as a basis for allocating jurisdiction. It is a 'first come, first served' approach to jurisdiction which can allow criminals to play the system by inviting prosecution in the jurisdiction which treats them most leniently. Furthermore, if criminal activities extend across more than one state, it is unclear why prosecution and sentencing should be confined to a single state. It may be that it is better to allocate different dimensions of the criminality to different jurisdictions.[126]

4 HARMONISATION AND INCREASED CRIMINALISATION THROUGH EU LAW

The procedures for harmonisation of the constituent elements of particular criminal offences and the sanctions for these offences are set out in Article 83 TFEU. The provision does not establish a general power for the Union to harmonise criminal law but rather sets out two classes of offences which may be subject to harmonising measures.

---

[123] Case C-150/05 *Van Straaten* [2006] ECR I-9327. For similar reasoning see Case C-288/05 *Kretzinger* [2007] ECR I-6441.

[124] Case C-367/05 *Kraaijenbrink* [2007] ECR I-6619.   [125] Mitsilegas, n. 85 above, 149–51.

[126] On the debate see M. Fletcher, 'The Problem of Multiple Criminal Prosecutions: Building an Effective EU Response' (2007) 26 *YBEL* 33; Mitsilegas, n. 85 above, 153–5.

The first class comprises a limited number of crimes listed in the Treaty because they are deemed both to be serious and to have a transnational dimension. There is an internal tension to the provision as these two dimensions can place differing demands. Article 83(1) TFEU has addressed this by allowing offences to be added to those explicitly mentioned through use of the assent procedure.

Article 83(1) TFEU

1. The European Parliament and the Council may, by means of directives adopted in accordance with the ordinary legislative procedure, establish minimum rules concerning the definition of criminal offences and sanctions in the areas of particularly serious crime with a cross-border dimension resulting from the nature or impact of such offences or from a special need to combat them on a common basis. These areas of crime are the following: terrorism, trafficking in human beings and sexual exploitation of women and children, illicit drug trafficking, illicit arms trafficking, money laundering, corruption, counterfeiting of means of payment, computer crime and organised crime.

   On the basis of developments in crime, the Council may adopt a decision identifying other areas of crime that meet the criteria specified in this paragraph. It shall act unanimously after obtaining the consent of the European Parliament.

In the second class of offences, criminal law is seen as a regulatory tool parasitic on a prior EU policy – be it protection of the Union budget, the common transport policy or environment policy – and which is assessed against how it contributes to the realisation of that policy.

Article 83(2) TFEU

2. If the approximation of criminal laws and regulations of the Member States proves essential to ensure the effective implementation of a Union policy in an area which has been subject to harmonisation measures, directives may establish minimum rules with regard to the definition of criminal offences and sanctions in the area concerned. Such directives shall be adopted by the same ordinary or special legislative procedure as was followed for the adoption of the harmonisation measures in question, without prejudice to Article 76[127].

The two classes of harmonisation are subject to some similar constraints. The emergency brake procedure applies to both so that a Member State can refer any proposal in either to the European Council if it believes it will affect fundamental aspects of its criminal justice system.[128] There are also national constitutional constraints. The German Constitutional Court in its *Lisbon Treaty* judgment stated that the Union should leave the German legislature free to determine which interests should be legally protected and which sanctions should be imposed on culpable conduct.[129] Finally, the EU institutions have set out their own commitment to

---

[127] This provision, it will be remembered, allows a proposal to be made either by the Commission or one-quarter of Member States.
[128] Article 83(3) TFEU.
[129] 2 BvE 2/08 *Treaty of Lisbon*, Judgment of 30 June 2009, para. 356. See pp. 627–8.

self-constraint. The Stockholm Action Programme, which sets out the action to be taken in the Area of Freedom, Security and Justice up until 2014 and the 2011 Commission Communication on EU Criminal Policy state that criminal law provisions should only be introduced as a last resort.[130]

However, beyond this, the dynamics of each class of offences are different.

(i) Euro-crimes

The Union has secondary legislation setting out the constituent elements and minimum penalties for a diverse array of crimes extending a little beyond those mentioned in Article 83(1) TFEU.[131] These include fraud and counterfeiting,[132] money laundering,[133] human trafficking,[134] terrorism,[135] corruption in the private sector,[136] drug trafficking,[137] sexual exploitation of children,[138] cybercrime,[139] organised crime[140] and racism and xenophobia.[141] This diversity raises questions about the rationale behind Union intervention. Chaves has noted that, heinous though many of those crimes may be, there is little to suggest that these crimes have significant and transnational dimensions which distinguish them from other crimes. Crimes such as rape, murder or robbery per se, for example, are not within EU's purview. Instead, she suggests that the Union is moving towards establishing a new form of 'Euro-crime' centred around a loose idea of organised crime in which the common and distinguishing feature of these offences is that they rely for their realisation upon a sense of common enterprise and prior infrastructure.[142]

---

[130] EU Council, *The Stockholm Programme: An Open and Secure Europe Serving and Protecting the Citizens,* Council Doc. 17024/09, 29; European Commission, *Towards an EU Criminal Policy: Ensuring the Effective Implementation of EU Policies Through Criminal Law,* COM(2011)573, 7–8.

[131] On these see S. Miettinen, *Criminal Law and Policy in the European Union* (Abingdon, Routledge, 2013) 145–75.

[132] Framework Decision 2001/413/JHA combating fraud and counterfeiting of non-cash means of payment [2001] OJ L149/1; Framework Decision 2000/383/JHA on increasing protection by criminal penalties and other sanctions against counterfeiting in connection with the introduction of the euro [2000] OJ L140/1, as amended by Framework Decision 2001/888/JHA [2001] OJ L329/3. There is a proposal to replace the latter by a Directive. European Commission, Proposal for a Directive on the protection of the euro and other currencies against counterfeiting by criminal law, and replacing Council Framework Decision 2000/383/JHA, COM(2013)42.

[133] Framework Decision 2001/500/JHA on money laundering, the identification, tracing, freezing, seizing and confiscation of instrumentalities and the proceeds of crime [2001] OJ L182/1.

[134] Directive 2011/36/EU on preventing and combating trafficking in human beings and protecting its victims [2011] OJ L101/1. Ireland is participating in this Directive but not the United Kingdom.

[135] Framework Decision 2002/ 475/JHA on combating terrorism [2002] OJ L164/3, as amended by Framework Decision 2008/919/JHA [2008] OJ L330/21.

[136] Framework Decision 2003/568/JHA of 22 July 2003 on combating corruption in the private sector [2003] OJ L192/54.

[137] Framework Decision 2004/757/JHA laying down minimum provisions on the constituent elements of criminal acts and penalties in the field of illicit drug trafficking [2004] OJ L335/8.

[138] Directive 2011/92/EU on combating the sexual exploitation of children and child pornography [2011] OJ L335/1. Both Ireland and the United Kingdom participate in this Directive.

[139] Directive 2013/40/EU on attacks against information systems [2013] OJ L218/8. Both Ireland and the United Kingdom participate in this Directive.

[140] Framework Decision 2008/841/JHA on the fight against organised crime [2008] OJ L300/42.

[141] Framework Decision 2008/913/JHA on combating certain forms and expressions of racism and xenophobia by means of criminal law [2008] OJ L328/55.

[142] It seems that this may be in part because the concept of organised crime is so malleable that it has become both a convenient container for further criminalisation and Union intervention, resulting in an over-extension of the concept. F. Calderoni, 'A Definition that Could not Work: The EU Framework Decision on the Fight against Organised Crime' (2008) 16 *European Journal of Crime, Criminal Law and Criminal Justice* 265.

M. Chaves, *European Criminal Law: Reshaping Criminal Justice Across the European Union?* (London, Mimeo, 2009)

[The Treaty] made reference to concepts of transnationality or seriousness of the criminality at stake. However, these concepts not only are not systematically addressed in the measures adopted as they often collapse at the light of specific examples. Take for instance the examples of private corruption and trafficking in human beings. Corruption for example does not necessarily need to be transnational, although trafficking in human beings most likely is. As for the seriousness of the offences, in principle, they both are serious offences, but this is a vague criteria. Corruption wise, how much is enough to be considered serious? Trafficking wise, would an offence of transporting two passengers in a private vehicle by the price of £500 each into UK territory be considered serious? Would the evaluation change if the payment was of £5000 or if the number of people illegally inserted in the UK was of two hundred instead of two?

The large majority of offences above, thus, require infrastructure in the sense of technology, means of transport, or telecommunication or of a network which allows for the completion of the offence. Trafficking in human beings, for example, requires the use of transport to move people and the setting up of physical structures to keep them. Likewise, terrorist acts traditionally also involve the use of materials, the construction of chemical or other type of weaponry able to cause severe bodily harm to others, and often perpetrators use sites to assemble and prepare for the crime. Likewise, the laundering of profits of crime involves necessary infrastructures such as particular businesses or the use of the financial system in general through which money can be moved and laundered. Furthermore, the large majority of these offences often involve more than one perpetrator to be effective. Organised crime, terrorism, trafficking in human beings, drugs or theft of works of art or money laundering, for example, are all offences that require usually more than one perpetrator and a certain degree of coordination. These two ideas are close to what Levi calls a contemporary legal construction or form of organised crime which, accordingly, have a close relationship to 'tools of later modernity', such as 'transnational air travel and communications, internet and the spread of information about weapons construction, globalisation of financial services and commerce including the arms trade and covert networking'.[143]

That said, the category has a slippery and indeterminate quality to it. It is possible for many of these offences to be carried out by isolated individuals. Furthermore, some of the offences harmonised did not exist in all Member States. In others, they often existed in a much more restricted form. Article 83(1) TFEU is used therefore to extend criminalisation of activities that were previously not criminal in some Member States. Chaves, after finding similar patterns with regard to the Framework Decisions on cybercrime, illicit drug trafficking and terrorism, provides the example of the Framework Decision on Human Trafficking, which existed prior to the Directive which has now been adopted on this.[144] Some Member States did not have such an offence and others had narrower offences, because Framework Decision 2002/629/JHA included as trafficking the recruitment, transportation, transfer, harbouring or subsequent reception of a person for the exploitation of labour or services – a very broad definition indeed.

[143] M. Levi, 'Organized Crime and Terrorism' in M. Maguire *et al.* (eds.), *The Oxford Handbook of Criminology* (4th edn, Oxford, Oxford University Press, 2007) 775.

[144] See n. 134 above.

M. Chaves, *European Criminal Law: Reshaping Criminal Justice Across the European Union?* (London, Mimeo, 2009)

Examples can be found with regard to trafficking in human beings, countries such as Estonia and Poland did not have criminal offences corresponding with the conducts described in the Framework Decision, while all other Member States already contained provisions relating to such acts.[145] Even in countries where such acts were already considered as offences, the definition of trafficking in the Framework Decision is broader than most pre-existing definitions in national laws and even in international instruments. This is because the EU introduced the additional general element of 'labour exploitation', while most legislation covered trafficking only for the purposes of sexual exploitation, prostitution or forced or slave labour.

Dutch law did not include in its definition of trafficking any other purpose beside sexual exploitation. However, with the Framework Decision, the provision was amended in order to include 'coerced or forced work or services, slavery and practices and bondage comparable to slavery'.[146] Likewise, Portuguese law, in the earlier versions of the Portuguese Penal Code, only considered trafficking of persons for the purpose of sexual exploitation.[147] However, in 2007 the crime was expanded in order to incorporate the purpose of labour exploitation and extraction of organs[148] thus complying with the Framework Decision.

Consequently, the harmonisation in this field is of a different kind from other areas of EU law. It does not seek to create definitions which are sufficiently uniform to allow free movement of goods or services but rather those which act as a starting point for a Member State to create new criminal offences or extend existing ones. An example is the new offence of 'conduct related to a criminal organisation' set out in the Framework Decision below.

Framework Decision 2008/841/JHA on the fight against organised crime[149]

Article 1
For the purposes of this Framework Decision:
1. 'criminal organisation' means a structured association, established over a period of time, of more than two persons acting in concert with a view to committing offences which are punishable by deprivation of liberty or a detention order of a maximum of at least four years or a more serious penalty, to obtain, directly or indirectly, a financial or other material benefit;
2. 'structured association' means an association that is not randomly formed for the immediate commission of an offence, nor does it need to have formally defined roles for its members, continuity of its membership, or a developed structure.

---

[145] European Commission, *Report based on Article 10 of Framework Decision on Combating Trafficking in Human Beings*, COM(2006)187, 6.

[146] Criminal Code, art. 250a, after changes introduced by the Act of 13 July 2002.

[147] Article 169 in the version of Decreto Lei 48/95 of 15 March 1995 and following the alterations of Lei 99/2001 of 25 August 2001.

[148] Lei 59/2007 of 4 September 2007.   [149] [2008] OJ L300/42.

Article 2

Each Member State shall take the necessary measures to ensure that one or both of the following types of conduct related to a criminal organisation are regarded as offences:

(a) conduct by any person who, with intent and with knowledge of either the aim and general activity of the criminal organisation or its intention to commit the offences in question, actively takes part in the organisation's criminal activities, including the provision of information or material means, the recruitment of new members and all forms of financing of its activities, knowing that such participation will contribute to the achievement of the organisation's criminal activities;

(b) conduct by any person consisting in an agreement with one or more persons that an activity should be pursued, which if carried out, would amount to the commission of offences referred to in Article 1, even if that person does not take part in the actual execution of the activity.

Article 3

1. Each Member State shall take the necessary measures to ensure that:
   (a) the offence referred to in Article 2(a) is punishable by a maximum term of imprisonment of at least between two and five years; or
   (b) the offence referred to in Article 2(b) is punishable by the same maximum term of imprisonment as the offence at which the agreement is aimed, or by a maximum term of imprisonment of at least between two and five years.
2. Each Member State shall take the necessary measures to ensure that the fact that offences referred to in Article 2, as determined by this Member State, have been committed within the framework of a criminal organisation, may be regarded as an aggravating circumstance.

The definition is vague and general. It could include three teenagers who have got together over a month to commit a number of burglaries, but it could also encompass the largest scale of Mafia-like activity. Whilst in the former case, it is clear that they should be prosecuted for burglary it is not clear why this liability should be exacerbated by virtue of Article 3 with potentially large jail terms. There is a concern that harmonisation in this area is leading to an unnecessary and unconstrained extension of repressive measures.[150] Herlin-Karnell has, furthermore, observed that there are not simply dangers in any ever-widening number of activities being criminalised. The characteristics of these offences, with their elements of organisation, collective action and possible transnational quality, have allowed the Union to justify measures not simply on the basis of stopping or punishing certain activity but also to curb *the risk* of such activity taking place. For these activities are seen as something pervasive and external to Member States, whose incidence is unclear. These qualities, in turn, justify greater intrusion, surveillance and policing than might otherwise be the case.[151]

---

[150] For findings similar to those of Chaves see A. Weyembergh, 'Approximation of Criminal Laws, the Constitutional Treaty and the Hague Programme' (2005) 42 *CMLRev.* 1567, 1588–90; T. Elholm, 'Does EU Criminal Cooperation Necessarily Mean Increased Repression?' (2009) 17 *European Journal of Crime, Criminal Law and Criminal Justice* 191.

[151] E. Herlin-Karnell, *The Constitutional Dimension of European Criminal Law* (Oxford, Hart, 2012) 175–7.

(ii) EU criminal law and regulatory effectiveness of other EU policies

The second class of offences has its roots in the EC pillar of the TEU prior to the Lisbon Treaty. The Court of Justice imposed duties on Member States to secure the effective functioning of policies within that pillar and take appropriate criminal sanctions which were effective enough to meet that duty.[152] Measures were, therefore, adopted requiring Member States to prohibit unauthorised use of firearms, facilitating illegal migration, insider dealing, ship pollution, environmental crimes and money laundering.[153] Article 83(2) TFEU establishes that the Union may set minimum rules on both the definition of offences and on sanctions in such cases.[154] However, there are two constraints. First, criminal measures may only be adopted where these are essential to ensuring the effective implementation of an EU policy. This would suggest that they can only be used as a measure of last resort where other measures have not been effective. Secondly, the area must already have 'been subject to harmonisation measures'. The gist of this phrase is that criminal measures can only be deployed within a prior legislative framework which has already been set out by EU legislation. However, it could have been expressed a lot more clearly. A narrow interpretation would be that they can only be adopted in respect of activities that breach a norm set out in prior EU legislation. A broader interpretation would allow for the possibility that where an area has been subject to partial harmonisation, criminal measures can be adopted touching on activities not fully regulated by an EU measure but which, nevertheless, operate within a context that is strongly informed by EU law.

5 EUROPEAN UNION RIGHTS OF VICTIMS

The final powerful strand of EU criminal law goes to the rights of victims. Article 82(2)(c) TFEU provides that the Union may provide minimum rules on the rights of victims of crime. The rights provided are extensive and are unusual for Union rights in that they apply not merely to transnational situations, such as the rights of a victim resident in a state of which they are not a national, or in a context which is defined by other provisions of EU law (i.e. when these set out certain offences and questions may arise as to the rights and needs of the victims of those offences). Instead, the central rights apply to any situation within the Union where there is a victim of a criminal offence. As a group, therefore, victims enjoy rights under EU law that other categories do not enjoy. We have, thus, already seen that EU fundamental rights are only granted to individuals where there is a prior legal context. Similarly, EU citizenship rights are only granted where there is a transnational dimension or where the violation deprives the citizen of the 'substance' of the right.[155] The other twist is that recognition of the rights of victims

---

[152] Case 68/88 *Commission* v *Greece* [1989] ECR 2965.

[153] Directive 91/477/EC on control of the acquisition and possession of firearms, article 16 [1991] OJ L256/51, as amended by Directive 2008/51/EC [2008] OJ L179/5; Directive 2003/6/EC on insider dealing and market manipulation, article 14(1) [2003] OJ L96/16; Directive 2002/90/EC defining the facilitation of unauthorised entry, transit and residence, article 3 [2002] OJ L328/17; Directive 2005/35/EC on ship-source pollution and on the introduction of penalties, particularly criminal penalties, for infringements, article 8(1) [2005] OJ L255/11; Directive 2008/99/EC on the protection of the environment through criminal law, article 5 [2008] OJ L328/28; Directive 2005/60/EC on the prevention of the use of the financial system for the purpose of money laundering and terrorist financing, article 39 [2005] OJ L309/15.

[154] Criminal measures continue to be adopted on the basis of other EU legal competences, however. In relation to Article 114 TFEU and the single market, therefore, see Regulation 98/2013/EU on the marketing and use of explosives precursors, article 11 [2013] OJ L39/1.

[155] See Chapter 11.

is something which has emerged within many European states only relatively recently, and their recognition is relatively haphazard.[156]

Experience elsewhere suggests also that there are ambivalences about how this category of rights is to be developed. On the one hand, this category suggests a greater empathy and recognition for those whose lives have been harmed or destroyed by the activity in question, and are placed in a vulnerable situation by virtue of the trial. Victims' rights, thus, allow victims greater agency and voice in a process which is both often traumatic for them and goes to a recent source of trauma.[157] On the other hand, victims' rights are also used not to empower victims but to justify greater criminalisation of activities, repressive measures against the accused and limitations on rights of due process as the administration acts in the name of victims to engage in all these.[158] Alongside this, and particularly pertinently in the case of the European Union, victims' rights can be used by a political system to justify identification with it. Aware that citizens will not identify with repressive measures carried out in the name of a vague public interest, use of the idea of the victim can generate both greater support for criminal measures and a political order in that it feeds both on the empathy that citizens feel for victims of crime and the awareness that the acts befalling victims of crime could also befall them.[159]

The central piece of legislation on the rights of victims of crime is Directive 2012/29/EU establishing minimum standards on the rights, support and protection of victims of crime.[160] The Directive, first, establishes a wide category of beneficiaries by setting out a broad notion of victim.

Directive 2012/29/EU, article 2(1)(a)

1. (a) 'victim' means:
    (i) a natural person who has suffered harm, including physical, mental or emotional harm or economic loss which was directly caused by a criminal offence;
    (ii) family members of a person whose death was directly caused by a criminal offence and who have suffered harm as a result of that person's death;[161]

There is no threshold with regard either to the quality of the crime or the harm suffered. Victims of all are granted equal rights. A person whose window is broken has the same entitlements as those subject to life-changing grievous abuse. This 'one size fits all' approach raises questions both about whether the procedure can be deployed by the former to press for disproportionate effects to be expended on minor offences, and about whether,

---

[156] On these divergences see European Commission, *Report from the Commission pursuant to Article 18 of the Council Framework Decision of 15 March 2001 on the Standing of Victims in Criminal Proceedings*, COM(2009)166.

[157] See e.g. J. Doak, 'Victims' Rights in Criminal Trials: Prospects for Participation' (2005) 32 *JLS* 294.

[158] Simon, n. 25 above, 77–105.

[159] M. Dubber, *Victims in the War on Crime: The Use and Abuse of Victims' Rights* (New York, New York University Press, 2006) 4–5.

[160] [2012] OJ L315/57. Ireland and United Kingdom participate in this Directive. The date for transposition is 16 November 2015.

[161] These are the spouse, those in a committed intimate relationship or living in a joint household and on a stable and continuous basis with the victim, the relatives in direct line, the siblings and the dependants of the victim. *Ibid.* article 2(1)(b).

conversely, it offers enough to those who have been left in the most terrible situation by the criminal act.

The Directive provides a number of categories of rights and support to victims: rights of information and support, a right to participate in the criminal proceedings, and a right to protection.

The headline principle for information and support is set out in article 3 of the Directive.

Directive 2012/29/EU, article 3(1)

1. Member States shall take appropriate measures to assist victims to understand and to be understood from the first contact and during any further necessary interaction they have with a competent authority in the context of criminal proceedings, including where information is provided by that authority.

There are two types of entitlements which fall under this heading: a right to understand and a right to be understood.

A right to understand is about the provision of information which enables the victim to chart what is taking place. The right to understand includes a right to receive information, without unnecessary delay, after their first contact with a competent authority – typically when they report the crime – about their rights and entitlements under the Directive.[162] It also includes a right to receive information about the case, in particular on any decision not to prosecute or investigate further; the time and place of the trial and nature of the charges brought; any final judgment; and the state of criminal proceedings, unless, exceptionally, it adversely affects the handling of the case.[163] This information shall include the reasons behind the judgment or the decision not to proceed unless it compromises some national legal duty of confidentiality.[164]

In some ways, the right to be understood comprises a more sweeping set of entitlements. It includes the right to be understood in a formal sense. There is, thus, the right to free interpretation and translation services where the victim does not speak the language of the proceedings. These will, as a minimum, be provided for interviews and questioning of them during the investigation, and where they have to participate in the court hearings.[165] It shall also extend to translation of information essential for victims to exercise their rights and of any decision not to proceed and the reasons for this.[166]

However, the right to be understood also embraces an approach which centres around responding to the needs of the victim. It thus includes, first, a right to written acknowledgment of their formal complaint and the basic elements of the criminal offence concerned.[167] This acknowledgment allows the victim to see whether they have been understood and acts as a baseline against which they can track subsequent process. Secondly, it includes a right not to receive information. This wish is binding on national authorities unless the victim is required to participate actively in the criminal proceedings.[168] Thirdly, it includes the right to be informed when the alleged offender (or offender) is released or escapes (certainly in all cases

---

[162] *Ibid.* article 4.   [163] *Ibid.* article 6(1) and (2).   [164] *Ibid.* article 6(3).   [165] *Ibid.* article 7(1).
[166] *Ibid.* article 7(3).   [167] *Ibid.* article 5(1).   [168] *Ibid.* article 6(4).

where there is a danger or risk of harm to the victim) and to be informed of any measures taken for the victim's protection.[169] This right shall not exist, however, if an identified risk to the offender would result from notification.[170] Finally, victims shall have a right to access confidential victim support services.[171] These services shall include the provision of information, advice and support to victims about their rights; information about referral to specialist support services; emotional and, where available, psychological support; advice relating to financial and practical issues arising from the crime and to the prevention of repeat victimisation, intimidation and retaliation.[172]

The second category of rights comprises rights of participation. These provide the substantive rights available to the victim to make demands of the criminal process. The ethos behind these rights is that the victim should have an active, independent voice within the process.

Directive 2012/29/EU

Article 10

1. Member States shall ensure that victims may be heard during criminal proceedings and may provide evidence. Where a child victim is to be heard, due account shall be taken of the child's age and maturity.
2. The procedural rules under which victims may be heard during criminal proceedings and may provide evidence shall be determined by national law.

Article 11

1. Member States shall ensure that victims, in accordance with their role in the relevant criminal justice system, have the right to a review of a decision not to prosecute. The procedural rules for such a review shall be determined by national law.
2. Where, in accordance with national law, the role of the victim in the relevant criminal justice system will be established only after a decision to prosecute the offender has been taken, Member States shall ensure that at least the victims of serious crimes have the right to a review of a decision not to prosecute. The procedural rules for such a review shall be determined by national law.

Beyond these rights, victims are to have access to legal aid where they are parties to the proceedings;[173] their expenses are to be reimbursed where they participate in proceedings;[174] their property is to be returned without delay where it is recovered;[175] and they are entitled to safeguards in restorative justice services which secure both their safety and their participation if they are willing.[176]

Perhaps the most challenging issue is compensation. The Directive provides that victims have a right to a decision on compensation from the offender within a reasonable time unless a decision is made in other legal proceedings. It also requires Member States to promote measures to secure adequate compensation to victims from offenders.[177] Alongside this, a right to compensation is provided for violent intentional crimes committed in Member States other than that where the victim is habitually resident by a separate Directive, Directive

---

[169] *Ibid.* article 6(5).   [170] *Ibid.* article 6(6).   [171] *Ibid.* article 8(1).
[172] *Ibid.* article 9(1).   [173] *Ibid.* article 13.   [174] *Ibid.* article 14.
[175] *Ibid.* article 15.   [176] *Ibid.* article 12(1).   [177] *Ibid.* article 16.

2004/80/EC.[178] However, the first set of requirements is vague, and refers simply to compensation from the offender, and the second is confined to a narrow range of crimes. The possibility of a broader right of reparation for the victim whether it be provided by the offender (who may not have such resources) or by public funds is largely kept off the table. And this is indeed the paradox of victims' rights, namely, that possibly the entitlement of most value to them is denied them.[179]

The third category of rights goes to the protection of victims and recognition of specific protection needs. This involves a series of general protection rights for all victims. This involves, first, protection for the victim and family members from retaliation, intimidation and repeat victimisation insofar as this does not compromise the rights of defence of the accused.[180] Secondly, contacts with the offender should be avoided within the premises of the criminal proceedings, unless these so require.[181] Thirdly, interviews are to be kept to a minimum and conducted without unjustified delay.[182] Medical examinations must also be kept to a minimum.[183] Finally, appropriate measures must be taken to protect the privacy of the victim.[184]

In addition, provision is made for victims with special protection needs. This is to be done on the basis of an individual assessment in each case.[185] Particular attention in making the assessment is to be paid to victims who have suffered considerable harm; victims of hate crimes; victims particularly vulnerable to and dependent on the alleged offender; and victims of crimes such as trafficking, terrorism and organised crime.[186]

In the case of adults with special protection needs, a particular sensitivity has to be shown in the interview process. It has to be done in premises designed for the purpose and carried out by professionals trained for that purpose. The interviews must generally be carried out by the same person and crimes involving gender-based violence or violence within an intimate relationship should be carried out by somebody of the same sex if the victim so wishes.[187] Within the courtroom, measures must be put in place to avoid contact between victims and offender during the giving of evidence; to allow evidence to be given virtually; to protect against unnecessary questioning on the victim's private life; and to allow evidence to be given without the presence of the public.[188]

Children are presumed to have specific protection needs.[189] They benefit from all the protections in the paragraph above. In addition, their interviews may be videoed and this video evidence will be sufficient to be used as evidence without the possibility for cross-examination of it.[190] Furthermore, a special representative should be appointed to represent the child where those with parental responsibility are precluded from representing the child.[191] Similarly, the child has a right to an independent lawyer where there might be a conflict of interest between them and those with parental responsibility.[192]

---

[178] Directive 2004/80/EC relating to compensation to crime victims [2004] OJ L261/15, article 1.

[179] On this issue within the US context see D. Beloof, 'The Third Wave of Crime Victims' Rights: Standing, Remedy, and Review' (2005) *Brigham Young University Law Review* 255, 342–50.

[180] Directive 2012/29/EU, article 18.

[181] *Ibid.* article 19.   [182] *Ibid.* article 20(a) and (b).   [183] *Ibid.* article 20(d).

[184] *Ibid.* article 21(1).   [185] *Ibid.* article 21(1) and (2).   [186] *Ibid.* article 22(3).

[187] *Ibid.* article 23(2).   [188] *Ibid.* article 23(3).   [189] *Ibid.* article 22(4).

[190] *Ibid.* article 24(1)(a). The giving of evidence outside the trial was held not to be a violation of the rights of defence in Case C-105/03 *Pupino* [2005] ECR I-5285.

[191] *Ibid.* article 24(1)(b).   [192] *Ibid.* article 24(1)(c).

FURTHER READING

E. Baker, 'Governing through Crime: The Case of the European Union' (2010) 7 *European Journal of Criminology* 187

E. Baker and C. Harding, 'From Past Imperfect to Future Perfect? A Longitudinal Study of the Third Pillar' (2009) 34 *European Law Review* 25

C. Eckes and T. Konstadines (eds.), *Crime within the Area of Freedom, Security and Justice: A European Public Order* (Cambridge, Cambridge University Press, 2012)

T. Elholm, 'Does EU Criminal Cooperation Necessarily Mean Increased Repression?' (2009) 17 *European Journal of Crime, Criminal Law and Criminal Justice* 191

M. Fichera, 'The European Arrest Warrant and the Sovereign State: A Marriage of Convenience' (2009) 15 *European Law Journal* 70

C. Harding and J. Beata Banach-Gutierrez, 'The Emergent EU Criminal Policy: Identifying the Species' (2012) 37 *European Law Review* 758

E. Herlin-Karnell, *The Constitutional Dimension of European Criminal Law* (Oxford, Hart, 2012)

V. Mitsilegas, *EU Criminal Law* (Oxford/Portland, Hart, 2009)

V. Mitsilegas, 'The Limits of Mutual Trust in Europe's Area of Freedom, Security and Justice: From Automatic Inter-State Cooperation to the Slow Emergence of the Individual' (2012) 31 *Yearbook of European Law* 319

S. Peers, *EU Justice and Home Affairs Law* (3rd edn, Oxford, Oxford University Press, 2012) chs. 9–11

B. van Bockel, *The Ne Bis in Idem Principle in EU Law* (Alphen aan den Rijn, Kluwer Law International, 2010)

15

The Internal Market

CONTENTS

1 INTRODUCTION

This chapter provides an overview of what the internal market is, and the current debates about what it should be. It provides background and context to the chapters on free movement which follow. The chapter is organised as follows.

Section 2 sets out the purposes of the internal market. Primarily, the internal market aims to integrate the national markets of the Member States into a single European market. It does this by removing regulatory barriers to trade between states. The reasons for pursuing this project are partly economic, but also social and political: for some, the market entrenches a form of individualism (ordoliberalism) that has strong roots in continental European philosophy, while for others, its main benefit is that it sucks Member States into deeper integration in other areas. More recently, it has come to be seen by many as a regulatory project, balancing social and economic interests.

Section 3 considers the legal tools used to build the internal market and the concepts underlying them. As well as free trade, a central idea in the internal market is that of 'undistorted competition'. If states have different rules on matters relevant to industry (for example, environmental or labour law), then companies in states with low regulatory burdens will have an advantage. This may be economically problematic, but is also seen as unfair. Harmonisation often aims to remove such distortions.

Section 4 discusses competence to harmonise. Harmonisation is the replacement of national laws by a common Union-wide law. The most important legal basis for internal market harmonisation is Article 114 TFEU, which is controversial because it appears to be very broad. In *Tobacco Advertising I*, the Court of Justice set some limits: distortions of competition can only be harmonised away when they are 'appreciable' or likely to become so. However, this is not very precise. Moreover, other cases show that, under certain conditions, Article 114 can be used to set up new agencies and regulatory bodies.

Sections 5 and 6 consider techniques of harmonisation and the problems they bring. Harmonisation is a difficult political and technical process. In recent years, the Union has been using the 'new approach', in which legislation concentrates on laying down general safety and health standards, while European standardisation agencies work these out in detail. This has been fairly successful, but attracts some democratic criticism: are these agencies accountable and do they take into account interests that are not scientific or economic? This last question is particularly important where EU law touches on matters that are politically sensitive, such as genetically modified organisms (GMOs). Many scholars take the view that decentralising much market regulation away from the representative bodies – the Council and Parliament – to the Commission and agencies has made decisions so technocratic and science-based that there is a danger that ethical and social concerns are no longer heard. Others argue that this is precisely the point: Member States want the Union to be an objective regulator, beyond the reach of populist whims. Section 6 also discusses how a parallel critique has been made of the Court of Justice: that it is too quick to set aside national measures in order to promote free movement, and does not give full enough consideration to the national values, preferences and interests which those measures may protect.

Section 7 discusses regulatory competition. Many internal market debates can be reduced to 'Should the Union regulate, or should the Member States?'. Regulatory competition is an important part of this question. If states can choose their own rules, some fear that they will lower standards in order to attract business. Other states will be forced to follow and there will be a 'race to the bottom', in which social and environmental policies are sacrificed to business interests. This view supports widespread harmonisation. Others argue that the race to the bottom does not happen in practice: businesses do not just want low standards. There are reasons why they may even prefer states with high standards and well-functioning social welfare systems. Finding the right compromise means preventing destructive competition, while still allowing states enough autonomy to experiment, reflect local preferences and learn from each other.

2 PURPOSE OF THE INTERNAL MARKET

For most of the history of the Union, its central policy has been the creation of the internal market (or single market, or common market, as it has been called at various times).[1] The reasons for this are diverse. The classical economic perception that because nations do not do

---

[1] See K. Mortelmans, 'The Common Market, the Internal Market and the Single Market: What's in a Market?' (1998) 35 *CMLRev.* 101; L. W. Gormley, 'Competition and Free Movement: Is the Internal Market the Same as a Common Market?' (2002) 13 *EBLRev.* 522.

everything equally well or efficiently, trade between nations can be beneficial for all, has of course always been important.[2] However, the internal market has ambitions beyond interstate trade. It aims to merge the markets of the Member States into one larger market, something which entails a greater degree of uniformity of structure and conditions. This is partly at odds with the simple trade-maximisation approach: instead of only capitalising on difference, the Union aims to reduce it. While such homogeneity may bring economic benefits, notably via economies of scale as firms become European rather than purely national operators, the integrative goals of the market reveal that it is not, and never has been, just an economic policy.

On the contrary, a number of normative agendas were prominent in defining and shaping the Treaty rules. First, economic integration was seen as an essential step towards social and political integration. The neofunctionalist analysis of European integration, associated with Haas, argued that because of the interconnection of policy areas, integration in one would lead inevitably to integration in another.[3] This theory is no longer dominant, or even widely accepted in its pure form, but it played a significant role in early support for the internal market. Even today it resonates. Many of the cases in the following chapters show how an apparently simple desire to facilitate interstate transactions has led to involvement of the Union in matters of broader social concern, be it with the families and working conditions of workers, or with the quality of foodstuffs. The following extract portrays a recent theory of integration which maintains some of these ideas, while also emphasising the role of Member States in steering integration.

A. Stone Sweet and W. Sandholtz, 'European Integration and Supranational Governance' (1997) 4 *Journal of European Public Policy* 297, 299–300

We claim that transnational activity has been the catalyst of European integration; but transnational exchange cannot, in and of itself, determine the specific details, or the precise timing, of Community rule-making. Instead it provokes, or activates, the Community's decision-making bodies, including the Council of Ministers. Member state governments often possess (but not always) the means to facilitate or to obstruct rule-making, and they use these powers frequently. Nevertheless, we argue, among other things, that as transnational exchange rises in any specific domain (or cluster of related domains), so do the costs, for governments, of maintaining disparate national rules. As these costs rise, so do incentives for governments to adjust their policy positions in ways that favor the expansion of supranational governance. Once fixed in a given domain, European rules – such as relevant treaty provisions, secondary legislation, and the European Court of Justice's (ECJ's) case law – generate a self-sustaining dynamic that leads to the gradual deepening of integration in that sector and, not uncommonly, to spillovers into other sectors. Thus, we view intergovernmental bargaining and decision-making as embedded in processes that are provoked and sustained by the expansion of transnational society, the pro-integrative activities of supranational organizations, and the growing density of supranational rules. And, we will argue, these processes gradually, but inevitably, reduce the capacity of the Member States to control outcomes.

---

[2] See D. Ricardo, *On the Principles of Political Economy and Taxation* (London, John Murray, 1821), also available at www.econlib.org/library/Ricardo/ricP.html, and S. Suranovic, 'The Theory of Comparative Advantage' in *International Trade Theory and Policy* (Center for International Economic Policy, George Washington University, 2007) ch. 40, available at http://internationalecon.com/Trade/Tch40/Tch40.php.

[3] See J. Ruggie, P. Katzenstein, R. Keohane and P. Schmitter, 'Transformations in World Politics: The Intellectual Contributions of Ernst B. Haas' (2005) 8 *Annual Review of Political Science* 271.

Secondly, many of the most ardent early supporters of the internal market were believers in ordoliberalism. This political view, with origins in early twentieth-century Germany, regards the regulation of economic activity as essentially about the regulation of public and private power.[4] On the one hand, competition law is necessary to prevent private power becoming dominant enough to challenge the state. But on the other hand, individual economic rights are a normative good in themselves and an important bulwark against tyranny.

M. Maduro, 'Reforming the Market or the State? Article 30 and the European Constitution:[5] Economic Freedom and Political Rights' (1997) 3 *European Law Journal* 55, 61–2

Neo-liberal or *'laissez-faire'* interpretations of the free movement rules and of the European Economic Constitution owe much to traditional ordo-liberal theories and their contribution in both the initial debate on European integration and in the provision of a coherent theoretical framework for an understanding of integration. The ordo-liberal aim is the creation of a free-market, liberal economy, protected through constitutional principles...The main concern is a political one: the protection of a free and equal society. 'Within society itself no power groups should be formed which would make it possible for others, individually or as groups, to be subjugated and exploited.' Ordo-liberals and other neo-liberals have been active participants in the project of European integration; they entrusted to Community law the process of constitutionalising a free market economy with undistorted competition.

...It should be recalled that these neo-liberal ideas developed as a reaction to recent German and European history. For Röpke, there was an inevitable connection between the aims of individual freedom and the avoidance of nationalism, on the one hand, and free trade and the prevention of state control of the economy, on the other. According to ordo-liberals and other neo-liberals, the failure of the initial device of separation of powers to achieve its aim of controlling power and government meant that a new device had to be created. That device was a federation of States with an international authority to limit governments' economic powers and assure international order without taking over the power of the States. The division of powers inherent in this form of federalism 'would inevitably act at the same time also as a limitation of the power of the whole as well as of the individual state'. Hence, a federation is seen more as a source of individual rights than as a source of common policies.

Trade facilitation, empowerment of individuals, and the integration of Europe all continue to influence market-building decisions today.

3 LEGAL FRAMEWORK OF THE INTERNAL MARKET

The umbrella Treaty article is Article 26 TFEU.

Article 26 TFEU

1. The Union shall adopt measures with the aim of establishing or ensuring the functioning of the internal market, in accordance with the relevant provisions of the Treaties.
2. The internal market shall comprise an area without internal frontiers in which the free movement of goods, persons, services and capital is ensured in accordance with the provisions of the Treaties...

---

[4] See D. Gerber, *Law and Competition in Twentieth Century Europe: Protecting Prometheus* (Oxford, Oxford University Press, 1998).
[5] Article 30 is now Article 34 TFEU.

One way of achieving the goals of Article 26 TFEU is by the development of Union-wide rules on matters which may affect interstate trade, such as product standards and consumer rights. Such harmonisation is discussed further in the next section. However, the requirement to abolish borders is also developed later in the Treaty in a number of specific Treaty Articles, which are the subject of the following chapters. These Articles prohibit restrictions on the free movement of goods, persons, services and capital. The essential question of all these Articles is what this prohibition means. What is free movement? What is a restriction on this? There are so many measures, public and private, which might tend to make us stay at home (trains still aren't free). Which should be caught and which not? There is an ongoing debate between two views. One is that only measures which make movement across borders harder than staying at home, or which discriminate against the foreign, should be caught: the idea of a restriction on movement between states entails some kind of comparison.[6] Advocate General Maduro considered in *Alfa Vita* how the Court of Justice should interpret the provisions in the Treaty on the free movement of goods.

Joined Cases C–158/04 and C–159/04 *Alfa Vita Vassilopoulos AE* v *Elliniko Dimosio, Nomarkhiaki Aftodioikisi Ioanninon*; *Carrefour Marinopoulos AE* v *Elliniko Dimosio, Nomarkhiaki Aftodioikisi Ioanninon* [2006] ECR I-8135, Advocate General M. Poiares Maduro

41. In such circumstances it is obvious that the task of the Court is not to call into question as a matter of course Member States' economic policies. It is instead responsible for satisfying itself that those States do not adopt measures which, in actual fact, lead to *cross-border situations being treated less favourably than purely national situations.*

42. In order to carry out such a review, it is necessary to rely on concrete criteria. Three principal criteria can be drawn from the relevant case-law.

43. Firstly, the Court maintains, in this respect, that any discrimination based on nationality, whether direct or indirect, is prohibited. For example, it is clear that a publicity campaign promoting the purchase of national products to the detriment of intra-Community trade constitutes a breach of Treaty rules.

44. Secondly, it is established that imposing supplementary costs on goods in circulation in the Community or on traders carrying out a cross-border activity creates a barrier to trade which needs to be duly justified...

45. Thirdly, any measure which impedes to a greater extent the access to the market and the putting into circulation of products from other Member States is considered to be a measure having equivalent effect within the meaning of Article [34 TFEU]...

46. It seems to me that a consistent approach emerges from this case-law. These three criteria, as they have been applied by the Court, amount in substance to identifying *discrimination against the exercise of freedom of movement.*

---

[6] G. Marenco, 'Pour une interpretation traditionelle de la notion de mesure d'effet équivalent à une restriction quantitative' (1984) *Cahiers du Droit Européen* 291; J. Snell, *Free Movement of Goods and Services in EC Law* (Oxford, Oxford University Press, 2002); G. Davies, *Nationality Discrimination in the European Internal Market* (The Hague, Kluwer Law International, 2003).

The Advocate General suggests that the Treaty internal market rules should aim to remove measures that have some specifically trade-negative effect, rather than those which just diminish economic activity generally.

The other view, put forcefully by Advocate General Jacobs and developed by several academic writers, is that comparison is irrelevant.[7] Any measure restricting cross-border movement is clearly caught, whether or not it has an equivalent domestic effect.

Case C-412/93 Société d'Importation Edouard Leclerc-Siplec v TF1 Publicité SA and M6 Publicité SA [1995] ECR I-179, Opinion of Advocate General Jacobs

39. Secondly, the exclusion from the scope of Article [34 TFEU] of measures which 'affect in the same manner, in law and in fact, the marketing of domestic products and those from other Member States' amounts to introducing, in relation to restrictions on selling arrangements, a test of discrimination. That test, however, seems inappropriate. The central concern of the Treaty provisions on the free movement of goods is to prevent unjustified obstacles to trade between Member States. If an obstacle to inter-State trade exists, it cannot cease to exist simply because an identical obstacle affects domestic trade. I have difficulty in accepting the proposition that a Member State may arbitrarily restrict the marketing of goods from another Member State, provided only that it imposes the same arbitrary restriction on the marketing of domestic goods. If a Member State imposes a substantial barrier on access to the market for certain products, for example, by providing that they may be sold only in a very limited number of establishments and a manufacturer of those products in another Member State suffers economic loss as a result, he will derive little consolation from the knowledge that a similar loss is sustained by his competitors in the Member State which imposes the restriction.

40. Equally, from the point of view of the Treaty's concern to establish a single market, discrimination is not a helpful criterion: from that point of view, the fact that a Member State imposes similar restrictions on the marketing of domestic goods is simply irrelevant. The adverse effect on the Community market is in no way alleviated; nor is the adverse effect on the economies of the other Member States, and so on the Community economy. Indeed the application of the discrimination test would lead to the fragmentation of the Community market, since traders would have to accept whatever restrictions on selling arrangements happened to exist in each Member State, and would have to adapt their own arrangements accordingly in each State. Restrictions on trade should not be tested against local conditions which happen to prevail in each Member State, but against the aim of access to the entire Community market. A discrimination test is therefore inconsistent as a matter of principle with the aims of the Treaty.

41. The question then is what test should be applied in order to determine whether a measure falls within the scope of Article [34 TFEU]. There is one guiding principle which seems to provide an appropriate test: that principle is that all undertakings which engage in a legitimate economic activity in a Member State should have unfettered access to the whole of the Community market, unless there is a valid reason for denying them full access to a part of that market...

42. If the principle is that all undertakings should have unfettered access to the whole of the Community market, then the appropriate test in my view is whether there is a substantial restriction on that access...

---

[7] S. Weatherill, 'After Keck: Some Thoughts on How to Clarify the Clarification' (1996) 33 *CMLRev.* 885; C. Barnard, 'Fitting the Remaining Pieces into the Goods and Persons Jigsaw' (2001) 26 *ELRev.* 35.

This extract, like the preceding one, concerns the law on goods, but the analyses are equally relevant to the other freedoms. Advocate General Jacobs is presenting a vision of the Treaty as a tool for deregulation and trade-facilitation per se. If this is not to result in the abolition of huge amounts of law, it is because measures which seem to be reasonable may, he proposes, remain.[8] The Treaty rules on free movement would then amount to a general proportionality review of national law affecting economic activity.[9] This might have the effect of creating a more dynamic and integrated European marketplace, but would expand the scope of EU law at the expense of national autonomy.[10] The debate over the scope of free movement is essentially about this.

A number of other legal tools also contribute to free movement. Article 30 TFEU prohibits customs duties between Member States, while Article 110 TFEU prohibits discriminatory taxation on foreign goods. Customs duties, although now rarely an issue, were the primary obstacle to movement in the early days of the Union. Article 110 continues to be important. It provides as follows.

Article 110 TFEU

No Member State shall impose, directly or indirectly, on the products of other Member States any internal taxation of any kind in excess of that imposed directly or indirectly on similar domestic products.

Furthermore, no Member State shall impose on the products of other Member States any internal taxation of such a nature as to afford indirect protection to other products.

The Court of Justice has interpreted this globally as imposing a rationality requirement on the taxation of goods, to prevent covert protectionism.

Case C-221/06 *Stadtgemeinde Frohnleiten* [2007] ECR I-9643

56. First of all, although it is settled case-law that, as it now stands, Community law does not restrict the freedom of each Member State to establish a tax system which differentiates between certain products, even products which are similar within the meaning of the first paragraph of Article [110 TFEU], on the basis of objective criteria, such differentiation is compatible with Community law, however, only if it pursues objectives which are themselves compatible with the requirements of the Treaty and its secondary legislation, and if the detailed rules are such as to avoid any form of discrimination, direct or indirect, against imports from other Member States or any form of protection of competing domestic products.

A particular issue is what kind of criteria may be used: do they have to be related to the physical product, or can they extend to the way it is made? This is of increasing importance as Member States seek to use tax policy to encourage respect for social interests and human

---

[8] *Ibid.*

[9] E. Spaventa, 'From Gebhard to Carpenter: Towards a (Non)economic European Constitution' (2004) 41 *CMLRev.* 743; M. Dougan, 'The Constitutional Dimension to the Case Law on Union Citizenship' (2006) 31 *ELRev.* 613.

[10] Spaventa, n. 9 above.

rights, or environmentally friendly production of goods such as wood and electricity. They increasingly wish to impose taxes linked to sustainability, carbon dioxide emissions, or good labour practices, none of which are reflected directly in the finished product. The reason to permit this is that it allows tax to be used as a progressive tool of social engineering. The reason to be suspicious is that it results in different taxes being imposed on apparently identical products and may be a back-door to protectionism. In *Outokumpu Oy*,[11] the Court of Justice seemed to cautiously open the door to social and environmental impact taxation. It found that tax criteria might include factors 'such as the nature of the raw materials used or the production processes employed'. A tax benefit for green electricity was therefore permitted.

Analogous issues arise in the context of the Directives on public procurement, an important part of the free movement acquis.[12] Here, states increasingly try to use their purchasing power to influence the social and environmental behaviour of suppliers, by requiring them to comply with conditions if they wish to supply public bodies. There is a growing scholarship on the legality of this.[13] Such demands may also amount to closet protectionism, requiring foreign suppliers to conform to local norms, even when producing in their home jurisdiction.

The public procurement Directives require public bodies to tender openly and Europe-wide for purchases above a certain threshold. This has admirable goals: the state is by far the largest purchaser of goods and services and has tended traditionally to purchase from favoured suppliers, who were usually national. Yet, the attempt to break open public purchasing markets has been a challenge, with intensely complicated procedural requirements employed in order to minimise discretionary space which might be used for secret favouritism. Despite such efforts, and the transaction costs they bring for public bodies, public markets are not yet considered to have been opened to the extent that private ones have. The difficulties and ambitions are outlined by Bovis.

C. Bovis, 'The Regulation of Public Procurement as a Key Element of European Economic Law' (1998) 4 *European Law Journal* 220, 224–5, 229

After all the attempts of European institutions to stimulate the demand side of public procurement in the Member States, one could justifiably question the relative slow progress and the underlying reasons behind such a recalcitrant rejection of the envisaged competitive regime in public markets. The answer seems simple, although cynical in terms of reference to commitment to European integration and the completion and functioning of a genuinely common market in Europe. By perpetuating discriminatory and preferential public purchasing, Member States pay attention to immediate needs relating to domestic/national priorities such as balance of payments, sustainability of strategic industries, employment and, last but not least, national pride. This exercise, in terms of the envisaged integrated

---

[11] Case C-213/96 *Outokumpu Oy* [1998] ECR I-1777.

[12] Directive 2004/18/EC on the coordination of procedures for the award of public works contracts, public supply contracts and public service contracts [2004] OJ L134/114; Directive 2004/17/EC coordinating the procurement procedures of entities operating in the water, energy, transport and postal services sectors [2004] OJ L134/1. These have now been repealed and new Directives are awaiting publication.

[13] S. Arrowsmith and P. Kunzlik (eds.), *Social and Environmental Policies in EC Procurement Law* (Cambridge, Cambridge University Press, 2009); C. McCrudden, *Purchasing Social Justice* (Oxford, Oxford University Press, 2007); C. Hilson, 'Going Local? EU Law, Localism and Climate Change' (2008) 33 *ELRev.* 194; G. Davies, 'Process and Production Method-Based Trade Restrictions in the EU' (2007–08) 10 *CYELS* 69.

public markets of the EU, represents a sub-optimal allocation of resources (human and capital) throughout the common market at the expense of the public sector, which pays more than it should for equivalent or even better products or deliveries. It is tantamount to geographical market segmentation imposed by the demand side on the supply side, with a view to determining and controlling the latter as far as its activities vis-à-vis the public sector are concerned....

Combating discrimination on grounds of nationality in public procurement and eliminating domestic preferential purchasing schemes could result in efficiency gains at European and national levels through three major effects which would influence the supply side. These include a trade effect, a competition effect and a restructuring effect. The trade effect is associated with the actual and potential savings that the public sector will be able to achieve through lower cost purchasing. This effect appears to have a static dimension. On the other hand, the competition effect relates to the changes of price behaviour of national firms which have been protected from competition by means of discriminatory procurement practices. Finally, the third effect reflects the restructuring dimension in the supply side as a result of increased competition. The restructuring effect is dynamic and refers to the long-term.

Making interstate trade easier has consequences for competition. The removal of borders exposes national firms to foreign competition. This generates lobbying for two kinds of rules. First, there is a consensus that the behaviour of firms in the European market requires regulation both in the interests of economic wellbeing (preventing, for example, the exploitation of consumers by Europe-wide monopolists), and of interfirm fairness (say, larger firms in one state dominating or crushing smaller ones elsewhere).[14] Hence, a European-wide competition law, the subject of Chapters 21 to 23, has always been a part of Union market-building. Secondly, the creation of interstate competition draws attention to the fact that the conditions under which businesses operate vary significantly from Member State to Member State. Prices and taxes vary, but so do regulations. Variations in, particularly, labour law and environmental rules may provide a significant advantage for firms located in one state rather than another, as it is often expensive to comply with social and environmental requirements. Industrial lobbies are quick to cry that such disparities create unfair competition. The firm in a state which requires six weeks paid holiday, a minimum wage and the recycling of waste may find itself unable to compete with a competitor located in a place where none of these things are required. This creates a political momentum for the replacement of diverse national rules by a common Union-wide one. Such political harmonisation has inevitably a somewhat ad hoc character. Some matters which are important to competitiveness lend themselves to harmonisation, notably environmental regulation of industry, on which a social and political consensus can often be reached, and where uniform standards are practically achievable. However, the creation of uniform tax rates has always been politically impossible (although a legal basis exists: see Articles 113 and 115 TFEU), while the creation of uniform wage levels is economically impossible. Thus, it seems that two of the most important factors affecting location-based competitiveness are largely outside the power of the Union to address.

---

[14] R. Van der Laan and A. Nentjes, 'Competitive Distortions in EU Environmental Legislation: Inefficiency versus Inequity' (2001) 11 *EJL and E* 131.

The economics of harmonisation tends to regard cost differences between states as less problematic.[15] Considering welfare as a whole, the loss to country Y when its industry migrates to a low cost jurisdiction is often outweighed by the benefit of cheaper products combined with the benefit to country X, to where the industry has moved. Moreover, where a competitive edge is obtained by matters such as loose environmental or social standards, this may simply reflect different preferences. Perhaps people in country X don't care as much about holidays or clean rivers? In that case, it is better if dirty and labour-intensive industry moves to X. On this view, the major – some argue the only – reason to adopt obligatory harmonisation is where there are interstate externalities.[16] These occur where a part of the cost of an activity is not taken into account in its production because the producer is able to 'dump' that cost on someone else. Thus, if industry in country X emits air pollution which makes the population of that country less healthy, but they think the benefits of increased industrial profit, or increased economic dynamism, are worthwhile, there is an argument that this is their free choice, to be respected. However, if prevailing winds blow that air pollution over to another state and make people ill there, then in fact country X is not 'internalising' the costs of its industry, and the low price which products from X bear is not their 'real' price. Here, there is an interstate externality which justifies interstate rules.[17]

The question of when harmonisation is appropriate is one of the most bitterly contested in EU law.[18] The economic approach outlined above assumes democracy: that the local regulation genuinely reflects the preferences of the population. Yet, preferences are not static, and a more ambitious, political approach to the Union sees it partly as a mechanism to develop preferences and change the world views of its citizens. The economic approach also ignores the political sustainability of a Union of widely diverging preferences. An irony of a narrowly economic approach to harmonisation may be that it leads to political stresses which result in greater protectionism and a diminished market – and so, in fact, less of the benefits of interstate trade. As a result, decisions to harmonise to remove what EU law calls 'distortions of competition' continue to be a complex intertwining of political, social and economic arguments.[19] As is discussed below, the legal conditions for such harmonisation are open enough to allow considerable legislative discretion.

The final tool in the internal market toolbox is the law on state aid. Allowing a national champion to fail often brings a high political price and the instinct of governments is to reach for their wallet. In general, this is prohibited by the Treaty, in Article 107 TFEU, which provides only limited derogations for exceptional situations, such as situations following a natural

---

[15] A. Ogus, 'Competition Between National Legal Systems: A Contribution of Economic Analysis to Comparative Law' (1999) 48 *ICLQ* 405.

[16] *Ibid.*

[17] J. N. Bhagwati and R. Hudoc (eds.), *Fair Trade and Harmonization: An Economic Analysis* (Cambridge, MA, Massachusetts Institute of Technology Press, 1996).

[18] See for overviews e.g. S. Woolcock, 'Competition Among Rules in the Single European Market' in W. Bratton, J. McCahery, S. Picciotto and C. Scott (eds.), *International Regulatory Competition and Coordination: Perspectives on Economic Regulation in Europe and the United States* (Oxford, Oxford University Press, 1996); R. van den Bergh, 'Regulatory Competition or Harmonization of Laws? Guidelines for the European Regulator' in A. Marciano and J.-M. Josselin, *The Economics of Harmonizing European Law* (Cheltenham, Edward Elgar, 2002); Z. Drabak, 'Limits to the Harmonisation of Domestic Regulations' (2008) 2 *Journal of International Trade and Diplomacy* 47; G. Wagner, 'The Economics of Harmonisation: The Case of Contracts' (2002) 39 *CMLRev.* 995.

[19] Van der Laan and Nentjes, n. 14 above; S. Weatherill, 'Why Harmonise?' in T. Tridimas and P. Nebbia, *European Union Law for the Twenty-First Century* (Oxford/Portland, Hart, 2004) 11.

disaster, or where a failure would have unacceptable social consequences, such as the failure of a bank. State aid is discussed further in Chapter 23.

4 COMPETENCE TO LEGISLATE

There are a number of Treaty Articles which provide a legal basis for legislation relevant to the internal market. However, the most important is Article 114 TFEU.

Article 114 TFEU

1. Save where otherwise provided in the Treaties, the following provisions shall apply for the achievement of the objectives set out in Article 26. The European Parliament and the Council shall, acting in accordance with the ordinary legislative procedure and after consulting the Economic and Social Committee, adopt the measures for the approximation of the provisions laid down by law, regulation or administrative action in Member States which have as their object the establishment and functioning of the internal market.
2. Paragraph 1 shall not apply to fiscal provisions, to those relating to the free movement of persons nor to those relating to the rights and interests of employed persons.

Article 115 provides analogous powers for harmonisation concerning free movement of persons and direct taxation, but by unanimity in the Council.

The leading case interpreting Article 114 continues to be the first Tobacco Directive case, *Tobacco Advertising I*.[20] In this case, the Court of Justice annulled a Directive based on Article 114 for the first time, on the grounds that the Directive exceeded what the legal basis allowed.[21] The Directive amounted to a ban on all tobacco advertising in media other than television (which was addressed in an earlier Directive). This included sponsorship of sport by tobacco firms, tobacco advertising in magazines, and even tobacco advertising on ashtrays, parasols and posters in cafes. The argument put forward for the Directive was that the laws on tobacco advertising varied from state to state, which resulted in obstacles to free movement and distortions of competition. A magazine with tobacco advertisements could be printed and sold in one state, but not exported to another. Advertising firms based in states which permitted tobacco advertising had a source of revenue denied to firms in other states, giving them a competitive advantage, as did sports competitions and teams in those states. The development of pan-European advertising campaigns was prevented by the different rules in different states.

However, there were a number of forceful objections to the Directive. First, the distortions of competition were claimed to be marginal. Theoretically, there might be advantages for firms in one state or another but these did not reach the level of a serious market problem. Secondly, while there were certainly some obstacles to movement resulting from different advertising laws, notably where magazines were concerned, the Directive went beyond addressing these and banned advertising in contexts where it was not obvious that this made any contribution at all to interstate trade. For example, it was unclear in what way the banning of tobacco

---

[20] Case C-376/98 *Germany v Parliament and Council (Tobacco Advertising I)* [2000] ECR I–8419.
[21] See generally J. Usher, annotation at (2001) 38 *CMLRev.* 1520; T. Hervey, 'Up in Smoke? Community (Anti)-Tobacco Law and Policy' (2001) 7 *ELRev.* 101.

advertisements in cinemas or cigar shops would make any kind of movement easier. Thirdly, for some of the goods on which advertising was banned, such as ashtrays and parasols, the level of interstate trade was negligible. Finally, the Directive was claimed to be a covert health protection measure. Rather than being primarily aimed at improving the operation of the market, it was really aimed at improving public health. Not only was this outside the remit of Article 114, but it was in fact prohibited, it was claimed, elsewhere in the Treaty, in Article 168(5) TFEU. This Article permits the Union to take public health measures but 'excluding harmonisation'.

Case C-376/98 Germany v Parliament and Council (Tobacco Advertising I) [2000] ECR I-8419

80. In this case, the approximation of national laws on the advertising and sponsorship of tobacco products provided for by the Directive was based on Articles [114, 53 and 62 TFEU] of the Treaty....

83. Those provisions, read together, make it clear that the measures referred to in Article [114(1) TFEU] of the Treaty are intended to improve the conditions for the establishment and functioning of the internal market. To construe that article as meaning that it vests in the Community legislature a general power to regulate the internal market would not only be contrary to the express wording of the provisions cited above but would also be incompatible with the principle embodied in Article [5 TEU] that the powers of the Community are limited to those specifically conferred on it.

84. Moreover, a measure adopted on the basis of Article [114 TFEU] of the Treaty must genuinely have as its object the improvement of the conditions for the establishment and functioning of the internal market. If a mere finding of disparities between national rules and of the abstract risk of obstacles to the exercise of fundamental freedoms or of distortions of competition liable to result therefrom were sufficient to justify the choice of Article [114 TFEU] as a legal basis, judicial review of compliance with the proper legal basis might be rendered nugatory. The Court would then be prevented from discharging the function entrusted to it by Article [19 TEU] of ensuring that the law is observed in the interpretation and application of the Treaty.

85. So, in considering whether Article [114 TFEU] was the proper legal basis, the Court must verify whether the measure whose validity is at issue in fact pursues the objectives stated by the Community legislature.

86. It is true, that recourse to Article [114 TFEU] as a legal basis is possible if the aim is to prevent the emergence of future obstacles to trade resulting from multifarious development of national laws. However, the emergence of such obstacles must be likely and the measure in question must be designed to prevent them...

88. Furthermore, provided that the conditions for recourse to Articles [114, 53 and 62 TFEU] as a legal basis are fulfilled, the Community legislature cannot be prevented from relying on that legal basis on the ground that public health protection is a decisive factor in the choices to be made. On the contrary, [Article 168 TFEU] provides that health requirements are to form a constituent part of the Community's other policies and Article [114(3) TFEU] expressly requires that, in the process of harmonisation, a high level of human health protection is to be ensured....

Elimination of obstacles to the free movement of goods and the freedom to provide services

96. It is clear that, as a result of disparities between national laws on the advertising of tobacco products, obstacles to the free movement of goods or the freedom to provide services exist or may well arise.

97. In the case, for example, of periodicals, magazines and newspapers which contain advertising for tobacco products, it is true, as the applicant has demonstrated, that no obstacle exists at present to their importation into Member States which prohibit such advertising. However, in view of the trend in

national legislation towards ever greater restrictions on advertising of tobacco products, reflecting the belief that such advertising gives rise to an appreciable increase in tobacco consumption, it is probable that obstacles to the free movement of press products will arise in the future.

98. In principle, therefore, a Directive prohibiting the advertising of tobacco products in periodicals, magazines and newspapers could be adopted on the basis of Article [114 TFEU] with a view to ensuring the free movement of press products, on the lines of Directive 89/552, Article 13 of which prohibits television advertising of tobacco products in order to promote the free broadcasting of television programmes.

99. However, for numerous types of advertising of tobacco products, the prohibition under Article 3(1) of the Directive cannot be justified by the need to eliminate obstacles to the free movement of advertising media or the freedom to provide services in the field of advertising. That applies, in particular, to the prohibition of advertising on posters, parasols, ashtrays and other articles used in hotels, restaurants and cafés, and the prohibition of advertising spots in cinemas, prohibitions which in no way help to facilitate trade in the products concerned.

100. Admittedly, a measure adopted on the basis of Articles [114, 53 and 62 TFEU] of the Treaty may incorporate provisions which do not contribute to the elimination of obstacles to exercise of the fundamental freedoms provided that they are necessary to ensure that certain prohibitions imposed in pursuit of that purpose are not circumvented. It is, however, quite clear that the prohibitions mentioned in the previous paragraph do not fall into that category....

Elimination of distortion of competition

106. In examining the lawfulness of a directive adopted on the basis of Article [114 TFEU] of the Treaty, the Court is required to verify whether the distortion of competition which the measure purports to eliminate is appreciable (Case C-300/89 *Titanium Dioxide* [1991] ECR I-2867).

107. In the absence of such a requirement, the powers of the Community legislature would be practically unlimited. National laws often differ regarding the conditions under which the activities they regulate may be carried on, and this impacts directly or indirectly on the conditions of competition for the undertakings concerned. It follows that to interpret Articles [114, 53 and 62 TFEU] as meaning that the Community legislature may rely on those articles with a view to eliminating the smallest distortions of competition would be incompatible with the principle, already referred to in paragraph 83 of this judgment, that the powers of the Community are those specifically conferred on it.

108. It is therefore necessary to verify whether the Directive actually contributes to eliminating appreciable distortions of competition.

109. First, as regards advertising agencies and producers of advertising media, undertakings established in Member States which impose fewer restrictions on tobacco advertising are unquestionably at an advantage in terms of economies of scale and increase in profits. The effects of such advantages on competition are, however, remote and indirect and do not constitute distortions which could be described as appreciable. They are not comparable to the distortions of competition caused by differences in production costs...[such as those in Case C-300/89 *Titanium Dioxide*].

110. It is true that the differences between certain regulations on tobacco advertising may give rise to appreciable distortions of competition. As the Commission and the Finnish and United Kingdom Governments have submitted, the fact that sponsorship is prohibited in some Member States and authorised in others gives rise, in particular, to certain sports events being relocated, with considerable repercussions on the conditions of competition for undertakings associated with such events.

111. However, such distortions, which could be a basis for recourse to Article [114 TFEU] of the Treaty in order to prohibit certain forms of sponsorship, are not such as to justify the use of that legal basis for an outright prohibition of advertising of the kind imposed by the Directive.

The Court of Justice provides a framework of legal principle which continues to define the scope of Article 114:[22]

(1) Measures based on that article must contribute to removing obstacles to interstate trade, or to removing distortions of competition.

(2) While there is no *de minimis* for obstacles to movement (even minor ones may be harmonised away), harmonisation to remove distortions is only possible when those distortions are 'appreciable'. The reason for this is that almost any differences between national laws have some kind of effect on business, and so could be claimed to cause some degree of market distortion. Without a minimum threshold for harmonisation, Article 114 would amount to an open-ended harmonisation power, which would be contrary to the principle that the Union only has conferred powers.[23]

(3) It is acceptable to harmonise to prevent obstacles arising, rather than removing already existing problems, but those future problems must be likely. One cannot harmonise on the basis of a theoretical possibility.

(4) Provided that a measure does in fact contribute to free movement or undistorted competition, it is not rendered invalid because it also contributes to public health. On the contrary, the Union is required to take other interests into account when deciding how obstacles and distortions should be removed. Article 168(5) TFEU is only a ban on harmonising public health using that Article, not on integrating public health considerations into internal market rules.

The Court of Justice applied these thoughts to the Directive on the basis of several findings of fact. First, the claimed distortions of competition were not significant. Secondly, a number of provisions of the Directive did not in fact contribute to free movement. The Court was unable to see how, for example, banning tobacco advertising in cinemas, or cigar shops, or on ashtrays or parasols, facilitated interstate trade.

This second finding is not entirely convincing. The trade in new or second-hand ashtrays or parasols, or for that matter in posters, may be small, even non-existent, but there is no reason in principle why it should not exist, and there will clearly be obstructions caused if tobacco advertising is permitted in some states and not others. A ban on tobacco advertising would prevent this problem from arising. Ironically, in fact, interstate trade in these goods may barely exist if tobacco advertising is permitted because they will be given away free for promotional reasons. However, without such advertising cafés may have to buy their parasols and ashtrays, and an interstate trade may well come into being. In any case, the Court's finding that no obstacles were being removed should probably be seen in the context of the rule that future obstacles must be likely. Since it had not been demonstrated that there actually was any present or likely future trade that was being obstructed – it is simply an imaginable possibility – the ban on these forms of advertising could not be based on Article 114.

---

[22] See for commentary e.g. M. Kumm, 'Constitutionalising Subsidiarity in Integrated Markets: The Case of Tobacco Regulation in the European Union' (2006) 12 *ELJ* 503; F. Duina and P. Kurzer, 'Smoke in Your Eyes: The Struggle over Tobacco Control in the European Union' (2004) 11 *JEPP* 57; J. Snell, 'Who has Got the Power: Free Movement and Allocation of Competences' (2003) 22 *YBEL* 323; A. Somek, *Individualism: An Essay on the Authority of EU Law* (Oxford, Oxford University Press, 2008) ch. 7; S. Weatherill, 'Competence Creep and Competence Control' (2004) 23 *YBEL* 1; T. Hervey, 'Up in Smoke? Community (Anti) Tobacco Law and Policy' (2001) 26 *ELRev.* 101.

[23] See Chapter 5.

Tobacco Advertising I has since been followed by a number of other cases also addressing the scope of Article 114 TFEU. These cases confirm the principles *of Tobacco Advertising I*, and clear up some ambiguities.

Tobacco Advertising II addressed the Directive adopted to replace the one annulled in *Tobacco Advertising I*.[24] The broad idea of the replacement Directive was the same, but it was more limited. It confined itself generally to printed media and radio, where it could be shown that there actually was cross-border trade in goods or cross-border provision of radio services, and to sponsorship of sports with some international aspect, and it moreover included a clause ensuring that products within its limited derogations (trade publications and third country publications) could be traded throughout the Union. It thus created a greater degree of uniformity than the previous Directive in the areas that mattered, while leaving other matters alone.

Nevertheless, objections were still raised, notably that all printed media and radio programmes were covered, while in fact many magazines and radio broadcasts were for an exclusively local market. Some radio transmissions were not even strong enough to reach a border.

The judgment applies the same principles as the previous one, but this time the Court of Justice found the Directive to be valid. This time it did confine itself to matters relevant to interstate trade. Local sports tournaments with no international aspect at all were excluded, as were the ashtrays and parasols for which apparently no market exists. The fact that the printed media and radio ban extended to local media was not seen by the Court as a problem. Cross-border radio and trade in magazines existed, and could be disturbed by variations in tobacco advertising rules. Harmonisation was therefore justified. However, to try and distinguish between what might be traded or heard across the border and what would not be was practically impossible and would distort the market in itself. Therefore a general approach was justified. An internal market Directive may regulate purely internal matters if this is an inseparable part of regulating cross-border ones.

The judgment also clarifies two further matters. First, a Directive does not have to pursue both the removal of obstacles to movement and undistorted competition. Either is enough. The first *Tobacco Advertising I* judgment had been a little unclear on this. Secondly, it is possible to harmonise public health matters under Article 114 TFEU provided this is part of genuine internal market regulation. *Tobacco Advertising I* had made clear that a contribution to public health was not excluded, but it might have been argued that this could not go so far as harmonisation. However, tobacco advertising rules *are* intended to protect public health, and they *were* harmonised in the second Tobacco Directive, and the Court found this to be acceptable. The Article 168 TFEU ban on harmonisation prevents that Article being used for this purpose, but it does not prevent incidental harmonisation within the context of the internal market.

The second post-*Tobacco Advertising I* case was *Swedish Match*.[25] This concerned a Directive banning tobacco for chewing. Sweden enjoys an exemption from this ban, as a result of the particular popularity of chewing tobacco in that country. However, this was not enough for the complainants in this case who wished to market the chewing tobacco in the United

---

[24] C-380/03 *Germany* v *Parliament and Council (Tobacco Advertising II)* [2006] ECR I-11573.
[25] C-210/03 *R* v *Secretary of State for Health ex parte Swedish Match* [2004] ECR I-11893.

Kingdom and, in a parallel case decided on the same day, Germany.[26] The Directive prevented this. They therefore challenged the validity of the Directive, saying a ban on a product did not contribute to the internal market. The Court of Justice disagreed, pointing out that without the Directive it was very likely that states would adopt different laws on the product, creating obstacles to trade. A pre-emptive approach, preventing these obstacles from arising, was appropriate.

This was taken further in *Vodafone*, which concerned the validity of a regulation setting a maximum on mobile phone roaming charges paid by consumers when using their phones in other Member States.[27] It was argued that this was not harmonisation, since none of the Member States had attempted to regulate these charges so there could be no question of problems arising from disparaties between national laws. On the contrary, critics argued that the regulation was just an attempt to regulate the behaviour of mobile phone companies, whose commercial choices were making mobile phone use abroad very expensive. As such, it was not harmonisation of national laws and therefore should not be based on Article 114. The Court of Justice, however, accepted the Commission's argument that it was likely that individual Member States would regulate such charges in the future, creating distortions of competition, and therefore pre-emptive harmonisation could be adopted using Article 114. A notable aspect of the case is that the Advocate General had concluded that there was no evidence that Member States were planning to adopt laws, so the test of 'likelihood' was not satisfied. As has been commented, it is extremely hard to know what kinds of laws Member States are going to adopt, and unless concrete plans and proposals are already in existence, the likelihood test becomes a very subjective and imprecise one.[28]

The other aspect of *Swedish Match* was that it involved a ban on a product. It is not obvious how banning something can facilitate interstate trade in that product. This same point can be made about the *Seal Products* case, which concerned a Regulation prohibiting the import of seal products into the EU.[29] If the point of that Regulation was just to protect seals, then, however worthy, it should not have been based on Article 114. The General Court nevertheless accepted that it was a legitimate internal market measure: some Member States felt very strongly about the ethics of seal culling and banned seal products on their national markets, while others did not, resulting in a situation where the internal market would effectively be divided. Any seal products that were imported would be saleable in some parts of the EU, and not others. The situation was complicated by the fact that it was not always easy to distinguish seal products from others. A ban therefore contributed to free trade, because it helped ensure that all products on sale in the internal market could be sold throughout that market. In its judgment the General Court allows a great deal of room for animal welfare considerations, yet integrates these smoothly with the core validity requirement that obstacles to trade should be removed.

---

[26] Case C-434/02 *Arnold André GmBH & Co. KG* v *Landrat des Kreises Herford* [2004] ECR I-11825.

[27] Case C-58/8 *Vodafone* [2010] ECR I-4999. See M. Brenncke, annotation of *Vodafone* (2010) 47 *CMLRev.* 1793; S. Weatherill, 'The Limits of Legislative Harmonization Ten Years after *Tobacco Advertising*: How the Court's Case Law has become a "Drafting Guide"' (2011) 12 *German Law Journal* 827, 841–2.

[28] Brenncke, n. 27 above, 1802; Weatherill, n. 27 above, 833.

[29] Regulation 2065/2003 [2003] OJ L309/1. Case T-526/10 *Inuit Tapiriit Kanatami*, Judgment of 25 April 2013.

Case T-526/10 *Inuit Tapiriit Kanatami*, Judgment of 25 April 2013

41. In that regard, it must be borne in mind that, according to case-law, provided that the conditions for recourse to Article [114 TFEU] as a legal basis are fulfilled, the Union legislature cannot be prevented from relying on that legal basis on the ground that the protection of animal welfare is a decisive factor in the choices to be made. Such a situation may be found, by analogy, in relation to public health protection (Case C-376/98 *Germany* v *Parliament and Council*...), and as regards consumer protection (*Vodafone*...).

42. Moreover, it should be noted that the protection of animal welfare is a legitimate objective in the public interest, the importance of which was reflected, in particular, in the adoption by the Member States of the Protocol on the protection and welfare of animals, annexed to the EC Treaty. Moreover, the Court has held on a number of occasions that the interests of the Union include the health and protection of animals.

43. As is apparent from recitals 9 and 10 in the preamble to the basic regulation, it is against that background that, aware of its obligations to pay full regard to the welfare requirements of animals when formulating and implementing its internal market policy under the Protocol, the Union legislature concluded that, to eliminate the present fragmentation of the internal market, it was necessary to provide for harmonised rules while taking into account animal welfare considerations.

44. In order to be effective, the measure envisaged in the present case had to constitute an appropriate response taking into account the reasons which led to the rules which existed or were planned in the various Member States. In that connection, it appears from recital 10 in the preamble to the basic regulation that, to restore consumer confidence while, at the same time, ensuring that animal welfare concerns are fully met, 'the placing on the market of seal products should, as a general rule, not be allowed'. In addition, the Union legislature took the view that, to allay the concerns of citizens and consumers regarding 'the killing and skinning of seals as such, it [was] also necessary to take action to reduce the demand leading to the marketing of seal products and, hence, the economic demand driving the commercial hunting of seals'.

45. As is apparent from recital 13 in the preamble to the basic regulation, the Union legislature took the view that the most effective means of preventing existing and expected disturbances of the operation of the internal market in the products concerned was to reassure consumers by offering them a general guarantee that no seal product would be marketed on the Union market, inter alia by banning the import of such products from third countries.

At the time of writing, this judgment is being appealed to the Court of Justice.

Banning products nevertheless remains a counter-intuitive contribution to market-building. It can best be understood by recognising that all products are part of a wider market, meaning that there are alternatives for the consumer: other tobacco products, or other forms of leather, in the examples above. Any product regulation limits what can be sold, and so entails a ban on non-complying products, but if the effect of that product delimitation is to steer consumers to freely tradeable alternatives then the regulation can be said to contribute to removing obstacles to trade and creating an open market.

The other major question on Article 114 arising in the case law concerns the meaning and scope of 'approximation'. Can this Article be used only for legislation which actually harmonises, or can it be used for measures which contribute to the process of harmonising, without engaging in it as such? The latter position appears to be correct, following the *Smoke Flavourings* case and the *ENISA* case.[30]

The first of these concerned the British passion for chemically flavoured potato crisps, some varieties of which used flavourings which were likely to be banned under EU food safety rules. Faced with this sacrifice of national culture at the altar of mere safety, the British claimed that the procedure which had been created to decide on such bans lacked a legal basis. This procedure was found in Regulation 1007/2009, which enabled the Commission to regulate food additives according to a number of principles and processes, of which an important element was that they would receive advice from the European Food Safety Authority. The Regulation was based on Article 114. The British Government argued that this Article could only be used to actually approximate national rules directly, not to create a system leading to such approximation, as the Regulation did.

Case C-66/04 *United Kingdom v Parliament and Council (Smoke Flavourings)* [2005] ECR I-10553

45. ...in Article [114 TFEU] the authors of the Treaty intended to confer on the Community legislature a discretion, depending on the general context and the specific circumstances of the matter to be harmonised, as regards the harmonisation technique most appropriate for achieving the desired result, in particular in fields which are characterised by complex technical features.

46. That discretion may be used in particular to choose the most appropriate harmonisation technique where the proposed approximation requires physical, chemical or biological analyses to be made and scientific developments in the field concerned to be taken into account. Such evaluations relating to the safety of products correspond to the objective imposed on the Community legislature by Article [114(3) TFEU] of ensuring a high level of protection of health.

47. Finally, it should be added that where the Community legislature provides for a harmonisation which comprises several stages, for instance the fixing of a number of essential criteria set out in a basic regulation followed by scientific evaluation of the substances concerned and the adoption of a positive list of substances authorised throughout the Community, two conditions must be satisfied.

48. First, the Community legislature must determine in the basic act the essential elements of the harmonising measure in question.

49. Second, the mechanism for implementing those elements must be designed in such a way that it leads to a harmonisation within the meaning of Article [114 TFEU]. That is the case where the Community legislature establishes the detailed rules for making decisions at each stage of such an authorisation procedure, and determines and circumscribes precisely the powers of the Commission as the body which has to take the final decision. That applies in particular where the harmonisation in question consists in drawing up a list of products authorised throughout the Community to the exclusion of all other products.

Article 114 can therefore be used to create mechanisms leading to harmonisation, as well as for immediate harmonisation.

This was taken a step further in *ENISA*. The European Network and Information Society Agency provided non-binding advice on technical matters concerning electronic communications, for

---

[30] Case C-217/04 *United Kingdom v Parliament and Council (ENISA)* [2006] ECR I-3771.

example, on current threats, or techniques for using electronic signatures, and so on. It was created by secondary legislation based on Article 114 and again the British Government argued that this went beyond approximation.

Case C–217/04 *United Kingdom* v *Parliament and Council* [2006] ECR I–3771

44. It must be added in that regard that nothing in the wording of Article [114 TFEU] implies that the addressees of the measures adopted by the Community legislature on the basis of that provision can only be the individual Member States. The legislature may deem it necessary to provide for the establishment of a Community body responsible for contributing to the implementation of a process of harmonisation in situations where, in order to facilitate the uniform implementation and application of acts based on that provision, the adoption of non-binding supporting and framework measures seems appropriate.

45. It must be emphasised, however, that the tasks conferred on such a body must be closely linked to the subject-matter of the acts approximating the laws, regulations and administrative provisions of the Member States. Such is the case in particular where the Community body thus established provides services to national authorities and/or operators which affect the homogeneous implementation of harmonising instruments and which are likely to facilitate their application.

The activities of ENISA took place in the context of a number of Directives on electronic communication and networks. These outlined the functions and goals which Member State agencies were to adopt and pursue for the objective of creating compatible and secure European information systems and networks. However, much detailed implementation was left to the national agencies. The Court of Justice therefore found that ENISA, by providing information on common approaches and problems, even in a non-binding way, helped states to develop standardised and compatible systems, and therefore made a contribution to a harmonisation process. Provided the activities of ENISA were closely linked to the matter being harmonised, this was sufficient to justify Article 114 as a legal base.

The scope of Article 114 is now reasonably clear. However, what is unaddressed is the ambiguity of the term 'appreciable' in *Tobacco Advertising I*. This is really the only word which prevents Article 114 from becoming a general power to harmonise national laws.[31] On the one hand, there seems no particular reason to fear that Article 114 will spiral out of control. Both the Council and Parliament must agree to legislation, and the Court of Justice is also likely to annul Directives which go too far.[32] Nevertheless, it is striking and, for many, problematic that the legal limit on harmonisation is so vague. One may still talk of limited Union powers, but hardly of well-defined ones.

Nor is 'appreciable' always an adequate limit. There are matters which cause very appreciable distortions of competition yet which we would not expect to see harmonised. The existence of different languages hinders trade and distorts competition in many and significant ways. It is beyond doubt that a common European language would contribute hugely to the internal market. Nothing in 'appreciable' provides an argument against a Directive legislating to make French the language of Europe.[33] Moreover, the appreciability threshold does not apply to the

[31] A. Dashwood, 'The Limits of European Community Powers' (1996) 21 *ELRev.* 113.
[32] *Ibid.*
[33] G. Davies, 'Subsidiarity: The Wrong Idea, in the Wrong Place, at the Wrong Time' (2006) 43 *CMLRev.* 63.

removal of obstacles to free movement. A fierce academic debate rages over whether the use of Article 114 to create a common European Contract Code would be appropriate.[34] There is much discussion over the extent to which differing laws on contracts hinder firms and individuals from doing business across borders, and whether a common code would make a significant difference. However, it seems likely that a common code would facilitate interstate contracts and business to at least some extent, and thus is prima facie possible under Article 114.

The objection to both these measures would be that they are disproportionate: the benefits to trade do not justify the cultural and social cost.[35] While the Court of Justice did not find the measures in *Tobacco Advertising II* or *Swedish Match* disproportionate, it is significant that it gave the matter explicit consideration. Proportionality is the other barrier to an open-ended Article 114.

What this all shows is the problem of containing purposive powers. Article 114 is not defined in terms of a particular area of activity – health, education, foodstuffs – but in terms of the achievement of goals – free movement and undistorted competition. These cut across other areas of activity, because so many different kinds of law may impact upon them. Areas of law which are not conventionally 'economic' may still affect cross-border trade or the costs of doing business, and so be subject to harmonisation using Article 114. Goal-oriented powers have thus an inherent tendency to spread.[36] As governments have always known, if the end justifies the means then much can be achieved.

Finally, a note must be made on the changes in the law since the judgments discussed above. They all took place in the context of the EC Treaty in which Article 3(g) provided that the Union would have 'a system ensuring that competition in the internal market is not distorted'. This provided the traditional intellectual background and support for the thesis that the 'establishment and functioning' of the internal market encompassed not only removing obstacles to movement, as explicitly mentioned in Article 26 TFEU, but also removing distortions of competition. However, in the new Treaties this clause has been cut out and moved to a Protocol.

Protocol No. 27 on the Internal Market and Competition

THE HIGH CONTRACTING PARTIES,

CONSIDERING that the internal market as set out in Article 3 of the Treaty on European Union includes a system ensuring that competition is not distorted,

HAVE AGREED that:
To this end, the Union shall, if necessary, take action under the provisions of the Treaties, including under Article 352 of the Treaty on the Functioning of the European Union. This protocol shall be annexed to the Treaty on European Union and to the Treaty on the Functioning of the European Union.

---

[34] S. Weatherill, 'Why Object to the Harmonisation of Private Law by the EC?' (2004) 12(5) *European Review of Private Law* 633; S. Weatherill and Stefan Vogenauer (eds.), *The Harmonisation of European Contract Law: Implications for European Private Laws, Business and Legal Practice* (Oxford, Hart, 2006); P. van den Bergh, 'Forced Harmonisation of Contract Law in Europe: Not to be Continued' in S. Grundmann and J. Stuyck (eds.), *An Academic Green Paper on European Contract Law* (Kluwer, The Hague, 2002) 245–64; M. van Hoecke and F. Ost (eds.), *The Harmonisation of European Private Law* (Oxford, Hart, 2000); A. Hartkamp and E. Hondius *et al.*, *Towards a European Civil Code* (3rd edn, The Hague, Kluwer Law International, 2004); P. Legrand, 'Against a European Civil Code' (1997) 60 *MLR* 44; M. Hesselink, *The Politics of a European Civil Code* (The Hague, Kluwer Law International, 2006); J.-J. Kuipers, 'The Legal Basis for a European Optional Instrument' (2011) 5 *European Review of Private Law* 545.

[35] Davies, n. 33 above.   [36] *Ibid.*

It remains to be seen whether this will impact on the Court of Justice and Commission's interpretation of Article 114 TFEU, which in itself is unchanged. On the one hand, a Protocol has the same legal status as a Treaty Article. Merely moving mention of distortions from the Treaty to a protocol should have no doctrinal consequences. In a recent case the Court of Justice indeed said that Article 114 'corresponds' to Article 95 EC, suggesting it sees no change in substance.[37]

Nevertheless, editing undistorted competition out of the Treaty itself represents a political perception that harmonisation of the internal market has perhaps gone too far, and should be brought under control. This is reinforced by the reference to Article 352 TFEU, which in contrast to Article 114 requires unanimity in the Council. Legal niceties apart, it is not unimaginable that this new mood will infect the institutions.

There would, however, be some irony in this. The major objections to the old Article 3(g) were from the traditional left rather than the free-market right, those who felt that unmitigated competition was no good thing and was being pursued too enthusiastically. Yet removing distortions prevents states from capitalising on low regulatory burdens to gain a competitive edge. Undistorted competition is a more fettered form of competition than competition without harmonisation would be. Were the Court of Justice to limit such harmonisation, while harmonisation to remove obstacles to movement continues, it would in fact be making the internal market an even more ruthlessly competitive place.

(5) TECHNIQUES OF REGULATION

(i) Old and new approaches

One of the fundamental obstacles to free trade between states is technical standards. These vary from state to state, with the result that a product made according to French law probably does not conform to the requirements of German or UK law. Manufacturers thus have a difficult time making products that they can freely trade throughout the European Union.

In the early days of the Union (when it was the European Economic Community), the approach to this problem was relatively straightforward. Wherever necessary, the Commission sought to propose legislation replacing national product standards with equivalent European ones. Common standards, combined with mutual recognition of inspections, removed the trade problem.[38] However, standards are a complex business, not only for complicated technical products, but even for apparently simple ones, such as toys, where one may have to think about paint types, strength, resistance to strain, and so on. Each piece of legislation was a time-consuming business, and the Community was simply not able to produce enough legislation to create a single market, particularly given the pace of product development and the constant introduction of new product types.[39]

In the mid-1980s a new approach was introduced, still called 'the new approach' today.[40] This was based on a much more minimalist legislative approach. Instead of detailed and

---

[37] Case C-128/11 *UsedSoft*, Judgment of 3 July 2012, para. 41.

[38] See General Programme on the Removal of Technical Obstacles to Trade [1969] OJ C76/1.

[39] Commission White Paper, *Completing the Single Market*, COM(85)310; *The Development of Standardisation: Action for Faster Technical Integration in Europe*, COM(90)456.

[40] For policy documents, details of legislation and background, see www.newapproach.eu and http://ec.europa.eu/enterprise/policies/european-standards/harmonised-standards/new-approach_en.htm.

technical legislation for each product type, Directives would be adopted for broad product categories, toys, machinery, and so on. These would lay down, at a high level of abstraction, general demands concerning the essential health and safety requirements that such products should meet. A selection of the requirements from Directive 2009/48/EC on toy safety provides a flavour of the style of these requirements, abstract almost to the point of being banal.

Directive 2009/48/EC of the European Parliament and of the Council of 18 June 2009 on the safety of toys, Annex II, Particular Safety Requirements

I. Physical and Mechanical Properties

1. Toys and their parts and, in the case of fixed toys, their anchorages, must have the requisite mechanical strength and, where appropriate, stability to withstand the stresses to which they are subjected during use without breaking or becoming liable to distortion at the risk of causing physical injury.

2. Accessible edges, protrusions, cords, cables and fastenings on toys must be designed and manufactured in such a way that the risks of physical injury from contact with them are reduced as far as possible.

3. Toys must be designed and manufactured in such a way as not to present any risk or only the minimum risk inherent to their use which could be caused by the movement of their parts....

5. Aquatic toys must be designed and manufactured so as to reduce as far as possible, taking into account the recommended use of the toy, any risk of loss of buoyancy of the toy and loss of support afforded to the child.

6. Toys which it is possible to get inside and which thereby constitute an enclosed space for occupants must have a means of exit which the intended user can open easily from the inside.

The responsibility of the Member States under new approach Directives is to ensure that products placed onto their domestic markets conform to the essential requirements in the Directive.[41] How exactly they do this is up to them. There are two important differences from the old approach. First, the new approach gives states a considerable freedom to standardise in different ways. There is no uniform approach. Thus, the virtues of experiment and diversity are maintained. Essential health and safety requirements can be satisfied by different regulatory styles and methods according to the traditions and preferences of the state. Secondly, the legislation only deals with essential health and safety requirements. Matters that are purely concerned with quality are not harmonised. Thus, the Union may legislate to ensure that sausages are safe, but under the new approach will not be concerned with how much meat a sausage has to contain.

This decision not to harmonise quality standards was made possible by the decision in *Cassis de Dijon*, where the Court of Justice decided that pure quality issues are not a sufficient

---

[41] On the new approach, see J. Pelkmans, 'The New Approach to Technical Harmonization and Standardization' (1987) 25 *JCMS* 249; European Commission, *Enhancing the Implementation of New Approach Directives*, COM(2003)240; A. McGee and S. Weatherill, 'The Evolution of the Single Market: Harmonisation or Liberalisation?' (1990) 53 *MLR* 578. See further M. Egan, *Constructing a European Market* (Oxford, Oxford University Press, 2001) ch. 4; S. Weatherill, 'Pre-emption, Harmonisation and the Distribution of Competence to Regulate the Internal Market' in C. Barnard and J. Scott (eds.), *The Law of the Single European Market: Unpacking the Premises* (Oxford/Portland, Hart, 2002); K. Armstrong, 'Governance and the Single European Market' in P. Craig and G. de Búrca (eds.), *The Evolution of EU Law* (Oxford, Oxford University Press, 1998).

reason to exclude foreign products from the market.[42] Germany may decide that German-made sausages should have more than 50 per cent meat, but it cannot use this requirement to exclude British ones that may have much less. The EU approach to quality requirements is now no longer based on compulsory quality standards, but on informing the consumers, who then decide for themselves what they prefer: Germany may, for example, require sausages to indicate on the packaging how much meat they contain. Since quality standards therefore no longer create (in principle) obstacles to trade, there is no need to harmonise them. This is the core insight of the new approach.

(ii) Mechanics of the new approach

The new approach does not rest on the broad-spectrum Directives alone. There are two other aspects which are in practice essential to its success. First, European standardisation is not abandoned. Rather, it is moved away from the legislative process to specialist standardisation agencies.[43] These create technical standards of a more detailed and specific type, although often less specific and detailed than under the old approach, still leaving a certain discretion and freedom in how to meet substantive requirements. The advantage of this outsourcing is that it decouples the making of standards (which can be slow and difficult) from the legislative process, so that this latter is no longer seized up. The Council and Parliament can agree on a general framework, and then let the experts deal with the details at their own pace. Moreover, the new European standards are voluntary: there is no obligation to adopt them. A state, or a manufacturer, may prefer to meet the requirements of the Directive in another way, and they are free to do so. However, they will then have to show that their products do in fact meet the health and safety requirements. It may be easier to simply follow the European standards, since if a producer does this it creates a strong presumption that the product conforms to the Directive. She should then be able to sell her goods throughout the Union without problem. The idea of a new European standard is therefore that it shows one way of manufacturing a product so that it is sufficiently safe and conforms to the relevant Directive, but it does not insist that this is the only way. Room for production-method innovation and deviation is allowed.

The second additional aspect of the new approach is its procedural requirements concerning certification. It is all very well to say that products conforming to the European standard, or complying with the Directive by another method, must be accepted by all Member States. This begs the question of who establishes that there actually is such conformity. The new approach comes with a certification system for products, but it is this system which has been at the root of its problems. The system is decentralised and Member States do not trust each other's implementation.

---

[42] Case 120/78 *Rewe-Zentral AG* v *Bundesmonopolverwaltung für Branntwein (Cassis de Dijon)* [1979] ECR 649. See pp. 773–83.

[43] For example European Committee for Standardisation (CEN), European Committee for Electrotechnical Standardisation (CENELEC) and European Telecommunication Standards Institute (ETSI). See European Commission Communication, *The Role of European Standardisation in the Framework of European Policies and Legislation*, COM(2004)674 final (18 October 2004); H. Schepel, *The Constitution of Private Governance* (Oxford/Portland, Hart, 2005) ch. 2; C. Frankel and E. Højbjerg, 'The Constitution of a Transnational Policy Field: Negotiating the EU Internal Market for Products' (2007) 14 *JEPP* 96; M. Austin and H. Milner, 'Strategies of European Standardization' (2001) 8 *JEPP* 411.

Commission Staff Working Document SEC(2007)173

1.2.2. What are the specificities of the New Approach?

As discussed above, instead of setting out detailed technical requirements in the legislation, New Approach directives limit themselves to defining essential requirements in relation to issues such as health, safety, consumer protection and the protection of the environment. The legislation fixes the level of safety which products must meet but does not pre-determine the technical solutions to achieve this level of safety. The choice of different solutions leading to the same result is therefore open to manufacturers.

Technical specifications, in the form of standards, coming under the framework of the New Approach directives, allow products to meet the essential requirements needed and are considered as an 'easy' way to meet compliance with the legislation (presumption of conformity). Use of standards guarantees the required level of safety of products, but use of harmonised standards is voluntary and a manufacturer may use any other technical solution which demonstrates that his product meets the essential requirements.

The directives also set out requirements for conformity assessment, which depending upon the product need to be done either by a third party testing, inspection or certification body or by the manufacturer himself. The different types of conformity assessment procedures were identified by Decision 93/465/EEC and are set out in the form of 'modules'. Each directive has chosen the modules which are considered to be appropriate for demonstrating conformity, taking into account the type of risk related to the particular product.

Certain modules require the intervention of third party conformity assessment bodies, known as notified bodies. These bodies are chosen ('designated') by Member States on the basis of certain minimum criteria (competence, impartiality, integrity, etc.) which are set out in the directives. They are then 'notified' to the Commission, after which they are authorised to carry out conformity assessment activities according to the procedures set out in the directives.

In addition to this, the Commission has also supported the development at European level of a new evolution at national level: Accreditation. In the past, Member States' public authorities approved products prior to them being placed on the market.

However, national testing and certification resources were not always sufficient and the national authorities began to use the services of private conformity assessment bodies. In order to ensure that these private bodies were able to provide the correct level of service, they were submitted to the control of a national public authority body: the national accreditation body. This was devised in all Member States as a means to ensure an appropriate level of credibility for test results and product certification or inspection.

Last but not least the New Approach introduced a common marking of conformity, which has become its most visible and well known element. The CE marking is in effect a declaration by the manufacturer that the product conforms to all the essential requirements of the relevant legislation and that it has been subject to the applicable conformity assessment procedures. Since products bearing the CE marking are presumed to be in compliance with the applicable directives and hence benefit from free circulation, the CE marking operates as a 'passport' to the whole EU market....

2.1. Performance of notified bodies and weaknesses in the notification process

Certain conformity assessment procedures require that a product is tested, inspected or certified by an independent third party, a 'notified body', before it is placed on the market. Notified bodies hence play an important role within the New Approach system to guarantee the safety of products on the market. Therefore, it is crucial to ensure that they have the necessary competence and capacity to carry out their tasks correctly. Furthermore, confidence in their competence is crucial to ensure EU wide recognition of certificates issued by these bodies.

Most notified bodies do a professional and complete job. However, sometimes certain notified bodies apply practices which can undermine the confidence of this type of work in the whole sector.

The 'modules' referred to above are different procedures by which a producer may show that her goods comply with the relevant Directive. These very often involve testing by an accredited 'notified body', a body authorised by the Member State of production to test and certify those products as complying with EU law. However, as the extract suggests, and goes on to explain in more detail, the major weakness of the new approach is a lack of trust between states on the performance and reliability of these bodies, leading to a reluctance to accept their results as proof of compliance.[44]

The core problem is that if standards leave room for variety, then it becomes a harder and less objective process to assess whether they are met. It is easier to objectively certify a teddy bear if every detail of its manufacture is specified than if the rules say 'it must be able to resist normal use by a child'. Clearly, bodies will take different approaches to measuring compliance. The problems this creates are magnified by the fact that there is no uniform European approach to accreditation of notified bodies, and these vary greatly in character and quality. They may be private companies, public authorities or quasi-public agencies. There are repeated complaints that the bodies are not of consistent quality, that market pressures encourage them to be over-easy with their certification, that not all Member States adequately supervise the notified bodies or are strict enough about accreditation.

Thus, the principle of the new approach is attractively easy: a producer contracts with a notified body to have her products tested and certified to show they comply with the Directive; the body does this, whereupon the producer attaches a CE mark to her product, and supplies the certification documents to the authorities of the state to which she is exporting and the goods are accepted onto their market. However, this relies on these authorities trusting the notified bodies of other states, which they often do not. Thus, despite a CE mark and evidence of certification, it is not at all uncommon for states to block market access on the grounds that the products are not in fact sufficiently safe. They may take the view that the way the producer has chosen to meet the Directive's requirements is not adequate, or that there is insufficient evidence of such compliance.

It may well be that if the producer litigates, then ultimately she will win.[45] National authorities are still often over-suspicious of foreign standards and notifying bodies and their refusals may be unjustified. However, litigation is slow and expensive. If producers have to use the courts regularly to gain market access, then the new approach has failed. In fact the picture is mixed; in many cases it works well, but too often it does not.[46]

---

[44] See G. Majone, *Mutual Trust, Credible Commitments and the Evolution of the Rules of the Single Market*, EUI Working Paper RSC No. 95/1 (Florence, European University Institute, 1995); Pelkmans, n. 41 above.

[45] See e.g. Case C-254/05 *Commission* v *Belgium* [2007] ECR I-4269.

[46] See J. Pelkmans, *Mutual Recognition in Goods and Services: An Economic Perspective*, ENEPRI Working Paper No. 16/2003 (Brussels, ENEPRI, 2003).

As a result of these concerns, the new approach is being updated. While trying to maintain its light legislative touch and flexibility, new legislation has been adopted aiming to improve trust surrounding the certification process. Regulation 765/2008/EC creates a Union framework for the operation, accreditation and supervision of conformity assessment bodies (notified bodies) in the hope that this will create a more uniform quality and approach, and therefore more trust and more effective interstate mutual recognition of certification.[47] It is perhaps an irony that minimising the harmonisation of products is only possible by increasing the harmonisation of procedure.

Alongside this, the old approach is not dead. Technical legislation usually provided for updating by the comitology process, so that it survives product development.[48] A significant number of products are therefore still subject to 'old style' Directives. The following section, particularly the extract from Joerges, discusses some of the more political aspects of the difference between these two parallel approaches to regulation.[49]

(iii) Minimum harmonisation

The new and old approaches are both about technical product standards, but much internal market harmonisation concerns production processes and the ironing out of distortions of competition, or less urgent aspects of product regulation such as consumer protection. Here the Union has other techniques which it uses to try and reach the right balance between harmonisation and local autonomy.

An approach often used is minimum harmonisation.[50] This lays down a minimum standard, but leaves Member States free to have stricter standards if they wish. Where this is applied to harmonisation of the conditions of competition it is relatively unproblematic in principle. The competitive impact of legal differences is not eliminated, but it is reduced. However, where minimum harmonisation is applied to matters related to tradable goods or services it raises legal problems. If a Member State chooses to maintain higher standards, is it entitled to apply these to imports or not? If so, then the Directive does not ensure free movement, and its purpose and validity may be questioned (if it is based on Article 114 TFEU at least; where it is based on other Treaty Articles such as those providing for environmental legislation, the matter becomes more complex).[51] Yet if not, then Member States are not in fact able to guarantee a higher level of protection on their territory, since they may only apply the higher standard to domestic producers, and not to imports. The minimum level may in practice become the actual level prevailing in the marketplace, rendering the option to maintain higher standards a little hollow.

The answer turns on the wording and context of each Directive. However, in general, the imperative that measures based on Article 114 facilitate free movement means that internal market Directives usually require Member States to admit products that meet the minimum standards. Thus, Member States may usually only apply stricter requirements to domestic

---

[47] Regulation 765/2008 setting out the requirements for accreditation and market surveillance relating to the marketing of products [2008] OJ L218/30.

[48] See pp. 144–51.   [49] See p. 695.

[50] M. Dougan, 'Minimum Harmonization and the Internal Market' (2000) 37 *CMLRev.* 853.

[51] *Ibid*; J. Jans and H. H. B. Vedder, *European Environmental Law* (3rd edn, Groningen, Europa Law Publishing, 2008).

production, and not to imports. One consequence of this is that domestic production may bear a heavier regulatory burden than imported goods. The Court of Justice confirmed in *Gallaher* that this is not to be seen as prohibited discrimination, but simply as an inevitable and acceptable result of the choice for minimum harmonisation.[52] *Gallaher* concerned the size of health warnings on cigarette packets. Directive 89/622/EC required these to cover at least 4 per cent of the packet, but allowed Member States to be stricter. The United Kingdom required 6 per cent but, as the Directive required, did not enforce this against imports. UK producers complained, without avail, that they were unfairly disadvantaged.

6 NON-ECONOMIC INTERESTS IN THE INTERNAL MARKET

Economic and non-economic interests cannot feasibly be separated. Economic activity inevitably impacts on the environment, society and individual safety and security. Nor does the Treaty intend that such matters should be considered in isolation. It explicitly demands an integrated approach. Article 7 TFEU provides that the Union shall ensure consistency between all its policies, and Articles 8 to 12 require anti-discrimination goals, social policy, the environment and consumer protection to be integrated into all other policies. Moreover, Article 114 TFEU enables both the Commission, in its proposals, and Member States, by means of derogations from harmonisation measures, to take into account and react to health, safety and environmental concerns.

Article 114(3)–(5) TFEU

3. The Commission, in its proposals envisaged in paragraph 1 concerning health, safety, environmental protection and consumer protection, will take as a base a high level of protection, taking account in particular of any new development based on scientific facts. Within their respective powers, the European Parliament and the Council will also seek to achieve this objective.
4. If, after the adoption of a harmonisation measure by the European Parliament and the Council, by the Council or by the Commission, a Member State deems it necessary to maintain national provisions on grounds of major needs referred to in Article 36, or relating to the protection of the environment or the working environment, it shall notify the Commission of these provisions as well as the grounds for maintaining them.
5. Moreover, without prejudice to paragraph 4, if, after the adoption of a harmonisation measure by the European Parliament and the Council, by the Council or by the Commission, a Member State deems it necessary to introduce national provisions based on new scientific evidence relating to the protection of the environment or the working environment on grounds of a problem specific to that Member State arising after the adoption of the harmonisation measure, it shall notify the Commission of the envisaged provisions as well as the grounds for introducing them.

The remainder of the Article provides for procedures to assess and police the derogations above.

The right balance between interests is, of course, always contested. This is the stuff of politics. However, an issue of current concern is the process of achieving that balance. An

---

[52] Case C-11/92 *R* v *Secretary of State for Health ex parte Gallaher Ltd* [1993] ECR I-3545.

accusation levelled at the Union is that it is deaf to voices other than scientific ones, and presents scientific analyses of health and safety and environmental issues as more objective and less contested than they in fact are, and also as more important than they in fact are: scientific perspectives are only a part of a picture in which moral and social and democratic preferences are also relevant.

This issue arose in the *Austrian GMOs* case, in which the region of Upper Austria sought to ban the release of GMOs on its territory.[53] To do this it needed a derogation from Directive 2001/18/EC, which it sought on the basis of Article 114(5) TFEU. This was refused by the Commission, and the Commission's view was upheld in both the General Court and Court of Justice. The Court emphasised that Article 114(5) TFEU could only be relied upon where there was new scientific evidence, problems specific to a Member State arising after the harmonisation measure had been adopted, and where those problems related to the working or natural environment. These were cumulative requirements: a failure on any ground made derogation impossible. The Austrian view was that its unique eco-systems, sizeable organic production and large number of small farms made it a special case. It was not so much that they had new evidence on the science, as that the consequences for an industry and society where naturalness and purity are especially important were particularly frightening. There was no room for this within Article 114(5). The Court of Justice's view is textually understandable – the Article is fairly clear – but it raises the question whether EU law is adapted to modern risk management, which has to face situations where threats to health and safety are bound up with ethics and social norms, or whether it is only suited for less controversial and more lumpen issues.

The same question may be asked about the EU legislative process. Chapter 5 goes into more detail on how this process deals with risk, and on the distinction between determining the acceptable level of risk, which is a political task for the legislator, and determining what the actual level of risk is, which is outsourced to the scientists in specialist agencies.[54] Yet, while this distinction makes apparent sense, it glosses the complexity of the decision-making process. In practice, the centrality of the scientific risk-assessment process may have the effect of marginalising legitimate ethical concerns or public doubts about scientific reliability. One of the ways in which this occurs results from the decision-making framework and practices of the Commission. Kritikos argues that it tends not to actively engage with non-scientific concerns, and structures its processes in a way that excludes them.[55] Although it has the power to take into account many interests, in practice it chooses as quantitative and expert-based an approach as possible. In particular, adoption of the distinction between questions of fact (what is the risk?) and value (what should be done about this risk?) has led to the exclusion of the vast majority of public concerns from the most influential stage of the decision-making model: the process of risk-framing. The result is that 'it is less the case that those critics who are currently excluded from decision-making…do not "possess" the "necessary" knowledge to participate; rather, what counts as knowledge has been defined in such a way as to exclude their potential contributions and legitimacy'.[56]

---

[53] Joined Cases C-439/05 P and C-454/05 P *Land Oberösterreich and Austria* v *Commission* [2007] ECR I-7141.

[54] Case T-13/99 *Pfizer Animal Health* v *Council* [2002] ECR II-3305.

[55] M. Kritikos, 'Traditional Risk Analysis and Releases of GMOs into the European Union: Space for Non-Scientific Factors' (2009) 44 *ELRev*. 405.

[56] D. Smith and S. Tombs, 'Of Course It's Safe, Trust Me!' in E. Coles, D. Smith and S. Tombs, *Risk Management and Society* (Dordrecht, Kluwer Academic Publishers, 2000) 68. Cited in Kritikos, n. 55 above.

An additional reason for concern about this alleged science bias arises from the role of technocratic agencies. Given that their views may in practice often be constitutive of legislative decisions, there is a fear of government by an undemocratic technocracy. Chapters 2 and 9 have more detail on this issue, and portray the fear that agencies may not be so much neutral as the embodiment of entrenched ideologies, isolated from alternative views.[57] Joerges has portrayed, by contrast, the advantages of the traditional comitology process. This is run by national experts who he suggests are more connected to the worlds of politics and democracy than their agency peers. As a result they are better able to take account of diverse political concerns.

C. Joerges, 'The Law's Problems with the Governance of the Single European Market' in C. Joerges and R. Dehousse (eds.), *Good Governance in Europe's Integrated Market* (Oxford, Oxford University Press, 2002) 1, 17–18

Committees were born of a strong national desire to retain control over the setting and consequences of European regulatory norms/standards. And they thus embody the functional and structural tensions that characterize internal market regulation. First, they hover between 'technical' and 'political' considerations, or between the functional needs and the ethical/social criteria that inform European regulation. Second, they often have very fluid compositions that reflect upon the regulatory goal of balancing rationalizing technical criteria against broader political concerns, and that also forcefully highlight schisms between the political interests of those engaged in the process of internal market regulation. Committees are deeply implicated in political processes, even when they have been established with the explicit role of supporting and overseeing the implementing powers delegated to the Commission. They are the fora for the balancing of a market integrationist logic against a Member State's interest in the substance and costs of consumer protection and cohesive economic development. As such, they often resemble mini-Councils.

Yet, it is precisely in the context of the market that the wisdom of this call for democratic responsiveness is sometimes questioned. There is an argument that market regulation should not be politicised, because the scientific and economic issues involved are a matter of technical competence more than political choices.

Support for this view has been most prominently provided by Giandomenico Majone, who has argued that the Union is not intended to be a place of political contestation, but a technocratic regulator in the service of the states. He fears below that the more agencies depart from a narrowly technical approach to their task, the more they will undermine their own credibility.

G. Majone, 'The Credibility Crisis of Community Regulation' (2002) 38 *Journal of Common Market Studies* 273, 285

One of the core insights of functionalist theories is that integration is most likely to occur within a domain shielded from the direct clash of political interests. For several decades, law and economics – the discourse of legal and market integration – provided a sufficient buffer to achieve results that could not be directly obtained in the political realm. It was generally admitted that the credibility and coherence of European regulatory law depends crucially on the perception that the Commission is able and willing to enforce the common rules in an objective and even-handed way.

[57] See pp. 78–80 and 384–8.

Follesdal and Hix, disagreeing with him, summarise his view as follows.

A. Follesdal and S. Hix, 'Why there is a Democratic Deficit in the EU: A Response to Majone and Moravcsik' (2006) 44 *Journal of Common Market Studies* 533, 537–8

…The EU governments have delegated regulatory policy competences to the European level – such as the creation of the single market, the harmonization of product standards and health and safety rules and even the making of monetary policy by the European Central Bank – to deliberately isolate these policies from domestic majoritarian government. From this perspective, the EU is a glorified regulatory agency, a 'fourth branch of government', much like regulatory agencies at the domestic level in Europe, such as telecoms agencies, competition authorities, central banks, or even courts.

Following from this interpretation, Majone asserts that EU policy-making *should not* be 'democratic' in the usual meaning of the term.…

Politicization would result in redistributive rather than Pareto-efficient outcomes, and so in fact undermine rather than increase the legitimacy of the EU.

The discussion above is about the EU legislative process, but a parallel debate exists about the effect of the internal market on Member States. Free movement law is often justified by the fact that it protects outsiders, the foreigner or foreign trader, doing business in a Member State which is not her own and where she has no political voice and may tend to be excluded by the domestic majority.[58] Yet a counter-criticism is made, which is that precisely by protecting these mobile outsiders the choices of the domestic majority as to their institutions, values and mechanisms for redistribution are undermined. Both of these arguments will become more concrete in the following chapters on free movement law, where the conflict between free movement and domestic law is a central theme.

F. De Witte, 'Transnational Solidarity and the Mediation of Conflicts of Justice in Europe' (2012) 18 *European Law Journal* 694, 702–3

[The exercise of free movement rights] structurally favours (in the most general terms) the much more mobile capital and the richer citizens over immobile labour and poorer citizens by making policy choices that go against the interests of such mobile actors unavailable. This process has been described in company law, labour law and regulation of the marketing of goods – where policy outcomes are structurally biased towards the interests of global (and mobile) capital. In those fields, collective choices are restricted by the need to respect individual agency of those who actually move. Such partial de-politicisation is problematic as such, given that collective agency was exactly meant to tame such (often the very same) particularistic interests, but more fundamentally because it shows that obligation of non-discrimination is not normatively neutral and may dislocate normative and redistributive commitments on the national level.

As well as its immediate effects in specific cases, the internal market has also been argued by Somek to embody a commitment to individualism which challenges the very fabric of

---

[58] M. Poiares Maduro, *We the Court* (Oxford/Portland, Hart, 1998).

social-democratic societies, tending to break the bonds of solidarity between citizens.[59] He makes a claim about the conflict between economic and social policy which goes to the heart of the internal market. Yet, by contrast with domestic politics, it has been argued that the EU prefers to deny such conflicts rather than to debate, or even accept, them.[60] Neither in the legislative process nor before the Court of Justice when it adjudicates on free movement is there an open enough expression of all the interests at stake, which go beyond the merely concrete and include questions of identity, justice and views about 'the good life', as de Witte has put it: rules about products, services and migration are also rules about how we want to live together.[61] This depoliticisation of value-laden policy choices challenges the legitimacy of the internal market, and of the EU as a whole.[62]

7 REGULATORY COMPETITION

Does the market actually need legislation? It is quite imaginable to build a market purely on the basis of a simple and directly effective rule of free movement. Member States would be required to accept onto their domestic markets any goods and services made according to the laws of other Member States. Such a rule is sometimes called a country of origin principle, or a principle of mutual recognition.[63] As will become evident from subsequent chapters, the case law on free movement embodies such a rule to a considerable extent.

The merits of this minimalist market would be that it apparently permits local regulatory diversity and autonomy. These should be valued as such. If populations are required to accept regulation that does not correspond to their preferences, then one gets what economists call a reduction in welfare. The population may not necessarily be less well off in narrowly financial terms, but they are less well off in terms of the things that they value, which are the things that matter, and which a competent economic policy aims to maximise. As was discussed earlier in the chapter, there is an argument that harmonisation should only be undertaken when local regulation is creating externalities; when the local population is getting what they want by imposing some of the costs on their neighbours.[64] The question of what comprises an externality is difficult: one could argue that getting wealthy creates externalities since research shows that other people become less happy when those near to them get richer, particularly if they do so by means that others feel to be unfair.[65] At this point, the economics of harmonisation collapses into little more than a consideration of what is fair and decent. However, there is a specific economic argument about a minimalist internal market which has attracted much commentary and continues to be central in policy debates. It is taken by different commentators to support different standpoints.

---

[59] Somek, n. 22 above; A. Somek, 'From Workers to Migrants, from Distributive Justice to Inclusion: Exploring the Changing Social Democratic Imagination' (2012) 18 *European Law Journal* 711.

[60] M. Dani, 'Rehabilitating Social Conflicts in European Public Law' (2012) 18 *European Law Journal* 621.

[61] F. de Witte, 'Sex, Drugs and EU Law: The Regulation of Moral and Ethical Diversity in EU Law' (2013) 6 *CMLRev.* 1545; Dani, n. 60 above.

[62] G. Davies, 'Democracy and Legitimacy in the Shadow of Purposive Competence' (2014) 20 *ELJ* (forthcoming).

[63] See e.g. G. Davies, *Services, Citizenship and the Country of Origin Principle*, Mitchell Working Paper No. 2/2007 (Edinburgh, Europa Institute, 2007).

[64] Ogus, n. 15 above.

[65] See B. Frey, *Happiness: A Revolution in Economics* (Cambridge, MA, Massachusetts Institute of Technology Press, 2008) 31, and generally ch. 3, 'How Income Affects Happiness' and ch. 5, 'How Inflation and Inequality Affect Happiness'.

The argument is that a market based on mutual recognition and free movement alone, or to an excessive extent, creates what is called regulatory competition. Sun and Pelkmans were among the first to frame the debate in the European context.

J.-M. Sun and J. Pelkmans, 'Regulatory Competition in the Single Market' (1995) 33 *Journal of Common Market Studies* 67, 68

Once the EC-1992 process had begun to take shape, a fundamental debate on the optimal regulatory strategy for the single market emerged. Following the advocacy of 'competition among rules' in the Padoa-Schioppa Report (1987) [a report published in 1987 on, among other things, the internal market] this debate came to be focused on the merits of, and potential for, 'regulatory competition'. There is now an emerging literature on regulatory competition, which is inspired by the literature on economic regulation and the economics of federalism. Crucial in the former is that regulation can only be economically justified if it remedies a market failure, while minimizing its (regulatory) costs.

The latter provides the economic underpinning of subsidiarity, in seeking the optimal economic assignment of regulatory competencies in a multi-layer structure of government.

The essence of regulatory competition is that if firms are able to locate in the state of their choice, produce there, and market their products throughout the Union, then they will be inclined to locate in the states with the most attractive business environment.[66] Since states need businesses to provide tax revenue and employment, states will be forced to make their regulation business-friendly. This has both advantages and disadvantages. The advantages are claimed to be that regulation will improve in quality. There will be a form of competition between states, and as with competition between producers, this will result in better products for the consumer. In this case the 'product' will be law, and the consumer will be the mobile firm, or individual. In general, a diversity of different national approaches to law will result in a more creative and dynamic legal Union than central harmonisation, and not only will individual states produce better laws, but they will learn from each other.[67]

Yet, the claimed downside of regulatory competition is that it forces states to take account of only some of those who are affected by regulation: mobile economic actors. The citizen's voice is lost. Laws become tailored to those who are able to threaten exit, while others are ignored.[68] In practice, this may lead to what is called a 'race to the bottom' as states impose ever lighter regulatory standards to attract businesses.[69] As one state cuts environmental or social obligations, other states will be forced to do the same or lose their tax and employment base, leading to a general lowering of standards. Harmonisation of the conditions of competition is seen as an essential balance to prevent this happening. Deakin provides an overview of these issues.

---

[66] See generally in the European context C. Barnard and S. Deakin, 'Market Access and Regulatory Competition' in C. Barnard and S. Deakin (eds.), *The Law of the European Single Market* (Oxford/Portland, Hart, 2005); N. Reich, 'Competition Between Legal Orders: A New Paradigm of EC Law?' (1992) 29 *CMLRev.* 459; Ogus, n. 15 above; S. Deakin, 'Legal Diversity and Regulatory Competition: Which Model for Europe?' (2006) 12 *ELJ* 440; H. Søndergaard Birkmose, 'Regulatory Competition and the European Harmonisation Process' (2006) *EBLRev.* 1075.

[67] See especially Deakin, n. 66 above.

[68] See A. O. Hirschmann, *Exit, Voice and Loyalty: Responses to Decline in Firms, Organizations and States* (Cambridge, MA, Harvard University Press, 1970); F. De Witte, 'Transnational Solidarity and the Mediation of Conflicts of Justice in Europe' (2012) 18 *European Law Journal* 694.

[69] See Barnard and Deakin, 'Market Access and Regulatory Competition', n. 66 above.

S. Deakin, 'Legal Diversity and Regulatory Competition: Which Model for Europe?'
(2006) 12 *European Law Journal* **440, 441–3**

Regulatory competition can be defined as a process whereby legal rules are selected and de-selected through competition between decentralised, rule-making entities, which could be nation states, or other political units, such as regions or localities. A number of beneficial effects are expected to flow from this process. Insofar as it avoids the imposition of rules by a centralised, 'monopoly' regulator, it promotes diversity and experimentation in the search for effective laws. In addition, by providing mechanisms for the preferences of the different users of laws to be expressed and for alternative solutions to common problems to be compared, it enhances the flow of information on what works in practice. Above all, it allows the content of rules to be matched more effectively to the preferences or *wants* of those consumers, that is, the citizens of the polities concerned. In some versions of the theory, the first two of these goals are, in essence, simply the means by which the third is achieved.

The idea of regulatory competition is not new, but it was first formalised within the framework of modern welfare economics in the mid-1950s, in relation to the issue of the production of local public goods. The timing is significant: Tiebout's celebrated article, entitled 'A pure theory of public expenditure', was, essentially, an application of theories of general equilibrium that were prevalent at the time. The article constructs a model in which competition operates on the basis of mobility of persons and resources across the boundaries of local government units within a sovereign state. In the model, local authorities compete to attract residents by offering packages of services in return for levying taxes at differential rates. Consumers with similar wants then 'cluster' in particular localities. The effect is to match local preferences to particular levels of service provision, thereby maximising the satisfaction of wants, while also maintaining diversity and promoting information flows between jurisdictions.

Tiebout's model is of wider interest because laws, like aspects of local public infrastructure, can be seen as indivisible public goods. By showing formally that they can be understood as products which jurisdictions *supply* in response to the *demands* of consumers of the laws, Tiebout demonstrated the relevance, even to public goods of this kind, of a market analogy. However, in Tiebout's 'pure theory', freedom of movement was *assumed* for the purpose of setting up the formal economic model. The model was aimed at showing that, *given* an effective threat of exit, spontaneous forces would operate in such a way as to discipline states against enacting laws that set an inappropriately high (or low) level of regulation. Tiebout's article did not set out the institutional conditions that would have to be met for the process of competition to occur in the 'real' world; in common with other applications of the general equilibrium model at this time, these conditions were simply assumed. However, the model could be, and was, used as a benchmark against which to judge institutional measures aimed at creating regulatory competition. Since the mid-1950s, the identification of these conditions has become the central question uniting various new-institutional movements in economics and law; it is no longer adequate simply to assume their existence. Sensitivity to the need to consider the institutional framework has not, however, avoided a tendency on the part of many analyses to present the 'pure model' of unfettered competition as the goal to which laws and institutions should be directed, and the debate over regulatory competition is no exception to this.

The most obvious institutional implication of the Tieboutian model is that regulatory competition, in its various forms, requires a particular division of labour between different levels of rule making. It cannot work unless effective regulatory authority is exercised by entities operating at a devolved or local level. Law-making powers should be conferred on lower-level units, subject only to the principle that there must be some level below which further decentralisation becomes unfeasible because of diseconomies of scale.

But even this gives rise to a need for a federal or transnational body that involves superintending the process of competition between the lower level units. Individual units could shut down competition unilaterally, either by placing barriers to the movement of the factors of production beyond their own territory, or by denying access to incoming capital, labour, and services, or both. Hence the central or federal authority has the task of guaranteeing effective freedom of movement. This task, in and of itself, may well require active interventions of various kinds.

Since, in the 'real' world, mobility of persons and of non-human economic resources is self-evidently more limited than it is in the world of pure theory, three prerequisites for making exit effective may be identified. One is the legal guarantee of freedom of movement – entry and exit – for persons and resources. The second is a requirement of non-discrimination, sometimes described in terms of 'mutual recognition' or the concept of 'most favoured nation' status in international economic law. The third is the acceptance of the presence of unwanted side effects of competition: 'externalities' or spill-over effects of various kinds. Even if there is in general a presumption against federal intervention and in favour of allowing rules to emerge through the competitive process, a space remains for harmonisation to protect standards against a 'race to the bottom'. Only the most Panglossian or willfully unobservant would deny that this problem exists; the controversy relates to how serious it is, and whether harmonisation at the federal level is the best way to deal with it.

The fear that regulatory competition makes it impossible for states to maintain high standards has been applied with particular force to welfare states. Fritz Scharpf is the most prominent scholar amongst those arguing that the disciplines of economic liberalism take away the capacity of states to maintain expensive welfare institutions. They are no longer able to impose the legal framework necessary to maintain these. Firms will migrate rather than pay for luxurious welfare systems via taxation or via worker-friendly social legislation. States are therefore forced to cut regulatory burdens.

F. Scharpf, 'The European Social Model: Coping with the Challenges of Diversity' (2002) 40 *Journal of Common Market Studies* 645, 648–9

[Having discussed the constraints on national policy resulting from the Euro rules, free movement, and state aid law]…compared to the repertoire of policy choices that was available two or three decades ago, European *legal* constraints have greatly reduced the capacity of national governments to influence growth and employment in the economies for whose performance they are politically accountable. In principle, the only national options which under European law remain freely available are supply-side strategies involving lower tax burdens, further deregulation and flexibilization of employment conditions, increasing wage differentiation and welfare cutbacks to reduce reservation wages. At the same time, governments face strong *economic* incentives to resort to just such strategies of competitive deregulation and tax cuts in order to attract or retain mobile firms and investments that might otherwise seek locations with lower production costs and higher post-tax incomes from capital. By the same token, unions find themselves compelled to accept lower wages or less attractive employment conditions in order to save existing jobs. Conversely, welfare states are tempted to reduce the generosity or tighten the eligibility rules of tax-financed social transfers and social services in order to discourage the immigration of potential welfare clients.

Scharpf goes on to argue that the only way to prevent economic freedom impacting destructively on welfare systems is to move welfare to a European level, but that this is not possible because of the diversity of different national systems. For him, if the European Union is to retain its social character, it faces a choice between a less demanding internal market or more social integration. He contrasts the situation with the United States, where the development of state welfare systems was initially prevented by regulatory competition considerations similar to those at work in Europe today.[70] However, after the New Deal in the 1930s, it became possible for the federal government to play a significant role in welfare, removing the local competitive element. It is that federal involvement which is neither existent, nor currently possible, in the Union today, he suggests.

Yet, many consider his fears exaggerated. The empirical evidence to date is ambiguous, and economists never tire of pointing out that there is very limited evidence that a race to the bottom often takes place. Whether or not it will depends on the specific circumstances.[71] It may well be that states consider it in their national interest to maintain high standards and that certain kinds of industry are even attracted by this. There is certainly plenty of evidence that a high-tax high-standard economic model can work. It may be easier to attract good employees to a state with high environmental and social standards, and a generous welfare net may not be a net burden on firms: otherwise they would perhaps be forced by the employment market to offer even more expensive private facilities and protection. On the whole, solidarity can be cost-effective.

In any case, we should beware of over-easy reliance on apparently 'social' arguments against regulatory diversity and for harmonisation. They are open to abuse.

G. Majone, 'The Common Sense of European Integration' (2006) 13 *Journal of European Public Policy* 607, 624

Moreover, as Revesz has pointed out, race-to-the-bottom arguments are incomplete because they fail to consider that there are more direct means of attracting foreign direct investments than lowering social standards. The advocates of harmonisation assume implicitly that states compete over only one variable, such as environmental quality. Given the assumption of a 'race', however, it is more reasonable to suppose that if harmonisation prevents competition on the environmental dimension, states would try to compete over other variables, such as worker safety, minimum wages or taxation of corporate profits. To avoid these alternative races, the central regulators would have to harmonise national rules so as to eliminate the possibility of any form of interstate competition altogether. This would amount to eliminating any trace of national autonomy, so that the race-to-the-bottom argument is, in the end, an argument against subsidiarity.

A number of writers have argued that there is a need to move beyond the simple opposition of a race to the bottom and regulatory diversity. The goal of policy should be to seek the ideal mix between these, summed up in a well known article by Esty and Gerardin as 'regulatory

---

[70] F. Scharpf, 'Democratic Legitimacy under Conditions of Regulatory Competition: Why Europe Differs from the United States' in K. Nicolaidis and R. Howse, *The Federal Vision* (Oxford, Oxford University Press, 2001) 355.
[71] See e.g. Ogus, n. 15 above; J.-M. Sun and J. Pelkmans, 'Regulatory Competition in the Single Market' (1995) 33 *Journal of Common Market Studies* 67.

co-opetition'.[72] Deakin has emphasised that harmonisation which reduces diversity so much that states can no longer experiment would be destructive. He introduces the idea of 'reflexive harmonisation' in which states learn from each other, and develop their own laws in the light of their neighbours. He sees a role for EU harmonisation as framing this process, facilitating communication between states and preventing competition which would, in practice, reduce state autonomy and ultimately diversity.

> **S. Deakin, 'Legal Diversity and Regulatory Competition: Which Model for Europe?'**
> **(2006) 12 *European Law Journal* 440, 444–5**
>
> The model of reflexive harmonisation holds that the principal objectives of judicial intervention and legislative harmonisation alike are two-fold: first, to protect the autonomy and diversity of national or local rule-making systems, while, second, seeking to 'steer' or channel the process of adaptation of rules at state level away from 'spontaneous' solutions that would lock in sub-optimal outcomes, such as a 'race to the bottom'. In this model, the process by which states may observe and emulate practices in jurisdictions to which they are closely related by trade and by institutional connections is more akin to the concept of 'co-evolution' than to convergence around the 'evolutionary peak' or end-state envisaged by Tiebout's general equilibrium model. The idea of co-evolution, borrowed from the modern evolutionary synthesis in the biological sciences, argues that a variety of diverse systems can coexist within an environment, with each one retaining its viability. It thereby combines diversity and autonomy of systems with their interdependence within a single, overarching set of environmental parameters.

Nevertheless, any legislative framework has to correspond to popular notions of fairness if it is to be legitimate and politically stable. There is only a limited tolerance for diverse conditions of competition within the Union, and harmonisation is often driven by a desire for uniformity that transcends nuanced policy thinking and comes from a much deeper constitutional and cultural place.[73]

FURTHER READING

C. Barnard and S. Deakin, 'Market Access and Regulatory Competition' in C. Barnard and J. Scott (eds.), *The Law of the European Single Market* (Oxford/Portland, Hart, 2005)

D. Chalmers, 'Risk, Anxiety and the European Mediation of the Politics of Life' (2005) 30 *ELRev.* 649

G. Davies 'Democracy and Legitimacy in the Shadow of Purposive Competence' (2014) 20 *ELJ* (forthcoming)

D. Gerber, *Law and Competition in Twentieth Century Europe: Protecting Prometheus* (Oxford, Oxford University Press, 1998)

A. O. Hirschmann, *Exit, Voice and Loyalty: Responses to Decline in Firms, Organizations and States* (Cambridge, MA, Harvard University Press, 1970)

G. Majone, *Europe as the Would-be World Power* (Cambridge, Cambridge University Press, 2009)

---

[72] D. Esty and D. Gerardin, 'Regulatory Co-opetition' (2000) 3 *JIEL* 235.

[73] See J. Weiler, *The State "Uber Alles": Demos, Telos and the German Maastricht Decision*, Jean Monnet Working Paper No. 95/6 (New York, Jean Monnet Center, 1995).

N. Nic Shuibhne, *The Coherence of EU Free Movement Law* (Oxford, Oxford University Press, 2013)

N. Nic Shuibhne (ed.), *Regulating the Internal Market* (Cheltenham, Edward Elgar, 2006)

K. Nicolaides and G. Schaffer, 'Transnational Mutual Recognition Regimes: Governance Without Global Government' (2005) 68 *Michigan Review of International Law* 267

M. Poiares Maduro, *We the Court* (Oxford/Portland, Hart, 1998)

F. Scharpf, 'Democratic Legitimacy under Conditions of Regulatory Competition: Why Europe Differs from the United States' in K. Nicolaidis and R. Howse (eds.), *The Federal Vision* (Oxford, Oxford University Press, 2001)

A. Somek, *Individualism: An Essay on the Authority of EU Law* (Oxford, Oxford University Press, 2008)

S. Weatherill, 'Why Harmonise?' in T. Tridimas and P. Nebbia (eds.), *European Union Law for the Twenty-First Century* (Oxford/Portland, Hart, 2004)

S. Weatherill, 'The Limits of Legislative Harmonization Ten Years after Tobacco Advertising: How the Court's Case Law has become a "Drafting Guide"' (2011) 12 *German Law Journal* 827

F. de Witte, 'Sex, Drugs and EU Law: The Regulation of Moral and Ethical Diversity in EU Law' (2013) 6 *Common Market Law Review* 1545

16

Economic and Monetary Union

CONTENTS

1 INTRODUCTION

This chapter considers economic and monetary union. It is organised in the following manner.

Section 2 considers the initial template for economic and monetary union. There are four elements to this template. There is to be, first, free movement of capital between Member States and between Member States and non-EU states. Secondly, an independent European Central Bank (ECB) is to have the exclusive right to authorise the issue of a single currency, the euro. Thirdly, states commit not to incur excessive government deficits. This is to be policed by a preventive mechanism in which the Council monitors medium-term budgetary policy by states, and a corrective mechanism, the Excessive Deficit Procedure, which allows the sanctioning of a Member State for running an excessive deficit. Fourthly, there is to be coordination of economic policy.

Section 3 considers the system of differentiated integration brought about by economic and monetary union. From 1 January 2014, eighteen Member States have the euro as the currency. Member States have, however, to meet certain criteria, the Convergence Criteria, before they can participate in the euro. Eight Member States, known as 'states with a derogation', have not met these criteria. In addition, Denmark and the United Kingdom have Protocols which allow them not to participate in the euro. Free movement of capital provisions apply to these ten states and they also participate in economic policy coordination. However, they are neither bound by ECB measures nor any Union measure which sanctions national governments in this field of activity for weak economic or fiscal performance. They can, furthermore, neither participate in ECB decision-making nor in the Euro Group, a group of euro area Finance Ministers who consider coordination of economic policy in relation to the euro.

Section 4 considers the effect of the sovereign debt crisis on these institutional arrangements. The crisis led to a perception that these arrangements were too rigid, too weak in terms of securing national compliance, and too limited in scope. There were three dominant types of reform. First, oversight and sanction of national economic and fiscal performance was extended and strengthened. The Excessive Deficit Procedure was refocused to concentrate as much on annual debt as on a euro area state's annual budget deficit. The Significant Observed Deviation procedure commits states to securing a balanced budget over the economic cycle. A significant observed deviation from the adjustment path towards this goal can lead to sanctions. States also commit not to incur macro-economic imbalances within their economies. States can, consequently, be sanctioned for incurring and failing to correct excessive macro-economic imbalances. The second type of reform is the provision of financial guarantees to euro area states experiencing difficulties conditional on their taking agreed steps. This is done through the European Stability Mechanism, which was established to offer up to €500 billion of support. The third reform involves the extension of the powers of the ECB. It has been granted significant new regulatory powers over the prudential supervision of banks. It has also, increasingly and controversially, become an informal lender of last resort to euro area states by purchasing their bonds on securities markets when nobody else will.

Section 5 considers the ECB and the European System of Central Banks (ESCB). The traditional decision-making bodies of the ECB are the Governing Council, which sets guidelines and interest rates, and the Executive Board, which manages day-to-day relations with national central banks (NCBs). The Governing Council comprises the Executive Board plus the Governors of the NCBs who participate in the euro. The Executive Board comprises the President and Vice-President of the ECB and four other members. A further body, the Supervisory Board, has been added in the field of prudential supervision. Formally, it merely prepares draft Decisions to be adopted by the Governing Council, but these will be deemed adopted unless the latter votes against the Draft. The ECB has three main tasks. It is responsible, first, for the authorisation of the issue of euros. The wider conduct of monetary policy is pursued through the ESCB, a network comprising the ECB and all NCBs in which the latter act on the ECB's instructions. The second significant task of the ECB is prudential supervision of all credit institutions within the euro area. Prudential supervision goes to the financial soundness of these credit institutions, and has been interpreted widely to include not just their solvency, exposure to risk and liquidity but also their authorisation and governance arrangements. Although the ECB is, in principle, responsible for the prudential supervision of all credit institutions within the euro area, a division is made between significant credit institutions – a minimum of three per state – for which it is responsible and less significant ones for which national authorities are responsible. The final role of the ECB is as a lender of last resort to euro area states through the Outright Monetary Transactions Programme.

Section 6 considers the European Stability Mechanism (ESM), the central vehicle of financial support for euro area states experiencing severe public financing difficulties. Set up by international treaty between the euro area states, its central decision-making body is a Board of Governors comprising national Finance Ministers. This is responsible, inter alia, for approving financial guarantees to states requesting support. Support is offered after an assessment of the financial needs of the state by the Commission and the ECB. Conditions are set out in a Memorandum of Understanding between the state concerned and the ESM which will have been negotiated with the Commission, ECB and International Monetary Fund (IMF). Its implementation will also be overseen by these. The ESM draws EU institutions into the world of redistributive politics and welfare policy in a manner which has generated a number of institutional concerns. These go, first, to the making of substantial commitments from the public purse with insufficient domestic parliamentary involvement. There are, secondly, concerns about the use of the EU institutions for significant tasks beyond the TEU framework. However, the biggest concern revolves around the lack of legal constraint surrounding the Memorandum of Understanding and the demands it can make of the citizenry receiving support.

Section 7 considers the framework governing general Union oversight and coordination of domestic economic, fiscal and welfare policy. The central arena for this is the European Semester for Economic Policy Coordination. The Semester involves assessment by the Council of the employment, economic, fiscal and welfare policies of each Member State against Union guidelines and indicators. This assessment will be made on the basis of earlier Recommendations by the Commission. Recommendations will then be made by the Council to individual states in the light of general policy orientations by the European Council. There is also provision for input into this process from the European Parliament, national parliaments and civil society. The scope of the Semester is so ambitious that it is difficult to assess its effects. However, in principle, these are to be felt in national budgets in the succeeding year, which are to take account of the guidance received from the Semester.

Section 8 considers the procedures for sanctioning euro area states who have engaged in a significant observed deviation from the agreed adjustment path towards realising a balanced budget; allowed excessive macro-economic imbalances to arise and failed to correct them; or run an excessive government deficit. The procedures are Byzantine. In all cases, they involve the assessment by the Commission of a significant observed deviation, excessive macro-economic imbalance or deficit; the finding by the Council that this is the case; a plan agreed with the state to rectify the issue; a finding that the state has failed to do this; and then sanctions. The sanctions are considerable, ranging from 0.1 per cent to 0.5 per cent of GDP. This raises doubts over whether they will ever be imposed. These procedures are, therefore probably best seen as providing new arenas for stronger Union involvement with national economic and fiscal policy where national performance has breached, in a persistent manner, certain thresholds of concern.

2 CENTRAL PILLARS OF ECONOMIC AND MONETARY UNION PRIOR TO THE CRISIS

(i) Delors Blueprint for economic and monetary union

Economic and monetary union is set out as one of the central tasks of the Union.

Article 3(4) TEU

4. The Union shall establish an economic and monetary union whose currency is the euro.

The creation of a single currency was first considered by the Heads of Government at The Hague in 1969. They established a working group under the chairmanship of the Prime Minister of Luxembourg, Pierre Werner, which produced a fully-fledged blueprint for the establishment of economic and monetary union by 1980.[1] The subsequent years of economic crisis and currency instability meant that this came to nothing. Instead, efforts turned to managing exchange rates. An initial attempt to manage exchange rates in 1972 in the so-called 'Snake' failed as a result of currency turmoil in the 1970s.[2] It was replaced in 1979 by the European Monetary System (EMS) and its exchange rate mechanism (ERM).[3] The currency of each Member State was assigned fixed central exchange rates as against every other participating currency and a notional composite unit of account, the ECU (European Currency Unit). The actual market exchange rate was to fluctuate around the central rate within strict bands (generally, of +/-2.5 per cent) with national central banks intervening to secure this.

The seminal moment for the establishment of economic and monetary union was the Hanover European Council in June 1988.[4] Flushed with the success of the Single European Act, the European Council entrusted the task of producing a report on how to achieve it to a committee chaired by the President of the Commission, Jacques Delors. The report of the Delors Committee, adopted at the Madrid European Council in 1990, set out the blueprint for the economic and monetary union we have today in the European Union.

---

[1] Supplement to *EC Bulletin*, 11–1970. On the history of economic and monetary union see the magisterial H. James, *Making the European Monetary Union* (Cambridge, MA, Harvard University Press, 2012).

[2] The Basel Agreement created a multilateral intervention mechanism in the foreign exchange market and the European Monetary Co-operation Fund the following year; Regulation 907/73 establishing a European Monetary Cooperation Fund [1973] OJ L89/2.

[3] *EC Bulletin*, 6–1978, 1.5.2. See also J. van Ypersele and J.-C. Koeune, *The European Monetary System: Origins, Operation and Outlook* (Brussels, European Commission, 1984).

[4] On the conditions which allowed this see K. McNamara, *The Currency of Ideas: Monetary Politics in the European Union* (Ithaca, NY, Cornell University Press, 1999).

Committee for the Study of Economic and Monetary Union, *Report on Economic and Monetary Union in the European Community* **(Luxembourg, 1989)**

22. A *monetary union* constitutes a currency area in which policies are managed jointly with a view to attaining common macroeconomic objectives. As already stated in the 1970 Werner Report, there are three necessary conditions for a monetary union:

   - the assurance of total and irreversible convertibility of currencies;
   - the complete liberalization of capital transactions and full integration of banking and other financial markets; and
   - the elimination of margins of fluctuation and the irrevocable locking of exchange rate parities.

   The first two of these requirements have already been met, or will be with the completion of the internal market programme. The single most important condition for a monetary union would, however, be fulfilled only when the decisive step was taken to lock exchange rates irrevocably....

23. ...The adoption of *a single currency*, while not strictly necessary for the creation of a monetary union, might be seen – for economic as well as psychological and political reasons – as a natural and desirable further development of the monetary union. A single currency would clearly demonstrate the irreversibility of the move to monetary union, considerably facilitate the monetary management of the Community and avoid the transactions costs of converting currencies. A single currency, provided that its stability is ensured, would also have a much greater weight relative to other major currencies than any individual Community currency....

25. *Economic union* – in conjunction with a monetary union – combines the characteristics of an unrestricted common market with a set of rules which are indispensable to its proper working. In this sense economic union can be described in terms of four basic elements: the single market within which persons, goods, services and capital can move freely; competition policy and other measures aimed at strengthening market mechanisms; common policies aimed at structural change and regional development; and macroeconomic policy coordination, including binding rules for budgetary policies....

   ...A coherent set of economic policies at the Community and national levels would be necessary to maintain permanently fixed exchange rates between Community currencies and, conversely, a common monetary policy, in support of a single currency area, would be necessary for the Community to develop into an economic union.

29. *Community policies in the regional and structural field* would be necessary in order to promote an optimum allocation of resources and to spread welfare gains throughout the Community...

30. *Macroeconomic policy* is the third area in which action would be necessary for a viable economic and monetary union. This would require an appropriate definition of the role of the Community in promoting price stability and economic growth through the coordination of economic policies. Many developments in macroeconomic conditions would continue to be determined by factors and decisions operating at the national or local level. This would include not only wage negotiations and other economic decisions in the fields of production, savings and investment, but also the action of public authorities in the economic and social spheres. Apart from the system of binding rules governing the size and the financing of national budget deficits, decisions on the main components of public policy in such areas as internal and external security, justice, social security, education, and hence on the level and composition of government spending, as well as many revenue measures, would remain the preserve of Member States even at the final stage of economic and monetary union.

   However, an economic and monetary union could only operate on the basis of mutually consistent and sound behaviour by governments and other economic agents in all member countries. In particular, uncoordinated and divergent national budgetary policies would undermine monetary stability and generate imbalances in the real and financial sectors of the Community....

31. ...Economic and monetary union would require the creation of a new monetary institution, placed in the constellation of Community institutions (European Parliament, European Council, Council of Ministers, Commission and Court of Justice). The formulation and implementation of common policies in non-monetary fields and the coordination of policies remaining within the competence of national authorities would not necessarily require a new institution; but a revision and, possibly, some restructuring of the existing Community bodies, including an appropriate delegation of authority, could be necessary.

32. A new monetary institution would be needed because a single monetary policy cannot result from independent decisions and actions by different central banks. Moreover, day-to-day monetary policy operations cannot respond quickly to changing market conditions unless they are decided centrally. Considering the political structure of the Community and the advantages of making existing central banks part of a new system, the domestic and international monetary policy-making of the Community should be organized in a federal form, in what might be called a *European System of Central Banks* (ESCB). This new System would have to be given the full status of an autonomous Community institution.

(ii) Four pillars of economic and monetary union prior to the crisis

The Delors Report suggested a number of dimensions to economic and monetary union which are, to a large extent, now replicated in Article 119 TFEU.

Article 119 TFEU

1. For the purposes set out in Article 3 of the TEU, the activities of the Member States and the Union shall include, as provided in the Treaties, the adoption of an economic policy which is based on the close coordination of Member States' economic policies, on the internal market and on the definition of common objectives, and conducted in accordance with the principle of an open market economy with free competition.

2. Concurrently with the foregoing, and as provided in the Treaties and in accordance with the procedures set out therein, these activities shall include a single currency, the euro, and the definition and conduct of a single monetary policy and exchange-rate policy the primary objective of both of which shall be to maintain price stability and, without prejudice to this objective, to support the general economic policies in the Union, in accordance with the principle of an open market economy with free competition.

It is worth unpacking these elements as they set out the architecture of economic and monetary union prior to the crisis, and still remain central elements of its architecture.

Free movement of capital: It has to be possible for people to make investments and payments for assets in different parts of the Union. National restrictions on payments and investments, which limit the movement of capital from one part of the Union to another, in principle, therefore have to be abolished. Alongside this, all currencies have to be fully convertible; that is to say there should be no limits on the amount of one legal tender that can be exchanged into another Union legal tender. Otherwise, it would be possible to limit the amount that could be invested in a state with another legal tender. To this end, Article 63 TFEU prohibits, subject to certain limited exceptions, restrictions on the free movement of capital and payments.

Article 63 TFEU

1. Within the framework of the provisions set out in this Chapter, all restrictions on the movement of capital between Member States and between Member States and third countries shall be prohibited.
2. Within the framework of the provisions set out in this Chapter, all restrictions on payments between Member States and between Member States and third countries shall be prohibited.

The provision has been interpreted in similar fashion to the other economic freedom. It catches any national measure which is liable to prevent or deter investment or payments from one Member State to another, be these measures which restrict capital going out of a state or capital coming in from another state.[5] As with the other economic freedoms, national measures will be found to be lawful if they pursue a legitimate public interest.[6] In addition to these, Article 65 TFEU allows Member States to impose restrictions on public policy and security grounds. It also allows Member States to take measures which provide for the differential fiscal treatment of non-residents, the prudential supervision of financial institutions and to combat tax evasion, albeit that these might restrict free movement of capital. All such restrictions must neither arbitrarily discriminate nor constitute a disguised restriction on free movement of capital.

A single currency whose issue is authorised only by the European Central Bank: The model of monetary union adopted by the Union requires a single currency issued by a central bank, the European Central Bank (ECB). Based in Frankfurt, this bank has a monopoly over the authorisation of the issue of the euro and over the setting of short-term interest rates as these set the terms at which it will lend money to financial institutions.[7]

Controls on national budget deficits: Excessive borrowing by one government creates costs for other governments.[8] If one state goes bankrupt other states will have to bail it out. Otherwise, as it cannot print money to service its needs, the only other possibility is for it to leave the monetary union to enable this, which will be difficult and costly. Furthermore, even if something so drastic does not happen, to counter inflationary pressures generated by excessive borrowing, the central bank may increase short-term interest rates, thus penalising governments who have not borrowed in this way.[9] The TFEU therefore prohibits excessive government deficits.

---

[5] Case C-112/05 *Commission* v *Germany* [2007] ECR I-8995; Joined Cases C-105–107/12 *Staat der Nederlanden* v *Essent and others*, Judgment of 22 October 2013.

[6] For example, Case C-452/01 *Ospelt and Schlössle Weissenberg Familienstiftung* [2003] ECR I-9743. Case C-35/11 *Test Claimants in the FII Group Litigation*, Judgment of 13 November 2012.

[7] Article 128 TFEU.

[8] A government or budget deficit is the amount by which government expenditure exceeds government income in a given year.

[9] For an accessible explanation see W. Buiter, 'The "Sense and Nonsense of Maastricht" Revisited: What have We Learnt about Stabilization in EMU?' (2006) 44 *JCMS* 687, 693–705.

Article 126(1) TFEU

1. Member States shall avoid excessive government deficits.

Excessive deficits were, in principle, to be either an annual government deficit of more than 3 per cent of GDP or a government debt of more than 60 per cent of GDP.[10] A simple injunction was not seen as sufficient to secure these ambitions, however. Pan-Union machinery was put in place, therefore, to oversee national budgetary policy. Known as the Stability and Growth Pact, this was formally established in 1997.[11] It comprises two arms. There is a preventive arm which is concerned to secure the budgetary policy of a Member State over the medium term. Each state is set a Medium Term Budgetary Objective (MTBO) which sets out a target, typically over three years, for where that state's budget should be. Each state should set out a programme to meet it which would be assessed annually by the Commission and the Council.[12] There is, then, a corrective arm: the Excessive Deficit Procedure. This provides for the Commission and the Council to find that a state's budget deficit in a particular year is excessive, and for the Council, ultimately, to sanction it in such cases.[13]

Coordination and surveillance of national economic policy: Other national economic policies were also seen as potentially disruptive of monetary union. If the European Central Bank wished to restrict demand by increasing interest rates, this could, for example, be frustrated if a state stimulated it by increasing public spending. Equally, there was a danger, if national economic policies were too different, that it would be difficult for the European Central Bank to institute a policy which worked for all parts of the euro area. There was, therefore, to be coordination of national economic policy within the Council.[14]

Article 120 TFEU

Member States shall conduct their economic policies with a view to contributing to the achievement of the objectives of the Union, as defined in Article 3 TEU, and in the context of the broad guidelines referred to in Article 121(2). The Member States and the Union shall act in accordance with the principle of an open market economy with free competition, favouring an efficient allocation of resources, and in compliance with the principles set out in Article 119.

---

[10] Article 126(2) TFEU; Protocol on the Excessive Deficit Procedure, Article 1.

[11] Resolution of the European Council on the Stability and Growth Pact [1997] OJ C236/1. For discussion see M. Heipertz and A. Verdun, *Ruling Europe: The Politics of the Stability and Growth Pact* (Cambridge, Cambridge University Press, 2010).

[12] Regulation 1466/97/EC on the strengthening of the surveillance of budgetary positions and the surveillance and coordination of economic policies [1997] OJ L209/1 as amended by Regulation 1055/2005 [2005] OJ L174/1 and Regulation 1175/2011 [2011] OJ L306/12.

[13] Regulation 1467/97 on speeding up and clarifying the implementation of the excessive deficit procedure [1997] OJ L209/6, as amended by Regulation 1056/2005 [2005] OJ L174/5 and Regulation 1177/2011 [2011] OJ L306/33.

[14] On the weakness of this coordination see D. Hodson, *Governing the Euro Area in Good Times and Bad* (Oxford, Oxford University Press, 2011) ch. 5.

Article 121 TFEU

1. Member States shall regard their economic policies as a matter of common concern and shall coordinate them within the Council, in accordance with the provisions of Article 120.
2. The Council shall, on a recommendation from the Commission, formulate a draft for the broad guidelines of the economic policies of the Member States and of the Union, and shall report its findings to the European Council.

   The European Council shall, acting on the basis of the report from the Council, discuss a conclusion on the broad guidelines of the economic policies of the Member States and of the Union.

   On the basis of this conclusion, the Council shall adopt a recommendation setting out these broad guidelines. The Council shall inform the European Parliament of its recommendation.
3. In order to ensure closer coordination of economic policies and sustained convergence of the economic performances of the Member States, the Council shall, on the basis of reports submitted by the Commission, monitor economic developments in each of the Member States and in the Union as well as the consistency of economic policies with the broad guidelines referred to in paragraph 2, and regularly carry out an overall assessment.

These legal and institutional arrangements for economic and monetary union cannot be seen in a vacuum. There is a mission set out in Article 128(3) TFEU underlying these institutional arrangements.[15]

Article 128(3) TFEU

3. These activities of the Member States and the Union shall entail compliance with the following guiding principles: stable prices, sound public finances and monetary conditions and a sustainable balance of payments.

It is highly unusual to entrench economic objectives – be this low inflation, sound public finances or sustainable balance of payments – in this way, so that they become constitutional imperatives. To tie the Union to such a narrow range of objectives seems both dogmatic and holding the Union's institutional arrangements open to fortune. Although the Treaties borrowed heavily from the successful post-War German monetary model, the commitment to low inflation was not so constitutionally entrenched there.[16] There is also a concern about fighting yesterday's wars. The concerns about high inflation, which dominated debates leading up to the decision to establish the euro, were not, therefore, the central challenge which Member States encountered following its institution and during the sovereign debt crisis.

---

[15] See also Articles 119(2) and 219 TFEU which make it a norm of exchange rate and monetary policy, and Article 127 TFEU which makes it the central objective of the ESCB.

[16] This point is powerfully made in M. Herdegen, 'Price Stability and Budgetary Restraints in the Economic and Monetary Union: The Law as Guardian of Economic Wisdom' (1998) 35 *CMLRev.* 9, 11–15.

3 DIFFERENTIATED OBLIGATIONS OF ECONOMIC AND MONETARY UNION

On 1 January 1999 eleven Member States adopted the euro as their currency. The group comprised Austria, Belgium, Finland, France, Germany, Ireland, Italy, Luxembourg, the Netherlands, Portugal and Spain. Since then a further six states – Estonia, Greece, Slovenia, Cyprus, Malta and Slovakia – have followed suit and adopted the euro with Latvia due to follow on 1 January 2014. To adopt the euro, each of these Member States had, in principle, to meet a series of economic conditions known as the convergence criteria. These are currently:[17]

- the annual government deficit should not exceed 3 per cent of GDP and the total government debt should not exceed 60 per cent of GDP;[18]
- an annual rate of inflation not more than 1.5 percentage points above the three best performing Member States;
- participation within the exchange-rate mechanism for at least two years, without devaluing against the euro;
- long-term nominal interest rates that are not more than 2 percentage points above the three best performing states in terms of price stability.[19]

States adjudged not yet to have met these criteria are not entitled to participate in the euro. They are known in the Treaties as 'states with a derogation.'[20] At least once every two years or at their own request, states with a derogation are considered as to whether they meet the criteria and should be invited to join the euro.[21] These currently include all the other Member States in the Union except Denmark and the United Kingdom. Denmark has notified the other states that it will not participate in the euro, and there is a Protocol acknowledging its position.[22] The position for the United Kingdom is slightly different. It has a Protocol granting it the right to decide at some future date whether it wishes to participate in the euro.[23] There is no sign that it will exercise that right. Although there are some slight differences, the obligations of Denmark,[24] the United Kingdom[25] and the states with a derogation[26] are similar.

- They are bound by the free movement of capital provisions.
- The euro is not legal tender within their jurisdictions. They are not bound by measures concerning use of the euro and they do not take part in the tasks of the European System of Central Banks (the network of central banks that administers the euro).
- Whilst a finding can be made that they have an excessive deficit, they cannot be required to take steps to remedy it or be sanctioned for failing to do so.
- They are guided by the Broad Economic Policy Guidelines unless these relate specifically to the euro area.

---

[17] The need for observance of these criteria is set out in Article 140 TFEU.
[18] Protocol on the excessive deficit procedure, article 1.
[19] The last three criteria set out in the Protocol on the convergence criteria, articles 1, 3 and 4.
[20] Article 139(1) TFEU.   [21] Article 140 TFEU.
[22] Protocol on Certain Provisions relating to Denmark.
[23] Protocol on Certain Provisions relating to the United Kingdom.
[24] Protocol on Certain Provisions relating to Denmark, Article 1.
[25] Protocol on Certain Provisions relating to the United Kingdom, Article 4. The central difference relates to excessive deficits. The United Kingdom makes no commitment to avoid excessive deficits whereas all the other states are constrained by this commitment.
[26] Article 139(2) TFEU.

These states do not take part in the governing arrangements of the European Central Bank or the appointment of its members.[27] As the euro area states do not run their monetary policy, there is no reason why they should contribute to the running of the monetary policy of the euro area states. More controversial is their exclusion from the Euro Group. Established as an informal group in 1999, this comprises the Finance Ministers of the euro area states, with the ECB and the Commission invited to participate, and was formally recognised by the Lisbon Treaty.[28] This group discusses questions related to the specific responsibilities these all share in relation to the single currency. The Group is extremely powerful.[29] It meets before Council meetings, and is seen as an ante-chamber for discussing questions of economy policy within the Union, pre-empting decisions that might subsequently be taken in the Council.

4 REVISED INSTITUTIONAL ARCHITECTURE AFTER THE CRISIS

(i) Earthquake of the European sovereign debt crisis

The starting date for the European sovereign debt crisis is usually taken as October 2009. The Greek authorities announced that the Greek budget deficit had been massively underestimated. It was not 3.7 per cent of GDP but 12.5 per cent of GDP. This prompted concerns in financial markets through late 2009 and early 2010 that Greece would not be able to sustain its public finances. Despite the adoption of an austerity plan by Greece in early 2010 seen as sufficient by the European Council, concerns continued to mount leading to borrowing becoming increasingly expensive for Greece. Unable to meet the demands of lenders, Greece was granted a loan of €110 billion by euro-zone states and the IMF in May 2010.

This heralded just the beginning of financial market anxiety about whether euro area states would be able to service their public finances. A pattern repeated itself from mid-2010 to mid-2013 whereby lending costs to certain euro area states would increase to the point where they would be unaffordable. These states would then be offered financial support through a variety of mechanisms by the other euro area states and the IMF dependent on their meeting a number of conditions aimed at rebalancing their public finances. Ireland received a support package, therefore, of €85 billion in November 2010; Portugal €78 billion in May 2011; Greece a second support package of €130 billion in March 2012; Spain up to €100 billion in July to recapitalise its banks; and Cyprus up to €10 billion in April 2013.[30] These measures alone were insufficient to shore up national public finances. From May 2010 to August 2012, the European Central Bank ran the Securities Market Programme which allowed it to buy, albeit through third parties, government bonds of states experiencing public financing difficulties. This purchase amounted to a loan as it was a purchase by the ECB of a commitment by that state to repay an

---

[27] They also do not take part in the formulation of the Broad Economic Policy Guidelines insofar as these relate specifically to the euro area. Article 136(2) TFEU.

[28] Article 137 TFEU; Protocol on the Euro Group.

[29] U. Puetter, 'Governing Informally: The Role of the Eurogroup in EMU and the Stability and Growth Pact' (2004) 11 *JEPP* 854. For a more extensive analysis of the powerful links between the ministers see U. Puetter, *The Eurogroup: How a Secretive Group of Finance Ministers Shapes European Economic Governance* (Manchester, Manchester University Press, 2006).

[30] Ireland and Spain have indicated that they will exit their programmes at the end of 2013.

amount. The intervention was considerable. €220 billion of bonds were purchased during this period, with the majority bought to help Italy and Spain.[31]

To describe the crisis simply as a struggle by certain euro area states to sustain their public finances is to miss the wider context of the dislocation in global financial markets which followed the collapse of Lehmann Brothers in Autumn 2008.[32] This dislocation simultaneously made it much more difficult for governments to borrow; switched off sectors of economic activity for many Member States, notably finance and property, thereby depriving governments of tax receipts; forced many governments to buy out bankrupt banks; and, finally, pushed down on economic growth by making it very difficult for commercial actors to borrow. This mix affected European states, within and outside the euro area, in different ways and at different levels of intensity. Its first effect was to lead, however, to a number of European states, all outside the euro area, experiencing public financial difficulties prior to the Greek sovereign debt crisis. Hungary, Latvia Romania and Iceland all experienced catastrophic collapses in their public finances in 2008 and had to seek help from the Union and/or international organisations. Furthermore, the 2008 crisis hit the public finances of all EU Member States. Total debt and annual budget deficits (as proportions of GDP) increased, respectively, from 62.3 per cent and 2.4 per cent in 2008, to 80 per cent and 6.4 per cent in 2010. Total debt continued to rise after that, so that it was 85.9 per cent in November 2013, even if budget deficits were tempered so that for the Union they were 3.9 per cent of GDP in 2012. The risk of a number of states not being able to service their debt led, in turn, to the spectre of a wider banking insolvency crisis. The *Wall Street Journal*, for example, estimated in February 2010 that French and German commercial banks had an exposure of US$900 billion to Greek, Portuguese and Irish borrowers.[33]

States across the Union relied on a combination of privatisations, cuts in public spending and tax increases to deal with this public finance crisis. This, in turn, had dramatic effects on their societies. In the first three months of 2009, over 2 million EU citizens were added to the unemployment figures. EU employment remains stubbornly high still in October 2013, with 10.9 per cent of the EU workforce being unemployed. Five states (Croatia, Portugal, Cyprus, Greece and Spain) had rates of over 15 per cent, with Spain having an unemployment rate of 26.7 per cent and Greece 27.3 per cent. The effects were particularly severe in those states which sought financial support. A detailed study found that in just one year, 2010, poverty increased in Greece from 20 per cent of all Greeks to 25.8 per cent, an increase of over one-quarter.[34] Alongside this, welfare provision was also reduced in many of these states just as need increased. This had some devastating effects. Suicides increased by 17 per cent between 2009 and 2010 in Greece with a further significant increase in 2011. HIV infection arose by

[31] Decision 2010/5/ECB establishing a securities markets programme [2010] OJ L124/8. On this programme see F. Eser and B. Schwab, *Assessing Asset Purchases within the ECB's Securities Markets Programme*, Working Paper 1587 (Frankfurt, ECB, 2013). This programme was discontinued in September 2012 to be replaced by that on Outright Monetary Transactions.

[32] On the stages of the crisis see F. Scharpf, 'Monetary Union, Fiscal Crisis and the Disabling of Democratic Accountability' in A. Schäfer and W. Streeck (eds.), *Politics in the Age of Austerity* (Cambridge, Polity Press, 2013); M. Drudi *et al.*, 'The Interplay of Economic Reforms and Monetary Policy: The Case of the Eurozone' (2012) 50 *JCMS* 881.

[33] See 'Exposure to Greece weighs on French, German banks', *Wall Street Journal*, 17 February 2010, available at http://online.wsj.com/article/SB10001424052748703798904575069712153415820.html.

[34] M. Matsaganis and C. Leventi, 'The Distributional Impact of the Greek Crisis in 2010' (2013) 34 *Fiscal Studies* 83.

52 per cent in 2011 with much of this rise due to increases in prostitution, and the lack of rehabilitation programmes for drug users (85 per cent were recorded as not on any programme).[35]

This has been associated, in turn, with a political crisis.[36] There has been political instability in all the states receiving public financial support with change of governments in all of
them; the growth of new social movements opposed to the direction taken by these states
(Democracia Real YA in Spain, the Indignant Citizens Movement in Greece, and Geração à
Rasca in Portugal); and the rapid growth of the radical left and, more worryingly, the radical right in some of them.[37] Of equal concern, from Autumn 2009, there was a sharp increase
in citizen distrust of both national governments and, particularly worryingly, with increased
suspicion of national parliaments in states at the heart of the maelstrom, namely, Portugal,
Greece, Ireland and Spain.[38] Alongside this, there have been strong divisions within the EU
institutions. Within the Council and European Council conflicts arose between lender states
and states receiving support. In September 2011, the Council delayed payment of €8 billion
to Greece because it was believed it was not doing enough to meet its commitments under the
agreed austerity plan.[39] In response, the Greek Economics Minister accused the other Member
States of scapegoating Greece for their own problems. Likewise, initial loans to Ireland had to
be renegotiated after outrage in Ireland at the terms of repayment.[40] There have also been conflicts between lender states. As a condition for its financial support, Finland asked Greece in
2011 for collateral in the form of loans received by Greece from other Member States which led
to protests from other lender states. There have also been tensions within the usually discrete
world of central banks. The Bundesbank, the German national central bank, publicly opposed
and criticised use of the Securities Market Programme.[41] Finally, there have been tensions
between national institutions. The offering of public financial support and the implementation
of the conditions required for that support have been challenged before the national constitutional courts of those states offering the support and those states receiving it.[42]

---

[35] A. Kentikelenis et al., 'Health Effects of Financial Crisis: Omens of a Greek Tragedy' (2011) 378 The Lancet 1457.
See also G. Quaglio et al., 'Austerity and Health in Europe' (2013) 113 Health Policy 13. These effects have not
been confined to Greece. Health care spending declined by 6.5 per cent in Ireland and 7.3 per cent in Estonia in
2010, OECD, Health at a Glance: Europe 2012 (Paris, OECD, 2012) 120.

[36] The causal relations are complicated and contested. See, however, A. Schäfer and W. Streeck, 'Introduction:
Politics in the Age of Austerity' and M. Berezin, 'The Normalization of the Right in Post-Security Europe' in
A. Schäfer and W. Streeck (eds.), Politics in the Age of Austerity (Cambridge, Polity Press, 2013).

[37] On the change in the political landscape in Greece see A. Katsonidou, 'The Euro Crisis and New Dimensions of
Contestation in National Politics' in B. de Witte et al. (eds.), The Euro Crisis and the State of European Democracy
(Florence, EUI, 2013).

[38] F. Roth et al., Crisis and Trust in National and European Union Institutions: Panel Evidence for the EU, 1999–
2012, RSCAS 2013/31 (Florence, EUI, 2013) 5–12.

[39] This was finally released after six weeks on 21 October 2011: see www.consilium.europa.eu/uedocs/cms_data/
docs/pressdata/en/ecofin/125488.pdf.

[40] This was a central issue at the Irish parliamentary elections in February 2011. L. O'Carroll, 'Ireland's Fine Gael
seeks renegotiation of bail out', Guardian, 27 January 2011, available at www.guardian.co.uk/business/ireland-
business-blog-with-lisa-ocarroll/2011/jan/27/ireland-seeks-renegotiation-of-bailout. This was in the end largely
conceded at the March 2011 European Council which allowed Ireland and Portugal the same terms as Greece.

[41] 'Bundesbank opposes ECB bond buying', Financial Times, 22 August 2011, available at www.ft.com/cms/s/0/
d1cd36b4-ccc6-11e0-b923-00144feabdc0.html#axzz2nY6Hk5Um.

[42] Case 3-4-1-6-12 Request of the Chancellor of Justice to Declare Article 4(4) of the Treaty Establishing the
European Stability Mechanism in Conflict with the Constitution, Supreme Court of Estonia, Judgment of 12 July
2012; 2 BvR 1390/12 et al. ESM Treaty(Temporary Injunctions), German Constitutional Court, Judgment of
12 September 2012; Acordão 187/2013 on Portuguese Budget, Portuguese Constitutional Tribunal, Judgment of
5 April 2013.

The radical changes in the environment led to a common perception that the institutional architecture for economic and monetary union established at Maastricht was inadequate. Reforms constellated around three trajectories: more extensive and intensive Union oversight of national economic and fiscal performance; significant financial support for states experiencing public financing differences, albeit on onerous terms; and increased powers for the ECB.

(ii) More extensive Union oversight and disciplining of national fiscal and economic performance

All Union governments believed that the Stability and Growth Pact was both too narrow and too weak, and this had contributed to the crisis. The Pact was too narrow in that focus had centred on the annual budget deficits of Member States. It did not look sufficiently at their total debt or whether performance was fiscally sustainable over the medium-term. It also did not look sufficiently at how wider economic performance could expose states to considerable risks, such as a collapse in their housing or banking sectors. It was felt to be weak on a number of levels. The Union procedures for sanctioning states for poor performance had not been deployed. In addition, there seemed insufficient domestic rules and processes to provide checks against states slipping into poor fiscal performance.[43]

Three sets of measures were put in place, therefore, to rectify these perceived governance failings. The first, in November 2011, was the 'six-pack', five Regulations and a Directive, which addressed all these issues.[44] This was seen as insufficiently strong by itself on two fronts. EU legislation alone was, first, incapable of securing the necessary commitment to sound public finances. This commitment had to be given a domestic constitutional or quasi-constitutional force. The procedure for sanctioning states for running an excessive budget deficit was, secondly, perceived as too weak. Set out in the TFEU, it could not, however, be amended by secondary legislation. The second measure, a Treaty amendment known as the 'fiscal compact', was therefore proposed. The Czech Republic and the United Kingdom were unhappy to sign such an amendment. An international treaty, the Treaty on Stability, Coordination and Governance in the Economic and Monetary Union (TSCG) was therefore signed, instead, between the other Member States in March 2012, and entered into force on 1 January 2013.[45] Finally, there is the 'two-pack'. This was adopted in May 2012, and involves two Regulations which provide for greater Union surveillance of national budgets: one for states

---

[43] All these criticisms are contained in the Report of the Task Force to the European Council, *Strengthening Economic Governance in the EU* (Brussels, European Council, 2010). This was co-authored by all national Finance Ministers, as well as the Commission and the President of the Euro Group, ECB and European Council. In like vein, by two senior Commission officials, see M. Buti and N. Carnot, 'The EMU Debt Crisis: Early Lessons and Reforms' (2012) 50 *JCMS* 899.

[44] Regulation 1173/2011 on the effective enforcement of budgetary surveillance in the euro area [2011] OJ L306/1; Regulation 1174/2011 on enforcement measures to correct excessive macro-economic imbalances in the euro area [2011] OJ L306/8; Regulation 1175/2011 amending Regulation 1466/97 on the strengthening of the surveillance of budgetary positions and the surveillance and coordination of economic policies [2011] OJ L306/12; Regulation 1176/2011 on the prevention and correction of macro-economic imbalances [2011] OJ L306/25; Regulation 1177/2011 amending Regulation 1467/97 on speeding up and clarifying the implementation of the excessive deficit procedure [2011] OJ L306/33; Directive 2011/85/EU on requirements for budgetary frameworks of the Member States [2011] OJ L306/41.

[45] The Treaty can be found at [2012] OJ C219/95. See P. Craig, 'The Stability, Coordination and Governance Treaty: Principle, Politics and Pragmatism' (2012) 37 *ELRev.* 231.

receiving financial support or experiencing severe financial difficulties[46] and the other for all other euro area states.[47]

Combined, these reforms do a number of things.

First, they broaden the horizons of Union policing. This is now centred around three ambitions: avoiding a wider notion of excessive budget deficits; securing a balanced budget; and avoiding macro-economic imbalances.

In relation to avoiding excessive government deficits, a stronger emphasis is to be placed not simply on ensuring that annual budget deficits are no greater than 3 per cent of GDP but also that total debt is brought down to 60 per cent of GDP. Both these requirements were present in the TFEU.[48] However, the one on total debt had not been policed. To that end, a new requirement was added. A state would not be running an excessive deficit, even if its budget deficit was more than 3 per cent of GDP and its debt greater than 60 per cent of GDP, if it brought these both down by one-twentieth of the difference between the actual deficit and these targets.[49] A state with a debt of 100 per cent of GDP would, for example, have to find 2 per cent of GDP to pay off the capital sum of the debt in addition to all its other needs, as this would represent 5 per cent of the difference (40 per cent) between its debt and the target of 60 per cent.

The duty on Member States to avoid macro-economic imbalances goes to wider vulnerabilities in their economies. Macro-economic imbalances are defined as:

> any trend giving rise to macroeconomic developments which are adversely affecting, or have the potential adversely to affect, the proper functioning of the economy of a Member State or of the economic and monetary union, or of the Union as a whole.[50]

Examples of these can be:

> internal imbalances, including those that can arise from public and private indebtedness; financial and asset market developments, including housing; the evolution of private sector credit flow; and the evolution of unemployment;...external imbalances, including those that can arise from the evolution of current account and net investment positions of Member States; real effective exchange rates; export market shares; changes in price and cost developments; and non-price competitiveness, taking into account the different components of productivity.[51]

There is a particular concern that states should not run excessive imbalances. These are

> severe imbalances, including imbalances that jeopardise or risks jeopardising the proper functioning of the economic and monetary union.[52]

As we shall see, excessive imbalances have particular legal consequences as a failure to rectify them can lead to sanctions.

The final duty is the balanced budget rule. Member States are to commit to having balanced budgets.

---

[46] Regulation 472/2013 on the strengthening of economic and budgetary surveillance of Member States in the euro area experiencing or threatened with serious difficulties with respect to their financial stability [2013] OJ L140/1.

[47] Regulation 473/2013 on common provisions for monitoring and assessing draft budgetary plans and ensuring the correction of excessive deficit of the Member States in the euro area [2013] OJ L140/11.

[48] See n. 10 above.

[49] Regulation 1467/97 on speeding up and clarifying the implementation of the excessive deficit procedure [1997] OJ L209/6, as amended by Regulation 1056/2005 [2005] OJ L174/5 and Regulation 1177/2011, article 2(1a). This is reiterated in Article 4 TSCG.

[50] Regulation 1176/2011, article 2(1).   [51] *Ibid.* article 4(3).   [52] *Ibid.* article 2(2).

Article 3(1) TSCG

1. The Contracting Parties shall apply the rules set out in this paragraph in addition and without prejudice to their obligations under European Union law:

   (a) the budgetary position of the general government of a Contracting Party shall be balanced or in surplus;

   (b) the rule under point (a) shall be deemed to be respected if the annual structural balance of the general government is at its country-specific medium-term objective, as defined in the revised Stability and Growth Pact, with a lower limit of a structural deficit of 0.5% of the gross domestic product at market prices. The Contracting Parties shall ensure rapid convergence towards their respective medium-term objective.[53]

To a non-economist, this provision is a little obscure. An annual structural balance is the budgetary position of the state once it has been cyclically-adjusted.[54] It is understood that in recessions welfare spending will increase and tax receipts fall, whilst the opposite is true in moments of economic boom. The balance is thus adjusted for where the state is on the economic cycle but the intention is that across the cycle there should not be a deficit lower than 0.5 per cent of GDP. Structural balances are notoriously difficult to determine as they require policy-makers to identify the point on the economic cycle: something which is beyond most policy-makers.[55]

Secondly, more extensive Union sanction procedures are introduced alongside the intention that it should be less easy for states to obstruct penalties. Alongside the Excessive Deficit procedure, two further procedures have been introduced to sanction states with similar levels of fines to that procedure. There is a procedure for sanctioning states who incur a significant observed deviation from the path towards meeting their Medium Term Budget Objective.[56] There is also a procedure to sanction states who allow excessive macro-economic imbalances to arise.[57]

The third element of the package is the introduction of domestic rules to reinforce the pursuit of these targets. The headline one is as follows.

Article 3(2) TSCG

2. The rules set out in paragraph 1 shall take effect in the national law of the Contracting Parties at the latest one year after the entry into force of this Treaty through provisions of binding force and permanent character, preferably constitutional, or otherwise guaranteed to be fully respected and adhered to throughout the national budgetary processes.

---

[53] The Czech Republic and the United Kingdom are not party to the TSCG. This does not apply to them.

[54] Article 3(3)(a) TSCG.

[55] In 1997, for example, the IMF calculated the deficit of France as 0.8 per cent of GDP whilst the Commission put it at 1.75 per cent. C. Bouthevillain and A. Quinet, 'The Relevance of Cyclically Adjusted Public Balance Indicators: The French Case', paper presented at Indicators of Structural Budget Balances Conference, Banca D'Italia Perugia, 26–28 November 1998, available at www.bancaditalia.it/studiricerche/convegni/atti/structural_bud_bal/iv/325-352_bouthevillain_and_quinet_2.pdf.

[56] Regulation 1466/97, article 6(2) and (3).

[57] Regulation 1176/2011, articles 7–10 and Regulation 1174/2011. All three sanctions procedures only apply to euro area states.

Alongside this, Member States have to put in place extensive systems to ensure that their statistics and public accounts are in order, and that they have procedures which allow reliable budgetary forecasting and planning.[58]

(iii) Formalisation of financial support to sustain euro area state public finances

Financial support was initially offered in 2010 to euro area states in difficulties through two instruments. A European Financial Stabilisation Mechanism was funded by all Union Member States, and could provide loans. Its total size was €60 billion.[59] Alongside this, an international agreement between euro area states established a facility, the European Financial Stability Facility, to provide a variety of forms of financial support. This was considerably larger, comprising a fund of €440 billion.

These were seen as only temporary measures. In addition, some non-euro area states were unhappy about contributing money to something which they perceived as a euro area problem. They were therefore replaced by the European Stability Mechanism Treaty, an international agreement between the euro area states. Comprising two international agreements, signed in 2011 and 2012, respectively, this came into force in September 2012. It comprises a shared commitment of €700 billion of which €500 billion can be offered as financial support to states experiencing difficulties. The European Stability Mechanism (ESM) is based in Luxembourg. It is run by a Board of Governors, comprising euro-zone Finance Ministers.

Article 3 ESM

The purpose of the ESM shall be to mobilise funding and provide stability support under strict conditionality, appropriate to the financial assistance instrument chosen, to the benefit of ESM Members which are experiencing, or are threatened by, severe financing problems, if indispensable to safeguard the financial stability of the euro area as a whole and of its Member States.

Financial support can only be offered where a state requests it.[60] However, the central point to note is that any support will be conditional, and these conditions have been found by states receiving support to be extremely draconian. They will be set out in a Memorandum of Understanding between that state and the ESM, with financial support typically being tapered so that funding becomes available as that state is adjudged to meet certain conditions.[61]

(iv) Extension of powers of European Central Bank

Prior to the crisis, the ECB had one central task: the running of monetary policy through setting short-term interest rates for the euro. This has now changed.

It has become a significant lender of financial support to some euro area states through the purchase of government bonds. The initial programme, the Securities Market Programme, was seen as both too limited in scale and too unconditional. In September 2012, the ECB

---

[58] Directive 2011/85.
[59] Regulation 407/2010 establishing a European Financial Stabilisation Mechanism [2010] OJ L118/1.
[60] Article 13(1) ESM.   [61] Article 13(3) and (4) ESM.

announced, therefore, a new programme, that on Outright Monetary Transactions (OMTs), which allowed for the unlimited purchase of the securities of euro area states for states already receiving support under the ESM Treaty. This momentous shift was announced not by a formal decision but by a Press Release.[62]

The other significant role carved out for the ECB by the crisis is a supervisory one. An ongoing concern during the crisis has been that weaknesses in the banking sector will undermine states' attempts to restore their public finances as they will be forced to spend large amounts recapitalising their banks. In June 2012, the Commission proposed a banking union for the euro area. This banking union has a number of elements,[63] but a central one is the establishment of a Single Supervisory Mechanism. Its ethos is set out below.

European Commission, *A Roadmap Towards a Banking Union*, COM(2012)510, 3

Further steps are needed to tackle the specific risks within the Euro Area, where pooled monetary responsibilities have spurred close economic and financial integration and increased the possibility of cross-border spill-over effects in the event of bank crises, and to break the link between sovereign debt and bank debt and the vicious circle which has led to over €4.5 trillion of taxpayer's money being used to rescue banks in the EU. Coordination between supervisors is vital but the crisis has shown that mere coordination is not enough, in particular in the context of a single currency and that there is a need for common decision-making. It is also important to curtail the increasing risk of fragmentation of EU banking markets, which significantly undermines the single market for financial services and impairs the effective transmission of monetary policy to the real economy throughout the Euro Area.

The Commission has therefore called for a banking union to place the banking sector on a more sound footing and restore confidence in the Euro as part of a longer term vision for economic and fiscal integration. Shifting the supervision of banks to the European level is a key part of this process, which must subsequently be combined with other steps such as a common system for deposit protection, and integrated bank crisis management.

To that end, the ECB has been given powers of prudential supervision over all banks in the euro area.[64] Historically, prudential supervision goes just to questions of whether a bank is financially sound. This has been interpreted widely. These powers include powers to authorise and revoke authorisation for all banks as well as to supervise the governance arrangements of credit institutions, as well as traditional elements which go to the liquidity, solvency and exposure to risk of these institutions.[65]

---

[62] European Central Bank, Press Release, 'Technical Features of Outright Monetary Transactions', 6 September 2012, available at www.ecb.europa.eu/press/pr/date/2012/html/pr120906_1.en.html.

[63] The banking union is also believed to require a single rule book providing a single set of rules for financial services, a single resolution mechanism which would provide a euro area mechanism to provide for the orderly winding up of a bankrupt bank, and strong guarantees for depositors, European Commission, *A Roadmap towards a Banking Union*, COM(2012)510.

[64] Regulation 1024/2013 conferring specific tasks on the European Central Bank concerning policies relating to the prudential supervision of credit institutions [2013] OJ L287/63.

[65] *Ibid.* article 4. The division of duties between national supervisors and the ECB is set out in article 6(4). For more detail on this see pp. 733–6.

(v) Composite architecture of economic and monetary union[66]

The EU law regime emerging from the crisis is unrecognisable from that prior to it. The idea that the Union would police national economic policies and structural balances or that the ECB would be the central supervisor of the banking sector within the euro area is undoubtedly compatible with the Treaties but was not anticipated by them. This shift has involved a move away from traditional EU law instruments to deployment of a variety of new legal and institutional tools, be these international treaties, such as the ESM and TSCG Treaties, or informal instruments such as the press release authorising the development of Outright Monetary Transactions.

This begs two questions in particular.

The first goes to the place of EU law in this process. This was raised most acutely in *Pringle*. Mr Pringle, it will be remembered, challenged the ESM Treaty on a number of grounds.[67] One was that participating states were breaching Article 125(1) TFEU, which provides that Member States shall not be liable for or assume the financial commitments of other Member States. He argued that the provision of financial support violated this 'no bail-out' provision as this was what was happening in practice through their provision of financial guarantees.

Case C-370/12 *Pringle* v *Government of Ireland*, Judgment of 27 November 2012

135. It is apparent from the preparatory work relating to the Treaty of Maastricht that the aim of Article 125 TFEU is to ensure that the Member States follow a sound budgetary policy...The prohibition laid down in Article 125 TFEU ensures that the Member States remain subject to the logic of the market when they enter into debt, since that ought to prompt them to maintain budgetary discipline. Compliance with such discipline contributes at Union level to the attainment of a higher objective, namely maintaining the financial stability of the monetary union.

136. Given that that is the objective pursued by Article 125 TFEU, it must be held that that provision prohibits the Union and the Member States from granting financial assistance as a result of which the incentive of the recipient Member State to conduct a sound budgetary policy is diminished....

137. However, Article 125 TFEU does not prohibit the granting of financial assistance by one or more Member States to a Member State which remains responsible for its commitments to its creditors provided that the conditions attached to such assistance are such as to prompt that Member State to implement a sound budgetary policy.

138. As regards the ESM Treaty, it is clear, first, that the instruments for stability support of which the ESM may make use...demonstrate that the ESM will not act as guarantor of the debts of the recipient Member State. The latter will remain responsible to its creditors for its financial commitments....

142. Secondly, the ESM Treaty does not provide that stability support will be granted as soon as a Member State whose currency is the euro is experiencing difficulties in obtaining financing on the market. In accordance with Articles 3 and 12(1) of the ESM Treaty, stability support may be granted to ESM Members which are experiencing or are threatened by severe financing problems only when such support is indispensable to safeguard the financial stability of the euro area as a whole and of its

---

[66] This phrase is taken from C. Chiti and P. Texeira, 'The Constitutional Implications of the European Responses to the Financial and Public Debt Crisis' (2013) 50 *CMLRev.* 683, 690–1.

[67] See pp. 61–2.

> Member States and the grant of that support is subject to strict conditionality appropriate to the financial assistance instrument chosen.
>
> 143. …the purpose of the strict conditionality to which all stability support provided by the ESM is subject is to ensure that the ESM and the recipient Member States comply with measures adopted by the Union in particular in the area of the coordination of Member States' economic policies, those measures being designed, inter alia, to ensure that the Member States pursue a sound budgetary policy.

The reasoning is curious. On the one hand, a formal reasoning is adopted. Recipient states are still liable for their debts and this is not displaced by the receipt of financial support. This reasoning is coherent but unconvincing. Any child knows that if they owe €10 to another child and I lend them €10 to pay off that other child, they may still be liable to that child if they do not use the money to pay off the debt, but there is no doubt that I have *assumed* the commitment (something prohibited by Article 125 TFEU) by substituting the debt to the other child with the debt to me.[68] However, *Pringle* does not then follow this reasoning consistently. The offer of financial support may still be illegal if it does not promote sound budgetary policy. A substantive argument, namely, the policy objective of the support, is used to differentiate between different commitments. This, of course, undermines the formal reasoning. This argument may possibly be persuasive in policy terms, where the 'no bail-out' provision is seen as being too rigid in current circumstances. However, the Court of Justice is not acting as a policy actor in which it decides when it is economically appropriate for states to support other states. This engagement with policy stands out in the judgment with the interpretive reasoning being very thin. The consequence, of course, is that EU law becomes relativised. Its meaning is given a flexibility and indeterminacy which allows it to be tailored to the circumstances.

The second concern revolves around the distinct qualities of this regime. Chiti and Texeira observe that solutions were adopted because they provided flexibility in the face of very difficult political circumstances. This adaptability has led, however, to the dynamics of EMU becoming increasingly different from other parts of the TFEU.

C. Chiti and P. Texeira, 'The Constitutional Implications of the European Responses to the Financial and Public Debt Crisis' (2013) 50 *Common Market Law Review* 683, 693–4

The new composite framework of the EMU, partly within and partly outside the EU legal order, has created the pre-conditions for a potential mismatch between the EU and the EMU institutional dynamics, which now relies on a multiplicity of bodies, both internal and external to the EU order, partly different from those governing the internal market project and the other fields of EU action. Moreover, it has accentuated the distinction between the euro area countries and the other EMU members, not only because it has envisaged that the two groups of States participate in partly different sets of rules,

---

[68] On the ESM violating this principle see R. Palmstorfer, 'To Bail Out or Not to Bail Out? The Current Framework of Financial Assistance for Euro Area Member States Measured Against the Requirements of EU Primary Law' (2012) 37 *ELRev.* 771; M. Ruffert, 'The European Debt Crisis and European Union Law' (2011) 48 *CMLRev.* 1777, 1785–1787.

but also and above all because it has provided the eurozone countries with a legal and institutional context favourable to the deepening and broadening of their integration, also thanks to the possibilities offered by recourse to international public law instruments.

It should be also pointed out that the differentiation of EMU within the EU does not only derive from the recourse to composite arrangements, but is also triggered by instruments internal to the EU framework. The conferral of banking supervision tasks on the ECB, for instance, was made on the basis of Article 127(6) TFEU, which is a provision with a dual nature, relating both to the EMU and to the single market in banking services. Since, however, the ECB's jurisdiction is limited to the euro area, the Member States from outside could only be associated to the ECB's banking supervision competences through bilateral agreements on 'close cooperation'.

The piece below indicates that this informalisation is manifested not only by new informal instruments but also pervades traditional decision-making processes. It carries many risks.[69]

M. Dawson and F. de Witte, 'Constitutional Balance in the EU after the Euro-Crisis' (2013) 76 *Modern Law Review* 817, 834–5

Such informalisation may not only lead to executive dominance, but inhibit individual and political self-determination by excluding the degree of transparency and consultation necessary for the genuine involvement of citizens in EU decision-making to take place. Uwe Puetter's account of institutional change during the euro crisis provides a stark example of this.[70] Puetter argues that given the increase in informal coordination, even relatively formal bodies, such as ECOFIN, increasingly adopt informal working methods that can lead to problems of intransparency. In interviews with ECOFIN officials, for example, Puetter points to the increasing importance of breakfast meetings where bi-lateral discussions occur either between Eurozone finance ministers exclusively or through the finance ministers of the most important governments.[71] Commonly during the crisis, such meetings not only produced broad policy discussions, but also produced precise agreements on language that would then be tabled in formal ECOFIN meetings. The respective finance ministers would then leave the meeting of ECOFIN in the hands of their deputies, confident that a majority in support of the informal position had already been secured.

There is little doubt that the European Council has also often acted in this manner since the crisis. As Puetter also points out, the outcomes of European Council meetings were often decided beforehand, their agendas and policy proposals formed as a result of bilateral meetings between the two most important players – the French and German heads of government. While the crisis itself demanded 'instant' responses to crisis situations – promoting the trend towards informalisation – such methods will do little to re-assure those who see the Union as pursuing a path of increasing intransparency and executive control.

[69] M. Poiares Maduro *et al.*, 'The Euro Crisis and the Democratic Governance of the Euro: Legal and Political Issues of a Fiscal Crisis' in M. Poiares Maduro *et al.* (eds.), *The Democratic Governance of the Euro*, RSCAS 2012/08 (Fiesole, EUI, 2012).

[70] U. Puetter, 'Europe's Deliberative Intergovernmentalism: The New Role of the Council and European Council in EU Economic Governance' (2012) 19 *JEPP* 161.

[71] ECOFIN is, of course, the Economic and Financial Affairs Configuration of the Council of Ministers.

5 EUROPEAN CENTRAL BANK AND EUROPEAN SYSTEM OF CENTRAL BANKS

(i) European Central Bank and its decision-making bodies

Historically, the ECB comprised two decision-making bodies: the Governing Council and the Executive Board.[72] The membership of each is set out in Article 283 TFEU.

Article 283 TFEU

1. The Governing Council of the European Central Bank shall comprise the members of the Executive Board of the European Central Bank and the Governors of the national central banks of the Member States whose currency is the euro.
2. The Executive Board shall comprise the President, the Vice-President and four other members.

    The President, the Vice-President and the other members of the Executive Board shall be appointed by the European Council, acting by a qualified majority, from among persons of recognised standing and professional experience in monetary or banking matters, on a recommendation from the Council, after it has consulted the European Parliament and the Governing Council of the European Central Bank.

    Their term of office shall be eight years and shall not be renewable.

    Only nationals of Member States may be members of the Executive Board.

The respective tasks of the two bodies are set out in Article 12 of the Protocol on the Statute of the European System of Central Banks (ESCB).

Protocol on the Statute of the European System of Central Banks, Article 12

12.1 The Governing Council shall adopt the guidelines and take the decisions necessary to ensure the performance of the tasks entrusted to the ESCB under these Treaties and this Statute.[[73]] The Governing Council shall formulate the monetary policy of the Union including, as appropriate, decisions relating to intermediate monetary objectives, key interest rates and the supply of reserves in the ESCB, and shall establish the necessary guidelines for their implementation.

   The Executive Board shall implement monetary policy in accordance with the guidelines and decisions laid down by the Governing Council. In doing so the Executive Board shall give the necessary instructions to national central banks. In addition the Executive Board may have certain powers delegated to it where the Governing Council so decides.

   To the extent deemed possible and appropriate and without prejudice to the provisions of this Article, the ECB shall have recourse to the national central banks to carry out operations which form part of the tasks of the ESCB.

The supreme decision-making body is, therefore, the Governing Council. It takes the decisions most readily associated with the ECB, notably the setting of short-term interest rates. The Executive Board, by contrast, is responsible for the preparation of the Governing Council

---

[72] Article 129(1) TFEU. See also Article 282(2) TFEU.
[73] The ESCB is described in more detail later. Its tasks are the definition and implementation of monetary policy within the euro area.

meetings, the management of the daily business and implementing policy through giving instructions to national central banks (NCBs).

This leads to complicated decision-making dynamics. The governors of the NCBs of the euro area form a large majority of the ECB's Governing Council's membership. With seventeen states participating in the euro, they comprise seventeen out of twenty-three members of the Governing Council. These governors are subject to national societal pressures and rely for their briefings primarily on their own staff.[74] Potentially, a coalition of NCB governors might be able to exercise a strong influence over the direction of the single monetary policy. For this reason, an ECB legal adviser has suggested that it is better to see the ECB as an organisation dominated by its component parts rather than an institution.[75]

The Treaties try to protect against this in two ways. First, the Executive Board prepares and sets the agenda for the meetings with the President of the Executive Board chairing those meetings.[76] Secondly, the voting membership of the Governing Council is capped at twenty-one, including the six members of the Executive Board. The rostrum of fifteen NCB governor votes is selected through a system of asymmetrical rotation, whereby in the future the governors of the NCBs of the large countries will exercise voting rights more frequently than those of smaller ones.[77]

A third body has been created in relation to the new ECB powers of prudential supervision of banks. This is the Supervisory Board. It comprises four ECB members chosen by the Governing Council of the ECB, and one representative from each of the competent authorities of the euro area states.[78] It will also have a Chair and a Vice Chair who will be a member of the ECB Executive Board.[79] All decisions of the Supervisory Board are taken by simple majority,[80] other than where the ECB is adopting Regulations which have to be adopted by qualified majority voting (QMV),[81] and all members are expected to act in the interest of the Union as a whole.[82]

Formally, the Supervisory Board is not a decision-making body. It merely carries out the preparatory work for Governing Council Decisions. It submits drafts Decisions to the Governing Council which are to be formally adopted by the law. However, these draft Decisions are deemed to be adopted unless the Governing Council objects within a period, which shall in no circumstances exceed ten working days.[83] This requirement of a reverse majority in the Governing Council to overturn a draft Decision of the Supervisory Board suggests that, in most cases, the latter will be the substantive decision-maker.

(ii) Independence and accountability of European Central Bank

The other guarantee provided against domestic (or pan-Union) political pressures lies in the independence granted to the ECB. The framers of the Treaties were persuaded by the academic

---

[74] Buiter observes the 'collegiate' presentation of the Governing Council's decisions on interest rates shields its members from the need to defend publicly their individual voting record; but it cannot provide effective protection from pressures that may be exercised by governments who may find out what has gone on behind the curtains. W. Buiter, 'Alice in Euroland' (1999) 37 *JCMS* 191–3, 195–6.

[75] C. Zilioli and M. Selmayr, 'The Constitutional Status of the European Central Bank' (2007) 44 *CMLRev.* 355, 359–60.

[76] Protocol on the Statute of the ESCB, articles 12(2) and 13, respectively.

[77] Protocol on the Statute of the ESCB, article 10(2).

[78] Regulation 1024/2013, article 26(1). The four ECB members are not allowed to participate in the monetary functions of the ECB, article 26(5).

[79] *Ibid.* article 26(3).   [80] *Ibid.* article 26(6).   [81] *Ibid.* article 26(7).

[82] *Ibid.* article 26(1).   [83] *Ibid.* article 26(8).

literature which drew a link between strong price stability and independent central banks.[84] They, thus, modelled the institutional settlement for the ECB on that of the German Bundesbank, with its federal structure and strong tradition of independence.[85] The central provision securing this is Article 130 TFEU.

Article 130 TFEU

When exercising the powers and carrying out the tasks and duties conferred upon them by the Treaties and the Statute of the ESCB and of the ECB, neither the ECB, nor a national central bank, nor any member of their decision-making bodies shall seek or take instructions from Union institutions, bodies, offices or agencies, from any government of a Member State or from any other body. The Union institutions, bodies, offices or agencies and the governments of the Member States undertake to respect this principle and not to seek to influence the members of the decision-making bodies of the ECB or of the national central banks in the performance of their tasks.[86]

The Treaty sets out a series of different institutional guarantees to protect this independence. The ECB is granted its own legal personality.[87] It can, furthermore, only be brought before the Court of Justice where to do so will not interfere with the performance of its tasks.[88] This will typically be in relation to administrative maladministration, such as breach of EU anti-fraud law, employment law or public procurement law.[89] The ECB is also to have organisational autonomy. It, thus, has financial and accounting independence.[90] There are, next, a series of guarantees to protect the personal independence of its decision-makers. The Executive Board's conditions of employment are set by the Governing Council.[91] Members of the Executive Board are to avoid conflicts of interest and to take the job on a full-time basis.[92] They are appointed for one eight-year non-renewable term.[93] Hope of reappointment will, thus, not be a factor which might lead the Board's members to heed to political pressures in their decision-making.[94]

---

[84] A review of the arguments can be found in R. Burdekin *et al.*, 'A Monetary Constitution Case for an Independent European Central Bank' (1992) 15 *World Economy* 231.

[85] On the institutional design of the ECB and the ESCB see R. M. Lastra, 'European Monetary Union and Central Bank Independence' and J. de Haan and L. Gormley, 'Independence and Accountability of the European Central Bank' in M. Andenas, L. Gormley, C. Hadjiemmanuil and I. Harden (eds.), *European Economic and Monetary Union: The Institutional Framework* (London, Kluwer Law International, 1997); R. Smits, *The European Central Bank: Institutional Aspects* (The Hague, Kluwer Law International, 1997); F. Amtenbrink, *The Democratic Accountability of Central Banks: A Comparative Study of the European Central Bank* (Oxford, Hart Publishing, 1999).

[86] The same text also appears in the Protocol on the Statute of the ESCB, Article 7.

[87] Article 282(3) TFEU; Protocol on the Statute of the ESCB, Article 9(1).

[88] Case C-11/00 *Commission* v *ECB* [2003] ECR I-7147.

[89] On this see C. Zilioli and M. Selmayr, 'The Constitutional Status of the European Central Bank' (2007) 44 *CMLRev.* 355, 370–2. The ECB is to be audited by the Court of Auditors, Protocol on the Statute of the ESCB, Article 27(2).

[90] See, generally, Protocol on the Statute of the ESCB, Articles 26–33.

[91] Protocol on the Statute of the ESCB, Article 11(3). Their removal from their positions is possible only following a decision of the Court of Justice, if they no longer fulfil the conditions required for the performance of their duties or if they have been guilty of serious misconduct. *Ibid.* Article 11(4).

[92] Protocol on the Statute of the ESCB, Article 11(2).

[93] Article 283(2) TFEU; Protocol on the Statute of the ESCB, Article 11(1).

[94] The Supervisory Board and its members are required to act independently, and not take instructions from third parties, Regulation 1024/2013, article 19(1). There are, however, none of the guarantees which exist in relation to the Executive Board.

The form of independence which has been most challenging for the ECB is financial independence. The Treaty sets aside for the ECB the financial resources (capital and foreign-reserve assets) required for the effective conduct of monetary operations, thus ensuring its financial independence from the EU institutions and the Member States.[95] In addition, neither the ECB nor NCBs are allowed to engage in lending activities to public institutions which might compromise that independence.

Article 123(1) TFEU

1. Overdraft facilities or any other type of credit facility with the European Central Bank or with the central banks of the Member States (hereinafter referred to as 'national central banks') in favour of Union institutions, bodies, offices or agencies, central governments, regional, local or other public authorities, other bodies governed by public law, or public undertakings of Member States shall be prohibited, as shall the purchase directly from them by the European Central Bank or national central banks of debt instruments.

In line with this, the TFEU confines contact between the political institutions and the ECB to that necessary to ensure that their respective policy stances are mutually understood. It gives the president of the Council and a member of the Commission the right to participate, without a vote, in meetings of the ECB's Governing Council.[96] Conversely, it requires that the President of the ECB be invited to meetings of the Euro Group[97] and to Council meetings whenever matters relating to the ESCB's field of competence are discussed.[98]

The flip side of this regime is the ECB's weak accountability in having to justify or explain its conduct or face the consequences for its mistakes.[99] There are certain reporting duties. It must publish quarterly reports on the activities of the ECB and present an Annual Report to the Parliament, European Council, Commission and Council.[100] The President and other members of the Executive Board can also at either their request or that of the European Parliament be heard by the competent committees of the European Parliament.[101] This weak accountability has been reinforced by resistance by the ECB to any duty to account on the ground that this would comprise its independence.[102] Thus, whilst Governing Council meetings are confidential, there was the possibility for the ECB to make its deliberations public.[103] It has refused to do so.[104]

In an extensive study, Amtenbrink analysed accountability within seven central banking systems.[105] He found the euro area accountability mechanisms to be uniquely feeble. The legal mandate for the ECB does not provide a clear yardstick against which ECB's monetary performance may be judged. Institutionalised contacts with the EU institutions are scarce. There is no override

---

[95] Protocol on Statute of the ESCB, Articles 28–30.   [96] Article 284(1) TFEU.
[97] Protocol on the Euro Group.   [98] Article 284(2) TFEU.
[99] On the nature of accountability within the Union see pp. 407–8.
[100] Protocol on the Statute of the ESCB, Article 15(1) and (3), respectively. On the latter see also Article 284(3) TFEU.
[101] Article 284(3) TFEU.
[102] For criticism see Buiter, n. 9 above, 191–6. See also the reply of Otmar Issing, a member of the ECB's Executive Board, 'The Eurosystem: Transparent and Accountable or "Willem in Euroland"' (1999) 37 *JCMS* 503.
[103] Protocol on the Statute of the ESCB, Article 10(4).
[104] Decision 2004/257/EC adopting the Rules of Procedure of the European Central Bank, article 23.1 [2004] OJ L80/33; Decision 2004/526/EC adopting the Rules of Procedure of the General Council of the European Central Bank, article 10(1) [2004] OJ L230/61.
[105] Amtenbrink, n. 85 above, ch. 4, in particular.

mechanism under which the political branches of government can intervene in the conduct of monetary policy or suspend the legal objectives of the central bank. The openness of the decision-making process is limited as a result of weak reporting requirements. Performance-based disciplining or dismissal was largely excluded. There was little transparency in its decision-making procedures. This combination of features was not present in other independent central banks.[106]

F. Amtenbrink, *The Democratic Accountability of Central Banks: A Comparative Study of the European Central Bank* (Oxford, Hart Publishing, 1999) 362 and 364

The unique position which the ECB holds even among the most independent of central banks is due to the fact that its entire legal basis has been enshrined in primary Community law. A change of the institutional structure requires a change of primary Community law itself. The restraining effect which the threat of an amendment of the legal basis can have on the behaviour of a central bank is virtually non-existent in the case of the ECB, as the probability of such a Treaty amendment is remote....

With regard to preconditions for democratic accountability, the legal basis of the ECB could be enhanced, introducing a clear yardstick for monetary policy and enhancing the arena in which the performance of the ECB is reviewed....Contrary to what is sometimes suggested, it should not be left to the ECB to define its objective [through its own interpretations of the Treaty's rather abstract price stability objective]. One suggestion could be to put the ECOFIN Council, the members of which are democratically legitimised through the respective Member States, in charge of defining the monetary policy objective in the form of a point target or a target range for inflation.

In the field of monetary policy, there is, indeed, no reason why political actors should not set the medium to long-term goals such as inflation targets, as this is a deeply political question on which institutions accountable to voters should have a voice.[107] The European Parliament has thus increasingly asked questions about the ECB's primary objectives, namely, its inflation target, and its relationship to wider economic policy.[108] In monetary policy, this lack of accountability was borne out of a tradition which prized the independence of central banks in that field. There was no such tradition in relation to the new prudential supervisory tasks acquired by the ECB. In recent years, these have been done by financial regulators who, whilst independent, are subject to a number of controls.[109] The British House of Lords described the issues in the following terms.

House of Lords, European Union Committee, *European Banking Union: Key Issues and Challenges* (7th Report, London, Stationery Office, 2012–13)

55. The principle of ECB independence is a necessary one in terms of the ECB's core monetary policy role. Effective banking supervision also requires independence, but independence in the supervisory context must be balanced by strong accountability mechanisms.

---

[106] *Ibid.* 359–63. See also the numerical index of central bank accountability in J. de Haan, F. Amtenbrink and S. Eijffinger, *Accountability of Central Banks: Aspects and Quantifications*, Tilburg University, Center for Economic Research Discussion Paper No. 98–54 (1998), which produces a particularly low mark for the ECB.

[107] L. Gormley and J. de Haan, 'The Democratic Deficit of the European Central Bank' (1996) 21 *ELRev.* 95.

[108] F. Amtenbrink and K. van Duin, 'The European Central Bank before the European Parliament: Theory and Practice after 10 Years of Monetary Dialogue' (2009) 34 *ELRev.* 561, 572–82.

[109] On these see M. Quintyn *et al.*, *The Fear of Freedom: Politicians and the Independence and Accountability of Financial Sector Supervisors*, IMF Working Paper 7/25 (Washington, IMF, 2007).

56. The ECB will become an exceptionally powerful institution if it takes on the proposed supervisory powers. Four principles of accountability need to be borne in mind:
    - That the ECB should be fully answerable to the Council and European Parliament for the supervisory decisions that it undertakes;
    - That an effective, calibrated and streamlined mechanism of accountability to national parliaments should be established, in particular in relation to individual supervision decisions that have a significant impact on an individual Member State's banking sector. It must be for national Parliaments to set out how any new accountability structures and frameworks should operate in practice;
    - That an effective appeals system should be established within the ECB, with a timely and appropriate system of external legal challenge;
    - That the accountability mechanism should be able to operate speedily and effectively at moments of acute crisis.

There is some responsiveness to these concerns.

First, the reporting duties existing in relation to monetary policy are reinforced in relation to supervisory policy. An Annual Report must be presented to the European Parliament, the Council, the Commission and the Euro Group.[110] The Chair of the Supervisory Board can be requested by the Euro Group to appear before it or by the European Parliament to appear at a hearing.[111] Furthermore, the ECB is to reply to questions on matters within this field put to it by either the Parliament or the Euro Group.[112] These powers are not significantly different from those in other fields of ECB activity.

Secondly, provision is made for inter-institutional arrangements between the European Parliament and the European Central Bank allowing European Parliamentary Committees to scrutinise the supervisory activities of the ECB.[113] These arrangements provide greater accountability on two issues in particular: hearings and transparency. They provide for the possibility of hearings and exchanges of view on all aspects of the ECB's work under the Single Supervisory Mechanism. If these bear on confidential matters MEPs will be bound by duties of confidentiality. The meetings themselves will also be confidential. The ECB is also to provide the relevant Parliamentary Committee with a comprehensive and meaningful record of Supervisory Board proceeding. If the Governing Council opposes a draft Decision, it must not provide details of the debate but must set out the reasons for the objection.

There is also some accountability to national parliaments. The Annual Report is to be provided to these.[114] The ECB is to answer questions put by these,[115] and the Chair or other members of the Supervisory Board can appear before a national parliament for an exchange of views.[116] To be sure, this is welcome, but it is limited. It amounts to little more than a duty to report. The House of Lords, thus, found the accountability mechanisms to be 'patently weak'.[117] To be sure,

---

[110] Regulation 1024/2013, article 20(2).   [111] *Ibid.* article 20(4) and (5).   [112] *Ibid.* article 20(6).

[113] *Ibid.* article 20(8) and (9). Inter-institutional Agreement between the European Parliament and the European Central Bank on the practical modalities of the exercise of democratic accountability and oversight over the exercise of the tasks conferred on the ECB within the framework of the Single Supervisory Mechanism [2013] OJ L320/1.

[114] Regulation 1024/2013, article 21(1).   [115] *Ibid.* article 21(2).   [116] *Ibid.* article 21(3).

[117] House of Lords, European Union Committee, *European Banking Union: Key Issues and Challenges* (7th Report, London, Stationery Office, 2012–13) para. 57.

it would be unrealistic to expect the ECB to have the same relationship with each of the national parliaments that it has with the European Parliament. However, individual decisions are likely to affect particular states insofar as they regulate a bank based in that state. It is clearly concerning that national parliaments have little comeback in such circumstances other than an ex post report which includes no duty to provide a full record of what took place.

(iii) Tasks of European Central Bank

The tasks of the ECB can be divided into three clusters: monetary policy; its role as a supervisor or regulator; and finally, its role as a lender.

(a) Monetary policy

Monetary policy is not undertaken exclusively by the ECB. Monetary policy is carried out through the European System of Central Banks (ESCB).[118] This is a composite organisation comprising the ECB and the national central banks (NCBs) of all twenty-eight Member States.[119]

Article 127(2) TFEU

2. The basic tasks to be carried out through the ESCB shall be:
   - to define and implement the monetary policy of the Union;
   - to conduct foreign-exchange operations consistent with the provisions of Article 219;[[120]]
   - to hold and manage the official foreign reserves of the Member States;
   - to promote the smooth operation of payment systems.

If monetary policy is to be defined and implemented through the ESCB, the ECB has a *primus inter pares* position within the ESCB. It has, first, a monopoly over the central tool of monetary policy, the authorisation of the issue of euros, and, thereby, the setting of short-term interest rates.

Article 128 TFEU

1. The European Central Bank shall have the exclusive right to authorise the issue of euro banknotes within the Union. The European Central Bank and the national central banks may issue such notes. The banknotes issued by the European Central Bank and the national central banks shall be the only such notes to have the status of legal tender within the Union.
2. Member States may issue euro coins subject to approval by the European Central Bank of the volume of the issue.

---

[118] Article 127 TFEU.
[119] Article 282 TFEU; Protocol on the Statute of the ESCB, Article 1. On the legal arrangements see B. Krauskopf and C. Steven, 'The Institutional Framework of the European System of Central Banks: Legal Issues in the Practice of the First Ten Years of Its Existence' (2009) 46 *CMLRev.* 1143.
[120] This provision governs exchange rate policy between the euro and other currencies.

The ECB is also the central decision-maker within the ESCB. It will be remembered that Article 12(1) of the Protocol on the Statute of the European System of Central Banks provides that it is the Governing Council of the ECB which adopts the guidelines and takes the decisions necessary to ensure the performance of the tasks entrusted to the ESCB. NCBs are consigned to an executory role. They are required, when acting within the framework of the ESCB, to act in accordance with the guidelines and under the instructions of the ECB.[121] Furthermore, they are constrained even when they act outside that framework, as the ECB can require them not to carry out these activities if it believes these interfere with the objectives and tasks of the ESCB.[122]

If the ECB is the dominant player within the setting and carrying out of monetary policy within the euro area, there are two constraints on its power.

The first is the reliance a decentralised system of NCBs for the execution of policy. This structure has led to an increased dependence on formal legal techniques, be these instructions or guidelines, to implement monetary policy, in situations where a unitary central bank would treat similar issues informally as purely internal affairs. This, in turn, raises the possibility of legal disputes between the ECB and NCBs. The Treaties, consequently, empower the ECB to commence enforcement proceedings before the Court of Justice against NCBs which fail to fulfil their ESCB-related obligations.[123] Conversely, ECB measures may be challenged by NCBs where these are addressed to them or of direct and individual concern to them.[124] Such legal challenges have not happened, and would be symptomatic of a dangerous breakdown of relations. However, the possibility of such proceedings indicates the operational reliance of the ECB on NCB goodwill.

The second constraint lies in the external relations of the euro. Notwithstanding the strong relationship between exchange rate policy and monetary policy, the Council can intervene extensively here, should it so wish.[125] It can conclude formal agreements on an exchange-rate system involving the euro and non-Union currencies[126] or, in the absence of this, adopt general orientations for exchange rate policy with these currencies.[127] It can also, on a proposal from the Commission, establish common positions on matters of particular interest for economic and monetary union within the respective international financial institutions and conferences.[128]

By contrast, the ECB competences appear modest. It can establish 'relations with central banks and financial institutions in other countries and, where appropriate, with international organisations'.[129] It is also responsible for the management of the revamped exchange rate mechanism (ERM II), which was introduced in January 1999 to link other Member State currencies to the

---

[121] Protocol on the Statute of the ESCB, Article 14.3.

[122] The Governing Council can only do this with a two-thirds vote cast, Protocol on the Statute of the ESCB, Article 14.4.

[123] Article 271 TFEU; Protocol on the Statute of the ESCB, Article 35.6.

[124] Article 263(1) and (4) TFEU; Protocol on the Statute of the ESCB, Article 35(1). On judicial review in relation to the ECB, see R. Smits, *The European Central Bank: Institutional Aspects* (The Hague, Kluwer Law International, 1997) 106–10; P. Craig, 'EMU, the European Central Bank, and Judicial Review' in P. Beaumont and N. Walker (eds.), *Legal Framework of the Single European Currency* (Oxford, Hart Publishing, 1999).

[125] On the possibility for conflict see C. Zilioli and M. Selmayr, 'The External Relations of the Euro Area: Legal Aspects' (1999) 36 *CMLRev*. 273; C. Zilioli and M. Selmayr, *The Law of the European Central Bank* (Oxford, Hart Publishing, 2001) ch. 5; and Smits, n. 124 above, Part III.

[126] Article 219(1) TFEU. The Council acts unanimously and has also to consult the Parliament.

[127] Article 219(2) TFEU.   [128] Article 138(1) TFEU.

[129] Protocol on the Statute of the ESCB, Article 23, first indent.

euro.[130] Participation in ERM II is voluntary for the non-euro area Member States, and, as of January 2014, only two currencies (the Danish krone and Lithuanian litas) participate in it. For each participating currency, a central rate of exchange is set against the euro. The actual exchange rate fluctuates within a band set at +/-2 per cent for the krone and +/-15 per cent for the litas around the central rate. An agreement between the European Central Bank (ECB) and the non-euro area NCBs demands intervention by these to keep the actual rates within the bands at all times.[131]

(b) Prudential supervision

The Treaties grant limited direct regulatory powers to the ECB. It has the power to make regulations, in particular, on minimum reserves to be held on account for credit institutions,[132] and on clearing and payment systems.[133] It can impose fines and periodic penalty payments on undertakings which do not comply with its Regulations.[134] However, the most significant field is prudential supervision: the field of banking regulation which goes to the financial soundness of banks. The ECB can be granted powers in this field by the Council,[135] and, in the light of the crisis, this is what happened with the adoption of Regulation 1024/2013/EU.[136] The Regulation establishes a Single Supervisory Mechanism (SSM).

Regulation 1024/2013, article 6

1. The ECB shall carry out its tasks within a single supervisory mechanism composed of the ECB and national competent authorities. The ECB shall be responsible for the effective and consistent functioning of the SSM.
2. Both the ECB and national competent authorities shall be subject to a duty of cooperation in good faith, and an obligation to exchange information.

   Without prejudice to the ECB's power to receive directly, or have direct access to information reported, on an ongoing basis, by credit institutions, the national competent authorities shall in particular provide the ECB with all information necessary for the purposes of carrying out the tasks conferred on the ECB by this Regulation.
3. Where appropriate and without prejudice to the responsibility and accountability of the ECB for the tasks conferred on it by this Regulation, national competent authorities shall be responsible for assisting the ECB, under the conditions set out in the framework mentioned in paragraph 7 of this Article, with the preparation and implementation of any acts relating to the tasks referred to in Article 4 related to all credit institutions, including assistance in verification activities. They shall follow the instructions given by the ECB when performing the tasks mentioned in Article 4.

---

[130] Resolution of the European Council on the establishment of an exchange-rate mechanism in the third stage of economic and monetary union [1997] OJ C236/5. See K. Rohde Jensen, 'Inside EU, Outside EMU: Institutional and Legal Aspects of the Exchange Rate Mechanism II' in ECB, *Legal Aspects of the European System of Central Banks: Liber Amicorum Paolo Zamboni Garavelli* (Frankfurt, ECB, 2005).

[131] Agreement of 16 March 2006 between the ECB and the national central banks of the Member States outside the euro area laying down the operating procedures for an exchange rate mechanism in stage three of Economic and Monetary Union (EMU) [2006] OJ C73/9.

[132] Protocol on the Statute of the ESCB, Article 19.   [133] Protocol on the Statute of the ESCB, Article 22.

[134] Regulation 2157/1999 on the powers of the ECB to impose sanctions [1999] OJ L264/21.

[135] Article 127(6) TFEU.   [136] See n. 64 above.

The tasks mentioned in article 4 go to the remit of the SSM. They take a broad view of prudential supervision. They include requirements as to how much of their own funds credit institutions should have; their levels of exposure of risk and how liquid they should be. There are powers to authorise and withdraw authorisation for credit institutions; powers to ensure that credit institutions have robust procedures in place, be these risk management arrangements, payment schemes or internal control mechanisms. There are also powers to carry out stress tests to see how robust credit institutions are, and the level of risk these can withstand. In all cases, the legal requirements are set by the EU legislature (i.e. the ordinary legislative procedure). However the SSM is responsible for supervising credit institutions to make sure these requirements are applied.

A framework is to be agreed between the ECB and national authorities allocating duties along certain principles.[137] The default position is that the ECB is exclusively responsible for all credit institutions.[138] However, for almost all supervisory duties a division takes place whereby national authorities have responsibility for 'less significant' credit institutions.[139] Significance is to be measured by the size of the credit institution, its importance for the economy of the Union or any participating state, and the significance of its cross-border activities. Minimum thresholds are set for this. In all cases, the three most significant credit institutions in any participating state will be deemed significant.[140]

In relation to these significant credit institutions, the ECB will issue regulations, guidelines and institutions to national authorities and after consulting with the national authorities, may exercise direct powers of its own over these banks. More generally, the ECB is to exercise oversight over the functioning of the system as a whole and may request information from national authorities on how they are performing their tasks within the SSM. Finally, the ECB, to enable it to perform its tasks, may request information from credit institutions, carry out investigations and, with authorisation from the relevant judicial authority, carry out on-site inspections of credit institutions.[141]

A central challenge for this supervisory system is the sheer size of the task relative to the resources of the ECB. As the excerpt below indicates, the competence and good faith of national authorities will be central to the operation of this new supervisory system, and these are not to be assumed.

House of Lords, European Union Committee, *European Banking Union: Key Issues and Challenges* (7th Report, London, Stationery Office, 2012–13)

40. The effectiveness of the SSM will be determined by the extent and nature of the supervisory regime. In other words which banks will be supervised, and to what degree? We were told that there were some 6000 banks in the euro area (and 8000 banks across the EU as a whole). The majority of witnesses argued

---

[137] Regulation 1024/2013, article 6(7).   [138] *Ibid.* article 4(1).

[139] *Ibid.* article 6(6). The main exception is authorisation and withdrawal of authorisation of credit institutions. A national authority is to consider this under national law and then, for all credit institutions, will pass its draft decision to the ECB which has ten days to object if it does not believe EU law is being met. *Ibid.* article 14.

[140] These are where the total value of the institution's assets exceeds €30 billion; the ratio of its assets as a proportion of the GDP of the state of establishment exceeds 20 per cent unless it has assets of less than €5 billion. The ECB may also consider a bank significant following a notification by the competent national authority after looking at the balance sheet of the credit institution. Finally, the ECB can, of its own initiative, consider a bank significant if the bank has subsidiaries in other participating states and significant cross-border assets or liabilities. *Ibid.* article 6(4).

[141] *Ibid.* article 6(5).

that all 6000 euro area banks should be brought within the Single Supervisory Mechanism, although Rosa Lastra, Professor in International Financial and Monetary Law, Queen Mary University of London, suggested a 'Champions League model' with only the larger institutions subject to European supervision.

41. There are sound reasons for an inclusive approach. Smaller and medium-sized EU banks, such as Northern Rock in the UK, or the *cajas* (regional savings banks) in Spain, found themselves at the centre of the financial crisis. Barclays pointed to the dangers created by the significant interdependence of banks that had come to light during the financial crisis. Others stressed the need for supervisory consistency across all banks. Mr Enria told us that, if banks of all sizes were not included, in a moment of distress there might be a flight of deposits from one set of banks to the other.

42. Given the resource implications and the need for expertise in national banking cultures, most acknowledged that it would not be possible for the ECB to be engaged in intensive supervision of all 6000 banks. Mr Pisani-Ferry suggested that a reasonable compromise would be for the ECB to have the necessary authority to cover all banks whilst delegating supervision where appropriate. Barclays described this as a 'hub and spoke' model, relying on national supervisors acting in effect as a branch of the ECB.

43. Such a system would require close and effective cooperation between the ECB and national supervisors. However, some witnesses foresaw tensions. Philip Whyte, Senior Research Fellow, Centre for European Reform, suggested that the ECB would have fewer qualms about closing down an insolvent German *Landesbank* than German authorities would have. Prior to the October 2012 Summit there had been much reporting of German objections to an inclusive model because of the impact on *Landesbanken* (regionally organised state-owned institutions specialising in wholesale banking). Ambassador Boomgaarden stressed that European supervision should concentrate on the systemically important banks, with the majority remaining under the national supervisory authorities.

44. The Summit Conclusions stated that 'the ECB will be able, in a differentiated way, to carry out direct supervision'. Mr Constâncio confirmed that the ECB would directly supervise the 25 or 30 most significant banks, and that supervision would be decentralised to national supervisors for other banks. However, national supervisors would act in accordance with approved guidelines and would be required to follow the ECB's instructions. In addition, the ECB would have authority to call in any banks that required more direct attention.

45. Mr Whyte was not clear how this compromise would work in practice. He was concerned that there would continue to be 'policies of forbearance driven by local political considerations'.

46. The Financial Secretary to the Treasury agreed that, initially, the ECB would be supervising the supervisors, but emphasised that this was an important first step. He also stressed that it was not proposed to create a set of institutions divorced from national supervisory authorities requiring 'a whole set of people to be magicked up from nowhere'.

47. It is unrealistic to expect the ECB to engage in intensive supervision of all 6000 euro area banks. Yet the dangers created by the significant interdependence of banks that came to light during the financial crisis demonstrate that it is not only large credit institutions that pose a threat to the financial sector. A sensible compromise would be for the ECB to direct the conduct of supervision by national supervisors, and for the ECB itself to focus on day-to-day supervision of only the largest cross-border and systemically important banks, but with the power quickly to assume responsibility for the supervision of smaller banks as required.

48. This model can only work if there is close and positive cooperation between the ECB and national supervisors. The ECB must also have the means to eliminate national supervisory bias where it occurs. The proposed supervisory arrangements must be stress-tested against conditions of acute crisis, setting out clearly who is in charge, the relationship between the parties involved, and how the chain of command will operate.

The other concern goes to Member States outside the euro area. The ECB will inevitably regulate banks either based in one of these states, or euro area banks with significant branches, subsidiaries, in these other states. In either case, ECB supervisory decisions will have repercussions for these other non-euro area states. The SSM, therefore, allows for non-euro area states to participate in it if these agree to abide by ECB guidelines, pass national legislation to ensure that their competent authority complies with ECB instructions, and agree to pass all the information to the ECB which is necessary for its tasks.[142] This participation poses one challenge. Non-euro area states are not represented on the Governing Council, the formal decision-maker. If such a state disagrees with a Governing Council decision objecting to a draft Decision of the Supervisory Board, it can express that disagreement within thirty days, and not be bound by the Governing Council's Decision.[143] Non-participating Member States, albeit that they are likely to be equally affected by the ESM, are less well-treated. There is a commitment to agree a Memorandum of Understanding establishing cooperation with those states. The content of that cooperation is left, however, undefined.[144]

(c) Lender of last resort

In September 2012, the ECB announced that it was replacing the Securities Market Programme under which it had purchased over €200 billion of bonds with that on Outright Monetary Transactions (OMTs).

European Central Bank, Press Release, 'Technical Features of Outright Monetary Transactions' (6 September 2012)

…the European Central Bank (ECB) has today taken decisions on a number of technical features regarding the Eurosystem's outright transactions in secondary sovereign bond markets that aim at safeguarding an appropriate monetary policy transmission and the singleness of the monetary policy. These will be known as Outright Monetary Transactions (OMTs) and will be conducted within the following framework:

Conditionality
A necessary condition for Outright Monetary Transactions is strict and effective conditionality attached to an appropriate European Financial Stability Facility/European Stability Mechanism (EFSF/ESM) programme. Such programmes can take the form of a full EFSF/ESM macroeconomic adjustment programme or a precautionary programme (Enhanced Conditions Credit Line), provided that they include the possibility of EFSF/ESM primary market purchases. The involvement of the IMF shall also be sought for the design of the country-specific conditionality and the monitoring of such a programme.

Coverage
Outright Monetary Transactions will be considered for future cases of EFSF/ESM macroeconomic adjustment programmes or precautionary programmes as specified above. They may also be considered for Member States currently under a macroeconomic adjustment programme when they will be regaining bond market access.

---

[142] *Ibid.* article 7(1) and (2).   [143] *Ibid.* article 7(7).   [144] *Ibid.* article 3(6).

Although not stated explicitly, the amount of purchases which can be made are unlimited. This has led some economists to argue that the ECB has allowed itself to become a lender of last resort. If nobody else will offer finances to a euro area state, it can lend as much as it takes for that state's finances to be sustained.[145] However, such a role is tied strongly to the political process. The Press Release makes clear that purchases will not be made as a way of undercutting the conditions attached to any financial support offered under the ESM. They will be subject to states meeting the conditions in any Memorandum of Understanding agreed under that mechanism. If this is to prevent states gaming the process by securing finance which does not require them to take measures to restabilise their public finances, it emphasises that this programme is simply about lending money to states who could otherwise not secure it.

This has proved to be controversial as, it will be remembered, Article 123(1) TFEU prohibits loans by the ECB to national governments. In particular, the last sentence prohibits 'the purchase directly from [national government] by the European Central Bank of debt instruments'. The ECB has got around this by purchasing these bonds not directly from national governments but on the securities markets from third parties. The legality of this has been called into question by the German Constitutional Court.

---

2 BvR 1390/12 *ESM Treaty (Temporary Injunctions)*, Judgment of 12 September 2012 (German Constitutional Court)

219. The current programme of European integration designs the monetary union as a stability community. As has been repeatedly emphasised by the Federal Constitutional Court..., this is the essential basis of the Federal Republic of Germany's participation in the monetary union. Not only with regard to currency stability, the treaties are parallel to the requirements of the Basic Law,...which makes compliance with the independence of the European Central Bank and the primary objective of price stability permanent constitutional requirements of a German participation in the monetary union (see Article 127(1), Article 130 TFEU); further central provisions on the design of the monetary union also safeguard the constitutional requirements in European Union law. This applies in particular to the prohibition of monetary financing by the European Central Bank, the prohibition of accepting liability (bail-out clause) and the stability criteria for sound budget management (Articles 123 to 126, Article 136 TFEU...).

220. In view of the transfer of monetary sovereignty to the European System of Central Banks, the German Bundestag's overall budgetary responsibility is safeguarded particularly by the fact that the European Central Bank subjects itself to the strict criteria of the TFEU and of the Statute of the European System of Central Banks with regard to the independence of the Central Bank and to the priority of monetary stability...In this context, an essential element of safeguarding the constitutional requirements...of the Basic Law in European Union Law is the prohibition of monetary financing by the European Central Bank....

278. ...an acquisition of government bonds on the secondary market by the European Central Bank aiming at financing the Members' budgets independently of the capital markets is prohibited as well, as it would circumvent the prohibition of monetary financing.

---

[145] P. de Grauwe, 'Stop this campaign against ECB policy', *Financial Times*, 22 October 2012, available at www. ft.com/cms/s/0/8e902142-1c32-11e2-a63b-00144feabdc0.html; W. Buiter and E. Rahbari, 'The European Central Bank as Lender of Last Resort for Sovereigns in the Eurozone' (2012) 50 *JCMS* 5 (Annual Review).

The issue was not addressed fully in this judgment. The German Constitutional Court returned to this in its *ECB/ESM* decision. It ruled that OMT could not be used as a means of getting around the procedural or substantive constraints set out in the ESM Treaty. The ECB did not have the power to engage in extensive purchases of bonds and such purchases also violated Article 123 TFEU. The German Constitutional Court ruled, however, that OMT would not be illegal if it could be seen as contributing and being subject to the constraints of the programmes established under the ESM Treaty.

---

2 BvR 3738/13 *ECB/ESM*, Judgment of 14 January 2014

59. The independence which the European Central Bank and the national central banks enjoy in the exercise of the powers conferred upon them (Art. 130, Art. 282 sec. 3 sentences 3 and 4 TFEU) diverges from the requirements the Basic Law states with regard to the democratic legitimation of political decisions. For Germany, the Federal Constitutional Court has expressly held that the democratic legitimation which emanates from the voters in the Member States is restricted by the transfer of monetary policy powers to an independent European Central Bank, and that this affects the principle of democracy. Nevertheless, this restriction is still compatible with democratic principles because it takes the tested and scientifically documented special character of monetary policy into account that an independent central bank is more likely to safeguard monetary stability, and thus the general economic basis for budgetary policies, than state bodies whose actions depend on money supply and value and which need to rely on short-term approval by political forces. The constitutional justification of the independence of the European Central Bank is, however, limited to a primarily stability-oriented monetary policy and cannot be transferred to other policy areas.

...

61. Pursuant to Art. 3 sec. 1 letter c TFEU, the European Union has the exclusive responsibility in the field of monetary policy for the Member States of the euro currency area. The Treaties do not define the term "monetary policy" (cf. ECJ, Judgment of 27 November 2012, Case C-370/12, *Pringle*). The responsibility in question is, however, substantiated by the Treaty on the Functioning of the European Union and the ESCB Statute.

62. The primary objective of the European System of Central Banks is to maintain price stability (Arts 127(1) & 282 (2) TFEU). The basic tasks of the System are, pursuant to Art. 127 (2) TFEU, to define and implement the monetary policy of the Union (first indent), to conduct foreign-exchange operations (second indent), to hold and manage the official foreign reserves of the Member States (third indent), and to promote the smooth operation of payment systems (fourth indent). The Statute of the European System of Central Banks and the European Central Bank specifies, in Chapter IV, the monetary functions and operations of the European System of Central Banks and authorises it to open accounts (Art. 17 ESCB Statute), to conduct open market and credit operations (Art. 18 ESCB Statute), to define minimum reserves (Art. 19 ESCB Statute), and to use other instruments of monetary control (Art. 20 ESCB Statute). Pursuant to Art. 22 ESCB Statute, the European Central Bank and the national central banks may also provide facilities, and the ECB may issue regulations, to ensure efficient and sound clearing and payment systems within the Union and with other countries. Art. 23 ESCB Statute authorises them to enter into external operations with other countries and international organisations, and Art. 24 ESCB Statute authorises them to enter into other auxiliary fiscal operations.

63. The monetary policy is to be distinguished – and thereby further defined – according to the wording, structure, and purpose of the Treaties from (in particular) the economic policy, which primarily falls into the responsibility of the Member States. Relevant to the delimitation are the immediate objective of an

act, which is to be determined objectively, the instruments envisaged to achieve the objective, and its link to other provisions...

64. As far as the classification from the point of view of the distribution of powers is concerned, it is thus crucial, first, whether the act directly pursues economic policy objectives. In the *Pringle* case, the Court of Justice has affirmed this with regard to the European Stability Mechanism, because its aim is the stabilisation of the euro currency area as a whole. The Court of Justice has held that such an act could not be treated as equivalent to an act of monetary policy for the sole reason that it might have indirect effects on the stability of the euro (cf. ECJ, Judgment of 27 November 2012..). On the basis of this case-law, purchases of government bonds may not qualify as acts of monetary policy for the sole reason that they also indirectly pursue monetary policy objectives.

65. However, what is relevant is not only the objective, but also the instruments used for reaching the objective and their effects. According to the case-law of the Court of Justice, acts of monetary policy are, for instance, the decision on key interest rates for the euro currency area and the release of the euro currency (cf. ECJ, [*Pringle*] Judgment of 27 November 2012,). In contrast, the grant of financial assistance "clearly" does not fall within monetary policy (cf. ECJ, Judgment of 27 November 2012....To the degree that the European System of Central Banks thus grants financial assistance, it pursues an economic policy that the European Union is prohibited from conducting

....

69. According to these principles, it is likely that the OMT Decision – if one bases the assessment on its wording – is not covered by the mandate of the European Central Bank. Based on an overall assessment of the delimitation criteria that the Federal Constitutional Court considers relevant, it does not constitute an act of monetary policy, but a predominantly economic-policy act. This is supported by its immediate objective (aa), its selectivity (bb), the parallelism with assistance programmes of the European Financial Stability Facility or the European Stability Mechanism (cc), and the risk of undermining their objectives and requirements (dd). Therefore, it is likely that the OMT Decision can also not be justified as an act to support the Union's economic policy (ee). Against this background, there are considerable doubts concerning its validity

...

85. Art. 123 TFEU and Art. 21.1. ESCB Statute forbid the purchase of government bonds "directly" from the emitting Member States, i.e. the purchase on the primary market. This prohibition is, however, not limited to this interdiction, but is an expression of a broader prohibition of monetary financing of the budget...Union law recognises the legal concept of bypassing as do the national legal systems. It is ultimately based on the principle of effectiveness ("effet utile") and has repeatedly been alluded to in the Court of Justice's jurisprudence (cf. most recently ECJ, Judgment of 20 June 2013 Case C-259/12, *Rodopi-M* 91).

86. Also in the present context, the Court of Justice has (in the *Pringle* case) largely focused on the objective pursued by the provision for the interpretation of Art. 125 TFEU...and thus conducted a teleological interpretation. It seems obvious that this must also apply to the interpretation of Art. 123 TFEU, and that the prohibition of the purchase of government bonds directly from the issuing Member States may not be circumvented by functionally equivalent measures....

87. In addition to the above-mentioned aspects, namely the neutralisation of interest rate spreads, selectivity, and the parallelism with EFSF and ESM assistance programmes, the following aspects – at least when taken together – also indicate that the OMT Decision aims at a circumvention of Art. 123 TFEU and violates the prohibition of monetary financing of the budget: The willingness to participate in a debt cut with regard to the purchased bonds (aa), the increased risk of such a debt cut regarding the purchased government bonds (bb), the option to keep the purchased government bonds to maturity

(cc), the interference with the price formation on the market (dd), and the encouragement of market participants to purchase the bonds in question on the primary market (ee).

...

99. The Federal Constitutional Court believes that these concerns regarding the validity of the OMT Decision, based on the interpretation used here, could be met by an interpretation in conformity with Union law. This would require that the content of the OMT Decision, when comprehensively assessed and evaluated, essentially complies with the above-mentioned conditions.

100. In the view of the Federal Constitutional Court, the OMT Decision might not be objectionable if it could, in the light of Art. 119 and Art. 127 etseq. TFEU, and Art. 17 etseq. of the ESCB Statute, be interpreted or limited in its validity in such a way that it would not undermine the conditionality of the assistance programmes of the European Financial Stability Facility and the European Stability Mechanism, and would only be of a supportive nature with regard to the economic policies in the Union. This requires, in light of Art. 123 TFEU, that the possibility of a debt cut must be excluded, that government bonds of selected Member States are not purchased up to unlimited amounts, and that interferences with price formation on the market are to be avoided where possible. Statements by the representatives of the European Central Bank in the proceedings before the Constitutional Court concerning the framework for the implementation of the OMT Decision (limited volume of a possible purchase of government bonds; no participation in a debt cut; observance of certain time lags between the emission of a government bond and its purchase; no holding of the bonds to maturity) suggest that such an interpretation in conformity with Union law would also most likely be compatible with the meaning and purpose of the OMT Decision.

Much will depend on how the Court of Justice rules on the reference. However the German Constitutional Court has put a gun to its head. The former cannot rule that the ECB can be a lender of last resort without the German Constitutional Court declaring OMT illegal. In principle, OMT is only to contribute to programmes agreed within the framework of the ESM Treaty, and then only in a modest way. This is of course a victory for national parliaments. All support must now go through procedures which, according to the German Constitutional Court, must be approved by the German parliament. Albeit good for parliamentary democracy and transparent debate, the concern with this is that national parliaments may not pay sufficient heed to either the concerns of citizens in other Member States or the risks to the stability of the euro area as a whole.

6 EUROPEAN STABILITY MECHANISM

Notwithstanding the presence of OMT, the central vehicle for financial support to euro area states experiencing severe public financing difficulties remains the European Stability Mechanism (ESM). Set up by an international treaty outside the formal TEU structures, the central decision-making body of the ESM is the Board of Governors.[146] This comprises the Finance Ministers of the euro area states with the Presidents of the ECB and Euro Group and the Commissioner in charge of economic and monetary affairs participating as observers.[147] The Board of Governors ordinarily votes by unanimity,[148] but can vote by QMV in an emergency

---

[146] Article 5(1) ESM.   [147] Article 5(3) ESM.   [148] Article 4(3) ESM.

procedure where the economic and financial sustainability of the euro area is threatened.[149] This QMV is an odd animal as it requires 85 per cent of the votes cast with voting weight determined by the state's financial contribution to the ESM, with Germany, for example, having 27.15 per cent and Estonia 0.19 per cent of the votes.[150]

Important decisions to be taken by the Board of Governors include calling in capital which has not been paid by the Member States[151] and increasing the size of the capital which may be lent.[152] The Board of Governors is above all to consider requests for financial support and the conditions attached to the grant of any such support.

Article 13 ESM

1. An ESM Member may address a request for stability support to the Chairperson of the Board of Governors. Such a request shall indicate the financial assistance instrument(s) to be considered. On receipt of such a request, the Chairperson of the Board of Governors shall entrust the European Commission, in liaison with the ECB, with the following tasks:
   (a) to assess the existence of a risk to the financial stability of the euro area as a whole or of its Member States, unless the ECB has already submitted an analysis under Article 18(2);[153]
   (b) to assess whether public debt is sustainable. Wherever appropriate and possible, such an assessment is expected to be conducted together with the IMF;
   (c) to assess the actual or potential financing needs of the ESM Member concerned.

2. On the basis of the request of the ESM Member and the assessment referred to in paragraph 1, the Board of Governors may decide to grant, in principle, stability support to the ESM Member concerned in the form of a financial assistance facility.

3. If a decision pursuant to paragraph 2 is adopted, the Board of Governors shall entrust the European Commission – in liaison with the ECB and, wherever possible, together with the IMF – with the task of negotiating, with the ESM Member concerned, a memorandum of understanding (an 'MoU') detailing the conditionality attached to the financial assistance facility. The content of the MoU shall reflect the severity of the weaknesses to be addressed and the financial assistance instrument chosen. In parallel, the Managing Director of the ESM shall prepare a proposal for a financial assistance facility agreement, including the financial terms and conditions and the choice of instruments, to be adopted by the Board of Governors.[154]

   The MoU shall be fully consistent with the measures of economic policy coordination provided for in the TFEU, in particular with any act of European Union law, including any opinion, warning, recommendation or decision addressed to the ESM Member concerned.

4. The European Commission shall sign the MoU on behalf of the ESM, subject to prior compliance with the conditions set out in paragraph 3 and approval by the Board of Governors....

7. The European Commission – in liaison with the ECB and, wherever possible, together with the IMF – shall be entrusted with monitoring compliance with the conditionality attached to the financial assistance facility.

---

[149] Article 4(5) ESM. This power exists only in relation to the grant and modalities of financial support, Articles 13–18 ESM.

[150] Article 4(7) and Annex II ESM. On this institutional imbalance see M. Dawson and F. de Witte, 'Constitutional Balance in the EU after the Euro-Crisis' (2013) 76 *MLR* 817, 828–35.

[151] Article 9 ESM.   [152] Article 10 ESM.

[153] This provides for a prior assessment by the ECB where there is concern about risks of financial contagion spreading to other euro area states.

[154] The Managing Director is the legal representative of the ESM and is appointed for a five-year term by the Board of Governors, Article 7 ESM. In December 2013, it was Klaus Regling, a German national.

This procedure has to be set against a context in which the ESM moves European integration in a robust way into contentious fields of redistributive activity. For creditor states, the levels of financial support being offered – at the expense of their own domestic public finances – are considerable. The ESM becomes a financial commitment to be weighed along pensions, education, social assistance and health. By contrast, the conditions attached to the financial support place powerful demands on the welfare and fiscal policies of those states receiving support. These states have to increase taxes, cut welfare and engage in privatisations. This world of tax and spend is, traditionally, the central topic of contestation of national elections.[155] The piece below suggests that not only does this destabilise the balance of power between Member States and European integration it also raises questions about the new institutional procedures to deal with these issues.

M. Dawson and F. de Witte, 'Constitutional Balance in the EU after the Euro-Crisis' (2013) 76 *Modern Law Review* 817, 825–6

Financial aid to Greece and future aid to Spain is made conditional on VAT increases, pension cuts, and the liberalisation of public services. Similarly, the Memoranda of Understanding that struggling Member States are asked to negotiate with a troika composed of the Commission, IMF and ECB list specific and detailed reforms in salient policy areas such as trade union rights, education, and healthcare. In Greece, for example, all collective agreements have been effectively rescinded as part of the implementation package request of the troika, which has been severely criticised by the ILO. Yet such processes occur outside the formal framework of the treaties, which explicitly prohibits Union competences in such policy areas. This is not only problematic from a purely juridical perspective, but also from a normative viewpoint. The Union's lack of competences was, after all, meant to stabilise the integration project by ensuring a substantive balance between economic objectives and the social values that make those economic objectives acceptable to the 'man on the street'.

Indeed, the Union's attempt to 'save' the eurozone risks undermining the substantive balance that sustains the legitimacy of the integration project. The circumvention of the limits to the competences of the Union is problematic for both structural and substantive reasons. In structural terms, it allows distributive norms to be decided in a forum that is incapable of offering a space of open contestation and communication, which is integral to its overall legitimacy. The Union is simply institutionally unable to 'do' redistributive policies or fiscal transfers. It lacks the robust political space that can come up with a criterion for distributive justice and can legitimise the redistributive choices made by articulating and incorporating the citizens' views and protecting competing values. Crudely put, it cannot offer a political space for discussion between German taxpayers and Greek recipients of public funds.

The first institutional concern to emerge arose in creditor state parliaments. On its face, the ESM allows a national Finance Minister to make large financial commitments on behalf of her state unchecked by any parliamentary constraints. This seemed to encroach on the traditional prerogative of national parliaments to ratify all such commitments through the domestic budgetary process. In both Germany and Finland, a constitutional precondition for ratification of

---

[155] This question was addressed at most length in Case 3–4–1–6–12 *Request of the Chancellor of Justice to Declare Article 4(4) of the Treaty Establishing the European Stability Mechanism in Conflict with the Constitution*, Supreme Court of Estonia, Judgment of 12 July 2012.

the ESM Treaty was, therefore, that the national parliament would have full information about the activities of the ESM, and the possibility to control any grant of financial support or any decision which might increase the commitments of these states, either absolutely or relative to the commitments of other Member States.[156]

The second concern revolves around the dominance of the Commission, ECB and IMF in the process. It is the Commission and the ECB who assess the request, check whether it meets the criteria for support. It is the Commission, the ECB and the IMF who negotiate the Memorandum of Understanding (MoU), with the requesting state setting out the conditions to be met for that support. Finally, it is these institutions which verify compliance by the recipient state with the conditions in the MoU. However, there is nothing in the TEU or TFEU which provides for the Commission or ECB to do any of these things. Indeed, it seems particularly odd that an institution, such as the ECB, set up primarily to authorise the issuing of money is now in charge of monitoring health policy or education policy in these recipient states.

These powers were challenged in *Pringle* on the ground that they breached the principle of conferred powers. The Court of Justice rejected this challenge. It stated that Member States could grant EU institutions new powers outside the framework of the EU Treaties provided that these did not conflict with any other Treaty norms and these powers did not alter the essential character of the respective institutions. In this regard, it did not believe the powers granted by the ESM did this. They were consistent with the role of the Commission as an institution which promotes the general interest of the Union and the ECB as an institution which supports the general economic policies of the Union.[157] These constraints are, however, very generic. They allow the Commission, in particular, to be used for any task desired by the Member States.[158] It can, of course, be argued that the ESM Treaty was ratified by Member States and their national parliaments. Concerns about the extent of institutional powers can be addressed there and if these wish to grant additional powers to EU institutions, then so be it. However, issues also arise as to how these new powers affect the exercise of existing duties. They may shift institutional attention and priorities away from TFEU responsibilities. The culture and values of the institutions may change. The ESM, for example, involves the ECB and the Commission being far more extensively involved with policing national governments. To be sure, the Commission already does that within the context of infringement proceedings, but when that institution's focus of relations with Member States goes to issues of compliance rather than those of agenda-setting, inevitably different dynamics will emerge. There is no sense any of this was considered.

---

[156] These were, of course, the conditions imposed in the German Constitutional Court's judgments in 2 BvR 1390/12 *ESM Treaty (Temporary Injunctions)*, Judgment of 12 September 2012, paras. 239–99. These had already, by and large, been put in place by a 2012 Act. See pp. 242–5. On the German debate see C. Callies, 'The Future of the Eurozone and the Role of the German Federal Constitutional Court' (2012) 32 *YBEL* 402; M. Wendel, 'Judicial Restraint and the Return to Openness: The Decision of the German Federal Constitutional Court on the ESM and the Fiscal Treaty of 12 September 2012' (2013) 14 *German Law Journal* 21; K. Schneider, 'Yes, But…One More Thing: Karlsruhe's Ruling on the European Stability Mechanism' (2013) 14 *German Law Journal* 53. On the debate within Finland see P. Leino and J. Salminen, 'The Euro Crisis and Its Constitutional Consequences for Finland: Is there Room for National Politics in EU Decision-Making' (2013) 9 *EuConst.* 451, 465–7.

[157] Case C-370/12 *Pringle* v *Government of Ireland*, Judgment of 27 November 2012, paras. 162–5. This is also discussed in Chapter 2. See pp. 61–2.

[158] In like vein see P. Craig, '*Pringle* and Use of EU Institutions Outside the EU Legal Framework: Foundations, Procedure and Substance' (2013) 9 *EuConst.* 263, 277–8. On the precedents for this and the wider legal debate see S. Peers, 'Towards a New Form of EU Law? The Use of EU Institutions Outside the EU Legal Framework' (2013) 9 *EuConst.* 37; B. de Witte and T. Beukers, 'The Court of Justice Approves the Creation of the European Stability Mechanism Outside the EU Legal Order: *Pringle*' (2013) 50 *CMLRev.* 805, 843–7.

The third concern goes to the checks and balances within the system. The ESM Treaty provides for disputes between Member States or between Member States and the ESM to be referred, in the first place, to the Board of Governors.[159] A Member State can contest any decision of the Board and refer it to the Court of Justice.[160] This is a very thin form of accountability. There are no duties on the ESM to consult with or to justify itself to anybody. There are no provisions on what occurs if misfeasance or negligence takes place. Even more acutely, the only accountability owed is one to national governments. This was once again challenged in *Pringle*. It was argued that the conditions required in any MoU could have a significant effect on the social rights recognised by the European Union Charter of Fundamental Rights (EUCFR).[161] There was no possibility for anybody whose rights were compromised to challenge the MoU before the Court of Justice. The ESM, thus, violated his fundamental right to effective judicial protection. The Court of Justice stated that there was no duty on the ESM to observe fundamental rights as this duty only applied to Member States when they are implementing EU law.[162] In this instance, they were acting outside the framework of EU law.[163]

The concern extends beyond protection of fundamental rights, important though this is. The legal status of the MoU is unclear. Questions about how it is to be interpreted and its binding qualities are all uncertain. The Greek Memorandum was, for example, revised five times between 2010 and 2012.[164] This leaves doubt about what is to be expected and a sense of cat and mouse where both parties can continually revisit the agreement if it does not deliver what was expected. Awareness of this led the Union to reinforce the MoU. States subject to financial support are now required by EU law to establish a macro-economic adjustment programme.[165] This programme is identical to that which must be agreed with the ESM.

Regulation 472/2013/EU, article 7(1)

1. Where a Member State requests financial assistance from one or several other Member States or third countries, the EFSM, the ESM, the EFSF or the IMF, it shall prepare, in agreement with the Commission, acting in liaison with the ECB and, where appropriate, with the IMF, a draft macroeconomic adjustment programme…

   The draft macroeconomic adjustment programme shall address the specific risks emanating from that Member State for the financial stability in the euro area and shall aim at rapidly re- establishing a sound and sustainable economic and financial situation and restoring the Member State's capacity to finance itself fully on the financial markets.

---

[159] Article 37(2) ESM.   [160] Article 37(3) ESM.

[161] These include workers' rights, right to health care and social assistance.

[162] Case C-370/12 *Pringle* v *Government of Ireland*, Judgment of 27 November 2012, paras. 191–4.

[163] The treatment of the Portuguese implementation of its Memorandum by the Portuguese Constitutional Tribunal is instructive. It found there had been an unlawful discrimination between public sector and private sector workers in the distribution of costs, *Acordão 187/2013 on Portuguese Budget*, Portuguese Constitutional Tribunal, Judgment of 5 April 2013.

[164] K. Tuori, *The European Financial Crisis: Constitutional Aspects and Implications*, Law Working Paper 2012/28 (Florence, EUI, 2012) 12.

[165] Regulation 472/2013 on the strengthening of economic and budgetary surveillance of Member States in the euro area experiencing or threatened with serious difficulties with respect to their financial stability [2013] OJ L140/1.

The guarantees provided in EU law are greater than under the ESM. The programme must respect national systems of collective bargaining.[166] The Member State must also seek the views of social partners as well as civil society organisations in drafting this programme.[167] As the procedure is contained in an EU Regulation, this programme is now also something which can be scrutinised by both national courts and the Court of Justice.

These future guarantees do not cover existing programmes agreed under the ESM. Furthermore, there is no commitment to respect social rights beyond that of collective bargaining. Arguably the greatest concern, however, goes to revision of the plan. The state receiving support has no control over this, and it seems to take place unconstrained by domestic democratic processes.

Regulation 472/2013, article 7(5)

5. The Commission, in liaison with the ECB and, where appropriate, with the IMF, shall examine with the Member State concerned the changes and updates that may be needed to its macroeconomic adjustment programme in order to take proper account, inter alia, of any significant gap between macroeconomic forecasts and realised figures, including possible consequences resulting from the macroeconomic adjustment programme, adverse spill-over effects and macroeconomic and financial shocks. The Council, acting by a qualified majority on a proposal from the Commission, shall decide on any change to be made to that programme.

A state entering a financial support arrangement is, therefore, making a Faustian Pact. If it might have some strong role over agreement of the original arrangement, it loses that role as the arrangement continues. It is to be consulted on subsequent changes but these will be determined by two sets of foreign executives: the Commission and the Finance Ministries of the other euro area states represented by their ministers in the Council. There is no accountability for this even to the European Parliament.

7 EUROPEANISATION OF ECONOMIC, EMPLOYMENT AND BUDGETARY POLICY THROUGH THE EUROPEAN SEMESTER

The crisis led to a perception that Union mechanisms of oversight were too weak insofar as they focused excessively on budget deficits and insufficiently on medium and long-term weaknesses in Member States' economic and fiscal performance. Their oversight was also insufficiently coordinated. It did not look sufficiently at how different elements of economic performance affected each other and economic performance overall. Finally, surveillance happened too late in the day. This prevented early planning and only allowed for correction when matters had gone awry.[168] To rectify this, an annual European Semester for Economic Policy Coordination was established in September 2010. This was formalised in Regulation 1466/97.

---

[166] *Ibid.* article 7(1).   [167] *Ibid.* article 8.
[168] European Commission, *Reinforcing Economic Policy Coordination*, COM(2010)250.

Regulation 1466/97, article 2a(1)

1. In order to ensure closer coordination of economic policies and sustained convergence of the economic performance of the Member States, the Council shall conduct multilateral surveillance as an integral part of the European Semester for economic policy coordination in accordance with the objectives and requirements set out in the TFEU.

The range of activities considered at the Semester is considerable. It includes:

- the formulation and surveillance of implementation of guidelines in the fields of economic and employment policy and the surveillance and examination of these;
- the submission and assessment of stability and convergence plans. These go to Member States' commitment to a balanced budget. It will be remembered that each state is to have a Medium Term Budget Objective, which sets out a cyclically adjusted deficit or surplus for it. This is revised every three years, and is something which it must work towards.[169] The stability programme is a programme of action submitted by euro area states setting out the measures and assumptions behind these for realising this;[170]
- the submission and assessments of national reform plans. These go to the Union growth strategy, Europe 2020. This strategy involves an Annual Growth Survey setting out challenges and priorities for the Union economy.[171] On the basis of this, each state adopts a national reform programme indicating which measures it will take to support the objectives set out in this survey;
- assessment of macro-economic imbalances in national economies.

The review, thus, covers all aspects of fiscal, economic and social policy, as well as commitments on matters such as climate change policy (typically handled in the national reform plans). The process of review is set out in article 2a of Regulation 1466/97.

Regulation 1466/97, article 2a(3)

3. In the course of the European Semester, in order to provide timely and integrated policy advice on macrofiscal and macrostructural policy intentions, the Council shall, as a rule, following the assessment of these programmes on the basis of recommendations from the Commission, address guidance to the Member States making full use of the legal instruments provided under Articles 121 and 148 TFEU, and under this Regulation and Regulation 1176/2011.

  Member States shall take due account of the guidance addressed to them in the development of their economic, employment and budgetary policies before taking key decisions on their national budgets for the succeeding years. Progress shall be monitored by the Commission.

---

[169] Regulation 1466/97, article 2a.
[170] *Ibid.* article 3(1) and (2). Similar programmes are set out by all non-euro area states, but these are called convergence programmes. *Ibid.* article 7(1) and (2).
[171] On this see http://ec.europa.eu/europe2020/index_en.htm.

Failure by a Member State to act upon the guidance received may result in:

(a) further recommendations to take specific measures;

(b) a warning by the Commission under Article 121(4) TFEU;

(c) measures under this Regulation, Regulation 1467/97 or Regulation 1176/2011.

Implementation of the measures shall be subject to reinforced monitoring by the Commission and may include surveillance missions under Article 11 of this Regulation.

The initial process of scrutiny is similar for all five fields of activity.[172] National policies are subject to Commission assessment as to compliance with Union Guidelines, indicators and so on. The Council shall then issue its own guidance to individual states based on the Commission's recommendations. These take place against a context where the European Council has issued general policy orientations on the direction and priorities of the Annual Growth Strategy. There is also provision for involvement of the European Parliament through a process known as the Economic Dialogue in which it can ask the president of any the other institution to appear before the Committee to discuss the orientations, results and recommendations of the Semester.[173] This is, however, an ex post control, which takes place after the surveillance has been carried out and the recommendations adopted. There is no requirement for any involvement of national parliaments but governments must disclose what parliamentary involvement took place in regard to stability programmes.[174] Practice suggests quite active national parliament involvement.[175] Finally, there is provision for stakeholders to be involved with the process on the main policy issues.[176]

The challenge for the Semester lies in its scope. As an exercise in policy planning and coordination, a European Parliament study found that it was too ambitious in nature and too unfocused in its priorities for there to be any sense of its wider significance.[177] As it is relatively novel, however, its effects are largely untested, and will be determined by how it is taken up in national budget policy. Member States are required to take account of the guidance and recommendations of the guidance received in the European Semester 'before taking key decisions on their national budgets for the succeeding years'.[178]

To facilitate Union oversight of this take-up, there is provision for a common budgetary timeline which allows monitoring of that budget by the Commission and the Euro Group. Euro area states are required to make public a draft budget for the forthcoming year by no later than 15 October.[179] This is to be presented to the Commission and the Euro Group.[180] The Commission shall then present an assessment of the draft Budget by 30 November to the Euro Group, who shall then discuss it.[181] The European Parliament can also ask the Commission to present its assessment to it.[182] Following this assessment, the state should adopt the budget by no later

---

[172] On the Semester and the wider system of fiscal governance to which it contributes see K. Armstrong, 'The New Governance of EU Fiscal Discipline' (2013) 38 *ELRev.* 601.

[173] Regulation 1466/97, articles 2a(4) and 2ab.   [174] *Ibid.* article 3(4).

[175] M. Hallerberg *et al.*, *An Assessment of the European Semester*, PE 475.121 (Brussels, European Parliament, 2012) 68–76.

[176] *Ibid.* article 2a(4).   [177] Hallerberg *et al.*, n. 175 above, 77–9.   [178] Regulation 1466/97, article 2a(3).

[179] Regulation 473/2013/EU on common provisions for monitoring and assessing draft budgetary plans and ensuring the correction of excessive deficit of the Member States in the euro area, article 4(2) [2013] OJ L140/11.

[180] *Ibid.* article 6(1).   [181] *Ibid.* article 7(1).   [182] *Ibid.* article 7(3).

than 31 December of that year.[183] Although none of the Commission's assessments are binding on that state, the challenge with the procedure is how it telescopes national parliament consideration of the budget. The Budget must remain a plan until 30 November, but must be ratified by the parliament within a month. There is, thus, very little time for that parliament to consider the draft budget in the light of the Commission's assessment and Euro Group discussions. In adopting their budgets, euro area states now have to satisfy two arenas: the supranational one of the Commission and the Euro Group and the national one of their domestic parliament. Undoubtedly, this will weaken domestic parliamentary influence over the budget. There is, in particular, a danger that a national government will use the support of the Commission and euro area states to push through last minute changes in its budget during the rushed period of December for its adoption by the national parliament.

8 SANCTION PROCEDURES FOR SIGNIFICANT OBSERVED DEVIATIONS FROM THE MTBO, EXCESSIVE IMBALANCES AND EXCESSIVE DEFICITS

A key part of the European Semester is that it puts in play two processes which can lead to sanctions for euro area states. This shifts the nature of these two processes and distinguishes them from other parts of the Semester, as they go far more to Union policing of national policy than to more general policy coordination. These processes are the assessment of national stability programmes and the assessment of the presence of macro-economic imbalances within national economies.

The assessment of each national stability programme is intensive and wide-ranging.

Regulation 1466/97, article 5(1)

1. Based on assessments by the Commission and the Economic and Financial Committee, the Council shall, within the framework of multilateral surveillance under Article 121 TFEU, examine the medium-term budgetary objectives presented by the Member States concerned in their stability programmes, assess whether the economic assumptions on which the programme is based are plausible, whether the adjustment path towards the medium-term budgetary objective is appropriate, including consideration of the accompanying path for the debt ratio, and whether the measures being taken or proposed to respect that adjustment path are sufficient to achieve the medium-term budgetary objective over the cycle.

If a 'significant observed deviation from the adjustment path' towards the MTBO is found as a consequence of this assessment, the Commission must address a warning. Within one month of this, the Council will adopt a recommendation (based on a Commission recommendation) setting out the necessary measures to be taken. A deadline for state action is set by the Council. This cannot be more than five months and can, if urgent action is warranted, be three months. If appropriate action is not taken by the state, the Commission will recommend the Council to find, by QMV, that no effective action has been taken. If the Council takes no action, and the position persists, the Commission, after one month, can recommend itself that no effective action has been taken. The Recommendation will be deemed to be adopted by the Council unless it votes against it by simple majority within ten days.[184]

---

[183] *Ibid.* article 4(3).   [184] This is all set out in Regulation 1466/97, article 6(2).

With macro-economic imbalances, the Commission sets out an annual report prior to the Semester detailing a series of indicators against which imbalances can be assessed both at a Union level and in individual Member States.[185] This report also identifies states which have crossed certain thresholds in relation to these indicators, and whether, as a consequence, that state may be affected by or be at risk of having a macro-economic imbalance.[186] This report will then be discussed by the Council and the Euro Group.[187] The Commission, taking account of these discussions, shall then carry out an 'in-depth review' of every state it considers may be affected or at risk of being affected by imbalances.[188] If the review finds that the state is experiencing imbalances, the Council, on a recommendation from the Commission, will make public recommendations to the state concerned about action to be taken.[189]

The situation is more serious if the Commission considers that the state is affected by *excessive imbalances*. In such circumstances, the Council may, on a recommendation from the Commission, adopt a recommendation establishing an excessive imbalance and recommending corrective action within a deadline.[190] This recommendation requires the state concerned to set out a corrective action plan with a timetable for action within that deadline.[191] The Council will then, on a report by the Commission, assess the adequacy of that correction action plan and set out a timetable for surveillance.[192] If it considers the plan to be insufficient, it can ask for a new plan to be provided.[193] The Commission will then monitor the plan.[194] On the basis of a Commission report to that effect, the Council will then take a decision where there is non-compliance: a decision that sets the scene for sanctions.[195]

The third sanctions procedure, the Excessive Deficit procedure, does not originate in the European Semester. It can begin at any time with the Commission having to write a report if it believes there is an excessive deficit or a risk of an excessive deficit.[196] The test is more fluid than simply identifying whether a state has exceeded a numerical threshold, namely 3 per cent of GDP for its annual budget deficit or 60 per cent of GDP for its debt, or is failing to bring down the difference between its actual deficits and these thresholds by one-twentieth per annum.[197] First, an excessive deficit will not be found to exist if this results from a severe economic downturn. This is interpreted to be wherever there is negative annual growth or an accumulated loss of output during a protracted period of low economic growth.[198] Secondly, there is an overarching condition. If the state's deficit is numerically close to its targets, the Commission can take account of a number of other features, namely, whether the deficit is temporary and whether it is exacerbated by financial spending on a number of headings, including obligations arising from European integration (i.e. towards the ESM) and contributions to fostering international solidarity.[199]

If, having written the report, it still believes an excessive deficit exists or may occur, it must then address an opinion to the Member State concerned and inform the Council accordingly.[200] The Council must then decide whether there is an excessive deficit after hearing the Member State.[201] The finding of an excessive deficit will result in the Council making recommendations (on a recommendation from the Commission) to the state to take a number of measures to bring the deficit to an end.[202] If no effective action is taken by the state concerned, these recommendations will be made public.[203]

---

[185] Regulation 1176/2011, article 3(1).   [186] *Ibid.* article 3(2).
[187] *Ibid.* article 3(5). The latter only discusses euro area states.   [188] *Ibid.* article 5(1).
[189] *Ibid.* article 6(1)–(3).   [190] *Ibid.* article 7(2).   [191] *Ibid.* article 8(1).   [192] *Ibid.* article 8(2).
[193] *Ibid.* article 8(3).   [194] *Ibid.* article 9.   [195] *Ibid.* article 10(4).   [196] Article 126(3) TFEU.
[197] See n. 10 above.   [198] Regulation 1467/97, article 2(1).   [199] *Ibid.* article 2(4).
[200] Article 126(5) TFEU.   [201] Article 126(6) TFEU.   [202] Article 126(7) TFEU.   [203] Article 126(8) TFEU.

All three procedures – Significant Observed Deviation, Excessive Imbalance and Excessive Deficit – share certain traits. They are, first, all byzantine. Secondly, they all rely on an initial finding of a failure of national economic or fiscal performance by the Council on the basis of an assessment and recommendation by the Commission. Thirdly, they all give a period for action to be taken during which time the state is monitored by the Commission. Fourthly, they all reach a point where the Council finds that the state has failed to take action required of it by the Council. The fifth shared trait is that this finding leads to financial penalties. However, the modalities for this vary between procedures. It leads automatically to the payment of an interest-bearing deposit of 0.1 per cent of GDP with the excessive imbalance procedure.[204] A further Council decision is required, within twenty days, in the case of the Significant Observed Deviation procedure, which leads to the levying of a non-interest bearing deposit of 0.1 per cent of GDP.[205] With the Excessive Deficit procedure, the Commission recommends within twenty days of the Council decision a fine of 0.2 per cent of GDP which will be deemed to be adopted unless the Council votes against it by QMV within ten days.[206]

Continued breach leads to further sanctions. States already punished under the Significant Observed Deviation procedure or where the Commission has identified 'particularly serious non-compliance with their budgetary obligations' have to pay a non-interest bearing deposit of 0.2 per cent of GDP on the simple finding of an excessive deficit by the Council.[207] Continuance of an excessive deficit can lead to further fines up to a ceiling of 0.5 per cent of GDP.[208] Under the Excessive Imbalance procedure, states subject to either two successive decisions of non-compliance with the terms of a correction action plan or two failures to provide a corrective action plan will have their deposit converted into a fine.[209]

There is a complete implausibility about this system of fines. Their potential size is eye-watering, running into billions of euros. It is difficult to believe that national governments would impose it on one another or that citizens of that state would tolerate such fines. There is also something paradoxical about fining a bankrupt state. If a state cannot manage its economy or public finances, it is going to struggle to pay this additional sanction. Leblond has thus noted that investors did not react negatively to a relaxation of the process, which took place between 2002 and 2004, and has suggested this was a sign that the markets did not believe the sanctions were credible and looked instead for other assurances of budgetary discipline.[210]

This problem was identified in both the 'six-pack' and the fiscal compact as one of overly high voting thresholds within the Council. A QMV vote was too high a barrier for the effective utilisation of these procedures given the incentives and pressures on national Finance Ministers not to vote for them within the Council.[211] The TSCG, therefore, set out the principle of reverse QMV. Commission recommendations are deemed to be adopted unless a QMV of states votes against them.

---

[204] Regulation 1174/2011, article 3(1) and (5).
[205] Regulation 1173/2011, article 4(1).   [206] *Ibid.* article 6(1).
[207] *Ibid.* article 5(1). The Commission can recommend that this be reduced, article 5(4).
[208] Regulation 1467/97, article 12.
[209] Regulation 1174/2011, article 3(2). These sanctions can be reduced or cancelled upon a Commission request. *Ibid.* article 3(6).
[210] P. Leblond, 'The Political Stability and Growth Pact is Dead: Long Live the Economic Stability and Growth Pact' (2006) 44 *JCMS* 969, 976–82.
[211] Notably in Article 126(6), (8), (9) and (11) TFEU. On this see D. Adamski, 'National Power Games and Structural Failures in the European Macroeconomic Governance' (2012) 49 *CMLRev.* 1319, 1322–3. It has been argued that the problem was rather that Finance Ministers are much more domestically constrained than is realised. D. Hodson, *Governing the Euro Area in Good Times and Bad* (Oxford, Oxford University Press, 2011) 60–74.

Article 7 TSCG

While fully respecting the procedural requirements of the Treaties on which the European Union is founded, the Contracting Parties whose currency is the euro commit to supporting the proposals or recommendations submitted by the European Commission where it considers that a Member State of the European Union whose currency is the euro is in breach of the deficit criterion in the framework of an excessive deficit procedure. This obligation shall not apply where it is established among the Contracting Parties whose currency is the euro that a qualified majority of them, calculated by analogy with the relevant provisions of the Treaties on which the European Union is founded, without taking into account the position of the Contracting Party concerned, is opposed to the decision proposed or recommended.

Similar patterns are present in the other two procedures where reverse QMV is applied to all parts of the process other than the initial identification of an excessive imbalance or a significant observed deviation, where a straightforward decision by QMV in the Council is required.[212] The assumption is that the Commission is bedevilled by fewer conflicts of interests in this process than the Council. It is thus easier for it to make a more dispassionate assessment of the risks, and this should be followed unless the overwhelming majority of states believe that a mistake has been made.

As the piece below suggests, it is not clear that this will lead to easier decision-making. Reverse QMV increases the damage to the Commission's reputation if states vote against it, and is thus likely to make it more cautious. More importantly, it provides incentives for the Commission to frame debates about a state's fiscal and economic performance in a manner which obscures the redistributive and welfare implications of what is taking place.

D. Chalmers, 'The European Redistributive State and a European Law of Struggle' (2012) 18 *European Law Journal* 667, 689–91

The processes are thus, in every way, analogous to regulatory processes in which agencies exercise sustained and focused authority over market actors. There is the intense focus on changing identified behavior through frequent interaction and the classic regulatory 'compliance pyramid' model of escalating responses (discussions, warnings, period for self-regulation, reversible sanctions, greater sanctions). Regulatory processes tend to lead to strong mutual dependence, which is likely to be intensified, as well as the associated conflicts, by the application of these techniques to economic and budgetary policy-making: fields marked by redistributive clashes and political salience. Indeed, this has already been seen in first application of the sanctions against Hungary in 2012. The response from that State and society was vigorous. It led to demonstrations in Budapest of two hundred thousand people.

---

[212] Regulation 1176/2011, article 7(2). With the Significant Observed Deviation procedure, the Council attempts to adopt the measures by QMV. If this is not possible within one month, resort is had to reverse QMV, Regulation 1466/97, article 6(2).

The regulatory style of policy-making is first present in the same division of labour between risk assessment and risk management as found in other areas of EU activity with the former seen as an expert process and the latter a political, evaluative one. The Commission is to assess domestic performance and the Council to take formal decisions on the basis of its assessments. This model is confounded by conflicts being as much about different ways of seeing the world as about preferences. The interplay between these in a process of struggle is central both to creativity and to the prevention of hegemonies. With regard, to the former, an opportunity is lost to exploit the collective European political imagination. There may be assessments and options beyond those held by the Commission and the national executive which would provide additional and possibly more fertile avenues for exploring how a State might improve its performance. The Commission has, indeed, had to relinquish risk assessment in other fields of EU law because of doubts about its competence. Issues of dominance are likely to tarnish the authority of the Commission's assessment. This model has not worked well elsewhere in EU law where risk assessment is seen as driving the formal decision-making process and has thus become highly politicised. In this field, there is a particular problem as States have their own assessments and statistics which have already been regularly deployed to contest the credibility of Commission assessments. More generally, the failure to politicize knowledge reinforces existing patterns of executive dominance insofar as these are the only domestic parties that can put forward their representation of the situation. Inevitably, this will lead to excluded parties seeing the process as ideologically tarnished insofar as it does not represent economic and fiscal performance through any other lens.

This regulatory ethos is likely, secondly, to be central to the mechanics of decision-making in a manner which limits political mobilisation. In all three processes voting within ECOFIN fluctuates between QMV and reverse QMV. If the latter formally strengthens the position of the Commission, it increases the political costs of defeat for it as this will involve rejection by a large majority of States. In all likelihood, it will seek, as it has done in other fields where reverse QMV rule has applied, to seek an informal consensus with COREPER before formally declaring its position. The evidence from elsewhere is that such consensus can only easily be achieved where a matter is framed in regulatory terms as realization of a common good – in this instance the meeting of a best practice which is both optimal for that State and poses least risks to other States. The reason is that voting positions by Member States within the Council (and therefore ECOFIN) are historically informed partly by individual self-interest and partly by arguments couched in terms of best practice. This framing allows the notion of the common good to be manipulated in a way that is compatible with different national preferences. If there is no idea of a common good to crystalise consensus, States focus, instead, more acutely on redistributive issues between them. There are, thus, strong incentives for the Commission to frame debates in these terms.

Conceiving this policy-making process as a regulatory one is an opaque way of framing it. It would be more honest to frame it in political economy terms, namely that it is a significant part of the process for organizing a State's economy and budget. This allows the arena to be seen more transparently as one which is both realizing collective goods (ie a strong economy) and is mediating redistributive conflicts between different social actors. The latter, of course, happen as any decision has significant redistributive consequences. Conceiving it more openly in this way would allow parties to identify more clearly its effects on them and thereby facilitate a more vibrant, pluralist, authoritative politics within this arena. Parties would mobilise to influence it, and this would, in turn, generate cross-cutting alliances and commonalities between domestic and transnational interests.

FURTHER READING

F. Amtenbrink, *The Democratic Accountability of Central Banks: A Comparative Study of the European Central Bank* (Oxford, Hart Publishing, 1999)

F. Amtenbrink and K. van Duin, 'The European Central Bank before the European Parliament: Theory and Practice after 10 Years of Monetary Dialogue' (2009) 34 *European Law Review* 561

K. Armstrong, 'The New Governance of EU Fiscal Discipline' (2013) 38 *European Law Review* 601

D. Chalmers, 'The European Redistributive State and a European Law of Struggle' (2012) 18 *European Law Journal* 667

C. Chiti and P. Texeira, 'The Constitutional Implications of the European Responses to the Financial and Public Debt Crisis' (2013) 50 *Common Market Law Review* 683

M. Dawson and F. de Witte, 'Constitutional Balance in the EU after the Euro-Crisis' (2013) 76 *Modern Law Review* 817

J. de Haan, C. Eijffinger and S. Waller, *The European Central Bank: Credibility, Transparency, and Centralization* (Cambridge, MA, MIT Press, 2005)

M. Ruffert, 'The European Debt Crisis and European Union Law' (2011) 48 *Common Market Law Review* 1777

A. Schäfer and W. Streeck (eds.), *Politics in the Age of Austerity* (Cambridge, Polity Press, 2013)

B. de Witte, A. Heritier and A. Trechsel (eds.), *The Euro Crisis and the State of European Democracy* (Florence, EUI, 2013)

C. Zilioli and M. Selmayr, *The Law of the European Central Bank* (Oxford, Hart Publishing, 2001)

C. Zilioli and M. Selmayr, 'The Constitutional Status of the European Central Bank' (2007) 44 *Common Market Law Review* 355

17

The Free Movement of Goods

CONTENTS

1 INTRODUCTION

Article 34 TFEU prohibits restrictions on the import of goods from other Member States. Case law has divided measures which may be restrictions into three categories, governed by three important cases, *Dassonville, Cassis de Dijon* and *Keck*. The structure of the chapter reflects this.

Section 2 discusses the umbrella notion of a restriction on imports, which is provided in *Dassonville*. This case established a very broad scope to Article 34, applying to any measure which impedes imports, however that effect is achieved. *Alfa Vita* even suggests that if a measure results in reduced sales of certain goods this may be enough to bring it within Article 34.

Section 3 discusses the application of Article 34 to product rules. The basis for this application is provided in *Cassis de Dijon*. Product rules are rules which require producers to change some aspect of the physical product or its packaging before it may be sold. Examples are rules which only allow the sale of foodstuffs made in certain ways, or which limit the kinds of containers that can be used for soft drinks. The Court of Justice held in *Cassis de Dijon* that even if these rules apply equally to imports and domestic products, they are nevertheless restrictions on imports.

(a) The reason for the ruling was that in practice it is very difficult to export to other Member States if one has to amend products to adapt to the different rules in each state.

(b) The judgment created a principle of 'mutual recognition' of the adequacy of other Member State laws. It established that goods should only be subject to the regulation of their country of production. The principles of country of origin regulation and mutual recognition are now applied throughout free movement law.

(c) It is possible to derogate from mutual recognition for legitimate and proportionate reasons, but this is strictly policed. It is often argued, for example, that permitting foreign products to be sold when these do not conform to national rules and expectations undermines consumer protection. However, the Court usually finds that labelling provides the consumer with sufficient information and protection, and is a lesser hindrance to trade.

Section 4 discusses *Keck* and the idea of 'selling arrangements'. These are rules which regulate the way products are sold. Examples are advertising and rules on shop opening times. The Court of Justice held in *Keck* that these are generally not restrictions on imports, as long as they do not have a greater effect on imports than on domestic products. Member States may therefore regulate selling arrangements however they like, so long as the effect on imports and domestic products is the same. *Keck* is criticised by many because even if selling arrangements do not have an unequal effect, they may still have the effect of hindering trade, by making marketing more difficult.

Some principles are common to all categories of restrictions on imports.

(a) Restrictions on imports which discriminate directly between national and foreign goods may only be saved by Article 36 TFEU. This is discussed in Chapter 20.

(b) Restrictions on imports which are equally applicable (equal on their face, although they may have some unequal effect) will not be prohibited if they are necessary for some legitimate public interest objective (often called a 'mandatory requirement') and are proportionate.

(c) Article 34 only applies insofar as measures affect imports. If Member States wish to burden domestic producers with heavy regulation this is a matter of purely national law. However, in exceptional situations stricter regulation of domestic production may actually give it a reputational advantage, and so be a hindrance to imports.

(d) Article 34 TFEU has never been clearly applied to a purely private measure, only to broadly public ones. However, the notion of 'public' catches all bodies and measures in which the state is implicated or has control, even if the measure is apparently implemented by a private organisation. Moreover, the Member State has a positive obligation to prevent private parties from obstructing free movement, for example, where demonstrators block roads. This may entail sensitive balancing between free movement and fundamental rights to free expression and to demonstrate.

Section 5 discusses Article 35 TFEU, which prohibits restrictions on exports. It has a different logic from Article 34 TFEU. It only applies to measures which have some greater negative effect on export sales than on domestic sales. As with Article 34, if these measures are equally applicable and serve a legitimate aim in a proportionate way, then they may be permitted.

2 GENERAL DEFINITION OF A MEASURE EQUIVALENT TO A QUANTITATIVE RESTRICTION

Article 34 TFEU provides that:

> Quantitative restrictions on imports and all measures having equivalent effect shall be prohibited between Member States.

A quantitative restriction is a limit on the amount of imports.[1] That limit may be constructed in various ways, by reference to value, or physical quantity, or some other factor. Examples could be a rule permitting only so many cars to be imported per year or limiting imports of cheese to a percentage of total domestic sales. Quantitative restrictions do not arise often any more: their prohibition is too clear.

The second part of Article 34 is rather more important in practice. This prohibits measures which do not actually set a limit to imports, but have the same effect as such a limit. These 'measures of equivalent effect' (MEQRs), as they are often called, result in imports being reduced just as if there was in fact an explicit limit.

The case law on Article 34 consists of attempts to define and explain what constitutes a MEQR. The problems of such a definition are twofold. First, a MEQR, by definition, produces its import-reducing effects by a more or less indirect path. That can make causation difficult to establish. The first problem is therefore to know, as a matter of fact, which measures actually do result in imports being reduced or are likely to do so. In some cases it may be obvious, but other cases are difficult. The Court of Justice has dealt with this by drawing broad-brush distinctions of convenience between the types of measures that may be expected to obstruct trade or not, as will be seen below in the discussions of *Dassonville* and *Keck*.[2] The second problem is to decide whether Article 34 is about combating rules with a protectionist effect, or about deregulating economic activity.[3] Many measures restrict or reduce economic activity generally: tax rises, rules on transport and advertising, labour regulation. Such measures are likely, therefore, to reduce imports too. However, they do not *specifically* reduce imports. They do not have any effect on imports that they do not also have on domestic production. On the whole, as will be seen below, the Court of Justice excludes such measures from Article 34, although the position is far from entirely clear and recent cases suggest a rethinking may be underway.[4]

In the current state of the law, measures potentially within Article 34 can be divided into three groups, each falling within a distinct legal regime. The most recent group consists of measures which concern the way goods are marketed or sold. Whether or not this type of measure is prohibited is decided according to the principles laid down in *Keck*, discussed later in this chapter.[5] Perhaps the most important group in practice consists of measures concerning the way products are produced or packaged – their physical specifications. Whether or not these measures contravene Article 34 is decided according to the principles laid down in

---

[1] See Case 2/73 *Riseria Luigi Geddo* v *Ente Nazionale Risi* [1973] ECR 865.

[2] Case 8/74 *Procureur du Roi* v *Benoit and Gustave Dassonville* [1974] ECR 837; Joined Cases C-267/91 and C-268/91 *Keck and Mithouard* [1993] ECR I-6097. See also G. Davies, 'The Court's Jurisprudence on Free Movement of Goods: Pragmatic Presumptions, Not Philosophical Principles' (2012) 2 *European Journal of Consumer Law/Revue Européenne de Droit de la Consommation* 25.

[3] See Chapter 15; Advocate General Tesauro in Case C-292/02 *Hünermund* v *Landesapotheker Baden-Württemburg* [1994] ECR I-6787.

[4] See pp. 759–63.   [5] See pp. 786–90.

Cassis de Dijon, also discussed below.[6] The third group consists of measures which affect imports or trade in some way, but do not fall within the other groups. These are measures which cannot be easily captured by the *Cassis* definition of a product rule or the *Keck* definition of a selling arrangement. The legality of this third group of measures is decided according to the principles in *Dassonville*.[7] In fact, this is the oldest of the three central goods cases, and is the case which provides the general umbrella definition of a MEQR. In the years immediately after it was decided, it was the starting point for all questions of free movement of goods. However, now that the specialised sub-regimes of *Cassis* and *Keck* are well established, *Dassonville* has become less important in practice. Nevertheless, a wave of recent cases relying on it to extend Article 34 to new areas show that its principles are in no way defunct.

(i) *Dassonville*

Mr Dassonville was a Belgian trader who bought Scotch whisky in France and imported it to Belgium for sale there. The reason why he did this was that whisky was much cheaper in France than in Belgium. The French, at the time of the case, did not have as high a disposable income as Belgians, and could not be persuaded to pay as much for whisky. Moreover, while whisky was a fairly well-established tipple in Belgium, it was less so in France, where it had to compete against domestic spirits and aperitifs. A common technique used to enter a new market is to sell the product at a low price initially, and whisky producers and retailers did precisely this. The hope was, of course, that eventually the French would come to love whisky and the price could be raised, and large profits finally made.

However, such market-specific pricing is made very difficult by Article 34, since what is called parallel trading quickly reduces the price differences. People like Mr Dassonville go and buy the goods in the cheap market and sell in the expensive one, until the prices converge. This is possible because, given Article 34, there should be no obstacles to the trading of goods between states.

Nevertheless, Mr Dassonville encountered a problem in the form of a Belgian law on 'designations of origin'. The law prohibited the import of products bearing such a 'designation of origin' without a certificate from the authorities of the state of production to prove that this designation was correct. Thus, whisky labelled as Scotch (from Scotland) could not be imported to Belgium without a certificate of origin from the British customs.

For retailers who imported their whisky directly from the United Kingdom this was not a problem, since the whisky would be delivered with the appropriate certificate if desired. However, such certificates were typically removed at the point of importation, and were no longer attached to the whisky by the time it was on sale within the country. Thus, when Mr Dassonville bought his whisky for a good price in France it came without a certificate. Moreover, it was difficult for him to obtain such a certificate since the goods had already left the United Kingdom. He was therefore in possession of Scotch whisky which could not be lawfully sold in Belgium according to Belgian law. He claimed that this law was a MEQR, and in the Court of Justice's judgment gave what continues to be the standard description of what a MEQR is.

---

[6] Case 120/78 *Rewe-Zentral AG* v *Bundesmonopolverwaltung fur Branntwein (Cassis de Dijon)* [1979] ECR 649, discussed at p. 773.

[7] Case 2/73 *Riseria Luigi Geddo* v *Ente Nazionale Risi* [1973] ECR 865.

Case 8/74 *Procureur du Roi v Benoît and Gustave Dassonville* [1974] ECR 837

5. All trading rules enacted by Member States which are capable of hindering, directly or indirectly, actually or potentially, intra-community trade are to be considered as measures having an effect equivalent to quantitative restrictions.

6. In the absence of a community system guaranteeing for consumers the authenticity of a product's designation of origin, if a Member State takes measures to prevent unfair practices in this connection, it is however subject to the condition that these measures should be reasonable and that the means of proof required should not act as a hindrance to trade between Member States and should, in consequence, be accessible to all community nationals.

7. Even without having to examine whether or not such measures are covered by Article [34 TFEU], they must not, in any case, by virtue of the principle expressed in the second sentence of that article, constitute a means of arbitrary discrimination or a disguised restriction on trade between Member States.

8. That may be the case with formalities, required by a Member State for the purpose of proving the origin of a product, which only direct importers are really in a position to satisfy without facing serious difficulties.

9. Consequently, the requirement by a Member State of a certificate of authenticity which is less easily obtainable by importers of an authentic product which has been put into free circulation in a regular manner in another Member State than by importers of the same product coming directly from the country of origin constitutes a measure having an effect equivalent to a quantitative restriction as prohibited by the Treaty.

There are four elements of this judgment worth noting: first, the definition in paragraph 5, which continues to be cited in almost unchanged terms, although with the words 'all trading rules' replaced in some judgments by the words 'all rules' or 'all measures'.[8] This definition is very broad. It extends a MEQR to include measures which have not yet had any actual effect, but may potentially do so, as well as those whose effect on trade is indirect. Article 34 TFEU applies to any measure which may somehow hinder interstate trade. Yet, the second aspect of the judgment mitigates this. The Court of Justice appears to accept in paragraph 6 that even measures which might fall within its own definition may be permitted if they are 'reasonable'. This notion was later developed and brought to fruition in *Cassis de Dijon*. As a result, even though paragraph 5 of the judgment establishes a broad scope of supervision of Article 34, some of the measures caught may in fact ultimately escape its prohibition.

Thirdly, the breadth of the definition can then be understood as an establishment of jurisdiction. By making Article 34 broad, the Court is granting itself equally broad powers to supervise national measures via the preliminary reference procedure, even if in some cases it will find those measures compatible with the Treaty. This was particularly important in a time where the internal market was in its infancy and national protectionist traditions were well-entrenched, while national judges were still often unfamiliar with EU law. Finally, one may note the emphasis in paragraphs 7 to 9 on discrimination. There is no mention of this in the

---

[8] See e.g. Case C-88/07 *Commission v Spain*, Judgment of 5 March 2009; Case C-319/05 *Commission v Germany* [2007] ECR I-9811; Joined Cases C-158/04 and C-159/04 *Alfa Vita v Elliniko Dimosio and Nomarchiaki Aftodioikisi Ioanninon* [2006] ECR I-8135; Case C-383/97 *Van der Loan* [1999] ECR I-731.

paragraph 5 definition, and yet the Belgian rule is finally ruled incompatible not because it makes all imports difficult, but because it makes imports from France harder than those from the United Kingdom (paragraph 9). The traditional view of free trade agreements, and of Article 34, that they are fundamentally about equal treatment of goods from different states,[9] is clearly influential here.

In practice, subsequent case law reflects much of this nuance, and the headline rule of *Dassonville* is not a complete representation of the law on Article 34 TFEU. Nevertheless, it has been influential, and Regan argues that it should never have been used, since it offers an interpretation which does not fit the text of the Article, nor the intention of the Treaty authors.

D. Regan 'An Outsider's View of "Dassonville" and "Cassis de Dijon": On Interpretation and Policy' in M. Poiares Maduro and L. Azoulai (eds.), *The Past and Future of EU Law* (Oxford, Hart, 2010) 465, 465–6

In *Dassonville*, the Court simply announces that all measures that have any tendency to reduce imports are 'measures having equivalent effect' to quantitative restrictions. The implicit argument seems to be: 'Quantitative restrictions reduce imports. Therefore any sort of measure that reduces imports has "equivalent effect"'. This is a bad argument. There are many ways to describe the effects of traditional quantitative restrictions (embargoes and quotas). They do reduce imports. More particularly still, they reduce imports, without reducing domestic production or sales, and their form is such as to ground a (rebuttable) presumption that they are not justified by any positive effects they may have on domestic non-economic values. We now have three descriptions of quantitative restrictions in terms of their effects. Which should the Court choose? The third, the most complete. The Court is going to condemn (presumptively) any measure whose effects fall within its chosen description of quantitative restrictions. So the description it chooses should be complete enough to explain why quantitative restrictions themselves are condemned (presumptively). The description the Court chooses in *Dassonville* fails this test. Only the third description passes this test. And even though it covers many fewer measures than *Dassonville*, the third description still encompasses not only border measures other than core quantitative restrictions (which Articles 31 and 32 of the Treaty of Rome, now repealed, suggest were probably the main thing the drafters were thinking about), but also facially discriminatory internal measures (which they may have been thinking about, with GATT Article III in mind), and arguably even the sort of facially neutral measures on products/packaging/labeling covered by *Cassis de Dijon*.

(ii) Limits of the notion of a MEQR

The situations to which *Dassonville* has been applied are diverse. Examples include government campaigns encouraging consumers to purchase domestic goods;[10] rules requiring electricity suppliers to purchase a percentage of their electricity from domestic wind farms;[11]

---

[9] See G. de Búrca, 'Unpacking the Concept of Discrimination in EC and International Trade Law' in C. Barnard and J. Scott (eds.), *The Law of the European Single Market* (Oxford, Hart, 2002) 181.

[10] Case 249/81 *Commission v Ireland* [1982] ECR 4005; Case 207/83 *Commission v United Kingdom (Marks of Origin)* [1985] ECR 1201.

[11] Case C-379/98 *Preussen Elektra* [2001] ECR I-2099.

obligations on petrol importers to maintain a reserve store;[12] requirements to obtain a licence to import certain goods,[13] even where the licence is a formality granted as of right;[14] public tenders requiring goods made according to national standards;[15] and procedures whereby alcoholic drinks could only be imported via certain state-controlled channels.[16] The most important common factor which these measures share is simply that in practice they hinder imports, or are likely to do so.[17] As the Court of Justice said in *Fra.Bo*, discussing the rule in *Dassonville*, 'the mere fact that an importer might be dissuaded from introducing or marketing the products in question in the Member State concerned constitutes a restriction on the free movement of goods for the importer'.[18] *Dassonville* is usually applied in a very pragmatic and non-theoretical way.

An additional factor linking most measures which the Court of Justice has found to be MEQRs is that they have some unequal effect: either they discriminate against imported products directly, or they create some specific hindrance to cross-border trade which they do not create for internal trade.[19] Even measures which seem at first glance to have equal effects often turn out to have some specifically import-restricting effect upon closer examination. In *Commission* v *Austria*, an Austrian rule prohibiting heavy goods traffic from an alpine motorway, on environmental grounds, was found to contravene Article 34 TFEU.[20] The rule applied without reference to nationality, but the Commission argued, without being contradicted, that most of the heavy trucks on that road were in fact transiting Austria, and were likely to be foreign or to be carrying foreign goods, while local freight traffic tended to use smaller vehicles.

Thus, although the definition in *Dassonville* does not make protectionism or discrimination part of the definition of a MEQR, in practice the Court of Justice has seemed reluctant to extend Article 34 to measures which have no specific cross-border impact, but just reduce trade or economic activity generally. However, several very recent cases call this into question, and suggest that the Court may be letting go of this implicit limit, applying Article 34 whenever access to a market is hindered.

One group of cases has involved rules concerning the use of goods. In *Mickelsson and Roos*, the Finnish Government prohibited the use of jet-skis except on designated waterways, and then did not designate any waterways, so that in practice jet-skis could not be used in Finland.[21] In *Commission* v *Portugal*, a Portuguese measure was successfully challenged which prohibited sticking tinted plastic to car windows to turn them into tinted windows.[22] Then in

---

[12] Case C-398/98 *Commission* v *Greece* [2001] ECR I-7915.

[13] Case C-54/05 *Commission* v *Finland* [2007] ECR I-2473. See also Case C-443/10 *Bonnarde* [2011] ECR I-9327.

[14] Case C-434/04 *Ahokkainen* [2006] ECR I-9171.

[15] Case 45/87 *Commission* v *Ireland* [1988] ECR 4929.

[16] Case C-170/04 *Klas Rosengren and others* v *Riksåklagaren* [2007] ECR I-4071. Also Case C-456/10 *ANETT*, Judgment of 26 April 2012.

[17] Tax measures are generally excluded from Article 34 TFEU; see Case C-383/01 *De Danske Bilimportører* [2003] ECR I-6065; Case 47/88 *Commission* v *Denmark* [1990] ECR 4509.

[18] Case C-171/11 *Fra.Bo*, Judgment of 12 July 2012, para. 22; *Bonnarde*, n. 13 above, para. 26.

[19] See G. Davies, *Nationality Discrimination in the European Internal Market* (The Hague, Kluwer Law International, 2003).

[20] Case C-320/03 *Commission* v *Austria* [2005] ECR I-9871.

[21] Case C-142/05 *Åklagaren* v *Mickelsson and Roos* [2009] ECR I-4273.

[22] Case C-265/06 *Commission* v *Portugal* [2008] ECR I-2245.

Commission v *Italy*, a challenge was brought to Italian rules which prohibited the towing of a trailer behind a motorcycle.[23]

In these three cases there was no outright prohibition on the importation or sale of a product, but a measure which indirectly achieved more or less the same effect. If something cannot be used (jet-skis, tinted window stickers or motorcycle trailers), then in practice trying to import and sell that product will be a hopeless venture. It will not be illegal, but no one will want to buy it.

Case C-110/05 *Commission* v *Italy* [2009] ECR I-519

33. It should be recalled that, according to settled case-law, all trading rules enacted by Member States which are capable of hindering, directly or indirectly, actually or potentially, intra-Community trade are to be considered as measures having an effect equivalent to quantitative restrictions and are, on that basis, prohibited by Article [34 TFEU].

34. It is also apparent from settled case-law that Article [34 TFEU] reflects the obligation to respect the principles of non-discrimination and of mutual recognition of products lawfully manufactured and marketed in other Member States, as well as the principle of ensuring free access of Community products to national markets ...

55. In its reply to the Court's written question, the Commission claimed, without being contradicted by the Italian Republic, that, in the case of trailers specially designed for motorcycles, the possibilities for their use other than with motorcycles are very limited. It considers that, although it is not inconceivable that they could, in certain circumstances, be towed by other vehicles, in particular, by automobiles, such use is inappropriate and remains at least insignificant, if not hypothetical.

56. It should be noted in that regard that a prohibition on the use of a product in the territory of a Member State has a considerable influence on the behaviour of consumers, which, in its turn, affects the access of that product to the market of that Member State.

57. Consumers, knowing that they are not permitted to use their motorcycle with a trailer specially designed for it, have practically no interest in buying such a trailer. Thus, Article 56 of the Highway Code prevents a demand from existing in the market at issue for such trailers and therefore hinders their importation.

58. It follows that the prohibition laid down in Article 56 of the Highway Code, to the extent that its effect is to hinder access to the Italian market for trailers which are specially designed for motorcycles and are lawfully produced and marketed in Member States other than the Italian Republic, constitutes a measure having equivalent effect to quantitative restrictions on imports within the meaning of Article [34 TFEU], unless it can be justified objectively.

The Court of Justice here finds that Article 34 TFEU requires both equal treatment and market access, suggesting that these are not the same: that free trade entails not just stopping discrimination against the foreign, but also removing other rules which may be obstructive to importers. Hence in this case the conclusion was based on the finding that the ban on use took away any reason for consumers to buy the goods, and so effectively prevented the goods

---

[23] Case C-110/05 *Commission* v *Italy* [2009] ECR I-519. See also Case C-142/09 *Lahousse* [2010] ECR I-11685; Case C-433/05 *Sandström* [2010] ECR I-2885. See also the special edition of the *European Journal of Consumer Law* dedicated to these cases ((2012) 2 *EJCL/REDC*, L. G. Gormley, P. Nihoul and E. Nieuwenhuyze (eds.)).

being sold, and, *ergo*, from being imported. Thus while the measure may perhaps have had an unequal effect – in general domestic producers do not make goods which cannot be used in their home state, so goods excluded from the market by the rules are more likely to originate abroad – the Court did not reason on this basis, ignoring comparison and instead focusing on absolute impact on sales. That raises the question whether a measure which merely reduced sales, rather than preventing them, would also be a MEQR.

One kind of measure which could reduce sales, by discouraging consumers from purchasing, would be a restriction on use, rather than the effective total ban that was at issue in *Commission* v *Italy*. In *Sandström* a Swedish rule restricting jet-skis to certain areas of water was challenged, but the Court of Justice found Article 34 not to be infringed. However, it was unclear whether this was because a mere restriction on use was not a MEQR, or whether it was because the restrictions were seen as proportionate environmental measures, providing justification.[24] The door is still open to bringing driving licences and gun licences within the scope of Article 34.

Moreover, *Alfa Vita* goes a step in this direction, using Article 34 to actually prohibit a measure which did not prevent sales, but merely diminished them. This case concerned Greek regulation of the operation of bakeries.[25] Greek law required all bakeries to have an operating licence, which was granted only if they complied with a number of physical requirements, such as having an area for kneading bread and a flour store. A number of supermarkets were prosecuted because they had bakery sections, but did not comply with these norms. Their defence was that they did not in fact make their own bread products, but bought frozen dough, or frozen part-cooked bread, which then simply had to be placed in the ovens for a while to complete its baking process. Thus, the bakery requirements were completely inappropriate to their activities, and imposed an unreasonable cost on their business. The sale of 'bake-off' bread products was burdened and therefore inhibited.

The Court of Justice agreed entirely, finding the rules to be a MEQR. They inhibited the sale of a product which might be imported. However, it did not address the question whether these bakery requirements had any import-specific effect, and there was no discussion of whether the 'bake-off' products were in fact imported or not. It is possible to argue that bread baked on the premises is inevitably a local product, whereas frozen bake-off products may be domestically produced but may equally be imported. Thus rules which favour the former at the expense of the latter will tend to support local products and discourage possible imports. However, the Court did not emphasise this possible inequality. By contrast, its reasoning was merely that by imposing an unreasonable cost on the sale of a product, the rules would inhibit or diminish its sale and therefore also its import.

The judgments in *Commission* v *Italy* and *Alfa Vita* therefore suggest that it is not necessary to show unequal effect to engage Article 34, although the fact that the rules in these cases probably did hit imports particularly hard must temper this conclusion somewhat. Moreover, while *Commission* v *Italy* concerns measures which effectively prevent sales entirely, *Alfa Vita* takes Article 34 further and applies it to a measure which merely inhibited sales by imposing a cost burden. If this is the law, and the fact that a measure has a potential sales-reducing effect is enough to make it a MEQR, then Article 34 is indeed broad.

---

[24] *Sandström*, n. 23 above; Davies, n. 2 above.
[25] Case C-188/04 *Alfa Vita* v *Elliniko Dimosio and Nomarchiaki Aftodioikisi Ioanninon* [2006] ECR I-8135.

It remains to be seen where the Court of Justice will go. The extension of Article 34 to any measure reducing sales, even without unequal effect, would enable its application to a huge range of measures, and potentially raise constitutional problems. It would require some new limit, for example a condition that a measure have a sufficiently 'direct' effect, or that its impact on sales be 'significant' or 'substantial'.[26] As yet the Court has not developed such concepts, and they are sufficiently vague that they might present problems of justiciability.[27] There are therefore good reasons to be sceptical that a true 'market access' approach to Article 34 will ever be implemented, or should be.[28] It may also be noted that *Alfa Vita* is in tension with cases in other areas of free movement, and with another pillar of the case law, *Keck*, a matter discussed further below.[29]

(iii) Form of a MEQR

The form of a MEQR has never been something of great significance. The Court of Justice looks at the effects, and does not limit Article 34 to any particular type of legal measure. National laws and regulations may be caught, but so may administrative practices without a formal legal basis.[30] Most notably, in the *AGM* case, the Court found a mere pronouncement by a public official to comprise a MEQR.[31] AGM, an Italian company, exported lifting machines to Finland. There was some doubt in Finland as to whether they complied with the safety requirements of Finnish law and of the relevant European standards. After negotiations with AGM, which agreed to make some alterations to the machines, the Finnish Government decided that no further action was necessary. However, there were clearly differences of opinion within the safety authorities, because the safety official who had initially investigated the machines, Mr Lehtinen, went on television in an interview and declared that the machines were dangerous, and did not comply with the relevant Directive. A storm of media interest followed, with newspaper reports about 'treacherous vehicle lifts', concern from the Finnish metalworkers union, and so on. Inevitably, sales of AGM machines were badly affected.

The Court was asked to consider whether Mr Lehtinen's statements could be a MEQR. It took into account the fact that he had initially been authorised by his superiors to appear in the interview, but that he was later removed from the case and disciplined for making public statements which did not conform to the official position. The extent to which his statements should therefore be attributed to the state was therefore arguable.

The discussion in the case took place in the context of article 4(1) of the relevant harmonisation Directive. That article provided that machinery complying with the Directive

---

[26] See S. Weatherill, 'After *Keck*: Some Thoughts on How to Clarify the Clarification' (1996) 33 *CMLRev.* 885; C. Barnard, 'Fitting the Remaining Pieces into the Goods and Persons Jigsaw' (2001) 26 *ELRev.* 35; A. Tryfonidou, 'Was *Keck* a Half-baked Solution After All?' (2007) 34 *LIEI* 167.

[27] See Davies, n. 2 above.

[28] J. Snell, 'The Notion of Market Access: A Concept or a Slogan?' (2010) 47 *CMLRev.* 437; G. Davies, 'Understanding Market Access: Exploring the Economic Rationality of Different Conceptions of Free Movement Law' (2010) 11 *German Law Journal* 671.

[29] See pp. 787–8; Case C-544/03 *Mobistar* [2005] ECR I-7723.

[30] Case 21/84 *Commission v France* [1985] ECR 1355; Case C-192/01 *Commission v Denmark* [2003] ECR I-9693; Case C-212/03 *Commission v France* [2005] ECR I-4213.

[31] Case C-470/03 *AGM-COS.MET Srl v Suomen Valtio and Tarmo Lehtinen* [2007] ECR I-2749; see N. Reich, '*AGM-COS.MET* or Who is Protected by EC Safety Regulation?' (2008) 31 *ELRev.* 85; S. De Vries, 'Annotation of *AGM*' (2008) 45 *CMLRev.* 569.

should benefit from free movement. It essentially translates Article 34 TFEU to this particular context.

Case C–470/03 AGM–COS.MET Srl v Suomen Valtio and Tarmo Lehtinen [2007] ECR I–2749

55. ...the referring court's first question should be reformulated so that the court essentially asks whether it is possible to classify the opinions expressed publicly by Mr Lehtinen as obstacles to the free movement of goods for the purposes of Article 4(1) of the Directive, attributable to the Finnish State.

56. Whether the statements of an official are attributable to the State depends in particular on how those statements may have been perceived by the persons to whom they were addressed.

57. The decisive factor for attributing the statements of an official to the State is whether the persons to whom the statements are addressed can reasonably suppose, in the given context, that they are positions taken by the official with the authority of his office.

58. In this respect, it is for the national court to assess in particular whether:
- the official has authority generally within the sector in question;
- the official sends out his statements in writing under the official letterhead of the competent department;
- the official gives television interviews on his department's premises;
- the official does not indicate that his statements are personal or that they differ from the official position of the competent department; and
- the competent State departments do not take the necessary steps as soon as possible to dispel the impression on the part of the persons to whom the official's statements are addressed that they are official positions taken by the State.

59. It remains to examine whether the statements at issue in the main proceedings, on the assumption that they are attributable to the Finnish State, infringe Article 4(1) of the Directive.

60. Any measure capable of hindering, directly or indirectly, actually or potentially, intra-Community trade is to be considered as an obstacle. That principle applies also where the interpretation of Article 4(1) of the Directive is concerned ...

65. Since the statements at issue described the vehicle lifts, in various media and in widely circulated reports, as contrary to standard EN 1493:1998 and dangerous, they are capable of hindering, at least indirectly and potentially, the placing on the market of the machinery.

66. In the light of the above considerations, the answer to Question 1 must be that statements which, by reason of their form and circumstances, give the persons to whom they are addressed the impression that they are official positions taken by the State, not personal opinions of the official, are attributable to the State. The decisive factor for the statements of an official to be attributed to the State is whether the persons to whom those statements are addressed can reasonably suppose, in the given context, that they are positions taken by the official with the authority of his office. To the extent that they are attributable to the State, statements by an official describing machinery certified as conforming to the Directive as contrary to the relevant harmonised standard and dangerous thus constitute a breach of Article 4(1) of the Directive.

It is long established that if the state were to campaign in favour of national products, using appeals to patriotism or chauvinism, or criticising foreign products, this would contravene

Article 34 TFEU.[32] It seems, following *AGM*, that the same principles apply to statements by individual officials where these are reasonably attributed to the state by their addressees, something which will encourage official organs to keep an even stricter rein on their functionaries. The Court went on to find that the normal principles of state liability applied, so that it was open to the national court to find the state liable to compensate AGM. EU law also permitted, but did not require, that officials such as Mr Lehtinen attract personal liability for behaviour amounting to a MEQR.

Cases such as *AGM* beg the question whether Article 34 TFEU has a *de minimis* threshold. Not every comment by a civil servant causes as much excitement as Mr Lehtinen's did. One can imagine discriminatory statements or acts by individuals or authorities that are wrongful in principle, but simply too insignificant to merit much concern. Does Article 34 apply?

(iv) *De minimis*

The Court of Justice's formal position has always been that there is no *de minimis* for the application of Article 34.

Joined Cases 177/82 and 178/82 *Van de Haar* [1984] ECR 1797

13. It must be emphasized in that connection that Article [34 TFEU] does not distinguish between measures having an effect equivalent to quantitative restrictions according to the degree to which trade between Member States is affected. If a national measure is capable of hindering imports it must be regarded as a measure having an effect equivalent to a quantitative restriction, even though the hindrance is slight and even though it is possible for imported products to be marketed in other ways.

Thus, if a measure is a MEQR within the *Dassonville* definition, it is not important that its effect is in fact very small.

However, a quasi-*de minimis* rule is introduced by the doctrine, consistently present in the case law on goods and on the other freedoms, that measures whose effect is too 'uncertain and indirect' will not be caught by the Treaty.

Case C-379/92 *Peralta* [1994] ECR I-3453

23. The national court enquires about the compatibility of the Italian legislation with Article [34 TFEU] insofar as it requires Italian vessels to carry costly equipment. It asks itself whether this makes imports of chemical products into Italy more expensive and therefore creates an obstacle prohibited by that article.

24. On this point, it is sufficient to observe that legislation like the legislation in question makes no distinction according to the origin of the substances transported, its purpose is not to regulate trade in goods with other Member States and the restrictive effects which it might have on the free movement of goods are too uncertain and indirect for the obligation which it lays down to be regarded as being of a nature to hinder trade between Member States.

---

[32] Case 249/81 *Commission v Ireland* [1982] ECR 4005; Case 207/83 *Commission v United Kingdom (Marks of Origin)* [1985] ECR 1201.

This is potentially important in the light of the recent market access cases discussed above.[33] In the event that Article 34 is increasingly applied in the future on the basis that a measure has the effect of reducing sales, the rule in *Peralta* could provide a useful counterbalance, preventing every tax rise or change to public transport becoming subject to Article 34.

(v) Internal situation

Article 34 TFEU only applies to measures hindering imports. If a measure does not apply to imports but only to domestic producers, then in general it will be outside Article 34.[34] Thus, in *Dassonville*, the Court of Justice found that applying the origin-certificates rule to imports was contrary to Article 34, but if the Belgian state had continued to apply that rule only to Belgian drinks brewed in Belgium and bearing origin marks from Belgian towns or regions, this would have been of no interest to EU law. It is true that this approach can lead to reverse discrimination, whereby EU law tolerates a situation in which domestic producers are more heavily burdened by law than importers. However, the Court is unconcerned by this:

> As regards the general principle of non-discrimination, it must be observed that community law does not apply to treatment which works to the detriment of national products as compared with imported products or to the detriment of retailers who sell national products.[35]

In some, relatively unusual, circumstances even though a measure does not apply to imports it may nevertheless create a problem or disadvantage for them and so comprise a MEQR. *Pistre* concerned French law on product designations, and the particular designation 'mountain ham'.[36] Apparently ham from pigs who have lived in the mountains is often particularly good, and so in marketing such ham, specific reference is made to its high altitude origin. To protect the consumer, French law regulated the use of such references. Ham could only be called 'mountain ham' if its production complied with a number of rules. However, in practice it was only possible to comply with these rules if the ham was French. They were so formulated that ham even from very high places in other countries would not comply.

Realising that this amounted to discrimination against imported goods, the French Government chose not to apply the rules to imports. It was therefore possible to sell Spanish or Scottish ham in France which bore the word 'mountain' on the package, or reference to a specific mountain area, without legal problems. In the case, therefore, it was not an importer, but a French producer who complained. He was being prosecuted for selling French ham bearing the word 'mountain' without complying with the rules associated with that name. In his defence he challenged the legality of the French rules. The French Government claimed that since these rules did not apply to imports, Article 34 was not relevant. The Court of Justice disagreed.

---

[33] T. Horsley, 'Unearthing Buried Treasure: Art. 34 TFEU and the Exclusionary Rules' (2012) 37 *ELRev.* 734.
[34] Case C-98/86 *Mathot* [1987] ECR 809.   [35] Case 355/85 *Driancourt* v *Cognet* [1986] ECR 3231, para. 11.
[36] Case C-321/94 *Pistre* [1997] ECR I-2343.

Case C–321/94 *Pistre* [1997] ECR I-2343

43. According to settled case-law, the prohibition laid down in Article [34 TFEU] covers all trading rules enacted by Member States which are capable of hindering, directly or indirectly, actually or potentially, intra-Community trade.

44. Accordingly, whilst the application of a national measure having no actual link to the importation of goods does not fall within the ambit of Article [34 TFEU], Article [34 TFEU] cannot be considered inapplicable simply because all the facts of the specific case before the national court are confined to a single Member State.

45. In such a situation, the application of the national measure may also have effects on the free movement of goods between Member States, in particular when the measure in question facilitates the marketing of goods of domestic origin to the detriment of imported goods. In such circumstances, the application of the measure, even if restricted to domestic producers, in itself creates and maintains a difference of treatment between those two categories of goods, hindering, at least potentially, intra-Community trade.

The Court found that the measure contravened Article 34 even though it only applied to domestic products – in fact precisely because it only applied to domestic products. By having a designation with which only domestic ham could comply, French law provided a marketing advantage to national ham over foreign ham. The mere creation of a distinction between national and foreign products may itself amount to a barrier to imports.[37] This was the case even though the importer was in fact subject to fewer requirements than the domestic producers, and thus at first glance was advantaged rather than disadvantaged.

EU law often also applies indirectly to internal situations, via national law. Sometimes national law prohibits reverse discrimination, meaning that a court faced with internal facts, as in *Pistre*, is required by national law to treat the litigant in the same way as they would were she an importer. This means that the court needs to know what EU law would say in the hypothetical situation that the measure is applied to imports. The Court answers such questions, because the answer is necessary for the national judge if she is to reach her decision. However, the actual situation in question, being internal, is not within the scope of EU law.[38]

A variation on the internal situation is the U-turn, whereby goods are exported and then reimported. This may simply be the result of several sales, from party to party. Sometimes goods are traded quite extensively before reaching the final consumer. However, it may be a deliberate construction, aimed at bringing the goods within Article 34 so that they can benefit from EU law and be exempted from burdensome national rules. In *Au Blé Vert*, the Court of Justice decided that reimports must be treated as imports, unless it could be shown that the goods were exported for the sole purpose of reimportation, in order to circumvent national legislation. This is doctrinally quite straightforward, but raises very difficult questions of evidence.[39] Where

[37] See G. Davies, 'Consumer Protection as an Obstacle to the Free Movement of Goods' (2007) 4 *ERA-Forum* 55.

[38] Case C-448/98 *Guimont* [2000] ECR I-10663; see C. Ritter, 'Purely Internal Situations, Reverse Discrimination, *Guimont*, *Dzodzi* and Article 234' (2006) 31 *ELRev.* 690.

[39] Case 229/83 *Association des Centres Distributeurs Leclerc v SARL 'Au Blé Vert'* [1985] ECR 1.

goods are sold to a trader abroad, and then resold to a new domestic trader, it is a considerable challenge to demonstrate that these were working together.[40]

(vi) Article 34 TFEU and private actors

In contrast to the other fundamental freedoms in the Treaty, the Court of Justice has never clearly applied Article 34 to a purely private measure.[41] Indeed, its usual position is that 'Articles [34 and 35 TFEU] concern only public measures and not the conduct of undertakings'.[42] Where companies or individuals act in a way that excludes foreign products, the Court has usually seen this as a matter for competition law.[43]

This apparent limit to Article 34 is mitigated somewhat by a broad conception of the public. For Article 34 to apply, a body does not have to be formally a part of the government. It is sufficient that it is carrying out a public duty on behalf of the state, or that it is controlled by the state. In *Apple and Pear Development Council*, a body representing fruit growers ran a 'buy English apples and pears' campaign. The council was not a public body, but it enjoyed public law privileges, such as the power to levy fruit growers.

Case 222/82 *Apple and Pear Development Council* [1983] ECR 4083

17. As the Court held in its judgment of 24 November 1982 in Case 249/81 *Commission* v. *Ireland,* a publicity campaign to promote the sale and purchase of domestic products may, in certain circumstances, fall within the prohibition contained in Article [34 TFEU]…, if the campaign is supported by the public authorities…[I]n fact, a body such as the development council, which is set up by the government of a Member State and is financed by a charge imposed on growers, cannot under Community law enjoy the same freedom as regards the methods of advertising used as that enjoyed by producers themselves or producers' associations of a voluntary character.

The Court refers here to the *Buy Irish* case, in which the Irish Government set up a marketing organisation to promote Irish goods.[44] This was clearly discrimination against foreign goods, but was it attributable to the Irish state? They argued that the body was incorporated as an independent company, acting on behalf of Irish producers, for whose actions the state could not be held accountable.

---

[40] Case C-322/01 *Deutscher Apothekerverband* v *DocMorris* [2003] ECR I-14887.

[41] See generally H. Schepel, 'Annotation of *Fra.Bo*' (2013) 9 *European Review of Contract Law* 186; V. Trstenjak and E. Beysen, 'The Growing Overlap of Fundamental Freedoms and Fundamental Rights in the Case-law of the CJEU' (2013) 38 *ELRev.* 293; C. Krenn, 'A Missing Piece in the Horizontal Effect "Jigsaw": Horizontal Direct Effect and the Free Movement of Goods' (2012) 49 *CMLRev.* 177; E. Lohse, 'Fundamental Freedoms and Private Actors' (2007) 13 *EPL* 159; S. Van den Bogaert, 'Horizontality' in C. Barnard and J. Scott (eds.), *The Law of the European Single Market* (Oxford, Hart, 2002) 123. See also pp. 813–20 and 859.

[42] Case 311/85 *Vereniging van Vlaamse Reisbureaus* v *ASBL Sociale Dienst van de Plaatselijke en Gewestelijke Overheidsdiensten* [1987] ECR 3801.

[43] See generally on the competition/free movement boundary W. Sauter and H. Schepel, *State and Market in EU Law* (Cambridge, Cambridge University Press, 2008) ch. 4; K. Mortelmans, 'Towards Convergence in the Application of the Rules on Free Movement and on Competition' (2001) 38 *CMLRev.* 613.

[44] Case 249/81 *Commission* v *Ireland* [1982] ECR 4005.

Case 249/81 *Commission v Ireland* [1982] ECR 4005

23. The first observation to be made is that the campaign cannot be likened to advertising by private or public undertakings…, or by a group of undertakings, to encourage people to buy goods produced by those undertakings. Regardless of the means used to implement it, the campaign is a reflection of the Irish government's considered intention to substitute domestic products for imported products on the Irish market and thereby to check the flow of imports from other Member States.

It is clear that the link between state and organisation does not need to be legally watertight, as long as it is demonstrably real. In this case it was the Irish state that was the object of the Commission's enforcement action, but given the way the Court in *Apples and Pears* draws a parallel between that case and the *Buy Irish* case, it seems likely that it would have been possible to apply Article 34 directly to the Buy Irish organisation itself. This is what happened in the *German Quality Products* case.[45] German producers complying with various quality rules were able to apply for the right to affix a mark to their goods, 'German Quality Product'. This was clearly not available to foreign goods, and so amounted to a discriminatory marketing scheme. It was found to violate Article 34 even though the scheme was operated by a non-governmental body, because that body was a product of statute, and so was essentially acting on behalf of and under the auspices of the state.

Fra.Bo is in several ways similar to *German Quality Products*.[46] It concerned a German body, DVGW, which certified water and gas pipe components as being fit for use and in compliance with the relevant German laws. The complaint was that part of its certification procedure was particularly inaccessible to foreign producers, including Fra.Bo, an Italian producer, making it harder for them to get certified and gain access to the German market. While the body in question was undoubtedly a private organisation, its certificates were recognised in German law, and it was the only body authorised to issue such certificates.

Case C-171/11 *Fra.Bo* v *DVGW*, Judgment of 12 July 2012

24. It is common ground that the DVGW is a non-profit, private-law body whose activities are not financed by the Federal Republic of Germany. It is, moreover, uncontested that that Member State has no decisive influence over the DVGW's standardisation and certification activities, although some of its members are public bodies.

25. The DVGW contends that, accordingly, Article [34 TFEU] is not applicable to it, as it is a private body. The other parties concerned consider that private-law bodies are, in certain circumstances, bound to observe the free movement of goods as guaranteed by Article [34 TFEU].

26. It must therefore be determined whether, in the light of inter alia the legislative and regulatory context in which it operates, the activities of a private-law body such as the DVGW has the effect of giving rise to restrictions on the free movement of goods in the same manner as do measures imposed by the State.

27. In the present case, it should be observed, firstly, that the German legislature has established, in Paragraph 12(4) of the ABVWasserV, that products certified by the DVGW are compliant with national legislation.

---

[45] Case C-325/00 *Commission v Germany (CMA)* [2002] ECR I-9977.
[46] See Schepel, n. 41 above.

28. Secondly, it is not disputed by the parties to the main proceedings that the DVGW is the only body able to certify the copper fittings at issue in the main proceedings for the purposes of Paragraph 12(4) of the ABVWasserV. In other words, the DVGW offers the only possibility for obtaining a compliance certificate for such products....

30. Thirdly, the referring court takes the view that, in practice, the lack of certification by the DVGW places a considerable restriction on the marketing of the products concerned on the German market. Although the ABVWasserV merely lays down the general sales conditions as between water supply undertakings and their customers, from which the parties are free to depart, it is apparent from the case-file that, in practice, almost all German consumers purchase copper fittings certified by the DVGW.

31. In such circumstances, it is clear that a body such as the DVGW, by virtue of its authority to certify the products, in reality holds the power to regulate the entry into the German market of products such as the copper fittings at issue in the main proceedings.

32. Accordingly, the answer to the first question is that Article [34 TFEU] must be interpreted as meaning that it applies to standardisation and certification activities of a private-law body, where the national legislation considers the products certified by that body to be compliant with national law and that has the effect of restricting the marketing of products which are not certified by that body.

Notwithstanding its private origins, DVGW was the bearer of public law privileges and power, in the form of unique certification rights, and it was these legal supports which gave it such power over access to the market. The result is thus quite consistent with previous case law. However, it is notable that the Court of Justice is ambiguous in its reasoning. Paragraphs 25 and 26 suggest that private law bodies are subject to Article 34 TFEU whenever they restrict free movement 'in the same manner as do measures imposed by the state' which seems like a broadening of the law – albeit not a clear one. When are private measures similar to public measures? If this just means that Article 34 applies when private bodies are linked to the state then the case adds nothing new. However, it could also be suggesting an effects-based approach, in which not the actor but the consequence of their actions is central, as appears to be the case in the other freedoms.[47] It may be that even private parties are subject to Article 34 if they have the power to do what laws so often do, and restrain or discourage other parties from engaging in cross-border contracts with each other.[48]

A different kind of situation, sometimes called indirect horizontal effect, arises where the state does not actively support market-closing measures, but simply refrains from taking action against them. This first occurred in *Commission v France*, in which the Court found that France had violated a combination of Articles 34 and 4(3) TEU (the duty of loyalty) by failing to remove French farmers who were blocking border crossings to prevent imported agricultural goods from reaching the French market.[49] The leading case, however, is now *Schmidberger*, in which the relevant principles have been most clearly developed. In *Schmidberger*, a group of Austrian demonstrators blocked motorways coming into Austria from Italy, as a protest against the pollution caused by transit traffic in Alpine valleys. This clearly restricted the import of goods by blocking freight traffic, and the Austrian Government therefore had an

---

[47] See pp. 818–19.

[48] G. Davies, 'Freedom of Movement, Horizontal Effect, and Freedom of Contract' (2012) 20 *European Review of Private Law* 805.

[49] Case C-265/95 *Commission v France (Spanish Strawberries)* [1997] ECR I-6959.

obligation as in *Commission* v *France* to clear the roads. However, this obligation had to be balanced against the fundamental right to association, which the protesters claimed would be violated by an unmitigated application of Article 34. The question, ultimately, was whether the Austrian Government had behaved in a proportionate and reasonable way in the light of the balance which needed to be struck. The Court found that it had, and provided a very clear framework for the balancing of free movement and fundamental rights.

Case C–112/00 *Schmidberger* v *Republic of Austria* [2003] ECR I-5659

57. In this way the Court held in particular that, as an indispensable instrument for the realisation of a market without internal frontiers, Article [34 TFEU] does not prohibit only measures emanating from the State which, in themselves, create restrictions on trade between Member States. It also applies where a Member State abstains from adopting the measures required in order to deal with obstacles to the free movement of goods which are not caused by the State.

58. The fact that a Member State abstains from taking action or, as the case may be, fails to adopt adequate measures to prevent obstacles to the free movement of goods that are created, in particular, by actions by private individuals on its territory aimed at products originating in other Member States is just as likely to obstruct intra-Community trade as is a positive act.

59. Consequently, Articles [34 and 35 TFEU] require the Member States not merely themselves to refrain from adopting measures or engaging in conduct liable to constitute an obstacle to trade but also, when read with Article [4(3) TEU], to take all necessary and appropriate measures to ensure that that fundamental freedom is respected on their territory. Article [4(3) TEU] requires the Member States to take all appropriate measures, whether general or particular, to ensure fulfilment of the obligations arising out of the Treaty and to refrain from any measures which could jeopardise the attainment of the objectives of that Treaty.

60. Having regard to the fundamental role assigned to the free movement of goods in the Community system, in particular for the proper functioning of the internal market, that obligation upon each Member State to ensure the free movement of products in its territory by taking the measures necessary and appropriate for the purposes of preventing any restriction due to the acts of individuals applies without the need to distinguish between cases where such acts affect the flow of imports or exports and those affecting merely the transit of goods....

69. It is apparent from the file in the main case that the Austrian authorities were inspired by considerations linked to respect of the fundamental rights of the demonstrators to freedom of expression and freedom of assembly, which are enshrined in and guaranteed by the ECHR and the Austrian Constitution...

77. The case thus raises the question of the need to reconcile the requirements of the protection of fundamental rights in the Community with those arising from a fundamental freedom enshrined in the Treaty and, more particularly, the question of the respective scope of freedom of expression and freedom of assembly, guaranteed by Articles 10 and 11 of the ECHR, and of the free movement of goods, where the former are relied upon as justification for a restriction of the latter.

78. First, whilst the free movement of goods constitutes one of the fundamental principles in the scheme of the Treaty, it may, in certain circumstances, be subject to restrictions for the reasons laid down in Article [36 TFEU] or for overriding requirements relating to the public interest, in accordance with the Court's consistent case-law since the judgment in Case 120/78 *Rewe-Zentral* (*'Cassis de Dijon'*) [1979] ECR 649.

79. Second, whilst the fundamental rights at issue in the main proceedings are expressly recognised by the ECHR and constitute the fundamental pillars of a democratic society, it nevertheless follows from the express wording of paragraph 2 of Articles 10 and 11 of the Convention that freedom of expression and freedom of assembly are also subject to certain limitations justified by objectives in the public interest, insofar as those derogations are in accordance with the law, motivated by one or more of the legitimate aims under those provisions and necessary in a democratic society, that is to say justified by a pressing social need and, in particular, proportionate to the legitimate aim pursued.

80. Thus, unlike other fundamental rights enshrined in that Convention, such as the right to life or the prohibition of torture and inhuman or degrading treatment or punishment, which admit of no restriction, neither the freedom of expression nor the freedom of assembly guaranteed by the ECHR appears to be absolute but must be viewed in relation to its social purpose. Consequently, the exercise of those rights may be restricted, provided that the restrictions in fact correspond to objectives of general interest and do not, taking account of the aim of the restrictions, constitute disproportionate and unacceptable interference, impairing the very substance of the rights guaranteed.

81. In those circumstances, the interests involved must be weighed having regard to all the circumstances of the case in order to determine whether a fair balance was struck between those interests.

82. The competent authorities enjoy a wide margin of discretion in that regard. Nevertheless, it is necessary to determine whether the restrictions placed upon intra-Community trade are proportionate in the light of the legitimate objective pursued, namely, in the present case, the protection of fundamental rights.

The Court of Justice went on to find that the Austrian authorities had not violated Article 34 TFEU. Their actions reflected a justified and proportionate approach to balancing free movement of goods and the right to demonstrate. The factors which influenced the Court in particular were that this was a lawful and peaceful demonstration, approved in advance, for a limited period of time (around thirty hours), and for the purpose of demonstrating a legitimate concern – the protection of the environment. Moreover, the authorities could show that they had considered whether limiting the place and time of the demonstration so that the effect on goods traffic was reduced was a realistic alternative, but had for reasonable grounds come to the conclusion that these would deprive the demonstration of its very purpose and so be an excessive restriction on the right to demonstrate. Finally, once the demonstration was approved the authorities tried to minimise disruption by diverting traffic to other possible routes. In short, the Austrian authorities were a model of good governance, balancing interests in a carefully reasoned way. *Schmidberger* can be contrasted with *Commission* v *France*, in which the demonstration was explicitly aimed at preventing imports as such yet the French authorities tolerated border closure for an extended and open-ended period, showed little concern about occasional violence by those involved, allowed a climate of fear and hostility to trade to develop and expressed complete passivity over the consequences.

Schmidberger has been criticised because the Court of Justice appears to put the 'fundamental freedom' embodied in Article 34, which is essentially about trade, on an equal level with the fundamental rights to free association and expression.[50] Despite the actual result, it has been argued that the case opens the door to a degradation of the status of fundamental rights. However, as the Court noted, the rights to free expression and assembly are not absolute, and neither is Article 34, so it is

[50] J. Morijn, 'Balancing Fundamental Rights and Common Market Freedoms in Union Law' (2006) 12 *ELJ* 15.

hard to see what the Court could have done other than look for an appropriate balance. However, whether the Court always takes such a rights-friendly stance needs to be considered in the light of recent cases in the field of services, *Laval* and *Viking*, discussed in Chapter 18.[51]

3 PRODUCT STANDARDS AND *CASSIS DE DIJON*

Germany, like a number of EU Member States, traditionally regulates products strictly, leading to a marketplace with a limited range of goods but high quality. This creates problems for importers located in less demanding states. Their goods, made according to different, or laxer, standards do not comply with local rules in many other states and so cannot gain access to the markets of these states. In the early days of European integration this was not seen as unfair. A 'when in Rome' approach was taken.[52] If importers wished to sell in state X they should comply with its rules. *Dassonville* was not generally considered to prohibit product standards if these were equally applicable to domestic and to foreign products.

However, this approach brings with it a number of problems. First, it requires producers to make their products according to a number of different standards, depending upon where they wish to export to. The idea that the internal market will enable consolidation of industry and economies of scale is undermined if factories have to run numerous separate production lines for different markets. Moreover, in practice, producers will not always do this, so that the realisation of an undivided European market will be impeded. Markets will remain local, as producers decide that it is too difficult or expensive to rework their goods to comply with local rules. The markets in smaller states will be particularly isolated, as potential profits are less and may not justify adapting production.

Traditionally such issues were to be dealt with by harmonisation. However, this did not turn out to be the easy and effective market-building tool that some had hoped, as product development and national regulation outpaced the capacity of the European institutions to harmonise.[53] It was in this context, and during a period of European political stagnation, that the Court of Justice intervened with its judgment in *Cassis de Dijon*.

German law required fruit liqueurs to possess at least 25 per cent alcohol. Cassis de Dijon, a blackcurrant liqueur, was made in France and typically contained between 15 and 20 per cent alcohol. As a result it could not be sold in Germany. A German importer, refused authorisation to import and sell *Cassis*, challenged this decision on the basis that it contravened Article 34 TFEU.

Case 120/78 Rewe-Zentral AG v Bundesmonopolverwaltung für Branntwein (Cassis de Dijon) [1979] ECR 649

8. In the absence of common rules relating to the production and marketing of alcohol... it is for the Member States to regulate all matters relating to the production and marketing of alcohol and alcoholic beverages on their own territory.

---

[51] See N. Nic Shuibhne, 'Margins of Appreciation: National Values, Fundamental Rights and EC Free Movement Law' (2009) 34 *ELRev.* 230; C. Kombas, 'Fundamental Rights and Fundamental Freedoms: A Symbiosis on the Basis of Subsidiarity' (2006) 12 *EPL* 433.

[52] The use of the phrase in this context is borrowed from K. Nicolaidis and G. Shaffer, 'Managed Mutual Recognition Regimes: Governance Without Global Government' (2005) 68 *Law and Contemporary Problems* 263.

[53] See Chapter 15.

Obstacles to movement within the community resulting from disparities between the national laws relating to the marketing of the products in question must be accepted insofar as those provisions may be recognized as being necessary in order to satisfy mandatory requirements relating in particular to the effectiveness of fiscal supervision, the protection of public health, the fairness of commercial transactions and the defence of the consumer.

9. The government of the Federal Republic of Germany, intervening in the proceedings, put forward various arguments which, in its view, justify the application of provisions relating to the minimum alcohol content of alcoholic beverages, adducing considerations relating on the one hand to the protection of public health and on the other to the protection of the consumer against unfair commercial practices.

10. As regards the protection of public health the German government states that the purpose of the fixing of minimum alcohol contents by national legislation is to avoid the proliferation of alcoholic beverages on the national market, in particular alcoholic beverages with a low alcohol content, since, in its view, such products may more easily induce a tolerance towards alcohol than more highly alcoholic beverages.

11. Such considerations are not decisive since the consumer can obtain on the market an extremely wide range of weakly or moderately alcoholic products and furthermore a large proportion of alcoholic beverages with a high alcohol content freely sold on the German market is generally consumed in a diluted form.

12. The German government also claims that the fixing of a lower limit for the alcohol content of certain liqueurs is designed to protect the consumer against unfair practices on the part of producers and distributors of alcoholic beverages.

    This argument is based on the consideration that the lowering of the alcohol content secures a competitive advantage in relation to beverages with a higher alcohol content, since alcohol constitutes by far the most expensive constituent of beverages by reason of the high rate of tax to which it is subject.

    Furthermore, according to the German government, to allow alcoholic products into free circulation wherever, as regards their alcohol content, they comply with the rules laid down in the country of production would have the effect of imposing as a common standard within the community the lowest alcohol content permitted in any of the Member States, and even of rendering any requirements in this field inoperative since a lower limit of this nature is foreign to the rules of several Member States.

13. As the Commission rightly observed, the fixing of limits in relation to the alcohol content of beverages may lead to the standardization of products placed on the market and of their designations, in the interests of a greater transparency of commercial transactions and offers for sale to the public.

    However, this line of argument cannot be taken so far as to regard the mandatory fixing of minimum alcohol contents as being an essential guarantee of the fairness of commercial transactions, since it is a simple matter to ensure that suitable information is conveyed to the purchaser by requiring the display of an indication of origin and of the alcohol content on the packaging of products.

14. It is clear from the foregoing that the requirements relating to the minimum alcohol content of alcoholic beverages do not serve a purpose which is in the general interest and such as to take precedence over the requirements of the free movement of goods, which constitutes one of the fundamental rules of the Community.

    In practice, the principal effect of requirements of this nature is to promote alcoholic beverages having a high alcohol content by excluding from the national market products of other Member States which do not answer that description.

It therefore appears that the unilateral requirement imposed by the rules of a Member State of a minimum alcohol content for the purposes of the sale of alcoholic beverages constitutes an obstacle to trade which is incompatible with the provisions of Article [34 TFEU].

There is therefore no valid reason why, provided that they have been lawfully produced and marketed in one of the Member States, alcoholic beverages should not be introduced into any other Member State; the sale of such products may not be subject to a legal prohibition on the marketing of beverages with an alcohol content lower than the limit set by the national rules.

15. Consequently, the first question should be answered to the effect that the concept of 'measures having an effect equivalent to quantitative restrictions on imports' contained in Article [34 TFEU] is to be understood to mean that the fixing of a minimum alcohol content for alcoholic beverages intended for human consumption by the legislation of a Member State also falls within the prohibition laid down in that provision where the importation of alcoholic beverages lawfully produced and marketed in another Member State is concerned.

The Court finds that the application of product standards to imports hinders their importation, as is obviously correct. Therefore such rules, applied to imports, are MEQRs.

The solution, however, is not to prohibit product standards as such. This would result in an unregulated European product market, undesirable for many reasons. By contrast, the Court begins paragraph 8 by noting that since there is no EU legislation harmonising alcohol levels (there is now, there was not then), it is quite legitimate for Member States to regulate this matter. It is thus not the existence of product standards as such that is the problem, but just their application to products imported from other Member States.

The trade-restricting effects of such application are dealt with by developing two ideas, which are the major contribution of *Cassis de Dijon* to EU law, and which are both among the most important legal developments since the Union's foundation.

The first of these is mutual recognition. The Court finds in paragraph 14 that if products comply with the laws of the Member State where they are produced, then there is no reason why they should not be sold in all other Member States. Each Member State is required to accept products made according to the laws of other Member States. What is good enough for France is good enough for Germany. The name subsequently given to this idea is 'mutual recognition', because Member States recognise as adequate each other's laws and regulations, and therefore do not impose additional requirements on products complying with these. This idea is immensely powerful and has become a general principle of EU law, applied not only to the free movement of goods, but throughout the internal market.[54] It provides a conceptual basis for accepting not just foreign products, but foreign qualifications, tests and certificates, official documents, and so on.[55] As a general rule, the foreign (from another Member State) must be recognised as functionally equivalent, at least in all really important respects, to the domestic.

The second idea is that of mandatory requirements. While the Court states that in principle goods from one state should be marketable in all others, it also concedes in paragraph 8 that there may sometimes be a need for derogation from this general principle. Sometimes the

[54] See Chapter 15.   [55] See Chapters 18 and 19.

application of standards to imports may be necessary to protect important interests such as consumer protection or public health. The name given to these, 'mandatory requirements', sounds somewhat odd in English, but has stuck and is still used, although the phrase 'public interest objectives' is now also used.

It is therefore the case that an equally applicable rule which would otherwise violate Article 34 may be saved if it can be shown that it is necessary to protect some public interest objective. There is therefore a balancing process involved, in which proportionality is the central concept. Cases subsequent to *Cassis* are in fact a litany of judicial attempts to decide whether a given general interest is, on the facts, sufficient to justify derogation from the mutual recognition rule. The following two sections go into more detail first on the general rule, and then the application of the mandatory requirement exceptions.

(i) Mutual recognition

It seems fairly intuitive that a factory located in a certain Member State should be subject to the rules and regulations of that state. It also seems fairly intuitive that a product on the supermarket shelves in a Member State should be subject to the rules and regulation in that state. Yet, if products are required to comply with the laws of both the state of production and the state of sale this can create impossible burdens. Imagine, for example, that France had a maximum alcohol limit of 20 per cent and Germany a minimum of 25 per cent; it would be impossible to manufacture in France for sale in Germany. Even without such extreme situations, the burden of complying with two sets of laws would impose cost and inconvenience on producers.

This is, of course, an import-specific problem. Goods sold domestically would face no problem because the state of production and state of sale would be the same. They would only have one set of laws to comply with. However, any goods traded between states would face at least two.[56] The application of product standards to imports would therefore not just make trade difficult, but it would often disadvantage imports relative to domestic production.

The solution is to construct a regime in which a given product (or service, the principle is generalised now) is only subject to one set of rules. If there has been harmonisation then this will provide that unique regulatory framework. However, in the absence of harmonisation the question is whether it is better to apply the rules of the state of sale or of production.

Given that product standards exist to protect the consumers of the products, and that the relevant consumers are in the state of sale, it might seem most logical to make these the relevant laws. On such a model, a factory located in France could gain exemption from local product regulations by declaring that it was manufacturing for export. However, this approach has great practical difficulties. First, it fragments the production process, by requiring producers to make different goods for different markets, as discussed above. Secondly, it is hard to supervise. On the whole, supervision of production facilities is easier than of the marketplace. A factory is fixed, hard to hide and easy to inspect. By contrast, if liqueurs have not been subject to any French laws or control because they were declared to be destined for the German market, then the German authorities will want to conduct very thorough controls

---

[56] See Case C-470/93 *Verein gegen Unwesen in Handel und Gewerbe Köln* v *Mars GmbH* [1995] ECR I-1923.

before admitting them, creating new and significant barriers to movement, and sometimes, given the openness of borders, being hard to enforce. There is a real risk that a choice for state of destination regulation would result in products or services actually escaping any effective supervision.

The Court of Justice in *Cassis* therefore made a choice for regulation by the country of origin. It is now a general rule of free movement law that products or services are primarily subject to the laws of their origin state, and should not, except where mandatory requirements apply, be subjected to further requirements based on destination state law.[57] Joerges has described *Cassis de Dijon* as creating a meta-norm which both parties to a free movement conflict (France and Germany in this case) can accept, and which mediates between their different laws.[58]

This approach has great legal elegance. It has been described as a principle of tolerance, akin to multiculturalism in products, because it requires Member States to accept products that are different from those they are used to domestically.[59] It embodies an idea of 'different but equal'. Moreover, in a few lines it provides a framework for an entire internal market.[60] Using the ideas in *Cassis* it is possible to implement trade between states while still allowing Member States to maintain their own laws and avoiding the need for harmonisation.

Yet, it is open to powerful criticism from various perspectives. It has been claimed that applying mutual recognition results in non-economic concerns being trumped by free trade; that it crushes diversity and replaces it by a deregulated and uniform marketplace;[61] and yet also that it is ineffective in creating free trade, that mutual recognition is too open-ended and abstract to be effectively applied by national courts and authorities.[62] It can even therefore be seen as a stalking horse for harmonisation, an approach to free movement that is apparently based on local diversity of regulation but by its very failure to create a market turns into a justification for centralised rules.[63]

The first criticism is that standards are not in fact equal in different states. While it may be true that all Member States generally ensure that their products are adequately safe, it is a fantasy to think that the quality guaranteed by different standards is the same. Some states have a *laissez-faire* approach to quality regulation, and are content to let the consumer decide

---

[57] See Case C-288/89 *Gouda v Commissariat voor de Media* [1991] ECR I-4007; Directive 2006/123/EC on services in the internal market [2006] OJ L376/36; see Chapter 18.

[58] See C. Joerges and J. Neyer, *Deliberative Supranationalism Revisited*, EUI Working Paper No. 2006/20 (Florence, European University Institute, 2006) 25.

[59] See Nicolaidis and Shaffer, n. 52 above, 317; G. Davies, 'Is Mutual Recognition an Alternative to Harmonisation: Lessons on Trade and Tolerance of Diversity from the EU' in F. Ortino and L. Bartels (eds.), *Regional Trade Agreements and the WTO* (Oxford, Oxford University Press, 2006) 265–80.

[60] For a very thorough discussion of the policy issues, see the special edition of the *Journal of European Public Policy* on mutual recognition: S. Schmidt (ed.), 'Mutual Recognition as a New Mode of Governance' (2007) 14(5) *JEPP*; K. Armstrong, 'Mutual Recognition' in C. Barnard and J. Scott (eds.), *The Law of the European Single Market* (Oxford, Hart, 2002) 225.

[61] See K. Alter and S. Meunier-Aitsahalia, 'Judicial Politics in the European Community: European Integration and the Pathbreaking *Cassis de Dijon* Decision' (1994) 26 *Comparative Political Studies* 535.

[62] See J. Pelkmans, 'Mutual Recognition in Goods: On Promises and Disillusions' (2007) 14 *JEPP* 699; Commission Report to the Council, Parliament and ESC, *Second Biennial Report on the Application of the Principle of Mutual Recognition in the Single Market*, COM(2002)419 final, 23 July 2002.

[63] See Davies, n. 59 above; W. Kerber and R. van den Bergh, 'Mutual Recognition Revisited: Misunderstandings, Inconsistencies, and a Suggested Reinterpretation' (2008) 61 *Kyklos* 447.

what she is prepared to pay for. Others are strict, as will be seen in the subsequent section. Admitting goods made according to foreign laws therefore undermines the quality standards in force in strict states. The populations of those countries are no longer able to express their collective preference for a certain kind of strictly regulated market in which low quality goods are prohibited. Trade trumps both local democracy and product quality.[64]

Moreover, mutual recognition has potential economic effects. The Court of Justice is quite clear that it is not the product rule as such which is contrary to Article 34 TFEU, but its application to imports. Thus, Germany is able to apply its 25 per cent rule to domestically made liqueurs, just not to foreign ones. But this puts German producers at a distinct disadvantage. Alcohol is a significant part of the cost of such liqueurs (one of the reasons for the conflict), so foreign liqueur will probably be cheaper. The German Government is then faced with the choice between abandoning its rule for domestic producers, and moving to a *laissez-faire* marketplace, or continuing to enforce the rule and risking domestic producers being priced out of the market. Ultimately, as the German Government argued in the case, there is a risk that the lowest standard state provides the de facto standard everywhere; their exports are the cheapest products in every shop in Europe. A regulatory race to the bottom is then feared as other states abandon their own rules. In fact, as discussed in Chapter 15, it is notable that this does not always, or even often, happen but the risk is real in some circumstances.

The discussion above may suggest that mutual recognition tends to sacrifice non-economic concerns in the cause of free trade. However, the principle is also criticised from a free trade perspective, with the claim being that in practice it is ineffective.[65] The problem is that applying *Cassis* entails balancing interests, since the possibility of derogations, the mandatory requirements, does exist. This balancing is so politically laden that it is seen as a heavy burden on national judges and authorities, who may well be inclined to defer to national laws and quickly concede their necessity when faced with governmental arguments to that effect.[66] Expecting national bodies to set aside national law to an extent sufficient to really create a single market is perhaps unrealistic. Thus, it can be argued that mutual recognition has not turned out to be the legal panacea it may seem, and leaves many obstacles to movement in place.[67] In practice, what often happens is that litigation over national product rules identifies a particular problem, at which point the Commission may begin the process of harmonisation. *Cassis de Dijon* itself did not lead to a European market in which alcohol products are freely traded on the basis of that mutual recognition. On the contrary, shortly afterwards harmonising legislation on alcohol levels was adopted.

Most of these abstract criticisms depend for their force upon the extent to which mandatory requirements actually limit the general rule of mutual recognition. It is thus these requirements, rather than the general principle, which have been the concrete subject matter of post-*Cassis* legal debate.

---

[64] Kerber and van den Bergh, n. 63 above; H.-C. von Heydebrand u.d. Lasa, 'Free Movement of Foodstuffs, Consumer Protection and Food Standards in the European Community: Has the Court Got it Wrong?' (1991) *ELRev.* 391.

[65] See Pelkmans, n. 62 above.

[66] See M. Jarvis, *The Application of EC Law by National Courts: The Free Movement of Goods* (Oxford, Oxford University Press, 1998) 220–1.

[67] See particularly N. Bernard, 'On the Art of Not Mixing One's Drinks: *Dassonville* and *Cassis de Dijon* Revisited' in M. Poiares Maduro and L. Azoulai (eds.), *The Past and Future of EU Law* (Oxford, Hart, 2010) 456.

(ii) Mandatory requirements

In *Cassis de Dijon*, the Court of Justice provided a list of the sorts of reasons which might justify restricting the free movement of goods. It mentioned the 'effectiveness of fiscal supervision, the protection of public health, the fairness of commercial transactions and the defence of the consumer'. This list was broadened in subsequent cases, and the category of mandatory requirements is now considered to be open-ended. A formulation which is often cited by the Court was used in *Bellamy and English Shop*, where the Court had to consider whether Belgium was justified in applying its food labelling laws to imported English foodstuffs, which the Belgians claimed was necessary to protect the consumer.

Case C-123/00 *Criminal Proceedings Against Bellamy and English Shop Wholesale* [2001] ECR I-2795

18. In that regard, it should be borne in mind that, in the absence of harmonisation of legislation, obstacles to free movement of goods which are the consequence of applying, to goods coming from other Member States where they are lawfully manufactured and marketed, rules that lay down requirements to be met by such goods (such as those relating to designation, form, size, weight, composition, presentation, labelling, packaging) constitute measures having equivalent effect which are prohibited by Article [34 TFEU], even if those rules apply without distinction to all products, unless their application can be justified by a public-interest objective taking precedence over the free movement of goods...

An equally applicable rule restricting movement may therefore be justified by any reason within the umbrella concept of the 'public interest'. The Court of Justice has set certain limits to this concept, such as the rule that purely economic reasons may not be relied upon,[68] and these limits are discussed further in Chapter 20. However, the class of legitimate justifications remains broad. Nevertheless, in practice the majority of cases have concerned consumer protection, while those concerning environmental protection also form an important group. These are looked at in the next two sections, to show how the Court determines what is justified and, in particular, what is proportionate.

The legal status of these judicially invented derogations is odd. Article 36 TFEU provides for exceptions to Article 34 where necessary to protect really important interests such as public health or security.[69] Yet when the Court of Justice referred to mandatory requirements in *Cassis*, it was not offering a broad interpretation of Article 36. On the contrary, it was creating a new class of exception to free movement, existing alongside and in addition to the exceptions in the Treaty.[70] These exceptions are in one sense broader than Article 36: they cover a wider range of interests. However, they are narrower than Article 36 in that they only apply to equally applicable measures.[71] Where a measure discriminates directly, an appeal to the doctrine of mandatory requirements may not be made.

---

[68] Case 72/83 *Campus Oil v Minister for Industry and Energy* [1984] ECR 2727; J. Snell, 'Economic Aims as Justifications for Restrictions on Free Movement' in A. Schrauwen (ed.), *The Rule of Reason: Rethinking Another Classic of European Legal Doctrine* (Groningen, Europa Law Publishing, 2005).

[69] See Chapter 20.

[70] See P. Craig and G. de Búrca, *EU Law* (4th edn, Oxford, Oxford University Press, 2006) 706–7.

[71] Case 788/79 *Gilli and Andres* [1980] ECR 2071.

(a) Consumer protection

The most common justification for applying national product rules to imports is the protection of the consumer. One of the most well-known examples is the *German Beer* case.[72] The Reinheitsgebot, a centuries-old German rule defining the ingredients permitted in beer, was challenged as contrary to Article 34. Many foreign beers used ingredients not on the list, varying from rice to various chemical additives, and so were denied access to the German market under the name beer – they could be sold under some other name, say 'rice-chemical alcoholic beverage', but this was clearly unattractive. The German Government claimed that the rule was necessary to prevent consumers being deceived about what they were buying: the German consumer had certain expectations, which beers made from non-conforming ingredients did not fulfil. The impure brew was simply not, in German eyes, beer.

Case 178/84 *Commission* v *Germany (German Beer)* [1987] ECR 1227

29. It is not contested that the application of article 10 of the Biersteuergesetz to beers from other Member States in whose manufacture raw materials other than malted barley have been lawfully used, in particular rice and maize, is liable to constitute an obstacle to their importation into the Federal Republic of Germany.

30. Accordingly, it must be established whether the application of that provision may be justified by imperative requirements relating to consumer protection.

31. The German government's argument that article 10 of the Biersteuergesetz is essential in order to protect German consumers because, in their minds, the designation 'Bier' is inseparably linked to the beverage manufactured solely from the ingredients laid down in article 9 of the Biersteuergesetz must be rejected.

32. Firstly, consumers' conceptions which vary from one Member State to the other are also likely to evolve in the course of time within a Member State. The establishment of the common market is, it should be added, one of the factors that may play a major contributory role in that development. Whereas rules protecting consumers against misleading practices enable such a development to be taken into account, legislation of the kind contained in article 10 of the Biersteuergesetz prevents it from taking place. As the court has already held in another context (Case 170/78 *Commission* v *United Kingdom*), the legislation of a Member State must not 'crystallize given consumer habits so as to consolidate an advantage acquired by national industries concerned to comply with them'.

33. Secondly, in the other Member States of the Community the designations corresponding to the German designation 'Bier' are generic designations for a fermented beverage manufactured from malted barley, whether malted barley on its own or with the addition of rice or maize. The same approach is taken in Community law as can be seen from heading no. 22.03 of the common customs tariff. The German legislature itself utilizes the designation 'Bier' in that way in article 9(7) and (8) of the Biersteuergesetz in order to refer to beverages not complying with the manufacturing rules laid down in article 9(1) and (2).

34. The German designation 'Bier' and its equivalents in the languages of the other Member States of the Community may therefore not be restricted to beers manufactured in accordance with the rules in force in the Federal Republic of Germany.

---

[72] Case 178/84 *Commission* v *Germany (German Beer)* [1987] ECR 1227.

35. It is admittedly legitimate to seek to enable consumers who attribute specific qualities to beers manufactured from particular raw materials to make their choice in the light of that consideration. However, as the court has already emphasized, that possibility may be ensured by means which do not prevent the importation of products which have been lawfully manufactured and marketed in other Member States and, in particular, 'by the compulsory affixing of suitable labels giving the nature of the product sold'. By indicating the raw materials utilized in the manufacture of beer 'such a course would enable the consumer to make his choice in full knowledge of the facts and would guarantee transparency in trading and in offers to the public'. It must be added that such a system of mandatory consumer information must not entail negative assessments for beers not complying with the requirements of article 9 of the Biersteuergesetz.

The Court of Justice accepted that consumers may have preferences, for example for pure beer, and that their ability to satisfy these preferences was important and deserved protection. However, it took the view that prohibiting the sale as 'beer' of any non-conforming product was disproportionate. Consumers could be adequately protected by a labelling requirement: if it was clear from the label which ingredients the beer contained and whether it was made according to the purity rules then this was sufficient consumer protection, and was more proportionate because it had a far lesser effect on interstate trade. It is easier for foreign beer producers to amend their labels than their product.

This is the Court's consistent approach. It insists that matters of quality and preference, rather than safety or health, do not need to be dealt with by bans, but can be more proportionately addressed by rules on labels.[73] Indeed, its usual standpoint is that protecting the quality of goods as such does not justify a restriction on free movement.[74] This is a coherent part of the Court's relatively liberal philosophy of consumer protection, which assumes that if adequate information is available to consumers they are then able to make their own decisions about quality.[75] This is by contrast with the more paternalistic approach reflected in the rules challenged in *Cassis* and *German Beer*, where the state determined what consumers could buy and what they could not.

This information-based approach assumes that consumers read labels, and are reasonably circumspect.[76] It is vulnerable to the criticism that in fact these assumptions are not true, and consumers will simply seize a product without realising that it is not quite what they are used to. There is a considerable scholarship on whether the information approach is a sensible and proportionate approach to consumer protection, or rather its sacrifice on the altar of free trade.[77]

---

[73] See e.g. Case 261/81 *Ran v De Schmedt* [1982] ECR 3961; Case 407/85 *Drei Glocken* [1988] ECR 4233; see also Case 788/79 *Gilli and Andres* [1980] ECR 2071. See also Joined Cases C-158/04 and C-159/04 *Alfa Vita v El-liniko Dimosio and Nomarchiaki Aftodioikisi Ioanninon* [2006] ECR I-8135, para. 23.

[74] Case C-161/09 *Kakavetsos-Fragkopoulos* [2011] ECR I-915, para. 54; *Alfa Vita*, n. 73 above, para. 23.

[75] See S. Weatherill, *EU Consumer Law and Policy* (Northampton, Edward Elgar, 2005); M. Radeideh, *Fair Trading in EC Law: Information and Consumer Choice in the Internal Market* (Groningen, Europa Law Publishing, 2005).

[76] See Case C-210/96 *Gut Springenheide* [1998] ECR I-4657; Case C-51/94 *Commission v Germany* [1995] ECR I-3599; Case 27/80 *Fietje* [1980] ECR 3839.

[77] See L. W. Gormley, 'The Consumer Acquis and the Internal Market' (2009) 20 *EBLRev.* 409; von Heydebrand u.d. Lasa, n. 64 above; C. Macmaolain, 'Waiter, There's a Fly in My Soup. Yes Sir, that's E120: Disparities Between Actual Individual Behaviour and Regulating Labelling for the Average Consumer in EU Law' (2008) 45 *CMLRev.* 1147; M. Radeideh, *Fair Trading in EC Law: Information and Consumer Choice in the Internal Market* (Groningen, Europa Law Publishing, 2005); H. Unberath and A. Johnston, 'The Double-headed Approach of the

This debate can be kept in perspective by remembering that it is only quality that is in issue. Where there is a genuine health risk, the Court of Justice is much more deferential to national rules.[78] Moreover, there is an issue of principle involved, which is addressed in paragraph 32 of the judgment above: consumer behaviour and expectations are not fixed, but changing, and so the law should not try to entrench them as they are, but provide a framework within which they can develop. The European consumer may be unused to diversity, but the goals of the internal market are that she should become used to this, and this means she will need to become someone used to making decisions on the basis of information, rather than having products selected for her by the state. Whether this is necessarily an improvement in quality of life is another issue, but it is a persuasive corollary of the free trade agreement which Article 34 TFEU represents.

In the judgment, this question of consumer change was framed around the issue of naming. The German Government had argued that impure beer was, in the eyes of the local consumer, not beer. The Court took this as an example of the kind of expectation which must not be crystallised in law, precisely because it has a trade-hindering effect.[79] The Court further suggested that what is 'beer' should be understood in the context of other national definitions and the EU customs definition. National product definitions no longer stand in isolation.

This has recurred in several cases. Italy challenged the phrase 'apple vinegar' saying that it was a fraud on consumers because vinegar was inherently made from grapes, while France challenged foreign foie gras which did not entirely conform to French rules.[80]

Case C-184/96 *Commission v France* [1998] ECR I-6197

23. So far as concerns the argument based on the necessity to prevent offences with respect to false descriptions, the Court, in its judgment in *Deserbais*, did not exclude the possibility that Member States could require those concerned to alter the denomination of a foodstuff where a product presented under a particular denomination is so different, as regards its composition or production, from the products generally known under that denomination in the Community that it cannot be regarded as falling within the same category (Case 286/86 *Ministère Public* v *Deserbais* [1988] ECR 4907).

24. Nonetheless, the mere fact that a product does not wholly conform to the requirements laid down in national legislation on the composition of certain foodstuffs with a particular denomination does not mean that its marketing can be prohibited.

If someone tried to market a generic paté as foie gras, it would be justifiable to prevent this on consumer protection grounds. However, the fact that foie gras is made in slightly different ways in other places is not enough to justify a prohibition on using the name.

ECJ Concerning Consumer Protection' (2007) 44 *CMLRev.* 1237; S. Weatherill, 'Recent Case Law Concerning the Free Movement of Goods: Mapping the Frontiers of Market Deregulation' (1999) 36 *CMLRev.* 51; S. Weatherill, *EU Consumer Law and Policy* (Northampton, Edward Elgar, 2005).

[78] See Chapter 20.

[79] See also Case C-358/01 *Commission* v *Spain* [2003] ECR I-13145, para. 52.

[80] Case 788/79 *Gilli and Andres* [1980] ECR 2071; Case C-166/03 *Commission* v *France (Gold)* [2005] ECR I-6535; Case C-12/00 *Commission* v *Spain (Spanish Chocolate)* [2003] ECR I-459; Case C-14/00 *Commission* v *Italy (Chocolate)* [2003] ECR I-513; Case C-358/01 *Commission* v *Spain* [2003] ECR I-13145; see also Case C-6/02 *Commission* v *France* [2003] ECR I-2389.

The concept of the informed and circumspect consumer defines the Court of Justice's approach to consumer protection, but leaves open the question of what information the consumer can be expected to process and understand, and how much information she needs. While labelling requirements are in general the legislative approach that states should follow, even these may be disproportionate under some circumstances. Because the label is a physical part of the product, national labelling rules are themselves product rules in the *Cassis* sense, and so must still be justified. Labelling requirements impose relatively low costs on producers, and so are preferable to rules about the product itself, but they do impose some costs, so that if the labelling rules are in some sense unreasonable then these too will be contrary to Article 34 TFEU.

There are two kinds of potential labelling problems. One is where the information to be displayed is in some sense discriminatory. The Court warned about this in *German Beer*. If, for example, non-conforming beer was required to bear a red stamp saying 'impure' then while this might not be very difficult to comply with, and while it might make matters clear to the consumer, it would nevertheless contravene Article 34 because it would have an unnecessarily negative effect on marketing of foreign beer, and so would be disproportionate. Something rather similar to this occurred in the *Irish Souvenirs* case, in which Ireland proposed that souvenirs not made in Ireland be stamped with their country of production or with the word 'foreign'.[81] A requirement to indicate the country of production, even if it applies to all goods, the Court has found, may have the effect of steering consumers towards national goods, while it is not in fact necessary information.[82]

The other kind of labelling problem is where the information to be displayed is pointless. When Belgium required medicinal labels to bear the 'notification number' which was associated with the application for approval to sell that medicine in Belgium, the Court found this to be disproportionate.[83] It imposed a small, but not trivial, burden on producers while realistically, what use was it to the consumer?

The protective approach to product regulation which was traditionally applied to the substance of the goods can also be seen in national rules on packaging and information. In *Clinique*, for example, the German Government objected to the marketing of cosmetics under that name, because it was too similar to *Klinik*, the German word for hospital.[84] Consumers might therefore think that the products were medically approved, and believe that they really would look younger or more beautiful if they used them.

The Court of Justice disagreed. In the circumstances (the products were sold not by pharmacists but in shops selling make-up), it felt the dangers did not justify the trade-hindering effects of the rule. The European consumer is expected to show a certain awareness and scepticism. If this is not yet always reality, that fact does not justify legislation entrenching passivity and naivety.

(b) Protection of the environment

Environmental issues are often dealt with under Article 36 TFEU, and are discussed further in Chapter 20. However, the protection of the environment has also been recognised as a

---

[81] Case 113/80 *Commission v Ireland (Irish Souvenirs)* [1981] ECR 1625.
[82] *Ibid.*; Case 207/83 *Commission v United Kingdom (Marks of Origin)* [1985] ECR 1201.
[83] Case C-217/99 *Commission v Belgium* [2000] ECR I-10251; Case C-55/99 *Commission v France* [2000] ECR I-11499.
[84] Case C-315/92 *Verband Sozialer Wettbewerb v Clinique Laboratories* [1994] ECR I-317.

mandatory requirement, especially in the context of recycling schemes and their effect on trade.

These recycling cases have been about soft drinks containers. In each case a state has imposed obligations on producers related to the types of containers they used for their drinks. In *Commission* v *Denmark*, a system was successfully challenged in which only certain types of soft drinks containers were permitted in Denmark, the goal being to make recycling more efficient and practical.[85] Since this dramatically limited the possibilities for importing soft drinks from elsewhere in Europe where many different kinds of containers were in use, the rule was disproportionate. The reasoning of the Court of Justice was that it was not necessary to limit the types of containers, since the goal of promoting recycling could be met by other means.

The case was heavily criticised.[86] While it is, of course, true that many different kinds of containers can be recycled, the point is that this is expensive. A recycling scheme is most efficient if it only has to deal with a limited range of packaging types. In reality, recycling will be successful if it is not too expensive, and so the Danish considered that their strict limits on container types were in fact an essential part of increasing the amount of recycling. That the Court did not consider economic reality, but merely the theoretical fact that other kinds of containers were in principle also recyclable, suggested that environmental protection was not being taken seriously, and would be subordinated to trade.

In more recent cases, the environment has been more successful. In *Radlberger Getränkegesellschaft*, the German Government amended its laws to require producers selling more than a certain proportion of soft drinks in non-reusable containers to set up a deposit-and-return scheme, whereby they would take back the waste packaging they generated, and deal with it themselves.[87] Since such a scheme costs money, producers using a large proportion of non-reusable packaging faced a cost burden which might hinder their access to the German market. The Court of Justice was particularly concerned about the fact that non-German producers used more non-recyclable packaging than German ones, so that they would be relatively more affected. Moreover, a return system is clearly more expensive if the goods have to be returned to a distant production location in another state than if production is local. The scheme therefore imposed a greater burden on more distant producers. In the light of this, the Court considered whether the environmental benefits outweighed these trade concerns.

Case C-309/02 *Radlberger Getränkegesellschaft mbH & Co.* v *Land Baden-Württemberg* [2004] ECR I-11763

75. In accordance with settled case-law, national measures capable of hindering intra-Community trade may be justified by overriding requirements relating to protection of the environment provided that the measures in question are proportionate to the aim pursued.

---

[85] Case 302/86 *Commission* v *Denmark* [1988] ECR 4607.

[86] See J. Scott, *EC Environmental Law* (London, Longman, 1998) 69–72, quoted in J. Holder and M. Lee, *Environmental Protection: Law and Policy* (Cambridge, Cambridge University Press, 2007) 179; H. Temmink, 'From Danish Bottles to Danish Bees: The Dynamics of Free Movement of Goods and Environmental Protection – A Case Law Analysis' (2000) 1 *YEEL* 61.

[87] Case C-309/02 *Radlberger Getränkegesellschaft* v *Land Baden-Württemberg* [2004] ECR I-11763; see also the almost identical Case C-463/01 *Commission* v *Germany* [2004] ECR I-11705, decided on the same day.

76. The obligation to establish a deposit and return system for empty packaging is an indispensable element of a system intended to ensure that packaging is reused.

77. With regard to non-reusable packaging, as the defendant in the main proceedings and the German Government state, the establishment of a deposit and return system is liable to increase the proportion of empty packaging returned and results in more precise sorting of packaging waste, thus helping to improve its recovery. In addition, the charging of a deposit contributes to the reduction of waste in the natural environment since it encourages consumers to return empty packaging to the points of sale.

78. Furthermore, insofar as the rules at issue in the main proceedings make the entry into force of a new packaging-waste management system conditional on the proportion of reusable packaging on the German market, they create a situation where any increase in sales of drinks in non-reusable packaging on that market makes it more likely that there will be a change of system. Inasmuch as those rules thus encourage the producers and distributors concerned to have recourse to reusable packaging, they contribute towards reducing the amount of waste to be disposed of, which constitutes one of the general objectives of environmental protection policy.

79. However, in order for such rules to comply with the principle of proportionality, it must be ascertained not only whether the means which they employ are suitable for the purpose of attaining the desired objectives but also whether those means do not go beyond what is necessary for that purpose.

80. In order for national rules to satisfy the latter test, they must allow the producers and distributors concerned, before the deposit and return system enters into force, to adapt their production methods and the management of non-reusable packaging waste to the requirements of the new system. While it is true that a Member State may leave to those producers and distributors the task of setting up that system by organising the taking back of packaging, the refunding of sums paid by way of deposit and any balancing of those sums between distributors, the Member State in question must still ensure that, at the time when the packaging-waste management system changes, every producer or distributor concerned can actually participate in an operational system.

81. Legislation, such as the VerpackV, that makes the establishment of a deposit and return system dependent on a packaging reuse rate, which is certainly advantageous from an ecological point of view, complies with the principle of proportionality only if, while encouraging the reuse of packaging, it gives the producers and distributors concerned a reasonable transitional period to adapt thereto and ensures that, at the time when the packaging-waste management system changes, every producer or distributor concerned can actually participate in an operational system.

In principle, therefore, the Court of Justice was prepared to accept rules which would not only have a significant effect on trade, but probably impact on importers much more than on domestic producers, because those rules did serve an important environmental goal. The only requirements that it imposed, in the name of proportionality, was that producers be given a reasonable amount of time to adapt to the new rules and that the system be so constructed that producers were in practice able to participate and comply. This rather procedural approach to proportionality is also found in other cases, where the Court has preferred to examine whether the state has taken account of all interests and considered alternatives, rather than engaging too deeply in the substantive policy choice.[88]

[88] Case C-28/09 *Commission v Austria*, Judgment of 21 December 2011; *Bonnarde*, n. 13 above. S. Prechal, 'Free Movement and Procedural Requirements: Proportionality Reconsidered' (2008) 35 *Legal Issues of Economic Integration* 201.

4 SELLING ARRANGEMENTS AND *KECK*

The acceptance in *Cassis* that equally applicable rules could be MEQRs led to cases testing the limits of this principle, applying it to any kind of measure which could be argued to have a negative effect on import quantities. Most well-known, the rules on Sunday trading in the United Kingdom were challenged as contrary to Article 34 TFEU: if shops could open on Sundays they could sell more goods, and some of those goods would be imported.[89] *Ergo*, requiring shops to close on Sundays limited imports.

This turns a Treaty Article that is apparently about goods into a tool for policing wider socio-economic regulation, which brings with it risks of constitutional discontent among the Member States. Moreover, it is inefficient. In the Sunday trading cases, the Court of Justice unsurprisingly found that the measures were justified by legitimate social goals, and therefore not contrary to the Treaty. All that was happening was that many creative cases were being brought, but they were not being won. Such a broad reading of the Treaty was not therefore opening up the internal market or increasing trade. It was just increasing work for the Court.

In *Keck*, the Court of Justice finally set a limit to the kinds of equally applicable rules which could be MEQRs. It excluded one group, which it called *selling arrangements*. These, it said, were simply outside the scope of the Treaty, as long as they were in fact equal in impact on both domestic goods and imports.

Joined Cases C–267/91 and C–268/91 *Keck and Mithouard* [1993] ECR I–6097

11. By virtue of Article [34 TFEU], quantitative restrictions on imports and all measures having equivalent effect are prohibited between Member States. The Court has consistently held that any measure which is capable of directly or indirectly, actually or potentially, hindering intra-Community trade constitutes a measure having equivalent effect to a quantitative restriction.

12. National legislation imposing a general prohibition on resale at a loss is not designed to regulate trade in goods between Member States.

13. Such legislation may, admittedly, restrict the volume of sales, and hence the volume of sales of products from other Member States, insofar as it deprives traders of a method of sales promotion. But the question remains whether such a possibility is sufficient to characterize the legislation in question as a measure having equivalent effect to a quantitative restriction on imports.

14. In view of the increasing tendency of traders to invoke Article [34 TFEU] as a means of challenging any rules whose effect is to limit their commercial freedom even where such rules are not aimed at products from other Member States, the Court considers it necessary to re-examine and clarify its case-law on this matter.

15. It is established by the case-law beginning with '*Cassis de Dijon*' that, in the absence of harmonization of legislation, obstacles to free movement of goods which are the consequence of applying, to goods coming from other Member States where they are lawfully manufactured and marketed, rules that lay down requirements to be met by such goods (such as those relating to designation, form, size, weight, composition, presentation, labelling, packaging) constitute measures of equivalent effect prohibited by Article [34 TFEU].

---

[89] See e.g. Case C-145/88 *Torfaen Borough Council v B & Q* [1989] ECR 3851; Case C-169/91 *Stoke-on-Trent and Norwich City Council v B & Q* [1992] ECR I-6635; for full discussion see C. Barnard, *The Substantive Law of the EU* (3rd edn, Oxford, Oxford University Press, 2010) 117–23.

This is so even if those rules apply without distinction to all products unless their application can be justified by a public-interest objective taking precedence over the free movement of goods.

16. By contrast, contrary to what has previously been decided, the application to products from other Member States of national provisions restricting or prohibiting certain selling arrangements is not such as to hinder directly or indirectly, actually or potentially, trade between Member States within the meaning of the *Dassonville* judgment, so long as those provisions apply to all relevant traders operating within the national territory and so long as they affect in the same manner, in law and in fact, the marketing of domestic products and of those from other Member States.

17. Provided that those conditions are fulfilled, the application of such rules to the sale of products from another Member State meeting the requirements laid down by that State is not by nature such as to prevent their access to the market or to impede access any more than it impedes the access of domestic products. Such rules therefore fall outside the scope of Article [34 TFEU].

18. Accordingly, the reply to be given to the national court is that Article [34 TFEU] of the EEC Treaty is to be interpreted as not applying to legislation of a Member State imposing a general prohibition on resale at a loss.

The rule that the Court of Justice lays down is that rules governing the way products are sold are not MEQRs within the meaning of *Dassonville* and Article 34 TFEU. Member States may therefore legislate however they like on matters such as advertising, shop opening hours, sales techniques and prices.[90] However, this is subject to the proviso that the measures taken must not have a greater effect on imports than they do on domestic goods or producers. If this is the case, then even measures concerning selling arrangements will be MEQRs. It has been made clear in later cases that the usual approach then applies: such measures will be prohibited unless they are justified by a mandatory requirement or a Treaty exception.[91]

The reasoning provided by the Court for this position is that, it says, rules on selling arrangements do not generally have the effect of preventing access to the market for imports, nor of impeding it any more than is the case for domestic products. If a shop has to close on Sundays, or advertising of certain goods is prohibited, this does not actually prevent those goods being sold. It may have some effect on their sales, but in general this effect is the same for domestic and foreign goods. The implicit contrast is with product rules, which do tend to prevent non-conforming products reaching the market, and which also tend to impact on foreign goods more than domestic.

Keck therefore interprets Article 34 to prohibit two things: (i) measures which have a greater effect on imports than on domestic products; and (ii) measures which effectively prevent certain imports from being sold.[92] This second category does not appear to be dependent upon showing any unequal effect, although it may be argued that in practice the complete exclusion of a class of goods from the marketplace almost invariably has the effect of protecting established, usually national, alternatives.

Keck therefore broadly reflects an inequality-based understanding of Article 34 TFEU. It is for this reason that *Alfa Vita*, discussed above,[93] is so surprising: the measure involved was

---

[90] See nn. 109–10 below for examples of the range of selling arrangements.
[91] See e.g. Case C-20/03 *Burmanjer* [2005] ECR I-4133; Case C-441/04 *A-Punckt Schmuckhandels* [2006] ECR I-2093.
[92] *Keck and Mithouard*, n. 2 above, paras. 16 and 17.   [93] See p. 762.

argued neither to be unequal in effect, nor to prevent access completely, but merely to reduce sales. *Alfa Vita* and *Keck* apply to different categories of measures, so there is no hard conflict, but there is a conceptual inconsistency. It is as if the idea of a MEQR underlying the law on selling arrangements is not the same as that underlying the law on other types of MEQR. This highlights the ongoing policy tensions surrounding Article 34, between those who would like to see it used to reduce all unjustified regulatory inhibition of economic activity *(Alfa Vita)*, and those who remain attached to a non-discrimination rule *(Keck)*.[94]

The tensions are captured in *Ker-Optika*, in a judgment which brings together and summarises the various lines of case law within Article 34. The case concerned a Hungarian rule preventing the sale of contact lenses by Internet, a selling arrangement of obviously unequal effect.

Case C-108/09 *Ker-Optika* [2010] ECR I-12213

47. According to settled case-law, all trading rules enacted by Member States which are capable of hindering, directly or indirectly, actually or potentially, trade within the European Union are to be considered as measures having an effect equivalent to quantitative restrictions and are, on that basis, prohibited by Article 34 TFEU.

48. It is also apparent from settled case-law that Article 34 TFEU reflects the obligation to comply with the principles of non-discrimination and of mutual recognition of products lawfully manufactured and marketed in other Member States, as well as the principle of ensuring free access of EU products to national markets.

49. Accordingly, measures adopted by a Member State the object or effect of which is to treat products coming from other Member States less favourably are to be regarded as measures having an effect equivalent to quantitative restrictions, as are rules that lay down requirements to be met by such goods, even if those rules apply to all products alike.

50. Any other measure which hinders access of products originating in other Member States to the market of a Member State is also covered by that concept.

51. For that reason, the application to products from other Member States of national provisions restricting or prohibiting certain selling arrangements is such as to hinder directly or indirectly, actually or potentially, trade between Member States for the purposes of the case-law flowing from *Dassonville*, unless those provisions apply to all relevant traders operating within the national territory and affect in the same manner, in law and in fact, the selling of domestic products and of those from other Member States. The application of such rules to the sale of products from another Member State meeting the requirements laid down by that State is by nature such as to prevent their access to the market or to impede such access more than it impedes the access of domestic products.

So if a measure impedes market access equally for foreign and domestic goods is it outside Article 34, following the logic of *Keck*, or within it, because it is nevertheless a restriction on market access, following the wording of *Commission v Italy*? Both views are contained within the extract above.[95] The ambiguous language of the case law on market access and Article 34 suggests an ongoing judicial struggle with this apparently principled choice.[96]

---

[94] See Chapter 15, pp. 671–3.   [95] *Ibid.*
[96] Snell, n. 28 above; P. Pecho, 'Good-Bye *Keck*: A Comment on the Remarkable Judgment in *Commission v Italy*' (2009) 36 *LIEI* 257.

Economists, however, might just finesse it: where measures have truly equal effects on all market actors they do not generally restrict market access at all, simply creating a universal cost which can be safely passed onto consumers without competitive consequences. Similarly, if a measure does in fact restrict market access, in the sense that it hinders new firms from entering a market, then it necessarily protects incumbents, and so has an inherently unequal effect. Moreover, in the internal market incumbents are disproportionately national, so that this inequality will also be protectionist. Hence a choice between market access or inequality as a basis for defining a MEQR may be a false one: it is the essence of measures with unequal effects that they restrict access for some, and it is the essence of restricting market access that it creates market inequality.[97]

Keck is not just a controversial case because of these doctrinal ambiguities, but also because its business sense has been doubted.[98] In reality, it has been argued, rules on advertising may have a greater effect on sales of goods than some product rules do. Adapting a product is not always expensive or difficult, while there may be contexts where an inability to advertise, or to sell via certain channels, or to offer certain kinds of discounts (all of which are selling arrangements) might seriously undermine a marketing campaign and make market access impractical. *Keck* is often considered to be a very formalistic approach to Article 34 TFEU. Instead of trying to distinguish between rules according to their actual effect on trade, it divides them into convenient, but somewhat arbitrary, groups which do not correspond to practical importance for the trader.

The advantage of this division is that it is relatively clear. In most cases it is easy to distinguish between a selling arrangement and a product rule, and both states and market actors are able to determine what their legal position is. An alternative interpretation of Article 34 which is sometimes put forward is that it should prohibit all measures which substantially restrict market access, relying on this effect to engage Article 34 and not *a priori* categories of measure. This interpretation is very close to the goals of the Article, and has an obvious integrationist appeal, but would result in a very open and vague rule. It is, moreover, open to question whether such an open norm would be effective in practice because it would be so difficult to apply in an apparently apolitical way, perhaps causing national judges to be shy of using it forcefully.[99]

There is also a principled defence of the categorisation created by *Keck*. Unlike product rules, selling arrangements do not impose a double burden on imports, nor do selling arrangements require products to be adapted at all, so there is no question of excluding non-conforming goods. There is a fundamental difference between the market effects of selling arrangements and the market effects of product rules, which does not make it entirely obvious that they should be treated in the same way.

Keck also needs to be seen in constitutional terms given the important limit it sets to the Union's capacity to second-guess state regulatory choices. Maduro's constitutional interpretation of *Keck* has been one of the most influential.[100] He notes that when states regulate economic

---

[97] Snell, n. 28 above; Davies, n. 28 above.

[98] L. Gormley, 'Two Years after *Keck*' (1996) 19 *Fordham International Law Journal* 866; Weatherill, n. 26 above. Cf. L. Rossi, 'Economic Analysis of Article 28 after the *Keck* Judgment' (2006) 7(5) *German Law Journal* 479.

[99] See D. Wilsher, 'Does *Keck* Discrimination Make Any Sense? An Assessment of the Non-discrimination Principle within the European Single Market' (2008) 33 *ELRev.* 3.

[100] M. Poiares Maduro, *We the Court* (Oxford, Hart, 1998).

activity this does not only have an effect on domestic actors, but also on foreign ones who want to participate in the domestic market. Yet, while domestic actors are represented in the law-making process via national democratic institutions, foreign actors, in general, are not. States therefore impose costs on non-domestic actors without taking this into account. In the context of an integrating Union in which states accept a certain degree of responsibility towards each other, this should be seen as a democratic problem. The justification for the Court of Justice's intervention in national economic regulation is therefore that it safeguards the interests of the unrepresented foreign actor.[101]

This logic explains the different approaches to product rules and selling arrangements, the one being presumptively contrary to Article 34 and the other presumptively compatible: when states regulate products they usually produce legislation reflecting local production norms – established tastes and products – and do not consider what is accepted or usual elsewhere, with the effect that their legislation tends to have a protectionist effect. However, where selling arrangements are concerned this is not the case. The legislator makes a trade-off between economic freedom and other interests, but in general the interests and concerns of the importer are exactly the same as those of the domestic producers. Both want, for example, freedom to advertise and set prices, and both want this for the same reasons. If the domestic producers are represented in the domestic democratic process then this serves as an adequate proxy for foreign producers, and there should usually be no need for a democratically-justified correction of national law by the Court of Justice.

In any case, *Keck* has resisted criticism from many commentators and is still a pillar of the Court's case law. Its apparent clarity and ease of use are among the major reasons for its resilience. Yet, while most of the time it is fairly easy to see whether a measure is a selling arrangement and whether it has an unequal effect, there are cases where this becomes very difficult.

(i) Notion of a selling arrangement

The distinction between a selling arrangement and a product rule was laid down in *Familiapress*.[102] A product rule is a measure which requires some physical aspect of the product or its packaging or labelling to be changed, while a selling arrangement is concerned only with the way in which goods are sold or marketed. Measures conforming to neither definition are to be considered under *Dassonville*.

The boundary between categories becomes difficult when measures are concerned with the sale of particular types of products, for example a rule restricting sale of alcohol with a percentage above 25 per cent to licensed shops. Is that a product rule, because it is to do with the amount of alcohol in the drink, or a selling arrangement, because it regulates the place where the product is sold? The Court of Justice seems to find rules like this to be product rules, because the obligation or burden that they contain is specifically linked to the physical characteristics of the product. There is thus a pressure, if not an absolute requirement, on producers to amend their product to avoid the burdensome rule.

---

[101] Cf. D. Regan, 'An Outsider's View of "Dassonville" and "Cassis de Dijon": On Interpretation and Policy' in M. Poiares Maduro and L. Azoulai (eds.), *The Past and Future of EU Law* (Oxford, Hart, 2010) 465.

[102] Case C-368/95 *Familiapress v Heinrich Bauer Verlag* [1997] ECR I-3689. See also Case C-159/00 *Sapod Audic* [2002] ECR I-5031.

For example, in *Schwarz*, an Austrian rule was in issue which prohibited the sale of un-wrapped bubble gum from vending machines.[103] This was said to be unhygienic. The Court found that this was a product rule because those 'importers wishing to put those goods up for sale in Austria have to package them'. A producer who wanted to sell bubble gum to vend-ing machine operators in Austria would have to make adjustments to her production process. Similarly, in *Dynamic Medien*, a rule prohibiting the sale by mail order of DVDs without an age-classification sticker was found to be a product rule, because the rule, while restricting the method of sale, was linked to a physical part of the packaging.[104]

By contrast, *Morellato* concerned an Italian law on semi-baked bread.[105] This is bread that is bought by shops as half-baked frozen dough. The shops then finish baking it in their own ovens. This enables them to sell warm fresh bread, without having all the facilities for making bread from scratch. The process is quite controversial in some countries, because it threatens the traditional artisanal baker, and enables all kinds of shops to apparently sell their own freshly-baked bread. It was in this context that Italy required shops selling bread made by this process to prepackage it in bags with labels clearly indicating its nature. The measures informed the consumer, but also distinguished the bread from bread made on the premises, which did not need to be packaged, allowing this latter to preserve some distinctive aura of naturalness.

The Court of Justice found that the measure was a selling arrangement.

Case C-416/00 *Morellato* [2003] ECR I-9343

32. The distinctive feature of the main proceedings is that the product put on sale by Mr Morellato was imported at a stage when its production process was not yet finished. In order to be able to market the product in Italy as bread ready for consumption, it was necessary to complete the baking of the pre-baked bread imported from France.

33. The fact that a product must, to a certain extent, be transformed after importation does not in itself preclude a requirement relating to its marketing from falling within the scope of application of Article [34 TFEU]. It is possible that, as in the main proceedings, the imported product is not simply a component or ingredient of another product but in reality constitutes the product that is intended for marketing as soon as a simple transformation process has been carried out.

34. In such a situation, the relevant question is whether the requirement for prior packaging laid down in the legislation of the Member State of import makes it necessary to alter the product in order to comply with that requirement.

35. In the present case, nothing in the file indicates that it was necessary for the pre-baked bread, as imported into Italy, to be altered in order to comply with that requirement.

36. In those circumstances, the requirement for prior packaging, since it relates only to the marketing of the bread which results from the final baking of pre-baked bread, is in principle such as to fall outside the scope of Article [34 TFEU], provided that it does not in reality constitute discrimination against imported products.

---

[103] Case C-366/04 *Georg Schwarz v Bürgermeister der Landeshauptstadt Salzburg* [2006] ECR I-10139.
[104] Case C-244/06 *Dynamic Medien Vertriebs GmbH* v *Avides Media AG* [2008] ECR I-1505.
[105] Case C-416/00 *Morellato* [2003] ECR I-9343.

As in *Schwarz* the product had to be packaged before it could be sold. There was thus a physical adjustment necessary. However, the difference was that in *Schwarz* the nature of the adjustment was such that it could only realistically be done by the producer. One could not expect vending machine operators to put balls of bubble gum in individual sealed plastic bags. *Schwarz* therefore imposed a production burden. However, in *Morellato*, there was no need for the producer of the semi-baked dough to change anything at all. While shops had to put the bread in bags, they had no need to get those bags from the dough producers, and the packaging had to be done by the shops, not by the producers, since, as the Court said, the production process was incomplete when the dough was delivered – it still had to be partly baked. Thus, although *Morellato* is superficially similar to *Schwarz* and *Dynamic Medien*, it is very different from the perspective of the producer of the imported product. These cases highlight that the question determining whether a measure is a selling arrangement or a product rule is whether that producer is required, or pressured, to change some physical aspect of the product that she ships.

A variation on *Morellato* was offered by *Alfa Vita*, in which 'bake-off' products were also considered.[106] Greek law required that vendors of these had to have all the facilities that were required of a normal bakery, which included areas for kneading bread and a flour store. Clearly such facilities were inappropriate in, for example, a supermarket, and the law was again an attempt to protect traditional bakeries. The Court of Justice, however, found that this could not be considered a selling arrangement because it aimed 'to specify the production conditions for bakery products'. It was not, unlike *Morellato*, about the circumstances of sale, but rather about the final stage of production.

On the other hand, the rule in *Alfa Vita* does not pressure the producer of the bake-off dough to change their product. This is probably why the case was decided without reference to *Cassis*, and not treated as a product rule. Nevertheless, the imposition of a cost imposed on vendors of bake-off bread (they had to maintain facilities) might tend to discourage them from selling it, so that it could have an effect on imports. Hence, it was treated as a general MEQR within *Dassonville*.

The same was the case for the rules at issue in the cases on use of goods, such as *Commission v Italy*.[107] Although these rules seemed to have much to do with sale, and the impact on sale was central to the Court of Justice's reasoning, nevertheless they were not selling arrangements, apparently for the simple reason that they did not in fact regulate the circumstances of sale.[108]

(ii) Unequal effect of selling arrangements

Where a selling arrangement has a greater effect on imported products than on domestic ones, it will fall within Article 34 TFEU, and will be prohibited unless justified. If it discriminates directly a justification must be sought in Article 36 TFEU, while if it is equally applicable but tends as a matter of fact to burden imports more then it may be saved by proportionate reliance on a mandatory requirement.

[106] Case C-188/04 *Alfa Vita v Elliniko Dimosio and Nomarchiaki Aftodioikisi Ioanninon* [2006] ECR I-8135. See p. 763.
[107] See p. 761.
[108] See also Case C-170/04 *Klas Rosengren and others v Riksåklagaren* [2007] ECR I-4071.

For some years after *Keck* was decided, this proviso was largely theoretical, with the Court of Justice being reluctant to investigate whether a measure might have some unequal effect.[109] There are good reasons for this. Restrictions on selling arrangements tend to keep markets static, but this tends to be to the advantage of incumbents and the disadvantage of market newcomers. Since the former are often national it can be argued that most selling arrangements in fact hurt importers most. An over-realistic approach to the proviso might therefore bring most selling arrangements back within Article 34 and once again extend that Article beyond the judicial and constitutional comfort zone.

Nevertheless, in several cases, most importantly *De Agostini* and *Gourmet International*, the Court has recognised that the above logic could apply, particularly where advertising is concerned.[110] The former case concerned television advertising aimed at children, and the latter case concerned advertising of alcohol in Sweden. Bans on these, claimed the litigants, preserved domestic incumbents at the expense of foreign 'wannabe' market entrants. In *De Agostini*, the Court left it to the national court to decide whether the rule did, as a matter of fact, affect importers more. By contrast, in *Gourmet*, it felt able to take a view itself.

Case C-405/98 *Konsumentombudsmannen (KO) v Gourmet International Products AB* [2001] ECR I-1795

19. The Court has also held ... that it cannot be excluded that an outright prohibition, applying in one Member State, of a type of promotion for a product which is lawfully sold there might have a greater impact on products from other Member States.

20. It is apparent that a prohibition on advertising such as that at issue in the main proceedings not only prohibits a form of marketing a product but in reality prohibits producers and importers from directing any advertising messages at consumers, with a few insignificant exceptions.

21. Even without its being necessary to carry out a precise analysis of the facts characteristic of the Swedish situation, which it is for the national court to do, the Court is able to conclude that, in the case of products like alcoholic beverages, the consumption of which is linked to traditional social practices and to local habits and customs, a prohibition of all advertising directed at consumers in the form of advertisements in the press, on the radio and on television, the direct mailing of unsolicited material or the placing of posters on the public highway is liable to impede access to the market by products from other Member States more than it impedes access by domestic products, with which consumers are instantly more familiar.

The key factor was the nature of the product. Alcoholic drinks are not usually bought only on price, but also on the basis of tradition, reputation, image and brand. Market entry is very difficult without the chance to speak directly to consumers via advertising.

Other recent examples of unequal selling arrangements include *DocMorris*, in which the Court of Justice found that a prohibition on Internet sales of pharmaceutical products had an

---

[109] See e.g. Case C-391/92 *Commission v Greece (Greek Milk)* [1995] ECR I-1621; Joined Cases C-69/93 and C-258/93 *Punto Casa v Sindaco del Comune di Capena* [1994] ECR I-2355.

[110] See also Case C-254/98 *Schutzverband v TK-Heimdienst* [2000] ECR I-151; Case C-531/07 *Fachverband der Buchund Medienwirtschafl*, Judgment of 30 April 2009; Case C-20/03 *Burmanjer* [2005] ECR I-4133; Case C-441/04 *A-Punckt Schmuckhandels* [2006] ECR I-2093; Case C-322/01 *Deutscher Apothekerverband v DocMorris* [2003] ECR I-14887; see also Case C-71/02 *Karner* [2004] ECR I-3025.

794 | European Union Law

unequal effect because it was inevitably pharmacies at a distance who would be most affected, and these were most likely to be foreign.[111] The physical pharmacy, inevitably domestic, was protected from pharmacies abroad wishing to supply products from other states. More recently, in *Fachverband*, the Court found that minimum book prices deprived imports, which might otherwise be cheaper than domestic goods, of an important competitive advantage.[112] Although the goal of the rule, protecting cultural diversity, was legitimate, a uniform price for domestic books and imports was disproportionate. The Court found that a minimum price could be set for imports, but it had to be one which reflected the possibility of cheaper production abroad.

5 ARTICLE 35 TFEU AND RESTRICTIONS ON EXPORTS

Article 35 TFEU is the equivalent of Article 34 for exports, and provides:

> Quantitative restrictions on exports, and all measures having equivalent effect, shall be prohibited between Member States.

The leading case until recently was *Groenveld*, which concerned a ban on the possession of horsemeat by sausage makers in the Netherlands.[113] This was to make Dutch sausages acceptable in states where horsemeat was prohibited, by removing any risk of contamination. The measure was therefore aimed at protecting exports. However, a sausage producer who wanted to branch out into horsemeat sausages attempted to overturn the rule by claiming that it contravened Article 35. Since he could not possess horsemeat, he could not export horsemeat sausages.

Although the Dutch rule could be conceived of as a product rule in the *Cassis* sense, limiting the way sausages are produced, the Court of Justice found that the measure fell outside Article 35, since it applied to all producers and products, whether aimed for the domestic market or for export.

Case 15/79 *Groenveld BV v Produktschap voor Vee en Vlees* [1979] ECR 3409

7. That provision concerns national measures which have as their specific object or effect the restriction of patterns of exports and thereby the establishment of a difference in treatment between the domestic trade of a Member State and its export trade in such a way as to provide a particular advantage for national production or for the domestic market of the state in question at the expense of the production or of the trade of other Member States.

This made clear that Article 35 has its own logic, and Article 34 reasoning cannot simply be transposed. A measure within Article 35 must provide some specific disadvantage for exports, by comparison with goods sold domestically, thereby encouraging domestic sales at the expense of export sales.

---

[111] Case C-322/01 *Deutscher Apothekerverband* v *DocMorris* [2003] ECR I-14887.
[112] Case C-531/07 *Fachverband der Buchund Medienwirtschafl* [2009] ECR I-3717.
[113] Case 15/79 *Groenveld BV* v *Produktschap voor Vee en Vlees* [1979] ECR 3409.

An example is *Ravil*, which concerned Italian rules on the sale of grated cheese.[114] The specific cheese in question, 'Grana Padano', could only be sold under that name in grated form if it had been grated within the region of production. If it was exported whole, and grated abroad, the name could not be used. This rule was enforced by means of bilateral conventions with other states, and it was one such with France that was at the centre of the case. The Court of Justice found that this was an Article 35 MEQR because it treated cheese which had been transported across a border for grating differently from cheese which had been transported within the Grana Padano region of Italy for grating, grating often being done not by the cheese producer but by the large retail firms who package and sell the grated cheese to consumers.

By contrast, *Gysbrechts* concerned a rule which applied without distinction between domestic sale and exports yet which the Court nevertheless found to be within Article 35.[115] It had long been assumed that equally applicable rules were not within Article 35, as a result of comments in *Groenveld* and the result in that case. It is now clear that this assumption was mistaken. Even an equally applicable rule may, as a matter of fact, disadvantage exports relative to domestic sales, contrary to Article 35.[116]

The rule in *Gysbrechts* prohibited those selling goods at a distance, for example by Internet, from requiring buyers to pay in advance or even to provide details of their payment card. Buyers were only required to pay once they had received the goods. This, of course, created a significant risk of non-payment. However, it is far simpler and cheaper for a firm to pursue a domestic customer for payment than one abroad. Thus, this rule had a more discouraging effect on sales abroad than on domestic sales.

Case C–205/07 *Gysbrechts*, Judgment of 16 December 2008

40. In that regard, the Court has classified as measures having equivalent effect to quantitative restrictions on exports national measures which have as their specific object or effect the restriction of patterns of exports and thereby the establishment of a difference in treatment between the domestic trade of a Member State and its export trade in such a way as to provide a particular advantage for national production or for the domestic market of the State in question, at the expense of the production or of the trade of other Member States.

41. In the main proceedings, it is clear, as the Belgian Government has moreover noted in its written observations, that the prohibition on requiring an advance payment deprives the traders concerned of an efficient tool with which to guard against the risk of non-payment. That is even more the case when the national provision at issue is interpreted as prohibiting suppliers from requesting that consumers provide their payment card number even if they undertake not to use it to collect payment before expiry of the period for withdrawal.

42. As is clear from the order for reference, the consequences of such a prohibition are generally more significant in cross-border sales made directly to consumers, in particular, in sales made by means of the Internet, by reason, inter alia, of the obstacles to bringing any legal proceedings in another Member State against consumers who default, especially when the sales involve relatively small sums.

---

[114] Case C-469/00 *Ravil* v *Bellon Import* [2003] ECR I-5053; see also Case C-388/95 *Belgium* v *Spain* [2000] ECR I-3123.

[115] Case C-205/07 *Gysbrechts* [2008] ECR I-9947.

[116] A. Dawes, 'A Freedom Reborn? The New Yet Unclear Scope of Article 29' (2009) 34 *ELRev.* 639.

43. Consequently, even if a prohibition such as that at issue in the main proceedings is applicable to all traders active in the national territory, its actual effect is nonetheless greater on goods leaving the market of the exporting Member State than on the marketing of goods in the domestic market of that Member State.

44. It must therefore be held that a national measure, such as that at issue in the main proceedings, prohibiting a supplier in a distance sale from requiring an advance or any payment before expiry of the period for withdrawal constitutes a measure having equivalent effect to a quantitative restriction on exports. The same is true of a measure prohibiting a supplier from requiring that consumers provide their payment card number, even if the supplier undertakes not to use it to collect payment before expiry of the period for withdrawal.

Article 35 therefore applies to all national measures which tend to make export sales more difficult or burdensome than domestic sales, whether or not this is by direct discrimination or simply as a matter of fact.[117] However, as with Article 34, equally applicable measures hindering exports may in principle be permitted if they are necessary to meet some mandatory requirement and are proportionate. In *Gysbrechts*, the Court found the prohibition on advance payment to be justified by consumer protection, while the prohibition on even asking for a payment card number was held to be disproportionate.

Finally, in *Jersey Potatoes*, the Court of Justice ruled that measures hindering the movement of potatoes from Jersey to the United Kingdom were contrary to Article 35.[118] The oddity of the case is that Jersey is not an independent Member State, and free movement of goods law only applies to it via a Protocol as a result of its special ties with the United Kingdom. For the purposes of EU law, United Kingdom-Jersey trade is not cross-border.[119] However, the Court's reasoning was that the potatoes sent to the United Kingdom might in some cases be exported on to other Member States. Extrapolating the reasoning it would seem that internal barriers to movement may fall within Article 35 where they may hinder export by, for example, making access to ports or roads more difficult.[120]

FURTHER READING

C. Barnard, 'What the *Keck*? Balancing the Needs of the Single Market with State Regulatory Autonomy in the EU (and the US)' (2012) 2 *European Journal of Consumer Law/Revue Européenne de Droit de la Consommation* 201

G. Davies, 'Understanding Market Access: Exploring the Economic Rationality of Different Conceptions of Free Movement Law' (2010) 11 *German Law Journal* 671

---

[117] See Case C-12/02 *Grilli* [2003] ECR I-11585.   [118] Case C-293/02 *Jersey Potatoes* [2005] ECR I-9543.

[119] See P. Oliver and S. Enchelmaier, 'Free Movement of Goods: Recent Developments in the Case Law' (2007) 44 *CMLRev.* 649.

[120] See similarly Case C-161/09 *Kakavetsos-Fragkopoulos* [2011] ECR I-915; Joined Cases C-1/90 and C-176/90 *Aragonesa* [1991] ECR I-4151; Case C-72/03 *Carbonati Apuani* [2004] ECR I-8027. See I. Kvesko, 'Is There Anything Left Outside the Reach of the European Court of Justice?' (2006) 33 *LIEI* 405.

G. Davies, 'The Court's Jurisprudence on Free Movement of Goods: Pragmatic Presumptions, Not Philosophical Principles' (2012) 2 *European Journal of Consumer Law/Revue Européenne de Droit de la Consommation* 25

S. Enchelmaier, 'The Awkward Selling of a Good Idea, or a Traditionalist Interpretation of *Keck*' (2003) 22 *Yearbook of European Law* 259

H.-C. von Heydebrand u.d. Lasa, 'Free Movement of Foodstuffs, Consumer Protection and Food Standards in the European Community: Has the Court got it Wrong?' (1991) 16 *European Law Review* 391

T. Horsley 'Unearthing Buried Treasure: Art. 34 TFEU and the Exclusionary Rules' (2012) 37 *European Law Review* 734

D. Regan 'An Outsider's View of "Dassonville" and "Cassis de Dijon": On Interpretation and Policy' in M. Poiares Maduro and L. Azoulai (eds.), *The Past and Future of EU Law* (Oxford, Hart, 2010) 465

N. Reich, 'The "November Revolution" of the European Court of Justice: *Keck*, *Meng* and *Audi* Revisited' (1994) 31 *Common Market Law Review* 459

J. Snell 'The Notion of Market Access: A Concept or a Slogan?' (2010) 47 *Common Market Law Review* 437

A. Tryfonidou, 'Was *Keck* a Half-baked Solution After All?' (2007) 34 *Legal Issues of Economic Integration* 167

S. Weatherill, 'After *Keck*: Some Thoughts on How to Clarify the Clarification' (1996) 33 *Common Market Law Review* 885

S. Weatherill, 'Recent Case Law Concerning the Free Movement of Goods: Mapping the Frontiers of Market Deregulation' (1999) 36 *Common Market Law Review* 51

J. Weiler, 'The Constitution of the Common Market Place: The Free Movement of Goods' in P. Craig and G. de Búrca (eds.), *The Evolution of EU Law* (Oxford, Oxford University Press, 1999) 349

D. Wilsher, 'Does *Keck* Discrimination Make Any Sense? An Assessment of the Non-discrimination Principle within the European Single Market' (2008) 33 *European Law Review* 3

18

The Free Movement of Services

CONTENTS

1 INTRODUCTION

Article 56 TFEU prohibits restrictions on the provision of services between Member States. Trade in services comprises the largest part of a modern economy, yet interstate trade is hindered by the high level of regulation applying to many service activities. EU law has taken a threefold approach to breaking down these barriers: the direct application of Article 56 by courts is now complemented by Directive 2006/123/EC on services in the internal market (Services Directive), and by sector specific regulation for many complex services of particular social or economic importance. This chapter addresses Article 56 and the Services Directive. It is organised as follows.

Section 2 provides an overview of why services markets are hard to integrate. Because services involve people interacting, they raise issues of power and knowledge inequalities, requiring protective legislation. Also, services are often of great social importance and some services arouse strong moral feelings.

Section 3 is concerned with defining the services to which Article 56 applies. A core aspect is that the services must be provided for remuneration. Genuinely non-economic services, such as free public education, are excluded. Yet, where the service consumer, or an insurer acting on her behalf, does pay for services, Article 56 applies, however socially sensitive the services may be. Health care has been subjected to Article 56 on this basis.

Section 4 considers prohibited restrictions on the free movement of services. The range of these is broad. The Court of Justice applies Article 56 to any measure which makes access to the service market of a state more difficult. Since *Gebhard* and *Alpine Investments*, it does not appear to be necessary to show that the measure promotes either domestic service providers or domestic transactions. Yet in *Mobistar*, the Court said that measures which merely impose costs, but have no unequal impact, are outside Article 56. A certain ambiguity about the limits of Article 56 remains.

Section 4(ii) is devoted to the application of Article 56 to non-state actors. The powers of the bodies governing sport, and of trade unions, have both been subjected to the principle that they must not be exercised in a way that unjustifiably hinders the movement of services. This has been deeply controversial. In particular, the right of trade unions to both protect their members against low-cost competition from other Member States and preserve levels of worker protection in their home state are seen as threatened. Yet, the Court of Justice notes that if non-state bodies do not have to respect Article 56, this greatly reduces its effectiveness, and allows an opening for nationality discrimination and protectionism.

Section 5 is about justifying restrictions on the movement of services. This is possible where the restrictions are equally applicable, and the restrictive measure is necessary for a good public interest reason. However, service providers cannot be subjected to all host state legislation. First, account must be taken of whether the interest concerned is already protected by measures in the home state. Secondly, in deciding whether a regulatory burden is proportionate it is important to remember that a service provider may only have weak bonds with the host state market, perhaps just a few clients. Over-regulation of them would then be disproportionate, the Court has found.

Section 6 considers the way Article 56 impacts on society beyond business. In particular, the free movement of services requires that many sensitive and important activities be looked at through an economic lens. Abortion, gambling and prostitution are legally provided for remuneration in some states, enabling reliance on Article 56 to challenge restrictive measures. These challenges will not necessarily be successful, but the mere fact that courts must place non-economic concerns in the context of a right to trade in services has been offensive to some, and may rebalance public reasoning so that the non-economic interests are marginalised.

Section 6(iii) focuses in more detail on Article 56 and welfare states. The case law on health care has been the most significant here, and provides patients with a right to go abroad to receive medical treatment at the expense of their home state. States claim this may add to the cost of health care and threaten budgets, and in response limited restrictions are permitted where hospital treatment is concerned. Nevertheless, both the general principle, and the procedural and transparency requirements which the Court has attached to it, are transformative, and are causing health care systems to rethink their financing and organisation. Some of the Court's reasoning has now been adopted in a Directive on patients' rights to cross-border health care.

Section 7 is about the Services Directive. This is the most significant recent development in the law on services. The Directive applies a strict country of origin principle to services, so that providers need hardly concern themselves with the rules of their host state. The only exceptions are the narrowly interpreted grounds of public policy, public security, public health and the environment. Yet, the Directive, the product of a dramatically controversial legislative process, is full of exclusions and limitations, so that there will be just as many situations to which it does not apply as to which it does, and the direct application of Article 56 will remain important.

2 REGULATING THE SERVICES MARKET

Creating a single market for services is difficult.[1] Service providers are people, or companies, and when they are active in host states they interact with a wide range of regulations. These may be to do with the actual service, but may also be to do with the nature of the provider: their qualifications, or legal form, or financial position. A comparison with goods may be helpful: imagine if sale of goods were to be made conditional not just on aspects of the product, but on aspects of the company producing it, their factory and work methods. The creation of free movement would become even more of a challenge.

It is, of course, natural for a state to apply their laws to all on their territory. The EU law rejection of this is counter-intuitive from a national perspective. Yet, it is equally natural for a service provider to find it deeply frustrating when she is forced to demonstrate compliance with all kinds of professional and technical regulation which essentially duplicates similar demands in her state of establishment. Nor is such duplication the only problem. Other local rules may impose costs and make it harder for her to do business in the way she is used to – according to her business model, as the Court of Justice has recently put it.[2] Examples might be a prohibition on a particular marketing method, such as cold-calling, or a tax on the equipment necessary for the service, advertising rules, or rules about the legal form of the service provider. These rules might not discriminate, nor have any protectionist intent, but they might nevertheless have the effect that some service providers decide it is just not worth entering that market, or that market entry should be on a smaller scale. Trade is inhibited.

This makes Article 56 TFEU constitutionally dangerous. If all law affecting a service provider imposes costs on her somehow, then all law deters her activities to some extent, and Article 56 might just become a tool for a general review of national legislative proportionality. One of the central issues of the free movement of services is, as with the other freedoms, how to define its limits in a way reflecting the right balance between purposive market-creation, and practical, attribution-respecting, limits to EU law. The Court of Justice has not yet created a *Keck* for services, a case which is accepted to draw such lines, perhaps partly because the types of restrictions which impact on services are less easy to categorise than is the case for goods.[3] Rather, the Court uses a variety of formulas and phrases to sum up the scope of

---

[1] European Commission, *The State of the Internal Market in Services*, COM(2002)441 final.

[2] Case C-518/06 *Commission* v *Italy*, Judgment of 28 April 2009.

[3] Although see the parallels drawn in W.-H. Roth, 'The European Court of Justice's Case Law on Freedom to Provide Services: Is *Keck* Relevant?' in M. Andenas and W.-H. Roth (eds.), *Services and Free Movement in EU Law* (Oxford, Oxford University Press, 2002) 1; V. Hatzopoulos, 'Annotation of *Alpine Investments*' (1995) 29 *CMLRev*. 1427; J. L. Da Cruz Vilaca, 'On the Application of *Keck* in the Field of Free Provision of Services' in M. Andenas and W.-H. Roth (eds.), *Services and Free Movement in EU Law* (Oxford, Oxford University Press, 2002) 25.

Article 56, not all of which are entirely consistent with each other. In particular, it is unclear whether regulation which has an entirely equal impact on domestic and cross-border services, and which merely imposes costs rather than actually preventing service provision, is caught by the Treaty.

The challenges for the Court of Justice and legislator are increased by the fact that services can be both economically and socially extremely sensitive. Partly this is a matter of scale. At one extreme, huge service industries like banking, telecoms and transport are of such importance to the wider economy that they demand intensive regulation and control. This makes transnational integration even harder, but it is difficult for a generalist court to tamper with complex national supervisory systems. In practice, free movement in this kind of industry is usually pursued via sector-specific legislation. Yet, services can equally be very local, very small-scale, and sometimes very traditional, which raises its own problems, often political. In France, the debate around the Services Directive focused on the image of a French plumber threatened by Polish competition. The ability to remain established in Poland, with associated low costs, while providing services in France, would enable the Polish plumbers to undercut the French, plunder the local market, and wipe out a class of small-scale artisanal service providers, it was claimed by opponents. This is globalisation brought down to a human scale, and all the more politically potent as a result.

Other services are hard to integrate, or adjudicate, because they are part of the structure of the state, or the fabric of national society. Health care, education and sport are examples. Breaking down national barriers to these affects the sense of national community and identity,[4] and so free movement has to be balanced against factors which are hard to voice, hard to weigh, impossible to quantify, and sometimes not easy to distinguish from unacceptable nationalism.[5]

Finally, services are about people doing things to, or for, each other. Some of the things people do enrage others: abortion, gambling, prostitution.[6] Adjudicating the free movement of these is always controversial. Other things that people do involve risk for others: lay clients buying complex professional services are vulnerable to exploitation by their provider, while providers of sex services may be vulnerable to their clients; services tend to involve unequal relationships. In all these cases, the Court of Justice is faced with human, moral and social concerns and interests which complicate its decision-making but cannot be ignored.

The Court is not the primary regulator of such issues: it supervises Member State legislation, and acknowledges the national margin of appreciation where choices of social or moral policy are concerned.[7] It shows no enthusiasm to be a social or moral arbiter as such. However, since free movement and non-discrimination are also values within the European legal system, it is forced to balance national priorities against EU priorities. Where matters such as the opening of the welfare state or trade in morally controversial services are concerned, there is no safe neutral position, only value-laden choices to be made.

---

[4] See M. Wright and T. Reeskens, 'Of What Cloth are the Ties that Bind? National Identity and Support for the Welfare State Across 29 European Countries' (2013) 20 *JEPP* 1443.

[5] See C. Hilson, 'The Unpatriotism of the Economic Constitution? Rights to Free Movement and the Impact on National and European Identity' (2008) 14 *ELJ* 156.

[6] See Case C-268/99 *Jany* v *Staatssecretaris van Justitie* [2001] ECR I-8615.

[7] See N. Nic Shuibhne, 'Margins of Appreciation: National Values, Fundamental Rights and EC Free Movement Law' (2009) 34 *ELRev.* 230.

3 CROSS-BORDER SERVICES

The free movement of services is regulated by Article 56 TFEU, which provides in its first paragraph:

> Within the framework of the provisions set out below, restrictions on freedom to provide services within the Union shall be prohibited in respect of nationals of Member States who are established in a Member State other than that of the person for whom the services are intended.

Article 57 TFEU then provides that:

> Services shall be considered to be 'services' within the meaning of the Treaties where they are normally provided for remuneration.

Subsequent Articles address aspects of certain specific services (transport, banking and insurance services) and aspects of the process of harmonisation and liberalisation.

A number of derogations are also provided. The free movement of services may be restricted on grounds of public policy, public security or public health, and it does not apply at all to the exercise of official authority. These derogations are found in the Treaty Chapter on freedom of establishment, and are applied to the services Chapter by Article 61 TFEU. They are discussed further in Chapter 20.

The free movement of services raises several issues of definition. What is a service? What is 'remuneration'? And, when does a service have a sufficient cross-border element to fall within Article 56 TFEU? These questions are addressed below.

(i) What is a service?

The distinction between goods and services is relatively simple. Goods are things that one can feel. Hence, electricity is treated by the Court of Justice as goods. The sale of e-books, however, would fall within the provision of services, since there is no tactile object being traded. If the book were on a CD, by contrast, then this CD would be a good.[8]

Sometimes the provision of a service is attached to the provision of a physical thing. Most notably, in *Schindler*, the Court found that buying a lottery ticket fell within the free movement of services, not goods, because the physical ticket was purely ancillary to the real substance of the transaction, which was the chance of winning a prize.[9] The customer paid in order to participate in the lottery – a service – not in order to own a piece of paper.

The distinction between services and establishment is less precise. If a person or company has a number of customers in another Member State to which they provide services, this will fall within Article 56. However, if their position in that Member State reaches a sufficient level of permanence and solidity that one might speak of them being 'established' there, then any

---

[8] Case 155/73 *Giuseppe Sacchi* [1974] ECR 409; L. Woods, *Free Movement of Goods and Services within the European Community* (Aldershot, Ashgate, 2004) 19.

[9] Case C-275/92 *HM Customs and Excise* v *Schindler* [1994] ECR I-1039. See also Case C-55/93 *Van Schaik* [1994] ECR I-4837; Case C-71/02 *Karner* v *Troostwijk* [2004] ECR I-3025; Case C-36/02 *Omega Spielhallen- und Automatenaufstellungs* v *Oberbürgermeisterin der Bundesstadt Bonn* [2004] ECR I-9609; Case C-97/98 *Jägerskiöld* v *Gustafsson* [1999] ECR I-7319; Case C-451/99 *Cura Anlagen* v *Auto Source Leasing* [2002] ECR I-3193.

restrictions on their activities will be seen as restrictions on freedom of establishment, not of services.[10] Deciding when a service provider is embedded enough that they become established entails looking at several factors.

Case C-215/01 *Schnitzer* [2003] ECR I-14847

27. The third paragraph of Article [57 TFEU] states that the person providing a service may, in order to do so, temporarily pursue his activity in the Member State where the service is provided, under the same conditions as are imposed by that State on its own nationals. Insofar as pursuit of the activity in that Member State remains temporary, such a person thus continues to come under the provisions of the chapter relating to services.

28. The Court has held that the temporary nature of the activity of the person providing the service in the host Member State has to be determined in the light not only of the duration of the provision of the service but also of its regularity, periodical nature or continuity. The fact that the activity is temporary does not mean that the provider of services within the meaning of the Treaty may not equip himself with some form of infrastructure in the host Member State (including an office, chambers or consulting rooms) insofar as such infrastructure is necessary for the purposes of performing the services in question.

(ii) Cross-border element

Article 56 TFEU provides that it applies whenever the service provider and service recipient are established in different Member States.[11] This covers several situations.[12] The most obvious is where the service provider (who must be an EU company or an EU citizen established in a Member State)[13] travels to another state, as in *van Binsbergen*, where a Dutch lawyer established in Belgium travelled to the Netherlands to see and represent clients.[14] However, Article 56 also applies where it is the recipient who travels. This was established in *Luisi and Carbone*, where two Italians wanted to go to Germany to receive medical services. Italian laws which obstructed this fell within Article 56.[15] It may even be the case that recipient and provider both travel, and meet in a third Member State.[16]

---

[10] Case 2/74 *Reyners v Belgium* [1974] ECR 631; Case C-55/94 *Gebhard v Consiglio dell'ordine degli avvocati eprocuratori di Milano* [1995] ECR I-4165.

[11] Wholly internal situations are thus excluded: see Case C-108/98 *RI-SAN v Commune de Ischia* [1999] ECR I-5219; Case 52/79 *Procureur du Roi v Debauve* [1980] ECR 833. Cf. Case 15/78 *SG Alsacienne v Koestler* [1978] ECR 1971.

[12] See G. Sampson and R. Snape, 'Identifying the Issues in Trade in Services' (1985) 8 *World Economy* 171, 172–3; P. Eeckhout, *The European Internal Market and International Trade: A Legal Analysis* (Oxford, Clarendon Press, 1994) 10; J. Snell, *Goods and Services in EC Law: A Study of the Relationship Between the Freedoms* (Oxford, Oxford University Press, 2002) 16–17. The situation is very similar in the central treaty regulating international trade in services, the General Agreement on Trade in Services (GATS), Article I(2).

[13] Case C-290/04 *FKP Scorpio* [2006] ECR I-9461; Case C-452/04 *Fidium Finanz v Bundesanstalt für Finanzdienstleistnugsaufsicht* [2006] ECR I-9521. As EU citizens, service providers and recipients enjoy the citizenship rights discussed in Chapter 11.

[14] Case 33/74 *Van Binsbergen v Bestuur van de Bedrijsvereniging voor de Metaalnijverheid* [1974] ECR 1299.

[15] Joined Cases 286/82 and 26/83 *Luisi and Carbone v Ministero del Tesoro* [1984] ECR 377. Also Case 186/87 *Cowan v Trésor Public* [1989] ECR 195.

[16] As is often the case with tour guides. See e.g. Case 180/89 *Commission v Italy* [1991] ECR 709; Case C-398/95 *Syndesmos ton en Elladi Touristikon kai Taxidiotikon Grafeion v Ypourgos Ergasias* [1997] ECR I-3091.

Equally important today is the situation where the service itself moves. Services provided over the Internet, telesales and the cross-border provision of telecoms and television are all commercially important examples of cross-border service provision in which neither provider nor recipient has to physically move. Thus, measures which prevent companies from cold-calling customers abroad, or which impose restrictions on the supply or receipt of television programmes from abroad, and many other examples of this type, have been found to fall within Article 56.[17]

The Court has also extended Article 56 beyond its literal wording. In *Vestergard*, a Danish company organised training courses for Danish workers on Greek islands. On the one hand, provider and recipients all travelled to another Member State, so there was clearly an international element to the service provision. However, both provider and recipient were established in Denmark, so the transaction was domestic.[18] Nevertheless, the Court applied Article 56.

Case C-55/98 *Skatteministeriet* v *Vestergard* [1999] ECR I-7641

18. Thirdly, it is important to point out that in order for services such as those in question in the main proceedings, namely the organisation of professional training courses, to fall within the scope of Article [56 TFEU], it is sufficient for them to be provided to nationals of a Member State on the territory of another Member State, irrespective of the place of establishment of the provider or recipient of the services.

19. Article [56 TFEU] applies not only where a person providing a service and the recipient are established in different Member States, but also whenever a provider of services offers those services in a Member State other than the one in which he is established, wherever the recipients of those services may be established.

This was taken a step further in *ITC*, where a German employment agency found a job in the Netherlands for its German client, who at that time lived in Germany. The Court of Justice found that Article 56 applied even though client, provider and payment all took place in Germany. The judgment does not indicate very clearly what reasoning was behind this, but the Advocate General, whose Opinion was followed, provides a useful analysis.

Case C-208/05 *ITC Innovative Technology Center GmbH* v *Bundesagentur für Arbeit* [2007] ECR I-181, Opinion of Advocate General Léger

118. Next, unlike the German Government, I am of the view that the situation at issue in the main proceedings does indeed involve a sufficient cross-border extraneous element.

119. I would point out in that regard that the Court of Justice has held that Article [56 TFEU] applies even where the provider and the recipient of the services are established in the same Member State, on condition that the services are being provided in another Member State.

---

[17] See e.g. Case 352/85 *Bond van Adverteerders* v *Netherlands* [1988] ECR 2085; Case C-422/01 *Försäkringsaktiebolaget Skandia* v *Riksskatteverket* [2003] ECR I-6817; Case C-243/01 *Gambelli* [2003] ECR I-13031; Case C-70/99 *Commission* v *Portugal (Flight Taxes)* [2001] ECR I-4845. See also Case C-18/93 *Corsica Ferries France* [1994] ECR I-1783; Case C-381/93 *Commission* v *France* [1994] ECR I-5145; Case C-384/93 *Alpine Investments* v *Minister van Financiën* [1995] ECR I-1141.

[18] See also Case C-381/93 *Commission* v *France* [1994] ECR I-5145.

120. In the case in the main proceedings, the cross-border dimension is made clear by the fact that the job searching, which forms an integral part of the activity of recruitment, was done by the private-sector agency in another Member State. It is, moreover, to be expected that, as part of the performance of a recruitment contract the service provider will have contacts with potential employers based in other Member States, in order to increase the chances of a successful recruitment.

121. Thus, the fact that a recruitment contract was concluded between a person seeking employment and a private-sector recruitment agency each of which are located in the same Member State does not in my view preclude the applicability of Article [56 TFEU] since the job searching, which is the main purpose of the recruitment activity, was undertaken in another Member State.

The Advocate General took the view that the actual service was the finding of a job, and this was done in the Netherlands – that was where the company went to look. It therefore appears, following *Vestergard* and *ITC*, that even a domestic service contract falls within Article 56 if an important part of the work for which the service provider is paid takes place abroad.

It is not necessary that the cross-border element be already realised. As is the case in goods, if a measure could restrict cross-border service provision, then the fact that no actual complainant can be found does not exclude a reference or an answer. Potential restrictions are also caught by Article 56.[19]

However, as with the other freedoms, if 'the relevant facts are confined within a single Member State' the Treaty will not apply to those facts.[20] Nevertheless, questions are sometimes referred in such cases, where a national judge is required by national law to 'grant the same rights to a national of a given Member State as those which a national of another Member State in the same situation would derive from European Union law'.[21] In such situations it is necessary to know the EU law position, and the Court of Justice therefore answers the question.[22]

(iii) Remuneration

Services provided out of charity, or without any desire for payment, are not covered by Article 56 TFEU. It is concerned with economic activity, and Article 57 TFEU provides that services must be 'normally provided for remuneration'. The word 'normally', although it has not been discussed by the Court of Justice, is probably intended to ensure that the occasional provision of a service for free in a generally commercial context (as part of a sales promotion, for example) does not result in essentially economic activities falling outside the Treaty.

Remuneration need not be money, as long as it can be valued in money.[23] Food and lodging has been found by the Court to be remuneration in the context of employment, and there is no

---

[19] Case C-6/01 *Anomar* v *Estado Português* [2003] ECR I-8621; Case C-398/95 *Syndesmos ton en Elladi Touristikon kai Taxidiotikon Grafeion* v *Ypourgos Ergasias* [1997] ECR I-3091; Case C-570/07 *Blanco Pérez* [2010] ECR I-4629. In like vein, Case C-384/93 *Alpine Investments* v *Minister van Financiën* [1995] ECR I-1141. See annotation by Hatzopoulos, n. 3 above.

[20] Case C-245/09 *Omalet* [2010] ECR I-13771, para. 12; Case C-108/98 *RI.SAN* [1999] ECR I-5219.

[21] *Omalet*, n. 20 above, para. 15.

[22] See also Case C-602/10 *Volksbank Romania*, Judgment of 12 July 2012.

[23] Case 154/80 *Staatsecretaris van Financiëen* v *Coöperative Aardappelenbewaarplaats* [1981] ECR 445; Case 324/82 *Commission* v *Belgium* [1984] ECR 1861; Case C-288/94 *Argos Distributors Ltd* v *CCE* [1996] ECR I-5311; Case C-258/95 *Söhne* v *Finanzamt Neustadt* [1997] ECR I-5577.

reason why it should take a different stance on services.[24] Nor does remuneration need to be paid by the recipient of the service.[25] If an insurance company pays for medical care abroad this is remuneration just as much as if the patient had paid herself, and is sufficient to bring that care within Article 56.

However, not every payment to the service provider is remuneration. In *Humbel*, the Court of Justice had to consider whether university education was a Treaty service.[26] Universities receive most of their funding from the state, but students paid a small contribution.

Case 263/86 *Humbel v Belgium* [1988] ECR 5365

17. The essential characteristic of remuneration thus lies in the fact that it constitutes consideration for the service in question, and is normally agreed upon between the provider and the recipient of the service.

18. That characteristic is, however, absent in the case of courses provided under the national education system…First of all, the State, in establishing and maintaining such a system, is not seeking to engage in gainful activity but is fulfilling its duties towards its own population in the social, cultural and educational fields…Secondly, the system in question is, as a general rule, funded from the public purse and not by pupils or their parents…

19. The nature of the activity is not affected by the fact that pupils or their parents must sometimes pay teaching or enrolment fees in order to make a certain contribution to the operating expenses of the system.

The Court makes an implicit contrast between payments which are essentially consideration for the services – where there is a transaction between payer and provider – and payments which are intended to fund or support the provider, for non-commercial motives.[27] One way of looking at this is to ask whether the service provider would consider the payer (here the state) to be her 'client', or to be acting on behalf of her client. In the case of free public education this would usually be a somewhat artificial perspective.

It is arguable that there must be some legal obligation to pay. In *Tolsma*, the Court of Justice had to consider whether busking on the highway fell within the ambit of Article 2 of the Sixth VAT Directive.[28] This is similarly phrased to Article 57 TFEU, as it provides that services provided by a taxable person must, in principle, be taxed if they are made for payment or consideration.[29] The Court of Justice held that money given by passers-by could not be seen as value provided for a service. Donations were voluntary and the passers-by did not request the music. Thus, it was difficult to find any legal relationship that provided a context for remuneration.

It should also be noted that in *Humbel*, the Court suggested that very small payments will not amount to remuneration. The function of the essentially symbolic fees which many states require students to pay is not really to pay for the education they receive, but to encourage the students to take their education seriously.

---

[24] Case 196/87 *Steymann v Staatssecretaris van Justitie* [1988] ECR 6159.

[25] Joined Cases C-51/96 and C-191/97 *Deliège v Asbl Ligue Francophone de Judo* [2000] ECR I-2549.

[26] Case 263/86 *Humbel v Belgium* [1988] ECR 5365.

[27] See also EFTA Case E-5/07 *Private Barnehagers Landsforbund v EFTA Surveillance Authority*, Judgment of 21 February 2008, available at www.eftacourt.int/press-publications/detail/article/case-e-507-private-barnehagers-landsforbund-v-efta-surveillance-authority/.

[28] Case C-16/93 *Tolsma v Inspecteur der Omzelbelastingen Leeuwarden* [1994] ECR I-743 on busking.

[29] Directive 77/388/EEC [1977] OJ L145/1.

In later cases, notably *Wirth*, the Court has suggested that as long as the state 'essentially' funds public education, this will fall outside Article 56 TFEU.[30] This suggests that if private payments, from students or their parents, or from scholarship funds, for example, amount to more than half of the total funds received for the service provided, then these payments will be remuneration and Article 56 will apply.

In education it is increasingly common for universities to have some courses, often Masters courses, which are paid for by students and run at a profit, while other courses are state-funded. This raises the question whether a specific course may fall within Article 56 even if most other courses provided by that institution do not. Will a generally non-economic organisation that dabbles in the market find itself subject to Article 56? Following the approach in competition law, one would expect that it is the nature of the particular activity or service which matters, rather than the institution as a whole.[31] The alternative would allow largely non-economic institutions to enter markets without being subject to their rules, creating quite serious risks of competitive distortions. In *Zanotti*, an LLM at a public Dutch university was involved, which had been paid for by the Italian student.

Case C-56/09 *Zanotti* [2010] ECR I-4517

32. …the Court has held that courses offered by educational establishments essentially financed by private funds, in particular by students and their parents, constitute services within the meaning of Article [57 TFEU] since the aim of those establishments is to offer a service for remuneration.

33. Therefore, courses essentially financed by persons seeking training or professional specialisation must be regarded as constituting services within the meaning of Article [57 TFEU].

34. It is for the national court to assess the facts and, in particular, the terms and conditions of the specialist course attended by the applicant in the main proceedings.

35. It follows that Article [56 TFEU] is applicable to facts such as those in the main proceedings where a taxpayer of a given Member State attends a university in another Member State which may be regarded as providing services for remuneration, that is to say, which is essentially financed by private funds, which it is for the national court to verify.

Although there is ambiguity in this extract, with some references apparently to the nature of the institution as a whole, on balance it seems to suggest that even in a largely state-financed institution individual courses which are provided for remuneration will be within Article 56. This is confirmed by the ultimate finding: the University of Leiden is state-owned and largely state financed, and most students just pay *Humbel*-type 'contributions'. However, this still leaves other constellations open to some doubt: whether Article 56 would apply, for example, if half the students on the course are being paid for by the state, while the other half are paying fees. On the one hand, a service paid for by an individual should not cease to be a service because someone else gets it free. On the other hand, the word 'normally' in Article 57 might conceivably play a role here.

---

[30] Case C-109/92 *Wirth* v *Landeshauptstadt Hannover* [1993] ECR I-6447; Case C-318/05 *Commission* v *Germany* [2007] ECR I-6957.
[31] Case 118/85 *Commission* v *Italy* [1987] ECR 2599; Case T-319/99 *FENIN* [2003] ECR II-357.

An odd tension in the case law is that while the motivation of the payer appears to be important in characterising services, the motivation of the provider is not.[32] The Court of Justice has ruled that there is no need for service providers to seek to make a profit, and the mere fact that they are providing very important public services, such as health or education, does not as such take them outside of Article 56.[33] Nor does it matter what legal or institutional form they have: they need not be a company or a business, but might be, for example, a school or a foundation.[34] They do not even have to be 'doing it for the money'. In *Jundt*, a university teacher received a fee for a guest lecture.[35] It was argued that his post was 'quasi-honorary'. The Court found this to be irrelevant, since he did in fact receive a payment in return for his teaching. The only question appears to be whether the service provider receives consideration for their activities.

One of the consequences of this case law is that the mechanism of funding public services becomes very important. In some Member States, health care is provided free on the basis of need, and is probably not therefore a Treaty service. In other Member States, the state guarantees universal health care by requiring residents to purchase medical insurance from private companies, in the context of a legislative framework in which insurance for the poor or sick is cross-subsidised by the richer and healthier. Because the actual medical care in such a system is paid for by insurers, Article 56 TFEU will apply. Similarly, if universities have high fees, but students can take out subsidised loans to pay them, then university education will probably be remunerated. If, on the other hand, the state funds universities directly, there will be no remuneration. In both cases the state ultimately pays, but the choice of mechanism determines the extent to which the Treaty applies.

This interaction of Article 56 and aspects of the welfare state is of great current importance, and has been the source of much case law. It is discussed further in section 6 below.

4 RESTRICTIONS ON THE MOVEMENT OF SERVICES

(i) Notion of a restriction on the provision of services

As with the other freedoms, the most complex and slippery aspect of the case law on services is the definition of a prohibited restriction. It has never been in doubt that direct and indirect nationality discrimination is prohibited within the sphere of Article 56 TFEU,[36] but the extent to which the prohibition does and should extend beyond this is less clear. In *Arblade*, the Court of Justice said:

---

[32] Cf. Case C-56/09 *Zanotti* [2010] ECR I-4517, para. 32.

[33] Case C-157/99 *Geraets-Smits* v *Stichting Ziekenfonds*; *Peerbooms* v *Stichting CZ Groep Zorgverzekeringen* [2001] ECR I-5473; Case C-158/96 *Kohll* v *Union des Caisses de Maladie* [1998] ECR I-1931. Cf. Articles 54 and 62 TFEU. See pp. 833–41.

[34] Case C-109/92 *Wirth* v *Landeshauptstadt Hannover* [1993] ECR I-6447; Case C-318/05 *Commission* v *Germany* [2007] ECR I-6957; G. Davies, 'Welfare as a Service' (2002) 29 *LIEI* 27, 29–30.

[35] Case C-281/06 *Jundt and Jundt* v *Finanzamt Offenburg* [2007] ECR I-12231.

[36] Article 57 TFEU, last para.; see e.g. Case 33/74 *Van Binsbergen* v *Bestuur van de Bedrijsvereniging voor de Metaalnijverheid* [1974] ECR 1310; Case 39/75 *Coenen* v *Sociaal-Economische Raad* [1975] ECR 1547; Case C-288/89 *Gouda* v *Commissariat voor de Media* [1991] ECR I-4007; Case C-17/92 *FDC* v *Estado Español and UPCT* [1993] ECR I-2239; Case C-294/97 *Eurowings* v *Finanzamt Dortmund-Unna* [1999] ECR I-7447. For definitions of discrimination in EU law, see pp. 481–2.

33. It is settled case law that Article [56] of the Treaty requires not only the elimination of all discrimination on grounds of nationality against providers of services who are established in another Member State, but also the abolition of any restriction, even if it applies without distinction to national providers of services and to those of other Member States, which is liable to prohibit, impede, or render less advantageous the activities of a provider of services established in another Member State where he lawfully provides similar services.

Although this makes clear that equally applicable measures may be caught by Article 56, it does not tell us how we are to understand 'prohibit, impede or render less advantageous'.[37] Is it necessary to show that an equally applicable measure may have some unequal impact – that it has a greater effect on the foreign or the cross-border than on the domestic? Or is Article 56 engaged simply whenever a measure may affect cross-border services, without any kind of comparison being involved?[38]

In *Gebhard*, the Court of Justice found that all national measures 'liable to hinder or make less attractive the exercise of fundamental freedoms' are to be seen as restrictions on movement.[39] The case was about establishment, but the formulation was general, and is very often cited for services too. It is even more open than *Arblade*, and suggests a broad scope to Article 56, in which comparison between the domestic or the foreign is irrelevant, the only question being whether some hindrance to service provision can be argued.

This view is also reflected in *Alpine Investments*.[40] A Dutch law prohibited Dutch companies from cold-calling customers, even those in other Member States where cold-calling was not prohibited. The aim was to prevent the Dutch financial services industry from getting a bad reputation, but frustrated Dutch providers who wanted to cold-call German clients claimed that the measure was a restriction on services. The Court of Justice agreed, for the very straightforward reason that:

28. ... such a prohibition deprives the operators concerned of a rapid and direct technique for marketing and for contacting potential clients in other Member States. It can therefore constitute a restriction on the freedom to provide cross-border services.

This suggests, as in *Gebhard*, a naive reading of Article 56 in which not discrimination, but factual barriers to trade are central: is there a service provider who finds doing business abroad is made more difficult by some national measure? Then, the measure is a restriction on services. This broad reading may be slightly tempered by the facts: it is arguable that a restriction on cold-calling has a greater effect on contact with distant clients than local ones, so that *Alpine* is really about a measure of unequal impact. However, the Court did not address this, and *Alpine* is usually cited as support for the view that Article 56 applies even to equal impact measures.

On the other hand, in *Mobistar*, the Court took a more precise and more limited approach to Article 56. *Mobistar* was about a tax on telecoms masts and pylons, necessary for the transmission of phone calls. It was argued that this hindered the provision of cross-border telecoms services, by imposing an additional cost on the necessary infrastructure. But the masts were just as necessary for domestic phone calls as for cross-border ones.

---

[37] Joined Cases C-369/96 and C-376/96 *Arblade* [1999] ECR I-8453; Case C-165/98 *Mazzoleni and ISA* [2001] ECR I-2189; Case C-49/98 *Finalarte* [2001] ECR I-7831.

[38] See generally S. Enchelmeier, 'Always at Your Service (Within Limits): The ECJ's Case Law on Article 56 TFEU (2006–11)' (2011) 36 *ELRev.* 615.

[39] Case C-55/94 *Gebhard v Consiglio dell'ordine degli avvocati eprocuratori di Milano* [1995] ECR I-4165.

[40] Case C-384/93 *Alpine Investments v Minister van Financiën* [1995] ECR I-1141.

C-544/03 *Mobistar v Commune de Fléron* [2005] ECR I-7723

29. According to the Court's case-law, Article [56 TFEU] requires not only the elimination of all discrimination on grounds of nationality, against providers of services who are established in another Member State, but also the abolition of any restriction, even if it applies without distinction to national providers of services and to those of other Member States, which is liable to prohibit or further impede the activities of a provider of services established in another Member State where he lawfully provides similar services.

30. Furthermore, the Court has already held that Article [56 TFEU] precludes the application of any national rules which have the effect of making the provision of services between Member States more difficult than the provision of services purely within one Member State.

31. By contrast, measures, the only effect of which is to create additional costs in respect of the service in question and which affect in the same way the provision of services between Member States and that within one Member State, do not fall within the scope of Article [56 TFEU].

The exclusion in paragraph 31 of the judgment contrasts with the broad concept of a restriction in *Gebhard* and *Alpine Investments*. However, there are other cases which take a similar approach to *Mobistar*, notably *Viacom Outdoor*.[41] This case concerned a tax on bill-posting in Genoa. The extra cost which this added to poster advertising in Genoa was argued to be a restriction on advertising services: it made it harder for agencies which arranged local advertising to attract foreign clients.

Case C-134/03 *Viacom Outdoor v Giotto Immobilier and others* [2005] ECR I-1167

37. With regard to the question of whether the levying by municipal authorities of a tax such as the advertising tax constitutes an impediment incompatible with Article [56 TFEU], it must first of all be noted that such a tax is applicable without distinction to any provision of services entailing outdoor advertising and public bill-posting in the territory of the municipality concerned. The rules on the levying of this tax do not, therefore, draw any distinction based on the place of establishment of the provider or recipient of the bill-posting services or on the place of origin of the goods or services that form the subject-matter of the advertising messages disseminated.

38. Next, such a tax is applied only to outdoor advertising activities involving the use of public space administered by the municipal authorities and its amount is fixed at a level which may be considered modest in relation to the value of the services provided which are subject to it. In those circumstances, the levying of such a tax is not on any view liable to prohibit, impede or otherwise make less attractive the provision of advertising services to be carried out in the territory of the municipalities concerned, including the case in which the provision of services is of a cross-border nature on account of the place of establishment of either the provider or the recipient of the services.

As in *Mobistar*, the Court ruled that the mere imposition of an equally applicable cost is not a restriction on services,[42] but in *Viacom* it made clear that this is because such costs do not, in its view, impede or make less attractive the provision of services. Using the language of

---

[41] See also Case C-177/94 *Perfili* [1996] ECR I-161.
[42] Cf. Case C-165/98 *Mazzoleni and ISA* [2001] ECR I-2189.

Gebhard, in paragraph 38, makes *Viacom* an interpretation of that case, rather than a rejection of it, in a way reminiscent of *Keck* and *Dassonville*.

A distinction may be made between *Mobistar* and *Viacom*, on the one hand, and *Alpine Investments*, on the other. *Alpine* concerned prohibition of a sales technique, which restricted access to a foreign market. Merely imposing a cost, the Court of Justice said in *Mobistar* and *Viacom*, does not. However, this distinction is vulnerable to criticism. In practice, costs may deter market entry in just the same way as regulation does: for companies it is all about cost. Equally, the business objection to restriction of a marketing technique may often be that it raises the costs of contacting customers. Distinguishing between mere cost burdens and access restrictions is somewhat artificial.[43]

Yet a line has to be drawn somewhere, and the distinction above is at least reasonably adjudicable. More importantly, *Mobistar* has some very solid policy behind it. If a mere cost burden that has an equal impact on domestic and foreign trade is a restriction on services, then almost every tax or regulation relevant to a service industry will fall within Article 56 TFEU. This is undesirable and unrealistic, and an unconvincing reading of the intention of Article 56. It is very reminiscent of the situation in goods pre-*Keck*. Thus, it is suggested that *Mobistar* is likely to be followed in similar situations, and should, like *Keck*, be treated as a specific exception to the general rule. Mere cost burdens, like mere selling arrangements, if they have an equal impact on national and foreign, domestic and cross-border, are not restrictions on trade.

In *Commission* v *Italy*, the Court of Justice took a new rhetorical path. Here it had to address a national rule which prohibited motor insurers from rejecting a client.[44] Such rules are quite common where socially important insurance is concerned, as they ensure universal access, even for individuals who may be bad risks, and who would be refused cover in a free market. However, insurance companies are not always happy, since they are obliged to accept clients who are likely to cost them money. In *Commission* v *Italy*, it was argued that foreign insurance companies would be deterred from offering insurance services in Italy by the acceptance obligation, and that it therefore amounted to a restriction on the free movement of services. The judgment does not substantively change the law, but offers an interestingly clear and practical analysis of Article 56.

Case C–518/06 *Commission* v *Italy*, Judgment of 28 April 2009

62. It is settled case-law that the term 'restriction' within the meaning of Articles [49 TFEU] and [56 TFEU] covers all measures which prohibit, impede or render less attractive the freedom of establishment or the freedom to provide services.

63. As regards the question of the circumstances in which a measure applicable without distinction, such as the obligation to contract at issue in the present case, may come within that concept, it should be borne in mind that rules of a Member State do not constitute a restriction within the meaning of the EC Treaty solely by virtue of the fact that other Member States apply less strict, or more commercially favourable, rules to providers of similar services established in their territory.

64. By contrast, the concept of restriction covers measures taken by a Member State which, although applicable without distinction, affect access to the market for undertakings from other Member States and thereby hinder intra-Community trade.

---

[43] Cf. V. Hatzopoulos, 'Annotation of *Alpine Investments*' (1995) 29 *CMLRev.* 1427.
[44] Case C-518/06 *Commission* v *Italy*, Judgment of 28 April 2009.

65. In the present case, it is common ground that the obligation to contract does not have any repercussions for the acceptance by the Italian authorities of the administrative authorisation, referred to in paragraph 13 of this judgment, which insurance undertakings having their head office in a Member State other than the Italian Republic obtain in the Member State in which they have their head office. It therefore leaves intact the right of access to the Italian market as regards third-party liability motor insurance resulting from that authorisation.

66. Nevertheless, the imposition by a Member State of an obligation to contract such as that at issue constitutes a substantial interference in the freedom to contract which economic operators, in principle, enjoy.

67. In a sector like that of insurance, such a measure affects the relevant operators' access to the market, in particular where it subjects insurance undertakings not only to an obligation to cover any risks which are proposed to them, but also to requirements to moderate premium rates.

68. Inasmuch as it obliges insurance undertakings which enter the Italian market to accept every potential customer, that obligation to contract is likely to lead, in terms of organisation and investment, to significant additional costs for such undertakings.

69. If they wish to enter the Italian market under conditions which comply with Italian legislation, such undertakings will be required to re-think their business policy and strategy, inter alia, by considerably expanding the range of insurance services offered.

70. Inasmuch as it involves changes and costs on such a scale for those undertakings, the obligation to contract renders access to the Italian market less attractive and, if they obtain access to that market, reduces the ability of the undertakings concerned to compete effectively, from the outset, against undertakings traditionally established in Italy.

71. Therefore, the obligation to contract restricts the freedom of establishment and the freedom to provide services.

The Court of Justice here explicitly notes, in paragraph 65, that foreign insurance companies are not excluded from the Italian market. They can receive authorisation to offer insurance services just as companies established in Italy can. The only effect on cross-border service provision of the 'obligation to contract' is that companies may incur extra costs, since they may have to rethink their business strategy. This, however, is enough to make the measure a restriction on the free movement of services. Access to the national market does not have to be prevented to engage Article 56. It is enough that it is 'affected' (paragraph 64) and this includes making such access more expensive.

This is not necessarily contrary to *Mobistar*. In *Commission v Italy*, the Court of Justice implies very strongly that the obligation to accept has an unequal impact. Companies based outside Italy will be disadvantaged relative to those established in Italy, whose business model already takes account of the Italian laws. The Court appears to be taking the approach that laws which are equally applicable, but in practice require foreign service providers to adapt their business models, will tend to be exclusionary, and therefore fall within Article 56.

It should be noted that the Italian rule required an amendment to the terms of the insurance contracts on sale. It was analogous to a product rule, in the *Cassis de Dijon* sense, and it is well established that requiring service providers to adapt their product to domestic rules is a restriction on trade.[45] Yet, the judgment goes further than this. A business model may include

---

[45] See W.-H. Roth, 'The European Court of Justice's Case Law on Freedom to Provide Services: Is *Keck* Relevant?' in M. Andenas and W.-H. Roth (eds.), *Services and Free Movement in EU Law* (Oxford, Oxford University Press, 2002) 1.

the way a service is advertised or sold. The suggestion is present that, consistently with *Alpine Investments*, a need to change these matters is also a restriction on trade. Implicit in *Commission* v *Italy* is that a service provider should be able to do business throughout the Union in the same way, and with the same products, as she provides in her home state, unless there is a very good reason justifying derogation from this rule.

Nevertheless, the mere fact of having to comply with host state law will not be enough to demonstrate a market access restriction. In *Commission* v *Italy (Lawyers' Fees)* Italian rules setting maximum lawyers' fees were challenged with reference to *Commission* v *Italy* and in *Volksbank Romania* a similar challenge was made to Romanian rules limiting the kinds of charges that credit organisations could apply.[46] While it would seem that both of these rules could in principle affect a business model, the Court of Justice found that there was no evidence that they actually did have this effect, or were even liable to (partly because the rules were, in both cases, less strict than they first seemed) and that therefore, in *Volksbank Romania*, the impact of the measures was too 'uncertain and indirect' to fall within Article 56. In both cases the Court used the language of competition in its reasoning, and, as in *Commission* v *Italy*, seemed to be looking for evidence that the rules affected the ability of the foreign provider to compete on the host state market.[47] Minimum fees, it is well established, can have this effect by taking away a competitive advantage which lower-cost foreign providers would otherwise enjoy.[48] Maximum fees, by contrast, can exclude market entry at the high end. However, there needs to be evidence that this is actually the case.

A restriction on services therefore seems to comprise any measure which affects access to the national market for services. This includes measures which disadvantage the foreign or the cross-border by comparison with the national or the domestic,[49] including measures which take away a competitive advantage that the foreign provider would otherwise enjoy.[50] It is also likely to include any measure which requires a service provider to amend their services or business model in order to provide those services in another state, since this will tend to affect their ability to compete.[51] It does not, if *Mobistar* is correct, include rules which merely impose a cost burden that has no unequal effect. However, experience with *Keck* indicates that this exception may shrink with time. Serious factual investigation often reveals unequal effects even where rules are apparently neutral,[52] and the discussion of business models in *Commission* v *Italy* indicates a certain judicial preparedness to engage with this commercial reality.

(ii) Horizontal application of Article 56 TFEU

Article 56 TFEU is, like the other free movement Articles, apparently addressed primarily to Member States. However, unlike the case with goods, Article 56 may also be directly applied

---

[46] Case C-565/08 *Commission v Italy* [2011] ECR I-2101; Case C-602/10 *Volksbank Romania*, Judgment of 12 July 2012.

[47] See *Commission v Italy*, n. 46 above, paras. 48–52; *Volksbank Romania*, n. 46 above, para. 80; Case C-518/06 *Commission v Italy*, n. 44 above, para. 70.

[48] Joined Cases C-94/04 and C-202/04 *Cipolla and others* [2006] ECR I-11421.

[49] See e.g. Case C-375/92 *Commission v Spain* [1994] ECR I-923; Case C-224/97 *Ciola v Land Vorarlberg* [1999] ECR I-2517; Case C-70/99 *Commission v Portugal (Flight Taxes)* [2001] ECR I-4845.

[50] *Cipolla and others*, n. 48 above.

[51] Case C-384/93 *Alpine Investments v Minister van Financiën* [1995] ECR I-1141; Case C-518/06 *Commission v Italy*, Judgment of 28 April 2009; *Volksbank Romania*, n. 46 above.

[52] See pp. 792–4.

to private actors under certain circumstances.[53] The reason why the Court of Justice allows this is that the Article would be deprived of some of its effectiveness if private actors were permitted to act in ways obstructing service provision by others. This is even more so as the trend of recent decades has been for states to outsource ever more of their regulatory functions to non-governmental bodies of different types. Yet, many private organisations represent the views and interests of individuals and constraining their freedom of choice and action is also a constraint on the capacity of those individuals to collectively express and act on their views and preferences, raising issues of fundamental rights.

The most common situation to have occurred in practice is where a private organisation is involved in regulating some area of activity. In *Walrave and Koch*, the rules of the International Cycling Union (ICU) were involved.[54] This non-governmental body organised and regulated international bicycling competitions, and made certain demands concerning the nationality of members of the support team. Because these team members received payment for their work, the matter fell within free movement law, and it was decided that they were self-employed providers of services rather than employed people. The claim was therefore made that the ICU rules restricted the freedom to provide services in other Member States, by preventing team members with the wrong nationality from taking part in international competitions. However, it was disputed whether Article 56 could be applied to the ICU, since it was a private body.

Case 36/74 Walrave and Koch v Association Union Cycliste Internationale [1974] ECR 1405

19. Since, moreover, working conditions in the various Member States are governed sometimes by means of provisions laid down by law or regulation and sometimes by agreements and other acts concluded or adopted by private persons, to limit the prohibitions in question to acts of a public authority would risk creating inequality in their application.

20. Although the third paragraph of Article [57 TFEU], and Articles [59 and 61 TFEU], specifically relate, as regards the provision of services, to the abolition of measures by the state, this fact does not defeat the general nature of the terms of Article [56 TFEU], which makes no distinction between the source of the restrictions to be abolished...

21. It is established, moreover, that Article [45 TFEU], relating to the abolition of any discrimination based on nationality as regards gainful employment, extends likewise to agreements and rules which do not emanate from public authorities.

22. Article 7(4) of Regulation No. 1612/68 in consequence provides that the prohibition on discrimination shall apply to agreements and any other collective regulations concerning employment...

23. The activities referred to in Article [56] are not to be distinguished by their nature from those in Article [45 TFEU], but only by the fact that they are performed outside the ties of a contract of employment.

24. This single distinction cannot justify a more restrictive interpretation of the scope of the freedom to be ensured...

---

[53] See generally J. Snell, 'Private Parties and Free Movement of Goods and Services' in M. Andenas and W.-H. Roth (eds.), *Services and Free Movement in EU Law* (Oxford, Oxford University Press, 2002) 211; S. Prechal and S. de Vries, 'Seamless Web of Judicial Protection in the Internal Market?' (2009) 34 *ELRev.* 5.

[54] Case 36/74 *Walrave and Koch* v *Association Union Cycliste Internationale* [1974] ECR 1405.

Several points emerge. First, Article 56 TFEU is applied to the rules of the ICU because these are part of the regulation of an area of economic activity. To exclude private agreements and rules, which are often an important part of the employment context, from the scope of Article 56 would allow private parties to create obstacles to movement, and create an arbitrary distinction between the rights of economic actors according to the particular mode of regulation prevailing in their industry and state. This view has particular force as states privatise ever more of their regulatory functions, and the distinction between public and private becomes ever less clear and principled.[55]

Secondly, the Court of Justice sees no reason to make a principled distinction between the free movement of workers and services. It is a technical matter whether an economic relationship is structured as one of employment or self-employed service provision, and this should not affect the scope of the freedom or the degree to which it may be restricted. Since the free movement of workers applies to all aspects of employment regulation and agreements, private or public, it would be arbitrary to exclude such matters from Article 56. This approach has continued in later cases, and the principles of horizontal application appear to be the same whether workers, services or establishment are concerned.[56]

This application of Article 56 TFEU to sport has been very controversial. Sport is, for many people, a matter of social and cultural importance. It can be socially cohesive, and provides a relatively harmless outlet for national identity and the urge to sublimate oneself to a greater whole. To subject it to economic law is not just to miss the point, but to actively threaten the values it embodies and the positive role that it can play in society.[57] Yet, sport is also economic: modern sporting competitions involve large amounts of money, and sportspeople are often well paid for their services.

The case law shows the Court of Justice trying to maintain a distinction between rules which are an inherent part of the regulation of sport, and should not be seen as restrictions on free movement, and those that are to do with the economic aspects of sporting activity and may be assessed in the light of free movement law. In *Deliège*, a judoka who had not been selected by the Belgian judo association to represent Belgium in the Olympics claimed that this restricted her freedom to provide services in another Member State. The process of selection limited participation, she argued, and thereby restricted the provision of services.[58] Clearly, she could not win, as this would have created sporting chaos, but rather than finding that there was a restriction which was justified, the Court of Justice found there to be no restriction at all. Its reasoning was that restrictions on participation were inherent to the organisation of a sporting event, and as such did not fall within Article 56.

---

[55] Case 90/76 *Van Ameyde* v *UCI* [1997] ECR 1091; J. Baquero Cruz, *Between Competition and Free Movement: The Economic Constitutional Law of the European Community* (Oxford/Portland, Hart, 2002) 123.

[56] Case C-281/98 *Roman Angonese* v *Cassa di Risparmio di Bolzano* [2000] ECR I-4139; Case C-415/93 *Union Royale Belge des Sociétés de Football Association and others* v. *Bosman and others* [1995] ECR I-4921; Case C-176/96 *Jyri Lehtonen and Castors Canada Dry Namur-Braine Asbl* v *Fédération royale belge des sociétés de basket-ball Asbl (FRBSB)* [2000] ECR I-2681; Case C-438/05 *International Transport Workers' Federation and Finnish Seamen's Union* v *Viking Line ABP and OÜ Viking Line Eesti* [2007] ECR I-10779.

[57] The Declaration on Sport attached to the Treaty of Amsterdam. See also the 'Helsinki Report' by the Commission. European Commission, *Report to the European Council with a View to Safeguarding Current Sports Structures and Maintaining the Social Function of Sport within the Community Framework*, COM(1999)644. For discussion, see S. Weatherill, 'European Football Law' in *Collected Courses of the 7th Session of the Academy of European Law* (Florence, Kluwer/European Union Institute, 1999) 339–82; S. Weatherill, 'The Helsinki Report on Sport' (2000) 25 *ELRev.* 282.

[58] Joined Cases C-51/96 and C-191/97 *Deliège* v *Asbl Ligue Francophone de Judo* [2000] ECR I-2549.

The General Court explained this idea in more detail in *Meca Medina*.[59] A Spanish and a Slovenian long-distance swimmer both tested positive for nandrolone, a banned substance. They were suspended for four years by FINA, the International Swimming Federation, acting under the rules of the International Olympic Committee, reduced on appeal to two years. The swimmers appealed to the Commission that the ban breached EU competition law and what is now Article 56 TFEU. When the Commission took no action, they brought their case before the General Court.

Case T–313/02 *Meca Medina and Majcen v Commission* [2004] ECR II–3291

37. …having regard to the objectives of the Community, sport is subject to Community law only insofar as it constitutes an economic activity within the meaning of Article 2 EC…

38. That is also borne out by Declaration on Sport No. 29, annexed to the final act of the Conference which adopted the text of the Amsterdam Treaty, which emphasises the social significance of sport and calls on the bodies of the European Union to give special consideration to the particular characteristics of amateur sport. In particular, that Declaration is consistent with the abovementioned case law insofar as it relates to situations in which sport constitutes an economic activity.

39. Where a sporting activity takes the form of paid employment or a provision of remunerated service, it falls, more particularly, within the scope of Article [45 TFEU] *et seq.* or of Article [56 TFEU] *et seq.*, respectively…

40. Therefore…the prohibitions laid down by those provisions of the Treaty apply to the rules adopted in the field of sport which concern the economic aspect which sporting activity can present. In that context, the Court has held that the rules providing for the payment of fees for the transfer of professional players between clubs (transfer clauses) or limiting the number of professional players who are nationals of other Member States which those clubs may field in matches (rules on the composition of club teams), or fixing, without objective reasons concerning only the sport or justified by differences in the circumstances between players, different transfer deadlines for players coming from other Member States (clauses on transfer deadlines) fall within the scope of those provisions of the Treaty and are subject to the prohibitions which they enact…

41. On the other hand, the prohibitions enacted by those provisions of the Treaty do not affect purely sporting rules, that is to say rules concerning questions of purely sporting interest and, as such, having nothing to do with economic activity…In fact, such regulations, which relate to the particular nature and context of sporting events, are inherent in the organisation and proper conduct of sporting competition and cannot be regarded as constituting a restriction on the Community rules on the freedom of movement of workers and the freedom to provide services. In that context, it has been held that the rules on the composition of national teams…or the rules relating to the selection by sports federations of those of their members who may participate in high-level international competitions…constitute purely sporting rules which therefore, by their nature, fall outside the scope of Articles [45 TFEU] and [56 TFEU]. Also among such rules are 'the rules of the game' in the strict sense, such as, for example, the rules fixing the length of matches or the number of players on the field, given that sport can exist and be practised only in accordance with specific rules. That restriction on the scope of the above provisions of the Treaty must however remain limited to its proper objective…

44. It is appropriate to point out that, while it is true that high-level sport has become, to a great extent, an economic activity, the campaign against doping does not pursue any economic objective. It is

---

[59] See also p. 1005.

intended to preserve, first, the spirit of fair play, without which sport, be it amateur or professional, is no longer sport. That purely social objective is sufficient to justify the campaign against doping. Secondly, since doping products are not without their negative physiological effects, that campaign is intended to safeguard the health of athletes. Thus, the prohibition of doping, as a particular expression of the requirement of fair play, forms part of the cardinal rule of sport.

45. It must also be made clear that sport is essentially a gratuitous and not an economic act, even when the athlete performs it in the course of professional sport. In other words, the prohibition of doping and the anti-doping legislation concern exclusively, even when the sporting action is performed by a professional, a non-economic aspect of that sporting action, which constitutes its very essence…

47. In view of the foregoing, it must be held that the prohibition of doping is based on purely sporting considerations and therefore has nothing to do with any economic consideration. That means, in the light of the case law and the considerations set out…above, that the rules to combat doping cannot…come within the scope of the Treaty provisions on the economic freedoms.

The General Court's judgment was later overturned by the Court of Justice, but not on grounds relevant to the extract above.

The other area where horizontal application of services law has been applied to significant effect, perhaps even more controversially, is labour regulation, in particular the activities of trade unions. This is the result of *Laval* and *Viking Line*.[60]

Of the two, *Laval* was decided a week later, but is the more concerned with service provision, whereas *Viking* is primarily about establishment. In *Laval*, the Court of Justice applied Article 56 TFEU to the law concerning trade unions. Swedish unions took industrial action against foreign employers using posted workers. The unions were trying to force the employers to sign Swedish collective agreements. The union fear was that otherwise the posted workers would receive lower pay and worse conditions, and would undercut local workers and undermine local standards. The employers, however, considered that their freedom to provide services was being restricted by the industrial action, which was effectively preventing them from carrying out their building projects. Citing cases on services, workers and establishment, the Court ruled as follows.

Case C-341/05 *Laval un Partneri Ltd* v *Svenska Byggnadsarbetareförbundet, Svenska Byggnadsarbetareförbundets avdelning 1, Byggettan and Svenska Elektrikerförbundet* [2007] ECR I-11767

98. Furthermore, compliance with Article [56 TFEU] is also required in the case of rules which are not public in nature but which are designed to regulate, collectively, the provision of services. The abolition, as between Member States, of obstacles to the freedom to provide services would be compromised if the abolition of State barriers could be neutralised by obstacles resulting from the exercise of their legal autonomy by associations or organisations not governed by public law…

---

[60] Case C-341/05 *Laval un Partneri Ltd* v *Svenska Byggnadsarbetareförbundet, Svenska Byggnadsarbetareförbundets avdelning 1, Byggettan and Svenska Elektrikerförbundet* [2007] ECR I-11767; Case C-438/05 *International Transport Workers' Federation and Finnish Seamen's Union* v *Viking Line ABP and OÜ Viking Line Eesti* [2007] ECR I-10779.

This application of Article 56 TFEU to trade unions raised fears because of its implications for union autonomy and the freedom of workers to fight for their interests, not least because they might perhaps be sued for damages if their action violated Article 56.[61] However, it was doctrinally hardly different from *Walrave*.[62] In the Swedish employment system, trade unions were an important part of the system of employment regulation, and via their role in collective bargaining, contributed to de facto regulation of labour terms and conditions.

However, in *Viking Line*, the Court of Justice appeared to go further, and suggest that the application of free movement law to private bodies is not dependent upon them playing some quasi-regulatory role. In *Viking Line*, it was Finnish trade unions that were objecting to free movement, but in this case they took industrial action to try and prevent a Finnish shipping company from reflagging a ship under a Latvian flag. The company wanted to employ workers under cheaper Latvian terms and conditions. It was therefore the freedom of the shipping company to choose their state of establishment that was being restricted by the unions. The Court reaffirmed that Article 49 TFEU must be interpreted to apply to private bodies, in terms almost identical to those in the paragraph above from *Laval*, and then continued as follows.

Case C-438/05 International Transport Workers' Federation and Finnish Seamen's Union v Viking Line ABP and OÜ Viking Line Eesti [2007] ECR I-10779

64. It must be added that, contrary to the claims, in particular, of ITF, it does not follow from the case-law of the Court...that that interpretation applies only to quasi-public organisations or to associations exercising a regulatory task and having quasi-legislative powers.

65. There is no indication in that case-law that could validly support the view that it applies only to associations or to organisations exercising a regulatory task or having quasi-legislative powers. Furthermore, it must be pointed out that, in exercising their autonomous power, pursuant to their trade union rights, to negotiate with employers or professional organisations the conditions of employment and pay of workers, trade unions participate in the drawing up of agreements seeking to regulate paid work collectively.

This is an important clarification *of Laval* and *Walrave*. Although there is a certain tension between paragraph 64 and the comment in the next paragraph that trade unions do in fact contribute to labour regulation, it appears that the Court is saying that Article 49 does not apply to private parties because they have some specific legally assigned role in economic activity, but merely because as a matter of fact they have the power to obstruct free movement.

---

[61] See C. Barnard, *Employment Rights, Free Movement under the EC Treaty and the Services Directive*, Mitchell Working Paper No. 5/08 (2008); N. Reich, 'Free Movement v Social Rights in an Enlarged Union: The *Laval* and *Viking* Cases before the ECJ' (2008) 9 *German Law Journal* 125; J. Malmberg and T. Sigeman, 'Industrial Actors and EU Economic Freedoms: The Autonomous Collective Bargaining Model Curtailed by the European Court of Justice' (2008) 43 *CMLRev.* 1115; C. Barnard, '*Viking* and *Laval*: An Introduction' in C. Barnard (ed.) (2007–08) 10 *CYELS* 463; A. Dashwood, '*Viking* and *Laval*: Issues of Horizontal Direct Effect' in C. Barnard (ed.), (2007–08) 10 *CYELS* 525; T. Novitz, 'A Human Rights Analysis of the *Viking* and *Laval* Judgments' in C. Barnard (ed.) (2007–08) 10 *CYELS* 541; S. Sciarra, '*Viking* and *Laval*: Collective Labour Rights and Market Freedoms in the Enlarged EU' in C. Barnard (ed.) (2007–08) 10 *CYELS* 563; C. Kaupa, 'Maybe Not Activist Enough? On the Court's Alleged Neoliberal Bias in its Recent Labor cases' in M. Dawson, B. de Witte and E. Muir (eds.), *Judicial Activism at the European Court of Justice* (Cheltenham, Edward Elgar, 2013) 56.

[62] Cf. H. Schepel, 'Constitutionalising the Market, Marketising the Constitution, and to Tell the Difference: On the Horizontal Application of the Free Movement Provisions in EU Law' (2012) 18 *ELJ* 177.

The application to unions is therefore not because of any particular legal status that they may enjoy, but because as a matter of fact the action they were undertaking was making establishment in Latvia harder. There seems no reason why the Court should take a different approach in the context of services.

Schepel has made two powerful criticisms of the doctrine in *Viking* and *Laval*. One is that the kind of balancing of interests that courts will have to make in order to see whether industrial action is justified is so imprecise that it will lead to legal uncertainty, which will result in poor application of the law, which will in turn lead ultimately to a reduced effectiveness of Article 56 – even though, ironically, effectiveness is the primary rationale for the decision that the Court of Justice provides. The other criticism is that it is wrong to see *Viking* and *Laval* as following on from *Walrave*: as he argues in the extract below, they have a quite different underlying philosophy.

H. Schepel, 'Constitutionalising the Market, Marketising the Constitution, and to Tell the Difference: On the Horizontal Application of the Free Movement Provisions in EU Law' (2012) 18 *ELJ* 177, 177–8

In constitutional scholarship, the issue of horizontal effect of fundamental rights is usually thought to arise when market outcomes seem to conflict with constitutional norms. Put this way, it is easy to see the trouble the concept gets into when entitlements to market outcomes are elevated to the status of fundamental rights. In a string of cases starting with the 1974 decision in *Walrave*, the Court of Justice has held that the economic freedom of private employers and other powerful organisations are limited by the free movement provisions of the Treaty that protect individuals from discrimination on grounds of nationality. In 2007, the Court held in *Viking* and *Laval* that the fundamental right of collective action of trade unions is limited by the provisions of the Treaty that guarantee employers the economic freedom to provide services and to establish themselves in other Member States. One could be forgiven for thinking that these cases represent radically different conceptions of the internal market: the first as the expression of the primacy of the polity over 'the market' through the imposition of public law values on principles of private law, the second as an act of neoliberal faith in imposing economic freedom on constitutionally protected social rights. Where the former cases seem to foreshadow the 'social market economy', the latter hark back to the days when the Treaty could be described as the 'most strongly free market-oriented constitution in the world'.[63] And yet, the Court decided the latter cases largely on the authority of the former under the same rubric of the 'horizontal direct effect of the fundamental freedoms'.

The seriousness of the potential problems depends partly on the precise extent of horizontal effect. All of the cases discussed in this section have concerned a private party who was not themselves engaged in cross-border provision of services, but was taking measures which prevented two other parties from doing so. Could the Treaty also be applied to one of the parties to the service provision, the recipient or the provider?[64] It seems now to be clear that if a private party prevents an Italian hairdresser from accessing Belgian clients then it will be

---

[63] C.-D. Ehlermann, 'The Contribution of EC Competition Policy to the Single Market' (1992) 29 *CML Rev.* 257, 273.
[64] See G. Davies, 'Freedom of Movement, Horizontal Effect, and Freedom of Contract' (2012) 20 *European Review of Private Law*, 805.

subject to the Treaty. But what if the Italian hairdresser herself refuses Belgian clients, or if a Belgian client refuses to go to an Italian hairdresser? Is this a restriction on free movement of services? On the one hand, it would seem clear that a cross-border provision of services is being prevented by a directly discriminatory choice. On the other hand, applying the Treaty to individual preferences like this would have a huge impact on individual autonomy, as well as being practically impossible to police. Moreover, if we cannot choose an Italian hairdresser, does this mean that the time will come when we cannot choose French cheese without discriminating illegally?

It is suggested that it is possible to draw a distinction between areas of free movement: people are different, and a rejection of discrimination against them is not new to policy. Discrimination in employment is prohibited already and where service relationships come close to employment in their substance it would make sense to take the same approach.[65] Yet could this go so far as to prohibit a private preference to do business with a national bank, or an Italian hairdresser? Conceptual tools which may help answer this difficult question could include the presence of market power, and the effect on the dignity of the individual.[66] It may be noted that Directives have already been adopted prohibiting discrimination on grounds of sex and race in the supply of goods and services.[67] The application of normative constraints to individual choices is something EU law has already begun to embrace.

5 JUSTIFYING RESTRICTIONS ON SERVICES

The analytical structure of the law on services is summarised in *Gebhard*:[68]

> 37. It follows, however, from the Court's case-law that national measures liable to hinder or make less attractive the exercise of fundamental freedoms guaranteed by the Treaty must fulfil four conditions: they must be applied in a non-discriminatory manner; they must be justified by imperative requirements in the general interest; they must be suitable for securing the attainment of the objective which they pursue; and they must not go beyond what is necessary in order to attain it.

Rephrasing this, it can be said that as with the law on the other freedoms, a restriction on services will be permitted if it is:

(i) equally applicable to the national and the foreign;
(ii) justified by some legitimate public interest objective; and
(iii) proportionate to that objective.

If a restriction on services is not equally applicable, but discriminates on its face, then it may only be saved by reliance on one of the Treaty exceptions.[69]

---

[65] *Angonese*, n. 56 above.   [66] See generally Davies, n. 64 above.
[67] Council Directive 2004/113/EC of 13 December 2004 implementing the principle of equal treatment between men and women in the access to and supply of goods and services [2004] OJ L373/37–43; Council Directive 2000/43/ EC of 29 June 2000 implementing the principle of equal treatment between persons irrespective of racial or ethnic origin [2000] OJ L180/22–6.
[68] Case C-55/94 *Gebhard* v *Consiglio dell'ordine degli avvocati eprocuratori di Milano* [1995] ECR I-4165.
[69] Case C-288/89 *Gouda* v *Commissariat voor de Media* [1991] ECR I-4007; see also p. 900.

The justifications which may be put forward for equally applicable measures are diverse, and the list is not closed.[70] Any good policy reason that is not discriminatory or purely economic is acceptable. The need to regulate a profession in the public interest, consumer protection and the protection of workers are examples.[71] However, the imposition of national laws on service providers is not justified where the interest concerned is protected by legislation in the state of establishment.[72] In *Guiot*, employers were required to pay social security payments for workers in Belgium. However, this applied not only if the company and its workers were established in Belgium, but also if the company was established in another Member State and had temporarily posted workers to Belgium to supply services there. The Court of Justice found that compulsory social security payments could be justified in general by the protection of workers, but imposing them on companies that might be making similar contributions in their home states, without taking any account of this, was disproportionate.[73]

Case C-272/94 *Guiot* [1996] ECR I-1905

14. National legislation which requires an employer, as a person providing a service within the meaning of the Treaty, to pay employer's contributions to the social security fund of the host Member State in addition to the contributions already paid by him to the social security fund of the State where he is established places an additional financial burden on him, so that he is not, so far as competition is concerned, on an equal footing with employers established in the host State.

15. Such legislation, even if it applies without distinction to national providers of services and to those of other Member States, is liable to restrict the freedom to provide services within the meaning of Article [56 TFEU].

16. The public interest relating to the social protection of workers in the construction industry may however, because of conditions specific to that sector, constitute an overriding requirement justifying such a restriction on the freedom to provide services.

17. However, that is not the case where the workers in question enjoy the same protection, or essentially similar protection, by virtue of employer's contributions already paid by the employer in the Member State of establishment.

Requiring a service provider to undergo police checks when similar ones have been performed in the home state is another example of an attempt to make a foreign provider jump through two sets of hoops, in violation of mutual recognition.[74]

It is also disproportionate to subject service providers to all the rules which would apply to them if they were established.[75] The logic of the internal market is that as far as possible

---

[70] S. O'Leary and J. Fernández-Mártin, 'Judicially Created Exceptions to Free Provision of Services' in M. Andenas and W.-H. Roth (eds.), *Services and Free Movement in EU Law* (Oxford, Oxford University Press, 2002); Snell, n. 12 above, 169–219.

[71] See Case C-288/89 *Gouda v Commissariat voor de Media* [1991] ECR I-4007, para. 14 for a long list.

[72] Case C-288/89 *Gouda v Commissariat voor de Media* [1991] ECR I-4007; Case 205/84 *Commission v Germany (German Insurance)* [1986] ECR 3755; Case C-439/99 *Commission v Italy (Trade Fairs)* [2002] ECR I-305. See also Case C-212/11 *Jyske Bank*, Judgment of 25 April 2013.

[73] Similarly, Joined Cases 62/81 and 63/81 *Seco v Etablissement d'assurance contre la vieillesse et l'invalidité* [1982] ECR 223; Case 3/88 *Commission v Italy* [1989] ECR 4035.

[74] Case 279/80 *Webb* [1981] ECR 3305; Case C-458/08 *Commission v Portugal* [2010] ECR I-11599. See also *Jyske Bank*, n. 72 above.

[75] Case 205/84 *Commission v Germany (German Insurance)* [1986] ECR 3755.

each economic actor should be subject to the law of their home state, and mutual recognition should ensure that other states recognise the adequacy of this law and permit that actor to do business on their national markets without further ado. Thus, if a company chooses to establish in state X it is reasonable that in principle it should comply fully with the regulation of X. However, if it is merely providing temporary services in X, then full compliance with the laws of X will almost always be a disproportionate demand. This would take away the regulatory distinction between services and establishment, and undermine the capacity of service providers to choose where to establish. In *Säger*, the German Government obstructed the provision of patent services in Germany by patent agents based in the United Kingdom.[76] They did not possess the qualifications required in Germany for the service they were providing. The Court of Justice did not object to the German rules as such: appropriate rules on qualifications are a way of protecting the consumer in a complex and technical field. However, it went on to hold as follows.

Case C-76/90 *Säger* v *Dennemeyer* [1991] ECR I-4221

...a Member State may not make the provision of services in its territory subject to compliance with all the conditions required for establishment and thereby deprive of all practical effectiveness the provisions of the Treaty whose object is, precisely, to guarantee the freedom to provide services. Such a restriction is all the less permissible where, as in the main proceedings, and unlike the situation governed by the third paragraph of Article [57 TFEU], the service is supplied without its being necessary for the person providing it to visit the territory of the Member State where it is provided.

A step further is to actually require a service provider to establish: some cases have involved national rules which restrict certain service activities to those who are established in that Member State, or have physical premises there, or who live there. In *Van Binsbergen*, a Dutch requirement that lawyers be established in the Netherlands in order to provide legal services was in issue, and in *Commission* v *Italy* a rule was challenged requiring debt collectors to have physical premises in each province where they were licensed.[77] The argument for such rules is usually about the need for supervision, but they are rarely justified. Given the fact that they effectively ban all cross-border provision of the service in question, and given that the requirements in question do not really do much to guarantee effective supervision in a world of modern communication, the general position is that a less restrictive and more proportionate approach should be found.

(i) Restrictions on marketing and prices

The way that a service is marketed and priced may be just as important to the commercial success of the service provider as the content or quality of the service. Moreover, where a market is dominated by established providers, an innovative marketing or pricing policy can help a new market player break in. The Court of Justice has therefore acknowledged that

---

[76] Case C-76/90 *Säger* v *Dennemeyer* [1991] ECR I-4221.
[77] *Van Binsbergen*, n. 36 above; Case C-134/05 *Commission* v *Italy* [2007] ECR I-6251.

rules which limit price competition may restrict trade.[78] Most notably, in *Cipolla*, it considered regional rules in Italy which fixed legal fees at a set level, and prohibited lawyers from charging less.[79]

Joined Cases C-94/04 and C-202/04 *Federico Cipolla and others* v *Rosaria Fazari, née Portolese and Roberto Meloni* [2006] ECR I-11421

59. That prohibition deprives lawyers established in a Member State other than the Italian Republic of the possibility, by requesting fees lower than those set by the scale, of competing more effectively with lawyers established on a stable basis in the Member State concerned and who therefore have greater opportunities for winning clients than lawyers established abroad...

60. Likewise, the prohibition thus laid down limits the choice of service recipients in Italy, because they cannot resort to the services of lawyers established in other Member States who would offer their services in Italy at a lower rate than the minimum fees set by the scale...

62. In order to justify the restriction on freedom to provide services which stems from the prohibition at issue, the Italian Government submits that excessive competition between lawyers might lead to price competition which would result in a deterioration in the quality of the services provided to the detriment of consumers, in particular as individuals in need of quality advice in court proceedings...

64. In that respect, it must be pointed out that, first, the protection of consumers, in particular recipients of the legal services provided by persons concerned in the administration of justice and, secondly, the safeguarding of the proper administration of justice, are objectives to be included among those which may be regarded as overriding requirements relating to the public interest capable of justifying a restriction on freedom to provide services, on condition, first, that the national measure at issue in the main proceedings is suitable for securing the attainment of the objective pursued and, secondly, it does not go beyond what is necessary in order to attain that objective.

65. It is a matter for the national court to decide whether, in the main proceedings, the restriction on freedom to provide services introduced by that national legislation fulfils those conditions. For that purpose, it is for that court to take account of the factors set out in the following paragraphs.

66. Thus, it must be determined, in particular, whether there is a correlation between the level of fees and the quality of the services provided by lawyers and whether, in particular, the setting of such minimum fees constitutes an appropriate measure for attaining the objectives pursued, namely the protection of consumers and the proper administration of justice.

67. Although it is true that a scale imposing minimum fees cannot prevent members of the profession from offering services of mediocre quality, it is conceivable that such a scale does serve to prevent lawyers, in a context such as that of the Italian market which, as indicated in the decision making the reference, is characterised by an extremely large number of lawyers who are enrolled and practising, from being encouraged to compete against each other by possibly offering services at a discount, with the risk of deterioration in the quality of the services provided.

68. Account must also be taken of the specific features both of the market in question, as noted in the preceding paragraph, and the services in question and, in particular, of the fact that, in the field of

---

[78] Case 82/77 *Van Tiggele* [1978] ECR 25; Case 231/83 *Cullet* [1985] ECR 305; Case C-442/02 *Caixabank France* [2004] ECR I-8961.

[79] See M. J. Frese and H. J. van Harten, 'How Extravagant the Fees of Counselors at Law Sometimes Appear: Competition Law and Internal Market Constraints to Fixed Remuneration Schemes' (2007) 34 *LIEI* 393. See also Case C-565/08 *Commission* v *Italy*, n. 46 above.

lawyers' services, there is usually an asymmetry of information between 'client-consumers' and lawyers. Lawyers display a high level of technical knowledge which consumers may not have and the latter therefore find it difficult to judge the quality of the services provided to them.

69. However, the national court will have to determine whether professional rules in respect of lawyers, in particular rules relating to organisation, qualifications, professional ethics, supervision and liability, suffice in themselves to attain the objectives of the protection of consumers and the proper administration of justice.

The argument that minimum prices prevent excessive competition leading to lower standards and thereby protect the consumer is a very common one, used in most professional contexts. What is striking about *Cipolla* is the extent to which the Court of Justice is prepared to critically examine this argument on the particular facts, and to question whether professional quality could be protected by less restrictive means. What is also interesting is that while it leaves the final answer to the national court to decide, the Court implies that facts specific to Italy or the local legal market may be relevant to that answer. It is therefore possible that a minimum price might be justified and proportionate in Italy, but not in another Member State, or even in one region of Italy but not in another, because of the different characteristics of the market for legal services in each area. Such a market-specific approach to proportionality is only politically sustainable because it is local judges who finally decide whether local rules are proportionate. Were the Court of Justice to rule that, for example, minimum prices were permissible in Italy but not in Germany, this would probably be seen as grossly unfair.

A variation on the theme of price control was found in *DKV*, where Belgian law prevented health insurers from imposing large increases in premiums.[80] The Court of Justice found that this certainly restricted access to the Belgian market, because it might force providers from other states to rethink their business strategies. However, it was sympathetic to the claim that the rules were necessary to protect consumers from price shocks, being particularly influenced by the fact that health insurance premiums might otherwise rise sharply precisely in the period where the insurance is most likely to be necessary – when people get older. While leaving the decision to the national court, the Court sketched its own vision of how the health insurance market works in a way that made it easy to find the rules justified.

In *Alpine Investments*, discussed above, the Court of Justice found a restriction on services to be present because cold-calling (making unsolicited telephone calls to potential clients) can be an effective marketing technique.[81] It did not expand on its reasoning, but in reality it is a particularly good technique for a non-established market actor, and the judgment reflects an integrationist use of Article 56 TFEU, as well as a very practical and business-oriented one.

Yet, the Court went on to find the restriction justified. It was argued that it was not for the Dutch Government to protect German consumers, particularly since Germany did not in fact prohibit cold-calling. However, the Court accepted Dutch arguments that in the particular branch of the financial services industry involved, customers were relatively vulnerable and allowing cold-calling could easily result in the Dutch finance industry getting a bad name, which was a legitimate thing to want to prevent. Moreover, the Dutch authorities could not just

---

[80] Case C-577/11 *DKV*, Judgment of 7 March 2013.
[81] Case C-384/93 *Alpine Investments* v *Minister van Financiën* [1995] ECR I-1141.

rely on their German peers to prevent customers being exploited, since it would be difficult for them to prevent or to regulate cold-calls coming from other states. The state of establishment was best placed to control the calls a company made, and therefore justified in taking a stance on this issue. *Alpine Investments* has an unusual fact-set, but establishes that restrictions on the export of services are no different from restrictions on import for the purposes of Article 56: they are equally prohibited but equally open to justification.[82]

Dermoestetica concerned a prohibition on advertising private medical or surgical care on national television. Advertising is particularly important for cross-border services, where the foreign provider, who may not have a local physical presence, has no other means of coming into contact with local clients. This suggests one reason why there is no *Keck* for services – because the effect of selling arrangements on goods and services is not necessarily the same. Nevertheless, the Court of Justice would have been prepared to find the restriction justified by public health were it not that similar advertising was permitted on local television. This inconsistency undermined the effectiveness of the measure, so that it was no longer, the Court found 'appropriate for the purpose of securing the attainment of the objective of public health'.[83]

(ii) Access to regulated industries and professions

The largest group of cases on services concern access to regulated professions and industries. Foreign service providers wishing to provide services in a highly regulated industry, such as the law, medicine, gambling, or private security, typically find that many measures stand in their way. One of the most common problems is obtaining recognition of foreign qualifications, which is dealt with in Chapter 19.[84] However, other aspects of authorisation and regulation have also been the subject of much case law.

Corsten is a relatively simple example. An architect working from the Netherlands contracted to arrange floor laying in Germany, but was fined when he did the work because he was not entered on the local German register of skilled traders. In order to go on this register, he had to submit various documents, pay a fee, and become a member of the local chamber of skilled trades, which entailed paying a subscription. The process also took some time, and he was not permitted to practise his trade in the area until it was completed.

Case C-58/98 *Corsten* [2000] ECR I-7919

45. Even if the requirement of entry on that Register, entailing compulsory membership of the Chamber of Skilled Trades for the undertakings concerned and therefore payment of the related subscription, could be justified in the case of establishment in the host Member State, which is not the situation in the main proceedings, the same is not true for undertakings which intend to provide services in the host Member State only on an occasional basis, indeed perhaps only once.

46. The latter are liable to be dissuaded from going ahead with their plans if, because of the compulsory requirement that they be entered on the Register, the authorisation procedure is made lengthier and more expensive, so that the profit anticipated, at least for small contracts, is no longer economically

---

[82] See also Case C-18/93 *Corsica Ferries France* [1994] ECR I-1783; Case C-379/92 *Peralta* [1994] ECR I-3453.
[83] Case C-500/06 *Corporacion Dermoestetica* [2008] ECR I-5785, para. 40.
[84] See pp. 866–73.

worthwhile. For those undertakings, therefore, the freedom to provide services, a fundamental principle of the Treaty, and likewise Directive 64/427 are liable to become ineffective.

47. In consequence, the authorisation procedure instituted by the host Member State should neither delay nor complicate exercise of the right of persons established in another Member State to provide their services on the territory of the first State where examination of the conditions governing access to the activities concerned has been carried out and it has been established that those conditions are satisfied.

48. Moreover, any requirement of entry on the trades Register of the host Member State, assuming it was justified, should neither give rise to additional administrative expense nor entail compulsory payment of subscriptions to the chamber of trades.

The Court of Justice highlights the importance of distinguishing between established persons and those providing services. Service providers may do very little business in their host state, and so even relatively light administrative burdens wipe out their profit and deter them from entering the market. The aim of the register was to ensure the quality of traders and protect consumers, which was legitimate, but proportionality demanded that where a service provider was concerned the procedure for register entry be as minimal and simple as possible. In particular, it must not add 'administrative expense' and nor must it delay the start of work – meaning that either a trader can begin work while the process of registration is underway, or registration must be available immediately. In *Commission* v *Belgium*, an apparently very simple administrative procedure was found to violate Article 56: all those providing services in Belgium who were established elsewhere were required to fill in a form once a year indicating their identity and the services they were providing.[85] The form was available online, and the procedure was free, and the Belgian Government estimated it took about half an hour per year to fill in. Nevertheless, since the Belgian Government could not show that the information was actually necessary to safeguard some public interest, it was disproportionate. It may have been relevant that although not much was being asked of service providers, there were criminal sanctions for a failure to comply.

Somewhat more burdensome demands have been involved in the considerable number of cases concerning private security firms.[86] These are highly regulated for understandable reasons, but the nature of the regulation is at times bizarre, and very often disproportionate. In *Commission* v *Italy*, security guards were required to swear an oath of allegiance to the Italian state, obviously disproportionate, and particularly irksome for the temporary service provider; while in *Commission* v *Belgium*, private security firms were required to be established in Belgium, and the managers and employees were required to live in Belgium.[87] Such territorial requirements have been the subject of many cases over the years, and are invariably disproportionate.[88] The proposed justification is that it enables better supervision of the firms and

---

[85] Case C-577/10 *Commission* v *Belgium*, Judgment of 19 December 2012.

[86] Case C-355/98 *Commission* v *Belgium* [2000] ECR I-1221; Case C-171/02 *Commission* v *Portugal* [2004] ECR I-5645; Case C-514/03 *Commission* v *Spain* [2006] ECR I-963; Case C-465/05 *Commission* v *Italy* [2007] ECR I-11091.

[87] Case C-465/05 *Commission* v *Italy* [2007] ECR I-11091; Case C-355/98 *Commission* v *Belgium* [2000] ECR I-1221.

[88] Case 33/74 *Van Binsbergen* v *Bestuur van de Bedrijsvereniging voor de Metaalnijverheid* [1974] ECR 1310; Case 39/75 *Coenen* v *Sociaal-Economische Raad* [1975] ECR 1547; Case 205/84 *Commission* v *Germany (German Insurance)* [1986] ECR 3755. Similarly Case C-299/02 *Commission* v *Netherlands* [2004] ECR I-9761.

individuals by the national authorities, but the Court has found that this can be achieved by less restrictive means. It is possible to communicate with authorities in other states, and it is possible to carry out checks on firms and individuals wherever they live or are established.[89]

A number of recent gambling cases have concerned the right to offer gambling services, such as lotteries or betting on horse-races, at a distance, usually over the Internet.[90] The Court of Justice accepts that this kind of service requires strict controls in the cause of preventing crimes such as fraud and money-laundering and preventing addiction to gambling by the public. These issues are discussed further in Chapter 20.[91] However, even justifiably protective measures can be prohibited restrictions on free movement if they have some discriminatory or protectionist element in the way they are applied. This was the case with horse-betting licences in *Commission* v *Italy*. Italy permitted a fixed number of these, but they were awarded and renewed without any publicity so that there was little turnover of licence holders, and for a new entrant it was difficult to obtain a licence. The Court found an obligation of transparency to be imposed on public authorities by Article 56 TFEU.[92]

Case C-260/04 *Commission* v *Italy* [2007] ECR I-7083

22. The Court has held that, notwithstanding the fact that public service concession contracts are, as Community law stands at present, excluded from the scope of Directive 92/50 [on public procurement] the public authorities concluding them are, nonetheless, bound to comply with the fundamental rules of the EC Treaty, in general, and the principle of non-discrimination on the grounds of nationality, in particular.

23. The Court then stated that the provisions of the Treaty applying to public service concessions, in particular Articles [49 and 56 TFEU], and the prohibition of discrimination on grounds of nationality are specific expressions of the principle of equal treatment.

24. In that regard, the principles of equal treatment and non-discrimination on grounds of nationality imply, in particular, a duty of transparency which enables the concession-granting public authority to ensure that those principles are complied with. That obligation of transparency which is imposed on the public authority consists in ensuring, for the benefit of any potential tenderer, a degree of advertising sufficient to enable the service concession to be opened up to competition and the impartiality of procurement procedures to be reviewed.

---

[89] Case C-393/05 *Commission* v *Austria* [2007] ECR I-10195; Case C-404/05 *Commission* v *Germany* [2007] ECR I-10239; Case C-383/05 *Talotta* v *Belgium* [2007] ECR I-2555; Case C-107/83 *Ordre des Avocats au Barreau de Paris* v *Klopp* [1984] ECR I-2971; Case 33/74 *Van Binsbergen* v *Bestuur van de Bedrijsvereniging voor de Metaalnijverheid* [1974] ECR 1310.

[90] E.g. Case C-186/11 *Stanleybet*, Judgment of 24 January 2013; Case C-46/08 *Carmen Media* [2010] ECR I-08149; Case C-316/07 *Stoß* [2010] ECR I-08069; Case C-258/08 *Ladbrokes* [2010] ECR I-04757; Case C-67/98 *Questore di Verona* v *Zenatti* [1999] ECR I-7289; Case C-42/02 *Lindman* [2003] ECR I-13519; Case C-6/01 *Anomar* v *Estado Português* [2003] ECR I-8621; Case C-243/01 *Gambelli* [2003] ECR I-13031; Joined Cases C-338/04, C-359/04 and C-360/04 *Placanica, Palazzese and Soricchio* [2007] ECR I-1891; Case C-42/07 *Liga Portuguesa de Futebol Profissional and Bwin International Ltd* v *Departamento de Jogos da Santa Casa da Misericórdia de Lisboa*, Judgment of 8 September 2009. See D. Doukas, 'In a Bet there is a Fool and a State Monopoly: Are the Odds Stacked Against Cross-border Gambling?' (2011) 36 *ELRev.* 243; S. Van den Bogaert, A. Cuyvers, '"Money for Nothing": The Case Law of the EU Court of Justice on the Regulation of Gambling' (2011) 48 *CMLRev.* 1175; J. Mulder, 'A New Chapter in the European Court of Justice Gambling Saga: A Stacked Deck?' (2011) 38 *LIEI* 243.

[91] See especially pp. 904–6.

[92] See M. Szydlo, 'The Process of Granting Exclusive Rights in the Light of Treaty Rules on Free Movement' (2011) 12 *German Law Journal* 1408.

A final group of cases concern measures which set restrictions on the nature of the service provider, rather than on their activities. For example, in *Sjöberg*, Sweden only allowed non-profit and public organisations to offer gambling services, and did not allow advertising of foreign gambling providers in Sweden unless these were also non-profit or public.[93] The Court of Justice found that the principle that profit and gambling should not be mixed was a fundamental part of the Swedish system of gambling regulation, served legitimate policy goals, and justified the measure. *Duomo*, by contrast, concerned an Italian rule that companies involved in tax collection (there was some outsourcing of this to the private sector) must have a minimum size.[94] Reasons were put forward for this, mainly that larger companies were less likely to go bankrupt with resulting loss of the collected revenue. However, the Court found that other measures could be found which were less restrictive, and did not absolutely exclude smaller actors.

(iii) Tax and investment issues

Tax is still a very national matter. In the current state of European integration, it can neither be levied nor spent in a way that takes no account of national boundaries, creating an unavoidable tension with free movement law, which pursues a Europe in which those boundaries are gone. What is simply practical and responsible tax policy, focused on those living and working in a given Member State, may look like nationality discrimination from another perspective. The necessary compromises have created a complex body of EU law which cannot be fully addressed here.

The underlying principles are no different from those applicable to other measures discussed above. It is just that in deciding what is justified, it is often necessary to have a detailed knowledge of how the tax system works. However, in some cases the facts are more accessible, and these provide a taste of how tax and the free movement of services interact.

Tax discrimination based on location is the most common problem.[95] The Spanish Government exempted winnings from a number of lotteries from tax, but all the relevant lotteries were organised by Spanish organisations.[96] Lottery winnings from lotteries established abroad were not exempted. This placed lotteries established abroad at a disadvantage on the Spanish market and discouraged them from offering their services there. The case is also an example of the well-established principle that it is not necessary to advantage every national operator in order to discriminate: advantaging some national businesses at the expense of foreign ones will suffice.[97]

In *Jundt*, it was tax on the provider rather than the recipient that was in issue.[98] The German Government exempted expense payments to part-time university teachers from tax, but only if the university in question was established in Germany. This was prohibited because it made the provision of services abroad less attractive than equivalent domestic provision and so amounted to a restriction on cross-border service provision.

---

[93] Case C-447/08 *Sjöberg* [2010] ECR I-06921.   [94] Case C-357/10 *Duomo*, Judgment of 10 May 2012.

[95] Case C-39/04 *Laboratoires Fournier SA* v *Direction des vérifications nationales et internationales* [2005] ECR I-2057; Case C-383/05 *Talotta* v *Belgium* [2007] ECR I-2555; Case C-330/07 *Jobra VermögensverwaltungsGesellschaft mbH* v *Finanzamt Amstetten Melk Scheibbs*, Judgment of 4 December 2008.

[96] Case C-153/08 *Commission* v *Spain*, Judgment of 6 October 2009.

[97] See also Case C-169/08 *Presidente del Consiglio dei Ministri* v *Regione Sardegna*, Judgment of 17 November 2009.

[98] Case C-281/06 *Jundt and Jundt* v *Finanzamt Offenburg* [2007] ECR I-12231.

Commission v *Belgium* is the mirror of *Jundt*.[99] Belgian laws required those employing building contractors not established in Belgium to withhold 15 per cent of any payment to them against possible tax liabilities of those contractors in Belgium. The contractors had to go through an administrative procedure to show they owed no tax before they could get this money. This deterred foreign contractors from working in Belgium. The justification of preventing tax fraud was not enough to convince the Court of Justice, which suggested, quite consistently with its case law, that a more proportionate approach would be for the authorities to exchange information with employers and contractors so that tax obligations could be enforced.

De Coster concerned indirect discrimination.[100] A tax was imposed on satellite dishes by the municipal authorities in a town in Belgium. This was claimed to be largely on aesthetic grounds: dishes are not pretty, and the tax was intended to discourage them. However, satellite dishes tend to be used to receive cross-border television transmissions, whereas most national programmes are transmitted by cable. Since there was no analogous tax on cable connections, the measure disadvantaged foreign television providers. The Court found that it could not be justified.

Case C-17/00 *De Coster* v *Collège des bourgmestre et échevins de Watermael-Boitsfort* [2001] ECR I-9445

38. As the Commission observed, there are methods other than the tax in question in the main proceedings, less restrictive of the freedom to provide services, which could achieve an objective such as the protection of the urban environment, for instance the adoption of requirements concerning the size of the dishes, their position and the way in which they are fixed to the building or its surroundings or the use of communal dishes. Moreover, such requirements have been adopted by the municipality of Watermael-Boitsfort, as is apparent from the planning rules on outdoor aerials adopted by that municipality and approved by regulation of 27 February 1997 of the government of the Brussels-Capital region.

The odd thing here is that the municipality had already adopted the measures proposed by the Court of Justice, and clearly considered that they were not enough. Yet, the Court uses their adoption as an argument against the tax. This perhaps shows two things. One is that the Court is very strict where unequal effects are involved, particularly if there is the suspicion of deliberate discrimination against foreign service providers. The other is that the Court may have been aware of the considerable unspoken social background to taxes such as these: satellite dishes are most popular among immigrant groups, and this colours the aesthetic arguments against them, however real these may be.

Laws requiring or deterring investment are usually treated as restrictions on the free movement of capital. However, *UTECA* provides an example where the provision of services is also involved.[101] The Spanish Government required television operators to use 5 per cent of their revenue to fund European films, and to use 60 per cent of that 5 per cent for films made in one

---

[99] Case C-433/04 *Commission* v *Belgium* [2006] ECR I-10653.
[100] Case C-17/00 *De Coster* v *Collège des bourgmestre et échevins de Watermael-Boitsfort* [2001] ECR I-9445.
[101] Case C-222/07 *UTECA* v *Administración General del Estado*, Judgment of 5 March 2009.

of the official languages of Spain. The Court of Justice rather surprisingly found that the first requirement was not a restriction on any of the freedoms. It seems likely that many television companies would be deterred from establishing in Spain by this rule. The second requirement, by contrast, was a restriction on capital, services and establishment. Spanish television operators would be less likely to buy, or finance the making of, non-Spanish films. Foreign suppliers or makers of films would therefore find their position on the Spanish market weakened. Nevertheless, the measures were found to be justified by the need to defend Spanish multilingualism. As with other culture and language cases, the Court shows a greater deference to national concerns than is usually the case.[102]

6 SERVICES AND THE MARKET SOCIETY

(i) Right to trade and socially sensitive services

Article 56 TFEU embodies a right to trade services. This applies even to services which have not traditionally been seen as tradeable or as primarily economic. Health care, education, sport and ethically sensitive services like abortion or gambling have traditionally been regulated from a primarily non-economic perspective.

It has been put to the Court of Justice that such services should not fall within Article 56 because of their special social, cultural or ethical importance. The Court has consistently rejected this.[103] In *Kohll*, speaking of rules on social security and health care, it said: 'The Court has held that the special nature of certain services does not remove them from the ambit of the fundamental principle of freedom of movement.'[104] Similarly, when it was argued in *Schindler* that gambling could not be regarded as a service because in some states it was illegal, the Court refused to take a moral stance.

Case C–275/92 HM Customs and Excise v Schindler [1994] ECR I-1039

32. In these circumstances, lotteries cannot be regarded as activities whose harmful nature causes them to be prohibited in all the Member States and whose position under Community law may be likened to that of activities involving illegal products (see, in relation to drugs, the judgment in Case 294/82 *Einberger* v *Hauptzollamt Freiburg* [1984] ECR 1177) even though, as the Belgian and Luxembourg Governments point out, the law of certain Member States treats gaming contracts as void. Even if the morality of lotteries is at least questionable, it is not for the Court to substitute its assessment for that of the legislatures of the Member States where that activity is practised legally...

---

[102] See also Case 379/87 *Groener* v *Minister for Education and the City of Dublin Vocational Educational Committee* [1989] ECR I-3967; Case C-424/97 *Salomone Haim* v *Kassenzahnärztliche Vereinigung Nordrhein* [2000] ECR I-5123; Case C-250/06 *United Pan-Europe Communications Belgium SA and others* v *Belgian State* [2007] ECR I-11135. See also Case C-506/04 *Graham J. Wilson* v *Ordre des avocats du barreau de Luxembourg* [2006] ECR I-8613.

[103] By contrast, it has been more reluctant to apply competition law. See Joined Cases C-159/91 and C-160/91 *Poucet* v *Assurances Générales de France and Caisse Mutuelle Régionale du Languedoc-Roussillon* [1993] ECR I-637. See generally W. Sauter and H. Schepel, *State and Market in European Union Law* (Cambridge, Cambridge University Press, 2009).

[104] Case C-158/96 *Kohll* v *Union des Caisses de Maladie* [1998] ECR I-1931.

It has applied the same logic to prostitution,[105] and most famously to abortion, in *Grogan*. A group of students in Ireland distributed pamphlets providing information on how to get an abortion in the United Kingdom. Abortion is constitutionally prohibited in Ireland.[106] The Irish authorities took steps to prohibit the distribution of the pamphlets, and the question was whether this amounted to a restriction on the free movement of services.

Case C–159/90 *Society for the Protection of the Unborn Child (SPUC)* v Grogan [1991] ECR I–4685

18. It must be held that termination of pregnancy, as lawfully practised in several Member States, is a medical activity which is normally provided for remuneration and may be carried out as part of a professional activity. In any event, the Court has already held in the judgment in *Luisi and Carbone* that medical activities fall within the scope of Article [57] of the Treaty.[107]

19. SPUC, however, maintains that the provision of abortion cannot be regarded as being a service, on the grounds that it is grossly immoral and involves the destruction of the life of a human being, namely the unborn child.

20. Whatever the merits of those arguments on the moral plane, they cannot influence the answer to the national court's first question. It is not for the Court to substitute its assessment for that of the legislature in those Member States where the activities in question are practised legally.

21. Consequently, the answer to the national court's first question must be that medical termination of pregnancy, performed in accordance with the law of the State in which it is carried out, constitutes a service within the meaning of Article [57] of the Treaty...

24. As regards, first, the provisions of Article [56] of the Treaty, which prohibit any restriction on the freedom to supply services, it is apparent from the facts of the case that the link between the activity of the students associations of which Mr Grogan and the other defendants are officers and medical terminations of pregnancies carried out in clinics in another Member State is too tenuous for the prohibition on the distribution of information to be capable of being regarded as a restriction within the meaning of Article [56] of the Treaty.

In fact, the Court of Justice managed to avoid a major conflict of values by finding that Article 56 did not apply because the students had no connection with the service providers.[108] They were acting out of non-commercial motives on their own initiative. The case implicitly introduces a 'directness' criterion into the concept of a restriction on services,[109] but the context was so politically sensitive and the facts so unusual that this extrapolation must remain uncertain.

However, the lasting importance of the case is in the confirmation that, however offensive or illegal a service may be in one state, if it is permitted in others then providers in those states

---

[105] See also Case C-268/99 *Jany* v *Staatssecretaris van Justitie* [2001] ECR I-8615.

[106] With nuances: see e.g. I. Bacik, 'The Irish Constitution and Gender Politics: Developments in the Law on Abortion' (2013) 28 *Irish Political Studies* 380.

[107] Joined Cases 286/82 and 26/83 *Luisi and Carbone* v *Ministero del Tesoro* [1984] ECR 377, para. 16.

[108] See D. R. Phelan, 'The Right to Life of the Unborn v Promotion of Trade in Services: The European Court and the Normative Shaping of the European Union' (1992) 55 *MLR* 670. Shortly after this case a Protocol was adopted protecting the Irish ban on abortion from EU law. See C. Barnard, *The Substantive Law of the EU* (2nd edn, Oxford, Oxford University Press, 2007) 362–6.

[109] *Ibid.* 361.

can rely on Article 56. Had the Irish Government taken sufficiently concrete steps to prevent Irish women going to the United Kingdom for paid abortions, Article 56 TFEU would have applied, the Irish Constitution notwithstanding.

This is not to say that national constitutional values will not be respected, or may not prevail. Both mandatory requirements and Treaty exceptions may justify a restriction on free movement and it is undoubtedly the case that where there is such strong national feeling as exists in Ireland over abortion, the Court of Justice will weigh this heavily.[110] However, the structure of the normative framework has been changed. After *Kohll*, *Grogan* and *Schindler*, moral, social and cultural perspectives are tested against economic rights, rather than economic rights being clearly subordinated to higher norms. This does not necessarily lead to different outcomes in cases, but it may encourage them: rhetorical reordering does influence the reasoning process, both in public debate and in judicial proceedings. Hervey has expressed this point.

T. Hervey, 'Buy Baby: The European Union and the Regulation of Human Reproduction' (1998) 18 *OJLS* 207, 230

[T]he ability and indeed duty to apply EC law hinders national courts from explicitly approaching issues concerned with moral or ethical choices. Rather, the application of EC law may encourage or at least enable national courts to resolve cases by applying economic concepts, for example, relating to trade in goods and services. The EU legal order, with its underlying principles of market openness, and conceptualization of individuals as market actors, might aid this type of approach.[111]

(ii) The market society

The fundamental fear – for others the hope – is that Article 56 TFEU will create a market society, in Polanyi's famous term, which inverts the relationship between the market and society.[112] Instead of the economy being embedded in social relations, social relations are embedded in the economic system.

A feature of the market society is that the contract is the central social relation. The contract is not only legally protected by Article 56 through its protection of the freedom to transact. Many social relations are recast as contractual relations. The provision of a medical operation, for example, is not seen, under Article 56, in terms of the Hippocratic ideal, whereby the doctor commits herself to the unconditional alleviation of suffering and not to exploit the patient, and the patient commits herself to the professional expertise of the doctor and to the doctor's judgement on what is best. Instead, the terms of the relationship are to be determined by the contractual document. This allows more room for the patient's desires. She can look around for operations not considered suitable by some doctors. She can doubt the chosen doctor's judgement. Similarly, the responsibilities of the doctor have altered. She may want to weigh the possibility and type of treatment against the cost. She is, after all, in competition with other doctors. Finally, she is only committed to treat those with whom she has a contractual arrangement.

---

[110] See pp. 902–3.

[111] T. Hervey, 'Buy Baby: The European Union and the Regulation of Human Reproduction' (1998) 18 *OJLS* 207, 230.

[112] The term was first used in K. Polanyi, *The Great Transformation* (2nd edn, Boston, MA, Beacon, 2001).

A second feature of the market society is that many collective goods become measured as a series of individual entitlements. Public health is no longer a public good, of which the level and distribution are to be decided collectively. As something which can be transacted, health becomes a series of individual rights.

Finally, the market society places a particular value on subjective preferences and desires. Subjective desire becomes a source of value. It is the justification for Article 56, which grants the individual a prima facie right to transact for what she desires. A desire will only be refused where the activity threatens some external good, which is seen as having a greater value. The prohibition of the selling of certain forms of other drugs, such as heroin or cocaine, is prohibited, therefore, precisely because the importance of maintaining public order and public health are seen to outweigh the value of the enjoyment the user derives from the drugs. The market society, however, does not attribute equal value to the desires of all individuals. The desire of the homeless to have a warm home is not accorded any value. Instead, value is only attached to preferences insofar as one is a market actor and can pay the market price for realisation of those preferences.

(iii) Article 56 TFEU and the welfare state

If the processes above are to be observed, then the most promising context is where Article 56 TFEU has interacted with the welfare state, and in particular health care.[113] This is the area where the law has intruded the furthest into a sensitive service area, embodying many non-economic values. The cases show, as suggested above, an increasing centrality for individual transactions and preferences above systemic considerations.[114] However, they also show pragmatism and compromise, and a willingness at least to listen to Member State fears, if not always to accept them. Nor can they be seen as a simple triumph of economic freedom over other values: in most cases, states oppose the use of Article 56 on largely budgetary (economic) grounds, while individuals plead for free movement using a normative and non-economic language in which their personal and medical circumstances are more central than any notion of economic liberty. Perhaps the far-reaching scope of the health care cases has been partly possible because it is the patients, rather than the providers, who have led the litigation, and have more easily claimed the moral high ground than a commercial service provider could have done.[115]

In any event, the law discussed below is leading to a reorganising of welfare structures and a redrawing of the boundaries of solidarity.[116] Individuals have been granted rights to exit their national system and receive services in other Member States, with consequences for the

---

[113] See e.g. G. de Búrca (ed.), *EU Law and the Welfare State* (Oxford, Oxford University Press, 2005); M. Dougan and E. Spaventa, *Social Welfare and EU Law* (Oxford, Hart, 2005); E. Spaventa, 'Public Services and European Law: Looking for Boundaries' (2002) *CYELS* 271; G. Davies, *The Process and Side-effects of Harmonisation of European Welfare States*, Jean Monnet Working Paper No. 2/06 (2006); M. Ross and Y. Borgmann-Prebil, *Promoting Solidarity in the European Union* (Oxford, Oxford University Press, 2010).

[114] See C. Newdick, 'Citizenship, Free Movement and Healthcare: Cementing Individual Rights by Corroding Social Solidarity' (2006) 43 *CMLRev.* 1645.

[115] But see pp. 840–1.

[116] See e.g. D. S. Martinsen and V. Vrangbaek, 'The Europeanisation of Health Care Governance: Implementing the Market Imperatives of Europe' (2008) 86 *Public Administration* 169; Davies, n. 113 above; J. Montgomery, 'The Impact of European Union Law on English Healthcare Law' in M. Dougan and E. Spaventa, *Social Welfare and EU Law* (Oxford, Hart, 2005) 145; M. Ferrera, 'Towards an Open Social Citizenship? The New Boundaries of Welfare in the European Union' in G. de Búrca (ed.), *EU Law and the Welfare State* (Oxford, Oxford University Press, 2005) 11.

budgets of their home state and the state they travel to. As well as this, institutions have also been granted the right to offer welfare services in other Member States, with consequences for the integrity and stability of pre-existing national institutions. This is primarily an issue of establishment, and is addressed in Chapter 19.[117] What follows focuses on the rights of individuals to seek services such as health care and education abroad.

This right took some time to emerge. Many public services are provided free and the Court of Justice has found these not to be remunerated, and so not to be Treaty services.[118] This was enough to prevent Article 56 and the welfare state meeting, and to raise a perception that this meeting would not occur.

One reason that this has changed in recent years is that public institutions such as schools, universities and hospitals are increasingly funded by private insurance or by the consumers of their services, so that Article 56 applies to at least some of their activities.[119] Yet another reason, which has been more important in the case law, is that the type of migration has changed: instead of individuals going abroad to receive free public services, in recent years individuals have been exiting their (free) domestic systems in order to pay for services abroad. Instead of the non-economic welfare state being a destination, it has become a hindrance.

This creates a role for Article 56. Whatever the character of the domestic welfare state, economic or not, where migrants pay for services abroad there is obviously a remunerated cross-border service in issue. The nature of the domestic system becomes quite irrelevant to this point. For example, in *Commission v Germany*, the Commission challenged German rules which made school fees tax deductible, but only if the school was in Germany.[120] This, of course, discouraged the sending of children to schools abroad. Germany argued that school education was not a service.

Case C-318/05 Commission v Germany [2007] ECR I-6957

71. It is undisputed that, in parallel with schools belonging to a public educational system whereby the State performs its task in the social, educational and cultural areas, the financing of which is essentially from public funds, there are schools in certain Member States which do not belong to such a system of public education and which are financed essentially from private funds.

72. The education provided by such schools must be regarded as a service provided for remuneration.

73. It should be added that, for the purposes of determining whether Article [56 TFEU] applies to the national legislation at issue, it is irrelevant whether or not the schools established in the Member State of the user of the service – in this case the Federal Republic of Germany – which are approved, authorised or recognised in that Member State within the meaning of that legislation, provide services within the meaning of the first paragraph of Article [57 TFEU]. All that matters is that the private school established in another Member State may be regarded as providing services for remuneration.

The mere fact that a state organises its public services in a non-economic way does not therefore protect that state from Article 56 TFEU: its citizens still have a right to go to other states where the services may be economic in character, and this right of exit may have far-reaching organisational consequences for the systems at home. This has been above all the case in the context of health care. The Dutch and UK Governments have both argued in the past that Article 56 could not be used by patients who wished to leave the Netherlands or United

---

[117] See p. 881.   [118] See pp. 805–8.   [119] *Ibid.*
[120] See also Case C-76/05 *Schwarz and Gootjes-Schwarz v Finanzamt Bergisch Gladbach* [2007] ECR I-6849.

Kingdom for health care abroad, because those countries provided health care to their citizens within a non-remunerated framework to which Article 56 did not apply (this has now changed in the Netherlands). In both cases, this argument was just as irrelevant as above.[121]

A right to go abroad for health care is, however, only half the story. The real question, which determines the domestic impact of that right, is what kind of national measures will be seen as impeding it. In particular, most national health systems or insurers have traditionally only paid for health care at home, and refused to cover the cost of treatment abroad, except perhaps in exceptional situations. A policy such as this discourages patients from exiting the system and encourages them to receive their health care at home. Is that sufficient to say that not paying for foreign treatment is a restriction on services?

In *Kohll*, the Court of Justice ruled that this is the case. Kohll, a Luxembourgeois national, applied for his daughter to have dental treatment in Germany. Under Luxembourg law, such treatment could be received free if provided in Luxembourg, but required prior authorisation from the sickness insurance fund if it were to be provided outside the country. Authorisation was refused on the grounds that the treatment was not urgent and could, in any case, be provided within Luxembourg. Kohll argued that this breached Article 56 as the dental treatment constituted a service under that provision.

Case C-158/96 Kohll v Union des Caisses de Maladie [1998] ECR I-1931

32. The Member States which have submitted observations consider, on the contrary, that the rules at issue do not have as their purpose or effect to restrict freedom to provide services, but merely lay down the conditions for the reimbursement of medical expenses.

33. It should be noted that, according to the Court's case law, [Article 56 TFEU] precludes the application of any national rules which have the effect of making the provision of services between Member States more difficult than the provision of services purely within one Member State.

34. While the national rules at issue in the main proceedings do not deprive insured persons of the possibility of approaching a provider of services established in another Member State, they do nevertheless make reimbursement of the costs incurred in that Member State subject to prior authorisation, and deny such reimbursement to insured persons who have not obtained that authorisation. Costs incurred in the State of insurance are not, however, subject to that authorisation.

35. Consequently, such rules deter insured persons from approaching providers of medical services established in another Member State and constitute, for them and their patients, a barrier to freedom to provide services.

The practical consequences of this judgment are displayed in the series of post-*Kohll* cases on health care, which have now been consolidated into Directive 2011/24 on patients' rights in cross-border health care (Patients' Rights Directive).[122] The cases and Directive confirm a

---

[121] Case C-157/99 *Geraets-Smits* v *Stichting Ziekenfonds*; *Peerbooms* v *Stichting CZ Groep Zorgverzekeringen* [2001] ECR I-5473; Case C-372/04 *Watts* v *Bedford Primary Care Trust* [2006] ECR I-4325.

[122] Directive 2011/24/EU on the application of patients' rights in cross-border health care. The cases in this area and the Directive need to be seen alongside Regulation 883/2004 which provides for a parallel regime, in which instead of being reimbursed as if they were being treated at home, a migrant patient is treated as if they were insured under the law of the treating state. See generally S. de la Rosa, 'The Directive on Cross-border Healthcare or the Art of Codifying Complex Case Law' (2012) 49 *CMLRev.* 15; M. Peeters, 'Free Movement of Patients: Directive 2011/24 on the Application of Patients' Rights in Cross-Border Healthcare' (2012) 19 *European Journal of Health Law* 29.

patient's right to exit the national system of health care and choose treatment abroad, subject to certain limitations.[123]

The three cases which substantially formed the law in this area, *Geraets-Smits and Peerbooms*, *Müller-Fauré* and *Watts*, share essentially the same fact pattern as *Kohll*.[124] A patient (Dutch in the first two cases, British in the third) approached their health insurer or health authority to ask for authorisation to go abroad for treatment, to ask for confirmation that the insurer or authority would pay the costs. This was refused in each case, whereupon the patient went anyway, and submitted the bill. The insurers or authorities refused to pay, the patient litigated, and the Court of Justice was ultimately asked to adjudicate on exactly when a state or insurer was permitted to refuse payment for treatment abroad and exactly when a patient could obtain it.

In all of these cases, the Member States argued that restrictions on treatment abroad could be justified by public health reasons. They claimed that the cost increases which might result from patient migration could be so dramatic that the stability and sustainability of the public health system would be threatened.

The reasons why costs might increase are several. First, the costs of treatment abroad may be higher than the cost of equivalent treatment domestically. Secondly, patients may go abroad for treatment that is not in fact medically effective, following their whims rather than medical science. Thirdly, a good domestic health system requires the maintenance of an expensive medical infrastructure. For the most efficient use of this there must be a stable and continuous flow of clients. If patients can go abroad then domestic hospitals may run at less than full capacity. Yet, states cannot close them, because each state wants to maintain the domestic capacity to treat its citizens. Hence, states may be forced effectively to pay twice, once for the unused domestic capacity, and once for the actual treatment abroad.

In all of the cases, the Court of Justice took the same approach: merely budgetary or economic arguments do not justify a restriction on free movement.[125] However, if states could show that the financial consequences would be so great that they would indeed threaten the stability and quality of the system, then this would justify restrictions. The question is when this would be the case.

The first two arguments for cost increase – expensive foreign treatment and luxury treatment – have not been accepted. The Court has noted that Member States are free to define

[123] See A.-P. van der Mei, 'Annotation of *Commission* v. *France* and *Elchinov*' (2011) 48 *CMLRev.* 1297; V. Hatzopoulos, 'Killing National Health and Insurance Systems but Healing Patients? The European Market for Health Care Services after the Judgments of the ECJ in *Van Braekel* and *Peerbooms*' (2002) 39 *CMLRev.* 683; M. Flear, 'Note on Müller-Fauré' (2004) 41 *CMLRev.* 209; M. Cousins, 'Patient Mobility and National Health Systems' (2007) 34 *LIEI* 183; K. Stoger, 'Freedom of Establishment and the Market Access of Hospital Operators' (2006) *EBLRev.* 1545; V. Hatzopoulos, 'Health Law and Policy: The Impact of the EU' in G. de Búrca (ed.), *EU Law and the Welfare State* (Oxford, Oxford University Press, 2005) 111; P. Koutrakos, 'Healthcare as an Economic Service under EC Law' in M. Dougan and E. Spaventa, *Social Welfare and EU Law* (Oxford, Hart, 2005) 105; Davies, n. 113 above.

[124] Case C-157/99 *Geraets-Smits v Stichting Ziekenfonds; Peerbooms v Stichting CZ Groep Zorgverzekeringen* [2001] ECR I-5473; Case C-385/99 *Müller-Fauré v Onderlinge Waarborgmaatschappij OZ Zorgverzekeringen* [2003] ECR I-4509; Case C-372/04 *Watts v Bedford Primary Care Trust* [2006] ECR I-4325; see also Case C-211/08 *Commission v Spain*; Case C-173/09 *Elchinov* [2010] ECR I-08889; Case C-512/08 *Commission v. France* [2010] ECR I-8833; Case C-8/02 *Leichtle v Bundesanstalt für Arbeit* [2004] ECR I-2641; Case C-368/98 *Vanbraekel v ANMC* [2001] ECR I-5363; Case C-444/05 *Stamatelaki v OAEE* [2007] ECR I-3185; Case C-56/01 *Inizan v Caisse Primaire d'Assurance Maladie des Hauts-de-Seine* [2003] ECR I-12403.

[125] See pp. 897–9.

the scope of health care for which their system will pay, and the rates that they will pay.[126] Provided they do this in a non-discriminatory, transparent and rational way, the existence of a defined health package will not in itself contravene Article 56.[127] These limits then apply equally to treatment abroad, so that the cost risk is avoided. If states determine that a hip operation costs €3,000 in their domestic system, they may, for example, rule that they will pay a maximum of €3,000 for the same operation abroad. They must not have a lower reimbursement tariff for foreign treatment, but it need not be higher. This is now the approach taken in the Patients' Rights Directive.[128]

This sounds reasonable, but defining the domestic health care package imposes considerable administrative burdens on states.[129] In *Geraets-Smits and Peerbooms*, a Dutch coma patient was refused authorisation for a treatment in Austria on the grounds that it was experimental and had not been proven to be effective. The Dutch system only paid for treatment that was considered 'normal'. Even after the patient had been cured by the Austrian treatment, the Dutch insurance fund continued to refuse reimbursement on this ground. They lost before the Court of Justice because the definition of 'normal' treatment appeared to be one deriving exclusively from domestic medical practice, rather than from medical science, which, as the Court noted, is inherently international. 'Only an interpretation on the basis of what is sufficiently tried and tested by international medical science' was compatible with Article 56. Thus, Member States which wish to effectively limit the treatment their patients can receive abroad must define the scope of their domestic care with reasonable precision and care.[130]

This applies also to costs. Treatment abroad may be limited to the costs of equivalent domestic care, but this requires establishing what domestic care actually costs. In many systems, this is no easy task. Where hospitals receive lump-sum funding, or a mix of lump-sum funding and per-patient or per-treatment funding, establishing what a given operation or treatment costs is extremely difficult, and any sum is likely to be open to legal challenge. If it is artificially low it will prevent patients going abroad, but attract foreign patients, burdening the domestic system. If it is artificially high, then patients will be able to accumulate large bills abroad. The Directive requires Member States to base both the amount they reimburse and the prices they charge on objective, non-discriminatory criteria, but this is more easily said than done.[131] Moreover, states are likely to find that compliance has consequences: as they establish transparent price lists and lists of available treatment, this will reveal the efficiencies and weaknesses of the system, and enable international comparison, with possible political impact.

The third argument for cost increase – the cost of infrastructure – was recognised by the Court of Justice in *Müller-Fauré*. Here it made a distinction between hospital care and non-hospital care. Where non-hospital care is concerned, it ruled that the infrastructure argument did not apply, and there is no justification for restricting foreign treatment. EU patients may now go wherever they want in the European Union for their consultations or minor treatments

---

[126] Case C-157/99 *Geraets-Smits v Stichting Ziekenfonds*; *Peerbooms v Stichting CZ Groep Zorgverzekeringen* [2001] ECR I-5473; Case C-385/99 *Müller-Fauré v Onderlinge Waarborgmaatschappij OZ Zorgverzekeringen* [2003] ECR I-4509; Case C-372/04 *Watts v Bedford Primary Care Trust* [2006] ECR I-4325.

[127] See cases at n. 126 above.

[128] Patients' Rights Directive, article 7.

[129] G. Davies, 'The Effect of Mrs Watts' Trip to France on the National Health Service' (2007) 18 *Kings Law Journal* 158; Case C-173/09 *Elchinov* [2010] ECR I-08889.

[130] *Elchinov*, n. 129 above.   [131] Patients' Rights Directive, articles 4 and 7.

and expect costs to be covered by their domestic system just as if they had had the treatment at home. By contrast, where hospital care is concerned the Court conceded that the potential cost risks were indeed far greater, and certain restrictions could be justified. This approach has been incorporated in the Directive, which provides that where treatment involves at least one night in hospital, or the use of expensive medical infrastructure, Member States may require patients to seek authorisation before treatment abroad.[132] That authorisation may be refused on various grounds, of which the most important, provided for in article 8, is that the treatment can be provided domestically within a 'medically justifiable' time.

This is particularly important because the most common reason for patient migration is not to receive better or different treatment but to avoid domestic waiting lists. Member States have a particular objection to this which is not to do with absolute cost increases, but to do with cost control. The UK Government's position in *Watts*, and as intervener in *Müller-Fauré*, was that it had a finite annual health care budget, and so needed to control the rate of treatment. If patients could avoid waiting lists, then apart from this being unethical (queue jumping) it would make this annual budget control impossible. It would also undermine planning: with a finite budget the state may wish to determine which treatments get priority, and make hip patients wait longer than heart patients, for example. Waiting lists, in the view of the United Kingdom, were part of a fair and effective health care system.[133]

The question of when a waiting time is 'medically justifiable' is thus very much at the heart of the law and policy. In the pre-Patients' Rights Directive case law, the Court of Justice had ruled that authorisation could be refused if treatment could not be provided without 'undue delay' and had interpreted this in a way putting the concerns of the patient, not the health care system, central.

Case C–385/99 *Müller-Fauré v Onderlinge Waarborgmaatschappij OZ Zorgverzekeringen* [2003] ECR I-4509

90. In order to determine whether treatment which is equally effective for the patient can be obtained without undue delay in an establishment having an agreement with the insured person's fund, the national authorities are required to have regard to all the circumstances of each specific case and to take due account not only of the patient's medical condition at the time when authorisation is sought and, where appropriate, of the degree of pain or the nature of the patient's disability which might, for example, make it impossible or extremely difficult for him to carry out a professional activity, but also of his medical history...

Putting the effect of illness on the patient's broader health, and on their career, into the concept of undue delay makes it fluid and contestable. Each case has to be looked at on its own facts, and it would no longer be possible for states or insurers to decide authorisation applications purely by looking at a tariff or standard times.[134] This makes it significant that the Patients' Rights Directive appears to have moved back to the narrower 'medically justifiable', which would seem to exclude wider considerations. Yet in article 9, which is about the administrative procedures for authorisations, the Directive provides that when considering applications for authorisation Member States shall take into account (a) the specific medical condition, and (b)

---

[132] *Ibid.* article 8.   [133] See Newdick, n. 114 above.   [134] Davies, n. 113 above .

urgency and individual circumstances. This seems somewhat broader than the substantive rule in article 8. There is certainly room here for the Court of Justice to maintain the *Müller-Fauré* line that even non-medical factors should be taken into account. At any rate it is clear that the mere fact that a patient does not have to wait any longer than other national patients is not decisive: medical justification is not determined purely by the institutional status quo.

Litigation on these points matters because both waiting times for treatment, and attitudes towards what is an acceptable waiting period, vary widely between Member States. The UK Government considered it not undue, nor medically problematic, to make the elderly Mrs Watts wait months for a hip replacement, largely because this was normal in the United Kingdom. Some doctors in other states will be shocked by this. The fact that perceptions of what is medically, and above all humanly, acceptable vary so much make it significant that this matter is now within the scope of EU law. Applying the logic of *Geraets-Smits* one might argue that it should not be answered just by reference to local habits and expectations, but also by reference to international scientific best practice. That would be demanding for Member States with long, and long-established, waiting times.

All of these points will, however, be academic if patients cannot enforce their rights, and this is why the Court of Justice and now the Patients' Rights Directive give procedural requirements a prominent place. The Directive contains a number of provisions ensuring that Member States publish clear and accessible information on what and how much will be reimbursed, that they provide speedy decisions based on objective criteria, and that they make it possible for patients to challenge these decisions in court.[135] The core ideas are still summarised best by the Court, whose approach has been adopted wholesale in the Directive.

Case C-157/99 *Geraets-Smits v Stichting Ziekenfonds; Peerbooms v Stichting CZ Groep Zorgverzekeringen* [2001] ECR I-5473

90. …a scheme of prior authorisation cannot legitimise discretionary decisions taken by the national authorities which are liable to negate the effectiveness of provisions of Community law, in particular those relating to a fundamental freedom such as that at issue in the main proceedings…Therefore, in order for a prior administrative authorisation scheme to be justified even though it derogates from such a fundamental freedom, it must, in any event, be based on objective, non-discriminatory criteria which are known in advance, in such a way as to circumscribe the exercise of the national authorities' discretion, so that it is not used arbitrarily…Such a prior administrative authorisation scheme must likewise be based on a procedural system which is easily accessible and capable of ensuring that a request for authorisation will be dealt with objectively and impartially within a reasonable time and refusals to grant authorisation must also be capable of being challenged in judicial or quasi-judicial proceedings.

As ever, the Court of Justice is concerned not just with abstract principle but with the effectiveness of EU law. Member States are likely to be just as concerned about these procedural demands as about the substantive rights of patients. As long as the number of patients migrating is small the issue is manageable, but the requirement for quick, objective and transparent decision-making is precisely what may make the right to receive medical services abroad a

---

[135] Patients' Rights Directive, articles 5 and 9.

reality for the many rather than the few. Whether this will happen continues to be the object of research. The factors which are likely to influence this include cultural and linguistic barriers (border areas between states sharing a language may see significant cross-border health care), physical distance (distant states such as the United Kingdom or Greece may see less for this reason), but also the presence of domestic waiting lists (so states with national health systems, which tend to have waiting lists, may have the greatest outflow). Views on the likely extent of patient migration in the future vary widely and remain speculative.[136]

As well as the above, the Directive contains provisions aimed at helping patients find their way in the foreign legal system, and protecting their rights to privacy and information. Contact points, cooperation between national medical authorities and domestic follow-up treatment after initial treatment abroad are all addressed.[137] It is a fairly comprehensive package, clearly aimed at promoting patient movement, not merely regulating it.

That has invited criticism that the character of national welfare organisation is being undermined. The promotion of exit benefits the elite who can use this right, and reduces their commitment to the national system, to the detriment of the mass; the prioritising of individual rights is essentially the pre-emption of a value choice about the right balance between the collective and the individual good, going beyond a guarantee of essential medical care and protecting individual choice, time and convenience in a way that brings costs for others; and the locus of all this within the law on services, and the free movement logic of economic exchange, makes the patient into a consumer, with a consequent change in the nature of their relationship with their doctors – treatment becomes more business than care.[138] Some of the dangers are pithily described by Newdick below.

C. Newdick, 'Disrupting the Community: Saving Public Health Ethics from the EU Internal Market' in J. van de Gronden, E. Szyszczak, U. Neergaard and M. Krajewski (eds.), _Health Care and EU Law_ (The Hague, Asser Press, 2011) 211, 211–13

EU Institutions have misconceived the relationship between the economics of free market individualism and the politics of social welfare in the EU. The consequence of this misconception is especially serious with respect to cross-border access to health care because of the risk of damaging public health ethics. Public health concerns collective policies to promote community health and often involves the distribution of rights and duties in society. Its _ethical_ dimension can be explained on a spectrum of values which puts at each extreme the objective of _freedom of choice_, _individual rights_ and _liberty_ on the one hand, and _democracy_, _equality_ and _community_ on the other. Each may be characterized as the 'liberal' and 'republican', presumptions of citizenship. Of course, there are dangers inherent at both extremes of the spectrum; as to unrestricted individualism, as much as blind communitarianism. Scharpf suggests that balance is preserved because they serve as 'mutual antidotes' against the other's excesses. 'Republican collectivism is moderated by the protection of individual liberties, whereas libertarian

---

[136] See the special edition of the _European Journal of Public Health_ on cross-border health care: (1997) 7 _EJPub Health Supplement_ 3, 1–50; see e.g. G. France, 'Cross-border Flows of Italian Patients within the European Union' (1997) 7 _EJPub Health Supplement_ 3, 18 (Italians were then the largest group of users of cross-border health care in the Union).

[137] Patients' Rights Directive, articles 4, 5 and 6.

[138] See D. da Costa Leite Borges, 'Making Sense of Human Rights in the Context of European Union Health-care Policy: Individualist and Communitarian Views' (2011) 7 _International Journal of Law in Context_ 335.

egoism is constrained by the institutions of collective determination.'[139] Recognising the pull in both directions, we can better understand the proper balance between them, especially with respect to cross-border access to health care in the EU.

Social welfare helps to measure the extent to which nation states lean towards one end of this political spectrum or the other. It is part of the fabric of constitutional norms and expectations within which governments balance the tensions between individual *market freedoms* and broader *civic virtues* and which permit a redistribution of resources to reflect social need. Redistribution is said to be warranted by virtue of the moral bond which 'connects the strong to the weak, the lucky and the unlucky, the rich and the poor, creating a union that transcends all differences of interest, drawing its strength from history, culture, religion, language and so on'.[140] As Esping-Andersen has so elegantly shown,[141] the way in which this understanding affects national welfare policy differs because the 'social contract' between government and governed varies from place to place. For example, contributory mechanisms of social insurance used in the 'Bismarkian' systems may be considered more regressive in terms of tax burdens than 'Beveridgean' systems in which benefits are financed from progressive taxation. Whichever model we examine, the politics of each describes the community-based sense of civic republicanism embedded within EU Member States and national policy-making is inevitably constrained by the political environment in which those systems have evolved.

In the EU, however, current institutional presumptions heavily predispose the European Court of Justice towards the *libertarian* end of this spectrum and the protection of individual rights. Its mission is to promote fair market competition among Member States. However, because 'political' and democratic components in EU decision-making are weak, *civic republican* values, and the forces which affect *national identity* may be neglected. As a result, claims of individuals and companies may override democratic national institutions and political legacies. This poses a problem for the doctrine of EU supremacy because it transforms '... the hierarchical relation between European and national law into a hierarchical relationship between liberal and republican constitutional principles. Subjective rights [of individuals] may override all countervailing national objectives, regardless of their salience as manifestations of democratic self-determination.'[142]

While not uncontested,[143] these views highlight how the apparently reasonable step-by-step progress of the case law can be seen as threatening to certain visions of social order, importing economic and individual values to places where they do not belong. The question now is whether the same process will be seen in education, where mobile individuals who are prepared to pay and entrepreneurial institutions prepared to sell combine to put pressure on traditional systems in an analogous way to the law on patients and health.[144]

---

[139] F. Scharpf, *Legitimacy in the Multilevel European Polity*, MPIfG Working Paper No. 1 (2009) 7.

[140] R. Bellamy, *The Liberty of the Post-Moderns? Market and Civic Freedom Within the EU*, LSE Europe in Question Discussion Paper No.1 (2009) 13.

[141] G. Esping-Andersen, *The Three Worlds of Welfare Capitalism* (Oxford, Polity Press, 1990).

[142] Scharpf, n. 139 above, 25.

[143] See e.g. C. Rieder, 'When Patients Exit, What Happens to Solidarity?' in M. Ross and Y. Borgmann-Prebil (eds.), *Promoting Solidarity in the European Union* (Oxford, Oxford University Press, 2010) 122; G. Davies, 'Health and Efficiency: Community Law and National Health Systems in the Light of *Müller-Fauré*' (2004) 67 *MLR* 94.

[144] A. Gideon, 'Higher Education Institutions and EU Competition Law' (2012) 8 *Competition Law Review* 169.

7 SERVICES DIRECTIVE

Directive 2006/123/EC on services in the internal market (Services Directive) is the product of one of the most publicised and controversial legislative processes that the Union has enjoyed.[145] The aim of the Directive is to finally break down the many barriers to interstate service provision and establishment. There is a perception that the complexity and sensitivity of many services has meant that case law has not succeeded in this task. Member States continue to rely on mandatory requirements to obstruct services, and providers must fight for their rights on a case-by-case basis. Yet, the original draft proclaimed its goals too proudly for the European Parliament and many Europeans and was not adopted. It explicitly chose a widely applicable country of origin principle as the foundation of the European services market, effectively abolishing the possibility of relying on mandatory requirements to impose restrictions. The spectre of uncontrolled regulatory competition was raised, and of economic interests trampling on non-economic concerns, and in the same period where the Union was struggling with its proposed Constitution this was a step too far for the legislator as well as for the public.[146]

The final version applies to a narrower range of services, with the most sensitive, such as health care, excluded. Moreover, it does not use the words 'country of origin'. However, as will be seen, in substance it does apply such a principle to the services within its scope, and does abolish mandatory requirements. The regulatory approach chosen differs from the original version more in rhetoric than in substance.[147]

The Services Directive has three aspects. First, it regulates the administrative and bureaucratic procedures relevant to services and establishment. Secondly, it elaborates the scope of the rights to provide and receive services and to establish in another Member State. Thirdly, it contains coordination provisions allowing and requiring states to exchange the information necessary for an effective regulation of service providers.

(i) Scope of application of Services Directive

The Directive applies to all services except those specifically excluded. However, these exclusions are so impressively numerous that it is almost easier to think about what the Directive does apply to. A list of examples is provided in recital 33: management consultancy; facilities management; advertising; recruitment services; real estate services; legal and fiscal advice; car rental; travel agencies; and tourism services such as those provided by tour guides or amusement parks.

---

[145] See M. Klamert, 'Of Empty Glasses and Double Burdens: Approaches to Regulating the Services Market à propos the Implementation of the Services Directive' (2010) 37 *LIEI* 111; C. Barnard, 'Unravelling the Services Directive' (2008) 41 *CMLRev.* 323; V. Hatzopoulos, 'Assessing the Services Directive' in C. Barnard (ed.) (2007–08) 10 *CYELS* 215; U. Neergaard, R. Nielsen and L. M. Roseberry (eds.), *The Services Directive: Consequences for the Welfare State and the European Social Model* (Copenhagen, DJØF Publishing, 2008); G. Davies, 'The Services Directive: Extending the Country of Origin Principle and Reforming Public Administration' (2007) 32 *ELRev.* 232.

[146] B. De Witte, *Setting the Scene: How Did Services Get to Bolkestein and Why?*, Mitchell Working Paper No. 3/2007 (2007); C. Barnard, 'Unravelling the Services Directive' (2008) 41 *CMLRev.* 323, 329–30.

[147] R. Craufurd Smith, *Old Wine in New Bottles? From the 'Country of Origin Principle' to 'Freedom to Provide Services' in the European Community Directive on Services in the Internal Market*, Mitchell Working Paper No. 6/2007 (2007).

By contrast, it does not apply to financial services; electronic communications services; transport services; temporary work agencies; health care services;[148] gambling; private security; most social services such as social housing or child care; notaries and bailiffs; or audio-visual services.[149] In addition, there are specific exclusions relating only to services, but not to establishment.[150] These include waste treatment; posted workers; social security; water distribution; and the registration of vehicles in other states.

There are also several areas upon which the Services Directive is said not to impinge or not to affect or not to concern; taxation, labour law, fundamental rights, criminal law, cultural or linguistic diversity and the liberalisation of services of general economic interest or private international law.[151] As a description of the Services Directive, these provisions are rather dubious. It is quite imaginable that the rest of the Directive could have significant implications for these matters. Education provided for remuneration, by example, is not excluded, and the free movement of educational services has obvious implications for cultural diversity. If these provisions are to have meaning, then presumably where the application of the Directive would have implications for such matters, for example labour law or fundamental rights, this would be a reason to set the Directive aside, or to interpret it differently.

In addition, the Services Directive is expressed to be residual. Article 3(1) provides that if it conflicts with other EU legislation concerning a specific service activity, the specific legislation will take precedence. Examples given include legislation on posted workers, social security and television broadcasting.

The Services Directive's limited scope means that services now fall broadly into one of three categories: those governed by the Directive, those governed by specific legislation and those governed by the case law and Article 56 TFEU directly. However, the situation is actually more complex than this. Even if a service falls within the Directive, then it will be necessary to look at the particular measure which is being challenged. It may be that this is addressed by the Directive, in which case that will apply and the case law will be of purely interpretative or contextual relevance. On the other hand, it may be that a service is involved which in itself is within the Directive (say management consultancy), but the measure being challenged involves labour law or taxation or the registration of a vehicle abroad, or is addressed by specific legislation, so that the Directive cannot be relied upon and the cases or the specific legislation are the proper source of law. Given that many cases involve a long list of measures which impede a particular services activity, it is quite likely that some will fall within the Directive and some without, so that we will see a body of case law in which the Directive and Article 56 are used alongside each other. This only increases the likelihood that they will exert an interpretative influence on each other.

(ii) Administrative simplification

Bureaucratic and administrative procedures have long been identified as a major obstacle to the free movement of services. A Commission survey of small and medium-sized enterprises found that 91 per cent of these believed that the highest priority should be given to simplification of these.[152] The time taken to complete the certification of translation, the fees, the

---

[148] See Case C-57/12 *Femarbel*, Judgment of 11 July 2013.
[149] Directive 2006/123/EC, article 2.   [150] *Ibid.* article 17.   [151] *Ibid.* articles 1–3.
[152] European Commission, Internal Market and Services Directorate-General, *Internal Market Scoreboard November 2000* (Brussels, 2000) 10–12.

non-constructive attitude of the authorities and the difficulties in lodging appeals were all seen as hindering the provision of services.[153]

Article 5(1) of the Services Directive accordingly provides that:

> Member States shall examine the procedure and formalities applicable to access to a service activity and to the exercise thereof. Where procedures and formalities examined under this paragraph are not sufficiently simple, Member States shall simplify them.

Articles 6, 7 and 8 go on to provide that service providers must be able to complete all formalities and procedures via a single point of contact, and that this must be possible electronically and at a distance. Thus, the vision of the Services Directive is that where an activity is legitimately regulated and service providers must complete formalities, instead of going from office to office filling in forms they can simply visit a single website or office and complete everything once.

It is not entirely clear what formalities are included here. 'Access to a service activity' could simply cover explicit authorisations to engage in that activity, for example, the obtaining of a licence or the membership of a professional regulatory body. However, the exercise of a service may involve renting premises, making noise and waste, or using transport and distributing advertising, all of which might involve other authorisations or procedures. Are they all covered? It is even arguable that 'access to a service activity' should be interpreted in the light of the case law to include any formality or procedure which may hinder market access. That could stretch from procedures associated with the buying of a house to those linked to the presence of family members.[154]

It appears that these provisions do not just apply to foreign service providers or established persons, but also to the national starting a business in her own state.[155] She is also engaging in a service activity in that state. In any case, even if this is not the case as a matter of law it will be as a matter of practice. Member States are unlikely to introduce a new streamlined bureaucracy for foreigners while imposing the old model on their own citizens. These provisions are therefore a limited harmonisation of the government–citizen relationship, changing the balance of power towards the citizen, and moving the mode of interaction from face-to-face towards the electronic.[156]

(iii) Right to provide and receive services

The Services Directive has a Chapter on establishment and one on services. The establishment provisions are discussed in Chapter 19.[157] The central provision on the free movement of services is article 16.

Services Directive, article 16

Freedom to provide services

1. Member States shall respect the right of providers to provide services in a Member State other than that in which they are established. The Member State in which the service is provided shall ensure free access to and free exercise of a service activity within its territory.

    Member States shall not make access to or exercise of a service activity in their territory subject to compliance with any requirements which do not respect the following principles:

---

[153] European Commission, *The State of the Internal Market for Services*, COM(2004)441 final, 18.
[154] See Barnard, n. 145 above, 336–40.   [155] Davies, n. 145 above. See also Barnard, n. 145 above, 341–2.
[156] Davies, n. 145 above.   [157] See pp. 890–1.

(a) non-discrimination: the requirement may be neither directly nor indirectly discriminatory with regard to nationality or, in the case of legal persons, with regard to the Member State in which they are established;

(b) necessity: the requirement must be justified for reasons of public policy, public security, public health or the protection of the environment;

(c) proportionality: the requirement must be suitable for attaining the objective pursued, and must not go beyond what is necessary to attain that objective...

Examples of prohibited requirements are included in article 16(2) and include the obligation to have an establishment within the Member State, to register with a professional body in that state, or to possess an identity document issued by that state.

This article therefore applies to any public measure imposing conditions on access to or exercise of a service activity. It seems plausible that this should be understood to encompass the same public measures which are considered to be 'restrictions on the free movement of services' in the Court of Justice's case law.[158] In that case, article 16 reproduces the case law with one striking difference: restrictions may only be justified by public policy, security, health or the environment. Other possible justifications, such as consumer protection, are no longer possible.

This is not entirely certain. In fact, article 16 largely reproduces the words of the Treaty, which also does not mention mandatory requirements. This did not prevent the Court of Justice discovering them to be implicit. Why should it not do the same here?[159] This is certainly a possibility, but article 16 needs to be contrasted with article 9 on establishment, which specifically includes the possibility to restrict establishment for an 'overriding reason relating to the public interest'. This suggests persuasively that article 16 is intended to be narrower, and not to encompass public interest derogations beyond the short list in article 16(l)(b).

The impact of this may be put in perspective: Member State attempts to rely on mandatory requirements usually fail except where the issue is serious, in which case public policy can usually be invoked. However, it remains the case that article 16 establishes a strong country of origin principle, with very limited exceptions, despite the political fears which this has always attracted, and despite the fact that the Court has never felt able to go quite so far.[160] The greatest substantive innovation of the Services Directive is that the judicially created doctrine of mandatory requirements is legislatively abolished as far as the free movement of services is concerned.

(iv) Administrative cooperation

The risks to the consumer which home state regulation entails are twofold. One is that the consumer will contract with a foreign provider, not realising that this provider is subject to laxer regulation than providers established in the consumer's home state. They may not receive the quality of service they expect from the type of provider they expected. The second risk is that providers in fact slip through the supervisory net. Their home state regulators have little idea

[158] Barnard, n. 145 above; see pp. 808–13.
[159] Which appears to be accepted in Case C-458/08 *Commission v Portugal* [2010] ECR I-11599.
[160] Cf. Hatzopoulos, n. 145 above.

exactly what the provider is doing when providing services abroad, and may not be very interested, while host state regulators are prohibited from interfering and imposing their own rules.

These fears are addressed by the later parts of the Services Directive. The Chapter on quality of services requires Member States to ensure that providers make a range of information available to service recipients, from the legal form and address of the provider to their indemnity insurance, where relevant, so that the recipient can have a clear idea of exactly what she is paying for, and from whom.[161] It also, quietly but importantly, requires Member States to remove all total prohibitions on commercial communication (broadly, advertising) by the regulated professions, although it permits continued regulation of this.[162] The philosophy is, just as with the Court of Justice's consumer case law, that consumer protection should primarily be achieved by clear and fair communication between all parties.[163]

Chapter VI of the Services Directive addresses administrative cooperation between national supervisory authorities. It requires these bodies to communicate with each other about service providers, providing information on those who might be a threat to recipients, for example because they are struck off or convicted or bankrupt.[164] This may raise human rights issues where concerns are communicated that later turn out to be misplaced: getting off the watch-list in other Member States will probably be harder than getting onto it. There is also a specific obligation on authorities not to relax their supervision of those established in their state merely because services are being provided in another state.[165] The logic of home state regulation requires that national authorities now protect the interests of consumers in other states.

The supervisory challenge raised by cross-border services is also addressed by a special emergency procedure, provided for in articles 18 and 35. This permits host states to take measures necessary for the safety of consumers, in exceptional circumstances. However, rather than acting unilaterally against service providers, they are to follow a mutual assistance procedure in which they ask the state of establishment to investigate the service provider and take appropriate measures. The state of establishment is obliged to do this 'within the shortest possible period'.[166] The host state may then take additional measures, but only if it can show that the measures taken by the state of establishment are insufficient. The Commission is to be informed, and will take a decision either confirming or rejecting the host state measures.

This procedure is an attempt to reconcile the country of origin principle with high levels of service safety. It concedes that host states need to be able to guarantee service safety on their territory, but creates a communicative and cooperative mechanism which attempts to achieve this goal as much as possible via home state control.

FURTHER READING

C. Barnard, *Employment Rights, Free Movement under the EC Treaty and the Services Directive*, Mitchell Working Paper No. 5/08 (2008)

C. Barnard, 'Unravelling the Services Directive' (2008) 41 *Common Market Law Review* 323

C. Barnard, 'Viking and Laval: An Introduction' in C. Barnard (ed.), *Cambridge Yearbook of European Legal Studies 2007–8* (Oxford, Hart, 2008) 463

[161] Services Directive, article 22. [162] *Ibid.* article 24. [163] See pp. 780–3.
[164] Services Directive, articles 28–33. [165] *Ibid.* article 30. [166] *Ibid.* article 35(2).

A. Biondi, 'Recurring Cycles in the Internal Market: Some Reflections on the Free Movement of Services' in A. Arnull, P. Eeckhout and T. Tridimas (eds.), *Continuity and Change in EU Law* (Oxford, Oxford University Press, 2008) 228

A. Dashwood, '*Viking* and *Laval*: Issues of Direct Horizontal Effect' in C. Barnard (ed.), *Cambridge Yearbook of European Legal Studies 2007–8* (Oxford, Hart, 2008) 525

G. Davies, *The Process and Side-effects of Harmonisation of European Welfare States*, Jean Monnet Working Paper No. 02/06 (2006)

S. Enchelmaier, 'Always at Your Service (Within Limits): The ECJ's Case Law on Article 56 TFEU (2006–11)' (2011) 36 *European Law Review* 615

V. Hatzopoulos, 'The Court's Approach to Services (2006–2012): From Case Law to Case Load?' (2013) 50 *Common Market Law Review* 459

V. Hatzopoulos, *Regulating Services in the European Union* (Oxford, Oxford University Press, 2012)

T. Hervey, 'Buy Baby: The European Union and Regulation of Human Reproduction' (1998) 18 *Oxford Journal of Legal Studies* 207

G. Marenco, 'The Notion of Restriction on the Freedom of Establishment and Provision of Services in the Case-law of the Court' (1991) 11 *Yearbook of European Law* 111

S. de la Rosa, 'The Directive on Cross-border Healthcare or the Art of Codifying Complex Case Law' (2012) 49 *Common Market Law Review* 15

H. Schepel, 'Constitutionalising the Market, Marketising the Constitution, and to Tell the Difference: On the Horizontal Application of the Free Movement Provisions in EU Law' (2012) 18 *European Law Journal* 177

E. Spaventa, 'From *Gebhard* to *Carpenter*: Towards a (Non)-Economic European Constitution' (2004) 41 *Common Market Law Review* 743

B. de Witte, *Setting the Scene: How Did Services Get to Bolkestein and Why?*, Mitchell Working Paper No. 3/07 (2007)

19

The Pursuit of an Occupation in Another Member State

1 INTRODUCTION

This chapter is about the right to pursue an occupation in another Member State. It is organised as follows.

Section 2 outlines the scope of this right. Article 45 TFEU provides a right to work in other Member States, while Article 49 TFEU provides a right to self-employment in other Member States. While these are separate Treaty provisions, the Court of Justice often interprets them in parallel. Beneficiaries are EU citizens (and companies in the case of Article 49) who engage in a more than marginal economic activity with some cross-border element. If the subject lives in one state and works in another, this is sufficiently cross-border.

Section 3 considers national measures which restrict access to an occupation. In the past, certain professions were often restricted to nationals, but more recent cases tend to concern refusals to recognise foreign qualifications, or measures which make establishment of a business or professional practice subject to various requirements: these may be to do with the legal form of the business, the qualifications of the owner or shareholders, local economic need, or limits on the number of establishments which one person or company may run. The Court of Justice's approach, as ever, is to permit only those justified by the public interest and proportionate. However, because access restrictions have the effect of excluding some people from labour and business markets, the Court has been strict, and has been prepared to review even non-discriminatory national rules.

Section 4 analyses restrictions on the exercise of an occupation. Discrimination in pay and conditions, in union rights and in tax benefits, are all prohibited by case law and secondary legislation. The Court of Justice also examines measures critically for proportionality where they are equally applicable but tend to protect incumbents and disadvantage market entrants. However, it has been reluctant to engage with national measures whose only effect is to hinder economic effect generally, without any inequality in their impact.

Section 5 discusses the free movement of companies. Freedom of establishment enables companies to incorporate in one state while doing all their business in another. They can then avoid burdensome company laws in their state of business. Member States have argued that this is an abuse of free movement, but the Court of Justice disagrees. It is part of free movement that economic actors can choose to establish themselves in the jurisdiction most advantageous for them.

Section 6 is about the Services Directive, which also addresses establishment. Its Chapter on establishment addresses a limited number of national measures, but takes a similar approach to the case law; states may not discriminate, and measures restricting the business activities of established persons must be justified and proportionate. However, it appears that the Directive applies these principles not only where the measures impact on cross-border establishment, but generally, so that those starting a business in their own state will also benefit.

2 TAKING UP AND PURSUIT OF AN OCCUPATION IN ANOTHER MEMBER STATE

A central feature of any market is the possibility for individuals and companies to relocate to any part of its territory which offers them economic opportunities. Two economic freedoms in EU law are pivotal to the realisation of this. The first is free movement of workers, for which the central provision is Article 45 TFEU.

Article 45 TFEU

1. Freedom of movement for workers shall be secured within the Union.
2. Such freedom of movement shall entail the abolition of any discrimination based on nationality between workers of the Member States as regards employment, remuneration and other conditions of work and employment.

3. It shall entail the right, subject to limitations justified on grounds of public policy, public security or public health:
   (a) to accept offers of employment actually made;
   (b) to move freely within the territory of Member States for this purpose;
   (c) to stay in a Member State for the purpose of employment in accordance with the provisions governing the employment of nationals of that State laid down by law, regulation or administrative action;
   (d) to remain in the territory of a Member State after having been employed in that State, subject to conditions which shall be embodied in regulations to be drawn up by the Commission.
4. The provisions of this Article shall not apply to employment in the public service.

The second freedom is that of establishment. The central provision governing this is Article 49 TFEU.

Article 49 TFEU

Within the framework of the provisions set out below, restrictions on the freedom of establishment of nationals of a Member State in the territory of another Member State shall be prohibited. Such prohibition shall also apply to restrictions on the setting-up of agencies, branches or subsidiaries by nationals of any Member State established in the territory of any Member State.

Freedom of establishment shall include the right to take up and pursue activities as self-employed persons and to set up and manage undertakings, in particular companies or firms within the meaning of the second paragraph of Article 54, under the conditions laid down for its own nationals by the law of the country where such establishment is effected, subject to the provisions of the Chapter relating to capital.

An important difference between the Articles is that Article 45 only applies to natural persons, whereas Article 49 also applies to legal persons such as companies.

Regarding natural persons, the reason for treating the employed and self-employed separately is not obvious, and this chapter will suggest that the two groups are best considered in parallel. Their separateness in the Treaty is a historical artefact which does not fully correspond to the current state of the law or of society.

The origins of the distinction lie in the circumstances surrounding the original EEC Treaty. At a time of full employment, there were no concerns about the labour market and thus an assumption that free movement of labour was unproblematic. By contrast, there was concern that free movement might undermine professionals, such as lawyers, accountants and doctors, much of whose activity was carried out on a self-employed basis. Legislative harmonisation was thus seen as a precondition for free movement of the self-employed.

However, in today's world the distinction appears anachronistic, and often problematic in practice. People move interchangeably between employment and self-employment, each being economically substitutable for the other. In addition, companies have a range of contracts with individuals working for them, of which only some fit easily into the traditional model of the contract of employment.

Moreover, the legal distinctiveness of the two categories has been eroded by EU citizenship. Regulation 492/211 confers on workers certain advantages and restrictions, most notably in the field of social benefits, but does not extend these to the self-employed.[1] These rights provided the most significant added value to the status of worker. However, both workers and the self-employed are EU citizens, and this fact has been used in recent years by both the Court of Justice and the EU legislator to assimilate their rights. In particular, the Citizenship Directive 2004/38/EC ensures that rights of entry, residence and expulsion, and rights to social benefits, are now the same for all categories of economically active migrant.[2] The distinction between economically active and non-active is more important today than the distinction between employed and self-employed.[3]

This constitutional and social convergence of the worker and the self-employed person may have influenced the Court of Justice. A central argument of this chapter is that Articles 45 and 49 TFEU are being interpreted in a similar manner, and using the same concepts and limits. In particular, both these provisions are being interpreted as being part of a more general right to pursue an occupation in another Member State.

Nevertheless, the free movement of persons, established or employed, cannot be understood in isolation from the free movement of services. The situations to which they are relevant often overlap: a measure which makes service provision from state X to other states harder will deter establishment in state X, and vice versa. Unsurprisingly, therefore, the Court has interpreted the law on services, establishment and workers largely in parallel. This chapter is therefore complemented by the chapter on free movement of services. In particular, the discussion of horizontal application of Article 56 TFEU is just as relevant to Articles 45 and 49,[4] while the discussion of abuse later in this chapter is applicable to the law on services.[5]

(i) Employment and self-employment

Article 45 governs movement of the employed, whereas Article 49 performs the same function for the self-employed. The distinction between the two was explored in some depth in *Trojani*. Trojani, a French man, was given accommodation in a Salvation Army hostel in Brussels and some pocket money, in return for which he carried out approximately thirty hours of work each week for the hostel. This arrangement had a social purpose, as it was perceived to be a rehabilitation programme. After two years, Trojani approached the Belgian authorities for social assistance. On refusal, he argued that he was a worker under Article 45 and therefore entitled to social assistance.

Case C–456/02 *Trojani* v *Centre public d'aide sociale* [2004] ECR 1–7573

15. …the concept of 'worker' within the meaning of Article [45 TFEU] has a specific Community meaning and must not be interpreted narrowly. Any person who pursues activities which are real and genuine, to the exclusion of activities on such a small scale as to be regarded as purely marginal and ancillary, must

---

[1] Regulation 492/2011 on freedom of movement for workers, replacing Regulation 1612/68 [1968] OJ Spec. Edn L257/2, 475.
[2] See pp. 475–81.
[3] Although see Joined Cases C–147/11 and C–148/11 *Czop and Punakova*, Judgments of 6 September 2012, and C. O' Brien, 'Social Blind Spots and Monocular Policy Making: The ECJ's Migrant Worker Model' (2009) 46 *CMLRev.* 1107.
[4] See pp. 813–20.   [5] See pp. 873–5.

be regarded as a 'worker'. The essential feature of an employment relationship is, according to that case law, that for a certain period of time a person performs services for and under the direction of another person in return for which he receives remuneration...

16. Moreover, neither the *sui generis* nature of the employment relationship under national law, nor the level of productivity of the person concerned, the origin of the funds from which the remuneration is paid or the limited amount of the remuneration can have any consequence in regard to whether or not the person is a worker for the purposes of Community law...

17. With respect more particularly to establishing whether the condition of the pursuit of real and genuine activity for remuneration is satisfied, the national court must base its examination on objective criteria and make an overall assessment of all the circumstances of the case relating to the nature both of the activities concerned and of the employment relationship at issue...

18. In this respect, the Court has held that activities cannot be regarded as a real and genuine economic activity if they constitute merely a means of rehabilitation or reintegration for the persons concerned...

19. However, that conclusion can be explained only by the particular characteristics of the case in question,[6] which concerned the situation of a person who, by reason of his addiction to drugs, had been recruited on the basis of a national law intended to provide work for persons who, for an indefinite period, are unable, by reason of circumstances related to their situation, to work under normal conditions...

20. In the present case, as is apparent from the decision making the reference, Mr Trojani performs, for the Salvation Army and under its direction, various jobs for approximately 30 hours a week, as part of a personal reintegration programme, in return for which he receives benefits in kind and some pocket money.

21. Under the relevant provisions [the national law] the Salvation Army has the task of receiving, accommodating and providing psycho-social assistance appropriate to the recipients in order to promote their autonomy, physical well-being and reintegration in society. For that purpose it must agree with each person concerned a personal reintegration programme setting out the objectives to be attained and the means to be employed to attain them.

22. Having established that the benefits in kind and money provided by the Salvation Army to Mr Trojani constitute the consideration for the services performed by him for and under the direction of the hostel, the national court has thereby established the existence of the constituent elements of any paid employment relationship, namely subordination and the payment of remuneration.

23. For the claimant in the main proceedings to have the status of worker, however, the national court, in the assessment of the facts which is within its exclusive jurisdiction, would have to establish that the paid activity in question is real and genuine.

24. The national court must in particular ascertain whether the services actually performed by Mr Trojani are capable of being regarded as forming part of the normal labour market. For that purpose, account may be taken of the status and practices of the hostel, the content of the social reintegration programme, and the nature and details of performance of the services...

27. ...the freedom of establishment provided for in Articles [49 TFEU] to [54 TFEU] includes only the right to take up and pursue all types of self-employed activity, to set up and manage undertakings, and to set up agencies, branches or subsidiaries...Paid activities are therefore excluded.

[6] Case 344/87 *Bettray* v *Staatssecretaris van Justitie* [1989] ECR 1621.

Trojani provides a useful and oft-cited summary of the preceding case law on the application of Article 45. The extract above should also be read alongside the following section.

The judgment makes clear that where a migrant works under the direction of another person in return for payment, she is regarded as an employee and falls under Article 45. The essence of a worker is that she has a boss and a wage. By contrast, if she earns her living independently through supplying goods or services to other persons, she is treated as self-employed and falls under Article 49.

(ii) Performance of significant economic activity in another Member State

To fall within either Articles 45 or 49 TFEU, the migrant must be engaging in activity which is economic in nature. Economic activity involves her 'satisfying a request by the beneficiary in return for consideration'.[7] In the case of employment, the migrant will be receiving consideration from the employer and providing services under the direction of the employer. In the case of the self-employed, the remuneration is usually received from the customer for whom the service is carried out.

The Court of Justice has enlarged this notion of economic activity in two ways. In *Steymann*, a migrant lived in a Bhagwan community and received food and lodging and pocket money in return for doing tasks and duties within the community. The Court accepted that remuneration need not be financial, but could be in kind, so that Steymann was a worker in the Treaty sense.[8]

Relationships involving an element of guardianship or social welfare may also constitute economic activity. Training will be considered economic activity if it is regarded as practical preparation directly related to the actual pursuit of an occupation, and the training period itself takes the form of economic activity.[9] Similarly, jobs which would otherwise be unviable, sponsored with public funds to enable individuals to enter or re-enter working life, have been classified as economic activity.[10] Within such schemes, however, the person must have been chosen on the basis of their ability to perform a particular activity. In *Bettray*,[11] a Dutch drug rehabilitation scheme which offered individuals employment as part of the treatment of weaning them off drugs was not considered economic activity. It was regarded instead as a form of treatment because the jobs were adapted to the physical and mental capabilities of each person.

In *Raccanelli*, the Court of Justice found that a Ph.D. student may or may not be a worker.[12] It depends on whether the key elements of the worker relationship are present: remuneration and subordination. A grant may count as remuneration, but whether the researcher is under the direction of the faculty in question, or is independent in their activities, is a question of fact for the national court.

To fall within the provisions, the degree of economic activity must be more than minimal. In *Levin*, the Court of Justice ruled that to fall within Article 45 a migrant had to pursue 'effective

---

[7] Case C-268/99 *Jany* v *Staatssecretaris van Justitie* [2001] ECR I-8615.
[8] Case 196/87 *Steymann* v *Staatssecretaris van Justitie* [1988] ECR 6159. See also Case C-456/02 *Trojani* v *Centre public d'aide sociale* [2004] ECR I-7573.
[9] Case C-109/04 *Kranemann* v *Land Nordrhein-Westfalen* [2005] ECR I-2421.
[10] Case C-1/97 *Birden* v *Stadtgemeinde Bremen* [1998] ECR I-7747.
[11] Case 344/87 *Bettray* v *Staatssecretaris van Justitie* [1989] ECR 1621.
[12] Case C-94/07 *Raccanelli* v *Max-Planck-Gesellschaft zur Förderung der Wissenschaften* [2008] ECR I-5939.

and genuine activities, to the exclusion of activities on such a small scale as to be purely marginal and ancillary'.[13] But this does not exclude work under a short-term contract,[14] part-time work or low-paid work. In the same case the Court offered an interpretation of Article 45 in its broader context which still stands:

> 15. ...Since part-time employment, although it may provide an income lower than what is considered to be the minimum required for subsistence, constitutes for a large number of persons an effective means of improving their living conditions, the effectiveness of Community law would be jeopardized if the enjoyment of rights conferred by the principle of freedom of movement for workers were reserved solely to persons engaged in full-time employment and earning, as a result, a wage at least equivalent to the guaranteed minimum wage in the sector under consideration.

Following this, in *Kempf*,[15] the Court held that a part-time music teacher who gave twelve hours of lessons a week was doing sufficient work to be covered by Article 45, even though she earned so little that she was forced to apply for benefits.

The minimum threshold for engaging Article 49 is a little more complex. In some cases the question may be whether an individual is established in a host state or providing services, and the intensity and scale of their economic activity will be relevant to this determination. This was discussed in Chapter 18.[16] However, if an individual is resident in a host state, so that there is no question that this is the centre of her activities, then the question may arise, as with Article 45, whether those activities are of a sufficient scale to classify her as economically active. The only words of guidance that the Court of Justice has provided are in *Gebhard*, in which it said that:

> 25. The concept of establishment within the meaning of the Treaty is therefore a very broad one, allowing a Community national to participate, on a stable and continuous basis, in the economic life of a Member State other than his State of origin and to profit therefrom, so contributing to economic and social interpenetration within the Community in the sphere of activities as self-employed persons.[17]

This was intended to distinguish establishment from services, but may also indicate the minimum criteria for establishment per se. There must be some non-trivial stability and continuity in the activities: one small or brief job performed for one client is not enough. In substance, it is suggested that the minimum level of economic activity will be interpreted in the same way as for Article 45.

The definition of 'worker' which emerges from these cases is unusual in EU law in not taking account of the personal circumstances of the individual, instead imposing a fixed test. That may have the consequence that a disabled person, working as much as they can, will have to cross the same threshold of 'genuine and effective activity' as an able-bodied person, and that someone engaging in informal, but arduous and necessary, care may not be a worker while someone who receives payment for the same work will be. This may seem quite reasonable

---

[13] Case 53/81 *Levin* v *Staatssecretaris van Justitie* [1982] ECR 1035.
[14] Case C-413/01 *Franca Ninni-Orasche* v *Bundesminister für Wissenschaft, Verkehr und Kunst* [2003] ECR I-13187.
[15] Case 139/85 *Kempf* v *Staatssecretaris van Justitie* [1986] ECR 1741.
[16] See pp. 802–3.
[17] Case C-55/94 *Gebhard* v *Consiglio dell'ordine degli avvocati e procuratori di Milano* [1995] ECR I-4165.

from an economic point of view, but it fits somewhat uneasily with cases such as *Levin* and *Kempf*, where the Court of Justice seems to be focusing far less on the economic contribution of the individual, and rather on what has been described as their 'genuine intention to work', treating worker status as recognition of effort and attitude rather than success.[18] It also fits uneasily with current anti-discrimination law, which generally requires recognition of the particular position of disabled people in the labour market.

C. O' Brien, 'Social Blind Spots and Monocular Policy Making: The ECJ's Migrant Worker Model' (2009) 46 *Common Market Law Review* 1107

It is here suggested that the application of the same 'worker' test to all people is inappropriate, and actually discriminatory. This problem is not solved by 'refining' the test by continually adding conditions. Instead, these entrench the problem by introducing extra sources of discrimination, as exemplified by the 'genuine and effective' requirement, and its refinement, that work be part of the 'normal labour market'. The meaning of 'genuine and effective' has been somewhat shrouded in ambiguity, with no suggestion that it may vary as between workers. If anything, the 'normal labour market' stipulation makes clear that there is no room for accommodating such differences. It squeezes social concerns out of the definitional process and shuts out any positive equality duty. It was possibly a knee-jerk reaction, to avoid the social obligations of host Member States 'going too far' after the widening application of the term 'worker' reached its fullest compass in *Steymann*. A German national who had worked as a plumber in the Netherlands, joined a religious community that provided for the material needs of its members, where he contributed to the life of the community through activities, including its fundraising activities. The community preserved an independence from surrounding society. This was clearly not a 'classic' employment relationship, yet it was 'impossible to rule out a priori the possibility that [the] work…in question constitutes an economic activity within the meaning of Article 2 of the Treaty'. The Court was soon faced with a 'less attractive' claimant than a religious plumber seeking a right to reside, this time an ex-drug addict, and circumvented its own reasoning.

The consequence was the *Bettray* principle that work should be part of the 'normal labour market'. That it departed from previous case law was implied in the Advocate General's statement that he did 'not think that [previous] case law can be directly transposed to the unusual circumstances of the present case'. It is a poorly elaborated, apparently foundation-free principle, applied without substantiating evidence. Bettray's activity under the Social Employment Law did exhibit 'the essential feature of an employment relationship', as he performed services under the direction of another person in return for remuneration, and Advocate General Jacobs did actually acknowledge his activities to have been 'substantial'. Furthermore, Bettray was classed under the Social Employment Law as a person whose productivity is expected to be a third of a 'normal' worker's. If working full time, that still suggests productivity capable of being compared to that of a 'normal' part time worker. This contrasts considerably with the (undetermined) amount of activity in *Steymann*.

The various elements called upon in 'ab-normalizing' Bettray's work include: physical/mental adaptations to work; unavailability for 'normal' work; selection of the work rather than the worker; and speculation about the noncommerciality of the labour. Each criterion makes clear that all workers are to be subjected to the same test for genuine and effective work; a test against which non-normal work

---

[18] E. Johnson and D. O'Keeffe, 'The Free Movement of Workers 1989–1994' (1994) 31 *CMLRev*. 1318, quoted in C. O' Brien, 'Social Blind Spots and Monocular Policy Making: The ECJ's Migrant Worker Model' (2009) 46 *CMLRev*. 1107, 1117.

is not valued, exacerbating the danger of disability discrimination. The significance attributed to the fact that the work had been adapted to the physical and mental possibilities of the persons in question is difficult to reconcile with notions of reasonable adjustments and positive discrimination as regards disability discrimination. Rather than allowing notions of genuine work to be altered to accommodate adapted work, it actually uses such adaptations as an indicator to rule out that work.

(iii) Cross–border element

In an analogous manner to the other freedoms, Articles 45 and 49 TFEU apply only to work or establishment with a cross-border aspect.[19] The usual situation is where the individual physically relocates to another Member State. However, Article 45 also includes the situation where the worker works in their home state, but lives in another. In *Hartmann*, a German worker living and working in Germany moved house, but not job, to France. The Court of Justice found that this was enough to give him the status of migrant worker.[20] In similar fashion, the Court has stated that where the economic activity of a person or company based in one Member State is entirely or principally directed towards the territory of another Member State, they fall within Article 49.[21]

The cross-border economic activity need not already be underway to engage Articles 45 and 49. Measures which prevent it starting are also caught, provided their effect is not too hypothetical.[22] These Articles therefore involve not merely the right to pursue an occupation in another Member State but also the right to *take up* that occupation. Article 45 therefore protects both workers and work-seekers.[23] In like vein, Article 49 covers restrictions on those who are self-employed as well as restrictions preventing EU citizens wishing to take up self-employment, but not yet self-employed. For example, in *Reyners*,[24] a Dutch national successfully challenged a Belgian measure permitting only Belgian nationals to practise as advocates in Belgium, which was preventing him practising as a lawyer in that state.

(iv) Right to pursue an occupation in another Member State

The common themes present in employment and self-employment, and the Court of Justice's clear inclination towards parallel development of the four freedoms,[25] suggest room for an explicit overarching right to take up and pursue an occupation in another Member State, which encompasses and structures both Articles 45 and 49. Such reasoning is present in the recent

---

[19] Case 175/78 *Saunders* [1979] ECR 1129; Case C-65/96 *Uecker and Jacquet* [1997] ECR I-3171; Case C-107/94 *Asscher* [1994] ECR I-1137.

[20] Case C-212/05 *Hartmann v Freistaat Bayern* [2007] ECR I-6303; see also Case C-336/96 *Gilly v Directeur des services fiscaux du Bas-Rhin* [1998] ECR I-2793; Case C-213/03 *Geven v Land Nordrhein-Westfalen* [2007] ECR I-6347; A. Tryonidou, 'In Search of the Aim of the EC Free Movement of Persons Provisions: Has the Court of Justice Missed the Point?' (2009) 46 *CMLRev.* 1591.

[21] Case 205/84 *Commission v Germany (German Insurance)* [1986] ECR 3755.

[22] See pp. 863–4.

[23] Case 53/81 *Levin v Staatssecretaris van Justitie* [1982] ECR 1035; Case C-281/98 *Roman Angonese v Cassa di Risparmio di Bolzano SpA* [2000] ECR I-4139.

[24] Case 2/74 *Reyners v Belgium* [1974] ECR 631.

[25] See A. Tryfonidou, 'Further Steps on the Road to Convergence Among the Market Freedoms' (2010) 35 *ELRev.* 35.

case of *Danish Company Cars*.[26] To avoid tax evasion, Denmark prohibited Danish residents from using company cars registered abroad for private purposes in Denmark. The Commission considered this to penalise those working abroad and therefore to breach Article 45, as Danish residents could use company cars registered in Denmark for private purposes. The Danish Government argued that the measure fell outside Article 45 as this Article related solely to conditions of employment.

Case C-464/02 Commission v Denmark (Danish Company Cars) [2005] ECR I-7929

34. The provisions of the Treaty on freedom of movement for persons are intended to facilitate the pursuit by Community citizens of occupational activities of all kinds throughout the Community, and preclude measures which might place Community citizens at a disadvantage when they wish to pursue an economic activity in the territory of another Member State...

35. Provisions which preclude or deter a national of a Member State from leaving his country of origin in order to exercise his right to freedom of movement therefore constitute an obstacle to that freedom even if they apply without regard to the nationality of the workers concerned...

36. However, in order to be capable of constituting such an obstacle, they must affect access of workers to the labour market...

37. The manner in which an activity is pursued is liable also to affect access to that activity. Consequently, legislation which relates to the conditions in which an economic activity is pursued may constitute an obstacle to freedom of movement within the meaning of that case law.

38. It follows that the Danish legislation at issue in this case is not excluded from the outset from the scope of Article [45 TFEU].

The case is, like *Alpine Investments, Rüffler, Bosman*[27] and the case law on Article 35 TFEU, about a restriction on exit, imposed by the home state. These are legally interesting because they can rarely be seen in terms of nationality discrimination. As a result, the Court of Justice is often forced into innovative legal formulations, usually relying on the fact that a measure makes cross-border movement less attractive than staying at home.[28] Accordingly, in the extract above the central objection is that the measure discouraged Danes from going abroad to work, since a job abroad would be relatively less advantageous for them. In paragraph 34, the Court places this in a cross-category context. The extract implies a right to pursue an occupation abroad which encompasses both Articles 45 and 49, and extends beyond mere equal treatment.

As a matter of convenience, the right to pursue an occupation abroad can be considered to have two aspects: the right to *take up* economic activities and the right to *pursue* these activities. This distinction often occurs in the language of the Court of Justice,[29] and is useful in understanding the kinds of situations which may arise.

---

[26] For similar reasoning in respect of Article 56 TFEU, see Case 143/87 *Stanton* v *INASTI* [1988] ECR 3877, paras. 13 and 14.

[27] Case C-384/93 *Alpine Investments* v *Minister van Financiën* [1995] ECR I-1141; Case C-544/07 *Rüffler*, Judgment of 23 April 2009; Case C-415/93 *Union Royale Belge des Sociétés de Football Association and others* v *Bosman and others* [1995] ECR I-4921.

[28] See pp. 484–7.

[29] Case 197/84 *Steinhauser* v *City of Biarritz* [1985] ECR 1819; Case C-311/06 *Consiglio Nazionale degli Ingegneri* v *Ministero della Giustizia and Marco Cavallera*, Judgment of 29 January 2009; Case C-464/02 *Commission* v *Denmark (Danish Company Cars)* [2005] ECR I-7929.

The right to take up activities concerns entry onto the market of another Member State. At its crudest, this would capture restrictions on residence in another Member State. It would also comprise anything that might prevent the migrant from commencing activity in that Member State. This would include restrictions on secondary establishment, which prevent traders with a central place of business opening up branches, agencies or subsidiaries in other Member States, restrictions on entering the labour market, such as prerequisites that one have a licence or join a trade union, which may be difficult to meet or, finally, requirements that a migrant have a qualification before she can pursue a particular activity. The nature of all these rules is that they reserve the occupation in question for those complying with certain criteria.

Restrictions on the pursuit of economic activity are restrictions on activities of the migrant once she is on the market of the host Member State. They do not determine who may engage in the occupation in question, but they create disadvantages for some of those who do so. They might involve discriminatory conditions of employment, discriminatory planning restrictions for the location of a business, or discrimination in the tax system or in access to credit. They may also include non-discriminatory regulation of economic activity which, because it imposes disproportionate burdens, hinders that activity.[30]

The distinction between restrictions on the taking up of activities and restrictions on the pursuit of activities is not always clear-cut. There are restrictions on the taking up of an activity that also apply to the pursuit of that activity. Qualifications are a case in point. They are necessary for entry onto a market as certain activities cannot be taken up without them. Yet, possession of qualifications will often also go to the pursuit of economic activity as they strengthen the trader's position in the marketplace by demonstrating recognition of a particular expertise. In a corollary manner, as *Danish Company Cars* suggests, restrictions on the pursuit of economic activity may be so onerous for the trader that they make it unviable for her to enter the market, and so perform the same role as restrictions on the taking up of activity.

These arguments should not be allowed to disguise the fact that in most cases the distinction is real and useful. It is different to be told by a state 'You cannot practise that profession' than to be permitted to do so but to find that some of the state's regulation is burdensome. The first is directed at the actor, the second at the activity. More important, the first kind of restriction is far more exclusionary. A measure which prevents the taking up of an occupation is therefore something that justifies intensive judicial scrutiny. Indeed, measures which exclude some players from the market have always concerned the Court of Justice, as the case law on goods and services also shows.[31]

Moreover, restrictions on taking up an occupation do not always lend themselves to a discrimination-based analysis. A comparison with other market participants is not always useful nor is it appropriate for an actor who cannot participate herself, while a comparison with other potential market participants is often far-fetched or evidentially challenging. There is thus a particularly strong case for restrictions on the right to take up activities falling within Articles 45 and 49 even where no discrimination has been shown.

The non-discrimination principle does become central, however, where restrictions on the pursuit of economic activities are concerned. It protects the competitive position of the migrant within the host state by ensuring that she is treated in a genuinely neutral manner vis-à-vis a state's own nationals. The non-discrimination principle safeguards the ideal that

---

[30] See pp. 877–83.   [31] See p. 787.

the migrant should prosper or fail in a single market only on the basis of the competitiveness of her activities. The application of the Treaty provisions to discriminatory restrictions on the pursuit of economic activity is, therefore, also uncontentious. By contrast, the arguments about whether Articles 45 and 49 should cover non-discriminatory restrictions on the pursuit of economic activity are more finely balanced. Such restrictions go not to market access or the competitive position of non-nationals, but to the general level of regulation within a Member State, and whether this is compatible with the Treaty. Extending Articles 45 and 49 to cover such measures would have significant market liberalising effects, but would also result in the extension of the reach of these Articles into almost all areas of regulation of economic life. Legislation as diverse as that covering general labour, the environment, consumers and health and safety could all be challenged on the grounds that it limits in some way the economic activity pursued by a migrant or migrant business in that host state. There is a significant danger of overreaching here, with EU law being perceived, particularly from a local perspective, as being both excessively deregulatory and excessively intrusive. For this reason, the Court of Justice has found it fairly easy to deal with the first two types of restriction: non-discriminatory restrictions on the taking up of activity and discriminatory restrictions on the pursuit of activity. By contrast, as we shall see, its case law on non-discriminatory restrictions on the pursuit of economic activity has been contradictory and uncertain. We now turn to each of these lines of reasoning.

3 RESTRICTIONS ON THE TAKING UP OF AN OCCUPATION

(i) Discriminatory restrictions on taking up an occupation

In some instances, Member States have reserved certain occupations to their own nationals. Because of the obvious discriminatory intent of such measures, the Court of Justice has chosen to strike them down as a violation of the non-discrimination principle. In *Reyners*,[32] a Belgian requirement that one have Belgian nationality to practise as an advocate was therefore condemned as a breach of Article 49 TFEU on the grounds that it discriminated against other EU nationals. Similar reasoning has been applied to companies,[33] and in respect of Article 45. In *French Merchant Navy*,[34] a French restriction limiting the proportion of non-national French merchant navy employees was found to breach Article 45 on the grounds of its discriminatory nature.

There are also slightly less direct requirements, which still work to protect locals. In *Angonese*, a bank in the German-speaking part of Italy made employment conditional upon a particular local certificate of bilingualism, refusing to accept other evidence.[35] The Court of Justice found this a violation of Article 45 because of its discriminatory effect on access to the posts, notwithstanding that instead of a public measure, a rule imposed by a private company was in issue. Article 45 is general, and applies equally to private and public employers and measures. More recently, in *Las*, the Court found it disproportionate to require by law that all

---

[32] Case 2/74 *Reyners* v *Belgium* [1974] ECR 631.
[33] Case C-299/02 *Commission* v *Netherlands* [2004] ECR I-9761.
[34] Case 167/73 *Commission* v *France (French Merchant Navy)* [1974] ECR 359.
[35] Case C-281/98 *Roman Angonese* v *Cassa di Risparmio di Bolzano SpA* [2000] ECR I-4139.

employment contracts with companies established in the Flemish-speaking part of Belgium be drafted exclusively in Flemish.[36]

Legal requirements that an employee actually speak the local language are in practice even more exclusionary. They could be argued to fall within Article 3 of Regulation 492/2011, which declares that Member State laws or practices shall not apply if their exclusive aim or effect is to limit the access of non-nationals to employment.[37] However, such requirements may of course be reasonable, and Article 3 goes on to explicitly permit language requirements where the linguistic knowledge is required by reason of the nature of the post. In such a case, although the requirement may adversely affect foreign applicants, it will not be treated as prohibited discrimination. In *Groener*,[38] a Dutch teacher challenged an Irish requirement that all full-time teachers in Irish state colleges were proficient in the Irish language. She argued that this did not fall within the exception, as teaching could be done in English. The Court of Justice nevertheless found the requirement to be lawful. It stated that any requirement of linguistic proficiency would be lawful if it was necessary for the implementation of a policy to protect and promote a language which is both the national language and the first official language, and the restriction was neither disproportionate to the aim pursued nor unnecessarily discriminatory towards other Member State nationals. In this case, the restriction was not disproportionate, as education was seen by the Court as central to the implementation of such a policy. In this instance, education included not merely teaching but also participation in the daily life of the school and the forging of relations with pupils. In such circumstances, the Court considered that even though teaching did not have to be done in Irish, the language could be central to other parts of school life.[39]

The vast majority of restrictions on the taking up of activity in another Member State are not explicitly directed at foreigners. In such instances, the Court looks at the restrictive effects of the measure rather than its discriminatory effects. We look at these below.

(ii) Equally applicable restrictions on taking up an occupation

One of the best-known cases in EU law is that of *Bosman*, which revolutionalised the European football industry. Bosman played football for Liège in Belgium. Following the end of his contract, relations between him and the club broke down. Under the footballing rules of the time, the club held on to the registration card that entitled him to play as a footballer. They sought to transfer him, with his consent, to Dunkerque in France. The sale broke down because there were doubts about Dunkerque's solvency and its ability to pay the transfer fee demanded by Liège. Despite his being out of contract, Liège refused to allow Bosman to move to Dunkerque until its demand for a transfer fee had been met. Bosman was therefore unable to work as a footballer: Liège would not use him, but they would not let him go to another team. He challenged the transfer system operating in football, which allowed clubs to restrict the movement of players post-contract by holding on to their registration card, arguing it violated Article 45 TFEU.

---

[36] Case C-202/11 *Las*, Judgment of 16 April 2013.
[37] Cf. posted workers in a recent situation: C. Barnard, '"British Jobs for British Workers": The Lindsey Oil Refinery Dispute and the Future of Local Labour Clauses in an Integrated EU Market' (2009) 38 *ILJ* 245.
[38] Case 379/87 *Groener* v *Minister for Education and the City of Dublin Vocational Educational Committee* [1989] ECR 3967.
[39] See also Case C-424/97 *Salomone Haim* v *Kassenzahnärztliche Vereinigung Nordrhein* [2000] ECR I-5123; Case C-506/04 *Wilson* v *Ordre des avocats du barreau de Luxembourg* [2006] ECR I-8613.

Case C–415/93 *Union Royale Belge des Sociétés de Football Association and others* v *Bosman and others* [1995] ECR 1–4921

94. …the provisions of the Treaty relating to freedom of movement for persons are intended to facilitate the pursuit by Community citizens of occupational activities of all kinds throughout the Community, and preclude measures which might place Community citizens at a disadvantage when they wish to pursue an economic activity in the territory of another Member State…

95. In that context, nationals of Member States have in particular the right, which they derive directly from the Treaty, to leave their country of origin to enter the territory of another Member State and reside there in order there to pursue an economic activity…

96. Provisions which preclude or deter a national of a Member State from leaving his country of origin in order to exercise his right to freedom of movement therefore constitute an obstacle to that freedom even if they apply without regard to the nationality of the workers concerned…

97. The Court has also stated in [Case 81/87 *Daily Mail*] that even though the Treaty provisions relating to freedom of establishment are directed mainly to ensuring that foreign nationals and companies are treated in the host Member State in the same way as nationals of that State, they also prohibit the Member State of origin from hindering the establishment in another Member State of one of its nationals or of a company incorporated under its legislation which comes within the definition contained in Article [54 TFEU]. The rights guaranteed by Article [49 TFEU] *et seq.* of the Treaty would be rendered meaningless if the Member State of origin could prohibit undertakings from leaving in order to establish themselves in another Member State. The same considerations apply, in relation to Article [45 TFEU], with regard to rules which impede the freedom of movement of nationals of one Member State wishing to engage in gainful employment in another Member State.

98. It is true that the transfer rules in issue in the main proceedings apply also to transfers of players between clubs belonging to different national associations within the same Member State and that similar rules govern transfers between clubs belonging to the same national association.

99. However…those rules are likely to restrict the freedom of movement of players who wish to pursue their activity in another Member State by preventing or deterring them from leaving the clubs to which they belong even after the expiry of their contracts of employment with those clubs.

100. Since they provide that a professional footballer may not pursue his activity with a new club established in another Member State unless it has paid his former club a transfer fee agreed upon between the two clubs or determined in accordance with the regulations of the sporting associations, the said rules constitute an obstacle to freedom of movement for workers….

103. It is sufficient to note that, although the rules in issue in the main proceedings apply also to transfers between clubs belonging to different national associations within the same Member State and are similar to those governing transfers between clubs belonging to the same national association, they still directly affect players' access to the employment market in other Member States and are thus capable of impeding freedom of movement for workers. They cannot, thus, be deemed comparable to the rules on selling arrangements for goods which in *Keck and Mithouard* were held to fall outside the ambit of Article [34 TFEU].

104. Consequently, the transfer rules constitute an obstacle to freedom of movement for workers prohibited in principle by Article [45 TFEU]. It could only be otherwise if those rules pursued a legitimate aim compatible with the Treaty and were justified by pressing reasons of public interest. But even if that were so, application of those rules would still have to be such as to ensure achievement of the aim in question and not go beyond what is necessary for that purpose.

The Court went on to find that the rules could not be justified by the need to maintain the financial and competitive balance between clubs, nor by the need to find and support young talent. These were good goals, but the Court was convinced they could be achieved by means less restrictive of free movement.[40]

Bosman applies the same logic to Articles 45 and 49[41] as has been applied, since *Cassis de Dijon*, to the case law on free movement of goods and freedom to provide services.[42] The provisions will not only catch measures which distinguish between nationals of different Member States. They will also catch certain equally applicable restrictions on employment and establishment. In cases where such a measure falls within either provision, it will only be lawful if it meets a number of conditions. It must be justified in the public interest; it must be applied in a non-discriminatory manner, it must be suitable for securing the attainment of the objective pursued; and it must not go beyond what is necessary to attain this objective.[43]

The same reasoning has been applied in the context of Article 49 in *Gebhard*, where the Court pronounced that any measure 'liable to hinder or make less attractive the exercise of fundamental freedoms' would be prohibited, unless it complied with the same justificatory requirements outlined in *Bosman*.[44] In *Gebhard*, as in *Bosman*, the reasoning was expressed to be general, applying to restrictions on the pursuit of an occupation as much as to restrictions on taking up an occupation. However, *Gebhard* concerned the right to use the title 'avvocato' in Italy, and a prohibition imposed upon Mr Gebhard from 'pursuing his professional activity' in Milan. As such it was about access to an activity, as was *Bosman*. The facts of these cases are somewhat narrower than the Court's conclusions. This is relevant because, as will be seen below, where restrictions on pursuit of an occupation are concerned it is not clear that the full potential scope of these judgments has actually been realised: in fact the Court of Justice does seem to use non-discrimination as a guiding and limiting idea.[45]

The application of Article 49 to equally applicable measures has, as with the other freedoms, been a powerful tool for opening up regulated professions to new competition. In *Hartlauer*, an Austrian rule made the setting up of an outpatient dental clinic conditional upon local 'need', which was determined by the relevant authority.[46] This was found to be a restriction on establishment which ultimately, because of various arbitrary elements in the authorisation procedure, was not justified. Similarly, rules in Greece permitting opticians to own only one shop, and Italian laws which prohibited either companies or non-pharmacists from owning pharmacies, were both found to comprise restrictions on establishment, albeit in the latter case

---

[40] See also Case C-325/08 *Olympique Lyonnais* [2010] ECR I-2177.

[41] Similar reasoning was first used in relation to Article 49 TFEU in Case 107/83 *Ordre des Avocats au Barreau de Paris* v *Klopp* [1984] ECR 2971.

[42] See p. 773 *et seq.*

[43] Case C-55/94 *Gebhard* v *Consiglio dell'ordine degli avvocati e procuratori di Milano* [1995] ECR I-4165; Case C-299/02 *Commission* v *Netherlands* [2004] ECR I-9761.

[44] Case C-55/94 *Gebhard* v *Consiglio dell'ordine degli avvocati e procuratori di Milano* [1995] ECR I-4165.

[45] See pp. 879–83.

[46] Case C-169/07 *Hartlauer Handelsgesellschaft mbH* v *Wiener Landesregierung, Oberösterreichische Landesregierung*, Judgment of 10 March 2009. See also Case C-315/08 *Grisoli* [2011] ECR I-139; Case C-217/09 *Polliseni* [2010] ECR I-175; Case C-570/07 *Blanco Perez*; Case C-72/10 *Costa*, Judgment of 16 February 2012; Case C-539/11 *Ottica*, Judgment of 26 September 2013. See for discussion R. Cisotta, 'Limits to Rights to Health Care and the Extent of Member States' Discretion to Decide on the Parameters of their Public Health Policies' in F. Benyon (ed.), *Services and the EU Citizen* (Oxford, Hart, 2013) 113.

justified.[47] Other unjustified restrictions have included those requiring businesses carrying on certain activities to have a certain minimum size,[48] and planning rules, such as those in *Commission* v *Spain*, which set a maximum size for shopping malls.[49]

As in *Bosman*, these cases concern rules which do not discriminate explicitly, and do not seem to have any greater effect on cross-border movement than domestic movement.[50] The only sense in which it could be argued that they are discriminatory is that they tend to entrench the status quo, and protect incumbents, who still tend to be disproportionately national in almost all industries, from new competition. Not that the Court of Justice uses this argument. Its objection is just that for some parties, establishment or employment will be, or could be, prevented. Indeed, in *Commission* v *Spain* it explicitly rejected the Commission's argument that the planning rules would have a greater effect on foreign operators than domestic ones since the former were more likely to want large shopping centres, yet nevertheless went on to find that there was a restriction on movement simply because the rules might prevent a foreign operator from establishing.

(iii) *De minimis*: limits of the right to take up an occupation

Bosman and the other cases in the preceding section concerned measures with a very direct and powerful effect. In *Graf*, the Court of Justice stated that measures affecting the taking up of economic activities in another Member State would not fall within Article 45 TFEU if their restrictive effects were too indirect or uncertain.[51] In that instance, an Austrian law entitling employees to two months' pay as compensation for loss of employment where they had been working for their employer for at least three years was challenged. This entitlement did not exist where it was the employee who gave notice. Graf left his company to work in Germany. He sued for the compensation, claiming that its absence acted as a disincentive to move job, and thus fell within Article 45. The Court disagreed.

Case C-190/98 *Graf* v *Filzmoser Maschinenbau* [2000] ECR I-493

22. Nationals of Member States have in particular the right, which they derive directly from the Treaty, to leave their country of origin to enter the territory of another Member State and reside there in order to pursue an economic activity...

23. Provisions which, even if they are applicable without distinction, preclude or deter a national of a Member State from leaving his country of origin in order to exercise his right to freedom of movement therefore constitute an obstacle to that freedom. However, in order to be capable of constituting such an obstacle, they must affect access of workers to the labour market.

---

[47] Case C-140/03 *Commission* v *Greece* [2005] ECR I-3177; Case C-531/06 *Commission* v *Italy*, Judgment of 9 May 2009; see also Joined Cases C-171/07 and C-172/07 *Apothekerkammer des Saarlandes*, Judgment of 19 May 2009.

[48] Case C-357/10 *Duomo*, Judgment of 10 May 2012.

[49] Case C-400/08 *Commission* v *Spain* [2011] ECR I-1915; Case C-338/09 *Yellow Cab* [2010] ECR I-13927.

[50] See C. Costello, 'Market Access All Areas? The Treatment of Non-Discriminatory Barriers to the Free Movement of Workers' (2000) 27(3) *LIEI* 267.

[51] *Ibid.*

24. Legislation of the kind at issue in the main proceedings is not such as to preclude or deter a worker from ending his contract of employment in order to take a job with another employer, because the entitlement to compensation on termination of employment is not dependent on the worker's choosing whether or not to stay with his current employer but on a future and hypothetical event, namely the subsequent termination of his contract without such termination being at his own initiative or attributable to him.

25. Such an event is too uncertain and indirect a possibility for legislation to be capable of being regarded as liable to hinder freedom of movement for workers where it does not attach to termination of a contract of employment by the worker himself the same consequence as it attaches to termination which was not at his initiative or is not attributable to him.

Graf may be contrasted with *Kranemann*,[52] where there was a challenge to the regulations governing travel expenses for trainee civil servants in the German state of Nordrhein-Westfalen. Travel expenses were reimbursed where the training was carried out within Germany, but not for that outside Germany. It was not clear whether this would dissuade many trainees from taking up training abroad. The Court of Justice, nevertheless, considered that the measure violated Article 45 TFEU, as it considered that it might deter trainees with limited financial resources from taking up training abroad. Two sorts of measure are, therefore, caught under this case law. The first are measures, such as that in *Bosman*, which prevent access to the market. Regardless of their aim, their extreme restrictive effects lead to their falling within Article 45 or 49. The second are measures such as those in *Graf* or *Kranemann*. The effect of such measures is not to prevent access to the market, but to deter an individual from taking up activities in another Member State because of the economic costs such activity would entail. In the latter case, *Graf* creates a *de minimis* rule, but *Kranemann* suggests that this will not be applied, or will be less rigorously applied, where the measure specifically targets movement between Member States.

(iv) Restrictions on secondary establishment

The taking up of business activity in another Member State can occur either through primary or secondary establishment. The former is where a trader relocates her central place of business to another Member State. By contrast, with secondary establishment, the trader remains in her home state, but sets up branches, agencies or subsidiaries in other Member States. Restrictions on secondary establishment inevitably prevent traders from other Member States setting up a business in the host state, as to do so would involve their having to abandon their place of business in their home state. This question was raised in *Klopp*, concerning a German lawyer practising law in Dusseldorf. He applied to register with the Paris Bar Council in order to practise in Paris, but was refused because of a general prohibition on anyone practising at the Paris Bar unless their principal office was in Paris and the other offices they worked from were in the environs of Paris.

---

[52] Case C-109/04 *Kranemann v Land Nordrhein-Westfalen* [2005] ECR I-2421.

Case 107/83 *Ordre des Avocats au Barreau de Paris* v *Klopp* [1984] ECR 2971

17. …under [the second paragraph of Article 49 TFEU] freedom of establishment includes access to and the pursuit of the activities of self-employed persons 'under the conditions laid down for its own nationals by the law of the country where such establishment is effected'. It follows from that provision and its context that in the absence of specific Community rules in the matter each Member State is free to regulate the exercise of the legal profession in its territory.

18. Nevertheless that rule does not mean that the legislation of a Member State may require a lawyer to have only one establishment throughout the Community territory. Such a restrictive interpretation would mean that a lawyer once established in a particular Member State would be able to enjoy the freedom of the Treaty to establish himself in another Member State only at the price of abandoning the establishment he already had.

19. That freedom of establishment is not confined to the right to create a single establishment within the Community is confirmed by the very words of Article [49 TFEU], according to which the progressive abolition of the restrictions on freedom of establishment applies to restrictions on the setting up of agencies, branches or subsidiaries by nationals of any Member State established in the territory of another Member State. That rule must be regarded as a specific statement of a general principle, applicable equally to the liberal professions, according to which the right of establishment includes freedom to set up and maintain, subject to observance of the professional rules of conduct, more than one place of work within the Community.

20. In view of the special nature of the legal profession, however, the second Member State must have the right, in the interests of the due administration of justice, to require that lawyers enrolled at a bar in its territory should practise in such a way as to maintain sufficient contact with their clients and the judicial authorities and abide by the rules of the profession. Nevertheless such requirements must not prevent the nationals of other Member States from exercising properly the right of establishment guaranteed them by the Treaty.

21. In that respect it must be pointed out that modern methods of transport and telecommunications facilitate proper contact with clients and the judicial authorities. Similarly, the existence of a second set of chambers in another Member State does not prevent the application of the rules of ethics in the host Member State.

The judgment suggests that it is unlikely that restrictions on secondary establishment can be justified. This position is supported by *Commission* v *France*,[53] where the French Government attempted to justify a similar prohibition on secondary establishment for doctors and dentists, on the grounds that patients will often wish to have access to the same doctor. The Court of Justice was equally dismissive, stating that even in general practices, recent developments resulted in practitioners belonging to group practices with the consequence that a patient could never ensure access to a particular practitioner. The argument in *Klopp* that effective supervision does not in fact require physical presence has been reinforced in the context of taxation in *Commission* v *Denmark*, where the Court pointed out that a Directive existed specifically to regulate mutual assistance between national tax authorities.[54] Denmark made certain tax breaks conditional upon incorporation in Denmark, saying this was necessary to

[53] Case 96/85 *Commission* v *France* [1986] ECR 1475. See also Case C-351/90 *Commission* v *Luxembourg* [1992] ECR I-3945.

[54] Case C-150/04 *Commission* v *Denmark* [2007] ECR I-1163.

prevent fraud, because the authorities could not verify tax claims made by companies based abroad. In a judgment entirely consistent with its information-based approach to the internal market, and with the philosophy of the Services Directive, the Court found this to be disproportionate.[55] If checking of claims was necessary, Denmark should seek to find ways to do this abroad, with the help of local authorities, rather than washing its hands of the matter. The case shows that Member States should not regard foreign establishments as beyond the supervisory pale, but rather should engage with authorities in other states to obtain the information that they need.

Most cases have concerned more hidden restrictions on secondary establishment. In *Stanton*,[56] a challenge was made to a Belgian requirement for the self-employed to pay social security contributions unless they were also employed in Belgium. The Court of Justice considered that such an exemption penalised those who extended their business activities across more than one Member State and whilst it was not discriminatory, as more Belgians were affected by it than any other nationality, it was nevertheless illegal as it restricted free movement. More recently, in *Commission* v *Portugal*,[57] a Portuguese requirement that private security firms be legally incorporated in Portugal was held to be an illegal restriction on secondary establishment as it prevented natural persons from other Member States setting up in Portugal.

(v) Restrictions on the use of diplomas and qualifications

By definition, professions deny access to an occupation, for they prevent that activity being pursued unless the individual submits to oversight of the professional body governing the activity in question and has the qualifications required for exercise of the profession. It might, therefore, be that the very presence of a profession is challenged under Articles 45 and 49 TFEU on the grounds that it prevents an individual taking up an economic activity. Early on, however, the Court of Justice ruled that Member States may be permitted to lay down professional rules relating to organisation, qualifications, professional ethics, supervision and liability,[58] and this has been repeated on a number of occasions since.[59] The Court has, instead, scrutinised the conditions imposed by these rules for the taking up of a profession, most notably the qualifications required before a migrant can enter a particular profession.

The central case is *Vlassopoulou*, concerning a Greek lawyer who completed her doctorate at the University of Tübingen, Germany, in 1982, and from 1983 until 1988 worked at a German law firm in Mannheim. In 1988 she applied to become a Rechtsanwalt, a German lawyer, but was refused on the grounds that she had neither studied law at a German university for two years, nor completed the First State exams, nor undergone the relevant period of training in Germany. She argued that this violated Article 49 as no account was taken of her Greek qualifications or her work experience in Germany.

---

[55] See pp. 780–3.
[56] Case 143/87 *Stanton* v *INASTI* [1988] ECR 3877. See also Joined Cases 154/87 and 155/87 *Rijksinstituut voor de sociale verzekering des zelfstandigen* v *Wolf* [1998] ECR 3897; Case C-53/95 *INASTI* v *Kammler* [1996] ECR I-703.
[57] Case C-171/02 *Commission* v *Portugal* [2004] ECR I-5645.
[58] Case 71/76 *Thieffry* v *Conseil de l'Ordre des Avocats à la Cour de Paris* [1977] ECR 765.
[59] Case 292/86 *Gullung* v *Conseil de l'Ordre des Avocats* [1988] ECR 111; Case C-55/94 *Gebhard* v *Consiglio dell'ordine degli avvocati e procuratori di Milano* [1995] ECR I-4165.

Case C-340/89 *Vlassopoulou* v *Ministerium für Justiz Bundes- und Europaangelegenheiten Baden-Wurttemberg* [1991] ECR I-2357

14. ...insofar as Community law makes no special provision, the objectives of the Treaty, and in particular freedom of establishment, may be achieved by measures enacted by the Member States, which, under Article [4(3) TEU], must take 'all appropriate measures, whether general or particular, to ensure fulfilment of the obligations arising out of this Treaty or resulting from action taken by the institutions of the Community' and abstain from 'any measure which could jeopardize the attainment of the objectives of this Treaty'. [The wording of this provision has since been slightly amended by the Lisbon Treaty.]

15. It must be stated in this regard that, even if applied without any discrimination on the basis of nationality, national requirements concerning qualifications may have the effect of hindering nationals of the other Member States in the exercise of their right of establishment guaranteed to them by Article [49 TFEU]. That could be the case if the national rules in question took no account of the knowledge and qualifications already acquired by the person concerned in another Member State.

16. Consequently, a Member State which receives a request to admit a person to a profession to which access, under national law, depends upon the possession of a diploma or a professional qualification must take into consideration the diplomas, certificates and other evidence of qualifications which the person concerned has acquired in order to exercise the same profession in another Member State by making a comparison between the specialized knowledge and abilities certified by those diplomas and the knowledge and qualifications required by the national rules.

17. That examination procedure must enable the authorities of the host Member State to assure themselves, on an objective basis, that the foreign diploma certifies that its holder has knowledge and qualifications which are, if not identical, at least equivalent to those certified by the national diploma. That assessment of the equivalence of the foreign diploma must be carried out exclusively in the light of the level of knowledge and qualifications which its holder can be assumed to possess in the light of that diploma, having regard to the nature and duration of the studies and practical training to which the diploma relates...

18. In the course of that examination, a Member State may, however, take into consideration objective differences relating to both the legal framework of the profession in question in the Member State of origin and to its field of activity. In the case of the profession of lawyer, a Member State may therefore carry out a comparative examination of diplomas, taking account of the differences identified between the national legal systems concerned.

19. If that comparative examination of diplomas results in the finding that the knowledge and qualifications certified by the foreign diploma correspond to those required by the national provisions, the Member State must recognize that diploma as fulfilling the requirements laid down by its national provisions. If, on the other hand, the comparison reveals that the knowledge and qualifications certified by the foreign diploma and those required by the national provisions correspond only partially, the host Member State is entitled to require the person concerned to show that he has acquired the knowledge and qualifications which are lacking.

20. In this regard, the competent national authorities must assess whether the knowledge acquired in the host Member State, either during a course of study or by way of practical experience, is sufficient in order to prove possession of the knowledge which is lacking.

21. If completion of a period of preparation or training for entry into the profession is required by the rules applying in the host Member State, those national authorities must determine whether professional

experience acquired in the Member State of origin or in the host Member State may be regarded as satisfying that requirement in full or in part.

22. Finally, it must be pointed out that the examination made to determine whether the knowledge and qualifications certified by the foreign diploma and those required by the legislation of the host Member State correspond must be carried out by the national authorities in accordance with a procedure which is in conformity with the requirements of Community law concerning the effective protection of the fundamental rights conferred by the Treaty on Community subjects. It follows that any decision taken must be capable of being made the subject of judicial proceedings in which its legality under Community law can be reviewed and that the person concerned must be able to ascertain the reasons for the decision taken in his regard.

There is a duty to take account of the qualifications and experience of the migrant in deciding whether to grant her access to the market.[60] A question emerging from *Vlassopoulou* is that concerning the types of proof that may be furnished by the migrant in order to demonstrate that she meets the required standard. The host state can only refuse access to the profession if there are 'objective differences' between its qualifications and the practical experience and qualifications of the migrant. Such an approach assumes a substitutability of knowledge, whereby if the migrant has the requisite standard of knowledge, no matter the source, she should be allowed to practise.

Subsequent case law has expounded on which knowledge and training must be taken into account by the host state authorities. In *Hocsman*,[61] a Spaniard applied to practise as a doctor in France. All his university training was from Argentina, whose diplomas France did not recognise as equivalent to its own. He had, however, worked for a number of years as a doctor in Spanish hospitals and as a urologist in French hospitals. The Court of Justice held that in making their decision the French authorities should have considered all the practical experience acquired by Hocsman not only in France, but also in Spain. They were also required to take into account all the diplomas and qualifications that certified a specialised knowledge, notwithstanding that these came from outside the European Union. The test imposes severe demands on the professional bodies. It will be difficult to vet the quality of practical experience not gained on their territory. It is even more difficult to know how to evaluate certification of an expertise from an institution whose standards are not trusted. Finally, they are required to provide some overall assessment on what may be a set of heterogeneous and eclectic experiences. Any decision will be difficult for the authority to make. Such requirements are not necessarily advantageous to the migrant, as this complexity results in any decision being difficult to review as it is difficult to point to a clear standard which is being breached.

Professional qualifications also facilitate the pursuit of an activity by demonstrating certification of a skill, thereby making the holder more marketable. It would be extremely complicated if different constraints were to apply to how Member States regulated access to a profession and how they regulated the broader use of professional qualifications. The Court of Justice has, therefore, a similar logic on all non-discriminatory restrictions on the

---

[60] See also Case C-345/08 *Pesla* [2009] ECR I-11677; Case C-422/09 *Vandorou* [2010] ECR I-12411; Case C-118/09 *Koller* [2010] ECR I-13627.

[61] Case C-238/98 *Hocsman v Ministre de l'Emploi et de la Solidarité* [2000] ECR I-6623.

recognition of non-national professional qualifications. In *Kraus*,[62] a German, who had completed an LLM at Edinburgh University, challenged a German requirement that administrative authorisation was necessary for use of higher education titles acquired abroad. The Court noted that qualifications were necessary both for access to a profession and, more generally, to facilitate the exercise of economic activity. Any conditions on the use of a title which hindered or made more difficult the exercise of the economic freedoms fell, in its view, within Article 49 TFEU. It refused to draw a distinction between titles necessary for access to a profession and other titles, but held that Member States could impose non-discriminatory restrictions on the use of titles to prevent fraud. An administrative authorisation for these purposes was lawful provided it was accessible, susceptible to judicial review, reasons were given for any refusal to approve a title, the administrative costs charged were not excessive and any sanctions imposed for the use of the title without authorisation were not disproportionately heavy.

Vlassopoulou now co-exists alongside Directive 2005/36/EC on the recognition of professional qualifications, which consolidates what had previously been a number of different Directives.[63] There are situations which do not fall within the Directive, to which the case law principles continue to apply, but it provides a fairly comprehensive regime.

The Directive governs the pursuit, either in an employed or self-employed capacity, of a regulated profession by EU nationals in a Member State other than that where they acquired their qualifications.[64] The Directive gives a nigh exhaustive definition of regulated professions, taking these to include any professional activity access to or the pursuit of which is subject to the possession of specific professional qualifications.[65] These professional qualifications may be attested by formal qualifications, a confirmation of competence or professional experience.[66] The central provision of the Directive, article 4(1), states that an EU national who has qualified abroad will have access to the host state market where her qualifications are recognised by that state.

Directive 2005/36/EC, article 4(1)

1. The recognition of professional qualifications by the host Member State allows the beneficiary to gain access in that Member State to the same profession as that for which he is qualified in the home Member State and to pursue it in the host Member State under the same conditions as its nationals.

Recognition is not acquired automatically. The Directive provides three routes to recognition, depending upon the professional activity being undertaken.

The first is the 'general system for the recognition of evidence of training'. This applies where access to or pursuit of a regulated profession in the host state is contingent upon possession of specific qualifications. The basic principle for such activities is mutual recognition of qualifications.

---

[62] Case C-19/92 *Kraus* v *Land Baden-Württemberg* [1993] ECR I-1663.
[63] [2005] OJ L255/22.   [64] *Ibid.* article 2(1).
[65] *Ibid.* article 3(1). The Directive also applies to a large number of occupations not fitting neatly into this definition. These are set out in Annex I.
[66] *Ibid.* article 3(1)(b).

> **Directive 2005/36/EC, article 13**
>
> 1. If access to or pursuit of a regulated profession in a host Member State is contingent upon possession of specific professional qualifications, the competent authority of that Member State shall permit access to and pursuit of that profession, under the same conditions as apply to its nationals, to applicants possessing the attestation of competence or evidence of formal qualifications required by another Member State in order to gain access to and pursue that profession on its territory. Attestations of competence or evidence of formal qualifications shall satisfy the following conditions:
>   (a) they shall have been issued by a competent authority in a Member State, designated in accordance with the legislative, regulatory or administrative provisions of that Member State;
>   (b) they shall attest a level of professional qualification at least equivalent to the level immediately prior to that which is required in the host Member State....
> 2. Access to and pursuit of the profession, as described in paragraph 1, shall also be granted to applicants who have pursued the profession referred to in that paragraph on a full-time basis for two years during the previous 10 years in another Member State which does not regulate that profession, provided they possess one or more attestations of competence or documents providing evidence of formal qualifications. Attestations of competence and evidence of formal qualifications shall satisfy the following conditions:
>   (a) they shall have been issued by a competent authority in a Member State, designated in accordance with the legislative, regulatory or administrative provisions of that Member State;
>   (b) they shall attest a level of professional qualification at least equivalent to the level immediately prior to that required in the host Member State....
>   (c) they shall attest that the holder has been prepared for the pursuit of the profession in question.

Member States may require applicants to take an aptitude test or complete an adaptation period of up to three years where the duration of the training undertaken is at least one year shorter than that in the host state, where the training is substantially different from that in the host state, or where the regulated profession in the host state comprises one or more regulated activities which do not exist in the corresponding home state and where the difference consists of specific training required by the host state which is substantially dissimilar to anything covered by the applicant's qualification. The applicant must be given the choice between either taking the aptitude test or undergoing the adaptation period except where the activity requires precise knowledge of national law, in which case the host state may choose which of the obligations to impose on the applicant.[67]

A difficult situation occurs where qualifications and training are not merely different in detail, but so fundamentally divergent that differences cannot just be made up by a little extra training. In this case the Directive does not provide a solution, but the Court of Justice has found that Member States must still consider how free movement can be protected, and a good solution may be to allow the migrant to practise a specific part of the protected profession, perhaps under their home title, to avoid confusion. Mr Nasiopoulos had qualified as a medical masseur-hydrotherapist in Germany, but this particular form of therapy was conducted in Greece, where he wished to establish, by physiotherapists, and reserved

---

[67] *Ibid.* article 14.

to them. Mr Nasiopoulos did not claim that he should be recognised as a physiotherapist or allowed to do all the things that they do, but argued that he should be allowed to carry out the specific therapy for which he was trained: he wanted what the Court has called 'partial recognition'.

Case C-573/11 *Nasiopoulos*, Judgment of 27 June 2013

20. Since the conditions for access to the profession of physiotherapist have not, to date, been harmonised at European Union level, the Member States remain competent to define such conditions since Directive 2005/36 does not restrict their powers on that point. They must, however, exercise their powers in this area in a manner which respects the basic freedoms guaranteed by the Treaty.

21. Thus, legislation of a host Member State which excludes all partial access to a regulated profession and, accordingly, is liable to hinder or make less attractive the exercise of freedom of establishment may be justified, inter alia, by overriding reasons relating to the public interest, provided that it does not go beyond what is necessary in order to attain the objective which it pursues.

22. With regard to the objective of legislation such as that at issue in the main proceedings, the overriding reasons relating to the public interest relied upon by the Governments which submitted observations are, firstly, consumer protection and, secondly, health protection.

23. As regards consumer protection, it must be noted that, indeed, partial recognition of professional qualifications could, theoretically, have the effect of fragmenting the professions regulated in a Member State into various activities. That would lead essentially to a risk of confusion in the minds of the recipients of services provided by professionals established in that Member State, which recipients might well be misled as to the scope of the qualifications associated with the profession of physiotherapist.

24. However, exclusion from even partial access to the profession of physiotherapist goes beyond what is necessary to achieve the objective of consumer protection.

25. As the Court has already pointed out in the judgment in [Case C-330/02] *Colegio de Ingenieros de Caminos, Canales y Puertos*, the legitimate objective of protection of consumers may be achieved through less restrictive means than total exclusion of even partial access to a profession, particularly the obligation to use the professional title of origin or the academic title both in the language in which it was awarded and in its original form, and in the official language of the host Member State.

The Court went on to make clear that these principles only applied where training was so different that the title acquired and the relevant host state title did not belong to the 'same profession', so that the Directive could not be applied. Partial recognition cannot be used as a path to avoid acquiring necessary extra knowledge where similar professional qualifications differ in content, thereby undermining the host state profession. It is also necessary, before engaging in partial recognition, to consider whether a particular aspect of a profession can safely and coherently be separated from the whole. In Mr Nasiopoulos's case that seemed to be so.

The second route concerns activities which require only general commercial or professional knowledge. These are listed in Annex IV of the Directive and include activities involving mainly industrial experience. Access to the market is premised upon mutual recognition of experience.

Directive 2005/36/EC, article 16

If, in a Member State, access to or pursuit of one of the activities listed in Annex IV is contingent upon possession of general, commercial or professional knowledge and aptitudes, that Member State shall recognise previous pursuit of the activity in another Member State as sufficient proof of such knowledge and aptitudes.

The length of time depends on the activity in question and whether any prior training has been carried out. There is less protection for these activities than for those in the first category. There are no checks on the equivalence of the experience or any exceptions to this requirement of mutual recognition.

The third category covers those professionals (doctors, vets, nurses, midwives, pharmacists, architects and dentists) who were previously regulated by sectoral Directives. These require not only evidence of formal qualifications, but also evidence that the applicant has satisfied minimum training conditions which are set out in the Directive.[68] A good example is the requirements set out for basic medical training.

Directive 2005/36/EC, article 24

1. Admission to basic medical training shall be contingent upon possession of a diploma or certificate providing access, for the studies in question, to universities.
2. Basic medical training shall comprise a total of at least six years of study or 5,500 hours of theoretical and practical training provided by, or under the supervision of, a university...
3. Basic medical training shall provide an assurance that the person in question has acquired the following knowledge and skills:
   (a) adequate knowledge of the sciences on which medicine is based and a good understanding of the scientific methods including the principles of measuring biological functions, the evaluation of scientifically established facts and the analysis of data;
   (b) sufficient understanding of the structure, functions and behaviour of healthy and sick persons, as well as relations between the state of health and physical and social surroundings of the human being;
   (c) adequate knowledge of clinical disciplines and practices, providing him with a coherent picture of mental and physical diseases, of medicine from the points of view of prophylaxis, diagnosis and therapy and of human reproduction;
   (d) suitable clinical experience in hospitals under appropriate supervision.

A different philosophy underlies each category. These may be described respectively as qualified mutual recognition; unqualified mutual recognition; and unqualified mutual recognition combined with partial harmonisation. The presence of these different approaches is generated in part by the wide range of activities covered by the Directive. Nevertheless, the absence of a single ethos is unsettling. Why is a different regime applied to engineers (the first approach) than to architects (the third approach)? The variety of activities may be a partial answer to that

---

[68] *Ibid.* article 21.

question, but it attracts further criticism. The principles determining the allocation of activities to each approach are unclear and, in turn, each approach covers a sweeping range of activities, many of which have demands that are not readily comparable.

(vi) Restrictions on grounds of abuse of free movement

In a number of situations individuals may be motivated to go abroad in order to avoid inconvenient rules in their home state. This occurs where individuals migrate in order to benefit from the family rights awarded to migrant citizens, and then come home at a later date, continuing to rely on their migrant status. It also occurs where companies relocate to a Member State with more convenient tax or incorporation rules, but continue to do business in their original state. In both these cases, the original state is inclined to regard the use of free movement as 'abusive' and to claim that reliance on free movement rights merely to avoid national law should not be permitted. As is discussed in Chapter 11, and below, the Court of Justice has not been sympathetic.[69] It is not abusive to allow the legal advantages of a particular location or relocation to influence decision-making, and nor is it abusive to engage in economic activity purely in order to benefit from the associated rights, as may happen where a student gets a job in order to obtain finance for their study: the reasons why someone migrates or works are irrelevant to their rights.[70]

Indeed, the context where abuse arguments have been the most numerous, particularly in recent years, is that of education and training. An early example was *Knoors*, where a Dutch citizen worked as a plumber in Belgium, and on his return to the Netherlands applied to have his experience recognised as equivalent to the Dutch plumbing qualification, as the Directive then in force permitted. The Dutch Government claimed that he had migrated purely to avoid having to study for the plumbing qualification which in the Netherlands was compulsory.

Case 115/78 J. *Knoors* v *Staatssecretaris van Economische Zaken* [1979] ECR 399

24. Although it is true that the provisions of the Treaty relating to establishment and the provision of services cannot be applied to situations which are purely internal to a Member State, the position nevertheless remains that the reference in Article [49 TFEU] to 'nationals of a Member State' who wish to establish themselves 'in the territory of another Member State' cannot be interpreted in such a way as to exclude from the benefit of Community law a given Member State's own nationals when the latter, owing to the fact that they have lawfully resided on the territory of another Member State and have there acquired a trade qualification which is recognized by the provisions of Community law, are, with regard to their state of origin, in a situation which may be assimilated to that of any other persons enjoying the rights and liberties guaranteed by the Treaty.

---

[69] See p. 506; see also Case C-456/12 *O and B*, Judgment of 12 March 2014; K. Engsig Sørensen, 'Abuse of Rights in Community Law: A Principle of Substance or Merely Rhetoric?' (2006) 43 *CMLRev.* 423; A. Kjellgren, 'On the Border of Abuse: The Jurisprudence of the European Court of Justice on Circumvention, Fraud and Other Misuses of Community Law' (2000) 11 *EBLRev.* 179; M. Evers and A. de Graaf, 'Limiting Benefit Shopping: Use and Abuse of EC Law' (2009) 18 *EC Tax Review* 279; R. de la Feria, 'Prohibition of Abuse of (Community) Law: The Creation of a New General Principle of EC Law Through Tax' (2008) 45 *CMLRev.* 395; K. Ziegler, '"Abuse of Law" in the Context of the Free Movement of Workers' in R. de la Feria and S. Vogenauer (eds.), *Prohibition of Abuse of Law: A New General Principle of EU Law?* (Oxford, Hart, 2011).

[70] Case C-46/12 *LN*, Judgment of 21 February 2013; Case 53/81 *Levin* [1982] ECR 1035.

25. However, it is not possible to disregard the legitimate interest which a Member State may have in preventing certain of its nationals, by means of facilities created under the Treaty, from attempting wrongly to evade the application of their national legislation as regards training for a trade.

The suggestion in this last paragraph, that there may be limits to the extent to which individuals can choose the jurisdiction that suits them best, has not been realised in practice.[71] Just as a state may, sometimes, be able to justify applying rules to migrants which restrict their movement, if necessary in order to protect important interests, they may in principle do this also to citizens engaging in U-turns. However, that does not mean that self-interested choices somehow nullify rights, and in practice the Court of Justice continues to respect the individual freedom of choice which is inherent in free movement.

Centros, a case on company migration which is discussed later in this chapter,[72] has become a central authority on this and contains the clear statement that 'the fact that a national of a Member State who wishes to set up a company chooses to form it in the Member State whose rules of company law seem to him the least restrictive and to set up branches in other Member States cannot, in itself, constitute an abuse of the right of establishment'.[73] That appears to reflect the Court's general approach to 'instrumental' use of free movement law.

N. Nic Shuibhne, *The Coherence of EU Free Movement Law* (Oxford, Oxford University Press, 2013) 91

The Court's sanctioning of the instrumental use of EU law short of fraudulent conduct – i.e. simply taking advantage of the possibilities created by free movement – was widely transposed from *Centros* to the case law on personal free movement. While some Advocates General did consider the relevance of intention or motivation, the Court's approach becomes more consciously consistent with the view that instrumental exercise (or 'legitimate circumvention'[74]) of free movement rights does not constitute abuse. For example, in *Ninni-Orasche*, the applicant, an Italian national living in Austria and married to an Austrian national, had worked for a short period in order to generate eligibility for study finance benefits in the host state.[75] To determine whether she was a worker within the meaning of EU law the national court was empowered by the Court of Justice to determine whether the relevant activity was purely marginal and ancillary. It was also emphasized that 'factors relating to the conduct of the person concerned before and after the period of employment are not relevant in establishing the status of worker'.

In recent years entrepreneurial higher education institutions have created a new locus for abuse arguments. The European School of Economics (ESE) was a UK institution which awarded degrees according to UK law, but which provided classes at a campus in Italy. Italian law, however, only recognised foreign degrees if the study for that degree had actually been undertaken in the degree-awarding state. In *Neri*, the Court of Justice found that this was an

---

[71] See N. Nic Shuibhne, *The Coherence of EU Free Movement Law* (Oxford, Oxford University Press, 2013) 85–100.
[72] See p. 887.   [73] Case C-212/97 *Centros* [1999] ECR I-1459, para. 27.
[74] De la Feria, n. 69 above, 403.   [75] *Ninni-Orasche*, n. 14 above.

unlawful restriction on the freedom of establishment of the ESE.[76] In *Khatzithanasis* and *Commission* v *Spain*, the Court took the same approach in similar situations, ruling that a failure to recognise qualifications as an optician or engineer just because the actual study was done in the home state was contrary to the Directive on professional qualifications then in force.[77] The requirement to recognise qualifications awarded by bodies in other Member States is not subject to an exception or condition to do with the physical place of study.

A limit was, however, reached in *Cavallera*.[78] In Italy, one may practise as an engineer after a university course in engineering, and the taking of a state exam. In Spain, a university course in engineering suffices. Mr Cavallera attempted to leverage this difference: he had obtained a university degree in engineering in Italy, and successfully obtained recognition of this in Spain as equivalent to a Spanish degree. This entitled him to practise as an engineer in Spain and he obtained certification to this effect. He then returned to Italy and argued that since he was entitled to practise as an engineer in Spain, his Spanish authorisation should be recognised and translated to an authorisation to practise in Italy, pursuant to the Directive on professional qualifications then in force. He would then have successfully avoided the Italian state examination. However, he lost his case. The Court of Justice found that the Directive did not grant any right to rely on a certificate authorising a person to practise a profession when that certificate did not attest to any course of study or examination at an institution in that state.[79]

4 RESTRICTIONS ON THE PURSUIT OF AN OCCUPATION

Restrictions on the pursuit of economic activity concern restrictions placed on the migrant, which occur once she has placed herself on the market of the host state, either through working for an employer or through self-employment within that state. The presumption is then that they will be subject to the law of that state but this is subject to the caveat that the law must contain no overt (direct) or covert (indirect) discrimination. Overt discrimination occurs where there is an express reference to nationality which disadvantages the migrant. Covert discrimination results where the conditions are on their face formally neutral, but are liable to adversely affect migrants to a disproportionate extent. This is considered to be the case where the conditions imposed essentially disadvantage migrant workers, or where they can more easily be satisfied by national workers than by migrant workers, or where there is a risk that they may operate to the particular detriment of migrant workers. In such circumstances, the measure will be illegal as a form of covert discrimination unless justified by some legitimate objective and proportionate to that objective.[80] Discrimination is considered pernicious in this field on two grounds. First, it places the migrant at a competitive disadvantage and thus acts to protect that state's market. Secondly, the migrant is not simply a business machine concerned

---

[76] Case C-153/02 *Neri* v *European School of Economics* [2003] ECR I-13555.

[77] Case C-151/07 *Theologos-Grigorios Khatzithanasis* v *Ypourgos Ygeias kai Koinonikis Allilengyis and Organismos Epangelmatikis Ekpaidefsis kai Katartisis (OEEK)*, Judgment of 4 December 2008; Case C-286/06 *Commission* v *Spain* [2008] ECR I-8025. See also Case C-274/05 *Commission* v *Greece* [2008] ECR I-7969.

[78] Case C-311/06 *Consiglio Nazionale degli Ingegneri* v *Ministero della Giustizia and Marco Cavallera*, Judgment of 29 January 2009.

[79] See e.g. Case C-118/09 *Koller* [2010] ECR I-13627.

[80] Case C-237/94 *O'Flynn* v *Adjudication Officer* [1996] ECR I-2617.

with accumulating profit. She is also a human being and thus discrimination constitutes an affront to her dignity and acts as an obstacle to her integration into the host society.

Alongside the prohibition of discrimination, the question arises whether a person or business can challenge host state regulation merely because it obstructs their activities, even without showing that a national or local business would be better off. The law and policy surrounding this question is addressed in (iii) below.

(i) Discrimination in labour markets

Discrimination between workers as regards remuneration and other conditions of employment is expressly prohibited by Article 45(2) TFEU. Regulation 492/2011 reiterates and elaborates this, and also provides in article 7(4) that:

> Any clause of a collective or individual agreement or of any other collective regulation concerning eligibility for employment, employment, remuneration and other conditions of work or dismissal shall be null and void insofar as it lays down or authorises discriminatory conditions in respect of workers who are nationals of the other Member States.

An example of this in action is *Erny*.[81] German employers provided extra contributions to part-time workers nearing retirement, and did so according to a formula which took account of their salary and the amount of tax they paid. However, frontier workers living in France were treated as if they were taxed at the German level, even though they in fact paid tax in France, and this had disadvantageous consequences for them. The contributions had come into being as part of a collective agreement, but the Court of Justice considered that neither the autonomy of the social partners, nor the practical difficulties of taking into account foreign tax levels, provided sufficient justification for the discriminatory effect. The clauses of the agreement were therefore null and void. What is notable is that the Court did not prescribe an alternative, but left it to the Member State or the social partners to come up with a better solution. On the one hand, this respects the autonomy of labour processes, but on the other it means that negotiations towards a collective agreement are framed by stringent Treaty obligations and the case law of the Court.

A good example of discrimination in work is *Köbler*.[82] Austrian law granted university professors an increased salary once they had completed fifteen years' service in the Austrian university system. This was not available to university professors who had served part of that time at universities outside Austria. Köbler was denied the increase on the grounds that he had spent some of this period in a German university and, as the scheme was designed to reward loyalty to the Austrian university system, it was considered that this period away meant he did not qualify. The Court of Justice found the measure to be illegal, as it discriminated in two ways. First, it penalised non-Austrians who were likely to have spent some time in universities elsewhere in the European Union. Secondly, it discriminated against Austrians who had exercised their rights under Article 45 TFEU and spent time abroad. Similar failures to take account of experience abroad, when domestic experience is rewarded, have been repeatedly

---

[81] Case C-172/11 *Erny*, Judgment of 28 June 2012.
[82] Case C-224/01 *Köbler* v *Austria* [2003] ECR I-10239.

condemned by the Court.[83] A variation on this theme was found in *Delay*, where a failure to take into account years of experience in a particular domestic job was also discriminatory, where that job was one that was primarily done by foreigners.[84] The case concerned language assistants in Italian universities. If they were lucky enough to obtain a permanent post, their years as a language assistant did not count towards their seniority, whereas under the Italian university rules experience in other comparable posts would have done.

Several types of discrimination have been the recurring subject of litigation before the Court of Justice: trade union rights, tax advantages and social advantages. With regard to trade union rights, provision is made in article 8 of Regulation 1612/68 for migrants to enjoy equality of treatment in respect of both membership of trade unions and exercise of those trade union rights.[85] A broad interpretation has been taken, so this right to equal treatment applies not merely to formally recognised trade unions, but also to any body to which workers pay contributions in return for defence and representation of their interests.[86] It also confers the right not only to equal protection from the union, but also the equal opportunity to govern the trade union, by standing for election for office.[87]

The migrant is entitled, by virtue of both Article 45(2) TFEU and secondary legislation,[88] to the same tax benefits in a Member State as its nationals who are working there.[89] This principle has not proved straightforward to apply. Tax benefits are intended to compensate for or diminish tax burdens. However, individuals are usually taxed in their place of residence. As a result, tax benefits are often also awarded only to residents. Yet, this is likely to especially adversely affect migrant workers, particularly frontier workers, and so may be indirectly discriminatory.

The Court of Justice addressed this problem in *Schumacker*, and found that since, in general, residents and non-residents were in objectively different positions with regard to taxation, differences in treatment with regard to tax benefits were not generally wrongful.[90] However, they found that there could be exceptions to this rule. Mr Schumacker earned the major part of his income in Germany, and it was taxed in Germany, while he earned no significant income in Belgium, where he lived. In those circumstances he should have the right to the same tax benefits as a German resident. This lays down a rule of thumb for a particular problem, but serves more to demonstrate the complexities of taxation than to provide a general framework for addressing them.[91]

Regulation 492/2011 also prohibits discrimination in 'social advantages' and housing.[92] However, these clauses have become considerably less important since the development of citizenship. Those relying on Articles 45 and 49 TFEU are also EU citizens, and can rely on

---

[83] Case C-429/92 *Ingetraut Scholz v Opera Universitaria di Cagliari and Cinzia Porcedda* [1994] ECR I-505; Case C-371/04 *Commission v Italy* [2006] ECR I-10257.

[84] Case C-276/07 *Nancy Delay v Università degli studi di Firenze, Istituto nazionale della previdenza sociale* [2008] ECR I-3635.

[85] [1968] OJ Spec. Edn L257/2, 475.

[86] Case C-213/90 *Association de Soutien aux Travailleurs Immigrés (ASTI) v Chambre des employés privés* [1991] ECR I-3507.

[87] *Ibid.* Case C-465/01 *Commission v Austria* [2004] ECR I-8291.

[88] Regulation 1612/68, article 7(2).

[89] Case 175/88 *Biehl v Administration des contributions du grand-duché de Luxembourg* [1990] ECR I-1779.

[90] Case C-279/93 *Finanzamt Köln-Altstadt v Schumacker* [1995] ECR I-225.

[91] I. Roxan, 'Assuring Real Freedom of Movement in EU Direct Taxation' (2000) 63 *MLR* 831, 847–50.

[92] Regulation 492/2011, articles 7(2), 9. See e.g. Case 32/75 *Anita Cristini v Société nationale des chemins de fer français* [1975] ECR 1085.

Article 18 TFEU and the Citizenship Directive 2004/38/EC to obtain equal treatment in matters relating to their life outside work.[93]

A different kind of situation arises where employees suffer disadvantages indirectly, as a result of benefits or burdens created for employers. *Petersen* concerned a German law which provided that development aid workers were exempt from tax, provided they worked for an organisation established in Germany. Mr Petersen was an aid worker in Benin who had residence in Germany, but was employed by a Danish organisation.

Case C-544/11 *Petersen*, Judgment of 28 February 2013

46. By establishing a difference in treatment for employees' income in this way, depending on the Member State in which their employer is established, the national legislation at issue in the main proceedings is liable to dissuade those employees from accepting work from an employer established in a Member State which is not the Federal Republic of Germany and thus constitutes a restriction on the free movement of workers, which is in principle forbidden by Article 45 TFEU....

59. ...the German Government argues that the tax advantage provided for by the national legislation at issue in the main proceedings pursues development-policy objectives, by enabling development aid organisations to benefit from lower labour costs. According to the German Government, the Member States must remain free specifically to promote in a targeted manner, by means of tax advantages and in accordance with their own priorities, activities in the context of the public cooperation of each Member State in the field of development. The fiscal incentive created by the national legislation at issue in the main proceedings is necessary in order to implement those objectives and the Federal Republic of Germany would not have sufficient means to honour its own commitments if it were also obliged to encourage the activities of organisations headquartered in other Member States.

60. In that regard, it is sufficient to state that the question submitted to the Court of Justice by the referring court concerns only the condition relating to the undertaking being established in Germany.

61. In its arguments relating to the pursuit of German development-policy objectives, the German Government does not explain why only those undertakings that are established in Germany may be deemed capable of pursuing activities aimed at achieving those objectives.

Discrimination on grounds of one's employer restricts free movement, and may amount to discrimination in employment.[94]

(ii) Discrimination in the pursuit of a business

Freedom of establishment includes the right to pursue business activities. The Court of Justice has understood this as involving anything connected with the running of the business. There must be no discrimination in anything which affects the running of the migrant's business in any way at all. In *Steinhauser*,[95] a German artist living in Biarritz in France applied to rent a fisherman's shed from the local authority but was refused on the grounds that he was not a French national. In its reference the national court noted that the letting of premises did not

---

[93] See Chapter 11.
[94] See also Case C-379/11 *Caves Krier Frères*, Judgment of 13 December 2012.
[95] Case 197/84 *Steinhauser* v *City of Biarritz* [1985] ECR 1819.

relate to a specific business activity and, therefore, implicitly raised the question of whether it fell outside Article 49 TFEU. The Court held that the measure constituted illegal discrimination within Article 49. It stated that as the renting of premises for business purposes furthers the pursuit of a business, it falls within Article 49. Insofar as the measure was discriminatory, it was illegal. The remit of Article 49 in particular is, therefore, very wide. Planning, tax, health and safety, environmental and labour laws all affect the running of business. They must all be couched and applied in a manner that does not discriminate against non-nationals or foreign companies.

In most cases it is indirect discrimination that is in issue, commonly as a result of rules referring to the location of establishment or employment. In *CIBA*, a Hungarian law was challenged which required companies to pay a training levy on all their employees, including those employed abroad, but which granted those companies a discount if they provided in-house training.[96] However, the discount was only granted where the training took place in Hungary. That disparity between benefit and burden might discourage companies from establishing subsidiaries abroad, the Court found, and so restricted secondary establishment.[97]

(iii) Equally applicable restrictions on the pursuit of an occupation

As discussed above,[98] regulation of the pursuit of an occupation covers a multitude of regulatory activities. Taxation laws or employment laws affect the employment relationship, and can make employment either more or less attractive in a Member State. These laws, as well as health and safety, environmental and planning laws, all affect business costs and therefore can also make establishment in another Member State less attractive. However, challenging these under EU law would have a number of effects. It would increase substantially the power of the Court of Justice and national courts, which would be required to rule on the appropriate level of regulation in these fields. In a corresponding vein, it would reduce the power of national and local authorities, who would only be able to legislate within the parameters set for them by the Court of Justice. It would also create uncertainty, as it would be unclear which laws affected the pursuit of an occupation, which could be justified in the public interest and which were pursued in a proportionate way. Finally, allowing non-discriminatory restrictions on the pursuit of economic activity to be challenged would introduce a strong deregulatory bias into EU law, as it would never be individuals pleading for more regulation but would, in all cases, be individuals challenging regulation they disliked for whatever reason. For these reasons, the Court of Justice's case law has been hesitant on whether non-discriminatory restrictions on the pursuit of economic activity should fall within either Article 45 or 49 TFEU.

The Article 45 case law on this question has been rather terse. One of the cases in which it nevertheless has been addressed is *Danish Company Cars*. It will be remembered that Denmark prohibited residents using company cars registered abroad in Denmark, to quell the fear that many of its residents would use this as a way of not paying Danish motor vehicle tax. Company cars are an employment benefit and therefore relate to the pursuit of employment rather than the taking up of employment. In the excerpt quoted earlier,[99] the Court stated that such

---

[96] Case C-96/08 *CIBA* [2010] ECR I-02911.
[97] Cf. Case C-186/12 *Impacto Azul*, Judgment of 20 June 2013.
[98] See p. 859.   [99] See p. 457.

restrictions could fall within Article 45 if they affected access to the labour market. It then considered whether this was the case.

Case C-464/02 *Commission v Denmark (Danish Company Cars)* [2005] ECR I-7929

45. It is settled case law that Article [45 TFEU] prohibits not only all discrimination, direct or indirect, based on nationality, but also national rules which are applicable irrespective of the nationality of the workers concerned but impede their freedom of movement.

46. It is clear that the original scheme, insofar as it remains applicable, could, on account of the obligation to register in Denmark a company car made available to the employee by an employer established in another Member State, deter such an employer from taking on an employee resident in Denmark for work which is not the employee's principal employment and, consequently, impede access to such employment by residents in Denmark.

47. As regards employees resident in Denmark who wish to pursue their principal employment in an undertaking established in another Member State, the amended scheme also impedes freedom of movement for those workers since it imposes additional costs in the form of a temporary registration tax.

48. Insofar as the undertaking established in another Member State bears those costs without being compensated, it is deterred from taking on an employee resident in Denmark in respect of whom the costs are higher than those borne for an employee who does not reside in that State.

49. It is true, as the Danish Government asserts, that the employer could attempt to adjust the salary of an employee resident in Denmark in order to offset the additional expense in question. In other words, he could try to pay to that employee a salary lower than that paid to an employee engaged in the same activity, but who resides in another Member State.

50. However, an employee resident in Denmark might already be deterred from seeking employment in another Member State faced with the prospect of receiving a salary lower than that of a comparable employee resident in that other Member State. As the Court ruled in paragraph 18 of Case 121/86 *Ledoux* [1988] ECR 3741, the fact that an employee is placed at a disadvantage in regard to working conditions compared to his colleagues residing in the country of their employer has a direct effect on the exercise of his right to freedom of movement within the Community...

52. Consequently, it must be held that the Danish legislation, both in its original version and in its amended version, constitutes a restriction on freedom of movement for workers.

The same reasoning has been applied to an analogous rule in the context of self-employed workers in *Nadin*.[100] In neither case was it possible to speak of nationality discrimination, but rather discrimination against migrants, against those who had exercised their EU rights to engage in economic activity in another Member State. This has been one of the major themes of the case law on equally applicable restrictions on employment and establishment.[101]

Where a measure does not specifically disadvantage movement, and in the absence of an argument that it disadvantages foreigners and is therefore discriminatory, the Court of Justice

---

[100] Joined Cases C-151/04 and C-152/04 *Nadin, Nadin-Lux and Durré* [2005] ECR I-11203.

[101] See e.g. Case C-464/05 *Geurts and Vogten* v *Administratie van de BTW, registratie en domeinen, Belgische Staat* [2007] ECR I-9325.

has tended to find no restriction to be present. An example is *Sodemare*.[102] Sodemare was a Luxembourg company, which, amongst other things, provided sheltered accommodation for elderly residents. It was refused approval to enter into contracts with public authorities in the region of Lombardy in Italy, which would have allowed it to be reimbursed for some of the health care services it provided. The reason was that under Lombard law, such contracts were only available to non-profit-making bodies. Sodemare challenged this, claiming that it violated Article 49 as it affected its ability to run its business in Italy.

Case C-70/95 *Sodemare v Regione Lombardia* [1997] ECR I-3395

32. ...as Community law stands at present, a Member State may, in the exercise of the powers it retains to organize its social security system, consider that a social welfare system of the kind at issue in this case necessarily implies, with a view to attaining its objectives, that the admission of private operators to that system as providers of social welfare services is to be made subject to the condition that they are non-profit-making.

33. Moreover, the fact that it is impossible for profit-making companies automatically to participate in the running of a statutory social welfare system of a Member State by concluding a contract which entitles them to be reimbursed by the public authorities for the costs of providing social welfare services of a health-care nature is not liable to place profit-making companies from other Member States in a less favourable factual or legal situation than profit-making companies in the Member State in which they are established.

34. In view of the foregoing, the non-profit condition cannot be regarded as contrary to Article [49 TFEU].

It has therefore been argued that Articles 45 and 49 TFEU are fundamentally, perhaps only, concerned with prohibiting discrimination. The first set of cases in this chapter, concerning restrictions on the taking up of an activity, are (arguably) in reality about discrimination since, by preventing migrants entering the market, these measures protect the Member State's own nationals from competition. The second set of cases, concerning restrictions on the pursuit of economic activity, are also about discrimination since they specifically disadvantage either nationals of other Member States, or those who have exercised their cross-border EU rights.[103] All these restrictions therefore create inequalities within the markets for employment and self-employment.

However, recent cases fit this framework a little uncomfortably. In *Caixa Bank France*, a challenge was made by the subsidiary of a Spanish bank to a French prohibition on the offering of certain types of bank account. French law prohibited remuneration or interest being offered on 'sight accounts'. These are accounts that allow instant withdrawals. The restriction applied to all banks and although it did not prevent foreign banks setting up in France, it did prevent them from carrying out these types of activity.

---

[102] See also Case C-221/85 *Commission* v *Belgium* [1987] ECR 719; Case 196/86 *Conradi and others* [1987] ECR 4469; L. Hancher, and W. Sauter, 'One Step Beyond? From *Sodemare* to *Docmorris*: The EU's Freedom of Establishment Case Law Concerning Healthcare' (2010) 47 *CMLRev.* 117.

[103] G. Marenco, 'The Notion of Restriction on the Freedom of Establishment and Provision of Services in the Case-law of the Court' (1991) 11 *YBEL* 111.

Case C-442/02 *Caixa Bank France* v *Ministère de l'Économie, des Finances et de l'Industrie* [2004] ECR I-8961

11. Article [49 TFEU] requires the elimination of restrictions on the freedom of establishment. All measures which prohibit, impede or render less attractive the exercise of that freedom must be regarded as such restrictions.

12. A prohibition on the remuneration of sight accounts such as that laid down by the French legislation constitutes, for companies from Member States other than the French Republic, a serious obstacle to the pursuit of their activities via a subsidiary in the latter Member State, affecting their access to the market. That prohibition is therefore to be regarded as a restriction within the meaning of Article [49 TFEU].

13. That prohibition hinders credit institutions which are subsidiaries of foreign companies in raising capital from the public, by depriving them of the possibility of competing more effectively, by paying remuneration on sight accounts, with the credit institutions traditionally established in the Member State of establishment, which have an extensive network of branches and therefore greater opportunities than those subsidiaries for raising capital from the public.

14. Where credit institutions which are subsidiaries of foreign companies seek to enter the market of a Member State, competing by means of the rate of remuneration paid on sight accounts constitutes one of the most effective methods to that end. Access to the market by those establishments is thus made more difficult by such a prohibition…

17. It is clear from settled case law that where, as in the case at issue in the main proceedings, such a measure applies to any person or undertaking carrying on an activity in the territory of the host Member State, it may be justified where it serves overriding requirements relating to the public interest, is suitable for securing the attainment of the objective it pursues and does not go beyond what is necessary to attain it…

The Court nevertheless found that the restriction could not be justified by the protection of consumers or the need to encourage long-term saving. These admirable goals, it asserted, could be met by less restrictive measures.

While the Court of Justice in *Caixa Bank France* speaks about foreign companies wishing to enter the French market, and the problems which the rule may cause them, the Court does not make it obvious that the rule would affect them more than it would an emerging French competitor. Nor does the Court make any such comparison part of its reasoning. The core of the objection is that the rule disadvantages would-be market entrants. This could be presented in terms of nationality discrimination, since incumbents are being protected and they are usually national. However, it seems that this is not the way the Court wants to frame the law.

The Court of Justice may therefore be moving towards a position that in substance is similar to its position concerning the free movement of goods. Restrictions which do not actually prevent an actor from entering the market are only likely to fall within Articles 45 and 49 TFEU if they discriminate against market entrants.[104] Equal impact market regulation will not be caught. In *Caixa Bank France*, therefore, offering rewards on a current account would be a central route for any new bank, be it foreign or French, to build up market share. The bank

---

[104] See Case C-405/98 *Konsumentombudsmannen (KO)* v *Gourmet International Products AB* [2001] ECR I-1795; see p. 787.

is denied this important marketing strategy, and in a market in which it cannot differentiate itself, it will struggle to win clients. The basis for such reasoning is that participation in the single market necessitates that Member States allow sufficiently vibrant competition on their markets. This is not unreasonable, but it is a very imprecise goal to realise. Secondly, measures will only actually violate Articles 45 and 49 if they are unjustifiably heavy-handed. Thus, *Caixa Bank France* involves a measure which deprives banks of an important marketing tool and element of a business model, namely, the right to offer interest on current accounts, and the reasons given for the deprivation are fairly weak.

The case may be contrasted with *DHL*, in which Belgium required operators of postal services to submit to an external complaints procedure. The Court of Justice took the view that imposition of such a procedure could not be said to hinder or discourage establishment in Belgium, since:

> First, that measure is applied, without discrimination on grounds of nationality, to all providers established in Belgium of postal services which are outside the scope of the universal service. Secondly, as the Advocate General stated in point 77 of his Opinion, operators cannot expect Member States not to have structures in place which afford legal protection for the interests of their customers and provide out-of-court procedures for settling disputes. Lastly, nearly all Member States have extended the external complaints schemes to providers of postal services which are outside the scope of the universal service.[105]

The fact that DHL considered the procedure to some extent burdensome and costly is suggested by the fact that they fought it in the Belgian courts. Nevertheless, the Court of Justice was clearly more influenced by the fact that the procedure seemed reasonable, probably of marginal impact on business, and common. The fact that lots of Member States do something is not usually accepted as a basis for finding it has no effects on trade. This is a *de minimis* ruling in all but name.

5 FREE MOVEMENT OF COMPANIES

(i) Discrimination and foreign companies

Freedom of establishment is granted not merely to EU citizens, but also to non-natural legal persons. In this respect, it is quite different from Article 45 TFEU on the free movement of workers. The beneficiaries of the right to establishment are set out in Article 54 TFEU.

Article 54 TFEU

Companies or firms formed in accordance with the law of a Member State and having their registered office, central administration or principal place of business within the Community shall, for the purposes of this Chapter, be treated in the same way as natural persons who are nationals of Member States.

'Companies or firms' means companies or firms constituted under civil or commercial law, including cooperative societies, and other legal persons governed by public or private law, save for those which are non-profit-making.

---

[105] Case C-148/10 *DHL* [2011] ECR I-09543, para. 62.

Companies have to be formed in accordance with the laws of one of the Member States and have their registered office, central administration or principal place of business within the European Union if they are to have the right to freedom of establishment. Therefore, whilst the prohibition on discrimination in Article 49 forbids discrimination on the grounds of national-ity in the case of individuals, it forbids discrimination on the grounds of the place of registered office, central administration or principal place of business in the case of companies.[106] As Marenco has pointed out, there is, however, an important difference between these grounds of discrimination and that of nationality.

G. Marenco, 'The Notion of Restriction on the Freedom of Establishment and Provision of Services in the Case-law of the Court' (1991) 11 *Yearbook of European Law* 111, 113–14

[T]here can never be more than a partial equivalence of the nationality condition and that of the company's registered office on a national territory. The former indeed uses a purely formal criterion, with no concrete or substantial content, to exclude equality of treatment. Thus it cannot be justified on economic grounds, which is where freedom of establishment operates. By contrast, the registered office as criterion of the connection of a company with a State is simultaneously a concrete situation which might justify a difference in treatment. Thus it cannot be equated purely and simply with nationality.

This emerges in Case 270/83 *Commission* v. *France* [[1986] ECR 273], which dealt with a French tax provision that denied tax credits in respect of dividends on shares in French companies held by branches or agencies of companies, the registered office of which was in another Member State. The Court, having found that this provision led to a difference in treatment between French companies and those in other Member States, took into consideration the French Government's arguments that this difference in treatment was in the circumstances justified by objective differences in the situations of the two types of company. While in the end finding in favour of the Commission, the Court observed, in refuting the French Government's arguments, that 'the possibility cannot altogether be excluded that a distinction based on the location of the registered office of a company or the place of residence of a natural person may, under certain circumstances, be justified in an area such as tax law'. The registered office is thus compared first with the nationality of physical persons and then with their residence. This double comparison reveals that the registered office condition plays a role at once formal and substantial.

(ii) Movement of companies and reincorporation

Companies may wish to move their principal place of business or head office to another Member State or to reincorporate in another Member State. This is something more than establishing a secondary establishment, which has been addressed in the previous sections. Such fundamental movement is about a company changing its core legal nature, going from incorporation in one Member State, under that Member State's laws, to incorporation in an-other Member State, in effect recreating itself. This is nevertheless a form of movement, and since it takes place for the same kind of economic reasons that companies engage in other

---

[106] Case 270/83 *Commission* v *France* [1986] ECR 273.

cross-border activities and arrangements it would seem the type of relocation of business activity that the single market is intended to stimulate. However, there is a double context which complicates matters.

The first difficulty is a formal legal one. The company's incorporation within its home Member State is the feature which allows it to claim rights under Article 49. If companies lose their legal personality within that state, either by dissolving or not meeting its corporate law requirements, they would lose their right to establish under Article 49.

The second is the policy context. Companies may wish to evade their fiscal and corporate responsibilities in Member States where they carry out their principal business by creating a legal shell in another Member State, which has lower fiscal obligations and less demanding corporate law (e.g. lower minimum capital requirements or less protection of minority shareholders). There are, moreover, incentives for Member States to attract these legal shells because, at very little cost to themselves, they can attract taxes that would otherwise go to the state where the company carries out its principal place of business. This can lead to a 'race to the bottom' where the tax base and basic company law requirements are eroded as states compete to attract investment.[107]

These issues were first addressed in the *Daily Mail* judgment. Under UK law, companies could not transfer their central management from the United Kingdom and still retain their legal personality without first obtaining the consent of the Treasury. The *Daily Mail* newspaper wished to transfer its central management to the Netherlands so that it might sell off some of its shares without being subject to UK capital gains tax. After negotiations with the Treasury broke down, it brought an action claiming that the UK regime breached Article 49. The case therefore raised both of the concerns outlined above.

The Court of Justice found that there was no violation of Article 49. The United Kingdom was not preventing the *Daily Mail* from emigrating and becoming a Dutch company, if it so wanted. Rather, the *Mail* wanted to remain a UK company, while moving its headquarters abroad, whereas UK law said that to be a UK company entailed that its headquarters were in the United Kingdom. Thus the case, in the view of the Court, was not so much about whether the *Daily Mail* could move, as about the right of the United Kingdom to define what it meant to be a UK company. In the absence of harmonisation of the rules concerning incorporation, this was for the United Kingdom to decide.

Case 81/87 *R v HM Treasury ex parte Daily Mail* [1988] ECR 5483

18. The provision of United Kingdom law at issue in the main proceedings imposes no restriction on transactions such as those described above [reincorporation in another Member State]. Nor does it stand in the way of a partial or total transfer of the activities of a company incorporated in the United Kingdom to a company newly incorporated in another Member State, if necessary after winding-up and, consequently, the settlement of the tax position of the United Kingdom company. It requires Treasury

---

[107] This is sometimes called the 'Delaware effect' after a so-called 'race to the bottom' in state company laws in the United States was believed to have been initiated by the State of Delaware in the 1960s. W. Gary, 'Federalism and Corporate Law: Reflections upon Delaware' (1974) 83 *Yale Law Journal* 663. On this within the European Union, see C. Barnard, 'Social Dumping and the Race to the Bottom: Some Lessons for the European Union from Delaware?' (2000) 25 *ELRev.* 57. See also pp. 697–702.

consent only where such a company seeks to transfer its central management and control out of the United Kingdom while maintaining its legal personality and its status as a United Kingdom company.

19. In that regard it should be borne in mind that, unlike natural persons, companies are creatures of the law and, in the present state of Community law, creatures of national law. They exist only by virtue of the varying national legislation which determines their incorporation and functioning.

20. As the Commission has emphasized, the legislation of the Member States varies widely in regard to both the factor providing a connection to the national territory required for the incorporation of a company and the question whether a company incorporated under the legislation of a Member State may subsequently modify that connecting factor. Certain States require that not merely the registered office but also the real head office, that is to say the central administration of the company, should be situated on their territory, and the removal of the central administration from that territory thus presupposes the winding-up of the company with all the consequences that winding-up entails in company law and tax law. The legislation of other states permits companies to transfer their central administration to a foreign country but certain of them, such as the United Kingdom, make that right subject to certain restrictions, and the legal consequences of a transfer, particularly in regard to taxation, vary from one Member State to another.

21. The Treaty has taken account of that variety in national legislation. In defining, in Article [54 TFEU], the companies which enjoy the right of establishment, the Treaty places on the same footing, as connecting factors, the registered office, central administration and principal place of business of a company…

22. It should be added that none of the Directives on the coordination of company law adopted under Article 54(3)(g) of the Treaty deal with the differences at issue here.

23. It must therefore be held that the Treaty regards the differences in national legislation concerning the required connecting factor and the question whether – and if so how – the registered office or real head office of a company incorporated under national law may be transferred from one Member State to another as problems which are not resolved by the rules concerning the right of establishment but must be dealt with by future legislation or conventions.

24. Under those circumstances, Articles [49 and 54 TFEU] cannot be interpreted as conferring on companies incorporated under the law of a Member State a right to transfer their central management and control and their central administration to another Member State while retaining their status as companies incorporated under the legislation of the first Member State.

Daily Mail has been recently confirmed in *Cartesio*. The facts were similar, but concerned Hungary and Italy rather than the United Kingdom and the Netherlands. The company Cartesio argued that *Daily Mail* was no longer good law in the light of subsequent cases, but the Court of Justice rejected this, repeating its arguments above in almost identical terms, and emphasising that it was for Member States to determine the conditions for incorporation in their jurisdiction, and the presence of headquarters was a perfectly legitimate condition. Nevertheless, although this did not arise in *Cartesio*, it would be wrong to think that conditions for incorporation are outside the scope of Article 49. If, for example, they discriminate, they will still violate the Treaty.[108]

---

[108] Case C-299/02 *Commission* v *Netherlands* [2004] ECR I-9761. See generally O. Mörsdorf, 'The Legal Mobility of Companies Within the European Union Through Cross-border Conversion' (2012) 49 *CMLRev.* 629.

This was the case in *VALE*, which concerned the Hungarian law on company conversion. Conversion is where one company ceases to exist, and a new one is formed, but it is recorded in the incorporation that the old company is the predecessor in law of the new one.[109] This can be important for matters such as the continuity of debts which the old company may have had. VALE was an Italian company originally, which removed itself from the Italian company register with the intention of converting to a Hungarian company, incorporated under Hungarian law. It was prepared to comply with all the requirement of Hungarian law, but conversion was still not possible, because Hungarian law simply did not allow cross-border conversions. Only a Hungarian company could convert to a new Hungarian company. The directors could start a new Hungarian company, but they could not have the old Italian VALE recorded as its predecessor in law.

This time the Court of Justice found the rules contrary to Article 49. While it was for Member States to determine whether and under what conditions company conversion was possible, 'Articles 49 TFEU and 54 TFEU require Member States which make provision for the conversion of companies governed by national law to grant that same possibility to companies governed by the law of another Member State which are seeking to convert to companies governed by the law of the first Member State'.[110] It went on to reject the force of the Hungarian Government's arguments about the procedural and documentary difficulties that a conversion from a non-Hungarian company would entail.

Most cases involve a different scenario however: where a company is incorporated in state X, but does most of its business in state Y. The reason for such a construction is often to avoid strict rules on incorporation in Y, and for this same reason state Y is usually inclined to view the incorporation in X as an abusive attempt to avoid its rules. These cases raise the concerns about regulatory competition raised above.

This scenario was addressed in *Centros*. Two Danish nationals registered a company in the United Kingdom. Although it never traded from the United Kingdom, it was registered there because the UK authorities impose no minimum share capital requirement for companies, whilst in Denmark there was a requirement of a minimum of 100,000 Danish kroner. They were refused permission to register a branch in Denmark and challenged this under Article 49. The Danish Government argued that there was no violation as they were simply refusing the setting up of a primary establishment and not the setting up of a branch. The Court of Justice disagreed.

Case C-212/97 *Centros v Erhvervs-og Selskabsstyrelsen* [1999] ECR I-1459

21. Where it is the practice of a Member State, in certain circumstances, to refuse to register a branch of a company having its registered office in another Member State, the result is that companies formed in accordance with the law of that other Member State are prevented from exercising the freedom of establishment conferred on them by Articles [49 and 54 TFEU].

22. Consequently, that practice constitutes an obstacle to the exercise of the freedoms guaranteed by those provisions.

---

[109] Case C-378/10 *VALE*, Judgment of 22 July 2012. See S. Rammeloo, 'Case C378/10 *VALE Építési Kft*, Freedom of Establishment: Cross-border Transfer of Company "Seat": The Last Piece of the Puzzle?' (2012) 19 *Maastricht Journal of European and Comparative Law* 563; Thomas Biermeyer, 'Case C-378/10, *VALE Építési Kft*, Judgment of the Court of Justice (Third Chamber) of 12 July 2012' (2013) 50 *CMLRev*. 571.

[110] *VALE*, n. 109 above, para. 46.

23. According to the Danish authorities, however, Mr and Mrs Bryde cannot rely on those provisions, since the sole purpose of the company formation which they have in mind is to circumvent the application of the national law governing formation of private limited companies and therefore constitutes abuse of the freedom of establishment. In their submission, the Kingdom of Denmark is therefore entitled to take steps to prevent such abuse by refusing to register the branch.

24. It is true that according to the case law of the Court a Member State is entitled to take measures designed to prevent certain of its nationals from attempting, under cover of the rights created by the Treaty, improperly to circumvent their national legislation or to prevent individuals from improperly or fraudulently taking advantage of provisions of Community law...

25. However, although, in such circumstances, the national courts may, case by case, take account – on the basis of objective evidence – of abuse or fraudulent conduct on the part of the persons concerned in order, where appropriate, to deny them the benefit of the provisions of Community law on which they seek to rely, they must nevertheless assess such conduct in the light of the objectives pursued by those provisions...

26. In the present case, the provisions of national law, application of which the parties concerned have sought to avoid, are rules governing the formation of companies and not rules concerning the carrying on of certain trades, professions or businesses. The provisions of the Treaty on freedom of establishment are intended specifically to enable companies formed in accordance with the law of a Member State and having their registered office, central administration or principal place of business within the Community to pursue activities in other Member States through an agency, branch or subsidiary.

27. That being so, the fact that a national of a Member State who wishes to set up a company chooses to form it in the Member State whose rules of company law seem to him the least restrictive and to set up branches in other Member States cannot, in itself, constitute an abuse of the right of establishment. The right to form a company in accordance with the law of a Member State and to set up branches in other Member States is inherent in the exercise, in a single market, of the freedom of establishment guaranteed by the Treaty.

28. In this connection, the fact that company law is not completely harmonised in the Community is of little consequence. Moreover, it is always open to the Council, on the basis of the powers conferred upon it by Article [50(3)(g) TFEU], to achieve complete harmonisation.

29. In addition...the fact that a company does not conduct any business in the Member State in which it has its registered office and pursues its activities only in the Member State where its branch is established is not sufficient to prove the existence of abuse or fraudulent conduct which would entitle the latter Member State to deny that company the benefit of the provisions of Community law relating to the right of establishment.

30. Accordingly, the refusal of a Member State to register a branch of a company formed in accordance with the law of another Member State in which it has its registered office on the grounds that the branch is intended to enable the company to carry on all its economic activity in the host State, with the result that the secondary establishment escapes national rules on the provision for and the paying-up of a minimum capital, is incompatible with Articles [49 and 54 TFEU], insofar as it prevents any exercise of the right freely to set up a secondary establishment which Articles [49 and 54 TFEU] are specifically intended to guarantee.

Centros reaffirms the right of companies to secondary establishment in other states. Whilst a company retains corporate status within its home Member State, other Member States must recognise it as validly incorporated under Article 54 TFEU and therefore entitled to the benefits of Article 49 TFEU. Needless to say, this does not meet the policy concerns about regulatory competition whereby companies will simply incorporate in the state whose fiscal and corporate regime is most favourable to them. Member States have attempted to prevent this practice in a number of cases before the Court of Justice.

In *Überseering*,[111] a challenge was made to the German law which stated that a company's legal capacity is governed by the law of the territory in which its central place of administration is based. What this meant in substance was that German law would only recognise the existence of a company whose administration and incorporation were in the same state. Überseering, however, had its central administration in Germany, but was incorporated in the Netherlands. Dutch law permitted this, but when Überseering sought to bring legal action in Germany over a business dispute it discovered that it had no standing because in the eyes of German law it did not exist. The Court of Justice found this to be a violation of Article 49. Where a company is validly incorporated in one Member State according to the laws of that state, other Member States are required to recognise that incorporation, notwithstanding that their own conditions for incorporation may be different. Not to recognise Überseering's Dutch legal status would be to greatly deter establishment in the Netherlands.

In *Inspire Art*,[112] the Netherlands rather clumsily attempted to avoid *Centros*. Companies incorporated abroad, but which conducted almost all their business in the Netherlands through branches or agencies, had to register their agencies or branches in the Netherlands as 'foreign companies'. These were then required to meet Dutch company law requirements on directors' duties and minimum share capital for companies. Inspire Art was a company which conducted almost all its business in objets d'art, but which had incorporated in the United Kingdom specifically to avoid these requirements. It challenged the obligation to satisfy them under Article 49 TFEU. The Dutch Government argued that Inspire Art was engaged in an abuse of Article 49 as it was deliberately incorporating in another Member State in which it did no business to evade and thereby undermine Dutch company law. The Court of Justice disagreed. It found that the formation of a company in one Member State for the sole purpose of enjoying the benefit of more favourable legislation was not abusive behaviour even where that company conducted all its activities in another Member State. Thus, insofar as the Dutch Government was imposing restrictions on companies validly incorporated within the European Union and thereby preventing them from trading in the Netherlands unless they met certain conditions concerning directors' duties and minimum share capital, it was engaged in a breach of Article 49.[113]

This case law reflects two potent dangers between which it is difficult to navigate. On the one hand, if companies could only trade in another Member State where they met all that state's company law requirements, there would be a grinding halt to economic activity across the Union. In effect, no foreign companies could operate in the state with the most restrictive company law as they would not meet these standards. On the other hand, allowing foreign

---

[111] Case C-208/00 *Überseering v NCC* [2002] ECR I-9919.

[112] Case C-167/01 *Kamer van Koophandel en Fabrieken voor Amsterdam v Inspire Art* [2003] ECR I-10195.

[113] There is substantial literature on this case law. See particularly M. Siems, 'Convergence, Competition, *Centros* and Conflicts of Law: European Company Law in the 21st Century' (2002) 27 *ELRev.* 47; W.-H. Roth, 'From *Centros* to *Überseering*: Free Movement of Companies, Private International Law, and Community Law' (2003) 52 *ICLQ* 177; E. Micheler, 'Recognition of Companies Incorporated in Other EU Member States' (2003) 52 *ICLQ* 521; C. Kersting and C. Philipp Schindler, 'The ECJ's *Inspire Art* Decision of 30 September 2003 and its Effects on Practice' (2003) 4(12) *German Law Journal* 1277.

companies who do not meet the Member State's company law standards to operate on local markets has the effect of completely undermining local company and tax laws, as it is easy and inexpensive for companies to locate in the state with the least onerous requirements.

6 SERVICES DIRECTIVE AND FREEDOM OF ESTABLISHMENT

Directive 2006/123/EC (Services Directive) applies not only to cross-border service provision but also to those establishing in a Member State. They benefit from the Directive's Chapter on establishment, as well as from its rules on administrative simplification. These latter, and the material scope of the Services Directive, were discussed in Chapter 18.[114]

The Chapter on freedom of establishment addresses three categories of national measures.[115] The first articles in this Chapter deal with authorisation schemes – rules which require that a person cannot establish or begin their activity without an authorisation. Such rules are fairly common in some Member States. Article 9 provides that such schemes are only permitted where they are non-discriminatory, justified by a public interest objective, and the goal cannot be met by a less restrictive measure. As is evident, this is neither more nor less than the existing case law would suggest. However, articles 9 to 13 provide some detail on the operation of authorisation schemes, with procedural requirements aimed at ensuring that they function in an accessible, fair, transparent and non-discriminatory way.

Article 14 then lists certain kinds of measure concerning established persons which are prohibited. These include discriminatory requirements, requirements concerning the nationality of shareholders or company directors, restrictions on secondary establishment or requirements that the establishment in the state be the primary establishment and market-need based restrictions. The Court of Justice has tended to prohibit such restrictions anyway, but the absence of grounds for derogation may make the Directive stricter, although this has to be weighed against the many exclusions from the Directive's scope.

Finally, article 15 provides a list of 'requirements to be evaluated'. These include limits on employee numbers or tariffs, requirements to have a particular legal form, or 'quantitative or territorial restrictions'. Any such requirements are only permitted if they are non-discriminatory, justified and proportionate. Once again, the Directive follows the case law of the Court.

The establishment Chapter is apparently weaker than the services Chapter. It only applies to certain specifically listed national requirements, and, apart from article 14, it permits these to be justified by any good public interest objective. Its approach to the legality of national measures is essentially a summary of the case law.

This difference between the approach to service and establishment reflects their different roles in the wider structure of the internal market. Home state regulation, which is the philosophy of the cases and of the Directive, entails that requirements imposed on service providers by their host state should be the exception, and so are subject to strict limits. By contrast, the home state approach entails that the established person has in principle made a choice to subject herself to the rules of her state of new establishment, and EU intervention should confine itself to rooting out discrimination against her, or particularly obstructive and disproportionate rules.

[114] See pp. 842–6.
[115] Directive 2006/123/EC on services in the internal market, articles 9–15.

However, the Chapter on establishment does add to the law in another way: it appears to apply to those establishing in their own state, as well as those coming from other states. Either might fall victim to many of the measures discussed (the authorisation requirements or rules on employee numbers or tariffs), and there is nothing in the Directive to suggest that only the cross-border person can rely on it. By contrast, that text appears to regulate the national measures in question in a general way. Thus, while the law on establishment is not made stricter by the Directive, it has been broadened. It is at least arguable that within the scope of the Directive's provisions on establishment, as is the case with the provisions on administrative simplification, wholly internal situations are no longer excluded. The defined group of national rules to which this Chapter applies is now subject to proportionality review at the request of any economic actor suffering disadvantage from them.

This is understandable. The alternative would be that the foreigner wishing to start his business would be exempted from all kinds of authorisation procedures and administrative requirements with which the national would still have to comply. This would create reverse discrimination. That may sometimes be an unavoidable side-effect of the case law, but it is bad policy to entrench it in legislation.[116] Secondly, any such entrenched distinction would create a motivation for artificial cross-border constructions: the Frenchman wanting to start a business in France would be better first starting a nominal business abroad and then coming home, or looking for a foreign 'partner'. As is usually the case with harmonising legislation, the Directive tries to avoid such problems by creating a uniform structure of rights for all economic actors, albeit within a limited sphere.

FURTHER READING

D. Ashiagbor, 'Unravelling the Embedded Liberal Bargain: Labour and Social Welfare Law in the Context of EU Market Integration' (2013) 19 *European Law Journal* 303

C. Costello, 'Market Access All Areas? The Treatment of Non-Discriminatory Barriers to the Free Movement of Workers' (2000) 27(3) *Legal Issues of Economic Integration* 267

S. Deakin, 'Reflexive Governance and European Company Law' (2009) 15 *European Law Journal* 224

L. Hancher and W. Sauter, 'One Step Beyond? From *Sodemare* to *Docmorris*: The EU's Freedom of Establishment Case Law Concerning Healthcare' (2010) 47 *Common Market Law Review* 117

A. Johnston and P. Syrpis, 'Regulatory Competition in European Company Law after *Cartesio*' (2009) 34 *European Law Review* 378

A. Kranz, 'The *Bosman* Case: The Relationship Between European Union Law and the Transfer System in European Football' (1999) 5 *Cambridge Journal of European Law* 431

G. Marenco, 'The Notion of Restriction on the Freedom of Establishment and Provision of Services in the Case-law of the Court' (1991) 11 *Yearbook of European Law* 111

C. O' Brien, 'Social Blind Spots and Monocular Policy Making: The ECJ's Migrant Worker Model' (2009) 46 *Common Market Law Review* 1107

A. Tryfonidou, 'In Search of the Aim of the EC Free Movement of Persons Provisions: Has the Court of Justice Missed the Point?' (2009) 46 *Common Market Law Review* 1591

---

[116] See G. Davies, *Services, Citizenship and the Country of Origin Principle*, Mitchell Working Paper No. 2/07 (2007).

20

Trade Restrictions and Public Goods

CONTENTS

1 INTRODUCTION

This chapter is about derogations from free movement, and their review by the Court of Justice. These derogations exist to protect important national interests – public goods – but they can also be used to disguise protectionism, which is why they are usually quite strictly reviewed.

Section 2 provides an introduction to the themes and context of the Treaty derogations. These Articles are at the heart of one of the most important current debates: whether globalisation unavoidably threatens non-economic interests and values, or whether reconciliation or compromise is possible. The Court uses a range of ideas and principles, from transparency to a margin of appreciation, in its search for the right approach.

Section 3 addresses the range of public goods which the Treaty protects. The explicit derogations are brief and limited, but the Court has extended them with its invention of the mandatory requirement, or the general public interest objective. The range of justifications which may be relied upon to restrict movement is now very broad, and only protectionist reasons, or purely economic reasons, have been excluded. This latter category is problematic: the distinction between an economic and a non-economic interest is often not clear. For example, protecting national budgets protects the health of public institutions, and so also protects interests such as public health and public security.

Section 4 is about the principles governing derogations. The Court will critically examine whether they are truly necessary, or whether the goals could be achieved by less restrictive measures. In making this decision it is influenced by the coherence of national policy: if the Member State shows itself to be inconsistent in protecting a particular interest then this undermines its claim that the threat is serious and action is necessary. This, however, ignores the political compromises which legislation and policy-making entail. Consistency may not always be a feasible governmental goal. In deciding whether less restrictive measures could be adopted the Court may itself investigate the question, or instruct the national court to, or it may adopt a procedural approach and ask whether the Member State adequately investigated other possibilities before it acted.

Sections 5 to 8 are about specific Treaty derogations and provide examples of how the Court applies them. It becomes apparent that while, for example, public health claims are often critically examined and tested strictly for proportionality, where public policy and security are involved the Court may be more deferential. Environmental reasons occupy their own unique position. The environment is not specifically mentioned in the Treaty derogations, but the Court is aware that current concerns require it to be taken seriously and measures protecting the environment are weighed heavily in the balance when they impact on trade.

2 BALANCING FREE MOVEMENT AGAINST OTHER INTERESTS

At the heart of many globalisation debates is the fear that we are living in a runaway world.[1] In this world, the free movement of different factors of production undermines local democracy. Investment and companies simply move elsewhere whenever faced with unattractive demands by the local population. The dedication to the pursuit of wealth means that insufficient attention is paid to damaging side-effects, such as harm to the environment, further impoverishment of poor regions or the marketing of unsafe food. Finally, local forms of culture become swamped by the pervasiveness of global branding. Such a view is a distortion of what generally takes place, yet, if there is a setting to provide a stage for these fears, it is that offered by the economic freedoms. These freedoms institutionalise such concerns by giving capital, goods, services and labour a legal right to move across borders. This is not an unfettered right. Even in the early EEC Treaty, there were a number of grounds on which Member States were permitted to restrict trade. As attitudes evolved and conflicts have become more diverse, the Court of Justice has extended the grounds on which Member States may restrict trade to include an extremely wide array of justifications. The accommodation of so many interests and values has prompted further challenges. Everything turns on the way the Court of Justice mediates between the economic freedom and the exception in question. As we shall see, it has used a few generic principles to do this. Measures must be effective. They must not arbitrarily discriminate. They must take account of the regulatory requirements that have already been met in other Member States. They must be the least restrictive of trade necessary to secure their objectives. However, the sheer diversity of the disputes and issues involved has inevitably led to the partial breakdown of these general principles, so that they are

---

[1] See e.g. K. Ohmae, *The Borderless World: Power and Strategy in the Interlinked Economy* (New York, Harper, 1990); J. Habermas, *The Postnational Constellation* (London, Polity, 2001) ch. 4.

applied in different ways in different areas and cases. This has generated its own uncertainties, leading to doubt about the relationship between the general principles that are supposed to apply across the board and the specialised case law that predominates in certain areas.

Alongside a substantive investigation, or instead of it, the Court of Justice increasingly relies on procedural principles to determine the legitimacy of derogations. The Court now regularly asks whether the Member State has taken appropriate measures in the process leading to its decision, and whether that decision is adequately open to challenge by those affected: Was there a detailed risk assessment? Was international scientific opinion taken into account? Are authorisation procedures transparent, quick and accessible, and can decisions be challenged in court? This proceduralisation reflects broader themes in market regulation, especially the ever more central role of risk management, and the emphasis of recent years on good governance.

In general, the trend in many technocratic areas of the internal market seems to be towards more intrusive review and a heavier evidential burden on Member States to prove their case. Yet, in more subjective and value-laden fields the notion of a national margin of appreciation has become ever more central. Here, the Court of Justice looks for signs of honest intent, but emphasises the continuing freedom of states to define their own values and public norms. Perhaps the broadest overarching theme is that within a framework of common principles, there is a differentiated approach to their application, and an ever greater repertoire of rules and ideas which the Court can use.

3 PUBLIC GOODS PROTECTED UNDER EU LAW

The TFEU makes only limited provision for the protection of public goods from free trade, such as the environment, public morality and public health. The most extensive provision is that in relation to free movement of goods.

> **Article 36 TFEU**
>
> The provisions of Articles 34 and 35 shall not preclude prohibitions or restrictions on imports, exports or goods in transit justified on grounds of public morality, public policy or public security; the protection of health and life of humans, animals or plants; the protection of national treasures possessing artistic, historic or archaeological value; or the protection of industrial and commercial property. Such prohibitions or restrictions shall not, however, constitute a means of arbitrary discrimination or a disguised restriction on trade between Member States.

In addition, Article 65 TFEU sets out circumstances in which Member States may derogate from Article 63, which provides for free movement of capital.

> **Article 65(1) TFEU**
>
> 1. The provisions of Article 63 shall be without prejudice to the right of Member States:
>   (a) to apply the relevant provisions of their tax law which distinguish between taxpayers who are not in the same situation with regard to their place of residence or with regard to the place where their capital is invested;

(b) to take all requisite measures to prevent infringements of national law and regulations, in particular in the field of taxation and the prudential supervision of financial institutions, or to lay down procedures for the declaration of capital movements for purposes of administrative or statistical information, or to take measures which are justified on grounds of public policy or public security.

In both instances, the grounds on which Member States can restrict trade are fairly limited. They are, however, more extensive than those provided for the other economic freedoms. Derogations from the Articles on free movement of workers, establishment and services are only provided for on grounds of public policy, public security and public health.[2] These, however, have been used more commonly as a form of migration control, to prevent persons entering the territory, than to stop undesirable economic activities.

Two more derogations allow for the protection of the special link between a Member State and its own nationals, reserving them an exclusive role in some aspects of the business of government. With regard to workers, therefore:

Article 45(4) TFEU

4. The provisions of this Article shall not apply to employment in the public service.

A parallel provision exists for services and establishment.

Article 51 TFEU

The provisions of this chapter [on establishment] shall not apply, so far as any given Member State is concerned, to activities which in that State are connected, even occasionally, with the exercise of official authority.

All the provisions above are both limited and static. Largely unchanged since they were first introduced into the EEC Treaty in 1957, it has been left to the Court of Justice to protect the mixed economy in a dynamic fashion that takes account of the changing nature of the integration process, developments in political value and the challenges posed by new technologies. In the *Cassis de Dijon* judgment, the Court of Justice indicated that a quid pro quo for the extension of the economic freedoms was an acceptance that Member States should be able to take measures to protect a wide array of public interests, which would otherwise be threatened by these provisions, on condition that the measures did not arbitrarily discriminate and were proportionate and necessary to securing the objective they pursued.[3] The 'mandatory requirements' established in *Cassis de Dijon* to protect these interests from

---

[2] Articles 45(3), 52(1) and 62 TFEU.
[3] Case 120/78 *Rewe-Zentrale AG* v *Bundesmonopolverwaltung für Branntwein (Cassis de Dijon)* [1979] ECR 649.

erosion by Article 34 TFEU have been applied in various guises to all the other economic freedoms.[4] The array of interests that have been successfully invoked to safeguard national legislation, using Treaty exceptions or mandatory requirements, may be grouped for convenience under four headings.

(i) *Market externalities.* Market externalities arise where a transaction fails to take account of somebody's interests and that person was not deemed to have a choice in the matter. Most obviously, these interests are third party interests, such as those of the wider public. Market externalities can also affect the interests of one of the parties directly involved in the transaction. The sale of a dangerous product is an example. In all cases, the transaction is associated with the risk of some undesirable physical impact. The Court of Justice has moved to protect against a wide variety of market externalities. These include damage to public health;[5] harm to the consumer;[6] destruction of the environment;[7] unfair competition; fraud;[8] abuse of creditors;[9] dangers to road safety;[10] violation of intellectual property rights;[11] harm to the health and safety of workers;[12] and damage to the national historic and artistic heritage and to cultural policy.[13]

(ii) *Civil liberties.* The Court of Justice has also moved to ensure that the economic freedoms do not compromise those political values which are central to protecting human dignity, autonomy and equality. In such circumstances, the Court is concerned not only with the material impacts of trade but also its symbolic impacts, namely, whether it is seen to undermine the standing of important constitutional values.[14] To this end, the Court has indicated that matters such as human dignity,[15] freedom of expression,[16] freedom of assembly,[17] the right to strike,[18] the sanctity of religious beliefs[19] and cultural pluralism[20] are all capable of justifying derogations.

---

[4] Case C-415/93 *Union Royale Belge des Sociétés de Football Association and others* v *Bosman and others* [1995] ECR I-4921 (workers); Case 205/84 *Commission* v *Germany (German Insurance)* [1986] ECR 3755 (services); Case 107/83 *Ordre des Avocats au Barreau de Paris* v *Klopp* [1984] ECR 2971 (establishment); Joined Cases C-515/99 and C-527–540/99 *Reisch and others* v *Bürgermeister der Landeshaupstadt Salzburg* [2002] ECR I-2157 (capital).

[5] See e.g. Case C-429/02 *Bacardi France* v *Télévision française 1* [2004] ECR I-6613.

[6] Case 220/83 *Commission* v *France* [1986] ECR 3663; Case C-262/02 *Commission* v *France* [2004] ECR I-6569.

[7] Case 302/86 *Commission* v *Denmark* [1988] ECR 4607; Case C-17/00 *De Coster* v *Collège des bourgmestre et échevins de Watermael-Boitsfort* [2001] ECR I-9445.

[8] Case C-243/01 *Gambelli* [2003] ECR I-13031.

[9] Case C-212/97 *Centros* v *Erhvervs- og Selskabsstyrelsen* [1999] ECR I-1459.

[10] Case C-55/93 *Van Schaik* [1994] ECR I-4837; Case C-451/99 *Cura Anlagen* v *Auto Service Leasing* [2002] ECR I-3193; Case C-110/05 *Commission* v *Italy*, Judgment of 10 February 2009.

[11] Case 262/81 *Coditel* v *Ciné-Vog Films* [1980] ECR 881.

[12] Case 155/80 *Oebel* [1981] ECR 1993; Case C-113/89 *Rush Portuguesa* v *Office national d'immigration* [1990] ECR I-1417; Case C-164/99 *Portugaia Construções* [2002] ECR I-787; Case C-445/03 *Commission* v *Luxembourg (Employment of Foreign Workers)* [2004] ECR I-10191.

[13] Case C-180/89 *Commission* v *Italy* [1991] ECR I-709; Case C-200/96 *Metronome Musik* v *Music Point Hokamp* [1998] ECR I-1953.

[14] See Case C-209/08 *Sayn Wittgenstein* [2010] ECR I-13693.

[15] Case C-36/02 *Omega Spielhallen -und Automatenaufstellungs-GmbH* v *Oberbürgermeisterin der Bundesstadt Bonn* [2004] ECR I-9609.

[16] Case C-71/02 *Karner* v *Troostwijk* [2004] ECR I-3025.

[17] Case C-112/00 *Schmidberger* v *Republic of Austria* [2003] ECR I-5659.

[18] Case C-438/05 *Viking* [2007] ECR I-10779; Case C-341/05 *Laval* [2007] ECR I-11767. But see pp. 817–20.

[19] Case C-275/92 *HM Customs and Excise* v *Schindler* [1994] ECR I-1039.

[20] Case C-288/89 *Gouda* v *Commissariat voor de Media* [1991] ECR I-4007.

(iii) *Socio-cultural preferences.* Many rules may reflect or embody societal and cultural preferences or traditions. For example, rules concerning the role of professional organisations in regulating local markets are not just about the maintenance of objective standards, but about the place of the skilled person and of non-governmental bodies in society.[21] Such rules are seen as contributing to trust and stability. Rules on the opening hours of shops, such as Sunday opening, are not just economic policy, but reflect choices about the place of economic activity in the national lifestyle.[22] The autonomy of sporting organisations and their freedom to determine rules is also the product of the particular role of sport in society and attitudes towards it,[23] just as the rules on ownership of land, which have often been the subject of litigation, have much to do with the societal desire to nurture rural communities and protect a particular quality of life.[24] Measures aimed at guaranteeing the availability of housing for the local poor, as in issue in *Libert*, would also fall within this group, and show that while preferences must be compatible with the Treaty if they are to justify derogation (so they may not be nationalistic or protectionist) the specific responsibility of a Member State for those within its territory is acknowledged.[25] The Court of Justice has recognised the legitimacy of a wide range of rules within this group, varying from those which are deeply rooted in culture, such as traditions on naming of children,[26] to mere policy choices, such as the internationalisation of the labour market.[27]

(iv) *Preservation of the machinery of the state.* The final category of cases relate to the Member State's capacity to supply the services that are necessary for the government of its territory. In such cases, the Court of Justice is not so much concerned to protect certain values or interests per se but, rather, it aims to safeguard the machinery of government that enables such protection. Member States may, therefore, keep in place measures derogating from the economic freedoms to maintain internal and external security;[28] cohesion of their tax systems;[29] order in society;[30] their systems of administration of justice;[31] and financial balance in their systems of education or social security.[32]

There is one group of interests that the Court of Justice will not protect: interests of a purely economic nature. In numerous cases it has repeated that purely economic reasons cannot

---

[21] Case 33/74 *Van Binsbergen v Bestuur van de Bedrijsvereniging voor de Metaalnijverheid* [1974] ECR 1299; Case C-71/76 *Thieffry v Conseil de l'Ordre des Avocats à la Cour de Paris* [1977] ECR 765; Case C-58/98 *Corsten* [2000] ECR I-7919; Case C-309/99 *Wouters and others v Algemene Raad van de Nederlandse Orde van Advocaten* [2002] ECR I-1577.
[22] Case C-145/88 *Torfaen Borough Council v B & Q* [1989] ECR I-3851.
[23] Case C-415/93 *Union Royale Belge des Sociétés de Football Association and Others v Bosman and others* [1995] ECR I-4921.
[24] Case C-370/05 *Festersen* [2007] ECR I-1129.   [25] Case C-197/11 *Libert*, Judgment of 8 May 2013.
[26] Case C-391/09 *Runevic* [2011] ECR I-03787.
[27] Case C-542/09 *Commission v Netherlands*, Judgment of 14 June 2012.
[28] Case 72/83 *Campus Oil v Minister for Industry and Energy* [1984] ECR 2727.
[29] Case C-204/90 *Bachmann v Belgian State* [1992] ECR I-249; Case C-300/90 *Commission v Belgium* [1992] ECR I-305.
[30] Case C-275/92 *HM Customs and Excise v Schindler* [1994] ECR I-1039.
[31] Case C-3/95 *Reisebüro Broede v Sandker* [1996] ECR I-6511.
[32] Case C-147/03 *Commission v Austria* [2005] ECR I-5969; Case C-73/08 *Bressol* [2010] ECR I-2735; Case C-158/96 *Kohll v Union des Caisses de Maladie* [1998] ECR I-1931.

justify restrictions on free movement.[33] The implication is that the type of interests protected by free movement are qualitatively of a higher order than purely economic matters, so these latter can never serve to restrict the former. However, in practice the idea of a purely economic reason is not tidily defined, since money impacts on other interests. Indeed, since the Member State's capacity to carry out policy is dependent to a large extent on its budget, and since the wellbeing of its citizens is dependent to a large extent on the state of the national economy, any economic reason can be repackaged as being about other interests, such as good public services, employee protection, or even public order, as the cases below show.

Within the concept of the economic reason there are two distinct types of reason, both unacceptable. One reason sometimes put forward for a measure is the desire to protect local businesses or industry, or the national or local economy.[34] The main reason to object to such measures is that they are implicitly protectionist. They aim to ensure that national economic actors are protected from foreign intrusion. This aim is not legitimate in the context of a market where Member States have committed to openness and non-discrimination. However, there is a very fine line between a quasi-protectionist measure and one serving legitimate goals. For example, in *Wolff and Müller*, a German law requiring foreign service providers to pay their employees the German minimum wage whilst providing services in Germany was claimed to breach Article 56 TFEU.[35] The Explanatory Memorandum made clear that the purpose of the law was to protect small and medium-sized enterprises from cheap competition. Yet, the measure also protected the employees of the service providers, and employees on the German market in general. For this reason, the Court of Justice ruled the measure to be lawful. The fact that one justification – protection from cheap competition – fails, does not mean that another justification – employee protection – cannot be put forward.

The other type of economic interest is where the Member State is trying to protect its own budget. For example, in *Kranemann*, the German Government paid travel expenses for trips taken by trainee civil servants only if these trips were within Germany, and claimed that this was necessary for budgetary reasons.[36] Similarly, in *Kohll* and the other health care cases, governments have argued that restrictions on patient migration should be imposed to prevent strain on health care budgets.[37] Neither argument was acceptable as such, since they posed purely economic interests against a fundamental freedom. However, in *Kohll* the Court of Justice acknowledged that if the economic effects were such that the health care system was threatened, then the economic concern in fact became a public health concern, which would be a legitimate reason for a restriction.[38] Analogously, in *Campus Oil* the Court permitted the Irish Government to require oil companies to purchase some of their oil from a national refinery.[39]

---

[33] Case 352/85 *Bond van Adverteerders* [1988] ECR 2085; Case C-158/96 *Kohll v Union des Caisses de Maladie* [1998] ECR I-1931; Case C-398/95 *Syndesmos ton en Elladi Touristikon kai Taxidiotikon Grafeion v Ypourgos Ergasias* [1997] ECR I-3091; Case C-171/08 *Commission v Portugal* [2010] ECR I-6817; Case C-172/11 *Erny*, Judgment of 28 June 2012; J. Snell, 'Economic Aims as Justifications for Restrictions on Free Movement' in A. Schrauwen, *The Rule of Reason: Rethinking Another Classic of Community Law* (Groningen, Europa Law Publishing, 2005) 37.

[34] Case C-367/98 *Commission v Portugal (Free Movement of Capital)* [2002] ECR I-473; Case C-452/01 *Ospelt v Schössle Weissenberg Familienstiftung* [2003] ECR I-9743.

[35] Case C-60/03 *Wolff and Müller v Felix* [2004] ECR I-9553. See also Case C-370/05 *Festersen* [2007] ECR I-1129.

[36] Case C-109/04 *Kranemann v Land Nordrhein-Westfalen* [2005] ECR I-2421.

[37] Case C-158/96 *Kohll v Union des Caisses de Maladie* [1998] ECR I-1931. See pp. 833–41.

[38] *Ibid.* See also Case C-141/07 *Commission v Germany* [2008] ECR I-6935.

[39] Case 72/83 *Campus Oil v Minister for Industry and Energy* [1984] ECR 2727.

This measure reduced imports, and its immediate reason was to ensure the viability of the state refinery – an economic reason. However, the Irish Government successfully argued that keeping the refinery operating was of strategic and security importance – legitimate reasons – and such operation could only be guaranteed by ensuring customers. Other interests which have been used to make concerns about money acceptable by presenting them as social, systemic or moral concerns, are the cohesion of the tax system, the protection of local agricultural communities and the effectiveness of fiscal supervision (prevention of tax avoidance).[40] The lack of clarity in all this is reflected in the Court of Justice's ruling that preventing a reduction in tax revenue, by contrast with avoidance, is in pursuit of an economic interest and cannot, therefore, justify restrictions.[41]

4 PRINCIPLES MEDIATING CONFLICTS BETWEEN FREE MOVEMENT AND PUBLIC GOODS

When applying Treaty exceptions, the starting point is that these are to be strictly and narrowly interpreted, and that they are EU law concepts. Member States cannot play a Treaty exception as a trump card. By contrast, it is for national judges and ultimately the Court of Justice to assess the state measure in the light of the constraints imposed by EU law. These points were made clear in *Van Duyn*, in which the United Kingdom wished to restrict the entry of a Dutch national on the grounds that she was a scientologist, and therefore a threat to public policy.

Case 41/74 *Van Duyn v Home Office* [1974] ECR 1337

18. ... It should be emphasized that the concept of public policy in the context of the Community and where, in particular, it is used as a justification for derogating from the fundamental principle of freedom of movement for workers, must be interpreted strictly, so that its scope cannot be determined unilaterally by each Member State without being subject to control by the institutions of the Community. Nevertheless, the particular circumstances justifying recourse to the concept of public policy may vary from one country to another and from one period to another, and it is therefore necessary in this matter to allow the competent national authorities an area of discretion within the limits imposed by the Treaty.

A strict review can only mean that the Court of Justice assesses the proportionality of the measure, rather than just looking at formal correctness. In that sense, *Van Duyn* embodies similar principles to those which *Gebhard* and other cases have applied to mandatory requirements. It will be remembered that in this latter context, the Court found that restrictions on free movement could be justified by public interest objectives provided that the measures were equally applicable and proportionate.[42]

---

[40] Case C-204/90 *Bachmann* [1992] ECR I-249; Case C-250/95 *Futura Participations and Singer* v *Administration des contributions* [1997] ECR I-2471; *Ospelt*, n. 34 above. See also Case C-544/11 *Petersen*, Judgment of 28 February 2013.
[41] Case C-35/98 *Staatssecretaris van Financiën* v *Verkooijen* [2000] ECR I-4071; Case C-436/00 *X and Y* v *Riksskatteverket* [2002] ECR I-10829.
[42] See p. 820.

The fundamental difference between relying on a Treaty exception and relying on a mandatory requirement/general public interest objective is therefore that mandatory requirements are only available for equally applicable measures, whereas Treaty exceptions do not have this restriction – although overt discrimination will still require explanation, which may be a significant hurdle.

This distinction is often regarded as somewhat arbitrary.[43] Why not just merge the two classes of exception into one? In *Danner*, a case concerning Finnish rules which applied a more generous fiscal regime to pension insurance schemes based in Finland, Advocate General Jacobs put the case for this:

> Once it is accepted that justifications other than those set out in the Treaty may be invoked, there seems no reason to apply one category of justification to discriminatory measures and another category to non-discriminatory restrictions. Certainly the text of the Treaty provides no reason to do so: Article [56 TFEU] does not refer to discrimination but speaks generally of restrictions on freedom to provide services. In any event, it is difficult to apply rigorously the distinction between (directly or indirectly) discriminatory and non-discriminatory measures. Moreover, there are general interest aims not expressly provided for in the Treaty (e.g. protection of the environment, consumer protection) which may in given circumstances be no less legitimate and no less powerful than those mentioned in the Treaty. The analysis should therefore be based on whether the ground invoked is a legitimate aim of general interest and if so whether the restriction can properly be justified under the principle of proportionality. In any event, the more discriminatory the measure, the more unlikely it is that the measure complies with the principle of proportionality.[44]

This line of reasoning is present in Opinions from other Advocates General too,[45] but the Court of Justice nevertheless maintains the distinction. Usually this is of little importance: measures which are not equally applicable are very hard to justify anyway, so the theoretical possibility of relying on mandatory exceptions would be unlikely to change the outcome of many cases. Moreover, there is a good symbolic argument for restricting the justifications open to overtly discriminatory measures. These are, after all, an affront to the basic principles of the Union. Yet, in some exceptional contexts an overt distinction between people, products or providers from different states may apparently serve a legitimate policy aim which is not comfortably within the Treaty exceptions. In these situations, the Court has been known to overlook its general rule and permit non-Treaty justifications to be invoked.[46]

In any case, whichever type of justification is invoked, the Member State or organisation pleading it must show that the measure in question is the right way of addressing the problem.

---

[43] P. Oliver, 'Some Further Reflections on the Scope of Articles 28–30 (ex 30–36) EC' (1999) 36 *CMLRev.* 783, 804–5; N. Notaro, 'The New Generation of Case Law on Trade and the Environment' (2000) 25 *ELRev.* 467, 489–91.

[44] Case C-136/00 *Danner* [2002] ECR I-8147.

[45] Opinion of Advocate General Leger in Case C-80/94 *Wielockx v Inspecteur der Directe Belastingen* [1995] ECR I-2493; Opinion of Advocate General Tesauro in Case C-120/95 *Decker v Caisse de maladie des employés privés* [1998] ECR I-1831; Opinion of Advocate General Poiares Maduro in Case C-446/03 *Marks & Spencer v Halsey* [2005] ECR I-10837.

[46] Case C-2/90 *Commission v Belgium (Walloon Waste)* [1992] ECR I-4431; Case C-379/98 *PreussenElektra* [2001] ECR I-2099; Case C-203/96 *Chemische Afvalstoffen Dusseldorp BV and others v Minister van Volkhuisvesting, Ruimtelijke Ordening en Milieubeheer* [1998] ECR I-4075; Case 113/80 *Commission v Ireland (Irish Souvenirs)* [1981] ECR 1625; Case C-120/95 *Decker* [1998] ECR I-1831; Case C-158/96 *Kohll v Union des Caisses de Maladie* [1998] ECR I-1931.

Broadly speaking this means that the measure must be a proportionate, non-discriminatory and procedurally fair response to the policy concern raised. The specific questions which the Court tends to pose are, however, whether it has been shown that action is necessary; whether the measure is effective; whether the measure respects non-discrimination and mutual recognition; whether a less restrictive policy option would also be possible; and whether the procedural rights of those affected are guaranteed.

(i) The measure must be necessary

Any measure must meet a real rather than imagined threat to the public good in question.[47] In *Commission* v *Denmark*,[48] Denmark prohibited foods being enriched with vitamins and minerals unless there was a nutritional need on the part of the Danish population for these additives. The Court of Justice held that such a restriction would only be lawful if it could be shown that the products posed a real risk to public health. The Court ruled that without the presence of a prior risk assessment to appraise the probability of the danger to public health, the products could not be shown to pose a real risk to public health.

In many cases there may be genuine scientific uncertainty about whether protective measures are necessary. Numerous health cases have, like *Commission* v *Denmark*, concerned the addition of vitamins to food, about the safety of which opinions vary widely. In *Greenham and Abel*, the Court of Justice followed positions it had taken in *Commission* v *Denmark* and *Sandoz*, and confirmed that in a situation of scientific uncertainty Member States may take legitimately varying positions, but are not relieved of the obligation to provide evidence for the position they choose.[49]

Case C-95/01 *Greenham and Abel* [2004] ECR I-1333

37. It is of course for the Member States, in the absence of harmonisation and to the extent that there is still uncertainty in the current state of scientific research, to decide on the level of protection of human health and life they wish to ensure and whether to require prior authorisation for the marketing of foodstuffs, taking into account the requirements of the free movement of goods within the Community.

38. That discretion relating to the protection of public health is particularly wide where it is shown that there is still uncertainty in the current state of scientific research as to certain nutrients, such as vitamins, which are not as a general rule harmful in themselves but may have special harmful effects solely if taken to excess as part of the general diet, the composition of which cannot be foreseen or monitored.

39. However, in exercising their discretion relating to the protection of public health, the Member States must comply with the principle of proportionality. The means which they choose must therefore be confined to what is actually necessary to ensure the safeguarding of public health; they must be proportionate to the objective thus pursued, which could not have been attained by measures less restrictive of intra-Community trade.

---

[47] Case C-212/08 *Zeturf* [2011] ECR I-5633.   [48] Case C-192/01 *Commission* v *Denmark* [2003] ECR I-9693.
[49] *Ibid.*; Case 174/82 *Sandoz* [1983] ECR 5094. See also Case C-446/08 *Solgar* [2010] ECR I-3973l; Case C-333/08 *Commission* v *France*. See N. Nic Shuibhne and M. Maci, 'Proving Public Interest: The Growing Impact of Evidence in Free Movement Case Law' (2013) 50 *CMLRev.* 965.

40. Furthermore, since Article [36 TFEU] provides for an exception, to be interpreted strictly, to the rule of free movement of goods within the Community, it is for the national authorities which invoke it to show in each case, in the light of national nutritional habits and in the light of the results of international scientific research, that their rules are necessary to give effective protection to the interests referred to in that provision and, in particular, that the marketing of the products in question poses a real risk to public health.

41. A prohibition on the marketing of foodstuffs to which nutrients have been added must therefore be based on a detailed assessment of the risk alleged by the Member State invoking Article [36 TFEU].

The judgment refers to public health, but the procedural and substantive principles above should apply to any area where the underlying issue is one of scientific fact, rather than preference. The details of the risk assessment process and its consequences are discussed in the section on public health, below.

By contrast, the question of necessity is less amenable to a scientific approach where moral or social values and interests are concerned. There may be fundamental disagreements not just about evidence, but about what is threatening to the public interest. *Omega Spielhallen* concerned a German ban on laser game arcades which involved 'playing at killing'. This ban restricted the free movement of goods and services. Most other Member States allowed these games, and the German measure reflected a particular national sensitivity to the moral issues involved.

Case C–36/02 *Omega Spielhallen* [2004] ECR I-9609

32. In this case, the competent authorities took the view that the activity concerned by the prohibition order was a threat to public policy by reason of the fact that, in accordance with the conception prevailing in public opinion, the commercial exploitation of games involving the simulated killing of human beings infringed a fundamental value enshrined in the national constitution, namely human dignity ...

33. It should be recalled in that context that, according to settled case-law, fundamental rights form an integral part of the general principles of law the observance of which the Court ensures, and that, for that purpose, the Court draws inspiration from the constitutional traditions common to the Member States and from the guidelines supplied by international treaties for the protection of human rights on which the Member States have collaborated or to which they are signatories. The European Convention on Human Rights and Fundamental Freedoms has special significance in that respect.

34. As the Advocate General argues in paragraphs 82 to 91 of her Opinion, the Community legal order undeniably strives to ensure respect for human dignity as a general principle of law. There can therefore be no doubt that the objective of protecting human dignity is compatible with Community law, it being immaterial in that respect that, in Germany, the principle of respect for human dignity has a particular status as an independent fundamental right.

35. Since both the Community and its Member States are required to respect fundamental rights, the protection of those rights is a legitimate interest which, in principle, justifies a restriction of the obligations imposed by Community law, even under a fundamental freedom guaranteed by the Treaty such as the freedom to provide services.

36. However, measures which restrict the freedom to provide services may be justified on public policy grounds only if they are necessary for the protection of the interests which they are intended to guarantee and only in so far as those objectives cannot be attained by less restrictive measures.

37. It is not indispensable in that respect for the restrictive measure issued by the authorities of a Member State to correspond to a conception shared by all Member States as regards the precise way in which the fundamental right or legitimate interest in question is to be protected. Although, in paragraph 60 of *Schindler*, the Court referred to moral, religious or cultural considerations which lead all Member States to make the organisation of lotteries and other games with money subject to restrictions, it was not its intention, by mentioning that common conception, to formulate a general criterion for assessing the proportionality of any national measure which restricts the exercise of an economic activity.

38. On the contrary, as is apparent from well-established case-law subsequent to *Schindler*, the need for, and proportionality of, the provisions adopted are not excluded merely because one Member State has chosen a system of protection different from that adopted by another State.

The Court of Justice strives here to bring the German ban within a wider European framework of respect for rights, to present it as a particular embodiment of a shared norm, rather than a fundamental value difference with other Member States. Yet at the same time, it accepts the German right to interpret and protect such fundamental values in their own way, even if other states do so differently.

This respect for Member State peculiarities is vital if derogations are to serve their goal of protecting the things that states legitimately care about. However, if the need for a measure is based on local and subjective preferences it can make that need hard to police, and could invite misuse of the exceptions. The central concept in preventing this is consistency.[50] Consistent policy is increasingly taken as a reasonable proxy for genuineness. Thus, where a Member State attempts to prevent the entry of goods or persons, claiming they are a threat to some domestic interest, but takes no measures against similar domestically made goods, or nationals with the same allegedly dangerous characteristic, then it undermines its own claim of a serious threat, and will no longer be taken seriously.

In *Conegate*,[51] pornographic rubber dolls were seized under the Customs Consolidation Act 1976, which prohibited the importation of obscene or indecent articles. However, British law on their domestic equivalents varied. In the Isle of Man and Scotland, the manufacture, sale and distribution of such articles were prohibited. In England and Wales, however, neither the manufacture nor sale was prohibited. The only controls were that such items could not be sold through the post, could not be displayed in a public place and had to be sold from licensed premises.

Case 121/85 *Conegate* v *Customs and Excise Commissioners* [1986] ECR 1007

14. ... In principle it is for each Member State to determine in accordance with its own scale of values and in the form selected by it the requirements of public morality in its territory.

15. However, although Community law leaves the Member States free to make their own assessments of the indecent or obscene character of certain articles, it must be pointed out that the fact that goods cause offence cannot be regarded as sufficiently serious to justify restrictions on the free movement

---

[50] See G. Mathisen, 'Consistency and Coherence as Conditions for Justification of Member State Measures Restricting Free Movement' (2010) 47 *CMLRev.* 1021.

[51] Case 121/85 *Conegate* v *Customs and Excise Commissioners* [1986] ECR 1007.

of goods where the Member State concerned does not adopt, with respect to the same goods manufactured or marketed within its territory, penal measures or other serious and effective measures intended to prevent the distribution of such goods in its territory.

16. It follows that a Member State may not rely on grounds of public morality in order to prohibit the importation of goods from other Member States when its legislation contains no prohibition on the manufacture or marketing of the same goods on its territory.

17. It is not for the Court ... to consider whether, and to what extent, the United Kingdom legislation contains such a prohibition. However, the question whether or not such a prohibition exists in a state comprised of different constituent parts which have their own internal legislation, can be resolved only by taking into consideration all the relevant legislation. Although it is not necessary, for the purposes of the application of the above-mentioned rule, that the manufacture and marketing of the products whose importation has been prohibited should be prohibited in the territory of all the constituent parts, it must at least be possible to conclude from the applicable rules, taken as a whole, that their purpose is, in substance, to prohibit the manufacture and marketing of those products.

The same logic has been applied in numerous cases, but with varying results. In *Henn and Darby*, the United Kingdom was able to restrict the import of pornographic magazines, because the Court of Justice took the view that production of similar domestic ones was also prohibited.[52] However, in *Adoui and Cornuaille*, Belgium could not deport French prostitutes because even though prostitution was illegal in Belgium, repressive measures were not in fact taken.[53] The comparison between the domestic and the foreign must clearly be one of substance, not just legal form. Yet, this does not mean they need to be treated identically. In *Van Duyn*, the Court pointed out that Member States could not deport their own nationals, so one could not demand identical treatment of foreign and domestic scientologists.[54] What is necessary, if the state is to make good its claim of a serious threat against which action is necessary, is evidence of a consistent policy reflecting that view.

Consistency has also been at the heart of the very large number of cases concerning gambling restrictions.[55] Gambling is sometimes reserved to national monopolies, or to providers who have obtained one of a limited number of licences. The reasons put forward are usually to do with preventing crime, money laundering and gambling addiction, and the general desire to limit what is seen as a socially undesirable activity. However, the suspicion is always present that the Member State is merely trying to keep the profit from gambling for itself, or for a few chosen partners. First, the Court of Justice repeatedly finds that the ambition to reduce gambling, while legitimate, will not justify restrictions if Member States simultaneously

---

[52] Case 34/79 *R v Henn and Darby* [1979] ECR 3975.

[53] Joined Cases 115/81 and 116/81 *Adoui and Cornuaille v Belgian State and City of Liège* [1982] ECR 1665; see also Case C-268/99 *Jany v Staatssecretaris van Justitie* [2001] ECR I-8615.

[54] Case 41/74 *Van Duyn v Home Office* [1974] ECR 1337.

[55] Case C-275/92 *HM Customs and Excise v Schindler* [1994] ECR I-1039; Case C-124/97 *Läärä v Kihlakunnansyyttäjä* [1999] ECR I-6067; Case C-243/01 *Gambelli* [2003] ECR I-13031; Case C-46/08 *Carmen Media* [2010] ECR I-8149; Joined Cases C-338/04, C-359/04 and C-360/04 *Placanica, Palazzese and Soricchio* [2007] ECR I-1891; Case C-258/08 *Ladbrokes* [2010] ECR I-4757; Case C-316/07 *Stoß* [2010] ECR I-8069; Case C-186/11 *Stanleybet*, Judgment of 24 January 2013; Case C-42/07 *Liga Portuguesa de Futebol Profissional and Bwin International Ltd v Departamento de Jogos da Santa Casa da Misericórdia de Lisboa* [2010] ECR I-22; D. Doukas, 'In a Bet there is a Fool and a State Monopoly: Are the Odds Stacked Against Cross-border Gambling?' (2011) 36 *ELRev.* 243.

allow, for example, a national lottery to advertise widely. Secondly, claims about the need to exert control over a business often closely linked to criminal activities, while potentially acceptable, must actually be based on factual problems, and not be mere assertions. *Zeturf* is but one example among many, but the judgment captures the issues fairly clearly. At issue was the exclusive right of the PMU, a state-controlled organisation, to take bets on horse racing in France.[56]

Case C–212/08 *Zeturf* [2011] ECR I–5633

66. It must be recalled at the outset in that context that, in so far as the authorities of a Member State incite and encourage consumers to participate in games of chance to the financial benefit of the public purse, the authorities of that State cannot invoke public and social policy concerns relating to the need to reduce opportunities for gambling in order to justify restrictions on the freedom to provide services.

67. The Court has nevertheless held that a policy of controlled expansion of gambling activities may be consistent with the objective of channelling them into controlled circuits by drawing bettors away from clandestine, prohibited betting and gaming to activities which are authorised and regulated. Such a policy may indeed be consistent both with the objective of preventing the use of gambling activities for criminal or fraudulent purposes and that of preventing incitement to squander money on gambling and of combating addiction to the latter, by directing consumers towards the offer emanating from the holder of the public monopoly, that offer being deemed to be protected from criminal elements and also designed to safeguard consumers more effectively against squandering of money and addiction to gambling.

68. In order to achieve that objective of channelling into controlled activities, it is common ground that authorised operators must represent a reliable, but at the same time attractive, alternative to non-regulated activities, which may as such necessitate the offer of an extensive range of games, advertising on a certain scale and the use of new distribution techniques.

69. It is specifically for the national court to determine, in the light of the facts of the dispute before it, whether the commercial policy of the PMU may be regarded, both with regard to the scale of advertising undertaken and with regard to its creation of new games, as forming part of a policy of controlled expansion in the betting and gaming sector, aiming, in fact, to channel the propensity to gamble into controlled activities.

70. In the context of that assessment, it is for the national court to determine, in particular, whether, first, criminal and fraudulent activities linked to gambling and, second, gambling addiction might have been a problem in France at the material time and whether the expansion of authorised and regulated activities would have been capable of solving such a problem. In particular, the Court has stated that if a Member State wishes to rely on an objective capable of justifying an obstacle to the freedom to provide services arising from a national restrictive measure, it is under a duty to supply the court called upon to rule on that question with all the evidence of such a kind as to enable the latter to be satisfied that the said measure does indeed fulfil the requirements arising from the principle of proportionality. In that regard the Commission argues that the national authorities have not, in contrast to the situation in *Placanica and others* and *Liga Portuguesa de Futebol Profissional and Bwin International*, demonstrated the reality of a black market for betting on horse racing.

---

[56] See G. Anagnostaras, 'Les Jeux Sont Faits: Mutual Recognition and the Specificities of Online Gambling' (2012) 37 *ELRev.* 191.

71. In any event, any advertising issued by the holder of a public monopoly must remain measured and strictly limited to what is necessary in order thus to channel consumers towards controlled gaming networks. Such advertising cannot, on the other hand, specifically aim to encourage consumers' natural propensity to gamble by stimulating their active participation in it, such as by trivialising gambling or giving it a positive image owing to the fact that revenues derived from it are used for activities in the public interest, or by increasing the attractiveness of gambling by means of enticing advertising messages holding out the prospect of major winnings.

A quite different conceptual issue arose in *Compassion in World Farming*.[57] The United Kingdom wished to restrict the export of young calves to Spain on grounds of animal welfare: they were destined to be reared in boxes for veal, which is prohibited in the United Kingdom. The United Kingdom lost because minimum conditions for the welfare of calves were laid down in secondary legislation, and Spain complied with this legislation. The United Kingdom was free to have stricter standards, but where legislation of this type exists a Member State must accept as adequate the standards of any Member State complying with it, notwithstanding that the first state may be stricter.

Yet, the case could have been resolved on other grounds: the threat to animal welfare was to occur in Spain, and was none of the United Kingdom's business. The Advocate General hinted at this, but the Court of Justice did not raise the issue, and implicitly accepted that in principle the threat against which action is necessary need not be domestic. This principle is of particular importance where environmental measures are concerned, and the Court has indeed accepted measures which aim to protect the environment in other Member States, as well as the global environment.[58] Action may be necessary to protect interests beyond the borders of the acting Member State.

(ii) The measure must be effective

In addition to addressing a genuine need, the measure must effectively protect the public good in question. The Court of Justice will generally not look to whether there are more effective instruments available but, rather, will be concerned merely that the measure contributes to protection of the public good. In *Commission* v *Belgium*, the Court of Justice ruled illegal a Belgian law stipulating that all goods to which nutrients had been added must be labelled with a notification number allocated to them by the Belgian authorities.[59] The Court contemplated that labelling a product with a notification number did not protect public health or the consumer as it did not inform the consumer of the nutritional content of the goods or whether the appropriate checks had been carried out. The measure was, measured against its stated goals, useless.[60]

---

[57] Case C-1/96 *Compassion in World Farming* [1998] ECR I-1251.
[58] See p. 925. See also G. Davies, 'Process and Production Method-based Restrictions on Trade in the EU' in C. Barnard (ed.), *Cambridge Yearbook of European Legal Studies* 2008 (Oxford, Hart, 2008) 69.
[59] Case C-217/99 *Commission* v *Belgium* [2000] ECR I-10251.
[60] See also Case C-55/99 *Commission* v *France* [2000] ECR I-11499.

A situation which has recurred in several cases is where a measure could be effective, but in fact is not, as a result of other aspects of national law and policy. For example, *Hartlauer* concerned Austrian rules which required new out-patient dental clinics to be authorised. This was said to be necessary to prevent an over-supply of dentists in a given area, which might have implications for quality and for local health budgets, and so ultimately for access to good dental care. However, the rules only applied to clinics which employed dentists, not to group practices, which were usually partnerships. The difference between a clinic and a partnership is one of business model – the employment model being traditionally regarded as threatening by professionals – but not of obvious importance to the customer.

Case C–169/07 *Hartlauer Handelsgesellschaft mbH* v *Wiener Landesregierung and Oberösterreichische Landesregierung*, Judgment of 10 March 2009

50. Consequently, it must be ascertained whether the restrictions at issue in the main proceedings are appropriate for ensuring attainment of the objectives of maintaining a balanced high-quality medical service open to all and preventing the risk of serious harm to the financial balance of the social security system. [The Court then accepted that a planning and authorisation system could in principle be a part of achieving these goals.] ...

54. In the present case, however, two series of considerations prevent the legislation in question from being accepted as appropriate for ensuring attainment of the above objectives.

55. First, it must be recalled that national legislation is appropriate for ensuring attainment of the objective pursued only if it genuinely reflects a concern to attain it in a consistent and systematic manner.

56. However, it follows from [national law], that a prior authorisation based on an assessment of the needs of the market is required for setting up and operating new independent outpatient dental clinics, whatever their size, and that the setting up of new group practices, by contrast, is not subject to any system of authorisation, regardless of their size.

57. Yet it appears from the order for reference that the premises and equipment of group practices and those of outpatient dental clinics may have comparable features and that in many cases the patient will not notice any difference between them.

58. Moreover, group practices generally offer the same medical services as outpatient dental clinics and are subject to the same market conditions.

59. Similarly, group practices and outpatient dental clinics may have comparable numbers of practitioners. It is true that the practitioners who provide medical services within group practices have the status of personally liable partner and are authorised to practise independently as dental practitioners, whereas the practitioners in an outpatient clinic have the status of employee. However, the documents before the Court do not show that that circumstance has any definite effect on the nature or volume of the services provided.

60. Since those two categories of providers of services may have comparable features and a comparable number of practitioners and provide medical services of equivalent volume, they may therefore have a similar impact on the market in medical services, and are thus liable to affect in an equivalent manner the economic situation of contractual practitioners in certain geographical areas and, in consequence, the attainment of the planning objectives pursued by the competent authorities.

61. That inconsistency also affects the attainment of the objective of preventing a risk of serious harm to the financial balance of the national social security system. Even supposing that the uncontrolled establishment of independent outpatient dental clinics may lead to a considerable increase in the

volume of medical services at constant prices to be paid for by that system, the Austrian Government has not put forward anything capable of explaining why the establishment of those clinics but not of group practices could have such an effect.

62. Moreover, the provision of dental care in those independent outpatient clinics is liable to prove more rational, in view of the way they are organised, the fact of having several practitioners, and the use in common of medical installations and equipment, which enable them to reduce their operating costs. They will thus be able to provide medical services in conditions that are less costly than those, in particular, of independent practitioners who do not have such opportunities. The provision of care services by those institutions may have the consequence of more efficient use of the public funds allocated to the statutory health insurance system.

63. In those circumstances, it must be concluded that the national legislation at issue in the main proceedings does not pursue the stated objectives in a consistent and systematic manner, since it does not make the setting up of group practices subject to a system of prior authorisation, as is the case with new outpatient dental clinics.

Hartlauer, with its emphasis on consistency, is very close in principle to the cases in the previous section. However, the Court of Justice's argument is slightly different. In this case it does not regard inconsistency as demonstrating that there is no real problem to be addressed, but rather that the measure is not actually going to effectively achieve its goal.[61] Nevertheless, the two issues blur into each other in many judgments, and this is not unreasonable: if a Member State undermines the effectiveness of its own measures, by acting in a way that conflicts with their stated policy goals, then this must also raise the question whether that state genuinely considers action to meet those goals to be necessary. Where inconsistency is taken as showing measures are not necessary the implicit accusation is that the Member State is being dishonest. Where inconsistency is taken as showing that measures will not be effective the implicit accusation is that the Member State is incompetent. Which of these is closer to the truth may vary from case to case. However, the basis of either is an assessment of the measure in its wider policy context. *Hartlauer* is an example of a moderately penetrating review of this.

A similar level of intensity was shown by the Court of Justice in *Festersen*. Danish law required owners of agricultural property to live on the property. If they did not, within a certain period of buying it, they could be required by law to sell the land. This is a restriction on the free movement of capital, because it discourages investment in land and property. However, the aim was stated to be to protect agricultural communities, the risk being that urban people, or foreigners, would buy up the houses and old farms and use them as holiday homes, so that traditional agricultural activities, and much of the local economy, would die out. This has arisen in several cases, and the Court acknowledges the Member State concerns.[62] Nevertheless, in *Festersen* it considered critically whether the measures taken were actually suitable to meet the stated goals.

---

[61] See also Case C-500/06 *Dermoestetica* [2008] ECR I-5785; Case C-570/07 *Blanco Perez* [2010] ECR I-4629.

[62] Case C-302/97 *Konle* [1999] ECR I-3099; Joined Cases C-515/99 and C-527–540/99 *Reisch and others* v *Bürgermeister der Landeshauptstadt Salzburg* [2002] ECR I-2157; Case C-452/01 *Ospelt* v *Schössle Weissenberg Familienstiftung* [2003] ECR I-9743.

Case C-370/05 *Festersen* [2007] ECR I-1129

27. As regards the condition relating to the pursuance of an objective in the public interest, the Danish Government submits that the national legislation seeks, first, to preserve the farming of agricultural land by means of owner-occupancy, which constitutes one of the traditional forms of farming in Denmark, and to ensure that agricultural property be occupied and farmed predominantly by the owners, second, as a town and country planning measure, to preserve a permanent agricultural community and, third, to encourage a reasonable use of the available land by resisting pressure on land.

28. Such objectives are themselves in the public interest and are capable of justifying restrictions to the free movement of capital. In addition, as the Danish Government and the Commission of the European Communities maintain, those objectives are consistent with those of the common agricultural policy which, under Article [39(1)(b) TFEU] aims 'to ensure a fair standard of living for the agricultural community' in the working-out of which, according to Article [33(2)(a) TFEU], account must be taken 'of the particular nature of agricultural activity, which results from the social structure of agriculture and from structural and natural disparities between the various agricultural regions'.

29. As regards the condition of proportionality, it is necessary to check whether the requirement that the acquirer take up his fixed residence on the agricultural property acquired constitutes, as submitted by the Danish and Norwegian Governments, an appropriate and necessary measure for the attainment of the objectives mentioned in paragraph 27 above.

30. As regards whether the national measure at issue in the main proceedings is appropriate, it must be observed that it contains only a residence requirement and is not coupled, for an acquirer of an agricultural property of less than 30 hectares, with a requirement to farm the property personally. Such a measure thus does not appear, in itself, to ensure the attainment of the alleged objective seeking to preserve the traditional form of farming by owner-occupiers.

31. It is true that, as regards the second aim assigned to the Law on agriculture, the residence requirement is likely to contribute, by definition, to preserving an agricultural community and it can be met even further by farmers who, in accordance with one of the general objectives of the Law on agriculture seeking to encourage the owner-occupancy form of farming, personally farm their own land.

32. However, in the light of the phenomena of both reduction of the number of farms and regrouping of farms, as is apparent from the written observations lodged before the Court, and which were not challenged at the hearing, the objective of preserving an agricultural community cannot be met where the acquisition is made by a farmer who is already resident on another farm. In such a situation, the residence requirement does not guarantee the attainment of that objective, and thus it does not appear that that requirement is, in actual fact, appropriate, in itself, for the purpose of attaining such an objective.

33. In relation to the third aim which the Law on agriculture seeks to attain, it must be found that the residence requirement can reduce the number of potential acquirers of agricultural property and, consequently, it is capable of reducing the pressure on that land. It can therefore be accepted that national legislation containing such a requirement, which seeks to avoid the acquisition of agricultural land for purely speculative reasons, and which is thus likely to facilitate the preferential appropriation of that land by persons wishing to farm it does pursue a public interest objective in a Member State in which agricultural land is, and this is not challenged, a limited natural resource.

The Court concludes that since there is only an obligation to live on the land, not to farm it, the measure is not suitable for protecting agricultural activities. Moreover, since the land might be bought by another farmer, as part of a consolidation of farms, a residence requirement here would also serve no purpose. However, the Court concedes that the residence rule will discourage some buyers, and this in itself might reduce pressure on agricultural land and make it easier for locals to buy and farm it.

Festersen and *Hartlauer* both concern policy areas which are dominated neither by science, as in food safety, nor by sensitive values, as where morality arguments are made. Rather, they are practical, reasonably comprehensible policy fields which lie within the judicial comfort zone, so we see the Court of Justice engaging in a factual analysis, and conclusion, which is slightly at odds with its role in the reference procedure. There is a risk with these apparently accessible national policy areas that the common sense judicial approach does not do justice to the full complexity of the policy and the factors involved.

Carmen Media shows how that complexity may be not just a policy matter, but a political one. The German region of Schleswig-Holstein had established a regional betting monopoly, with the aim of controlling the supply of gambling in order to prevent addiction and 'squandering' money. This might have been fine, but was undermined by the fact that it did not cover all forms of gambling, and the rules on casinos and arcade games were actually being relaxed, with a significant increase in supply in recent years. Yet Schleswig-Holstein argued that this could not be blamed on them: some forms of gambling were regulated by the German Länder, but others were at least partly under the control of the federal government. The conflicting policies came from different levels of government, which had constitutionally protected spheres of competence. The Court of Justice acknowledged this, but found it irrelevant.

Case C–46/08 *Carmen Media* [2010] ECR I–8149

64. ... the case-law of the Court of Justice also shows that the establishment, by a Member State, of a restriction on the freedom to provide services and the freedom of establishment on the grounds of such an objective is capable of being justified only on condition that the said restrictive measure is suitable for ensuring the achievement of the said objective by contributing to limiting betting activities in a consistent and systematic manner....

67. In the present case, after stating that bets on competitions involving horses and automated games can be exploited by private operators which hold an authorisation, the referring court has also established that, in regard to casino games and automated games, even though such games present a higher risk of addiction than bets on sporting competitions, the competent public authorities are pursuing a policy of expanding supply. Thus, the number of casinos has risen from 66 to 81 between 2000 and 2006, while the conditions under which automated games may be exploited in establishments other than casinos, such as gaming arcades, restaurants, cafes and places of accommodation, have recently been the subject of major relaxations.

68. In that respect, on the basis of such findings, it must be acknowledged that the referring court may legitimately be led to consider that the fact that, in relation to games of chance other than those covered by the public monopoly at issue in the main proceedings, the competent authorities thus pursue policies seeking to encourage participation in those games rather than to reduce opportunities for gambling and to limit activities in that area in a consistent and systematic manner has the effect that

the aim of preventing incitement to squander money on gambling and of combating addiction to the latter, which was at the root of the establishment of the said monopoly, can no longer be effectively pursued by means of the monopoly, with the result that the latter can no longer be justified having regard to Article [56 TFEU].

69. As for the fact that the various games of chance concerned are partially within the competence of the Länder and partially within the competence of the federal State, it should be recalled that, according to consistent case-law, a Member State may not rely on provisions, practices or situations of its internal legal order in order to justify non-compliance with its obligations under EU law. The internal allocation of competences within a Member State, such as between central, regional or local authorities, cannot, for example, release that Member State from its obligation to fulfil those obligations.

70. It follows from the above that, whilst EU law does not preclude an internal allocation of competences whereby certain games of chance are a matter for the Länder and others for the federal authority, the fact remains that, in such a case, the authorities of the Land concerned and the federal authorities are jointly required to fulfil the obligation on the Federal Republic of Germany not to infringe Article [56 TFEU]. It follows that, in the full measure to which compliance with that obligation requires it, those various authorities are bound, for that purpose, to coordinate the exercise of their respective competences.

The demand that levels of government coordinate their policies before they can legitimately rely on a derogation from the Treaty is substantively understandable, but has potentially far-reaching implications for the domestic political order.

(iii) Arbitrary discrimination and mutual recognition

Measures taken in derogation from the freedoms must of course comply with general principles of EU law, such as fundamental rights.[63] One of the most important of these in practice is the principle of non-discrimination. This is expressly referred to in the second sentence of Article 36 TFEU, which prevents 'arbitrary discrimination', but the principle applies across the freedoms.[64] It entails that Member States may not use derogations for covert protectionism, and requires them to take full account of protective measures which may be in place in other Member States, and which may make their own measures less necessary.

An extreme example is found in the *Newcastle Disease* case. This highly infectious viral disease affects birds including chickens and turkeys, and after an outbreak on the continent the British Government imposed restrictions on the import of poultry products from mainland Europe. At first glance this seemed like a reasonable animal health measure. However, the Commission and France presented the facts in a way which told a different story. The timing of the measure, the political pressure preceding it, the absence of any scientific basis for it, and the fact that measures taken by France to combat Newcastle Disease had been summarily dismissed as inadequate by the United Kingdom were all relevant.

[63] Case C-260/89 *ERT* v *DEP* [1991] ECR I-02925; see Chapter 6.
[64] See Article 18 TFEU. C-447/08 *Sjöberg and Gerdin* [2010] ECR I-06921.

Case 40/82 *Commission v United Kingdom (Newcastle Disease)* [1984] ECR 283

36. As the Court has already observed ... in Case 34/79 *Henn and Darby*, the second sentence of Article [36 TFEU] is designed to prevent restrictions on trade mentioned in the first sentence of that article from being diverted from their proper purpose and used in such a way as either to create discrimination in respect of goods originating in other Member States or indirectly to protect certain national products.

37. Certain established facts suggest that the real aim of the 1981 measures was to block, for commercial and economic reasons, imports of poultry products from other Member States, in particular from France. The United Kingdom Government had been subject to pressure from British poultry producers to block these imports. It hurriedly introduced its new policy with the result that French Christmas turkeys were excluded from the British market for the 1981 season. It did not inform the Commission and the Member States concerned in good time, as the letter in which the Commission was informed of the new measures – which took effect on 1 September 1981 – was dated 27 August 1981. It did not find it necessary to discuss the effects of the new measures on imports with the Community Institutions, with the Standing Veterinary Committee or with the Member States concerned.

38. It should be noted, in this context, that when the United Kingdom abandoned, in 1964, the policy of non-vaccination and compulsory slaughter conducted till then in Great Britain, in order to adopt a policy of control of Newcastle disease by vaccination, this change of policy was thoroughly prepared by an elaborate report of a committee of experts, by various studies and by prolonged discussions among veterinary experts. The evidence available in the present case does not suggest that any comparable effort was made before the Government decided, in 1981, to reintroduce the policy which it had applied before 1964. The deduction must be made that the 1981 measures did not form part of a seriously considered health policy.

39. This conclusion is reinforced by the way in which the United Kingdom dealt with French demands that French poultry products should be readmitted to Great Britain after the French Republic had fulfilled the three conditions laid down by the United Kingdom Government, namely that the exporting country should be totally free from outbreaks of Newcastle disease, should prohibit vaccination and should apply a policy of compulsory slaughter in the event of any future outbreak of the disease. By refusing French imports on the ground that France had not closed its frontiers to poultry imports from non-member countries where vaccine was still in use, the United Kingdom added in fact a fourth condition to the three which it had previously stated in its letter to the Commission of 27 August 1981, and which it still states in its defence in the present case as the only applicable conditions.

The ban on arbitrary discrimination also covers less colourful stories. In *Rewe*, a German policy on apple disease was examined, which subjected imported apples to phytosanitary checks, while German apples were subjected to a different regime in which the trees were checked.[65] This resulted in different cost burdens on German and imported apples. However, the Court of Justice found this to be permitted differentiation, not arbitrary discrimination: the fact was that it was not possible to conduct checks on trees outside Germany, and this difference justified the different approach to controls.

Nevertheless, had the Member States of origin conducted such tree checks and offered evidence of the results Germany would have been obliged to accept them. The principle of mutual

---

[65] Case 4/75 *Rewe-Zentralfinanz GmbH* v *Landwirtschaftskammer Bonn* [1975] ECR 843.

recognition is a specific expression of non-discrimination, and is often relevant to derogations, particularly where testing and certification are concerned. This principle prevents the
importing state duplicating measures which have already been taken by the exporting state.
This principle was confirmed in *Biologische Producten*,[66] where a Dutch law requiring prior
authorisation for the marketing of all toxic plant protection products by the Dutch authorities was challenged on the grounds that the product in question had already been subject to
extensive laboratory analyses in France.

Case 272/80 *Frans–Nederlandse Maatschappij voor Biologische Producten* [1981] ECR 3277

14. Whilst a Member State is free to require a product of the type in question, which has already received
approval in another Member State, to undergo a fresh procedure of examination and approval, the
authorities of the Member States are nevertheless required to assist in bringing about a relaxation of
the controls existing in intra-Community trade. It follows that they are not entitled unnecessarily to
require technical or chemical analyses or laboratory tests where those analyses and tests have already
been carried out in another Member State and their results are available to those authorities, or may at
their request be placed at their disposal.

15. For the same reasons, a Member State operating an approval procedure must ensure that no
unnecessary control expenses are incurred if the practical effects of the control carried out in the
Member State of origin satisfy the requirements of the protection of public health in the importing
Member State. On the other hand, the mere fact that those expenses weigh more heavily on a trader
marketing small quantities of an approved product than on his competitor who markets much greater
quantities, does not justify the conclusion that such expenses constitute arbitrary discrimination or a
disguised restriction within the meaning of [Article 30].

The requirement to accept foreign tests as adequate is premised on them being equivalent to
the national ones. This may not always be so. If the Member State can establish that there are
important differences, so that the tests do not in fact satisfy the (legitimate and proportionate)
domestic needs, then they may impose additional tests. But while this is simple in principle it
may be complex in practice.[67] The procedures used by different Member States will rarely be
identical. Thus, establishing equivalence between different standards in often highly complex
and technical areas will be difficult.[68] The principle of equivalence places an exacting burden
on the national judge. This is not only true where product standards are concerned, but also
where the adequacy of supervision by other Member State regulatory authorities is in issue.
Member States should regard supervision by the home state as rendering their own supervision superfluous unless they can show that it leaves gaps in protection which must be filled,
but this is once again often a complex matter.[69] One response to that complexity is to take a

---

[66] Case 272/80 *Frans-Nederlandse Maatschappij voor Biologische Producten* [1981] ECR 3277. See also Case C-432/03 *Commission v Portugal* [2005] ECR I-9665.
[67] See p. 691.
[68] European Commission, *Second Biennial Report on the Application of the Principle of Mutual Recognition in the Single Market*, COM(2002)419 final, 17–21.
[69] Case C-243/01 *Gambelli* [2003] ECR I-13031; Case C-393/05 *Commission v Austria* [2007] ECR I-10195; Case C-404/05 *Commission v Germany* [2007] ECR I-10239.

procedural approach to reviewing Member State measures, asking primarily whether they have complied with principles of good governance in their approach to issues of equivalence. This is increasingly adopted by the Court of Justice, and discussed further below.[70]

Mutual recognition is at its most powerful where objective, factual issues are concerned and documents from different states can be easily compared. By contrast, where authorisations are concerned these may be based on different policy considerations, making them non-comparable. In the gambling cases the issue has arisen whether an authorisation to provide gambling services from one Member State should automatically entitle the holder to offer these in other Member States. The Court of Justice in *Stoß* explains why mutual recognition should not apply in this case:

Case C–316/07 *Stoß* [2010] ECR I-8069

111. In that respect, it should however be noted that, having regard to the discretion ... which Member States have in determining, according to their own scale of values, the level of protection which they intend to ensure and the requirements which that protection entails, the Court had regularly held that assessment of the proportionality of the system of protection established by a Member State cannot, in particular, be influenced by the fact that another Member State has chosen a different system of protection.

112. Having regard to that margin of discretion and the absence of any Community harmonisation in the matter, a duty mutually to recognise authorisations issued by the various Member States cannot exist having regard to the current state of EU law.

113. It follows in particular that each Member State retains the right to require any operator wishing to offer games of chance to consumers in its territory to hold an authorisation issued by its competent authorities, without the fact that a particular operator already holds an authorisation issued in another Member State being capable of constituting an obstacle.

Because the underlying conditions for obtaining a licence may vary significantly from state to state they cannot be treated as interchangeable or equivalent.[71] Mutual recognition, at least in the context of Treaty derogations, is not intended to undermine the substantive policy choices of Member States.[72]

(iv) The measure must be the least restrictive option

Even if action has been shown to be necessary, and the measure has been shown to be effective, it must still be no more restrictive of movement than is necessary. An example of this principle being applied is *De Peijper*.[73] In this case, where any pharmaceutical was marketed in the Netherlands, a file had to be presented to the authorities setting out details of its composition, packaging and preparation. This file had to be certified by the manufacturer. Centrafarm was importing valium from the United Kingdom, which was produced by Hoffman La Roche.

---

[70] See pp. 921–3. Also Case C-333/08 *Commission v France* [2010] ECR I-757.
[71] See Doukas, n. 55 above; Anagnostaras, n. 56 above.
[72] Cf. p. 777.   [73] Case 104/75 *Officier van Justitie* v *De Peijper* [1976] ECR 613.

Hoffman La Roche refused to give Centrafarm the documentation, as it also sold valium on the Dutch market. When Centrafarm was prosecuted, it argued that although the Dutch authorities were entitled to take measures to protect public health, the requirement for it to obtain documentation from a competitor was unnecessarily restrictive.

Case 104/75 *Officier van Justitie v De Peijper* [1976] ECR 613

17. National rules or practices do not fall within the exception specified in [Article 36 TFEU] if the health and life of humans can be as effectively protected by measures which do not restrict intra-Community trade so much.

18. In particular [Article 36 TFEU] cannot be relied on to justify rules or practices which, even though they are beneficial, contain restrictions which are explained primarily by a concern to lighten the administration's burden or reduce public expenditure, unless, in the absence of the said rules or practices, this burden or expenditure clearly would exceed the limits of what can reasonably be required …

23. With regard to the documents relating to a specific batch of a medicinal preparation imported at a time when the public health authorities of the Member State of importation already have in their possession a file relating to this medicinal preparation, these authorities have a legitimate interest in being able at any time to carry out a thorough check to make certain that the said batch complies with the particulars on the file.

24. Nevertheless, having regard to the nature of the market for the pharmaceutical product in question, it is necessary to ask whether this objective cannot be equally well achieved if the national administrations, instead of waiting passively for the desired evidence to be produced to them – and in a form calculated to give the manufacturer of the product and his duly appointed representatives an advantage – were to admit, where appropriate, similar evidence and, in particular, to adopt a more active policy which could enable every trader to obtain the necessary evidence.

25. This question is all the more important because parallel importers are very often in a position to offer the goods at a price lower than the one applied by the duly appointed importer for the same product, a fact which, where medicinal preparations are concerned, should, where appropriate, encourage the public health authorities not to place parallel imports at a disadvantage, since the effective protection of health and life of humans also demands that medicinal preparations should be sold at reasonable prices.

26. National authorities possess legislative and administrative methods capable of compelling the manufacturer or his duly appointed representative to supply particulars making it possible to ascertain that the medicinal preparation which is in fact the subject of parallel importation is identical with the medicinal preparation in respect of which they are already informed.

27. Moreover, simple co-operation between the authorities of the Member States would enable them to obtain on a reciprocal basis the documents necessary for checking certain largely standardized and widely distributed products.

28. Taking into account all these possible ways of obtaining information the national public health authorities must consider whether the effective protection of health and life of humans justifies a presumption of the non-conformity of an imported batch with the description of the medicinal preparation, or whether on the contrary it would not be sufficient to lay down a presumption of conformity with the result that, in appropriate cases, it would be for the administration to rebut this presumption.

29. Finally, even if it were absolutely necessary to require the parallel importer to prove this conformity, there would in any case be no justification under [Article 36 TFEU] for compelling him to do so with the help of documents to which he does not have access, when the administration, or as the case may be, the Court, finds that the evidence can be produced by other means.

The Court of Justice here accepted that Member States may need information on products which might be a risk to health, but pointed out that there may well be different ways of achieving this goal, and it is not legitimate for states to simply choose the method which imposes the least financial or administrative burden on them. The Court considered critically whether the various aspects of the Dutch scheme could not be made less burdensome for importers: Is it necessary to ask for documents when similar documents are already on file? Is it reasonable to expect an importer to obtain information from a competitor, when the state could obtain that information from authorities in other states? *De Peijper* is an example of the 'least restrictive option' rule being applied literally and thoroughly. As will be discussed below, this is not always the case.

The degree to which the Court of Justice can engage in *De Peijper*-like correction of the legislator depends on the complexity and subjectivity of the facts, but also on more subtle governance considerations. The principle that a measure must be the least restrictive option assumes a distinction between the objectives of a measure and the means used to pursue those objectives. The principle is not used to control the former. It does not decide on the level of protection, but is used instead to assess the latter by evaluating whether the means were the least restrictive necessary to secure these ends. Such analysis relies on the identification of a coherent series of ends or functions for the legislation, which the administration is assumed to be pursuing. The assumption of coherent or unitary objectives ignores the possibility of intra-institutional conflicts within ministries, and inter-institutional conflicts between different arms of government. The purpose of legislation may simply be to broker a compromise between different objectives; it may be deliberately contradictory. There is a danger that a judge may ignore this balance, by focusing on just one aim of the legislation and then declaring other aspects of the legislation unnecessary to that aim, and therefore illegal. Such analysis also obscures the distinction between policies and decisions. Whilst decisions are taken with regard to a particular factual situation, policies extend beyond the immediate scenario and deal with scenarios where facts are uncertain, and risk endemic. It may not be appropriate to attribute fixed objectives to them as circumstances change.

These tensions have led the Court of Justice not to apply the principle mechanistically. The intensity and form of the review has varied according to the type of subject matter reviewed.[74]

The Court has been most faithful to the strict *De Peijper* approach in its treatment of market externalities. In this field, one tends to find that the Court examines with some thoroughness whether the adopted measure was the least restrictive of trade necessary to secure its objectives.[75] It is here, therefore, that one finds most judicial intrusion into national policy-making.[76] The difficulty in distinguishing between ends and means has led the Court of Justice to curtail many policy options and set out fairly strict parameters as to what policy objectives are permissible in these fields. It is also in this field that its procedural bent has come most to the fore, as the section on public health below shows, and where it most explicitly puts the evidential burden on the restricting state. In *Leichtle*, concerning health care rules which

---

[74] G. de Búrca, 'The Principle of Proportionality and Its Application in EC Law' (1993) 13 *YBEL* 105.

[75] Case 124/81 *Commission* v *United Kingdom* [1983] ECR 203; Case C-67/97 *Bluhme* [1998] ECR I-8033.

[76] See e.g. Case C-322/01 *Deutscher Apothekerverband* v *DocMorris* [2003] ECR I-14887; Joined Cases C-338/04, C-359/04 and C-360/04 *Placanica, Palazzese and Soricchio* [2007] ECR I-1891; Case C-143/06 *Ludwigs–Apotheke München Internationale Apotheke* v *Juers Pharma Import-Export GmbH* [2007] ECR I-9623; Case C-421/09 *Humanplasma* [2010] ECR I-12869.

impacted on free movement of services, the Court said that 'the reasons which may be invoked by a Member State by way of justification must be accompanied by an analysis of the appropriateness and proportionality of the restrictive measure adopted by that State' and went on in the next paragraph to find that the Member State had failed to supply evidence demonstrating the necessity of its measures.[77] An even stronger statement is found in *Commission* v *Austria*, where heavy goods trucks were prohibited on certain stretches of motorway, on air quality grounds.[78] Having accepted the need for measures, and that the measures in question were effective, the Court then said:

> As the Court stated in Case C-320/03 *Commission* v *Austria*, paragraph 87, before adopting a measure so radical as a total traffic ban on a section of motorway constituting a vital route of communication between certain Member States, the Austrian authorities were under a duty to examine carefully the possibility of using measures less restrictive of freedom of movement, and discount them only if their inappropriateness to the objective pursued was clearly established.[79]

It went on to find that Austria was in breach of Article 28 TFEU purely because it had not demonstrated that alternative, less restrictive measures, could not be effective. This puts a strict burden of proof on Member States, and an almost procedural obligation to make policy in a certain kind of way.

The position is more complicated with regard to measures protecting local socio-cultural preferences and traditions. These are often quirky and particularistic. Their value lies not so much in realising some general goal, but in reinforcing the identity of a community or region. As a consequence, it is very difficult to separate the institutions and legislation protecting these traditions and preferences from the tradition itself. It is also very difficult for the Court of Justice to provide a general statement about the nature and value of the tradition to act as a standard for review. This has led to a variety of approaches being present in the judgments. In many cases in this field, a fairly marginal standard of review is adopted. In *UTECA*, concerning Spanish rules requiring film companies to reserve a percentage of their income for financing films in local languages, the Court asked itself whether the measure went beyond what was necessary to protect 'Spanish multilingualism' and noted '[t]he documents submitted to the Court do not contain any material which might lead to the conclusion that such a percentage is disproportionate in relation to the objective pursued', an apparent reversal of the usual burden of proof.[80] In *Sayn Wittgenstein*, where an Austrian ban on the use of noble titles was claimed to reflect a constitutional commitment to equality, the Court accepted the measure without discussion of evidence or alternatives, on the basis that it did not appear to go further than was necessary.[81] By contrast, in other cases within this general field, such as *Bosman*, the Court has been more rigorous, engaging in examination of less restrictive alternatives.[82] The difference between the groups is probably explained by the degree to which the Court actually accepts that it is social preferences and values which are at stake: in that case a hands-off, evidence-light approach can be justified. By contrast, where it sees the measures as primarily

---

[77] Case C-8/02 *Leichtle* v *Bundesanstalt für Arbeit* [2004] ECR I-2641.

[78] Case C-28/09 *Commission* v *Austria*, Judgment of 21 December 2011.

[79] *Ibid.* para. 140.

[80] See e.g. Case C-434/04 *Ahokainen* [2006] ECR I-9171; Case C-192/01 *Commission* v *Denmark* [2003] ECR I-9693.

[81] Case C-209/08 *Sayn Wittgenstein* [2010] ECR I-13693.

[82] Case C-415/93 *Union Royale Belge des Sociétés de Football Association and others* v *Bosman and others* [1995] ECR I-4921.

pragmatic economic or social policy, it is more critical. The difficulty with this distinction, however, is that the function and importance of a measure is often contested: whether *Bosman* was primarily about the economics of the football industry or the preservation of a social institution is still debated.

Gambling is an example of a policy area where many concerns meet and the difficulty in finding just the right approach is manifest. Restrictions often serve, to some extent, subtle social, cultural and policy goals. The presence of a national lottery monopoly, for example, may mean that the government can exert influence over marketing and other commercial behaviour, as well as contributing to social cohesion. The fragmentation of the industry might result in both upscale and distinctly down-market gambling businesses emerging, which in the long-term could present a regulatory and social challenge. Yet Member States have not shown themselves to be good at explaining such things, and before the Court of Justice tend to focus on the more measurable and objective goals, such as the prevention of fraud and crime, perhaps feeling on safer legal ground with such issues.[83] However, the consequence has been to put the cases firmly in the evidence-based group, often to the detriment of state rules. The Court, following the lead of Member States, has focused on the more concrete and pragmatic issues, and engaged in intrusive review. While it has repeatedly found that administrations have a margin of appreciation because of the particular moral, social and cultural features associated with gambling,[84] it has nevertheless often found national measures to be unduly restrictive after a thorough examination of their logic.

In *Gambelli*,[85] Italian legislation granted a monopoly in the making of sporting bets to a state enterprise, CONI. Gambelli was prosecuted for breaching this monopoly by taking sporting bets for Stanley, an English bookmaker. In Italy, such activity was illegal and was punishable by a term of imprisonment of between six months and three years.

Case C-243/01 *Gambelli* [2003] ECR I-13031

72. Finally, the restrictions imposed by the Italian legislation must not go beyond what is necessary to attain the end in view. In that context the national court must consider whether the criminal penalty imposed on any person who from his home connects by Internet to a bookmaker established in another Member State is not disproportionate in the light of the Court's case law ... especially where involvement in betting is encouraged in the context of games organised by licensed national bodies.

73. The national court will also need to determine whether the imposition of restrictions, accompanied by criminal penalties of up to a year's imprisonment, on intermediaries who facilitate the provision of services by a bookmaker in a Member State other than that in which those services are offered by making an Internet connection to that bookmaker available to bettors at their premises is a restriction that goes beyond what is necessary to combat fraud, especially where the supplier of the service is subject in his Member State of establishment to a regulation entailing controls and penalties, where

---

83 Cf. Case C-447/08 *Sjöberg and Gerdin* [2010] ECR I-6921.
84 Case C-275/92 *HM Customs and Excise* v *Schindler* [1994] ECR I-1039; Case C-124/97 *Läärä* v *Kihlakunnansyyttäjä* [1999] ECR I-6067; Case C-67/98 *Questore di Verona* v *Zenatti* [1999] ECR I-7289; Joined Cases C-338/04, C-359/04 and C-360/04 *Placanica, Palazzese and Soricchio* [2007] ECR I-1891; Case C-42/07 *Liga Portuguesa de Futebol Profissional and Bwin International Ltd* v *Departamento de Jogos da Santa Casa da Misericórdia de Lisboa*, Judgment of 8 September 2009; Case C-258/08 *Ladbrokes* [2010] ECR I-4757.
85 Case C-243/01 *Gambelli* [2003] ECR I-13031.

the intermediaries are lawfully constituted, and where, before the statutory amendments effected by Law No. 388/00, those intermediaries considered that they were permitted to transmit bets on foreign sporting events.

74. As to the proportionality of the Italian legislation … even if the objective of the authorities of a Member State is to avoid the risk of gaming licensees being involved in criminal or fraudulent activities, to prevent capital companies quoted on regulated markets of other Member States from obtaining licences to organise sporting bets, especially where there are other means of checking the accounts and activities of such companies, may be considered to be a measure which goes beyond what is necessary to check fraud.

The final field concerns the protection of the machinery of the state. This raises institutionally sensitive matters, as the economic freedoms are being invoked to challenge the national government's right and capacity to govern. The position of the Court of Justice depends on the sensitivity of the matter. In areas perceived to be less sensitive and where the government is capable of reorganising itself to realise the same goals, such as protection of the coherence of the fiscal system, the Court just looks at whether the measure is the least restrictive necessary to secure its objectives, quite commonly suggesting alternative approaches to preventing tax evasion, such as a greater reliance on cooperation between national tax authorities, rather than the automatic application of punitive rules and rigid presumptions wherever the mere possibility of tax evasion is present.[86] In areas which are both more sensitive and where judicial intervention is less frequent, such as national security, a more marginal form of review is taken. The Court does not look to see whether the measure is the least restrictive necessary so much as at the bona fides of the measure. In *Campus Oil*, the Irish Government required importers of petroleum to obtain a minimum of 35 per cent of their needs from the one Irish refinery, which had been set up to ensure an orderly supply of petrol onto the Irish market.[87] The Court of Justice found this minimum purchasing requirement to be lawful on the grounds that securing non-interruption of petrol supplies was essential to a state's security. It had been argued, however, that refineries could not secure a supply of oil, and maintenance of reserves would be a less restrictive way of securing this. A less onerous system of supporting the refinery than through a purchasing commitment might have been for the Irish Government to subsidise the refinery directly. The Court was dismissive of these arguments. It noted that having an independent refining capacity prevented a state being dependent upon foreign refineries and thus removed one threat to its security.

This does not give Member States a *carte blanche*. In *Commission* v *Greece*, the Court of Justice examined a Greek obligation on those marketing petrol to hold minimum stocks of petrol. It was unimpressed by a provision that allowed companies to transfer these obligations to refineries, so long as they had purchased petrol from those refineries in the last year.[88] The Court found that this requirement of prior purchase was not the least restrictive means available to secure petrol supply and was therefore illegal. The explanation for this stricter measure

---

[86] Case C-212/11 *Jyske Bank*, Judgment of 25 April 2013; Case C-383/10 *Commission* v *Belgium*, Judgment of 6 June 2013; Case C-155/08 *Passenheim-van Schoot* [2009] ECR I-5093; Case C-137/11 *Partena*, Judgment of 27 September 2012.

[87] Case 72/83 *Campus Oil* v *Minister for Industry and Energy* [1984] ECR 2727.

[88] Case C-398/98 *Commission* v *Greece* [2001] ECR I-7915.

of review can be found in the sheer protectionist nature of the measure and its lack of relationship to public security. It had less to do with ensuring stocks were maintained than with providing a subsidy to those who purchased petrol from Greek refineries.

Higher education is an aspect of the state that has been the subject of a large number of recent cases, many involving student migration and grants, but some also involving the problems which arise when the universities of a small country are flooded by students from a neighbouring large one. This has been the situation faced, or feared, in Belgium and Austria. Belgium introduced a quota for medical students who were not resident in Belgium, claiming that otherwise there would be a shortage of medical personnel staying in Belgium after their studies, raising a public health issue. This was litigated in *Bressol*, where the Court of Justice referred the question back to the national court after giving it detailed instructions on the kinds of evidence of a serious threat that it should insist the Belgian Government present.[89] The Austrians introduced rules making it harder for those with foreign qualifications to obtain a place at Austrian universities, and justified this, among other reasons, with the desire to safeguard the 'homogeneity' of the Austrian higher education system. Again, the Court imposed a high burden of proof on the state.

Case C-147/03 *Commission v Austria (Access to Universities)* [2005] ECR I-5969

63. Moreover, it is for the national authorities which invoke a derogation from the fundamental principle of freedom of movement for persons to show in each individual case that their rules are necessary and proportionate to attain the aim pursued. The reasons which may be invoked by a Member State by way of justification must be accompanied by an analysis of the appropriateness and proportionality of the restrictive measure adopted by that State and specific evidence substantiating its arguments.

64. In the present case, the Republic of Austria simply maintained at the hearing that the number of students registering for courses in medicine could be five times the number of available places, which would pose a risk to the financial equilibrium of the Austrian higher education system and, consequently, to its very existence.

65. It must be pointed out that no estimates relating to other courses have been submitted to the Court and that the Republic of Austria has conceded that it does not have any figures in that connection. Moreover, the Austrian authorities have accepted that the national legislation in question is essentially preventive in nature.

66. Consequently, it must be held that the Republic of Austria has failed to demonstrate that, in the absence of Paragraph 36 of the UnistG, the existence of the Austrian education system in general and the safeguarding of the homogeneity of higher education in particular would be jeopardised. The legislation in question is therefore incompatible with the objectives of the Treaty.

The Court of Justice is particularly critical of the fact that the Austrian Government is taking a 'preventive' measure, acting on the basis of a potential problem without showing quantitative evidence that this problem will be, or has been, realised.[90] Yet it can be difficult to produce convincing evidence of future flows of students. It is also hard for a Member State to accept

---

[89] Case C-73/08 *Bressol* [2010] ECR I-2735.

[90] See N. Nic Shuibhne and M. Maci, 'Proving Public Interest: The Growing Impact of Evidence in Free Movement Case Law' (2013) 50 *CML Rev.* 965.

that it should just wait and see, and only act once its higher education system is clearly struggling and failing to cope, since the reality of legislation and policy-making is that it cannot be put in place in an instant, and anticipating and preventing problems would normally be seen as good practice. On the other hand, one of the reasons why the Court is probably reluctant to be tolerant of state claims is that the risk of exclusionary and nationalistic action is quite real: if Member States are allowed to act on the basis of an unquantified potential risk then it is extremely likely that cross-border access to education – or indeed health, for the same evidential issues have arisen in that context[91] – will be widely restricted. Potential threats to movement justify limits to national policies,[92] but potential threats to national policy do not justify limits to movement.

Something which emerges from the cases above is that the proportionality principle is not always applied in the same way in the case law, which invites criticisms of inconsistency by the Court of Justice. Yet although the variation is real, it is inevitable that the interface between the economic freedoms and a great many diverse public interests will generate heterogeneous tensions, and apparent inconsistency may be a price worth paying if the alternative is insensitivity to national concerns. A more defining, and more precise, criticism is that the case law is too 'decisionistic', in that it is too preoccupied with outcomes,[93] and should be more concerned with the process of policy formation and decision-making. The emphasis on evidence and proof in cases such as *Leichtle, Commission* v *Austria (Heavy Goods Trucks)* and *Commission* v *Austria (Access to Universities)*, and the growing importance given to consistency in the judgments, both suggest that the Court is moving, albeit in small steps, in this direction.[94] Majone explains below the merits of the procedural approach.

G. Majone, *Evidence, Argument and Persuasion in the Policy Process* (New Haven, CT, Yale University Press, 1989) 17–18

A ... limitation of decisionism is its exclusive preoccupation with outcomes and lack of concern for the processes whereby the outcomes are produced. A lack of concern for process is justified in some situations. If the correctness or fairness of the outcome can be determined unambiguously, the manner in which the decision is made is often immaterial; only results count. But when the factual or value premises are moot, when there are no generally accepted criteria of rightness, the procedure of decision-making acquires special significance and cannot be treated as purely instrumental.

Even in formal decision analysis the explicit recognition of uncertainty forces a significant departure from a strict orientation toward outcomes. Under conditions of uncertainty different alternatives correspond to different probability distributions of the consequences, so that it is no longer possible to determine unambiguously what the optimal decision is. Hence, the usual criterion of rationality – according to which an action is rational if it can be explained as the choosing of the best means to achieve given objectives – is replaced by the weaker notion of consistency. The rational decision maker is no longer an optimiser, strictly speaking. All that is required now, and all that the principle of maximising expected utility guarantees, is that the choice be consistent with the decision maker's

---

[91] See p. 836. [92] See p. 805; Case 8/74 *Dassonville* [1974] ECR 837.

[93] For more specific arguments that EU law should be concerned with process in this field, see J. Scott, 'Of Kith and Kine (and Crustaceans): Trade and Environment in the EU and WTO' in J. Weiler (ed.), *The EU, NAFTA and the WTO: Towards a Common Law of International Trade* (Oxford, Oxford University Press, 2000).

[94] S. Prechal, 'Free Movement and Procedural Requirements: Proportionality Reconsidered' (2008) 35 *LIEI* 201.

valuations of the probability and utility of the various consequences. Notice that consistency is a procedural, not a substantive, criterion.

Exclusive preoccupation with outcomes is a serious limitation of decisionism, since social processes seldom have only instrumental value for the people who engage in them. In most areas of social activity, the processes and rules that constitute the enterprise and define the roles of its participants matter quite apart from any identifiable 'end state' that is ultimately produced. Indeed in many cases it is the process itself that matters most to those who take part in it.

(v) The measure must be procedurally fair

A condition for the legitimacy of a restriction is that the rights of the parties affected are sufficiently protected: that the powers of the national authorities imposing the restriction are defined in an objective and transparent way; that the parties affected have access to sufficient information to assess and challenge the measures; that courts have jurisdiction to consider these challenges; and that the systems for doing all these are reasonably accessible and speedy. The logic of these principles is that rights are only meaningful if they can be enforced and defended. In this light they are no more than is necessary or sensible to make the law effective. Yet they can be quite constraining and troublesome for Member States.[95]

An example is *French Vitamins*. In this case the Commission challenged French legislation which provided that food containing added nutrients that were not on an approved list endorsed by the French authorities had to be subject to a procedure of prior authorisation before it could be marketed. The procedure for this authorisation was often lengthy and took no account of regulatory tests carried out in other Member States.

Case C-24/00 *Commission v France (French Vitamins)* [2004] ECR I-1277

24. It [the French legislation] does not contain any provision ensuring the free movement of fortified foodstuffs lawfully manufactured and/or marketed in another Member State and for which a level of human health protection equivalent to that ensured in France is guaranteed, even if such products do not wholly satisfy the requirements of that legislation.
25. However, the Court has held that national legislation which makes the addition of a nutrient to a foodstuff lawfully manufactured and/or marketed in other Member States subject to prior authorisation is not, in principle, contrary to Community law, provided that certain conditions are satisfied ...
26. First, such legislation must make provision for a procedure enabling economic operators to have that nutrient included on the national list of authorised substances. The procedure must be one which is readily accessible and can be completed within a reasonable time, and, if it leads to a refusal, the decision of refusal must be open to challenge before the courts ...
27. Secondly, an application to obtain the inclusion of a nutrient on the national list of authorised substances may be refused by the competent national authorities only if such substance poses a genuine risk to public health ...

[95] See the section on welfare states at p. 837.

36. As is clear from paragraph 26 of this judgment, a procedure which requires prior authorisation, in the interest of public health, for the addition of a nutrient authorised in another Member State complies with Community law only if it is readily accessible and can be completed within a reasonable time and if, when it is refused, the refusal can be challenged before the courts.

37. As regards first the accessibility of the procedure in question in this case, a Member State's obligation to provide for such a procedure in the case of any national rule which on grounds of public health makes the addition of nutrients subject to authorisation cannot be fulfilled if that procedure is not expressly provided for in a measure of general application which is binding on the national authorities ...

38. By stating in their reply of 31 December 1998 to the reasoned opinion their intention of clarifying the French legislation by setting out in a legislative text the procedure for authorising the use of nutrients, the French authorities have recognised that, at least at the end of the period prescribed by the reasoned opinion, the national legislation did not formally provide for that procedure.

39. Whilst the French Government has prepared a notice to economic operators on the detailed rules for incorporating nutrients in foodstuffs for daily consumption which, it submits, fulfils that function, it is not apparent from the documents before the Court that such notice, assuming that it meets the requirements of Community law, was in force at the end of the period prescribed by the reasoned opinion.

40. Secondly, the examples provided by the Commission in its application reveal that applications for authorisation submitted by economic operators were not dealt with either within a reasonable period or according to a procedure which was sufficiently transparent as regards the possibility of challenging refusal to authorise before the courts.

41. Thus, in the case of the application for authorisation relating to the drink Red Bull, the applicant waited nearly seven months for acknowledgement of receipt of its application and more than two years to be informed of the decision to refuse it.

French Vitamins applies general principles of administrative due process, such as duties of transparency, efficiency and judicial accountability.[96] However, none of these will achieve the intended results if they are purely applied to the process of appealing, and not to the decision itself and the powers behind that decision. A recurring problem in the case law is that national authorities have vague and discretionary powers. These make it hard to formulate a precise objection to a decision, and make it unlikely that a national court will uphold that objection. For this reason the Court of Justice has consistently objected to imprecise powers, even in sensitive policy fields.

In *Église de Scientologie de Paris*,[97] French law required any direct foreign investment, subject to highly limited exceptions, to have prior authorisation from the French authorities. The French Government argued that this was necessary on grounds of public policy. The French authorities were accused, however, of exercising their discretion in an arbitrary manner.

[96] See also Case C-372/04 *Watts* [2006] ECR I-4325; Case C-333/08 *Commission v France* [2010] ECR I-757.
[97] Case C-54/99 *Église de Scientologie de Paris* v *Prime Minister* [2000] ECR I-1335.

Case C-54/99 *Église de Scientologie de Paris* v *Prime Minister* [2000] ECR I-1335

20. In the case of direct foreign investments, the difficulty in identifying and blocking capital once it has entered a Member State may make it necessary to prevent, at the outset, transactions which would adversely affect public policy or public security. It follows that, in the case of direct foreign investments which constitute a genuine and sufficiently serious threat to public policy and public security, a system of prior declaration may prove to be inadequate to counter such a threat.

21. In the present case, however, the essence of the system in question is that prior authorisation is required for every direct foreign investment which is such as to represent a threat to public policy [and] public security, without any more detailed definition. Thus, the investors concerned are given no indication whatever as to the specific circumstances in which prior authorisation is required.

22. Such lack of precision does not enable individuals to be apprised of the extent of their rights and obligations deriving from [Article 63 TFEU]. That being so, the system established is contrary to the principle of legal certainty.

Analogous reasoning is found in a large number of cases concerning investment restrictions.[98] Concern over who may own or influence strategic industries is justifiable, but catch-all authorisation schemes are unacceptable: restrictions must be based on specific, objective criteria; these criteria must be known in advance; authorisations must be accessible and speedy, given the particular importance of time to investment issues; and they must be open to challenge in court.[99]

Nevertheless, it is not the case that the Court of Justice rejects any role for discretion in decision-making. Where interests are complex and non-quantifiable it may be unavoidable, and the test then is whether it is sufficiently constrained to ensure that it is exercised in a fair and non-discriminatory way.[100]

Case C-470/11 *Garkalns*, Judgment of 19 July 2012

41. In those circumstances, it must be ascertained whether the restriction on the freedom to provide services imposed by the national legislation at issue in the main proceedings is appropriate for achieving the objective of protecting consumers against the risks linked to betting and gaming and whether it does not go beyond what is necessary to achieve that objective.

42. In addition, in order to be consistent with the principle of equal treatment and to meet the obligation of transparency which flows from that principle, an authorisation scheme for betting and gaming must be based on objective, non-discriminatory criteria known in advance, in such a way as to circumscribe the exercise by the authorities of their discretion so that it is not used arbitrarily.

43. In order to enable the impartiality of the authorisation procedures to be monitored, it is also necessary for the competent authorities to base each of their decisions on reasoning which is

---

[98] Case C-222/97 *Trummer and Mayer* [1999] ECR I-1661; Case C-483/99 *Commission v France* [2002] ECR I-4781; Case C-503/99 *Commission v Belgium* [2002] ECR I-4809; Case C-174/04 *Commission v Italy (Free Movement of Capital)* [2005] ECR I-4933; Joined Cases C-282/04 and C-283/04 *Commission v Netherlands (Direct and Portfolio Investments)* [2006] ECR I-9141; Case C-567/09 *Woningstichting Sint Servatius*, Judgment of 1 October 2009.

[99] *Ibid.*   [100] See also Case C-197/11 *Libert*, Judgment of 8 May 2013.

accessible to the public, stating precisely the reasons for which, as the case may be, authorisation has been refused.

44. In that connection, the Court has held that it is for the national courts to ensure, in the light, in particular, of the actual rules for applying the restrictive legislation concerned, that that legislation genuinely meets the concern to reduce opportunities for gambling and to limit activities in that domain in a consistent and systematic manner.

45. In the case under consideration, it cannot be denied that, as is apparent from the order for reference, in allowing authorisation to open an amusement arcade to be refused on grounds of substantial impairment of the interests of the State and of the residents of the administrative area concerned, the national legislation at issue in the main proceedings confers a broad discretion on the administrative authorities, particularly for the purposes of assessing the interests which that legislation is intended to protect.

46. Discretion, such as that at issue in the main proceedings, could be justified if the national legislation itself were genuinely intended to meet the concern to reduce opportunities for gambling and to limit activities in that domain in a consistent and systematic manner, or to ensure that local residents can live in peace or even, generally, to preserve public order, by conferring on the local authorities, for that purpose, a certain discretion in applying the rules relating to the organisation of betting and gaming.

47. In order to assess the proportionality of the national legislation at issue, it is therefore for the national court to verify, in particular, that the State strictly supervises the activities related to betting and gaming; that the refusal of the local authorities to authorise the opening of new establishments of that type genuinely pursues the declared objective of protecting consumers; and that the criterion of 'substantial impairment of the interests of the State and of the residents of the administrative area concerned' is applied without discrimination.

A slightly different kind of problem arose in *French Processing Aids*.[101] This case was very similar to *French Vitamins*, except that it concerned authorisation for foods containing additives to do with processing (for example, preservatives), rather than vitamins. The particular problem in this case was that thanks to contradictory national legal measures it was not quite clear what the legal position was, and what those marketing imported foodstuffs were exactly required to do. The Court of Justice found that the various laws and decrees 'have created a situation of legal uncertainty which itself constitutes an unjustified obstacle to Article 28 EC'.[102] Once again, if people cannot know their rights, they will not be able to protect them.

5 ENVIRONMENTAL PROTECTION

Protection of the environment has been used to justify a number of types of national restriction.[103] Member States are permitted to take measures prohibiting environmentally harmful activities where the ecological costs of an activity are obvious and high. A French prohibition on the burning of waste oils was, therefore, found to be compatible with Article 56 TFEU on the grounds that it protected the environment. In like vein, the Court of Justice has approved measures that ban chlorofluorocarbons or other ozone-depleting substances.[104] Member States

---

[101] Case C-333/08 *Commission* v *France* [2010] ECR I-757.   [102] *Ibid.* para. 111.   [103] See also pp. 783–5.
[104] Case C-341/95 *Bettati* v *Safety Hi-Tech* [1998] ECR I-4355; Case C-284/95 *Safety Hi-Tech* v *S and T* [1998] ECR I-4301.

must still show, however, that there are no other, less restrictive means of protecting the environment. In *Aher-Waggon*, a challenge was made to German restrictions on permissible noise emissions from aircraft.[105] These measures were stricter than those permitted by EU legislation. It was argued that there were less restrictive means of limiting noise, such as restricting the amount of flights or planning restrictions on the sites of airports. The Court, nevertheless, upheld the German restriction because it was convinced that these other options were not in fact feasible.

Member States can also take measures to protect biodiversity. The most interesting case is *Bluhme*.[106] The case suggests that biodiversity is to be protected under the heading of protection of the health of animals rather than that of protection of the environment, and that Member States are to be given considerable leeway to protect fauna or flora. It concerned a Danish law allowing only Læsø brown bees to be kept on the island of Læsø in Denmark. Bluhme argued that this restriction, which was in order to protect the dissolution of the local brown bee population through mating with other bees, could not be justified ecologically as the brown bee was not a distinct species in its own right.

Case C-67/97 *Bluhme* [1998] ECR I-8033

33. ... the Court considers that measures to preserve an indigenous animal population with distinct characteristics contribute to the maintenance of biodiversity by ensuring the survival of the population concerned. By so doing, they are aimed at protecting the life of those animals and are capable of being justified under Article [36 TFEU].

34. From the point of view of such conservation of biodiversity, it is immaterial whether the object of protection is a separate subspecies, a distinct strain within any given species or merely a local colony, so long as the populations in question have characteristics distinguishing them from others and are therefore judged worthy of protection either to shelter them from a risk of extinction that is more or less imminent, or, even in the absence of such risk, on account of a scientific or other interest in preserving the pure population at the location concerned.

35. It does, however, have to be determined whether the national legislation was necessary and proportionate in relation to its aim of protection, or whether it would have been possible to achieve the same result by less stringent measures ...

36. Conservation of biodiversity through the establishment of areas in which a population enjoys special protection, which is a method recognised in the Rio Convention, especially Article 8a thereof, is already put into practice in Community law [in particular, by means of the special protection areas provided for in Council Directive 79/409/EEC of 2 April 1979 on the conservation of wild birds [1979] OJ L103/1, or the special conservation areas provided for in Directive 92/43/EC].

37. As for the threat of [the disappearance] of the Læsø brown bee, it is undoubtedly genuine in the event of mating with golden bees by reason of the recessive nature of the genes of the brown bee. The establishment by the national legislation of a protection area within which the keeping of bees other than Læsø brown bees is prohibited, for the purpose of ensuring the survival of the latter, therefore constitutes an appropriate measure in relation to the aim pursued.

---

[105] Case C-389/96 *Aher-Waggon* v *Federal Republic of Germany* [1998] ECR I-4473.
[106] Case C-67/97 *Bluhme* [1998] ECR I-8033.

The judgment is unusual in placing the Member State restriction in the context of international conventions. Environmental protection is an atypical ground for derogation because it is also an EU goal. There is not always a simple balance to be made between the Union interest in movement and the national interest in a restriction. Rather, the Union may have as great an interest as the Member State in the restriction, particularly where the environmental concerns are not strictly local as is the case with biodiversity and climate change.

An example of this latter goal justifying an apparently discriminatory measure is *PreussenElektra*. The German Government required electricity retailers to buy a proportion of their electricity from wind farms in Germany, the aim being to stimulate such farms and make them viable, and so reduce global warming. Such a measure is clearly both protectionist and directly discriminatory, but it is also, arguably, one of the most practical ways of stimulating a domestic green energy sector, particularly since the law on state aids imposes constraints on direct subsidy. The Court of Justice's judgment was, like that in *Bluhme*, notably context-aware and discursive. The cases suggest that where current environmental crises are in issue, the Court may take a less hostile approach to Member State derogations than is normally the case.

Case C–379/98 *PreussenElektra* [2001] ECR I–2099

70. Secondly, the case law of the Court also shows that an obligation placed on traders in a Member State to obtain a certain percentage of their supplies of a given product from a national supplier limits to that extent the possibility of importing the same product by preventing those traders from obtaining supplies in respect of part of their needs from traders situated in other Member States....

72. However, in order to determine whether such a purchase obligation is nevertheless compatible with Article [34 TFEU], account must be taken, first, of the aim of the provision in question, and, second, of the particular features of the electricity market.

73. The use of renewable energy sources for producing electricity, which a statute such as the amended Stromeinspeisungsgesetz is intended to promote, is useful for protecting the environment insofar as it contributes to the reduction in emissions of greenhouse gases which are amongst the main causes of climate change which the European Community and its Member States have pledged to combat.

74. Growth in that use is amongst the priority objectives which the Community and its Member States intend to pursue in implementing the obligations which they contracted by virtue of the United Nations Framework Convention on Climate Change, approved on behalf of the Community by Council Decision 94/69/EC of 15 December 1993 (OJ 1994 L 33, p. 11), and by virtue of the Protocol of the third conference of the parties to that Convention, done in Kyoto on 11 December 1997, signed by the European Community and its Member States on 29 April 1998 (see inter alia Council Resolution 98/C 198/01 of 8 June 1998 on renewable sources of energy (OJ 1998 C 198, p. 1), and Decision No. 646/2000/EC of the European Parliament and of the Council of 28 February 2000 adopting a multiannual programme for the promotion of renewable energy sources in the Community (Altener) (1998 to 2002) (OJ 2000 L 79, p. 1)).

75. It should be noted that that policy is also designed to protect the health and life of humans, animals and plants.

76. Moreover, as stated in the third sentence of the first subparagraph of Article [11 TFEU], environmental protection requirements must be integrated into the definition and implementation of other Community policies ...

77. In addition, the 28th recital in the preamble to Directive 96/92 expressly states that it is 'for reasons of environmental protection' that the latter authorises Member States in Articles 8(3) and 11(3) to give priority to the production of electricity from renewable sources.

78. It should also be noted that, as stated in the 39th recital in its preamble, the directive constitutes only a further phase in the liberalisation of the electricity market and leaves some obstacles to trade in electricity between Member States in place.

79. Moreover, the nature of electricity is such that, once it has been allowed into the transmission or distribution system, it is difficult to determine its origin and in particular the source of energy from which it was produced.

80. In that respect, the Commission took the view, in its Proposal for a Directive 2000/C 311 E/22 of the European Parliament and of the Council on the promotion of electricity from renewable energy sources in the internal electricity market (OJ 2000 C 311 E, p. 320), submitted on 10 May 2000, that the implementation in each Member State of a system of certificates of origin for electricity produced from renewable sources, capable of being the subject of mutual recognition, was essential in order to make trade in that type of electricity both reliable and possible in practice.

81. Having regard to all the above considerations, the answer to the third question must be that, in the current state of Community law concerning the electricity market, legislation such as the amended Stromeinspeisungsgesetz is not incompatible with Article [34 TFEU].

It is not clear from the judgment whether a Treaty derogation or a mandatory requirement is being relied upon. This is partly because the Treaty does not in fact contain an environmental exception, the free movement of goods derogation, Article 36 TFEU, referring instead to the life and health of humans, animals and plants. This could be interpreted to cover all kinds of environmental harm, but it is sometimes an uncomfortable stretch, leading the Court of Justice in this case to choose studied ambiguity. The absence of a clear naming of the environment in Article 36 is distinctly old-fashioned, but the Court is clearly not going to allow this to have undesirable consequences.

That is very evident in *Commission* v *Austria*, where a ban on heavy goods traffic on certain roads was in issue. The judgment makes clear that the protection of the environment is clearly in no sense a less powerful or important basis for a derogation than is public health, merely because the latter is in the Treaty and the former is not.

Case C–28/09 *Commission* v *Austria (Heavy Goods Trucks)*, Judgment of 21 December 2011

119. It is settled case-law that national measures liable to obstruct intra-Community trade may be justified on one of the public-interest grounds set out in Article 30 EC, such as the protection of human health and life, or one of the overriding requirements relating inter alia to protection of the environment, provided that the measures in question are proportionate to the objective sought.

120. It should be recalled that the protection of health and the protection of the environment are essential objectives of the European Union. Article 2 EC states that the Community has, as one of its tasks, to promote 'a high level of protection and improvement of the quality of the environment' and Article 3(1)

(p) EC states that the activities of the Community are to include a contribution to the attainment of 'a high level of health protection'.

121. Furthermore, in accordance with Articles 6 EC and 152(1) EC, the requirements of environmental protection and public health must be taken into account in the definition and implementation of Community policies and activities. The transversal and fundamental nature of those objectives is also reaffirmed in Articles 37 and 35 respectively of the Charter.

122. As to the relationship between the objectives of protection of the environment and protection of health, it is apparent from Article 174(1) EC that the protection of human health is one of the objectives of Community policy on the environment. Those objectives are closely linked, in particular in connection with the fight against air pollution, the purpose of which is to limit the dangers to health connected with the deterioration of the environment. The objective of protection of health is therefore already incorporated, in principle, in the objective of protection of the environment.

123. In those circumstances, the arguments of the Republic of Austria on protection of health need not be considered separately from those on protection of the environment.

Another type of environmental restriction which has been considered by the Court of Justice concerns the transportation of waste. In *Walloon Waste*, the Court considered a Wallonian ban on the import of waste from anywhere outside that region of Belgium.[107] The Court accepted the measure was justified on the basis of the proximity principle, namely, that waste should be disposed of as close to the place of production as possible. The ecological basis for such a principle is that it avoids the environmental costs and risks of transporting the waste and establishes a principle of environmental equity. Clean places are not to bear the environmental costs generated by dirty places. However, the judgment is contentious. The reach of the proximity principle is unclear. *Walloon Waste* covered a regional restriction, but it is far harder to justify a similar national restriction, as that would permit waste to be transported over long distances. More fundamentally, the principle is unsatisfactory as an instrument for allocating environmental costs.[108] Most industrial waste is produced in locations far away from where the good is consumed and, in an integrated European economy, it is not really fair to expect the people who live close to the factory to bear the full cost of disposal. The inevitable duplication of facilities associated with such a principle, in addition, increases the risk of waste facilities being placed in locations which, in ecological terms, are far from ideal and deprives operators of the most suitable sites for waste disposal.

The operation of the proximity principle is made more difficult by the use of different reasoning for waste for recovery. In *Afvalstoffen Dusseldorp*,[109] an application to export two loads of oil filters for processing was refused by the Dutch authorities on the grounds that, under Dutch law, export of waste for recovery was only permitted if there were superior processing techniques abroad or there was insufficient capacity in the Netherlands. The Court of Justice noted that such an export restriction provided an advantage for national facilities. It

---

[107] Case C-2/90 *Commission v Belgium (Walloon Waste)* [1992] ECR I-4431.

[108] P. von Wilmowsky, 'Waste Disposal in the Internal Market: The State of Play after the ECJ's Ruling on the Walloon Import Ban' (1993) 30 *CMLRev.* 541, 547–7; D. Chalmers, 'Community Policy on Waste Management: Managing Environmental Decline Gently' (1994) 14 *YBEL* 257, 280–4.

[109] Case C-203/96 *Chemische Afvalstoffen Dusseldorp BV and others v Minister van Volkhuisvesting, Ruimtelijke Ordening en Milieubeheer* [1998] ECR I-4075.

enabled the Dutch undertaking, AVR Chemie, which recovered the waste, to operate in a profitable manner and to use the filters as a cheap source of fuel. The Court found that there was no evidence of a health risk resulting from transport, and so no justification for the restriction on export of waste with an economic value. From an ecological perspective, however, the transport risks for both forms of waste are the same, and there is still the danger of dirty regions offloading waste onto clean regions. Advocates of the proximity principle have therefore been highly critical of *Dusseldorp*.[110] It may be that the reasons for the distinction are more pragmatic, economic ones. Waste for recovery is a large and growing industry. Preventing its development on a European scale might bring some environmental benefits, but would also bring significant economic costs.[111]

6 PUBLIC HEALTH

The exception most frequently invoked before the Court of Justice is that of public health. In its initial case law, the Court simply looked at the answers provided by international science. If there was doubt or international science ruled something unsafe, a Member State would be justified in banning the product. Increasingly, this test appeared unsatisfactory.[112] In many scenarios knowledge developed, so what had formerly appeared certain was now less so. In other scenarios, it would be unrealistic to assume zero risk as this would be something that science could never certify. Therefore, the Court of Justice has increasingly moved towards a proceduralist test of whether a sufficiently rigorous risk assessment has been carried out. An example of this new approach is *Dutch Vitamins*.[113] With a couple of exceptions, Dutch legislation prohibited the addition of a number of vitamins to foods. The Dutch argument was not that these vitamins were dangerous in themselves, but that ingestion of excess quantities could be dangerous. In this, they relied on general studies. There was no study that estimated the likelihood of risk. For this reason, the Court of Justice found the Dutch legislation to be illegal. It stated its general approach in the following manner.

Case C-41/02 Commission v Netherlands (Dutch Vitamins) [2004] ECR I-11375

45. It is clear from [Article 191 TFEU] that the protection of human health is one of the objectives of the Community policy on the environment, that that policy aims at a high level of protection and is to be based inter alia on the precautionary principle, and that the requirements of that policy must be integrated into the definition and implementation of other Community policies. In addition, it follows from the case law of the Court that the precautionary principle may also apply in policy on the protection of human health which, according to [Article 168 TFEU] likewise aims at a high level of protection ...

---

[110] N. Notaro, 'The New Generation Case Law on Trade and Environment' (2000) 25 *ELRev*. 467.

[111] Movements of waste within the European Union are now governed exclusively by Regulation 259/93 on the supervision and control of shipments of waste [1993] OJ L30/11. This retains the distinction made in the case law, however: Case C-324/99 *DaimlerChrysler* v *Land Baden-Württemberg* [2001] ECR I-9897. For discussion, see G. van Calster, 'The Free Movement of Waste after *DaimlerChrysler*' (2002) 27 *ELRev*. 610.

[112] Case 272/80 *Frans-Nederlandse Maatschappij voor Biologische Producten* [1981] ECR 3277.

[113] Case C-41/02 *Commission* v *Netherlands (Dutch Vitamins)* [2004] ECR I-11375. See also Case C-319/05 *Commission* v *Germany* [2007] ECR I-9811; Case C-88/07 *Commission* v *Spain*, Judgment of 5 March 2009.

46. However, in exercising their discretion relating to the protection of public health, the Member States must comply with the principle of proportionality. The means which they choose must therefore be confined to what is actually necessary to ensure the safeguarding of public health; they must be proportional to the objective thus pursued, which could not have been attained by measures which are less restrictive of intra-Community trade.

47. Furthermore, since [Article 36 TFEU] provides for an exception, to be interpreted strictly, to the rule of free movement of goods within the Community, it is for the national authorities which invoke it to show in each case, in the light of national nutritional habits and in the light of the results of international scientific research, that their rules are necessary to give effective protection to the interests referred to in that provision and, in particular, that the marketing of the products in question poses a real risk for public health …

48. A prohibition on the marketing of foodstuffs to which nutrients have been added must therefore be based on a detailed assessment of the risk alleged by the Member State invoking [Article 36 TFEU] …

49. A decision to prohibit the marketing of a fortified foodstuff, which indeed constitutes the most restrictive obstacle to trade in products lawfully manufactured and marketed in other Member States, can be adopted only if the real risk for public health alleged appears sufficiently established on the basis of the latest scientific data available at the date of the adoption of such decision. In such a context, the object of the risk assessment to be carried out by the Member State is to appraise the degree of probability of harmful effects on human health from the addition of certain nutrients to foodstuffs and the seriousness of those potential effects …

50. In assessing the risk in question, it is not only the particular effects of the marketing of an individual product containing a definite quantity of nutrients which are relevant. It could be appropriate to take into consideration the cumulative effect of the presence on the market of several sources, natural or artificial, of a particular nutrient and of the possible existence in the future of additional sources which can reasonably be foreseen …

51. In a number of cases, the assessment of those factors will demonstrate that there is much uncertainty, in science and in practice, in that regard. Such uncertainty, which is inseparable from the precautionary principle, affects the scope of the Member State's discretion and thus also the manner in which the precautionary principle is applied.

52. It must therefore be accepted that a Member State may, in accordance with the precautionary principle, take protective measures without having to wait until the existence and gravity of those risks become fully apparent.… However, the risk assessment cannot be based on purely hypothetical considerations …

53. A proper application of the precautionary principle requires, in the first place, the identification of the potentially negative consequences for health of the proposed addition of nutrients, and, secondly, a comprehensive assessment of the risk for health based on the most reliable scientific data available and the most recent results of international research …

54. Where it proves to be impossible to determine with certainty the existence or extent of the alleged risk because of the insufficiency, inconclusiveness or imprecision of the results of studies conducted, but the likelihood of real harm to public health persists should the risk materialise, the precautionary principle justifies the adoption of restrictive measures.

Dutch Vitamins suggests that, following a risk assessment, if the Member State finds a likelihood of real harm then, based on the precautionary principle, it can ban the good.

This leaves open the question whether Member States may impose restrictions for reasons of nutrition. This is a particular concern as the dangers posed by obesity mount in the European population. In *Sandoz*, permission was sought to market muesli bars to which vitamins A and D had been added. Authorisation was refused on the grounds that although these vitamins were necessary for a healthy life, too much of them could be dangerous. The Court of Justice held that Member States could ban a substance if there was a danger that it could be taken to excess as part of the general nutrition, and the individual amounts consumed could neither be monitored nor foreseen.[114] In *French Vitamins*, a broader ban was involved. The French authorities refused to allow vitamins or nutrients to be added to food unless there was a nutritional need.[115] The Court found this restriction to be unlawful. The blanket ban was not based on specific dangers, but just on the general view that such additives were not necessary. This fact could not, in itself, justify a ban. Even very small concrete risks can justify measures, but purely nutritional aspects of food are reserved to the sovereignty of the consumer.[116]

Restrictions on nutritional content can only be imposed, therefore, if the nutritional content of the good is felt to lead to some harm or be part of some threat to public health. An argument to this effect could certainly be made with respect to fat or carbohydrate levels in food, and it would not be difficult to produce relevant scientific evidence. The approach in *Sandoz* could be used to justify regulation of food aimed at combating obesity. Just like vitamins A and D, fats and carbohydrates are essential in some quantities, and dangerous in excess. Nevertheless, the politics and economics of such regulation would clearly be quite different, as the rules would have a far broader effect, and would also be difficult to adopt in a coherent and consistent way – many traditional and natural foods are as fatty as processed ones. The Court of Justice has not closed the door to the use of food law to attack obesity, but the demands of proportionality and consistency would make such a policy challenging.

A criticism of the case law is that it is too narrow. By focusing exclusively on demonstrable threats it chooses a test that is different from that chosen by many consumers when they decide whether food is safe or not. The latter weave in considerations such as how the food is produced, by whom and the effect on the environment. Trust in the producer, ideas about naturalness and purity, and mistrust of scientific progress, may all influence the consumer in her judgments about the risks food poses to her.[117] These may not be factors for which expert evidence can be produced, but they are relevant to consumers, so should they not be relevant to the law?

B. Wynne, 'Scientific Knowledge and the Global Environment' in M. Redclift and T. Benton (eds.), *Social Theory and the Global Environment* (London, Routledge, 1994) 169, 175–6

[I]t is now commonplace to find the inevitable limitations of scientific knowledge recognized as a fact of life which policy-makers and publics should learn to accept. Thus scientific uncertainty is widely discussed as the cross which policy-makers have to bear, and the main obstacle to better and

---

[114] Case 174/82 *Sandoz* [1983] ECR 5094.

[115] Case C-24/00 *Commission v France (French Vitamins)* [2004] ECR I-1277. See also Case C-192/01 *Commission v Denmark* [2003] ECR I-9693.

[116] For a measure held lawful that constituted a minuscule risk to health, see Case C-121/00 *Hahn* [2002] ECR I-9193.

[117] See G. Davies, 'Morality Clauses and Decision-making in Situations of Scientific Uncertainty: The Case of GMOs' (2007) 6 *World Trade Review* 249.

more consensual or authoritative policies. Yet much of this debate still assumes that if only scientific knowledge could develop enough to reduce the technical uncertainty, then basic social consensus would follow, assuming that people could be educated into the truth as revealed by science.

There are two main sociological strands of criticism of this dominant conventional perspective. The interests-oriented strand would note that even within the constraints of an accepted natural knowledge consensus, legitimate social interests – and hence favoured policies – can be in conflict. A perspective from the sociology of knowledge would go further, to argue that dominant interests control expertise and hence shape the available knowledge to reinforce their interests.

A more radical strand would suggest that beneath the level of conflicting explicit preferences or interests lies a deeper sense in which scientific knowledge tacitly reflects and reproduces normative models of social relations, cultural and moral identities, as if these are natural. Thus, for example, the level of intellectual aggregation of environmental data and variables such as radio caesium in the environment, when used to establish and justify restrictions on farmers operating in that environment, is effectively prescribing that degree of social or administrative standardization of the farmers. In other words, at a deeper level than explicit interests the form in which scientific knowledge is practically articulated prescribes important aspects of their social relations and identities. In research on the interactions of scientists and farmers after Chernobyl, this point came out as the farmers' detailed and differentiated local knowledge of the environment and what it meant for optimal farming methods, even in the same valley, were denied by scientific knowledge whose 'natural' form aggregated and deleted them into single, uniform data categories combining and homogenising several different valleys and many farmers. As one farmer caught by the Chernobyl restrictions lamented in this respect: 'this is what they can't understand; they think a farm is a farm and a ewe is a ewe. They think we just stamp them off a production line or something'.

The other question to arise is one concerning the administration of health restrictions. Whilst sampling of imports will often be permitted on grounds of public health, the Court of Justice has shown itself to be unsympathetic to systematic analysis. It was held disproportionate, in the absence of fraud or irregularities, for the French authorities to inspect three out of four consignments of Italian wine, and the Court, in its interim measures, ordered the French to inspect no more than 15 per cent of the consignments.[118] Conversely, a Directive authorising national authorities to check one in three consignments was not considered to be dispropor-tionate.[119] This is an area, however, where there can clearly be very little certainty, as the number of inspections that may be permissible will depend upon the nature of the goods and other circumstances, such as whether there has been a recent outbreak of a particular disease.

7 PUBLIC POLICY, PUBLIC SECURITY AND PUBLIC MORALITY

Public policy, public security and public morality are treated as separate headings in the Trea-ty. Historically, they have also been treated differently in the case law. Public policy and public security have been treated, on the one hand, as interchangeably protecting the fundamental

---

[118] Case 42/82 *Commission* v *France* [1983] ECR 1013.
[119] Directive 77/93/EEC [1977] OJ L26/20. Case 37/83 *Rewe-Zentrale* v *Landwirtschaftskammer Rheinland* [1984] ECR 1229.

interests of a society.[120] Public morality has been concerned to secure the central values of a society.[121] However, there is no morality exception provided except for free movement of goods, so where morals questions arise in other fields they are treated as public policy matters. *Omega* concerned a German prohibition on a laser game, where people simulated killing each other, on the grounds that it violated the German constitutional provision protecting human dignity.[122] The measure was concerned with the protection of a fundamental value and was essentially about the moral standards of society. The Court of Justice, nevertheless, treated the matter as one of public policy, showing the fluidity and interchangeability of the concepts. Such fluidity is also evident in *Josemans*, where a Dutch policy restricting drugs tourism was in issue.[123] The Court noted the differing opinions of the parties on whether public policy or security were relevant grounds for the restriction, without actually settling the issue, merely noting that:

> 65. It must be pointed out that combating drug tourism and the accompanying public nuisance is part of combating drugs. It concerns both the maintenance of public order and the protection of the health of citizens, at the level of the Member States and also of the European Union.
>
> 66. Given the commitments entered into by the European Union and its Member States, there is no doubt that the abovementioned objectives constitute a legitimate interest which, in principle, justifies a restriction of the obligations imposed by European Union law.

The use of the phrase 'public order' is notable, since this has recurred in other cases, and it has been suggested that there is a move towards an umbrella 'European public order' exception whereby Member States are free to take measures to protect the central interests, symbols and values of their societies, and the Court of Justice engages in a more marginal form of appraisal.[124] An example of judicial rhetoric which might support this idea is found in *Ladbrokes*, yet another gambling case.[125]

Case C-258/08 *Ladbrokes* [2010] ECR I-4757

18. Article 46(1) EC allows restrictions justified on grounds of public policy, public security or public health. A certain number of overriding reasons in the public interest which may also justify such restrictions have been recognised by the case-law of the Court, including, in particular, the objectives of consumer protection and the prevention of both fraud and incitement to squander money on gambling, as well as the general need to preserve public order.

19. In that context, moral, religious or cultural factors, as well as the morally and financially harmful consequences for the individual and for society associated with betting and gaming, may serve to

---

[120] Case C-100/01 *Ministre de l'Intérieur v Olazabal* [2002] ECR I-10981.

[121] Case 34/79 *R v Henn and Darby* [1979] ECR 3975.

[122] Case C-36/02 *Omega Spielhallen- und Automatenaufstellungs v Oberbürgermeisterin der Bundesstadt Bonn* [2004] ECR I-9609. See p. 902.

[123] Case C-137/09 *Josemans* [2010] ECR I-13019.

[124] G. Straetmans, 'Note on Case C-124/97 *Läärä* and Case C-67/98 *Zenatti*' (2000) 37 *CMLRev.* 991, 1002–5.

[125] Case C-258/08 *Ladbrokes* [2010] ECR I-4757.

justify a margin of discretion for the national authorities, sufficient to enable them to determine what is required in order to ensure consumer protection and the preservation of public order.

20. The Member States are free to set the objectives of their policy on betting and gambling according to their own scale of values and, where appropriate, to define in detail the level of protection sought. The restrictive measures that they impose must, however, satisfy the conditions laid down in the case-law of the Court, in particular as regards their proportionality.

The particular moral, cultural and religious particularities of the Member States are acknowledged as justifying unique standpoints, and yet the use of the 'margin of appreciation' concept makes clear that this is within a broader EU framework of what is acceptable, and the framing concept that the Court of Justice chooses (perhaps counter-intuitively for moral and religious questions) is that of public order, albeit coupled with consumer protection.

Despite any margins of discretion, there are still constraints which Member States must observe. The central issues are usually the necessity of the measure, and the coherence of the national policy, as discussed above. *Conegate, Adoui, Van Duyn, Henn and Darby* and the gambling cases were all about public policy or morality.[126]

Public security is an even stronger governmental card, which judges are traditionally shy of challenging. The Court of Justice is primarily concerned to establish that the measure actually serves the right aim. In *Commission* v *Greece*, a challenge was brought to Greek rules on the storage of petroleum.[127] Oil companies operating in Greece were required to maintain a store of petroleum in Greece, which was justified by the national security interest in a domestic oil reserve. However, they could also transfer this reserve to a national refinery (that is to say, the refinery would maintain a store on their behalf) but only if and to the extent that they had purchased oil from this refinery in the last year. The Court was comfortable with the obligation to maintain national stores, but the creation of a system which protected and benefited national refineries appeared to have nothing to do with the storage goal, and could not be justified by Article 36 TFEU.

In *Commission* v *France*, public policy was used, unusually, to justify inaction rather than action. French farmers had blocked cross-border roads and ports to prevent imports of agricultural products, which they regarded as unfair, or at any rate undesirable, competition. The French Government, to the despair of its trading partners, did nothing. The blockades happened several times over a period of years, sometimes going on for weeks at a time, and occasionally involving eruptions of violence against foreign trucks, goods and drivers. One of the arguments put forward by the French Government in its defence was that public feeling was so strong, particularly among the farmers but also in the general population, that if it were to use the police to clear roads and reopen ports this might lead to a breakdown of public order. The government was afraid of provoking demonstrations and riots and losing control.

Having found that the French Government had not taken sufficient measures to guarantee the free movement of goods, the Court of Justice went on to consider whether these arguments in defence could be accepted.

[126] See pp. 903–4. [127] Case C-398/98 *Commission* v *Greece* [2001] ECR I-7915.

Case C-265/95 Commission v France (Spanish Strawberries) [1997] ECR I-6959

54. The above finding is in no way affected by the French Government's argument that the situation of French farmers was so difficult that there were reasonable grounds for fearing that more determined action by the competent authorities might provoke violent reactions by those concerned, which would lead to still more serious breaches of public order or even to social conflict.

55. Apprehension of internal difficulties cannot justify a failure by a Member State to apply Community law correctly.

56. It is for the Member State concerned, unless it can show that action on its part would have consequences for public order with which it could not cope by using the means at its disposal, to adopt all appropriate measures to guarantee the full scope and effect of Community law so as to ensure its proper implementation in the interests of all economic operators.

57. In the present case the French Government has adduced no concrete evidence proving the existence of a danger to public order with which it could not cope.

58. Moreover, although it is not impossible that the threat of serious disruption to public order may, in appropriate cases, justify non-intervention by the police, that argument can, on any view, be put forward only with respect to a specific incident and not, as in this case, in a general way covering all the incidents cited by the Commission.

59. As regards the fact that the French Republic has assumed responsibility for the losses caused to the victims, this cannot be put forward as an argument by the French Government in order to escape its obligations under Community law.

60. Even though compensation can provide reparation for at least part of the loss or damage sustained by the economic operators concerned, the provision of such compensation does not mean that the Member State has fulfilled its obligations.

The Court of Justice suggests that if feeling on an issue is sufficiently strong that a Member State is essentially unable to enforce EU law, or would be unable to deal with the consequences of such enforcement, this might justify non-action. The same could presumably be translated to positive acts: if a Member State takes measures restricting free movement because it otherwise fears consequences with which it cannot cope, this could also be legitimate. However, the judgment shows that such arguments will be regarded with great suspicion, and measures will be very strictly limited to what is necessary. Such a breakdown of order justification will be truly exceptional.

Part of the reason for such strictness is not just the cost for EU policy of national derogations, but the cost for individuals. Free movement is presented as a 'fundamental freedom' of Europeans which must be valued, but traditional human rights can be equally relevant. Where Member States do derogate, a condition for the legitimacy of their action is that any measure should respect both fundamental rights[128] and general principles of law. This is often particularly relevant to procedural questions, where Member States make exercise of EU rights conditional upon procedures which may be inaccessible, arbitrary or otherwise unfair.[129]

---

[128] Case C-112/00 *Schmidberger* v *Republic of Austria* [2003] ECR I-5659.
[129] See pp. 922–5.

8 PUBLIC SERVICE AND OFFICIAL AUTHORITY

The exclusion of public service and the exercise of official authority from the free movement of workers, services and establishment may originally have been intended to have the scope that it now has: applying to functions which go to the heart of public power, and which demand a particular loyalty to the state, such as the judiciary, armed forces, and senior or sensitive posts in the national or regional administration. However, the growth of welfare states meant that in most Member States a large proportion of the workforce was in some sense a state employee. Member States made opportunistic arguments for a formalist approach to the exclusions, catching all those paid by the state, however menial or non-sensitive their role. The Court of Justice consistently rejected this. The attraction for states of a broad exclusion was partly that some public service functions have traditionally been used to manage unemployment, an increase in the number of state functionaries being a politically acceptable way to provide jobs. In some cases, such jobs were part of broader social engineering. State employees may be posted to various areas of the state, so that public jobs were not only about reducing unemployment but also about redeploying the population to areas where their social or economic impact might be more beneficial, for example, taking unemployed urban youth and transferring them to aging and underpopulated rural areas. Member States therefore wanted to keep as much control as possible over their employees and employment policies.[130] Nevertheless, the very fact of the scope and size of the modern state meant that bowing to a broad interpretation of the exclusion would do significant, perhaps fatal, harm to the concept of a single market for occupational activity.

A useful description of what 'official authority' entails is found in *Commission* v *Germany*. Here it was argued that the special traffic privileges granted to ambulances, and the nature of the working relationship they enjoyed with the police in emergency situations, meant that ambulance services should be considered to fall within official authority. The Court of Justice disagreed.

Case C-160/08 *Commission* v *Germany (Ambulance Services)* [2010] ECR I-3713

73. According to the first paragraph of Article 45 EC, in conjunction with Article 55 EC, the provisions relating to the freedom of establishment and the freedom to provide services do not extend to activities which in a Member State are connected, even occasionally, with the exercise of official authority.

74. As the Advocate General stated at point 51 of her Opinion, such activities are also excluded from the scope of directives which, like Directives 92/50 and 2004/18, are designed to implement the provisions of the Treaty relating to the freedom of establishment and the freedom to provide services.

75. It is necessary, therefore, to determine whether the ambulance service activities at issue in the present case are among the activities referred to in the first paragraph of Article 45 EC.

76. In that regard, it must be borne in mind that, as derogations from the fundamental rules of freedom of establishment and freedom to provide services, Articles 45 EC and 55 EC must be interpreted in a manner which limits their scope to what is strictly necessary in order to safeguard the interests which they allow the Member States to protect.

77. Moreover, it has consistently been held that the review of the possible application of the exceptions laid down in Articles 45 EC and 55 EC must take into account the fact that the limits imposed by those articles on the exceptions referred to fall within European Union law.

---

[130] See Case 149/79 *Commission* v *Belgium (No. 2)* [1982] ECR 1845.

78. According to settled case-law, the derogation provided for under those articles must be restricted to activities which, in themselves, are directly and specifically connected with the exercise of official authority.

79. As the Advocate General noted at point 58 of her Opinion, such a connection requires a sufficiently qualified exercise of prerogatives outside the general law, privileges of official power or powers of coercion.

80. In the present case, it must first be observed that a contribution to the protection of public health, which any individual may be called upon to make, in particular by assisting a person whose life or health are in danger, is not sufficient for there to be a connection with the exercise of official authority.

81. As regards the right of ambulance service providers to use equipment such as flashing blue lights or sirens, and their acknowledged right of way with priority under the German Highway Code, they certainly reflect the overriding importance which the national legislature attaches to public health as against general road traffic rules.

82. However, such rights cannot, as such, be regarded as having a direct and specific connection with the exercise of official authority in the absence, on the part of the providers concerned, of official powers or of powers of coercion falling outside the scope of the general law for the purposes of ensuring that those rights are observed, which, as the parties agree, is within the competence of the police and judicial authorities.

83. Nor can matters such as those raised by the Federal Republic of Germany – concerning special organisational powers in the field of the services delivered, the power to request information from third parties and the deployment of other specialist services, or even involvement in the appointment of civil service administrators in connection with the services at issue – be regarded as reflecting a sufficiently qualified exercise of official powers or of powers falling outside the scope of the general law.

84. As the Federal Republic of Germany also asserted, the fact that the provision of public ambulance services entails collaboration with the public authorities and with professional staff on whom official powers have been conferred, such as members of the police force, does not constitute evidence that the activities of those services have a connection with the exercise of official authority either.

85. The same applies to the fact, also maintained by the Federal Republic of Germany, that agreements relating to the service contracts at issue come within the scope of public law and that the activities concerned are carried out on behalf of those public-law bodies which take on responsibility for public emergency services.

86. It follows from this that the Court cannot accept that Articles 45 EC and 55 EC are applicable to the activities at issue in the present case.

The core concepts are clearly the possession of state-like powers or authorities, of which powers of coercion are the most obvious example. By contrast, the mere possession of privileges such as the right to break the highway code or have flashing lights on a car does not, alas, suffice.

A question which has arisen quite often is how close to that public power the activity has to be. In *Peñarroja Fa*, it was argued that a court translator, as part of the court system, producing documents with legal force on behalf of a judge, should be seen as part of official authority. The Court of Justice developed the idea that the connection with public power must be direct, and the activity must be truly a part of that power, not just ancillary to it.

Case C-372/09 *Peñarroja Fa* [2011] ECR I-1785

43. In the case before the referring court, it is apparent from the documents placed before the Court that the duty of a court expert translator, at issue in the main proceedings, is to provide to a high standard an impartial translation from one language to another, not to give an opinion on the substance of the case.

44. The translations carried out by such an expert are therefore merely ancillary steps and leave the discretion of judicial authority and the free exercise of judicial power intact, so that – as submitted by Mr Peñarroja Fa, the French Government, the European Commission and the EFTA Surveillance Authority – such translation services cannot be regarded as activities connected with the exercise of official authority.

In *Commission* v *Portugal* it was argued that vehicle testing therefore did fall within official authority, since the businesses involved actually conducted the tests and issued certificates which were necessary if the vehicle was to be allowed on the road; their activities were the very stuff of state coercive power. Yet the Court of Justice disagreed, on the basis that they were directly supervised by a public authority, rendering them apparently mere servants of power, not bearers of it.

C-438/08 *Commission v Portugal* [2009] ECR I-10219

36. Thus, according to settled case-law, the derogation for which that article provides must be restricted to activities which, in themselves, are directly and specifically connected with the exercise of official authority, which excludes from being regarded as 'connected with the exercise of official authority', within the meaning of that derogation, functions that are merely auxiliary and preparatory vis-à-vis an entity which effectively exercises official authority by taking the final decision.

37. The Court has defined further the distinction between activities of private bodies constituting simple preparatory tasks and those constituting a direct and specific connection with the exercise of official authority by finding that, even where private bodies exercise the powers of a public authority, drawing the conclusions from the inspections which they carry out, Article 45 EC cannot be relied on where the applicable legislation lays down that those private bodies are to be supervised by the public authority. The Court has found that private bodies carrying out their activities under the active supervision of the competent public authority, responsible, ultimately, for inspections and decisions of those bodies, cannot be considered to be 'connected directly and specifically with the exercise of official authority' within the meaning of Article 45 EC.

38. According to the indications contained in the application and in the defence, the carrying out of roadworthiness tests on vehicles in Portugal falls within the competence of a public establishment, the Public Institute for Mobility and Transport by Land, which can, however, have recourse to private bodies in order to carry out those inspections. The decision whether or not to certify the roadworthiness of vehicles is taken by the private vehicle inspection body without any intervention by the public administrative authority.

39. As is moreover apparent from the defence, the activity of vehicle inspection establishments is organised in two stages. The first stage of that activity consists in carrying out technical inspections, that is, in verifying whether the vehicles inspected comply with the technical standards applicable and drawing up a report of the inspection recording the details of the tests carried out and the results obtained. The

second stage of that activity includes certification of the inspection carried about by affixing a badge to the vehicle or, conversely, the refusal of such certification.

40. The tasks within the first stage are of a technical nature and thus unrelated to the exercise of official authority. On the other hand, the second stage, involving the certification of roadworthiness, includes the exercise of public authority powers, in that it concerns the drawing of legal conclusions from the roadworthiness test.

41. In that regard, it should, none the less, be pointed out that the decision whether or not to certify roadworthiness, which essentially only records the results of the roadworthiness test, on the one hand, lacks the decision-making independence inherent in the exercise of public authority powers and, on the other hand, is taken in the context of direct State supervision.

42. It follows from Article 2 of Directive 96/96 that, where the Member State entrusts the management of roadworthiness testing establishments to private bodies, it none the less continues to exercise direct supervision over them.

43. It is, in effect, for the Member State, pursuant to the first sentence of that article, to designate competent establishments, to put in place an authorisation procedure and to keep those establishments under direct supervision. Pursuant to the second sentence of Article 2, which mentions the precautions to be taken in the case of conflict of interests between the testing and repair of vehicles, the Member States must, in particular, ensure the objectivity and high quality of the vehicle testing. It follows from the use of the expression '[i]n particular' that Directive 96/96 seeks the strict realisation by the State of those two specific qualitative objectives, namely the objectivity and the high quality of the roadworthiness testing of vehicles, in the case of conflict of interests but, all the more, in the execution of its task of supervising the private vehicle inspection establishments described in the first sentence of Article 2 of Directive 96/96.

44. In addition, as the Commission has pointed out, without being contradicted by the Portuguese Republic, the private vehicle inspection bodies, in connection with their activities, have no power of coercion, the right to impose penalties for failure to comply with the rules on vehicle inspection belonging to the police and judicial authorities.

45. Consequently, the activities of the private vehicle roadworthiness testing bodies concerned in this case do not fall within the exception provided for in Article 45 EC. It is thus necessary to examine whether the regime for access to vehicle inspection implemented by the Portuguese Republic can be justified.

The Court went on to find that the conditions imposed on businesses wanting to engage in vehicle testing were overly restrictive, and not justified.

As well as restricting the core concept of public service and official authority, which are interpreted in parallel, the Court of Justice has made clear that they must be applied to specific functions, rather than to institutions as a whole. *Commission* v *Italy* concerned the Italian national research centre, in which all posts were reserved for Italians.[131] Part of the justification was that senior and management posts involved advising the government and contributing to policy formation. The Court accepted this, but found that it did not justify extending the exclusion to all researchers. The judgment had the consequence that foreign researchers might come up against a ceiling to their career, since unlike their Italian colleagues they could be legitimately denied promotion to the reserved senior posts. However, the Court emphasised that such discrimination must

---

[131] Case 225/85 *Commission* v *Italy* [1987] ECR 2625.

be kept to a minimum, and did not justify, for example, only employing foreigners on short-term contracts. Where foreigners were employed they were entitled to equality of conditions, and this must be reconciled with their more limited promotion prospects to the greatest extent possible.

Finally, the concept of public service may include work for private employers, if these are engaged in the service of the state and exercising public law powers.[132] This is quite logical: if the activities of a private organisation may be official authority, then the employees carrying out those activities may be expected to fall within the concept of public service. However, the privatisation of public functions means there are many difficult lines now to be drawn, and adds another layer of complexity to this particular derogation. The preference for distinctions based on the interests at stake, rather than formal public or private status, is consistent with the wider approach of free movement law, and in particular with the ruling in *Bosman* that public policy derogations from free movement could, in principle, be relied upon by private parties.[133]

FURTHER READING

A. Arcuri, *The Case for a Procedural Version of the Precautionary Principle: Erring on the Side of Environmental Protection*, Global Law Working Paper 10/04 (New York, Hauser Global Law School, 2004)

C. Barnard, 'Derogations, Justifications and the Four Freedoms: Is State Interest Really Protected?' in C. Barnard and O. Odudu, *The Outer Limits of European Law* (Oxford, Hart, 2009)

G. Davies, 'Process and Production Method-based Restrictions on Trade in the EU' in C. Barnard (ed.), *Cambridge Yearbook of European Legal Studies* (Oxford, Hart, 2008)

N. Georgiadis, *Derogation Clauses: The Protection of National Interests in EC Law* (Brussels, Bruylant, 2006)

J. Gerards, 'Pluralism, Deference and the Margin of Appreciation Doctrine' (2011) 17 *European Law Review* 80

W. Haslehner, '"Consistency" and Fundamental Freedoms: The Case of Direct Taxation' (2013) 50 *Common Market Law Review* 737

C. Macmaolain, 'Free Movement of Foodstuffs, Quality Requirements and Consumer Protection: Have the Court and the Commission Both Got it Wrong?' (2001) 26 *European Law Review* 413

G. Mathisen, 'Consistency and Coherence as Conditions for Justification of Member State Measures Restricting Free Movement' (2010) 47 *Common Market Law Review* 1021

N. Nic Shuibhne and M. Maci, 'Proving Public Interest: The Growing Impact of Evidence in Free Movement Case Law' (2013) 50 *Common Market Law Review* 965

J. Scott, 'Of Kith and Kine (and Crustaceans): Trade and Environment in the EU and WTO' in J. Weiler (ed.), *The EU, NAFTA and the WTO: Towards a Common Law of International Trade* (Oxford, Oxford University Press, 2000)

J. Scott, 'Mandatory or Imperative Requirements in the EU and WTO' in C. Barnard and J. Scott, *The Law of the European Single Market: Unpacking the Premises* (Oxford, Hart, 2002)

J. Snell, 'Economic Aims as Justifications for Restrictions on Free Movement' in A. Schrauwen, *The Rule of Reason: Rethinking Another Classic of Community Law* (Groningen, Europa Law Publishing, 2005)

---

[132] Case C-47/02 *Anker* [2003] ECR I-10447; Case C-405/01 *Colegio de Oficiales de la Marina Mercante Española* v *Administración del Estado* [2003] ECR I-10391.

[133] Case C-415/93 *Union Royale Belge des Sociétés de Football Association and others* v *Bosman and others* [1995] ECR I-4921.

EU Competition Law: Function and Enforcement

1 INTRODUCTION

This section of the book contains a survey of the main competition law provisions. Competition law forbids price fixing cartels among competitors and other agreements that restrict competition (Article 101 TFEU) and prohibits monopolies from abusing their position (Article 102 TFEU). Firms that infringe these rules may be fined by the Commission, and victims of such acts may seek damages. Law enforcement is discussed in Chapter 21 and the two Treaty provisions are discussed in Chapter 22. Competition law also monitors Member States' regulation of markets and can be applied to prohibit anti-competitive legislation, as well as promote competition in markets where national law has prevented competition. In this context, there are overlaps between the enforcement of competition law and the rules regulating the internal market discussed in Chapters 15 to 20. In Chapter 23 we look specifically at the state aid rules in the Treaty (Articles 107 to 109 TFEU) which limit the Member States' discretion to grant subsidies and other advantages to national firms. In light of the ongoing economic crisis the regulation of state aid is particularly poignant. There are two online chapters on competition law: Chapter 25 considers the role of EU law in markets subjected to heavy state regulation and traces the deregulatory impact of EU law intervention. Finally, Chapter 26 considers the EU's merger policy.

When the EEC Treaty was negotiated, there was considerable pressure by Americans, but also by segments of Europe's academic community, that competition law should be included in the Treaty.[1] However, at that time, the 'culture of competition' had yet to emerge in most Member States, who traditionally favoured cartel arrangements, state intervention and the promotion of national champions.[2] Indeed, some Member States only introduced national competition laws as late as the 1990s, and even today in some countries enforcement is emerging or unstable.[3] Thus, when provisions were first introduced to curb restrictive practices in the coal and steel sector (by Articles 65 and 66 of the ECSC Treaty), these were an innovation for the Member States.[4] Originally the purpose of introducing competition law into the EEC Treaty was to complement the internal market rules by preventing businesses from partitioning the internal market and by encouraging competition across borders.[5] Today, the need for EU competition law as a means of securing economic welfare is widely accepted and the rules are enforced robustly by the Commission.

The present chapter considers why competition law is important and how it is enforced. It is organised as follows.

Section 2 is a review of the debates about the objectives of EU competition law. It shows that there are divided opinions on two fronts: first, between those who consider that the application of competition law should focus on maximising economic welfare and those who take the view that competition law is about the pursuit of economic and non-economic considerations; and secondly that even among those who think that economics offers a superior paradigm for applying competition law, there are differences of opinion about how to best deploy economic thinking. This section of the chapter is essential reading for an understanding of the subject,

---

[1] D. J. Gerber, *Law and Competition in Twentieth Century Europe* (Oxford, Oxford University Press, 1998) ch. 9.

[2] H. G. Schröter, 'Cartelization and Decartelization in Europe, 1870–1995: Rise and Decline of an Economic Institution' (1996) 25 *Journal of European Economic History* 129. An exception was West Germany's competition law drafted in 1957.

[3] Examples of latecomers include: Ireland and Italy in 1990, the Netherlands in 1997, Luxembourg in 2004. The enforcement of competition law in Italy is advanced in part but certain markets remain closed to competition. See L. Berti and A. Pezzoli, *Le Stagioni dell'Antitrust* (Milan, EGEA, 2010). Furthermore, in exchange for receiving financial aid from the Union, a number of Member States have been required to strengthen their competition laws. For an overview see G. Monti, Independence, Interdependence and Legitimacy: The EU Commission, National Competition Authorities and the European Competition Network, EUI Department of Law Research Paper 2014/01.

[4] Jean Monnet, *Mémoires* (Paris, Fayard, 1976) 356–7, 411–13 (also noting US pressure to implement anti-cartel laws).

[5] G. Marenco, 'The Birth of Modern Competition Law in Europe' in A. von Bogdandy, P. Mavroidis and Y. Mény (eds.), *European Integration and International Coordination: Studies in Transnational Economic Law in Honour of C.-D. Ehlermann* (The Hague, Kluwer, 2002) esp. 297–8.

because, as will be seen in Chapter 23, these differences can have a significant impact on how competition law is applied and enforced.

Section 3 examines the enforcement powers of the European Commission. It explains how the Commission investigates cases, the procedures for reaching a decision, and the penalties that may be imposed if an infringement is found. Attention is given to the effectiveness of the enforcement scheme as well as to its legitimacy, measured by how well it safeguards the fundamental rights of those under investigation.

Section 4 considers the significance of Regulation 1/2003. This Regulation 'entrusted the national competition authorities with a key role in ensuring that the EU competition rules are applied effectively and consistently, in conjunction with the Commission'.[6] It was a significant and controversial measure. It gave greater prominence to national competition authorities, and changed the role of the Commission. Ten years since its coming into force the system has not suffered major failures, but its impact requires closer analysis, not least for the centralising tendencies that are emerging.

Section 5 reviews the rules relating to the private enforcement of EU competition law. It considers the contribution of the Court of Justice, the legislative proposals made by the Commission, and assesses the value and role of private enforcement.

2 AIMS OF EU COMPETITION LAW

There is considerable debate regarding the functions of competition law. Today, the majority view is that competition law should be enforced against firms whose behaviour harms consumers. Against this, there are two alternative views. One is that competition law should not be concerned with an outcome (consumer welfare or efficiency) but with maintaining the competitive process. Another view is that competition law can be enforced to attain a wider set of economic and non-economic ambitions; for example, it may be enforced to promote national industries, to safeguard employment, or to protect the environment. In (i) below, we sketch a justification of the role of competition law derived from the discipline of economics, which supports the majority view. In some jurisdictions (most notably the United States), scholars argue that competition law should be interpreted solely according to what economic theory dictates.[7] This mainstream view is contingent upon advances in economics, so that lawyers are called upon to reflect new learning in the application of the law. In (ii), we consider the alternative points of view. In (iii), we turn to explore how far these competing approaches have influenced EU competition law enforcement, and in (iv) we explore how far economic downturns may affect the application of competition law.

(i) Economics of competition

From an economic perspective, competition law should prohibit commercial practices that damage the operation of markets. Accordingly, the principal measuring stick of a good competition

---

[6] European Commission, *Report on the Functioning of Regulation 1/2003* COM(2009)206 final, para. 28.

[7] R. H. Bork, *The Antitrust Paradox* (New York, The Free Press, 1978, reprinted 1993); R. A. Posner, *Antitrust Law* (2nd edn, Chicago, IL, University of Chicago Press, 2000). The major debate here is whether this is best achieved with a consumer welfare standard or a total welfare standard. See for example R. D. Blair and D. D. Sokol, 'Welfare Standards in US and EU Antitrust Enforcement' (2003) 81 *Fordham Law Review* 2497.

law is how well it sustains an efficient economic order by prohibiting conduct that reduces efficiency; efficiency is a multilayered term.

M. de la Mano, *For the Customer's Sake: The Competitive Effects of Efficiencies in European Merger Control*, Enterprise Papers No. 11 (Brussels, Enterprise Directorate-General, 2002) 8–14

Economists generally distinguish between three broad classes of efficiencies all of which are relevant for the analysis of competition: allocative, productive (or technical) and dynamic (or innovation) efficiency.

Allocative efficiency: Allocative efficiency is achieved when the existing stock of (final and intermediate) goods are allocated through the price system to those buyers who value them most, in terms of willingness to pay or willingness to forego other consumption possibilities. At an allocatively efficient outcome, market prices are equal to the real resource costs of producing and supplying the products.

Productive (or technical) efficiency: Productive efficiency is a narrower concept than allocative efficiency, and focuses on a particular firm or industry. It addresses the question of whether any given level of output is being produced by that firm/industry at least cost or, alternatively, whether any given combination of inputs is producing the maximum possible output. Productive efficiency depends on the existing technology and resource prices. The state of technology determines what alternative combinations of resources can produce a given amount of output. Resource prices determine which combination of resources is the most efficient one in that it gives rise to the lowest production cost. Productive efficiency is achieved when output is produced in plants of optimal scale (or minimum efficient scale) given the relative prices of production inputs.

Dynamic (or innovation) efficiency: Allocative and productive efficiency are static notions concerned with the performance of an economy, industry or firm at a given point in time, for a given technology and level of existing knowledge. Dynamic efficiency in antitrust economics is connected to whether appropriate incentives and ability exist to increase productivity and engage in innovative activity over time, which may yield cheaper or better goods or new products that afford consumers more satisfaction than previous consumption choices.

The distinction between static (allocative or productive) efficiency and dynamic efficiency is based on the idea that the latter leads to improvements in the available technology or the discovery of new production processes or products. In other words, dynamic efficiency is related to the ability of a firm, industry or economy to exploit its potential to innovate, develop new technologies and thus expand its production possibility frontier.

These definitions provide us with the main tools to evaluate the performance of industry. Suppose that manufacturers of escalators agree among each other to raise prices. The implementation of this agreement serves to raise prices well above cost (allocative inefficiency), it reduces demand so that the manufacturers are not using their resources optimally (productive inefficiency) and since the firms cooperate in a way that is mutually beneficial, the incentive to innovate is reduced (dynamic inefficiency). This example typifies the kinds of considerations an economist makes to test if behaviour by firms is to be challenged as anti-competitive. It has also been suggested that there is a further economic harm: cartels are well-organised political players who can lobby successfully for legislative measures to exclude rivals.[8] This particular concern is also found in monopolies.

M. de la Mano, *For the Customer's Sake: The Competitive Effects of Efficiencies in European Merger Control*, Enterprise Papers No. 11 (Brussels, Enterprise Directorate-General, 2002) 8–14

Further, monopoly rents will tend to be dissipated as firms, in order to establish or defend a dominant position, are willing to spend anything up to the value of their monopoly profits. Such expenditures may take various forms: excess advertising, research and development (R&D), investment in excess capacity or brand proliferation in order to deter entry from rival firms, lobbying to secure government quotas or licences, etc. Often this expenditure is in itself entirely unproductive (e.g. lobbying) although other expenditures may partly lead to consumer benefits (as in the case of R&D that results in innovations). These examples imply that the costs of market power through weakened productive efficiency may be at least as important as its adverse impact on allocative efficiency.

The upshot is that competition law should be mostly concerned with manifestations of market power, where the likelihood of inefficient outcomes is higher. However, diagnosing market power and identifying harmful practices has evolved, and we trace this history briefly here.

In the 1960s, some economists believed that there was a direct causal relation between market structure and economic performance, whereby the fewer the firms (and thus the more concentrated the market), the less competitive the industry. This view (often labelled the 'Harvard School' view, as the main proponents were Harvard economists) influenced the development of US antitrust law (called antitrust rather than competition law, as its earliest actions were against cartels established in the form of trusts) until the 1970s, when the economic mood swung away from this exclusively structural understanding of markets.[9] One of the major policy consequences of this approach was that mergers were viewed with suspicion and conduct likely to exclude rivals was also of concern as both strategies would serve to exclude rivals, increasing concentration and thereby worsening economic performance. This led to aggressive antitrust enforcement.

In the 1970s, the 'Chicago School' championed a different set of opinions about how markets worked and advocated a more lax degree of scrutiny.[10] Their arguments can be summarised in the following manner. First, while it is true that a firm with a large market share may be tempted to behave anti-competitively by reducing output and increasing prices, this kind of behaviour will send a signal to other market players that there is unmet demand in the market, and invite

---

[8] G. Amato, *Antitrust and the Bounds of Power* (Oxford, Hart, 1997).

[9] F. M. Scherer and G. Ross, *Industrial Market Structure and Economic Performance* (3rd edn, Boston, MA, Houghton Mifflin, 1990) ch. 1 for a review of this approach. See the policy prescriptions in C. Kaysen and D. F. Turner, *Antitrust Policy: An Economic and Legal Analysis* (Cambridge, MA, Harvard University Press, 1959).

[10] H. Hovenkamp, 'Antitrust Policy After Chicago' (1986) 84 *Michigan Law Review* 213; F. H. Easterbrook, 'Workable Antitrust Policy' (1986) 84 *Michigan Law Review* 1696; B. Hawk, 'The American Antitrust Revolution: Lessons for the EEC?' (1988) *ECLR* 53. For a more critical perspective see E. M. Fox and L. A. Sullivan, 'Antitrust – Retrospective and Prospective: Where are We Coming From? Where are We Going?' (1987) 62 *New York University Law Review* 936.

the entry of new firms. This new entry will bring prices down and reintroduce the degree of competition necessary to satisfy consumer desires. In other words, while acknowledging that market structure may affect economic performance, the Chicago School added the rider that if economic performance led to unmet consumer demand, this would cause the entry of other firms. This economic dynamic meant that competition law was largely unnecessary unless new entry was hampered, and the greatest reason why entry was hampered was national legislation limiting business freedom, not the anti-competitive behaviour of business. Absent barriers for new competitors, the market would heal itself. Secondly, while the Harvard School lamented the increasing concentration of firms, the Chicago School argued that concentrated markets were more efficient because firms would be able to exploit economies of scale (that is, it is relatively cheaper for one firm to manufacture millions of cars than for several firms to manufacture a thousand cars each). Thirdly, the Chicagoans believed that law enforcers were more likely to damage the competitive process by their intervention because of their ignorance about how markets worked.

The Chicago and Harvard views can diverge significantly in their prescriptions for competition law enforcement. For example, a Harvard School approach would suggest that high prices by a monopoly are illegal but a Chicago School approach would indicate that high prices invite new entry, which would render the market competitive in the long run. The Chicago School is probably the most influential school of thought in competition law. It set out a coherent view of competition law enforcement, embedded in confidence that markets work best without excessive regulation by states or courts. However, the Chicago School model is currently contested by 'post-Chicago' economic theories.[11]

M. S. Jacobs, 'An Essay on the Normative Foundations of Antitrust Economics' (1995–1996) 74 _North Carolina Law Review_ 219, 222–5

A post-Chicago School of economics has arisen, working within the efficiency model, but starting from assumptions and ending with an enforcement methodology markedly different from Chicago's...Both agree that economics is 'the essence of antitrust' and that protecting consumer welfare, conceived in allocative efficiency terms, should be the exclusive goal of competition law. Both eschew the subjective inquiries that they ascribe to the overtly political approaches of the past, and both assert that unless business conduct raises prices or reduces output it should be left alone, regardless of the political or distributive consequences.

The new debate involves contending visions of the workings of the market mechanism and of the proper model for antitrust enforcement. Chicagoans believe that markets tend toward efficiency, that market imperfections are normally transitory, and that judicial enforcement should proceed cautiously, lest it mistakenly proscribe behavior that promotes consumer welfare. Post-Chicagoans, by contrast, believe that market failures are not necessarily self-correcting, and that firms can therefore take advantage of imperfections, such as information gaps or competitors' sunk costs, to produce inefficient results even in ostensibly competitive markets. They argue that the distortions to competition made possible by market imperfections should prompt enforcement authorities to scrutinize a wider variety of

---

[11] See H. Hovenkamp, 'Post-Chicago Antitrust: A Review and Critique' (2001) _Colum. Bus. L. Rev._ 257; L. A. Sullivan and W. S. Grimes, _The Law of Antitrust: An Integrated Handbook_ (2nd edn, St Paul, MN, West Publishing, 2006), a textbook written taking into account many post-Chicago insights; R. Pitofsky (ed.), _How the Chicago School Overshot the Mark_ (Oxford, Oxford University Press, 2008).

conduct than Chicagoans would examine. On the doctrinal level, this debate has produced conflicting answers to some of antitrust's most pressing questions: the relevant measures of market power, the competitive effects of tying arrangements and other vertical restraints, the economic plausibility of predatory pricing schemes, and the durability of cartels and oligopolies.

On its surface, the nature of this debate confirms the view that antitrust analysis has taken a decidedly technological turn…What apparently divide the parties are not their political ideologies or interpretations of history, but differing evaluations of the efficiency implications of their respective theories and methodologies. Indeed, some post-Chicagoans characterize their work not as an alternative to Chicago thinking but as a refinement of it, an effort to provide decisionmakers with a more accurate picture of the marketplace and more sensitive tools for detecting inefficient behavior.

These appearances, however, are deceptive. The parties' shared commitment to efficiency and the debate's specialized vocabulary mask deep divisions regarding the normative assumptions most appropriate to competition policy. The contending economic models reflect very different views of human nature, firm behavior, and judicial competence. While Chicagoans assume that the desire to maximize profits drives firms to compete away market imperfections and destabilizes collusive activity, post-Chicagoans believe that strategizing firms can create or perpetuate market imperfections that can seriously hamper competitive balance. Similarly, while Chicagoans presuppose that markets promote efficient business behavior and that judges untrained in economics are ill-equipped to identify and measure market imperfections, post-Chicagoans have less trust in markets and more confidence in the judiciary's ability to distinguish between competitive and anticompetitive conduct. Post-Chicagoans have shown that the neoclassical price model [based on assumptions that individuals have rational preferences and act based on all relevant information to maximise income (firms) or utility (consumers)] is not the only method for analyzing the efficiency questions central to antitrust. They have demonstrated that economists equally loyal to the goal of consumer welfare can disagree markedly with price theorists about the means most conducive to allocative efficiency. In doing so, however, they have revealed, albeit unintentionally, the inability of economics to furnish empirical or theoretical criteria for resolving the differences between their model and Chicago's. Their work has produced a stalemate in economic theory that effectively requires antitrust decisionmakers, most of whom accept the legitimacy of the economic model, to probe the technocratic surface of the current debate and evaluate the conflicting beliefs about firms, markets, and governments embedded in its foundation. Ironically, far from having marginalized the role of value choice in antitrust discourse, the ascendancy of economic models underscores its enduring importance.

The post-Chicago approach leads to suggestions for competition law enforcement that are different from the Chicago model. For example, under a Chicago approach, predatory pricing (that is, prices set at a level below the cost of production) is only unlawful when the predator is able to cause all rivals to exit and monopolise the market. In contrast, under post-Chicago theories, predatory pricing can be held to be unlawful even if the predator does not monopolise the market. Instead, predatory pricing may be a way of hurting competitors to 'discipline' them (for example, if a firm is well established in the United Kingdom and its competitor mainly sells in Germany, predatory pricing might be used by the UK firm should the German firm try to penetrate the UK market, the aim being not the destruction of the German competitor, but the maintenance of separate markets) or to establish a reputation as a tough competitor (for example, in a market where entry is relatively easy, one bout of predatory pricing against a new entrant may discourage other firms from entering, even when it might be economically rational to enter).[12] Jacobs suggests that these differences of opinion about what is economically rational belie a series of value assumptions about how markets work. Therefore, competition law cannot be founded upon economics; rather it is premised upon the assumptions we make about how market players operate. On this argument, a competition authority chooses an economic theory that supports those assumptions.

A further, similar, challenge to the Chicago School approach comes from behavioural economics. This approach to economics rejects the assumption of mainstream economic theory that actors behave rationally, and this has an effect on how one regulates markets. In the specific context of antitrust, irrationality may manifest itself on the side of consumers (who mishandle information, or make decisions based on factors like loyalty or an over-inflated perception of risk) and producers (who may similarly read market signals poorly). For instance, it has been suggested that firms entering new markets assume they will be successful, when in reality few manage to make any lasting inroads: this suggests that the Chicagoan view that low entry barriers reduce the risk of anti-competitive behaviour might be too limited if new entrants fail to bring discipline to the market. This means more sophisticated evidence is required to test if there is market power.[13]

A final economic issue to consider is the role of dynamic efficiency. We might object to the pharmaceutical sector being monopolised by one firm, but what if this is the only way to concentrate enough resources to obtain life-saving drugs in the future? How much can we suffocate competition today in favour of greater consumer benefits tomorrow? Some have taken the view that innovation occurs so frequently that competition law should not be overly concerned about firms that monopolise a high technology market, while others have taken the view that innovation can only take place if new entrants are protected by competition law regulating the firms that monopolise the market.[14] There is no consensus on the best competition policy to facilitate innovation, although 'antitrust economists recognise that dynamic net efficiency gains from continuing innovation may far outweigh the static gains from marginal-cost pricing'.[15] However, competition authorities have tended to focus on allocative and productive efficiency.[16]

---

[12] A. Kate and G. Neils, 'On the Rationality of Predatory Pricing: The Debate Between Chicago and Post-Chicago' (2002) *Antitrust Bulletin* 1. However, these new approaches have not been very successful. For a discussion of why this may be so, see N. Giocoli, 'Games Judges Don't Play: Predatory Pricing and Strategic Reasoning in US Antitrust', *Supreme Court Review* (forthcoming), available at http://papers.ssrn.com/sol3/papers.cfm?abstract_id=1676095.

[13] A. Tor, 'The Fable of Entry: Bounded Rationality, Market Discipline, and Legal Policy' (2002) 101 *Michigan Law Review* 482.

[14] See D. S. Evans and R. Schmalensee, 'Some Economic Aspects of Antitrust Analysis in Dynamically Competitive Industries' in A. B. Jae, J. Lerner and S. Stern (eds.), *Innovation Policy and the Economy* (Cambridge, MA, NBER and MIT Press, 2002) vol. 2; G. Monti, 'Article 82 EC and New Economy Markets' in C. Graham and F. Smith (eds.), *Competition, Regulation and the New Economy* (Oxford, Hart, 2004); J. D. Balto and R. Pitofsky, 'Challenges of the New Economy: Issues at the Intersection of Antitrust and the New Economy' (2001) 68 *Antitrust Bulletin* 913.

[15] M. de la Mano, *For the Customer's Sake: The Competitive Effects of Efficiencies in European Merger Control*, Enterprise Papers No. 11 (Brussels, Enterprise Directorate-General, 2002) 14.

[16] Although dynamic efficiency considerations played a role in the *Microsoft* decision, where the firm indicated the risk that the European Commission's action would undermine dynamic efficiency (summary at: [2007] OJ L32/23; full text available at http://ec.europa.eu/competition/index_en.html); and in Joined Cases C-501/06P, C-513/06P, C-515/06P and C-519/06P *GlaxoSmithKline Services Unlimited* v *Commission* [2009] ECR I-9291, where the ECJ confirmed that dynamic efficiencies may be pleaded under Article 101(3) TFEU.

It is worth closing with the following consideration: the post-Chicago and behavioural antitrust approaches, and the concerns over dynamic efficiency pose sound qualifications to a Chicago-based perspective but they have not led to major changes in enforcement policy. The reason for this has largely to do with considerations of institutional design.

W. E. Kovacic, 'The Intellectual DNA of Modern Competition Law for Dominant Firm Conduct: The Chicago/Harvard Double Helix' (2007) 1(1) *Columbia Business Law Review* **1, 36–7, 72**

Antitrust rules should not outrun the capabilities of implementing institutions. Among other points, Areeda and Turner [founding authors of the leading multi-volume treatise on US antitrust law] argued that antitrust rules and decision-making tasks must be administrable for the central participants in the antitrust system (courts, enforcement agencies, the private bar, and business managers); that special substantive and procedural screens should be used to ensure that suits initiated by private antitrust plaintiffs were consistent with larger social aims; and that remedies should be carefully linked to the harm caused by the specific practices found to have constituted improper behavior....

Post-Chicago scholars often falter because they make unduly hopeful assumptions about the capacity of the key implementing institutions of the antitrust system to apply the insights of Post-Chicago analysis skillfully. By this view, non-interventionist presumptions are endorsed not because they inevitably make sound assumptions about the harms of specific forms of business behavior, but instead because they make more accurate assumptions about the limitations of courts and enforcement agencies.

In other words, the conservative economic approach of the Chicago School is supported in large part because it is legally workable given the institutional setting for law enforcement in the United States. In particular, jury trials caution against the use of complex economic theories, treble damage awards for antitrust offences often invite spurious claims that courts must ward off,[17] and the level of expertise and capacity of an antitrust authority limits the degree to which it can regulate certain complex markets where specific regulators have a comparative advantage.[18]

(ii) Politics of competition law

The debates about the economics of competition law often seem technical and non-political. However, as Jacobs argued above, there is an inherent political dimension to competition law, even when analysed through an economic perspective. Debates about the role of competition law run through the history of US competition law.

---

[17] *Brunswick Corp.* v *Pueblo Bowl-O-Mat, Inc.* 429 US 477 (1977), denying damages when the conduct in question was pro-competitive.
[18] E.g. *Verizon* v *Trinko* 540 US 398 (2004), refusing to extend the scope of antitrust law on the facts because there is a dedicated telecommunications regulator tasked with promoting competition.

E. M. Fox and L. A. Sullivan, 'Antitrust – Retrospective and Prospective: Where are We Coming From? Where are We Going?' (1987) 62 *New York University Law Review* 936, 942, 956–9

Many economists, especially those with Chicago leanings, think that because antitrust is about markets, as is microeconomics, antitrust law should be economics. They react as though the law is out of kilter whenever it diverges from their particular economic insight; and they so react regardless of whether the law diverges because empirical processes have not validated factual assumptions, or because the law has identified social goals other than or in addition to allocative efficiency.

Law is not economics. Nor were the antitrust laws adopted to squeeze the greatest possible efficiency out of business.

Finally, the producer-plus-consumer-welfare paradigm presses the analyst to think only in terms of aggregate outcomes or wealth of the nation. But this concept is static and outcome-oriented, while the antitrust laws are dynamic and process-oriented. They protect not an outcome, but a process – competition. Antitrust laws set fair rules of the game. They give rights of access and opportunity. The antitrust laws preserve and foster dynamic interactions among those in the market. They deal not with aggregate national wealth, but with the expectations and behavior of the people who participate in the markets.

The American debate is particularly instructive in setting out the competing values that animate competition policy. As Fox has suggested more recently, the real point of debate presently is between those who consider that antitrust law should only be enforced when one proves a harmful economic outcome (or at most the strong likelihood of a harmful economic outcome) and those who believe that it should also be enforced when certain actions weaken the competitive process.[19]

Moreover, Fox and Sullivan locate competition law within the perspective of a liberal economic order, which has a particular affinity to the origins of EU competition law. In its early years, EU competition law was influenced by German scholarship and German officials played a key role in the development of competition law. Underpinning the German approach to competition was a unique economic philosophy: ordoliberalism.[20]

W. Möschel, 'Competition Policy from an Ordo Point of View' in A. Peacock and H. Willgerodt (eds.), *German Neo-liberals and the Social Market Economy* (London, Macmillan, 1989) 146

The actual goal of the competition policy of Ordo-liberalism lies in the protection of individual economic freedom of action as a value in itself, or vice versa, in the restraint of undue economic power. Franz Böhm once illuminated this idea by the aphoristic formula, 'the one who has power has no right to be free and the one who wants to be free should have no power'. Economic efficiency as a generic

---

[19] E. M. Fox, 'Against Goals'(2013) 81 *Fordham Law Review* 2157.

[20] See also D. J. Gerber, *Law and Competition in Twentieth Century Europe* (Oxford, Oxford University Press, 1998) ch. 7; W. Möschel, 'The Proper Scope of Government Viewed from an Ordoliberal Perspective: The Example of Competition Policy' (2001) 157(1) *Journal of Institution and Theoretical Economics* 3.

term for growth, for the encouragement and development of technical progress and for allocative efficiency, is but an indirect and derived goal. It results generally from the realisation of individual freedom of action in a market system...

This is contrary to the various concepts of utilitarianism. In this respect the Ordo-liberal competition policy is obviously related to the intellectual traditions of idealist German philosophy, particularly that of Immanuel Kant...Modern currents in the American anti-trust law which lean directly upon wealth maximisation, [like] Richard Posner's constrained utilitarianism...are obviously incompatible with the Ordo-liberal system of values. Ordo-liberalism treats individuals as ends in themselves and not as means of another's welfare.

Here, the dislike of market power is not based primarily on fears of inefficiency, rather on concerns that firms with market power can stifle the freedom of other economic operators, and this leads to inefficiency. Like Fox and Sullivan, the process of competition, favouring access and opportunities for new businesses, is valued. This vision has had a strong influence in the development of EU competition law.[21] Protecting the competitive process or competitive outcomes does not make a significant practical difference in most cases (e.g. both condemn cartels and mergers that create a dominant player). The major difference (as we will examine more closely in the following chapter) is over exclusionary conduct. Taking predatory pricing again, an economic approach would condemn it only if it is likely that the conduct harms welfare, while an approach protecting the competitive process would condemn it a step before: once it is likely that the conduct excludes market players. One criticism that may be made of the latter approach is that it is not always clear how to translate the notion of competitive process when faced with a set of facts: to a certain extent every contract reduces competition (if I agree to sell all my books to you, nobody else can buy them), but it is hard to find a test by which one decides what degree of reduction is sufficiently meaningful to merit prohibition, and there is a risk that one slides into taking a very formalist approach which applies the prohibition too aggressively.[22]

Originally the Commission enforced competition law informed by this approach, but it is currently recalibrating its rules to focus more on examining the effects of suspicious conduct. Those that support the old policy have three major concerns: first, the absence of any debate at EU level about the choice to abandon the model of competition based on safeguarding the competitive process and favouring an economic approach; secondly, that an economic approach may lead to reduced enforcement, especially against the most powerful firms, while harming smaller players; and thirdly, that the mainstream economic approach focuses on allocative efficiency (i.e. measuring the direct impact on consumers today) at the expense of promoting dynamic efficiency.[23]

---

[21] D. Gerber, 'Constitutionalising the Economy: German Neo-Liberalism, Competition Law and the "New" Europe' (1994) 42 *American Journal of Comparative Law* 25, 69–74.

[22] C. Ahlborn and C. Grave, 'Walter Eucken and Ordoliberalism: An Introduction from a Consumer Welfare Perspective' (2006) 2(2) *Competition Policy International* 197.

[23] I. L. O. Schmidt, 'The Suitability of the More Economic Approach for Competition Policy: Dynamic vs. Static Efficiency' (2007) *ECLR* 408; Bundeskartellamt/Competition Law Forum, 'A Bundeskartellamt/Competition Law Forum Debate on Reform of Article 82: A Dialectic on Competing Approaches' (2006) 2 *ECJ* 211; R. Zäch and A. Künzler, 'Freedom to Compete or Consumer Welfare: The Goal of Competition Law according to Constitutional Law' in R. Zäch, A. Heinemann and A. Kellerhals (eds.), *The Development of Competition Law* (Cheltenham, Edward Elgar, 2009).

(iii) Aims of EU competition policy

It was only in the late 1980s that EU competition policy took shape. This happened as a result of five factors. First, the neoliberal economic policies championed by Reagan in the United States and Thatcher in the United Kingdom began to affect governments and industries across Europe, and the economic liberalisation called for by the Single European Act necessitated a stronger role for competition law to ensure that the transformation from a mixed economy to a free market occurred smoothly. Secondly, the Court of Justice, since the 1960s, had ruled on a number of competition law cases and established strong precedents that consolidated the Commission's powers. Thirdly, the staff morale at the Directorate-General (DG) for Competition (charged with enforcing competition law in the Union) was considerably strengthened by the economic and legal backing that emerged in the 1980s. Fourthly, the personalities of the competition Commissioners were instrumental in strengthening this DG. Two competition commissioners, Peter Sutherland (1985–1989) and Sir Leon Brittan (1989–1993), were instrumental in pursuing and extending the free market logic, often leading to clashes between the views espoused by DG Competition and those of the Commission President, Jacques Delors. Finally, in 1990, the Commission obtained powers to regulate mergers in the Union. With the economic restructuring that was taking place as a result of economic liberalisation, this placed EU competition law at the heart of the Union's transformation to a neoliberal market economy.[24]

Two aspects of this evolution are worthy of note. First, the increased emphasis on the benefits of efficient markets undermined concerns about economic power and economic freedom that were seminal in the early development of EU competition law. Secondly, the Commissioner for competition policy can have a direct role in influencing the general direction of competition policy. For instance, Sir Leon Brittan's advocacy of free markets was instrumental in the early success of the implementation of the merger rules. His successor, Karel van Miert (1993–1999), however, was less convinced than his predecessor about grounding competition law in free market terms, as this quotation from one of his speeches indicates:

> Let me make one thing clear straight away: the application of competition principles is not an end in itself. Competition policy is a tool which can be used to help achieve the fundamental aims of the Community. The Commission's competition policy does not operate in a vacuum. It has to take account of its repercussions in other areas of Commission policy, such as industrial policy, regional policy, social policy and the environment. But this is not a one way process. Competition policy also makes its own contribution to the formulation and implementation of policy in those areas. The point is sometimes overlooked by those who criticize the institutional framework of European competition policy, such as the advocates of a European Cartel Office.[25]

His replacement, Mario Monti (1999–2004), an economics professor, steered competition policy back along the lines taken by Sutherland and Brittan, and the Commissioners who have followed him (Neelie Kroes (2004–2010) and Joaquim Almunia (since 2010)) have more or less

---

[24] L. McGowan, 'Safeguarding the Economic Constitution: The Commission and Competition Policy' in N. Nugent (ed.), *At the Heart of the Union: Studies of the European Commission* (2nd edn, Basingstoke, Macmillan Press, 2000) 151–3; R. Buch-Hansen and A. Wigger, *The Politics of European Competition Regulation: A Critical Political Economy Perspective* (Abingdon, Routledge, 2011).

[25] Karel van Miert, *The Competition Policy of the New Commission*, EGKartellrechtsforum der Studienvereinigung Kartellrecht Brussels 11/5/1995, available at http://europa.eu.int/comm/competition/index_en.html.

continued to follow this policy line. In particular, the speeches of these Commissioners make regular reference to the benefits consumers obtain as a result of competition law enforcement, whether this is lower prices as a result of dismantling a cartel, or more choice as a result of removing certain contract terms.[26] However, it should be recalled that competition law (and indeed, the economic provisions in the Treaty) are there also for the development of a strong European industry.[27] And a closer study of the development of the Community shows that an even broader range of objectives have influenced EU competition law.

R. Wesseling, *The Modernisation of EC Antitrust Law* (Oxford/Portland, Hart, 2000) 48–9

Initially, the antitrust law provisions were inserted into the Treaty in view of their role in the process of market integration. The antitrust rules were no more than the private counterpart to the rules, enshrined in Arts 28–30 EC which guaranteed freedom to trade across borders without hindrance from the Community's Member States. The framers of the Treaty wanted to preclude private undertakings replacing the prohibited public obstacles to inter-state trade. The first period of Community antitrust policy [1958–1973][28] saw the Commission enforcing the rules with constant reference to ensuring the free flow of goods, thus promoting market integration.

Subsequently, in the second period [1973–1985], antitrust policy was employed to establish a broader Community industrial policy. Exemptions for the antitrust rules were granted to forms of (trans-national) co-operation between undertakings which the Commission considered desirable, to promote either integration (*Eurocheque*) or broader Community policy aims (for example employment in crisis sectors). Thus, a Community industrial policy was gradually developed on the basis of the Treaty's antitrust rules.

The momentum generated by the Commission's '1992 programme' then provided the occasion for expanding the scope of Community antitrust policy even further [in the third period commencing in 1985]. With continued reference to the needs of market integration, the Commission acquired powers under the Merger Regulation to regulate the structure of markets. Furthermore it extended the enforcement of the antitrust rules to the public sectors of the various Member States. While reference was still made to the underpinning of Community antitrust law in economic integration, the socio-political implications of integration by competition (law) became ever more apparent. In this respect the control of corporate mergers and the gradual liberalisation of public economic sectors, both highly political exercises, which commenced by the end of the 1980s, symbolise the altered character of Community antitrust law enforcement.

Although the system was originally devised for promoting market integration, antitrust policy is now also – and mainly – directed at promoting the various objectives of the Community enshrined in Article 2 EC. Absent a clear hierarchy between those objectives, priorities are selected on a case by case basis. Agreements between undertakings have been exempted from the prohibition in Article 81(1) EC when their negative effect on the intensity of competition on the relevant market was outweighed by positive consequences for European industry's competitiveness, or for social and economic cohesion. Likewise, mergers are sometimes held compatible with the common market, in spite of the significant reduction in the degree of competition they engender, when the Commission considers that they may contribute

---

[26] See e.g. M. Monti, 'European Competition for the 21st Century' (2001) *Fordham Corporate Law Institute* 257, 257–8.

[27] European Commission, *A Pro-active Competition Policy for a Competitive Europe*, COM(2004)293 final, esp. ch. 2.

[28] The author uses the same time periods as J. Weiler, 'The Transformation of Europe' (1991) 100 *Yale Law Journal* 2403.

to one or more of the objectives laid down in Article 2 EC. While it is not submitted that the majority of antitrust issues is settled on the basis of extra-competition elements, it is evident from the Commission decisions, endorsed by the European Courts, that the Commission is able to pursue 'flanking' policies on the basis of its enforcement of the antitrust rules.

This review suggests that a wide range of policy issues affect competition law decisions, and that competition law objectives might at times take second place to other Community values. On the one hand, we might be sympathetic to the use of competition law to sustain other Community policies, but this would be to forget that there are other, direct means to achieve them, and that using competition law may not be the most effective means.[29] Secondly, legal certainty for market participants is undermined if competition law is modified to achieve other objectives. Lastly, there is a risk that by securing other policies, markets may not develop efficiently and thereby harm consumers. These concerns, among others, led the Commission to try and concentrate on regulating markets only when there was harm to consumer welfare. However, as we illustrate in this and the following chapters, there remain episodes where competition is enforced for the pursuit of other goals.

(iv) Impact of the economic crisis

In recent history, two events have shaken the Commission's commitment to a consumer-welfare oriented enforcement style. The first can now be laid to rest as a storm in a teacup: in the Treaty Establishing a Constitution for Europe the draftsman had inserted a provision setting out the objectives of the Union for the first time. Among the objectives it identified the following: 'an internal market where competition is free and undistorted'.[30] After the rejection of this Treaty by a number of national referenda, the French President seized the opportunity to remove the reference to competition as an objective of the Union (see Article 3(3) TEU), which was a move in response to a perception that one of the reasons the Treaty was rejected was the over-emphasis on markets at the expense of the social dimension.[31] Whatever political gain was secured, from a legal perspective this is irrelevant: the Union's competences remain unchanged.[32] And since then there has been no alteration of the Commission's policy or of the stance taken by the Court of Justice.[33]

The second event which has a much more significant impact on competition enforcement is the economic recession the world has found itself in since 2008. Should this lead

---

[29] L. Kaplow, 'On the Choice of Welfare Standards in Competition Law' in D. Zimmer (ed.), *The Goals of Competition Law* (Cheltenham, Edward Elgar, 2012).

[30] Constitutional Treaty, Article I-3-2.

[31] See the anger in *Statement by European Commissioner for Competition Neelie Kroes on Results of June 21–22 European Council, Protocol on Internal Market and Competition*, Memo 07/250, 27 June 2007, available at http://europa.eu/rapid/press-release_MEMO-07--250_en.htm.

[32] For a fuller discussion, see G. Monti, 'EU Competition Law from Rome to Lisbon: Social Market Economy' in C. Heide-Jorgensen, C. Bergqvist, U. Neergard and S. T. Poulsen (eds.), *Aims and Values in Competition Law* (Copenhagen, DJØF Publishing, 2013). A number of authors have mistakenly stated that the Lisbon Treaty amended former Article 3(1)(g) EC, however this provision was not amended in any way, but simply moved to Article 3(1)(b) TFEU, clarifying the EU's exclusive competence in the field of competition policy.

[33] In the second edition of this work we had speculated that the ECJ might respond to this amendment, but has ignored it; see in particular Case C-52/09 *Telia Sonera* [2011] ECR-527.

to less strict competition law enforcement? The rhetoric from the Commission is that competition law enforcement is part of the solution to the economic crisis. Firms cannot be allowed to form cartels as a means of surviving the crisis: some firms should exit the market if they are not competitive, to allow the more efficient firms to serve consumers best. Nor can merger control be made more lenient to support politically important industries. The former Competition Commissioner, Neelie Kroes, described this approach as 'tough love'.[34] The justification of this stance is the following: first, in the aftermath of the global recession of 1929 the US Government had supported a relaxation of antitrust laws but an influential study came to the conclusion that this made matters worse, not better.[35] Secondly, the Commission reflected back on its own management of the oil crisis in the 1970s and concluded that its lax approach to competition law, which included allowing the formation of so-called crisis cartels (i.e. agreements between manufacturers to reduce output collectively so as to ensure that all firms survived) was a failure because it did not force industries to adjust.[36] Furthermore, Wigger and Buch-Hansen have suggested that while crises normally lead to policy changes, the present crisis has not made an impression for five reasons. First, the policy approach has been to fix the current economic system rather than rethink it; secondly, this approach has the backing of major industrial and financial interest groups as well as politicians; thirdly, no concrete alternative to the current economic system has been identified. The fourth and fifth reasons are given in the extract below.

A. Wigger and H. Buch-Hansen, 'Explaining (Missing) Regulatory Paradigm Shifts: EU Competition Regulation in Times of Economic Crisis' (2013) New Political Economy 1, 18

Fourth, the Commission, enjoying significant powers and a considerable degree of operational autonomy from Member State governments, has been able to take a proactive approach in acting as a neoliberal crisis manager, interfering with national-level crisis management and prescribing ever more vigorous neoliberal policies. By being strategically selective, it has privileged the interests of organised financial capital and national crisis strategies compatible with neoliberal ideas. The relative strength of the DG, namely its institutional independence, discretionary powers and resources as well as ensuing business support, allowed it to oppose fundamental institutional change, thereby marginalising more radical solutions from the outset and thus the possibility for a regulatory paradigm shift.

The fifth and final factor relates to the absence of a wider shift in the regulation of economic activities…Recent studies in the fields of EU financial services regulation, EU trade policies and international tax policies as well as the budget austerity programmes orchestrated by the EU–IMF tandem more generally suggest that neoliberalism is currently being reworked and extended in various regulatory fields rather than being abandoned. Against the backdrop of the prevalence of a neoliberal crisis management filling merely regulatory gaps in the financial sector, a paradigm shift in the field of EU competition regulation is also unlikely at this stage.

---

[34] Neelie Kroes, 'Competition, the Crisis and the Road to Recovery', address at Economic Club of Toronto, Speech/09/152, 30 March 2009.

[35] H. L. Cole and L. E. Ohanian, 'New Deal Policies and the Persistence of the Great Depression: A General Equilibrium Analysis' (2004) 112 *Journal of Political Economy* 779.

[36] OECD Global Forum on Competition, *Crisis Cartels* (DAF/COMP/GF(2011)11) 109–20.

Turning to enforcement, the only visible relaxation of the antitrust rules has been with respect to the Commission's fining policy in cartel cases. Here the Commission has reduced fines on undertakings if they show that in the given economic circumstances the fine would cause irretrievable damage to their business, such that, first, the assets would disappear from the market and, secondly, this would lead to an 'increase in unemployment or deterioration in the economic sectors upstream and downstream of the undertaking concerned'.[37] This provision balances the aim of fines (deterrence) with the aim of avoiding social losses from insolvency, and in a scenario of economic crisis the social costs are higher as re-entry into the market is more difficult. However, there has not been a significant amount of cases to which this fine reduction was applied.[38]

3 ENFORCEMENT BY THE COMMISSION

The Commission's powers were originally set out in Regulation 17/62, which was in force between 1962 and 2004, and have been expanded by Regulation 1/2003, which is in force from 1 May 2004.[39] As intimated above, while in 1962 one did not expect much from competition policy, today it has 'a kind of rock star status'[40] because of the active way these powers are exercised.

The cases the Commission takes up have two sources. First, the Commission may start an investigation on its own initiative, triggered by press reports, or its investigation of an economic sector under the powers provided in Regulation 1/2003, article 17. Secondly, some cases arise from complaints made by private parties or 'confessions' made by undertakings that have infringed the rules. However, the Commission has no obligation to reach a decision on every complaint or confession it receives: it may prioritise cases on the basis of whether there is a Union-wide interest.[41] This is so where the parties commit important violations, where the case gives rise to novel points of law, or where the practices in question have a significant effect on market integration.[42] Given the powers of national competition authorities to apply EU competition law, this provides a further basis for declining to take up a case.

The enforcement procedure, which is administrative in character, is divided into two stages.[43] In the first stage, the Commission gathers evidence to determine whether there has been an infringement. In the second stage, it makes its concerns known to the parties being investigated and after a hearing issues a decision.[44]

---

[37] Case T-352/09 *Novácke chemické závody a.s.* v *Commission*, Judgment of 12 December 2012, para. 192.

[38] P. Kienapfel and G. Wils, 'Inability to Pay: First Cases and Practical Experiences' (2010) 3 *Competition Policy Newsletter* 3.

[39] Regulation 17/62 First Regulation implementing Articles 81 and 82 [1959] OJ Special Edn 062, 57; Regulation 1/2003 on the implementation of the rules on competition laid down in Articles 81 and 82 [2003] OJ L1/1.

[40] R. D. Kelemen, *Eurolegalism: The Transformation of Law and Regulation in the European Union* (Cambridge, MA, Harvard University Press, 2011) 143.

[41] Case T-24/90 *Automec Srl* v *Commission (Automec II)* [1992] ECR II-2223; but reasons must be given, see T-427/08 *CEAHR* v *Commission* [2010] ECR II-5865.

[42] Commission Notice on cooperation within the Network of Competition Authorities [2004] OJ C101/42, paras. 14, 15 and 54.

[43] For a detailed exposition, see C. S. Kerse and N. Kahn, *EU Antitrust Procedure* (6th edn, London, Sweet & Maxwell, 2012). See also Commission Regulation 773/2004 of 7 April 2004 relating to the conduct of proceedings by the Commission pursuant to Articles 81 and 82 of the EC Treaty [2004] OJ L123/18, setting out in more detail the practicalities of the proceedings; and a helpful guide is also DG Competition's *Manual of Procedure for the Application of Articles 101 and 102 TFEU* (March 2012).

[44] Joined Cases C-238/99P, C-244/99P, C-245/99P, C-247/99P, C-250–252/99P and C-254/99P *Limburgse Vinyl Maatschappij NV and others* v *Commission* [2002] ECR I-8375, paras. 181–3.

(i) First stage: investigation

In order to obtain information to determine whether an undertaking has infringed competition law, the Commission has two powers. First, it may require undertakings to hand over information and carry out interviews; secondly, it has power to inspect business premises and private homes to seize relevant documents.

(a) Requests for information and interviews

Regulation 1/2003, article 18(1) empowers the Commission to require undertakings to hand over information, but only that which is related to the infringement.[45] The Commission may make a simple request (to which reply is not compulsory, but a fine is payable if incorrect information is supplied intentionally or negligently),[46] or issue a decision requiring information to be provided. The information normally consists of documents setting out how the undertaking has acted. The Commission had also recently begun to rely on statements made to it by the parties.[47] Regulation 1/2003 codifies this practice in article 19(1), which empowers the Commission to interview any person who consents to be interviewed, but there are no penalties if the information provided is incorrect or misleading.

In supplying information, there is a risk that the undertaking is providing proof that it has infringed competition law. This would run counter to the undertaking's right against self-incrimination and in a challenge to a request for information by the Commission, the Court of Justice recognised this right in part. First, the right not to incriminate oneself only applies to requests where the addressee is required to reply, under pain of a fine; in cases of a simple request, this protection is not available, because the undertaking has no duty to reply.[48] Secondly, even in cases of requests made under pain of a fine, the right is limited.

Case 374/87 *Orkem* v *Commission* [1989] ECR 3283

28. In the absence of any right to remain silent expressly embodied in Regulation No. 17 [now Regulation 1/2003], it is appropriate to consider whether and to what extent the general principles of Community law, of which fundamental rights form an integral part and in the light of which all Community legislation must be interpreted, require, as the applicant claims, recognition of the right not to supply information capable of being used in order to establish, against the person supplying it, the existence of an infringement of the competition rules...

33. In that connection, the Court observed recently that whilst it is true that the rights of the defence must be observed in administrative procedures which may lead to the imposition of penalties, it is necessary to prevent those rights from being irremediably impaired during preliminary inquiry procedures which may be decisive in providing evidence of the unlawful nature of conduct engaged in by undertakings and for which they may be liable. Consequently, although certain rights of the defence relate only to contentious proceedings which follow the delivery of the statement of objections, other rights must be respected even during the preliminary inquiry.

---

[45] Case C-36/92 P *SEP* v *Commission* [1994] ECR I-1911, para. 21.
[46] Regulation 1/2003, article 23(1).
[47] E.g. *Pre-insulated Pipes* [1999] OJ L24/1, para. 24; *Zinc Phosphate* [2003] OJ L153/1, paras. 57 and 59.
[48] Case C-407/04P *Damline SpA* v *Commission* [2007] ECR I-835, paras. 33–6.

34. Accordingly, whilst the Commission is entitled, in order to preserve the useful effect of Article [18 of Regulation 1/2003], to compel an undertaking to provide all necessary information concerning such facts as may be known to it and to disclose to it, if necessary, such documents relating thereto as are in its possession, even if the latter may be used to establish, against it or another undertaking, the existence of anti-competitive conduct, it may not, by means of a decision calling for information, undermine the rights of defence of the undertaking concerned.

35. Thus, the Commission may not compel an undertaking to provide it with answers which might involve an admission on its part of the existence of an infringement which it is incumbent upon the Commission to prove.

On the facts of the case, the Court of Justice held that some of the information sought by the Commission infringed the applicant's rights. For example:

> [b]y requiring disclosure of the 'details of any system or method which made it possible to attribute sales targets or quotas to the participants' and details of 'any method facilitating annual monitoring of compliance with any system of targets in terms of volume or quotas', the Commission endeavoured to obtain from the applicant an acknowledgment of its participation in an agreement intended to limit or control production or outlets or to share markets.

Likewise, the Commission cannot ask parties how many meetings they had with their competitors that infringed Article 101 TFEU. However, it is possible to obtain documentary information concerning agreements entered into, or factual information, for example about which undertakings were present in certain meetings.[49] Following *Orkem*, parties have challenged the Commission's requests for information as infringing the privilege against self-incrimination, with occasional success.[50] The Court of Justice has not changed the position taken in *Orkem*, and a helpful explanation is found in Advocate General Geelhoed's Opinion.

Case C-301/04P *Commission* v *SGL Carbon* [2006] ECR I-5915, Opinion of Advocate General Geelhoed

67. …the interplay between the fundamental rights of legal persons and competition enforcement remains a balancing exercise: at stake are the protection of fundamental rights versus effective enforcement of Community competition law. Article [101 TFEU] is a fundamental provision which is essential for the accomplishment of the tasks entrusted to the Community and, in particular, for the functioning of the internal market. Article [101 TFEU] forms part of public policy. If the Commission is no longer empowered to request the production of documents its enforcement of competition law in the Community legal order will become heavily dependent on either voluntary cooperation or on the use of other means of coercion as for example dawn raids. It is self-evident that the effective enforcement with reasonable means of the basic tenets of the Community public legal order should remain possible, just as it is evident that the rights of the defence should be respected too. In my view, the latter is the case. As case-law now stands, a defendant is still able, either during the administrative procedure or in the proceedings before the Community courts, to contend that the documents produced have a different meaning from that ascribed to them by the Commission.[51]

---

[49] *Austrian Banks* [2002] OJ L56/1, para. 488.
[50] E.g. Case T-112/98 *Mannesmannröhren-Werke AG* v *Commission* [2001] ECR II-729, para. 71.
[51] The ECJ took the same view; see paras. 39–49 of the judgment.

While the General Court considers that the approach reflects the jurisprudence of the European Court of Human Rights (ECtHR) on the right against self-incrimination, commentators have been less convinced.[52] There are two points of debate. The first is whether the judgments of the Court of Justice are in conformity with those of the ECtHR. Here the Court of Justice appears to take the view that they are, on the ground that when asking for documents one is seeking information which is available independently of the person. If they are not, then the second issue is whether the right against self-incrimination developed in the context of human rights law should apply with equal vigour to the enforcement of economic laws. According to Advocate General Geelhoed, 'it is not possible simply to transpose the findings of the European Court of Human Rights without more to legal persons or undertakings'.[53]

The Court of Justice also protects the privacy of communications between an undertaking and its lawyers, and information passing between lawyer and client need not be disclosed. This rule is justified by the view that the lawyer collaborates in the administration of justice and is required to provide, independently and confidentially, any legal assistance the client needs.[54] However, the Court curtails lawyer-client privilege in one way: it only protects communication by independent lawyers, not in-house lawyers. The rationale for this is that in many Member States in-house lawyers are not subject to professional codes of discipline.[55] Furthermore, the information that is privileged only extends to matters linked with the subject matter of the investigation, which will normally be material written after the investigation.[56] It may include working documents prepared by the undertaking to aid the lawyers in preparing the defence.[57]

(b) Inspections

The Commission's most draconian means to secure information about a possible competition law infringement are its powers to enter business premises of the parties under investigation and seize the relevant information. These procedures are colloquially referred to as 'dawn raids'.[58]

---

[52] See Case T-112/98 *Mannesmannröhren-Werke AG* v *Commission* [2001] ECR II-729, para. 77. The leading cases are *Funke* v *France* [1993] 16 EHRR 297; *Saunders* v *United Kingdom* (1997) 23 EHRR 313. For comment see I. van Bael and J.-F. Bellis, *Competition Law of the European Community* (4th edn, The Hague, Kluwer Law International, 2005) 107, opining that national courts which are signatories to the ECHR might interpret the ECHR more strictly than the ECJ; A. McCulloch, 'The Privilege Against Self-incrimination in Competition Investigations' (2006) 26(2) *Legal Studies* 211, criticising the distinction between factual questions and admissions of infringement.

[53] Case C-301/04P *Commission* v *SGL Carbon* [2006] ECR I-5915, Opinion of Advocate General Geelhoed, para. 63. See further S. Douglas-Scott, 'A Tale of Two Courts: Luxembourg, Strasbourg and the Growing Human Rights Acquis' (2006) 43 *CMLRev.* 629.

[54] Case 155/79 *AM&S Europe Ltd* v *Commission* [1982] ECR 1575, para. 24. See generally J. Faull, 'Legal Professional Privilege: The Commission Proposes International Negotiations' (1985) 10 *ELRev.* 119.

[55] While the President of the Court of Justice (Case C-7/04P(R)) noted that, given changes in the regulation of the profession in many Member States, the exclusion may be obsolete (paras. 125–6), the General Court has confirmed the approach of the ECJ in Cases T-125 and T-253/03 *Akzo Nobel Chemicals Ltd and Akcros Chemicals Ltd* v *Commission* [2007] ECR II-3523.

[56] See Case 155/79 *AM&S Europe Ltd* v *Commission* [1982] ECR 1575.

[57] *Akzo* [2007] ECR II-3523, paras. 123–4.

[58] J. Joshua, 'The Element of Surprise' (1983) *ELRev.* 3.

Regulation 1/2003, articles 20(1), (2), 21(1)

Article 20

1. In order to carry out the duties assigned to it by this Regulation, the Commission may conduct all necessary inspections of undertakings and associations of undertakings.
2. The officials and other accompanying persons authorised by the Commission to conduct an inspection are empowered:
   (a) to enter any premises, land and means of transport of undertakings and associations of undertakings;
   (b) to examine the books and other records related to the business, irrespective of the medium on which they are stored;
   (c) to take or obtain in any form copies of or extracts from such books or records;
   (d) to seal any business premises and books or records for the period and to the extent necessary for the inspection;
   (e) to ask any representative or member of staff of the undertaking or association of undertakings for explanations on facts or documents relating to the subject-matter and purpose of the inspection and to record the answers...

Article 21(1)

1. If a reasonable suspicion exists that books or other records related to the business and to the subject-matter of the inspection, which may be relevant to prove a serious violation of Article [101 TFEU] or Article [102 TFEU]... are being kept in any other premises, land and means of transport, including the homes of directors, managers and other members of staff of the undertakings and associations of undertakings concerned, the Commission can by decision order an inspection to be conducted in such other premises, land and means of transport.

The Commission must specify the subject matter and purpose of its investigation 'not merely to show that the proposed entry onto the premises of the undertakings concerned is justified but also to enable those undertakings to assess the scope of their duty to cooperate whilst at the same time safeguarding their rights of defence'.[59] Article 21 is an innovation and provides for searches into private homes, but these require prior authorisation from a national court where the premises are located.

The Commission's power to search premises is controversial when judged against fundamental rights standards. Article 8 of the European Convention of Human Rights (ECHR) incorporates a right to private and family life. A derogation from this right is specified in Article 8(2) ECHR, which states that infringements of privacy are justified only when necessary, inter alia, for the economic wellbeing of the country or the prevention of crime. To benefit from the derogation in Article 8(2), the interference with the right to privacy must be based on accessible legal rules, the interference must have a legitimate aim, and there must be effective protection against abuse by the investigators.[60] The Court of Justice originally held that privacy rights recognised by the ECHR only applied to searches of private homes, not business premises, although a similar right to privacy of business premises was held to exist as a general

[59] Joined Cases 46/87 and 227/88 *Hoechst AG* v *Commission* [1989] ECR 2859, para. 19.
[60] Kerse and Kahn, n. 43 above, 166; *Société Colas Est and others* v *France* (2004) 39 EHRR 17.

principle of EU law which protects all private persons against 'arbitrary or disproportionate intervention by public authorities'.[61]

This narrow interpretation of an undertaking's right to privacy under Community law must now be reconsidered as a result of two developments in the case law of the ECtHR. First, in *Niemetz* v *Germany*, the ECtHR held that the right to private life does not merely encompass private homes but also business premises, when this is necessary to protect the individual against arbitrary interference by public authorities.[62] Secondly, in *Société Colas Est and others* v *France*, the ECtHR held that in competition cases, prior judicial authorisation is required when conducting inspections so as to afford adequate and effective safeguards against abuse.[63]

Applied to EU competition law, the *Niemetz* case suggests that Article 8 rights can no longer be distinguished on the basis that they only apply to private homes. This means that inspections are only lawful if they benefit from the derogation in Article 8(2) ECHR. Regulation 1/2003, articles 20 and 21 inspections normally satisfy the first two requirements established by the ECtHR for Article 8(2) ECHR (the rules are transparent and the purpose is the suppression of anti-competitive behaviour). However, the principal doubt about the legality of the Commission's inspection procedures is whether there is effective protection against abuse, particularly in light of the *Société Colas Est* ruling. However, the Court of Justice in *Roquette Frères* did not consider judicial authorisation to be necessary, unless the Member State where the inspection is due to take place requires judicial authorisation. The main justification for not requiring prior judicial authorisation is that it is possible to seek judicial review after the event, on the grounds that, in the circumstances, a dawn raid was arbitrary, disproportionate or excessive.[64] If the Court of Justice agrees with the applicant that the Commission abused its powers, then the Commission would be prevented from using, for the purposes of proceeding in respect of an infringement of the Community competition rules, any documents or evidence which it might have obtained in the course of that investigation.[65] The Court of Justice's ruling was later codified in Regulation 1/2003.

Regulation 1/2003, article 20(6)–(8)

6. Where the officials and other accompanying persons authorised by the Commission find that an undertaking opposes an inspection ordered pursuant to this Article, the Member State concerned shall afford them the necessary assistance, requesting where appropriate the assistance of the police or of an equivalent enforcement authority, so as to enable them to conduct their inspection.

7. If the assistance provided for in paragraph 6 requires authorisation from a judicial authority according to national rules, such authorisation shall be applied for. Such authorisation may also be applied for as a precautionary measure.

8. Where authorisation as referred to in paragraph 7 is applied for, the national judicial authority shall control that the Commission decision is authentic and that the coercive measures envisaged

---

[61] C-94/00 *Roquette Frères* v *Directeur général de la concurrence, de la consommation et de la répression des frauds* [2002] ECR I-9011.

[62] *Niemetz* v *Germany* [1993] 16 EHRR 97, para. 31; *Veeber* v *Estonia (No. 1)* [2004] 39 EHRR 6.

[63] *Société Colas Est and others* v *France* (Application no. 37971/97) [2002] ECHR 418, Judgment of 16 April 2002, para. 49.

[64] Joined Cases 97–99/87 *Dow Chemical Ibérica and others* v *Commission* [1989] ECR 3165, para. 16.

[65] C-94/00 *Roquette Frères* v *Directeur général de la concurrence, de la consommation et de la répression des frauds* [2002] ECR I-9011, para. 49.

are neither arbitrary nor excessive having regard to the subject matter of the inspection. In its control of the proportionality of the coercive measures, the national judicial authority may ask the Commission, directly or through the Member State competition authority, for detailed explanations in particular on the grounds the Commission has for suspecting infringement of Articles [101 TFEU] and [102 TFEU]…as well as on the seriousness of the suspected infringement and on the nature of the involvement of the undertaking concerned. However, the national judicial authority may not call into question the necessity for the inspection nor demand that it be provided with the information in the Commission's file. The lawfulness of the Commission decision shall be subject to review only by the Court of Justice.

However, it has been argued that this falls short of the requirements for derogation stipulated by the ECtHR's case law because a judicial warrant need not be obtained in all cases, and the scope for judicial scrutiny by the national judge in article 20(8) is limited.[66] Accordingly, dawn raids may be challenged, either at national level, questioning national courts' authorisations of Commission inspections,[67] or at Community level, for compatibility with the protection of the undertaking's fundamental rights in the absence of judicial authorisation.

(ii) Second stage: adjudication

Once the information is gathered, two steps precede the Commission's decision. First, the Commission issues a statement of objections and the parties have access to the Commission's file to see the evidence upon which the allegations are based. Secondly, the parties have the right to a hearing. The rationale for these procedures is to guarantee the parties rights to defend themselves.

(a) Statement of objections and access to the file

After proceedings have begun, the Commission must notify the parties of the infringements that it believes have been committed. This document is known as the statement of objections.

Regulation 1/2003, article 27(1)

1. Before taking decisions…the Commission shall give the undertakings or associations of undertakings which are the subject of the proceedings conducted by the Commission the opportunity of being heard on the matters to which the Commission has taken objection. The Commission shall base its decisions only on objections on which the parties concerned have been able to comment. Complainants shall be associated closely with the proceedings.

---

[66] A. Riley, 'The ECHR Implications of the Investigation Provisions of the Draft Competition Regulation' (2002) 51 *ICLQ* 55, 76–7.

[67] As in Case C-94/00 *Roquette Frères* v *Directeur général de la concurrence, de la consommation et de la répression des fraudes* [2002] ECR I-9011, appeal against an order of a local judge to empower the Commission to conduct an investigation on the appellant's premises.

As the final sentence of article 27(1) makes clear, the Commission can only issue a decision on grounds set out in the statement of objections. Originally, the Commission would only allow the defendants access to incriminating evidence, which was unsatisfactory because the parties would not be able to see documents that would have been useful for their defence. However, in 1982, the Commission developed a practice to give access to all the documents it used in preparing the case (except for documents containing business secrets of other undertakings, other confidential information and internal documents of the Commission)[68] which was made compulsory by the General Court.[69] Following this judgment, the rights to access were specified in a Notice,[70] and now the right to access the file is enshrined in Regulation 1/2003.[71]

Regulation 1/2003, article 27(2)

2. The rights of defence of the parties concerned shall be fully respected in the proceedings. They shall be entitled to have access to the Commission's file, subject to the legitimate interest of undertakings in the protection of their business secrets. The right of access to the file shall not extend to confidential information and internal documents of the Commission or the competition authorities of the Member States. In particular, the right of access shall not extend to correspondence between the Commission and the competition authorities of the Member States, or between the latter. Nothing in this paragraph shall prevent the Commission from disclosing and using information necessary to prove an infringement.

A key principle of EU law is 'equality of arms': the party accused of an infringement has access to the Commission's entire file (save for the documents protected by article 27(2)) and it is not for the Commission to decide which documents to pass on.[72]

(b) Oral hearing

Hearings are normally attended by the following: the parties accused, complainants, Commission representatives and representatives of the national competition authorities. They are moderated by a hearing officer. This Commission official is independent of DG Competition and reports directly to the Commissioner for competition. He or she is not involved in the preparation of the case and has the task of ensuring 'that the hearing is properly conducted and contributes to the objectivity of the hearing itself and of any decision taken subsequently'.[73]

---

[68] Case T-23/99 *LR AF 1998* v *Commission* [2002] ECR II-1705, para. 170.

[69] Case T-7/89 *Hercules* v *Commission* [1991] ECR II-1711, paras. 52–3.

[70] In 1997, the current version is Commission Notice on the internal rules of procedure for processing requests for access to the file in cases pursuant to Articles 81 and 82 of the EC Treaty [2005] OJ C325/7.

[71] And recognised by the ECJ, see e.g. Joined Cases 204/00P etc. *Aalborg Portland A/S and others* v *Commission* [2004] ECR I-123, paras. 68–77.

[72] Case T-30/91 *Solvay SA* v *Commission* [1995] ECR II-1775, paras. 81–3. For a critique see C. D. Ehlermann and B. J. Drijber, 'Legal Protection of Enterprises: Administrative Procedure, in Particular Access to the File and Confidentiality' [1996] *ECLR* 375.

[73] Decision of the President of the European Commission of 13 October 2011 on the function and terms of reference of the hearing officer in certain competition proceedings [2011] OJ L275/29.

The hearing is composed of arguments by the Commission and the accused, and is followed by questions from those present.[74] Before the hearing the defendant will have had several exchanges of view with DG Competition. However, it has been said that the hearing is useful because it is the only time for the defendant to set out its case to the national authorities, to the Commission's legal service, and to representatives of other Directorates-General.[75]

After the hearings, the Commission prepares a decision acting as a collegiate body. Draft decisions are reviewed by the Advisory Committee which is composed of representatives of Member States' competition authorities.[76] The Commission must take the 'utmost account' of the Committee's views but is not bound to follow them.[77] For most competition cases, the Commission operates with a 'written procedure' whereby the draft decision is circulated to all Commissioners and is adopted if there are no objections.[78] For controversial cases however, there are debates among the Commissioners, and lobbying is not uncommon.[79] The decisions must be fully reasoned to allow the parties to see which findings of fact and of law led the Commission to its conclusion.[80] This is necessary to afford the parties the opportunity of challenging the Commission's decision in the courts.

(iii) Penalties for infringement

Once an infringement is established, the Commission has a wide range of powers, which may be divided into two categories. First, the Commission has powers to bring the infringement to a close and to remedy the anti-competitive effects of the anti-competitive practice.

Regulation 1/2003, article 7(1)

1. Where the Commission, acting on a complaint or on its own initiative, finds that there is an infringement of Article [101 TFEU] or of Article [102 TFEU]…it may by decision require the undertakings and associations of undertakings concerned to bring such infringement to an end. For this purpose, it may impose on them any behavioural or structural remedies which are proportionate to the infringement committed and necessary to bring the infringement effectively to an end. Structural remedies can only be imposed either where there is no equally effective behavioural remedy or where any equally effective behavioural remedy would be more burdensome for the undertaking concerned than the structural remedy. If the Commission has a legitimate interest in doing so, it may also find that an infringement has been committed in the past.

In a cartel case, for example, the Commission will normally demand that the undertakings bring the agreement to an end so that the damage to competition does not continue. It may also order parties to change their behaviour vis-à-vis competitors, a sanction which has been imposed upon dominant undertakings to oblige them to supply competitors.[81] However, the Commission cannot impose obligations that are not necessary to bring the infringement to an

---

[74] For detail see Regulation 773/2004 [2004] OJ L123/18. [75] Van Bael and Bellis, n. 52 above, 1096.
[76] Regulation 1/2003, article 14. [77] *Ibid.* article 14(5).
[78] Van Bael and Bellis, n. 52 above, 1103.
[79] 'Brussels braces for a lobbying invasion', *Financial Times*, 3 October 2005.
[80] Case 41/69 *ACF Chemiefarmia* v *Commission* [1970] ECR 661, paras. 76–81.
[81] See e.g. Case T-201/04 *Microsoft* v *Commission* [2007] ECR II-3601.

end. In one case the General Court held that requiring members of a cartel to stop fixing prices was legitimate, but asking them to inform customers that they may renegotiate the contracts that had been signed when the cartel inflated prices was unnecessary, because the contracts in question were only of a year's duration and because if parties to a cartel suffer losses, this is a matter to be addressed by the national court.[82]

Article 7 adds a novel remedy: empowering the Commission to impose 'structural remedies'. This can entail a demand that a company be broken up into two or more smaller units – a remedy so draconian it is likely to be used sparingly. The final sentence of article 7 allows the Commission to make decisions against infringements that have occurred in the past but only if there is a legitimate interest: for example, clarifying a point of law or issuing a decision to facilitate follow-on damages claims.[83]

The second category of powers the Commission has is penalising the undertaking for breaching competition law. Fines not exceeding 1 per cent of the undertaking's turnover may be imposed for procedural infringements (for example, supplying incorrect or misleading information),[84] and fines not exceeding 10 per cent of the undertaking's turnover may be imposed for intentional or negligent infringements of Articles 101 and 102 TFEU.[85] The Commission's approach to fines should be read together with its policy on leniency applications and settlements. In this way, we can gain a sense of the Commission's enforcement strategy as a whole.

(a) Fining policy

In the early days, the fines were fairly low but they have increased gradually. In 1980 the Commission declared that fines would be increased as a means of deterring undertakings,[86] and in 1991, it announced that in appropriate cases it would apply the highest penalty possible: 10 per cent of the undertaking's turnover.[87] The gradual increase can be seen as a sensible policy in that in the early years undertakings were unfamiliar with their obligations under the competition rules, but as the culture of competition spread, and as the deadline for achieving a single market neared, the fines were increased. The current policy targeting cartels has led to ever greater fines. Between 2009 and mid-2013 the Commission imposed fines for infringements of Article 101 TFEU amounting to €6.5 billion.[88] The highest fines to date (€1,470,515,000) were imposed in 2012 on undertakings that took part in a cartel in the TV and monitor tubes cartel.[89]

---

[82] Case T-395/94 *Atlantic Container Line* v *Commission* [2002] ECR II-875, paras. 410–16.

[83] Case 7/82 *GVL* v *Commission* [1983] ECR 483, para. 24.

[84] Regulation 1/2003, article 23(1).

[85] *Ibid.* article 23(2).

[86] *Pioneer* [1980] OJ L60/21; affirmed in Joined Cases 100–103/80 *Musique diffusion française and others* v *Commission* [1983] ECR 1825, paras. 105–9.

[87] European Commission, *Twenty-first Report on Competition Policy* (1991), para. 139 (e.g. *Fine Art Auction Houses*, Decision of [2005] OJ L200/92, but here Christie's escaped without a fine because of its cooperation and Sotheby's fines were reduced by 40 per cent because of its cooperation); *Pre Insulated Pipe Cartel* [1999] OJ L24/1, para. 176.

[88] Source: http://ec.europa.eu/competition/cartels/statistics/statistics.pdf (before the parties appealed against the fine, the precise figure was €7,040,649,074; after the appeals concluded the precise total shrunk to €6,555,439,074).

[89] 'Commission fines producers of TV and computer monitor tubes €1.47 billion for two decade-long cartels', Press Release IP/12/1317, 5 December 2012.

However, the Commission is often criticised for imposing fines arbitrarily, in particular due to the vagueness of article 23(3) of Regulation 1/2003, which merely provides: 'in fixing the amount of the fine, regard shall be had both to the gravity and duration of the infringement'. In response to calls for greater transparency, the Commission issued Guidelines on the method of setting fines in 1998, which were updated in 2006.[90] The current Guidelines reflect the Commission's practice and take into account the rulings of the Court of Justice;[91] but also aim to provide for tougher fines to deter the undertaking in question as well as all undertakings in the market. The Guidelines indicate that the Commission will first determine a 'basic amount' for the fine, which is then adjusted by considering aggravating or mitigating circumstances. We consider these two steps in turn.

The basic amount is set by reference to the value of the sales of the goods to which the infringement relates, having regard to the gravity of the infringement. For 'very serious' infringements (e.g. price fixing and market sharing) the basic amount will be up to 30 per cent of the value of the sales. Under the 2006 Guidelines, this figure is then multiplied by the number of years that the undertaking has infringed competition law.[92] Under the 1998 Guidelines, in contrast, an addition was made depending on the duration of the agreement. The change is significant in two respects. First, it places greater emphasis on the duration of the cartel, and secondly, it serves to raise the fine considerably. For example, under the old Guidelines, in a cartel lasting three years where the basic amount was €20 million, the Commission would add 50 per cent for duration, making the total fine €30 million. Under the new Guidelines the same infringement would lead to a fine of €60 million (€20 million x 3). In addition, an 'entry fee' is added to the basic amount (of between 15 and 25 per cent of the value of sales) to cartels that involve price-fixing, market sharing or output limitation, irrespective of duration.[93]

The basic amount is adjusted both (a) upwards if there are aggravating circumstances (for example, repeated infringements, for which the fine will be increased by 100 per cent for each previous infringement;[94] refusal to cooperate with the investigation; instigating the infringement); and (b) downwards in the presence of attenuating circumstances (for example, a passive role in the infringement; termination as soon as the investigation begins; the existence of reasonable doubt as to the legality of the practice).[95]

Two themes can be detected in the Commission's fining Guidelines. Deterrence features most prominently. The second theme focuses on sales as a proxy for how much each member stood to gain from the cartel, thereby imposes a more accurate fine on each member of the cartel. It can thus be said to lead to fairer fines as between cartel members. This is in response to one frequent ground on which fines are appealed: discrimination between cartel offenders.[96]

The European Courts have upheld the legality of the Commission's Guidelines.

---

[90] Guidelines on the method of setting fines imposed pursuant to Article 23(2)(a) of Regulation 1/2003 [2006] OJ C210/2.

[91] See further P. Manzini, 'European Antitrust in Search of the Perfect Fine' (2008) 31(1) *World Competition* 3; C. Veljanovski, 'Cartel Fines in Europe: Law, Practice and Deterrence' (2007) 30(1) *World Competition* 65.

[92] 2006 Guidelines, n. 90 above, para. 19.

[93] *Ibid.* para. 25.   [94] *Ibid.* para. 28.

[95] For an example of the application of the previous Guidelines, see Joined Cases T-236/01, T-239/01, T-244–246/01, T-251/01 and T-252/01 *Tokai Carbon Co. Ltd and others* v *Commission* [2004] ECR II-1181, paras. 291–315.

[96] E.g. in Case T-18/03 *CD Contact Data GmbH* v *Commission* [2009] ECR II-01021, the fine imposed was reduced to ensure compliance with the principle of equal treatment.

Case T-279/02 *Degussa AG v Commission* [2006] ECR II-897[97]

74. As regards the validity of Article 15(2) of Regulation No. 17 [now Article 23(2) of Regulation 1/2003] in the light of the principle that penalties must have a proper legal basis, as that principle has been recognised by the Community judicature in accordance with the guidance provided by the ECHR and the constitutional traditions of the Member States, it must be stated that, contrary to what the applicant maintains, the Commission does not have unlimited discretion in setting fines for infringements of the competition rules.... 76. While it is true that those two criteria [the 10 per cent ceiling and the consideration of gravity and duration] leave the Commission wide discretion, the fact remains that they are criteria which have been adopted by other legislatures for similar provisions, allowing the Commission to adopt sanctions taking account of the degree of illegality of the conduct in question. It must therefore be held, at this stage, that Article 15(2) of Regulation No. 17, while leaving the Commission a certain discretion, lays down the criteria and limits to which it is subject in the exercise of its power in regard to fines.

77. In addition, it must be pointed out that, in setting fines pursuant to Article 15(2) of Regulation No. 17, the Commission is bound to comply with the general principles of law, in particular the principles of equal treatment and proportionality, as developed by the case-law of the Court of Justice and the Court of First Instance.... 81. Furthermore, it is settled case-law that the Commission may at any time adjust the level of fines if the proper application of the Community competition rules so requires, since such an alteration of an administrative practice may then be regarded as objectively justified by the objective of general prevention of infringements of the Community competition rules. The recent increase in the level of fines, alleged and criticised by the applicant, cannot therefore, in itself, be regarded as unlawful under the principle that penalties must have a proper legal basis, since it remains within the statutory limits laid down by Article 15(2) of Regulation No. 17, as interpreted by the Community Courts.

82. Moreover, it should be borne in mind that, for the sake of transparency and in order to increase legal certainty on the part of the undertakings concerned, the Commission has published the Guidelines in which it sets out the method of calculation which it undertakes to apply in each individual case. In that regard, the Court of Justice has also held that, in adopting such rules of conduct and announcing by publishing them that they will henceforth apply to the cases to which they relate, the Commission imposes a limit on the exercise of its discretion and cannot depart from those rules under pain of being found, where appropriate, to be in breach of the general principles of law, such as equal treatment or the protection of legitimate expectations. In addition, although the Guidelines do not constitute the legal basis of the Decision, they determine, generally and abstractly, the method which the Commission has bound itself to use in assessing the fines imposed by the Decision and, consequently, ensure legal certainty on the part of the undertakings. It follows that, contrary to the applicant's assertions, the adoption by the Commission of the Guidelines, in so far as it fell within the statutory limits laid down by Article 15(2) of Regulation No. 17, cannot be regarded as marred by lack of competence and merely contributed to defining the limits of the exercise of the discretion which the Commission already had under that provision.

83. Consequently, in view of the various considerations set out above, a prudent trader, if need be by taking legal advice, can foresee in a sufficiently precise manner the method and order of magnitude of the fines which he incurs for a given line of conduct. The fact that that trader can, in advance, know precisely the level of the fines which the Commission will impose in each individual case cannot

---

[97] It was affirmed on appeal but only a summary of the judgment is provided: Case C-266/06P *Evonik Degussa v Commission* [2008] ECR I-81*.

constitute a breach of the principle that penalties must have a proper legal basis, since, due to the gravity of the infringements which the Commission is required to penalise, the objectives of punishment and deterrence justify preventing undertakings from being in a position to assess the benefits which they would derive from their participation in an infringement by taking account, in advance, of the amount of the fine which would be imposed on them on account of that unlawful conduct.

The confirmation of the Commission's powers is a boost in its fight against cartels because these powers allow it to design a fining policy that it considers necessary to deter undertakings to create cartels. However, the Commission's wide discretion has led to criticism from lawyers that the Notice on the method of setting fines does little to increase transparency and consistency.[98] Furthermore, critics have said that the courts do not exercise a sufficiently robust standard of review when fines are appealed.[99] On the other hand, economists consider that the current policy may not do enough to deter. Most cartels that are caught are on the verge of breaking up, so the more stable cartels remain undetected. Further, the number of investigations is still too low, so while the fine is high, the probability of being subject to the fine remains low. One study of US antitrust, where discovery and penalties are stronger than those in the Union, estimated that only one in six cartels is detected.[100] A more recent study concluded that fines are at least five times too small to deter.[101] In these circumstances it still pays to engage in restrictive practices because the expected gains are greater than the expected penalties.[102]

(b) Leniency policy

Pursuant to the Commission's leniency policy, the first undertaking that informs the Commission of the existence of an anti-competitive practice of which it is a member, and whose information allows the Commission to carry out an inspection or find an infringement under Article 101 TFEU, obtains immunity from any fine. However, if an undertaking collaborates with the Commission during the investigation by providing important evidence that strengthens the Commission's case, this may result in a reduction in the fine of between 20 and 50 per cent, the reduction being more significant for those who collaborate first.[103] The aim

[98] R. Richardson, 'Guidance Without Guidance: A European Revolution in Fining Policy?' (1999) *ECLR* 360.

[99] I. Forrester, 'A Challenge for Europe's Judges: The Review of Fines in Competition Cases' (2011) 36 *ELRev.* 185; E. Barbier de la Serre and E. Lagathu, 'The Law on Fines Imposed in EU Competition Proceedings: Faster, Higher, Harsher' (2013) 4(4) *Journal of European Competition Law and Practice* 325.

[100] P. G. Bryant and E. W. Eckard, 'Price Fixing: The Probability of Getting Caught' (1991) 73 *Review of Economics and Statistics* 531 is the seminal work. Recent research has obtained similar results. E. Combe *et al.*, *Cartels: The Probability of Getting Caught in the European Union*, Bruges European Economic Research Papers, Working Paper No. 12 (2008), available at http://ssrn.com/abstract=1015061. But see N. H. Miller, 'Strategic Leniency and Cartel Enforcement' (2009) 99 *American Economic Review* 750, suggesting that the probability is now 20–27 per cent, which is reassuring because it means that the leniency policies and the increases in penalties since the early 1990s have had some impact.

[101] J. M. Connor and R. H. Lande, 'Cartels as Rational Business Strategy: Crime Pays' (2012) 34 *Cardozo Law Review* 427.

[102] M. P. Schinkel, 'Effective Cartel Enforcement in Europe' (2007) 30 *World Competition* 539.

[103] Notice on immunity from fines and reduction of fines in cartel cases [2006] OJ C298/17. For comment on earlier drafts of this document, see N. Levy and R. O'Donoghue, 'The EU Leniency Programme Comes of Age' (2004) 27 *World Competition* 75.

of this policy is to give members of a cartel the incentive to bring the existence of cartels to the attention of the Commission.[104] The prize for being the first to do so is designed to encourage cartel members to blow the whistle, which can save Commission resources, as it may be able to rely solely on the evidence supplied by the 'whistleblower' to reach a decision that competition law has been infringed. The policy began in 1996 and has been effective in increasing the number of successful cartel infringement decisions brought by the Commission, if judged by the number of times fines have been reduced.[105] A significant proportion of cartel cases have been initiated by a leniency application (over half of the cartel cases decided between 2005 and 2008),[106] although the Commission stresses that it does not depend solely on leniency applications to uncover cartels.[107] These results match those of a comparable US programme, which has been described as 'the single greatest investigative tool available to anti-cartel enforcers'.[108]

Two factors that may undermine the initial success of the Commission's leniency policy have been addressed recently.[109] First, national competition authorities can enforce EU competition law, and Member States have different (or no) leniency policies.[110] If an undertaking provides evidence of a cartel to one competition authority, but the cartel is then prosecuted by a competition authority without a leniency programme or one with less generous reductions in fines, the benefits of confessing vanish. This may deter parties from stepping forward.[111] This has been tackled by the European Competition Network designing a Model Leniency Programme, and a significant number of Member States have used (or are planning to use) this model as a basis for designing national leniency policies.[112] Furthermore, in 2012 the programme was enhanced in that all leniency applicants who apply for leniency to the Commission may also send a summary leniency application to all Member State competition authorities and the summary form is standardised.[113] A better approach would have been to allow a single leniency application to be recognised throughout the EU, but this would likely have required legislative action, while the model programme may be applied by national authorities without statutory intervention.

Secondly, leniency policies do not affect the quantum of damages payable if cartel members are sued by undertakings harmed by the infringement of competition law. Confession raises the chances of liability, and if private litigation increases in the Union, this may deter parties from coming forward. The money saved by confessing to the existence of a cartel, which might never have been discovered by competition authorities, can be lost when the undertaking is

---

[104] And some have gone even further, suggesting that the Commission should pay whistleblowers. See A. Riley, 'Beyond Leniency: Enhancing Enforcement in EC Antitrust Law' (2005) 28 *World Competition* 377.

[105] Kerse and Kahn, n. 43 above, 417, report that since 1998 the leniency notice was applied in eighteen out of twenty cartel decisions.

[106] *Report on Competition Policy 2005* SEC(2006)761 final, para. 174; *Report on Competition Policy 2006*COM(2007)358 final, para. 8; *Report on Competition Policy 2007*COM (2008)368 final, para. 6.

[107] *Report on Competition Policy 2007*COM(2008)368 final, para. 6.

[108] S. D. Hammond, 'When Calculating the Cost and Benefits of Applying for Corporate Amnesty, How Do You Put a Price Tag on an Individual's Freedom?', 8 March 2001, www.usdoj.gov/atr.

[109] For a critical account, see P. Billiet, 'How Lenient is the EC Leniency Policy? A Matter of Certainty and Predictability' (2009) *ECLR* 14.

[110] See L. Brokx, 'A Patchwork of Leniency Programmes' (2001) *ECLR* 35.

[111] The Commission suggests this is not a significant problem. S. Blake and D. Schnichels, 'Leniency Following Modernisation: Safeguarding Europe's Leniency Programmes' (2004) 2 *Competition Policy Newsletter* 7.

[112] Commission Staff Working Document, Annex to *Commission Report on Competition Policy 2007*, SEC(2008)2038, para. 449.

[113] Commission Staff Working Document accompanying *Report on Competition Policy* (2012) 8.

sued for damages.[114] We address this below when studying private enforcement, and as will be seen the Commission and the Court of Justice disagree on the best solution.

A related policy remains to be mentioned: cartel settlements.[115] Parties secure a discount on the fine up to 10 per cent if they agree not to contest the Commission's proposed infringement findings. The aim is to save resources that go into preparing the case for oral hearing and subsequent appeals. Practitioners report that the Commission gives fairly clear ideas about the estimated fines it proposes to apply so that parties can decide if it is worth settling; however, the discount is not as generous as that found in other legal systems, which may reduce its attractiveness.[116] It is of course possible to benefit from both leniency and settlement policies.

(iv) Commitment decisions

Over 90 per cent of competition cases are closed without a formal decision.[117] Originally, there was little transparency for informal decisions. The Commission had considerable discretion in deciding whether to close cases informally or press on with a final decision, and it has been criticised for not exercising this discretion in a predictable manner.[118] For undertakings, informality has the obvious advantage that fines and the publicity of an investigation (which may give rise to damages claims) are avoided. The disadvantages, however, are over-enforcement, on the one hand (e.g. without a full hearing the Commission may abuse its powers by accusing parties of a non-existent infringement); or under-enforcement on the other (informal closures avoid the imposition of fines and are privately negotiated between parties and Commission).[119] Furthermore, from an enforcer's point of view, if the parties did not comply, the Commission's only solution would be to restart an investigation afresh. In an attempt to increase transparency of its settlements practice, and to strengthen its enforceability, the Council formalised this practice, creating a new category: commitment decisions.

Regulation 1/2003, article 9(1)

1. Where the Commission intends to adopt a decision requiring that an infringement be brought to an end and the undertakings concerned offer commitments to meet the concerns expressed to them by the Commission in its preliminary assessment, the Commission may by decision make those commitments binding on the undertakings. Such a decision may be adopted for a specified period and shall conclude that there are no longer grounds for action by the Commission.

---

[114] P. C. Zane, 'The Price Fixer's Dilemma: Applying Game Theory to the Decision of Whether to Plead Guilty to Antitrust Crimes' (2003) *Antitrust Bulletin* 1.

[115] Commission Regulation 622/2008 of 30 June 2008 amending Regulation 773/2004, as regards the conduct of settlement procedures in cartel cases [2008] OJ L171/3.

[116] S.-P. Brankin, 'The First Cases Under the Commission's Cartel Settlement Procedure: Problems Solved?' (2011) 32(4) *ECLR* 5 for an informative insider's perspective. M. P. Schinkel, 'Bargaining in the Shadow of the European Settlement for Cartels' (2011) 56(2) *Antitrust Bulletin* 462.

[117] In 2000 there were 38 formal decisions and 362 settlements; in 2001, 54 decisions and 324 settlements; in 2002, 33 decisions and 363 settlements; and in 2003, 24 decisions and 295 settlements (*Twenty-third Report on Competition Policy* (2003) 62). For a review of the settlement practice under Regulation 17/62 see I. van Bael, 'The Antitrust Settlement Practice of the EC Commission' (1986) 23 *CMLRev.* 61.

[118] Kerse and Kahn, n. 43 above, 357.

[119] For a discussion of these concerns, see G. Bruzzone and G. Boccaccio, 'Taking Care of Modernisation After the Startup: A View from a Member State' (2008) 31 *World Competition* 89.

Proposed decisions to accept commitments must be published, inviting comments from third parties as a way of gaining information about the competitive impact of the commitment[120] and consulting the Advisory Committee.[121] Increased transparency and consultation may lead to more predictable use of settlement procedures, however a number of concerns have arisen with this new procedure, not least because the Commission uses it in non-cartel cases far more frequently than expected. Further concerns arose after the *Alrosa* judgment. The Commission received a notification of an agreement between two competitors in the market for diamonds by which one (Alrosa) agreed to sell all its diamonds for export to the other (De Beers). After a series of proceedings De Beers offered a commitment to phase out the agreement, which the Commission accepted. Alrosa was dissatisfied with the outcome and argued that the commitment was disproportionate, for less aggressive commitments would have sufficed to resolve the competition concerns.[122]

Case C-441/07P *Commission v Alrosa* [2010] ECR I-5949

35. ...Article 9 of the Regulation is based on considerations of procedural economy, and enables undertakings to participate fully in the procedure, by putting forward the solutions which appear to them to be the most appropriate and capable of addressing the Commission's concerns.

36. As observed by the parties and by the Advocate General...the principle of proportionality, as a general principle of European Union law, is...a criterion for the lawfulness of any act of the institutions of the Union, including decisions taken by the Commission in its capacity of competition authority....

48. Undertakings which offer commitments on the basis of Article 9 of Regulation No. 1/2003 consciously accept that the concessions they make may go beyond what the Commission could itself impose on them in a decision adopted under Article 7 of the Regulation after a thorough examination. On the other hand, the closure of the infringement proceedings brought against those undertakings allows them to avoid a finding of an infringement of competition law and a possible fine.

49. Moreover, the fact that the individual commitments offered by an undertaking have been made binding by the Commission does not mean that other undertakings are deprived of the possibility of protecting the rights they may have in connection with their relations with that undertaking.

50. It must therefore be concluded that the Commission is right to submit that in the judgment under appeal the General Court wrongly considered that the application of the principle of proportionality must be assessed, in the case of decisions taken under Article 9 of Regulation No. 1/2003, by reference to the way in which it is assessed in connection with decisions taken under Article 7 of that Regulation despite the different concepts underlying those two provisions.

Accordingly, in commitment decisions the parties forfeit the accuracy of the article 7 remedy in favour of a more convenient procedure. The problems with this line of argumentation are many.[123] Principal among these is that the Commission has superior bargaining power and

---

[120] Regulation 1/03, article 27(4).

[121] *Ibid.* article 14(1) (the composition of the committee is described above at p. 965).

[122] There is an added complexity: the Commission had moved against this agreement in two ways: against De Beers for breach of Article 102 TFEU and against both undertakings for breach of Article 101 TFEU. There were ongoing negotiations on the Article 101 commitments when De Beers then proposed to settle under Article 102. The attentive reader will also have noticed that the agreement here looks like a cartel, and article 9 procedures should not normally apply to such cases, see Regulation 1/2003, recital 13.

[123] F. Wagner von Papp, 'Best and Even Better Practices in Commitment Procedures After Alrosa' (2012) 49 *CMLRev.* 929, offering the most comprehensive critique.

thus can extract significant concessions that go beyond what is strictly necessary, and there is no doubt that the Commission proposes commitments to the parties, contrary to what the Court of Justice intimates.[124] Not only can the Commission threaten a formal procedure with fines, but parties may fear that non-cooperation today damages their future dealings with the Commission. Furthermore, parties prefer commitments because there is no finding of infringement so they escape likely damages actions. Given the lax standard of judicial review (only misuse of powers by the Commission would serve to quash a decision) it means one relies on self-restraint by the enforcer. To remedy this critique the Commission has developed a practice of assessing the proportionality of the remedy in detail. However, further concerns remain. The fact that commitment decisions are appeal-proof may stimulate the enforcer to use this procedure even for cases where the law is not clear, meaning that rather than exploring in detail the soundness of the legal theory (and risking judicial assessment of that) the Commission can expand the reach of the competition rules. We show the concrete effects of this risk in Chapter 22.

(v) Commission's procedures: an assessment

One theme that emerges from the discussion above is how the significant powers that may be exercised need to be kept in check by reference to the fundamental rights of the parties under investigation. The source of these fundamental rights has evolved: at first these were general principles of EU law, often interpreted by reference to the jurisprudence of the ECtHR, and more recently the source of rights has been the European Union Charter of Fundamental Rights (EUCFR). In evaluating the compatibility of EU competition procedures with fundamental rights, one should distinguish two lines of analysis: one is whether the exercise of the various powers noted above is carried out in such a way that fundamental rights are complied with. As discussed above, there is some doubt as to whether this is the case, but it is telling that the European Courts and Commission make genuine attempts to ensure the law evolves to safeguard these rights.[125] The second point is whether the institutional set-up by which the Commission investigates, prosecutes and reaches a decision is compatible with fundamental rights.[126] We examine this debate here.

Article 6(1) ECHR provides that when persons face criminal charges they are entitled to 'a fair and public hearing by an independent and impartial tribunal established by law'. One might object that article 23(5) of Regulation 1/2003 provides that fines are administrative in nature, but this is to overlook the case law of the ECtHR which provides that formal classifications are irrelevant and that a wide range of penalties may be described as criminal, by reference to the penalty imposed and whether it aims to sanction and deter the infringer. Accordingly, most assume that Commission procedures are criminal in nature.[127] However, the ECtHR has also held that there are different degrees of criminal charges, and for non-hardcore

---

[124] DG Competition, *Antitrust Manual of Procedures* (2012) ch. 16, p. 7.

[125] See generally I. van Bael, *Due Process in EU Competition Proceedings* (The Hague, Kluwer, 2011).

[126] This is a long-standing debate, see F. Montag, 'The Case for Radical Reform of the Infringement Procedure under Regulation 17' (1998) *ECLR* 428; C. D. Ehlermann and M. Marquis (eds.), *European Competition Annual 2009: The Evaluation of Evidence and its Judicial Review in Competition Cases* (Oxford, Hart, 2011).

[127] Case C-272/09P *KME v Commission*, Judgment of 8 December 2011, Opinion of Advocate General Sharpston, para. 64; Editorial Comments, 'Towards a More Judicial Approach? EU Antitrust Fines under the Scrutiny of Fundamental Rights' (2011) 48(5) *CMLRev.* 1405, 1408.

criminal charges the imposition of penalties by agencies may be appropriate provided that the agency's decisions are subjected to judicial review. In *Menarini Diagnostics* v *Italy*, the ECtHR ruled that Italy's antitrust procedures, which are similar to those of the Commission, comply with Article 6(1) ECHR in that the decision of the competition authority was susceptible to judicial review by a court that had full jurisdiction.[128] One might thus legitimately assume that the same applies to the Commission, so that undertakings in competition cases do not require the full set of procedural guarantees that are afforded to, say, those accused of theft.[129] If so, the question then is how far the General Court has full jurisdiction. This is where the debate is most heated at the moment, and the Court of Justice has attempted to respond to the *Menarini* judgment in a recent appeal against a Commission decision imposing fines on members of a cartel.

Case C–272/09P, *KME* v *Commission*, Judgment of 8 December 2011

93. The judicial review of the decisions of the institutions was arranged by the founding Treaties. In addition to the review of legality, now provided for under Article 263 TFEU, a review with unlimited jurisdiction was envisaged in regard to the penalties laid down by regulations.

94. As regards the review of legality, the Court of Justice has held that whilst, in areas giving rise to complex economic assessments, the Commission has a margin of discretion with regard to economic matters, that does not mean that the Courts of the European Union must refrain from reviewing the Commission's interpretation of information of an economic nature. Not only must those Courts establish, among other things, whether the evidence relied on is factually accurate, reliable and consistent but also whether that evidence contains all the information which must be taken into account in order to assess a complex situation and whether it is capable of substantiating the conclusions drawn from it.

95. With regard to the penalties for infringements of competition law, the second subparagraph of Article 15(2) of Regulation No. 17 provides that in fixing the amount of the fine, regard is to be had both to the gravity and to the duration of the infringement.

96. The Court of Justice has held that, in order to determine the amount of a fine, it is necessary to take account of the duration of the infringements and of all the factors capable of affecting the assessment of their gravity, such as the conduct of each of the undertakings, the role played by each of them in the establishment of the concerted practices, the profit which they were able to derive from those practices, their size, the value of the goods concerned and the threat that infringements of that type pose to the European Community.

97. The Court has also stated that objective factors such as the content and duration of the anti-competitive conduct, the number of incidents and their intensity, the extent of the market affected and the damage to the economic public order must be taken into account. The analysis must also take into consideration the relative importance and market share of the undertakings responsible and also any repeated infringements.

98. This large number of factors requires that the Commission carry out a thorough examination of the circumstances of the infringement.

---

[128] *Menarini Diagnostics* v *Italy* (Application no. 43509/08), Judgment of 27 September 2011.
[129] W. P. J. Wils, 'Antitrust Enforcement Powers and Procedural Rights and Guarantees: The Interplay between EU Law, National Law, the Charter of Fundamental Rights of the EU and the European Convention on Human Rights' (2011) 34 *World Competition* 189.

99. In the interests of transparency the Commission adopted the Guidelines, in which it indicates the basis on which it will take account of one or other aspect of the infringement and what this will imply as regards the amount of the fine.

100. The Guidelines, which, the Court has held, form rules of practice from which the administration may not depart in an individual case without giving reasons compatible with the principle of equal treatment, merely describe the method used by the Commission to examine infringements and the criteria that the Commission requires to be taken into account in setting the amount of a fine.

101. It is important to bear in mind the obligation to state reasons for Community acts. That is a particularly important obligation in the present case. It is for the Commission to state the reasons for its decision and, in particular, to explain the weighting and assessment of the factors taken into account. The Courts must establish of their own motion that there is a statement of reasons.

102. Furthermore, the Courts must carry out the review of legality incumbent upon them on the basis of the evidence adduced by the applicant in support of the pleas in law put forward. In carrying out such a review, the Courts cannot use the Commission's margin of discretion – either as regards the choice of factors taken into account in the application of the criteria mentioned in the Guidelines or as regards the assessment of those factors – as a basis for dispensing with the conduct of an in-depth review of the law and of the facts.

103. The review of legality is supplemented by the unlimited jurisdiction which the Courts of the European Union were afforded by Article 17 of Regulation No. 17 and which is now recognised by Article 31 of Regulation No. 1/2003, in accordance with Article 261 TFEU. That jurisdiction empowers the Courts, in addition to carrying out a mere review of the lawfulness of the penalty, to substitute their own appraisal for the Commission's and, consequently, to cancel, reduce or increase the fine or penalty payment imposed.... 106. The review provided for by the Treaties thus involves review by the Courts of the European Union of both the law and the facts, and means that they have the power to assess the evidence, to annul the contested decision and to alter the amount of a fine. The review of legality provided for under Article 263 TFEU, supplemented by the unlimited jurisdiction in respect of the amount of the fine, provided for under Article 31 of Regulation No. 1/2003, is not therefore contrary to the requirements of the principle of effective judicial protection in Article 47 of the Charter.

This judgment leaves something to be desired on two fronts. First, the General Court's power with respect to fines is much more significant than its power when it comes to a review of the facts, which raises questions about whether the Court really has full jurisdiction across the board. Secondly, the Court restates a long-held view that while for factual findings the Court can examine the correctness in detail, in certain complex economic matters it defers to the Commission's judgment (paragraph 94). Commentators have viewed this approach as unsatisfactory on two grounds: first, it is not always clear which kinds of issue merit more in-depth review and which ones do not; secondly, this passage seems to be evidence that the court lacks full jurisdiction.[130] On the other hand, the judgment has been welcomed because it appears to require the General Court to consider much more closely than it has done in the past whether the level of fine set is appropriate.

The debate on the nature of judicial review has developed in an unsatisfactory manner because no court has yet arrived at a clear conception of what an appropriate level of judicial scrutiny means. This has not been helped by one judge explaining that when faced with the

---

[130] I. van Bael, *Due Process in Competition Proceedings* (The Hague, Kluwer, 2011) 357–63.

review of complex economic assessments the court applies an 'intense – though marginal – review'.[131]

As a reaction to this it has been argued that a more fruitful approach would be to allow the Court of Justice to retain the present marginal review of delicate economic policy issues (for which the Commission is constitutionally better placed) and instead consider reforming the decision-making organism so that there is a functional separation between prosecution and decision-making. Rendering the decision-maker independent in this way would serve to legitimise the exercise of the Commission's discretionary powers for there would be no confirmation bias.[132] On the other hand, the current dialectic between the Commission and the General Court appears satisfactory in most cases.

C. Harding and J. Joshua, *Regulating Cartels in Europe: A Study of Legal Control of Corporate Delinquency* (2nd edn, Oxford, Oxford University Press, 2010) 219–20

[The General Court] has fashioned for itself a distinctive role as a court of review…Moreover, its review of virtually every aspect of the Commission's procedure has been painstaking. In effect, this has encouraged appeals by undertakings to such an extent that the Court has an almost automatic role in dealing with the Commission's cartel decisions. It would not be an exaggeration to say that it has for practical purposes almost turned itself into a trial court in this context…In effect, therefore, the separation of powers complaint…has been addressed. In the majority of cartel cases, the Commission's formal decision has evolved into a summative statement of the case for the prosecution, which is then judicially tested before the [General Court]. Since the dust has settled on this development, from the middle of the 1990s both the Commission and the Court appear to have settled into a comfortable relationship, within which the former prepares its cases carefully, and the latter confirms most of the prosecution case…the cartels still have their day in court, with the prospect of appeal to the Court of Justice if they wish to continue the legal battle.

However, Harding and Joshua are concerned with the fact that this legal development has occurred as a result of powerful corporate actors, who have explored the judicial process in the light of clear infringements of EU competition law, and who often make repetitive legal arguments. And while the appeals by these large firms have led to the creation of considerable procedural safeguards for their interests, the Court of Justice has had little opportunity to explain what rights those injured by anti-competitive behaviour have. One possible reaction to this assessment is that the Court's review of the Commission's decisions appears to vary from case to case. In some merger cases the Court appears to be very willing to probe in depth the soundness of the economic theories used,[133] while in cartel and abuse of dominance cases the Court appears to be less exacting in its review.[134]

---

[131] M. Jaeger, 'The Standard of Review in Competition Cases Involving Complex Economic Assessments' (2011) 2(4) *Journal of European Competition Law and Practice* 295, 300. The judge was simply referring to para. 94 in *KME*, noting how this has been the basis for several detailed reviews of the economic evidence brought by the Commission. Yet, the choice of language is rather unfortunate. Likewise, later the learned judge's suggestion that marginal review be limited to matters of 'economic policy' (313) appears too narrow, for what he appears to mean is the application of economic theory by the Commission, its discretion in selecting a theory of harm.

[132] R. Nazzini, 'Administrative Enforcement, Judicial Review and Fundamental Rights in EU Competition Law: A Comparative Contextual-Functionalist Perspective' (2012) 49(3) *CMLRev.* 971.

[133] See e.g. Case C-12/03P *Commission v Tetra Laval* [2005] ECR I-987.

[134] See e.g. Case T-201/04, *Microsoft Corp. v Commission* [2007] ECR II-3601. For discussion see I. Forrester, 'A Challenge for Europe's Judges: The Review of Fines in Competition Cases' (2011) 36 *ELRev.* 185; D. Bailey, 'Scope of Review under Article 81 EC' (2004) 41 *CMLRev.* 1327; A. Fritzsche, 'Discretion, Scope of Judicial Review and Institutional Balance in European Law' (2010) 47 *CMLRev.* 361.

(vi) Commission's performance

A further long-standing criticism of the Commission's procedures is the potentially political nature of the decision-making process.

> **L. Laudati, 'The European Commission as Regulator: The Uncertain Pursuit of the Competitive Market' in G. Majone (ed.), *Regulating Europe* (London, Routledge, 1996) 231, 235–6**
>
> The degree of independence of an antitrust enforcement institution is determined by two elements: the structural independence from political authority, and separation of investigatory, prosecutorial and decision-making functions. The Community antitrust enforcement has a low level of independence in both respects....
>
> When the Community system was established, it was believed that placing the powers to execute the competition laws in the hands of the Commission would minimize political interference with enforcement by the Member States. The Commission has, however, become a highly political body, and political considerations play a significant role in its competition enforcement decisions. National antitrust officials acknowledge that pressure from national governments may influence the Commission's decisions because the Commission must have the cooperation of national governments in order to fulfil its mission. Thus the Commission exerts considerable effort to reconcile national policies with Community policy.
>
> Moreover, DG IV [now, DG Competition] cannot act independently of the other DGs since final decisions are made by the full Commission. Political pressure from other DGs is felt constantly, owing to the broad economic implications of competition decisions. Such pressure, in general, runs against the negative decisions by DG IV, particularly with regard to mergers. Moreover, it forces DG IV to take account of policy considerations other than competition policy...This type of pressure has grown in recent years owing to the increasingly important role of competition law, and the economic recession and high levels of unemployment throughout the Community.
>
> For instance, DG III (industrial policy) and DG IV (social policy) frequently take positions at odds with those of DG IV. Other DGs likely to intervene regulate specific sectors of the economy – for example DG XIII (telecommunications) and DG XVII (energy). This does not mean that all communication among the DGs is contentious. Rather, collaboration and consultation regularly occur between rapporteurs of DG IV and those of other DGs, especially DG III, because of their familiarity with the various sectors. But if DG III staff believe that a merger should be cleared and their counterparts believe the opposite, the staff members of each DG must convince their Commissioner of the merits of their position. Commissioners themselves then resolve the dispute.
>
> Another fault of the system is that it requires Commissioners with no expertise in competition law and severe time constraints to apply complex laws and economic analysis to facts in all cases, then make the final decision. It is doubtful whether all Commissioners are professionally qualified to perform this function. Critics point out that, in practice, most competition decisions are adopted with little or no debate, as written proposed decisions are circulated to each cabinet of each Commissioner and considered to be adopted if no objections are made within a limited period.
>
> An additional problem results from a lack of clarity as to the standards being applied in deciding antitrust cases. As stated above, policy areas other than competition are considered, especially industrial and social policy. However, parties with competition matters before the Commission have no substantive or procedural rules to follow regarding the presentation of evidence on such policy issues, even though these matters could have significant impact on the outcome of their cases. This raises due process concerns.

Laudati's comments strengthen the views of Wesseling (discussed in section 2 of this chapter) by noting how the interference of other EU objectives is inevitable, given the institutional make-up of the Commission and the Commission's own political energies and understanding of how the Community project impacts upon the development of competition law. Of course, not every competition decision is keenly debated by the College of Commissioners – much competition law enforcement is the routine supervision of business practices where wider Community interests are affected marginally, but in significant cases that establish a new precedent or apply to novel markets, other Commissioners' views (whether based upon their portfolio or their national interests) become more prominent. It is fair to say, however, that as a whole, the Commission's enforcement of competition law is like that of any other independent agency: while it must be sensitive to the political context, by and large it exercises its powers autonomously. Indeed, competition enforcement by the Commission is highly regarded worldwide.[135]

4 RESETTLEMENT OF COMPETITION REGULATORY AUTHORITY

(i) Modernisation

Concentrating the task of enforcement with the Commission brought certain advantages: a single regulator, a uniform approach to competition (although stricter national competition laws could still apply provided the Commission had not acted),[136] and DG Competition gained experience in handling disputes. However, there were two drawbacks in concentrating enforcement in the hands of the Commission. The first, as we saw above, is that the Commission could act in a politically motivated manner. In the mid-1990s it was argued that competition enforcement should be delegated to a separate 'European Cartel Office' to enhance the independence of the decision-making process, but this suggestion is now unlikely to be implemented.[137] The second problem is that the Commission considered that its limited resources had become insufficient to deal with all competition problems coming to its attention. This was because parties were able to notify the Commission of their plans and evaluating these proposals was time-consuming and diverted efforts away from a proactive enforcement strategy.[138] This enforcement pattern was neither in the interests of business nor in the interests of the proper enforcement of competition law.

Since the 1970s, the Commission has attempted to ameliorate this, first by issuing comfort letters. These were administrative letters written in response to a notified agreement indicating that the Commission did not think the agreement restricted competition. The comfort letter was not a formal decision and thus could be issued more quickly. However, its non-binding character gave parties little legal security where the agreement was challenged in national courts. The second solution was to draft Block Exemption Regulations. These provide that if an agreement meets certain specified criteria, it benefits from automatic exemption, without notification. The weakness of this approach is that it creates a straitjacket effect: the parties

---

[135] See generally Monti, n. 3 above.

[136] Case 14/68 *Walt Wilhelm* v *Bundeskartellamt* [1969] ECR 1. On the difficulties of this see R. Wesseling, 'Subsidiarity in Community Competition Law over National Law' (1997) 22 *ELRev.* 19.

[137] S. Wilks and L. McGowan, 'Disarming the Commission: The Debate Over a European Cartel Office' (1995) 32 *JCMS* 259.

[138] 40,000 notifications were received. *Ninth Report on Competition Policy* (1979) 15–16.

use the relevant Block Exemption as the basis for their contractual relations and structure the agreement according to its terms, which might skew their commercial desires. Requiring parties to sacrifice commercial practicality in order to gain legal security seemed to some too high a price to pay.[139]

In the early 1990s the Commission attempted a third solution, often referred to as a programme of decentralisation. It encouraged national competition authorities to enforce EU competition law and invited private parties to use national courts to enforce competition law. The Commission argued that national competition authorities had a common task of protecting competition and the national authorities should use EU competition law to regulate markets, allowing the Commission to take action in cases of particular significance to the Community.[140] However, encouraging decentralised enforcement though soft law Notices failed to galvanise national authorities and courts and the Commission still had a worryingly heavy caseload, due to increase with impending enlargement, preventing it from setting its enforcement priorities. More drastic reforms were needed.

In 1999, the Commission published a *White Paper on Modernisation*, which proposed reform along the following lines: to abolish the system of notification, to declare Article 101(3) TFEU directly effective, and to compel national competition authorities to apply EU competition law.[141] These significant changes were agreed by the Council and came into effect on 1 May 2004 under Regulation 1/2003.[142]

Regulation 1/2003, article 1

1. Agreements, decisions and concerted practices caught by Article [101(1)] of the Treaty which do not satisfy the conditions of Article [101(3)] of the Treaty shall be prohibited, no prior decision to that effect being required.
2. Agreements, decisions and concerted practices caught by Article [101(1)] of the Treaty which satisfy the conditions of Article [101(3)] of the Treaty shall not be prohibited, no prior decision to that effect being required.

The implication of article 1 is profound: parties who before would have submitted a request for exemption and had to wait endlessly for a response must now decide for themselves whether their agreement infringes the competition rules. This represents a switch from an ex ante notification-based system of competition enforcement to an ex post deterrence-based system. Abolishing the right of parties to notify an agreement means that the Commission is now free to focus on the more serious infringements.

---

[139] The first Block Exemption was implemented in 1967: Regulation 67/67 on exclusive purchase agreements [1967] OJ L84/67.

[140] Commission Notice on cooperation between national competition authorities and the Commission in handling cases falling within the scope of Articles [101 TFEU] and [102 TFEU] [1997] OJ C313/1; Commission Notice on cooperation between national courts and the Commission in applying Articles [101 TFEU] and [102 TFEU] [1993] OJ C39/6.

[141] *White Paper on Modernisation of the Rules Implementing Articles [101 TFEU] and [102 TFEU]* [1999] OJ C132/1.

[142] Regulation 1/2003 on the implementation of the rules on competition laid down in Articles 81 and 82 of the Treaty [2003] OJ L1/1.

The other plank of the reform is to require national competition authorities to enforce EU competition law, thereby decentralising enforcement of EU competition law.

Regulation 1/2003, article 3

1. Where the competition authorities of the Member States or national courts apply national competition law to agreements, decisions by associations of undertakings or concerted practices within the meaning of Article [101(1)] which may affect trade between Member States within the meaning of that provision, they shall also apply Article [101] to such agreements, decisions or concerted practices. Where the competition authorities of the Member States or national courts apply national competition law to any abuse prohibited by Article [102], they shall also apply Article [102].
2. The application of national competition law may not lead to the prohibition of agreements, decisions by associations of undertakings or concerted practices which may affect trade between Member States but which do not restrict competition within the meaning of Article [101(1)], or which fulfil the conditions of Article [101(3)] or which are covered by a Regulation for the application of Article [101(3)]. Member States shall not under this Regulation be precluded from adopting and applying on their territory stricter national laws which prohibit or sanction unilateral conduct engaged in by undertakings.
3. Without prejudice to general principles and other provisions of Community law, paragraphs 1 and 2 do not apply when the competition authorities and the courts of the Member States apply national merger control laws nor do they preclude the application of provisions of national law that predominantly pursue an objective different from that pursued by Articles [101] and [102].

This provision obliges national competition authorities (NCAs) to apply Articles 101 and 102 TFEU and to give EU competition law priority over national competition law. 'Enforcement of Articles [101 and 102] is now a shared responsibility, not just in theory but in practice. At both political and practical level the modernisation regime requires Member States to adopt a commitment to the enforcement of Community law in this area far in excess of anything to date.'[143] In effect, Regulation 1/2003 turns the NCA into a Union competition authority. There are three exceptions to the obligation of the NCA to give priority to EU competition law. The first is in the final sentence of Regulation 1/2003, article 3(2), which allows the authority to apply stricter national competition law that regulates unilateral behaviour. As we will see in the following two chapters, EU competition law only regulates unilateral behaviour when the firm has a dominant position. In contrast, some Member States have competition laws that are wider in scope. The second exception is that national merger law is unaffected. The final exception is that national laws, which pursue non-competition objectives, may be enforced to prohibit a practice which is unobjectionable from a competition perspective, for example consumer protection legislation.

From the perspective of undertakings, Regulation 1/2003 reduces compliance costs because very similar competition rules apply across the EU. Therefore, their practices will be scrutinised uniformly regardless of which competition authority handles the investigation. From the perspective of the Commission, this creates a battalion of competition authorities with ample resources, thereby improving the enforcement of competition law.

[143] Kerse and Khan, n. 43 above, 47.

(ii) Commission's new role

The Commission no longer has to review every agreement notified to it. It can now set its own agenda in a legal environment where the majority of competition enforcement will be carried out by national authorities. The Commission has carried out three main tasks.

First, the Commission has increased enforcement against cartels which operate internationally, as well as focusing on industries where a few firms hold market power. This is significant because in the past the Commission was criticised for focusing on harmless business conduct that was notified to it,[144] whereas now it can direct enforcement in line with economic theory and focus on the more important infringements.[145] However, this is somewhat misleading because a closer look at the statistics reveals that the Commission had already begun to focus on cartels around the year 2000, largely because of improved internal working practices, and because the wider Block Exemptions led to fewer notifications. The absence of a significant increase in the Commission's output in the period since 2004 is not easy to explain.[146]

The second task for the Commission is to provide guidance in novel cases to facilitate the work of national competition authorities. The Commission will continue the process of drafting Notices and Guidelines (begun in the late 1990s), which are not binding but are an expression of how the Commission would handle a case and bound to influence the national authorities. These instruments will be of increasing importance for undertakings because they are now unable to notify agreements to gain exemption and require as much information as possible to determine for themselves whether their planned business practices are lawful. In exceptional circumstances, however, parties may be able to obtain individual guidance from the Commission.

Regulation 1/2003, recital 38

(38) Legal certainty for undertakings operating under the Community competition rules contributes to the promotion of innovation and investment. Where cases give rise to genuine uncertainty because they present novel or unresolved questions for the application of these rules, individual undertakings may wish to seek informal guidance from the Commission. This Regulation is without prejudice to the ability of the Commission to issue such informal guidance.

The Commission's powers to grant this guidance are not expressly provided for in the Regulation, and a Notice on Informal Guidance has been published which suggests that guidance will be offered when parties engage in business practices where there is no precedent or other informal guidance to help the undertakings determine whether their proposed action infringes EU competition law.[147] Guidance letters resemble comfort letters which were issued under the old regime, but these new letters will only be issued sparingly. In addition to soft law measures, the Commission may also take formal decisions.

---

[144] D. Neven, P. Papandropoulos and P. Seabright, *Trawling for Minnows: European Competition Policy and Agreements Between Firms* (London, CEPR, 1998).

[145] M. Monti, 'European Competition Policy: Quo Vadis?', 10 April 2003, http://ec.europa.eu/competition/index_en.html.

[146] Monti, n. 3 above, and W. P. J. Wils, 'Ten Years of Regulation 1/2003: A Retrospective' (2013) 4(4) *Journal of European Competition Law and Practice* 1.

[147] [2004] OJ C101/78.

> **Regulation 1/2003, article 10**
>
> Where the Community public interest relating to the application of Articles [101 TFEU] and [102 TFEU]...so requires, the Commission, acting on its own initiative, may by decision find that Article [101 TFEU]...is not applicable to an agreement, a decision by an association of undertakings or a concerted practice, either because the conditions of Article [101(1) TFEU]...are not fulfilled, or because the conditions of Article [101(3) TFEU]... are satisfied.
>
> The Commission may likewise make such a finding with reference to Article 82 of the Treaty.

There is a risk that article 10 could be used for reasons other than merely clarifying the law. The provision is triggered by the need to serve the *Community's public interest*. This is sufficiently wide to allow the Commission to decide that a particular practice does not infringe Article 101 TFEU because of some public policy reason unrelated to competition law. Given the institutional make-up of the Commission, the risk is present, even though the recitals to the Regulation suggest that the purpose of article 10 is to shed light on areas where the law is unclear.[148] To date, no decision has been issued under article 10. Instead of using these methods the Commission has used its powers as *amicus curiae* to intervene in cases in national courts.[149]

The Commission's third task is to coordinate the network of national competition authorities, and we consider this novel role in the following section.

(iii) European Competition Network

To ensure the successful functioning of national enforcement, each Member State must designate the competition authority responsible for the application of Articles 101 and 102 TFEU,[150] and the NCA must be able to impose meaningful remedies, including interim measures, prohibition orders, imposing penalties and accepting commitments.[151] This harmonises the sanctions of all NCAs to guarantee the effective enforcement of EU competition law. However, in addition to empowering each NCA, successful enforcement requires considerable coordination among the NCAs and the Commission. Therefore, as early as 2002 the European Competition Network (ECN) was created, comprising all NCAs and the Commission. The ECN is not a competition authority, but a forum for cooperation for the NCAs. Its principal tasks when it was originally designed were the following: first, to coordinate enforcement so that there is an efficient allocation of cases among the network; and secondly, to develop mechanisms for cooperation during investigations and means of ensuring consistency in the application of competition rules.

(a) Case allocation

Regulation 1/2003 envisaged that each case should be handled by a single authority,[152] but the detailed implementation was left to soft law instruments, setting out in detail how cases

---

[148] Regulation 1/2003, recital 14.
[149] *Ibid.* article 15(3) provides for this power. The interventions are available at http://ec.europa.eu/competition/court/antitrust_amicus_curiae.html.
[150] *Ibid.* article 35(1).   [151] *Ibid.* article 5.   [152] *Ibid.* recital 18.

may be allocated. Three alternatives are envisaged: enforcement by one NCA, enforcement by several NCAs, or enforcement by the Commission.[153] The Network serves as a platform for case reallocation. One agency will initiate a procedure and will inform the others of it. Normally the agency that initiates the case keeps it but other agencies may claim to be better placed. An authority is well placed when the practice in question affects its territory, where it is able to impose effective remedies and when it has access to the information necessary to prove the infringement.[154] Parallel action is envisaged when this might be better for bringing the infringement to an end, or where this might allow for more effective remedies.[155] Finally, the Notice provides that the Commission may be better placed in three scenarios: when the activity affects three or more Member States; when the competition complaint is closely linked to other EU law prohibitions so that it is more efficient for the Commission to intervene; or when the case 'requires the adoption of a Commission decision to develop [EU] competition policy when a new competition issue arises or to ensure effective enforcement'.[156]

Thus far there have been very few reallocations. However, a legal concern arises in instances of parallel proceedings: suppose there is a price-fixing agreement among manufacturers of widgets and prices are fixed in Bulgaria and Hungary. May the two NCAs decide to divide up the case so that each prosecutes it? Arguably this is advantageous because then the two authorities may impose a fine each for the effects of the cartel in their jurisdiction. However, it is arguable that this prosecution infringes the undertakings' right not to be prosecuted twice for the same offence. The Court of Justice has addressed this concern in *Toshiba*, but here the facts were slightly different: the Commission and the Czech NCA had prosecuted and fined a cartel, but the Czech NCA had done so for activities that had taken place in the Czech Republic before that country's accession to the EU. In these circumstances, the right not to be prosecuted twice did not arise.[157] However, the Court intimated that parallel application of EU law by two NCAs could be allowed because even if the agencies were addressing the same conduct, they were protecting two different effects: the Bulgarian NCA could tackle the effects of the cartel in its territory, and the Hungarian one the effects in its territory. A contrary view is that while this may be expedient, it undermines the rights of the firms under investigation: the justifications for prohibiting a second prosecution are in order to discipline the prosecutor so that it has all the evidence before proceeding; a single prosecution also spares the defendant the burdens of defending the issue twice. Furthermore, allowing multiple prosecutions of the same price-fixing cartel misses the key enforcement gap: many NCAs appear to have no power to impose fines for effects that occur outside their Member State. This is particularly problematic because the reason they must apply EU competition law in the first place is that the practice has an effect on trade among Member States.[158]

(b) Cooperation within the Network

Once a case is allocated, there are also provisions to assist the NCA: the Commission or any other NCA may transmit information to the NCA in charge, and it is even possible that one

---

[153] Commission Notice on cooperation within the Network of Competition Authorities [2004] OJ C101/43.
[154] *Ibid.* paras. 6–11.   [155] *Ibid.* para. 12.
[156] *Ibid.* para. 15.   [157] Case C-17/10 *Toshiba*, Judgment of 14 February 2012.
[158] For further discussion, see G. Monti, 'Managing Decentralised Antitrust Enforcement' (2014) 51(1) *CMLRev.* 261;
G. di Federico, 'EU Competition Law and the Principle of *Ne Bis in Idem*' (2011) 17(2) *European Public Law* 241.

NCA carries out investigations in its Member State on behalf of the NCA in charge of prosecuting the case.[159] Some concerns have been expressed that this transmission of information may not contain sufficient safeguards, but so far there have been very few instances where these powers have been exercised.[160]

Finally, before a decision is rendered by an NCA, the Commission may check it.

Regulation 1/2003, article 11(4), (6)

4. No later than 30 days before the adoption of a decision requiring that an infringement be brought to an end, accepting commitments or withdrawing the benefit of a block exemption Regulation, the competition authorities of the Member States shall inform the Commission. To that effect, they shall provide the Commission with a summary of the case, the envisaged decision or, in the absence thereof, any other document indicating the proposed course of action. This information may also be made available to the competition authorities of the other Member States. At the request of the Commission, the acting competition authority shall make available to the Commission other documents it holds which are necessary for the assessment of the case. The information supplied to the Commission may be made available to the competition authorities of the other Member States. National competition authorities may also exchange between themselves information necessary for the assessment of a case that they are dealing with under Article [101] or Article [102] of the Treaty....

6. The initiation by the Commission of proceedings for the adoption of a decision shall relieve the competition authorities of the Member States of their competence to apply Articles [101 TFEU] and [102 TFEU]...If a competition authority of a Member State is already acting on a case, the Commission shall only initiate proceedings after consulting with that national competition authority.

Article 11(4) is designed to allow other NCAs to express their views on the decision and, more significantly, it is a way for the Commission to check that the NCA does not use the law in a political manner to favour national industry. As an additional safeguard against national bias in a planned decision, article 11(6) allows the Commission to remove the case from the NCA and decide it itself. The latter provision is a drastic measure, and the Commission has so far used less drastic (but also less transparent) means of advising NCAs on the approach they should take.[161]

(iv) Modernisation in practice

What has been observed is that the two main tasks for the ECN have not taxed it, but the ECN has been active on other fronts: it appears to be a site where members seek practical advice about how to analyse markets, and where collaborative projects are entered into to improve enforcement. To some, this environment provides an ideal site for experimentalist governance.

---

[159] See Regulation 1/2003, articles 11(3), 12 and 22(4).
[160] D. Reichelt, 'To What Extent Does the Co-operation within the European Competition Network Protect the Rights of Undertakings?' (2005) 42 *CMLRev.* 745.
[161] Monti, n. 3 above.

Y. Svetiev, 'Networked Competition Governance in the EU: Delegation, Decentralization or Experimentalist Governance?' in C. F. Sabel and J. Zeitlin (eds.), *Experimentalist Governance in the European Union: Towards a New Architecture* (Oxford, Oxford University Press, 2010) 84, 103

...the new network has features that can make it an important mechanism for disseminating learning about regulatory interventions by national authorities and the Commission, reviewing such interventions, and using the information gathered so as to advance the identified objectives of competition law and the metrics used to gauge their attainment. Finally, the residual powers of intervention vested in the Commission need not be viewed as instruments of command and control, both because, if exercised, they are checked by requirements for justification and peer review, and because they may play a different role in building up implementation capacity among the network members....

Alternatively, the obligation to report initiatives and decisions from specific interventions can provide a key learning tool for members of the network. For example, interventions by authorities considered to have greater implementation capacity and credibility (such as the United Kingdom, France, Germany and Italy) can be used by the smaller and less credible authorities to inform their own decision-making.

This optimistic approach is countered by those who fear that the system is too informal to work in a legitimate manner. The club-like qualities of the ECN may well ensure better decision-making but at the expense of a transparent forum for deliberation. And opacity brings the risk of domination, whether by the Commission or another NCA, dictating enforcement priorities, thus NCAs work for the EU's competition policy.[162] Moreover, others have argued that more procedural harmonisation is necessary to make cooperation work well.[163] The Commission's first review of Regulation 1/2003 suggests that, while there is scope for improvement, decentralised enforcement has been a success.[164]

European Commission, *Report on the Functioning of Regulation 1/2003*, COM(2009)206 final

24. Enforcement of the EC competition rules has vastly increased since the entry into application of Regulation 1/2003. By the end of March 2009, more than 1,000 cases have been pursued on the basis of the EC competition rules in a wide variety of sectors.

25. Work sharing between the enforcers in the network has generally been unproblematic. Five years of experience have confirmed that the flexible and pragmatic arrangements introduced by Regulation

---

[162] S. Wilks, 'Agency Escape: Decentralization or Dominance of the European Commission in the Modernization of Competition Policy?' (2005) 18 *Governance* 431.

[163] C. Gauer, 'Does the Effectiveness of the EU Network of Competition Authorities Require a Certain Degree of Harmonisation of National Procedures and Sanctions?' in C.-D. Ehlermann and I. Atanasiu (eds.), *European Competition Law Annual 2002: Constructing the EU Network of Competition Authorities* (Oxford, Hart, 2004).

[164] For a more critical assessment, see G. Bruzzone and G. Boccaccio, 'Taking Care of Modernisation After the Startup: A View from a Member State' (2008) 31 *World Competition* 89; A. Schwab and C. Steinle, 'Pitfalls of the European Competition Network: Why Better Protection of Leniency Applicants and Legal Regulation of Case Allocation is Needed' (2008) *ECLR* 523.

1/2003 and the Network Notice work well. Discussions on case-allocation have come up in very few cases and have been resolved swiftly.

26. Cooperation mechanisms for fact-finding purposes within the ECN have worked well overall. The possibility to exchange and use information gathered by another competition authority enhances the overall efficiency within the network and is a pre-condition for a flexible case-allocation system. Moreover, the power of national competition authorities to carry out inspections or other fact-finding measures on behalf of another national competition authority, while encountering some limitations as a result of the diversity of national procedures, has been used actively in appropriate cases and has contributed to effective enforcement...

28. By the end of the reporting period, the Commission had been informed of more than 300 envisaged decisions by the national competition authorities on the basis of Article 11(4). None of these cases resulted in the Commission initiating proceedings pursuant to Article 11(6) to relieve a national competition authority of its competence for reasons of coherent application. Experience indicates that national competition authorities are generally highly committed to ensuring consistency and efforts undertaken in the ECN have successfully contributed to this aim. Pursuant to Article 11(4), a practice of informally discussing the national authority's proposed course of action at services' level and within the confines of confidentiality in the network has been developed. Stakeholders are largely satisfied with the results of application of the EC competition rules within the ECN.

29. The ECN has proven to be a successful forum to discuss general policy issues. Constant dialogue between the network members on all levels over the last years has significantly contributed to coherent application of the EC competition rules.

30. While Regulation 1/2003 does not compel Member States to adopt a specific institutional framework for the implementation of EC competition rules, many Member States have reinforced or reviewed their enforcement structures to optimise their effectiveness.

31. Regulation 1/2003 does not formally regulate or harmonise the procedures of national competition authorities, meaning that they apply the same substantive rules according to divergent procedures and they may impose a variety of sanctions. Regulation 1/2003 accommodates this diversity. It has also given rise to a significant degree of voluntary convergence of Member States' laws that has been supported by policy work in the ECN.

32. The ECN Model Leniency Programme illustrates how the ECN is able to combine its forces and jointly develop a new vision to address real and perceived deficits in the existing system. The work within the ECN has been a major catalyst in encouraging Member States and/or national competition authorities to introduce and develop their own leniency policies and in promoting convergence between them. Today, only two Member States do not have any kind of leniency policy in place. The Model Programme foresees that the ECN will evaluate the state of convergence of the leniency programmes by the end of 2008. The assessment will form the basis for a reflection on whether further action is needed in this field.

33. Notwithstanding, divergences of Member States' enforcement systems remain on important aspects such as fines, criminal sanctions, liability in groups of undertakings, liability of associations of undertakings, succession of undertakings, prescription periods and the standard of proof, the power to impose structural remedies, as well as the ability of Member States' competition authorities to formally set enforcement priorities. This aspect may merit further examination and reflection.

Here we have a tension: on the one hand, insiders report that the Network members cooperate amicably and productively.[165] But this raises concerns about absence of legitimacy: who actually decides the case, the NCA or the ECN? When does peer review become peer pressure? And who is accountable for the Network's deliberations? These procedural concerns lead to legitimate questions of whether the quality of decisions is actually improved by the ECN.

(v) Modernisation and the courts

It was inevitable, given the incomplete nature of Regulation 1/2003 that the Court of Justice would become involved. What is striking is the vigour with which the Court has tested national arrangements and limited NCAs. This case law is in tension with the flexibility some would like to see develop. The most striking judgment, with far-reaching impact, is *VEBIC*. This was a simple cartel case but the Court was asked to investigate if the Belgian competition procedures were adequate. The legislation designated the Belgian NCA to function like an administrative court, and within it were two bodies: a prosecutor and a decision-maker. This was to ensure compliance with fundamental rights. Parties could appeal, but on such appeals the NCA (which was the lower court) was understandably not allowed to act as respondent. Instead, a minister responsible for the economy could make written observations in support of the NCA's decision.

Case C-439/08 *VEBIC* [2010] ECR I-12471

57. Although Article 35(1) of the Regulation leaves it to the domestic legal order of each Member State to determine the detailed procedural rules for legal proceedings brought against decisions of the competition authorities designated thereunder, such rules must not jeopardise the attainment of the objective of the Regulation, which is to ensure that Articles 101 TFEU and 102 TFEU are applied effectively by those authorities.

58. In that regard, as the Advocate General has remarked in point 74 of his Opinion, if the national competition authority is not afforded rights as a party to proceedings and is thus prevented from defending a decision that it has adopted in the general interest, there is a risk that the court before which the proceedings have been brought might be wholly 'captive' to the pleas in law and arguments put forward by the undertaking(s) bringing the proceedings. In a field such as that of establishing infringements of the competition rules and imposing fines, which involves complex legal and economic assessments, the very existence of such a risk is likely to compromise the exercise of the specific obligation on national competition authorities under the Regulation to ensure the effective application of Articles 101 TFEU and 102 TFEU.

59. A national competition authority's obligation to ensure that Articles 101 TFEU and 102 TFEU are applied effectively therefore requires that the authority should be entitled to participate, as a defendant or respondent, in proceedings before a national court which challenge a decision that the authority itself has taken. . . .

62. Under Article 35(1) of the Regulation, the competition authorities designated by the Member States may include courts. Under Article 35(2), when enforcement of EU competition law is entrusted to

---

[165] K. Dekeyser and M. Jaspers, 'A New Era of ECN Cooperation' (2007) 30 *World Competition* 3. For a more theoretical analysis, see G. Majone, 'The Credibility Crisis of Community Regulation' (2000) 38(2) *JCMS* 273; I. Maher, 'Regulation and Modes of Governance in EC Competition Law: What is New in Enforcement?' (2007–2008) 31 *Fordham International Law Journal* 1713.

national administrative and judicial authorities, the Member States may allocate different powers and functions to those different national authorities, whether administrative or judicial.

63. In that regard, in the absence of EU rules, the Member States remain competent, in accordance with the principle of procedural autonomy, to designate the bodies of the national competition authority which may participate, as a defendant or respondent, in proceedings brought before a national court against a decision that the authority itself has taken, while at the same time ensuring that fundamental rights are observed and that EU competition law is fully effective.

The key point is the Court of Justice's repeated insistence on effectiveness. This may pose significant limits on the possibilities of NCAs to explore alternative means of handling. For example, the Court may challenge the design of leniency policies: in *Schenker* it reminded a national authority that immunity from a fine should be an exceptional reward only when cooperation is 'decisive in detecting and actually suppressing the cartel';[166] in *Donau Chemie*, it found that the criteria to determine whether a plaintiff should be able to have access to the leniency documents must be set at national level having regard to the effectiveness of leniency programmes.[167] It is not clear how far-reaching the judgment in *VEBIC* might be: can one challenge an NCA because its fining policies are not sufficiently high when the NCA imposes fines for the effects of an anti-competitive practice only in its territory?[168] Can it be used to challenge the funding of an NCA, if it is found that insufficient resources are afforded to ensure effective enforcement?

Furthermore, the Court of Justice has also eroded some of the powers NCAs may be afforded; for example, an NCA cannot make a decision stating that a given practice does not infringe competition law.[169] It has also expanded the reach of EU competition law in two ways: first (in *Expedia*), by ruling that if an agreement is contrary to Article 101 TFEU because it restricts competition by object, then there is necessarily an effect on trade and so EU law applies; secondly (in *Allianz Hungaria*), by allowing itself to provide an interpretation of Hungarian competition law even when the issue appeared to be purely domestic. This appears to harmonise national and EU law by means of preliminary rulings.[170] These centralising tendencies make the case for further legislative harmonisation, to avoid piecemeal reconstruction of NCA powers and procedures.

5 PRIVATE ENFORCEMENT

It has been argued that private litigation in competition law should be welcomed for two reasons: first, victims of competition law infringements are compensated (public law enforcement merely prevents further harm); secondly, private litigants increase the number of enforcement

---

[166] Case C-681/11 *Schenker & Co. and others*, Judgment of 18 June 2013, para. 47.

[167] Case C-536/11 *Donau Chemie*, Judgment of 6 June 2013.

[168] This is a live issue because the practice in many NCAs is to limit fines to local effects, even if the practice is caught by EU competition law. See Monti, n. 158 above.

[169] Case C-375/09 *Prezes Urzędu Ochrony Konkurencji i Konsumentów v Tele2 Polska sp. z o.o., devenue Netia SA* [2011] ECR I-3055, see discussion in Chapter 22, pp. 1025–6, and the note by S. Brammer (2012) 49(3) *CMLRev.* 1163.

[170] Case C-32/11 *Allianz Hungária Biztosító and others*, Judgment of 14 March 2013, Opinion of Advocate General Cruz-Villalón, para. 47.

actions, widening the application of competition law.[171] The Commission has long campaigned for private parties to bring competition cases in national courts, originally as a means of reducing the Commission's heavy caseload.[172] Recently, private enforcement (especially damages claims against undertakings who infringe EU competition law) has been promoted in an effort to complement the Commission's deterrence-based enforcement strategy. We begin by explaining the contribution of the Court of Justice in galvanising damages claims before turning to the ongoing legislative efforts.

(i) An EU law right to damages

It has long been clear that Articles 101(1) and 102 TFEU have direct effect,[173] opening the way for parties to seek damages. However, there was very little litigation because of uncertainties about the nature of a claim for damages and because a national court could not decide on the application of Article 101(3) (which left it with little room for applying Article 101). The second problem, as we saw above, was resolved by Regulation 1/2003, which establishes the direct effect of Article 101(3), and the first was resolved in 2001 by the Court of Justice in a dispute that arose from a pub lease. Mr Crehan made a contract with Inntrepreneur for the lease of two pubs. The lease contract included a beer tie, providing that Crehan would buy his beer exclusively from Courage. The business was unsuccessful and Crehan abandoned the leases. He sought damages for the loss of a business from Inntrepreneur on the basis that the beer tie prevented him from buying cheaper beer which would have allowed him to make a profit. In the English courts, doubts arose as to whether a party privy to an anti-competitive agreement could claim damages. The Court of Justice enthusiastically affirmed that Crehan could claim damages. When the case returned to the English courts, the Court of Appeal awarded Crehan £131,336 in damages for the losses he suffered, but on appeal to the House of Lords the claim failed.[174]

Case C–453/99 *Courage v Crehan* [2001] ECR I–6314

24. …any individual can rely on a breach of Article [101(1) TFEU] before a national court even where he is a party to a contract that is liable to restrict or distort competition within the meaning of that provision.

25. As regards the possibility of seeking compensation for loss caused by a contract or by conduct liable to restrict or distort competition, it should be remembered from the outset that…the national courts whose task it is to apply the provisions of Community law in areas within their jurisdiction must ensure that those rules take full effect and must protect the rights which they confer on individuals.

26. The full effectiveness of Article [101 TFEU] and, in particular, the practical effect of the prohibition laid down in Article [101(1) TFEU] would be put at risk if it were not open to any individual to claim damages for loss caused to him by a contract or by conduct liable to restrict or distort competition.

---

[171] *White Paper on Productivity and Enterprise: A World Class Competition Regime*, Cm. 5233 (2001) ch. 8.

[172] European Commission, *Thirteenth Report on Competition Policy* (1983) paras. 217–18; Commission Notice of 23 December 1992 on cooperation between national courts and the Commission in applying Articles 85 and 86 of EEC Treaty [1993] OJ C39/6.

[173] Case 127/73 *BRT v SABAM* [1974] ECR 313.

[174] *Crehan v Inntrepreneur* [2004] EWCA Civ 637; *Inntrepreneur Pub Company (CPC) and others* v *Crehan* [2006] UKHL 38.

27. Indeed, the existence of such a right strengthens the working of the Community competition rules and discourages agreements or practices, which are frequently covert, which are liable to restrict or distort competition. From that point of view, actions for damages before the national courts can make a significant contribution to the maintenance of effective competition in the Community.

28. There should not therefore be any absolute bar to such an action being brought by a party to a contract which would be held to violate the competition rules.

29. However, in the absence of Community rules governing the matter, it is for the domestic legal system of each Member State to designate the courts and tribunals having jurisdiction and to lay down the detailed procedural rules governing actions for safeguarding rights which individuals derive directly from Community law, provided that such rules are not less favourable than those governing similar domestic actions (principle of equivalence) and that they do not render practically impossible or excessively difficult the exercise of rights conferred by Community law (principle of effectiveness).

30. In that regard, the Court has held that Community law does not prevent national courts from taking steps to ensure that the protection of the rights guaranteed by Community law does not entail the unjust enrichment of those who enjoy them.

31. Similarly, provided that the principles of equivalence and effectiveness are respected, Community law does not preclude national law from denying a party who is found to bear significant responsibility for the distortion of competition the right to obtain damages from the other contracting party. Under a principle which is recognised in most of the legal systems of the Member States and which the Court has applied in the past, a litigant should not profit from his own unlawful conduct, where this is proven.

32. In that regard, the matters to be taken into account by the competent national court include the economic and legal context in which the parties find themselves and, as the United Kingdom Government rightly points out, the respective bargaining power and conduct of the two parties to the contract.

33. In particular, it is for the national court to ascertain whether the party who claims to have suffered loss through concluding a contract that is liable to restrict or distort competition found himself in a markedly weaker position than the other party, such as seriously to compromise or even eliminate his freedom to negotiate the terms of the contract and his capacity to avoid the loss or reduce its extent, in particular by availing himself in good time of all the legal remedies available to him.

This judgment should be studied from two perspectives. From a narrow perspective focusing on the facts of the case, it should be noted that the English courts had never doubted that a right to damages for breach of competition law was available.[175] Rather, the question that had been referred to the Court of Justice was whether a party privy to an anti-competitive agreement should be able to seek compensation, because the principle of illegality in English law meant that those implicated in an illegal venture lost the right to damages for loss suffered. The Court of Justice paid little attention to this question.[176]

From a wider perspective, the judgment is a general statement establishing an EU law right to damages. This is significant because it gives the European and national courts a shared role in shaping the law. The most helpful analysis has been provided by Asimmakis Komninos who has elaborated a framework developed by former Advocate General van Gerven.[177] He

---

[175] In the United Kingdom, for example, the House of Lords in *Garden Cottage Foods* v *Milk Marketing Board* [1984] AC 130 assumed damages to be available.

[176] G. Monti, 'Anticompetitive Agreements: The Innocent Party's Right to Damages' (2002) 27 *ELRev.* 282.

[177] W. van Gerven, 'Of Rights, Remedies and Procedures' (2000) 37 *CMLRev.* 501.

distinguishes three elements of a damages claim: constitutive, executive and procedural. The first relates to the nature of the claim itself, which must be identical among the Member States. Executive elements include matters like the test for causation, defences and damages. The rules pertaining to these issues can be designed by national courts and legislatures subject to two principles of EU law: first that the rules are effective to safeguard the right, and secondly, that they are equivalent to comparable claims that are made in national law. Procedural matters (e.g. limitation periods and rules of evidence) can also be designed by national courts subject to a more lenient scrutiny under EU law.[178]

In *Manfredi*, the Court of Justice took further steps to explain the right to damages and the role of national courts relating to the executive and procedural conditions. This was a damages claim by Italian consumers who had purchased liability insurance for motor vehicles at inflated prices after insurers had colluded. It was a follow-on claim after the Italian competition authority had found an infringement of Italian competition law (the wording of which is very close to Article 101 TFEU). However, the plaintiff claimed damages based on Article 101 TFEU because a claim for damages for breaches of Italian competition law rests with the Court of Appeal, while a claim under Article 101 TFEU can be taken to a small claims court, which is less formal, cheaper and quicker at delivering judgment. The Court of Justice agreed that it was plausible to find that the cartel affected trade between Member States, allowing the application of Article 101 TFEU. It then gave some guidance on the role of national courts, suggesting that in the absence of Community rules on matters such as the jurisdiction of national courts, limitation periods, and the measure of damages, it was up to Member States to ensure that plaintiffs received adequate safeguards 'provided that such rules are not less favourable than those governing similar domestic actions (principle of equivalence) and that they do not render practically impossible or excessively difficult the exercise of rights conferred by Community law (principle of effectiveness)'.[179] The Court elaborated somewhat on the measure of damages.

Joined Cases C-295–298/04 *Vincenzo Manfredi and others* v *Lloyd Adriatico Assicurazioni SpA and others* [2006] ECR I-6619

61. It follows that any individual can claim compensation for the harm suffered where there is a causal relationship between that harm and an agreement or practice prohibited under Article [101 TFEU]....

93. ...in accordance with the principle of equivalence, it must be possible to award particular damages, such as exemplary or punitive damages, pursuant to actions founded on the Community competition rules, if such damages may be awarded pursuant to similar actions founded on domestic law.

94. However, it is settled case-law that Community law does not prevent national courts from taking steps to ensure that the protection of the rights guaranteed by Community law does not entail the unjust enrichment of those who enjoy them.

95. Secondly, it follows from the principle of effectiveness and the right of any individual to seek compensation for loss caused by a contract or by conduct liable to restrict or distort competition that injured persons must be able to seek compensation not only for actual loss (*damnum emergens*) but also for loss of profit (*lucrum cessans*) plus interest.

---

[178] A. P. Komninos, *EC Private Antitrust Enforcement* (Oxford, Hart, 2008) 170–6.

[179] Joined Cases C-295–298/04 *Vincenzo Manfredi and others* v *Lloyd Adriatico Assicurazioni SpA and others* [2006] ECR I-6619, para. 62.

> 96. Total exclusion of loss of profit as a head of damage for which compensation may be awarded cannot be accepted in the case of a breach of Community law since, especially in the context of economic or commercial litigation, such a total exclusion of loss of profit would be such as to make reparation of damage practically impossible.

The relevant Italian court has now rendered a judgment that among other matters awards the claimant 'double damages' as a means of giving effect to the Court of Justice's judgment, but it has been suggested that this is not what the Court intended.[180] Further guidance is probably needed on the quantum of damages, and it is significant that the Court of Justice suggests that claimants have a right to seek damages for loss of profit as well, although the difficulties in showing a causal link between an infringement of competition law and the loss of a chance to make profit seem insurmountable, and it is likely that most claimants will settle for a claim of actual loss (i.e. the overcharge caused by the cartel).[181]

According to Komninos, the Court of Justice in *Manfredi* also set out the constitutive conditions of the claim in paragraph 61: damages are available when there is harm, a competition law violation, and a causal link between the violation and the harm.[182] If this is correct, then two consequences follow. First, there is no need for the plaintiff to prove fault (liability is strict). Secondly, and more significantly, it means that both direct and indirect buyers may claim damages. Think, for example, of a cartel in the market for MP3 players sold by manufacturers to high street shops. The high street shop pays an inflated price, and as a result, they try and pass on some of that higher cost to consumers in the form of higher prices. It appears that a claim for damages may be brought by the shops (direct purchasers) and each individual buyer (indirect purchasers).

While the Court of Justice has made a major contribution in establishing certain elements to facilitate damages claims, the Commission has taken the view that further legislative efforts are required to ensure that the right to damages is exercised widely.

(ii) Commission initiatives

It is very complicated for the Commission to initiate action to facilitate damages actions: the European Parliament is supportive but warns of the risk of US-style litigation, and Member States are divided. The 2005 *Green Paper on Damages Actions* was criticised for being too aggressive; the 2008 *White Paper on Damages Actions* addressed this by stating that proposals would be 'balanced measures that are rooted in European legal culture and traditions',[183] but was criticised as not bold enough;[184] the first Directive proposed in 2009 was rejected even before it was made public, and at the time of writing there is a Proposed Directive on certain rules governing actions for damages under national law for infringements of the competition

---

[180] See P. Nebbia, 'So What Happened to *Manfredi*?' (2007) *ECLR* 591, for a strong critique of the Italian court's decision.

[181] E.g. *Devenish Nutrition Ltd and others v Sanofi and others* [2007] EWHC 2394 (Ch).

[182] Komninos n. 178 above, 175.   [183] *Ibid.* 2.

[184] Editorial Comments, 'A Little More Action Please! The White Paper on Damages Actions for Breach of the EC Antitrust Rules' (2008) 45 *CMLRev.* 609.

law provisions of the Member States and of the EU.[185] The title is informative: this is a helter-skelter attempt to address some of the issues, and not a comprehensive codification. This is the best the Commission feels able to do given political opposition to other aspects of its earlier proposals. We consider the main aspects below.

It addresses access to evidence in two ways. First, it introduces a discovery procedure whereby claimants may request documents held by the defendant or others when the claimant can show that that person holds evidence that is 'relevant' to making the claim and specifies the evidence as precisely as possible, and when the court receiving the request for discovery considers the request is proportionate.[186] Secondly, it proposes to overturn the approach of the Court of Justice towards leniency documents. Article 6 provides that leniency corporate statements and settlement submissions will not be disclosed. This is to be welcomed, because the Court of Justice instead has held that one should examine on a case-by-case basis whether disclosure of leniency documents should be allowed: on one side considering the usefulness of these documents for claimants, on the other considering that leniency policy might be undermined if access to the leniency file is made too easy (as undertakings may stop making leniency applications for fear of damages claims). This has led to conflicting approaches in national courts, but the Commission's proposal removes this uncertainty. It remains to be seen whether the discovery procedures are sufficient to afford parties the information needed to show an infringement and prove their losses. Further protection is also afforded for those who have been awarded full immunity as a result of a leniency application: their liability is normally limited to the losses caused to their direct purchasers, so they are not jointly liable for losses caused by the cartel as a whole.[187]

Follow-on damages actions were already facilitated by Regulation 1/2003: article 16 provided that if the Commission brings a successful action against an anti-competitive practice, then this decision binds national courts. Thus, the plaintiff does not have to prove the infringement again, only that she has suffered damage as a result. This saves considerable resources for litigants in what are often complex cases. Article 9 of the proposed Directive would make any decision of any NCA or any judgment of any national court binding on other national courts. This has already been implemented unilaterally in the United Kingdom and Germany,[188] and while it is controversial, it probably has little value: as matters stand, most NCAs appear to penalise cartels only for the effects they have in their Member State, so it is unlikely that claimants will find much value in decisions rendered in other Member States.[189]

The proposed Directive seeks to facilitate claims by indirect purchasers. The practical difficulties they face can be illustrated with an example. If the cartel causes the price to rise by €2 and the claimant resells the goods to the indirect purchaser at a price that is €1 higher than before the cartel, then he has passed on half of the overcharge, with the

---

[185] COM(2013)404 final. See also *Impact Assessment Report*, Commission Staff Working Document (2013) 203.
[186] Proposed Directive, article 5.   [187] *Ibid.* article 11(2).
[188] Likewise for investigations by NCAs; e.g. UK Competition Act 1998, s.58(1) provides that findings of *fact* by the Office of Fair Trading are binding in court proceedings; s.58A (inserted by Enterprise Act 2002, s.20) provides that findings of *infringements* of Articles 101 TFEU and 102 TFEU are binding on courts; s.47A (inserted by Enterprise Act 2002, s.18) provides for a follow-on action for damages in the Competition Appeals Tribunal where there has been a finding of an infringement of UK or EU competition law by the OFT or the European Commission; this is without prejudice to bringing an action in the normal courts.
[189] Monti, n. 158 above.

direct and indirect purchasers suffering €1 of damage each, if we calculate loss only based on the overcharge. The proposal is that while the indirect purchaser has the burden to prove that the loss was passed to it, this is deemed to have occurred if the defendant has committed an infringement, if this has resulted in an overcharge to the direct purchaser, and if the claimant bought from the direct purchaser. Furthermore, the court may estimate the share of the overcharge. Of course, the defendant can introduce evidence to show that the overcharge was not passed on. The proposal concomitantly allows the defendant to raise a passing-on defence when direct purchasers seek damages. These provisions are designed to ensure that direct and indirect buyers are compensated equitably, while placing the burden of bringing evidence on the defendant. The risk is that the defendant does not really know how much of the overcharge the direct buyer can pass on; however, the risk of the defendant paying twice over is mitigated by article 13 by which national courts must consider related proceedings. Ideally here the best solution is case-management, requiring that direct and indirect purchaser lawsuits are brought together, but the proposed Directive does not go this far.[190]

In the withdrawn proposed Directive of 2009, there had been provisions requiring Member States to facilitate collective redress through group actions and representative actions.[191] However, opposition from the European Parliament saw this element dropped from the current proposal.[192] The Parliament had three concerns in particular: the risk of abusive litigation; that opt-out class actions, which the Directive sought to facilitate (that is, class actions that are taken on behalf of a large group of consumers, say all those that bought insurance policies at inflated prices because of a cartel among insurers, by a representative of the class and each member is included in the action unless they actively opt out) infringe individual autonomy and are contrary to Article 6 ECHR; and that any class action initiative should cover consumer claims in other fields as well (e.g. product liability).[193] In response, the Commission has issued a Communication and a Recommendation in an attempt to encourage Member States to adopt analogous procedures for class actions.[194] At the time of writing, it remains to be seen if the Commission will opt for a bolder legislative initiative, but given that national sensitivities appear hard to overcome it is more likely that national initiatives will dominate the landscape, which means that claimants in some Member States will find easier routes to redress than others.

---

[190] An alternative solution, which is adopted in US federal law, is to allow suits only by direct purchasers, with no passing-on defence. It is claimed that this creates the right incentives for claimants. W. M. Landes and R. A. Posner, 'Should Indirect Purchasers have Standing to Sue under the Antitrust Laws? An Economic Analysis of the Rule in Illinois Brick' (1979) 46 *University of Chicago Law Review* 602; N. Reich, 'The "Courage" Doctrine: Encouraging or Discouraging Compensation for Antitrust Injuries?' (2005) 35 *CMLRev.* 35; C. Petrucci, 'The Issues of the Passing-on Defence and Indirect Purchasers' Standing in European Competition Law' (2008) *ECLR* 33.

[191] Proposed Directive, articles 4–6.

[192] European Parliament Resolution of 26 March 2009 on the *White Paper on Damages Actions for Breach of the EC Antitrust Rules*, P6_TA-PROV(2009)0187. The Parliament also disagreed with a number of other proposals in the White Paper.

[193] European Parliament Resolution of 2 February 2012 on 'Towards a Coherent European Approach to Collective Redress' (2011/2089(INI).

[194] Commission Communication, Towards a Horizontal Framework for Collective Redress, COM(2013)401 final; Commission Recommendation of 11 June 2013 on common principles for injunctive and compensatory collective redress mechanisms in the Member States concerning violations of rights granted under Union law [2013] OJ L201/60.

(iii) Assessment

Of the fifty-four prohibition decisions issued by the Commission between 2006 and 2012, fifteen have led to follow-on actions: most in three Member States (United Kingdom, Germany and the Netherlands) and almost none were brought by consumers or small or medium-sized firms.[195] While this makes a case for harmonisation, there are tensions between Member States that are worried about fomenting a litigation culture and those eager to facilitate claims.[196] This explains the slow progress and the timidity of the proposed Directive. It means that Member States will likely be the main players who design procedures to facilitate claims.[197]

Furthermore, one might doubt whether damages actions are desirable in competition law at all. Insofar as the aim of deterrence is concerned, public enforcement is a superior form of deterrence for a number of reasons. First, antitrust authorities have more effective investigatory and sanctioning powers, in particular with the network of NCAs being developed. Secondly, private plaintiffs are motivated by profit and not necessarily motivated to bring claims against practices that injure the public interest, whereas NCAs will tend to bring claims of most value to the economy. Thirdly, private enforcement is more costly because NCAs are repeat players, who specialise in competition law and thus the marginal cost of additional actions is lower.[198] But this view has, however, come under fire, with the argument that NCAs are superior being questioned on the basis that while private enforcement is imperfect, it is not an argument against allowing those who are able to mount an action to do so, and the risk that private parties will litigate unmeritorious claims is one which affects all private litigation, and which can be tempered by judges striking out worthless claims.[199] The Commission's justification seems to be that the estimated cost to antitrust victims ranges between €25 and €69 billion,[200] and that 'EU-wide infringements are becoming more and more frequent'.[201] However don't these findings suggest that the Commission should focus on measures to improve public enforcement?

FURTHER READING

G. Amato, *Antitrust and the Bounds of Power* (Oxford, Hart, 1997)

S. Bishop and M. Walker, *The Economics of EC Competition Law* (3rd edn, London, Sweet and Maxwell, 2010)

I. van Bael, *Due Process in EU Competition Proceedings* (The Hague, Kluwer, 2011)

S. Brammer *Co-operation between National Competition Agencies in the Enforcement of EC Competition Law* (Oxford, Hart, 2009)

---

[195] A. Howard, 'Too Little, too Late? The European Commission's Legislative Proposal on Anti-Trust Damages Actions' (2013) *Journal of European Competition Law and Practice* 455.

[196] J. S. Kortmann and C. R. A. Swaak, 'The EC White Paper on Antitrust Damage Actions: Why the Member States are (Right to be) Less than Enthusiastic' (2009) *ECLR* 340.

[197] This has happened already in Germany and there is an ongoing reform process in the United Kingdom. For discussion, see A. Higgins and A. Zuckerman, *Class Actions in England? Efficacy, Autonomy and Proportionality in Collective Redress*, University of Oxford Legal Research Paper Series No. 93/2013 (2013).

[198] W. P. J. Wils, 'Should Private Antitrust Enforcement be Encouraged in Europe?' (2003) 26 *World Competition* 473.

[199] C. A. Jones, 'Private Antitrust Enforcement in Europe: A Policy Analysis and a Reality Check' (2004) 27 *World Competition* 13.

[200] *Impact Assessment Report*, n. 185 above, paras. 42–3.   [201] *Ibid.* para. 32.

R. Buch-Hansen and A. Wigger, *The Politics of European Competition Regulation: A Critical Political Economy Perspective* (Abingdon, Routledge, 2011)

D. J. Gerber, *Law and Competition in Twentieth Century Europe* (Oxford, Oxford University Press, 1998)

D. J. Gerber 'Two Forms of Modernization in European Competition Law' (2008) *Fordham International Law Journal* 1235

C. Heide-Jorgensen, C. Bergqvist, U. Neergard and S.T. Poulsen (eds.), *Aims and Values in Competition Law* (Copenhagen, DJØF Publishing, 2013)

C. S. Kerse and N. Kahn, *EC Antitrust Procedure* (5th edn, London, Sweet & Maxwell, 2012)

A. P. Komninos, *EC Private Antitrust Enforcement* (Oxford, Hart, 2008)

W. Sauter, *Competition Law and Industrial Policy in the EU* (Oxford, Oxford University Press, 1997)

J. S. Venit, 'Brave New World: The Modernization and Decentralization of Enforcement under Articles 81 and 82 of the EC Treaty' (2003) 40 *Common Market Law Review* 545

S. B. Völker, 'Rough Justice? An Analysis of the European Commission's New Fining Guidelines' (2007) 44 *Common Market Law Review* 1285

R. Wesseling, *The Modernization of EC Antitrust Law* (Oxford/Portland, Hart, 2000)

S. Wilks, 'Agency Escape: Decentralization or Dominance of the European Commission in the Modernization of Competition Policy?' (2005) 18 *Governance* 431

W. P. J. Wils, 'Should Private Antitrust Enforcement be Encouraged in Europe?' (2003) 26 *World Competition* 473

W. P. J. Wils, 'Ten Years of Regulation 1/2003: A Retrospective' (2013) 4(4) *Journal of European Competition Law and Practice* 1

22

Antitrust and Monopolies

CONTENTS

1 INTRODUCTION

In this chapter we review the two principal provisions that implement the competition policy whose aims and enforcement structure were discussed in Chapter 21. Article 101 TFEU applies to agreements between undertakings and declares these agreements void when they are found to restrict competition; Article 102 TFEU applies to dominant undertakings and forbids them from abusing their position. Since the end of the 1990s, the Commission has been engaged in a series of reform initiatives to the application of competition law, in response to criticisms that its approach was insufficiently grounded in economics and was overly aggressive.[1] Explaining and evaluating this process of reform is the central theme of this chapter, which is organised in the following way.

Section 2 covers three legal issues that are common to both Articles: the meaning of an undertaking, the concept of an effect on trade between Member States, and judge-made rules that exclude the application of competition law.

Section 3 is a review of the key issues that have arisen in the application of Article 101. It is divided into three parts. First, we explore how this provision applies to activities that undermine the key aims of EU competition law (the protection of the consumer and the integration of markets). In particular we study how this provision tackles cartels, whose agreements cause them to act as a monopoly and reduce consumer welfare. A former Competition Commissioner characterised them as 'cancers on the open market economy'.[2] Catching and punishing cartels is at the heart of the functions of all competition authorities.[3] This subsection of the chapter should be read together with section 3 of Chapter 21 which explains the powers the Commission has to find cartels and to penalise them. The task in this chapter is to examine how widely the meaning of the concepts of agreement and concerted practice have been used to catch collusion. Secondly, we consider how the Commission and European Courts determine whether agreements that are not obviously anti-competitive (for example, joint ventures and distribution agreements) are evaluated under Article 101(1) and consider different views on what the legal or economic standard for assessment is. Thirdly, we study how Article 101(3) is applied to exempt anti-competitive agreements and explore the debate between a narrow and a wide interpretation of this exemption. The bulk of the Commission's energies over the past forty years of competition law enforcement have been devoted to Article 101 cases, and a daunting number of decisions have been published. However, in this chapter we will limit ourselves to analysing a small representative sample of decisions in close detail.

Section 4 examines Article 102 TFEU by first discussing the concept of abuse in general terms, followed by a case study on predatory pricing and related pricing practices. The key points are the breadth of the concept of dominance, and the policy underpinning the abuse doctrine. The Court of Justice's approach is to impose on dominant undertakings a special responsibility not to distort competition but seems to place little emphasis on testing whether a suspected abuse is successful in harming competition or in causing harm to economic welfare. The Commission is hoping to redirect this case law to consider the anti-competitive effects more fully and we chart this 'work in progress' here by explaining the new approach and considering how far the case law of the Court of Justice to date is sympathetic to this innovation.

Section 5 is a brief account of hidden developments. As we noted in Chapter 21, the Commission has the power to issue commitment decisions: it is worth noting that these decisions

---

[1] The most significant stimulus was a presentation to DG Competition by a distinguished antitrust practitioner: B. E. Hawk, 'System Failure: Vertical Restraints and EC Competition Law' (1995) 32 *CMLRev.* 973.

[2] M. Monti, 'Fighting Cartels Why and How?', speech 11–12 September 2000, available at http://europa.eu/rapid/press-release_SPEECH-00-295_en.htm.

[3] OECD, *Hard Core Cartels: Recent Progress and Challenges Ahead* (OECD, 2003); European Commission, *Report on Competition Policy 2004*, SEC(2005)805 final, 29.

are increasing in frequency and here the approach appears to deviate from the formal stance the Commission and the Court of Justice take. The implications of this development are that we have two parallel (and not entirely consistent) approaches to competition law.

2 SCOPE OF APPLICATION OF EU COMPETITION LAW

(i) Undertakings

EU competition law applies to 'undertakings', a term that 'encompasses every entity engaged in an economic activity, regardless of the legal status of the entity or the way in which it is financed'.[4] Its meaning is independent of any national law definitions of what constitutes a company. Rather, it is effects-based: the question is whether the entity in question, when doing a specific task, has an economic impact on the market by offering goods or services. It means that an economic entity may be treated as an undertaking when it performs certain functions, but fall outside the scope of competition law when pursuing other roles.[5] Inventors,[6] opera singers,[7] barristers,[8] sporting associations,[9] agricultural cooperatives[10] and multinational corporations can all act as undertakings. Employees however, are not undertakings,[11] nor are agents who operate on behalf of their principal and take no financial risk.[12] In recent years, as governments have increasingly contracted out the provision of public services, questions have arisen as to whether entities engaged in the provision of these types of services (for example, emergency ambulance services and air traffic control) should be regulated by competition law. This issue is discussed in Chapter 24, which is available online.

Subsidiaries may have independent legal personality, but for the purposes of competition law a subsidiary is treated as a single economic entity along with the parent company where the subsidiary has no ability to determine its conduct on the market.[13] Whether parent and subsidiary constitute a single economic entity is a question of fact. Relevant considerations include the number of shares that the parent has in the subsidiary (where a majority shareholding will give rise to a presumption that the parent controls the subsidiary),[14] the composition of the board of directors, and whether the subsidiary carries out the parent's instructions. Whether parent and subsidiary are one undertaking or two has considerable practical implications: first, if they are two undertakings then Article 101 TFEU applies, while if there is one undertaking, it is classified as an intra-firm agreement, to which Article 101 does not apply.

---

[4] Case C-41/90 *Höfner and Elser* v *Macrotron GmbH* [1991] ECR I-1979, para. 21.

[5] For example, the European Organisation for the Safety of Air Navigation (Eurocontrol) does not act as an undertaking when it controls traffic, but is an undertaking if it abuses its monopsony power when purchasing goods on the market. See Case C-113/07 *Selex Sistemi Integrati* v *Commission and Eurocontrol* [2009] ECR I-2207.

[6] *Reuter/BASF* [1976] OJ L254/40.   [7] *RAI/UNITEL* [1978] OJ L157/39.

[8] Case C-309/99 *Wouters* [2002] ECR I-1577.

[9] *The Distribution of Package Tours During the 1990 World Cup* [1992] OJ L326/31.

[10] Case C-250/92 *Gøttrup Klim* v *DLG* [1994] ECR I-5641.   [11] Case C-22/98 *Becu* [1999] ECR I-5665.

[12] See Guidelines on Vertical Restraints [2000] OJ C291/1, paras. 12–20.

[13] Case C-73/95P *Viho Europe* v *Commission* [1996] ECR I-5457.

[14] Compare Case C-73/95 *Viho Europe BV* v *Commission* [1996] ECR I-5457 (100 per cent shareholding meant the parent and subsidiary was a single economic entity) with *Gosmé/Martell-DMP* [1991] OJ L185/23 (50 per cent ownership of a joint venture insufficient to treat the two as a single entity) and Case T-228/97 *Irish Sugar* v *Commission* [1999] ECR II-2669 (subsidiary in which Irish Sugar held 51 per cent of the shares held to be a separate undertaking).

As a result, an undertaking may evade the application of Article 101 by buying firms with whom it would normally contract if it finds that the burden of complying with Article 101 is too onerous. Parker Pen embarked on this strategy, owning all its distributors in certain Member States and orchestrating distribution through them. The effect of this was to partition the market, as each subsidiary was only allowed to sell in the territory allocated to it by Parker Pen. Viho (a Dutch wholesaler) complained because it wished to buy Parker products in Germany for resale in the Netherlands, but was unsuccessful in obtaining the goods from Parker's German subsidiary. Had Parker prohibited an independent distributor in Germany from selling to Viho, this would have constituted an agreement in breach of Article 101, but as it was an internal measure, the Court of Justice held that it was not caught by Article 101 because Parker and its subsidiaries formed a single economic unit.[15] Parker's strategy had been the result of an earlier Commission decision (spurred by an earlier complaint from Viho) that its contracts with an independent distributor in Germany infringed Article 101 by prohibiting the German distributor from exporting Parker products.[16] In response, Parker Pen established its own distribution network, avoiding the finding of an agreement but dividing the market, thereby undermining one central aim of EU competition law.

A second significant reason for determining whether parents and subsidiaries are a single economic unit is that a parent is responsible for acts by its wholly owned subsidiary. This rule was used in *ICI* v *Commission* (*Dyestuffs*) to impose a penalty on foreign parents for a cartel carried out in the Union by subsidiaries even if the parent company had no presence in the European Union.[17] Thirdly, a number of crucial determinations in competition law proceedings depend upon calculating the turnover or market shares of the undertaking concerned. For instance, a fine is calculated in part based upon the turnover of the undertaking (and this figure will include the turnover of the entire economic entity).[18] It means that the fine can be increased significantly because the turnover of the whole corporate group may be taken into account. These two points are particularly important because there is a presumption that the parent and a wholly owned subsidiary are a single undertaking, which parties have challenged regularly but unsuccessfully.[19]

Case C–501/11P *Schindler Holding Ltd and others* v *Commission*, Judgment of 18 July 2013

108. The presumption that decisive influence is exercised over a subsidiary wholly or almost wholly owned by its parent company is intended, in particular, to strike a balance between, on the one hand, the importance of the objective of combating conduct contrary to the competition rules, in particular

---

[15] Case C-73/95P *Viho Europe* v *Commission* [1996] ECR I-5457, paras. 15–18.

[16] *Viho/Parker Pen* [1992] OJ L233/27; affirmed in Case T-66/92 *Herlitz* v *Commission* and Case T-77/92 *Parker* v *Commission* [1994] ECR II-531 and II-549.

[17] Case 48/69 *ICI* v *Commission* [1972] ECR 619. This approach may be criticised because the Court merely considered whether the parent was able to exercise control over the subsidiary, and not whether it had in fact exercised control. See D. G. Goyder, *EC Competition Law* (4th edn, Oxford, Oxford University Press, 2003) 499–500.

[18] Regulation 1/2003 on the implementation of the rules on competition laid down in Articles 81 and 82 of the Treaty, article 23(2) [2003] OJ L1/1. Furthermore, damages claims may be brought against parent and subsidiary, and the penalty increases for recidivism may apply if one part of the corporate group has infringed competition law before.

[19] The seminal case is Case C-97/08P *Akzo Nobel NV* v *Commission* [2009] ECR I-8237. See also Case C-179/12P *Dow Chemical Company* v *Commission*, Judgment of 26 September 2013, considering parental liability in a 50/50 joint venture.

to Article [101 TFEU], and of preventing a repetition of such conduct and, on the other hand, the requirements flowing from certain general principles of European Union law such as the principle of the presumption of innocence, the principle that penalties should be applied solely to the offender and the principle of legal certainty as well as the rights of the defence, including the principle of equality of arms. It follows that such a presumption is proportionate to the legitimate aim pursued.

109. Furthermore, first, the aforesaid presumption is based on the fact that, save in quite exceptional circumstances, a company holding all, or almost all, the capital of a subsidiary can, by dint merely of holding it, exercise decisive influence over that subsidiary's conduct and, second, it is within the sphere of operations of those entities against which the presumption operates that evidence of the lack of actual exercise of that power to influence is generally apt to be found. The presumption is, however, rebuttable and the entities wishing to rebut it may adduce all factors relating to the economic, organisational and legal links tying the subsidiary to the parent company that they consider to be capable of demonstrating that the subsidiary and the parent company do not constitute a single economic entity, but that the subsidiary acts independently on the market.

On the facts of this appeal, the Court of Justice also noted that the parent had devised a compliance programme to avoid competition infringements thereby suggesting that it 'did in fact supervise the commercial policy of its subsidiaries'.[20] Note how a substantive question of what an undertaking is takes on procedural significance.

(ii) Effect on trade between Member States

EU Competition law does not apply unless the practice in question has an appreciable effect on trade between Member States. The Court of Justice has set out a wide definition of 'effect on trade', which corresponds to the test deployed in disputes concerning the internal market generally.[21]

Case 56/65 *Société Technique Minière* v *Maschinenbau Ulm* [1966] ECR 234, 249

For this requirement to be fulfilled it must be possible to foresee with a sufficient degree of probability on the basis of a set of objective factors of law or of fact that the agreement in question may have an influence, direct or indirect, actual or potential, on the pattern of trade between Member States. Therefore, in order to determine whether an agreement which contains a clause 'granting an exclusive right of sale' comes within the field of application of Article [101 TFEU], it is necessary to consider in particular whether it is capable of bringing about a partitioning of the market in certain products between Member States and thus rendering more difficult the interpenetration of trade which the Treaty is intended to create.

Two weeks after this judgment the Court of Justice expanded this formula by holding that determining whether an agreement has an effect on trade does not require an evaluation as to whether the effect is positive or negative. Even agreements which increase trade are

---

[20] Case C-501/11P *Schindler Holding Ltd and others* v *Commission*, Judgment of 18 July 2013, para. 114.
[21] For an overview, see J. Faull, 'Effect on Trade Between Member States' (1999) *Fordham Corporate Law Institute* 481.

caught.[22] The aim of the 'effect on trade between Member States' phrase is purely to determine whether EU law applies, and is not used to appraise the agreement. The test is extremely broad: agreements within one Member State may affect trade – for instance a cartel
among Dutch roofing felt manufacturers was held to affect trade between Member States
because it restricted the ability of exporters to penetrate the Dutch market;[23] an agreement
concerning goods that are not traded across borders may have a potential effect on trade
if there is evidence to suggest that cross-border trade could increase;[24] an effect may be
indirect when an agreement fixes prices for a raw material which is not exported but which
is used in the manufacture of a product which is exported;[25] or when a product is sold with
a warranty that is only valid in the Member State where the product is bought.[26] Lastly, an
effect on trade may also arise when the agreement relates to trade outside the EU. Thus, a
distribution agreement whereby Yves Saint Laurent contracted with a firm to distribute its
goods in Russia, Ukraine and Slovenia (at the time not a Member State) and prohibited the
distributor from reimporting them into the Union, could have an 'appreciable effect on the
pattern of trade between the Member States such as to undermine attainment of the objectives of the common market'.[27]

On the one hand, the Commission welcomed this wide definition of an effect on trade as it
extended the reach of EU competition law, but on the other hand, it also posed a risk because it
meant that every agreement, even with players of insignificant size, would fall under Article 101,
which would prevent the Commission from dealing with the more serious infringements. The
Court of Justice attempted to unburden the Commission by holding that Article 101 TFEU
would only apply if the effect on trade was appreciable, thus an agreement with undertakings
that have small market shares would not be subject to Article 101 because its interstate effects
are *de minimis*.[28] In 2004, in order to ensure consistency among national authorities in their
determination of when to apply EU competition law, the Commission published a Notice on
the effect of trade between Member States that establishes the NAAT (no appreciable affecta-
tion of trade) test.[29] According to this test, agreements are incapable of appreciably affecting
trade when the parties' aggregate market share does not exceed 5 per cent, and in horizontal
agreements the turnover of both parties is less than €40 million, while for vertical agreements
the turnover of the supplier does not exceed €40 million. The Commission will not institute
proceedings in these cases and the intention of the Notice is to influence national authorities
to follow suit. However, agreements below these thresholds may still be caught by national
competition law.[30]

---

[22] Joined Cases 54/64 and 58/64 *Consten and Grundig* v *Commission* [1966] ECR 299.
[23] Case 246/86 *Belasco and others* v *Commission* [1989] ECR 2117, paras. 33–8.
[24] Case 107/82 *AEG* v *Commission* [1983] ECR 3151, para. 60.
[25] Case 123/83 *BNIC* v *Clair* [1983] ECR 391, para. 29.   [26] *Re Zanussi SpA Guarantee* [1978] OJ L322/26.
[27] Case C-306/96 *Javico International and Javico AG* v *Yves Saint Laurent Parfums SA* [1998] ECR I-1983, para. 25.
[28] Case 5/69 *Völk* v *Vervaecke* [1969] ECR 295.
[29] Commission Notice: Guidelines on the effect on trade concept contained in Articles 81 and 82 of the Treaty
[2004] OJ C101/81, para. 2.4.
[30] It is not clear why the Commission invented this test since agreements between operators with little market power
are already, in certain circumstances, excluded from the application of Article 101 TFEU when deemed to be of
minor importance on the basis that they are incapable of damaging competition substantially. See Commission
Notice on agreements of minor importance which do not appreciably restrict competition under Article 81(1)
[2001] OJ C368/13.

(iii) Excluded agreements

All economic activities fall to be regulated by EU competition law, but the Treaty provides for certain exceptions: for example, national security;[31] agriculture;[32] and providers entrusted with the provision of services of general economic interest.[33]

Alongside the economic sectors where exclusion was a matter of legislative choice, the Court of Justice has also identified certain fields where EU competition law is excluded. Agreements resulting from negotiations between employers and workers in the context of collective bargaining are excluded.[34] In the seminal case establishing this exclusion, a decision was taken by an organisation representing employers and workers in the wholesale trade of building materials in the Netherlands to establish a single pension fund for all employees in that sector. The fund would be responsible for managing the employees' supplementary pension scheme. The organisation of these supplementary funds was approved by Dutch law but the defendants, undertakings operating in the relevant sector, refused to make the relevant contributions. They had obtained a more advantageous private pension scheme, and considered that the decision by the employers and workers to make affiliation to a fund compulsory was restrictive of competition in two ways: it prevented undertakings from finding alternative pension schemes, and excluded insurers from the relevant market. In spite of the anti-competitive effects, the Court of Justice ruled that the agreement fell outside the scope of Article 101(1). The basis for this was that the Union is tasked with both ensuring competition and also developing a policy in the social sphere, and these two conflicting objectives had to be balanced. The Court found that restrictions of competition would be inherent in collective agreements between organisations representing employers and workers and that the application of competition law would damage collective attempts to improve the conditions of employment.[35] The judgment can be praised for consistency with the so-called 'European social model'. This imprecisely defined phrase is often used to explain that the EU's internal market project is not merely about the creation of economic wealth, but also about the safeguard of the interests of employees. However, the Court of Justice does not subject the pension scheme in question to a proportionality test; it does not consider whether this kind of pension arrangement is the least restrictive way of achieving the improvement of working conditions, nor does the Court take into consideration the possibility that Article 101(3) could have exempted these agreements.[36] Instead, the social policy considerations trump the

---

[31] Article 346 TFEU (ex Article 296 EC) (a provision invoked in mergers in the defence sector).

[32] Article 42 TFEU (ex Article 36 EC) provides that agriculture is covered to the extent that the Council determines, taking into account the aims of the Common Agricultural Policy. See Regulation 26/62 [1959–62] OJ 129. The provisions of the exclusions in this Regulation have been read restrictively, see e.g. Case 71/74 *FRUBO* v *Commission* [1975] ECR 563.

[33] Article 106(2) TFEU (ex Article 86(2) EC). See Chapter 23 for discussion.

[34] See also Case C-67/96 *Albany International BV* v *Stichting Bedrijfspensioenfonds Textielindustrie* [1999] ECR I-5751, paras. 52–60; Case C-219/97 *Maatschappij Drijvende Bokken BV* v *Stichting Pensioenfonds voor de Vervoer- en Havenbedrijven* [1999] ECR I-6121, paras. 40–7.

[35] Joined Cases C-115/97, C-116/97 and C-117/97 *Brentjens' Handelsonderneming BV* [1999] ECR I-6025, paras. 55–61.

[36] Advocate General Jacobs in this case (para. 193) had in fact acknowledged that the Court of Justice and Commission had in the past taken employment considerations into account in Article 81(3) (referring to Case 26/76 *Metro* [1977] ECR 1875, para. 43; Case 42/84 *Remia* [1985] ECR 2545, para. 42; *Synthetic Fibres* [1984] OJ L207/17, para. 37; and *Ford/Volkswagen* [1993] OJ L20/14, para. 23) while the Commission in its submissions insisted that such considerations were irrelevant in deciding on the application of the exemption.

competition policy considerations. Subsequent developments have called into question the validity of this judgment.[37]

A more well established, and wider exclusion was designed in *Wouters*. The Dutch Bar Association prohibited partnerships between lawyers and accountants ('multidisciplinary partnerships') by the so-called '1993 Regulation'. The 1993 Regulation (which was characterised as a decision by an association of undertakings) was challenged by lawyers wishing to work for an accountancy firm. It clearly restricted competition by preventing the creation of a new form of business. However, the Dutch Bar Association considered that multidisciplinary practices threatened the obligations of professional conduct because unlike lawyers, accountants had an obligation to audit clients and report their results to interested third parties. Thus the professional obligations of the two professions clashed.

Case C-309/99 *Wouters v Algemene Raad van de Nederlandse Orde van Advocaten* [2002] ECR I-1577

105. The aim of the 1993 Regulation is therefore to ensure that, in the Member State concerned, the rules of professional conduct for members of the Bar are complied with, having regard to the prevailing perceptions of the profession in that State. The Bar of the Netherlands was entitled to consider that members of the Bar might no longer be in a position to advise and represent their clients independently and in the observance of strict professional secrecy if they belonged to an organisation which is also responsible for producing an account of the financial results of the transactions in respect of which their services were called upon and for certifying those accounts.

106. Moreover, the concurrent pursuit of the activities of statutory auditor and of adviser, in particular legal adviser, also raises questions within the accountancy profession itself ...

107. A regulation such as the 1993 Regulation could therefore reasonably be considered to be necessary in order to ensure the proper practice of the legal profession, as it is organised in the Member State concerned.

108. Furthermore, the fact that different rules may be applicable in another Member State does not mean that the rules in force in the former State are incompatible with Community law. Even if multidisciplinary partnerships of lawyers and accountants are allowed in some Member States, the Bar of the Netherlands is entitled to consider that the objectives pursued by the 1993 Regulation cannot, having regard in particular to the legal regimes by which members of the Bar and accountants are respectively governed in the Netherlands, be attained by less restrictive means.

109. In light of those considerations, it does not appear that the effects restrictive of competition such as those resulting for members of the Bar practising in the Netherlands from a regulation such as the 1993 Regulation go beyond what is necessary in order to ensure the proper practice of the legal profession.

The Court of Justice returned to consider the scope of application of competition law in a dispute that arose between two swimmers, on the one hand, and the International Olympic Committee (IOC) and international swimming federation (FINA), on the other. The swimmers were given a two-year ban because a drugs test revealed that they had taken a banned substance,

---

[37] The ECJ refused to apply the principle in the context of the fundamental freedoms (Case C-438/05 *International Transport Workers' Federation and Finnish Seamen's Union v Viking Line ABP* [2007] ECR I-77) and public procurement (Case C-271/08 *Commission v Germany* [2010] ECR I-7091).

Nandrolone, but they considered the anti-doping rules were too strict and argued that the IOC's decision setting out the doping rules was restrictive of competition.

Case C–519/04P *Meca–Medina and Majcen* v *Commission* [2006] ECR I–6991

42. ... [T]he compatibility of rules with the Community rules on competition cannot be assessed in the abstract. Not every agreement between undertakings or every decision of an association of undertakings which restricts the freedom of action of the parties or of one of them necessarily falls within the prohibition laid down in Article [101(1) TFEU]. For the purposes of application of that provision to a particular case, account must first of all be taken of the overall context in which the decision of the association of undertakings was taken or produces its effects and, more specifically, of its objectives. It has then to be considered whether the consequential effects restrictive of competition are inherent in the pursuit of those objectives and are proportionate to them.

43. As regards the overall context in which the rules at issue were adopted, the Commission could rightly take the view that the general objective of the rules was, as none of the parties disputes, to combat doping in order for competitive sport to be conducted fairly and that it included the need to safeguard equal chances for athletes, athletes' health, the integrity and objectivity of competitive sport and ethical values in sport.

44. In addition, given that penalties are necessary to ensure enforcement of the doping ban, their effect on athletes' freedom of action must be considered to be, in principle, inherent itself in the anti-doping rules.

45. Therefore, even if the anti-doping rules at issue are to be regarded as a decision of an association of undertakings limiting the appellants' freedom of action, they do not, for all that, necessarily constitute a restriction of competition incompatible with the common market, within the meaning of Article [101(1) TFEU], since they are justified by a legitimate objective. Such a limitation is inherent in the organisation and proper conduct of competitive sport and its very purpose is to ensure healthy rivalry between athletes....

47. It must be acknowledged that the penal nature of the anti-doping rules at issue and the magnitude of the penalties applicable if they are breached are capable of producing adverse effects on competition because they could, if penalties were ultimately to prove unjustified, result in an athlete's unwarranted exclusion from sporting events, and thus in impairment of the conditions under which the activity at issue is engaged in. It follows that, in order not to be covered by the prohibition laid down in Article [101(1) TFEU], the restrictions thus imposed by those rules must be limited to what is necessary to ensure the proper conduct of competitive sport.

48. Rules of that kind could indeed prove excessive by virtue of, first, the conditions laid down for establishing the dividing line between circumstances which amount to doping in respect of which penalties may be imposed and those which do not, and second, the severity of those penalties.

Applying this standard the Court of Justice concluded that banning Nandrolone was justified and that banning athletes whose tests reveal a Nandrolone content higher than 2 nanogrammes per millilitre of urine was a practice that did not go beyond that which was necessary to ensure that sporting events take place and function properly.[38] Conversely, when the Portuguese

---

[38] S. Weatherill, 'Anti-Doping Revisited: The Demise of the Rule of "Purely Sporting Interest"' (2006) *ECLR* 645; another example may be found in a decision of the New Zealand Commerce Commission, Decision 580 New Zealand Rugby Football Union Incorporated, 2 July 2006, available at www.comcom.govt.nz. For comment, see R. Adhar, 'Professional Rugby, Competitive Balance and Competition Law' (2007) *ECLR* 36.

Accountancy Association (OTOC) imposed procedures that raised entry barriers to undertakings wishing to offer educational services for accountants (and thereby favouring the educational services offered by OTOC) the Court of Justice found that the exclusion in *Wouters* was inapplicable because while ensuring the quality of education was a legitimate objective, exclusion of providers without an appropriate procedure was a disproportionate way of addressing the public policy concern – it would be possible to monitor the performance of different service providers instead, which would not harm competition.[39]

These cases present a puzzle: how widely should they be construed? At its most restrictive, it may be said that these cases are about excluding only ethical rules from the scope of competition law.[40] Alternatively, it has been suggested that these cases identify certain restrictions of competition that are ancillary to the main regulatory function of the body whose decision is being questioned, without being limited to ethical considerations.[41] A third, broader, interpretation is that these judgments exclude certain restrictive agreements when there are valid public policy reasons for so doing.[42] On the latter view, an agreement among pubs to eliminate 'happy hours' when alcohol is cheaper as a means of protecting public health might be justified. This wider interpretation draws legitimacy from the realities of self-regulation in modern society, when private bodies are often encouraged or even required to take the public interest into account when making commercial decisions. Further judicial refinement is required to establish the appropriate limits of this strand of case law, not least because it blurs the line between Article 101(1) and the exemption provision in Article 101(3).[43] However, the cases are problematic: on the one hand, the competition rules are a fundamental building block of the EU's 'economic constitution' and should only be displaced exceptionally, by primary legislation, not by judges. On the other hand, recent revisions of the Treaty have widened the non-economic interests pursued by the European Union (e.g. environmental protection and the protection of services of general interest) so that the judiciary plays a key role in balancing the relationship between competing values, and these judgments afford it the ability to balance competing objectives.

3 ARTICLE 101 TFEU: RESTRICTIVE PRACTICES

Article 101 TFEU

1. The following shall be prohibited as incompatible with the common market: all agreements between undertakings, decisions by associations of undertakings and concerted practices which may affect trade between Member States and which have as their object or effect the prevention, restriction or distortion of competition within the common market, and in particular those which:
   (a) directly or indirectly fix purchase or selling prices or any other trading conditions;
   (b) limit or control production, markets, technical development, or investment;

---

[39] Case C-1/12 *Ordem dos Técnicos Oficiais de Contas* v *Autoridade da Concorrência*, Judgment of 23 February 2013, paras. 95–9.

[40] E. Loozen, 'Professional Ethics and Restraints of Competition' (2006) 31 *ELRev.* 28.

[41] R. Whish, *Competition Law* (6th edn, Oxford, Oxford University Press, 2008) 126–32.

[42] G. Monti, *EC Competition Law* (Cambridge, Cambridge University Press, 2007) 110–20.

[43] See A. P. Komninos, *Non-competition Concerns: Resolution of Conflicts in the Integrated Article 81*, EC Working Paper (L) 08/05 (Oxford Centre for Competition Law and Policy, 2005) Part IV, available at www.competition-law.ox.ac.uk/competition/portal.php; G. Monti, 'Article 81 EC and Public Policy' (2002) 39 *CMLRev.* 1057, 1086–90.

    (c) share markets or sources of supply;

    (d) apply dissimilar conditions to equivalent transactions with other trading parties, thereby placing them at a competitive disadvantage;

    (e) make the conclusion of contracts subject to acceptance by the other parties of supplementary obligations which, by their nature or according to commercial usage, have no connection with the subject of such contracts.

2. Any agreements or decisions prohibited pursuant to this article shall be automatically void.

3. The provisions of paragraph 1 may, however, be declared inapplicable in the case of:
   - any agreement or category of agreements between undertakings,
   - any decision or category of decisions by associations of undertakings,
   - any concerted practice or category of concerted practices,
   - which contributes to improving the production or distribution of goods or to promoting technical or economic progress, while allowing consumers a fair share of the resulting benefit, and which does not:

    (a) impose on the undertakings concerned restrictions which are not indispensable to the attainment of these objectives;

    (b) afford such undertakings the possibility of eliminating competition in respect of a substantial part of the products in question.

We provide a thumbnail sketch of this Article before considering it in more detail in the sections that follow. Paragraphs (1) and (3) should be read successively: paragraph (1) declares that agreements which restrict competition are unlawful, subject to the exception in paragraph (3) which provides that anti-competitive agreements that yield certain benefits may be lawful.[44]

If an agreement restricts competition under paragraph (1) and is not exempted under paragraph (3) then, following paragraph (2), it is automatically void. Under EU law, agreements in breach of Article 101 are prohibited.[45] The Commission may require the undertakings to bring the infringement to an end,[46] and impose fines.[47] At national level, parties to a void agreement are unable to enforce the agreement in national courts,[48] and may be sued for damages by parties who suffer harm as a result of anti-competitive practices.[49]

(i) Agreements, decisions and concerted practices

Three distinct types of cooperation fall under Article 101 TFEU. An *agreement* represents a consensus between parties to act in a certain manner; it need not be inscribed in a binding

---

[44] See Regulation 1/2003 on the implementation of the rules on competition laid down in Articles 81 and 82 of the Treaty, recital 4, articles 1, 5 and 6 [2003] OJ L1/1.

[45] Regulation 1/2003 on the implementation of the rules on competition laid down in Articles 81 and 82 of the Treaty, article 1 [2003] OJ L1/1.

[46] Regulation 1/2003 on the implementation of the rules on competition laid down in Articles 81 and 82 of the Treaty [2003] OJ L1/1, article 7.

[47] Regulation 1/2003 on the implementation of the rules on competition laid down in Articles 81 and 82 of the Treaty, article 23(2) [2003] OJ L1/1.

[48] Case C-126/97 *Eco Swiss China Time Ltd* v *Benetton* [1999] ECR I-3055, a precedent which allows a party in breach to avoid paying damages where the agreement is held to infringe Article 101 TFEU (the so-called 'Euro-defence'). See generally G. Monti, 'EU Competition Law and European Private Law' in C. Twigg-Flesner (ed.), *The Cambridge Companion to European Union Private Law* (Cambridge, Cambridge University Press, 2010).

[49] Case C-126/97 *Courage Ltd* v *Crehan* [2001] ECR I-6297.

contract,[50] and need not be in writing.[51] A *concerted practice* is a term used to catch forms of collusion that fall short of agreement, but where the parties substitute practical cooperation for the risks of competition, affecting the conditions of competition on the market.[52] An example is a situation where undertakings meet to exchange information about the prices they intend to charge and their sales volumes – information which makes coordination of behaviour likely because after the meeting each player takes into consideration what others have disclosed when planning their strategy. There is no agreement because specific conduct has not been determined, but the post-market behaviour of each is influenced by the information received and it is likely that prices are higher and output less than if each had determined their business conduct independently. Often cartels operate over a long period of time and are sustained by a mixture of agreements and concerted practices, whereby targets are agreed upon and then regular meetings are held where key information is disclosed to 'oil' the operation of the agreement.[53] Thus, concerted practices differ in form from agreements because of their intensity, but both are collusive devices having the same effect: coordinating the behaviour of the participants.

A trade association is designed to protect the interests of its members. A *decision* by an association is a provision in the rules of a trade association or a decision reached by a trade association, which affects the members. For example, the Law Society of a Member State may decide to fix the remuneration for lawyers, or an agricultural association may coordinate prices on behalf of its members.[54] In appropriate circumstances, a non-binding recommendation (for example, on prices to be charged by members of the association) may also constitute a decision where it is likely to affect members' pricing determinations.[55]

(a) Cartels

There are four conditions for a successful cartel: the major suppliers of the product in question take part; they agree on how to coordinate their behaviour (for example, by agreeing upon how to set prices or allocating geographical markets to each other); there is a mechanism to detect and punish cartel members who 'cheat' by cutting prices below the cartel price; there are high entry barriers to prevent competitors entering the market thereby reducing the cartel's profitability.[56] With these factors present, the cartel is able to behave like a monopoly, reducing output and increasing prices. There is evidence that some cartels have broken down because parties were unable to agree or coordinate behaviour,[57] but when there is a high level of trust among members, cartels can last for a considerable length of time. As we saw in

---

[50] See the 'gentlemen's agreement' in Cases 41, 44 and 45/69 *ACF Chemiefarma NV v Commission* [1970] ECR 661.

[51] *Polypropylene* [1986] OJ L230/1, para. 81.

[52] The seminal authorities defining concerted practices are Cases 48–57 *ICI v Commission (Dyestuffs)* [1972] ECR 619, para. 64; Cases 40–48, 50, 54–56, 111, 113 and 114/73 *Cooperatiëve Vereniging 'Suiker Unie' UA v Commission* [1975] ECR 1663.

[53] *Polypropylene* [1986] OJ L230/1, para. 87.

[54] See e.g. Case C-309/99 *Wouters v Algemene Raad van de Nederlandse Orde van Advocaten* [2002] ECR I-1577; Case C-250/92 *Gøttrup-Klim Grovvareforeninger v Dansk Landbrugs Grovvareselskab AmbA* [1994] ECR I-5641.

[55] *Fenex* [1996] OJ L181/28, paras. 32–42.

[56] On the economics of cartels, see M. Motta, *Competition Policy* (Cambridge, Cambridge University Press, 2004) ch. 4.

[57] See e.g. *Zinc Producer Group* [1984] OJ L220/27 for a partial breakdown, and D. T. Armentano, *Antitrust and Monopoly: Anatomy of a Policy Failure* (New York, John Wiley and Sons, 1982) ch. 5.

Chapter 21, EU competition law creates an additional source of instability for cartels: leniency programmes give incentives for cartel members to expose the existence of a cartel as a way of escaping the Commission's significant penalties.[58] Cartel-busting is a core activity for the Commission and the European Courts have facilitated this task in two ways: first, by setting out wide definitions of the terms 'agreement' and 'concerted practice'; secondly, by allowing the Commission to consider the pattern of collusion by several undertakings over a period of time as being a single infringement characterised in part by agreements and partly by concerted practices. The Court of Justice consolidated these methods in a series of judgments resulting from the polypropylene cartel decision where the Commission found that several undertakings active in the European petrochemical industry had participated in a cartel between 1977 and 1983. The parties had set up a system of target prices and devised a system to limit output to share the market according to agreed quotas. One cartel member, Anic, held a market share between 2.7 and 4.2 per cent and was fined 750,000 ECU. The Commission appealed against the decision to the General Court, which annulled the Commission's decision in part, on the basis that the Commission had failed to establish the correct duration of Anic's involvement in the cartel and had reduced the fine accordingly. Anic cross-appealed seeking further reduction or an annulment of the decision in its entirety, inter alia, on the basis that the Commission had failed to characterise the infringement either as an agreement or as a concerted practice. In affirming the General Court's decision the Court established several important criteria for identifying agreements and concerted practices. These principles have continued to inform the Commission's cartel enforcement strategy since.

Case C–49/92 *Commission v Anic Partecipazioni SpA* [1999] ECR I–4125

108. The list in Article [101(1)] of the Treaty is intended to apply to all collusion between undertakings, whatever the form it takes. There is continuity between the cases listed. The only essential thing is the distinction between independent conduct, which is allowed, and collusion, which is not, regardless of any distinction between types of collusion. Anic's argument would break down the unity and generality of the prohibited phenomenon and would remove from the ambit of the prohibition, without any reason, certain types of collusion which are no less dangerous than others....

109. The Court observes first of all that ... the [General Court] held that the Commission was entitled to categorise as agreements certain types of conduct on the part of the undertakings concerned, and, in the alternative, as concerted practices certain other forms of conduct on the part of the same undertakings. The [General Court] held that Anic had taken part in an integrated set of schemes constituting a single infringement which progressively manifested itself in both unlawful agreements and unlawful concerted practices....

112. Secondly, it must be observed that, if Article [101] of the Treaty distinguishes between 'concerted practices', 'agreements between undertakings' and 'decisions by associations of undertakings', the aim is to have the prohibitions of that article catch different forms of coordination and collusion between undertakings.

113. It does not, however, follow that patterns of conduct having the same anti-competitive object, each of which, taken in isolation, would fall within the meaning of 'agreement', 'concerted practice' or 'a

---

[58] See pp. 969–71.

decision by an association of undertakings', cannot constitute different manifestations of a single infringement of Article [101(1)] of the Treaty.

114. The [General Court] was therefore entitled to consider that patterns of conduct by several undertakings were a manifestation of a single infringement, corresponding partly to an agreement and partly to a concerted practice.

115. Thirdly, it must be borne in mind that a concerted practice, within the meaning of Article [101(1)] of the Treaty, refers to a form of coordination between undertakings which, without having been taken to a stage where an agreement properly so called has been concluded, knowingly substitutes for the risks of competition practical cooperation between them.

116. The Court of Justice has further explained that criteria of coordination and cooperation must be understood in the light of the concept inherent in the provisions of the Treaty relating to competition, according to which each economic operator must determine independently the policy which he intends to adopt on the market.

117. According to that case-law, although that requirement of independence does not deprive economic operators of the right to adapt themselves intelligently to the existing and anticipated conduct of their competitors, it does however strictly preclude any direct or indirect contact between such operators, the object or effect whereof is either to influence the conduct on the market of an actual or potential competitor or to disclose to such a competitor the course of conduct which they themselves have decided to adopt or contemplate adopting on the market, where the object or effect of such contact is to create conditions of competition which do not correspond to the normal conditions of the market in question, regard being had to the nature of the products or services offered, the size and number of the undertakings and the volume of the said market.

118. It follows that, as is clear from the very terms of Article [101(1)] of the Treaty, a concerted practice implies, besides undertakings' concerting together, conduct on the market pursuant to those collusive practices, and a relationship of cause and effect between the two.

119. The [General Court] therefore committed an error of law in relation to the interpretation of the concept of concerted practice in holding that the undertakings' collusive practices had necessarily had an effect on the conduct of the undertakings which participated in them.

120. It does not, however, follow that the cross-appeal should be upheld. As the Court of Justice has repeatedly held, if the grounds of a judgment of the [General Court] reveal an infringement of Community law but the operative part appears well founded on other legal grounds, the appeal must be dismissed.

121. For one thing, subject to proof to the contrary, which it is for the economic operators concerned to adduce, there must be a presumption that the undertakings participating in concerting arrangements and remaining active on the market take account of the information exchanged with their competitors when determining their conduct on that market, particularly when they concert together on a regular basis over a long period, as was the case here, according to the findings of the [General Court].

122. For another, a concerted practice, as defined above, falls under Article [101(1)] of the Treaty even in the absence of anti-competitive effects on the market.

123. First, it follows from the actual text of Article [101(1)] that, as in the case of agreements between undertakings and decisions by associations of undertakings, concerted practices are prohibited, regardless of their effect, when they have an anti-competitive object.

124. Next, although the concept of a concerted practice presupposes conduct of the participating undertakings on the market, it does not necessarily imply that that conduct should produce the concrete effect of restricting, preventing or distorting competition.

125. Lastly, that interpretation is not incompatible with the restrictive nature of the prohibition laid down in Article [101(1)] of the Treaty since, far from extending its scope, it corresponds to the literal meaning of the terms used in that provision.

126. The [General Court] therefore rightly held, despite faulty legal reasoning, that, since the Commission had established to the requisite legal standard that Anic had participated in collusion for the purpose of restricting competition, it did not have to adduce evidence that the collusion had manifested itself in conduct on the market....130. Fourthly, it is clear from the settled case-law of the Court of Justice that an agreement within the meaning of Article [101(1)] of the Treaty arises from an expression, by the participating undertakings, of their joint intention to conduct themselves on the market in a specific way.

131. A comparison between that definition of agreement and the definition of a concerted practice shows that, from the subjective point of view, they are intended to catch forms of collusion having the same nature and are only distinguishable from each other by their intensity and the forms in which they manifest themselves.

132. It follows that, whilst the concept of an agreement and of a concerted practice have particularly different elements, they are not mutually incompatible. Contrary to Anic's allegations, the [General Court] did not therefore have to require the Commission to categorise either as an agreement or as a concerted practice each form of conduct found but was right to hold that the Commission had been entitled to characterise some of those forms of conduct as principally 'agreements' and others as 'concerted practices'.

133. Fifthly, it must be pointed out that this interpretation is not incompatible with the restrictive nature of the prohibition laid down in Article [101(1)] of the Treaty. Far from creating a new form of infringement, the arrival at that interpretation merely entails acceptance of the fact that, in the case of an infringement involving different forms of conduct, these may meet different definitions whilst being caught by the same provision and being all equally prohibited.

134. Sixthly, it must be observed that, contrary to Anic's allegations, such an interpretation does not have an unacceptable effect on the question of proof and does not infringe the rights of defence of the undertakings concerned.

135. On the one hand, the Commission must still establish that each form of conduct found falls under the prohibition laid down in Article [101(1)] of the Treaty as an agreement, a concerted practice or a decision by an association of undertakings.

136. On the other hand, the undertakings charged with having participated in the infringement have the opportunity of disputing, for each form of conduct, the characterisation or the characterisations applied by the Commission by contending that the Commission has not adduced proof of the constituent elements of the various forms of infringement alleged.

These passages consolidate the definitions of agreement and concerted practice. The Court of Justice eases the Commission's burden of proof significantly in the context of concerted practices by holding that it can presume that a concerted practice has been implemented, and there is no need to prove anti-competitive effects resulting from the concerted practice. Moreover, several important consequences materialise as a result of the ruling that collusion constitutes a single infringement. The first is that the Commission is allowed to escape the limitation period of five years, which runs from the day when the infringement ceases.[59] Had each bout of

---

[59] Regulation 1/2003 on the implementation of the rules on competition laid down in Articles 81 and 82 of the Treaty, article 25(1) [2003] OJ L1/1.

collusion constituted a separate infringement, all acts would not have been punished and the deterrence value of competition law would have been dented. The second consequence is that the Commission's evidentiary burden is lightened significantly by not having to define each element of coordination as an agreement or a concerted practice. However, as the passages above make clear, the Commission must establish evidence of each instance of collusion and must allow the undertaking to respond and dispute the Commission's finding. The third consequence is that by characterising the infringement as a single conspiracy, a participant is responsible for all of the cartel's actions, even if it did not take part in all of them. This means that a cartel is a 'conspiracy' by its members, and as a result even those with small market shares, whose participation is limited, contribute to the overall conspiracy.[60] Even Anic, with a small market share, contributed to the conspiracy. However, the Commission must prove that the undertaking intended to contribute to the common objectives pursued by all participants and that it was aware of the conduct planned by them or that it could have foreseen such conduct.[61]

These principles should not be taken to mean that an undertaking can never escape liability when it is involved in a long-running cartel but does not participate in all the cartel's actions. Recently the General Court in *BASF* had an opportunity to give guidance on how to apply Article 101 to long-running cartels. This concerned collusion in the market for chlorine chloride: a global cartel to fix prices and allocate territories between 1992 and 1994, and a European cartel designed to continue the global cartel between 1994 and 1998. The Commission's decision treated the two parts of the cartel as a single infringement because if the two were separate agreements then the global cartel would not have been caught as it had ended five years before the investigation started and fell outside the limitation period. As a result, the parties' fines would have been reduced. On appeal, the parties questioned the Commission's characterisation of the two agreements as a single infringement and the General Court found that while the global agreement involved North American manufacturers and was designed to divide the American and European markets, the European agreement did not involve the North American firms and was designed to divide the European market. Nor was there any evidence that the effect of the global agreement continued beyond the date when it had formally ceased. Accordingly there had been two separate infringements.[62]

J. Joshua, 'Single Continuous Infringement of Article 81 EC: Has the Commission Stretched the Concept Beyond the Limit of its Logic?' (2009) 5(2) *European Competition Journal* **451, 471–2**

The CFI concluded that, to establish a single violation, (i) there had to be a common plan or economic aim and (ii) the arrangements had to be 'complementary', in the sense of interacting to realise the intended set of anti-competitive effects within the framework of a single objective. For the Court, the European and global infringements were each continuous infringements on their own. To justify combining them into one, account had to be taken of all the circumstances, such as period of

---

[60] See e.g. Case T-23/99 *LR af 1998 A/S* v *Commission* [2002] ECR II-1705, where an infringement was found even though the undertaking took no active role.

[61] Case C-49/92 *Commission* v *Anic Partecipazioni SpA* [1999] ECR I-4125, para. 87 and paras. 203–7.

[62] Joined Cases T-101/05 and T-111/05 *BASF AG and UCB SA* v *Commission* [2007] ECR II-4949. See also D. Bailey, 'Single, Overall Agreement in EU Competition Law' (2010) 47 *CMLRev.* 473.

application, the content and methodology of the agreements and, 'correlatively', their objective. In the CFI's judgment, the Commission had failed to demonstrate sufficient interdependence between the global and the later EU cartel: the Europeans had not adhered to the global arrangement in order to divide up the EEA market, the control methods were dissimilar and they only began to allocate the European market amongst themselves after the global arrangement had failed ... Durable as the single infringement concept has proved, it was certainly never intended as a slogan to substitute for robust legal or factual assessment. Nor, without more detailed analysis, is it determinative of the issue of whether a given course of conduct constitutes a single conspiracy or multiple conspiracies. But if the distinction between a single and many conspiracies is clear enough conceptually, its empirical application is beset with difficulty. Overturning the decision on the facts, the Court basically confirmed the generic 'totality of the evidence' approach of the previous case law. Although the CFI has made it clear in *BASF* that meeting the interdependency requirement is not going to be a walkover for the Commission, it would be helpful to have some workable guidance. The assessment is an empirical one, but it should not be left to the Commission's discretion how to treat a given set of facts. An objective rule would free the Commission from suspicion that the approach it takes is driven by the desired outcome.

In sum, the policy behind the Court of Justice's case law is to send a message to parties to a cartel that once they agree to conspire against the interests of the Community, they will be held responsible for the entirety of the conduct to which they have assented. The aim is to maximise the deterrence of competition law. The only way out for an undertaking is to either make a leniency application confessing the presence of the agreement, or to publicly distance itself from what has been agreed, but then risk retaliation from the undertakings.[63] The sole consolation for a minor participant is that the fact that it has not taken part in all aspects of an anti-competitive agreement, or that it played a minor role, will be taken into consideration when calculating the fine.[64]

So far we have considered the definition of agreements and concerted practices. It is also important to bear in mind the evidence that may be used to establish the existence of co-operation. In the majority of cases, the Commission obtains hard evidence in the form of memorandums or recordings of conversations that prove collusion. However, collusion can be established by inference from the conduct of the parties. The Court approved of this method early on,[65] and the limits upon the use of indirect evidence were set out in the *Wood Pulp* case.[66] The Commission decided that forty producers of wood pulp had colluded to fix prices between 1975 and 1981. For some aspects of the cartel, collusion was proven by documentary evidence of the undertakings' membership to certain trade associations, but for some, no documentary evidence supported a finding of collusion. The Court ruled that in principle a cartel could be inferred from the way undertakings behave only if their common behaviour has no

---

[63] See D. Bailey, 'Publicly Distancing Oneself from a Cartel' (2008) 32 *World Competition* 177.

[64] Case C-49/92 *Commission v Anic Partecipazioni SpA* [1999] ECR I-4125, para. 90.

[65] Cases 48–57 *ICI v Commission (Dyestuffs)* [1972] ECR 619; while the Commission's decision was also based on concrete evidence of collusion the Court focused solely on the circumstances of the market. See also Case 172/80 *Züchner v Bayerische Vereinsbank* [1981] ECR 2021.

[66] Joined Cases C-89/85, C-104/85, C-114/85, C-116/85, C-117/85 and C-125–129/85 *A. Ahlström Osakeyhtiö and others v Commission (Wood Pulp)* [1993] ECR I-1307, paras. 70–2; A. Jones, 'Woodpulp: Concerted Practice and/ or Conscious Parallelism?' (1993) *ECLR* 273.

other explanation than that the parties must have come to an agreement to behave in that way. However, on the facts, two Court-appointed experts reported that the parallel behaviour by the undertakings could be explained by reasons other than a pre-existing agreement to align their commercial strategies and the case failed. Since *Wood Pulp*, the Commission has not used economic evidence to infer the existence of an agreement, but has relied upon tangible evidence seized during searches of the cartel members' premises. While documents are hard to find, it is preferable for the Commission to bring a case based on hard evidence rather than having to argue that it can infer an agreement from the way parties behave on the market. This is because it would have to show that the parallel behaviour has no other explanation except prior collusion, and alternative plausible reasons for parallel behaviour can often be found.[67]

(b) Distinguishing between agreement and unilateral action

A key aim of EU competition law has been market integration. The paradigmatic example of how this is implemented is the early decision in *Consten and Grundig*. Grundig wished to distribute its electric goods in France and appointed Consten as exclusive distributor for that territory and took steps to guarantee that no other wholesaler was able to sell into France. An economist would justify Grundig's actions on the basis of the free-rider rationale: Consten's isolation gives it an incentive to market the goods aggressively knowing that it can recoup the promotional costs, as free-riders (who would wait for Consten to promote the goods and then sell them in France at prices lower than those which Consten would set, since they would not have to recover any promotional costs) could be kept out. Moreover, the distribution system could have enhanced inter-brand competition (that is, competition between Grundig's electronic goods and those of other brands). However, neither the Commission nor the Court of Justice accepted this argument, considering it more important that parallel imports (i.e. goods flowing from one Member State to another) should be allowed.

Joined Cases 54/64 and 58/64 *Consten and Grundig v Commission* [1966] ECR 299, 340

An agreement between producer and distributor which might tend to restore the national divisions in trade between Member States might be such as to frustrate the most fundamental [objectives] of the Community. The Treaty, whose preamble and content aim at abolishing the barriers between States, and which in several provisions gives evidence of a stern attitude with regard to their reappearance, could not allow undertakings to reconstruct such barriers. Article [101(1)] is designed to pursue this aim, even in the case of agreements between undertakings placed at different levels of the distribution process.

The Court emphatically rejected the applicants' arguments that the economics of the free-rider were relevant, in stark contrast to the US courts, which have embraced the free-rider rationale.[68] Gyselen explains and critiques the EU position.

---

[67] For a contrary position, see L. Kaplow, *Competition Policy and Price Fixing* (Princeton, NJ, Princeton University Press, 2013) advocating greater use of economic evidence.

[68] *Continental TV* v *GTE Sylvania* 433 US 36, 54–5 (1977).

L. Gyselen, 'Vertical Restraints in the Distribution Process: Strength and Weakness of the Free Rider Rationale under EEC Competition Law' (1984) *Common Market Law Review* 646, 649, 666–7

The free rider rationale is for EEC competition lawyers certainly the most intriguing one among the available defences of vertical restraints because it is conceptually antithecal to the parallel importer rationale, which has dominated the assessment of the restraints on competition in a distribution network ever since *Grundig Consten*. Parallel imports may indeed give rise to free rides from one exporting dealer to the promotional or servicing efforts of one local dealer. In the EEC Commission's eyes, however, the free rider is a hero because his sales foster the free movement of the brand within the common market and thus contribute to market integration. Consequently, restraints which limit his room for manoeuvre are subject to close scrutiny and will often fail to qualify for an exemption under Article [101(3)]. Ever more frequently the Commission is urged to alleviate its sacred parallel importer rationale and to give appropriate weight to the free rider rationale....

One could argue that the Commission should not be so much concerned with the free movement of one brand but rather with the free movement of all branded goods constituting one relevant market. Does not the establishment of a Common Market also, and in particular, mean more intense interbrand competition on the larger scale of ten [now 25] composite territories, even at the price of reduced transfrontier traffic of the individual brands which are launched on the Common Market?

The Commission's interference with a brand's price levels in the distinct national markets, out of a concern for price harmonisation, has also been criticised as being *ultra vires*. The Commission is said to seek the achievement of so-called 'positive' integration goals ... by means of 'negative' integration instruments. This raises the quasi-constitutional question whether antitrust promotion of parallel imports, which aims at evening out price differentials, amounts to undue pre-emption of sovereign national powers in the price policy area.

The urgency of this approach has led the Commission to try and stretch the notion of agreement to ensure market segmentation is prohibited even if the activity appears unilateral. We can distinguish between two strands in the case law.

In the first, manufacturers sent notices to their distributors exhorting them not to export,[69] or printing the words 'export prohibited' on invoices.[70] These requests were not part of the distribution contract and the parties argued they were unilateral requests. However, it was held that these tactics constitute export bans that are part of the agreement between manufacturers and distributors and which were tacitly accepted by the distributor continuing to buy goods from the manufacturer.[71] This case law has been criticised in that payment of an invoice does not necessarily represent an agreement by the distributor, but the Court of Justice 'glosses over' such technicalities to apply Article 101 to secure an integrated market.[72]

---

[69] See e.g. Joined Cases 32/78 and 36–82/78 *BWM Belgium* v *Commission* [1979] ECR 2435; *Bayo-n-ox* [1990] OJ L21/71; *Volkswagen* [1998] OJ L124/60, affirmed by the General Court, Case T-62/98 *Volkswagen AG* v *Commission* [2000] ECR II-2707 and Court of Justice, Case C-338/00P *Volkswagen AG* v *Commission* [2003] ECR I-9189.

[70] *Sandoz Prodotti Farmaceutici SpA* [1987] OJ L222/28, paras. 25–6, upheld in Case 227/87 *Sandoz* v *Commission* [1990] ECR I-45. See also *Tipp-Ex* [1987] OJ L222/1, upheld in Case 279/87 *Tipp-Ex* v *Commission* [1990] ECR 261 and J. E. Thompson, 'Case Note on *Sandoz* and *Tipp-Ex*' (1990) 27 *CMLRev.* 589.

[71] See e.g. *Konica* [1988] OJ L78/34, paras. 34–6.

[72] J. Shaw, 'The Concept of an Agreement in Article 85 EEC' (1991) *ELRev.* 262.

The second set of cases is well illustrated by *Ford v Commission*.[73] Ford originally supplied both right- and left-hand drive cars to its German distributors; then, in an effort to prevent British purchasers from importing lower priced cars from Germany into the United Kingdom, it ceased to supply right-hand drive cars in Germany. Ford insisted that the fact that it ceased selling right-hand drive cars in Germany was merely a unilateral act on its part, but the Court held that the decision to withdraw right-hand drive cars was part of the contractual relations between Ford and its dealers. Thus, to be admitted into the Ford network in Germany a dealer would be required to accept Ford's policy, including its policy on preventing parallel imports.[74] The ruling in *Ford* may be criticised in that the dealers in Germany objected to the decision, but continued their commercial relations with Ford because it would have been commercially impossible to terminate the contract with Ford given the vast sums expended in developing the dealer network.[75] In these circumstances, it seems inappropriate to speak of an agreement between Ford and its dealers.[76]

In the first type of case the Court of Justice read the manufacturer's action as a demand for a particular line of conduct by the distributors, while in the second, it interpreted the distribution network as a whole and found that the measures designed to prevent parallel trade were part of the agreement. In both, the Commission stretched the meaning of agreement to prevent restrictions on parallel trade. However, the limits of the Commission's ability to stretch the scope of Article 101 were limited by the Court's *Bayer* judgment. Bayer AG is the parent company of one of the main European chemical and pharmaceutical groups. It manufactured a drug to treat cardio-vascular disease (Adalat), sold by its wholly owned subsidiaries in the Member States. National health authorities fix the price of medicines and at the time of the dispute the prices fixed by the Spanish and French health authorities were 40 per cent lower than the prices in the United Kingdom. As a result, wholesalers in Spain and France exported Adalat to the United Kingdom, causing considerable losses for Bayer UK. In response, the Bayer group changed its delivery policy, ceasing to fulfil all the large orders placed by wholesalers in Spain and France. The Commission ruled that Bayer France and Bayer Spain had made an agreement with the wholesalers in France and Spain providing for an export ban. Bayer disputed this, acknowledging that it had embarked on a policy to restrict sales from Spain and France to the United Kingdom but denying that this policy was implemented by any agreement with the wholesalers. The Court of Justice agreed with Bayer.

Joined Cases C-2/01P and C-3/01P *Bundesverband der Arzneimittel-Importeure eV and Commission v Bayer* [2004] 4 CMLR 13

97. ... the [General Court] set out from the principle that the concept of an agreement within the meaning of Article [101(1)] of the Treaty centres around the existence of a concurrence of wills between at least two parties, the form in which it is manifested being unimportant so long as it constitutes the faithful

---

[73] Cases 25/84 and 26/84 *Ford v Commission* [1985] ECR 2725; see also Case 107/82 *AEG Telefunken v Commission* [1983] ECR 3135 and *Tipp-Ex* [1987] OJ L222/1.

[74] Cases 25/84 and 26/84 *Ford v Commission* [1985] ECR 2725, para. 21.

[75] P. Jakobsen and M. Broberg, 'The Concept of Agreement in Article 81 EC: On the Manufacturers' Right to Prevent Parallel Trade within the European Community' (2002) 23 *ECLR* 128, 130.

[76] C. Brown, 'Bayer v Commission, the ECJ Agrees' (2004) 25 *ECLR* 388, arguing that after *Bayer*, the correctness of *Ford* can be questioned.

expression of the parties' intention. The Court further recalled ... that for there to be an agreement within the meaning of Article [101(1)] of the Treaty it is sufficient that the undertakings in question should have expressed their common intention to conduct themselves on the market in a specific way.

98. Since, however, the question arising in this case is whether a measure adopted or imposed apparently unilaterally by a manufacturer in the context of the continuous relations which it maintains with its wholesalers constitutes an agreement within the meaning of Article [101(1)] of the Treaty, the [General Court] examined the Commission's arguments ... to the effect that Bayer infringed that article by imposing an export ban as part of the ... continuous commercial relations [of Bayer France and Bayer Spain] with their customers, and that the wholesalers' subsequent conduct reflected an implicit acquiescence in that ban....

100. Concerning the appellants' arguments that the [General Court] should have acknowledged that the manifestation of Bayer's intention to restrict parallel imports could constitute the basis of an agreement prohibited by Article [101(1)] of the Treaty, it is true that the existence of an agreement within the meaning of that provision can be deduced from the conduct of the parties concerned.

101. However, such an agreement cannot be based on what is only the expression of a unilateral policy of one of the contracting parties, which can be put into effect without the assistance of others. To hold that an agreement prohibited by Article [101(1)] of the Treaty may be established simply on the basis of the expression of a unilateral policy aimed at preventing parallel imports would have the effect of confusing the scope of that provision with that of Article [102] of the Treaty.

102. For an agreement within the meaning of Article [101(1)] of the Treaty to be capable of being regarded as having been concluded by tacit acceptance, it is necessary that the manifestation of the wish of one of the contracting parties to achieve an anti-competitive goal constitute an invitation to the other party, whether express or implied, to fulfil that goal jointly, and that applies all the more where, as in this case, such an agreement is not at first sight in the interests of the other party, namely the wholesalers.

103. Therefore, the [General Court] was right to examine whether Bayer's conduct supported the conclusion that the latter had required of the wholesalers, as a condition of their future contractual relations, that they should comply with its new commercial policy.

However, price uniformity in a diverse Union is a dangerous aspiration as the purchasing power of a person resident in the United Kingdom or Germany is likely to be higher than that of a person in Poland or Portugal. If price homogeneity leads to a convergence towards the average price, goods in poorer countries will become unaffordable.[77] The *Bayer* judgment is significant because while in the past the Court of Justice had supported the increasingly wide meaning that the Commission gave to the notion of 'agreement', it has now said that enough is enough and retreated from a teleological approach to a formalist, literal interpretation of the meaning of 'agreement'. The Court is willing to widen the meaning of Treaty Articles, but not to breaking point. It is also part of a pattern in the relationship between the Commission and the Court of Justice: while in the early years the Court supported the Commission's bold interpretations, more recently, in particular since the creation of the General Court, both courts have interpreted the Treaty more literally and subjected the Commission to stricter review.[78]

---

[77] B. Bishop, 'Price Discrimination under Article 86: Political Economy in the European Court' (1981) 44 *MLR* 282.

[78] *Parker Pen* (Case T-77/92 *Parker* v *Commission* [1994] ECR II-531 and II-549), is another illustration of the General Court refusing to adopt an expansive interpretation of the reach of competition law, and after *Bayer* the Court quashed another decision that took too expansive a view of the notion of agreement, Case T-208/01 *Volkswagen AG* v *Commission* [2003] ECR II-5141.

(ii) Object or effect the restriction, distortion or prevention of competition

(a) Background

The case law on parallel trade in pharmaceuticals is also useful in examining the Court of Justice's stance on what agreements harm competition. In *GlaxoSmithKline* (hereinafter *GSK*) we find a clear divergence between the General Court and the Court of Justice on this key question. The dispute arose when GSK, a producer of pharmaceuticals, inserted a clause in its contracts with Spanish wholesalers to ensure that they did not export the medicines to other Member States. The commercial rationale for GSK's practice is that medicines are bought by national health authorities and these buy medicines at different prices: in some, like Spain, the price is low because the government wants to guarantee availability of medicines, while in the United Kingdom the price is higher because the government wishes to reward pharmaceutical firms and encourage future innovation. Given low transport costs, there is a clear incentive for wholesalers in Spain to export to the United Kingdom, and an obvious interest in GSK to prevent these exports because they harm profits in the UK market. The Commission found the agreement had as its object the restriction of competition, a result which was to be expected given that the agreement served to partition the internal market.[79] From an economic perspective, the parallel trader does not bring any benefits to consumers. In fact, by reducing the revenue to the pharmaceutical companies, their research and development strategies are hindered. On this basis, the Commission's policy harms the development of new drugs.[80] On appeal, the General Court ruled that the prevention of parallel trade was not sufficient to find a restriction of competition.

Case T–168/01 GlaxoSmithKline Services Unlimited v Commission [2006] ECR II–2969

118. In effect, the objective assigned to Article [101(1) TFEU], which constitutes a fundamental provision indispensable for the achievement of the missions entrusted to the Community, in particular for the functioning of the internal market, is to prevent undertakings, by restricting competition between themselves or with third parties, from reducing the welfare of the final consumer of the products in question. At the hearing, in fact, the Commission emphasised on a number of occasions that it was from that perspective that it had carried out its examination in the present case, initially concluding that the General Sales Conditions clearly restricted the welfare of consumers, then considering whether that restriction would be offset by increased efficiency which would itself benefit consumers.

119. Consequently, the application of Article [101(1)TFEU] to the present case cannot depend solely on the fact that the agreement in question is intended to limit parallel trade in medicines or to partition the common market, which leads to the conclusion that it affects trade between Member States, but also requires an analysis designed to determine whether it has as its object or effect the prevention, restriction or distortion of competition on the relevant market, to the detriment of the final consumer … [T]hat analysis, which may be abridged when the clauses of the agreement reveal in themselves the existence of an alteration of competition, as the Commission observed at the hearing, must, on the other hand, be supplemented, depending on the requirements of the case, where that is not so....

---

[79] *Glaxo Wellcome* [2001] OJ L302/1.
[80] For greater detail see P. Rey and J. S. Venit, 'Parallel Trade and Pharmaceuticals: A Policy in Search of Itself' (2004) 29 *ELRev.* 176.

121. While it has been accepted since then that parallel trade must be given a certain protection, it is therefore not as such but, as the Court of Justice held, in so far as it favours the development of trade, on the one hand, and the strengthening of competition, on the other hand, that is to say, in this second respect, in so far as it gives final consumers the advantages of effective competition in terms of supply or price. Consequently, while it is accepted that an agreement intended to limit parallel trade must in principle be considered to have as its object the restriction of competition, that applies in so far as the agreement may be presumed to deprive final consumers of those advantages.

However, on appeal, the Court of Justice returned to the position it took in *Consten and Grundig* (which we discussed above). The Court ruled that nothing in the case law or in the text of Article 101 supported the position of the General Court.

Joined Cases C–501/06P, C–513/06P, C–515/06P and C–519/06P *GlaxoSmithKline Services Unlimited* v *Commission*, Judgment 6 October 2009

63. First of all, there is nothing in that provision to indicate that only those agreements which deprive consumers of certain advantages may have an anti-competitive object. Secondly, it must be borne in mind that the Court has held that, like other competition rules laid down in the Treaty, Article [101 TFEU] aims to protect not only the interests of competitors or of consumers, but also the structure of the market and, in so doing, competition as such. Consequently, for a finding that an agreement has an anti-competitive object, it is not necessary that final consumers be deprived of the advantages of effective competition in terms of supply or price.

64. It follows that, by requiring proof that the agreement entails disadvantages for final consumers as a prerequisite for a finding of anti-competitive object and by not finding that that agreement had such an object, the General Court committed an error of law.

The debate between the two courts is illustrative of the current controversy over the standard by which one assesses the anti-competitive nature of agreements. According to the General Court, a consumer welfare standard is preferred. This is in line with the Commission's current policy as well. In contrast, the Court of Justice's position reflects a different understanding of competition. The Court's statement that one is engaged in protecting 'competition as such' is opaque and leads to two competing interpretations.

On the one hand, it may be that the Court is using Article 101(1) to safeguard the economic freedom of market participants.[81] The Court is therefore saying that the notion of a restriction of competition needs no link to economic consequences. This is supported by the approach taken in *Allianz Hungária*: there were agreements between insurance companies and repair garages whereby the more insurance policies a garage sold, the better a price it would receive from the insurance company on repairs that it carried out. The commercial logic of this arrangement is simple: the more insurance policies are sold, the more money the garage makes on repairs. But the Court considered it would be possible to condemn it as a restriction by

---

[81] This is the view suggested by one of the co-authors of this book. G. Monti, *EC Competition Law* (Cambridge, Cambridge University Press, 2007).

object because national law requires that those who sell insurance should be independent of the insurance companies, and therefore this contract would run counter to the expectations of the policy-holders and so 'disrupt the proper functioning of the car insurance market'.[82] This is more a matter of consumer protection than a concern for competition authorities, but it fits with a narrative that sees the Court of Justice identify a wide range of practices as harmful.

On the other hand, the Court in *GSK* may have taken the view that when the competitive process is stifled, this is likely to have harmful effects on economic welfare. From this perspective, the difference between the two courts is not one of perspective, but of method: the General Court wishes to see proof of the likely economic impact of the agreement, while the Court of Justice considers that predicting the future in such a deterministic way is risky, and prefers to base its analysis on the premise that action that restricts economic freedom is likely to reduce efficiency. There is support for this in the *BIDS* judgment, where after concluding that an agreement among beef slaughterhouses that some of them would cease production was a restriction of competition by object, the Court indicated the kinds of anti-competitive effects that would likely result: higher prices as a result of reduced supply and foreclosure of new entrants as a result of the firms exiting the market agreeing to destroy their facilities.[83]

This debate between the European Courts has important practical implications: having to establish that a practice is likely to cause harm to consumer welfare raises the amount of evidence needed by the Commission to establish an infringement. In contrast, it is easier to condemn the wider kinds of harm that competition law addresses; and as we see below this also explains the present preference for prosecuting agreements by finding anti-competitive object.

(b) Agreements restrictive of competition by object

Article 101 TFEU distinguishes between agreements whose object is the restriction of competition and those which have as an effect the restriction of competition.[84] In considering infringements by object, two distinct considerations need to be kept in mind. The first is the definition of a restriction by object. It includes agreements which 'by their very nature' are 'injurious to the proper functioning of normal competition'.[85] Some of the agreements which are covered by this can be derived from the Court of Justice's analysis in the cases discussed above: agreements that fix prices or facilitate other forms of collusion with similar repercussions, and agreements that serve to partition the market.[86]

The second question is how one goes about establishing that an agreement has in fact an anti-competitive object, and here the Court's statements have been far from illuminating. In *T-Mobile*, the issue arose in the context of a concerted practice after a single meeting of operators of mobile phones in the Netherlands where they discussed reducing the remunerations paid to dealers for certain mobile phone contracts. In addition to confirming that there was no need to

---

[82] Case C-31/11 *Allianz Hungária Biztosító Zrt. and others* v *Gazdasági Versenyhivatal*, Judgment of 14 March 2013, para. 47. This judgment has received scathing criticism, see P. Harrison, 'The Court of Justice's Judgment in *Allianz Hungária* is Wrong and Needs Correcting' (2013) 1 *CPI Antitrust Chronicle* (May).

[83] Case C-209/07 *Competition Authority* v *Beef Industry Development Society Ltd* [2008] ECR I-8637, paras. 37–8.

[84] Agreements may 'restrict, distort or eliminate' competition but the analysis is the same for all three effects. For convenience we will henceforth only refer to 'agreements' but the analysis applies to all forms of cooperation.

[85] Case C-8/08 *T-Mobile Netherlands BV* v *Raad van bestuur van de Nederlandse Mededingingsautoriteit*, para. 29.

[86] Joined Cases C-501/06P, C-513/06P, C-515/06P and C-519/06P *GlaxoSmithKline Services Unlimited* v *Commission*, Judgment of 6 October 2009, paras. 60–1.

show consumer harm to establish that the agreement restricts competition, the Court had this to say about the concept of agreements restrictive by object.

Case C–8/08 *T-Mobile Netherlands BV v Raad van bestuur van de Nederlandse Mededingingsautoriteit* [2009] ECR I–4529

27. With regard to the assessment as to whether a concerted practice is anti-competitive, close regard must be paid in particular to the objectives which it is intended to attain and to its economic and legal context. Moreover, while the intention of the parties is not an essential factor in determining whether a concerted practice is restrictive, there is nothing to prevent the Commission of the European Communities or the competent Community judicature from taking it into account.

28. As regards the distinction to be drawn between concerted practices having an anti-competitive object and those with anti-competitive effects, it must be borne in mind that an anti-competitive object and anti-competitive effects constitute not cumulative but alternative conditions in determining whether a practice falls within the prohibition in Article [101(1) TFEU]. It has ... been settled case-law that the alternative nature of that requirement, indicated by the conjunction 'or', means that it is necessary, first, to consider the precise purpose of the concerted practice, in the economic context in which it is to be pursued. Where, however, an analysis of the terms of the concerted practice does not reveal the effect on competition to be sufficiently deleterious, its consequences should then be considered and, for it to be caught by the prohibition, it is necessary to find that those factors are present which establish that competition has in fact been prevented or restricted or distorted to an appreciable extent.

29. Moreover, in deciding whether a concerted practice is prohibited by Article 101 TFEU, there is no need to take account of its actual effects once it is apparent that its object is to prevent, restrict or distort competition within the common market. The distinction between 'infringements by object' and 'infringements by effect' arises from the fact that certain forms of collusion between undertakings can be regarded, by their very nature, as being injurious to the proper functioning of normal competition ...

30. Accordingly, contrary to what the referring court claims, there is no need to consider the effects of a concerted practice where its anti-competitive object is established.

31. With regard to the assessment as to whether a concerted practice, such as that at issue in the main proceedings, pursues an anti-competitive object, it should be noted ... that in order for a concerted practice to be regarded as having an anti-competitive object, it is sufficient that it has the potential to have a negative impact on competition. In other words, the concerted practice must simply be capable in an individual case, having regard to the specific legal and economic context, of resulting in the prevention, restriction or distortion of competition within the common market. Whether and to what extent, in fact, such anti-competitive effects result can only be of relevance for determining the amount of any fine and assessing any claim for damages.

These paragraphs are very difficult to interpret. Paragraph 31 is perhaps the most illuminating because it suggests that the assessment is about the capacity of the agreement to have an anti-competitive effect: this explains why some economic analysis is required. On the facts of the case, it is significant, for example, that all major providers had conspired, which is necessary for a successful horizontal cartel. It follows that, as Odudu has remarked, a finding that an agreement is restrictive by object merely generates a presumption of illegality because the parties may deny the claim that in the economic context the agreement will necessarily have harmful effects.[87] If the parties are successful in rebutting the presumption, it follows from paragraph 28 that the plaintiff may still prevail if it shows that the agreement has in fact caused harmful effects. If this interpretation is correct, then some of the Court of Justice's statements are misleading; in particular, while the Court is keen to distinguish the concepts of object and effect, it is best to see them as interlinked because when analysing a restriction by object one is always considering the capacity for anti-competitive harm.

(c) Agreements having an anti-competitive effect

The methodology for determining whether an agreement has an anti-competitive effect is also problematic because the Commission has been too quick to find anti-competitive effects,[88] in spite of the Court of Justice at times reminding the Commission that close analysis is warranted.[89] Before the coming into force of Regulation 1/2003, when parties had the opportunity to notify agreements, some even advised the parties to avoid doing so because the Commission would too easily find a restriction and then take too long to issue an exemption.[90] Others argued that the Commission should apply a more sophisticated approach systematically.[91]

The Commission has now revised its approach in response to the critiques it received. In 2004 it published Guidelines on the Application of Article 81(3) [now 101(3) TFEU]. These suggest that an economic appraisal will be carried out to determine whether an agreement has the effect of increasing prices or harming consumers in other ways. The intention of the Guidelines is to indicate that henceforth a narrower interpretation of Article 101(1) will be followed. However, this approach has left commentators confused, with some arguing that the Commission intends to carry out a detailed economic balance of the pro- and anti-competitive effects of an agreement under Article 101(1) leaving only borderline cases for evaluation under Article 101(3),[92] but others suggesting that an agreement will infringe Article 101(1) when the agreement gives the undertakings market power which may be used to harm consumers.[93] In sum, *some* economic analysis must be performed before determining that an

---

[87] O. Odudu, 'Restriction of Competition by Object: What's the Beef?' (2008) *Competition Law* 11.

[88] *Télévision par satellite (TPS)* [1999] OJ L90/6 offers the best example, where an agreement is declared to infringe Article 101(1) but then when considering Article 101(3) the Commission notes that the agreement improves competition.

[89] The leading cases in this respect are Case T-374/94 *European Night Services* v *Commission* [1998] ECR II-3141; Case 56-65 *Société Technique Minière* v *Maschinenbau Ulm GmbH* [1966] ECR 235; Case 26/76 *Metro SB-Großmärkte GmbH & Co. KG* v *Commission* [1977] ECR 1875; Case 258/78 *Nungesser* v *Commission* [1982] ECR 2015; Case 161/84 *Pronuptia de Paris GmbH* v *Schilgallis* [1986] ECR 353; Case C-234/89 *Delimitis* v *Henninger Bräu AG* [1991] ECR I-935.

[90] The *TPS* decision, n. 88 above, is telling: the exemption decision was issued a few months before the agreement was due to expire! See C. Bright, 'EU Competition Policy: Rules, Objectives and Deregulation' (1996) 16 *OJLS* 535; A. Brown, 'Notification of Agreements to the EC Commission: Whether to Submit to a Flawed System' (1992) 17 *ELRev.* 323.

[91] The seminal contribution is R. Joliet, *The Rule of Reason in Antitrust Law: American, German and Common Market Laws in Comparative Perspective* (The Hague, Faculté de Droit and Martinus Nijhoff, 1967). See also V. Korah, 'The Rise and Fall of Provisional Validity: The Need for a Rule of Reason in EEC Antitrust' (1981) *Northwest Journal of International Law and Business* 320; I. Forrester and C. Norall, 'The Laicization of Community Competition Law: Self-Help and the Rule of Reason' (1984) 21 *CMLRev.* 11.

[92] J. Bourgeois and J. Bocken, 'Guidelines on the Application of Article 81(3) of the EC Treaty, or How to Restrict a Restriction' (2005) 32 *LIEI* 111.

[93] P. Nicolaides, 'The Balancing Myth: The Economics of Article 81(1) and (3)' (2005) 32 *LIEI* 123.

agreement has anti-competitive effects, but we are still uncertain as to how much is needed before the burden shifts to the defendant to justify the practice under Article 101(3). In part the uncertainty results from the observations we made above: what does it mean to restrict competition? If one is looking for likely harm to consumer welfare, this would entail a more intense consideration than if one merely looks for damage to the functioning of markets. Furthermore, if all the analysis of effects is done under Article 101(1), what is the scope for Article 101(3)?[94]

The Commission's new approach was also bolstered by the General Court in a significant judgment that requires the party alleging an infringement of Article 101(1) to provide more refined evidence of the anti-competitive effects than the Commission has provided in some cases to date. At issue was a 'roaming' agreement between O2 and T-Mobile which was designed to help O2 secure a foothold in the German market while it was constructing its own network. The Commission first found that this restricted competition at wholesale and retail level, but when examining the agreement under Article 101(3) it found that the agreement would improve competition in the relevant markets. It exempted the agreement but for a period shorter than that which the parties had originally stipulated, so they sought (and obtained) annulment of the Commission's decision. The significance of this judgment is the legal standard set by the Court of Justice.

Case T–328/03 O2 (Germany) GmbH & Co. OHG v Commission [2006] ECR II–1231

68. [I]n a case such as this, where it is accepted that the agreement does not have as its object a restriction of competition, the effects of the agreement should be considered and for it to be caught by the prohibition it is necessary to find that those factors are present which show that competition has in fact been prevented or restricted or distorted to an appreciable extent. The competition in question must be understood within the actual context in which it would occur in the absence of the agreement in dispute; the interference with competition may in particular be doubted if the agreement seems really necessary for the penetration of a new area by an undertaking.

69. Such a method of analysis, as regards in particular the taking into account of the competition situation that would exist in the absence of the agreement, does not amount to carrying out an assessment of the pro- and anti-competitive effects of the agreement and thus to applying a rule of reason, which the Community judicature has not deemed to have its place under Article [101(1) TFEU].

70. In this respect, to submit, as the applicant does, that the Commission failed to carry out a full analysis by not examining what the competitive situation would have been in the absence of the agreement does not mean that an assessment of the positive and negative effects of the agreement from the point of view of competition must be carried out at the stage of Article [101(1) TFEU]. Contrary to the defendant's interpretation of the applicant's arguments, the applicant relies only on the method of analysis required by settled case-law.

71. The examination required in the light of Article [101(1) TFEU] consists essentially in taking account of the impact of the agreement on existing and potential competition and the competition situation in the absence of the agreement, those two factors being intrinsically linked.

---

[94] This is the reason why the European Courts regularly refused to import the rule of reason from US antitrust. Case T-112/99 *Métropole télévision (M6) and others* v *Commission* [2001] ECR II-2459, paras. 74–7.

Applied to the facts of the case, the General Court found first that the Commission had failed to examine the competitive effects without the agreement.

Case T–328/03 O2 (Germany) GmbH & Co. OHG v Commission [2006] ECR II–1231

77. Working on the assumption that O2 was present on the mobile communications market, the Commission did not therefore deem it necessary to consider in more detail whether, in the absence of the agreement, O2 would have been present on the 3G market. It must be held that that assumption is not supported in the Decision by any analysis or justification showing that it is correct, a finding that, moreover, the defendant could only confirm at the hearing. Given that there was no such objective examination of the competition situation in the absence of the agreement, the Commission could not have properly assessed the extent to which the agreement was necessary for O2 to penetrate the 3G mobile communications market. The Commission therefore failed to fulfil its obligation to carry out an objective analysis of the impact of the agreement on the competitive situation.

78. That lacuna cannot be deemed to be without consequences. It is apparent from the considerations set out in the Decision in the analysis of the agreement in the light of the conditions laid down in Article [101(3) TFEU] as regards whether it was possible to grant an exemption that, even in the Commission's view, it was unlikely that O2 would have been able, individually, without the agreement, to ensure from the outset better coverage, quality and transmission rates for 3G services, to roll out a network and launch 3G services rapidly, to penetrate the relevant wholesale and retail markets and therefore be an effective competitor (recitals 122 to 124, 126 and 135). It was because of those factors that the Commission considered that the agreement was eligible for exemption.

79. Such considerations, which imply some uncertainty concerning the competitive situation and, in particular, as regards O2's position in the absence of the agreement, show that the presence of O2 on the 3G communications market could not be taken for granted, as the Commission had assumed, and that an examination in this respect was necessary not only for the purposes of granting an exemption but, prior to that, for the purposes of the economic analysis of the effects of the agreement on the competitive situation determining the applicability of Article [101 TFEU].

The key insight from this judgment is that the Commission's evidentiary burden is raised: it is insufficient for it to show that the agreement affects the economic freedom of one of the parties: one has to demonstrate a causal link between the agreement and subsequent restrictions of competition.

M. Marquis, 'O2 (Germany) v Commission and the Exotic Mysteries of Article 81(1) EC' (2007) *European Law Review* 27, 44–5

[I]t is questionable whether the nature of the counterfactual test is truly different from an analysis that 'weighs' the agreement's pro-competitive and anti-competitive effects ... One could argue that the counterfactual test loses its meaning if the pro-competitive impact of the agreement cannot be weighed against its anti-competitive effects. What is to be compared with the counterfactual, *non-agreement* scenario if it is not the agreement's *net* impact on competition (or more precisely, its net impact on price and output)? If account is not taken of the agreement's pro-competitive effects as well as its restrictive effects, then the comparison becomes distorted and illogical.

The good news is that, regardless of the 'no balancing' doctrine, the CFI appears willing or indeed eager to apply an analysis under Art. 81(1) that is economically rigorous and commercially realistic. Thus, for example, the Commission's view that national roaming agreements restricted competition 'by definition' was rejected as a generalisation that had no specific bearing on the agreement at issue. Furthermore, the Court took very seriously – within the context of Art. 81(1), and consistently with *Société Technique Minière* – the structure of the market and the prospect that roaming could enhance O2's competitive position vis-à-vis the incumbent. This approach has important implications for the network industries, where liberalisation has resulted in lopsided competitive conditions, and above all for rapidly evolving sectors such as electronic communications, where the legacy of a dominant incumbent may potentially distort the development of emerging markets.

In short, the CFI seems to be applying the kind of searching inquiry that it applied in *European Night Services*, and it seems to be carrying out an assessment that looks suspiciously like balancing. Whatever it is called, it is a positive development, and the CFI's judgment provides further confirmation of what the ECJ has often asserted over the last 40 years, namely that there are boundaries to the concept of 'restriction of competition'. To be regretted is the lingering confusion – in the CFI's jurisprudence and in the Commission's Art. 81(3) Guidelines – regarding the division of labour between Art. 81(1) and 81(3). Much clarity could be achieved if the European Courts explicitly embraced the distinction described earlier between a consumer welfare test under Art. 81(1) and an assessment of productive/dynamic efficiency gains under Art. 81(3).

Taking the Guidelines and the judgment together, one may say that in testing for an anti-competitive effect the Commission will be more cautious: first asking if the parties have enough market power to cause harm, then considering the kinds of anti-competitive effects that may result from the agreement (e.g. reduced output or foreclosure), and finally asking whether in the given market context there is a causal link between the agreement and the likely harmful effects. However, as we discuss below, Marquis' suggestion that Article 101(3) is only about efficiencies can be contested.

(iii) Role of Article 101(3) TFEU

As indicated above, the procedure whereby exemption decisions were the exclusive competence of the Commission and were only available if the agreement was notified has come to an end with Regulation 1/2003. The effect of this reform is that Article 101 changed from a provision enforced primarily via an ex ante notification system to one that is enforced ex post and is based on deterrence: parties must assess for themselves whether the agreement falls foul of competition law. It follows that when a competition authority or a claimant challenges a restrictive practice, they have the burden of proving that the agreement infringes Article 101(1), and the defendant has the burden of proof in relation to Article 101(3). However, having eliminated the procedural delays that characterised the notification system, Regulation 1 has led to a potentially worse procedural nightmare: suppose a national competition authority reviews a practice and wishes to issue a decision stating that it may be exempted, can it do so? In *Tele 2*, the Polish competition authority wished to issue a decision that the undertaking whose conduct had been examined had not breached Article 102 TFEU. The Court of Justice held that the authority could not issue such decision.

> **Case C-375/09** *Prezes Urzędu Ochrony Konkurencji i Konsumentów* v *Tele2 Polska sp. z o.o., devenue Netia SA* [2011] ECR I-3055
>
> 27. Empowerment of national competition authorities to take decisions stating that there has been no breach of Article 102 TFEU would call into question the system of cooperation established by the Regulation and would undermine the power of the Commission.
> 28. Such a 'negative' decision on the merits would risk undermining the uniform application of Articles 101 TFEU and 102 TFEU, which is one of the objectives of the Regulation highlighted by recital 1 in its preamble, since such a decision might prevent the Commission from finding subsequently that the practice in question amounts to a breach of those provisions of European Union law.
> 29. It is thus apparent from the wording, the scheme of the Regulation and the objective which it pursues that the Commission alone is empowered to make a finding that there has been no breach of Article 102 TFEU, even if that article is applied in a procedure undertaken by a national competition authority.
> 30. Consequently, the answer to the first question is that Article 5 of the Regulation must be interpreted as precluding a national competition authority, in the case where, in order to apply Article 102 TFEU, it examines whether the conditions for applying that article are satisfied and where, following that examination, it forms the view that there has been no abuse, from being able to take a decision stating that there has been no breach of that article.

The same reasoning would apply to Article 101 TFEU. It is an awkward ruling because it means the best a competition authority can do is to issue a document stating that the case has been dropped, but it gives little comfort to the undertakings. Furthermore, while the Commission is empowered to declare agreements lawful, it has not yet exercised this power once since the coming into force of Regulation 1/2003. This leaves courts as the sole actors who could consider exemption under Article 101(3). The result of this procedural state of affairs is that since 2004 we have not seen any decisions finding that the conditions for applying this Article have been satisfied, only that they have failed. Thus we have shifted from a system where undertakings suffered the results of delayed decisions to one where they suffer from the absence of any decision whatsoever. Having noted this procedural marginalisation of Article 101(3) we turn to interpreting the provision.

(a) Individual exemptions

Four conditions must be satisfied for an agreement to benefit from an exemption: (1) it must improve the production and distribution of goods or promote technical and economic progress; (2) consumers must receive a fair share of the benefits identified in (1); (3) the restrictions of competition must be necessary to achieve the said benefits; (4) the agreement must not eliminate competition on the market. There is also a fifth implicit requirement by which the benefits outweigh the harm to competition. In theory, all agreements can qualify.[95]

The first condition is the most controversial because its scope is uncertain: does it mean that an agreement is exempted because it yields economic efficiency (the narrow view), or does it also mean that an agreement may be exempted if it makes a contribution to other matters

---

[95] Case T-17/93 *Matra Hachette* v *Commission* [1994] ECR II-595.

of interest to the Community (the wide view)?[96] For example, can the fact that an agreement enhances employment in a poor European region be a relevant consideration in determining whether it can be exempted? Or an agreement that strengthens a weak European industry against strong rivals from overseas? Neither the decisions of the Commission, nor the European Courts' judgments have provided an unambiguous answer to this question, although most commentators have suggested that non-economic factors play some role in influencing the decision to exempt an agreement, and others have also insisted that this is correct as a matter of law.[97] The Commission has indicated that Article 101(3) can only serve agreements which enhance economic efficiency, and that it is not to be used to exempt agreements that support other interests.[98] This position is somewhat out of line with the approach that has been taken in the past. In a decision concerning the Conseil Européen de la Construction d'Appareils Domestiques (CECED), an association representing manufacturers of domestic appliances, including washing machines, agreed to phase out from the market certain types of washing machines with low energy efficiency. The agreement was found anti-competitive by object because it prevented parties from manufacturing or exporting certain types of washing machines and thus restricted consumer choice. The agreement would also raise production costs for those manufacturers who had not yet developed more energy efficient models. However, the Commission found the following reasons for exempting the agreement.

CECED [2000] OJ L187/47

47. The agreement is designed to reduce the potential energy consumption of new washing machines by at least 15 to 20% (relative to 1994 data on models of washing machines) ...

48. Washing machines which, other factors being constant, consume less electricity are objectively more technically efficient. Reduced electricity consumption indirectly leads to reduced pollution from electricity generation. The future operation of the total of installed machines providing the same service with less indirect pollution is more economically efficient than without the agreement....

51. CECED estimates the pollution avoided at 3.5 million tons of carbon dioxide, 17,000 tons of sulphur dioxide and 6,000 tons of nitrous oxide per year in 2010, working on the basis of average emission values. Although such emissions are more efficiently tackled at the stage of electricity generation, the agreement is likely to deliver both individual and collective benefits for users and consumers.

(a) Individual economic benefits

52. The level at which the minimum performance standard is set provides a fair return within reasonable pay-back periods to a typical consumer for higher initial purchase costs derived from the more stringent standard in fact set out by CECED. Savings on electricity bills allow recouping of increased costs of

---

[96] For detail on the differences between these two see R. Whish, *Competition Law* (6th edn, Oxford, Oxford University Press, 2008) 151–7.

[97] R. B. Bouterse, *Competition and Integration: What Goals Count?* (The Hague, Kluwer Law International, 1994) chs. 1–4; R. Wesseling, *The Modernisation of EC Antitrust Law* (Oxford, Hart, 2000) esp. 105–12; C. Townley, *Article 81 EC and Public Policy* (Oxford, Hart, 2009). Contra, see O. Odudu, 'The Wider Concerns of Competition Law' (2010) 30(3) *Oxford Journal of Legal Studies* 599.

[98] Communication from the Commission, Notice: Guidelines on the application of Article 81(3) of the Treaty [2004] OJ C101/97.

upgraded, more expensive machines within nine to 40 months, depending mainly on frequency of use and electricity prices....

(b) Collective environmental benefits

56. The Commission reasonably estimates the saving in marginal damage from (avoided) carbon dioxide emissions (the so-called 'external costs') at EUR 41 to 61 per ton of carbon dioxide. On a European scale, avoided damage from sulphur dioxide amounts to EUR 4,000 to 7,000 per ton and EUR 3,000 to 5,000 per ton of nitrous oxide. On the basis of reasonable assumptions, the benefits to society brought about by the CECED agreement appear to be more than seven times greater than the increased purchase costs of more energy-efficient washing machines. Such environmental results for society would adequately allow consumers a fair share of the benefits even if no benefits accrued to individual purchasers of machines.

This decision gives a wide interpretation of economic efficiency, noting that the considerable environmental benefits which the agreement generates are enough to exempt the agreement. On the one hand, the decision may be read as suggesting that other Union policies affected the decision to exempt (see in particular paragraph 56). On the other hand, the decision might simply be read as stating that because the agreement reduces energy bills, consumers are better off because even though the price of washing machines rises, the electricity bills are low enough to compensate for this (see paragraph 52). Thus it can be read as espousing both the wide and narrow interpretation of Article 101(3). This ambiguity also characterises earlier decisions which suggest that a decision to exempt may be influenced by a range of non-efficiency related competition factors, for example relieving unemployment,[99] promoting environmental goals[100] and helping the creation of stronger European industry in the face of competition from firms in the United States and Japan.[101]

CECED is also interesting for its interpretation of the second condition in Article 101(3): that consumers should benefit. On the one hand, the benefits should accrue to those who buy the goods, and thus gain directly by the agreement. However, in *CECED* the Commission was willing to consider collective benefits to society as a whole as 'consumer benefits' which is an overly wide interpretation. Another interesting analysis of the consumer benefit criteria was offered by the Court of Justice in *Asnef-Equifax* v *Ausbanc*.[102] Spanish banks agreed to set up an electronic register of credit information that would disclose the credit history of potential customers. The effect was that each bank was aware of each potential client's credit history and took this into account when negotiating further loans. The Court held that it was unlikely that this agreement would restrict competition, but also added some reflections on how one might go about analysing the consumer benefit test in Article 101(3). It suggested that two groups of consumers benefit: those who get loans on better terms, and those who do not get loans because of their bad credit scores, and this is a benefit because it avoids

---

[99] See e.g. *Stichting Baksteen* [1994] OJ L131/15, paras. 27–8; *Synthetic Fibres* [1984] OJ L207/17, para. 37.

[100] See e.g. *Philips/Osram* [1994] OJ L378/37.

[101] See e.g. *Optical Fibres* [1986] OJ L236/30; *Olivetti/Canon* [1988] OJ L52/60; *Bayer/BPCL* [1988] OJ L150/35. See Bouterse, n. 97 above.

[102] Case C-238/05 *Asnef-Equifax, Servicios de Información sobre Solvencia y Crédito, SL* v *Asociación de Usuarios de Servicios Bancarios (Ausbanc)* [2006] ECR I-11125.

over-indebtedness. That persons who are unable to obtain a service as a result of an anti-competitive agreement can be seen as deriving a benefit requires further reflection: would one say, for example, that a cartel to fix the prices of cigarettes benefits smokers who therefore smoke less? Furthermore, in *GSK*, the Court agreed that a restriction on competition today which would facilitate research and development for future drugs could be exempted.[103]

The third condition is that the agreement must only contain restrictions that are indispensable to achieve the benefits identified by the first two criteria. This means that if the benefits can be achieved in a less restrictive way, then an exemption will not be granted. In *CECED*, for example, the Commission considered whether there were any other ways of reducing energy consumption. One less restrictive alternative could have been for the parties to agree to inform consumers in more detail about the energy costs of each washing machine and allow the consumer to make the choice. This would be less restrictive of competition than withdrawing certain models. However, the Commission decided that informing the consumer would not have been as effective. Thus the restriction agreed by the parties was necessary to achieve the relevant benefits.

The relevance of the final criteria is explained by the Commission: 'Ultimately, the protection of rivalry and the competitive process is given priority over potentially pro-competitive efficiency gains which could result from restrictive agreements.'[104] Therefore, if an agreement were to result in the parties not competing at all, then an exemption will not be granted. In *CECED*, there was no elimination of competition because the parties were able to compete on features like price, brand image and technical performance.[105]

In sum, there remains a tension between the Commission's recent policy of considering that efficiency is the sole basis for exemption, and the Court of Justice insisting that a wider basis for exemption is to be tolerated. At the time of writing, the Dutch competition authority is exploring how far agreements safeguarding the environment may be exempted. Its findings may provide lessons for the Commission's policy.[106]

(b) Block Exemptions

Block Exemption Regulations provide that all agreements meeting certain predefined criteria would merit exemption as a group. The 'old style' Block Exemptions defined a type of agreement and provided lists of clauses which parties were allowed to insert in the agreement (white lists) and lists of clauses which if present would deny the agreement the benefit of a Block Exemption (black lists).[107] The advantage of falling within the scope of a Block Exemption was that the parties did not need to notify the agreement, but this was at the expense of flexibility resulting from long black lists. Moreover, some Block Exemptions were said to be commercially unrealistic and to have been of no use in structuring certain types of agreement. The Commission has now redesigned Block Exemptions to make these more business friendly and more effectively based upon economic analysis. The first Block

---

[103] Joined Cases C-501/06P *GlaxoSmithKline Services Unlimited v Commission* [2009] ECR I-9291.
[104] Guidelines on Article 81(3), para. 105.   [105] *CECED* [2000] OJ L187/47, para. 64.
[106] Authority for Consumer and Markets, *Position Paper on Competition and Sustainability* (July 2013), available at www.acm.nl/en/.
[107] See e.g. Regulation 1983/83 on exclusive distribution [1983] OJ L173/1.

Exemption to be drafted in this way is that for vertical restraints, and a brief overview is provided below.[108]

Vertical restraints are agreements between undertakings operating at different levels of trade (for example, a distribution contract between a manufacturer and a retailer), which restrict the parties' behaviour. For example, a manufacturer of plasma TVs may decide to sell these only to a selected type of retail outlet whose staff are competent to give consumers advice. These contracts may restrict the number of outlets selling the plasma TVs (and so stifle intra-brand competition among retail outlets) but their redeeming virtue is that the selected retailers are better placed to satisfy consumer demand by providing valued pre-sale service. Provided there is healthy competition among rival brands of TV sets (inter-brand competition), then vertical restraints will enhance consumer welfare.[109] There may, however, be three anti-competitive risks that materialise with vertical restraints: first, if all manufacturers use similar distribution contracts this may facilitate collusion among them because they can monitor each other's prices more easily; secondly, vertical restraints that encourage unnecessary promotion by retailers may reduce consumer welfare;[110] and thirdly, vertical restraints might foreclose market access for new entrants (say, because the new entrant finds that there are no more outlets willing to distribute his goods).[111]

Anti-competitive risks tend to arise when there is market power, and the Block Exemption Regulation is designed with this in mind.[112] Parties may benefit from the Block Exemption only if they meet the condition specified in article 3: that the market share held by the supplier and the buyer does not exceed 30 per cent of the relevant market on which the supplier sells or the buyer purchases the contract goods or services. Parties that fall within this threshold are free to enter into whichever distribution contracts they wish save for a small number of 'black listed' clauses set out in articles 4 and 5. For instance, the manufacturer cannot impose a minimum price at which distributors may sell the goods (which might facilitate collusion), and the manufacturer cannot prevent the dealer from selling the contract goods in question in another Member State when these are ordered by a customer there (this is based on the crucial importance of the market integration goal). Finally, the Commission (or a national competition authority (NCA)) may remove the benefit of the Block Exemption if the benefits to consumers do not materialise.[113] While this has hardly been used, it is a helpful mechanism to regulate vertical restraints that do not live up to their promise. The Regulation is accompanied by Guidelines that explain how the Commission will apply Article 101 TFEU to agreements that

---

[108] The Commission's earlier approach to regulating vertical restraints had been criticised harshly. See B. E. Hawk, 'System Failure: Vertical Restraints and EC Competition Law' (1995) 32 *CMLRev.* 973; D. Neven, P. Papandropolous and P. Seabright, *Trawling for Minnows: European Competition Policy and Agreements Between Firms* (London, CEPR, 1998) 42–3.

[109] For a detailed account of the economics see M. Motta, *Competition Policy* (Cambridge, Cambridge University Press, 2004) ch. 6; P. W. Dobson and M. Waterson, *Vertical Restraints and Competition Policy* (London, OFT, 1996); L. G. Tesler, 'Why Should Manufacturers Want Fair Trade?' (1960) 3 *Journal of Law and Economics* 86.

[110] W. S. Comanor, 'Vertical Price-Fixing, Vertical Market Restrictions, and the New Antitrust Policy'(1985) 98 *Harvard Law Review* 983, esp. 991–2 and 100–2.

[111] S. C. Salop, 'Analysis of Foreclosure in the EC Guidelines on Vertical Restraints' (2000) *Fordham Corporate Law Institute*177, 191–2.

[112] Regulation 330/2010 of 20 April 2010 on the application of Article 101(3) of the Treaty on the Functioning of the European Union to categories of vertical agreements and concerted practices [2010] OJ L102/1.

[113] Regulation 330/2010, article 6 empowers the Commission to issue a decision to withdraw the benefit of the exemption in a relevant market, while Regulation 1/2003, article 29 empowers the Commission and national authorities to withdraw the benefit of exemption from a particular agreement.

fall outside the scope of the Block Exemption (e.g. when the market share threshold is not met) and these provide for an economics-based appraisal of vertical restraints.[114]

This Regulation has been very successful in limiting the intervention of competition law in this field.[115] Having said that, there are also instances where it appears that non-competition considerations result in an aggressive approach. In *Pierre Fabre*, the Court of Justice held that an agreement forbidding distributors in France from selling cosmetics online was a restriction of competition by object.[116] This is in spite of the fact that the undertaking held a 20 per cent share of the market and all other cosmetics manufacturers had already agreed to allow online sales, so it is hard to see what damage Pierre Fabre was likely to cause. Moreover, the French NCA which had originally brought the case felt compelled to review in detail the terms of the distribution contracts of all cosmetics manufacturers to ensure that online retailers had a good chance to exploit this sales channel. This regulatory approach seems to be more about facilitating online trade than about removing competitive restraints.[117]

4 ARTICLE 102 TFEU: ABUSE OF A DOMINANT POSITION

Enterprises holding significant market power should receive considerable scrutiny by competition authorities. From an economic perspective, firms that dominate a market have the kind of economic power that normally reduces efficiency because there are no competitive pressures to prevent dominant firms from raising prices and reducing output.[118] Moreover, large firms may exercise market power to consolidate their dominance, or even to expand their influence into the political domain.[119]

Article 102 TFEU

Any abuse by one or more undertakings of a dominant position within the common market or in a substantial part of it shall be prohibited as incompatible with the common market insofar as it may affect trade between Member States.

Such abuse may, in particular, consist in:

- directly or indirectly imposing unfair purchase or selling prices or other unfair trading conditions;
- limiting production, markets or technical development to the prejudice of consumers;
- applying dissimilar conditions to equivalent transactions with other trading parties, thereby placing them at a competitive disadvantage;
- making the conclusion of contracts subject to acceptance by the other parties of supplementary obligations which, by their nature or according to commercial usage, have no connection with the subject of such contracts.

---

[114] Commission Notice: Guidelines on vertical restraints [2010] OJ C 130/1.

[115] V. Korah and D. O'Sullivan, *Distribution Agreements Under the EC Competition Rules* (Oxford, Hart, 2002) ch. 8.

[116] Case C-439/09 *Pierre Fabre Dermo-Cosmétique SAS* v *Président de l'Autorité de la concurrence and Ministre de l'Économie, de l'Industrie et de l'Emploi* [2011] ECR I-9419.

[117] G. Monti, 'Restraints on Selective Distribution Agreements' (2013) 36(4) *World Competition* 489, reviewing the decision-making practices of the French competition authority.

[118] See Chapter 21 for a review of the economic analysis underlying this.

[119] See R. A. Posner, 'The Social Costs of Monopoly and Regulation' (1975) 83 *Journal of Political Economy* 807; R. Pitofsky, 'The Political Content of Antitrust' (1979) 127 *U Penn. L Rev.* 105; G. Amato, *Antitrust and the Bounds of Power* (Oxford, Hart, 1997) ch. 7.

When the Commission seeks to establish an infringement of Article 102 TFEU, it must show the following: that an undertaking is dominant in a given market; that it has abused its dominant position; that the abuse has an effect on trade between Member States; and the absence of any objective justification for the abuse.[120] Four examples of abuse are listed in Article 102 TFEU, but this list is not an exhaustive catalogue. As will be seen, the Commission and Court of Justice have found an ever-increasing number of practices abusive.

Compared to the voluminous case law under Article 101 TFEU, the abuse prohibition has been applied relatively infrequently (approximately sixty decisions by the Commission) but the Commission and the Court's case law has received the most scathing criticism for fettering the economic freedom of dominant firms unnecessarily and for being incoherent.[121] In response to this criticism, and in line with the more economics-oriented approach of contemporary competition law, the Commission embarked on a controversial reform process.[122] We start by considering the current law and the criticisms it has elicited before turning to examine the main traits of the new approach.

(i) Dominance

A dominant undertaking need not monopolise the entire market. Such an extreme degree of dominance is possible when an undertaking is given a monopoly by the Member State, for instance if the Member State grants the right to operate job centres exclusively to one undertaking.[123] But the concept of dominance is much wider than that.[124]

J. Temple Lang, 'Some Aspects of Abuse of a Dominant Position in EC Antitrust Law' (1979) 3 *Fordham International Law Forum* 1, 9–12

A dominant position exists when the dominant enterprise is able to use its economic power to obtain benefits or to practise behaviour which it could not obtain or practise in conditions of reasonably effective competition, i.e., that dominant power is power of which unfair advantage can be taken, or power which is great enough to be 'abused'.... This principle also implies a link between the concept of dominance and the concept of abuse....

It is the ability to contain competition, not the ability to ignore it, which is characteristic of dominance. Dominant firms can overcome competition, but very few of them can disregard it. The power to plan and choose a controlled response to competitors' efforts, sufficient to ensure no significant long term loss of market share, is typical of dominant firms. As market leader a dominant

---

[120] The interpretation of the requirement of an effect on trade between Member States is considered in Chapter 21, and the same approach is taken in Article 102 TFEU.

[121] B. Sher, 'The Last of the Steam Powered Trains: Modernising Article 82' (2004) 25 *ECLR* 243; C.-D. Ehlermann and M. Marquis (eds.), *European Competition Law Annual 2007: A Reformed Approach to Article 82 EC* (Oxford, Hart, 2008).

[122] P. Lowe, 'DG Competition's Review of the Policy on Abuse of Dominance' (2003) *Fordham Corporate Law Institute* 163.

[123] Case C-41/90 *Höfner and Elser* v *Macrotron GmbH* [1991] ECR I-1979.

[124] The Court's definition is: 'A position of economic strength enjoyed by an undertaking which enables it to prevent effective competition being maintained on the relevant market by giving it the power to behave to an appreciable extent independently of its competitors, customers and ultimately of its consumers': Case 27/76 *United Brands* v *Commission* [1978] ECR 207, para. 65.

firm is often able to adopt a strategy advantageous to itself and disadvantageous for the rest of the industry, without using overtly exclusionary practices, which will maintain its market in spite of some competition. Such a strategy may be adopted on the dominant firm's own initiative or in response to competitors' actions. Since dominance does not mean absence of competition, or even absence of effective competition, clearly it does not mean freedom to disregard competition. It follows that dominance can exist even if the dominant firm is compelled to react to its competitors' activities.

Accordingly, dominance means that an undertaking has the power to harm the competitive process, either by harming consumers (for example, through higher prices) or by harming competitors (for example, by offering discounts to customers who would otherwise buy the competitor's goods). From this perspective, it can be said that there are different degrees of dominance: some undertakings are so powerful that they face no competitive constraint, while some dominant undertakings may face competition from others, but are strong enough to keep the smaller competitors at bay. Dominance is measured in two steps: first, by considering the undertaking's market share; and secondly, by other factors used to confirm the undertaking's position vis-à-vis its competitors, customers and consumers.[125]

(a) Market shares

Market shares are used as a preliminary filter to determine whether there is dominance. Their significance was explored in *Hoffmann-La Roche*.[126] The Commission found that Roche held a dominant position in a number of vitamin markets and had abused it by entering into distribution contracts that granted purchasers fidelity rebates; that is, part of the purchase price was paid back to the buyer if they bought their vitamin requirements exclusively or almost exclusively from Roche, thereby excluding other vitamin suppliers. The Court of Justice confirmed that Roche was dominant, noting that by holding a substantial market share for some time (when smaller competitors were unable to meet the demand of Roche's customers) it was free to act independently of competitors. Subsequent case law suggests that a market share of 50 per cent can give rise to a presumption of dominance.[127] In many cases the dominant firm has held market shares in excess of 50 per cent while its competitors all have had considerably smaller market shares.[128] However, a market share between 40 and 50 per cent has also been sufficient to identify a dominant position once other factors were taken into consideration.[129]

(b) Additional factors

Dominance does not exist if entry is easy. A firm with a 90 per cent share of the market is not dominant if, as soon as it raised the price of its goods, other firms would enter its market and

---

[125] Case 322/81 *Nederlandsche Banden-Industrie Michelin NV* v *Commission* [1983] ECR 3461, para. 31.

[126] Case 85/76 *Hoffmann-La Roche & Co. AG* v *Commission* [1979] ECR 461, paras. 39–41.

[127] Case 62/86 *AKZO* v *Commission* [1991] ECR I-3359, para. 60.

[128] See e.g. Case 322/81 *Nederlandsche Banden-Industrie Michelin NV* v *Commission* [1983] ECR 3461 (dominant firm with a market share of approximately 57–60 per cent and the others with market shares between 4 and 8 per cent).

[129] Case 27/76 *United Brands* v *Commission* [1978] ECR 207, paras. 109–10; Case T-219/99 *British Airways* v *Commission*, Judgment of 17 December 2003, paras. 211–24.

sell their goods at more competitive prices. As a result, a definition of dominance requires an analysis of whether there are any barriers to entry. But this notion is not without controversy. Economists have been divided between those who take a wide conception of entry barriers (any factor that allows the existing company to raise price), and a narrower conception of entry barriers (only those costs that a new entrant must incur that were not faced by the existing firms).[130] The wider the concept used, the more likely it is that one finds dominance. However the application of this debate in competition law has been criticised: '[w]hat matters … is not what might happen in some year far off in the future but what will actually happen now and in the near future. Rather than focusing on whether an "entry barrier" exists according to some definition, analysts should explain how the industry will behave over the next several years'.[131] In this light, the wide range of factors identified by the Court of Justice as indicators of dominance can be explained by the Court's concern about whether in the relatively short term other firms can enter to compete against the dominant undertaking. In *Michelin*, the Court approved the Commission's decision that Michelin held a dominant position in the market for new tyres for certain types of vehicles. It found that this position was abused because Michelin entered into distribution agreements with tyre retailers in the Netherlands which restricted the retailer's freedom to source tyres from competitors because it was given financial incentives in the form of quantity rebates if it purchased more Michelin tyres. In this passage the appellant's challenge against the finding of dominance was rejected by the Court.

Case 322/81 *Nederlandsche Banden-Industrie Michelin NV* v *Commission* [1983] ECR 3461

55. … it should first be observed that in order to assess the relative economic strength of Michelin NV and its competitors on the Netherlands market the advantages which those undertakings may derive from belonging to groups of undertakings operating throughout Europe or even the world must be taken into consideration. Amongst those advantages, the lead which the Michelin group has over its competitors in the matters of investment and research and the special extent of its range of products, to which the Commission referred in its Decision, have not been denied. In fact in the case of certain types of tyre the Michelin group is the only supplier on the market to offer them in its range.

56. That situation ensures that on the Netherlands market a large number of users of heavy-vehicle tyres have a strong preference for Michelin tyres. As the purchase of tyres represents a considerable investment for a transport undertaking and since much time is required in order to ascertain in practice the cost-effectiveness of a type or brand of tyre, Michelin NV therefore enjoys a position which renders it largely immune to competition. As a result, a dealer established in the Netherlands normally cannot afford not to sell Michelin tyres.

57. It is not possible to uphold the objections made against those arguments by Michelin NV, supported on this point by the French government, that Michelin NV is thus penalized for the quality of its products and services. A finding that an undertaking has a dominant position is not in itself a recrimination but simply means that, irrespective of the reasons for which it has such a dominant position, the

---

[130] R. Schmalensee, 'Ease of Entry: Has the Concept been Applied Too Readily?' (1987) 56 *Antitrust Law Journal* 41; P. Geroski and A. Jacquemin, 'Industrial Change, Barriers to Mobility and European Industrial Policy' (1985) 1 *Economic Policy* 170, 182–3.

[131] D. E. Carlton, 'Why Barriers to Entry and Barriers to Understanding' (2004) 94 *American Economic Review* 466, 469.

undertaking concerned has a special responsibility not to allow its conduct to impair genuine undistorted competition on the common market.

58. Due weight must also be attached to the importance of Michelin NV's network of commercial representatives, which gives it direct access to tyre users at all times. Michelin NV has not disputed the fact that in absolute terms its network is considerably larger than those of its competitors or challenged the description, in the Decision at issue, of the services performed by its network whose efficiency and quality of service are unquestioned. The direct access to users and the standard of service which the network can give them enables Michelin NV to maintain and strengthen its position on the market and to protect itself more effectively against competition.

59. As regards the additional criteria and evidence to which Michelin NV refers in order to disprove the existence of a dominant position, it must be observed that temporary unprofitability or even losses are not inconsistent with the existence of a dominant position. By the same token, the fact that the prices charged by Michelin NV do not constitute an abuse and are not even particularly high does not justify the conclusion that a dominant position does not exist. Finally, neither the size, financial strength and degree of diversification of Michelin NV's competitors at the world level nor the counter poise arising from the fact that buyers of heavy-vehicle tyres are experienced trade users are such as to deprive Michelin NV of its privileged position on the Netherlands market.

The judgment provides an extensive list of factors that contributed to give Michelin a competitive advantage over its rivals. In addition, the Court of Justice has found that a dominant position might be protected by ownership of intellectual property rights (which prevent others from duplicating the dominant undertaking's products);[132] by access to capital; by considerable costs of entry; by economies of scale necessary to penetrate the market;[133] or by a well organised distribution system, advertising and brand recognition.[134] The criticism that by considering these factors one is merely describing the efficiency of the dominant firm, and using those efficiencies as a means to determine dominance, is rejected by the Court at paragraph 57 of *Michelin*: dominance is not unlawful, but dominant undertakings have a special responsibility not to hinder competition. But this has not assuaged those who think that the too-wide definition of dominance, combined with this passage, places a Damoclean sword over dominant undertakings whose commercial freedom is detrimentally affected by this obligation, paradoxically restricting the very kind of competition that dominant firms are said to endanger.[135]

(ii) Abuse of dominance: general principles

The types of abuse may be classified in two categories: exploitative and exclusionary. The first includes abuses that aim to harm the customer of the dominant undertaking (for example, excessive prices). However, the Commission has shown little interest in punishing exploitative abuses. The major reason for not intervening against firms that exploit market power is that it is difficult to identify the parameters for intervention. In any market where an undertaking has *some* market

---

[132] See e.g. Case 22/78 *Hugin Kassaregister AB* v *Commission* [1979] ECR 1869; Case T-30/89 *Hilti* v *Commission* [1991] ECR II-1439 (affirmed in Case C-53/92P *Hilti* v *Commission* [1994] ECR I-667).

[133] Case 27/76 *United Brands* v *Commission* [1978] ECR 207.

[134] Case T-203/01 *Michelin* v *Commission*, Judgment of 30 September 2003.

[135] S. Turnbull, 'Barriers to Entry, Article 86 and the Abuse of a Dominant Position' (1996) *ECLR* 96.

power, prices are higher than marginal cost.[136] However, if EU competition law were to apply to all prices above marginal cost, virtually all undertakings would be subject to scrutiny. Clearly, only exorbitantly high prices require regulation, although the Court's case law has provided little clear guidance to identify what constitutes an excessive price. In *United Brands*, the Court of Justice suggested that a price is excessive when it bears no reasonable relation to the economic value of the product in question. This could be measured by comparing the selling price with the cost of production.[137] This standard suggests that dominant firms are entitled to sell at a price somewhat above the cost of production, but not excessively beyond it. Quite how the line between a reasonably high and an unreasonably high price is to be drawn is not explained. As a result, the Commission has not prioritised exploitative abuses in its enforcement plans.[138] That said, the Commission has initiated investigations over excessive prices in economic sectors that have only recently been liberalised, where the transition to a competitive market is also monitored by national regulators that have the power to control prices. These investigations have often resulted in commitment decisions and price adjustments monitored by national regulators.[139]

The second category of abuse, exclusionary, covers abuses that are designed to impact negatively on rivals. There are two justifications for extending the application of Article 102 TFEU to exclusionary abuses.[140] On the one hand, these abusive practices are designed to safeguard the undertaking's dominant position and to facilitate subsequent exploitation of dominance.[141] For instance, United Brands, dominant in the market for bananas, fought to exclude other banana manufacturers from the European market as a way of maintaining its power over customers. Another justification for treating exclusionary abuses as anti-competitive is that by eliminating or weakening competitors, the dominant firm denies the opportunities of other economic actors to participate on the market. These rivals may have been capable of bringing new goods into the market or developing the market in other ways. The risk with this second justification of penalising exclusionary conduct is that it gives the appearance that the Commission protects smaller undertakings rather than consumers. This is so for two reasons: the first is that a finding of an infringement is made very easy by the Court of Justice's case law (there is no need to show likely consumer harm, nor indeed a need to show that the exclusionary tactic was or will be successful); and the second is that the undertakings under scrutiny find it difficult to justify their actions once these have been judged to constitute an abuse.

The controversial judgment in *British Airways* serves as a clear example of what many see as the overly aggressive approach adopted by the Union.[142] The Commission had condemned

---

[136] See S. Bishop and M. Walker, *The Economics of EC Competition Law* (2nd edn, London, Sweet and Maxwell, 2002) ch. 2, 43–4.

[137] Case 27/76 *United Brands v Commission* [1978] ECR 207, paras. 250–2.

[138] European Commission, *XXIVth Report on Competition Policy* (1994) para. 207.

[139] See Case COMP/39.388 *German Electricity Wholesale Market*, Decision of 26 November 2008; Case COMP/39.402 *RWE Gas Foreclosure*, Decision of 19 March 2009.

[140] But some see no good reason for applying Article 102 TFEU to exclusionary abuses, notably R. Joliet, *Monopolization and Abuse of Dominant Position* (Liège, Université de Liège, 1970).

[141] T. G. Kattenmaker and S. C. Salop, 'Anticompetitive Exclusion: Raising Rivals' Costs to Achieve Power Over Price' (1986) 96 *Yale Law Journal* 20.

[142] For strong critique of the policy towards these practices, see J. Kallaugher and B. Sher, 'Rebates Revisited: Anticompetitive Effects and Exclusionary Abuse under Article 82' (2004) 25 *ECLR* 263; for a defence of these cases see L. Gyselen, 'Rebates: Competition on the Merits or Exclusionary Practice?' in C.-D. Ehlermann and I. Atanasiu (eds.), *European Competition Law Annual : What is an Abuse of a Dominant Position?* (Oxford/Portland, Hart, 2006).

BA's strategy of offering travel agents extra commissions when they promoted BA tickets on the basis that this was discriminatory, designed to induce loyalty and served to exclude competing airlines.[143]

Case C–95/04P *British Airways plc. v Commission*, **Judgment of 15 March 2007**

Criteria for assessing exclusionary effects

68. It follows that in determining whether, on the part of an undertaking in a dominant position, a system of discounts or bonuses which constitute neither quantity discounts or bonuses nor fidelity discounts or bonuses within the meaning of the judgment in *Hoffmann-La Roche* constitutes an abuse, it first has to be determined whether those discounts or bonuses can produce an exclusionary effect, that is to say whether they are capable, first, of making market entry very difficult or impossible for competitors of the undertaking in a dominant position and, secondly, of making it more difficult or impossible for its co-contractors to choose between various sources of supply or commercial partners.

69. It then needs to be examined whether there is an objective economic justification for the discounts and bonuses granted. In accordance with the analysis carried out by the [General Court] ... an undertaking is at liberty to demonstrate that its bonus system producing an exclusionary effect is economically justified.

70. With regard to the first aspect, the case-law gives indications as to the cases in which discount or bonus schemes of an undertaking in a dominant position are not merely the expression of a particularly favourable offer on the market, but give rise to an exclusionary effect.

71. First, an exclusionary effect may arise from goal-related discounts or bonuses, that is to say those the granting of which is linked to the attainment of sales objectives defined individually....

73. It is also apparent from the case-law that the commitment of co-contractors towards the undertaking in a dominant position and the pressure exerted upon them may be particularly strong where a discount or bonus does not relate solely to the growth in turnover in relation to purchases or sales of products of that undertaking made by those co-contractors during the period under consideration, but extends also to the whole of the turnover relating to those purchases or sales. In that way, relatively modest variations – whether upwards or downwards – in the turnover figures relating to the products of the dominant undertaking have disproportionate effects on co-contractors....

75. Finally, the Court took the view that the pressure exerted on resellers by an undertaking in a dominant position which granted bonuses with those characteristics is further strengthened where that undertaking holds a very much larger market share than its competitors. It held that, in those circumstances, it is particularly difficult for competitors of that undertaking to outbid it in the face of discounts or bonuses based on overall sales volume. By reason of its significantly higher market share, the undertaking in a dominant position generally constitutes an unavoidable business partner in the market. Most often, discounts or bonuses granted by such an undertaking on the basis of overall turnover largely take precedence in absolute terms, even over more generous offers of its competitors. In order to attract the co-contractors of the undertaking in a dominant position, or to receive a sufficient volume of orders from them, those competitors would have to offer them significantly higher rates of discount or bonus.

---

[143] *Virgin/British Airways* [2000] OJ L30/1; affirmed by the CFI Case T-219/99 *British Airways* v *Commission* [2003] ECR II-5917. See further G. Monti, *EC Competition Law* (Cambridge, Cambridge University Press, 2007) 162–72 and O. Odudu, 'Case Note on BA v Commission' (2007) 44 *CMLRev.* 1781.

Applying these standards to the facts of the case, the Court of Justice confirmed that BA had abused its dominant position: the bonuses were drawn up individually for each travel agent; they were based upon the total number of tickets sold, and not on those sold over a given level, so selling a few extra BA tickets meant a significant increase in bonus payments, so that it was often more worthwhile selling a few extra BA tickets rather than selling some other airlines' tickets; BA's size was such that other competitors lacked 'a sufficiently broad financial base to allow them effectively to establish a reward scheme similar to BA's'.[144] It may be argued that this is insufficient to sustain a finding of abuse; for instance, there was no evidence that BA's scheme meant that its prices were below cost, in which case BA was simply more efficient than its rivals, or at least lucky to have been the first on the market and benefited from a statutory monopoly for several years giving it a significant advantage over new entrants.

The Court of Justice's approach in this case did little to reduce the criticisms that EU competition law protects competitors, and not competition,[145] but there is a rational basis for this approach, as Professor Fox has indicated:

> It is a principle of freedom of non-dominant firms to trade without artificial obstacles constructed by dominant firms, and carries an assumption that preserving this freedom is important to the legitimacy of the competition process and is likely to inure to the benefit of all market players, competitors and consumers.[146]

The reader should note the similarity between the Court of Justice's appraisal here and the approach it takes in Article 101 cases like *GlaxoSmithKline* and *T-Mobile*, discussed earlier: in both instances, the Court is committed to safeguarding the competitive process, not solely competitive outcomes.

(iii) Predatory pricing

The tension between penalising dominant firms because of the possible harm they might cause to the competitive process and the possible benefits of certain forms of behaviour by dominant undertakings is particularly relevant in the context of below-cost pricing, often referred to as predatory pricing. Below-cost pricing can be a benevolent strategy to enter a market, by reducing prices so as to invite customers, but it may also constitute a predatory strategy designed to drive other competitors out of the market, whereby the predator endures losses until the prey exits the market. Below-cost pricing is often practised selectively, targeting those customer groups where the benefits of below-cost pricing is greatest. The seminal predatory pricing case concerns Akzo, a dominant manufacturer of benzonyl peroxide (a chemical used in two lines of business, flour additives and plastics). It became concerned that one of its competitors, ECS, who had originally sold benzonyl peroxide in the flour sector, was expanding its sales in the plastics sector. Intent on safeguarding its profits, Akzo threatened ECS with retaliation, sold benzonyl peroxide at very low prices to ECS's customers in the flour market, while

---

[144] Case C-95/04P *British Airways plc.* v *Commission*, Judgment of 15 March 2007, para. 76.

[145] But see H. Schweitzer, 'Parallels and Differences in the Attitudes Towards and Rules regarding Market Power: What are the Reasons?' in C.-D. Ehlermann and M. Marquis (eds.), *European Competition Law Annual 2007: A Reformed Approach to Article 82 EC* (Oxford, Hart, 2008).

[146] E. M. Fox, 'What is Harm to Competition? Exclusionary Practices and Anticompetitive Effect' (2002) 70 *Antitrust Law Journal* 37, 395.

maintaining a higher price for its regular customers, and engaged in other commercial tactics designed to woo customers away from ECS in an effort to persuade ECS to abandon the plastics sector. The Court of Justice established the parameters to determine when low prices are to be deemed predatory.

Case C–62/86 *AKZO Chemie BV* v *Commission of the European Communities* [1991] ECR I–3359

69. It should be observed that, as the Court held in its judgment in Case 85/76 *Hoffmann-La Roche* v *Commission* [1979] ECR 461, paragraph 91, the concept of abuse is an objective concept relating to the behaviour of an undertaking in a dominant position which is such as to influence the structure of a market where, as a result of the very presence of the undertaking in question, the degree of competition is weakened and through recourse to methods which, different from those which condition normal competition in products or services on the basis of the transactions of commercial operators, has the effect of hindering the maintenance of the degree of competition still existing in the market or the growth of that competition.

70. It follows that Article [102] prohibits a dominant undertaking from eliminating a competitor and thereby strengthening its position by using methods other than those which come within the scope of competition on the basis of quality. From that point of view, however, not all competition by means of price can be regarded as legitimate.

71. Prices below average variable costs (that is to say, those which vary depending on the quantities produced) by means of which a dominant undertaking seeks to eliminate a competitor must be regarded as abusive. A dominant undertaking has no interest in applying such prices except that of eliminating competitors so as to enable it subsequently to raise its prices by taking advantage of its monopolistic position, since each sale generates a loss, namely the total amount of the fixed costs (that is to say, those which remain constant regardless of the quantities produced) and, at least, part of the variable costs relating to the unit produced.

72. Moreover, prices below average total costs, that is to say, fixed costs plus variable costs, but above average variable costs, must be regarded as abusive if they are determined as part of a plan for eliminating a competitor. Such prices can drive from the market undertakings which are perhaps as efficient as the dominant undertaking but which, because of their smaller financial resources, are incapable of withstanding the competition waged against them.

While complex economic theories of predatory pricing suggest that price predation is possible, the Court of Justice's approach appears too wide-ranging.[147] First, it does not take into account that below-cost pricing can be a pro-competitive strategy when a firm is entering a new product market, where low prices are necessary to generate initial sales.[148] Secondly, the judgment may dent dominant firms' competitive edge: why should Akzo not be entitled to increase its market share? Thirdly, intention was inferred by internal memoranda indicating the desire to undercut ECS, but the desire to undermine competitors is the prime instinct of any company,

---

[147] See P. Bolton, J. F. Brodley and M. H. Riordan, 'Predatory Pricing: Strategic Theory and Legal Policy' (2000) 88 *Georgetown Law Journal* 2239; A. Kate and G. Niels, 'On the Rationality of Predatory Pricing' (2002) *Antitrust Bulletin* 1.

[148] The point was recognised in theory in Case T-83/91 *Tetra Pak* v *Commission* [1994] ECR II-755, para. 147, but the scope for justification is very narrow.

dominant or not, so the probative value of this approach to intention is unclear. Fourthly, the judgment requires no showing that the predatory pricing campaign is likely to be success-ful:[149] for prices below average variable cost the Court appears to assume that the predator will be able to recover the lost profits it suffers because it will later be able to raise prices, but there is no showing that this is a likely effect; for prices above average variable cost but below average total cost, the Court finds harm by assuming that this pricing behaviour, coupled with a plan to exclude rivals, will most likely injure a rival as efficient as the dominant undertaking and so harm the competitive process.

In a subsequent application of the *Akzo* test by the Commission, WIN (Wanadoo Interactive which, following a merger, was at that time a part of France Télécom) was found to have set predatory prices 'as part of a plan to pre-empt the market in high-speed internet access during a key phase in its development'.[150] On appeal to the Court of Justice, the parties claimed that a finding of predatory pricing should only succeed if there was proof that the predator would be able to recoup the losses incurred during the predatory pricing campaign. This would be to add a further requirement to the *Akzo* test that would make one more convinced that predatory pricing was likely to harm consumers. While the Advocate General was sympathetic, the Court confirmed that there was no need to establish recoupment.

Case C-202/07P *France Télécom SA* v *Commission* [2009] ECR I-2369

110. Accordingly, contrary to what the appellant claims, it does not follow from the case law of the Court that proof of the possibility of recoupment of losses suffered by the application, by an undertaking in a dominant position, of prices lower than a certain level of costs constitutes a necessary precondition to establishing that such a pricing policy is abusive. In particular, the Court has taken the opportunity to dispense with such proof in circumstances where the eliminatory intent of the undertaking at issue could be presumed in view of that undertaking's application of prices lower than average variable costs.

111. That interpretation does not, of course, preclude the Commission from finding such a possibility of recoupment of losses to be a relevant factor in assessing whether or not the practice concerned is abusive, in that it may, for example where prices lower than average variable costs are applied, assist in excluding economic justifications other than the elimination of a competitor, or, where prices below average total costs but above average variable costs are applied, assist in establishing that a plan to eliminate a competitor exists.

112. Moreover, the lack of any possibility of recoupment of losses is not sufficient to prevent the undertaking concerned reinforcing its dominant position, in particular, following the withdrawal from the market of one or a number of its competitors, so that the degree of competition existing on the market, already weakened precisely because of the presence of the undertaking concerned, is further reduced and customers suffer loss as a result of the limitation of the choices available to them.

Since *Akzo*, the Court of Justice has failed to explain how a dominant undertaking may justify an aggressive price strategy when its dominant position is challenged by competitors. The General Court has suggested that a dominant firm may respond aggressively with price cuts that are not below cost, provided that the prices are (1) the result of a decision to protect one's position;

---

[149] Case C-333/94P *Tetra Pak* v *Commission* [1996] ECR I-5951, para. 44.
[150] Case COMP/38.233 *Wanadoo Interactive*, Decision of 16 July 2003, article 1.

(2) based on efficiencies; and (3) are in the interest of consumers.[151] However, the application of this standard is difficult. The Court suggests that the dominant firm may merely protect its position and not improve it, although it will be difficult to foresee whether a defensive practice leads the dominant firm to increase its market share (if you cut prices to save your sales you might also attract new customers). The condition that the dominant undertaking's practice must be efficient is not easy to prove, and it is not clear in the case law why low prices are not seen as beneficial to consumers. Thus dominant undertakings may respond to 'meet competition' but the circumstances in which a dominant firm will succeed in justifying its practices are extremely limited.[152] Perhaps asking whether dominant undertakings can benefit from a meeting competition defence is to approach the abuse doctrine in Article 102 TFEU from the wrong perspective. A meeting competition defence is appropriate if the aim is to promote economic efficiency, thereby allowing dominant firms to defend themselves when they are able to exclude less efficient rivals.[153]

(iv) Reform

Practitioners have regularly criticised the jurisprudence under Article 102: first, the abuse case law has arisen pragmatically in response to individual disputes and without a systematic enforcement policy. As a result, the Commission and European Courts in individual cases have operated without 'any clear general analytical or intellectual framework'.[154] Secondly, the influence of economic thinking, which has increasingly affected other areas of competition law, has not had the same impact on the application of Article 102. Instead the case law is (according to economists) based on formalistic distinctions, like the notion of loyalty rebates, and simple price-cost tests. These criticisms apply at two levels: first, each case is judged poorly; secondly, the function of Article 102 is distorted because the Commission can protect competitors without considering the likely effects of the practices it prohibits. However, reviewing the case law from a historical perspective, David Gerber suggests that the jurisprudence is not without wealth or value.[155]

> **D. J. Gerber, 'Law and the Abuse of Economic Power in Europe' (1987) 62 *Tulane Law Review* 57, 100–5**
>
> **A. Conceptual Structure**
> In Community law the broad principle of competitive distortion is the central mechanism for giving content to the abuse concept. It is generally applied, however, according to a developing set of case-law principles fashioned to protect particular interests. These application principles protect, for example, the interests of consumers and small and medium-sized firms. They also protect dominant enterprises

---

[151] Case T-228/97 *Irish Sugar plc* v *Commission* [1999] ECR II-2969, para. 189.
[152] P. Andrews, 'Is Meeting Competition a Defence to Predatory Pricing?' (1998) *ECLR* 9; D. Ridyard, 'Domco's Dilemma: When is Price Competition Anti-Competitive?' (1999) *ECLR* 345.
[153] E. Elhauge, 'Why Above-Cost Price Cuts to Drive Out Entrants are Not Predatory – and the Implications for Defining Costs and Market Power' (2002) 112 *Yale Law Journal* 681, Part IV.
[154] J. T. Lang, R. O'Donoghue, 'Defining Legitimate Competition: How to Clarify Pricing Abuses under Article 82 EC' (2002) 26 *Fordham International Law Journal* 83.
[155] *Ibid.*

by providing that conduct which otherwise would be a violation of Article 86 may be justified under certain circumstances. Analysis generally begins, therefore, with the issue of whether conduct 'distorts competition' and then turns to case law to determine whether the competitive distortion harms interests whose protection is required under existing guidelines ...

B. The Application of Abuse Law Concepts

Both systems [German and European] have also identified competitive unfairness as a category of abuse. Here the abuse concept is used to prevent dominant firms from using their power to achieve an unfair advantage in competition with other firms, such as, for example, through predatory pricing. In German law competitive unfairness is included within the concept of impediment abuse, whereas the European Commission applies Article 86 to such conduct because it distorts competition to the detriment of smaller competitors and, in the long run, consumers.

Both systems have encountered, however, significant difficulties in conceptualizing competitive unfairness for purposes of judicial application. Each has turned primarily to the intuitively appealing idea of competition on the merits in order to provide a fairness standard, but this method of giving content to the abuse concept has not been finally accepted in either system, and there are many who doubt its viability. These doubts relate to whether the merit competition notion has sufficient analytical power to make justifiable and reasonably predictable distinctions among the various types of conduct available to economically powerful firms. Neither system has yet had sufficient experience with this concept to warrant final conclusions about its effectiveness. Nevertheless, the fact that both systems have chosen to rely on it in using the abuse concept to combat competitive unfairness means that the future of the idea of unfairness as part of abuse law may well depend on the amenability to judicial application of the concept of merit competition.

A third category of practices that are considered abusive in both systems includes those by which dominant producers exercise control over firms that distribute their products. In both systems loyalty rebates, exclusive dealing contracts, and similar control measures may be abusive ... Under Community law, such control mechanisms are found abusive when they distort competition to the detriment of consumers and interfere with the freedom of small and medium-sized firms. This analysis refers directly to the power that a dominant producer may have over distributors as well as to its effects. The result has been the development of flexible and judicially applicable principles to guide business behavior ...

C. Methods of Interpretation

In Community law the decision in *Continental Can* to interpret abuse teleologically – i.e., by reference to the objectives of the Community – has determined the structure and development of abuse law, because it established the concept of competitive distortion as the analytical starting point. In addition, the court often fashions its application principles according to its perception of the systemic needs of the Community. For example, the court's application of the abuse concept to loyalty rebates is based on the perceived need to protect the structure of competition by protecting the competitive freedom of small and medium-sized firms. Although the court occasionally also finds guidance by analogizing to the examples provided in Article 86, the teleological method has been the dominant means of ascribing meaning to abuse in Community law.

Despite criticism for failure fully to utilize more predictable methods of interpretation, the European Court has fashioned a body of legal principles with sufficient integrity and coherence to have achieved general acceptance. Its success in doing so is clearly related, however, to a general consensus concerning the basic objectives of Articles 85 and 86 – principally, the elimination of barriers to trade within the Community – as well as to the articulation of Community objectives in the governing treaty ...

D. The Process of Legal Development

... Although basic principles of analysis in Community abuse law were provided through the authority of outside experts,[156] the subsequent development of the law has been primarily the product of adjudication by the European Court. The court has established a basic framework for giving content to the abuse concept and has consistently applied this framework and the ideas generated thereby to new fact situations. Consequently, it is the court's central role that has dominated the developmental process.

The Commission has shaped this development through both policy and enforcement decisions. Its identification and articulation of Community policy goals has been particularly influential because of the court's focus on using the abuse concept to achieve the fundamental objectives of the Community. Moreover, not only has the Commission's enforcement policy determined the fact situations which would reach the court, but its decisions have also established lines of conceptual development which the court has later adopted.

One helpful lesson which we might draw from Gerber's analysis is that to understand the law in this field, less attention should be paid to legal nuances and to economic edicts, but greater focus should be placed upon matching the abuse doctrine to EU policies, with an understanding that the Commission has regularly used Article 102 TFEU as a tool to achieve a vast array of Community objectives, and the Court of Justice gave this approach unstinting support in the early years but has since the 1990s exercised a more stringent form of judicial review.[157] From this angle, a richer synthesis of abuse might be attained by matching the decisions with Community policies: cases which support the aims of safeguarding small and medium-sized undertakings and of market integration are both seen as engines for developing, in the long term, the interests of consumers.

However, the reformers were eager to intervene. In late 2005, DG Competition published a Discussion Paper on Exclusionary Abuse which indicated that it sought to redirect its policy by using a more economics-oriented framework.[158] This stimulated a lively debate.[159] The outcome of these reflections is a paper issued in 2009 entitled *Guidance on the Commission's Enforcement Priorities in Applying Article 82 of the EC Treaty [now Article 102 TFEU] to Abusive Exclusionary Conduct by Dominant Undertakings*.[160] This paper should be studied from two angles.[161]

---

[156] This alludes to a report prepared by academics for the Commission: *Memorandum sur le Problème de la Concentration dans le Marché Commun* (1 December 1965), reprinted in (1966) *Revue trimestrelle de droit européen* 651.

[157] See generally A. Arnull, *The European Union and Its Court of Justice* (Oxford, Oxford University Press, 1999) noting a general trend whereby the Court of Justice supports the expansion of EU competition law doctrines in the early years but applies a stricter approach from the mid-1980s.

[158] Discussion Paper on the Application of Article 82 of the Treaty to Exclusionary Abuses (December 2005), available at http://ec.europa.eu/comm/competition/antitrust/art82/index.html.

[159] See e.g. C.-D. Ehlermann and I. Atanasiu (eds.), *European Competition Law Annual 2003: What is an Abuse of a Dominant Position?* (Oxford, Hart, 2004); Ehlermann and Marquis, n. 121 above; J. Vickers, 'Abuse of Market Power' (2005) 115 *Economic Journal* F244. See also EAGCP, 'An Economic Approach to Article 82' (July 2005), available at http://ec.europa.eu/dgs/competition/economist/eagcp_july_21_05.pdf.

[160] [2009] OJ C45/7.

[161] G. Monti, 'Article 82 EC: What Future for the Effects-Based Approach?' (2009) 1(1) *Journal of European Competition Law and Practice* 2; H. Schweitzer, 'Recent Developments in EU Competition Law (2006–2008): Single-Firm Dominance and the Interpretation of Article 82' (2009) *European Review of Contract Law* 175.

First, it is designed to set the tone for the Commission's overall enforcement strategy, which will focus on behaviour likely to harm consumers and indicates a shift away from merely protecting competition as such. This is a major change of position and sets the Commission on a collision course with the Court of Justice, as only the latter can determine the scope of Article 102 TFEU. However, the way the Commission avoids this clash is not by denying the correctness of the case law, but by saying that while potentially more abuse cases could be brought, the Commission will exercise its prosecutorial discretion by only taking those cases where, in addition to establishing abuse under the legal parameters set out by the Court, the Commission also finds that the abuse is likely to result in consumer harm. From this perspective, the title of the Guidance is telling, if a little misleading: in contrast to other soft law notices, which usually contain guidelines, this one simply indicates enforcement priorities. In this way the Commission does not appear to be rewriting the case law. This is a very astute move from the Commission: incapable of overruling the Court of Justice's case law, it supplements the current elements of abuse (harm to the competitive process) with new ones (likely foreclosure of competitors and likely consumer harm). In the long run, the European Courts may feel compelled to endorse these new elements and so incrementally a novel abuse doctrine will materialise. It is less easy to see a scenario where the Court of Justice will be asked to reject the enforcement standard being proposed by the Commission. Parties who are condemned will more likely question the evidence of consumer harm (as Intel did),[162] and the victims of those dominant undertakings who escape conviction are unlikely to be able to use the Court to require the Commission to ascertain an infringement absent likely consumer harm given the Commission's wide prosecutorial discretion. That said, national courts may continue to follow the precedents set by the Court of Justice and so there may be a tension between the interpretation of abuse at national and EU level. Finally, one must pause and consider why a successful competition authority should publish a document by which it makes it more difficult for it to prosecute abuse cases. This shows how sensitive certain members of DG Competition are to stakeholder criticism and to ensuring that the Commission utilises 'best practices' in applying competition law.

The second perspective through which to study the Guidance Paper is to test how the current tests for abuse are affected. For instance, in considering predatory pricing abuses, one might reasonably conclude that the new approach would hinge on proving that the predator will be able to gain from this strategy by raising prices, and so insist on recoupment. However, the Commission's approach is somewhat broader.

Guidance on the Commission's Enforcement Priorities in Applying Article 82 of the EC Treaty [now Article 102 TFEU] to Abusive Exclusionary Conduct by Dominant Undertakings [2009] OJ C45/7

68. ... [t]he Commission will generally investigate whether and how the suspected conduct reduces the likelihood that competitors will compete. For instance, if the dominant undertaking is better informed about cost or other market conditions, or can distort market signals about profitability, it may engage in predatory conduct so as to influence the expectations of potential entrants and thereby deter entry. If the conduct and its likely effects are felt on multiple markets and/or in successive periods of possible entry, the dominant undertaking may be shown to be seeking a reputation for predatory conduct. If the

---

[162] See n. 137 below.

targeted competitor is dependent on external financing, substantial price decreases or other predatory conduct by the dominant undertaking could adversely affect the competitor's performance so that its access to further financing may be seriously undermined.

69. The Commission does not consider that it is necessary to show that competitors have exited the market in order to show that there has been anticompetitive foreclosure. The possibility cannot be excluded that the dominant undertaking may prefer to prevent the competitor from competing vigorously and have it follow the dominant undertaking's pricing, rather than eliminate it from the market altogether. Such disciplining avoids the risk inherent in eliminating competitors, in particular the risk that the assets of the competitor are sold at a low price and stay in the market, creating a new low cost entrant.

70. Generally speaking, consumers are likely to be harmed if the dominant undertaking can reasonably expect its market power after the predatory conduct comes to an end to be greater than it would have been had the undertaking not engaged in that conduct in the first place, that is to say, if the undertaking is likely to be in a position to benefit from the sacrifice.

71. This does not mean that the Commission will only intervene if the dominant undertaking would be likely to be able to increase its prices above the level persisting in the market before the conduct. It is sufficient, for instance, that the conduct would be likely to prevent or delay a decline in prices that would otherwise have occurred. Identifying consumer harm is not a mechanical calculation of profits and losses, and proof of overall profits is not required. Likely consumer harm may be demonstrated by assessing the likely foreclosure effect of the conduct, combined with consideration of other factors, such as entry barriers. In this context, the Commission will also consider possibilities of re-entry.

These passages indicate that the Commission will consider the likely effect of predatory pricing on consumer welfare, but without requiring proof that prices will rise allowing the predator to recover the costs incurred. Instead, the major difference between the case law and the Guidance Paper is that, in the latter, the Commission is aware that mere proof of below-cost pricing is insufficient, and it identifies a number of scenarios where predation is more likely to prove a successful exclusionary strategy: predation by reputation, or disciplining rivals; these have been discussed by economists as plausible scenarios for exclusion. Thus in the future the Commission plans to only condemn below-cost pricing in a scenario where it is realistic to expect that such prices foreclose rivals.

The proposed change in rebate cases like *British Airways* or *Michelin* would be more profound, however. The Commission proposes to apply a standard similar to that for predatory pricing cases, with a slight difference which is best illustrated by an example. Suppose a retailer of car tyres sells 100 units a week, and without rebates they know that 60 consumers will buy Michelin. This means that of the 100 sales, 60 are non-contestable (the retailer must stock at least 60 Michelin branded tyres). It means that rivals of Michelin can only, at best, sell 40 tyres (this is the contestable part of the market, where there can be competition). Now, suppose Michelin offers the retailer a discount if they buy 80 Michelin tyres. The Commission will apply the amount of the discount to the 20 extra tyres and work out what the 'effective price' for those 20 tyres is. (This makes sense because the retailer would have bought the first 60 tyres even at the usual price, so the discount only affects his decision to buy the additional 20.) If this 'effective price' is below Michelin's costs then it will be taken as a sign that the discounts are exclusionary because a firm as efficient as Michelin cannot afford to sell tyres at such a price.[163] This approach is significantly more attentive to trying to infer likely exclusionary effects, but it is also more resource-intensive.[164]

(v) Response by the Court of Justice

How the Court of Justice will respond to the new policy will become clear in the next few years as the case law accumulates; at the time of writing we can detect two trends, rejection and timid acceptance.

Rejection is found in the first case the Court of Justice ruled upon after issuing the Guidance Paper: *TeliaSonera*. It was a reference from the Swedish courts in a case of price squeeze. This is a practice which may occur when the dominant player is vertically integrated, as in telecommunications markets. In this case the dominant firm (a former state monopoly) held a monopoly position in upstream markets (in this case the local loop, that is, the final connection between each house and the nearest local telephone exchange). New entrants wishing to sell retail services (in this case broadband Internet access) had to contract with the incumbent, who is also active on the retail market. On the facts, the dominant firm sold an ADSL wholesale package which a new Internet service provider could buy and offer its own retail services through. From a business perspective, the dominant firm would have no incentive to facilitate the entry of downstream competition, but the EU's liberalisation Directives require that access to the upstream market must be granted to create competition downstream. It remains possible for the dominant firm to make life difficult for the new entrant. For example, the wholesale price for the ADSL product can be set so high that it is not profitable for the new entrant to stay in business, or the dominant firm can set a very low retail price that also has the effect of squeezing the profits of the new entrant. Catching this exclusionary practice is very important because otherwise the market for telecommunications will not be opened to competition. Furthermore, it is not always possible for national regulatory authorities in charge of this sector to tackle this with the powers they have.[165] However, from a competition law perspective, there are two ways of addressing this concern using existing tools. First, if high wholesale prices are set, this can be said to constitute a constructive refusal to deal: the new entrant needs access to the wholesale infrastructure and a very high price denies access. This abuse is well established. Secondly, if the dominant undertaking sets very low retail prices instead, then, as we saw above, the predatory pricing rules exist. Accordingly, in the United States, the Supreme Court ruled that there is no third abuse of price squeeze, existing categories of abuse suffice.[166] The Court of Justice, however, took the opposite view.

---

[163] Guidance Paper, n. 160 above, paras. 37–45.

[164] This approach was applied for the first time in Case COMP/C-3/37.900 *Intel*, Decision of 13 May 2009. However this is an awkward one: first the Commission established the anti-competitive nature of rebates applying the established case law; secondly, it also applied the methodology in the Guidance Paper, n. 160 above. At the time of writing an appeal is pending (Case T-206/09).

[165] In other similar cases the regulator had been unable to intervene, see e.g. Case C-280/08P *Deutsche Telekom v Commission* [2010] ECR I-9555. For discussion, see G. Monti, 'Managing the Intersection of Utilities Regulation and EC Competition Law'(2008) 4(2) *Competition Law Review* 123.

[166] *Pacific Bell* v *LinkLine Communications* 555 US 438 (2009).

Case C-52/09 *Konkurrensverket v TeliaSonera Sverige AB* [2011] ECR I-527

21. Article 102 TFEU is one of the competition rules referred to in Article 3(1)(b) TFEU which are necessary for the functioning of that internal market.

22. The function of those rules is precisely to prevent competition from being distorted to the detriment of the public interest, individual undertakings and consumers, thereby ensuring the well-being of the European Union....

31. A margin squeeze, in view of the exclusionary effect which it may create for competitors who are at least as efficient as the dominant undertaking, in the absence of any objective justification, is in itself capable of constituting an abuse within the meaning of Article 102 TFEU.

32. In the present case, there would be such a margin squeeze if, inter alia, the spread between the wholesale prices for ADSL input services and the retail prices for broadband connection services to end users were either negative or insufficient to cover the specific costs of the ADSL input services which TeliaSonera has to incur in order to supply its own retail services to end users, so that that spread does not allow a competitor which is as efficient as that undertaking to compete for the supply of those services to end users.

33. In such circumstances, although the competitors may be as efficient as the dominant undertaking, they may be able to operate on the retail market only at a loss or at artificially reduced levels of profitability.

34. It must moreover be made clear that since the unfairness, within the meaning of Article 102 TFEU, of such a pricing practice is linked to the very existence of the margin squeeze and not to its precise spread, it is in no way necessary to establish that the wholesale prices for ADSL input services to operators or the retail prices for broadband connection services to end users are in themselves abusive on account of their excessive or predatory nature, as the case may be.

The Court of Justice then went on to explain that normally margin squeeze is calculated by reference to the costs and prices of the dominant firm, by asking this question: if the dominant firm had to pay the wholesale price to sell its retail products, would its profits be adversely affected? If yes, then there is a price squeeze because a competitor as efficient as the dominant firm would be unable to make sufficient profits on the market.

This case is a rejection of the Guidance Paper in three respects. First, it restates that the aim of the competition rules is to safeguard the public interest, and so not only the welfare of consumers. Secondly, in the Guidance Paper price squeeze had been treated as a form of refusal to deal, while here (and contrary to the advice of the Advocate General) it is a stand-alone abuse.[167] Thirdly, the Court retains its concern about ensuring equality of opportunity among rivals, which in this case allows one to use Article 102 TFEU to supplement the Commission's regulatory efforts in the telecoms sector.[168]

In contrast, commentators have indicated that *Post Danmark* reflects a greater willingness to be led by the Commission's initiative.[169] Post Danmark and the complainant

---

[167] Case C-52/09 *Konkurrensverket v TeliaSonera Sverige AB* [2011] ECR I-527, Opinion of Advocate General Mazák, para. 18, making reference to the Guidance Paper, n. 160 above, para. 80.

[168] G. A. Hay and K. McMahon, 'The Diverging Approach to Price Squeezes in the United States and Europe' (2012) 8(2) *Journal of Competition Law and Economics* 259; see also G. Faella and R. Pardolesi, 'Squeezing Price Squeeze Under EC Antitrust Law' (2010) 6(1) *European Competition Journal* 255; J.-Y. Art, 'Highway 102: A Nice Turn with Still some Miles to Go' (2011) 2(3) *Journal of European Competition Law and Practice* 183.

[169] E. Rousseva and M. Marquis, 'Hell Freezes Over: A Climate Change for Assessing Exclusionary Conduct under Article 102 TFEU' (2012) *Journal of European Competition Law and Practice* 32.

(Forbruger-Kontakt) operate in the market for the delivery of unaddressed mail (e.g. catalogues) where the largest clients are three supermarkets (Spar, SuperBest and Coop). There
was a bout of price competition towards the end of 2003 to secure these contracts and Post
Danmark won this, but it was alleged this was done unfairly for two reasons: first, because
it offered different prices to different supermarkets (so harming competition between supermarkets); secondly, because it offered the complainant's customers discounts that it did not
give to its own customers (so harming its competitor's chances of securing the contracts).
The Danish court was content with the first finding (Article 102(1)(c) TFEU specifically
provides that harming downstream rivals may be an abuse), but they were less certain as
to whether above-cost discounts, without evidence of a strategy to eliminate competitors,
could ever be considered an abuse.

Case C–209/10 *Post Danmark A/S* v *Konkurrencerådet*, Judgment of 27 March 2012

22. … not every exclusionary effect is necessarily detrimental to competition. Competition on the merits
    may, by definition, lead to the departure from the market or the marginalisation of competitors that are
    less efficient and so less attractive to consumers from the point of view of, among other things, price,
    choice, quality or innovation. …

24. In that regard, it is also to be borne in mind that Article [102 TFEU] applies, in particular, to the conduct
    of a dominant undertaking that, through recourse to methods different from those governing normal
    competition on the basis of the performance of commercial operators, has the effect, to the detriment
    of consumers, of hindering the maintenance of the degree of competition existing in the market or the
    growth of that competition. …

36. Moreover, it is common ground that, in the present case, the prices offered to the Spar and SuperBest
    groups were assessed as being at a higher level than those average total costs, as estimated by those
    authorities. In those circumstances, it cannot be considered that such prices have anti-competitive
    effects.

37. As regards the prices charged the Coop group, a pricing policy such as that in issue in the main
    proceedings cannot be considered to amount to an exclusionary abuse simply because the price charged
    to a single customer by a dominant undertaking is lower than the average total costs attributed to
    the activity concerned, but higher than the average incremental costs pertaining to the latter, as
    respectively estimated in the case in the main proceedings.

38. Indeed, to the extent that a dominant undertaking sets its prices at a level covering the great bulk
    of the costs attributable to the supply of the goods or services in question, it will, as a general rule,
    be possible for a competitor as efficient as that undertaking to compete with those prices without
    suffering losses that are unsustainable in the long term.

39. It is for the court making the reference to assess the relevant circumstances of the case in the main
    proceedings in the light of the finding made in the previous paragraph. In any event, it is worth noting
    that it appears from the documents before the Court that Forbruger-Kontakt managed to maintain
    its distribution network despite losing the volume of mail related to the three customers involved and
    managed, in 2007, to win back the Coop group's custom and, since then, that of the Spar group.

40. If the court making the reference, after carrying out that assessment, should nevertheless make a
    finding of anti-competitive effects due to Post Danmark's actions, it should be recalled that it is open
    to a dominant undertaking to provide justification for behaviour that is liable to be caught by the
    prohibition under Article [102 TFEU].

The Court of Justice first echoes the Guidance by stating that excluding inefficient rivals is not anti-competitive, and that the detriment to consumers is the focus of inquiry; it then suggests that an effects-based approach may be utilised to establish whether below-cost pricing is an abuse of dominance; furthermore, the Court notices that in reality the anticipated exclusion has not yet occurred, which sends a strong signal to competitors that arguing a risk of exclusion when the facts show that competition is lively is something of a paradox. However, this optimistic reading of the judgment can be challenged: on the facts the competition authority had no evidence of exclusionary intent and so it could not convict. The Court of Justice here opens an alternative route by which an abuse may be found, and this runs against the Commission's policy of restricting the scope of application of Article 102 TFEU. Thus, what the previous case law might have lacked in economic sophistication, it made up for by having a safe harbour: no predation outside the parameters set out in *AKZO*. This is now eliminated because proof of effects may be deployed instead. Accordingly, the judgment opens the possibility of more litigation rather than less. Moreover, the judgment is not consistent with earlier case law that condemned above-cost price abuses, and rather than trying to distinguish that case law (as the Advocate General sought to do) the Court failed to engage with the real puzzle thrown up by the Guidance Paper: may the Court approve of this document by cutting down the scope of the concept of abuse by overruling earlier case law, and if not, how can the application of Article 102 be reformed against the established case law?

5 HIDDEN SIDE OF COMPETITION LAW ENFORCEMENT

In Chapter 21 we noted that Regulation 1/2003 formalised a procedure by which parties subject to an investigation could offer commitments to the Commission to vary their conduct and thereby eliminate the Commission's competition concerns. There we addressed the procedural concerns with this decision: absence of meaningful judicial review; the Commission's relatively stronger bargaining position, with the concomitant risk that parties make unnecessary commitments; and the doubtful precedential value of these decisions. Here we suggest that the procedural weaknesses have allowed the Commission to develop an alternative enforcement strategy by applying new and possibly questionable theories of anti-competitive conduct, and solving cases with far-reaching remedies.[170] This applies in particular to cases involving Article 102 TFEU.

The approach of commitments in energy markets provides a good case study. The Commission has tried to liberalise electricity and gas markets for some twenty years, but with little result: all EU markets remain dominated by the former state monopolist who remains vertically integrated, and this makes it hard for new entrants.[171] Commitments have been used to complement the deregulatory efforts. In Italian gas markets (where all supply is imported), ENI is dominant in the transmission markets (pipelines that take gas into Italy) as well as the wholesale and retail gas markets. The Commission accused ENI of making access to the transmission

---

[170] Y. Botteman and A. Patsa, 'Towards a More Sustainable Use of Commitment Decisions in Article 102 TFEU Cases' (2013) 1(2) *Journal of Antitrust Enforcement* 347.

[171] Communication from the Commission: Inquiry pursuant to Article 17 of Regulation 1/2003 into the European Gas and Electricity Sectors, COM(2006)851 final. This summarises the remaining barriers to open markets and was the basis of all subsequent investigations.

market for new entrants more difficult by the following strategies: refusing to offer capacity on its pipelines; making some capacity available on inconvenient terms; and strategically choosing to under-invest in increasing transmission capacity, all to protect its monopoly in the downstream markets. ENI then agreed to divest some of its transmission capacity and the Commission approved this remedy because the new owner would have no interest in protecting downstream profits and their incentives would be to use the transmission capacity in the most efficient way.[172] Note that the Commission has never attempted to secure a structural remedy in prohibition decisions, while they are frequently found in commitment decisions; furthermore, some of the suspected abuses are not well settled in the case law (e.g. under-investment). Similarly, in the German market the Commission managed to secure structural remedies so that E.ON (one of the major electricity players in Germany) agreed to divest generation capacity because it was suspected that it was under-exploiting these to create scarcity in the market and so raise prices of its electricity. It was also suspected of deterring new entrants in the market for electricity generation, inter alia, by offering shares in E.ON's generation projects. The Commission considered these to be individual abuses of a collective dominant position.[173] Again, a far-reaching remedy is imposed on theories of abuse that are not too well established in the case law. However, these two decisions serve the Union's energy policy well because they open the two national markets to new entrants.

The criticisms that are made of this style of intervention are that the Commission uses commitments to advance a range of policy goals that are regulatory in nature; moreover, that the Commission completes the liberalisation of the sector that had not been agreed to politically by the Member States.[174] Furthermore, it has been noted that these decisions are 'a new phenomenon, a peculiar "negotiated antitrust" characterised by weak cases with extensive remedies'.[175] Against this concern about overly aggressive enforcement, it has been argued that this kind of approach may be justified because it is more appropriate as a method of regulating markets well.

D. A. Crane, 'Antitrust Antifederalism' (2008) 96(1) *California Law Review* 1, 32

To be sure, there are good reasons to treat the monopolist who built a better mousetrap more favorably than the one who blew up the competitor's factory. But most monopolists do not fall neatly into one category or the other. Most secured and maintained their position through some complex combination of skill, foresight, industry, accident, luck, shrewdness, strategic behavior, manipulation, and interrelated industry features such as government-sponsored entry barriers, first-mover advantages, network effects, entrenched customer preferences due to risk-aversion and switching costs, and so forth. Even if one could define the monopolization offense in a conceptually satisfying way, one lacks the tools to apply the standard reliably given the complexity of industrial markets.

Rather than think of monopolization as a criminal and tortious affront to some competition norm, one could think about how to manage the behavior and structure of dominant corporations so as to

---

[172] Case COMP/39.315 *ENI*, Decision of 29 September 2010.
[173] Case COMP/39.*388 E.ON: German Electricity Wholesale Market*, Decision of 26 November 2008.
[174] H. Von Rosenberg, 'Unbundling Through the Back Door ... the Case of Network Divestiture as a Remedy in the Energy Sector' (2009) 30 *ECLR* 237.
[175] M. Sadowska, 'Energy Liberalization in an Antitrust Straitjacket: A Plant Too Far?' (2011) 34(3) *World Competition* 449, 471.

capture the efficiencies inherent in large aggregations of capital while minimizing the inefficiencies attendant to market power ... The crime-tort model is comparatively ill-suited for advancing consumer welfare and economic efficiency. Many commercial practices can simultaneously help and hurt consumers. For example, tying contracts that require a customer to purchase a patented product together with an unpatented product can be good for some sets of consumers but not for others since they can entail raising the price to some consumers and lowering the price to others. Asking after the fact whether such price discrimination conformed to some ephemeral legal norm and awarding damages if it did is unhelpful. What is needed is a technical appraisal of the practice and expertly designed rules to make its implementation as efficient and consumer-friendly as possible.

Crane is not writing to advocate commitment decisions, but notes the comparative advantage of the regulatory style they embody. Presently, as a result of the economic crisis, many Member States are redesigning independent regulatory agencies and merging competition authorities with other regulators.[176] It might be that this reconfiguration allows the agencies to refine this style of enforcement (as they will collaborate with utilities regulators more intensely) while developing more legitimate procedures.

FURTHER READING

P. Akman, *The Concept of Abuse in EU Competition Law: Law and Economic Approaches* (Oxford, Hart, 2012)

C.-D. Ehlermann and M. Marquis (eds.), *European Competition Law Annual 2007: A Reformed Approach to Article 82 EC* (Oxford, Hart, 2008)

G. Van Gerven and E. Navarro Varona, 'The Wood Pulp Case and the Future of Concerted Practices' (1994) 31 *CMLRev.* 575

L. Kjølbe, 'The New Commission Guidelines on the Application of Article 81(3): An Economic Approach to Article 81' (2004) *ECLR* 566

G. Monti, *EC Competition Law* (Cambridge, Cambridge University Press, 2007)

M. Motta, *Competition Policy* (Cambridge, Cambridge University Press, 2004)

R. Nazzini, *The Foundations of European Competition Law: The Objective and Principles of Article 102* (Oxford, Oxford University Press, 2011)

R. O'Donoghue and A. J. Padilla, *The Law and Economics of Article 102 TEU* (2nd edn, Oxford, Hart, 2012)

O. Odudu, *The Boundaries of EC Competition Law* (Oxford, Oxford University Press, 2006)

P. Rey and J. S. Venit, 'Parallel Trade and Pharmaceuticals: A Policy in Search of Itself' (2004) 29 *European Law Review* 176

E. Rousseva, *Rethinking Exclusionary Abuses in EU Competition Law* (Oxford, Hart, 2010)

C. Townley, *Article 81 EC and Public Policy* (Oxford, Hart, 2009)

J. Vickers, 'Abuse of Market Power' (2005) 115 *Economic Journal* F244

A. Witt, 'The Commission's Guidance Paper on Abusive Exclusionary Conduct: More Radical than it Appears?' (2010) 35(2) *European Law Review* 214

---

[176] W. E. Kovacic and D. A. Hyman, 'Competition Agency Design: What's On the Menu?' (2012) 8(3) *European Competition Journal* 527.

23

State Aid Law

CONTENTS

1 INTRODUCTION

As we noted in Chapter 16 one of the results of economic and monetary union is that the EU has considerable influence in national budgets. In this chapter we consider a specific power that the Union has had since the very beginning to control state spending: those rules that prohibit Member States from granting economic advantages to firms. In trade law, these forms of intervention go under the name of subsidies. In contrast, the EU refers to state aids because, as we show below, this term allows one to control a wider range of state intervention, for example tax exemptions or loans on preferential terms. These powers are highly controversial because they control the way states use their budgets to pursue their economic and social policies.

In section 2 we summarise the state aid rules and place them in context. Here we note that the rules make little sense when seen as part of the competition law family and make more sense if they are seen as complementing the provisions of the Treaty pertaining to the internal market. However, even then the rationale for state aid law is perhaps best explained either by paternalism or by political considerations. We also identify the key policy considerations that have informed the Commission, in particular the most recent initiatives (the State Aid Action Plan of 2005 and State Aid Modernisation of 2012) that are designed to strengthen state aid enforcement, on the one hand, and enhance the EU's industrial policy, on the other.

In section 3 we look at the most contested aspect of state aid law, the definition of state aid. We note that in determining the boundaries of this concept the Court of Justice is torn between a wide approach whereby all harmful effects of national policies are caught and a narrower approach whereby some space is left for Member States to implement national policy. It is a matter of regret that this delicate policy-balancing exercise is carried out in defining the meaning of certain words and phrases and not more openly.

In section 4 we consider the structure of enforcement and supervision in state aid law. We explain the notification procedures and note the limited powers that the Commission has to enforce the law on state aid, both when it comes to discovering infringements of EU law and when it comes to punishing Member States which have infringed the rules. The limited scope for private enforcement suggests that a more effective system is necessary and we examine how far recent policy proposals may go in this respect.

In section 5 we explore what state aid may be allowed. Since 2005, the Commission has sought to reconsider its approach to ensure state assistance was provided where it was most effective. In 2008 this reflection was affected by the banking crisis which led to the unprecedented need for states to rescue banks, and by the subsequent economic crisis, which led the Commission to rethink its state aid policy further. The upshot is that there is now a more coherent framework for state aid regulation, with the result that national expenditure is channelled to safeguard the interests of the EU. Issues pertaining to financing for services of general interest are explored in Chapter 24, which is available online.

2 ROLE OF STATE AID LAW IN THE EU

In brief, the rules on state aid provide (in Article 107(1) TFEU) that aid is forbidden when it restricts competition and has an effect on trade between Member States. However, the Commission may authorise certain types of state aid if these fall within the exemptions provided in Article 107(2) and (3) TFEU. These rules are enforced by imposing on Member States an obligation to notify state aid and on the Commission a duty to assess these measures once notified (Article 108 TFEU).

(i) Justifications for state aid control

As we will discuss in section 3 below, neither the Commission, nor the European Courts, has placed much emphasis on explaining the precise anti-competitive effects of state aids. After all, if Member State A grants a subsidy to its beef industry, the other Member States should say 'thank you' and encourage that Member State to grant that subsidy for as long as possible.[1] This is because the other states may respond by reallocating resources away from beef production into other markets. Everyone appears to be better off.

However, there are situations where the cross-border externalities are negative and this can make an economic case for state aid. First, turning to the example above again, if Member State A did not have a comparative advantage in the beef industry, then the subsidy is inefficient and so should be kept in check. This suggests that state aids can reduce efficiency, but they are not distortive of competition in an antitrust sense. It has also been suggested that state aid rules prevent subsidy wars whereby Member States compete to give more and more subsidies to their firms. Again, this is undesirable because it is wasteful, but it is not necessarily anti-competitive. However, this justification of state aid control is odd within the context of the EU because there is no coordination on corporate taxation, so merely closing off the state aid route does not remove all attempts to subsidise industries.[2]

A competition-law based explanation for forbidding state aid is that it can be used to finance a predatory pricing campaign to exclude other rivals, or can be used to weaken rivals. However, this harm depends on specific market configurations. Doubtless some would welcome the requirement that the Commission develop a theory of anti-competitive harm before applying the state aid rules, because this would render them much less widely applicable. For instance, some have suggested that state aid should only be caught if it is likely to harm a competitor as efficient as the beneficiary.[3] Applying this test, few measures would fall within Article 107 TFEU: although in most cases the beneficiary is in a better position, this is not likely to allow it to reduce consumer welfare.[4]

Another line of argument that supports state aid rules is paternalism: states are likely to spend money unwisely at times, so a regime that keeps some external check on the ways Member States use their budget may be desirable. This is not so much because of the lack of wise politicians, more to do with the ability of private interest groups to twist economic policy to favour their interests. Research has shown that the allocation of state aid is largely determined by political factors as opposed to economic ones.[5] According to some this may be the better way to explain the institutional design of the EU state aid rules: they are forbidden unless they genuinely confer a benefit.[6]

This overview supports the view that state aid law should not be examined through the lens of conventional competition law, because it has closer affinities to the internal market rules in the EU Treaties. In other words, the harm that the rules cause is to the normal

---

[1] A. O. Sykes, 'The Questionable Case for Subsidies Regulation: A Comparative Perspective' (2010) 2(2) *Journal of Legal Analysis* 473.

[2] D. Spector, 'State Aids: Economic Analysis and Practice in the European Union' in X. Vives (ed.), *Competition Policy in the EU: Fifty Years on from the Treaty of Rome* (Oxford, Oxford University Press, 2009) 183. However, as we see below, EU state aid law increasingly controls national tax regimes. See C. H. Panayi, 'State Aid and Tax: The Third Way?' (2004) 32 *Intertax* 283.

[3] C. Ahlborn and C. Berg, 'Can State Aid Control Learn from Antitrust?' in A. Biondi, P. Eeckhout and J. Flynn (eds.), *The Law of State Aid in the European Union* (Oxford, Oxford University Press, 2004).

[4] See e.g. Case C-279/08P *Commission v The Netherlands* [2011] ECR I-07671, para. 132, agreeing that a mere strengthening of the position of the beneficiary suffices to show harm to competition.

[5] D. J. Neven, 'The Political Economy of State Aids: Econometric Evidence for the Member States' in D. J. Neven and L. H. Röller (eds.), *The Political Economy of Industrial Policy: Does Europe Have an Industrial Policy* (Berlin, Sigma, 2000).

[6] See Spector, n. 2 above.

functioning of the market. One disadvantage of this approach to state aid control is that almost any aid can be prohibited, as the line between good and bad aids becomes more difficult to draw.

(ii) Commission's state aid policy

It was not until the 1990s that the Commission began to prioritise state aid enforcement, thus challenging national policies.[7] This was part of a broader 'public turn' in enforcement, as the Commission also tackled undertakings that had been provided privileged positions by the state, thereby deregulating a number of economic sectors, like telecommunications and energy.[8] Having secured a legitimate space for state aid policy, and having had its approach supported but also circumscribed by the Court of Justice, the Commission was well placed to move to a second phase where it would give its enforcement policy more coherence. To the extent that data is available, it appears to demonstrate a correlation between increased state aid enforcement and a reduction of state aid: there has been a downward trend since the 1980s (when aid was 2 per cent of GDP), down to 1 per cent of GDP in the 1990s and down to 0.5 per cent of GDP since 2004, save for a spike upwards in 2006.[9] In the last five years the numbers are skewed upwards because of the massive amounts committed to rescue the financial sector, but also downwards because the recession and fiscal discipline makes states less able to spend.

In 2005 the Commission launched a major policy document, the State Aid Action Plan. Its key theme is found in its subtitle: 'less and better targeted state aid'.[10] The first prong entails stronger enforcement powers, while the second suggests that state aid should not be banned entirely but redirected. In particular, the Commission has pushed for Member States to move their spending away from specific industries and towards horizontal policies. Horizontal aid includes aid for research, development and innovation, safeguarding the environment, fostering energy saving and promoting the use of renewable energy sources, regional development, aid to SMEs, job creation and the promotion of training. These schemes (as opposed to aid to a named beneficiary) are said to be more likely to contribute to Union objectives and are also less likely to be distortive of competition. Around 87 per cent of state aid is now granted for horizontal measures.[11]

The reorientation of national state aid policy to serving the EU's agenda is even more pronounced in the current reform programme.

Communication from the Commission, State Aid Modernisation, COM(2012)209 final

12. Modernised State aid control should facilitate the treatment of aid which is well-designed, targeted at identified market failures and objectives of common interest, and least distortive ('good aid').

---

[7] M. G. Ross, 'State Aids: Maturing into a Constitutional Problem' (1995) 15 *Yearbook of European Law* 79.

[8] D. J. Gerber, *Law and Competition in Twentieth Century Europe* (Oxford, Oxford University Press, 1998) ch. 10.

[9] European Commission, *State Aid Scoreboard*, COM(2012)778 final, 7.

[10] Commission State Aid Action Plan, Less and Better Targeted State Aid: A Roadmap for State Aid Reform 2005–2009, COM(2005)107 final.

[11] Commission Staff Working Paper, *Facts and Figures on State Aid in the EU Member States*, SEC(2012)443 final, 11–13.

This shall ensure that public support stimulates innovation, green technologies, human capital development, avoids environmental harm and ultimately promotes growth, employment and EU competitiveness. Such aid will best contribute to growth when it targets a market failure and thereby complements, not replaces, private spending. State aid will be effective in achieving the desired public policy objective only when it has an incentive effect, i.e. it induces the aid beneficiary to undertake activities it would not have done without the aid. And State aid will have the greatest impact on growth only when it is designed in a way which limits competition distortions and keeps the internal market competitive and open. Therefore State aid control is crucial in order to improve the efficiency and effectiveness of public spending taking the form of State aid, with the overarching objective of spurring more growth in internal market, for which a necessary condition is developing competition. State aid which does not target market failures and has no incentive effect is not only a waste of public resources but it acts as a brake to growth by worsening competitive conditions in the internal market.

13. State aid control already underpins the Europe 2020 flagships. For example, the broadband guidelines provide conditions for efficient State support to broadband rollout, supporting the achievement of the objectives of 'Digital agenda for Europe'. Public support to develop infrastructure is also instrumental to the achievement of smart, upgraded and fully interconnected transport and energy networks as foreseen by 'Resource efficient Europe'. The framework for State aid to research, development and innovation facilitates the achievement of 'Innovation Union' as well as 'An industrial policy for the globalisation era' objectives. The enforcement of 'polluter pays' principle as well as a possibility to provide aid in order to encourage companies to go beyond mandatory EU environmental standards or to promote energy efficiency provided for in the Environmental aid guidelines are one of the tools to implement 'Resource efficient Europe' flagship. The possibility to support training with State funds contributes to the goals of 'An agenda for new skills and jobs'. Rescue and restructuring aid guidelines allow State aid to ailing companies only under strict conditions and if it results in their return to long-term viability, encouraging thereby exit of inefficient firms and bracing the companies for global competition, contributing to 'An industrial policy for a globalised era'. The link between the Europe 2020 objectives and flagship initiatives on the one hand, and State aid rules on the other, should be further developed to streamline the Commission's instruments and to encourage Member States to direct scarce public resources to common priorities.

14. By putting an emphasis on the quality and the efficiency of public support, State aid control can also help Member States to strengthen budgetary discipline and improve the quality of public finances – resulting in a better use of taxpayers' money. It is particularly important in order to achieve smart fiscal consolidation, reconciling the role of targeted public spending in generating growth with the need to bring budgets under control. There is therefore also a need to embed State aid control and more general competition concerns in the EU Semester procedure.

15. Robust State aid control is also essential to ensure a well functioning single market. Such robust control goes hand in hand with the effective implementation of EU internal market rules and is of particular relevance in markets that have only recently been opened and where large incumbents aided by the State still play a major role, such as transport, postal services or, in more limited cases, energy. State aid modernisation can improve the functioning of the internal market through a more effective policy aimed at limiting distortions of competition, preserving a level playing field and combating protectionism. This role of State aid becomes more important now as we need to mobilise the full potential of the internal market for growth.

This stance is quite different from the early days of state aid enforcement when the frameworks for assessing which aid should be authorised 'emerged directly from Member State preferences'.[12] Having noted the Commission's entrepreneurship, it must be recalled that other stakeholders can also act as policy entrepreneurs. One telling example is how the Assembly of European Regions steered the agenda over state support for regional airports (which came up in the context of the *Ryanair/Charleroi* case discussed below) and appeared to have secured a policy change that favoured the use of state aid to support regional development.[13] Lobbying and high level politics are an inextricable feature of state aid enforcement.[14] Having said that, the strategies of Member States change as state aid law becomes institutionalised: whereas resistance against the Commission was once possible, now that the legitimacy of state aid control is much more well-established, Member States must channel their strategies through the prism of the Commission's policy. This strengthens the enforcement hand of the Commission even if, as we detail below, the formal powers it has are weak.[15]

3 MEANING OF STATE AID

The definition of what measures constitute state aid is highly contested. This is for procedural and substantive reasons. At a procedural level, once a measure is found to be state aid, then the Member State must notify it to the Commission and wait for approval; moreover, the Commission may determine that the aid cannot be given or may only be granted if modified, and the Member State must report to the Commission on the implementation of the aid.[16] It should also be borne in mind that national courts play a central role in the definition of state aid: the only segment of the state aid rules to have direct effect is Article 108(3) TFEU (the duty to notify aid), and parties will seek to enforce this obligation as a means of securing a remedy (whether repayment of tax, or damages). This gives the Court of Justice a key role in determining the contours of the notion of state aid through preliminary rulings.

> ### Article 107(1) TFEU
>
> 1. Save as otherwise provided in the Treaties, any aid granted by a Member State or through State resources in any form whatsoever which distorts or threatens to distort competition by favouring certain undertakings or the production of certain goods shall, in so far as it affects trade between Member States, be incompatible with the internal market.

---

[12] M. P. Smith, 'Autonomy by the Rules: The European Commission and the Development of State Aid Policy' (1998) 36(1) *JCMS* 55, 59.

[13] D. C. Christopoulos, 'Relational Attributes of Political Entrepreneurs: A Network Perspective' (2006) 13(5) *JEPP* 757, 763–6.

[14] W. Bishop, 'From Trade to Tutelage: State Aid and Public Choice' in I. Govaere, R. Quck and M. Brockners (eds.), *The European Union in Trade and Competition Law in the EU and Beyond* (Cheltenham, Edward Elgar, 2011).

[15] For an absorbing account, see P. Le Galès, 'Est Maître Celui Qui Les Organise: How Rules Change when National and European Policy Domains Collide' in A. Stone Sweet, W. Sandholts and N. Fligstein (eds.), *The Institutionalisation of Europe* (Oxford, Oxford University Press, 2004).

[16] This reporting obligation was used to determine that a Member State could appeal even against a Commission Decision that had found that a measure was state aid but had authorised it. The Member State's interest in having the decision quashed on the definition of aid is that it relieves it from having its measures reviewed by the Commission. Case C-279/08P *Commission* v *Netherlands* [2011] ECR I-07671.

At a substantive level, the precise boundaries of this provision have been contested. Since the early days the Court has maintained the view that its approach to interpreting this provision is by considering the effects of the measures in question.[17] However, as we will see from the case-law below, this approach has been tempered by the recognition that certain national policy considerations justify a narrower approach. The search for a balance between regulating all measures that affect the market and the respect for national policy characterises the case law.[18]

Looking at the case law in the round, the following elements must be shown for this provision to apply: (i) an intervention by the Member State or through state resources; (ii) the intervention gives the recipient an advantage; (iii) the intervention is selective (for example, it is available only for specific companies or industry sectors, or to companies located in specific regions); (iv) an effect on trade and a restriction of competition.

(i) Intervention by the Member State or through state resources

(a) Necessary involvement of state resources

The first criterion is potentially very broad, for the test reads that the Member State may intervene either by committing resources, or in some other way (recall Article 107(1) TFEU speaks of intervention by the state *or* through state resources). This literal interpretation was rejected by the Court of Justice. In one of the seminal cases, a German law provided that national labour law protections were not applicable to ships registered in Germany but employing non-EU crew members. It is obvious that this measure is a form of state intervention that gives the ship owners who recruit non EU-workers a competitive advantage over those who recruit EU nationals because they face lower costs. However, the Court held that the measure did not require the expenditure of state resources and so was not state aid.

Joined Cases C-72/91 and C-73/91 *Firma Sloman Neptun Schiffahrts AG v Seebetriebsrat Bodo Ziesemer der Sloman Neptun Schiffahrts AG* **[1993] ECR I-887**

19. ...only advantages which are granted directly or indirectly through State resources are to be regarded as State aid within the meaning of Article [107(1) TFEU]. The wording of this provision itself and the procedural rules laid down in Article [108 TFEU] show that advantages granted from resources other than those of the State do not fall within the scope of the provisions in question. The distinction between aid granted by the State and aid granted through State resources serves to bring within the definition of aid not only aid granted directly by the State, but also aid granted by public or private bodies designated or established by the State....

21. The system at issue does not seek, through its object and general structure, to create an advantage which would constitute an additional burden for the State or the abovementioned bodies, but only to

---

[17] Case 173/73 *Italy* v *Commission* [1973] ECR 709.
[18] Case 61/79 *Amministrazione delle finanze dello stato* v *Denkavit* [1980] ECR 1205, 1288, where the Court recognised this consequence.

alter in favour of shipping undertakings the framework within which contractual relations are formed between those undertakings and their employees. The consequences arising from this, in so far as they relate to the difference in the basis for the calculation of social security contributions, mentioned by the national court, and to the potential loss of tax revenue because of the low rates of pay, referred to by the Commission, are inherent in the system and are not a means of granting a particular advantage to the undertakings concerned.

This approach has also served to exclude Italian legislation that exempted the post office from the statutory duty to grant its employees contracts of indefinite duration,[19] and the exclusion of small and medium-sized undertakings from the national laws of unfair dismissal.[20] In a further controversial development, the Court of Justice also excluded the provisions of a German electricity law. This required electricity distributors to purchase (at a fixed minimum price) electricity generated from renewable sources. In addition, generators of electricity from conventional sources had to pay extra to the distributors for the costs incurred. The effect of this measure was certainly to benefit the generators of renewable energy, but the Court nevertheless held that this was not state aid.

Case C-379/98 *PreussenElektra AG* v *Schhleswag AG* [2001] ECR I-2099

59. In this case, the obligation imposed on private electricity supply undertakings to purchase electricity produced from renewable energy sources at fixed minimum prices does not involve any direct or indirect transfer of State resources to undertakings which produce that type of electricity.

60. Therefore, the allocation of the financial burden arising from that obligation for those private electricity supply undertakings as between them and other private undertakings cannot constitute a direct or indirect transfer of State resources either.

61. In those circumstances, the fact that the purchase obligation is imposed by statute and confers an undeniable advantage on certain undertakings is not capable of conferring upon it the character of State aid within the meaning of Article [107(1) TFEU].

62. That conclusion cannot be undermined by the fact, pointed out by the referring court, that the financial burden arising from the obligation to purchase at minimum prices is likely to have negative repercussions on the economic results of the undertakings subject to that obligation and therefore entail a diminution in tax receipts for the State. That consequence is an inherent feature of such a legislative provision and cannot be regarded as constituting a means of granting to producers of electricity from renewable energy sources a particular advantage at the expense of the State.

63. In the alternative, the Commission maintains that, in order to preserve the effectiveness of Articles [107 and 108 TFEU], read in conjunction with Article [4(3) TEU], it is necessary for the concept of State aid to be interpreted in such a way as to include support measures which, like those laid down by the amended Stromeinspeisungsgesetz, are decided upon by the State but financed by private undertakings. It draws that argument by analogy from the case-law of the Court of Justice to the effect that Article 101 TFEU, read in conjunction with Article 4(3) of the Treaty, prohibits Member States from introducing

---

[19] Joined Cases C-52–54/97 *Epifanio Viscido* v *Ente Poste Italiane* [1998] ECR I-2629.
[20] Case C-189/91 *Kirsammer-Hack* v *Nurhan Sidal* [1993] ECR I-6185.

measures, even of a legislative or regulatory nature, which may render the competition rules applicable to undertakings ineffective.

64. In that respect, it is sufficient to point out that, unlike Article 101 of the Treaty, which concerns only the conduct of undertakings, Article 107 of the Treaty refers directly to measures emanating from the Member States.

65. In those circumstances, Article 107 of the Treaty is in itself sufficient to prohibit the conduct by States referred to therein and Article 4(3) of the TEU, the second paragraph of which provides that Member States are to abstain from any measure which could jeopardise the attainment of the objectives of the Treaty, cannot be used to extend the scope of Article 107 to conduct by States that does not fall within it.

In both of the cases above the Commission had argued in favour of a wide interpretation under which both measures would have fallen within the scope of Article 107 TFEU.[21] There are two responses to these judgments: one is that the Court of Justice showed some sensitivity to national policy measures and so tempered the breadth of the state aid rules. This is particularly convincing in the context of labour relations, for had the Court ruled otherwise it would have meant that the Commission would become competent to evaluate 'the entire social and economic life of a Member State'.[22] The second is that the case law risks undermining the rules on state aid, for it seems quite easy to circumvent the application of Article 107(1), and this is especially so after *Preussen Elektra* since one can force private parties to pay the beneficiary and omit the deployment of state resources. Moreover, the definition leads to some odd results. In *Essent*, electricity customers paid a surcharge that went to a body controlled by the state who then distributed these funds to the energy producers. This then was state aid because the funds were channelled through the state.[23] The distinction between this and *Preussen Elektra* is not persuasive.[24]

(b) State involvement

As observed above, measures are state aid if the Member State's resources are engaged. However, this is not sufficient. It must also be shown that the state is involved in the adoption of the measure in question. This is not an issue when the advantage is allocated by central or local government, but state involvement must be proven when a third party is responsible for the measure. In *Pearle*, an association of opticians in the Netherlands asked the Central Industry Board for Skilled Trades (a trade association) to finance a collective advertising campaign for opticians' businesses. The Board did this by imposing a levy on all opticians. The plaintiffs considered this levy was illegal state aid and sought their money back.

---

[21] Joined Cases C-72/9' and C-73/91 *Firma Sloman Neptun Schiffahrts AG v Seebetriebsrat Bodo Ziesemer der Sloman Neptun Schiffahrts AG* [1993] ECR I-887, para. 17.

[22] *Epifanio Viscido*, n. 19 above, Opinion of Advocate General Jacobs, para. 16.

[23] C-206/06 *Essent Netwerk Noord and others* [2008] ECR I-5497. *Preussen Elektra* was also distinguished in Case C-262/12 *Vent de Colère and others*, Judgment of 19 December 2013, where the excess charges paid by consumers were held by a public entity before being passed on to the beneficiaries.

[24] See generally K. Talus, *EU Energy Law and Policy: A Critical Account* (Oxford, Oxford University Press, 2013) 142–4.

Case C–345/02 Pearle BV, Hans Prijs Optiek Franchise BV and Rinck Opticiëns BV v Hoofdbedrijfschap Ambachten [2004] ECR I–7139

36. Even if the Board is a public body, it does not in the circumstances of the case appear that the advertising campaign was funded by resources made available to the national authorities. On the contrary, the judgment making the reference makes it clear that the monies used by the Board for the purpose of funding the advertising campaign were collected from its members who benefited from the campaign by means of compulsory levies earmarked for the organisation of that advertising campaign. Since the costs incurred by the public body for the purposes of that campaign were offset in full by the levies imposed on the undertakings benefiting therefrom, the Board's action did not tend to create an advantage which would constitute an additional burden for the State or that body.

37. Furthermore, the file clearly shows that the initiative for the organisation and operation of that advertising campaign was that of the NUVO, a private association of opticians, and not that of the Board. As the Advocate General pointed out ... the Board served merely as a vehicle for the levying and allocating of resources collected for a purely commercial purpose previously determined by the trade and which had nothing to do with a policy determined by the Netherlands authorities.

Establishing the role of the state is particularly difficult in cases where the funds are in the hands of a company where the state is a shareholder. Here the question of whether the state is responsible for an investment made by the company hinges on the degree of control the state has in the company's activities.[25]

(ii) Intervention gives the recipient an advantage

In determining whether the Member State's financing confers an advantage, one asks whether under 'normal market conditions' that undertaking would have secured a comparable advantage.[26] One way of testing for this is to ask if the measures taken by the state are like those which would have been taken by a private investor. If so, then the state has made an economically rational investment and so there is no advantage because the undertaking would likely have secured a similar advantage from private funds. This test was first developed in cases where the state invests in a company: would a private investor have taken the same kind of risk, considering the likely returns of this investment? This test is controversial: the state will often invest in its companies for reasons other than profit, but which may make economic sense – saving a company is better than having to deal with the social fallout from insolvency, for example. However the Court of Justice has insisted that when one compares public and private investors, the only criterion is the expected economic gains from the investment.[27]

This approach, known as the 'private investor test' has been applied to a wide range of measures where the state participates in the market. For example, loans and the terms of the loan can be analysed by considering whether a private investor would have made the loan, and if so whether on terms similar to those set by the state. It is even applicable when the state is

---

[25] See Case C-482/99 *France v Commission (Stardust Marine)* [2002] ECR I-4397.
[26] Case C-342/96 *Spain v Commission* [1999] ECR I-02459, para. 412.
[27] Case 303/88 *Italy v Commission* [1991] ECR I-1603; Case C-278/92 *Spain v Commission* [1994] ECR I-4103.

owed money but does not clam it because it considers it more prudent to allow the undertaking to keep the money and invest it. There are practical difficulties in applying this test, and in many instances the Commission has been criticised for failing to take into account all the evidence.[28] An interesting illustration is the *Ryanair/Charleroi* Decision. Here, the Walloon region in Belgium (the owner of Charleroi airport) and Brussels South Charleroi Airport (BSCA, a public undertaking controlled by the Walloon region) offered a number of inducements for Ryanair to land its planes at Charleroi. The Walloon region offered reduced landing charges, while BSCA offered payments for (among others) hotel costs, training staff and bonuses for new routes that Ryanair opened from Charleroi. The commercial logic of the transaction was that by giving Ryanair incentives to invest in the airport, there would be benefits to both the airport and the region. The Commission took the view that the measures of the two actors should be assessed separately. It held that the measures taken by the Walloon region were carried out in the exercise of its public functions, and so could not be assessed using the private investor test. BSCA's activities were instead assessed using the private investor test and the Commission ruled that the risk taken by BSCA was excessive. Some of the aid was authorised, but some was to be recovered. On appeal, the General Court quashed the decision. First, it held that the two entities should have been regarded as a single actor because of the close legal and economic links between them. Then the Court turned to the question of how to assess the measures taken by the Walloon region.

Case T–196/04 *Ryanair Ltd* v *Commission* [2008] ECR II-3643

85. While it is clearly necessary, when the State acts as an undertaking operating as a private investor, to analyse its conduct by reference to the private investor principle, application of that principle must be excluded in the event that the State acts as a public authority. In the latter event, the conduct of the State can never be compared to that of an operator or private investor in a market economy....

88. Contrary to what is stated by the Commission ... it must be held that the actions of the Walloon Region were economic activities. The fixing of the amount of landing charges and the accompanying indemnity is an activity directly connected with the management of airport infrastructure, which is an economic activity.

89. On that point, the airport charges fixed by the Walloon Region must be regarded as remuneration for the provision of services within Charleroi airport, notwithstanding the fact ... that a clear and direct link between the level of charges and the service rendered to users is weak....

91. Accordingly, the provision of airport facilities by a public authority to airlines, and the management of those facilities, in return for payment of a fee the amount of which is freely fixed by that authority, can be described as economic activities; although such activities are carried out in the public sector, they cannot, for that reason alone, be categorised as the exercise of public authority powers. Those activities are not, by reason of their nature, their purpose or the rules to which they are subject, connected with the exercise of powers which are typically those of a public authority.

92. The fact that the Walloon Region is a public authority and that it is the owner of airport facilities in public ownership does not therefore in itself mean that it cannot, in the present case, be regarded as an entity exercising an economic activity....

---

[28] See e.g. Case C-483/99 *Commission* v *France* [2002] ECR I-04781 and Case T-98/00 *Linde* v *Commission* [2002] ECR II-03961.

98. When examining the measures at issue, the Commission should have differentiated between the economic activities and those activities which fell strictly under public authority powers. In addition, whether the conduct of an authority granting aid complies with national law is not a factor which should be taken into account in order to decide whether that authority acted in accordance with the private investor principle or granted an economic advantage in contravention of Article 87(1) EC. It does not follow from the fact that an activity represents in legal terms an exemption from a tariff scale laid down in a regulation that that activity must be described as non-economic....

101. The mere fact that, in the present case, the Walloon Region has regulatory powers in relation to fixing airport charges does not mean that a scheme reducing those charges ought not to be examined by reference to the private investor principle, since such a scheme could have been put in place by a private operator.

It follows that excessive formalism is unhelpful: states are hybrid entities, sometimes performing state functions but increasingly they are also market actors. Furthermore, the decision also contains a flaw that the judgment did not cure: as noted earlier, the deal made commercial sense, and had any other airline offered similar traffic to any other airport it would have received similar treatment by the authorities. It follows that the anti-competitive impact is not that one airline has an edge over the others. Rather, competition among airports is distorted by one region spending to enhance its airport at the expense of others.[29]

In cases where the state does act as a public authority, the private investor test is not applicable but then the advantage is self-evident because but for the state's intervention there is no other way that the undertaking would have benefited in the same way. A good illustration is the reduction in social security contributions arranged by France in certain underperforming economic sectors.[30] The French Government argued that the benefit received by the undertakings merely compensated them for the costs incurred in favour of their employees. The Court of Justice rejected this on two grounds: first by noting simply that the offsetting of costs did not remove the advantage, for according to well-established case law an advantage includes a measure that mitigates the charges which are normally included in the budget of an undertaking.[31] Secondly, the Court also noted that the agreements between employers and employees that had been renegotiated did not only entail costs, but were designed to boost the competitiveness of the undertaking in the longer term. Accordingly it would be invidious to see those expenses as costs without also considering the expected gains the undertakings would make. On this ground the claim that the reduced charges were compensating a loss became less convincing.[32]

(iii) Intervention is selective

Applying the selectivity test requires one to distinguish between general measures of economic policy and measures that benefit certain undertakings at the expense of others in a comparable situation. For instance, if the rate of company taxation is cut for everyone, this is a general

[29] F. Gröteke and W. Kerber, *The Case of Ryanair: EU State Aid Policy on the Wrong Runway*, Marburger volkswirtschaftliche Beiträge No. 2004/13.
[30] Case C-251/97 *France v Commission* [1999] ECR 6639.
[31] Case 30/59 *De Gezamenlijke Steenkolenmijnen in Limburg v High Authority* [1961] ECR 1, 19.
[32] Case C-251/97 *France v Commission* [1999] ECR 6639, para. 46.

measure, even if it confers on all firms in that country a comparative advantage over firms located elsewhere. On the other hand, if a tax exemption is given to doctors then this is selective and qualifies as state aid.[33] The Court of Justice goes beyond appearances and looks at the operation of schemes. For example, in *Kimberly Clark* the Court ruled that a scheme, which appeared generally applicable, was in fact selective because of the wide discretion enjoyed by the body in charge of administering it, so that certain undertakings would receive advantages and others not.[34] One of the major difficulties in applying this test is that it is not always clear how the test is to be applied. It is convenient to distinguish two scenarios: geographical selectivity and material selectivity.

(a) Geographical selectivity

What happens when the local government of a region takes a measure designed to benefit those doing business there? The legislature of the Azores archipelago, for example, decided to support the local economy by imposing a lower rate of tax on firms in the Azores than on firms elsewhere in Portugal. Was this a general measure because it was determined by the government of a region? In answering this question the Court of Justice distinguished three scenarios.

Case C-88/03 *Portugal v Commission* [2006] ECR I-7115

64. In the first situation, the central government unilaterally decides that the applicable national tax rate should be reduced within a defined geographic area. The second situation corresponds to a model for distribution of tax competences in which all the local authorities at the same level (regions, districts or others) have the autonomous power to decide, within the limit of the powers conferred on them, the tax rate applicable in the territory within their competence. The Commission has recognised, as have the Portuguese and United Kingdom Governments, that a measure taken by a local authority in the second situation is not selective because it is impossible to determine a normal tax rate capable of constituting the reference framework.

65. In the third situation described, a regional or local authority adopts, in the exercise of sufficiently autonomous powers in relation to the central power, a tax rate lower than the national rate and which is applicable only to undertakings present in the territory within its competence.

66. In the latter situation, the legal framework appropriate to determine the selectivity of a tax measure may be limited to the geographical area concerned where the infra-State body, in particular on account of its status and powers, occupies a fundamental role in the definition of the political and economic environment in which the undertakings present on the territory within its competence operate.

67. As the Advocate General pointed out in paragraph 54 of his Opinion, in order that a decision taken in such circumstances can be regarded as having been adopted in the exercise of sufficiently autonomous powers, that decision must, first of all, have been taken by a regional or local authority which has, from a constitutional point of view, a political and administrative status separate from that of the central government. Next, it must have been adopted without the central government being able to directly intervene as regards its content. Finally, the financial consequences of a reduction of the national tax rate for undertakings in the region must not be offset by aid or subsidies from other regions or central government.

---

[33] Case C-172/03 *Wolfgang Heiser v Finanzamt Innsbruck* [2005] ECR I-1627.
[34] Case C-241/94 *France v Commission* [1996] ECR I-4551.

> **68.** It follows that political and fiscal independence of central government which is sufficient as regards the application of Community rules on State aid presupposes, as the United Kingdom Government submitted, that the infra-State body not only has powers in the territory within its competence to adopt measures reducing the tax rate, regardless of any considerations related to the conduct of the central State, but that in addition it assumes the political and financial consequences of such a measure.

On the facts, the case fell under the third heading and the Court of Justice found that the measures were in effect subsidised by the central government, so the measure was selective.[35] This approach is relatively clear but constitutionally controversial.[36] In particular, it requires the Court of Justice or national courts to investigate on questions that are deeply sensitive, such as whether the Basque Country is sufficiently autonomous that its corporation tax is a general measure.[37] Nevertheless the judgment in *Azores* is to be welcomed, especially given that in some Member States we have asymmetric devolution (that is, some regions have greater independence than others) so that a fact-intensive inquiry is appropriate.

(b) Material selectivity

If the measures apply to the whole territory of a Member State, selectivity is normally easier to ascertain when some undertakings are excluded. Measures that benefit only small or only large undertakings are selective.[38] Measures benefiting only certain manufacturers, or public undertakings, are also selective.[39] It should be noted that there is no requirement that the beneficiaries of the measure and those that are excluded are actual or potential competitors. This is probably justified by the role state aid law plays in fostering the internal market: the Court of Justice could not find that a measure benefitting an entire industry sector would constitute state aid when it would have adverse effects on competitors in other Member States, thus tax measures favouring Italian road hauliers, or a reduction in Belgian social security contributions for employers in determined sectors, are both examples of selective measures.[40] The concern, however, is that it becomes very difficult to implement any advantage-conferring policy that is not selective in scope. This would mean that a considerable amount of national legislation should be reviewed by the Commission: for example, most tax legislation contains exemptions of one sort or another but it cannot be that every such exemption is a state aid.

---

[35] Case C-88/03 *Portugal* v *Commission* [2006] ECR I-7115, paras. 71–9.

[36] R. Greaves, 'Autonomous Regions, Taxation and EC State Aid Rules' (2009) 34 *ELRev.* 779.

[37] Joined Cases C-428–434/06 *Unión General de Trabajadores de La Rioja (UGT-Rioja) and others* v *Juntas Generales del Territorio Histórico de Vizcaya and others* [2008] ECR I-06747.

[38] Respectively, see Case C-409/00 *Spain* v *Commission* [2003] ECR I-01487 and Case C-200/97 *Ecotrade* v *Altiforni e Ferriere di Servola* [1998] ECR I-07907.

[39] Respectively, see Case 248/84 *Germany* v *Commission* [1987] ECR 04013 and Case C-222/04 *Cassa di Risparmio di Firenze and others* [2006] ECR I-00289.

[40] See Case C-6/97 *Italy* v *Commission* [1999] ECR I-02981; Case C-75/97 *Belgium* v *Commission* [1999] ECR I-03671. For an example of indirect selectivity, see Case 173/73 *Italy* v *Commission* [1974] ECR 709. For discussion, B. Kurcz and D. Vallindas, 'Can General Measures be … Selective? Some Thoughts on the Interpretation of a State Aid Definition' (2008) 45 *CMLRev.* 159, suggesting that there seems little real scope for general measures.

To counter this risk the Court of Justice has tried to develop an approach by which a scheme which is selective on its face may not constitute state aid when the selection is justified by the scheme in question.[41] The scope of this justification is contested, and a spate of litigation has served to sharpen the focus. In *Adria-Wien Pipeline*, Austrian legislation granted an energy tax rebate to goods manufacturers, to the exclusion of service providers. This was selective in that some persons in Austria benefited and others did not, but is this enough?

Case C-143/99 *Adria-Wien Pipeline GmbH and Wietersdorfer and Peggauer Zementwerke GmbH* v *Finanzlandesdirektion für Kärnten* [2001] ECR I-8365

42. According to the case-law of the Court, a measure which, although conferring an advantage on its recipient, is justified by the nature or general scheme of the system of which it is part does not fulfil that condition of selectivity.

43. The Austrian Government points out that the introduction of the energy taxes and their rebate was not adopted as an isolated measure but in the context of the Strukturanpassungsgesetz of 1996, which provides for an overall package of measures intended to consolidate the budget. That package, composed of general socially balanced measures affecting all socio-professional groups, should be considered as a whole.

44. The Austrian Government also points out that, frequently in this type of overall package, new measures affecting a category of operators disproportionately are not fully applicable to that category during the implementation phase. The justification for restricting energy tax rebates to undertakings manufacturing goods lies in the very fact that they are proportionately more affected than others by those taxes....

49. Second, any justification for the grant of advantages to undertakings whose activity consists primarily in the production of goods is not to be found in the nature or general scheme of the taxation system established under the Strukturanpassungsgesetz of 1996.

50. For one thing, undertakings supplying services may, just like undertakings manufacturing goods, be major consumers of energy and incur energy taxes above 0.35% of their net production value – the threshold above which undertakings manufacturing principally goods are eligible for the energy tax rebate.

51. There is nothing in the national legislation at issue to support the conclusion that the rebate scheme restricted to undertakings which primarily manufacture goods is a purely temporary measure enabling them to adapt gradually to the new scheme because they are disproportionately affected by it, as the Austrian Government maintains.

52. For another thing, the ecological considerations underlying the national legislation at issue do not justify treating the consumption of natural gas or electricity by undertakings supplying services differently than the consumption of such energy by undertakings manufacturing goods. Energy consumption by each of those sectors is equally damaging to the environment.

53. It follows from the foregoing considerations that, although objective, the criterion applied by the national legislation at issue is not justified by the nature or general scheme of that legislation, so that it cannot save the measure at issue from being in the nature of State aid.

54. Besides, as the Commission has rightly observed, the statement of reasons for the bill which led to the enactment of the national legislation at issue indicates that the advantageous terms granted to undertakings manufacturing goods were intended to preserve the competitiveness of the manufacturing sector, in particular within the Community.

---

[41] Case 173/73 *Italy* v *Commission* [1974] ECR 709, para. 33.

While the arguments were unsuccessful in this case, the point to note is that the answer to whether a measure is selective or not hinges on the objectives of the measure. This test is quite difficult to apply: neither the temporary protection afforded to some undertakings, nor the environmental considerations pleaded were proven on the facts. But, if they were, would this matter? The dominant view is that arguments to justify an apparent selection are only applicable in cases where the selectivity is designed to ensure the regulatory system in question works, and it is not a means of introducing public policy justifications. For example, in *GIL Insurance*, British tax legislation imposed a higher tax rate on insurance sold together with certain goods or services. The Court of Justice found that this was driven by the concern that many sellers in this market were manipulating the price of the insurance and that the higher tax rate was designed to deter this. Accordingly the selectivity was justified to preserve the functioning of the tax system.[42] This can be contrasted with the assessment in *British Aggregates*. The British Government imposed a tax on 'aggregates' (these are building materials, made of fragments of rock, sand and gravel) but exempted substitutes that were recycled or byproducts. It was estimated that the tax (so-called aggregated levy, AGL) would reduce the demand of virgin aggregates by 20 per cent, and the government sought to justify the tax regime by reference to the environmental costs of aggregate extraction. The General Court was sympathetic to this approach, but the Court of Justice did not consider that the selectivity was justified, because the environmental motivation was not inherent in the scheme, and required the General Court to think again.[43]

Case T–210/02 RENV *British Aggregates Association* v *Commission*, Judgment of 7 March 2012

84. ...a distinction must be made between, on the one hand, the objectives attributed to a particular tax regime and which are extrinsic to it and, on the other, the mechanisms inherent in the tax system itself which are necessary for the achievement of such objectives, since, as basic or guiding principles of the tax system in question, those objectives and mechanisms could support such justification, which it is for the Member State to demonstrate.

85. ...the environmental objective of the AGL is essentially designed to encourage a shift in demand for 'primary' aggregates in the construction industry towards 'secondary' aggregates, which are the by-products of or waste from other processes, as well as towards 'recycled' aggregates, although that general definition does not distinguish between the various materials from which such aggregates can be obtained. The criteria determining the 'normal' nature of the taxation provided for under the AGL and that objective are thus the basic or guiding principles of the Act, on the basis of which any justification for tax differentiation must be assessed.

86. In the light of the matters put forward by the applicant, the Commission and the United Kingdom have failed to demonstrate that the tax differentiation associated with the exemption of clay, slate, china clay, ball clay and shale aggregate is justified on the basis of the 'normal' taxation principle underpinning the AGL or on the basis of the environmental objective of the AGL.

87. That tax differentiation clearly derogates from the normal taxation rationale of the AGL, in so far as aggregates from the exempted materials all constitute, at least potentially, 'aggregates' that are subject to commercial exploitation within the meaning of the Act.

---

[42] Case C-308/01 *GIL Insurance Ltd and others* v *Commissioners of Customs and Excise* [2004] ECR I-4777.
[43] Case C-487/06P *British Aggregates Association* v *Commission* [2008] ECR I-10515, paras. 81–92.

88. Moreover, that tax differentiation is likely to undermine the environmental objective of the AGL in two respects.

89. In the first place, subject to evidence to the contrary, which has not, to date, been produced by the Commission or the United Kingdom, the exemption of clay, slate, china clay, ball clay and shale aggregate risks creating even greater demand in the construction industry for 'primary' aggregates of that type rather than for 'secondary' aggregates – namely the by-products of or waste from certain processes, including those derived from other alternative but taxed materials – and thus intensifying the extraction of those 'primary' aggregates, which would be contrary to the environmental objective of the AGL, designed as it is to encourage the use of those 'secondary' aggregates alone, and to avoid their being tipped as waste or stockpiled. In that regard, except for the general assertion that those materials 'traditionally' or 'generally' do not constitute aggregates, the Commission and the United Kingdom were unable to cast doubt on the applicant's argument that there are in the United Kingdom a number of quarries producing ('primary') shale and slate aggregate, which would thus be likely to profit from that exemption in the manner described above.

90. In the second place, there can, to that extent, no longer be any guarantee of an effective and consistent shift in that demand towards the use of 'secondary' aggregates of all categories of material, namely the by-products of and waste from certain processes or 'recycled' aggregates, so as to avoid those 'secondary' aggregates being tipped as waste and to encourage the more efficient extraction of 'primary' aggregates as a whole, not only those derived from certain exempt materials. Yet such an outcome would be manifestly incompatible with the environmental objective of the AGL as invoked by the United Kingdom. Furthermore, in those circumstances, the potentially beneficial impact on the environment in the light of that same objective – first to exhaust existing stocks of 'secondary' aggregates of clay, slate, china clay, ball clay and shale – is not sufficient to justify the tax differentiation established since that impact is not limited in time and thus – subject to evidence to the contrary, not produced by the United Kingdom in this instance – risks creating similar problems of stocks of aggregate waste derived from other materials subject to the levy, demand for which has since been diverted elsewhere, which would also be contrary to the environmental objective of the AGL.

The puzzle here is that while the Court of Justice appeared to have insisted that environmental goals were not to be considered in testing for whether a measure was selective (such analysis should be carried out under Article 107(3) TFEU) the General Court appears to retain the view that the justifications for selectivity are wider.[44] The wider approach favours Member States because it allows them to implement measures more quickly than if state aid notifications are required and also gives them the space to implement national policies for which they have received a democratic mandate. There is a balance to be struck between giving states leg-room and making sure that any negative externalities measures cause in other Member States are kept in check by a supranational entity. This is irresolvable because at its root lies an incomplete transfer of competences of economic policy to the Union. One possible way out could be

---

[44] The Court of Justice also appears to take a narrower approach in Case C-279/08P *Commission v Netherlands* [2011] ECR I-07671. See the excellent discussion in W. Sauter and H. Vedder, 'State Aid and Selectivity in the Context of Emissions Trading: Comment on the NOx Case' (2012) 37(3) *ELRev.* 327, noting that when the EU legislates on emissions trading it can balance a range of factors, but such balancing is not allowed when the Member State implements that policy.

for state aid law enforcement to focus on those measures that cause the most damage to other trading partners, but as we see below, the Court has also favoured a wide interpretation of the restrictive effects of state aid.

(iv) Effect on trade and restriction of competition

We can examine the final requirements together, because the Court of Justice applies very low standards for both elements. This position harks back to the discussion in section 2 above as to the nature of the state aid prohibition. As noted there, the role of state aid law has less to do with the anti-competitive impact of a measure (i.e. it does not look to whether the aid gives the beneficiary market power to harm its rivals) and more to do with ensuring a level playing field or preventing costly subsidies.

(a) Overly broad standards

In order to show harm to competition it suffices that an undertaking is put in a better position than its competitors, so the competitive conditions on the market are not vital. Similarly, an effect on trade may be shown merely by proof that the beneficiary operates across borders, or where the beneficiary does not export, but the increased production that results from state aid means there are less imports. And the effects of trade may also be potential. In *Heiser*, the Court of Justice considered whether small amounts of aid to medical practitioners in Austria could affect competition and trade.

Case C–172/03 *Wolfgang Heiser* v *Finanzamt Innsbruck* [2005] ECR I–1627

30. The Austrian Government also submits that the effect of the measure at issue in the main proceedings on trade between Member States is not very marked given the particular nature of medical care which is primarily provided locally.

31. However, those arguments do not establish that the second condition [relating to the effect on trade] is not fulfilled.

32. According to the Court's case-law, there is no threshold or percentage below which it may be considered that trade between Member States is not affected. The relatively small amount of aid or the relatively small size of the undertaking which receives it does not as such exclude the possibility that trade between Member States might be affected....

35. Accordingly, since it is not inconceivable ... that medical practitioners specialising in dentistry, such as Mr Heiser, might be in competition with their colleagues established in another Member State, the second condition for the application of Article [107(1) TFEU] must be considered to be fulfilled....

55. As regards the fourth condition ... that the intervention by the State must distort or threaten to distort competition, it must be borne in mind that aid, that is to say aid which is intended to release an undertaking from costs which it would normally have had to bear in its day-to-day management or normal activities, distorts the conditions of competition.

56. The argument of Mr Heiser and the Austrian Government that the fourth condition is not fulfilled on the ground that the medical practitioners who benefit from a measure such as that at issue in the main proceedings do not face competition based on prices, cannot be upheld.

57. Even if, as Mr Heiser and the Austrian Government point out, the choice of a medical practitioner by patients may be influenced by criteria other than the price of the medical treatment, such as its quality and the confidence placed in the medical practitioner, the fact none the less remains that that price is liable to have an influence, or even a substantial influence, on the choice of medical practitioner by the patient. That is so where, inter alia, as is clear from the case-file put before the Court, in the case of medical practitioners not under contract such as Mr Heiser, the patient has to pay more than 50% of the cost of the treatment out of his own pocket.

While the case law does not exclude a finding that these two criteria are not met,[45] the very expansive approach has two adverse effects: first, it makes it harder for the Commission to focus on the more harmful state measures; and secondly, it should be in the context of these two criteria that the policy debate about the appropriate scope of the state aid rules should be carried out rather than in the definition of advantage and selectivity.

(b) *De minimis* aid

The Court of Justice's refusal to entertain a *de minimis* rule in state aid law means that the Commission would be unable to prioritise its enforcement strategies. Since 1992 the Commission has tried to find a way of introducing a *de minimis* rule. In 1998 an Enabling Regulation was agreed, which empowers the Commission to establish that certain types of state aid are exempted from the notification requirement.[46] This served as the legal basis for a *de minimis* Regulation, which sets the *de minimis* threshold at €200,000.[47]

The legality of this Regulation may be questioned.[48] In particular, the Court of Justice has exclusive competence to define the notion of aid. Even though the Court appears to have approved of the Commission's approach, this was when the threshold was only €100,000.[49] It might have been simpler had it been declared that *de minimis* measures may be state aid but that, given their limited impact, they are exempted automatically. However, with this approach one would still have to ensure that the aid fitted under one of the grounds for exemption. At the time of writing the Commission wishes to widen the scope of the *de minimis* rule further.[50]

---

[45] Cases C-15/98 and C-105/99 *Italy and Sardegna Lines* v *Commission* [2000] ECR I-08855, where the Commission failed to take into account that the market had not been opened to competition, and then applied in Case N356/2002 Network Rail, Decision of 17 July 2002.
[46] Council Regulation 994/98 on the application of Articles 92 and 93 of the Treaty establishing the European Community to certain categories of horizontal State aid [1998] OJ L142/1.
[47] Commission Regulation 1998/2006 on the application of Articles 87 and 88 of the Treaty to *de minimis* aid [2006] OJ L379/5.
[48] M. Berghofer, 'The New De Minimis Regulation: Enlarging the Sword of Damocles?' (2007) *EstAL* 11.
[49] Case C-351/98 *Spain* v *Commission* [2002] ECR I-8031.
[50] At the time of writing it had issued a consultation on the second draft of the new *de minimis* Regulation replacing Regulation 1998/2006.

4 ENFORCEMENT AND SUPERVISION

(i) Commission supervision

In the beginning the Commission was not provided with a procedural regulation to formalise how it could exercise its competences. Nevertheless, the Commission, accompanied by the Court of Justice, developed a set of procedural practices in a piecemeal fashion. Regulation 659/99 (amended marginally in 2013) codifies the Commission's practice.[51] However, this is incomplete, and the rights of third parties, for example, are still largely governed by the case law of the Court of Justice.[52]

The Commission procedure has two phases. In phase 1 (based on Article 108(3) TFEU) the Commission considers the measure in question in a relatively brief span of time, and at the end of its inquiry it may reach three conclusions: the measure is not aid; the measure is state aid, but it is compatible with the Treaty; the measure is state aid and raises serious concerns as to its compatibility such that closer inquiry is warranted. Phase 2 (based on Article 108(2) TFEU) is a longer procedure with no formal time limits. At the end of its inquiry the Commission may reach one of three decisions: authorising the measure (either because it turns out not to have been state aid at all or because it is compatible with the Treaty); authorising the aid subject to certain conditions or a negative decision holding that the aid may not be granted.

The Regulation identifies four different kinds of situations and sets out procedures for each: (i) new aid, which consists of measures a Member State has notified to the Commission prior to granting the aid; (ii) existing aid (for example, aid that has already been approved); (iii) unlawful aid (aid which is implemented without notification, or before notification or in breach of a condition set by the Commission); (iv) misused aid (where the beneficiary misuses the aid). It may come as a surprise that the Commission may authorise both new aid and unlawful aid. While in the context of unlawful aid the Commission also has powers to require the Member State to submit information, to put an end to the aid pending the Commission's review, or even issue a recovery order when the measure in question is clearly state aid, these powers are too weak to serve as an adequate deterrent. Likewise the procedure for misuse of aid is weak, because it requires a formal investigation and provisional recovery is not available. In contrast, when the Member State is diligent it finds that it has a duty to cooperate with the Commission and review all existing aid measures, and discuss any changes. The more a state cooperates, the greater the burdens.

It is not surprising that the Commission was eager to use the current State Aid Modernisation initiative to strengthen enforcement. However, the outcome still falls short of what is necessary.[53] Its principal new powers are the following. First, it may request information from other Member States or undertakings when assessing complex cases, and it may impose fines on undertakings that furnish incorrect or misleading information.[54] However, no penalties are

---

[51] A. Sinnaeve and P. J. Slot, 'The New Regulation on State Aid Procedures' (1999) 36 *CMLRev.* 1153.

[52] K. Norlander and D. Went, 'Checks and Balances in EU State Aid Procedures: Should More be Done to Protect the Rights of Aid Recipients and Third Parties?' (2010) 11(3) *ERA Forum* 361.

[53] For a critique, see A. Bartosch, 'The Procedural Regulation in State Aid Matters: A Case for Profound Reform' (2007) *European State Aid Law Quarterly* 474.

[54] Regulation 743/2013 amending Regulation 659/1999 laying down detailed rules for the application of Article 93 of the EC Treaty [2013] OJ L204/15, articles 6a and 6b.

available for Member States who fail to cooperate, only the tacit threat that the decision will be made irrespective of their cooperation. Secondly, it may launch EU-wide inquiries where certain measures or certain instruments appear to distort competition across the EU or where certain existing aids are no longer compatible.[55] This replicates the procedure for sector inquiries in antitrust law, which have been successful in allowing the Commission to identify priority sectors for intervention. Thirdly, also replicating antitrust rules, it formalises the cooperation between national courts and the Commission, allowing the courts to request information and the Commission to send written or oral comments.[56]

One significant gap in the rules, according to the Commission, is that increasingly aid is implemented via lawful channels that do not require notification. It found that roughly 88 per cent of aid granted to industry and services is granted on the basis of previously approved aid schemes or under Block Exemption. As a result, in 2011 Directorate General (DG) Competition stepped up its monitoring efforts, but the results are not encouraging.

> ### State Aid Scoreboard, COM(2012)778 final, 12
>
> Although investigation of a number of cases is still on-going, there seems to be an overall increase in the number of problematic cases. More than one-third of the cases monitored in 2011/2012 have raised problems of varying types and gravity (non-notified modification of schemes, individual aid exceeding the maximum thresholds, compatibility conditions not properly reflected in the national legal basis etc.). Keeping in mind the possible bias introduced by the limited number of cases monitored so far (compared to the great number of existing aid schemes), the compliance rate seems to vary across the Member States and the different types of aid. The Commission will systematically follow up all irregularities. At the same time, Member States must step up their efforts to better comply with State aid rules.

(ii) Enforcement

(a) Recovery

The major power that the Commission has to enforce the state aid rules is to order recovery of unlawful aid. This power had originally been identified by the Court of Justice,[57] and is now codified in the Regulation. Recovery means that the Member State takes back (with interest[58]) the advantage it has meted out. While this obligation will frustrate the government's policy and may cause some degree of political embarrassment, the delays between the grant of the aid and the time recovery is ordered may well mean that the measure achieves its desired effect anyway, even if only in part. Moreover, the Member State loses little since money is returned to its coffers. This leads one to be somewhat sceptical about the value of this kind of remedy. Finally, recovery of state aid is in the hands of the Member State, and national procedures to organise such recovery are not always in place to cover this eventuality, nor are state organs particularly eager to prioritise measures that harm national policy. In spite of these structural

---

[55] *Ibid.* article 20a.   [56] *Ibid.* article 23a.
[57] Case 70/72 *Commission* v *Germany (Khlengesetz)* [1973] ECR 813.
[58] Regulation 659/1999, article 14(2).

weaknesses, the rate of recovery by Member States has improved considerably: in 2004, 75 per cent of illegal or incompatible aid had yet to be recovered, but this was down to 25 per cent by December 2012.[59] This may in part be due to the Commission issuing guidance to aid states in implementing their recovery obligation,[60] but is also likely the result of the sovereign debt crisis creating incentives for states to recover funds.

Recovery does not deter Member States from granting state aid, but it is said that it re-establishes the *status quo ante*. That is to say, the beneficiary is put back in the position before the aid was awarded.[61] This may be so in some cases, but not always: there remains the risk that the advantage has led to even greater benefits accruing to the beneficiary, or to losses for its competitors that the recovery order cannot cover. These further harms may be addressed by private enforcement, but as we discuss below this is not well developed. As a result, it seems necessary for the remedy to be reformed substantially if it should serve to deter and restore the *status quo ante*. A provocative set of suggestions was made by Sir Jeremy Lever: the state aid should be paid back to the EU, not to the Member State, and the Union should then use these sums to recompense the undertakings that were harmed by the grant of the state aid. This might be costly to implement and politically impossible to obtain, but it serves to show the massive gap that exists between the current rules on recovery and a system that would, in reality, secure optimal enforcement.[62]

The Commission must issue a recovery decision,[63] and while the specific implementation is left to national procedures, these must allow for 'immediate and effective execution of the Commission's decision'.[64] While it is for the Member State to identify the beneficiaries and the amount to be recovered,[65] the Commission tends to do this in its decisions.[66] Given the mul-tifarious ways in which state aid might be granted, recovery has to be adapted. For example, when the aid is in the form of a state guarantee, recovery is the difference between the interest rate on the loan that would have been paid absent the guarantee and that which was paid as a result of the guarantee. In cases where no loan would have been made absent the guarantee, this means the loan itself is invalid.[67] When the aid is a tax exemption then the beneficiary should be ordered to repay the equivalent of the tax exemption received.[68]

Attempts by Member States to escape the obligation to recover aid have been unsuccessful: national procedures cannot stand in the way of the duty to recover;[69] insolvency does not ex-tinguish the duty to recover (the state should register its claim in insolvency proceedings);[70] and the transfer of the beneficiary's assets means that the buyer may be the new beneficiary and duty bound to repay the aid. This is particularly so when it appears that the divestiture of assets was

---

[59] Staff Working Document accompanying the Commission on Competition Policy 2012, SWD(2013)159 final, 5.
[60] See e.g. Notice from the Commission, Towards an effective implementation of Commission decisions ordering Member States to recover unlawful and incompatible state aid (Recovery Notice) [2007] OJ C272/4.
[61] Case 142/87 *Tubemuse* [1990] ECR I-959.
[62] J. Lever, 'The EC State Aid Regime: The Need for Reform' in A. Biondi, P. Eeckhout and J. Flynn (eds.), *The Law of State Aid in the European Union* (Oxford, Oxford University Press, 2004).
[63] Regulation 659/1999, article 14(1).   [64] *Ibid.* article 14(3).
[65] Case C-441/06 *Commission v France* [2007] ECR I-08887 or C-480/98 *Spain v Commission* [2000] ECR I-08717, paras. 25 and 26.
[66] Recovery Notice [2007] OJ C272/4 32, 37.   [67] Decision 2005/786 [2005] OJ L296/19, para. 107.
[68] C-193/91 *Finanzamt München III v Mohsche* [1993] ECR I-02615, para. 17.
[69] See e.g. Case 308/88 *Italy v Commission* [1991] ECR I-1433; Case 94/87 *Commission v Germany* [1989] ECR 175.
[70] Case C-331/09 *Commission v Poland* [2011] ECR I-02933; Recovery Notice, n. 66 above, paras. 63–7.

designed specifically to avoid repayment.[71] Nor have Member States fared any better in pleading that principles of EU law nullify the recovery decision. In a number of cases it was argued that the beneficiary's legitimate expectations would be harmed by the recovery order. However, the Court of Justice has not been sympathetic, ruling that a diligent businessman would be able to determine whether the state had followed the correct procedures to ensure that aid was lawful under EU law.[72] The plea of legitimate expectations only works when the Commission (or another EU institution) gave the beneficiary reason to believe the aid is lawfully granted, it cannot work when the Member State reassures the beneficiary. The Commission has, in some cases, decided not to impose recovery orders when it considered that the case law of the Court of Justice led the beneficiary to consider that the measure in question was not state aid.[73]

(b) Private enforcement

As indicated above, the only part of the state aid rules that has direct effect is the final sentence of Article 108(3) TFEU which provides that Member States may not grant state aid until the Commission has authorised it, and this obligation is also applicable to state aid that has not been notified at all.[74] Moreover, the breach of EU law that results from the failure to notify before granting the aid remains even if, at a later date the Member State notifies the aid and this is approved by the Commission.[75]

But what can national courts do? First, they are empowered to issue declarations that a certain measure is state aid. This empowers them to strike down national legislation.[76] Secondly, the court may order that aid that has been paid out is recovered. The view taken is that recovery restores the *status quo ante*, so it is plausible that a competitor who is injured by the aid has standing to seek recovery to protect their interests.[77] However, to date the majority of claims have been beneficiaries or states litigating to oppose recovery.[78] For example, in *Residex* the would-be beneficiary of a state guarantee sued when the Member State refused to honour it. The Member State argued that the guarantee it had issued was in breach of state aid to escape liability. Thus, state aid rules were used by the state as a defence against a contract claim, not the kind of litigation one would seek to promote to strengthen state aid enforcement.[79] Furthermore, the continuing uncertainty over the meaning of state aid also hampers the effective use of national courts. Perhaps the most dramatic illustration is the *CELF* saga. This concerned subsidies granted between 1980 and 2002 to an exporter in order to promote the sale of French books abroad. The question of whether this measure was state aid and, if so, if it merited exemption, was the

---

[71] Case C-415/03 *Commission v Greece* [2005] ECR I-03875. In contrast ,when shares are sold, then normally the seller of the shares remains the person liable for the recovery order. See generally, G. Monti, 'Recovery Orders in State Aid Proceedings: Lessons from Antitrust?' (2011) 10(3) *European State Aid Law Quarterly* 415.

[72] Case C-5/89 *Commission v Germany* [1990] ECR I-3437.

[73] See e.g. Decision 2005/565 [2005] OJ L190/13, para. 66 (on the basis of the *Adria Wien* judgment discussed above).

[74] Case 120/70 *Lorenz v Germany* [1973] ECR 1471.

[75] Case C-39/94 *SFEI v La Poste* [1996] ECR I-3577.

[76] This is how the notorious *British Aggregates* litigation began: *R (on the Application of BAA) v HM Treasury* [2002] EWHC 926 (Admin). As noted above the case may just have been resolved by the General Court.

[77] Recovery Notice, n. 66 above, para. 30.

[78] Study on the Enforcement of State Aid Law at National Level (2006, updated 2009).

[79] Case C-275/10 *Residex Capital IV*, Judgment of 8 December 2011 and see C-1/09 *CELF and ministre de la Culture et de la Communication* [2010] ECR I-02099 where the competitor made a request that aid be recovered.

subject of several exchanges between the Commission and the General Court. By 2009 CELF was insolvent, and to add to its woes a recovery order was issued at the request of the original complainant. The Court of Justice was asked to advise (twice) on the duties of the national courts in light of the tortuous and lengthy path the measure had pursued, and both times it confirmed the duty of the courts to secure repayment of the aid: the uncertainty over the Commission's position did not constitute an exceptional circumstance to prevent enforcement of the duty to notify. This can serve to deter the Member State, because the notification process cannot be circumvented, and recovery prevents the expected benefits of the aid from maturing.[80]

As we have noted, in some cases, the state aid is granted by a tax exemption. The question has arisen as to what the best means of protecting competitors harmed by this form of state aid is: can they avoid paying, or if they have paid, can they get their money back?

Joined Cases C–393/04 and C–41/05 *Air Liquide Industries Belgium SA v Ville de Seraing and Province de Liège* [2006] ECR I–5293

41. In that respect, the Court has held that national courts are involved in the system for reviewing State aid only through the direct effect attributed by case-law to the prohibition on putting State aid into effect, in accordance with the third sentence of Article 108(3) TFEU. The Court has in particular stated that it is for the national courts to uphold the rights of the persons concerned in the event of a possible breach by national authorities of the prohibition on putting aid into effect.

42. With regard to the measures which may or must be taken to ensure this legal protection, the Court has stated that, where such a breach is invoked by individuals, national courts must take all the consequential measures, in accordance with national procedures, as regards both the validity of measures giving effect to the aid and the recovery of financial support granted in disregard of Article 108(3) TFEU.

43. The Court has also held that those liable to pay a tax cannot rely on the argument that the exemption enjoyed by other businesses constitutes State aid in order to avoid payment of that tax. It follows that, even if the exemption at issue in the main proceedings constitutes aid within the meaning of Article 107 TFEU the fact that the aid may be unlawful does not affect the legality of the tax itself.

44. The last sentence of Article 108(3) TFEU lays down an obligation the aim of which is to ensure that aid is not granted until the Commission has declared it compatible with the common market. In this context, the powers of national courts are essentially preventive and cannot exceed those conferred on the Commission where it takes a decision on the legality of State aid following a substantive assessment.

45. Finally, it should be pointed out that an extension of the circle of potential recipients to other undertakings would not make it possible to eliminate the effects of aid granted in breach of Article 108(3) TFEU but would rather, on the contrary, lead to an increase in the effects of that aid.

46. It would be otherwise if the tax and the envisaged exemption were an integral part of an aid measure. For a tax to be regarded as forming an integral part of an aid measure, it must be hypothecated to the aid measure under the relevant national rules, in the sense that the revenue from the tax is necessarily allocated for the financing of the aid and has a direct impact on the amount thereof and, consequently, on the assessment of the compatibility of that aid with the common market. However, a tax cannot be hypothecated to an exemption from payment of that same tax for a category of businesses. Application of a tax exemption and its extent do not depend on the tax revenue.

---

[80] Case C-1/09 *CELF and ministre de la Culture et de la Communication* [2010] ECR I-02099, and for discussion see T. Jaeger, 'CELF II: Settling into a Weak *effet utile* Standard for Private State Aid Enforcement' (2010) 1(4) *Journal of European Competition Law and Practice* 319.

On the facts the tax was not hypothecated to the exemptions. This confirms that the aim of the recovery order is really designed to restore competition in the market, and not to protect the beneficiary fully. This might be criticised because it does not really create much of an incentive to seek a remedy if the reward is low. The response that breaches of state aid law allow injured parties to secure damages is not a meaningful answer given the difficulties in proving a causal nexus between the state aid and the injury.

5 EXEMPTIONS

(i) Overview

Not all state aid is forbidden.

Article 107(2) and (3) TFEU

2. The following shall be compatible with the internal market:
   (a) aid having a social character, granted to individual consumers, provided that such aid is granted without discrimination related to the origin of the products concerned;
   (b) aid to make good the damage caused by natural disasters or exceptional occurrences;
   (c) aid granted to the economy of certain areas of the Federal Republic of Germany affected by the division of Germany, in so far as such aid is required in order to compensate for the economic disadvantages caused by that division. Five years after the entry into force of the Treaty of Lisbon, the Council, acting on a proposal from the Commission, may adopt a decision repealing this point.
3. The following may be considered to be compatible with the internal market:
   (a) aid to promote the economic development of areas where the standard of living is abnormally low or where there is serious underemployment, and of the regions referred to in Article 349, in view of their structural, economic and social situation;
   (b) aid to promote the execution of an important project of common European interest or to remedy a serious disturbance in the economy of a Member State;
   (c) aid to facilitate the development of certain economic activities or of certain economic areas, where such aid does not adversely affect trading conditions to an extent contrary to the common interest;
   (d) aid to promote culture and heritage conservation where such aid does not affect trading conditions and competition in the Union to an extent that is contrary to the common interest;
   (e) such other categories of aid as may be specified by decision of the Council on a proposal from the Commission.

The distinction between these two subsections is that aid must be authorised if it fulfils the criteria of Article 107(2), while the Commission retains discretion when it comes to measures considered under Article 107(3).

The first two grounds in Article 107(2) are designed to address extreme scenarios, for example allowing the state to issue food or travel vouchers to disadvantaged consumers, or to assist firms affected by floods, earthquakes or even acts of terrorism. The key concern of the

Commission in these settings is to ensure the proportionality of the aid so that the Member State does not misuse these provisions to support the growth of the industries benefitting from the assistance, but only resolves the concerns caused by an exceptional event.[81] The final basis is construed narrowly: it only applies to the kinds of disadvantages suffered by the former East Germany that were the result of the geographical division of Germany. Therefore the mere fact that the regions of the former East Germany are less economically developed as a result of different economic policies is not a basis for authorising aid under this provision.[82]

It is in the domain of discretionary exemptions (Article 107(3) TFEU) where most of the aid has been granted and authorised. Already in the *Philip Morris* judgment in 1980, the Court of Justice had recognised that the Commission's assessment was to be carried out in the context of the Union as a whole.[83] Here the Court endorsed the compensatory justification principle that had been developed by the Commission: aid is authorised if the beneficiary makes a contribution to the interests of the EU over and above that which it would have made absent the state aid.[84]

However, one of the main criticisms of the Commission's approach to determining state aid exemptions under Article 107(3) has been that the approach lacks structure and is also subject to lax scrutiny by the Court of Justice. This means that sometimes aid may be granted when it makes no contribution to the interests of the EU, while at other times it may be denied even if it yields benefits.[85] If we recall the decision-making context, whereby the College of Commissioners takes decisions to authorise aid, one can legitimately fear that decisions to authorise state aid may be more based on political considerations than a systematic assessment of the expected benefits of state intervention.[86] In response to this criticism the Commission launched the State Aid Action Plan, by which the Commission sought to improve its assessment. We turn to the substantive reform in (ii), and to the procedural reform in (iii).

(ii) Better targeted aid and Europe 2020

The Commission now operates a new framework to test whether state aid should be authorised:[87]

(1) Is the aid measure aimed at a well-defined objective of common interest?
(2) Is the aid well designed to deliver the objective of common interest (i.e., does the proposed aid address a market failure or other valid objective)? In particular:

---

[81] Case C-278/00 *Greece* v *Commission* [2000] ECR I-8787, where there was no connection between the Chernobyl nuclear disaster and the assistance given to settle debts owed by agricultural cooperatives.

[82] See Case C-156/98 *Germany* v *Commission* [2000] ECR I-06857 and C-277/00 *Germany* v *Commission* [2004] ECR I-03925.

[83] Case C-730/79 *Philip Morris* [1980] ECR 2671.

[84] Thus, for aid under Article 107(3)(a) TFEU one looks at the impact in the EU: C-114/00 *Spain* v *Commission* [2002] ECR I-07657, para. 81; for aid under Article 107(3)(b) the aid must complement some sort of transnational European programme: Joined Cases 62/87 and 72/87 *Exécutif regional wallon* v *Commission* [1988] ECR I-01573.

[85] L. Hancher, T. Ottervanger and P.-J. Slot (eds.), *EU State Aids* (4th edn, London, Sweet & Maxwell, 2012) pp. 146–7.

[86] S. Bishop, 'State Aids: Europe's Spreading Cancer' (1995) *ECLR* 331.

[87] See Case C-34/2006 *North Rhine-Westphalia DTT*, Decision of 23 October 2007.

- is the aid measure an appropriate instrument?
- is there an incentive effect, that is, does the aid change the behaviour of firms?
- is the aid measure proportional, that is, could the same change in behaviour be obtained with less aid?

(3) Are the distortions of competition and effect on trade limited, so that the overall balance is positive?

This approach sets out a 'social welfare' standard for assessing state aid, which is open to exploring all positive and negative effects of state aid policy.[88] Before assessing it, we first explain how this test operates in practice. It is convenient to focus on a case study, which concerns aid granted by Spain to Industria de Turbo Propulsores to support experimental research in developing jet engines. This was the first detailed assessment of an R&D project after the new approach was announced.[89] In tackling the first question, the Commission considered whether there was a reason why the market was not providing that kind of research. It found that there was a market failure because of asymmetric information: the project in question is of a long duration and benefits are only seen ten to fifteen years after the start, so normally financial institutions shy away from funding these projects. Moreover, ITP was a new player and it did not benefit from internal cash flow from previous projects. The Commission agreed that there was a market failure but stated that this was a borderline case: there was evidence that other companies in the market had managed to fund their own projects; furthermore ITP should soon be mature enough to be able to benefit from cash flow from earlier projects and overcome the market failure. This analysis is interesting because it may well create a precedent whereby ITP can no longer be designated as beneficiary of further aid. Having identified a market failure the first limb of the test above was satisfied: the project would yield a benefit in the common interest.

The Commission then turned to the question of whether the aid was well designed and focused on the incentive effect. It found that without the aid, ITP would not have been able to make the investment. But it was also noted that ITP had been quite active in R&D in the past, and so the Commission turned to explore whether there were alternatives for ITP. It found, however, that the company indeed relied on securing the aid as a means of starting the project and that it saw no alternative for a project of this scale. Taking into account the way the company planned its strategy, the aid was found to be appropriate and to have an incentive effect. We might pause to note that the bulk of the assessment is done without considering alternative scenarios: in other cases the Commission asks what would have occurred *but for* the aid,[90] but here this was not done – perhaps because the internal documents were sufficiently credible to show that absent the aid the project had no chances. The aid was also considered proportionate because it would be kept to a minimum, and furthermore it was found that the Member State would receive a return when the loan was repaid. This seems an important factor in measuring the proportionality of the aid, even if its effects merely show that the state burden is less as a result.

The Commission was rather brief on the harm to competition: in light of ITP's small market share relative to its main rivals it was unlikely that the measure would affect competition

---

[88] P. Lowe, 'Some Reflections on the European Commission's State Aid Policy' (2006) 2(2) *Competition Policy International* 67.

[89] For discussion, see P. Nicolaides and I. Rusu, 'The "Binary" Nature of the Economics of State Aid Law' (2010) 37(1) *Legal Issues of Economic Integration* 25.

[90] Case N541/2006 *Fiat*, Decision of 13 June 2007.

whether by damaging the incentives of rivals to invest, or creating market power. This meant that when it came to 'balancing' the answer was self-evident: the benefits were clear, the harm to competition hardly proven, so the aid was authorised.

One striking aspect of this approach is that while no detailed economic assessment is done at the stage of defining the harm caused by the state aid, considerable effort is spent looking for the benefits of state aid intervention. It has led one economist to conclude that 'aid not solving a well-defined market failure should be banned, even in the absence of any distortion'.[91] The Commission acts more like an auditor, asking how far the state's money is well spent. Furthermore, it is not yet apparent how this approach can properly be said to balance positive and negative effects: in most cases it seems as if the effects are either overwhelmingly positive or the aid is unnecessary so one does not need to carry out the balance at all.[92] This approach is also puzzling because the Commission has not proposed to raise its standard of proof in identifying the anti-competitive effects of aids first.[93] Rather, it has merely raised the standard of proof of the Member State, requiring considerably more data and analysis before authorising the aid. These not inconsiderable administrative costs may well deter Member States from implementing certain measures and may direct states to only grant aid if it falls within the scope of the General Block Exemption Regulation (GBER) (see below). If this were so it would lead to suboptimal results. These concerns have led some to raise the more fundamental argument that the Commission lacks the competence to steer state aid policy in this direction: the economic tools do not fit the Treaty provisions, and the policy of less aid is not selected in a democratic manner.[94] However, the response is that state aid law has always been applied in such a way as to consider the EU interest: the modernised approach is just a more sophisticated way of finding out whether the aid yields benefits for the Union as a whole.

It is remarkable how the Commission has managed the state aid rules, not least because of the relatively weak enforcement tools available. It remains to discuss how the Commission achieved this.

M. Blauberger, 'Of Good and Bad Subsidies: European State Aid Control through Soft Law and Hard Law' (2009) 32(4) *West European Politics* 719

Two factors have been responsible for the Commission's ability to act as a supranational entrepreneur of positive integration: vague Treaty rules and heterogeneous Member State interests. EC Treaty rules reflect the conflicting policy goals in the field of state aid and they entrust the Commission to balance them in concrete cases. The ECJ has limited the scope of European state aid control and checks the Commission's practices for procedural correctness, but it largely follows a policy of 'judicial self-restraint' with regard to the underlying assessment of admissible state aid. Member states' conflicting views on national state aid policies meant that they were initially unwilling to agree upon secondary rules, and later were unable to counter the Commission's increasingly complex and detailed vision

---

[91] Spector, n. 2 above, 200.   [92] Nicolaides and Rusu, n. 89 above.

[93] For this important criticism see Monopolkommission, *The More Economic Approach in European State Aid Control* (8 July 2008), available at www.monopolkommission.de/haupt_17/chapteriv_h17.pdf.

[94] C. Kaupa, 'The More Economics Approach: A Reform Based on Ideology?' (2009) 2 *European State Aid Law Quarterly* 311.

of 'good' state aid policy. Essentially, the Commission's strategy can be described as one of 'lesser evil' from the Member States' perspective. Compared to case-by-case control, state aid soft law has improved legal certainty, and, rather than being exclusively oriented toward competition, it left some scope for the design of national state aid policies. Compared to the remaining uncertainties under soft law, particularly those arising from lengthy Commission investigations, directly applicable BERs further clarify the remaining possibilities of national policy makers and relieve them from burdensome notification procedures. In exchange, the Commission gains influence on national state aid policies.

Obviously there are limits to the Commission's entrepreneurship: some stem from the fact that within the Commission there are competing visions on the role of state aid law, others from the reality that when Member States are relatively united in opposing a Commission initiative, then the Commission will back down. It is also plausible that the new rules facilitate creative compliance: that is, Member States appear to follow the Commission's line but in reality use the aid for other reasons. The ex post monitoring of state aid in 2011 noted above suggests that this may well be the case.

The current SAM programme builds on the framework described above and seeks to transpose the economic analysis described above across all kinds of state aid, with a view to ensuring consistency. The Commission is particularly eager to promote state expenditure in projects that help meet the targets set out in the EU's industrial policy, the so-called Europe 2020 programme, for example, aid to facilitate developments in electronic communications.

(iii) Better targeted aid enforcement

As we saw in Chapter 22, one efficient way of handling recurring and unproblematic scenarios is to issue Block Exemptions. Powers to proceed in this way were conferred on the Commission in 1998.[95] Ten years later the Commission consolidated all existing Block Exemptions in a single legal instrument: the General Block Exemption Regulation (GBER).[96]

The GBER applies to a wide category of measures (including regional aid, aid for environmental protection and for research and development).[97] It is divided into two sections: Chapter 1 and Chapter 2. Chapter 1 sets out conditions that all aid should fulfil. The principal ones are the following. The aid must be below a given threshold (for example, €7.5 million per undertaking per investment project in the field of investment aid for environmental protection).[98] The aid must be transparent (which serves to exclude aid in the form of a capital injection, i.e. cash in exchange for equity).[99] The Member State must monitor and report on the

---

[95] There is judicial support for the Commission's Block Exemptions, see Case C-110/03 *Belgium* v *Commission* [2005] ECR I-2801.

[96] Commission Regulation 800/2008 declaring certain categories of aid compatible with the common market in application of Articles 87 and 88 of the Treaty (General Block Exemption Regulation) [2008] OJ L214/3.

[97] The full list is found in *Ibid*. article 1: (a) regional aid; (b) SME investment and employment aid; (c) aid for the creation of enterprises by female entrepreneurs; (d) aid for environmental protection; (e) aid for consultancy in favour of SMEs and SME participation in fairs; (f) aid in the form of risk capital; (g) aid for research, development and innovation; (h) training aid; (i) aid for disadvantaged or disabled workers.

[98] General Block Exemption Regulation, article 6(1)(b).

[99] *Ibid*. article 5.

implementation of the aid, which is to ensure that the funds are not misused.[100] And there must be an incentive effect.

Commission Regulation 800/2008 declaring certain categories of aid compatible with the common market in application of Articles 87 and 88 of the Treaty (General Block Exemption Regulation), article 8 [2008] OJ L214/3

1. This Regulation shall exempt only aid which has an incentive effect.
2. Aid granted to SMEs [small and medium-sized enterprises], covered by this Regulation, shall be considered to have an incentive effect if, before work on the project or activity has started, the beneficiary has submitted an application for the aid to the Member State concerned.
3. Aid granted to large enterprises, covered by this Regulation, shall be considered to have an incentive effect if, in addition to fulfilling the condition laid down in paragraph 2, the Member State has verified, before granting the individual aid concerned, that documentation prepared by the beneficiary establishes one or more of the following criteria:
   (a) a material increase in the size of the project/activity due to the aid;
   (b) a material increase in the scope of the project/activity due to the aid;
   (c) a material increase in the total amount spent by the beneficiary on the project/activity due to the aid;
   (d) a material increase in the speed of completion of the project/activity concerned;
   (e) as regards regional investment aid referred to in Article 13, that the project would not have been carried out as such in the assisted region concerned in the absence of the aid.

It is not entirely clear how detailed the Member State's scrutiny of the documentation has to be, and one does not have to be a cynic to suggest that this formality can easily be satisfied. Nevertheless it is unusual to find this requirement in a Block Exemption, where normally formal criteria are used, and the risk of under-enforcement is not really an issue. What is missing instead is any means to revoke the benefit of the exemption if it is found that the aid does not yield the benefits that were anticipated, although perhaps success or failure are hard to measure.

Chapter 2 explains in detail the kinds of expenditures that qualify (for example, aid to increase the level of environmental protection resulting from its activities in the absence of Community standards); the kinds of costs that are eligible to be covered by the aid (for example, the extra investment costs needed); and the aid intensity, that is to say the percentage of the eligible costs that can be supported by state aid (this is 35 per cent for the aid to increase the level of environmental protection).[101] This means that the beneficiary has to fund the remainder from own resources, which is an astute move because it creates an incentive to find resources in-house.

Under the State Aid Modernization programme the Commission wishes to expand this approach by broadening the scope of the GBER to other categories. It has already secured a widening of its powers to issue Block Exemptions in the fields of aid for innovation, aid for culture and heritage conservation, aid to compensate damages caused by natural disasters, aid

---

[100] *Ibid.* articles 10 and 11.   [101] *Ibid.* article 18.

to forestry as well as certain types of aid for transport and for broadband infrastructure.[102] A proposal for a wider GBER is awaited.

(iv) Rescuing banks

Between October 2008 and October 2011 the volume of financial support to the financial sector was €4.5 trillion (36.7 per cent of EU GDP).[103] Compared to the high of 2 per cent of GDP spent on state aids in the 1980s, the involvement of Member States in rescuing banks is astonishing. It is impossible to address all the details here, but the key elements of the Commission's approach can be set out briefly.

First, the Commission agreed that the measures taken to save banks merited exemption on the basis of Article 107(3)(b): they remedied a serious disturbance in the economy of the Member States in question. However, it also indicated that it would apply, by analogy, the kinds of criteria that it had developed in situations where the Commission monitored aid to rescue other kinds of struggling firms. In practice, this meant that the Commission authorised the state aid quickly (and so reassured the financial markets) but only on the condition that the Member State would later on explain what measures would be taken to mitigate the effects of the state aid. This two-stage procedure is unusual but wise: it gave the right market signals (banks would be saved) and allowed the Member State (and the Commission) some time to explore how the negative effects of the aid could be dealt with. However, a counter-argument is that if the legal basis for rescuing aid is Article 107(3)(b) then there is no good reason why there should be any conditions attached to the measure: the reason the state must act is that it faces an emergency and so the aid should not have any strings attached.

Secondly, the Commission, in cooperation with governments and the European Central Bank, learned about the kinds of measures that were necessary to rescue banks and created legal frameworks that allowed for the measures to be implemented and monitored. For example, in early 2009 one of the issues that surfaced is that a number of banks held so-called 'toxic assets'. That is to say, some of the assets held by banks had no value, and this hindered their capacity to trade. Governments agreed to buy these assets at a price higher than the market price so as to relieve the banks of them. The guidance from the Commission set out principles by which this procedure should be carried out to qualify for exemption: (i) the costs of handling these assets should be shared between the state and the bank; (ii) the identification of the impaired assets must be done in a transparent manner and validated by the national supervisory authority; (iii) for banks that are in distress or have already received some other forms of aid, then there must be a restructuring plan following the exit of the toxic assets.[104] In authorising aid measures, it was noted that almost all were approved. This might raise concerns about whether the Commission implemented its policies robustly, but it

---

[102] Regulation 733/2013 amending Regulation 994/98 on the application of Articles 92 and 93 of the Treaty establishing the European Community to certain categories of horizontal State aid, article 1 [2013] OJ L204/11.

[103] International Monetary Fund, *European Union: Publication of Financial Sector Assessment Program Documentation – Technical Note on Progress with Bank Restructuring and Resolution in Europe*, IMF Country Report No. 13/67 (March 2013) 7.

[104] Communication from the Commission on the treatment of impaired assets in the Community banking sector [2009] OJ C72/1.

is likely that the Member States consulted the Commission prior to notification, to avoid any objections.[105]

Thirdly, and most controversially, the Commission made the grant of state aid to banks subject to a duty on banks to restructure. This had been known to the beneficiaries from the start but it was only in July 2009 that the precise framework was established to guide banks.[106] This provides that the banks must present a strategy for restructuring their business to ensure that they are viable, and should pay the costs themselves (which is achieved mostly by restricting the dividend payments banks make to their shareholders). The aim is twofold: first, making sure that the banks are viable in the long term and can sustain further shocks; secondly, that the state aid that has been granted does not create a moral hazard risk. That is to say, banks may take risks in the future again, knowing that they will be saved by the Member States. Having to suffer the costs and the burdens of restructuring is a means of deterring risk taking. The restructuring measures include the requirement to sell off some assets to allow for the emergence of new banks or the entry of new competitors. This is an imaginative and controversial remedy: it is not clear that by granting state aid to a bank in difficulty that this foreclosed market access to other firms. On the contrary, given the perilous state of the market it is not clear that anyone would take the risk of entering the market. The measure requested by the Commission thus serves to create competition that was not there before. This is a desirable effect, but it is also open to the criticism that it goes further than necessary to reverse the anti-competitive effects. Finally, the Commission also requires the beneficiary from using the state aid to make better offers to customers as this would distort competition further. Some examples will serve to illustrate how these principles have been applied.

First, we consider the restructuring of the Royal Bank of Scotland.[107] This bank had received the largest amount of state aid in the EU, in a variety of forms (recapitalisations, guarantees, impaired assets assistance). It was required to divest a business that accounts for 5 per cent of banking services for retail and small and medium-sized customers, which included 318 branches and 6,000 staff. The aim of this divestiture was to create a new player in the British market that would compete seriously with the four leading banks. The purchaser cannot have a market share above 14 per cent on that market, thus preventing one of the other large British banks from acquiring it. As indicated above, this kind of remedy is remarkable for two reasons. First, there was no indication that the state aid had in fact prevented the emergence of competition: the reason the British market was highly concentrated had more to do with banking policy over the past twenty years than with the state aid. Secondly, the remedy interferes with the British regime for merger control, by forbidding certain acquirers from buying the assets. In addition, RBS also undertook to sell off a number of other assets, so as to reduce its balance sheet. This is designed to address the moral hazard concern. Furthermore, RBS also undertook not to acquire competitors, or use the state aid benefits to gain any advantage on the market (for example, advertising that its products are supported by a state guarantee). And finally RBS must adhere to the remuneration code of the Financial Services Authority.

---

[105] D. Zimmer and M. Blaschczok, 'The Role of Competition in European State Aid Control during the Financial Markets Crisis' (2011) 32(1) *ECLR* 9.

[106] Commission Communication on the return to viability and the assessment of restructuring measures in the financial sector in the current crisis under the state aid rules [2009] OJ C195/9.

[107] Case N422/2009 *RBS Restructuring Plan* [2010] OJ C119/1.

Secondly, we look to the restructuring plan for Bayern LB.[108] This bank received state aid in the form of a capital injection, a risk shield and a number of state guarantees. The restructuring plan includes a reduction of the balance sheet by 50 per cent (as compared with the bank's size in 2008); the reduction of risky activities abroad (for example, international project finance and real estate). The Commission considered that these measures would be likely to ensure that the bank is viable in the long term, and will focus on lending to the real economy in its region. It also considered that the plan, which included a repayment schedule for the aid received, ensured that the regional savings banks that own Bayern LB, would make a sufficient contribution to the repayment.

The Commission took stock of the impact of its decisions between 2008 and 2011. It concluded that its policies were on the right track: banks had become gradually less reliant on state aid, and markets had become less unstable. However, it also noted that there may still be the need for state aid, so that the processes and procedures that it had established needed to be extended.[109] It also noted that the measures implemented by states and banks under the Commission's supervision were no substitute for wider legislative measures to regulate financial markets in the EU.[110] However, not everyone is convinced of the wisdom of the Commission's state aid policy.

**A. Heimler and F. Jenny, 'The Limitations of European Union Control of State Aid'
(2012) 28(2) *Oxford Review of Economic Policy* 347, 364**

[T]hese behavioural measures unnecessarily constrain the market-response possibilities of aid-receiving banks and effectively reduce competition, instead of enhancing it. In particular, mergers and aggressive pricing benefit consumers and should not be prohibited unless they lead to violation of the antitrust laws. In some way, the Commission, instead of protecting competition (i.e. asking what would happen to the market if a particular bank were not granted the aid) is making sure that the bank would not need more aid in the future, forgetting that this is the objective of the once-and-for-all clause. Furthermore, just prohibiting mergers or aggressive pricing is hardly likely to affect ex ante moral hazard in corporate strategies...

As for other ex post measures taken to reduce moral hazard on the part of the managers of the aided financial institutions, the Commission is equally ineffective. Through behavioural constraints affecting the action of managers, the Commission is trying to ensure stability over excessive risk-taking. The approach is in some way simplistic and a bit naive. For example, in the Commerzbank case the Commission imposed limitations on managers' compensation and severance packages. The reason for this cap is unclear. If the constraint imposed by the Commission is binding, then good managers of subsidized institutions would leave for better jobs elsewhere, leading to worse results overall and to a slower recovery of the aided company. If the constraint is not binding it is, of course, useless. As a result, capping managers' pay does not lead to speedier recovery; on the contrary.

---

[108] 'State aid: Commission approves restructuring aid to Bayern LB subject to repayment of 5 billion of aid European Commission', IP/12/847, 25 July 2012 (at the time of writing the full text of this Decision is not yet available).

[109] Communication from the Commission on the application, from 1 August 2013, of state aid rules to support measures in favour of banks in the context of the financial crisis ('Banking Communication') [2013] OJ C216/1.

[110] European Commission Staff Working Paper, *The Effects of Temporary State Aid Rules Adopted in the Context of the Financial and Economic Crisis* (October 2011).

In addition to the effectiveness of these measures, others have also doubted their legal soundness, and criticise the Commission for a 'market structuring tendency'.[111] Others, however, have been more supportive, indicating that the Commission pragmatically adjusted to the crisis by adapting existing frameworks in a manner that was flexible enough to allow banks to be rescued, but also ensured that state aid control was exercised.[112] Whether the measures taken are a success will require evaluation at a later time. It is not, however, particularly clear by what benchmark success should be measured. The sole consideration should be to ask if the banking industry has been stabilised, but as we noted above, a number of other policies have been pursued: ensuring lending to small and medium-sized businesses, addressing moral hazard considerations, and enhancing competition in concentrated markets. It remains to be said that the Commission's strategy as a policy entrepreneur was excellent: it gave itself considerable policy space to regulate financial markets, and has turned the issues of moral hazard and the regulation of banks into an issue that requires further regulatory efforts at Union level, some of which have already been implemented.[113] Finally, the story of the Commission's pragmatic and opportunistic response to the financial crisis is part of a wider narrative about the incomplete nature of the European Union.

FURTHER READING

C. Ahlborn and D. Piccinin, 'The Application of the Principles of Restructuring Aid to Banks during the Financial Crisis' (2010) *European State Aid Law Quarterly* 47

K. Bacon (ed.), *European Community Law of State Aid* (2nd edn, Oxford, Oxford University Press, 2013)

A. Bartosch, 'The Procedural Regulation in State Aid Matters: A Case for Profound Reform' (2007) *European State Aid Law Quarterly* 474

A. Bartosch, 'Is there a Need for a Rule of Reason in European State Aid Law? Or How to Arrive at a Coherent Concept of Material Selectivity' (2010) 47 *Common Market Law Review* 729

A. Biondi, P. Eeckhout and J. Flynn (eds.), *The Law of State Aid in the European Union* (Oxford, Oxford University Press, 2004)

M. Blauberger, 'Of Good and Bad Subsidies: European State Aid Control through Soft Law and Hard Law' (2009) 32(4) *West European Politics* 719

F. De Cecco, *State Aid and the European Economic Constitution* (Oxford, Hart Publishing, 2012)

L. Hancher, T. Ottervanger and P.-J. Slot (eds.), *EU State Aids* (4th edn, London, Sweet & Maxwell, 2012)

C. Kaupa, 'The More Economics Based Approach: A Reform Based on Ideology?' (2009) 3 *European State Aid Law Quarterly* 311

P. Nicolaides, 'The Incentive Effect of State Aid: Its Meaning, Measurement, Pitfalls and Applications' (2009) *World Competition* 579

---

[111] Zimmer and Blaschczok, n. 105 above.

[112] H. Gilliams, 'Stress Testing the Regulator: Review of State Aid to Financial Institutions after the Collapse of Lehman' (2011) 36(1) *ELRev.* 3.

[113] See e.g. the single supervisory mechanism, Regulation 1024/2013 of 15 October 2013 conferring specific tasks on the European Central Bank concerning policies relating to the prudential supervision of credit institutions and the ongoing talks on banking union [2013] OJ L287/63. See p. 721.

M. P. Smith, 'Autonomy by the Rules: The European Commission and the Development of State Aid Policy' (1998) 36(1) *Journal of Common Market Studies* 55

D. Spector, 'State Aids: Economic Analysis and Practice in the European Union' in X. Vives (ed.), *Competition Policy in the EU: Fifty Years on from the Treaty of Rome* (Oxford, Oxford University Press, 2009)

D. Zimmer and M. Blaschczok, 'The Role of Competition in European State Aid Control During the Financial Market Crisis' (2011) *European Competition Law Review* 9

Index